DSM-IV Classifications

DISORDERS NEEDING FURTHER STUDY

The DSM-IV Task Force judged that these disorders do not currently have sufficient supporting data for inclusion in DSM-IV and therefore require further study. In fact, only a few of th___ ___ly meet criteria, while others will be excluded from further consideration. Many of th___ ___scussed in one or more appropriate chapters

Postconcussional ___ order

The key features ___ disorder are specific cognitive impairments as w___ ___xc___ ___tigue, disordered sleep, and headaches f___ ___ng ___uma that resulted in a concussion. (Se___ ___ted ___ in Chapter 15.)

Mild Neurocogn___ive

The key feature of t___ ___ is an impairment in neurocognitive fun___ ___at is the result of a general medical condition ___apter 15.)

Caffeine Withd___ ___

The key feature of this disorder is the experience of headaches, fatigue, anxiety, nausea, or vomiting after the abrupt cessation of caffeine consumption following prolonged daily use of the substance. (See related material in Chapter 12.)

Postpsychotic Depressive Disorder of Schizophrenia

The key feature of this disorder is a major depressive episode that occurs only during the residual phase of schizophrenia. (See related material in Chapter 7.)

Simple Deteriorative Disorder (Simple Schizophrenia)

The key feature of this disorder is the development of prominent negative symptoms (e.g., alogia, avolition) in the absence of positive symptoms (e.g., hallucinations, delusions) over the course of 1 year. (See related material in Chapter 14.)

Premenstrual Dysphoric Disorder

The key features of this disorder are marked anxiety or depressed mood, affective lability, and decreased interest in activities. These symptoms regularly occur during the week preceding menses and are never prese___ ___ week following it. (See Chapter 3.)

Minor Depressive Disorder

The key feature of this disorder is one or more periods of depressive symptoms that have the same duration as a major depressive episode but fewer and less seve___ symptoms. (See related material in Chapter 7.)

Recurrent Brief Depressive ___ ord___

The key feature of this disorder is one or more periods of depressive symptoms. The symptoms are equal in number and degree of impairment to those seen in a major depressive episode, but they last for less than 2 weeks. (See related material in Chapter 7.)

Mixed Anxiety–Depressive Disorder

The key featur___ ___ this disorder is the presence of persis-___ ___oric mood as well as a number of ___s ___ffect for at least 1 month. (See Chapter 6.)

Dissociative Trance Disorder

The key feature of this disorder is an involuntary state of trance that is not considered normal within the person's culture or religion and causes significant distress or impairment. (See Chapter 6.)

Binge-Eating Disorder

The key feature of this disorder is the repeated occurrence of binge eating. The person has impaired control over the binging and is distressed by it. Compensatory behaviors, such as those typical of bulimia nervosa, are absent.

Depressive Personality Disorder

The key feature of this disorder is a pervasive pattern of depressive thoughts and behaviors that develops by early adulthood and occurs in a variety of contexts. The symptoms are not better accounted for by dysthymia and do not occur only during major depressive episodes. (See related material in Chapters 7 and 13.)

Passive-Aggressive Personality Disorder (Negativistic Personality Disorder)

The key feature of this disorder is a pattern of negativistic attitudes and the use of passive means to resist occupational and social demands. This pattern develops by early adulthood and occurs in a variety of contexts. (See Chapter 13.)

___ ___ent Disorders

___ ___ designed to assist in the ___ ___d the assignment of psycho-logica___ ___tures of these disorders are abnormal physical m___ ___s or characteristics such as tremors, muscle rigidity or spasms, pacing, fidgety behav-___ ___normal posture that are judged to be side effects ___ ___ollowing diagnoses have ___ ___ry: Neuroleptic-Induced Parkinsonism, Neuroleptic Malignant Syndrome, Neuroleptic-Induced Acute Dystonia, Neuroleptic-Induced Acute Akathisia, Neuroleptic-Induced Tardive Dyskinesia, Medication Induced Postural Tremor, Medication-Induced Movement Disorder Not Otherwise Specified. (See related material in Chapter 15.)

1995

0534203582

Adapted from: American Psychiatric Association. (1994). *Diagnostic and statistical manual of mental* ___

Abnormal Psychology
An Integrative Approach

Abnormal Psychology
An Integrative Approach

David H. Barlow
University at Albany
State University of New York

V. Mark Durand
University at Albany
State University of New York

Brooks/Cole Publishing Company

I(T)P™ An International Thomson Publishing Company

Pacific Grove • Albany • Bonn • Boston • Cincinnati • Detroit • London • Madrid • Melbourne
Mexico City • New York • Paris • San Francisco • Singapore • Tokyo • Toronto • Washington

Sponsoring Editor: *Marianne Taflinger*
Project Development Editor: *Joanne Tinsley*
Marketing Manager: *Carolyn Crockett*
Marketing Representative: *James Grott*
Signing Representative: *Tammy Goldfeld*
Editorial Assistant: *Laura Donahue*
Production Coordinator: *Marjorie Z. Sanders*
Production: *Stacey C. Sawyer, Sawyer & Williams*
Manuscript Editor: *Patterson Lamb*
Permissions Editor: *May Clark*

Interior Design: *Katherine Minerva*
Interior Illustration: *Illustrious*
Cover Design: *Vernon T. Boes*
Cover Photo: *Mike Granberry, Carole Newman & Associates*
Photo Coordination: *Larry Molmud*
Photo Researcher: *Susan Friedman*
Indexer: *Lois Oster*
Typesetting: *Graphic World*
Color Separation: *Color Associates*
Cover Printing: *Phoenix Color Corporation, Inc.*
Printing and Binding: *Quebecor Printing/Hawkins*

For more information, contact:

BROOKS/COLE PUBLISHING COMPANY
511 Forest Lodge Road
Pacific Grove, CA 93950
USA

International Thomson Publishing Europe
Berkshire House 168-173
High Holborn
London WC1V 7AA
England

Thomas Nelson Australia
102 Dodds Street
South Melbourne, 3205
Victoria, Australia

Nelson Canada
1120 Birchmount Road
Scarborough, Ontario
Canada M1K 5G4

International Thomson Editores
Campos Eliseos 385, Piso 7
Col. Polanco
11560 México D. F. México

International Thomson Publishing GmbH
Königswinterer Strasse 418
53227 Bonn
Germany

International Thomson Publishing Asia
221 Henderson Road
#05-10 Henderson Building
Singapore 0315

International Thomson Publishing Japan
Hirakawacho Kyowa Building, 3F
2-2-1 Hirakawacho
Chiyoda-ku, Tokyo 102
Japan

Printed in the United States of America.

10 9 8 7 6 5 4 3 2 1

Library of Congress Cataloging-in-Publication Data

Barlow, David H.
    Abnormal psychology: an integrative approach / David H.
Barlow, V. Mark Durand.
        p.   cm.
    Includes bibliographical references and index.
    ISBN 0-534-20358-2
    1. Psychology, Pathological. 2. Mental illness. I. Durand,
Vincent Mark. II. Title.
    RC454.B345 1995   94-35287
    616.89—dc20   CIP

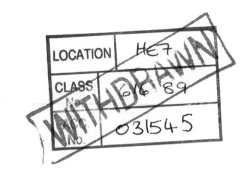

Credits continue on p. 799.

I dedicate this book to my mother, Doris Elinor Barlow-Lanigan
for her multi-dimensional influence across my life span.

D.H.B.

To Wendy and Jonathan,
whose patience, understanding, and love provided
me the opportunity to complete such an ambitious project.

V.M.D.

About the Authors

David H. Barlow is a world-renowned psychologist recognized as a leader and pioneer in the field of clinical psychology. He is Distinguished Professor at the University at Albany—State University of New York where he has served as the Director of Clinical Training and currently serves as the Co-Director of the Center for Stress and Anxiety Disorders and as Director of the Phobia and Anxiety Disorders Clinic. Previously, he was the Founding Director of the Brown University Clinical Psychology Internship program from 1975–1979 and the University of Mississippi Medical School Psychology Residency Program from 1969–1975. He received his B.A. from the University of Notre Dame, his M.A. from Boston College, and his Ph.D. from the University of Vermont.

PHOTO COURTESY OF UNIVERSITY AT ALBANY/MARK SCHMIDT

He is a Fellow of the American Psychopathological Association, the American Psychological Society, and the American Psychological Association, both Division 12 and Division 25. In honor of his excellence in scholarship, he was awarded the National Institute of Mental Health Merit Award. In 1988 he received an Award for Excellence in Research from the State University of New York. In 1989 he was awarded the Distinguished Scientist Award from the Society for a Science of Clinical Psychology of the American Psychological Association. He has published over 300 scholarly articles and books in his career to date.

David H. Barlow has served in a number of leadership positions in his field: President of the Division of Clinical Psychology of the American Psychological Association, President of the Association for the Advancement of Behavior Therapy, Vice President of the Society for the Experimental Analysis of Behavior, and on the Board of Directors for the American Association of Applied and Preventive Psychology.

He has served as editor of the *Journal of Applied Behavior Analysis* from 1980–1983 and *Behavior Therapy* 1983–1986 and as series editor of "Treatment Manuals for Practitioners" with Guilford Press. He was the guest editor of *The Journal of Abnormal Psychology* special issue: "Diagnosis, Dimensions & DSM-IV: The Science of Classification." In addition, he's also been associate editor of the *Journal of Consulting and Clinical Psychology.*

During his career he has served on the editorial boards of nineteen different journals.

David H. Barlow has written, edited, or co-authored 18 different books, the chief ones of which are *Anxiety and Its Disorders,* Guilford Press; *Clinical Handbook of Psychological Disorders: A Step-by-Step Treatment Manual,* 2nd ed., Guilford Press; *Single-Case Experimental Designs: Strategies for Studying Behavior Change,* 2nd ed., Allyn & Bacon (with Michel Hersen); *The Scientist Practitioner: Research and Accountability in Clinical and Educational Settings* (Allyn & Bacon) (with Steve Hayes and Rosemery Nelson); and *Mastery of Your Anxiety and Panic,* Graywind Publications (with Michelle Craske).

From 1990 to 1994, he had the unique opportunity to serve as one of three psychologists on the DSM-IV Task Force, which was responsible for reviewing the work of over 1000 mental health professionals who participated in the creation of the new DSM-IV.

At present he is the chair of the American Psychological Association's Task Force on Psychological Intervention Guidelines, which is creating a template for the construction of clinical practice guidelines. He is also co-chair of the Anxiety and Panic Disorder panel at the Agency for Health Care Policy and Research. Currently his research program continues to focus on the nature and treatment of anxiety and related emotional disorders. At leisure he plays golf, skis, and retreats to his home in Nantucket, where he loves to write, walk on the beach, and visit with his island friends.

About the Authors

V. Mark Durand is a nationally recognized researcher in the area of developmental disabilities and is currently an Associate Professor of Psychology at the University at Albany—State University of New York. He received his B.A., M.A., and Ph.D. all in psychology at the State University of New York–Stony Brook. While at the University at Albany, he has administered ten different federal research and training grants in the areas of functional communication, assistive technology, home-school training, and improving the problem behaviors of children and adults with severe disabilities. He has served as the Associate Director of Clinical Training for the doctoral psychology program at the University at Albany—State University of New York from 1987–1990 and is currently Director of the Albany Center for the Study of Developmental and Behavioral Disabilities.

He was awarded the University Award for Excellence in Teaching at the University at Albany—State University of New York in 1991 and the Distinguished Reviewer of the Year in 1989 for the *Journal of the Association for Persons with Severe Handicaps.*

Mark Durand has served on the editorial boards of *Analysis and Intervention in Developmental Disabilities,* the *Journal of the Association for Persons with Severe Handicaps,* and the *Journal of Applied Behavior Analysis.* And he has served as a reviewer for numerous journals, including *American Journal of Mental Retardation, Behavioral Assessment, Behavior Modification, Behavior Therapy, Journal of Abnormal Psychology, Journal of Applied Behavior Analysis, Journal of Autism and Developmental Disorders, Journal of Social and Clinical Psychology, Psychological Assessment: A Journal of Consulting and Clinical Psychology, Research in Developmental Disabilities, School Psychology Review,* and *The Behavior Analyst.*

He's written numerous scholarly articles, four books—the chief one of which is *Severe Behavior Problems: A Functional Communication Training Approach*, Guilford Press—and dozens of book chapters concerning functional communication, educational programming, and behavior therapy.

Mark has a growing reputation worldwide, having developed a unique treatment for severe behavior problems, one that is currently mandated by a number of states. In addition, he has developed an assessment tool that is used throughout the world and has been translated in more than five languages. He has also had the distinction of being the keynote speaker for the Australian National Conference on Behaviour Modification in 1993. He has been called on to consult with the Departments of Education for numerous states, as well as the U.S. Department of Justice and the U.S. Department of Education. His current research program covers many areas, including how mood affects behavior problems and the development of new models for serious problems such as self-injurious behavior. In his leisure time, he enjoys jogging, soccer, playing with his son, Jonathan, and long drives with his wife, Wendy.

PHOTO COURTESY OF UNIVERSITY AT ALBANY/MARK SCHMIDT

Brief Contents

Contents

Preface

Every once in a while something dramatic happens in science. For example, evolutionary biologists used to assume that the process of evolution was gradual. Then evidence emerged that evolution seems to take place in fits and starts and is almost certainly influenced by cataclysmic environmental events such as meteor impacts. And, even though geologists have only recently discovered the forces of plate tectonics, these findings have revolutionized their field.

We believe that something similar is happening in psychopathology, although it may not be apparent to those of us who work in this field every day. Up to now the science of psychopathology has been essentially compartmentalized. Psychopathologists examined the separate effects of psychological, biological, and social influences. This approach is also used in the popular press, where, frequently, new accounts appear describing, for example, a newly discovered gene, a biological dysfunction, or the social context of early childhood experiences as a "cause" of a psychological disorder. This thinking is also reflected in current abnormal psychology textbooks, in which discussions of causality and treatment are similarly compartmentalized. Thus we have the familiar format "the psychoanalytic views of this disorder are . . . the biological views of this disorder are. . . . " Similarly, often in a separate chapter, we see "psychoanalytic treatment approaches for this disorder are . . . cognitive behavioral treatment approaches for this disorder are . . . biological treatment approaches for this disorder are. . . ."

We believe this approach is no longer useful. A recent explosion of knowledge has demonstrated that one cannot study genetic and neuroscientific contributions to psychopathology without understanding that psychological and social factors directly affect neurotransmitter function and even genetic expression. Similarly, one cannot study behavioral, cognitive, or emotional processes without an appreciation of the contribution of biological and social factors to psychological and psychopathological expression. Thus, we have chosen to eliminate the traditional compartmentalized approach to psychopathology, which, in any case, was usually a source of confusion to our students.

New Approach

We have written what we hope will be the first of a new generation of abnormal psychology textbooks that present the subject matter in an integrative multidimensional approach. For example, the background of one-dimensional approaches to psychopathology—such as psychoanalytic, social learning, behavioral, and biological approaches—are presented as historical trends in the first chapter (along with supernatural models). When considered narrowly, these one-dimensional models are no longer scientifically viable; however, they form an important backdrop to the study of psychopathology. In Chapter 2, a chapter not found in abnormal psychology textbooks to date, we present current evidence of the reciprocal influences of biology on behavior as well as psychological and social influences on biology. We attempt to use examples that will catch the student's eye: for example, genetic contributions to divorce and the effects of early social and behavioral experience on later brain function and structure. This theme is carried throughout the chapters on disorders, in which we attempt to weave together the strands of multidimensional influences into unified models of etiology and treatment. We also underscore the fact that psychological science has verified the existence of the unconscious as exemplified in the phenomenon of implicit memory and blind sight, which may have parallels in dissociative experiences. Although these unconscious processes problably do not much resemble the seething caldron of conflicts envisioned by Freud, a number of psychoanalytic concepts have been verified and have substantially contributed to our understanding of some disorders—for example, the somatoform and dissociative disorders discussed in Chapter 6. In addition, we delineate the rich contributions to psychopathology from the often neglected area of emotion theory. We weave together scientific findings from the study of emotions with discoveries from behavioral, biological, cognitive, and social areas in an attempt to create an integrated tapestry of psychopathology.

You, our colleagues, are aware that our field has greater understanding of some disorders than others. But we hope you will share our excitement in conveying to the student what we currently know about causes and treatment of psychopathology and how far we have yet to go to understand these complex interactions.

Therapy as Inseparable

In keeping with our integrative theme we have resisted the temptation to parcel out descriptions of treatment in a separate chapter that would, it seems to us, communicate that treatment processes and procedures are independent of psychopathology. It is our belief that approaches to treatment are inseparable from the psychopathology that is the target of treatment. This is reflected in the growing specificity of our treatments, both psychosocial and pharmacological, for various disorders and the emerging evidence of the effectiveness of these treatments compared to psychological or pharmacological placebos. A special glossary of commonly used treatment procedures has been included to provide students with a broader frame of reference, in addition to the material in the chapter.

Life-Span Developmental and Cultural Influences

It is also our firm belief that no modern textbook on abnormal psychology can neglect to integrate the important influences of life-span developmental factors on the manifestation and treatment of psychopathology. To highlight our focus on the life span, we have incorporated into each chapter many of the disorders typically included in other texts in a "disorders of childhood" chapter. Therefore, for example, childhood anxiety is discussed in the anxiety disorders chapter. We hope this organization, which is consistent for the most part with changes in DSM-IV, gives students an appreciation of the need to study psychopathology from childhood through adulthood for each disorder.

In addition, in each disorder chapter we have noted findings on developmental and cultural considerations within a "statistics and course" section for the particular disorders. We also discuss specific developmental and cultural factors as appropriate within causation and treatment discussions.

Clinical Cases with a Rich, Believable Context

We have tried to enrich the book by using detailed clinical case material as vehicles for explaining scientific findings on causes and treatment of psychopathology. Furthermore, since we both run active clinics and have for years, 95% of the cases in this book are our own cases. We opted for this approach believing that we could provide a rich, believable context for the scientific findings in the book by discussing some of the nuances of case material from our files that illustrate the complexity as well as the human tragedy of psychopathology. To utilize this material most chapters start off with a case description. Most discussion of scientific findings relevant to the disorder in question is discussed in the context of, or with reference to, the case or cases described. For example, in Chapter 1 we discuss the case of Judy, an adolescent girl suffering from blood-injection-injury phobia, to illustrate how conditioning, biological, and social factors alone cannot completely account for the onset of her severe disorder.

Scientist-Practitioner Approach

We go to some length to describe the utility as well as the ideal of a scientist-practitioner approach to psychopathology. As life-long scientist-practitioners, we conceptualize this approach, as do many of you, as something more than simply being aware of scientific findings as they apply to psychopathology. Rather, we attempt to illustrate how all clinicians working in this area have contributed to our corpus of scientific knowledge through astute and systematic clinical observations, functional analyses wtihin the context of individual case studies, and systematic observations of series of cases in clinical settings, sometimes referred to as clinical replication series. In Chapter 6, for example, we illustrate how early psychoanalytic theorists provided important information on dissociative phenomena that has stood the test of time. Formal methods yielding this type of important data are described in Chapter 4; in this chapter, the reader learns how abstract research designs are being used in a real-life research program.

DSM-IV

This book went to press just as the fourth edition of the *Diagnostic and Statistical Manual* was made available. Thus the book contains the final DSM-IV criteria, including what are, in some cases, substantial changes from the draft criteria published in March 1993. For example, a totally different criteria set for dysthymia was adopted for the published version of DSM-IV. In addition, one of us (DHB) had the interesting experience of sitting on the DSM-IV Task Force. While much has been said and will be said about the mix of political and scientific considerations that resulted in DSM-IV, we have our own impressions. We as psychologists have often been concerned about some of the turf issues involved in what has become, for better or worse, the nosological standard in our field. Based on previous DSM editions, there was good reason for this concern, since scientific findings were eschewed in favor of the personal opinions of members of a committee. However, in the case of the DSM-IV Task Force, in most instances professional turf issues were left at the door while the Task Force almost endlessly debated the data. This process produced enough new information in the form of integrative reviews, reanalysis of existing databases, and new data from field trials to fill every psychopathology journal for a year. A sampling of these papers and data will be publihed in a series of four volumes accompanying the DSM-IV. Being part of this process was, from a scholarly point of view, both stimulating and exhausting.

Since membership in the subworkgroups (devoted to each specific disorder, such as panic disorder or hypochondriasis), the workgroups (devoted to classes of disorders—for instance, mood disorders, anxiety disorders), and the Task Force (with overall responsibility for the development of the nosology) comprised hundreds of people, at least half of whom were psychologists, one can say that for a period of four years there truly existed an invisible college of psychopathology.

In this book you will find highlights of the various debates and discussions that went into the creation of the nomenclature. For example, in Chapter 3 we present summaries of the data and discussion on two disorders that did not make it into the final criteria: premenstrual dysphoric disorder and mixed anxiety depression. We hope this discussion illustrates for the student the process of creating diagnoses as well as the mix of data and inference that are part of this process. The inside front cover of the book lists all the proposed disorders with insufficient data to appear in DSM-IV. Some of these disorders, pending further scientific elaboration, will undoubtedly appear in the next edition.

This textbook also reflects the intense and continuing debate on categorical vs. dimensional approaches to classifying psychopathology, and it discusses some of the compromises the Task Force arrived at to accommodate data on these issues. For example, Chapter 13, on personality disorders, includes a discussion on why it does not seem possible at the present time to dimensionalize personality disorders, even though almost everybody in the field agrees that ultimately this will be the preferred organizational approach.

Coverage of Disorders

In Chapters 5 through 16, we cover the major psychological disorders. Coverage focuses on three broad categories: clinical description, causal factors, and treatment and outcomes. Within the clinical descriptions, we include considerable discussion of case studies and DSM-IV criteria to give the full picture of each of the disorders. We also include statistical data, such as prevalence and incidence rates, sex ratio, age of

onset, and the general course or pattern for the disorder as a whole. Within the causal factors, we delve into the integrative multidimensional approach, exploring biological, psychological, and social dimensions and how they may interact to cause a particular disorder. Finally, treatment and outcomes are, as noted, discussed within the context of disorders for a realistic depiction of the treatment process.

Legal and Ethical Issues

Our closing chapter on mental health services and society pulls together many of the approaches and themes that run throughout the text. Thus we begin with a case study of an individual who has had direct experience with many of the legal and ethical issues and with the delivery of mental health services. This chapter is written with the scientist-practitioner in mind. In addition, we have tried to provide a historical perspective that gives real understanding of societal and cultural influences on today's perspectives and on their potential to influence our future perspectives.

Special Note on the Photo Program

In collaboration with our editors we have also decided to go down a somewhat different road by including many real photos of real clients diagnosed with some of the psychological disorders. In every case, we have made certain that we have the individual's permission to use his or her photo; in cases where we felt individuals might not truly understand our purpose, we have chosen to respect their privacy and have not used their photos. It is our sincere hope by showing the faces of people struggling with these disorders, faces that reflect both genders and most races, cultures, and stages of development, that we can communicate the hardship and struggle attendant on these disorders and help reduce the stigma, anxiety, and isolation commonly experienced in our society by people with these disorders.

Finally, communicating knowledge and discoveries in the exciting field of psychopathology is a task that you, the instructors, and we, the authors of this book, share. Since we have all chosen this particular field for our life's work, this task is a challenge that none of us takes lightly. In the spirit of collegiality we would greatly appreciate comments from you on the content and style of this book and how we can improve it in the future.

Like participating in the creation of DSM-IV, writing this book has been both a stimulating and exhausting task. Creating a book such as this, particularly one that attempts to take a new approach, could not be done without invaluable assistance from our colleagues in the field. All our colleagues listed read one or more chapters and/or provided extraordinarily perceptive critical comments by correcting our errors, pointing us to new information, and, on occasion, providing new insights to help us come ever closer to our goal of a successful integrative model of the disorder in question. Among these individuals we would like to single out a small group that read large sections of the book and therefore played a unique role in helping us to realize our overall integrative perspective. These individuals include: Linda Craighead, with her long experience teaching abnormal psychology and her particularly astute scholarly perspectives on eating and emotional disorders; Ann Kring, one of the brightest up-and-coming young scientists in the area of schizophrenia; and finally Don Fowles, truly a Talmudic scholar of abnormal psychology, who provided incisive commentary on every paragraph we wrote that was unparalleled in our careers or those of our colleagues at Brooks/Cole. Some of our colleagues or former colleagues at Albany (such as Michele Craske, Bruce Dudek, Beverly Rodriguez, Scott Lilienfeld, Elga Wulfert, Michele Carter, and Tracy Sbrocco) contributed to specific chapters, and we are greatly indebted to them.

Finally, this book would not have begun and certainly would not be finished without the inspiration and coordination of Marianne Taflinger, our senior editor at Brooks/Cole, who convinced us that we could truly accomplish something new and different and then put her heart and soul into the process. One additional person has left her mark throughout the pages of this book. We owe a great deal to Joanne Tinsley who, as our developmental editor, combined the unique qualities of attention to minute details of each sentence with an overall perspective on effectively communicating our views for the book. She is truly a woman of letters.

In the production process, many individuals worked as hard as we did on completing this project in the relatively brief period of two years. Irene Farruggio worked tirelessly to type much of the book as well as oversee its integration and production; her professionalism and accuracy are unparalleled. Amy Bach, Bill Korotitsch, and Jennifer Lackmann corrected seemingly endless errors, noted by themselves or others, and participated in seemingly endless decisions on photos, art, and content of the book. A part of them is in this book, and we hope their later careers will be enriched by their experience. Special thanks also to Professor Michael Gelder, Drs. David Clark, and Paul Salkovskis for their hospitality and incisive comments during DHB's sabbatical at Oxford University, where several chapters of this book were written, and to Judith Sumida, my eternally optimistic secretary in that setting, who convinced me of the importance of stopping for tea.

David H. Barlow
Nantucket Island

V. Mark Durand
Somewhere in front of a computer screen

Reviewers

An essential part of writing any textbook is receiving feedback from both teachers and experts in specific areas. We are pleased to thank the people listed below who, in their roles as reviewers, provided invaluable information that helped shape both the form and content of this book.

Dr. Brenda Allen, *Smith College*

Dr. John J. Allen, *University of Arizona*

Dr. Frank Andrasik, *University of West Florida*

Dr. Theodore R. Bashore, *University of Northern Colorado*

Dr. Michael Bailey, *Northwestern University*

Dr. Andrew Baum, *University of Pittsburgh*

Dr. J. Gayle Beck, *State University of New York at Buffalo*

Dr. Deborah C. Beidel, *Medical University of South Carolina*

Dr. Mary Beirne-Smith, *University of Alabama-Tuscaloosa*

Dr. Ed Blanchard, *State University of New York at Albany*

Dr. Charles M. Borduin, *University of Missouri-Columbia*

Dr. Karen Obremski Brandon, *State University of New York at Binghamton*

Dr. Thomas H. Brandon, *State University of New York at Binghamton*

Dr. Kelly D. Brownell, *Yale University*

Dr. Jim Calhoun, *University of Georgia*

Dr. Mary Lynne Calhoun, *University of North Carolina-Charlotte*

Dr. Cameron Camp, *University of New Orleans*

Dr. Michael Cary, *Syracuse University*

Dr. Linda Craighead, *University of North Carolina-Chapel Hill*

Dr. William Dement, *Stanford University*

Dr. Mitchell Earleywine, *University of Southern California*

Dr. Matthew Enos, *Harold Washington University*

Professor Jean W. Foss, *University of New Orleans*

Dr. Don Fowles, *University of Iowa*

Dr. Sherryl Goodman, *Emory University*

Dr. Robert E. Hales, *University of California, San Francisco*

Dr. Michael Havens, *University of Wyoming*

Dr. Brian Hayden, *Brown University*

Dr. William Iacono, *University of Minnesota*

Dr. Colleeen B. Jamison, *California State University, Los Angeles*

Dr. Ann M. Kring, *Vanderbilt University*

Dr. Arnold LeUnes, *Texas A & M University*

Dr. Robert W. McCarley, *Harvard Medical School*

Dr. Greg Miller, *University of Illinois*

Dr. Jodi Mindell, *St. Joseph's University*

Dr. Merrill Mitler, *Scripps Clinic*

Dr. Scott Monroe, *University of Oregon*

Dr. Leslie Morey, *Vanderbilt University*

Dr. Kim Mueser, *Dartmouth College*

Dr. Beth Ober, *University of California, Davis*

Dr. Jordan Peterson, *Harvard University*

Dr. Lynn Rehm, *University of Houston*

Dr. Ken Sher, *University of Missouri-Columbia*

Dr. David Spiegel, *Stanford University School of Medicine*

Dr. Tom Widiger, *University of Kentucky*

Dr. John Wincze, *Brown University*

Dr. Michael Zinser, *University of Colorado*

Prospectus Reviewers

Dr. Peter Finn, *Indiana University*

Dr. Ken Sher, *University of Missouri-Columbia*

Dr. Timothy Strauman, *University of Wisconsin*

Dr. Tom Wrobel, *University of Michigan-Flint*

Art Consultation

Dr. Michael Havens, *University of Wyoming*

Dr. Lori Marino, *Emory University*

Dr. Tom Widiger, *University of Kentucky*

Continuity Reviewer

Dr. Don Fowles, *University of Iowa*

A clear and complete insight into the nature of madness,
a correct and distinct conception of what constitutes
the difference between the sane and the insane has
as far as I know, not yet been found.
Schopenhauer
The World as Will and Idea

1

Past and Future Conceptions of Abnormal Behavior

Today you may have gotten out of bed, eaten something for breakfast, gone to class, studied, and, at the end of the day, enjoyed the company of your friends before dropping off to sleep. It probably did not occur to you that there is a large group of physically healthy people who may not be able to get out of bed, or eat, or attend class or study, or enjoy themselves, or even sleep normally. Some people may experience a number of these problems at the same time. What these individuals have in common is a **psychological disorder,** which can be defined as a psychological dysfunction associated with distress or impairment in functioning that is not a typical or culturally expected response. We will examine exactly what this means in some detail in the following pages, but before doing so, let's look at one individual's situation.

The Case of Judy

Judy was a 16-year-old female who was referred to the Anxiety Disorders Clinic that one of us runs after a series of fainting episodes that had been increasing in frequency of late. About 2 years previously she had begun taking her first biology class. Shortly thereafter, the teacher used a movie depicting a dissection of a frog to illustrate various points concerning anatomy. This was a particularly graphic film with vivid images of blood, tissue, and muscle. About halfway through the film, Judy felt a bit lightheaded and left the room. Still, the film images did not leave her. She continued to be bothered by them and occasionally would feel a bit queasy. Because of this reaction, she began to avoid situations where she might encounter the sight of blood or injury. She even avoided any magazines that might have these kinds of pictures. But her avoidance did not stop there. She also found it difficult to be in the presence of things like raw meat or Band–Aids because they tended to bring the feared images to mind. Eventually, anything her friends or parents would say that conjured up an image of blood or injury caused her to feel lightheaded. It got so bad that if one of her friends said "Cut it out," she would feel faint.

About 6 months before her visit to the clinic, she actually began to faint when she unavoidably encountered a triggering object or situation. She went to her family physician, who could find nothing wrong with her. Nor could several other physicians. By the time she was

1

referred to our clinic she was fainting five to ten times a week, often in class at school. This behavior was very disruptive in school because the other students would flock around her trying to help and class would be interrupted. Since nothing was "wrong" with her, the principal suspended her from school assuming she was just being manipulative, even though she was an honor student.

Judy was suffering from what we now call *blood-injury-injection phobia.* Her reaction was quite severe, thereby meeting the criteria for phobia, a psychological disorder characterized by marked and persistent fear of an object or situation. But many people with Judy's condition have similar reactions that are *not* as severe when they are about to receive an injection, or if they are confronted with the sight of someone who is injured, whether blood is present or not. Have you yourself ever felt queasy at the sight of blood? For people who experience a reaction as severe as Judy's, this phobia can be very disabling, often causing them to avoid certain careers such as medicine or nursing. In addition, if they are so fearful of needles and injections that they avoid them, they put their health and well-being at risk, since occasional injections are necessary for medical or dental reasons.

What Is Abnormal Behavior?

Having read about the real-life problems faced by Judy, let's now look more closely at the definition of *psychological disorder,* or abnormal behavior; to repeat, it is a psychological dysfunction associated with distress or impairment in functioning that is not a typical or culturally expected response. The criterion that the disorder or behavior be associated with "distress or impairment" seems clear—that would be the case if the individual with the disorder were extremely upset, or if the disorder were negatively affecting the person's ability to function. And the criterion that the response not be typical or culturally expected is clear as well: for example, after the death of a loved one a typical response would be grief. In some countries or subcultures, a culturally expected response from a sick person would be for him or her to experience a trance after seeing a traditional healer. Neither of these would be considered abnormal behavior. On the other hand, if you experience grief or go into a trance for no apparent reason, this behavior might meet one criterion for a psychological disorder. But what exactly is a "psycho-

logical disorder"? To understand it best, you should know how we have arrived at this definition. Over the years, many different criteria have been considered—among them statistics, distress, societal norms, impairment, and dysfunction—and we will look at each. Each has resulted in considerable debate, and each alone has been found wanting. As such, our current definition draws from many of the criteria.

At times, something has been considered abnormal because it occurred infrequently or rarely. This is a *statistical definition* of abnormality because it means, simply, that something deviates from the average. The more the deviation, the more abnormal it is. You might say that someone is abnormally short or abnormally tall, meaning that person deviates substantially from average height. But this obviously doesn't work very well as a definition of disorder. Many people are far from the average in their behavior, but few would consider that they have a disorder. Sometimes we call them talented or eccentric. Many artists, movie stars, and athletes might fall in this category. For example, it's not "normal" to masturbate in public; but Madonna does it on stage and is paid millions of dollars. The novelist J. D. Salinger, who wrote *Catcher in the Rye,* retreated to a small town in New Hampshire and refused to see any outsiders for years; but he continued writing. The singer Boy George dressed as a woman on stage. These individuals are not only well paid, but they generally seem to enjoy their careers. In most cases, the more productive you are in the eyes of society, the more eccentricities society will tolerate. Also, a condition could be "normal" because most people have it and still be a deviation—for example, dental cavities in our culture or parasites in some tropical cultures. In Judy's case, remember that many people feel queasy at the sight of blood, but this alone would not meet the criteria for a psychological disorder.

If simply being different from other people doesn't define abnormal behavior, what about distress or suffering? Could we create a definition of psychological disorder based on distress (a distress definition)? One could certainly say that Judy was very distressed and even suffered with her phobia. Would personal suffering or distress then be a definition for abnormality? The difficulty here is that there are many times when it is quite "normal" to be distressed. For example, if someone close to you dies, it would be normal to be very distressed. If you *never became* distressed in this circumstance, you might have what we call a *pathological grief reaction* and be referred for treatment if a number of other signs were also present. The human condition is such that suffering and distress are very much a part of life. This is not likely to change. Furthermore, there are some disorders where, by definition, suffering and distress are not present. Consider the person who feels extremely elated and

Some people deviate from the average on certain traits, such as height, but it does not mean they have a disorder.

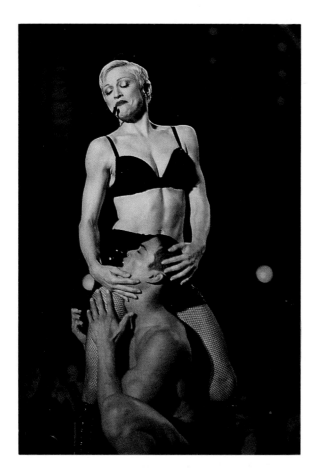

Artists and entertainers, such as Madonna, may behave in unusual ways that are tolerated and even encouraged by society.

may act impulsively—behaviors and feelings that may be part of a "manic" episode. One of the major difficulties with this problem, as we'll see in Chapter 7, is that these people enjoy the manic state so much that they are reluctant to begin treatment or stay in treatment very long. Thus, defining psychological disorder by distress doesn't seem to work, although the concept of "distress" may contribute to a good definition.

Some people have suggested that a behavior is abnormal if in doing it you are violating the norms that society sets up (*societal norms* definition), even if a number of people are sympathetic to your point of view. This definition of abnormal behavior is very useful in considering important cultural differences in psychological disorders. For example, entering a trance state and believing you are possessed would be a psychological disorder in most Western cultures but would not be a disorder in many third world societies where it is culturally accepted and expected. A cultural perspective will be an important point of reference throughout this book. But this societal norms definition can and has been misused, especially in dictatorships (Sedgwick, 1982; Ausabel, 1971). Before the fall of communism, the psychiatric profession in the Soviet Union was condemned by the World Psychiatric Association because some Soviet psychiatrists were committing to mental institutions individuals who disagreed politically with the Soviet communist system. If a prominent Soviet citizen believed that the rights of the individual were more important than the interests of the state as determined by the government, that citizen

Refusing to follow the social norms of the day is not a definition of a psychological disorder.

was judged to be psychologically impaired and eligible for commitment. Only recently has this practice changed and worldwide condemnation lifted. Nazi Germany is an example of a situation in which many individuals in a society embraced a societal norm that was meant to condemn an entire race; though many accepted it during those times, the brutal, sadistic behavior of the Nazi army and its sympathizers was hardly what one might call normal.

More recently, the concept of *impairment in functioning,* either at work, at home, or socially, has become one of the criteria for defining psychological disorder, as is the case in our definition. (*Maladaptive* is another word sometimes used to indicate impairment in functioning.) While not entirely satisfactory, the concept of impairment is useful. For example, many people consider themselves shy or lazy. This doesn't mean that they're abnormal. But if you are so "shy" that you find it impossible to go out on a date or even interact with people, and you make every attempt to avoid interactions even though you would like to make friends, then your social functioning is impaired. Or maybe you're so "lazy" that you can't accomplish even important tasks and, furthermore, you don't seem to have any interest in accomplishing anything even though you know it's important. Here again, some impairment is present. Most people suffering with this

type of impairment would readily agree to seek help if only they knew where. Judy was clearly impaired with her phobia, but many people with the same reaction, although less severe, are not impaired. This difference illustrates an important point. Most psychological disorders are simply extreme expressions or exaggerations of otherwise normal emotions, behaviors, and cognitive processes.

A related criterion is *dysfunction,* also part of our current definition (Wakefield, 1992). Psychological dysfunction refers to a breakdown in one's cognitive, emotional, or behavioral functioning. Thus, to be dysfunctional your reaction cannot simply be an expected or culturally sanctioned response to an event—for example, grief in response to the death of a close family member. In other words, if all your friends agreed that some person who asked you for a date was really dangerous for some reason, then it would not be "dysfunctional" for you to be fearful and avoid the date. In fact, your emotional reaction would be quite adaptive. On the other hand, if you wanted to go out on a date that should be fun but you were experiencing fear, your emotions would not be functioning properly. It is also important to note that dysfunction does *not* refer to deviant political behavior or to a conflict between the individual and society. But to experience only dysfunction is not enough to meet the criteria for a disorder. For example, you might have a "dysfunction" in one kidney, or perhaps donate one of your kidneys to a sister without affecting your well-being (Wakefield, 1992).

This, then, brings us back to our definition of abnormal behavior and psychological disorder. To have a disorder you must experience (psychological) dysfunction *and* severe distress or impairment. Also, your reactions would not normally be expected or culturally appropriate.

For those individuals displaying psychotic behavior—that is, who are hallucinating and totally out of touch with the reality around them, as is common in schizophrenia and some other severe disorders—a dysfunction in cognitive systems is present and society has set up guidelines (imperfect at best) to decide when the impairment is sufficiently severe to warrant intervention. Most people would readily agree that psychotic disorders are dysfunctional and associated with substantial impairment in functioning. For Judy, a dysfunction was also present, fainting at the sight of blood, and this dysfunction caused her significant distress and impairment. But the fact that many people experience a mild version of this reaction (queasiness at the sight of blood) and have some distress without meeting the criteria for disorder demonstrates that knowing where to draw the line between normal and abnormal is often difficult. For this reason, these problems are often considered as on a *continuum* or as a *dimension* rather than as categories that are either present or absent. We will return to this important issue when we discuss classification in Chapter 3. In any case, this book is not about mild problems or "glitches" in everyday life. Rather, it is about severe psychological disorders that would occur on the very end of a continuum from mild to severe.

To take the problem of defining abnormal behavior a step further, consider this: What if Judy passed out often but, after a while, neither her classmates nor her teachers were concerned or even noticed because she would regain consciousness rather quickly? Furthermore, what if Judy continued to get good grades? Would she still have a disorder because she faints all the time at the sight of blood? Would it be impairing? dysfunctional? distressing? What would you decide?

Finally, we might add that instances where patterns of sexual arousal differ from heterosexual ones have posed many problems to definitions of abnormality over the years. Homosexuality used to be right up there on the list of disorders. But the realization arose among those devising our systems of classification that this was not a psychological disorder in the usual sense, since one could function at a very high level and without distress. Homosexuality was then dropped from the classification system. The only way someone with homosexual arousal patterns could meet the criteria for a disorder would be for this pattern of arousal to be severely distressing to the individual. The implication of this description is that mental health professionals may well attempt to eliminate the distress rather than alter the homosexual arousal pattern itself, a strategy that is more usually adopted these days.

In conclusion, attempting to define what is normal and abnormal in the realm of behavior is fraught with pitfalls. But behavioral, emotional, or cognitive dysfunctions that are unexpected in their context and associated with personal distress or substantial impairment in functioning comes closest to a satisfactory definition. And this definition can be useful across cultures and subcultures if we pay very careful attention to what is "functional" or "dysfunctional" in a given culture. Jerome Wakefield (1992), in a very thoughtful analysis of the matter, ends up using the shorthand definition of "harmful dysfunction." It is a variant of this "harmful dysfunction" approach that is most often used in current diagnostic practice (as outlined in the fourth edition of the *Diagnostic and Statistical Manual* [DSM-IV] [American Psychiatric Association, 1994] which contains the current listing of criteria for psychological disorders). And it is this approach that will guide our thinking in this book.

A number of terms are often used as synonyms for *psychological disorder;* it is important that you be aware of them because you will no doubt come across

All of us experience distress and suffering at some time in our lives; but this does not work as a definition of a psychological disorder.

them in this and other writings on the subject. In addition to *abnormal behavior* and *abnormality,* the terms *mental disorder* and *mental illness* are roughly equivalent to the term *psychological disorder;* however, the term *mental illness* is less often used today because it implies a disease or medical origin for the problem that the more neutral term *mental disorder* does not. The term **insanity,** or insane, has also been used to refer to abnormal behavior; however, this term is really appropriate only when used in a legal sense to indicate the condition of an individual who is legally irresponsible or incompetent.

Understanding Psychological Disorders

Just as the definition of psychological disorder has evolved over the years, so too have the ways in which people have tried to understand it. Depending on the times, some of these efforts to understand psychological disorders might be considered rather unsophisticated, based largely on impression, superstition, and fads; others are more systematic, based more on careful, measured observation. The latter have grown more prevalent as scientific approaches have evolved, and it is from these that we have the most to gain in terms of understanding abnormality. **Psychopathology** refers to the field concerned with the scientific study of psychological disorders.

Within this field, one finds a number of specially trained professionals including clinical and counseling psychologists, psychiatrists, psychiatric social workers, and psychiatric nurses. **Clinical** and **counseling psychologists** receive the Ph.D. (or sometimes the Psy.D., doctor of psychology, or Ed.D., doctor of education) degree and follow a course of study, lasting approximately 5 years, that prepares them to carry on research into the causes and treatment of psychological disorders as well as to diagnose, assess, and treat these disorders utilizing psychosocial treatments. Clinical and counseling psychologists differ from psychologists with other specialty training, such as experimental psychologists or social psychologists, who concentrate on investigating the basic determinants of behavior but do not assess or treat psychological disorders. In addition, although there is a great deal of overlap, counseling psychologists tend to study and treat adjustment and vocational issues encountered by relatively healthy individuals. Clinical psychologists usually concentrate on more severe psychological disorders.

Psychiatrists first attend medical school earning an M.D. degree and then specialize in psychiatry during a 3- to 4-year period of residency training. Psychiatrists also investigate the nature and causes of psychological disorders, often from a biological point of view, and diagnose and treat psychological disorders. Many psychiatrists emphasize drugs or other biological treatments, although most utilize psychosocial treatments as well.

Psychiatric social workers typically earn a master's degree in social work where they develop expertise in collecting information relevant to the social and family situation of the individual with a psychological disorder. Social workers also treat psychological disorders, often concentrating on family problems associated with these disorders. **Psychiatric nurses** are nurses who may have advanced degrees such as a master's or even a Ph.D. degree and who specialize in the care and treatment of patients with psychological disorders, usually in hospitals as part of a treatment team.

The most important development in the recent history of the study of psychopathology has been the adoption of scientific methods to learn more about the nature of psychological disorders as well as their causes and treatment. As such, most of the mental health professionals described above would take a scientific approach to their clinical work and therefore earn the title **scientist-practitioner** (Barlow, Hayes, & Nelson, 1984). Mental health practitioners may function as scientist-practitioners in one of three ways. First, they may keep up with the latest scientific developments in their field and therefore use the most current diagnostic and treatment procedures in the course of their practice. In this sense they are consumers of the science of psychopathology to the advantage of their patients. Second, the scientist-practitioner evaluates his or her own assessment or treatment procedures to see if they work. In this way scientist-practitioners can be accountable not only to their patients but to the government agencies and insurance companies who are paying for the treatments in that they can demonstrate clearly that their treatments are working and doing some good. Third, the scientist-practitioner might actually conduct research, often in research clinics or hospitals, that produces new information on the nature of disorders and/or their treatment. In this way mental health professionals who are true scientist-practitioners become immune to fads and trends that plague our field, often at the expense of the well-being of patients and their families. For example, new "miracle cures" for psychological disorders that seem to pop up several times a year in newspapers or other sources would never be used by a scientist-practitioner unless he or she had sound scientific reasons to believe that these methods would help people suffering from psychological disorders.

Such sound scientific reasons would flow from research into psychological disorders. The study of psychological disorders basically falls into three categories: attempts to describe them, attempts to determine their causes, and attempts to treat them (see Figure 1.1). These three categories represent an organizational structure that you will see repeatedly throughout the book, one that will be formally evident in the specific disorder chapters, beginning with Chapter 5. But even before then, these categories are relevant, and a general overview of them here will give you a more immediate perspective on our efforts to understand abnormality.

Figure 1.1 Three major categories make up the study and discussion of psychological disorders.

Clinical Description

In hospitals and clinics we often say that a patient "presents" to a clinic with a specific problem or set of problems, or we discuss "the presenting problem." **Presents** is a traditional term used by clinicians that is a shorthand way of indicating the problem first noted as the reason for coming to the clinic. We have already described Judy's presenting problem. This represents the first step in determining Judy's **clinical description,** the unique combination of behaviors, thoughts, and feelings of an individual that make up a given psychological disorder. The word *clinical* simply refers to the types of problems or disorders that you would find in a clinic or hospital as well as activities connected with assessing and treating the disorder. Throughout this text you will read excerpts from many more individual cases, most of them from our own personal files.

What is important about the clinical description? Clearly, one important function is illustrating what makes the disorder different from normal behavior or from other disorders. In addition, statistical data can add to the clinical description. For example, how many people in the population as a whole have the disorder? This figure is called the **prevalence** of the disorder. Statistics on how many new cases occur during a given period of time, such as a year, represent the **incidence** of the disorder. Other statistics include the *sex ratio,* what percentage of people with the disorder are male and female, and the typical *age of onset,* which often differs from disorder to disorder.

In addition to "looking" different and having a different age of onset and possibly a different sex ratio and prevalence, most disorders follow a somewhat different pattern, or **course.** That is, some disorders such as schizophrenia (see Chapter 14) follow a *chronic course,* meaning that they tend to last a long time, sometimes one's whole life. Other disorders like mood disorders (see Chapter 7) follow an *episodic course* in that the individual tends to recover within a few months only to suffer a recurrence of the disorder at a later time. This pattern may repeat throughout one's life. Still other disorders may run a *time-limited course,* meaning the disorder will improve on its own in a relatively short period of time. Closely related to differences in the course of disorders are differences in onset. Some disorders have an *acute onset,* meaning that they begin suddenly; others seem to develop gradually over an extended period of time, sometimes called an *insidious onset.* It is important to know the typical course of a disorder so that we can know what to expect in the future and how best to deal with the problem the person is having. This is an important part of the clinical description. For example, if someone is suffering from a mild disorder with acute onset that we know is time

limited, we might advise the individual not to bother with treatment knowing that the problem will be over soon enough and there is no need to spend money on treatment. This would be analogous to someone's suffering from a common cold. On the other hand, if the disorder is likely to last a long time (become chronic), the individual with the problem would want to know so that he or she could seek treatment and take other appropriate steps. The future course of a disorder is called the **prognosis.** So we might say, "the prognosis is good," meaning the individual should recover or "the prognosis is guarded," meaning the probable outcome doesn't look good.

As part of the description, the patient's age may be very important. A specific psychological disorder occurring in childhood may present very differently from the same disorder in adulthood or old age. Children experiencing severe anxiety and panic often assume that they are physically ill because they have difficulty understanding that there is nothing physically wrong. They also lack some of the specific thoughts and feelings experienced by adults with anxiety and panic. For this reason, children are often treated for a medical disorder because they "look" different from adults with the psychological disorder even though they have basically the same disorder as adults.

Thus, in describing a psychological disorder it is important that we consider and describe the stage of life the individual is in. We call the study of changes in behavior over time *developmental psychology,* and we refer to the study of these changes in abnormal behavior as **developmental psychopathology.** When you think of developmental psychology, you probably picture researchers studying the behavior of children. However, because changes occur throughout our lifetime, researchers also study developmental changes in adolescents, adults, and older adults. This focus of study across the entire age span is referred to as *life-span developmental psychopathology.* The field is relatively new but is an area that is expanding rapidly.

Causal Factors

Another important facet of psychological disorders that we will examine very closely is the study of **etiology** or causation. Etiology refers to why a disorder begins (what causes it) and must include consideration of a number of factors or dimensions. These factors include biological dimensions, psychological dimensions, and social dimensions. Since the etiology of psychological disorders is such an important part of this book, we will devote an entire chapter (Chapter 2) to a description of how we study etiology.

Treatment and Outcomes

Finally, treatment often forms an important part of the study of psychological disorders. If we are successful in treating a disorder with a new drug or a new psychosocial treatment, it may give us some hints about the nature of the disorder and its causes. For example, if a drug with a specific known effect within the nervous system works for a certain psychological disorder, it would suggest to us that something about that function in the nervous system might either be causing the disorder or at least helping to maintain the disorder. Similarly, if a psychosocial treatment, designed to help clients regain a sense of control over their lives, is effective with a certain disorder, it might suggest that a diminished sense of control may be an important psychological component of the disorder being treated.

As we shall see in the next chapter, psychology is never that simple. Also, to assume that because a treatment works we should learn something about the cause of the disorder is something of a logical fallacy. This is because the *effect* does not necessarily imply the *cause*. To use a common example, you might take an aspirin to relieve a tension headache you developed during a grueling day of taking exams. But that does not mean that the tension headache was caused by a lack of aspirin in the first place. Nevertheless, many people seek treatment for their psychological disorders, and treatment can provide some interesting hints about the nature of the disorder.

In the past, textbooks such as this one have placed an emphasis on describing psychosocial treatment approaches in a very general sense with little attention to the disorder being treated. For example, mental health professionals might be thoroughly trained in a single theoretical approach such as psychoanalysis or behavior therapy (both described later in the chapter) and use these approaches irrespective of the disorder being treated. More recently, as our science has advanced, we have developed specific and effective psychosocial treatments for the various psychological disorders that do not always adhere neatly to one theoretical approach or another. These treatments have grown out of a deeper understanding of the psychological disorder in question. For this reason there are no *separate* chapters in this book on types of treatment approaches such as psychodynamic, cognitive behavioral, or humanistic. Rather, the latest and most effective treatments for specific disorders, both drug and psychosocial, will be described in the context of the chapters on the disorders to which they are applicable. Since outcome from treatment sometimes sheds light on the nature of the disorders, as noted above, information on treatments and their effectiveness will be woven into what we know about the description and causes of the disorder, in keeping with the integrative multidimensional perspective of this book.

We'll turn for the balance of this chapter to a survey of early attempts to understand abnormal behavior. Throughout that discussion, you will see many attempts to describe and treat abnormal behavior, and more still to comprehend its causes. Being familiar with the history of attempts to understand abnormal behavior will give you a better perspective on current approaches. In Chapter 2, we will examine some exciting contemporary ways to view causation and treatment; then in Chapter 3 we will discuss in some detail our current efforts to describe, or classify, abnormal behavior. In Chapter 4, we will review research methods, our systematic efforts to get at the truths underlying description, cause, and treatment that allow us to function as scientist-practitioners. From Chapters 5 through 16, we will examine the specific disorders themselves; our discussion will be organized in each case around the by-now familiar triad of description, cause, and treatment. Finally, in Chapter 17, we will examine legal, professional, and ethical issues relevant to psychological disorders and their treatment today. With that overview in mind, let us turn to the past.

The Past: Historical Conceptions of Abnormal Behavior

For thousands of years the human race has been preoccupied with explaining and controlling problematic behavior. But our efforts to understand and control this behavior always derive from prevailing theories or models of behavior that happen to be popular at the time. The purpose of these models is to answer the question "Why are they acting like that?" Three major models or theories have guided humankind over the years in the attempt to explain patterns of abnormal behavior. These models date back to the beginnings of civilization, but they were formalized by the intellectual founders of Western civilization, the ancient Greeks. The underpinnings or basic assumptions of these models are that the "mind" and the "body" are two separate entities. In ancient Greece and over the years, the "mind" was often called the "soul" or the "psyche." Although many, even in those times, thought that the mind could influence the body and, in turn, the body could influence the mind, most philosophers looked for causes of abnormal behavior in one entity or the other. This split gave rise to two traditions of thought or theorizing on the causes of abnormal behavior that can best be described as a **biological model** and a **psychological model.**

In addition, throughout all of our history and before our history began, the human race has supposed that agents outside of our bodies or social environment also influence our behavior, thinking, and emotions. These agents could be divinities, demons, spirits, or other phenomena such as magnetic fields or the influence of the moon or the stars. These "outside the body" influences most usually refer to divinities or demons and are the driving forces behind the **supernatural model.** These three models—the supernatural, the biological, and the psychological—were with us before history was recorded and continue to be with us today.

We will describe each of these models and the influence they have had throughout history on our conceptions of psychological disorders. We will begin with the supernatural model and then turn to the biological and psychological models.

Conflicting Tides of Opinions in the Middle Ages

For most of our recorded history, deviant behavior was considered an extension of the battleground between good and evil in the world. When confronted with unexplainable, irrational behavior, philosophies and techniques for dealing with evil were often the treatment of choice. When people were beset by sufferings and upheavals on all sides, and when the future of humanity looked particularly bleak, the perception of evil in the world grew. One of these periods began during the last 25 years of the 14th century and extended for several hundred years thereafter.

Barbara Tuchman, a noted historian of our time, has chronicled the latter half of the 14th century in her book *A Distant Mirror* (1978). She very ably captures the conflicting tides of opinion on the origins and treatment of insanity during that period. If the insane were royalty or nobility, firsthand accounts of their condition are often available. She notes the case of a well-known nephew of Queen Philippa of England who, although "tall, young, strong, dark and lively" was, in fact, a "raving maniac" who had to be confined in a castle with both hands and feet tied most of the time for a period of 30 years (p. 514). The necessity of restraining and confining strong, violent, or aggressive patients would continue into the middle of our own century, since few alternatives were available.

Most people suffering from psychological disorders, however, were not potentially dangerous. And what Tuchman documents is that, even during the worst of times in our history, many assumed that

Exorcisms were sometimes performed to rid "possessed" individuals of psychological disorders thought to be caused by evil spirits.

People with psychological disorders were sometimes treated with sympathy and kindness because their condition was thought to be caused by mental or emotional stress. Treatment consisted of providing a restful and healthy environment.

"madness" was due to natural causes and deserved humane treatment. This view reflected one strong current that, for most of this period, was the prevailing opinion. Many people held the enlightened view that insanity was caused by mental or emotional stress and that, as a natural phenomenon, it was curable (Alexander & Selesnick, 1966; Maher & Maher, 1985a). Mental depression and anxiety were recognized as illnesses (Schoeneman, 1977; Kemp, 1990), although the symptoms of depression, such as despair and lethargy, were often considered by the church to be the sin of acedia or sloth (Tuchman, 1978). The most common treatments were rest, sleep, and the provision of a healthy and happy environment. Other treatments included baths, ointments, and various potions. During the 14th and 15th centuries, the insane were often moved from house to house in medieval villages, along with others who were physically deformed or disabled, as neighbors took turns caring for them. We now know the advantage of this medieval practice of keeping people who have psychological disturbances in their own environment among family and friends (see Chapter 17). We will return to these views when we discuss biological and psychological models below.

An alternative and equally strong current of opinion, however, put the causes and treatment of psychological disorders squarely in the realm of the supernatural. Usually, evil demons were cited as the cause. Treatments included *exorcism,* the use of vari-

ous religious rituals to rid the victim of evil spirits, or, perhaps, shaving the pattern of a cross in the hair of the victim's head. Other approaches included securing sufferers to a wall near the front of a church so that they might benefit from hearing Mass.

Unexplainable phenomena have often been attributed to the supernatural, but it was during this 25-year period at the end of the 14th century that religious and lay authorities gave credence to these popular superstitions. Also during this time, society as a whole began to believe in the reality and power of demons and witches. The Catholic church had split in two and a second center, complete with a Pope (Pope Clement I), emerged in Avignon, in the south of France, to compete with Rome. In reaction to this schism, the Roman church fought back against the evil that must have been behind this heresy.

Also at this time society turned increasingly to magic and sorcery to solve their problems. The theological faculty at the University of Paris near the end of the century declared, from their position of authority, that "ancient errors and evils almost forgotten were emerging with a renewed vigor to infect society" (Tuchman, 1978, p. 319). They drew up a series of statements or articles establishing the authenticity and existence of the black arts and rejected very strongly any opinions that questioned the existence of witches. Therefore the church, having declared that witches exist, decided it was time to become more aggressive with them.

It followed naturally that during these turbulent times, bizarre behavior of people afflicted with psychological disorders was seen as the work of the devil and witches. It also followed that these individuals, possessed as they were by evil spirits, were probably responsible for any misfortune experienced by the townspeople. This linkage inspired drastic action against the possessed, including exorcisms and torture, that was to continue for centuries.

A more enlightened opinion existed among some thinkers, even during that black period. One of the chief advisers to the king of France, a bishop and philosopher named Nicholas Oresme, suggested that the source of some bizarre behavior, rather than being the demons increasingly blamed near the end of the 14th century, could be the disease of *melancholy* (depression). Oresme suggested that much of the evidence for the existence of sorcery and witchcraft, particularly among the insane, was obtained by confessions of people who were being tortured and who, quite understandably, would confess to anything.

The case of King Charles VI of France illustrates the conflict of opinions on the care of individuals with psychological disorders during the Middle Ages.

The Case of King Charles VI

The conflicting currents of this and subsequent centuries are reflected in the handling of the severe psychological disorder experienced by one of the central figures in the late 14th century, King Charles VI of France. In the summer of 1392, the king, who was under a great deal of stress and had been observed speaking in a disorganized manner, was on his way with his army to attack the Province of Brittany. A nearby aide dropped his lance with a loud clatter and the king, who was on horseback, suddenly thought he was under attack. Flailing wildly with his sword he proceeded to attack his own army, killing several prominent knights before being subdued from behind. The attack on Brittany was immediately called off, and the army marched back to Paris. The king's lieutenants and advisers concluded that he was mad.

During the years to follow, at his worst the King would hide in a corner of his castle believing he was made of glass or roam the corridors howling like a wolf. At other times he couldn't remember who or what he was. He became fearful and enraged whenever he saw his own royal coat of arms; he would try to destroy it if it were brought near him. Unfortunately, this fear and rage extended to his queen. If the queen came near him he would shout, "Who is that woman, the sight of whom torments me? Find out what she wants and free me from her demands if you can that she may follow me no more"

(Tuchman, 1978, p. 513). His sister-in-law, however, seemed to be able to calm him down, an effect that made some people in the castle think that she had bewitched him.

At one of the worst times in history, the people of Paris were devastated that their leader was apparently "mad." Speculating on the causes of his condition, some thought that it reflected God's anger at the king's failure to take up arms to end the schism in the Catholic church; others thought it was God's warning *against* taking up arms; still others thought it was divine punishment for heavy taxes (a conclusion some people might make today). But most believed the cause was sorcery. Contributing to this belief was a great drought that had dried up the ponds and rivers that summer, causing cattle to die of thirst. Merchants claimed their worst losses in 20 years.

Naturally the king was afforded the best of care available in France at that time. The most famous healer in the land was a 92-year-old physician who had traveled widely in the Arab lands studying illnesses and their treatment. According to his reputation, no illness was unknown to him. His treatment program for the king included moving him to one of his residences in the country where the air was thought to be the cleanest in the land. There the physician prescribed rest, relaxation, and recreation. After some time, the king seemed to recover. The physician recommended that the king not be burdened with the responsibilities of running the kingdom, claiming that, if he had few worries or irritations, gradually his mind would strengthen and further improve.

Unfortunately, the physician died and the insanity of King Charles VI returned more seriously than before. This time, however, he came under the influence of the conflicting crosscurrent of supernatural causation. "An unkempt evil-eyed charlatan and pseudo-mystic named Arnaut Guilhem was allowed to treat Charles on his claim of possessing a book given by God to Adam by means of which man could overcome all affliction resulting from original sin" (Tuchman, 1978, p. 514). Guilhem insisted that the king's malady was caused by sorcery, but his treatments failed to effect a cure.

A variety of remedies and rituals of all kinds were tried but none worked. High-ranking officials and doctors of the university called for the "sorcerers" to be discovered and punished. "On one occasion, two Augustinian friars, after getting no results from magic incantations and a liquid made from powdered pearls, proposed to cut incisions in the king's head." When this was not allowed by the king's council, the friars accused those who opposed their recommendation of sorcery (Tuchman, 1978, p. 514). Even the king himself, during his lucid moments, came to believe that the source of madness was evil and sorcery. "In the name of Jesus Christ" he cried weeping in his agony, "if there is any one of you who is an accomplice in this evil I suffer, I beg him to torture me no longer but let me die!" (Tuchman, 1978, p. 515).

The obsession with sorcery and witches as causes of madness and other evils in the world continued into the 15th century. Attribution to evil continued to be a popular explanation for unexplainable behavior even after the founding of our own country, as evidenced by the Salem witch trials.

These conflicting crosscurrents of natural and supernatural explanations for mental disorders have been represented more or less strongly in various historical works, depending on the sources consulted by historians. Some historians of psychopathology assumed that demonic influences were the predominant explanations of abnormal behavior during the Middle Ages (for example, Zilboorg & Henry, 1941). Others assumed that supernatural causes had little or no influence. As we see in the case of King Charles VI, both influences were strong, sometimes alternating within the same case over the course of the disorder.

What if Judy had lived during these turbulent times? It is quite possible that she would have been seen as possessed. With this "diagnosis," she might have been subjected to one of the prevailing treatments of the day, an exorcism. In this practice, through prayers and rituals, the unfortunate individual is to be freed of demonic possession. Some of you may remember the movie *The Exorcist,* in which a young girl, behaving very strangely, was screened for every possible mental and physical disorder before authorities reluctantly resorted to an exorcism.

In the Supernatural Realm

What are the consequences of seeking supernatural causes for psychological disorders? First, with a perceived connection between evil deeds and sin on the one hand and psychological disorders on the other, one logical conclusion was that the individual was largely responsible for his or her behavior. If so, then the disorder might well be a punishment for evil deeds. Does this sound familiar? One doesn't have to look beyond the acquired immune deficiency syndrome (AIDS) epidemic to see a very similar belief among some in our society in the 1990s. Specifically, since the human immunodeficiency virus (HIV) is most prevalent among practicing homosexuals, many people believe that this virus is the visitation of a divine punishment for abhorrent behavior. This view is slowly dissipating as the AIDS virus spreads to other "less sinful" segments of our population, but it still persists.

"Possession," however, is not always connected with sin. In contemporary times and also, occasionally, in medieval times, possession by evil spirits has been seen as involuntary. The possessed individual is held blameless. Furthermore, exorcisms at least have the virtue of being relatively painless. Most exorcisms involve the saying of a few prayers and other related rituals directed at the evil spirits. Interestingly, they sometimes work, as do other forms of faith healing for reasons we will explore in subsequent chapters. But what if exorcisms did not work? In the Middle Ages, our hopeless patients would often be in for something much worse. If evil spirits remained after exorcisms, some authorities thought that steps were necessary to make the body uninhabitable by evil spirits. Thus, many people were subjected to confinement, beatings, and other forms of torture (Kemp, 1990).

Somewhere along the way a creative "therapist" of this period decided that hanging people over the edge of a pit full of poisonous snakes might scare the evil spirits right out of their bodies (to say nothing of terrifying the people themselves). Strangely, this approach sometimes worked. That is, the most disturbed, oddly behaving individuals would suddenly come to their senses and experience a period of relief from their symptoms, if only temporarily. Naturally, this was reinforcing to the "therapist" and led to the placement of snake pits in many institutions of the

Établissement hydrothérapique de M. Émile Duval. — La salle des douches. (Voir le Courrier de l'Exposition.)

In the past, hydrotherapy—whereby individuals would be dunked in ice cold water or subjected to repeated showers and hosings—was used to "shock" the individual into coming to his or her senses.

day. It also led to a host of other approaches based on the hypothesized therapeutic element of "shock," such as dunkings in ice cold water. We will discuss modern-day shock treatments such as electroconvulsive therapy later in the chapter.

Mass Hysteria

Another fascinating phenomenon in the Middle Ages was the occurrence of *mass hysteria,* characterized by large-scale outbreaks of strange behavior. To this day these outbreaks puzzle historians and mental health practitioners. At that time, they lent support to the notion of possession. In Europe, whole groups of people were afflicted simultaneously by a compulsion to run out in the streets, dance, shout, rave, and jump around in patterns that would resemble a particularly wild disco late at night, but without the music. This became known by several names including *Saint Vitus's Dance,* or *Tarantism.*

The most interesting part of this phenomenon was that many people behaved in this strange way all at once. In an attempt to explain the inexplicable, several reasons were offered for this behavior. In addition to possession, one reasonable guess was reaction to insect bites. Another possibility is what we now might call "mass hysteria." Consider the following example.

One Case of Mass Hysteria

During a period of one week, numerous males began screaming for help and running to local clinics in a state of panic. They were shouting that they could feel their genitals retracting into their bodies. If their organs totally retracted, they firmly believed they would die, and they feared that this occurrence was imminent. Family and friends attempted to comfort them during these periods, affording them temporary relief. Nevertheless, these individuals went to enormous extremes to prevent their genitals from retracting. Among other strategies, they constructed various contraptions that they attached to their genitals to hold them in place. Anxiety over this event typically passed in a few hours. Recurrences also passed fairly quickly if help and support were available from family and friends. Occasionally, women in the same city also became panicky fearing that their nipples, breasts, or labia would retract.

This is not something out of the Middle Ages. This event occurred in 1967 in Singapore, among the large ethnic Chinese population (Ngui, 1969; Tan,

During episodes of mass hysteria, groups of individuals begin acting in an emotional and unusual manner.

1969). The name of this condition, still encountered occasionally, is *koro*. Individuals suffering from koro usually relate the onset of their condition to some sexual sin or misdemeanor occurring during their past—continuing the supernatural tradition as an explanation of psychological disorders.

Other examples of mass hysteria seem to exist today. Consider the following case.

A Second Case of Mass Hysteria

One Friday afternoon an alarm sounded over the public address system of a community hospital calling all physicians to the emergency room immediately. Arriving in a fleet of ambulances were 14 students and three teachers from a local school who reported dizziness, headache, nausea, and stomach pains. Some were vomiting. Most were hyperventilating as they entered the emergency room.

All the students and teachers came from four classrooms, two on each side of the hallway. The incident began when one student reported smelling something funny that seemed to be coming from a vent. That student, a 14-year-old girl, fell to the floor crying and complaining that her stomach hurt and her eyes were stinging. Soon many of the students and most of the teachers in the four adjoining classrooms, who could see and hear what was happening, experienced similar symptoms. Of 86 susceptible people (82 students and 4 teachers in the four classrooms), 21 patients (17 students and 4 teachers) experienced symptoms severe enough to be evaluated at the hospital. Inspections of the school building by public health authorities revealed no apparent cause for the reactions, and physical examinations by teams of physicians revealed no physical abnormalities. All patients were sent home and quickly recovered (Rockney & Lemke, 1992).

Occasionally mass hysterical reactions are considered to be examples of possession. Mass hysteria may simply be another demonstration or manifestation of the phenomenon of *emotion contagion,* in which the experience of an emotion seems to spread to those

LA PANIQUE

Emotions are contagious; an emotion such as fear can spread quickly.

around us (Hatfield, Cacioppo, & Rapson, 1993). If someone around you becomes very frightened or very sad, chances are, for the moment, you will also feel emotions of fear or sadness. When this experience escalates into full-blown panic, whole communities can be affected (Barlow, 1988). People are also very suggestible when they are in states of high emotion. Therefore, if one person identifies a "cause" of the problem, others will probably believe readily that their reactions have the same "cause." In popular language, this shared response is sometimes referred to as "mob psychology."

The Moon and the Stars

The need to explain the unexplainable and mysterious was not restricted to possession in the Middle Ages. Another hypothesis explaining psychological disorders became widely popular in the 16th century. Paracelsus, a Swiss physician who lived from 1490 to 1541, rejected notions of possession by the devil, suggesting instead that the movements of the moon and stars had profound effects on people's psychological functioning. This influential theorizing led to the word *lunatic,* which is derived from the Latin word for moon, *luna.* Today you might still hear some of your friends explain something crazy they did last night by saying, "It must have been the full moon."

Somewhat later, Anton Mesmer (1734–1815) put his faith in the planets as the major determinant of human behavior and emotion, perhaps reflecting the greater knowledge of the solar system at that time. Specifically, he hypothesized that the planets interacted with a personal "magnetism" present in our bodily fluids. Though Mesmer is also widely regarded as the father of hypnosis, many of his practices were considered as outrageous then as they would be now. Eventually he was banished from the city of Paris, where most of his work took place. The controversy was aroused by his practice of bringing patients into a dark room and seating them around a large vat of chemicals. Rods extending from the vat touched the bodies of the patients. Many of these patients suffered from "hysteria," which referred almost exclusively to physical difficulties such as paralysis of the arms or legs or other illness without any organic basis (see Chapter 6). Mesmer would enter the room in flowing, colorful robes with a wand in his hand and pronounce the patients "cured." Often, many of them *were* cured, leading to great interest in "mesmerism" (Boring, 1950).

The belief of Mesmer and Paracelsus that heavenly bodies affected human behavior is by no means obsolete. Despite many jokes, millions of people around the world are convinced that their behavior is influenced by the stages of the moon or the position of the stars. This belief is most noticeable today in the practice of astrology, whose adherents hold that your behavior and major events in your life can be predicted by your day-to-day relationship to the position of the stars. However, no serious evidence has ever emerged confirming this connection.

Early therapists such as Mesmer attempted to cure their patients through strong suggestions, often while the patients were in a hypnotic state.

Concluding Comments

What remains of the supernatural tradition in psychopathology? It is alive and well, although this belief is relegated, for the most part, to small religious sects in this country or to more primitive cultures around the world. Organized religions in most parts of the world would look to psychological and medical science for answers to the major psychological disorders. In fact, the Catholic church requires that all health care avenues be exhausted before "spiritual" solutions such as exorcism can be considered. Nonetheless, miraculous cures sometimes occur with exorcism, "magic" potions and rituals, or other approaches that seem to have little connection with modern scientific treatment. It is fascinating to explore the reasons for these "cures" when they do occur, and we will return to this topic in subsequent chapters. But these cases are relatively rare, and almost no one would advocate these approaches as the treatment of choice for severe psychological disorders except, perhaps, as a last resort.

Biological Traditions

To examine a second approach to treating mental disorders, we look back approximately 100 years to the turn of the century. At this point in our history, what would have become of individuals and their emotional and behavioral problems? Fortunately for most of them, their behavior would no longer have been attributed to the influence of supernatural forces. This was the age that brought discovery of the cause of syphilis and a new emphasis on brain pathology. This one discovery of the cause of syphilis helped turn conceptions of psychopathology 180 degrees. In the unending search for causation, emphasis was shifted from external supernatural forces to internal malfunctioning of the brain. In this age, Judy might have been diagnosed as having an illness or brain disorder or some other physically based problem. Judy's problem, along with other psychological disorders, would require the proper medical treatment of the day including bed rest, a healthy diet, exercise, and other medical ministrations as indicated.

Seeking physical causes of mental disorders can be traced to the early biological traditions. Important among them were a man, Hippocrates; a disease, syphilis; and the early consequences of considering psychological disorders as biologically caused.

Hippocrates

Four hundred years before Christ, the father of modern medicine, Hippocrates (460–377 B.C.), and his associates suggested that psychological disorders could be treated much as any other disease. Our knowledge of Greek medicine in these times comes from a body of work called the *Hippocratic Corpus* written between 450 and 350 B.C. (Maher & Maher, 1985a). Hippocrates himself did not actually write all of this work, although he seems to have been the leader of the group who did. Practicing in ancient Greece, Hippocrates and his associates did not limit their notion of the causes of psychopathology to the general concept of "disease." They also believed that psychological disorders might be caused by brain pathology or head trauma and would be influenced by heredity (genetics). These are remarkably astute deductions for the time; and many have been proven true within the last century or two. Hippocrates considered the brain to be the seat of wisdom, consciousness, intelligence, and emotion. Therefore, disorders involving these functions would logically be located in the brain.

Of course, modern biological treatments such as sophisticated drugs were not available at that time; but for disorders such as melancholia (depression), one of Hippocrates' three major categories of mental disorder (the others being mania and phrenitis, or brain fever), he would prescribe rest, proper nutrition, and exercise as well as sobriety. The basic assumption underlying this approach, which holds true today, is that if you take good care of your body, your "mind" has a better chance of healing itself. The recently discovered scientific basis for the positive effects of stress-reducing interventions will be reviewed in Chapter 9. Some of the specific treatments mentioned by Hippocrates would be quite useful today also. For example, exercise, which he advocated, has been shown to be effective for patients having difficulty breaking out of a major depressive episode (see Chapter 7). While retaining his biological views of causation, Hippocrates also recognized the importance of psychological and interpersonal contributions to psychopathology, such as the sometimes negative effects of family stress; on some occasions he removed patients from their families.

In Rome, the physician Galen (129–198 A.D.) adopted the ideas of Hippocrates and his associates and developed them further into a powerful and influential school of thought within the biological tradition. The Hippocratic-Galenic tradition extended well into the 19th century. One of the more interesting and influential legacies of this approach was the *humoral theory* of mental (and physical) disorders. Hippocrates assumed that normal brain functioning was related to four bodily fluids or *humors*. These humors were blood, black bile, yellow bile, and phlegm. Each humor emanated from a different organ in the body. Blood came from the heart, black bile (also called *melancholer*) from the spleen, phlegm from the brain, and choler or yellow bile from the liver. These four humors, in turn, were related to the Greeks' conception of the four basic qualities: heat, dryness, moisture, and cold. Each of the humors was associated with one of these four qualities. Excesses in one or more of the humors could be treated by regulating the environment to increase or decrease heat, dryness, moisture, and cold depending on the humor that was out of balance. Attempting to restore the balance in the humors is one reason his physician moved King Charles VI to the less stressful countryside (Kemp, 1990). Physicians believed that too much or too little of one of the humors would result in disease. Too much black bile might be the cause of melancholia (depression). In fact, the term *melancholer,* which means black bile, is still used today in its derivative form *melancholy* to refer to some aspects of depression. This was, perhaps, the first example of theorizing that psychological disorders are caused by a *chemical imbalance,* a concept that is current today and reappears throughout this book.

Terms derived from these four humors are also common today to describe personality traits. For example, *sanguine,* which refers to an excess of the humor blood, describes someone who is cheerful and hopeful. *Melancholic,* of course, means depressed. *Phlegmatic* refers to traits of apathy and sluggishness but can also mean being calm and composed under stress. If you are *choleric* you are hot tempered and easily angered or irritated. In addition to depression, which was thought to result from black bile flooding the brain, other disorders, such as insomnia or delirious states, were thought to be caused by excessive blood in the brain (Maher & Maher, 1985a).

Treatments were derived explicitly from these theories. In addition to rest, good nutrition, and exercise, two treatments were developed that directly affected the balance of humors in the body. One treatment referred to as bleeding or bloodletting removed a carefully measured amount of blood from the body, often by the use of leeches. A second, commonsensical approach to altering humors within the body was to induce vomiting. A variety of substances to induce vomiting, called *emetics,* were recommended. In a well-known treatise on depression published in 1621, called *Anatomy of Melancholy,* Burton recommended, among other substances, tobacco and a half-boiled cabbage to induce vomiting (Burton, 1621/1977).

Hippocrates also coined the term *hysteria,* which, it turns out, was one of his less-distinguished contributions to psychopathology, although he learned about this concept from the Egyptians. They had identified a group of disorders, now called *somatoform disorders;* individuals experiencing these have physical symptoms that appear to be the result of some organic pathology but for which no organic cause can be found, such as paralysis or some kinds of blindness. Since these disorders were found predominantly in women, the Egyptians (and Hippocrates) wrongly assumed that they were *restricted* to women. Furthermore, they also suggested a cause. The assumption was that the woman's uterus, if not in use at the time, would wander

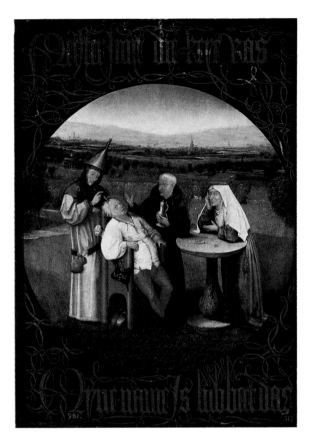

Removing blood from patients, or bloodletting, was an early treatment meant to restore the balance of humors in the body.

to various parts of the body in a futile search for conception (in Greek, the word *hysterian* means uterus). Depending on where in the body the uterus wandered, it would cause numerous physical symptoms. The prescribed cure was sometimes marriage or occasionally fumigation of the vagina in hopes of luring the uterus back to its natural position (Alexander & Selesnick, 1966). In just a few centuries, knowledge of physiology disproved the roaming uterus theory, but, interestingly, the tendency to stigmatize women who tend to be dramatic and attention seeking as "hysterical" continued unabated well into the 1970s. At this time, mental health professionals became sensitive to the prejudicial stereotype this term implied. As you will see in Chapter 6 these disorders (and the personality traits associated with them) are not limited to one sex or the other.

The Discovery of Syphilis

The biological tradition waxed and waned in the ensuing centuries after Hippocrates and Galen, but was reinvigorated in the 19th century by the discovery of the nature and cause of syphilis, a sexually transmitted disease caused by a bacterial microorganism entering the brain. Behavioral and cognitive symptoms of what we now know as an advanced case of syphilis include beliefs that everyone is plotting against you (delusion of persecution) or that you are God (delusion of grandeur) as well as other bizarre behavior. These symptoms are very similar to the hallucinations and lack of touch with reality characteristic of *psychotic behavior.* However, researchers recognized that a subgroup of patients with these apparently psychotic symptoms deteriorated steadily, becoming paralyzed and dying within 5 years. This course of events was in contrast to most psychotic patients, who remained fairly stable. In 1825 this condition was designated a disease because of the consistent symptoms (presentation) and the consistent course resulting in death. The disease was called *general paresis,* although the connection with syphilis was not yet known. Gradually, through the century, the relationship between general paresis and syphilis was established. Also discovered was the specific bacterial microorganism infecting the brain that caused syphilis. The presentation by the famous French physiologist, Louis Pasteur, of the germ theory of disease around 1870 facilitated this conceptualization and discovery. His theory stated that all of the symptoms of a specific disease were caused by a germ (bacterium) that had invaded the body.

More important, a cure for general paresis was discovered. After physicians observed a surprising recovery in patients with general paresis who had contracted malaria, a number of these patients were deliberately injected with the blood of a soldier who was ill with malaria. Many of them recovered because of the effects of the high fever, which "burned out" the syphilis bacteria. Obviously, this type of experiment would not be possible today for ethical reasons. Ultimately, clinical investigators discovered penicillin as a treatment for syphilis; but with the malaria cure, "madness" and associated behavioral and cognitive signs for the first time were traced directly to an infection that could be cured. Many mental health professionals of the time then assumed that a similar cause and cure might be discovered for all psychological disorders.

The Biological Tradition in the 19th Century

The biological tradition flourished in the Western world in the 19th century. Its champion in America was also the most influential American psychiatrist during the middle of the 19th century, Dr. John P. Grey (Bockoven, 1963). Beginning in 1854 Dr. Grey was appointed superintendent of the largest state hospital for the insane in America—the Utica State Hospital in New York. He also became editor of the *American Journal of Insanity,* which was the precursor of the current *American Journal of Psychiatry,* the flagship journal of the American Psychiatric Association. Grey's position was

that insanity was *always* due to physical causes. Therefore the mental hospital should be a place where the mentally ill patient was treated as physically ill. This treatment included, once again, emphasis on rest, diet, and proper room temperature and ventilation—approaches used in previous centuries by therapists in the biological tradition. Grey even invented the rotary fan in order to ventilate his large hospital.

Under Grey's leadership the conditions of hospitals greatly improved. In combination with other reformers, Grey helped hospitals move toward becoming humane and livable institutions, but they also became large impersonal institutions where individual attention was not possible. In fact, leaders in psychiatry at the end of the last century were alarmed at the increasing size and impersonal nature of mental hospitals and recommended that they be downsized so that patients could be treated more individually. It was to be almost 100 years more before the community mental health movement achieved any success in reducing the population of mental hospitals, with the very controversial policy of "deinstitutionalization," in which patients were released from hospitals and institutions into communities. Unfortunately, this policy has resulted in as many negative consequences as positive ones. One negative consequence is the large increase in the number of chronically disabled patients homeless on the streets of our major cities.

The Development of Biological Treatments

On the positive side, the resurgence of interest in biological causation of psychological disorders was to lead, ultimately, to a greatly increased understanding of biological contributions to psychopathology. It also led to the development of new treatments. In the 1930s physical interventions based on shock or brain surgery began to be used more frequently. The effects of most of these interventions, along with new drugs, were discovered quite by accident. For example, insulin was occasionally given to increase the appetite of psychotic patients who were not eating, but clinicians observed that insulin also seemed to calm them down. In 1927 a Viennese physician, Manfred Sakel, began using higher and higher dosages until, finally, patients convulsed and became comatose (Sakel, 1958). Some of those who convulsed actually recovered, much to the surprise of everybody, and their recovery was attributed to the convulsions. Administering insulin to the point of convulsion became known as *insulin shock therapy,* but it was abandoned because it was too dangerous. Other methods of producing convulsions had to be found.

In the 1920s, Joseph von Meduna had observed that schizophrenia was very rarely found in epileptics (an observation that ultimately did not prove to be true), and some of his followers concluded that inducing brain seizures might cure schizophrenia. Following earlier suggestions on the possible benefits of applying electric shock directly to the brain—notably, by two Italian physicians, Cerlette and Bini—a surgeon in 18th century London treated a depressed patient by administering six small shocks directly through his brain, producing convulsions (Hunt, 1980). The patient recovered. Though greatly changed, the use of shock treatment is still with us today, much to the distress of many who disagree with its use. In Chapter 7 the controversial modern uses of *electroconvulsive therapy* (ECT) are described. But it is interesting to note that even now we have very little knowledge of how ECT works.

A more important treatment in the biological tradition emerged in the 1950s. At that time, the first effective drugs for severe psychotic disorders were developed in a systematic way. Prior to that time a number of medicinal substances such as opium (the syrup of poppies) had been used as sedatives along with countless herbs and folk medicines (Alexander & Selesnick, 1966). But the discovery of *rauwolfia serpentina* and, later, another class of drugs called *neuroleptics* (or *major tranquilizers*) proved useful for the first time in diminishing hallucinatory and delusional thought processes of psychotic patients as well as controlling their agitation and aggressiveness. Neuroleptics are antipsychotic drugs that also produce some neurological symptoms such as tremors and shaking as side effects.

The accidental discovery of rauwolfia serpentina illustrates the most common way that new pharmacological agents are discovered. Rauwolfia is derived from the snakeroot plant. This plant, found in tropical areas of the Orient, has roots that zigzag along the ground like snakes (hence the name *serpentina*) and was used as an antidote for snake bite. It had also been used in those areas of the world for centuries as a treatment for insanity and thus became known as the "insanity herb." In the 1930s the Western world discovered that the drug derived from this plant could lower a person's blood pressure and reduce agitation. Soon, rauwolfia, renamed *reserpine*, was tried on agitated psychotic patients; it controlled their agitation and aggressiveness to some extent and became one of the miracle drugs of the 1950s. In the 1950s still other classes of drugs were discovered and introduced, such as *benzodiazepines* (or *minor tranquilizers*), drugs that seemed to reduce anxiety. By the 1970s, the benzodiazepines (known by such brand names as Valium and Librium) were among the most widely prescribed drugs in the world. As drawbacks and side effects of these drugs were discovered, along with their limited effectiveness, prescriptions decreased somewhat (we'll discuss the benzodiazepines again in Chapters 5 and 12).

Throughout the centuries, the use of new drugs to treat psychological disorders has followed a similar pattern. As Alexander and Selesnick (1966) point out, "The general pattern of drug therapy for mental illness has been one of initial enthusiasm followed by disappointment" (p. 287). As an illustration, bromides, a class of sedating drugs, were used at the end of the 19th and the beginning of the 20th century to treat anxiety or other psychological disorders. By the 1920s they were reported as being effective for many serious psychological and emotional symptoms. By 1928, one of every five prescriptions in the United States was for bromides. Then, their side effects, including various undesirable physical symptoms, became more widely known, and experience began to show that their overall effectiveness was relatively modest. Disillusionment set in, and these drugs largely disappeared from the scene.

The use of neuroleptics has also decreased somewhat as more attention has been focused on the many problems associated with this class of drugs and their descendants. However, the positive effects of these drugs on some patients' psychotic symptoms such as hallucinations, delusions, and agitation revitalized the search for biological contributions to psychological disorders as well as a search for new and more powerful drugs.

Consequences of the Biological Tradition

In the last two decades, a much deeper knowledge of the biochemistry of the brain has led to the development of many new and useful drugs. Many of these new drugs will be discussed in subsequent chapters. However, in the 19th century, the ideas of John P. Grey and his colleagues, ironically, reduced or eliminated interest in treating mental patients. They thought that mental disorders were due to some as yet undiscovered brain pathology and were therefore incurable. Thus, it was a waste of time to bother with treatment. The only available course of action was to hospitalize these patients. In fact, there are examples around the turn of the century of nurses who had documented clinical success in treating mental patients but were prevented from treating others for fear of raising hopes among their family members that the patients could be cured. In place of treatment, interest in diagnosis, legal questions concerning responsibility of the patient for his or her acts during periods of insanity, and the study of brain pathology itself predominated.

The dominant figure in this tradition at the turn of the century and one of the founding fathers of modern psychiatry was Emil Kraepelin (1856–1926). Kraepelin was also extremely influential in advocating the major ideas of the biological tradition but was little involved in treatment. He made his lasting contribution in the area of diagnosis and classification (see Chapter 3). Kraepelin (1913) was one of the first to see psychological disorders as distinct from one another with each having, perhaps, a different age of onset, running a different time course, presenting with somewhat different clusters of symptoms, and probably having a different cause. Many of his descriptions of schizophrenic disorders are still useful today.

By the end of the 1800s, the beginning of a scientific approach to psychological disorders and their classification had been established with the search for biological underpinnings. Furthermore, treatment was based on humane principles. But there were many drawbacks, the most unfortunate being that active intervention and treatment were all but eliminated in some settings. Lack of treatment would not have been a problem if no effective methods had existed, but there were some very effective treatment approaches in the last century. It is to these that we now turn.

Psychological Traditions

It is a large leap from evil spirits to brain pathology as causes of psychological disorders. In the intervening decades, where were psychological approaches? Where was the body of thought that put psychological development, both normal and abnormal, in an interpersonal and social context? In fact, this approach has had a long and distinguished tradition dating back to ancient Greece and beyond. Plato, for example, thought that the two causes of maladaptive behavior were the nature of the social and cultural influences in one's life and the learning that took place in that environment. If something was wrong with the environment, such as abusive parents, this faulty upbringing would cause one's impulses and emotions to overcome reason. The best treatment was to reeducate the individual through rational discussion so that the power of reason would overcome the powers of impulse and emotion (Maher & Maher, 1985a). This approach was very much a precursor to modern day **psychosocial treatment,** which has as its focus not only psychological factors but social and cultural ones as well. Other well-known early philosophers, such as Aristotle, also emphasized the influence of the social environment and early learning on later psychopathology. These philosophers wrote about the importance of fantasies, dreams, and cognitions, thus anticipating, to some extent, later developments in psychoanalytic thought and cognitive science. These leaders also advocated humane and responsible care for the psychologically disturbed.

The Rise of Moral Therapy

As we have seen, psychosocial approaches were rarely evident during the Middle Ages (with some exceptions). Not until the first half of the 18th century did a strong psychosocial approach to mental disorders predominate. This approach was called **moral therapy.** The basic tenets of moral therapy included treating patients as normally as possible in a setting that encouraged and reinforced normal social interaction (Bockoven, 1963). Thus, emphasis was placed on providing them with many opportunities for appropriate social and interpersonal contact. Relationships were carefully nurtured. Individual attention was readily available with a clear emphasis on positive consequences for appropriate interactions and behavior. The staff would make a point of modeling this behavior. A regular series of lectures on various interesting subjects was also provided for the patients. Restraint or seclusion was eliminated.

Once again, there is little that is new under the sun. Moral therapy has roots deep in our history and traditions, dating back to Plato and beyond. As far back as the 12th century, the Jewish philosopher Maimonides stated:

> One who suffers from melancholia may rid himself of it by listening to singing and all kinds of instrumental music, by strolling through beautiful gardens and splendid buildings, by gazing upon beautiful pictures and other things that enliven the mind and dissipate gloomy moods. (Kemp, 1990, p. 123)

But moral therapy itself can be said to have originated with the well-known French psychiatrist, Philippe Pinel (1745–1826) (Zilboorg & Henry, 1941). Pinel's early experience with the introduction of a humane, socially facilitative atmosphere in institutions produced the same types of "miraculous" results described above. But it wasn't actually Pinel's idea. A former patient, long since recovered, was working in the Parisian hospital, La Bicêtre, when Pinel took over. This former patient, Pussin, had already instituted the remarkable reforms, remembering, perhaps, what it was like when he was shackled as a patient. Pussin persuaded Pinel to go along with the changes. Much to Pinel's credit, he did, first at La Bicêtre and then at the women's hospital Salpétrière (Weiner, 1979; Maher & Maher, 1985b).

After William Tuke (1732–1822) followed Pinel's lead in England, Benjamin Rush (1745–1813), often considered the founder of American psychiatry, introduced moral, or "psychological," therapy to America with his early work at the Pennsylvania Hospital. Moral therapy then became the treatment of choice in the leading hospitals, such as the Boston State Hospital (currently the Massachusetts Mental Health Center), the Hartford Retreat (currently the Institute for Living in Hartford, Connecticut), the Worcester State Hospital, and the Pennsylvania Hospital in Philadelphia.

In these early years, the term *moral* really meant *emotional* or *psychological* rather than referring

Philippe Pinel (1745–1826) was one of the pioneers in making mental institutions more humane, in part by removing chains and shackles from individuals with severe psychological disorders.

to some authorized code of conduct. Moral therapy produced seemingly extraordinary results, even for those patients who had to be placed in institutions. A direct examination of old records revealed that as many as 75% of all patients with disorders lasting a year or less were discharged, seemingly cured, from institutions practicing moral therapy.

Moral therapy was also associated with remarkable reform within the institutions housing the mentally ill. Special institutions for these populations called *asylums* began appearing in the 16th century. More often these institutions were referred to as *mad-houses*. One of the earliest such asylums was Saint Mary's of Bethlehem in London established in 1547, a name that was soon contracted to the abbreviated form "Bedlam." Even today you will hear the phrase "that place was bedlam" referring to some situation where there was a great deal of noise or confusion. These early institutions were more like prisons than hospitals. It was the rise of moral therapy in Europe and the United States that made institutions habitable and even thera-peutic. The noted author Charles Dickens, who visited Boston State Hospital in 1842, was quite impressed with moral therapy. He observed a wide variety of activities available to patients, including carriage rides in the open air, fishing, gardening, and several kinds of indoor-outdoor games. He was quite amazed that

patients were routinely given sharp objects such as tools for gardening as well as knives and forks for dinner. In most institutions, even today, these objects would be removed for fear that patients would hurt themselves or others.

Dr. John S. Butler, for whom Butler Hospital in Providence, Rhode Island, is named, was the superin-tendent of several major hospitals in New England between 1839 and 1872. Dr. Butler routinely examined, in great detail, the family and personal history of his patients in order to determine possible early influences that might have led to later psychopathology. Butler (1887) provides an example of the early use of selective positive reinforcement, a procedure we will describe in some detail in subsequent chapters. If a woman tore her dress, rather than ordering restraint or seclusion, he would ignore her destructive behavior and provide her with a new dress that was particularly bright and pretty. As soon as she had the dress on, Butler would personally compliment her on her improved appear-ance and note how pleased he was to have her in his presence looking so well. Coming from an authority figure, this individual attention, delivered consistently and humanely, was quite effective in motivating the patient not to tear her dress again. Such approaches are used liberally in the psychosocial treatment and reha-bilitation of schizophrenic and psychotic patients as

Dorothea Dix (1802–1887) spent much of her life campaigning for reform in the treatment of the insane; she also began the mental hygiene movement.

well as with individuals with severe behavior disorders associated with mental retardation and developmental disabilities.

In 1933, the well-known public figure Horace Mann, who was also the chairman of the board of trustees of the Worcester State Hospital, reported on 32 patients who had essentially been given up as incurable. These patients were successfully treated with moral therapy, cured, and released to their families. He also noted that, of 100 patients who were viciously assaultive before treatment, no more than 12 continued to be assaultive within a year after beginning treatment. Forty patients had routinely torn off any new clothes provided by attendants; only eight continued this behavior after a period of treatment. These were remarkable statistics then, and would be remarkable even today (Bockoven, 1963).

Reform in the Asylums and the Decline of Moral Therapy

Unfortunately, by the middle of the 19th century, these humane approaches were beginning to disappear because of a convergence of factors. First, it was widely recognized that moral therapy worked best when the number of patients in an institution was 200 or fewer, allowing for a great deal of individual attention. After the Civil War, enormous waves of immi-

grants arrived in the United States, yielding their own populations of mentally ill. Patient loads in existing hospitals increased to 1,000, 2,000, or more. Since these immigrant groups were not thought to deserve the same privileges as "native" Americans (who had immigrated 50 or 100 years earlier), they were not afforded moral treatments, even if sufficient numbers of hospital personnel existed.

Ironically, a second reason for the decline of moral therapy comes from an unlikely source. In the middle of the century, the great crusader Dorothea Dix (1802–1887) campaigned endlessly for reform in the treatment of the insane. A school teacher who had worked in various institutions, she had firsthand knowledge of the deplorable conditions imposed on the insane. She made it her life work to inform the American public and their leaders of these abuses so that the care of individuals with psychological disorders could be greatly improved. Her work became known as the **mental hygiene movement.**

In addition to improving the standards of care in these institutions, she also observed the large number of mentally disturbed individuals living on the streets of our towns and cities, barely surviving. A good part of her crusade was to make sure that all individuals in need of care received it, including the homeless. Through her efforts, humane care became more widely available in American institutions. As her career drew to a close, she was rightly acknowledged as one of the heroes of the 19th century by the American people.

Unfortunately, one of the unforeseen consequences of Dorothea Dix's heroic efforts was an additional and substantial increase in the populations of institutions. This influx led to a rapid transition from moral therapy to custodial care because of inadequate numbers of hospital staff. Dorothea Dix reformed our asylums and single-handedly spearheaded the construction of numerous new institutions in this country and abroad. However, even she, with her tireless efforts and advocacy, could not ensure sufficient staffing of these new hospitals to allow the continuation of the individual attention necessary for the administration of moral therapy. A final reason for the demise of moral therapy was the decision by the new leaders in American psychiatry and others around the world, in the middle of the 19th century, that mental illness was caused by brain pathology and, therefore, was incurable.

Psychosocial Approaches in the 20th Century

The psychological tradition lay dormant for a time, only to reemerge in several very different forms or models in the 20th century. Among many schools of thought, two major approaches dominated the century.

The first approach was **psychoanalysis,** originated by Sigmund Freud (1856–1939), with its elaborate theory on the structure of the mind and the role of unconscious processes in determining abnormal behavior. The second was the **behavioral model,** associated with John B. Watson, Ivan Pavlov, and B. F. Skinner. This model focused on the role of learning and adaptation in the development of psychopathology. We will review briefly the roots and nature of these models, keeping in mind that each of these approaches, along with views on the biological causation of psychopathology reviewed above, is limited if viewed alone, without consideration of the multifaceted nature of psychopathology. But each of these models makes contributions that have become integral to our knowledge of psychopathology. Therefore, it is important to understand the foundation of each approach.

Psychoanalytic Theory

Have you ever felt as if someone placed a spell on you? Have you ever been mesmerized by a look across the classroom from a beautiful woman or man, or a stare from a rock musician as you sat down in front at a large concert? If so, you have something in common with the patients of Anton Mesmer (1734–1815) and with millions of people since that time who have been hypnotized.

Mesmer was considered an oddity and maybe a charlatan, but other distinguished scientists and physicians became very interested in his powerful methods of suggestion. One of the best known was Jean Charcot (1825–1893), head of the Salpêtrière Hospital in Paris, the same hospital where Philippe Pinel had introduced psychological treatments several generations earlier. As a distinguished neurologist, Charcot demonstrated the power of some of the techniques of mesmerism with a number of psychological disorders and did much to legitimize the fledgling study of hypnosis. Significantly, in 1885 a young man whose name was Sigmund Freud came to study with Charcot.

After returning to Vienna from France, Freud teamed up with Joseph Breuer (1842–1925), who had experimented with a somewhat different hypnotic procedure. While his patients were in the highly suggestible state of hypnosis, Breuer asked them to discuss their problems, conflicts, and fears in as much detail as they could. Breuer observed two extremely important phenomena during this process. First, patients often would become extremely emotional as they talked about their problems and conflicts and would feel quite relieved and improved after emerging from their hypnotic state. Second, seldom would they have "insight" or understanding of the relationship between their emotion-laden problems and their psychological disorder. In fact, it was difficult or impossible for them to recall some of the details of the problems they had discussed under hypnosis. In other words, the material seemed to be beyond the awareness of the patient, referred to as being in the **unconscious** mind. With this observation, Breuer and Freud had "discovered" the unconscious and its seeming influence on the production of psychological disorders. This was

Jean Charcot (1825–1893) studied the process of hypnosis and influenced Sigmund Freud to consider the power of psychosocial approaches to psychological disorders.

Joseph Breuer (1842–1925) described and treated the "hysterical symptoms" in Anna O. and worked closely with Sigmund Freud to develop the theory of psychoanalysis.

Anna O., whose real name was Bertha Pappenheim (1859–1936), was one of the most famous cases in the history of psychopathology.

one of the important developments in the history of psychopathology.

A close second was the finding that it is therapeutic to recall and relive emotional trauma that has been made unconscious (in a process called **repression**) and release some of the emotional tension of which patients have become unaware. This release of emotional material became known as **catharsis.** Developing a fuller understanding of the relationship of this emotional material to earlier events was referred to as **insight.** We shall see throughout this book, but particularly in Chapters 5 and 6 on anxiety and somatoform disorders, that the existence of "unconscious" mental processes and the importance of "processing" emotion-laden information has been reaffirmed and verified.

These findings were based on case observations. Some of the observations were made in a surprisingly systematic way for those times. One excellent example was Breuer's classic description of his treatment of "hysterical" symptoms in Anna O. in 1895 (Breuer & Freud, 1957). Anna O., one of the most famous cases in the history of psychopathology, was a bright, attractive, young woman who was perfectly healthy until she reached 21 years of age. Shortly before her problems began, her father developed a serious and chronic illness that led to his death. Throughout his

illness Anna O. had cared for him and had felt it necessary to spend endless hours at his bedside. Five months after her father became ill, Anna noticed that during the day her vision was blurring and that from time to time she was having difficulty moving her right arm and both legs. Soon additional symptoms appeared. She began to experience some difficulty speaking, and her behavior itself became very erratic. Shortly thereafter she consulted Dr. Breuer.

In a series of treatment sessions, Breuer dealt with one symptom at a time through hypnosis and subsequent "talking through," tracing each symptom to its hypothetical causation in circumstances surrounding the death of her father. One at a time these "hysterical" behaviors such as paralysis or blurred vision disappeared, but only when treatment was administered to each respective behavior. This process of treating one behavior at a time fulfills one of the basic requirements for drawing scientific conclusions about the effects of treatment in an individual case study, as we will see in Chapter 4. We will return to the fascinating case of Anna O. in Chapter 6.

Freud was to take some of these basic observations and expand them into the most comprehensive theory yet constructed on the development and structure of our personalities. He also speculated on where this development could go wrong to produce psychological disorders.

Freud wrote prolifically; his collected works fill volumes. (Other psychoanalysts have also made significant contributions to this theory.) Many of Freud's views changed as the years went by. In some cases, what he thought later in his career bears little resemblance to his early theory. Nevertheless, Freud's work introduced fresh and influential principles of mental functioning that remained constant through his writings and that are still held by psychoanalysts today.

Psychoanalytic theory has had unprecedented influence; what follows is a brief and basic outline of it. Our concern here is with three major facets of Freud's theory: first, the *structure of the mind* and the distinct functions of personality that sometimes clash with one another; second, the process by which the mind defends itself from these clashes or conflicts, referred to as *defense mechanisms;* and third, *the stages of early psychosexual development* that provide grist for the mill of our inner conflicts.

The Structure of the Mind.   The mind, according to Freud, has three major parts or functions: the *id, ego,* and *superego*. These terms, like many terms from psychoanalysis, have found their way into our common vocabulary, so you may be aware of the words themselves. You may not, however, be aware of their meaning.

The **id** is the source of our strong sexual and aggressive feelings or energies. The id is basically the animal within us; if left totally unchecked, it would make us all rapists or killers. The energy or drive within the id is the **libido.** Even today some individuals will describe their own low sex drive by saying they have no libido. A less important source of energy or drive, not as well conceptualized by Freud, is the death instinct or **thanatos.** Much like matter and antimatter, these two basic drives toward life and fulfillment on the one hand and death and destruction on the other are continually in opposition.

The id operates according to the **pleasure principle,** with an overriding goal of maximizing pleasure and eliminating any tension or conflicts associated with achieving this pleasure. The goal of pleasure, which is particularly prominent in childhood, often comes up against society's rules and regulations, as we shall see below. The id has its own characteristic way of processing information or thinking; referred to as **primary process,** this type of thinking is very emotional, irrational, illogical, and filled with fantasies and preoccupations of sex, aggression, selfishness, and envy.

Fortunately for all of us, in Freud's view, the id's selfish and sometimes dangerous drives do not go unchecked. In fact, only a few months into life, we recognize the necessity of adapting our basic demands

Sigmund Freud (1856–1939) is considered to be the founding father of psychoanalysis.

to the real world. In other words, we must find a way to meet our basic needs without offending everyone around us. Put yet another way, we must act realistically. The part of our mind that ensures that we act realistically is called the **ego** and it operates according to the **reality principle** instead of the pleasure principle. The cognitive operations or thinking style of the ego are characterized by logic and reason and are referred to as secondary process, as opposed to the illogical and irrational primary process of the id.

The third important structure within the mind, the **superego,** refers to what we might call "conscience." This concept is fairly easy to grasp since it represents the principles of morality instilled in us by our parents and our culture. It is the voice within you that nags at you when you know you're doing something wrong. Since the primary purpose of the superego is to counteract the potentially dangerous aggressive and sexual drives of the id, the basis for conflict is readily apparent.

The role of the ego is to mediate conflict between the id and the superego. For this reason, the ego has to coordinate everything. This is because the ego must juggle the demands of the id and the superego with the realities of the world. The ego is often referred to as the executive or manager of our minds. If the ego is successful, we can go on to the higher intellectual and creative pursuits of life. If the ego is unsuccessful and the id or superego becomes too strong, conflict will overtake us and psychological disorders will develop. Because these conflicts are within our mind, they are referred to as **intrapsychic conflicts.**

Now think back to the case of Anna O., in which Breuer observed that patients (including Anna O.) could not always remember important but unpleasant emotional events. Based on these and other observations, Freud conceptualized the mental structures described above to explain these unconscious processes. Freud believed that the id and the superego were almost entirely unconscious. Only the secondary processes of the ego were fully available to our awareness. Furthermore, the ego makes up a relatively small part of the mind.

Have you ever had a slip of the tongue? Maybe you were speaking to your friend Gail, but called her Carol by mistake? Or maybe you were talking about your exam tomorrow and you said "I've got to get ready for the *game* tomorrow" instead? You might conclude that you were simply thinking about your friend Carol for a moment and it slipped out, or that you were thinking about the football game on Saturday rather than your exam. To Freud, these little slips were much more than that. Slips of the tongue were reliable signs of the workings of the unconscious mind. The trick was to interpret them properly. In fact, Freud wrote a book devoted in large part to slips of the tongue (Freud, 1938).

Defense Mechanisms.   The ego is fighting a continual battle to stay on top of the warring factions of the mind. But occasionally, the residue of these conflicts results in such anxiety that it threatens to overwhelm the ego. The anxiety becomes a *signal* that alerts the ego to marshal any of an array of **defense mechanisms,** unconscious protective processes that keep primitive emotions associated with conflicts in check so that the ego can continue its coordinating function. Although Freud first conceptualized defense mechanisms, it was his daughter, Anna Freud, who developed these ideas more fully, as described shortly.

Some defense mechanisms are normal and adaptive. For example, have you ever done poorly on a test because the professor was unfair in her grading? And then when you got home you yelled at your brother or perhaps even your dog? This would be an example of the defense mechanism of *displacement.* When using displacement the ego "decides" that expressing primitive anger and rage at your professor might not be in your best interest, whereas your brother or dog don't have the authority to affect you in an adverse way. Therefore, your anger is "displaced" to your brother or

dog. Some people react to dangers and crises by making jokes. Using humor in this way can be a defense mechanism. Others may redirect energy from conflict or underlying anxiety into a more constructive outlet such as work, and they may work better and more efficiently because of it. This process is called *sublimation.* Another name for defense mechanisms could be *coping procedures,* since defense mechanisms are basically indirect ways of coping with conflicts by masking the dangerous emotions associated with them.

More severe internal conflicts that produce a lot of anxiety or other emotions can trigger self-defeating defensive processes or symptoms. Phobic and obsessive symptoms would be especially common self-defeating defensive reactions. These symptoms, according to Freud, represent an insufficient or inadequate attempt to deal with an internally dangerous situation. Typically, these symptoms incorporate elements of the danger. For example, a dog phobia may develop in connection with the activation of infantile fear of castration. That is, a man's internal conflict involves a fear of being attacked and castrated, but this fear is expressed as a fear of being attacked and bitten by a dog, even if he "knows" the dog is harmless.

Indeed, some experts think that characteristic defense mechanisms or coping procedures should be identified for all individuals with psychological disorders to aid in deciding on the best treatment. The DSM-IV is experimenting with this procedure by placing an "axis" of defense mechanisms in the appendix so clinicians can determine whether identifying defense mechanisms or coping procedures that might accompany psychological disorders is helpful. Definitions of some adaptive and some unadaptive defense mechanisms are presented in Table 1.1.

Defense mechanisms have been studied scientifically. Investigators such as George Vaillant (Vaillant, Bond, & Vaillant, 1986) and Gavin Andrews (Pollack & Andrews, 1989) have confirmed the potential importance of these coping styles in the study of psychopathology. For example, different psychological disorders seem to be associated with different defense mechanisms (Pollack & Andrews, 1989), something that might be important to know in planning treatment. Vaillant (1976) noted that the use of "healthy" defense mechanisms, such as humor and sublimation, correlated with psychological health. Thus the concept of defense mechanisms or coping styles continues to make an important contribution to the study of psychopathology.

Psychosexual Stages of Development.
Freud also theorized that we pass through a number of **psychosexual stages of development** during infancy and early childhood that have a profound impact on our later development. The inclusion of these stages marks

Table 1.1   Some Examples of Adaptive and Unadaptive Defense Mechanisms

Adaptive	*Unadaptive*
Affiliation—The individual deals with emotional conflict or internal or external stressors by turning to others for help or support. This involves sharing problems with others but does not imply trying to make someone else responsible for them.	**Passive-aggression**—The individual deals with emotional conflict or internal or external stressors by indirectly and unassertively expressing aggression toward others. There is a facade of overt compliance masking covert resistance, resentment, or hostility. Passive-aggression often occurs in response to demands for independent action or performance or the lack of gratification of dependent wishes but may be adaptive for individuals in subordinate positions who have no other way to express assertiveness more overtly.
Sublimation—The individual deals with emotional conflict or internal or external stressors by channeling potentially maladaptive feelings or impulses into socially acceptable behavior (for example, contact sports to channel angry impulses).	**Projection**—The individual deals with emotional conflict or internal or external stressors by falsely attributing to another his or her own unacceptable feelings, impulses, or thoughts.
Suppression—The individual deals with emotional conflict or internal or external stressors by intentionally avoiding thinking about disturbing problems, wishes, feelings, or experiences.	**Splitting**—The individual deals with emotional conflict or internal or external stressors by compartmentalizing opposite affect states and failing to integrate the positive and negative qualities of self or others into cohesive images. Because ambivalent affects cannot be experienced simultaneously, more balanced views and expectations of self or others are excluded from emotional awareness. Self and object images tend to alternate between polar opposites: exclusively loving, powerful, worthy, nurturant, and kind; or exclusively bad, hateful, angry, destructive, rejecting, or worthless.

Source: Adapted from *DSM-IV*, APA, 1994.

Freud as one of the first to take a developmental perspective on the study of abnormal behavior—an idea we will look at in more detail throughout this book. The stages, referred to as the oral stage, the anal stage, the phallic stage, the latency stage, and the genital stage, specify different and distinctive patterns of gratifying our basic needs and satisfying our drive for physical pleasure. For example, the oral stage, typically extending for approximately 2 years from birth, is characterized by a central focus on the need for food. Therefore the lips, tongue, and mouth in the act of sucking, necessary for feeding, become the focus of libidinal drives and, therefore, the principal source of pleasure. Freud hypothesized that, if we did not receive appropriate gratification during a specific stage or if a specific stage left a particularly strong impression (which he termed **fixation**), an individual's personality might reflect that impression throughout his or her adult life. For example, fixation at the oral stage might result in excessive thumb sucking and focus on oral stimulation through eating, chewing pencils, biting finger nails, and so on. Adult personality characteristics theoretically associated with fixation at this stage include dependency and passivity or, in reaction to these tendencies, rebelliousness and cynicism.

One of the most interesting and frequently referenced conflicts arising out of our psychosexual stages occurs during the phallic stage characterized by early genital self-stimulation. In the well-known Greek tragedy *Oedipus Rex,* Oedipus is forced by fate to kill his father and, unknowingly, to marry his mother. Freud asserted that all young boys relive this fantasy when genital self-stimulation is accompanied by images of sexual interactions with their mothers. These fantasies, in turn, are accompanied by strong feelings of envy and perhaps anger toward their fathers, with whom they identify but whose place they wish to take. Furthermore, strong fears develop that the father may take revenge against the son for the son's lust by removing his penis—thus, the phenomenon of **castration anxiety.** This fear and anxiety, in turn, helps the boy keep his lustful impulses toward his mother in check. The battle of the lustful impulses on the one hand and castration anxiety on the other creates a conflict that is internal, or intrapsychic. This conflict is called the **Oedipus complex.** The phallic stage passes uneventfully if several things happen. First, the child must resolve his ambivalent relationship with his parents and reconcile the simultaneous anger and love he has for his father. If this happens he may go on to channel his libidinal impulses into heterosexual relationships while retaining harmless affection for his mother.

The counterpart conflict in girls, called the **Electra complex,** is even more controversial. In this conflict, Freud viewed the young girl as wanting to replace her mother and possess her father. Central to

Freud's daughter, Anna Freud (1895–1982), contributed to the field of psychoanalysis with her study of defense mechanisms.

this possession is the girl's desire for a penis, so as to be more like her father and brothers; hence the term *penis envy.* According to Freud, the conflict is successfully resolved when females develop healthy heterosexual relationships and look forward to having a baby, which is construed as a healthy substitute for having a penis. Needless to say, this particular theory has provoked marked consternation over the years among individuals who view it as sexist and demeaning. It is important to remember that this is *theory,* not fact; no systematic research exists to support it.

In Freud's view all nonpsychotic psychological disorders resulted from underlying unconscious conflicts, anxiety that resulted from those conflicts, and the implementation of ego defense mechanisms. Freud grouped these disorders under the term **neuroses,** or *neurotic disorders,* from an old term referring to disorders of the nervous system.

Later Developments in Psychoanalytic Thought

During the remainder of the 20th century, psychoanalytic theories have been greatly modified and developed in a number of different directions. These directions depended mostly on new thinking from students or followers of Freud. Some of these theorists would simply take one component of psychoanalytic theory and develop it more fully. Other theorists broke with Freud and went in entirely new directions.

Anna Freud (1895–1982), Freud's daughter, further developed one aspect of psychoanalysis, concentrating on the defensive reactions of the ego and the way in which these reactions determine our behavior. In so doing, she became the first proponent of the modern-day field of **ego psychology** or **self-psychology.** Her book, *Ego and the Mechanisms of Defense* (1946), is still influential. According to her perspective, the individual slowly accumulates adaptational capacities, skill in reality testing, and defenses. Abnormal behavior develops when the ego is deficient in regulating functions such as delaying and controlling impulses or in marshaling appropriate normal defenses to strong internal conflicts.

Another development, quite popular today, is referred to as **object relations.** In this school of thought are theorists such as Melanie Klein and Otto Kernberg. Kernberg's work on borderline personality disorder, a severe disorder in which some behavior "borders" on being out of touch with reality or psychotic, has been widely noted (see Chapter 13).

Object relations is the study of how children incorporate the images, memories, and sometimes values of a person who was very important to them, and to whom they were (or are) emotionally attached. *Objects* in this sense refers to these important people in the child's environment, and the process of incorporation is called *introjection*. These introjected objects can become an integrated part of the ego, or may assume conflicting roles in the determination of one's identity or self. For example, your parents may have conflicting views on relationships or careers, which, in turn, may be different from your own partially developed point of view. To the extent that these positions have been partially incorporated, the potential for conflict arises. One day you may feel one way about your career direction, and the next day you may feel quite differently. In object relations theory, one tends to see the world through the eyes of the person incorporated into one's self. The study of how these disparate images come together to make up one's identity, and the conflicts that may emerge, is the focus of the object relations theorists.

Other theorists broke away from Freud. Carl Jung (1875–1961) and Alfred Adler (1870–1937) were actually students of Freud who came to reject his ideas and form their own schools of thought. Jung, rejecting many of the sexual aspects of Freud's theory, also introduced the notion of the **collective unconscious.** Jung speculated that there exists a source of wisdom accumulated by society and culture over the millennia that is stored deep in our memories and passed down from generation to generation. Jung also suggested that spiritual and religious drives are as much a part of human nature as sexual drives and, with his emphasis on the spiritual and the collective unconscious, drew the attention of mystics. Jung emphasized the importance of enduring personality traits such as *introversion* (the tendency to be shy and withdrawn) and *extraversion* (the tendency to be friendly and outgoing).

Adler focused his theories on feelings of inferiority and the striving for superiority; hence the term *inferiority complex*. Unlike Freud, both Jung and Adler also believed in the basic positive quality of human nature and in a strong drive toward self-actualization. By removing barriers to both internal and external growth, Jung and Adler believed that the individuals would improve and flourish.

Others took psychoanalytical theorizing in different directions, emphasizing development over the life span and the influence of culture and society on personality. Names such as Karen Horney (1885–1952) and Erich Fromm (1900–1980) are associated with these ideas, but the best-known theorist would be Erik Erikson (1902–1994). Erikson's greatest contribution was in specifying his own theory of development across the life span. He described in some detail the crises and conflicts that accompanied eight specific stages of development. For example, the last of these stages, called *mature age*, begins at approximately age 65. During this stage, Erikson speculated that individuals review their lives and attempt to make sense of them. At this point we experience the satisfaction of having completed some lifelong goals as well as the despair of having failed at others. Scientific developments have borne out the wisdom of considering psychopathology from the point of view of the developmental stages of one's life.

Psychoanalysis and Psychodynamic Psychotherapy

Many of the techniques of psychoanalytic psychotherapy, or psychoanalysis, are designed to reveal the nature of unconscious mental processes and conflicts. Freud developed techniques of **free association,** in which patients were instructed to say whatever came to mind without concern for the usual socially required censoring. Free association is intended to facilitate exploration of emotionally charged material that may be repressed because it is too painful or threatening to bring into consciousness. Freud would have his patients lie on a couch and he would sit behind them so they would not be distracted by looking at him. This is how the couch became such a symbol of psychotherapy. Other techniques include **dream analysis,** an activity still quite popular today. In this pro-

cedure the content of dreams, supposedly reflecting the primary process thinking of the id, was systematically related to symbolic aspects of unconscious conflicts. Using thoughts and feelings from free association and the content of dreams, the therapist interprets the material and relates it to various unconscious conflicts. This interpretation is often made more difficult because the patient may *resist* the efforts of the therapist to uncover these repressed and sensitive conflicts and *deny* that the interpretations of the therapist are accurate. The goal of this stage of therapy is for the therapist to assist the patient in gaining insight into the nature of the conflicts.

The relationship between the therapist, called the **psychoanalyst,** and the patient also becomes very important. It is in the context of this relationship as it evolves that therapists are often able to discover the nature of the patient's intrapsychic conflict. This is because patients come to relate to the therapist very much as they did toward important figures in their childhood, particularly their parents. This phenomenon is called **transference.** Some patients may feel resentful toward the therapist but can verbalize no good reason for it. Possibly they are reenacting an important period from childhood when they felt resentful toward one of their parents. More often the patient will fall deeply in love with the therapist, reflecting strong positive feelings that might have existed earlier for a parent. Therapists are trained to deal with these feelings whatever the mode of therapy, and it is strictly against all ethical canons of the mental health professions to accept any overtures from patients leading to relationships outside of therapy.

There is also the phenomenon of **countertransference,** in which therapists project some of their own personal issues and feelings, most often positive feelings, onto the patient. Therapists are also taught to be sensitive to the emergence of these feelings.

Analyzing the nature of these unconscious conflicts and attempting to resolve them, as well as restructuring the personality to put the ego back in charge, would require therapy four to five times a week for periods of from 2 to 5 years in classical psychoanalysis. In this approach, reduction of "symptoms" (psychological disorders) is relatively inconsequential, since symptoms are mere expressions of underlying intrapsychic conflicts arising out of psychosexual developmental stages. Thus, eliminating a phobia or depressive episode would be of little use if one did not deal adequately with the underlying conflict, since another set of "symptoms" would almost certainly emerge (called *symptom substitution*). Because of the extraordinary expense involved and the lack of evidence that classical psychoanalysis is effective in alleviating psychological disorders, this approach is seldom used today.

In more recent years psychoanalytic psychotherapy has undergone many transformations. Classical psychoanalysis still exists, particularly in some of our large cities, but many psychotherapists employ a loosely related set of approaches referred to as **psychodynamic psychotherapy.** Although an emphasis on conflicts and unconscious processes remains, including efforts to identify representations of trauma and active defense mechanisms, the new approaches most often contain an eclectic mixture of tactics, with a social and interpersonal focus. Two additional features characterize psychodynamic psychotherapy. First, it is significantly briefer than classical psychoanalysis. Second, psychodynamic therapists have deemphasized the goal of personality reconstruction, substituting a focus on relieving the suffering associated with psychological disorders.

Conclusions

Psychoanalysis, at least in its pure form, is of more historical than current interest, and classical psychoanalysis as a treatment has been diminishing in popularity for years. In 1980 the term *neurosis*, implying as it did a specific (psychoanalytic) view of the causes of psychological disorders, was dropped from the official diagnostic system of the American psychiatric system, the DSM.

Among the major criticisms of psychoanalysis is that it is basically unscientific, relying on reports by the patient of events that might have happened years ago. These events have been filtered through the experience of the observer and then interpreted by the psychoanalyst in ways that certainly could be questioned and might differ from one analyst to the next. Finally, there has been no careful measurement of any of these psychological phenomena, nor is there any obvious way to prove or disprove the basic hypotheses of psychoanalysis. However, measurement and the ability to prove or disprove a theory are the foundations of a scientific approach to these problems.

Nevertheless, psychoanalytic concepts and observations have made many valuable contributions, not only to the study of psychopathology and psychodynamic psychotherapy but also to the history of ideas in Western civilization. The observation of unconscious mental processes, the notion that basic emotional responses are often triggered by hidden or symbolic cues, and the understanding that memories of events in our lives can be repressed and otherwise avoided in a variety of ingenious ways have become increasingly supported by more careful scientific studies of psychopathology. These concepts along with the importance of various coping styles or defense mechanisms will appear repeatedly throughout this book.

These revolutionary ideas have brought us a long way from witch trials or incurable brain pathology.

In the world of Freud, pathological anxiety emerges in connection with some of our deepest and darkest instincts. Before Freud, the source of good and evil, of urges and prohibitions, was conceived as external and spiritual, usually in the guise of demons confronting the forces of good. Since Freud, we ourselves have become the battleground for these forces and we are inexorably caught up in the battle, sometimes for better and sometimes for worse.

Humanistic Theory: Self-Growth Influences

We have already seen that Jung and Adler broke sharply with Freud. Their fundamental disagreement concerned the very nature of humanity. Freud's theories portrayed life as a battleground where we are continually on the brink of being overwhelmed by our darkest forces. Jung and Adler, on the other hand, emphasized the positive, optimistic side of human nature. Jung talked about setting goals, looking toward the future, and realizing one's full potential. Adler believed that human nature reaches its fullest potential when we contribute to other individuals and to society as a whole. He conceptualized a striving in all of us to reach superior levels of intellectual and moral development. Nevertheless, these two theorists retained a strong emphasis on many of the principles of psychodynamic thought. The general philosophies of Jung and Adler were picked up in the middle of the century by personality theorists such as Carl Rogers (1902–1987), Abraham Maslow (1908–1970), and Fritz Perls (1893–1970) and became known as humanistic psychology.

Self-actualizing became the watchword for this movement. The underlying assumption was that all of us could reach our highest potential, in all areas of functioning, if only we had the freedom to grow. Inevitably, a variety of conditions arise in life that may block this tendency toward growth and actualization. Since any person is basically good and whole, most of these blocking tendencies originate outside the individual. Difficult conditions in living, stressful life experiences, or interpersonal experiences may move you farther away from your true self.

In describing the structure of personality, Abraham Maslow was the most systematic. He suggested that we have a **hierarchy of needs** beginning with the most basic physical needs for food and sex, and ranging to the very top of the hierarchy where needs of self-actualization, love, and self-esteem are apparent. Social needs such as friendship fall somewhere in between. Maslow hypothesized that we could not progress up the hierarchy until we had satisfied the needs at a lower level.

From the point of view of therapy, the most influential figure in the humanistic approach is Carl Rogers (1902–1987). Rogers originated client-centered therapy, later to be known as **person-centered therapy** (Rogers, 1961). In this therapeutic approach, the therapist takes a passive role. By making as few interpretations as possible, the therapist hopes to give the individual a chance to develop during the course of therapy, unfettered by threats to the self. Humanistic therapy puts great faith in the ability of human relations to foster this growth. **Unconditional positive regard,** which is the complete and almost unqualified acceptance of the client's feelings and actions, is critical to the humanistic approach. **Empathy** reflects the importance of a sympathetic and full understanding of the individual's particular view of the world. The hoped-for result of this therapy is that clients will be more straightforward and honest with themselves and will access their innate tendencies toward growth.

As with psychoanalysis, the humanistic approach has had a substantial effect on our culture and, in particular, on theories of interpersonal relationships. For example, the human potential movements so popular in the 1960s and 1970s were a direct result of humanistic theorizing. This approach also reemphasized the importance of the therapeutic relationship in quite a different way from Freud's conception. Rather than seeing the relationship as a means to an end (transference), humanistic therapists believed that relationships, including the therapeutic relationship, were the single most positive influence in facilitating human growth.

Nevertheless, the humanistic model has contributed relatively little new information to the field of psychopathology. One reason for this is that proponents of humanistic approaches, with some exceptions, were less interested in doing research that would discover or create new knowledge. Rather, they stressed the unique, nonquantifiable experiences of each individual, emphasizing that people are more different than alike. As Maslow noted, the humanistic model found its greatest application among relatively normal functioning individuals without psychological disorders. The practice of person-centered therapy on more severe psychological disorders has decreased substantially over the decades, although certain variations of this approach have periodically arisen in some areas of psychopathology (for example, see mental retardation in Chapter 15).

The Behavioral Model

As psychoanalysis was sweeping the world in the beginning of the 20th century, other events were ongoing in Russia and the United States that would eventually provide an alternative psychological model every bit as powerful as psychoanalysis. This model, initially referred to as the **behavioral model,** has come to be known by other names as well, including the **cognitive-behavioral** or **social learning model.** As

with other models described previously, major contributions to our knowledge of psychopathology have come from this approach. More important, what accompanied this model was the systematic development of a more scientific approach to psychological aspects of psychopathology. Because substantive contributions always become dated as our knowledge advances, it is the latter contribution that is more crucial.

Pavlov and Classical Conditioning.

The beginnings of classical conditioning can be traced to a scientific laboratory in St. Petersburg, Russia, where Ivan Petrovich Pavlov (1849–1936), a well-known professor of physiology, was engaged in groundbreaking research on the process of digestion. This research was to win Pavlov the Nobel Prize in medicine and physiology in 1904.

In the course of this research, Pavlov did something that all brilliant scientists do occasionally. He observed an event that was not only unexpected but also unrelated to the central purpose of his research, and he decided to stop everything and investigate it. While Pavlov and his assistants were studying various aspects of the process of digestion in dogs, including salivation, they noticed that the dogs began salivating *before* the food was even in sight. Specifically, hearing the assistants who fed the dogs coming down the hall was often sufficient to set off the beginnings of the digestive response. If you have a dog or cat and use an electric can opener to open their pet food, you have probably noticed the same thing. Your dog or cat will come running—and probably begin salivating—to the sound of the can opener before the pet can actually see or smell the food.

Pavlov decided to investigate these reactions systematically and thereby initiated the study of **classical conditioning,** a type of learning in which a neutral stimulus is paired with a response until it elicits

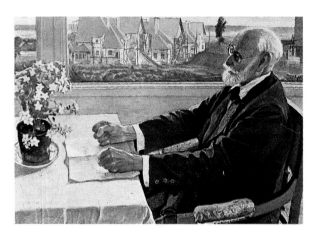

Pavlov (1849–1936) discovered the process of classical conditioning, which plays an important role in many emotional disorders.

that response. The origins of the word *conditioning* (or *conditioned response*) are really a bit of an accident occurring in translation from the original Russian. What Pavlov was really talking about was a *conditional* response that occurred only on the "condition" of the presence of a particular event or situation (stimulus)—in this case, the footsteps of the laboratory assistant around feeding time. Conditioning is one way we learn or acquire new information, particularly information that is somewhat emotional in nature. This process is not as simple as it first seems, and we continue to uncover many more facts about the complexity of this type of learning (Rescorla, 1988). But it can be quite automatic.

Before we turn to the actual process of classical conditioning, let's look at a powerful present-day example of it. Psychologists working in oncology units have studied a phenomenon well known to many cancer patients, their nurses and physicians, and their families. Chemotherapy, a common treatment for some forms of cancer, has some side effects. One of the side effects is severe nausea and vomiting. But it is common for these patients to experience severe nausea and, occasionally, vomiting, at times other than their treatments. Specifically, they may experience this reaction upon seeing the medical personnel who administered the chemotherapy or any equipment associated with the treatment itself, even on days when their treatment is not being delivered (Morrow & Dobkin, 1988). For some patients, this reaction can become associated with a wide variety of stimuli that resemble people or things present during chemotherapy—anybody in a nurse's uniform or even the sight of the hospital itself. The strength of the response to similar objects or people is usually a function of *how* similar these objects or people are. This phenomenon is called stimulus generalization since the response "generalizes" to similar stimuli. In any case, this particular reaction, obviously, is very distressing and uncomfortable, particularly if it is associated with a wide variety of objects or situations. Psychologists have had to develop specific treatments to overcome this response; they are described more fully in Chapter 9 (Redd & Andrykowski, 1982).

The Process of Classical Conditioning.   In the process of classical conditioning, whether the stimulus is food—meat powder—as it was in Pavlov's laboratory, or chemotherapy, the classical conditioning process begins with a stimulus that would elicit a response in almost anyone and requires no learning. Thus, there are no "conditions" that need to be present for the response to occur. For these reasons, the chemotherapy or meat powder would be called the *unconditioned stimulus* (UCS). The natural or unlearned response to this stimulus—in this case,

salivation or nausea—would be called the *unconditioned response* (UCR). Now the learning comes in. As we have already seen, any person or object that might become *associated* with the unconditioned stimulus (chemotherapy or the meat powder) would then acquire the power to elicit the same response; but now the response, because it was elicited by the conditional or *conditioned stimuli* (CS), is termed a *conditioned response* (CR). Thus, the nurse who was associated with the chemotherapy becomes a conditioned stimulus. The nauseous sensation, which is almost the same as would be experienced during chemotherapy, becomes the conditioned response.

With very powerful unconditioned stimuli, such as chemotherapy, this response can be learned in one trial. However, most learning of this type requires repeated pairing of the unconditioned stimulus (for example, chemotherapy) and the conditioned stimulus (for instance, nurses' uniforms, hospital equipment, and so on). When Pavlov began to investigate this phenomenon, he substituted a metronome for the footsteps of his laboratory assistants, so that he could quantify the stimulus more accurately and therefore, study the approach more precisely. What he also learned is that presentation of the CS (for example, the metronome) *without* the meat powder for a long enough period of time would eventually eliminate the conditioned response to the meat powder. In other words, the dog learned that the metronome no longer meant that a meal might be on the way. This process was called **extinction.**

Remember that Pavlov was a physiologist. Therefore, it was quite natural for him to study these processes in a laboratory and to be quite scientific about it. Being scientific required that he be very precise in measuring and observing these relationships and ruling out alternative explanations. While this is a common approach in biology, it was not at all common in psychology at that time. For example, it was impossible for psychoanalysts to measure precisely, or even observe, unconscious conflicts. Even early experimental psychologists such as Edward Titchener (1867–1927) emphasized the study of the process of **introspection.** Introspecting subjects would simply report on their inner thoughts and feelings after experiencing certain stimuli, but the results of this "armchair" psychology were inconsistent and discouraging to many experimental psychologists.

Watson and the Rise of Behaviorism. Strongly influenced by the work of Pavlov, a young American psychologist, John B. Watson (1878–1958), decided that psychology based on introspection was heading in the wrong direction. He declared that psychology could be made as scientific as physiology. This point of view is reflected in a now famous quote from a seminal article published by Watson in 1913: "Psychology as the behaviorist views it, is a purely objective experimental branch of natural science. Its theoretical goal is the prediction and control of behavior. Introspection forms no essential part of its methods" (Watson, 1913, p. 158). Watson concluded that psychology needs introspection or other nonquantifiable methods no more than do the sciences of chemistry and physics (p. 158). This, then, was the beginning of behaviorism and, like most revolutionaries, Watson took it to extremes. For example, he wrote that "thinking," for purposes of science, could be equated with subvocal talking, and that one need only measure movements around the larynx to study this process objectively.

Most of Watson's time was spent developing behavioral psychology as a radical empirical science, but he did dabble briefly in the study of psychopathology. In 1920, he and Rosalie Rayner presented an 11-month-old boy named Albert with a harmless fluffy white rat to play with. Albert was not afraid of the small animal and enjoyed playing with it. However, every time Albert reached for the animal, the experimenters made a loud noise behind him. After only five trials, Albert began showing the first signs of fear if the white rat came near. The experimenters then determined that Albert displayed mild fear of any white furry object, even a Santa Claus mask with a white fuzzy beard. You may not think that this is surprising, but keep in mind that this was one of the first examples ever recorded in the laboratory of actually producing fear of an object not previously feared.

Another student of Watson's, Mary Cover Jones, thought that if fear could be learned or classically conditioned in this way, perhaps it could also be unlearned or "extinguished." She worked with a boy named Peter, 2 years, 10 months old, who was already quite afraid of furry objects, something he had learned on his own. Mary Cover Jones decided to bring a white furry rabbit into the room where Peter was playing for a short time each day. She also arranged for other children, who she knew did not fear rabbits, to be in the same room. She noted that Peter's fear gradually diminished. Each time it diminished, she would then bring the rabbit closer and closer. Eventually Peter was touching and even playing with the rabbit (Jones, 1924a; 1924b), and the fear had not returned years later.

The Beginnings of Behavior Therapy.

The implications of Jones's research were largely ignored for two decades, given the prevailing fervor associated with more psychoanalytic conceptions of the development of fear. But in the late 1940s and 1950s, a pioneering psychiatrist from South Africa, Joseph Wolpe, became dissatisfied with prevailing psychoanalytic interpretations of psychopathology and began

Mary Cover Jones (1896–1987), pictured here at Vassar College, was one of the first psychologists to overcome a phobia in a child using behavioral techniques.

looking for something else. He turned to the work of Pavlov and became familiar with the remainder of the field of behavioral psychology. He developed a variety of procedures derived directly from these principles to treat his patients, many of whom suffered from phobias. The best-known technique he developed was termed **systematic desensitization.** In principle, it was really very similar to the treatment of little Peter. Specifically, individuals with phobias of various objects and situations were gradually introduced to these objects or situations so that their fear could extinguish; that is, they would have a chance to "test reality" and see that nothing bad really happened in the presence of the phobic object or scene. Wolpe also added another element by having his patients do something that was *incompatible with fear* while they were in the presence of the feared object or situation. The response Wolpe chose was *relaxation* because it was convenient. Furthermore, because he could not always reproduce the phobic object in his office, he would have patients carefully and systematically *imagine* the phobic scene. For example, Wolpe would treat a young man with phobias of dogs by training him to relax deeply and then have him imagine he was looking at a dog across the park. Gradually, he could imagine the dog across the park while in a relaxed state, experiencing little or

Joseph Wolpe (1915–) was one of the founding fathers of behavior therapy.

no fear, and Wolpe would have him imagine that he was somewhat closer to the dog. Eventually the young man would imagine that he was actually touching the dog. During this time he would remain in a very relaxed, almost trancelike state in an attempt to inhibit his fear.

Wolpe reported great success with this technique. Systematic desensitization was one of the first wide-scale applications of the new science of behaviorism to psychopathology. Wolpe, working together with other pioneers in this area such as Hans Eysenck and Stanley Rachman in London, came to call this approach **behavior therapy.**

B. F. Skinner and Operant Conditioning. Sigmund Freud's influence and reputation ranged far beyond psychopathology, reaching into many aspects of our culture and intellectual history. Only one other behavioral scientist has had a similar impact. Burrhus Frederick (B. F.) Skinner (1904–1990) published a book in 1938 entitled *The Behavior of Organisms*. This book laid out, in a comprehensive manner, the principles of **operant conditioning,** a type of learning in which responses are modified as a function of the consequence of the response. In this book, Skinner observed early on that a large part of our behavior was not automatically elicited by an unconditioned stimulus (UCS) and that, somehow, we must account for this. In the ensuing years, Skinner did not confine his ideas to the laboratories of experimental psychology. He ranged far and wide in his writings describing, for example, the potential applications of a science of behavior to our culture. Some of the best-known examples of his ideas on society and

culture are found in the book *Walden Two* (Skinner, 1948), which depicts a fictional society run on the principles of operant conditioning. In another well-known work, *Beyond Freedom and Dignity* (1971), Skinner lays out a more broadly conceived statement of problems facing our culture and potential solutions based on his own view of a science of behavior.

Skinner was strongly influenced by Watson's vision of the need to develop a science of human behavior based on observable events and relationships among those events. The work of psychologist Edward L. Thorndike (1874–1949) also influenced Skinner. Thorndike is best known for the *law of effect,* which states that behavior is either strengthened (likely to be repeated more frequently) or weakened (likely to occur less frequently) depending on the consequences of that behavior.

What B. F. Skinner did was to take these very simple notions that Thorndike had developed in the animal laboratories, using food as a reward, and develop them in a variety of complex ways to apply to much of our behavior. For example, if a 5-year-old boy starts singing at the top of his lungs in McDonald's, much to the annoyance of the people around him, it is unlikely that his behavior was automatically elicited by an unconditioned stimulus (UCS). Also, chances are he will be less likely to do it in the future if his parents scold him, or perhaps take him out to the car to sit for a bit, or consistently reinforce more appropriate behavior. On the other hand, if the parents think his behavior is cute and laugh, chances are he will do it again.

Skinner coined the term *operant* conditioning because behavior "operates" on the environment and changes the environment in some way. For example, the 5-year-old boy's behavior affected his parents' behavior and probably the behavior of other customers in McDonald's as well. Therefore, he changed his environment. Most things that we do socially provide the context for other people to respond to us in one way or another, thereby providing consequences for our behavior. The same is true about our physical environment, although the consequences may be longer term (polluting the air eventually will poison us). Skinner preferred the term **reinforcement** to reward because it connoted the effect on the behavior. Skinner once said that he found himself a bit embarrassed to be talking continually about reinforcement, much as Marxists used to see the "class struggle" everywhere. But he would point out that all of our behavior is governed to some degree by reinforcement, and reinforcement could be arranged in an endless variety of ways, referred to as **schedules of reinforcement.** Skinner wrote a whole book on different schedules of reinforcement (Ferster & Skinner, 1957). He also downplayed punishing consequences as being relatively ineffective in the long run and underscored that the primary way to develop new behavior is for positive reinforcing consequences to follow desired behavior.

The subjects of Skinner's research were most often animals—mostly pigeons and rats. Using his newly developed principles, Skinner and his disciples could actually teach these animals a variety of esoteric tricks such as dancing, playing Ping-pong, or playing a toy piano. To do this he used a procedure called **shaping.** Shaping refers to a process of reinforcing successive approximations to a final behavior or set of behaviors. If you want a pigeon to play Ping-pong, first you provide it with a pellet of food every time it moves its head slightly toward a Ping-pong ball tossed in its direction. Gradually you require the pigeon to move its head ever more closely to the Ping-pong ball until it begins touching the ball. Finally, receiving the food pellet becomes contingent on the pigeon's actually hitting the Ping-pong ball back with its head.

Much like Watson, Skinner did not see the need to go beyond observable and quantifiable behavior to establish a satisfactory science of behavior. He did not deny the influence of biology on behavior nor did he deny the existence of subjective states of emotion or cognition. Rather, he simply chose to explain these phenomena as relatively inconsequential side effects of a particular history of reinforcement. The work of Pavlov, Watson, and Skinner contributed directly to the beginnings of behavior therapy (for example, Wolpe, 1958), an approach in which scientific principles of psychology are applied to clinical problems. These ideas have made substantial contributions to modern-day psychosocial treatments and will appear repeatedly in this book.

Conclusions

The behavioral model of psychopathology, with its firm base in the developing science of psychology, has also made major contributions to the understanding and treatment of psychopathology. These contributions will be apparent in the chapters to follow. Nevertheless, this model, in isolation, is incomplete and inadequate to account for what we now know about psychopathology. In the past there was little or no room for biology in this model, since disorders were considered to be, for the most part, environmentally determined reactions. The development of psychopathology across the life span was largely ignored. Similarly, recent advances in our knowledge of how information is processed both in and out of awareness have added a layer of complexity. Integrating the various dimensions requires a new model of psychopathology. It is to this integrated model of psychopathology that we now turn.

B. F. Skinner (1904–1990) studied a form of learning he came to call *operant conditioning*, which has had substantial influence in the field of psychopathology.

The Future: The Scientific Method and a Multidimensional Integrative Approach

Shakespeare wrote, "What's past is prologue." We have just reviewed three different traditions or ways of thinking about causes of psychopathology: the supernatural, the biological, and the psychological. The psychological, in turn, was subdivided into two major historical components: psychoanalytic and behavioral.

Views on supernatural contributions to psychopathology are still with us. We see this influence in the many superstitions still prevalent, including beliefs in the effects of the moon and the stars on our behavior. However, this tradition, at present, has little influence on scientists or professionals. Biological, psychoanalytic, and behavioral models, on the other hand, continue to contribute to our knowledge of psychopathology. We will review these contributions in the next chapter.

Each of these traditions, however, has had at least one if not two important failings. First, the methods of science were not often brought to bear on the theories or treatments emanating from one tradition or another. This is most often because scientific approaches to psychopathology and its treatment that would have produced the evidence necessary to confirm or disconfirm the theories and treatments had not been developed. Lacking this evidence, society was subjected to various fads and superstitions of the times that were widely believed but were ultimately proved to be untrue or useless. Many times new fads superseded truly useful theories and treatment procedures. We saw this trend at work in the "discovery" of the drug reserpine, which, in fact, had been around for thousands of years, only to go in and out of favor. King Charles VI was subjected to a variety of procedures, some of which have proven to be useful while others were fads or even harmful. The ways in which we use scientific methods to confirm or disconfirm findings in psychopathology will be described in Chapter 4. Second, health professionals of the day tended to look at psychological disorders very narrowly from their own point of view. John Grey assumed that psychological disorders were the result of a brain disease and that psychological or social factors had no influence whatsoever. John Watson assumed that all behaviors, including disordered behavior, were the result of psychological and social influences and that the contribution of biological factors was inconsequential.

Two developments have come together as never before to shed light in the 1990s on the nature of psychopathology. These developments are, first, the increasing sophistication of our scientific tools or methodology as we investigate the nature of psychopathology, and second, the realization, as a result of our scientific investigations, that no one influence—biological, behavioral, cognitive, emotional, or social—

ever occurs in isolation. Literally, every time we think, feel, or do something, our brain and the rest of our body are hard at work contributing to these thoughts, feelings, or actions. Perhaps not as obvious, however, is the fact that our thoughts, feelings, and actions are inevitably influencing the function and even the structure of our brain, sometimes in a permanent way. In other words, our behavior, both normal and abnormal, is the product of a continual interaction of psychological, biological, and social influences.

The view that psychopathology is multiply determined had its early adherents. Perhaps the most notable was Adolf Meyer (1866–1950), often considered the dean of American psychiatry. While most professionals of his era held narrow views of the cause of psychopathology, Meyer steadfastly emphasized the equal contributions of biological, psychological, and social/cultural determinism. Although Meyer had some proponents over the years, it was to be 100 before the field fully recognized the wisdom of his advice.

By the late 1980s a veritable explosion of knowledge about psychopathology was occurring and it became clear that a new model was needed. This model would have to consider advances in knowledge from biology and psychology as well as the study of social influences on behavior. This approach to psychopathology would also have to integrate findings from all these areas with our rapidly growing understanding of how we experience life, and the events of life, at different developmental periods from infancy to old age. In the remainder of this book we will explore some of these reciprocal influences and the reasons the only currently valid model of psychopathology is a multidimensional integrative one.

Summary

- In this chapter we have seen how difficult it is to come up with a clear definition of abnormal behavior. The working definition in this book refers to a psychological dysfunction associated with distress or impairment in functioning. It is also important to note that the behavior is not simply the expected response that most people in that culture would make in a similar situation, such as experiencing grief after the death of a loved one.

- Historically, there are three prominent traditions to account for abnormal behavior. In the *supernatural* tradition, abnormal behavior and psychological disorders were attributed to agents outside our bodies or social environment, such as demons, spirits, or the influence of the moon and the stars. During the Middle Ages, many people viewed these as causes of abnormal behavior, although an equally strong tide of opinion at that time attributed mental disorders to natural causes. In the *psychological* tradition dating back to the ancient Greeks, disorders were attributed to faulty psychological development as well as to the interpersonal and social context of the disorders. In the *biological* tradition, abnormal behavior was most often seen as resulting from a chemical imbalance or a disease process.

• Two major difficulties were encountered in reviewing these historical traditions. First, since scientific approaches to abnormal behavior capable of proving or disproving theories or establishing knowledge had not been developed, various fads of the day were invoked to explain psychological disorders and guide treatment. For example, both drug and psychosocial treatments for specific psychological disorders later proven effective were often passed over in favor of the latest fad. Second, individuals working in one tradition or another tended to adopt a very narrow approach, ignoring influences from other traditions.

• We now realize that no one contribution to psychological disorders ever occurs in isolation. Our behavior, both normal and abnormal, is a product of a continual interaction of psychological, biological, and social influences.

Key Terms

behavioral model (23, 31)
behavior therapy (34)
biological model (8)
castration anxiety (27)
catharsis (24)
classical conditioning (31)
clinical description (7)
clinical psychologist (6)
cognitive-behavioral (or social learning) model (31)
collective unconscious (28)
counseling psychologist (6)
countertransference (29)
course (7)
defense mechanisms (26)
developmental psychopathology (7)
dream analysis (29)
ego (25)
ego psychology / self-psychology (28)
Electra complex (27)
empathy (31)
etiology (7)
extinction (32)

fixation (27)
free association (29)
hierarchy of needs (30)
id (25)
incidence (7)
insanity (5)
insight (24)
intrapsychic conflicts (26)
introspection (32)
libido (25)
mental hygiene movement (22)
moral therapy (20)
neuroses (28)
object relations (28)
Oedipus complex (27)
operant conditioning (34)
person-centered therapy (31)
pleasure principle (25)
presents (7)
prevalence (7)
primary process (25)
prognosis (7)
psychiatric nurse (6)
psychiatric social worker (6)
psychiatrist (6)

psychoanalysis (23)
psychoanalyst (29)
psychodynamic psychotherapy (30)
psychological disorder (1)
psychological model (8)
psychopathology (6)
psychosexual stages of development (26)
psychosocial treatment (20)
reality principle (25)
reinforcement (34)
repression (24)
schedules of reinforcement (34)
scientist-practitioner (6)
self-actualizing (30)
shaping (35)
superego (25)
supernatural model (9)
systematic desensitization (33)
thanatos (25)
transference (29)
unconditional positive regard (31)
unconscious (23)

*The spirit within nourishes, and the mind, diffused through
all the members, sways the mass and mingles
with the whole frame.*
Virgil
Aeneid, bk IV, 1. 726

2

A Multidimensional Integrative Approach to Psychopathology

Remember Judy from Chapter 1? When we left her, we knew she suffered from blood-injury-injection phobia, but we did not know why. Here we will address that issue. In this chapter we review the actual components of a multidimensional integrative approach to psychopathology. Biological dimensions include causal factors from the fields of genetics and neuroscience. Psychological dimensions include causal factors from behavioral and cognitive processes that vary widely, including such contributors as learned helplessness, social learning, prepared learning, and even unconscious processes—but in a different guise from those in the days of Freud. Emotional influences contribute in a variety of ways to psychopathology, as do social and interpersonal influences. Finally, the role of developmental influences is a factor in any discussion of causes of psychological disorders. In this chapter you will become familiar with these areas of influence as they relate to psychopathology, and learn about some of the latest developments within each that are relevant to psychological disorders. But keep in mind our conclusions in the last chapter. None of these influences operates in isolation. Each—whether from a biological or psychological dimension—is strongly influenced by interactions with the others, and all are affected by development. As such, these influences weave together in various complex and

intricate ways in the creation of a psychological disorder.

We describe briefly why we have adopted a multidimensional integrative model of psychopathology. Then we preview various causal influences and their interactions with each other, using Judy's case as a backdrop for understanding. After that we look in more depth at specific causal influences in psychopathology, examining both the latest research and integrative ways of viewing what we know.

One-Dimensional or Multidimensional Models

If people say that psychopathology is caused by a chemical imbalance, or by conditioning, they are adopting a linear or one-dimensional causal model. This description is simply an attempt to trace the origins of something, such as behavior, to a single underlying cause. If you were to hear that schizophrenia or phobia is caused by a chemical imbalance, or by inadequate child rearing due to overwhelming conflicts among family members, this would be an example of a linear causal model. In psychology and psychopathology, you will still encounter this type of thinking occasionally;

but for most scientists and clinicians, abnormal behavior is considered the product of a system of different influences. A system or feedback loop may have inputs at many different points, but each of these inputs becomes part of the feedback loop or system and can no longer be considered independent. You could describe this perspective on causality as *systemic,* which derives from the word *system;* this type of causal modeling implies that any particular influence contributing to psychopathology cannot be considered out of context. Context, in this case, is both the biology and the behavior of the individual as well as his or her cognitive, emotional, social, and cultural environment, since any one component of the system inevitably affects the other components.

What Caused Judy's Phobia?

Keeping a multidimensional model in mind, let's look at what might have caused Judy's phobia.

1. *Behavioral influences.* The cause of Judy's phobia might seem clear on the surface. She saw a particularly graphic movie complete with scenes of blood and injury and had a bad reaction to it. Her reaction, an unconditioned response, then became associated with a number of situations similar to the scenes in the original movie, depending on how similar they were. But Judy's reaction reached such an extreme that even hearing someone say "Cut it out" would evoke her queasy feeling. Is the cause of Judy's phobia a straightforward case of classical conditioning? It might seem so, but one puzzling question arises. Why didn't the other kids in Judy's class develop the same phobia? As far as Judy knew, nobody else even felt queasy!

2. *Biological influences.* We now know that a lot more is involved in the development of blood-injury-injection phobia than a simple conditioning experience, although, clearly, conditioning and stimulus generalization make a contribution. We have learned fairly recently (Ost, 1992; Marks, 1988; Thyer, Himle, & Curtis, 1985) some interesting things about this phobia.

Do you ever have queasy feelings at the sight of blood? If you have the same sort of sensation that Judy did, even if it isn't as severe, chances are your mother, or father, or someone else in your immediate family has the same reaction. The tendency of the phobia to run in families is extremely high for blood-injury-injection phobia, perhaps higher than for any other psychological disorder. In a recent study, 61% of the family members of individuals with this phobia had a similar condition, although somewhat milder in most cases (Ost, 1992).

Physiologically, Judy was experiencing a *vasovagal syncope,* which is a common cause of fainting. Here is what happens during a vasovagal syncope. When Judy saw the film she became mildly distressed, as many people would, and experienced an associated increase in her heart rate and blood pressure, of which she probably was not aware. Then her body took over: it immediately compensated by decreasing her vascular resistance, lowering her heart rate, and, eventually, lowering her blood pressure. The amount of blood reaching her brain then diminished to the point that she lost consciousness. "Syncope" actually means sinking feeling or swoon due to low blood pressure in your head. If Judy had quickly put her head between her legs she might have avoided fainting, but it happened so quickly she had no time to use this strategy.

One possible cause of this compensatory reaction is the *sinoaortic baroreflex arc.* The baroreflex is a mechanism the body has to compensate for sudden increases in blood pressure (Adler, France, & Ditto, 1991). Activation of this baroreflex *lowers* blood pressure, causing the syncope. The interesting thing about vasovagal syncope is that the tendency to overcompensate seems to be *inherited,* a trait that may account for this phobia's being one of the most strongly familial psychological disorders of which we are aware. Probably genes explain why this reaction runs in families.

You might think, then, that we have discovered the cause of blood-injury-injection phobia, and that all we need to do is to develop a pill to regulate the baroreflex. But we know that there are many people with rather severe syncope reaction tendencies who *do not* develop phobias. They seem to cope with their reaction in various ways, including tensing their muscles whenever they confront pictures or scenes of blood. Tensing your muscles very quickly raises blood pressure and prevents the fainting response. Furthermore, there seem to be some people with little or no syncope reaction who develop the phobia anyway (Ost, 1992). Therefore blood-injury-injection phobia is more complicated than it seems. If we say that a biological dysfunction (an overactive vasovagal reaction probably due to a particularly sensitive baroreflex mechanism) causes blood-injury-injection phobia, or if we say that traumatic experiences (seeing a gruesome film) and subsequent conditioning factors cause blood-injury-injection phobia, we would be right on both counts.

To cause phobia, a complex *interaction* must occur between behavioral and biological factors, but inheriting a strong syncope reaction definitely puts you at risk for developing this phobia. Other influences are at work as well.

3. *Emotional influences.* Judy's case illustrates how genes can increase the chance that you would develop a specific type of phobia. Her example is a good illustration of biology influencing behavior. But behavior, thoughts, and feelings can also influence biology, sometimes dramatically. Judy experienced fear and anxiety when she saw or heard about blood and injury, but we have already mentioned that many

people seem to experience vasovagal syncope *without* the strong emotions of fear and anxiety. What role did these emotions play in the development of Judy's phobia and where did they come from? Experiencing this unexpected sensation of fainting was very frightening to Judy as it would be to many people. But emotions of fear and anxiety can have dramatic effects on physiological responses such as blood pressure, heart rate, and respiration, particularly if we know rationally that there is nothing to fear, as Judy did. In Judy's case, rapid increases in heart rate caused by her emotions may have triggered a stronger and more intense baroreflex. Emotions also changed the way she thought about situations involving blood and injury and motivated her to behave in ways she didn't want—to avoid all situations where she might confront stimuli connected with blood and injury, even if it was important that she not avoid them. Emotions play a substantial role in the development of many disorders, as we shall see throughout this book.

4. *Social influences.* We have now examined, briefly, examples of the influence of biology on behavior and emotions and the influence of behavior and emotions on biology. But we are all social animals, meaning that by our very nature we tend to live in groups such as families. We also know that social and cultural factors make direct contributions to biology and behavior.

Judy's friends and family rushed to her aid when she fainted. Did their support help or hurt? Her principal rejected her and dismissed her problem. What effect did his behavior have on her phobia?

5. *Developmental influences.* One more influence affects us all—*time.* With the passage of time, many things about ourselves and our environments change in important ways. We know we change when we age. The passage of time is not really a contributing cause of abnormal behavior, but influences over time are important to consider when we study causes. This is because the different processes affecting behavior will exert more or less influence as time passes. To go back to our example of Judy's blood phobia, it is possible that she was previously exposed to other situations involving blood. An important question to ask is this: Why did this problem develop when she was 16 years old and not younger? Is it possible that her susceptibility to having a vasovagal reaction was highest in her teenage years? It may be that the timing of her physiological reaction along with the viewing of the disturbing biology film provided just the right (but unfortunate) combination to initiate her severe phobic response.

Conclusions

Fortunately for Judy, she responded very well to a brief but intensive treatment administered at one of our clinics and was back in school within seven days. This treatment, which lasted little more than a week, consisted of gradually exposing Judy, with her full cooperation, to words, images, and situations involving or depicting blood and injury. We would begin with something mild such as the phrase "cut it out." By the end of the week she was witnessing surgical procedures at the local hospital. Judy required close therapeutic supervision during this program. At one point while riding home with her parents from an evening session, she had the bad fortune to drive by a car accident where she saw an injured and bleeding accident victim. After going home and going to bed she began dreaming about bloody accident victims coming through the walls of her bedroom. This experience required her to call the clinic and receive emergency intervention to reduce her distress, but it did not slow her progress. Programs of this type for treating phobias and related anxiety disorders are described more fully in Chapter 5. It is the issue of etiology or causation that concerns us here.

As you can see, looking at causes of abnormal behavior is a complex and fascinating process. In the case of Judy, focusing on biological processes or behavioral conditioning factors would not have been sufficient for us to develop a full picture of the causes of her disorder. We also had to consider a variety of other influences and how they might interact. A more in-depth discussion follows, examining the research underlying the many biological, psychological, and social influences that must be considered in discussing the causes of any psychological disorder.

Genetic Contributions to Psychopathology

Do you look like your mother . . . or your father? These questions were very interesting to your parents, who attempted to make this determination within hours after you were born. You'll probably do the same thing if you have children. What causes you to look like one or both of your parents or perhaps your grandparents? Obviously it would be your genes that you inherit from your parents and your ancestors before them. Ever since Gregor Mendel's pioneering work in the 19th century, we have known that our physical characteristics such as hair color and eye color and, to a certain extent, height and weight are determined, or at least strongly influenced, by our genetic endowment. With the exception of identical twins, no two people have exactly the same genetic makeup. Furthermore, other factors in our environments influence our physical appearance. Our weight and even our height to some extent are affected by nutritional as well as social and cultural factors, as we see later in the chapter when we discuss a case of an individual with psychosocial dwarfism. Consequently, our genes, for the most part, seldom determine our physical development in any absolute way but rather provide some constraints or boundaries to our development. Exactly where we go within these constraints or boundaries is dependent on environmental influences.

While this is true for most of our characteristics, it is not true for all of them. Some of our characteristics are very strongly determined by one or more **genes.** Examples would be our hair or eye color. There is little or no room for a large number of other genes or for the environment to influence our *natural* hair and eye color. There are some rare disorders that are determined in this same kind of way. Among them is Huntington's chorea, a degenerative brain disease that appears in a person's early to middle age with the highest frequency of onset occurring during the early 40s. This disease has been traced to a genetic defect that causes deterioration in a specific area of the brain, the basal ganglia. Huntington's chorea results in broad-based changes in personality, cognitive functioning, and particularly motor behavior. The term *chorea* refers to involuntary shaking or jerkiness throughout the body. We have not yet discovered a way to environmentally influence the course of this disorder.

Another example of genetic influence would be a form of mental retardation known as phenylketonuria (PKU). This disorder, present at birth, is caused by the inability of the body to metabolize (break down) a chemical compound, phenylalanine, that is commonly found in many foods. Like Huntington's disease, PKU is caused by a defect in a single gene with little contribution from other genes or the environmental background. PKU is inherited when both parents are carriers of the gene and pass it on to the child.

Given the genetic determination of PKU, how would you think we could best intervene to prevent or correct this disorder? One possibility, of course, would be genetic counseling in which people carrying these genes would be advised not to marry or not to have children if they do marry if the risk for a PKU baby were high enough. Fortunately, in the case of PKU, researchers have discovered a much simpler way. We can change the environment to interact with and affect the genetic expression of this disorder. Specifically, by detecting PKU early enough (which is now routinely done), we can simply restrict the amount of phenylalanine in the baby's diet until the child develops to the point that amounts of phenylalanine found in a normal diet do not hurt the baby's brain. This level of development usually occurs at about 6 or 7 years of age. Disorders such as Huntington's chorea and PKU, in which cognitive impairment of various kinds is the prominent characteristic, are covered in more detail in Chapter 15.

Every person has a unique set of genes unlike those of anyone else in the world (except for identical twins). Since there is some room for the environment to influence our development within the constraints set by our genes, you can see that there are many reasons for the development of individual differences.

What about our personalities? What about our behavior and traits, our likes and dislikes? Do genes have any influence on personality and behavior and, by extension, abnormal behavior? This is the age-old question in psychology. This is the issue of nature (genes) versus nurture (upbringing and other environmental influences) and the answers that are beginning to emerge, with the help of new scientific methods and technology, are fascinating. Before discussing these discoveries, let's review briefly what we know about genes.

The Nature of Genes

We have known for a long time that all normal human cells have 46 chromosomes arranged in 23 pairs. One chromosome in each pair comes from your father and one from your mother. Since we can actually see these chromosomes (through a microscope), we can tell when one is faulty and in some cases predict what problems a faulty chromosome will cause. For example, Down's syndrome results when an extra inherited chromosome hooks up on the 21st pair of chromosomes resulting in a *trisomy* (three chromosomes). Down's syndrome is a well-known condition resulting in mental retardation and certain recognizable facial characteristics, such as a somewhat flattened face and slightly slanted eyes. (These characteristics led early Western scientists to coin the term *Mongoloid* to describe people with this condition, since, to Western scientists, they looked like people from central Asia. The culturally insensitive nature of this labeling has resulted in the elimination of the term from popular usage.)

The first 22 pairs of chromosomes provide programs for the development of our body and brain, but the last pair, called the *sex chromosomes,* determine an individual's sex. In females, both of the chromosomes in the 23rd pair are called *X chromosomes.* In males, the mother contributes an X chromosome but the father, instead of contributing an X chromosome, contributes a *Y chromosome.* This one difference is responsible for the development of our gender. Anomalies or abnormalities in the sex chromosomal pair can cause some individuals to have ambiguous sexual characteristics.

The DNA molecules containing genes have a certain structure discovered only a few decades ago. This structure has been referred to as a "double helix." The shape of a helix is like a spiral ladder or a stairway

(*Left*) Recent technical advances allow scientists to isolate and study DNA. (*Right*) The DNA molecules containing genes are structured in what is called a *double helix*, which resembles a spiral ladder.

on a ship. A double helix is two spirals intertwined, turning in opposite directions. Located on this double spiral are simple pairs of molecules bound together and arranged in different orders. For example, on the X chromosome there are approximately 160 million of these base pairs. The ordering of the base pairs determines how the body develops and works.

If something is wrong or defective in the ordering of these molecules on the double helix, we then have a "defective gene." This defective gene may or may not lead to problems. If it is a single dominant gene, such as the type that controls hair or eye color, the effect can be quite noticeable. A *dominant gene* is one of a pair of genes that determines a particular trait. A *recessive gene* on the other hand, must be paired with another recessive gene to determine a trait. When we have a dominant gene, using Mendelian laws of genetics, we can predict fairly accurately how many offspring will develop a certain trait, characteristic, or disorder, depending on whether one or both of the "parents" carries that dominant gene. We have already discussed Huntington's chorea and PKU as examples of disorders that are caused by identifiable genes (either dominant or recessive).

But most of the time predictions are not so simple. Much of our development and, interestingly, most of our behavior, personality, and even IQ, to the extent that they are influenced by genes, are probably influenced by many genes, each contributing only a tiny effect. For this reason most scientists have decided that we must look for patterns of genetic control across these genes using procedures called *quantitative genetics* (Plomin, 1990). Quantitative genetics basically sums up all the tiny effects across many genes without necessarily telling us which genes are responsible. We'll look at the actual methods used by researchers to study

the influence of genes in Chapter 4. Here our interest is more on what these scientists are finding.

New Developments in the Study of Genes and Behavior

Scientists have now examined, in a preliminary way, the genetic contribution to psychological disorders and related behavioral patterns. The best estimates for genetic contribution to enduring personality traits and cognitive abilities in humans hovers around 50%. For example, it now seems quite clear that the heritability of IQ scores is between 30% and 70% (Plomin, 1990) (but probably closer to 70% than 30%). This estimate is based on a landmark study by Bouchard, Lykken, McGue, Segal, and Tellegen (1990), who studied 100 sets of twins or triplets reared apart. In regard to intelligence, they found that 70% of the variance in IQ in twins who were adults was associated with genetic variation, whether they grew up together or apart. In twins who were children, it was closer to 50%. They point out that the higher estimate in adults compared to children suggests that one can influence the *rate* of intellectual development more easily than the ultimate *level* of intellectual development reached in adulthood. The same calculation for personality traits such as shyness or activity levels ranges between 30% and 50% (Plomin, 1990; Bouchard et al., 1990; Kagan, Reznick, & Snidman, 1988b).

What about psychological disorders? Here, too, the evidence indicates that genetic factors contribute to the full range of these disorders but account for less than half the explanation. The percentage of identical twins who both have schizophrenia is less than 50% (Gottesman, 1991). Similar or lower rates exist for other psychological disorders.

Genetic contributions to behavior are evident in twins brought up in different households. The twins in the picture were raised apart. When they finally met, they discovered that they had both become firemen and shared many other personality characteristics and interests.

Important for our purposes here are the general conclusions reached by behavioral geneticists on the role of genes and psychological disorders. The first conclusion is that *no individual genes* have been identified that relate to the major psychological disorders studied in this book. This point is important because occasionally reports appear in the press citing a specific gene as responsible for some disorder or other. For example, in 1987 a report appeared claiming that a gene linked to bipolar disorder had been found in a group of closely related Amish families (see Chapter 7). But this result was found to be incorrect and could not be replicated. Similar reports appear periodically for schizophrenia. It is possible that some specific genes may be found to be associated with certain psychological disorders, and we discuss in Chapter 4 one major effort underway to identify these. But all the evidence points the other way. The conclusions of most behavioral geneticists are that genetic contributions to psychological disorders come from many genes that each make relatively small contributions to the disorders. Nevertheless it is extremely important that we recognize this influence and make every attempt to track it down. Advances in gene mapping and molecular genetics (the study of the actual structure of genes) are helping us to do this, although it is very difficult.

From this research are coming revolutionary new developments that border on science fiction and are fascinating. One new development is the ability to "knock out" certain genes in organisms through breeding or other methods. These procedures might, in the future, prevent genetically determined diseases associated with individual genes. Because psychological disorders are the product of multiple genes, however, each contributing a small amount, it is unlikely that this technology would ever be useful in reducing a person's vulnerability to psychological disorders. In any case, such a step is decades in the future.

The more important question for now is how this multiple, broad-based genetic influence interacts with the environment and what the implications are, not only for the development of psychological disorders but also for treatment. It is this last area, to which we now turn, that holds the most interest and the most promise.

Gene-Environment Interactions

In 1983, the distinguished neuroscientist Eric Kandel speculated that the process of learning affects more than behavior. He suggested that the very genetic structure of cells may actually be changed as a result of learning. This change would happen if genes that were inactive or dormant interact with the environment in such a way that they become active. In other words, the environment may occasionally "turn on" certain genes. It is, possibly, this type of mechanism that leads to changes in the number of receptors at the end of a neuron, which, in turn, would affect biochemical functioning in the brain.

Although Kandel was not the first to propose this idea, it had enormous impact. Most of us assume that the brain, much like other parts of the body, may well be influenced by environmental changes during development. But we assume that once maturity is reached, the structure and function of our internal organs and most of our physiology is pretty much set or, in the case of the brain, "hardwired." The competing idea is that the brain and its functions are "plastic" and subject to continual change as a function of interactions with the environment, even at the level

Eric Kandel, a prominent neuroscientist, has been one of the pioneers in establishing the effects of learning and related psychological processes on biological functioning.

of genetic structure. Now there is evidence supporting that view.

Greenough, Withers, and Wallace (1990) have observed that animals raised in rich, complex environments requiring a lot of motor activity develop structures in the part of their brain controlling motor activity (the cerebellum) that are different from these brain structures in animals raised in impoverished environments where little activity is possible. One effect of a complex environment is an increased number of connections among neurons in the brain. More important, it seems that these complex environments activate a previously inactive set of genes that actually *control other genes* responsible for the developing structure of the brain. Thus far this effect has been observed only in certain sections of the brain, but there is every reason to think that it will be observed throughout the brain. In order to explore gene-environment interactions as they relate to psychopathology, we can look at two models of interaction: diathesis-stress and reciprocal gene-environment.

Diathesis-Stress Model

For years, scientists have assumed a specific method of interaction between genes and the environment. In this model, called the **diathesis-stress model,** individuals inherit, from multiple genes, tendencies to express certain traits or behaviors, which may then be activated under conditions of stress. Each inherited tendency is a *diathesis,* which means, literally, a condition that makes one susceptible to developing a disorder. When the right kind of life event, such as a certain type of stressor, comes along, the disorder develops. Take the example of Judy, the adolescent with blood-injury-injection phobia. Based on a diathesis-stress model, she would inherit a *tendency* to faint at the sight of blood. This would be the diathesis, which means vulnerability. But this tendency would not become a reality until certain environmental events occurred that triggered the tendency. For Judy, this would be the sight of an animal being dissected when she was in a situation in which escape, or at least closing her eyes, was not acceptable. The "stress" of seeing the dissection under these conditions activated her genetic tendency to faint. Together, these factors led to her development of a disorder. If she had not taken biology, she might have gone through life without ever knowing she had this tendency, at least to that extreme, although she might have felt a bit queasy when encountering minor cuts and bruises.

One might also take the case of an individual who inherits a vulnerability to become highly addicted to alcohol. This inherited vulnerability might make him substantially different from a close friend who does not have the same set of genes. During college, both engage in extended drinking bouts, but only the individual with the "addictive" genes begins the long downward spiral into alcoholism. His friend doesn't.

Both examples illustrate the diathesis-stress model of the development of psychopathology (see Figure 2.1). The *diathesis* would be the genetic tendency. Most often this tendency is described as a **vulnerability.** Having this vulnerability doesn't mean that you will develop the disorder. The stressor is the particular life event that triggers the genetic vulnerability. The smaller the vulnerability, the greater will be the life stress required to produce a disorder. Conversely, with greater vulnerability, less life stress will be required to produce a disorder. This model of gene-environment interactions has been very popular, although it is greatly oversimplified in view of what we have already reviewed about the relationship of the environment to the structure and function of the brain.

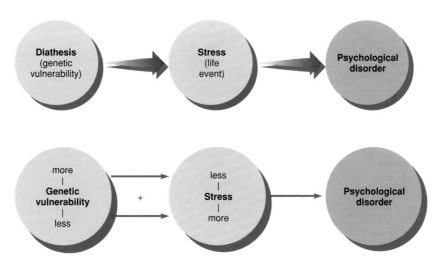

Figure 2.1 Diathesis-stress model

Reciprocal Gene-Environment Model

Nevertheless, it seems that even this diathesis-stress model, in its straightforward and simplistic form, may not describe what is happening. There is now some evidence that genetic endowment may actually *increase the probability* that the individual will encounter stressful life events. For example, people with a genetic vulnerability to develop certain disorders, such as blood-injury-injection phobia, may also have an element to their personality—let's say "impulsiveness"—that makes them more likely to be involved in minor accidents of some sort that would result in their seeing blood. In other words, they may be "accident prone" because they are continually rushing to complete things or to get places without regard for their physical safety. These people, then, might have a genetically determined tendency to create the very environmental risk factors that trigger a genetic vulnerability for them to develop blood-injury-injection phobia. This model, called the **reciprocal gene-environment model** (see Figure 2.2), has been proposed only recently (Rende & Plomin, 1992), but there is some evidence that it applies to the development of depression (Bebbington et al., 1988; McGuffin, Katz, Aldrich, & Bebbington, 1988; McGuffin, Katz, & Bebbington, 1988).

McGue and Lykken (1992) have even applied the reciprocal gene-environment model to some fascinating data on the influence of genes on the divorce rate. We all think we know why divorces occur. People simply marry the wrong partner. Some people, of course, may be more likely to stick it out, perhaps because their religion forbids divorce or they have negative feelings about divorce for other reasons. But it all depends on finding the ideal partner. Right? Not necessarily! For example, if you and your spouse

each has an identical twin, and both identical twins have previously been divorced, the chance that *you* will be divorced increases greatly. Furthermore, if not only your identical twins have been divorced, but also your parents and your spouse's parents, then the chance that you will divorce is 77.5%. On the other hand, if none of your family members on either side have been divorced, the probability you will be divorced is only 5.3%.

Of course, this is the extreme example, but McGue and Lykken (1992) demonstrated that the probability of your divorcing doubles over the probability in the population at large if your fraternal twin is also divorced, but increases *sixfold* if your identical twin is divorced. Is a gene responsible for divorce? Obviously there is no one gene that would cause divorce. Almost certainly the tendency to divorce, to the extent that it is genetically determined, is related to various traits or personality features we tend to inherit, such as being "high-strung," "impulsive," or "short-tempered." But another possibility is that some personality trait that is largely inherited makes it *more likely* that we will choose a spouse who will be incompatible. To take a simple example, if you are passive and unassertive, you may well choose a strong, dominant mate who turns out to be impossible to live with. You get divorced but then find yourself attracted to another individual with the same personality traits who is also impossible to live with. This kind of pattern seems to occur, and some people write it off to poor judgment. Social, interpersonal, psychological, and environmental factors play the major role in whether we stay married, but just possibly, your genes contribute something to the making of your own environment.

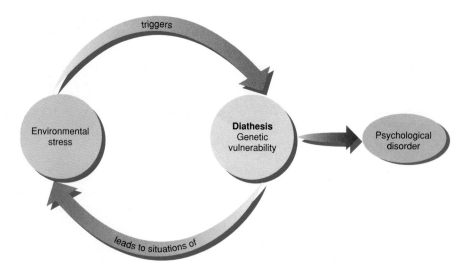

Figure 2.2   The reciprocal gene-environment model. According to the reciprocal gene-environment model of causation, the individual's genetic vulnerability, or diathesis, toward a certain disorder may make it more likely that he or she will encounter the stressful life events that in turn trigger the genetic vulnerability.

In summary, a very complex reciprocal interaction between genes and the environment seems to exist, and there is no psychological disorder where this interaction does not play an important role. Our genetic endowment *does* influence our behavior, our emotions, and our cognitive processes. Environmental events, in turn, seem to affect our very genetic structure. It is not nature (genes) and it is not nurture (environmental events) that influences the development of our behavior and personalities. It is a complex interaction of the two.

Neuroscience and Its Contributions to Psychopathology

Central to any understanding of our behavior, emotions, and cognitive processes is knowing how the nervous system and especially the brain work. We turn now to the field of **neuroscience,** where the focus is on understanding the role of the nervous system. To comprehend the cutting-edge research in this field, we first need an overview of how the brain and the nervous system function. Our nervous system is divided into the **central nervous system,** consisting of the brain and the spinal cord, and the **peripheral nervous system,** consisting of the somatic nervous system and the autonomic nervous system.

Central Nervous System

The central nervous system (CNS) processes all the information received from our sense organs, and reacts to this information if necessary. It sorts out the information, such as a certain taste or a new sound, that is relevant and the information that isn't; checks the memory banks to determine why the information is relevant; and decides on and implements the right reaction, whether it be answering a question or possibly playing a Chopin etude. This is a lot of work, and it is exceedingly complex work. The spinal cord is part of the central nervous system, but its primary function is to send messages to and receive messages from the other major component of the CNS and the most complex organ in our bodies: the brain. To accomplish the incredibly complex tasks of controlling our every thought and action, the brain contains an average of 140 billion nerve cells, called **neurons.** The neurons actually carry on the transmission of information, not only in the brain but throughout the nervous system. Understanding how neurons work is important because current research has implicated some of the workings of these neurons as contributing to psychopathology.

The typical neuron contains a central cell body with two different kinds of branches. One set of branches extending from the cell body are called **dendrites.** Dendrites receive messages in the form of chemical impulses from other nerve cells. These impulses are received by numerous **receptors** on the dendrites and converted into electrical energy for transmission *within* the neuron. The other branch, called an **axon,** transmits these impulses to other neurons. Any one nerve cell may have multiple connections. Since there are billions of these nerve cells in the brain alone, you can see how complicated this system becomes, far more complicated than the most powerful computer ever built (or likely to be built for some time).

Nerve cells are not actually connected. There is a small space through which the impulse must pass to get to the next neuron. The space between the axon of one neuron and the dendrite of another is called the **synaptic cleft** (see Figure 2.3). What happens in this space is of great interest to psychopathologists. The chemicals that are released from the axon of one nerve cell and actually transmit the impulse to the receptors of another nerve cell are called **neurotransmitters.** Only in the past several decades have we begun to understand the complexity of neurotransmitters. Now, using equipment and techniques far more sensitive than we have ever had before, scientists have identified many different types of neurotransmitters.

Major neurotransmitters that are often implicated in psychopathology include *norepinephrine* (also known as noradrenaline), *serotonin, dopamine,* and *gamma aminobutyric acid* or *GABA.* You will see these terms many times in this book. Excesses or insufficiencies in some of these neurotransmitters have been associated with different groups of psychological disorders. For example, a reduction in levels of the neurotransmitter GABA has been associated with excessive anxiety (Costa, 1985). Early research (Snyder, 1976, 1981) linked increases in dopamine activity to schizophrenia. Other early research has linked high levels of norepinephrine (Schildkraut, 1965) and possibly low levels of serotonin (Siever, Davis, & Gorman, 1991) to depression. However, later research described below has indicated that these early interpretations are probably much too simplistic. There are many types and subtypes of neurotransmitters and receptors that are just being discovered and they interact in a very complex manner. In view of the importance of this area, we will return to the subject of neurotransmitters shortly.

Structure of the Brain

In this section we review briefly different structures in the brain (see Figure 2.4). Having an outline or

Figure 2.3 The synaptic cleft. Neurotransmitters released into the synaptic cleft transmit the chemical nerve impulse from one neuron to another.

overview is useful because many of the structures described here are mentioned in the context of specific disorders in subsequent chapters. One way to view the brain is to see it in two parts—the brain stem and the forebrain or telencephalon. The lower and more ancient part of the brain is the *brain stem*. This structure is found in most animals and handles most of the automatic functions necessary to stay alive. These functions include breathing, sleeping, and moving around in a coordinated way. The more advanced part of the brain that has evolved more recently and most fully in humans is the *forebrain*. Structures in the brain are often called by Latin or Greek names based on their shape or some other characteristic.

The lowest part of the brain stem, called the *hindbrain*, contains several structures including the *medulla*, the *pons*, and the *cerebellum*. This part of the brain regulates many of the "automatic" activities of our body such as breathing, the pumping action of the heart (heartbeat), and digestion. The cerebellum controls motor coordination. Recent research suggests that abnormalities in the cerebellum may be associated

with the psychological disorder autism (Courchesne, 1991; see Chapter 16).

The *midbrain* coordinates movement with sensory input. The midbrain also contains parts of the *reticular activating system (RAS),* which contributes to processes of arousal and tension. For example, the RAS has substantial input into whether we are awake or asleep.

At the very top of the brain stem is the *diencephalon; encephalon* is Greek for head or brain and *di* means in the middle or between. This name refers to the location of the structure "between" the forebrain and the brain stem. The major structures in the diencephalon are the *thalamus* and *hypothalamus,* both of which are involved very broadly with the regulation of our behavior and emotion. The diencephalon functions primarily as a relay between the forebrain and the remaining lower areas of the brain stem. Some anatomists consider the diencephalon part of the forebrain.

The second part of the brain is the forebrain, or *telencephalon.* Telencephalon means "end" or top of

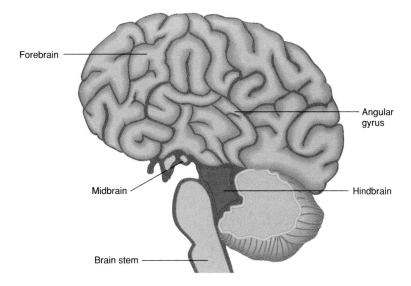

Figure 2.4   Structures of the brain

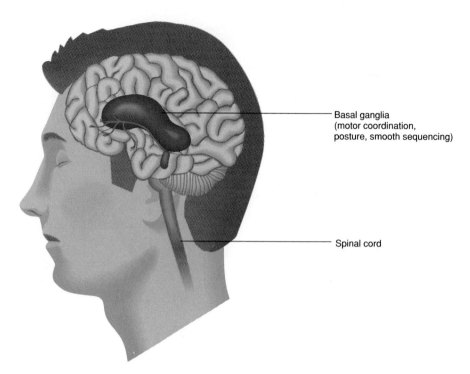

Basal ganglia
(motor coordination,
posture, smooth sequencing)

Spinal cord

Figure 2.4   *(continued)*

the brain. At the base of the telencephalon, sandwiched between the rest of the forebrain and the diencephalon is the *limbic system. Limbic* means border. This area of the brain, including such structures as the *hippocampus* (sea horse), *cingulate gyrus* (girdle), *septum* (partition), and *amygdala* (almond), figures prominently in much of psychopathology. It is this section of the brain that, in part, regulates our emotional experiences and expressions and, to some extent, our ability to learn and to control our impulses. This part of the brain is also involved with our basic drives of sex and aggression as well as hunger and thirst.

Another area at the base of the telencephalon is the *basal ganglia*, including the *caudate nucleus* (tailed nucleus). Parts of this area seem to control motor behavior because damage to these structures may change our posture or make us twitch or tremor. We will review some very interesting findings on the relationship of this area to obsessive-compulsive disorder later in the chapter.

The largest part of the forebrain is the *cerebral cortex,* which contains over 80% of all the neurons in the central nervous system. This is the part of the brain that provides us with our distinctly human qualities and allows us to look to the future and plan, to reason, and to create. The cerebral cortex is divided into two hemispheres. Although the hemispheres look very much alike structurally and operate relatively independently (both hemispheres are capable of perceiving, thinking, and remembering), recent research indicates that each has somewhat different "specialties." The left

hemisphere seems to be chiefly responsible for verbal and other cognitive processes. The right hemisphere seems to be better at perceiving the world around us and creating images. It is possible that one hemisphere or the other may play a differential role in some specific psychological disorders. For example, current theories about dyslexia (a learning disability involving reading) suggest that it may be a result of the two hemispheres not specializing adequately or communicating properly between themselves (Gladstone, Best, & Davidson, 1989).

Each hemisphere is conventionally divided into four separate areas or lobes: *temporal, parietal, occipital,* and *frontal* (see Figure 2.5). Each of these lobes or areas is associated with different processes. To provide a somewhat oversimplified summary, the temporal lobe is associated with recognizing various sights and sounds. The temporal lobe is also believed to be involved with long-term memory storage. The parietal lobe is responsible for recognizing various sensations of touch. The occipital lobe integrates and makes sense of various visual inputs. Actually, these three lobes, located toward the back (posterior) of the brain, are all involved in a somewhat integrated way in processing various sensations of sight, touch, hearing, and other signals from our senses.

The frontal lobe is the most interesting from the point of view of psychopathology. The frontal lobe carries most of the weight of our thinking and reasoning abilities as well as memory. It also enables us to relate to the world around us and the people in it, and to

Frontal lobe (the site of thinking, reasoning, remembering, and social abilities)

Parietal lobe (recognizes sensations of touch)

Occipital lobe (integrates visual sensations)

Temporal lobe (recognizes sensations of sound and memory)

Figure 2.5   The four lobes of the human cerebral cortex. Each lobe is associated with different processes.

behave as "social" animals. When studying areas of the brain for clues to psychopathology, most researchers center on the frontal lobe as well as the limbic system and the basal ganglia.

Peripheral Nervous System

The peripheral nervous system is the second part of the nervous system. The chief responsibility of the peripheral nervous system in coordination with the brain stem is to make sure that the body is working properly. The two major components of the peripheral nervous system are the **somatic nervous system** and the *autonomic nervous system*. The *somatic nervous system* controls the muscles. Problems with this part of the peripheral nervous system might make it difficult for us to engage in any voluntary movement, including talking. The **autonomic nervous system (ANS)** is divided into the **sympathetic nervous system (SNS)** and **parasympathetic nervous system (PNS).** The primary duty of the ANS is to regulate the cardiovascular system (for example, heart, blood vessels) and the endocrine system (for instance, pituitary and adrenal glands, as well as thyroid and gonadal glands), and perform various other functions, including aiding digestion and regulating body temperature.

The **endocrine system** works a bit differently from other systems in the body and plays a major role in some areas of psychopathology, such as anxiety and sexual disorders. Each of the glands produces its own chemical messenger, called a hormone, and releases this hormone directly into the blood stream. The adrenal glands produce epinephrine (or adrenalin) in response to stress, as well as salt-regulating hormones; the thyroid gland produces thyroxine, which facilitates energy metabolism and growth; the pituitary gland is a master gland that produces a variety of regulatory hormones; and the gonadal glands produce sex hormones such as estrogen and testosterone. The endocrine system is closely related to the immune system; it is also implicated in a variety of disorders, particularly the stress-related physical disorders discussed in Chapter 9.

The sympathetic and parasympathetic divisions of the ANS often operate in a complementary fashion. The sympathetic division is primarily responsible for mobilizing the body during times of stress or danger. Generally, this division of the ANS regulates expenditure of energy by rapidly activating the organs and glands under its control. When the sympathetic division goes on alert, our hearts beat faster, thereby increasing the flow of blood to our muscles; our respiration increases, allowing more oxygen to get into our blood and our brains; and our adrenal glands are stimulated. All this helps mobilize us for action. If we are threatened by some immediate danger such as a mugger coming at us on the street, we will be able to run away more quickly or defend ourselves with greater strength than if our sympathetic nervous system had not innervated our internal organs. When you read in the newspaper of a woman lifting a heavy object to free a trapped child, you can be sure that her sympathetic nervous system was working overtime. This system mediates a substantial part of what is called our "emergency" or "alarm" reaction, discussed later in this chapter and in Chapter 5.

One of the functions of the parasympathetic system, on the other hand, is to balance the sympathetic system. In other words, we could not operate in a state of hyperarousal and preparedness forever, so the parasympathetic system takes over after a while, renormalizing our arousal as well as facilitating the storage of energy by helping the digestive process.

One brain connection that is implicated in some psychological disorders involves the hypothalamus and the endocrine system. The hypothalamus connects to the adjacent pituitary gland, which is the master or coordinator of the endocrine system. The pituitary gland in turn may stimulate the adrenal glands located on top of the kidneys, specifically the cortical part of the adrenal glands. As noted above, surges of epinephrine tend to energize us, or arouse us to get our bodies ready for some threat or challenge. You may have heard athletes mention that their adrenalin was really flowing. This means they were really aroused or "up" for the game. The cortical part of the adrenal

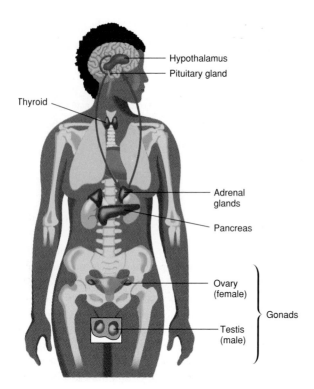

Hypothalamus
Pituitary gland
Thyroid
Adrenal glands
Pancreas
Ovary (female)
Gonads
Testis (male)

Figure 2.6 The endocrine system and the HYPAC axis. Shown here are the major glands of the endocrine system. The HYPAC axis is shown in the (blue) arrow. The pituitary gland controls the release of the stress hormone cortisol and has been implicated in several psychological disorders.

glands also produces the stress hormone **cortisol.** The name of this system in the brain is the **hypothalamic-pituitary-adrenalcortical axis** or **HYPAC axis** (see Figure 2.6). This axis has been implicated in several psychological disorders and will be mentioned in several of the disorder chapters (Chapters 5, 7, and 9, for example).

This brief overview should help you understand the structure and function of the brain and nervous system. Newly developed methods and procedures for studying brain structure and function that involve taking "pictures" of the working brain are discussed in Chapter 3. Here we focus on what these methods have determined about the nature of psychopathology.

Functions of Neurotransmitters

The different biochemical substances in the brain and nervous system responsible for carrying messages from one neuron to another are receiving intense attention in the study of psychopathology. It is important to emphasize that these substances were discovered only in the last several decades; and only in the past few years have we developed the extraordinarily sophisticated procedures necessary to study these neurochemi-

cals. Among these procedures are methods of estimating the extent of specific neurotransmitter activity by measuring by-products of this activity found in cerebrospinal fluid (the fluid within the brain and the spinal cord), accessed by lumbar puncture. These by-products are called **metabolites,** and neuroscientists have a pretty good idea of which metabolites are associated with which neurotransmitter, although the relationship is not always precise.

One way to think of these neurotransmitters would be as narrowly defined currents flowing through the ocean of the brain. Sometimes they run parallel with other currents, only to go their separate ways once again. Often they seem to meander aimlessly, looping back on themselves before moving on. Neurotransmitters are much like currents in the brain. Neurons that are more sensitive to one type of neurotransmitter, such as serotonin, tend to cluster together and form paths from one part of the brain to the other. Often these paths overlap with paths of other neurotransmitters, but, as often as not, they end up going their separate ways (Dean, Kelsey, Heller, & Ciaranello, 1993). There are literally thousands of these currents in the brain, perhaps tens of thousands, and we are just beginning to discover and map them. These neurotransmitter currents are called **brain circuits.** Recently neuroscientists have discovered a number of them that seem to play a role in different psychological disorders.

An appreciation of the various neurotransmitter systems is important for another reason. Almost all drug therapies for various psychological disorders work by either increasing or decreasing the flow of various neurotransmitters. There are many ways in which drugs accomplish this feat. Some drugs directly inhibit or block the production of a neurotransmitter. Other drugs increase the production of competing biochemical substances that may deactivate the neurotransmitter. Yet other drugs do not affect neurotransmitters directly, but block the neurotransmitter from reaching the next neuron by closing down (occupying) the receptors in that neuron. Finally, after a neurotransmitter is released, it is quickly drawn back into the neuron from the synaptic cleft. This process is called **reuptake.** Some drugs work by blocking the reuptake process, thereby causing continued stimulation along the brain circuit.

There are many neurotransmitters and many brain circuits along which they flow. New neurotransmitters are being discovered every year, and we are finding that existing neurotransmitter systems need to be subdivided into separate systems. Therefore, this area of study is a very dynamic one that is in a state of considerable flux at this time. Consequently, the neuroscience of psychopathology is a very exciting area of study, but research findings that seem very relevant to psychopathology today may no longer be true tomorrow. Many years of study will be required before it is all sorted out.

You may still read reports that certain psychological disorders are *caused* by either excesses or deficiencies in certain neurotransmitter systems (biochemical imbalances). For example, an abnormality in activity of the neurotransmitter serotonin was often described as causing depression, while abnormalities in the neurotransmitter dopamine have been implicated in schizophrenia. At one point, not so long ago, we thought this might be the case, but increasing evidence indicates that ascribing such direct causation was an enormous oversimplification. We are now learning that variations in activity of neurotransmitter systems have more general and less specific effects. Often these effects seem to be related to the way that humans process information (Depue, in press; Depue, Luciana, Arbisi, Collins, & Leon, in press). Changes in neurotransmitter activity may make people *more* or *less* likely to exhibit certain kinds of behavior in certain situations *without causing the behavior directly*. In addition, it seems that broad-based disturbances in our functioning, as is the case with psychological disorders,

Computer-generated model of serotonin

are almost always associated with the *interaction* of the various neurotransmitters in the brain rather than with alterations in the activity of any one neurotransmitter system (Depue & Spoont, 1986; Depue & Zald, 1993). In other words, these currents intersect often enough that changes in one result in changes in the other, often in an unpredictable way.

Research on neurotransmitter function focuses primarily on observing what happens when neurotransmitter activity levels change. We can do this in several ways. We can introduce substances called **agonists** that effectively *increase* the activity of a neurotransmitter by mimicking its effects, substances called **antagonists** that *decrease* or block a neurotransmitter, or occasionally substances called **inverse agonists** that produce effects *opposite* to those produced by the neurotransmitter. By systematically manipulating the production of the neurotransmitter in different parts of the brain, scientists are able to learn more about its effects. The next sections describe the four neurotransmitter systems most often mentioned in connection with psychological disorders.

Serotonin

The technical name for **serotonin** is **5-hydroxytryptamine (5-HT).** Serotonin-sensitive cells in the central nervous system seem to begin in the midbrain (see *Figure 2.7*). Approximately six major circuits or "ascending projections" spread from this area, looping around various parts of the brain (Azmitia, 1978). Because of the widespread nature of these projections, many of them ending up in the cortex, serotonin is believed by scientists to influence a great deal of our behavior, particularly the way we process information (Depue & Spoont, 1986; Spoont, 1992). Among the behavioral functions influenced by serotonin is our ability to coordinate our motor activities to accomplish a specific goal. We may decide we want to get up and walk across the room. When we do, serotonin activity increases significantly. Serotonin activity also influences our tendency to explore as opposed to withdraw from new situations as well as to act in either a more or less inhibited way in response to situations we may encounter or people we may meet (low serotonin activity is associated with less inhibi-

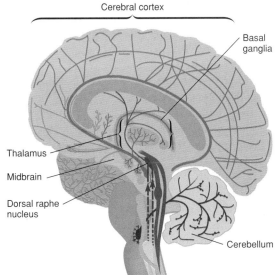

Cerebral cortex

Basal ganglia

Thalamus

Midbrain

Dorsal raphe nucleus

Cerebellum

Figure 2.7 PET scan showing distribution of serotonergic neurons in the human brain. (*Bottom*) The diagram shows the general distribution of serotonergic neurons.

Michele Spoont has theorized on the role of the neurotransmitter serotonin in brain function.

Computer-generated model of GABA

tion). Serotonin also seems to moderate and regulate our eating, sexual, and aggressive behaviors, important factors in much of psychopathology.

Considering everything we know about serotonin, Michele Spoont (1992) has proposed that its primary function is to facilitate the processing of information coming to the brain from all sources, both internal and external, and to stabilize this information flow. By stabilizing the information flow the serotonin system regulates our behavior, moods, and thought processes. Extremely low activity levels of serotonin are associated with instability, impulsivity, and the tendency to overreact to situations. For example, low serotonin activity has been associated with aggression and even suicide (as well as impulsive overeating and sexual behavior). From these findings, serotonin has correctly been conceptualized as a moderator or inhibitor of behavior (Depue & Spoont, 1986). However, we now think that these associations do not *necessarily* happen if serotonin activity is low. Other currents in the brain or other psychological or social influences may well compensate for low 5-HT activity. Therefore, low serotonin activity may make us more *vulnerable* to certain problematic behavior but may not *cause* it directly. The same view is emerging with other neurotransmitter systems. To add to the complexity, our awareness of the number of different types and subtypes of receptors sensitive to serotonin is proliferating. For example, serotonin has slightly different effects depending on the type or subtype of receptors that are affected. Several different classes of drugs seem to have their primary effects on this system, including the tricyclic antidepressants such as imipramine, known by its brand name Tofranil, and

a new class of serotonin reuptake blockers including the drug Prozac. These drugs are used with a number of psychological disorders but particularly the anxiety and mood disorders.

Benzodiazepine-GABA

One of the more exciting developments in recent years was the discovery of a strong circuit in the brain labeled the **benzodiazepine-GABA system (BZ-GABA).** This system was named, partly, after a class of drugs, the benzodiazepines or minor tranquilizers. You have probably heard of them by their trade names, such as Valium or Librium or, more recently, Xanax. We have known since the 1950s that these drugs seem to result in at least a temporary reduction of anxiety in both animals and humans, but only in 1977 was a particular receptor in a neuron discovered that seemed to be specifically sensitive to the benzodiazepine class of drugs (Mohler & Okada, 1977; Squires & Braestrup, 1970). The neurotransmitter in this system is **gamma aminobutyric acid** or **GABA.** GABA reduces postsynaptic activity that in turn inhibits a wide variety of behaviors and emotions, but its major effect is on generalized anxiety. Benzodiazepines make it easier for GABA molecules to attach themselves to the receptors of these specialized neurons. Thus, the higher the level of benzodiazepine, the more GABA will become attached to neuron receptors and the calmer we will become (to a point). In view of the existence of these specialized neurons and the neurotransmitter GABA, neuroscientists assume that we must have within us substances very much like the benzodiazepine class of drugs—in other words, natural benzodiazepines. However, we have yet to discover them.

As with other neurotransmitter systems, we now know that the benzodiazepine-GABA system is not specific to anxiety but has a much broader influence. Similarly to the 5-HT system, the BZ-GABA system rides on a large number of circuits distributed widely throughout the brain. This system seems to reduce overall arousal somewhat and temper our emotional responses. For example, in addition to reducing anxiety, minor tranquilizers are also used to relax muscle groups that may be subject to spasms, and to reduce the

Computer-generated model of norepinephrine

Computer-generated model of dopamine

possibility of convulsions (anticonvulsant effect). Over and above sedative and muscle relaxant effects, this system seems to reduce levels of anger, hostility, and aggression and, perhaps, even positive emotional states such as "eager anticipation" and pleasure (Lader, 1975; Bond & Lader, 1979). Thus, this system may specifically act to process information relevant to arousal associated with emotional and physical states.

We are also learning that the BZ-GABA system may not be unitary, and that we might have to break it down into a number of subsystems. It now seems that there are different types of GABA receptors that act in different ways, with perhaps only one of the subtypes having an affinity for the benzodiazepine component (Gray, 1985; Hoehn-Saric, 1982). Therefore, the conclusion that this system is "responsible" for anxiety seems just as out of date as concluding that the 5-HT system is responsible for depression.

Norepinephrine

A third important neurotransmitter system in the study of psychopathology is the noradrenergic system (or norepinephrine system). The neurotransmitter in this system is **norepinephrine** (also known as **noradrenaline**). We have already seen that epinephrine and norepinephrine (referred to as catecholamines) are part of our peripheral nervous system. Catecholamines are secreted by our adrenal glands. But norepinephrine is also a major neurotransmitter found in our central nervous system, particularly the brain. We now realize that the noradrenergic system, much like other systems, breaks down into a number of subsystems. Norepinephrine seems to stimulate at least two groups (and probably a lot more) of receptors called *alpha adrenergic* and *beta adrenergic receptors*. Someone in your family may be taking a widely used class of drugs called *beta blockers,* particularly if he or she has hypertension or difficulties regulating his or her heart rate. As the name indicates, these drugs block the beta receptors so that their response to a surge of norepinephrine is reduced, thereby keeping the blood pressure and heart rate down.

In the central nervous system, a number of circuits have been identified with heavy concentrations of noradrenergic neurotransmitters. One major circuit begins in the hindbrain in an area of the pons called the *locus coeruleus*. This area of the brain controls basic bodily functions such as respiration and is found even in animals far down on the phylogenetic scale. One major noradrenergic circuit extends from the locus coeruleus to the limbic system and on to the cerebral cortex as well as down into the brain stem. Work by innovative neuroscientists, such as Redmond (1977, 1979) and Gray (1982, 1985), suggests that this particular current controls our emergency reactions or alarm responses. As noted above, these responses occur when we suddenly find ourselves in some very dangerous situation, suggesting that this particular noradrenergic circuit may bear some relationship to states of panic (Charney et al., in press). More likely, however, is that this system, with all its varying circuits coursing through the brain, acts in a more general way to regulate or modulate certain behavioral tendencies and is not *directly* involved in specific patterns of behavior or in psychological disorders.

Dopamine

One final major neurotransmitter system is the dopaminergic system. The neurotransmitter in this system is **dopamine,** which has been implicated in psychological disorders such as schizophrenia. Remember the "wonder" drug reserpine (the snakeroot drug) mentioned in Chapter 1 that reduced symptoms of psychotic behaviors associated with schizophrenia? This drug and other more modern antipsychotic drugs affect a number of neurotransmitter systems, but their greatest impact may be on the dopaminergic system by blocking dopamine receptors, thereby lowering dopaminergic activity (for example, Snyder, Burt, & Creese, 1976). Thus, it is possible that the dopaminergic system might be too active in schizophrenia. We will explore this hypothesis in some detail in Chapter 14.

On the other hand, dopamine, in its various circuits throughout specific regions of the brain, also seems to have a more general effect. This effect is probably best described as a *switch* that turns on various brain circuits that may be associated with certain types of behavior. Once the switch is turned on, other neurotransmitters may then act to inhibit or facilitate emotions or behavior (Oades, 1985; Spoont, 1992).

Circuits of the dopaminergic system merge and cross with 5-HT serotonin circuits at many points and therefore influence many of the same behaviors. For example, dopamine activity is associated with exploratory, outgoing, pleasure-seeking behaviors while serotonin is associated with inhibition and constraint; thus, in a sense they balance each other (Depue et al., in press). Once again, the dopaminergic system is more complex than we originally thought. We have discovered at least five different receptor sites selectively sensitive to dopamine thus far (Dean, Kelsey, Heller, & Ciaranello, 1993). One of a class of drugs that affects the dopaminergic system specifically is L-DOPA, which is a dopamine agonist (increases levels of dopamine). One of the systems that dopamine switches on is our locomotor system. This system regulates our ability to move in a coordinated way and, once turned on, is influenced by the 5-HT system. Because of these connections, deficiencies in dopamine have been associated with disorders such as Parkinson's disease, in which a marked deterioration in motor behavior occurs including tremors, rigidity of muscles, and difficulty with judgment. L-DOPA has been successful in reducing some of these motor disabilities in Parkinson's disease.

Implications of Brain Structure and Function for Psychopathology

This overview of the structure and function of the brain and nervous system allows us to begin seeing the implications of this knowledge for theories of psychopathology. Identifiable lesions (or damage) localized in various structures of the brain do not, for the most part, result in psychological disorders with their mix of emotional, behavioral, and cognitive symptoms. Brain damage of this sort, even if it is widespread, most often results in motor or sensory deficits. These types of disorders are usually the province of the medical specialty of neurology, and neurologists often work in concert with neuropsychologists (see Chapter 3).

New and exciting findings on brain structure and function that are relevant to psychopathology are appearing almost monthly. Many of these findings have to do with *specific* contributions of the structure and functioning of the brain and various psychological disorders. But psychopathologists are also beginning to theorize about the more *general* role of brain function on the development of personality, and how different types of biologically driven personalities might be more vulnerable to developing certain types of psychopathological disorders.

One general theory has been proposed by Cloninger (1986). We should say at the outset that this theory is overly simplistic and already dated. But it is easy to describe and does provide an example of how science in this area is proceeding. Therefore, this type of theory is a glimpse of the future. Cloninger associates neurotransmitters in the brain with specific behavioral tendencies or traits. Building on the important work of pioneers like Hans J. Eysenck and Jeffrey Gray, Cloninger has investigated three basic personality traits called *harm avoidance, novelty seeking,* and *reward dependence.* Harm avoidance refers to a tendency to be very cautious and apprehensive, novelty seeking to be quite impulsive, and reward dependence to be very much influenced by approval and other positive consequences on behavior and to seek out these types of rewards. Cloninger proposes that these three traits may interact with each other to produce our personalities. What is particularly interesting about Cloninger's model, however, is his next step. He proposes that each of these three traits is strongly related to various neurotransmitter circuits in the brain. High harm avoidance and a tendency to appear anxious, apprehensive, and perhaps inhibited is associated with *high* serotonergic activity. High novelty seeking and impulsivity is associated with *low* dopaminergic activity. High reward dependence is associated with *low* noradrenergic activity. These traits and the underlying influences of the neurotransmitter system are depicted in Figure 2.8. For example, Cloninger suggests that individuals high in the trait of harm avoidance but low in the traits of reward dependence and novelty seeking would probably always be on the lookout for danger and threats and would overestimate the risks encountered in day-to-day living. Over time, these individuals would appear to be chronically anxious and socially introverted.

More sophisticated and comprehensive (and complex) theories along these lines have been proposed by leading neuroscientists such as Richard Depue (in press). As Depue and his colleagues point out, any model connecting a specific personality trait to only one neurotransmitter is not adequate and will require addition of other modulating factors. The fact that a number of the neurotransmitters modulate the flow of information in the brain and the finding that these neurotransmitters are widely distributed in the brain suggest that any changes in levels of neurotransmitters may have widespread effects on behavior, emotion, and personality (Depue et al., in press).

Neuroscience and Psychopathology

Another look into the future can suggest how these findings from neuroscience will contribute to our study

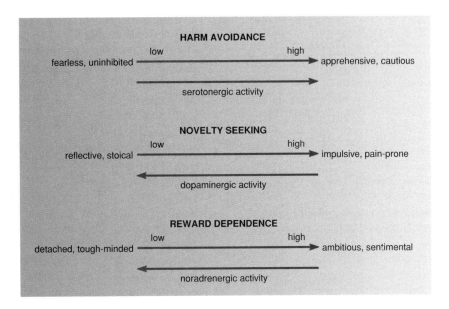

Figure 2.8 Cloninger's three heritable personality traits and their underlying neurobiological systems (adapted from Cloninger, 1986)

of psychopathology. Procedures for studying images of the functioning brain have recently been applied to a specific psychological disorder, *obsessive-compulsive disorder (OCD)*. This is a severe anxiety disorder in which individuals suffer from intrusive, frightening thoughts—for example, that they might have become contaminated with poison and will poison their loved ones if they touch them. To prevent this drastic consequence, these people engage in compulsive rituals such as very frequent washing to try to wash off the imagined poison and therefore prevent what they're thinking about from happening.

In trying to understand this disorder, a number of investigators have used brain imaging methods and

have found some intriguing differences in the brains of patients with OCD compared to people without it. Though they have found no differences in the size or structure of the brain, they have found increased activity, compared to normals, in one part of the frontal lobe of the cerebral cortex called the orbital surface. Activity is also present in the cingulate cortex and, to a lesser extent, the caudate nucleus. This brain circuit extends from the orbital section of the frontal area of the cortex, through the caudate nucleus, to parts of the thalamus. Activity in these areas seems to be correlated; that is, if one area is active, the other areas seem to be active also. These areas also define the location of several pathways of neurotransmitters, but one of the

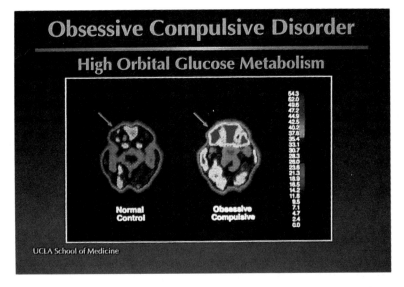

Brain function differs from normal in individuals with obsessive-compulsive disorder but "normalizes" once again after effective psychosocial treatment.

strongest concentrations of neurotransmitters serving this area is serotonin (also called *5-HT*, as mentioned previously).

Remember that one of the roles of serotonin seems to be to moderate our reactions. Our eating behavior, sexual behavior, and aggression are under better control with adequate levels of serotonin. Sometimes these behaviors go out of control when 5-HT levels are low. Research on this particular brain circuit, based mostly on experimental work with animals, demonstrates that lesions (damage) to this area of the brain that interrupt serotonin circuits seem to impair abilities to ignore irrelevant external cues and make organisms overreactive. Thus, if we were to experience damage or interruption in this brain circuit, we might find ourselves acting on every thought or impulse that enters our head.

Sometimes interesting glimpses of the workings of the human brain come from natural experiments arising out of unfortunate accidents. Occasionally people incur brain damage after accidents or brain tumors that affect only small and specific parts of the brain. Observing these phenomena is how scientists began studying brain function. In helping these people to recover, scientists can also examine what specific behavioral or personality changes occur and correlate those changes with the parts of the brain that have been damaged.

To explore what might be happening inside the brain of someone with obsessive-compulsive disorder, Thomas Insel, a biologically oriented psychopathologist, reviewed the most current literature. Insel (1992) describes a case originally reported by Eslinger and Damasio (1985) of a man who had been a successful accountant, husband, and devoted father of two before undergoing surgery for a brain tumor. He made a good recovery from surgery and seemed to be fine, but in the year following his treatment, his business failed. He also separated from his family. Although his scores on IQ tests were as high as ever and all his mental functions, such as memory, were intact, he was unable to keep a job or even be on time for an appointment. What was he doing that was causing all these problems? He was engaging in lengthy and uncontrollable compulsive rituals. Most of his days were consumed with washing, dressing, and rearranging things in the single room where he now lived. In other words, he had classic obsessive-compulsive symptoms. The area of his brain that was damaged by removal of the tumor was a small area of his orbital frontal cortex.

This new information seems to support very strongly a biological cause for psychopathology—in this case OCD. You might think there would be no need to consider social or psychological influences here. Maybe there is some wisdom to the strategy of adopting a one-dimensional or linear causal model where we can trace all psychopathology to certain brain circuits. But Insel and other neuroscientists are very cautious when interpreting these findings. First, this case involves only one individual. Other individuals with the *same* lesion might react differently. Also, the brain imaging studies described above are often inconsistent with each other on many important details. Sometimes it is difficult to pinpoint just where the increased or decreased activity is occurring because people's brains differ somewhat in their structure much as our physical size or facial features differ. Finally, studies that have been reported so far using brain imaging techniques have often cited interesting results, such as different-looking brain functions in patients with panic disorder, but other scientists or even the same scientists attempting to replicate the results have not been successful. Therefore, much more work will have to be done, and perhaps technology will have to be improved further, before we can really be confident about this particular brain circuit and its relation to OCD. It is also possible that activity in this particular brain circuit may simply be a *result* of the repetitive thinking and ritualistic behavior that characterizes OCD, rather than contributing to a cause. To take a simplistic example, if you were late for class and began running, massive changes would occur throughout your body and brain. If you were then examined with brain scans by someone who did not know you had just sprinted to class, your brain functions would look different from those of the brain of a person who walked to class. If you were doing very well in the class, the scientist might conclude, wrongly, that your unusual brain function "caused" your intelligence.

Although it may be decades before we make substantial progress in isolating, with any confidence, brain circuits of neurotransmitters associated with various psychological disorders, it is almost certain that these circuits will be found some day. But what causes these brain circuits to arise in the first place, and how can we change them? Part of the answer may lie with psychosocial influences, discussed next.

Psychosocial Influences on Brain Structure and Function

At the same time that psychopathologists are exploring the causes of psychopathology, whether in the brain or the environment, people are suffering and require the best treatments we have at this time. But sometimes the effects of treatment also tell us something about the nature of psychopathology. For example, if you think that obsessive compulsive disorder is caused by a specific brain (dys)function or by learned anxiety to scary or repulsive thoughts, this view would determine your choice of treatment, as noted in Chapter 1.

Directing your treatment at one or the other of these theoretical causes of the disorder, and observing whether your patient gets better, should also give you some hints about the accuracy of your theory on the cause of the disorder. This is a common strategy in studying psychopathology, but it has one overriding weakness. If you successfully treat a patient's particular feverish state or toothache with aspirin, the result does not mean that the fever or toothache was initially caused by an aspirin deficiency, because an effect does not imply a cause. Nevertheless, this line of evidence gives us some hints about causes of psychopathology, particularly when it is combined with other, more direct experimental evidence.

If you were to treat someone who had OCD, knowing that she might have a somewhat faulty brain circuit, what treatment would you choose? Maybe you would recommend brain surgery. In fact brain surgery (or psychosurgery) to correct severe psychopathology is an option still chosen today on occasion, particularly in the case of OCD when the suffering can sometimes be severe (Jenike et al., 1991). For the accountant described previously, the removal of his brain tumor *seems* to have inadvertently eliminated an inhibitory part of the brain circuit implicated in OCD. We know that very precise surgical lesions can be done in certain areas of the brain. Perhaps surgery on this brain circuit could dampen the runaway activity that seems to occur in or near this particular area of the brain. Other forms of psychosurgery have had beneficial effects on certain patients. This result would probably be welcome if all other treatments have failed, although psychosurgery is used very seldom and has not been studied systematically.

Nobody would want to do surgery if other, less intrusive treatments were available. To use the analogy of a television set that has developed a "disorder" of going fuzzy, if you had to go into the back of the set to rearrange and reconnect wires and change tubes every time your set got fuzzy, the correction would be a major undertaking. Alternatively, if you could simply turn a knob in front and eliminate the fuzziness, the correction would be simpler and less risky. The development of drugs affecting neurotransmitter activity has given us one of those knobs. We now have drugs that, while not a "cure" or even an effective treatment in all cases, do seem to be beneficial in treating OCD. As you might suspect, most of these drugs act by increasing serotonin activity in one way or another.

But is it possible to get at this brain circuit in another way? Is it possible that a psychological treatment might be powerful enough to affect this circuit directly? The answer now seems to be yes. One of the studies using brain imaging suggested the existence of this circuit in patients who had not been treated and took an additional, very important scientific step.

Lewis R. Baxter and his colleagues (Baxter et al., 1992) treated patients with a cognitive-behavioral therapy known to be effective with OCD called exposure and response prevention (described more fully in Chapter 5.) They then *repeated* the brain imaging after treatment. In a bellwether finding, widely noted in the world of psychopathology, Baxter and his colleagues discovered that the brain circuit had been *changed* (normalized) with a psychological intervention. Is psychotherapy another knob on the TV set with which we can directly change brain circuits? Much more research needs to be done in this area, but this finding is only one stream of evidence supporting the powerful effects of psychosocial factors on brain structure and function.

At this point we will consider just two examples of this phenomenon. Other examples of the influence of psychosocial variables on brain structure and function will appear in subsequent chapters.

Psychosocial Dwarfism (Kaspar Hauser Syndrome)

At a medical clinic in a well-known city, a young boy, appearing to be about 8 years old, presented for a medical evaluation. Detailed physical and psychological examination revealed a mental and social age of 8 years with physical development in the same age range.

This boy was born to a mother who was killed shortly thereafter in an automobile accident. The boy's father had been someone with whom the mother had had a passing affair. He was killed in the same accident. The boy's legal father, to whom the mother was married at the time he was born, remarried another woman when the patient was approximately 3 years old. Three other half-brothers and sisters, who were the legal children of this father, were also in the home.

The boy's stepmother began a course of physical and psychological abuse that will make you cringe. For years the boy was locked in a closet day and night and spent most of his time sitting in his own excrement. He was deprived of food and water. On occasion his brothers and sisters would sneak food to him. On occasions when he was let out, he would sneak food and water any way he could. Sometimes he drank out of the toilet bowl; sometimes he would eat out of the garbage can. Once a week he would be tied up and severely beaten with a broomstick. The mother would make the brothers and sisters do the beating. If they refused, she would beat them. The boy's arm and skull had been fractured in several places. The arm had never been set. The extreme nature of this abuse stunted the child's intellectual, emotional, and social growth. But one other surprising finding emerged from this study, a finding since documented, tragically, in a number of similar cases. The abuse stunted physical growth and

Left: Normally developed 16-year-old. *Center:* A 16-year-old boy suffering from psychosocial dwarfism, in which severe psychological stress contributes to the stunting of physical growth and maturation. *Right:* Same boy at age 19.3 years after rescue.

maturation. In fact, this 8-year-old boy was really 16 years old. "Rescue" from his house, which was perhaps more hostile than the worst prisoner-of-war camp, resulted in the boy's exhibiting an enormous growth spurt of 13 inches in 3 years. It was almost as if growth hormones had been dammed up in his pituitary gland all these years. In fact, pituitary function had been markedly inhibited during the years of abuse. While the boy never reached normal height, even at age 16 he was able to recover a large percentage of his growth. Intellectual and social functioning improved far less dramatically (Money, Annecillo, & Hutchison, 1985; Money, 1992).

More common is a condition often seen in young children called *failure to thrive,* which accounts for up to 5% of all pediatric hospital admissions. The prevalence is estimated at 10%–20% in rural settings (Drotar & Sturm, 1991). Although many of these non-thriving children have identifiable medical conditions responsible for their lack of development, a substantial number fall into the category of nonorganic or psychosocial failure to thrive, known officially as Feeding Disorder of Infancy or Early Childhood. Reduced caloric intake, for whatever reason, always plays a role, but the causes of reduced caloric intake lie in the dysfunctional psychosocial setting. This disorder is one of the eating disorders (see Chapter 8).

AIDS and the Immune System

Consider one more example of psychosocial influences from a very different context. One of the

most stressful times in the life of any individual occurs when she is told that she is about to die. In our times, this is happening every day to individuals stricken with acquired immune deficiency syndrome (AIDS), which is caused by the human immune deficiency virus type 1 (HIV-1). As most people now know, there is a period of time of greatly varying length between acquiring the virus and actually developing the symptoms of AIDS. But the stress of learning that you are carrying the AIDS virus can be devastating.

Recently a group of clinical scientists (Antoni et al., 1991) sought to learn whether they could reduce this stress by administering a psychosocial stress reduction treatment to a group of individuals who were concerned that they might be carrying the HIV virus. This program was administered during the period of several weeks before testing for HIV-1. To examine whether this treatment had any effect, only half of the group received the stress reduction program; the other half received the usual medical and psychological care. Unfortunately, many individuals in this group learned that they had the HIV virus. However, those who had undergone the psychosocial stress reduction procedures, unlike their counterparts, did *not* show substantial increases in anxiety and depression. Furthermore, and more important, they actually demonstrated *increases* in their immune system functioning as measured by such indices as T-Helper/Inducer cells (CD4) and natural killer (NK) cells, as well as other indices of immune functioning. It is too early to know whether these changes will result in increased survival time but other studies reviewed in Chapter 9 suggest that maybe this will happen.

The stress reduction results are consistent with a long line of research showing that psychosocial factors have profound influence on our immune systems. In the case of AIDS this is essential information. Because there is no cure, strengthening the immune system and delaying the onset of the disease itself for as long as possible is extremely important, particularly since recent evidence suggests that some experimental drugs—for example, Azidothymidine (AZT)—do not slow the progression of the disease (*Science,* 1993). It now seems that the development of cancer may be subject to similar psychosocial influences, and a new field of study called *psychoncology* has emerged to study these influences (Schneiderman, Antoni, Irsonson, LaPerriere, & Fletcher, 1992; Antoni & Goodkin, in press).

Changing the immune system, of course, is not the same as directly changing the structure and function of the central nervous system, but the immune system is profoundly influenced by the brain and its functioning. Changes in behavior and cognitive processes shown to affect the immune system are most likely mediated by the central nervous system, discussed further in Chapter 9.

Interactions of Psychosocial Influences and Neurotransmitters

Several recent experiments illustrate the interaction of psychosocial factors and neurotransmitters. Some experiments even indicate that psychosocial factors directly affect levels of neurotransmitters. For example, Insel, Champoux, Scanlan, and Suomi (1986) raised two groups of rhesus monkeys identically except for the ability they had to control things in their cages. One group had free access to toys and food treats, but the second group got these toys and treats only when the first group did. In other words, the second group had the same number of toys and treats but they could not choose when they got them. Therefore, they had less control over their environment. In psychological experiments we say that the second group was "yoked" with the first group because their treatment depended entirely on what happened to the first group. In any case, the first group grew up with a sense of control over things in their lives and the second group didn't, replicating results from a similar study.

Later in their lives, all these monkeys were administered a benzodiazepine inverse agonist. You will remember that this is a neurochemical that has the *opposite* effect of the neurotransmitter GABA. Therefore, the effect is an extreme burst of anxiety. The few times this neurochemical has been administered to people, usually scientists administering it to each other, the recipients reported the experience to be one of the most horrible sensations they had ever endured. Of course, it lasts only a short time.

When this substance was injected in the monkeys an interesting thing happened. The group that had been raised with little control over their environment ran to a corner of their cage where they crouched displaying severe anxiety and panic. But the group that had a sense of control behaved quite differently. They did not seem to be anxious at all. Rather, they seemed to be angry and aggressive, even attacking other monkeys near them. Thus, the very same level of a neurochemical substance, acting as a neurotransmitter, had very different effects depending on the psychological histories of the monkeys. Mineka, Gunnar, and Champoux (1986) in a similar but more complex experiment also demonstrated the crucially important effects of early experiences on later behavior.

The Insel et al. (1986) experiment is an example of a significant interaction between neurotrans-

(*Left*) Depending on their early psychological experiences, rhesus monkeys reacted either with anger or fear when injected with a specific neurotransmitter. (*Right*) Thomas Insel, the lead investigator in this study, conducts research on the interaction of psychosocial factors and neurotransmitters at the National Institute of Mental Health.

William Greenough and his associates discovered that raising rats in a complex environment that required a lot of learning and motor behavior later affected the structure of the rats' brains, demonstrating again the influence of psychological factors on biological development.

mitters and psychosocial factors. Other experiments suggest that psychosocial influences directly affect the functioning and perhaps even the structure of the central nervous system. Scientists have observed that psychosocial factors routinely change the levels of many of our neurotransmitter systems, including norepinephrine and serotonin (Anisman, 1984; Maser & Gallup, 1974). It also seems that the structure of neurons themselves, including the number of receptors on a cell, can be changed by learning and experience (Kandel, 1983; Paul & Skolnick, 1978, 1981).

We are now beginning to learn how this happens. As noted previously, William Greenough and his associates (Greenough et al., 1990), studying the cerebellum, which coordinates and controls motor behavior, discovered that rats raised in a rich environment requiring a lot of learning and motor behavior develop a different structure in their nervous system from rats that are "couch potatoes." The active rats had a greatly increased number of connections between nerve cells in the cerebellum and also grew many more dendrites. The researchers also observed that certain kinds of learning *decreased* the connections between neurons in other areas. Therefore, it seems that the very structure of our nervous system is constantly changing as a result of learning, and that some of these changes are permanent.

Conclusion

Scientists are beginning to discover the specific brain circuits involved in psychological disorders. These brain circuits are very complex systems identified by specific pathways of neurotransmitters traversing certain areas of the brain. Discovery of these brain circuits suggests that the structure and function of the nervous system plays a major role in psychopathology. But other research suggests that these brain circuits are strongly influenced by psychological and social factors and that we may not be born with them. Furthermore, both biological interventions, such as drugs, and psychological interventions seem capable of altering the circuits. Therefore, we cannot consider the nature and cause of psychological disorders without examining both biological and psychological factors.

Behavioral and Cognitive Influences

In this section we discuss some of the enormous progress that has been made in understanding behavioral and cognitive influences in psychopathology. To return to the case of Judy, it would be just as out of date to say that her blood phobia was caused by a conditioned response as it would be to say that it was caused by a brain dysfunction. Scientists have discovered that conditioning processes are more than simple random associations. They represent complex ways in which we process information, as we shall see below.

Some of this new information has come from the recently established field of **cognitive science** (for example, Baddeley, 1986), a field concerned with how we acquire and process information as well as how we store and ultimately retrieve it (one of the processes involved in memory). Scientists have also discovered that a great deal goes on inside our heads of which we are not necessarily aware. Since, technically, these cognitive processes are "unconscious," some of these findings recall the unconscious mental processes that are so much a part of Freud's theory of psychoanalysis (although these unconscious processes do not look much like the ones Freud envisioned). A brief account of modern-day thinking shows us what is happening during the process of classical conditioning.

Conditioning and Cognitive Processes

During the 1960s and 1970s, behavioral scientists in the animal laboratories studying the basic processes of classical conditioning began to uncover the complexity of this process (Rapee, 1991). Robert Rescorla (1988) concluded that simply pairing two events closely in time (such as the meat powder and the metronome in Pavlov's laboratories) is not really what's important in this type of learning. At the very least, it is a vast oversimplification of what happens. Rather, a variety of different judgments and cognitive processes enter into determining the final outcome of this learning, even in lower animals such as rats.

As one simple example, Pavlov would have predicted that if the meat powder and the metronome were paired, say, 50 times, then a certain amount of learning would take place. But Rescorla and others discovered that if one animal never saw the meat powder at any time except for the 50 trials following the metronome sound, while the meat powder was brought to the other animal many times *in between* the 50 times it was paired with the metronome, the two animals would learn something very different. That is, even though the metronome and the meat powder would have been paired 50 times for each animal, the metronome would be *much less meaningful* to the second animal. Put another way, the first animal learned that the sound of the metronome meant meat powder would be next; the second animal learned that sometimes the meat came after the sound and sometimes it came without the sound. Finding that the two different conditions produce two different learning outcomes is really a commonsense notion, but it demonstrates, along with many other, far more complex scientific findings, that basic classical (and operant) conditioning paradigms really facilitate the learning of the *relationship* among events in the environment. This type of learning makes it possible to develop some working ideas about your world that allow you to make appropriate judgments. You can then respond in a way that will either benefit you or at least not hurt you. In other words, complex cognitive as well as emotional processing of information is involved when conditioning occurs (yes, even in animals).

Learned Helplessness

Along similar lines Martin Seligman, also working with animals, described the phenomenon of **learned helplessness.** Learned helplessness occurs when rats, or other animals, encounter conditions over which they discover they have no control whatsoever. If rats are confronted with a situation in which they receive occasional foot shocks, they can function very well if they learn they can cope with these shocks by doing something to avoid them (say pressing a lever). But if the animals learn that their behavior has no effect whatsoever on their environment—sometimes they get shocked and sometimes they don't, no matter what they do—they become very "helpless." In other words, they give up attempting to cope and seem to develop the animal equivalent of depression.

Seligman drew some important conclusions from these observations. He theorized that the same phenomenon may happen with people who are faced with uncontrollable stress in their lives. Subsequent work revealed this to be true, but only under one

Martin Seligman first described the concept of learned helplessness after observing that rats who had no control over whether they received a foot shock seemed to abandon all efforts to cope with the shock and developed the animal equivalent of depression.

important condition. People will become depressed if they "decide" or "think" there is little they can do about the stress in their lives, even if it seems to others that there *is* something they could do. In other words, the people make an *attribution* that they have no control over the stress in their lives and they get depressed (Abramson, Seligman, & Teasdale, 1978; Miller & Norman, 1979). This has become an important psychological theory of depression, which we will revisit in Chapter 7. It illustrates, once again, the necessity of recognizing that ways in which information is processed about events in the environment differ from person to person. These cognitive differences are an important component of psychopathology.

Social Learning

Another influential psychologist, Albert Bandura (1973, 1986), observed that organisms, including lower animals, do not have to actually *experience* certain events in their environment to learn effectively. Rather, they can learn just as much by watching someone else experience a given situation and observing what happens to the other person. Once again, this is a rather commonsense notion that came to be known as **modeling** or **observational learning.** What is important about this process is that, even in animals, this type of learning requires a symbolic integration of the experiences of others with judgments of what might happen to the observer. In other words, even an animal that is not very intelligent by human standards, such as a rat, must infer the conditions under which its own experiences would be very similar to those of the animal it is observing. Bandura expanded these observations into a network of ideas where behavior, cognitive factors, and environmental influences converged to produce the complexity of behavior that confronts us. He also began specifying in some detail the importance of the social context of our learning. That is, much of what we learn depends on our interactions with other people around us.

The basic idea in all this work is that cognitive processes mediate our behavior. Therefore, a careful analysis of these processes may well produce the most accurate scientific predictions of behavior. Concepts of probability learning, information processing, and attention have become increasingly important in psychopathology (Martin, 1983; Martin & Levey, 1985).

Prepared Learning

Finally, it has become clear that biology and, probably, our genetic endowment influence *what* we learn. This conclusion is based on the fact that we learn to fear some objects much more easily than others. In other words, we learn fears and phobias selectively (Seligman, 1971; Mineka, 1985b). Why would this be? One possibility is a concept called **prepared learning:** The idea here is that we have become *highly prepared* for learning about certain types of objects or situations over the course of evolution because this learning contributes to the survival of the species. Even without any contact, we are more likely to learn to fear snakes or spiders than rocks or flowers, even if we know rationally that the snake or spider is harmless. On the other hand, in the absence of experience, we are less likely to fear guns or electrical outlets even though these are potentially much more deadly. Why would we so readily learn to fear snakes or spiders? Again, one possibility is that, back at the time when our ancestors lived in caves, those who tended to avoid all snakes and spiders ended up having less contact with deadly varieties and therefore survived in greater numbers, passing their genes down to us. This learning then contributed to the survival of the species. This is just a theory, of course, but at the present time it seems the most likely explanation.

We also seem to have something within us that facilitates learning the connection between a certain signal and an event in the environment that is threatening to us. In other words, certain UCSs (unconditioned stimuli) and CSs (conditioned stimuli) "belong" to one another. Have you ever gotten sick on cheap wine or bad food? If you have, chances are you won't touch that wine or food again. This very quick or "one-trial" learning also occurs in animals who eat something that is bad or perhaps contains some poison. It is easy to see how survival might be associated with the capacity to learn quickly to avoid poisoned food. Thus the sight or taste of certain foods (the CS) and nausea or other gastrointestinal reactions is an association that is learned very quickly. On the other hand, if animals were shocked instead of poisoned when they ate certain foods, they would not learn this association nearly as quickly. Perhaps these selective associations are also facilitated by our genes (Cook, Hodes, & Lang, 1986; Garcia, McGowan, & Green, 1972).

Cognitive Science and the Unconscious

Advances in cognitive science have also revolutionized our conceptions of the unconscious. Using procedures primarily from the new field of cognitive science, we now know that much goes on inside our heads of which we are not aware. But this unconscious is not necessarily the seething caldron of primitive emotional conflicts envisioned by Freud. Rather, we simply seem able to process and store information, and act on that information, without having the slightest awareness of what the information is or why we are acting on it. Does this sound surprising? Consider briefly these two examples.

Lawrence Weiskrantz (1992) has described a phenomenon called *blind sight* or *unconscious vision.* He describes a case of a young man who, for medical reasons, had a small section of his visual cortex (the center for the control of vision in his brain) surgically removed. Though the operation was considered a success, the young man lost the left side of his visual field. Later, during routine tests, one of the physicians raised his hand into the left side of the patient's visual field. Much to the shock of his doctors, he reached out and touched it. Subsequently, scientists determined that he could not only reach for objects in this "blind" area of his vision but could also distinguish among objects and perform most of the functions usually associated with sight. Yet, when asked about his abilities he would say, "I couldn't see anything, not a darn thing," and that all he was doing was guessing.

The phenomenon in this case, of course, is associated with real brain damage. Much more interesting, from the point of view of psychopathology, is that the same thing seems to occur in healthy individuals who, for example, have been hypnotized (Hilgard, 1992; Kihlstrom, 1992). That is, normal individuals, provided with hypnotic suggestions that they are blind, will be able to function visually but will have no awareness or memory of their visual abilities. This condition illustrates a process of *dissociation* between behavior and consciousness. This process forms the basis for the dissociative disorders discussed in Chapter 6.

A second example, which has more relevance for psychopathology, has been called **implicit memory** (Graf, Squire, & Mandler, 1984; Kihlstrom, Barnhardt, & Tataryn, 1992). Implicit memory refers to a condition in which individuals are clearly acting on the basis of things that have happened to them in the past, but they can't remember the events that are causing them to act that way. (If you have good memory of the events, which is usually the case when we talk about our memories, it is called *explicit memory.*) But implicit memory can be very selective for only certain events or circumstances. You may have seen an episode of *Star Trek* in which some of the crew were acting in a frightened and unusual way after a seemingly uneventful trip to a nearby planet. Only gradually did they recover memories of being captured and experimented on. Their frightened and unusual behavior seemed to be due to memories of their capture of which they were not aware. This situation represents the process of implicit memory at work. Clinically, we have already seen an example of implicit memory at work in the context of a psychological disorder in the case of Anna O. in Chapter 1. Remember that this was the classic case first described by Breuer and Freud (1957) as demonstrating the existence of the unconscious. Anna O. remembered events surrounding her father's death and the connection of these events to her paralysis only after therapy. Thus, it seems that Anna O.'s behavior (her occasional paralysis) was connected to implicit memories of her father's death. Many scientists have concluded that Freud's speculations on the nature and structure of the unconscious went beyond reality, but science has now demonstrated the existence of "unconscious" processes; we must confront these processes in the study of psychopathology.

What methods do we have for studying the unconscious? In recent decades, psychologists, confident in the establishment of a science of behavior, have moved back into the *black box* (a term common in psychology to refer to unobservable feelings and cognitions inferred by self-report of the individual). They have moved into the black box with new methods and new technology in an attempt to make the unobservable observable. There are several methods for studying the unobservable (unconscious), all of them made possible by advances in technology. One of them is the Stroop color-naming paradigm.

In the Stroop paradigm, subjects are shown a variety of words, each of which is printed in a different color. They are shown these words very quickly and asked to name the colors in which the words are printed while ignoring the meaning of the words. Delays in color naming occur when the meaning of the word attracts the subject's attention, despite his or her efforts to concentrate on the color of the word—that is, the meaning of the word *interferes* with the subject's ability to process information about the color of the word. Experimenters have determined that people with certain psychological disorders, like Judy, will be much slower at naming the colors of words associated with their problem (for example, blood, injury, dissect) than

words that have no relation to the disorder. Thus, psychologists can now uncover particular patterns of emotional significance, even if the subject may not be able to verbalize them or may not be aware of them. These developments in our understanding of the nature of psychopathology will come up repeatedly as we discuss specific psychological disorders. Once again, it is important to note that these findings support Freud's ideas about the unconscious, up to a point. But this conception is also very different from Freud's because no assumptions are made about an elaborate structure existing within the mind that is continually in conflict (for instance, id, ego, superego). As cognitive science advances, the necessity of assuming the existence of an unconscious with such a complex array of functions and structure seems less important.

Cognitive-Behavioral Therapy

When scientists such as Bandura and Seligman began to discover the important contributions of cognitive processes to behavioral development, others began to integrate cognitive procedures and techniques directly into therapy. At this point the approach called **cognitive-behavioral therapy** came into being. Among its originators was Aaron T. Beck (1976), who developed methods to deal with faulty attributions and attitudes associated with learned helplessness and depression (see Chapter 7). Albert Ellis (1962), in an approach he called **rational-emotive therapy,** also focused directly on the irrational beliefs that he believed were at the root of maladaptive feelings and behavior.

Cognitive-behavioral approaches to treatment will be described in some detail in later chapters, particularly in Chapter 5 on anxiety disorders, Chapter 7 on mood disorders, and Chapter 9, where we describe

Aaron T. (Tim) Beck, the originator of cognitive therapy

Charles Darwin (1809–1882) described the fight or flight reaction in animals, as exemplified in one of his books by this picture of a cat terrified at the sight of a dog.

stress reduction procedures. In general, therapists applying cognitive-behavioral approaches will examine in some detail the types of thinking processes ongoing in individuals who are anxious, depressed, or stressed. This probing is often accomplished by asking patients to monitor the thoughts they are having during periods of distress. An individual suffering from depression might decide before taking a particular course in college that she almost certainly will do very poorly in the course. She then may become more depressed thinking about all the negative implications of her poor performance. The thoughts might occur even though she has a straight A average, indicating that her anxieties are unrealistic and irrational. Individuals with severe anxiety might be continually focusing, in an unrealistic way, on dangers that might be inherent in otherwise normal situations. Many times individuals with these types of "depressive" or "anxious" thoughts are not aware of their inappropriate and negative thinking since the thoughts can be very automatic or "unconscious."

Therapy is directed at elucidating these thoughts and working to develop a different set of attitudes and attributions. Patients in cognitive-behavioral therapy will also be assigned specific behavioral tasks such as entering fearful situations where they can work on their emotional and cognitive reactions. Procedures to change arousal or activity levels such as relaxation procedures or exercise may also be a component of therapy. Thus, cognitive-behavioral approaches are continually targeting both cognitive aspects of the problem (attributions and attitudes) and behavioral aspects (avoiding situations that provoke unrealistic anxiety or perhaps feelings of depression, increasing activity, or improving social skills). Cognitive-behavioral therapies are usually brief, taking between 10 and 20 sessions. The specific ways in which cognitive behavioral approaches are applied to specific disorders will be spelled out in more detail in the appropriate chapter.

Emotional Influences

To some degree we are all experts on emotion. We experience emotions every day. We also see emotion displayed in movies or hear our friends talking about their loves, hates, and fears. Despite our familiarity with emotion, it is, ironically, an area about which psychologists know relatively little. When you experience an emotion and tell your friends about it, you are reporting on an internal subjective feeling state, but emotions are far more complex than what you feel. Consider the emotion of fear. Have you ever found yourself in a really dangerous situation? Have you ever almost crashed your car, and you knew for several seconds beforehand that this was going to happen? Have you ever been swimming in the ocean and realized that you were out too far or that you were caught in some currents? Or have you ever almost fallen off a high place such as a cliff or a roof? If so, you might have felt an incredible surge of "arousal." If, somehow, you could have stood to one side and watched yourself, you would have noticed a number of reactions. These reactions would be fundamentally the same responses noticed by Darwin in his careful observations of animals over 100 years ago. "With all or almost all animals, even with birds, terror causes the body to tremble. The skin becomes pale, sweat breaks out, and hair bristles. The secretions of the alimentary canal and of the kidneys are increased, and they are involuntarily voided, owing to the relaxation of the sphincter muscles, as is known to be the case with man, and as I have seen with cattle, dogs, cats, and monkeys. The breathing is hurried. The heart beats quickly, wildly, and violently; but whether it pumps the blood more efficiently through the body may be doubted, for the surface seems bloodless" (Darwin, 1872, p. 77).

Do these responses serve any purpose? The fact that this reaction seems to be "programmed" in all animals, including us, suggests that it probably does serve a useful function. For this behavior and the overwhelming emotions associated with it represent our alarm reaction that is activated during potentially life-threatening emergencies. This strong behavioral tendency is called the **flight or fight response.** If you are out in the ocean and caught in currents, your almost instinctual tendency will be to attempt to escape by struggling toward shore. You might realize rationally that you're best off just floating in the current until it runs its course, and then, more calmly, swimming in later. But somewhere, down deep within us, our ancient instincts for survival won't let us do this. Therefore, because struggling against ocean currents will only wear you out, the chances are greater that you will drown. On the other hand, this same reaction in other situations might momentarily give you the strength to lift the back of a car to help your trapped brother or enhance your ability to fight off an attacker. The whole purpose of the physical rush of adrenalin that we feel while in extreme danger is to mobilize us to escape the danger, or to fight it off (flight-fight).

The Physiology of Fear

How do these physical reactions prepare us to respond this way? The great physiologist Walter Cannon (1929) speculated on the reasons, and these reasons have been elaborated by Beck and Emery (1985). Your cardiovascular system becomes activated. Your blood vessels constrict, thereby raising arterial pressure and decreasing the blood flow to your extremities (your fingers and toes, etc.). Excess blood is redirected to the skeletal muscles, where the blood is more available to the vital organs that may be needed in an emergency. Often people seem "white with fear"; that is, they blanch with fear as a result of decreased blood flow to the skin. "Trembling with fear" with your hair standing on end may be the result of shivering and piloerection (in which body hairs stand erect). Both of these reactions conserve heat during periods when your blood vessels are constricted. These defensive adjustments can also produce the commonly observed "hot" and "cold" spells that occur during extreme fear. Breathing becomes more rapid and usually deeper to provide necessary oxygen to rapidly circulating blood. Increased blood circulation carries oxygen to the brain; thus cognitive processes and sensory functions are stimulated. This helps you to be more alert and to think more quickly during emergencies. An increased amount of glucose (sugar) is also released from the liver into the bloodstream to further energize various crucial muscles and organs, including the brain. Pupils dilate, presumably to allow a better view of the situation. Hearing becomes more acute and digestive activity is suspended, resulting in a reduced flow of saliva (the "dry mouth" of fear). There is often pressure to urinate and defecate and occasionally to vomit. In the short term, voiding the body of all waste material or the necessity of engaging in digestive processes will further prepare the organism for concentrated action and activity. This activity will also protect you if you happen to have ingested any poisonous substances during the emergency.

It is easy to see why this alarm or emergency reaction is so fundamentally important. Millennia ago, when our ancestors lived in caves, those individuals with a strong emergency reaction would tend to live through attacks and other emergencies, more so than those with a weak emergency response. The survivors of those harrowing periods passed their genes down to us through the ages.

Definitions of Emotional Phenomena

The emotion of fear, then, is not just a subjective feeling of terror. It is also a strongly motivated behavior (escaping or fighting) and a complex physiological response. For these reasons, to *define* emotion is difficult, but most emotion theorists would agree that emotion is an *action tendency* (Lang, 1979, 1985). That is, an **emotion** is a tendency to behave in a certain way (for example, escape) elicited by an external event (a threat) and a feeling state (terror) accompanied by a (possibly) characteristic physiological response (Ortony & Turner, 1990; Lazarus, 1991; Izard, 1992; Oatley & Jenkins, 1992). One purpose of the feeling state would be to *motivate* us to carry out the behavior. Thus if we do escape, our terror, which is unpleasant, will be decreased. Decreasing unpleasant feelings motivates us to escape. How do you think this works with anger, or love? What is the feeling state? What is the behavior?

At this point it is useful to consider some other terms you will encounter in this book. Emotions are usually thought to be short-lived, temporary states of several minutes to, perhaps, several hours, occurring in response to some external event. A more persistent period of emotionality is often referred to as **mood.** Thus, in Chapter 7 we will describe enduring or recurring states of depression or excitement (mania) as mood disorders. But anxiety disorders, described in Chapter 5, may also be characterized by enduring or chronic anxiety and, therefore, could also be called mood disorders. Alternatively, both anxiety disorders and mood disorders could be called emotional disorders, a term not formally used in psychopathology. This is only one example of occasional inconsistencies in terminology that have arisen over the years in abnormal psychology.

One other emotion-related term you will see occasionally, particularly in Chapters 3 and 14, is **affect.** Affect refers to the momentary emotional tone accompanying what we say or do at a given point in time. For example, if you just got an A+ on your test but you look sad, your friends might think it strange and want an explanation. This is because your *affect* is not appropriate to what happened.

The Components of Emotion

Emotion theorists tend to concentrate on one of three components of emotion: behavior, physiology, or cognitive processes. Emotion theorists who concentrate on behavior tend to think that basic patterns of emotion differ from one another in fundamental ways. Anger may differ from sadness not only in how it feels as well as behaviorally, but also physiologically. These theorists also emphasize that emotion is one way of communicating or sending a signal from one member of the species to another. One function of the emotion of fear is to motivate immediate and decisive action such as running away. But if you *look* scared, your appearance will quickly communicate the possibility of danger to your friends, who may not be aware that a threat is imminent. This communication will increase their chance for survival since they will be able to respond more quickly to the threat when they see it. This important function of emotion may be one reason emotions are contagious, as we observed in Chapter 1 when talking about mass hysteria (Hatfield, Cacioppo, & Rapson, 1993).

Other scientists have concentrated on the physiology of emotions. Most notable among these is Cannon (1929), who viewed emotion as primarily a brain function. Research in this tradition suggests that areas of the brain associated with emotional expression are generally more ancient and primitive than areas associated with higher cognitive processes such as reasoning. Other research suggests there may be direct neurobiological connections between these ancient areas of the brain and parts of the eye (the retina) that allow emotional activation without the influence of higher cognitive processes (Moore, 1973; Zajonc, 1984). In other words, you may experience various emotions quickly and directly without necessarily thinking about them or being aware of why you feel the way you do.

Finally, a number of prominent theorists concentrate on studying the cognitive aspects of emotion. Notable among these theorists is Richard S. Lazarus (for example, Lazarus, 1968, 1991), who theorizes that changes in a person's world are appraised in terms of their potential impact on that person. The type of appraisal you make will determine the emotion that you experience. For example, you might see somebody holding a gun in a dark alley, appraise the situation as dangerous, and experience fear. But if you saw a museum tour guide displaying a (rare) gun in a museum, you might make a very different appraisal and experience interest. Lazarus would suggest that, thinking and feeling (emotion) cannot be separated. But other cognitive scientists are concluding that although cognitive and emotional systems interact and overlap, they are fundamentally separate systems (Teasdale, 1993). All these components of emotion, behavior, physiology, and cognition are important, and emotion theorists continue to study their interaction.

Anger and Your Heart

When we discussed what caused Judy's blood phobia, we observed that behavior and emotion may strongly influence biology. Scientists have recently made some important discoveries in this regard concerning the familiar emotion of anger. We have known for years that negative emotions such as hostility and anger seem to increase a person's risk of developing heart disease (Chesney, 1986; MacDougall, Dembroski, Dimsdale, & Hackett, 1985). In fact, sustained hostility with angry outbursts contributes more strongly to death from heart disease than other well-known risk factors including smoking, high blood pressure, and high cholesterol levels (Williams, Haney, Lee, Kong, & Blumenthal, 1980).

How exactly does this happen? Recently Ironson and her colleagues (1992) studied this question. They asked a number of people with heart disease to imagine something that had made them very angry in the past. Sometimes these events had occurred many years ago. In one case, an individual who had spent time in a Japanese prisoner-of-war camp during World War II became angry every time he thought about it. What made him particularly angry was hearing about reparations paid by the United States government several years ago to Japanese Americans who had been held in internment camps in the United States during the war. Ironson et al. compared the experience of anger to other stressful events that increased heart rate but were *not* associated with anger. For example, some participants imagined making a speech while defending themselves against a charge of shoplifting. Others figured out difficult problems in arithmetic trying to beat a time limit. The subjects' heart rates in these angry and stressful situations were then compared to increases in their heart rates as a result of exercise (riding a stationary bicycle). The investigators found that the ability of the heart to pump blood through the body efficiently dropped significantly while the subjects were angry but not while they were stressed or exercising. In fact, *remembering* being angry was sufficient to cause the anger effect. If they were *really* angry, their heart-pumping efficiency would drop even more, putting them at risk for dangerous disturbances in heart rhythms (arrhythmias).

This study is the first to actually uncover the precise mechanism (decreased pumping efficiency) by which the emotion of anger affects the heart, at least in people who have already developed some heart disease. Other studies such as one by Williams et al. (1980) demonstrated that anger affects people without heart disease, also. Medical students who experienced a lot of anger were seven times as likely to have died by the age of 50 than were students in the same class who had lower levels of hostility.

Shall we conclude that too much anger causes heart attacks? In one sense we could say that it does, but this conclusion would be another example of the one-dimensional type of causal modeling mentioned earlier. Increasing evidence, including the studies just mentioned, suggests that anger and hostility contribute to heart disease, but so do many other factors, including a genetically determined biological vulnerability. We will discuss cardiovascular disease in Chapter 9.

The Role of Emotions in Psychopathology

We have seen how emotions can have a direct and dramatic impact on our functioning. Specifically, the emotion of anger seems to directly affect, in a negative way, the functioning of the heart and may contribute to the physical disorder of cardiovascular disease. Other emotions seem to play a more direct role in psychological disorders. In Chapter 5 we will study the phenomenon of *panic* and its relationship to anxiety disorders. One of the interesting possibilities that investigators are exploring is that a panic attack is simply our normal emotion of fear occurring at the wrong time. That is, it occurs when there is nothing really to be afraid of.

Emotions play a central role in other disorders, such as mood disorders. There is one group of patients who become overly excited and joyful. These individuals think they have the world on a string and that they can do anything they want and spend as much money as they want because everything will turn out all right. Every little event occurring during their day is the most wonderful and exciting experience they have ever had. These individuals are suffering from *mania*, which is part of a very serious mood disorder to be discussed in Chapter 7. Most often, individuals suffering from mania will alternate periods of excitement with periods of extreme sadness and distress when they feel that all is lost and that the world is a dark, gloomy, and hopeless place. Unlike people experiencing mania, individuals in a state of extreme sadness/distress are unable to experience any pleasure in life and often find it difficult even to get out of bed in the morning and move around. If things become particularly hopeless, these individuals are at risk for committing suicide. This emotional state is *depression*, a defining feature of many mood disorders.

Thus, basic emotions of fear, anger, sadness/distress, and excitement may all contribute to psychological disorders and may even come to define many anxiety and mood disorders. Emotions and mood also affect our cognitive processes: If one's mood is positive,

then one's associations, interpretations, and impressions also tend to be positive (Bower, 1981; Gilligan & Bower, 1984). Your impression of people you first meet or even your memories of past events will be colored to a great extent by your current mood. If your mood is consistently negative or depressed, then your memories of past events are likely to be unpleasant. This is a well-known part of our experience. The cheerful optimist is said to see the world through rose-colored glasses or make a judgment that the bottle is half full. On the other hand, the pessimist or someone who is depressed sees the bottle as half empty. This topic is a rich area of investigation for cognitive scientists (Eysenck, 1992; Teasdale, 1993), particularly those interested in the close interconnection of cognitive and emotional processes. Cognitive-behavioral treatments, as noted above, address directly the cognitive aspect of (faulty) emotional responding.

Social and Interpersonal Influences

Given the welter of neurobiological and psychological variables impinging on our lives, is there any room for influence from social, interpersonal, and cultural factors? This subject has not received as much attention as psychological or biological influences, but studies are beginning to demonstrate the substantial power and depth of social influences. In fact, researchers have now established that social or cultural influences can kill you. Consider the following example.

Voodoo and the Evil Eye

In many cultures around the world there is a phenomenon referred to as "fright disorders." These disorders have their origins in observable fear reactions or exaggerated startle responses. One example would be the occurrence of a disorder in Latin American cultures called *susto*. Susto is characterized by various anxiety-based symptoms such as insomnia, irritability, phobias, and marked somatic symptoms of sweating and increased heart rate (tachycardia). But the causes of susto across these Latin American cultures are the same. The individual is suddenly badly frightened, or is the object of black magic or witchcraft. In some cultures this influence is called the "evil eye" (Tan, 1980; Good & Kleinman, 1985). Within certain cultures, fright disorder can result in death. Cannon (1942), examining the phenomenon of voodoo death, suggested that the sentence of death by a medicine man may create an intolerable autonomic arousal in the subject, who has little opportunity to

Voodoo and other culturally specific practices can sometimes cause death.

cope with this event due to total lack of social support. Ultimately the condition leads to damage to internal organs and death. Thus, from all accounts, an individual who is functioning in a perfectly healthy and adaptive way, from a physical and psychological point of view, suddenly is dying because of marked changes in his social environment.

Similar phenomena occur in many cultures around the world. In Iran, fright disorder is almost always attributed to problems in the social environment—such as interpersonal conflict—that make people more susceptible to fright in the first place.

Social Effects on Health and Behavior

Does something like fright disorder happen in Western cultures? The answer now seems clear. A large number of studies have demonstrated that the greater the number and frequency of social relationships and contacts, the less likely you are to die. Conversely, the lower you score on a "social index" measuring the richness of your social life, the shorter your life will be. Studies documenting this finding have been reported in the United States (Berkman & Syme, 1979; House, Robbins, & Metzner, 1982; Schoenbach et al., 1986) as well as in other Western countries such as Sweden and Finland. These studies take into account existing physical health and other risk factors for dying young, such as high blood pressure, high cholesterol levels, and smoking habits, and still produce the same result.

There is also a variety of studies showing that social relationships seem to protect individuals against many physical and psychological disorders, such as high blood pressure, depression, alcoholism, arthritis,

and low birth weight in newborns (Cobb, 1976; House, Landis, & Umberson, 1988). What could account for this? Once again it seems that social and interpersonal factors influence psychological and neurobiological variables, sometimes to a substantial degree. Thus, one cannot really study psychological and biological aspects of psychological disorders without taking into account the social and cultural context of the disorder.

The necessity of this multidimensional point of view shows up time and again. Consider several more examples. Cohen, Kaplan, Cunnick, Manuck, and Rabin (1992) examined the effects of stable or unstable social environments on the immune response in monkeys. In the socially stable condition, monkeys got to live with the same group for over two years. This is important not just because they make "friends" but also because they are able to organize themselves into social hierarchies. A second group, the unstable group, was reorganized every month and was never with the same group of monkeys twice in a row. This constant shifting resulted in persistent social disruption and agitation. For monkeys in the social instability condition, the immune response became suppressed, making them more susceptible to disease processes. However, if the monkeys made attempts to overcome these social instabilities by forming whatever social affiliations they could in their group, their immune response function was not as severely suppressed. In monkeys, social affiliative behavior means keeping in close physical contact with other animals, and engaging in a lot of mutual grooming behavior.

Another experiment with primates illustrates the dangers of ignoring social context. A large group of monkeys was injected with amphetamines, a central nervous system stimulant (Haber & Barchas, 1983). Surprisingly, this drug had no reliable effect on the behavior of the monkeys as a group on the average. However, when the investigators divided the monkeys into socially dominant and socially submissive individuals, dramatic effects appeared. Amphetamine administration increased *dominant* behaviors in primates who were high in the social hierarchy, but increased *submissive* behaviors in monkeys who were low in the social hierarchy. Thus, the effects of a biological factor (the drug) on psychological characteristics (behavior) were uninterpretable unless one considered the social context of the experiment.

Returning to human studies, how do social relationships have such a profound impact on our physical and psychological characteristics? We don't know for sure, but there are some intriguing hints. Some people think interpersonal relationships give meaning to life and that individuals with something to live for seem to be able to overcome some physical deficiencies, and even delay death. You may know an elderly individual who far outlives his or her time in order to see a grandchild graduate from college or witness some other significant family event. Once it happens, the person dies. Another common observation, particularly in elderly males, is that, if one spouse in a long-standing marital relationship dies, the other will often die soon after, regardless of health status of the survivor at the time the spouse dies. It is also possible that social relationships facilitate health-promoting behaviors, such as restraint in the use of alcohol and drugs, getting proper sleep, or seeking appropriate health care (House, Landis, & Umberson, 1988).

Sometimes naturally occurring events, either positive or negative, afford scientists an opportunity to study the impact of social networks on functioning. Steinglass, Weissub, and Kaplan De-Nour (1988) studied residents of an Israeli community in the Sinai Peninsula when it was dismantled and evacuated as part of the peace negotiations with Egypt. These investigators found that believing one was embedded firmly in a social context was just as important as actually having a social network. Long-term (mal)adjustment was best predicted in those who *perceived* that their social network was disintegrating, whether it actually did or not.

To take another example, there is now a study suggesting that whether you live in the city or the country is associated with your chances of developing the very severe disorder schizophrenia. Lewis et al. (1992) found that the incidence of schizophrenia was 38% greater in men who had been raised in cities compared to those raised in rural areas. We have known for a long time that there is more schizophrenia in the city than the country. But researchers thought that people with schizophrenia drifted into the inner cities *after* developing schizophrenia, or that other factors endemic in our cities, such as greater drug use or unstable family relationships, might be the real culprit rather than just being in a city. But Lewis et al. carefully controlled for influences such as drug use, unstable families, and so on, and it now seems there may be something about living in cities over and above those influences that contributes to the development of schizophrenia. We do not yet know what it is. This finding, if it is replicated and shown to be true, may

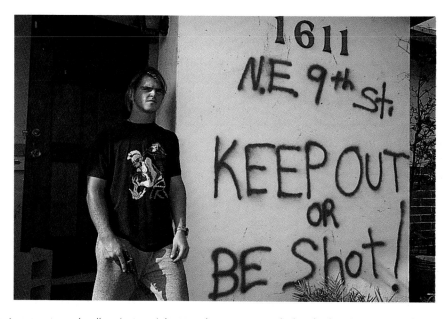

Unstable social environments and collapsing social networks, as occurred after the hurricane several years ago in Miami, may cause severe stress.

Strong social relationships and interpersonal networks may contribute to a long and happy life.

be very important in view of the mass migration of individuals, particularly in third world countries, to overcrowded urban areas. Will these migrations cause an epidemic of schizophrenia?

Social and Interpersonal Influences in the Elderly

Finally, social and interpersonal factors may affect the expression of physical and psychological disorders somewhat differently depending on the particular age range of the group. Grant, Patterson, and Yager (1988) studied 118 men and women 65 years old or older who were living independently in the community. Subjects with fewer meaningful contacts and less social support from relatives evidenced consistently higher levels of depression and reports of unsatisfactory quality of life. However, if these individuals became physically ill, their families mobilized to the extent that they had more substantial social support than those who were not physically ill.

This finding raises the unfortunate possibility that it might be advantageous for elderly individuals to become physically ill. An illness would allow them to reestablish the type of social support that makes life worth living for them. If further research indicates that this is true, mobilizing the families of these individuals *before* they get ill might improve their physical health and also lift an enormous burden from health care costs.

The study of older adults is growing at a rapid pace. The Census Bureau has estimated that by the year 2080 the number of people aged 85 or older

will grow from the current 3.3 million to 18.7 million. With this growth in the upper end of the population will come a corresponding increase in the number of older adults with mental health problems. Unfortunately, coupled with the predicted rise in older adults is the current trend to exclude those with psychological disorders from the nursing home system. Since both health and mental health services are available in most nursing homes, and since mental health services are less available elsewhere, many of these people will not receive appropriate mental health care (Gatz & Smyer, 1992). As you can see, understanding and treating the disorders experienced by older adults is a timely and important task for the 1990s.

Social Stigma

Other factors make imperative the consideration of social and cultural issues in the study of psychopathology. Psychological disorders continue to carry a substantial stigma in our society. To be anxious or depressed is to be weak and cowardly. To be schizophrenic is to be unpredictable and crazy. For physical injuries in times of war, we award medals. For psychological injuries, the unfortunate soldiers earn scorn and derision as anyone knows if he or she saw the movies *Patton* or *Born on the Fourth of July*. Many patients with psychological disorders do not seek reimbursement from their health insurance policies for fear that someone in the company where they work will learn about their illness. The very fact that this stigma exists tends to reduce the amount of social support that would be available if one were physically ill, thereby decreasing the chance that the individual will recover. Some of the consequences of society's attitudes toward psychological disorders are discussed in Chapter 17.

Interpersonal Psychotherapy (IPT)

Recently a new form of psychotherapy with proven effectiveness for some disorders has been developed. It emphasizes the resolution of interpersonal problems and stressors for individuals with psychological disorders. As developed by Myrna Weissman and her late husband, Gerald Klerman (Klerman, Weissman, Rounsaville, & Chevron, 1984), interpersonal psychotherapy grew out of the approach of the American psychiatrist Harry Stack Sullivan. Sullivan, trained as a Freudian, put great emphasis in his therapy on current interpersonal relationships, in addition to interpersonal experiences during particular psychosexual stages of growth in childhood.

In the therapy developed by Weissman, Klerman, and their colleagues, life stresses precipitating the psychological disorder, such as a depressive disorder, are identified and the patient and therapist work together on current interpersonal problems that are either the source of the life stress or are intimately connected with it. Typically these include one or more of four interpersonal issues. One of the most common issues would be dealing with interpersonal role disputes such as marital conflict. Experiencing the death of a loved one and making the necessary adjustments would be a second common area of focus. Acquiring a new relationship through marriage or changing a job provides a third source of interpersonal stress. Finally, a fourth area is identifying and correcting deficits in social skills that make it difficult to form relationships, particularly intimate relationships, which are so important to all of us. Interpersonal therapy, like cognitive-behavioral therapy, is brief, typically taking from 10 to 15 sessions, and has proven highly effective for problems such as depression.

The Incidence of Psychological Disorders Around the World

Behavioral and mental health problems are occurring in third world countries in increasing numbers. These problems are being exacerbated by political strife, technological change, and massive movements from rural to urban areas. An important study from the Center for the Study of Culture and Medicine headed by Arthur Kleinman reveals that 10% to 20% of all primary medical services in poor countries are being sought by patients with psychological disorders. Principal among these are anxiety and mood disorders (including suicide attempts) as well as alcoholism, drug abuse, and childhood developmental disorders. Record numbers of young men are committing suicide in Micronesia. Levels of alcoholism among adults in Latin America have risen to 20%. Although there are successful treatments for disorders such as depression and addictive behaviors, they can't be administered in these countries for there are almost no mental health professionals there. In China, over one billion people are served by approximately 3,000 mental health professionals. In the United States 200,000 mental health professionals serve 250 million people and yet only one in four people in our country with a psychological disorder has ever received treatment of any kind. These are shocking statistics, suggesting that social and cultural factors in psychological disorders play more than a role in causation. They also play a substantial role in the maintenance of these disorders, since most societies have not yet developed the resources nor the type of positive constructive approaches that would provide the social context in which the disorders could be alleviated and ultimately prevented. Changing society's attitude is just one of the challenges facing us in the next century.

Developmental Stages Across the Life Span

Life-span developmental psychopathologists have pointed out that we sometimes look at psychological disorders using a snapshot approach: We slice out a particular point in a person's life and assume that this represents the whole person. The inadequacy of this way of looking at people should be clear. Think back on your own life over the past few years. The person you were, say, three years ago, is much different from the person you are now. And the person you will be three years from now will also change in important ways. To completely understand psychopathology, we must begin to appreciate how disorders change with time.

Important developmental changes occur at all points in your life. Adulthood, rather than being a relatively stable period, is a dynamic time with important changes occurring into old age. Erik Erikson's view of behavior is more in keeping with this life-span view. He suggests that we go through eight major crises throughout the course of our lives (Erikson, 1982). Each of these crises or conflicts occurs at times that are determined by both our biological maturation and the social demands made at particular times in our lives. Unlike Freud, who envisioned no developmental stages beyond adolescence, Erikson believes that the developmental progression extends beyond the age of 65. Older adulthood, for example, is characterized as looking back over one's life and viewing it as either meaningful, happy, and productive, or as a major disappointment. Although aspects of Erikson's theory of psychosocial development have been criticized for being too vague (Shaffer, 1993), it is illustrative of the more comprehensive approach to human development being advocated by life-span developmentalists.

The Principle of Equifinality

Just as there may be many reasons someone would have a fever, a particular behavior or disorder may have a number of causes. The **principle of equifinality** is used in developmental psychopathology to indicate that there may be a number of paths to a given outcome (Cicchetti, 1991) and that we must consider the whole path and not just the outcome. There are many examples of this principle in psychopathology. For example, a delusional syndrome may be one facet of the disorder of schizophrenia, but it also can arise from amphetamine abuse. Delirium—which involves difficulties in concentrating and focusing attention—often occurs in older adults following surgery and can also be the result of thiamine deficiency or renal (kidney) disease. Autism can sometimes occur in children whose mothers are exposed to rubella during pregnancy, but it can also occur in children whose mothers experience difficulties during labor.

These different paths can also result from psychological factors interacting with biological components during various stages of development. How one copes with impairment due to organic causes may have a profound effect on one's overall functioning. For example, people with documented brain damage may have different levels of disorder. Those who have a healthy system of social support consisting of family and friends as well as highly adaptive personality characteristics, such as marked confidence in their abilities to overcome challenges, may experience only mild behavioral and cognitive disturbance despite known organic pathology. Others will be incapacitated. This example may be clearer if you think of people you know with physical disabilities. Some people paralyzed from the waist down due to accident or disease (paraplegics) have worked around their disabilities to become superb athletes or extremely accomplished business people or artists. Others with the same condition have become depressed and hopeless; they have either withdrawn from life or, even worse, ended their lives. Even the content of delusions and hallucinations and the degree to which they are frightening or difficult to cope with will be determined in part by psychological and social factors.

Now researchers have begun to explore not only what makes people experience particular disorders but also what protects others from having the same difficulties. If you are interested in why someone would be depressed, for example, you would first look at people who display depression. Another way to look at this problem is to study people who are in similar situations and who come from similar backgrounds but who are not depressed. An excellent example of this approach is the research on "resilient" children. This work suggests that individual personalities and social factors may protect some children from being impacted negatively from stressful experiences, such as living in families during childhood development in which one or both parents have a psychiatric disturbance (Garmezy & Rutter, 1983). The presence of a caring adult friend or relative can offset the negative stresses brought on by this environment. Additionally, the child's own ability to understand and cope with unpleasant situations can protect him or her from these stresses. Those of you who were brought up in violent or otherwise dysfunctional families yet who have successfully gone on to college might want to look back for the factors that served to protect you from these adversities. Perhaps if we better understood why some people did not encounter the same problems as others in similar circumstances, we could better understand the particular disorder, begin to assist those who had the disorder, and even prevent some cases from occurring at all.

Conclusions

We have examined, in this chapter, modern-day approaches to psychopathology and we have found it complex indeed. After reading the brief overview contained in this chapter (even though it doesn't seem brief), we have seen that contributions from (a) psychoanalytic theory, (b) behavioral and cognitive science, (c) emotional influences, (d) social and cultural influences, (e) genetics, (f) neuroscience, and (g) life-span developmental factors all must be considered as we think about psychopathology. Even though our knowledge is incomplete, you can see why we could never go back to the type of one-dimensional thinking that was present in the various historical traditions described in Chapter 1. When we come to chapters covering specific psychological disorders, we will return to cases very much like that of Judy and consider them from this multidimensional integrative perspective. But first we must explore the processes of assessment and diagnosis used in the measurement and classification of psychopathology.

Summary

- Examining the causes of abnormal behavior is complex and fascinating. You can say that psychological disorders are caused by nature (biology), and that psychological disorders are caused by nurture (psychosocial factors); and you would be right on both counts but also wrong on both counts.

- For biological, psychological, and social factors *all* contribute to psychological disorders and no one factor is more of a cause than another factor.

- We have reviewed evidence in this chapter that our genetic structure may make us vulnerable to the development of psychological disorders, but these vulnerabilities are not associated with specific dominant genes as is hair or eye color but with the summation of small contributions from many different genes. Within the nervous system, levels of neurotransmitter and neuroendocrine activity interact in very complex ways to modulate and regulate emotions and behavior and contribute to psychological disorders.

- On the other hand, behavioral and cognitive influences reflecting the learning and adaptation that each of us experiences as we go through life not only contribute to psychological disorders but may also directly modify brain functioning, brain structure, and even genetic expression.

- Similarly, emotional and social and interpersonal influences make profound contributions to psychological disorders and can also affect biology in a number of important ways.

- Considerations of each of these dimensions will reappear as we discuss the causes of various psychological disorders in subsequent chapters. For this reason we need to consider all relevant dimensions, specifically genetic contributions, the role of the nervous system, behavioral and cognitive influences, emotional influences, social and interpersonal influences, and developmental factors, and how these multiple dimensions influence and interact with each other. Thus, we have arrived at a multidimensional integrative model of the causes of psychological disorders.

Key Terms

affect (67)
agonists (53)
antagonists (53)
autonomic nervous system (ANS) (51)
axon (47)
benzodiazepine-GABA system, (BZ-GABA) (54)
brain circuits (52)
central nervous system (47)
cognitive science (62)
cognitive-behavioral therapy (65)
cortisol (52)
dendrites (47)
diathesis-stress model (45)
dopamine (55)
emotion (67)
endocrine system (51)

flight or fight response (66)
gamma aminobutyric acid (GABA) (54)
genes (42)
hypothalamic-pituitary-adrenalcortical axis (HYPAC axis) (52)
implicit memory (64)
inverse agonists (53)
learned helplessness (63)
metabolites (52)
modeling/observational learning (63)
mood (67)
neurons (47)
neuroscience (47)
neurotransmitters (47)
norepinephrine (*also* noradrenaline) (55)

parasympathetic nervous system (PNS) (51)
peripheral nervous system (47)
prepared learning (64)
principle of equifinality (74)
rational-emotive therapy (65)
receptors (47)
reciprocal gene-environment model (46)
reuptake (52)
serotonin (5-hydroxytryptamine/5-HT) (53)
somatic nervous system (51)
sympathetic nervous system (SNS) (51)
synaptic cleft (47)
vulnerability (45)

It is not the illness but the human being that needs help.
As a doctor I am not concerned with the illness
but with the human being.
Georg Groddeck
The Meaning of Illness

3

Clinical Assessment and Diagnosis

The processes of clinical assessment and diagnosis are central to the study of psychopathology and, ultimately, to the treatment of psychological disorders. **Clinical assessment** refers to a systematic evaluation and measurement of psychological, biological, and social factors in an individual presenting with a possible psychological disorder. **Diagnosis** is the process of determining whether the particular problem that is distressing the individual meets all the criteria for a psychological disorder. These criteria are set forth in the *Diagnostic and Statistical Manual of Mental Disorders (fourth ed.) (DSM-IV)* (American Psychiatric Association, 1994). In this chapter we examine in some depth the development of the DSM into a widely used classification system for abnormal behavior. First, however, we explore the processes of clinical assessment and diagnosis within the context of two cases from one of our clinics. Then we review the many types of assessment techniques available to the clinician. Finally, we turn to issues surrounding diagnosis and the related challenges of classification.

The Case of Frank

Frank was referred to one of our clinics for evaluation and possible treatment of severe distress and anxiety centering on his marriage. He arrived at the clinic neatly dressed in his work clothes (he was a mechanic). He reported that he was 24 years old and that this was the first time he had ever seen a mental health professional. He wasn't sure that he really needed to be here (or wanted to be here), but he felt as if he were beginning to "come apart" a little bit due to his marital difficulties. He figured that it certainly wouldn't hurt to come once to see whether it would help. What follows is a transcript of parts of that interview.

Therapist: What sorts of problems have been troubling you during the past month?

Frank: I'm beginning to have a lot of marital problems. I was married about 9 months ago, but I've been really tense around the house and we've been having a lot of arguments.

Therapist: Is this something recent?

Frank: Well, it wasn't too bad at first, but it's been worse lately. I've also been really uptight in my job, and I haven't been getting my work done.

Note that we always begin by asking the patient to describe for us, in a relatively open-ended way, the major difficulties that brought him or her to the office in the first place. When dealing with adults, or children old enough (or verbal enough) to tell us their story, this strategy tends to break the ice. It also allows us to relate details of the patient's life revealed later in the interview to the central problem as seen through the patient's eyes.

After Frank described his major problem in some detail, the therapist then asked him about his marriage, his job, and other current life circumstances. Frank reported that he had worked steadily in an auto body repair shop for the past 4 years and that, 9 months previously, he had married a 17-year-old woman. After getting a better picture of his current situation, we returned to his feelings of distress and anxiety.

Therapist: When you feel uptight at work, is it the same kind of feeling you have at home?

Frank: Pretty much; I just can't seem to concentrate, and lots of times I lose track of what my wife's saying to me, which makes her mad and then we'll have a big fight.

Therapist: Are you thinking about something else when you lose your concentration, such as your work, or maybe other things?

Frank: Oh, I don't know; I guess I just worry a lot.

Therapist: What do you find yourself worrying about most of the time?

Frank: Well, I worry about getting fired and then not being able to support my family. A lot of the time I feel like I'm going to catch something—you know, get sick and not be able to work. Basically I guess I'm afraid of getting sick and then failing at my job and in my marriage, and having my parents and her parents both telling me what an ass I was for getting married in the first place.

During the first 10 minutes or so of the interview, Frank seemed to be quite tense and anxious and would often look down at the floor while he talked, glancing up only occasionally to make eye contact. Sometimes his right leg would twitch a bit. Although it was not easy to see at first because he was looking down, Frank was also closing his eyes very tightly for a period of 2 to 3 seconds. It was during these periods when his eyes were closed that his right leg would twitch.

The interview proceeded for the next half hour, exploring marital and job issues. It became increasingly clear that Frank was feeling inadequate and anxious about handling situations in his life. By this time he was talking freely and looking up a little more at the therapist, but he was continuing to close his eyes and twitch his right leg slightly.

Therapist: Are you aware that once in a while you're closing your eyes while you're telling me this?

Frank: I'm not aware all the time, but I know I do it.

Therapist: Do you know how long you've been doing that?

Frank: Oh, I don't know, maybe a year or two.

Therapist: Are you thinking about anything when you close your eyes?

Frank: Well, actually I'm trying *not* to think about something.

Therapist: What do you mean?

Frank: Well, I have these really frightening and stupid thoughts, and . . . it's hard to even talk about it.

Therapist: The thoughts are frightening?

Frank: Yes. I keep thinking I'm going to take a fit, and I'm just trying to get that out of my mind.

Therapist: Could you tell me more about this fit?

Frank: Well, you know, it's those terrible things where people fall down and they froth at the mouth, and their tongues come out, and they shake all over. You know, seizures. I think they call it epilepsy.

Therapist: And you're trying to get these thoughts out of your mind?

Frank: Oh, I do everything possible to get those thoughts out of my mind as quickly as I can.

Therapist: I've noticed you moving your leg when you close your eyes. Is that part of it?

Frank: Yes, I've noticed if I really jerk my leg and pray real hard for a little while the thought will go away. (Nelson & Barlow, 1981, p. 19)

What's wrong with Frank? The first interview revealed an insecure young man experiencing substantial stress as he questions whether he is capable of handling marriage and a job. On the other hand, he reports that he loves his wife very much and wants the marriage to work and that he is attempting to be as conscientious as possible on his job, a job from which he derives a lot of satisfaction and enjoyment. Also, for some reason, he is having thoughts about seizures that trouble him.

Now let's consider one more case for purposes of illustration.

The Case of Brian

Brian was 20 years old and had recently been discharged from a tour of duty in the Army. He was referred by a psychiatrist in another state for evaluation of sexual problems. What follows is a greatly abbreviated transcript.

Therapist: What seems to be the problem?
Brian: I'm a homosexual.
Therapist: You're a homosexual?
Brian: Yes, and I want to be straight. Who wants to be queer?
Therapist: Do you have any homosexual friends or lovers?
Brian: No, I wouldn't get near them.
Therapist: How often do you engage in homosexual behavior?
Brian: Well, I haven't as of yet, but it's no secret that I'm homosexual, and it's just a matter of time before it happens, I suppose.
Therapist: Do you have somebody specifically in mind? Are you attracted to somebody?
Brian: No, but others are attracted to me. I can tell by the way they look at me.
Therapist: The way they look at you?
Brian: Yes, the look in their eyes.
Therapist: Has anyone ever actually approached you or said anything to you about being homosexual?
Brian: No, not to me; they wouldn't dare. But I know they talk about me behind my back.
Therapist: How do you know that?
Brian: Well, sometimes the guys will be talking in the next room and the only thing they could be talking about is that I'm queer. (Nelson & Barlow, 1981, p. 20)

Where do we go from here? How do we determine whether Frank has a psychological disorder or if he is simply one of many young men suffering the normal stresses and strains of a new marriage who,

perhaps, could benefit from some marital counseling? And what about Brian? Where do you think he got those ideas? The purpose of this chapter is to illustrate how mental health clinicians address these types of questions in a systematic way, assessing patients in order to study the basic nature of psychopathology as well as to make diagnoses and plan treatment.

Assessing Psychological Disorders

The process of clinical assessment in psychopathology can be likened to a funnel (Peterson, 1968; Hawkins, 1979). The clinician begins by collecting a lot of information across a broad range of the individual's functioning to determine where the source of the problem may lie. After collecting this information and getting a preliminary idea of the overall functioning of the person, the clinician begins to narrow the focus by ruling out problems in some areas and concentrating more specifically on other areas where problems seem to exist.

To understand the different ways clinicians assess psychological problems, we need to know three

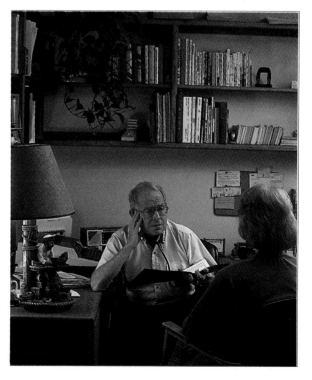

Mental health professionals meeting a patient for the first time will focus on the current problem that brings the person to treatment.

basic concepts that can help us determine the value of our assessments: reliability, validity, and standardization (see Figure 3.1). The techniques used to assess psychological disorders are subject to a number of strict requirements, not the least of which is some evidence (research) that they actually do what they are designed to do. One of the more important requirements of these assessments is that they be *reliable.* **Reliability** refers to the degree to which a measurement is consistent. Imagine how upset you would be if you had stomach pain, and you went to four different but competent physicians and got four different diagnoses and four different treatments. Which one would be correct? The diagnoses made by these physicians would be said to be unreliable, because two or more "raters" did not agree on the conclusion. We expect, in general, that presenting the same symptoms to different physicians will result in similar diagnoses. If you go to four mental health professionals, you should reasonably expect that the types of conclusions they make will be in general agreement. One way psychologists improve their reliability is by carefully designing their assessment devices and then conducting research on them to ensure that two or more raters will get the same answers (called *interrater reliability*). They also determine whether these techniques are stable across time. In other words, if you go to a clinician on Tuesday and are told you have an IQ of 110, you should expect a similar result if you take the same test again on Thursday. This is another type of reliability known as *test-retest reliability*. We will return to this concept of reliability when we talk of diagnoses and classification, later in the chapter.

Another important aspect of assessment is its **validity,** which is whether something measures what it is designed to measure. In other words, does a technique assess what it is supposed to assess? Comparing the results of one assessment measure with the results of others allows you to begin to determine its validity. This comparison is called *concurrent* or *descriptive validity.* Another form of validity—called *predictive validity*—is how well your assessment tells you what will happen in the future. For example, does the assessment predict who will succeed in school and who will not, which is one of the goals of an IQ test?

Finally, many assessments are standardized. **Standardization** is the process by which a certain set of standards or norms is determined for a technique in order to make its use consistent across different measurements. The standards might apply to procedures to follow during testing, during scoring, and during evaluation of data. The assessment may be given to large numbers of people who differ on important factors such as age, race, gender, socioeconomic status, and diagnosis, and the scores are then used as a standard, or norm, for comparison purposes. For

Figure 3.1   Concepts that determine the value of our assessments

example, if you are an African-American male, 19 years old and from a middle-class background, your score on a psychological test should be compared to scores of others like you and not to scores of very different people, such as a group of women of Asian descent who are in their 60s and from lower-middle-class backgrounds. What is "average" for young men on that particular test may not be average for other groups. The issues of reliability, validity, and standardization are important for all forms of assessment used for psychological problems.

Clinical assessment can be broken down into a number of strategies and procedures. All individuals with possible psychological disorders who seek out mental health professionals undergo many of these procedures. Their use helps clinicians acquire the information they need to better understand their patients and to assist them. Procedures that fall under the heading of clinical assessment include a *clinical interview* and, within the context of the interview, a *mental status exam* that can be administered to every individual either formally or informally; *behavioral observation and assessment; psychological tests* (if needed); and, often, a thorough *physical examination.*

Psychological tests include specific tests to determine cognitive, emotional, or behavioral responses that might be associated with a specific disorder, or more generalized tests assessing long-standing personality features. In addition, specialized areas of psychological testing include *intelligence testing* to determine the structure and patterns of cognitive abilities and *neuropsychological testing* to determine the possible contribution of specific brain damage or dysfunction to the patient's condition. If the latter type of specialized testing is indicated, it may be supplemented by the newer neurobiological procedures that use imaging to assess brain structure and function.

The Clinical Interview

The clinical interview is one of the most common assessment tools used by psychologists, psychiatrists, and other mental health professionals. The interview is used to gather information on present and past behavior, attitudes, and emotions as well as a detailed history of the problem and of the individual's life in general. Typically, clinicians focus on the current problem that brings the person to treatment and elicit more detail concerning the nature of the problem at present. Clinicians also determine the history of the specific problem, including when it first started and any other events (for example, life stress, trauma, physical illness) that might have occurred about the same time. In addition, most clinicians will gather at least some information on the patient's current and past interpersonal and social history, including current family makeup (for instance, married, divorced, number of children, college student currently living at home) and the history of the individual's upbringing. Information on sexual development, religious attitudes (current and past), relevant cultural concerns (such as stress induced by discrimination), and educational history are also routinely collected. The first tactic employed by most clinicians during a clinical interview is called a **mental status exam,** a strategy that is a useful means for organizing information obtained during an interview.

The Mental Status Exam

In essence, the mental status exam is an assessment technique that involves the systematic observation of somebody's behavior. This type of observation occurs when any one person interacts with another. All of us, clinicians and nonclinicians alike, are continually performing pseudo-mental status exams in the course of our daily lives. The trick for clinicians, of course, is to organize their observations of other people in a way that gives them sufficient information to determine whether a psychological disorder might be present (Nelson & Barlow, 1981). Mental status exams can be very structured and detailed (Wing, Cooper, & Sartorius, 1974), but for the most part, they are performed relatively quickly by experienced clinicians in the course of interviewing or observing a patient. Typically, the exam covers five categories: appearance and behavior, thought processes, mood and affect, intellectual functioning, and sensorium.

1. Appearance and behavior. When evaluating a person's appearance and behavior, the clinician notes any overt behaviors such as Frank's leg twitch. Also, the clinician observes the individual's dress, physical appearance, posture, and facial expression. For example, very slow and effortful motor behavior, sometimes referred to as *psychomotor retardation,* may indicate severe depression.

2. Thought processes. Any time clinicians hear a patient talk they're getting a good idea of that person's thought processes. They might look for several things here. For example, what is the rate or flow of speech? Does the person talk really fast or really slow? What about continuity of speech? In other words, does the patient make sense when he or she talks or is one idea presented after another, sometimes with no apparent connection? In some patients with schizophrenia this speech pattern can be quite noticeable and is referred to as *looseness of association.* To make this determination and gather appropriate information, clinicians sometimes ask very specific questions. If the patient shows difficulty with continuity or rate of speech they might ask, "Can you think clearly or is there some problem putting your thoughts together? Do your thoughts tend to be mixed or very slow?"

In addition to the rate or flow of speech and the continuity of speech, what about the content? Is there any evidence of *delusions* (distorted views of reality)? Typical delusions would be *delusions of persecution,* where someone thinks people are after him and out to get him all the time, or *delusions of grandeur,* where one individual thinks she is all powerful in some way. The individual might also have *ideas of reference,* where everything everyone else does somehow relates back to him. *Hallucinations* are things a person sees or hears but which really aren't there. For example, the clinician might say, "Let me ask you a couple of routine questions that we ask everybody. Do you ever see things or maybe hear things when you know there is nothing there?"

Now think back to the case of Brian. Extensive questioning of Brian revealed no evidence of any homosexual arousal patterns, fantasies, or behavior. In fact, he had been quite active heterosexually over the past several years and had strong patterns of heterosexual fantasies. What would you say about Brian's thought processes during the interview? What kinds of ideas was he expressing? Notice the conclusion he drew when he happened to see other men looking at him. What did he think when a group of men happened to have a conversation he was not part of? This would be an example of ideas of reference. That is, Brian thought everything that anyone else did or said *referred* to him. In fact, his strongly held conviction that he was a homosexual had no basis in reality. It was a delusion.

3. Mood and affect. Determining mood and affect are important parts of the mental status exam. *Mood* refers to the predominant feeling state of the individual. Does the person appear to be "down in the dumps" or perhaps continually elated? Does she talk in a depressed or hopeless fashion? How pervasive is this mood? Are there times when the depression seems to go away? *Affect,* on the other hand, refers to the feeling state that accompanies what we say at a given point in time. Most of the time our affect is what we would call "appropriate." That is, we laugh when we say something funny or look sad when we talk about something sad. If you have a friend who has just told you her mother had died and she laughed about it, or if your friend has just won the lottery and she is crying, you would think it strange to say the least. A mental health clinician would note that your friend's affect is "inappropriate." On the other hand, you might observe your friend talking about a range of happy and sad things with no affect whatsoever. If this were the case, a mental health clinician would say the affect is "blunted" or "flat." Observations of mood and affect play an important role in the clinician's assessment of a person's emotional and psychotic disorders.

4. Intellectual functioning.   Clinicians make a rough estimate of others' intellectual functioning just by talking to them. Do they seem to have a reasonable vocabulary? Can they talk in abstractions and metaphors (as most of us do much of the time)? How is their memory? We usually make some gross or rough estimate of intelligence that is noticeable only if it deviates from normal, such as concluding the person is above or below average intelligence.

5. Sensorium.   *Sensorium* refers to others' general awareness of their surroundings. Do they know what the date is, what time it is, where they are, who they are, and who you are? Most of us, of course, are fully aware of these facts. People with permanent brain damage or dysfunction, or temporary brain damage or dysfunction often due to drugs or other toxic states, may not know the answer to these questions. If the patient knows who he or she is and who the clinician is and has a good idea of the time and place, the clinician would say that the patient's sensorium is "clear," that she is *oriented times three* (which refers to person, place, and time) (see Figure 3.2).

What can we conclude from this informal series of behavioral observations? Basically, they allow the clinician to make a preliminary determination of the areas of the patient's behavior and condition that may need to be assessed in more detail and perhaps more formally, using psychological tests. If psychological disorders remain a possibility, the clinician may begin to hypothesize which disorders might be present. This process, in turn, provides more focus for the assessment and diagnostic activities to come. If the sensorium is not clear, clinicians would assess in greater detail for cognitive impairment disorders or for substance abuse. If intellectual functioning seems quite low and is accompanied by memory impairment, the clinician might want to assess intellectual or neuropsychological functioning in a more structured way using sophisticated assessment procedures devised for this purpose. With these tests, he or she could determine whether the patient's state is temporary, perhaps associated with head trauma or some other recent event, or whether it represents long-standing cognitive deficits associated with inferior intellectual functioning.

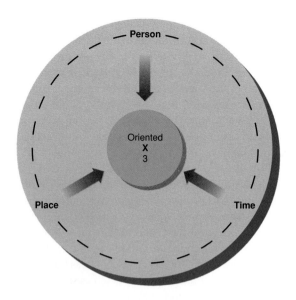

Figure 3.2   Oriented times three. Clinicians can determine patients' general awareness of their surroundings by gauging their awareness of self, place, and time. If a patient is fully aware of each of these, he or she is considered "oriented times three."

Observations of depressed, elated, or anxious mood would direct the clinician toward emotional disorders. Inappropriate affect and disordered thought processes could possibly be associated with schizophrenic disorders. Of course, these conclusions would be preliminary since each of these observations could have many other explanations. However, this process is the way clinicians begin.

Returning to our cases, what have we learned from this mental status exam (see Figure 3.3)? With Frank, observation of a persistent motor behavior in the form of a twitch led to the discovery of an association or a functional relationship (see below) with some troublesome thoughts regarding seizures. Beyond this, his appearance seemed reasonably appropriate, and the flow and content of his speech seemed reasonable; his intelligence was well within normal limits and he was oriented times three. He did display an anxious mood; however, his affect was appropriate to what he was saying. These observations suggested that we direct the remainder of the clinical interview and additional assessment and diagnostic activities to cover more carefully the possible existence of a disorder characterized by intrusive, unwanted thoughts and the tendency to attempt to resist them—in other words *obsessive-compulsive disorder.*

And what of Brian? He also was oriented times three, and his intelligence was well within normal limits. In addition, he was dressed appropriately and did not display any unusual motor behaviors or abnormali-

Observations during mental status exam   →   Subsequent focus

The Case of Frank

Persistent twitch
Appearance appropriate
Flow/content of speech reasonable
Intelligence within normal limits
Oriented times three
Anxious mood
Affect appropriate

Possible existence of disorder characterized by intrusive unwanted thoughts / tendency to attempt to resist these thoughts

The Case of Brian

No unusual motor behavior
Appearance appropriate
Speech suggests delusional ideas of reference
Intelligence within normal limits
Oriented times three
Normal mood
Affect appropriate

Possible existence of psychotic disorder such as schizophrenia

Figure 3.3 The mental status exam

ties of mood and affect. However, the content of his verbalizations *suggested* the possibility of delusional ideas of reference, a feature common to some psychotic disorders such as schizophrenia. Therefore, while not neglecting other areas, the clinician would be particularly careful to focus assessment and diagnostic activities in this area. Clinicians have long since learned that even the most paranoid delusional-sounding reports may well be based in fact. One of us once worked with a 14-year-old girl who had been diagnosed as a paranoid schizophrenic after a brief evaluation in the emergency room. She had reported, hysterically, that everyone was talking about her and her parents were out to get her. It turned out that her parents "tricked" her into the hospital by telling her they were taking her to the mall. She had been truant and oppositional, and everyone *was* talking about her. After she calmed down, it became clear that the content of what she said was true—she wasn't delusional. This anecdote also illustrates the importance of keeping an open mind during assessment and not jumping to conclusions.

Most often the patient has a pretty good idea of his or her major concerns in a general sense ("I'm depressed; I'm phobic"); occasionally the problem reported by the patient may not, after assessment, be the major issue in the eyes of the mental health clinician. The cases of Brian and Frank illustrate this well since both individuals came in complaining of distress relating to a particular issue (marital problems and homosexuality). But the clinician decided, on the basis of the initial interview, that the major focus of the difficulties lay elsewhere. In neither case was the patient attempting to hide anything from the clinician. Frank did not think his intrusive thoughts were the major problem; additionally, talking about them was very difficult for him since they were quite frightening. Brian was quite honestly not aware that his inferences or conclusions about what might be happening were not correct. Thus, he was somewhat "out of touch with reality" or lacked "insight."

These two examples illustrate the importance of conducting the clinical interview in such a way as to create in the patient a sense of trust and empathy. For this reason, psychologists and other mental health professionals are trained extensively in methods to put patients at ease and facilitate communication. These methods include nonthreatening ways of seeking information as well as appropriate listening skills. Information provided by patients to psychologists and psychiatrists is protected by laws of "privileged communication" or confidentiality in most states. That is, even if authorities want to know the information the therapist has received from the patient, they cannot have access to it without the expressed consent of the patient. The only exception to this rule occurs when the clinician judges that, because of the patient's condition, some harm or danger either to the patient or someone else is imminent (see Chapter 17). At the outset of the initial interview, the therapist should inform the patient of the confidential nature of their conversation and the (quite rare) conditions under which that confidence would not hold.

Despite these assurances of confidentiality and the clinician's interview skills, patients still sometimes have difficulty volunteering sensitive information. From our own files, there is a case of a young male in his early 20s who came to therapy once a week for 5 months. He was requesting help with what he viewed as deficient interpersonal skills and interpersonal anxieties that were impeding his ability to relate to other people. Only after 5 months, and quite by chance one day, during a particularly emotional session, did he volunteer his hidden secret. He was strongly sexually attracted to small boys and confessed that he found the feet of small boys or any associated objects such as socks and shoes to be nearly irresistible. In fact, he had accumulated a large collection of small socks and shoes well hidden in his home. This individual had no reason to hold back this information from the therapist. Confidentiality had been assured and the therapist was there to help. But the patient found it almost impossible to volunteer this information. There may well have been signs that something else was going on with this patient during the 5 months that he received treatment, but if there were, the therapist missed them.

Semistructured Clinical Interviews

Until relatively recently most therapists, after training, developed their own methods of interviewing to collect necessary current and historical information from patients. Different patients seeing different psychologists or other mental health professionals might encounter markedly different types and styles of interviews. Interviews that follow no systematic format are referred to as *unstructured*. Other interviews, called *semistructured interviews,* are made up of questions that have been carefully phrased and tested to elicit useful information in a consistent manner. By following these interview schedules, clinicians can be sure they have inquired about the most important aspects of particular disorders. Clinicians may also depart from a semistructured interview to follow up specific issues when this seems important—thus the label *semi*structured. Because the wording and sequencing of questions has been carefully worked out over a number of years, the clinician can feel confident that a semistructured interview is designed to accomplish its purpose. The disadvantage, of course, is that it robs the interview of some of the spontaneous quality of two people having a conversation about a problem. Also, if applied too rigidly, this type of interview may inhibit the patient

from volunteering otherwise useful information not directly relevant to the questions being asked. For these reasons, fully structured interviews administered wholly by a computer have not caught on, although they are used in some settings.

Many semistructured interviews have been developed lately and are being used routinely by an increasing number of mental health professionals. Some are quite specialized and probe certain problems in depth. Others are more general. An example of a general structured interview is the *Structured Clinical Interview for DSM-III-R (SCID)* (Spitzer, Williams, Gibbons, & First, 1989), which covers a number of disorders. This general interview is very useful in general outpatient clinics but, to make it manageable, only the minimum amount of information on each of the major disorders is collected. More specialized structured interviews would include the *Anxiety Disorders Interview Schedule for DSM-IV (ADIS-IV)* (DiNardo, Brown, & Barlow, 1994) developed at one of our clinics, the Center for Stress and Anxiety Disorders in Albany, New York, to cover, in depth, anxiety and related disorders as defined in DSM-IV. Another good example is the *Schedule for Affective Disorders and Schizophrenia (SADS),* which, as the name implies, inquires more deeply into mood and schizophrenic disorders (Schleyer, Aaronson, Mannuzza, Martin, & Fyer, 1990).

For purposes of illustration, the questions from the ADIS-IV inquiring into the possible existence of obsessive-compulsive disorder are presented in Table 3.1 (p. 86). This is the anxiety disorder suspected in the case of Frank, who reported intrusive thoughts about seizures. How do you think Frank would answer these questions?

The section on schizophrenia from the SADS interview is presented in Table 3.2 (p. 88). How do you think Brian would have answered these questions? Both the wording and the order of the questions is designed to develop the maximum possible amount of information so as to assist the clinician in drawing conclusions about the patient's condition and, perhaps, making a diagnosis.

Physical Examination

During the initial interview the clinician should determine whether the patient has had a recent physical exam. Many patients with problems first go to their family physician and are given a physical. If the patient presenting with psychological problems has not had a physical exam in the past year, a clinician might recommend one, with particular attention to the medical conditions known to be associated sometimes with the specific psychological problem. Many problems presenting as disorders of behavior, cognition, or mood may, on careful physical examination, have a clear relationship to a temporary toxic state. This toxic state could be caused by bad food or the wrong amount of medicine or by the onset of a medical condition. For example, thyroid difficulties, particularly hyperthyroidism (overactive thyroid gland), may well produce symptoms that mimic certain anxiety disorders such as generalized anxiety disorder. On the other hand, hypothyroidism (underactive thyroid gland) might produce symptoms consistent with depression. Certain psychotic symptoms, including delusions or hallucinations, might be associated with the development of a brain tumor. Similarly, ingestion of certain drugs, legal or illegal, may produce symptoms of psychological disorders. Cocaine intoxication (and sometimes, withdrawal from cocaine) often produces panic attacks. Many patients presenting with panic attacks to mental health professionals are reluctant to volunteer information about their cocaine abuse and addiction. This omission may lead clinicians to make an inappropriate diagnosis and recommend improper treatment.

Usually, psychologists and other mental health professionals are well aware of the variety of medical conditions or drug use and abuse that may contribute to psychological problems described by the patient. If a current medical condition or substance abuse situation exists, the clinician must ascertain whether these are merely coexisting problems or some causal relationship is present. Usually he or she accomplishes this by looking at the onset of the problem. If a patient has suffered from severe bouts of depression for the past 5 years, but within the past year also developed hypothyroid problems or began taking a sedative drug, then one would be unlikely to conclude that the depression was caused by the medical or drug condition. On the other hand, if the depression developed simultaneously with the initiation of sedative drugs and diminished considerably when sedative drugs were discontinued for a time, one would be likely to conclude that the depression was part of a substance-induced mood disorder.

Behavioral Assessment
The mental status exam we described above is one way to begin to sample how people think, feel, and behave, and how these actions might contribute to or explain their problems. **Behavioral assessment** takes this process one step further by *formally* assessing an individual's thoughts, feelings, and behavior in specific situations or *contexts* and then using this information to explain why he or she is having difficulties at this time. The process of observing the way people behave under certain conditions takes several forms, but in general it involves directly observing people—such as watching how a couple discusses their disagreements over child discipline—rather than inferring their feelings, thoughts, or behavior indirectly—for example, by the way they draw a picture.

For those individuals not old enough or "skilled" enough to report about their problems and experiences, clinical interviews provide limited assessment information. Young children or individuals who are not verbal due to the nature of their disorder or to cognitive deficits or impairments are not good candidates for clinical interviews. In addition, some people for various reasons may not always report accurately on their problems or the situations in their lives that provide a context for their problems. Sometimes people deliberately withhold information from clinicians because it is embarrassing or because they aren't aware that it is important. Much valuable time can be lost or, more seriously, an improper treatment can be implemented when pertinent information isn't presented to the clinician. To gather more detailed information important for investigating the nature of the disorder as well as planning treatment, the clinician needs a precise, accurate, ongoing picture of the individual's behavior or emotional state as it occurs in his or her day-to-day life. In other words, in addition to talking with a client in an office about a problem, some clinicians go to the person's home or workplace or even into the local community to observe the person and the reported problems directly. Others will set up role-play simulations in a clinical setting to see how people might behave in these situations in their daily lives. These techniques are subsumed under the general heading of behavioral assessment.

In behavioral assessment *target behaviors* are identified and observed with the goal of then determining the factors that seem to influence them. It may seem easy to identify what is bothering a particular person (that is, the target behavior), but even this aspect of assessment can be difficult. Remember that Frank came into therapy with the complaint of being tense and having marital problems. Yet as the interview went on, it became clear that one of his more significant problems involved his thoughts of having a seizure. Identifying problems and what influences them is done in a variety of ways. In addition to interviews, commonly used behavioral assessment techniques include observation of specific behaviors and the use of checklists and rating scales.

Observing Specific Behaviors
Precise and direct observation of behavior can sometimes lead to more accurate portraits of the problems people experience. Occasionally, these observations can be most illuminating. Recently, the mother of a child with a severe conduct disorder came to one of our clinics for assistance. During an initial interview, this woman told the clinician, after much prodding, that her son "didn't listen to her" and that he sometimes had an "attitude." The boy's school teacher, however, painted a very different picture of this young boy: She spoke candidly of his verbal

Table 3.1   Sample Questions for Assessing Obsessive-Compulsive Disorder

I. Initial Inquiry

a. Currently, are you bothered by thoughts, images, or impulses that keep recurring to you that seem inappropriate or nonsensical but that you can't stop from coming into your mind?

YES _____   NO _____

If YES, specify: _____

_____

b. Currently, do you feel driven to repeat some behavior or to repeat something in your mind over and over again to try to feel less uncomfortable?

YES _____   NO _____

If YES, specify: _____

_____

Obsessions:

For each obsession, make separate ratings of Persistence/Distress and Resistance using the scales and suggested queries below.

Persistence/Distress:

How often does _____ enter your mind?; how distressing is it to you when _____ enters your mind? (Time frame?)

0	1	2	3	4	5	6	7	8
Never/ no distress		Rarely/ mild distress		Occasionally/ moderate distress		Frequently/ marked distress		Constantly/ extreme distress

Resistance:

How often do you attempt to get rid of _____ by ignoring, suppressing, or trying to neutralize it/them with some thought or action?

0	1	2	3	4	5	6	7	8
Never		Rarely		Occasionally		Frequently		Constantly

	Current		
OBSESSION	Persistence/ distress	Resistance	Comments
a. Doubting (e.g., locks, turning appliances off, completion/ accuracy of tasks)	_____	_____	_____
b. Contamination (e.g., contracting germs from doorknobs, toilets, money, etc.)	_____	_____	_____
c. Nonsensical impulses (e.g., shouting/undressing in public)	_____	_____	_____
d. Aggressive impulses (e.g., hurting self or others intentionally, destroying objects)	_____	_____	_____
e. Sexual (e.g., obscene thoughts or images)	_____	_____	_____
f. Religious/Satanic (e.g., blasphemous thoughts/impulses)	_____	_____	_____

Table 3.1 *(continued)*

OBSESSION	Current		
	Persistence/distress	Resistance	Comments
g. Accidental harm to others (e.g., poisoning or hurting someone unknowingly)	_____	_____	_____
h. Horrific images (e.g., mutilated bodies)	_____	_____	_____
i. Nonsensical thoughts/images (e.g., numbers, letters, songs)	_____	_____	_____
j. Other	_____	_____	_____
k. Other	_____	_____	_____

For each compulsion, make ratings of frequency using the scale and suggested queries below.

Frequency:

How often are you driven to perform such actions as _____? (Time frame?)

0	1	2	3	4	5	6	7	8
Never		Rarely		Occasionally		Frequently		Constantly

COMPULSION	Current	
	Frequency	Comments
a. Counting (e.g., certain letters or numbers, other objects in the environment)	_____	_____
b. Checking (e.g., locks, appliances, driving routes, important papers, waste baskets)	_____	_____
c. Washing	_____	_____
d. Hoarding (e.g., newspapers, garbage, trivial items)	_____	_____
e. Internal repetition (e.g., phrases, words, prayers)	_____	_____
f. Adhering to certain rules or sequences (e.g., assuring symmetry, ritualistic acts, adhering to a specific routine for daily activities)	_____	_____
g. Other	_____	_____
h. Other	_____	_____

Source: Adapted from DiNardo, Brown, & Barlow, 1994.

One-way mirrors are sometimes used by psychologists to observe behavior in a more natural context.

violence—of his threats toward other children and to the teacher herself, threats that were taken very seriously. To get a clearer picture of the situation at home, the clinician visited one afternoon. Approximately 15 minutes after the visit began, the boy got up from the kitchen table without removing the drinking glass he was using. When his mother (quite meekly) asked him to put the glass in the sink, he picked it up and threw it across the room, sending broken glass throughout the kitchen. He giggled and went into his room to watch TV. "See," she said, "He doesn't listen to me!"

Obviously, this mother's description of her son's behavior at home didn't give a good picture of what he was really like. It also didn't accurately portray how she did or did not respond to his violent outbursts. Without this observation at home, the clinician's assessment of the problem and recommendations for treatment would have been much different. Clearly this behavior was more serious than just disobedience. We developed strategies to teach the mother how to make requests of her son and how to follow up if he was violent.

To go back to our initial case of Frank and his anxiety about his marriage, how do we know he is telling us the "truth" about his relationship with his wife? Is what he is *not* telling us important? What would we find if we observed Frank and his wife interacting in their home, or if they carried on a typical conversation in front of us in a clinical setting? Similarly, is Brian delusional about people's beliefs that he is a homosexual, or do others view him this way when he is out in public? What would you hear if you listened in on conversations about Brian at his workplace? Most clinicians assume that a more complete picture of a person's problems can be obtained through direct observation in naturalistic environments.

Frequently, going into a person's home, workplace, or school isn't possible or practical. To approximate these naturalistic observations, clinicians sometimes set up analog settings. For example, one of us studies the self-hitting (called *self-injurious behavior*)

Table 3.2   Psychotic Disorders: Schizophrenia

BEGIN CARD 024 (02401
02403)
DUP. COLS. (04-16)

	Optional Specifics	RDC	DSM-III-R
ACTIVE PHASE			
HALLUCINATIONS, DELUSIONS, OR FORMAL THOUGHT DISORDER:			
SOME OF THESE ITEMS MAY HAVE TO BE ANSWERED ON THE BASIS OF YOUR OBSERVATION OF THE SUBJECT (IF THE EPISODE IS CURRENT) OR BY USING ADDITIONAL SOURCES OF INFORMATION (FOR A PAST EPISODE).			
1.a. Has there ever been a time when you saw things that other people couldn't see, or you smelled odors others couldn't, or tasted strange things, or had strange feelings in your body?	12 _____ (2417)		
(What did you see/smell/taste/feel?)			
HALLUCINATIONS: _____			
_____			
_____			
b. Has there ever been a time when you heard voices that other people couldn't hear?	12 _____ (2418)		
HYPNAGOGIC AND HYPNOPOMPIC PHENOMENA AND MERELY HEARING ONE'S NAME CALLED ARE NOT CONSIDERED TO BE HALLUCINATIONS			

Table 3.2   *(continued)*

	Optional Specifics	RDC	DSM-III-R

2. Has there ever been a time when you had beliefs or ideas that you were convinced were true, but that you later found out were not true and that other people didn't seem to share or understand (such as that people were out to get you, or that your thoughts were being broadcast on television)?

(Tell me about these.)

DELUSIONS: _____

_____

_____

_____

                                      12 _____ (2419)

3.a. Was there ever a time when people had trouble understanding what you were saying because your speech was mixed up, or because you didn't make sense in the way you were talking?

Formal thought disorder, incoherence, or marked loosening of associations   12 _____ (2420)

b. Has there been a time when you did something to call attention to yourself—like dressing in some odd way or doing something strange?

(Tell me about this.)

BIZARRE BEHAVIOR/CATATONIA: _____

_____

_____

Odd, bizarre, catatonic, or grossly disorganized behavior   12 _____ (2421)

c. Was there ever a time when you seemed to react to things with different emotions than other people or felt "numb" emotionally (when you were not on medication)?

(How bad did this get?)

Blunted, flat, or inappropriate affect   12 _____ (2422)

> IF NO TO ALL SPECIFIC PSYCHOTIC SYMPTOMS, SKIP TO ANXIETY DISORDERS, PG. _____

4.   IF HAD AUDITORY HALLUCINATIONS, ASK:

a. Did you ever hear a voice which was speaking to you?   12 _____ (2423)

(What was it saying?)

AUDITORY HALLUCINATIONS: _____

_____

_____

b. Content was non-affective (i.e., mood-incongruent or unrelated to depression or elation).   12 _____ (2424)

c. Voice kept up a running commentary on subject's behavior or thoughts.   12 _____ (2425)

d. Did you ever hear two or more voices that were talking to each other?   12 _____ (2426)

Source: Schleyer et al., 1990.

of children with autism (a disorder we'll examine in Chapter 16 that is characterized by social withdrawal and communication problems) by placing the children in simulated classroom activities such as sitting alone at a desk, working in a group, and being asked to complete a difficult task (Durand & Crimmins, 1988). Observing how they behave in these different situations helps us determine why they hit themselves and design a successful treatment to eliminate the behavior. David Wolfe (1991) uses contrived situations to assess emotional reactions of parents with a history of abuse toward their children. By asking parents to have their child put away favorite toys, which in turn usually results in behavior problems by the child, the therapist can see how the parents respond to these difficult situations. These observations are later used to develop treatments.

The ABCs of observation.

Observational assessment usually focuses on the "here and now." Therefore, attention is usually directed to the immediate *behavior,* its *antecedents*, and its *consequences* (Baer, Wolf, & Risley, 1968). To use the example of the young boy, an observer would note that the sequence of events was (a) his mother's request to perform a task (to put his glass in the sink) (antecedent), (b) the boy's throwing of the glass (behavior), and (c) his mother's lack of response (consequence). This *A*ntecedent-*B*ehavior-*C*onsequence sequence (the "ABCs") might suggest that the boy was being reinforced for his violent outburst by not having to clean up his mess. And because there was no negative consequence for his behavior in this situation (his mother didn't scold or reprimand him), he will probably act violently the next time he doesn't want to do something (see Figure 3.4).

The type of observation just described would be an example of a relatively *informal observation*. At the time of the home visit, the clinician took rough notes about what occurred. Later, in his office, he elaborated on the notes. A problem with this type of observation is that it relies on the observer's recollecting what happened in the past as well as his or her interpretation of the events. More *formal observation* would involve specifically identifying the behaviors to be observed in such a way that they are *observable* and *measurable* (called an *operational definition*). It would be hard for two people to agree on what "having an attitude" would

look like. An operational definition might further specify this as "any time the boy does not comply with his mother's reasonable requests." Once the target behavior has been selected and defined, an observer would write down each time it occurred, along with what happened just before (antecedent) and just after (consequence). The goal of collecting this information is to see whether there are any obvious patterns of behavior and then to design a treatment based on these patterns.

People can also observe their own behavior to find patterns, a technique known as **self-monitoring** or self-observation. People who try to quit smoking may write down the number of cigarettes they smoke and the times and places where they smoke. This observation can tell them exactly how big their problem is (for example, they smoke two packs a day) and what situations lead them to smoke more (for example, talking on the phone). Because the person with the problem is in the best position to observe his own behavior throughout the day, clinicians will often ask a client to self-monitor his behavior to get more detailed information on the problem.

Checklists and rating scales.

A more formal and structured way to observe behavior is through checklists and *behavior rating scales*. These are used as an assessment prior to treatment and then are often used periodically during treatment to assess changes in the patient's behavior. There are many such instruments available to assist with assessing a variety of behaviors. One of them, the *Brief Psychiatric Rating Scale* (Overall & Hollister, 1982) can be completed by staff and assesses 18 general areas of concern. Each symptom is rated on a 7-point scale, from 0 (not present) to 6 (extremely severe). The rating scale includes such items as *somatic concern* (preoccupation with physical health, fear of physical illness, hypochondriasis), *guilt feelings* (self-blame, shame, remorse for past behavior), and *grandiosity* (exaggerated self-opinion, arrogance, conviction of unusual power or abilities). The *Child Behavior Checklist* (Achenbach & Edelbrock, 1983) assesses the presence of a wide range of problem behaviors typically observed in children with conduct and other disorders. Age and sex norms are available for this instrument, and it can be given to both parents and teachers to complete for a particular child.

Reactivity

In an early experience with direct observation, one of us spent several hours in a classroom observing a young boy diagnosed with attention deficit disorder. The task was to count the number of times the boy got out of his seat and walked around the room—which was defined as any time his buttocks left the chair. Despite every effort to try to conceal the fact that we

Figure 3.4   The ABCs of observation

were observing him, the boy soon learned what was occurring and, with a great big grin, he began to vigorously bounce up and down in his chair. Over 600 instances of "out-of-seat" behavior were recorded that day! This example illustrates—to an extreme—a phenomenon known as **reactivity.** Any time you observe people behave, the mere act of your observation may cause them to change their behavior (Kazdin, 1979).

To test reactivity, you can tell a friend you are going to record every time she says the word *like.* Just before you tell her of your intent, however, count the times she uses this word in a 5-minute period. You will probably find that she uses the word much less often when you are recording it. Your friend will "react" to the observation by changing her behavior. The same phenomenon will also occur if you observe your own behavior, or self-monitor. Behaviors people want to increase, such as talking more in class, will tend to *increase,* and behaviors people want to decrease, such as smoking, will tend to *decrease* when they are self-monitored (Cavior & Marabotto, 1976; Sieck & McFall, 1976). Clinicians sometimes depend on the reactivity of self-monitoring to increase the effectiveness of their treatments.

Psychological Testing

We are confronted with "psychological tests" in the popular press almost every week: "12 Questions to Test Your Relationship," "New Test Inside to Help You Assess Your Lover's Passion," "Are You a Type 'Z' Personality?" Although we may not want to admit it, many of us have probably purchased a magazine at some point to take one of these types of tests. Many are no more than entertainment, designed to make you think about the topic (and to make you buy magazines). They are typically made up for the purposes of the article and include questions that, on the surface, seem to make sense. We are interested in these tests because we do want to understand why we and our friends behave the way we do. Could it be that your roommate doesn't clean up the dishes because he or she has a type "Z" personality?

In contrast, the tests used to assess psychological disorders must meet the strict standards we mentioned previously. They must be reliable—so that two or more people administering the same test to the same person will come to the same conclusion about the problem—and they must be valid—so that they measure what they say they are measuring. Next we review some of these formal assessments and their relative strengths and weaknesses with regard to issues of reliability and validity.

Projective Testing

We saw in Chapter 1 how Freud brought to our attention the presence and influence of unconscious

processes in psychological disorders. At this point we should ask, if people aren't aware of these thoughts and feelings, how do you assess them? To address this intriguing problem, psychoanalytic workers developed several assessment measures known as **projective tests.** They include a variety of methods in which ambiguous stimuli—such as pictures of people or things—are presented to the person, who is then asked to describe what he or she sees. The theory here is that people "project" their own personality and unconscious fears on to other people and things—in this case the ambiguous stimuli—and without realizing it, reveal their unconscious thoughts to the therapist.

Because these tests are based in psychoanalytic theory they have been, and remain, controversial. Even so, the use of projective tests is quite common, with a majority of clinical facilities reported to administer them at least occasionally and a comparable number of doctoral clinical programs providing training in their use (Durand, Blanchard, & Mindell, 1988). Three of the more widely used of these are the *Rorschach inkblot test,* the *Thematic Apperception Test,* and the *sentence-completion method.*

Over 80 years ago, a Swiss psychiatrist named Herman Rorschach developed a series of inkblots, initially to study perceptual processes, then later to diagnose psychological disorders. These inkblots are now known as the *Rorschach inkblot test,* one of the early projective tests. The current form of the Rorschach inkblot test includes 10 inkblot pictures that serve as the ambiguous stimuli (see Figure 3.5). The

Figure 3.5 This inkblot resembles the ambiguous figures presented in the Rorschach inkblot test.

examiner presents the 10 inkblots, one by one, to the person being assessed, who responds by telling what he or she sees. Those of you interested in trivia will appreciate the following: Rorschach originally used 35 inkblots, but his publisher would not pay for printing more than 10. Also, a printer's error caused the inkblots to have shading, a feature Rorschach later incorporated into the interpretation scheme (Exner & Clark, 1978). In other words, much of the current form of the test was derived by accident!

Though Rorschach advocated a scientific approach to studying the answers to the test (Rorschach, 1951), he died at the age of 38, before he had fully developed his method for systematic interpretation of his test. Unfortunately, much of the early history of the use of the Rorschach can be characterized as extremely controversial because of the lack of data on reliability or validity, among other things. Until relatively recently, therapists would administer the test any way they saw fit, prompting the comment that "there are perhaps as many Rorschachs as there are examiners" (Exner & Clark, 1978, p. 147). One of the most important tenets of assessment is that examiners give or administer the same test in the same way each time, that is, according to standardized procedures. If you provide encouragement to someone for more detailed answers during one testing session but do not give additional help during a second testing session, you may get different responses. The variation in responses might be the result of your administering the test differently on the two occasions—and be totally unrelated to problems with the test or administration by another person (interrater reliability).

To respond to the concerns about reliability and validity, John Exner developed a standardized version of the Rorschach inkblot test, called the *Comprehensive System* (Exner, 1974, 1978, 1986; Exner & Weiner, 1982). Exner's system of administering and scoring the Rorschach specifies such things as how the cards should be presented, what the examiner should say, and how responses should be recorded. Variations in these steps can potentially lead to different responses by the client. Recent work on this new system indicates that the test, when used in a standard way, may indeed be a useful assessment device for identifying some forms of psychopathology (Acklin, McDowell, & Orndoff, 1992). Research on the use of the Rorschach remains limited, however; a recent review of research on the Rorschach with African-Americans revealed just seven published studies in the past 60 years (Frank, 1992). Despite efforts such as Exner's to standardize the administration of the test, many clinicians continue to use and interpret the results of the Rorschach test in their own idiosyncratic way, reducing its reliability and validity. This problem comes up with all the projective tests.

The *Thematic Apperception Test* (TAT) is perhaps the best known of projective tests, after the Rorschach. It was developed in 1935 by Morgan and Murray at the Harvard Psychological Clinic (Bellak, 1975). The TAT consists of a series of 31 cards (see Figure 3.6); 30 of the cards have pictures on them and there is one blank card, although only 20 cards are typically provided at each administration. Unlike the Rorschach, which involves asking for a fairly straight-forward description of what the test taker sees, the instructions for the TAT ask the person to tell a dramatic story about the picture. The tester presents the pictures and tells the client, "This is a test of imagination, one form of intelligence." The person being assessed can "give freer rein to his or her imagination" and can "let your imagination have its way, as in a myth, fairy story, or allegory" (Stein, 1978, p. 186). Again, like the Rorschach, the TAT is based on the notion that people will project their unconscious mental processes into their stories about these pictures.

Several variations of the TAT have been developed to be used with different groups. A Children's Apperception Test (CAT) and a Senior Apperception Technique (SAT) have been designed so that this test can be used for people across the life span. In addition, modifications of the test have evolved for use with a variety of racial and ethnic groups, including

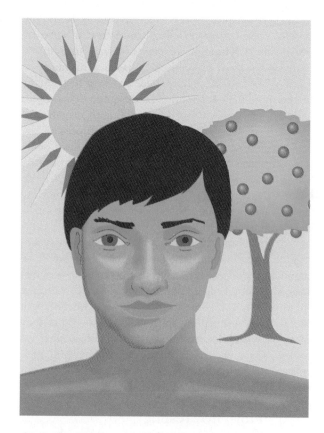

Figure 3.6 Thematic Apperception Test. Example of a possible card.

African-Americans, Native Americans, and people from India, South Africa, and the South Pacific Micronesian culture (Bellak, 1975). These modifications have included changes not only in the appearance of people in the pictures but also in the situations that are likely to be encountered by these different groups.

Unfortunately, unlike recent trends in the use of the Rorschach, the use of the TAT and its variants continues to be characterized by individualized administrations and interpretations. Interpretation of the stories people tell about these pictures depends on the examiner's frame of reference as well as what the patient may say. It is not surprising, therefore, that there is little reliability across raters using this system (Lundy, 1985). Despite these problems, the TAT is still widely used, and some clinicians continue to report that they find it valuable in guiding their diagnostic and treatment decisions.

Other projective tests use other means besides pictures to assess unconscious processes. In one technique, the *sentence-completion method,* the test taker is given a series of incomplete sentences and asked to complete them. The Rotter Incomplete Sentence Blank (Rotter & Rafferty, 1950) provides a series of sentences such as these:

I like _____.

Back home _____.

What annoys me _____.

I secretly _____.

As with the other projective techniques, the responses to these sentences are used to assess aspects of the responder that may not come out in more overt forms of questioning.

Another assessment technique uses drawings to extract responses from people. In a typical example, a person is given a blank sheet of paper and pencil, and is asked to "draw a person." Several of the characteristics of the drawing that are assessed include whether the person drew someone of the same or different gender, and the presence of certain details such as hands, feet, and the size of the head. Again, like the TAT, interpretations of these drawings often differ substantially from person to person.

Overall evaluation of projective tests.

Despite their popularity and the increasing availability of standard ways of administering these tests, most clinicians who use projective tests do so using their own, individualistic methods of administration and interpretation. When used as "ice breakers" or ways of getting people to open up and talk about how they feel about things going on in their lives, the ambiguous stimuli in these tests can be valuable tools. However, their relative lack of reliability and validity make them less useful as diagnostic tests (Anastasi, 1988). Concern over the inappropriate use of projective tests should alert readers to the importance of the scientist-practitioner approach to these issues. Clinicians are not only responsible for knowing how to administer these tests but also need to be aware of the research that suggests they have limited usefulness as a means of diagnosing psychopathology.

Personality Inventories

When we introduced this section, we mentioned the types of "psychological tests" usually published in mainstream magazines. The questions on these tests typically "make sense" when you read them. This is called having *face validity.* In other words, the wording of the questions seems to fit with the type of information desired. But is this necessary? A prominent psychologist, Paul Meehl, presented his position on this issue over 45 years ago, and subsequently influenced a whole field of study on **personality inventories** (Meehl, 1945). Put simply, Meehl pointed out that what is necessary from these types of tests is not whether the questions necessarily make sense on the surface, but, rather, what the answers to these questions predict. If we find that people who have schizophrenia tend to respond to the following statement—I have never been in love with anyone—with a "true," then it doesn't matter whether we have a theory of love and schizophrenia. If people with certain disorders tend, as a group, to answer a variety of questions in a certain way, we can use this pattern of answers to help predict who else has this disorder. The content of the question becomes irrelevant. The importance lies in what the answers to these questions predict.

The power of prediction underlies the most widely used personality inventory in the United States—the *Minnesota Multiphasic Personality Inventory (MMPI).* The MMPI was developed in the late 1930s and early 1940s and was first published in 1943 (Hathaway & McKinley, 1943). In stark contrast to the projective tests, which rely heavily on theory to provide an interpretation, the MMPI and similar inventories are based on an *empirical* approach, that is, the collection and evaluation of data. The administration of the MMPI is relatively straightforward. The individuals being assessed read the statements and answer either TRUE or FALSE as each statement relates to them. Following are some statements and answers from the MMPI:

I cry easily.   TRUE
I am happy most of the time.   FALSE
I believe I am being followed.   TRUE
Someone has been trying to
    poison me.   TRUE

Obviously, there is little room for interpretation of MMPI responses, unlike the types of responses from projective tests such as the Rorschach and the TAT. A problem with administering the MMPI, however, is the time and tediousness of responding to the 550 items on the original version and now the 567 items on the MMPI-2. Individual responses are *not* examined; instead, the pattern of responses is reviewed to see if it resembles patterns from people who have specific disorders (for example, a pattern similar to a group with schizophrenia). Fortunately, clinicians can have these responses computer scored; the program also includes an interpretation of the results, thereby reducing problems of reliability.

The answers to the first two questions above suggest that this person may have some depression. Similarly, the answers on the last two questions suggest paranoia and/or suspiciousness. What may not be as obvious is that persons with paranoia consistently tend to answer all the questions as indicated above and are included in the MMPI's Scale 6 (Paranoia) (Butcher, Graham, Williams, & Ben-Porath, 1990). The way these trends are determined is to give the test to a large group of people who have received the diagnosis of "paranoia," then see how they answer the questions. Their responses are compared to the responses of others with different diagnoses, and patterns of answers are devel-

oped for use in identifying new people—a method known as *empirical criterion keying* (Graham, 1990).

One concern that arose early in the development of the MMPI was the potential of some people to answer in ways that would downplay their problems; skilled individuals would ascertain the intent of some of the statements—Someone has control over my mind—and "fake" answers. To assess this possibility, the MMPI includes three additional scales that determine the validity of each administration. For example, on the "L" or Lie Scale, one statement is, "I have never had a bad night's sleep." Answering "true" to this is an indication that the person may be falsifying answers in order to look good. The other two scales are the "F" or Infrequency scale, which measures false claims about psychological problems or determines whether the person is answering randomly, and the "K" or Defensiveness scale, which assesses whether the person sees himself in unrealistically positive ways (see Table 3.3).

Figure 3.7 is an MMPI *profile* or summary of scores from an individual being clinically assessed. Before we tell you why this 27-year-old man (we'll call him James S.) was being evaluated, let's take a look at parts of his MMPI profile to see what it tells us about him. The first three data points represent scores on the L, F, and K scales; the high scores on these scales were

Table 3.3   The MMPI Validity and Standard Scales

Scale	Name	Description
Validity Scales		
?	Cannot say	This scale evaluates the extent of the test taker's cooperativeness with the test. It is simply the total number of the items the test taker did not answer.
L	Lie scale	Some individuals tend to distort their answers to give the impression that they are excessively virtuous. An example would be to answer false to the question, "At times I feel like swearing."
F	Infrequency scale	Some individuals exaggerate the extent of their problems; this scale assesses this tendency. The idea behind this scale is that those people who exaggerate will endorse ideas across a broad range of problems, some of which are incompatible, while some are in excess of what is typically reported by people who do have these problems.
K	Subtle defensiveness	This is a measure of test defensiveness—the willingness of people to disclose information on the test. For example, an answer of false on the following question would be an item on this scale: "Criticism or scolding hurts me terribly."
Standard Scales		
Hs	Hypochondriasis	Described as an abnormal concern over bodily health, this scale measures the degree of bodily complaints claimed by an individual. Hypochondriasis is a disturbance involving an unrealistic interpretation of physical signs or sensations as abnormal, which leads the person to fear that he or she has a serious disease.
D	Depression	This scale measures the extent to which the person has a negative frame of mind, a low morale, feelings of hopelessness and helplessness, general dissatisfaction, and, sometimes, preoccupation with death and suicide. This scale is considered to be a mood scale and is therefore sensitive to momentary emotional states.
Hy	Hysteria	The original intent of this scale was to create a measure of what we would today call *conversion disorder*. Individuals develop physical symptoms that appear to allow them to evade responsibilities and to escape from stressful and unpleasant situations.

interpreted to mean that James S. made a naive attempt to look good for the evaluator and may have been trying to fake an appearance of having no problems.

Another important part of his profile is the very high score on the "Pd" or Psychopathic deviation scale. This scale measures the tendency to behave in antisocial ways (see Chapter 13 for more on antisocial personality disorder). The interpretation of this score is that James S. is "aggressive, unreliable, irresponsible; unable to learn from experience; may initially make a good impression but then psychopathic features will surface in longer interactions or under stress." Why was James S. being evaluated? James S. (not his real name) is a young man with a long criminal record that reaches back into his childhood. He was being evaluated as part of his trial for kidnapping, raping, and murdering a middle-aged woman. Throughout his trial, he made up a number of contradictory stories to make himself look innocent (remember his high scores on the L, F, and K scales), including blaming his brother. Fortunately, there was overwhelming evidence of his guilt in this tragic event, and he was sentenced to life in prison. His own true/false answers on the MMPI resembled those of others who act in violent and antisocial ways.

The MMPI is one of the most extensively researched assessment instruments in psychology, with over 8,000 research references published regarding its use (Anastasi, 1988). The original standardization sample—the group of people who responded to the statements and set the "standard" for answers—included a large group of people from Minnesota who had no psychological disorders, and several groups of people who had particular psychological disorders. A more recent version of this test—the *MMPI-2*—was developed as problems arose over time with the original version, problems in part due to the original selective sample of people as well as the wording of questions (Helmes & Reddon, 1993). For example, some of the questions were sexist. One item on the original version asks the respondent to say whether she has ever been sorry that she was a girl (Worell & Remer, 1992). Another item states, "Any man who is willing to work hard has a good chance of succeeding." Other items were criticized for being insensitive to cultural diversity. Items dealing with religion, for example, referred almost exclusively to Christianity (Butcher, Graham, Williams, & Ben-Porath, 1990). The MMPI-2 has revised these types of items. The MMPI has also

Table 3.3 *(continued)*

Scale	Name	Description
Validity Scales		
Pd	Psychopathic deviation	The common denominator across subjects seemed to be that they had low anticipation of the consequences of their behavior; they were lacking in their ability to form warm and stable bonds to others, to appreciate social customs and abide by societal rules, and to profit from experiences that had negative consequences.
MF	Masculinity/femininity	The underlying construct for this scale was not a clinical syndrome but an attempt to assess the personality features that distinguish homosexual men with "feminine" interests.
Pa	Paranoia	Patients fitting this category manifested various signs of paranoia including ideas of reference, feelings of persecution, grandiose self-concepts, hypersensitivity, rigid thinking, and suspiciousness.
Pt	Psychasthenia	This scale was originally developed to assess a disorder called *psychasthenia*, which today would be considered one of the anxiety disorders—obsessive-compulsive disorder. Individuals classified as having psychasthenic tendencies were described as having excessive self-doubts leading to tension, difficulties in making choices, various fears, obsessive preoccupations, compulsive urges and acts, vague anxieties, and feelings of low self-confidence and insecurity.
Sc	Schizophrenia	People who score high on this scale tend to be rated as being very suspicious and as having unusual thought content. This is considered one of the weaker diagnostic scales.
Ma	Hypomania	Measures the milder aspects of an elevated mood that often is accompanied by a flight of ideas, affective lability, and psychomotor excitement. Hypomania indicates heightened activity levels with accompanying symptoms or traits such as easy distractibility, insomnia, overoptimism, occasional grandiosity, suspiciousness, and irascibility.
Si	Social introversion	This scale was designed to evaluate an individual's degree of introversion–extroversion. Many researchers and clinicians believe there are strong constitutional and biological factors contributing to the introversion–extroversion dimension of personality.

Source: Adapted from Butcher & Williams, 1992; Friedman, Webb, & Lewak, 1989; Graham, 1990.

Figure 3.7   An MMPI profile (from MMPI, 1982)

been standardized with a sample that is more similar to the 1980 U.S. Census figures, including African-Americans and Native Americans for the first time. In addition, new items have been added that deal with more contemporary issues such as Type A personality, low self-esteem, and family problems.

A number of clinicians continue to use the original MMPI and plan to do so until more research has been done on MMPI-2. The initial research on the revised version looks good, however, and a growing number of published research studies support its usefulness (Butcher & Graham, 1989; Graham, Timbrook, Ben-Porath, & Butcher, 1991; Chojnacki & Walsh, 1992). For example, a recent study of 29 Vietnam combat veterans with posttraumatic stress disorder (PTSD) indicated that the MMPI-2 was comparable to the original version of the MMPI in correctly identifying this group from groups of veteran psychiatric inpatients, veteran substance abusers, and

nonveterans—all without PTSD (Litz et al., 1991). Research has also begun on ethnic differences in responses on the MMPI-2 (for example, Hutton, Miner, Blades, & Langfeldt, 1992).

Reliability of the MMPI is excellent when it is interpreted according to standardized procedures, and there are thousands of studies on the original MMPI that attest to its validity with a range of psychological problems (Anastasi, 1988). A word of caution here. Just as with any other form of assessment, some clinicians take it on themselves to look at an MMPI profile and, based only on their own clinical experience and judgment, interpret the scales. By not relying on the standard means of interpretation, this practice compromises the instrument's reliability and validity.

In addition to the MMPI, there are numerous other personality measures in use including the *Symptom Check List-90 Revised (SCL-90 R)* (DeRogatis, 1977), in which respondents indicate their degree of distress on 90 physical and psychological symptoms; and the *Millon Multiaxial Clinical Inventory (MMCI)* (Millon, 1986), which is designed to distinguish people on one or more of DSM's personality disorders. Although these measures do not have as extensive a body of research behind them as that supporting the MMPI, they do have empirical support for their clinical use. Like the MMPI, they are an efficient means of collecting information about individuals, they have standard formats so that clinicians can collect reliable information with them, and they also provide relatively unambiguous information that can be reliably interpreted.

Intelligence Testing

"She must be very smart. I hear her IQ is 180!" What is "IQ"? What is "intelligence"? And how are they important in psychopathology? As many of you know by now from your introductory psychology course, intelligence tests were developed for one specific purpose—to predict who would do well in school. In 1904, a French psychologist, Alfred Binet, and a colleague, Theodore Simon, were commissioned by the French government to develop a test that would identify children who were "slow learners" and who would benefit from remedial help. The two psychologists identified a series of tasks that presumably measured the skills children would need to succeed in school including tasks of attention, perception, memory, reasoning, and verbal comprehension. Binet and Simon gave their original series of tasks to a large number of children; they then eliminated those tasks that were not successful in identifying the slow learners from the children who did well in school. After several revisions and sample administrations, they had a test that was relatively easy to administer and that did what it was designed to do—predict academic success. In 1916, Lewis Terman of Stanford University translated a revised version of this test for use in the United States; it became known as the *Stanford-Binet.*

The test provided a score, known as an **intelligence quotient**, or *IQ*. Initially, IQ scores were calculated by using the child's *mental age* (MA), which is the age level at which the child scored on the test. For example, if a child passed all the questions on the 7-year-old level and none of the questions on the 8-year-old level, then he or she received a mental age of 7. This mental age was then divided by the child's *chronological age* (CA) and multiplied by 100 to get the IQ score. However, there were problems with using this type of formula for calculating an IQ score. For example, a 4-year-old needed to score only one year above his or her chronological age to be given an IQ score of 125, although an 8-year-old had to score two years above his or her chronological age to be given the same score (Bjorklund, 1989). Current tests use what is called a *deviation IQ.* A person's score is compared only to scores of others of the same age. The IQ score, then, is really an estimate of how much a child's performance in school will deviate from the average performance of others of the same age.

In addition to the revised version of the Stanford-Binet (Thorndike, Hagen, & Sattler, 1986), there is another widely used set of intelligence tests, developed by psychologist David Wechsler. The Wechsler tests include versions for adults (*Wechsler Adult Intelligence Scale-Revised–WAIS-R*), children (*Wechsler Intelligence Scale for Children-Third Edition–WISC-III*), and for young children (*Wechsler Preschool and Primary Scale of Intelligence-Revised–WPPSI-R*). All these tests are broken down into *verbal scales* (which measure vocabulary, information for facts, short-term memory, and verbal reasoning skills) and *performance scales* (which assess psychomotor abilities, nonverbal reasoning, and ability to learn new relationships).

One of the biggest mistakes made by nonpsychologists (and a distressing number of psychologists) is to confuse IQ with intelligence. IQ is a score on one of the intelligence tests we just described. An IQ score significantly higher than average means only that the person has a significantly greater than average chance of doing well in our educational system. On the other hand, receiving a score that is significantly lower than average suggests that the person will probably not do well in school. Does a lower than average IQ score mean that a person is not "intelligent"? Not necessarily. First of all, there are numerous reasons that an IQ score might be low. If the IQ test is administered in English and that is not the person's native language, the results of the test will be affected.

Perhaps more important, however, is the lack of general agreement about what constitutes intelligence (Weinberg, 1989). Remember that the IQ tests used tasks that tap abilities such as attention, perception, memory, reasoning, and verbal comprehension abilities. But does this list of skills represent the totality of what we consider intelligence? Some recent theorists believe that what we think of as intelligence involves much more, including the ability to adapt to your environment, the ability to generate new ideas, and the ability to process information efficiently (Sternberg, 1988). We will discuss disorders that involve some level of cognitive impairment such as occurs in delirium and mental retardation, and IQ tests are typically used in assessing these disorders. Keep in mind, however, that we will be discussing IQ and not necessarily intelligence. In general, however, IQ tests tend to be reliable, and to the extent that they predict academic success, they are also valid assessment tools.

Neuropsychological Testing

From the psychological perspective sophisticated tests have been developed that can also pinpoint the location of brain dysfunction. Fortunately, these techniques are available and relatively inexpensive. In **neuropsychological testing** individuals are tested on their abilities in areas such as receptive and expressive language, attention and concentration, memory, motor skills, perceptual abilities, and learning and abstraction in such a way that the clinician can make educated guesses about the person's performance and the possible existence of brain impairment. In other words, this method of testing assesses brain dysfunction by observing its effects on the person's ability to perform certain tasks. Although you do not see damage, you can see its effects.

One fairly simple but less sophisticated neuropsychological test often used with children is the *Bender Visual-Motor Gestalt Test.* In this test, a child is given a series of pictures on which are drawn a variety of lines and shapes. The task is for the child to copy what is drawn on the card. Errors in copying these shapes are then recorded. This test is *age-normed,* meaning that different scores are standardized for different ages. Younger children who do not have organic impairment will make more mistakes than older children. The errors on the test are compared to test results of other children of the same age, and if the number of errors exceeds a certain amount, then brain dysfunction is suspected. This test is less sophisticated than other neuropsychological tests because the nature or location of the problem cannot be determined with this test. The Bender Visual-Motor Gestalt Test can be useful for psychologists, however, because it provides a simple screening instrument that is easy to administer and that can detect possible problems.

Two of the most popular and more advanced tests of organic damage that allow you to make more precise determinations of the location of the problem are the *Luria-Nebraska Neuropsychological Battery* (Golden, Hammeke, & Purisch, 1980) and the *Halstead-Reitan Neuropsychological Battery* (Reitan & Davison, 1974). These offer a much more elaborate battery of tests to assess a variety of skills. For example, the Halstead-Reitan Neuropsychological Battery includes the *Rhythm Test* (which asks the person to compare rhythmic beats to test sound recognition, attention, and concentration), the *Strength of Grip Test* (which compares the grip of the right versus the left hand), and the *Tactile Performance Test* (which requires the test taker to place wooden blocks in a form board while blindfolded, to test learning and memory skills).

Many of the skills assessed in neuropsychological testing are also assessed in intelligence tests. There is a great deal of overlap in these two approaches; however, neuropsychological testing also involves the assessment of such skills as motor and sensory abilities. For example, one of the intelligence tests described previously, the Wechsler Adult Intelligence Scale (WAIS), is included as part of the Halstead-Reitan

A first-grade Hispanic child in a standard psychological testing situation

Neuropsychological Battery. Research on the validity of these neuropsychological tests suggests that they may be useful for detecting organic damage. One study found that the Halstead-Reitan and the Luria-Nebraska test batteries were equivalent in their abilities to detect damage and were about 80% correct (Goldstein & Shelly, 1984). However, these types of studies raise a problem: the issue of **false positives** and **false negatives** (Boll, 1985). For any assessment strategy, there will be times when the test will show that there is a problem when none exists (false positives), and times when no problem will be found when indeed some difficulty is present (false negatives). The possibility of false results is particularly troublesome for tests of brain dysfunction; if a clinician fails to find damage that exists, he or she might miss an important medical problem that needs to be treated. Fortunately, these tests are used primarily as screening devices and are routinely paired with other assessments to improve the likelihood that real problems will be found.

These tests do well with regard to measures of reliability and validity. On the downside, they can require a number of hours to administer and are therefore not used routinely unless brain damage is suspected.

Pictures of the Brain: Neuroimaging

For over a century we have known that many of the things that we do, think, or remember are partially controlled by certain specific areas of our brain. In 1861, the famous surgeon Paul Broca was caring for a man who was hospitalized for an inability to speak intelligently. Before the man died, Broca examined him carefully; subsequent to death he performed an autopsy. The finding of a lesion (damage) in the third frontal convolution of the cerebral cortex convinced Broca, and eventually the rest of the scientific world, that this was the speech center of the brain. Broca proceeded to map out brain function further by systematically destroying parts of the brain in animals and noting the effects on behavior (Boring, 1950). These findings convinced his colleagues that the human brain must be explored and mapped much as the world was explored and mapped centuries earlier. But how to do it? Could this be done without inflicting serious damage and even death on subjects? Until recently, if someone had a specific behavioral or cognitive anomaly, we had to wait until death and perform an autopsy, much as Broca did, to determine the precise area of the brain that might have been damaged. Now that has changed.

In recent years we have developed the ability to look inside the brain and take increasingly accurate "pictures" of its structure and function, a technique called **neuroimaging** (Andreasen & Swayze, 1993; Baxter, Guze, & Reynolds, 1993). Neuroimaging can be divided into two categories. One category includes procedures that examine the *structure* of the brain, such as the size of various parts or whether there is any damage. In a second category are procedures that examine the actual *functioning* of the brain by mapping brain activity as indicated by blood flow or other metabolic activity.

Imaging of Brain Structure

The first technique, developed in the early 1970s, utilizes multiple X-ray exposures of the brain from different angles. That is, X-rays are passed directly through the head. As with any X-rays, these are partially blocked or attenuated more by bone and less by brain tissue. The degree of attenuation or blockage is picked up by detectors in the opposite side of the head. A computer then reconstructs pictures of various "slices" of the brain. This procedure is called **computerized axial tomography (CAT)** or **CAT scan.** Sometimes it is abbreviated further to *CT scan.* It is relatively noninvasive and has proven very useful in identifying abnormalities in the structure or shape of the brain as well as revealing the location of these abnormalities. CAT scans are particularly useful in locating brain tumors, injuries, or other structural or anatomical abnormalities. One difficulty, however, is that these scans involve repeated X-radiation, which poses some risk to the patient (Baxter et al., 1993).

More recently a procedure has been developed that has somewhat greater resolution (specificity and accuracy) than a CAT scan without the inherent risks of X-rays. This scanning technique is called nuclear **magnetic resonance imaging (MRI).** For the brain to be scanned, the patient's head is placed in a high-strength magnetic field through which radio frequency signals are transmitted. These signals "excite" the brain tissue, altering the protons in the hydrogen

atoms in the brain. The alteration, along with the time it takes the protons to "relax" or return to normal, is measured. If some part of the brain is slightly damaged, the signal will be lighter or darker (Andreasen & Swayze, 1993). Technology now exists that allows the computer to peel away layers of the brain (on the computer screen) enabling very precise examination of the structure. MRI is more expensive and takes as long as 45 minutes as opposed to 15 minutes for CAT scans, but this is changing as technology improves. Newer versions of MRI procedures may take as little as 10 minutes. Another disadvantage of MRI at present is that someone undergoing this procedure must be placed totally inside a narrow tube with a magnetic coil surrounding his or her head. People who are somewhat claustrophobic often cannot tolerate an MRI.

While these neuroimaging procedures are very useful for examining damage to the brain, only recently have they been used in attempts to determine any structural or anatomical abnormalities that might be associated with various psychological disorders. Some tantalizing preliminary studies are beginning to appear; these will be reviewed in subsequent chapters on specific disorders.

Imaging of Brain Functioning

Recently, experimental MRI procedures called *echo-plonar MRI* have been developed that work much more quickly than the regular MRI (Cohen, Rosen, & Brady, 1992). Using sophisticated computer technology, these procedures take only milliseconds and, therefore, with repeated images, can actually take pictures of the brain at work, recording its changes from one second to the next. In other words, echo-plonar MRI can measure the functioning of the brain.

Two additional procedures, recently developed but more widely used, are also capable of measuring the actual functioning of the brain as

Magnetic resonance imaging of the brain of a person with a psychological disorder

PET scans comparing brain activity of a drug abuser using PCP, an individual with schizophrenia, and a person with a normal brain.

opposed to its structure. The first is called **positron emission tomography (PET).** Subjects undergoing a **PET scan** are injected with a tracer substance attached to radioactive isotopes. This substance interacts with blood, oxygen, or glucose. When parts of the brain become active, blood, oxygen, and/or glucose rush to these areas of the brain, creating "hot spots" picked up by detectors. Thus, we can learn what parts of the brain are working and what parts are not. To obtain clear images, the individual undergoing the procedure must remain stationary for 40 seconds or more. These images can be superimposed on MRI images so that investigators can know the precise location of the active areas. PET scans are also useful in supplementing MRI and CAT scans in localizing the sites of trauma due to head injury or stroke as well as in localizing

brain tumors. More important, PET scans are used increasingly to look at varying patterns of metabolism that might be associated with different disorders. Recent PET scans have demonstrated that many patients with early Alzheimer's type dementia show reductions in glucose metabolism in the parietal lobes. Other intriguing findings have been reported for obsessive-compulsive disorder and bipolar disorder (see Chapters 5 and 7). Equipment for PET scanning is very expensive. The cost is about $6 million to set up a PET facility and $500,000 a year to run it. Therefore, these facilities are available only in large medical centers.

A second procedure used to assess brain functioning is called **single photon emission computed tomography,** or **SPECT.** SPECT works very much like PET although a different tracer substance is

(a)

(b)

(c)

This horizontal section of the brain in (a) shows how a SPECT of a brain of a person with schizophrenia reveals parietal lobe anomaly at a glance. The nature of these differences becomes clearer as the SPECT images become MRI images in photos (b) and (c). SPECT images show the metabolic activity that is occurring or not occurring and thus show the relationship between brain function and behavior. MRI images are high-resolution images that show variations in tissue and act as almost living photographs of the human brain.

used and it is somewhat less precise or accurate. SPECT is also less expensive, however, and requires far less sophisticated equipment to pick up the signals. For this reason it is used more frequently.

Although we have learned little to date, brain imagery procedures hold enormous potential for illuminating the contribution of neurobiological factors to psychological disorders.

Psychophysiological Assessment

Yet another method for assessing brain structure and function specifically and nervous system activity more generally is called **psychophysiological assessment.** As the term implies, *psychophysiology* refers to measurable changes in the nervous system reflecting emotional or psychological events. These procedures are used by psychologists and other mental health professionals. The measurements may be taken either directly from the brain or, more peripherally, from other parts of the body.

Brain Waves

Frank complained of fear that he might have seizures. If we had any reason to suspect that he might really be experiencing seizures (for example, periods of memory loss; reports from his wife of bizarre, trancelike behavior, if only for a short period of time) it would be important for him to have an exam called an **electroencephalogram** (EEG). The purpose of an electroencephalogram—in which electrical activity in the head related to the firing of a specific group of neurons is measured—would be to assess brain wave activity. Brain wave activity is the low voltage electrical current ongoing in the brain, most usually from the cortex. A person's brain waves can be assessed in both waking and sleeping states. In an EEG, electrodes are placed directly on various places on the scalp to record the different low voltage currents.

We have learned much about EEG patterns in the past decades (Fein & Callaway, 1993). Usually we measure *ongoing* electrical activity in the brain. When brief periods of EEG patterns are recorded in response to specific events, such as hearing a psychologically meaningful stimulus, the response is called an *event-related potential* (ERP) or evoked potential. We have learned that EEG patterns are often affected by psychological or emotional factors and can be an index of these reactions, or a psychophysiological measure. In a normal, healthy, but relaxed adult, waking activities are characterized by a very regular pattern of changes in voltage that we term *alpha waves.* Many types of stress-reduction treatments attempt to *increase* the frequency of the alpha waves patients experience, often by relaxing the patients in some way (see Chapter 9). The alpha wave pattern is associated with relaxation and calmness. During sleep we know that we pass through several different stages of brain activity, at least partially identified by EEG patterns. During the deepest, most relaxed stage of sleep, typically occurring one to two hours after a person falls asleep, EEG recordings will begin showing a pattern of *delta waves.* The pattern of these brain waves is slower and more irregular than that of the alpha waves and is perfectly normal for this stage of sleep. We will see in Chapter 5 that panic attacks occurring while a person is sound asleep come almost exclusively during the delta wave stage. If frequent delta wave activity occurred during the waking state, it might indicate dysfunction of localized areas of the brain.

Extremely rapid and irregular "spikes" on the EEG recordings of someone who is awake may reflect significant seizure disorders, depending on the pattern. EEG recording is one of the primary diagnostic tools for identifying seizure disorders. Individuals with documented seizure disorders are usually treated by neurologists although psychologists often play a role in treatment.

Psychophysiological assessment of other bodily responses may also play a role in assessment. These responses include heart rate, respiration, or *electrodermal responding* (skin conductance), formerly referred to as galvanic skin response (GSR), which is a measure of sweat gland activity controlled by the peripheral nervous system. Remember from Chapter 2

The administration of an electroencephalogram, a psychophysiological test to measure brain wave activity that the peripheral nervous system, and in particular the sympathetic division of the autonomic nervous system (ANS), is very responsive to stress and emotional arousal. When the organs and glands under control of the ANS are activated by psychological factors, such as stress or drugs, measurement of the activity of those organs and glands is called psychophysiological assessment. We often examine the psychophysiological responsivity of severely phobic patients in our Anxiety Disorders Clinic. For patients suffering from agoraphobia, a very severe fear of leaving a safe place or a safe person, we devise a real-life behavioral task. Since agoraphobics find it difficult to leave a safe place, the behavioral task directs them to walk as far as they can along a specific course leading away from the clinic toward a busy and crowded downtown area, a route that is increasingly anxiety provoking. Typically, agoraphobics carry a small map of the mile-long course, which is divided into 20 approximately equal distances or stations. When they reach each station, they are instructed to write down on a form how anxious they feel at that station on a self-report scale of 0 to 100 (where 0 equals complete relaxation and 100 represents maximum anxiety). The scale is called a *Subjective Units of Disturbance* or *SUDS scale.*

To measure psychophysiological responding, these individuals are fitted with a portable and rather unobtrusive device that measures heart rate while they are walking. The electrodes are placed at appropriate points in the chest area, and the wire leads run down the sleeve with the monitoring device itself typically fitting into a pocket or purse. Results from one of these tests comparing phobics to nonphobics who walked the same course are presented in Figure 3.8. As you can see,

the individuals with agoraphobia seem to have been more aroused and anxious than the other group, as measured by heart rate, during this behavioral task. However, in one of the unpredictable twists and turns that research sometimes takes, it turned out that these patients were *not* really responding with higher heart rates to the phobic situations. When we measured their heart rates *while they were at rest,* we discovered that phobic and other anxious patients are *chronically* aroused and anxious, and they carry this chronic overarousal with them into any test situation. Therefore, if you simply look at how much their heart rates *increase* while they are in a phobic situation over and above their heart rates at rest, you will find that their *actual response* is no greater than that of nonphobics. This finding, which has been replicated many times, indicates that one of the hallmarks of anxiety is chronic overarousal, which then becomes an important target for treatment through either psychological methods (for example, relaxation or meditation) or tranquilizing drugs.

On the other hand, assessing psychophysiological *responding* to emotional stimuli is very important in some other disorders, one being posttraumatic stress disorder. Stimuli such as sights and sounds associated with the trauma evoke strong psychophysiological responding, even if the patient is not fully aware of the nature of the trauma because he or she has repressed memories of it.

Psychophysiological assessment is also used with many other disorders. For example, sexual arousal can be assessed through direct measurement of penile circumference in males or vaginal blood flow in females in response to erotic stimuli, usually movies or slides (see Chapter 11). Sometimes the individual might be unaware of specific patterns of sexual arousal. Brian, for instance, thought he was homosexual. Direct physiological measures of his arousal to various types of standardized erotic stimuli indicated that he had no signs of homosexual arousal patterns and demonstrated exclusive heterosexual arousal patterns. This information then played a role in his diagnosis and treatment.

Physiological measures are also important in the assessment and treatment of other conditions such as headaches and hypertension (Blanchard, Martin, & Dubbert, 1988; Blanchard, 1992); they form the basis for the treatment we call biofeedback. In biofeedback, as we shall see in Chapter 9, levels of physiological responding, such as blood pressure readings, are "fed back" to the patient (provided to the patient on a continuous basis) by meters or gauges so that the patient can try to regulate these responses.

Nevertheless, physiological assessment is not without its limitations. A person must have a great deal of skill and some technical expertise to utilize these procedures. Even when administered properly, the

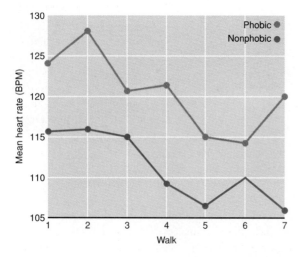

Figure 3.8 Mean heart rate of both groups during seven walks. Those in the phobic group were more aroused and anxious during the walks than were those in the nonphobic group (from Holden & Barlow, 1986).

measures often produce inconsistent results, either because of procedural or technical difficulties or the nature of the response itself. Consider heart rate. The heart does many things for us. Primarily, it keeps us alive by pumping blood and oxygen throughout the body. This function becomes more pronounced when we are engaging in exercise since the heart must work harder to get blood and oxygen to various parts of the body. When our patient with agoraphobia walks down the street, her heart must be concerned with these issues. In addition, her heart may reflect emotional activation as she develops panic or anxiety. The difficult task for the psychophysiologist is separating out that part of the reaction due to anxiety or emotion from the everyday functioning of the heart. For this reason, and because the technology is relatively expensive, only clinicians specializing in certain disorders where these measures are particularly important are likely to use psychophysiological recording equipment. This type of recording is more often used in theoretical investigations of the nature of certain psychological disorders, particularly emotional disorders (Barlow, 1988).

Diagnosing Psychological Disorders

In the last several years we have seen enormous changes in how we think about classifying psychopathology. Because these developments affect so much of what we do, including the organization and chapter headings of this and every other abnormal psychology book, we will examine quite carefully the process of diagnosis and classification as it is used in psychopathology. To begin, we discuss reasons for diagnosing and classifying individuals and some of the different strategies available to us. The concepts of reliability and validity as they pertain to diagnosis are presented, followed by a section on our current system of classification, the DSM-IV, and its history. After discussing criticisms of DSM-IV, we illustrate the process of creating a new diagnosis.

Thus far we have looked at the functioning of Frank and Brian on a very individual basis. That is, we have examined closely their behavior, cognitive processes, and mood by means of our observations as well as structured interviewing, behavioral assessment, and psychological tests. These operations basically tell us what is *unique* about these individuals and how they may differ from other individuals.

It is also very important for us to learn how Frank and Brian may be *similar* to other people in terms of the problems they are presenting. There are several reasons for this. If there were people in the past who came in with the same problems or psycho-

logical profiles, we can go back and find a lot of information from them that might be applicable to Frank and Brian. We can see how the problems began for those other individuals, what factors seemed to contribute to the beginning of the problem, and how long the problem or disorder lasted. Did the problem in the other people just go away on its own, or did it need treatment? If the problem didn't go away on its own, what kinds of factors or issues in the individual's current world were maintaining the problem or keeping it going? Most important, what treatments seemed to work to relieve the problem for those other individuals? Obviously this would be very important information to have. These general statements are very useful because they summarize a wealth of clinical and research information, enabling the clinician or investigator of psychopathology to make certain inferences about what is going to happen or what treatments are going to work. In other words, the clinician can establish a *prognosis,* a term we mentioned in Chapter 1 as referring to the likely future course of a disorder under certain conditions. If you can make these kinds of general conclusions, you don't have to start at square one every time someone new comes into your office.

Both strategies are essential in the study and treatment of psychopathology. If we are trying to determine what is unique about an individual with a given psychological disorder, we are using what is known as an **idiographic strategy.** The uniqueness could be in terms of his or her own personality, cultural background, or individual circumstances. This information is necessary to tailor our treatment for that person. On the other hand, to take advantage of the information already accumulated on a particular problem or disorder, we must be able to determine a general class or grouping of problems to which the presenting problem belongs. This is known as a **nomothetic strategy.** In other words, we are attempting to name or classify the problem. When we identify a specific psychological disorder, such as a mood disorder, in the clinical setting, the process is called making a *diagnosis.* Another example of identifying a general class or grouping of problems would be determining a particular personality profile on a psychological test such as the MMPI. Before proceeding we need to define some additional terms more precisely.

Terminology

Since classification is such an integral part of science and, indeed, our human experience, a number of terms or names have been created to describe different aspects of classification (Millon, 1991). The term **classification** itself is very broad and simply refers to any effort to construct groups or categories and to assign objects or people to these categories on the basis of their shared attributes or relations, a nomothetic strategy. If the process of classification is used in a scientific context, it is most often called **taxonomy.** Taxonomy refers to classifying entities—such as insects or rocks or, if the subject is psychology, behaviors—for scientific purposes. If you are applying a taxonomic system to psychological or medical phenomena or other clinical areas, you would use the word **nosology.** The term **nomenclature** refers to the names or labels of the disorders that make up the nosology (e.g., anxiety disorders, mood disorders). Most mental health professionals use a nosological system contained in the **Diagnostic and Statistical Manual of Mental Disorders (fourth ed.) (DSM-IV)** (American Psychiatric Association, 1994). This is the official system of nosology in the United States and is used widely throughout the world.

Issues Regarding Classification

Much of what we have said about classification is common sense. Indeed, classification is at the heart of any science. If we could not order and label objects or experiences, scientists could not communicate with each other and our knowledge would not advance. Without a system of classification, each individual would have to develop his or her own personal system, which, of course, would have no applicability outside the mind of that person. In your biology or geology courses, when you deal with insects or rocks, the ideas of classification are very fundamental. Insects and rocks are organized and classified in various ways. Knowing how one species of insects differs from another allows us to study its functioning and origins.

When we are dealing with human behavior or human behavioral disorders, however, the process of classification is much more controversial. Some people have questioned whether it is even proper or ethical to attempt to classify human behavior. For them, the value of a nomothetic approach is questionable; the only important goal is an idiographic one, knowing what is individual or unique about a person. Even among those who recognize the necessity of classification or nosology, major controversies have arisen in several areas. Within the realm of psychopathology, questions arise concerning what is normal or abnormal, something, you will recall, we struggled with in Chapter 1. Also, what determines which behaviors or cognitions are part of one disorder and not another? Some think it might be better just to talk about behavior or feelings on a continuum from happy to sad, or fearful to nonfearful, rather than attempting to create categories of mania, depression, or phobia. Of course, classifying behavior or people, for better or worse, is something that we all do. Few of us talk about our own emotions or those of our friends by using a number on a scale (where 0 is totally unhappy and 100 is totally happy), although there is some evidence that this might be more ac-

curate. ("How do you feel about that?" "About 65.") Rather, we talk about ourselves and our friends as being happy, sad, angry, depressed, or fearful. Since there have been many new developments in recent years, we spend some time next describing issues involved in our system of nosology.

Categorical and Dimensional Approaches

In view of the need to avoid reinventing the wheel every time we see a new set of problem behaviors and to look for general principles of psychopathology, what are the different ways we can organize and classify human behavior? We have already alluded to two possibilities: One is creating distinct *categories* of disorders that would presumably have little or nothing in common with one another. For example, you either hear voices talking to you from the refrigerator (auditory hallucination) and have other symptoms of schizophrenia, or you don't. Alternatively, we could quantify the various attributes of a psychological disorder along several *dimensions*, coming up with some kind of composite score. An MMPI profile would be a good example. Another example would be "dimensionalizing" depression on a continuum of severity from feeling mildly depressed in the morning (something most of us experience once in a while) to feeling so hopeless and depressed that suicide is the only answer. Which system is better? In fact, each has its strengths and each its faults. We'll look at both.

The **classical** (or pure) **categorical approach** to nosology has its origins in the work of Emil Kraepelin and the biological tradition in the study of psychopathology. Here we assume, for example, that every diagnosis has a clear underlying pathophysiological cause, such as a bacterial infection or a malfunctioning of the endocrine system, and each disorder is fundamentally different from every other disorder. When diagnoses are thought of in this way, the causes need not be pathophysiological. They could be psychological or cultural, but there would still be basically only one set of causative factors per disorder and this would not overlap at all with other disorders. Since each disorder is fundamentally different from the others, you would simply need one set of defining criteria and everybody in that category would have to meet those criteria. If your criteria for a major depressive episode were (a) the presence of depressed mood, (b) significant weight loss or weight gain when not dieting, and (c) diminished ability to think or concentrate, plus 7 additional specific symptoms, then, in order to be diagnosed with depression, every individual would have to meet all 10 criteria. If that were the case, according to the classical categorical approach, the clinician would know the cause of the disorder.

Classical categorical approaches have become quite useful in medicine. It is extremely important that a physician be able to make accurate diagnoses. If a patient has developed a fever accompanied by stomach pain, it will be important to determine rather quickly if the cause is the stomach flu or an infected appendix. This determination is not always easy, but physicians are trained to examine the signs and symptoms closely and usually reach the correct conclusion, resulting in an understanding of the cause of the symptoms (for instance, infected appendix) and effective treatment (surgery). But if someone is depressed or anxious, does the same type of underlying cause exist? As we saw in Chapter 2, probably not. Most psychopathologists believe that psychological and social factors interact with biological factors to produce a disorder. Therefore, despite the beliefs of Kraepelin and other early biological investigators, the mental health field has not adopted a classical categorical model of psychopathology since there is not any one clear, underlying, identifiable cause such as a bacterial infection or organ deterioration. As Frances and Widiger (1986) point out, the classical categorical approach is clearly an inappropriate strategy for dealing with the complexity that we find among psychological disorders.

A second strategy is a **dimensional approach.** Using this, we would note the variety of cognitions, moods, and behaviors with which the patient presents and quantify them on some scale as described above. For example, on a scale of 1 to 10, a patient might be rated as severely anxious (10), moderately depressed (5), and mildly manic (2) to create a profile of emotional functioning (10, 5, 2). While dimensional approaches have been attempted in the past, they are relatively unsatisfactory. Most theorists can't agree on how many dimensions are required to best represent psychopathology. Some respected theorists say one dimension is enough; others have identified as many as 33 (Millon, 1991).

A third strategy for organizing and classifying behavioral disorders has found increasing support in recent years as an alternative to classical categorical or dimensional approaches. It is a categorical approach but with a twist—it basically combines some of the features of each of the former approaches. Called a **prototypical approach,** this alternative identifies certain essential characteristics of an entity sufficiently to allow you (and others) to classify it; but it also allows

Dogs look very different, one from the other, but they are all classified as dogs.

for certain "nonessential" variations that do not necessarily change the classification. For example, if someone were to ask you to describe a dog, you could very easily give a general description of a dog (the essential, categorical characteristics), but you might not describe exactly any one individual dog. In other words, dogs come in different colors, sizes, and even species (the nonessential, dimensional variations); but they all share certain central characteristics that would be sufficient to allow you reliably to classify dogs, as compared to cats. Thus, requiring a dog to meet a certain number of "prototypical" criteria while, perhaps, meeting only some of an additional number of criteria would be adequate for your purposes. Of course, this system in itself is not perfect since there is a greater blurring at the boundaries of categories. For example, is a hyena basically a dog or a cat or neither? If you're not sleeping (a nonessential characteristic of depression and anxiety), are you depressed or anxious? This system, however, has the advantage of fitting best with the current state of our knowledge of psychopathology and is relatively user friendly. The approaches to classifying human behavior are shown in Figure 3.9.

When applied to psychological disorders, classifying simply means that many of the different possible features or properties of the psychological disorder are listed, and any one member of the category

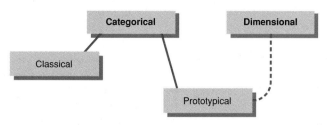

Figure 3.9 Approaches to classifying human behavior

must meet enough of them (but not all of them) to fall into that category. Consider the criteria defining a major depressive episode in DSM-IV listed below.

Criteria for Major Depressive Episode

A. Five (or more) of the following symptoms have been present during the same 2-week period and represent a change from previous functioning; at least one of the symptoms is either (a) depressed mood or (b) loss of interest or pleasure.

Note: Do not include symptoms that are clearly due to a general medical condition, or mood-incongruent delusions or hallucinations.

1. depressed mood most of the day, nearly every day, as indicated by either subjective report (for instance, feels sad or empty) or observation made by others (e.g., appears tearful). *Note:* In children and adolescents, can be irritable mood.
2. markedly diminished interest or pleasure in all, or almost all, activities most of the day, nearly every day (as indicated either by subjective account or observation made by others)
3. significant weight loss when not dieting or weight gain (for example, a change of more than 5% of body weight in a month) or decrease or increase in appetite nearly every day. *Note:* In children, consider failure to make expected weight gains.
4. insomnia or hypersomnia nearly every day
5. psychomotor agitation or retardation nearly every day (observable by others, not merely subjective feelings of restlessness or being slowed down)
6. fatigue or loss of energy nearly every day
7. feelings of worthlessness or excessive or inappropriate guilt (which may be delusional) nearly every day (not merely self-reproach or guilt about being sick)
8. diminished ability to think or concentrate or indecisiveness nearly every day (either by subjective account or as observed by others)
9. recurrent thoughts of death (not just fear of dying), recurrent suicidal ideation without a specific plan, or a suicide attempt or a specific plan for committing suicide

As you can see, this definition has many nonessential symptoms; but if you have either depressed mood or marked loss of interest or pleasure in most activities, *and* you have at least four of the remaining eight symptoms, you would come close enough to the prototype to meet criteria for a major depressive episode. Notice also that one person might have depressed mood, significant weight loss, insomnia, psychomotor agitation, and loss of energy, while another person also meeting the criteria for major depressive episode might have markedly diminished interest or pleasure in activities, fatigue, feelings of

worthlessness, difficulty thinking or concentrating, and suicidal ideation. Notice that each of these individuals would have the requisite number of five symptoms that would bring them close to the prototype. However, they would actually look very different since they would share only one symptom. This is a good example of a prototypical category. It is this approach on which our current nosological system, the DSM-IV, is based.

Reliability

Whether we talk about our behavior and emotions in terms of dimensions or categories, any system of classification should accomplish several very important goals. First, it should describe specific subgroups of symptoms or dimensions of behavior that are there for all to see and can be readily identified, at least by experienced clinicians. In the case of psychological disorders, if two clinicians interviewed the patient at separate times on the same day (and assuming that the patient has not changed during the day), the two clinicians should be able to see, and perhaps measure, the same set of behaviors and emotions that make up the problem. Thus the psychological disorder can be identified *reliably*. We discussed this concept earlier in the chapter. Obviously, if the disorder was not readily apparent to both clinicians, the resulting diagnosis might represent a bias in the way one looked at things. For example, if someone dressed in a flashy way came into your room where a group of your friends were gathered, her clothes might provoke some comment. After she left one of your friends might say, "She looked kind of sloppy tonight." Another friend might comment, "No, that's just a real funky look; she's right in style." Perhaps a third friend would say, "Actually I thought she was dressed kind of neatly." You might begin to wonder if they had all seen the same person. In any case there would be no *reliability* to their observations and, if you are interested in getting your friends to agree on someone else's appearance, you would have to develop a much more careful set of definitions on which you could agree concerning how someone was dressed.

As noted above, nosological systems that are not reliable are subject to bias by clinicians making diagnoses. One of the most unreliable categories in our nosology is the whole area of personality disorders—chronic, traitlike sets of inappropriate behaviors and emotional reactions that characterize a person's way of interacting with the world. While great progress has been made in diagnosing these, it is still very difficult to determine the presence or absence of this type of disorder during one interview. As illustration, Morey and Ochoa (1989) asked 291 mental health professionals to submit a description of an individual with a personality disorder that they had recently seen, along with their diagnosis. Morey and Ochoa also collected from these clinicians detailed information on the actual signs and symptoms present in these patients. In this way, they were able to determine whether the actual diagnosis made by the clinicians matched the objective criteria for the diagnosis as determined by the symptoms. In other words, was the clinician's diagnosis accurate based on the presence of symptoms that actually define the diagnosis?

These investigators found substantial bias in making diagnoses. In the case of borderline personality disorder, for example, for some reason clinicians who were either less experienced or female diagnosed this condition more frequently than the criteria indicated. More experienced clinicians or male clinicians diagnosed the condition less frequently than the criteria indicated. Also, if the patients were white, female, or poor, they were diagnosed with borderline personality more often than the criteria indicated. While bias among clinicians is always a potential problem, the more reliable the nosology, the less chance there is for bias to creep in during diagnosis.

Validity

In addition to being reliable, a system of nosology must be *valid*. Earlier in the chapter we described validity as a determination of whether something measures what it is designed to measure. When applied to diagnostic systems, there are several different types of validity. For one, the system should have **construct validity.** This means that the signs and symptoms chosen as the criteria for the presence of the diagnostic category "hang together" consistently or correlate, and that they identify something that differs from other categories. Someone meeting the criteria for depression should be "discriminable" from someone meeting criteria for social phobia. This discriminability might be evident not only in presenting symptoms but also in the course of the disorder and possibly in the most effective treatment. It may also predict the extent to which the disorder would be found in the family of the patient (familial aggregation) (Cloninger, 1989; Blashfield & Livesley, 1991).

In addition, the diagnosis should be useful to the clinician in that it tells the clinician what is likely to happen with the prototypical patient. Thus, it may predict the future course of the disorder and the likely response to one treatment or another. This type of validity is often referred to as *predictive validity,* or sometimes **criterion validity** when the outcome or course is the criterion by which we judge the usefulness of the category.

The last type of validity we will cover here is **content validity.** Content validity simply means that if you create criteria for a diagnosis of social phobia, it should reflect the way most experts in the field think of social phobia as opposed to, say, depression. In other words, you need to get the label right.

Diagnosis Before 1980

The classification of psychopathology, as th ___ ad- age goes, has a long past but a very recent history. Observations of depressed, phobic, or psychotic features stretch back to the earliest recorded observations of human behavior. Many of these observations were so detailed and complete that we could make a diagnosis today of the individuals they described. Nevertheless, only recently have we attempted the very difficult task of creating a formal nosology that would be useful for scientists and clinicians around the world. As late as 1959 there were at least nine different systems of varying usefulness for classifying psychological disorders worldwide, but only three of the nine systems listed "phobic disorder" as a separate category (Marks, 1969). One reason for this confusion is that creating a useful nosology is easier said than done.

Early efforts to classify psychopathology arose out of the biological tradition, particularly the work of Emil Kraepelin as described in Chapter 1 and mentioned above. Kraepelin first identified what we now know as the disorder of schizophrenia. His term for the disorder at the time was *dementia praecox*. Dementia praecox refers to deterioration of the brain that sometimes occurs with advancing age (dementia) and develops earlier than it is supposed to, or "prematurely" (praecox). This label (later changed to *schizophrenia*) reflected Kraepelin's belief that brain pathology was the cause of this particular disorder. Kraepelin's landmark 1913 book (*Textbook of Psychiatry*) described not only dementia praecox but also bipolar disorder, then called *manic depressive psychosis*. Kraepelin also described a variety of organic

Emil Kraepelin (1856–1926), one of the first psychiatrists to attempt to classify psychological disorders from a biological point of view

Robert L. Spitzer was responsible for radically revising the diagnostic and statistical manual to be more reliable and valid. This greatly increased its utility and usage both in North America and around the world.

brain syndromes. Other well-known figures in their time, such as Pinel, characterized psychological disorders, including depression (melancholia), as separate entities; but Kraepelin's theorizing that psychological disorders were basically biological disturbances had the greatest impact on the development of our nosology and led to an early emphasis on classical categorical strategies.

It was not until 1948 that the World Health Organization (WHO) added a section classifying mental disorders to the sixth edition of the *International Classification of Diseases, Injuries, and Causes of Death,* a name now "shortened" to the *International Classification of Diseases and Health Related Problems (ICD).* However, this early system did not have much influence. Nor did the first *Diagnostic and Statistical Manual (DSM-I)* published in 1952 by the American Psychiatric Association. Only in the late 1960s did systems of nosology begin to have some real influence on mental health professionals. In 1968 the American Psychiatric Association published a second edition of its *Diagnostic and Statistical Manual (DSM-II).* In 1969 WHO published the eighth edition of the ICD. Nevertheless, these systems lacked precision, often differing substantially from one another and relying heavily on unproven theories of etiology not widely accepted by all mental health professionals. To make matters worse, the systems had very little reliability. Two mental health practitioners looking at the same patient often came to very different conclusions based on the nosology at that time. Even as late as the 1970s many countries such as France and Russia had their own systems of nosology. In these countries, the same disorders would be labeled and interpreted very differently.

DSM-III

The year 1980 brought a landmark in the history of nosology: the publication of the third edition of the *Diagnostic and Statistical Manual (DSM-III)* (American Psychiatric Association, 1980). Under the leadership of Robert Spitzer, DSM-III departed radically from its predecessors. Three changes stood out. First, the DSM-III attempted to take an atheoretical approach to diagnosis. This approach relied on precise descriptions of the disorders as they presented to clinicians rather than on theories of etiology, whether psychoanalytic or biological. With this focus, the DSM-III became a tool that clinicians utilizing a variety of different points of view could use. For example, rather than being classified under a broad category called "neurosis" with descriptions of intrapsychic conflicts and defense mechanisms as part of the definitions, *phobia* was assigned its own category within a new broader group of disorders termed the *anxiety disorders.*

The second major change appearing in the DSM-III was the specificity and detail with which the criteria for identifying a disorder were listed. This specificity made it possible to study the reliability and validity of the criteria. While not all the categories in DSM-III (and its revision published in 1987, DSM-III-R) achieved the level of reliability and validity we would hope for, this system was a vast improvement over what came before.

Third, DSM-III (and III-R) provided for individuals with possible psychological disorders to be rated on five different dimensions, or *axes.* The disorder itself, such as a schizophrenic or mood disorder, was represented only on the first axis. More enduring (chronic) disorders of personality were listed on Axis II. Axis III comprised physical disorders and conditions. On Axes IV and V the clinician rated, in a dimensional fashion, the amount of psychosocial stress that the person had been experiencing (Axis IV) as well as the person's current level of adaptive functioning (Axis V). With this arrangement, the clinician could gather information describing the individual's functioning in a number of different areas rather than stopping, in a very narrow fashion, with the disorder itself.

Problems with DSM-III and III-R

Despite the conceptual advances present in DSM-III and its revision, DSM-III-R (American Psychiatric Association, 1987), a number of problems remained. First, the reliability of some of the diagnostic categories was often unacceptably low. Researchers discovered that, even under optimal conditions, experienced interviewers watching video tapes could not always agree on whether a disorder was present. This lack of consensus occurred more for some disorders, such as somatoform disorders or personality disorders, than for others (for example, Hyler, Williams, & Spitzer, 1982; Spitzer, Forman, & Nee, 1979). Even among disorders where reliability was better, such as the anxiety disorders, it was difficult for clinicians to agree on the presence or absence of some specific disorders such as generalized anxiety disorder or even simple phobia (DiNardo, O'Brien, Barlow, Waddell, & Blanchard, 1983; DiNardo, Moras, Barlow, Rapee, & Brown, 1993). One might think that identifying a phobia would be a fairly straightforward task, but clinicians often could not agree if it was severe enough to be a disorder. This lack of consensus is just one example of the complexity confronting a clinician or clinical researcher attempting to categorize psychopathology.

In addition, many of the criteria for DSM-III and III-R, although empirically based and potentially measurable, were simply derived by committee consensus (Spitzer, 1991). That is, a group of experts would sit in a room in an attempt to decide what criteria should be part of the diagnosis and what criteria would not. Decisions by consensus sometimes produce strange results. As we will see in Chapter 5, one of the criteria for panic disorder in DSM-III-R was four panics in a 4-week period. Why was it four? Did this refer to some study indicating that having three panics in a 4-week period is qualitatively different from having four or five? Of course not. This was simply the result of a committee offering a "ball park" figure on what sounded reasonable. Of course, members of this committee knew the figure was nothing more than a convenient number. But tens of thousands of other clinicians, utilizing these diagnostic criteria, were operating under the assumption that these were hard and fast criteria and that a person either had panic disorder or didn't, despite cautions published in the DSM itself. Such a mind-set reflects a tendency by some, often inexperienced, clinicians to "reify" a diagnostic category, which means to take it too literally. This is a mistake. Systems of nosology are simply our best working estimate of the optimal ways of classifying psychopathology at any one time and should not be taken as some permanent gold standard.

In spite of these shortcomings, DSM-III and III-R had a substantial impact. Maser, Kaelber, and Weise (1991) surveyed the international usage of various diagnostic systems and found that DSM-III had become very popular for a number of reasons. Primary among these was its precise descriptive format as well as its neutrality with regard to presuming a cause for diagnosis. The multiaxial format, which emphasizes a broad consideration of the whole individual rather than a narrow focus on the disorder alone, has also been very useful to clinicians. For these reasons, more clinicians around the world were using DSM-III-R at the begin-

ning of the decade than the ICD system, which was designed to be more applicable internationally.

DSM-IV

By the late 1980s, clinicians and researchers realized that a consistent, worldwide system of nosology was needed. The 10th edition of the ICD (ICD-10) was to be implemented in 1993 and the United States is required by treaty obligations to use the ICD-10 codes in all matters related to health. To abide by treaty obligations, and to make the ICD-10 and DSM as compatible as possible, work proceeded on both the ICD-10 and the fourth edition of the DSM (DSM-IV) more or less simultaneously. Concerted efforts were made through regular meetings to share research data and other information that would contribute to the goal of setting up an empirically based worldwide system of nosology for psychological disorders.

In creating DSM-IV, a task force of experts in the area was constituted. This DSM-IV task force decided to move as far away as possible from relying on a consensus of experts. Any changes in the diagnostic system of DSM-IV were to be based on sound scientific data. The revisers attempted to review the voluminous literature in all areas pertaining to the diagnostic system. They also made efforts to identify large sets of data that might have been collected for other reasons but that, with reanalysis, would be useful to DSM-IV. Finally, 12 different independent studies or field trials were conducted to examine the reliability and validity of alternative sets of definitions or criteria or, in some cases, to examine the possibility of creating a new diagnosis. A description of one of these field trials,

Allen Francis chaired the task force that produced the fourth edition of the *Diagnostic and Statistical Manual (DSM-IV)*, a project that lasted from its inception in 1988 through its publication in 1994 and involved the work of hundreds of mental health professionals.

examining the feasibility of creating a new diagnosis, mixed anxiety depression, is presented shortly.

Perhaps the most substantial change in DSM-IV is the elimination of any remnants of the distinction between organically based disorders and psychologically based disorders that was present in previous editions. Based on findings reviewed in Chapter 2 we now know that even disorders associated with known brain pathology have substantial psychological and social influences affecting their expression. Similarly, disorders previously described as psychological in origin certainly have biological components and contributions and, most likely, identifiable brain circuits.

The multiaxial system remains the same in DSM-IV but there are some changes in the five axes. Specifically, only personality disorders are now coded on Axis II. Mental retardation, pervasive developmental disorders, learning disorders, motor skills disorders, and communication disorders, previously coded on Axis II, are now all coded on Axis I. Axis IV, on which the clinician rated the amount of psychosocial stress that the person has been experiencing, was not reliable or useful to clinicians and has been modified. The new Axis IV is used for reporting psychosocial and environmental problems that might be impacting the disorder. Axis V is essentially the same as in III-R. In addition, optional axes have been included for rating dimensions of behavior or functioning that some clinicians may find important. The axes on defense mechanisms or coping styles have already been described in Chapter

1. Additional axes exist for social and occupational functioning as well as for relational functioning; on these, one might describe the quality of marital and other interpersonal relations that provide the interpersonal context for the disorder (see Table 3.4). Finally, a number of new disorders have been introduced in DSM-IV, and an additional set of disorders present in DSM-III-R have either been deleted or subsumed into other DSM-IV categories. (A summary table of the new disorders in DSM-IV appears on the front endsheets of this text.)

DSM-IV and Frank

Using the case of Frank, initial observations indicate that the psychological disorder identified on Axis I would be an anxiety disorder, specifically obsessive-compulsive disorder. However, he might also have a long-standing set of personality traits that would lead him systematically to avoid contact with people. If so, he might be a candidate for a diagnosis of schizoid personality disorder on Axis II. Unless he had an identifiable medical condition, nothing would be diagnosed on Axis III. Job and marital difficulties would constitute a problem coded on Axis IV. On this axis are noted psychosocial or environmental problems that are not part of the disorder but might be making it worse. In Frank's case his difficulties with work would be noted by checking occupational problems and specifying threat of job loss. Problems with the primary support group would also be noted with a specification

Table 3.4   Proposed Axes for Further Study

Three additional axes have been placed in the appendix of DSM-IV for further study for possible inclusion in subsequent editions of the DSM. Research on the usefulness of these axes will continue for the next several years.

Defensive Functioning Scale

As described in Chapter 1, defense mechanisms (or coping styles) are conceptualized as psychological processes that protect the individual from emotional conflicts as well as internal or external stressors. These defense mechanisms are automatic or unconscious in that the individual may not be aware of their use. Some examples of adaptive and unadaptive defense mechanisms are provided on Table 1.1. With this axis clinicians should use up to seven specific defense mechanisms, starting with the most prominent—meaning the coping style used most frequently—and then indicate whether the defenses are adaptive or unadaptive.

Social and Occupational Functioning Assessment Scale (SOFAS)

Social and occupational functioning is a very important part of any individual's life and must be considered in the clinical formulation of any psychological disorder. In addition, it is important to note changes in social and occupational functioning as a result of treatment. In other words, changes in features of the disorder itself, such as panic attacks and panic disorder, would be less important if the changes did not result in a general relief from the impairment in social and occupational functioning associated with the onset of the disorder. Social and occupational functioning will be rated by the clinician on a 0–100 scale, where a score of 100 indicates superior functioning in a wide range of activities while a score of 1 would reflect an inability to maintain even minimal personal hygiene.

Global Assessment of Relational Functioning (GARF) Scale

Just as social and occupational functioning is an important consideration, so is functioning in a network of interpersonal relationships including family, friends, and significant others. In this scale, the clinician will rate, also on a 0–100 scale, the degree to which the family or other personal relationships provide the necessary social and emotional support for the individual.

Source: Adapted from DSM-IV, APA, 1994.

of marital difficulties. On Axis V the clinician would rate the highest overall level of Frank's functioning currently on a 0–100 scale, where 100 indicates superior functioning in a wide variety of situations. At present, Frank would receive a score of 55 on this scale, indicating moderate interference with functioning at home and at work.

This multiaxial system helps the clinician consider a range of important information that might have an impact on predictions concerning the likely course of the disorder or, perhaps, choice of treatment. For example, two people such as Frank might present with obsessive-compulsive disorder but look very different on Axes II through V; these differences would greatly affect the clinician's recommendations on treatment strategies for the two cases.

Social and Cultural Considerations in DSM-IV

DSM-III and IV have attempted to facilitate a more complete picture of the individual with their multiaxial approach specifying, among other things, levels of stress in the individual's environment. Furthermore, DSM-IV is experimenting to correct a previous omission by including a plan to integrate important social and cultural influences on diagnosis. Based on this plan, the disorder will be described from the perspective of the patient's personal experience as well as his or her primary social and cultural reference group, such as Hispanic or Chinese. The following outline has been suggested to accomplish these goals (Mezzich et al., 1993).

A. What is the primary cultural reference group of the patient? For recent immigrants to the country as well as other ethnic minorities, how involved are they with their "new" culture versus their old culture? Have they mastered the language of their "new" country (for example, English in the United States) or is language a continuing problem?

B. Does the patient use terms and descriptions from his or her "old" culture to describe the disorder? For example *ataques de nervios* in the Hispanic subculture is a type of anxiety disorder close to panic disorder. Does the patient accept Western models of disease or disorder in which treatment is available in health care systems or does she also have an alternative health care system in her culture (for instance, traditional herbal doctors in Chinese subcultures)?

C. What does it mean to be "disabled"? What kinds of "disabilities" are acceptable in a given culture and which are not? For example, is it acceptable to be physically ill but not anxious or depressed? What are the typical family, social, and religious supports in the culture? Are they available to the patient?

D. Does the clinician understand the first language of the patient as well as the cultural significance of the disorder?

Illustrations showing inclusion of these cultural considerations in making diagnoses and planning treatment are used throughout this book.

DSM-IV: Criticisms

Since the collaboration among groups creating the ICD-10 and DSM-IV was largely successful, it is clear that DSM-IV (and the closely related ICD-10 mental disorder section) will be the most advanced, scientifically based system of nosology the world has yet had. Nevertheless, we still cannot assume that this system is final, or even correct in many cases.

Everyone would agree that the scientific basis of our nosology can be improved greatly. First, the very basic issue of establishing reliable diagnoses would seem to be straightforward, but sometimes it is very difficult. Our science also faces enormous challenges in establishing reasonably valid and useful categories or dimensions of psychopathology. For example, we know very little about the long-term course of psychopathology since studies examining such courses are difficult to carry out.

Second, we know little about etiology or the causes of disorders. And yet, any system of nosology inevitably will have to consider etiology as a primary issue in constructing an adequate diagnostic system. Only recently have we come to the conclusion that the etiology of psychological disorders is multifaceted and complex for all the reasons reviewed in Chapter 2. Sorting out the relative contributions of biological, psychological, and social contributions will occupy all of us for a long time to come. Third, no nosological system can be entirely atheoretical, or without any theoretical bias. Criteria reflecting the biases of biologically as opposed to psychologically oriented investigators inevitably creep into the final criterion sets, which, in turn, influence future research findings (Schacht, 1985). From a scientific point of view, adopting a theoretical stance is not always bad. Theories are very useful tools that help scientists determine and better understand the nature of something such as psychopathology. As we create and test more specific theories on how best to organize and classify psychopathology, our knowledge also becomes more specific and focused. This is how our science progresses (Morey, 1991).

At present we have a "fuzzy" system that blurs at the edges, making diagnostic decisions relatively difficult at times. As a consequence, individuals are often assigned more than one psychological disorder at the same time, sometimes as many as three or four. (Several disorders existing simultaneously is referred to as a state of **comorbidity.**) Multiple diagnoses occur more often than is desirable. How can we conclude anything about the course of a disorder or response to treatment or the likelihood of associated disorders or problems if we are dealing with combinations of three or four disorders instead of one? We are not even sure of the answers to these difficult questions when only one disorder is present. It may be that, in the future, people requiring an assignment of three or four disorders may form an entirely new class in our nosological system. Resolution of these tough problems simply awaits the long slow process of science.

Two other sets of criticisms center on current nosology as represented by DSM-IV and ICD-10. First, there is a very strong emphasis on reliability in our system, sometimes at the expense of validity. This focus is understandable, since reliability has been so difficult to achieve. But it is not so hard to achieve if you are willing to sacrifice validity. If the sole criterion for establishing depression was to hear the patient say at some point during the course of an interview, "I feel depressed," one could theoretically achieve perfect reliability (unless the clinician didn't hear the client, which sometimes happens). But this achievement would be at the expense of validity, since many people with very different psychological disorders will occasionally say they are depressed. Thus, clinicians could agree that the statement was present but it would be of little use (Meehl, 1989; Carson, 1991). Second, as Carson (1991) points out, methods of constructing our nosology have a way of perpetuating disorders handed down to us from past decades, even if these disorders might be fundamentally flawed. Carson (1991) makes a strong argument that it might be better to start fresh every once in a while and create a whole new system of disorders based on emerging scientific knowledge rather than simply fine-tune old disorders, but this is very unlikely to happen.

The criticisms presented here are just a sampling in the very theoretically complex area of categorizing psychopathology. For all these reasons, any nosological system should be considered nothing more than a work in progress.

In addition to the frightful complexity involved in attempting to categorize psychopathology and human behavior in general, the systems are also subject to misuse, some of which can be dangerous and harmful. One of the more obvious abuses is the tendency to *reify* diagnostic categories. Diagnostic categories are really just a convenient method for organizing observations of human behavior and emotions, but if we reify the category, we literally make it a "thing" or imbue it with a meaning that in reality does not exist. Diagnostic categories are just conveniences to help communication among professionals and to assist in treatment planning and in the study of psychopathology. They may change from time to time with the advent of new

knowledge. Therefore, any diagnostic category such as schizophrenia cannot be written in stone. If we find a case on the fuzzy borders between diagnostic categories, we should not expend all our energy attempting to force the behavioral disorder into one category or another. It is a mistaken assumption that everything has to fit neatly somewhere because these categories have their own reality.

The Special Problem of Labeling

A related problem that occurs any time we categorize people is the problem of **labeling.** You may remember Kermit the Frog from Sesame Street sharing with us that "it's not easy being green." The reason it's not easy is that there is something in human nature that will take a label, even one as superficial as skin color, and characterize the totality of that individual with that label ("He's green . . . he's different from me"). We see the same phenomenon among psychological disorders. Furthermore, if the disorder is associated with some impairment in cognitive or behavioral functioning, the label picks up negative connotations. As these negative connotations become known, the label itself becomes pejorative. There have been many attempts over the years to categorize mental retardation. Most of the categories were based on the severity of the impairment or highest level of developmental ability that the individual could reach. But we have had to change the "labels" for these categories of cognitive impairment periodically as the stigma associated with them builds up. One early categorization described levels of severity as moron, idiot, and imbecile. When these terms were introduced they were rather neutral, simply describing the severity of a person's cognitive and developmental impairment. But as they began to be used in common language, they picked up negative connotations and were used as insults. As these terms gradually became pejorative, it was necessary to eliminate them from the categorical lexicon and come up with a new set of classifying labels that were less pejorative. One of the more recent developments is to categorize mental retardation functionally in terms of the levels of support needed by these individuals. In other words, a person's degree of mental retardation is determined by how much assistance he requires (i.e., "intermittent," "limited," "extensive," or "pervasive") rather than by his IQ score (Luckasson et al., 1992).

Once labeled, individuals with a disorder may tend to identify with the negative connotations associated with the label. This association will affect their self-esteem and self-concept. Attempts to document the detrimental effects of labeling have produced mixed results (Segal, 1978); but if you think of your own reactions to the mentally ill, you probably will agree that the tendency to generalize inappropriately from the label does happen. To counteract this tendency, we

Franklin Delano Roosevelt (1882–1945) overcame the label of a "cripple" (he was paralyzed from the waist down) to become President of the United States.

have to remember that terms in psychopathology do not describe people but rather patterns of behavior that may or may not occur in certain circumstances. Thus, whether the disorder is medical or psychological, we must resist the temptation to identify the person with the disorder (John is a diabetic versus John is a person who has diabetes).

Creating a Diagnosis

During the extensive deliberations involving thousands of people that led to the publication of DSM-IV, a number of potentially new diagnostic categories were considered for inclusion in this nosological system. Since one of this book's authors was involved in this process as a member of the task force, two brief examples might help illustrate how diagnostic categories come into being.

Mixed Anxiety-Depression

For years, reports have come from family physicians, clinics, and hospitals about large numbers of individuals complaining of minor aches and pains that prove to have no physical basis. These settings (family physicians' offices, clinics, and so on) are called *primary care settings* because they are usually the first places a person will go with a problem before being referred to a mental health specialist. People coming to

these primary care clinics also complain of feeling uptight and tense, down in the dumps, and anxious. Physicians and other health care professionals examining these individuals report that they present with classic symptoms of both anxiety and depression but that the symptoms are not frequent enough or severe enough to meet criteria for an existing anxiety or mood disorder.

The DSM-IV task force became concerned about issues like this for several reasons. First, since there are many individuals presenting with some minor symptoms of a given disorder, it is important to set "thresholds" high enough that only people who clearly have the problem and are suffering some impairment will qualify for the category. "Thresholds" refer to the minimum number of criteria required to meet the definition of a disorder. The primary reason for this concern with thresholds is that there are substantial legal and policy implications contingent on receiving a diagnosis. That is, if one presents with a psychological disorder that clearly qualifies for a diagnosis, one becomes part of the loosely organized medico-legal system and is eligible to ask (or sue) the government or private insurance companies for reimbursement or perhaps disability payments. Ultimately this money comes from the people already burdened by skyrocketing health care costs. Clearly, if too many people are included in the diagnostic system, even those with only minor symptoms who are not particularly impaired and just "feel down" from time to time or who don't like their job and want disability (an all-too-common occurrence in mental health clinics) the health care system would be severely strained and have fewer resources to treat more seriously impaired cases. On the other hand, if people are experiencing considerable suffering and impairment in functioning, then there is an important need that these people be covered in any health care system.

For these reasons, minor complaints of dysphoric mood, characterized by vague complaints of anxiety and depression, were not considered sufficiently severe to constitute a formal diagnosis. But in 1989, Klerman, reporting on a large study by Wells et al. (1989), found that patients presenting with these symptoms *were* impaired in a number of areas, even when compared with normal controls, as well as patients with chronic medical conditions, based on data from questionnaires and structured interviews. Substantial impairment was present in areas of physical and social functioning. This impairment not only was causing patients to miss work but was also interfering with their functioning in the home; it was *worse* than the impairment of many patients with chronic medical conditions. The evidence also suggested that these individuals were already imposing an *enormous* burden on the health care system by appearing in large numbers at community clinics and the offices of family doctors. Barrett, Barrett, Oxman, and Gerber (1988), assessing patients from a rural primary care practice, found that as many as 14.4% of patients appearing in this practice presented with principal complaints of anxiety and depression. Other studies also supported this finding (Katon & Roy-Byrne, 1991). Finally, evidence suggested that these people were at greatly increased risk of developing more severe mood or anxiety disorders.

Therefore, we concluded that it might be very valuable to identify these people and find out more about the course of their problems as well as factors that might contribute to the etiology or maintenance of the problem. The authors of the ICD-10, recognizing that this phenomenon was prevalent in other parts of the world, had created a category of mixed-anxiety depression, but they had not determined the appropriate definition of the category or created any *criteria* that would allow further examination of this potential disorder. Therefore a study was undertaken to explore the possibility of creating a new diagnostic category (Zinbarg et al., in press).

This study had three specific goals. First, if these individuals were evaluated carefully by mental health professionals using semistructured interviews (the Anxiety Disorders Interview Schedule, see Table 3.1) would the interviewers find patients like this? Or would these individuals, on careful examination, meet the criteria for already existing disorders that had been overlooked by health professionals not well trained in identifying psychological disorders? Second, if these individuals did exist, were they really more prevalent in medical primary care settings than in outpatient mental health settings? Third, if these individuals did exist, what set of criteria (for example, types and number of symptoms) would best identify them?

The study to answer these questions was conducted simultaneously in seven different sites around the world. Results indicated that people presenting with a number of anxious and depressed symptoms, who *did not meet* criteria for an existing anxiety or mood disorder (because they did not have the right mix and/or severity of anxious or depressed symptoms), were common in primary care settings. Furthermore, they were substantially impaired in their occupational and social functioning and were experiencing a great deal of distress. Additional analysis revealed that such people could be discriminated from people with existing anxiety or mood disorders based on their symptoms. Specifically, they presented with a set of emotional and behavioral symptoms that fall into a general category of *negative affect*. Symptoms in this category can be discriminated from pure anxiety symptoms or pure depressive symptoms; they include behaviors such as difficulty sleeping and difficulty concentrating. These behaviors are often part of either an anxiety or mood disorder but are not specific to either. The concept of negative affect and the symptoms it comprises are described more fully in Chapter 7. In any case, because these people appeared both anxious and depressed, the potential new category possessed content validity.

This study also established some of the criteria important in determining *construct validity* for the new category of mixed anxiety-depression. However, since the category is so new, we do not have information on additional criteria important in establishing construct validity, such as course, response to treatment, and the extent to which the disorder aggregates in families. Also, we do not yet know the reliability of the diagnosis or anything about predictive validity. Since we have just identified this category, it is too early to have collected that type of information. Therefore, the decision of the DSM-IV task force was to place this new category in the Appendix of DSM-IV, a place reserved for new diagnoses under study. It is likely to become a full diagnostic category in future editions, but more research needs to be done first.

Premenstrual Dysphoric Disorder

We selected premenstrual dysphoric disorder for illustration because it presents a very different issue that must be considered in the creation of any diagnostic category: the issue of bias and stigmatization. Considerations of this extremely controversial category actually began well before the publication of DSM-III-R in 1987. At that time (and long before, actually) clinicians had identified a small group of women who seemed to present with severe and sometimes incapacitating emotional reactions associated with the late luteal phase of their menstrual period (Rivera-Tovar, Pilkonis, & Frank, 1992). Subsequently, proposals were made to consider inclusion of this category in the DSM-III-R. In view of the suffering and impairment associated with this emotional condition, the proponents argued, these women deserved the attention, care, and financial support that inclusion in a diagnostic category would provide. In addition, as with mixed-anxiety depression, the creation of this category would promote a substantial increase in research into the nature and treatment of this problem.

Nevertheless, arguments against the creation of the category were marshaled along several fronts. First, from the scientific point of view, opponents noted that there was relatively little information in either the clinical or research literature on this topic. What information existed was insufficient to warrant the creation of a new diagnostic category. More important, substantial objections were raised over the possibility that what could be a "normal" endocrinological stage experienced by all or most women would be stigmatized as a psychiatric disorder. Furthermore, this disorder, obviously, would exist only in women (Gallant & Hamilton, 1988). The seeming historical similarities with the once widely accepted category of "hysteria" described in Chapter 1 were also noted. (Remember that this "disorder," characterized by a variety of incapacitating physical complaints, without a medical basis, was thought to be caused by the wandering of a woman's uterus.) Others raised questions about whether the disorder, if it existed, would best be conceptualized as an endocrinological or gynecological rather than a mental disorder. Since the disorder occurs only in women, why not include a comparable male disorder associated with, for example, aggressiveness related to excessive male hormones?

The DSM-III-R task force decided to place this disorder in the Appendix of DSM-III-R in the hope of promoting further study on it. The committee also focused on differentiating this syndrome from the more common symptoms of premenstrual syndrome (PMS) with its less severe and specific premenstrual symptomatology. One way of accomplishing this differentiation was to come up with a different name. The result was the term *late luteal phase dysphoric disorder* (LLPDD).

After the publication of DSM-III-R, LLPDD attracted a great deal of research attention. By 1991 some observers estimated that one research article per month on LLPDD was appearing (Gold et al., in press). A variety of scientific findings began to accrue to support the inclusion of this disorder in DSM-IV. For example, the rather vague, diffuse, and less severe symptoms of premenstrual syndrome (PMS) occur in 20% to 40% of women (Severino & Moline, 1989). However, only a very small proportion of them suffer from the more severe and incapacitating symptoms associated with LLPDD. Rivera-Tovar and Frank (1990) found the prevalence to be approximately 4.6%. In addition, a substantial number of women with no other psychological disorder meet the criteria for LLPDD. Among other findings supporting the inclusion of this disorder in DSM-IV are abnormalities in several biological systems that are associated with clinically significant premenstrual dysphoria (Gold et al., in press) and the revelation that several different types of treatment show some promise of being effective against LLPDD (for example, Stone, Pearlstein, & Brown, 1991). Hurt and colleagues, in a reanalysis of data from 670 women, recommended a set of criteria for this disorder that were not very different from those proposed in DSM-III-R (Hurt et al., 1992).

Several additional research findings indicated that the name *late luteal phase dysphoric disorder* was not entirely accurate. For example, recent research indicates that the symptoms may not be exclusively related to the endocrine state of the late luteal phase. Therefore, the name has been changed to *premenstrual dysphoric disorder*.

Nevertheless, arguments against including this disorder in the diagnostic system remain. Most of them revolve around stigmatization, as recognition of this disorder might confirm the cultural belief that menstruation and resulting disability may make women less fit for positions of responsibility. There have been several cases where accusations of the less severe condition of PMS have been used against a mother in child custody cases in an attempt to win custody for the father (Dalton, 1979). Also, elevating these symptoms to the category of a disorder might sustain and strengthen religious and cultural taboos associated with the menstrual cycle. These taboos range from prohibition of sexual intercourse to actual banishment from regular living quarters. In one religion, Orthodox Judaism, women are required to take a ritual communal bath called the mikvah after each period to cleanse themselves of menstrual impurities. Only then can they resume physical and sexual contact with their husbands (Reik, 1964).

Those arguing against the disorder also point out that some of the symptoms making up the disorder are associated with anger. But they suggest that anger would not be inappropriate in a male. Only in a female does society presume that anger signifies something is wrong.

What would you do? Would you include this condition as a disorder in order to ensure that women suffering from the problem receive the attention and treatment that they seem to need? Or would you be more concerned with the potential for misuse of the diagnosis, particularly the social stigmatization? It is interesting that many women with this disorder are themselves quite comfortable with the label. Some women presenting with other psychological disorders, such as depression, who think they have PMS refuse to accept the suggestion that they have a "psychiatric disorder," insisting that it is really premenstrual syndrome (Rapkin, Chang, & Reading, 1989). Early in 1994 the DSM-IV task force decided not to elevate this disorder to full diagnostic status but to retain it in the Appendix as a disorder needing further study. Among other problems, the committee wanted to see more epidemiological data using the new criteria and to examine more carefully the relation of this problem to existing mood disorders.

Conclusions

The process of creating diagnoses and changing the criteria for existing diagnoses will continue as our science advances. New findings on brain circuits, cognitive processes, or cultural factors that affect our behavior as well as their interaction could "date" diagnostic criteria relatively quickly. Nevertheless, the enormous international effort that went into the construction of DSM-IV and ICD-10 is not likely to be repeated soon. At present, the best estimates are that attempts will not be made to update the system for another 10 to 15 years. With this in mind we can turn our attention to the current state of our knowledge about the variety of major psychological disorders. Beginning with Chapter 5 we will attempt to predict where the next major scientific breakthroughs affecting diagnostic criteria and definitions of disorders will take place. But first, we will review the all-important area of research methods and strategies used in the field of psychopathology to establish new knowledge.

Summary

- In this chapter we have reviewed methods for diagnosing specific psychological disorders in individuals who are distressed, and strategies for assessing and measuring psychological, biological, and social factors that may make up the disorder.

- All methods for diagnosing and assessing psychological disorders must possess two characteristics. First, they must be reliable, meaning that two or more mental health professionals will get the same answers when administering a diagnostic interview or a psychological test (interrater reliability) or that the interview or psychological test will be stable over time (test-retest reliability). Second, the diagnostic interview or test must be valid, meaning that the test or interview assesses what it is designed to assess.

- To assess various aspects of psychological disorders we may interview the patient in a systematic way to obtain reports from the patient of the problems he or she is suffering. More formal and systematic observations of behavior are called behavioral assessment.

- A variety of psychological tests exist that are designed to assist in assessing psychological disorders.

- In addition, we may assess more biological aspects of psychological disorders through neuropsychological tests that are instruments designed to identify possible areas of brain dysfunction. If we wish to examine brain structure and function more directly, pictures of the brain or brain imaging procedures can be used. Finally, psychophysiological assessment refers to measurable changes in the nervous system reflecting emotional or psychological events that might be relevant to a psychological disorder.

- Clinical assessment and diagnosis are central to the study of psychopathology and constitute a necessary first step in planning appropriate treatment for an individual with a psychological disorder.

- Before 1980, systems for classifying psychological disorders—called *nosologies*—were relatively unsystematic. Beginning with the publication of the third edition of the *Diagnostic and Statistical Manual* in 1980, descriptions of disorders became more detailed and systematic. The most widely used system of classifying psychological disorders in North America at the current time is the fourth edition of the DSM (DSM-IV). While this system is the best to date in terms of scientific underpinnings, it is far from perfect and research continues on the most useful way to classify psychological disorders.

Key Terms

behavioral assessment (85)

classical categorical approach (104)

classification (103)

clinical assessment (77)

comorbidity (111)

computerized axial tomography
(CAT)/CAT scans (99)

construct validity (107)

content validity (107)

criterion (predictive) validity (107)

diagnosis (77)

Diagnostic and Statistical Manual,
fourth edition (DSM-IV) (104)

dimensional approach (105)

electroencephalogram (101)

false positives/false negatives (98)

idiographic strategy (103)

intelligence quotient (97)

labeling (112)

magnetic resonance imaging
(MRI) (99)

mental status exam (81)

neuroimaging (99)

neuropsychological testing (98)

nomenclature (103)

nomothetic strategy (103)

nosology (103)

personality inventories (93)

positron emission tomography
(PET)/PET scan (100)

projective tests (91)

prototypical approach (105)

psychophysiological assessment
(101)

reactivity (91)

reliability (80)

self-monitoring (90)

single photon emission computed
tomography (SPECT) (100)

standardization (80)

taxonomy (104)

validity (80)

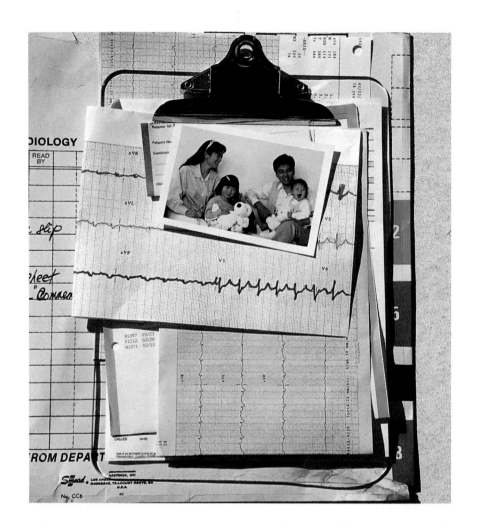

To a person uninstructed in natural history, his country or seaside stroll
is a walk through a gallery filled with wonderful works of art,
nine-tenths of which have their faces turned to the wall.

Thomas Henry Huxley

On the Educational Value
of the Natural History Sciences (1854)

4

Studying Abnormal Behavior: Research Methods

Behavioral scientists explore human behavior in the same way scientists study the path of a comet or the nature of the AIDS virus: They use the scientific method. As we've already seen, abnormal behavior, with its interaction of biological and psychological dimensions, is a challenge to study. Rarely are there any simple answers to questions such as "Why do some people have hallucinations?" or "How do you treat someone who is suicidal?"

In addition to the obviously complex nature of human behavior, another factor that makes an objective study of abnormal behavior difficult is the inaccessibility of many important aspects of this phenomenon. We can't "get inside the minds" of people who display abnormal behavior; instead, we must devise ways to do so indirectly. Fortunately, some very creative individuals have taken on this challenge and have developed many ingenious methods for studying human behavior in a scientific way.

In this chapter we look at some of the ways behavioral scientists study abnormal behavior. A multitude of methods have been developed to discover *what* behaviors constitute problems, *why* people engage in these behavioral disorders, and *how* to treat these problems. Some of you will go on and ultimately contribute to this important area of study by applying the methods described in this chapter. There are many

critical questions regarding abnormal behavior that have yet to be answered, and we hope that some of our readers will be inspired to take them on. However, even for those of you who may not become behavioral scientists, understanding research methods is extremely important. At some time in your lives, you or somebody you know may need the services of a psychologist, psychiatrist, or some other mental health provider. You may have questions such as these:

- Should childhood aggression be a concern, or is it just a phase that my child will grow out of?
- The "Today" show just reported that increased exposure to sunlight will alleviate depression. Should I forego seeing a therapist and buy a ticket to Hawaii?
- I read a story about the horrors of shock therapy. Should I advise my next-door neighbor not to let her daughter have this treatment?
- My brother has been in therapy for three years but doesn't seem to be any better. Should I tell him to look elsewhere for help?
- My mother is still in her fifties but seems to be forgetting things. Friends tell me this is natural as you grow older. Should I be concerned?

To answer such questions you need to be a good *consumer* of research. You should be able to understand the correct ways to obtain information—that is, research methodology—to ensure that you are dealing with fact and not fiction. Knowing the difference between a "fad" and what is an established approach to a problem can be the difference between months of suffering and a quick resolution to a disturbing problem.

Important Concepts in Research

As we have said from the start, in this book we will examine several aspects of abnormal behavior. First, "*What* are the problems that cause distress and impair functioning?" Second, "*Why* do people behave in unusual ways?" And third, "*How* do we help them behave in more adaptive ways?"

The first question asks about the nature of the problems people report; we will explore research

Research on abnormal behavior requires a great deal of expertise and creativity to "get inside the minds" of people with psychological disorders.

strategies—for example, epidemiological research—that help us better understand these disorders.

The second question considers the causes, or *etiology,* of abnormal behavior. For example, we know that the loss of someone we love can cause depression. We also have evidence that maternal abuse of alcohol during pregnancy can cause cognitive and physical deficits in children, a disorder known as *fetal alcohol syndrome*. Strategies for studying the etiology of the disorders described will be explored.

Finally, we are also concerned about helping people who have these disorders; thus we will describe how researchers evaluate treatments. Before we discuss specific strategies, however, we must introduce several general considerations for evaluating research.

Basic Components of a Research Study

The basic research process is really very simple. You start with an educated guess about what you want to study and what you expect to find—called a **hypothesis.** Then you decide how you want to go about testing this hypothesis (the **research design**), what aspects of the people you are studying you want to measure (called the **dependent variable**), and what you think will be influencing the behaviors of the people you study (called the **independent variable**). Finally, two forms of validity that are specific to research studies—*internal* and *external validity*—need to be considered. **Internal validity** is the extent to which we can be confident that it is the independent variable that is causing the dependent variable to change. **External validity** is how well the results relate to things outside your study, that is, how well the findings of the study describe similar individuals who were not among the study subjects. Although we will discuss a variety of different research strategies, they all have these basic elements. Table 4.1 shows the essential components of a research study.

Hypotheses

A close friend of one of the authors lost his younger brother in a motorcycle accident. At the funeral there was a tremendous amount of grief and bitterness because of the senseless loss of this fine young man. The family wanted to know why—what was the purpose, what was the reason for this tragedy?

We as human beings look for order and purpose in the world. We want to know why the world works as it does, why people behave the way they do. Kegan (cited in Lefrancois, 1990) describes us as "meaning-making" organisms—constantly striving to

Table 4.1   The Basic Components of a Research Study

Component	Description
Hypothesis	An educated guess or statement to be proven or disproven by data.
Research design	The plan for proving or disproving the hypothesis. Affected by the question addressed, by the hypothesis and by practical consideration.
Dependent variable	Some aspect of the phenomenon that is measured and is expected to be changed or influenced in the study.
Independent variable	In an experimental design, that aspect that is manipulated by the experimenter. In all research, the variables that are thought to be influencing behavior.
Internal validity	The extent to which the results of the study can be attributed to the independent variable.
External validity	The extent to which the results of the study can be generalized or applied outside the immediate study.

make sense of what is going on around us. It is interesting to note that our brains work the same way with such processes as vision. We often see only parts of things—the side of a person's head, the way she walks down a hall. Yet the brain is able to take these parts and put them together to make a whole (your best friend).

The search for meaning and order is also carried on in the field of abnormal behavior. Almost by definition, abnormal behavior seems to defy the regularity and predictability that we seem to want from the world. It is this departure from the norm that makes the study of abnormal behavior so intriguing to many. In an attempt to make sense of these phenomena, behavioral scientists construct *hypotheses* about abnormal behavior—statements to be proven or disproven by data—and then test them. Hypotheses are nothing more than educated guesses about the world. You believe that watching violent television programs will cause children to be more aggressive. You think that bulimia is influenced by media depictions of "ideal" female body types. You suspect that when someone is abused as a child he is likely to become a spouse and child abuser later on. All these concerns are potentially testable hypotheses about different phenomena people experience.

Once a scientist has an idea about what should be studied, the next step is to put it in words that are unambiguous and in a form that is testable. A recent study of depression among women can serve as an example. Kenneth Kendler and his associates (Kendler, Kessler, Neale, Heath, & Eaves, 1993) studied 680 female-female twins (both identical and fraternal twins) across several years to examine incidents of depression. These researchers posed the following hypothesis: "The probability that a woman will experience an episode of major depression is influenced by a number of 'risk factors,' such as premature loss of a parent, stressful life events, previous episodes of depression,

and genetic influences." The hypothesis is stated in a way that suggests the researchers already know the answer to their research question. Obviously, they don't know what they will find until the study is completed, but phrasing the hypothesis in this way allows it to be testable. If, for example, major depression isn't predicted by any of these risk factors, they can all be proven wrong; if only one of the risk factors is involved, then the other factors could be proven wrong. This concept of **testability** (the ability to confirm or disconfirm the hypothesis) is important for science because it allows us to say, in this case, either (a) depression is predicted by these multiple influences so let's study them more, or (b) depression is not predicted by these multiple influences, so let's look elsewhere.

When they are developing an experimental hypothesis, researchers also specify dependent and independent variables. A *dependent variable* is what is expected to change or be influenced by the study. In the field of abnormal psychology, we typically measure some aspect of the disorder such as overt behaviors, indirect measures of thoughts and feelings, or biological measures. In Kendler's study the main dependent variable was episodes of major depression as measured by structured interviews of the kind we described in Chapter 3. The researchers measured incidents of major depression across several years to try to predict what would cause these episodes. The factors that were thought to cause depression—including stressful life events, previous episodes of depression, and genetics—are the *independent variables* in this study. Independent variables are those factors thought to be influencing or affecting the dependent variables. Again, in this case, independent variables such as stressful life events and genetics were thought to influence the dependent variable—episodes of depression. In treatment studies, the treatment itself is what is expected to influence behavior and is therefore the independent variable.

Internal and External Validity

Suppose Kendler in his study of depression among twins found that, unknown to him, many of the women had been taking antidepressant drugs during the entire time he was studying them. Being on these drugs probably would have changed the number of episodes of depression they experienced, in a way not related to factors such as stressful life events or genetics—thereby completely changing the meaning of his results. This situation is called a **confound** and relates to internal validity. A confound is any factor occurring in your study that makes the results uninterpretable. In the Kendler study, we wouldn't know how the antidepressant drug taking affected the results or how these results would relate to women not taking such drugs. The degree to which confounds are present in a study is a measure of *internal validity*. Internal validity is the extent to which the results can be explained by the independent variable. The unexpected drug taking in Kendler's study would have been a confound and would have made the study internally *in*valid because it would have reduced the researcher's ability to explain the results as being based on the independent variables of stressful life events, previous depressive episodes, or genetics.

Scientists use many strategies to ensure internal validity in their studies, three of which we discuss here—control groups, randomization, and analog models. A **control group** is a group of people who are similar to the experimental group in every way with the exception that the experimental group is exposed to the independent variable change while the control group is not. Because researchers can't prevent people from being exposed to many things around them that could affect the outcomes of the study, they try to compare people who receive the treatment with people who go through similar experiences except for the treatment (control group). Control groups help rule out alternative explanations for results—strengthening internal validity.

A second strategy to help ensure internal validity in research is the use of **randomization,** the process of assigning people to different research groups in such a way that each person has an equal chance of being placed in any group. Placing people in groups at random (either by flipping a coin or using a random number table) helps improve internal validity by eliminating any systematic bias in the groups. We will see later that people sometimes "put themselves in groups" and that this self-selection can affect the study results. Perhaps a researcher is treating people with depression and offers them the option of either being in the treatment group, which will mean coming into the clinic two times per week for two months, or being in a wait-list control group, which means they will wait until some later time to be treated. The researcher is

likely to find that those who are most severely depressed will not be motivated to come to treatment sessions so frequently and will choose the wait-list group. If the treated group looks less depressed after several months, it could be because of the treatment or because the groups started out differently. Placing people in groups at random helps avoid these potential problems.

A third way behavioral scientists improve internal validity is to use **analog models,** which involve replicating aspects of the phenomenon under study in the controlled conditions of the laboratory. In other words, an analog model is designed to represent aspects of abnormal behavior that are similar or comparable (analogous) to the phenomenon you want to study. If a researcher were interested in the binge eating seen in people with bulimia and in analyzing their thoughts and feelings as they eat a great deal of food in a short amount of time, she could ask volunteers to agree to binge eat in the laboratory. She could question them before they ate, while they were eating, and after they finished, to learn whether eating in this way made them feel more or less anxious, guilty, and so on. If she were not looking for people with bulimia, she could get volunteers of any age, gender, race, or background. Using such a group would allow her to rule out other possible influences on the subjects' attitudes about eating that she might not be able to dismiss if she had to select only people with bulimia. In this way, such "artificial" studies can help improve internal validity.

In a research study, internal and external validity often seem to be opposing forces. On the one hand, we want to be able to control as many different things as possible so as to conclude that the independent variable—the aspect of the study manipulated—was responsible for the changes in the dependent variables—the aspects of the study expected to change. On the other hand, we want the results of the study to apply to people other than the subjects of the study and to settings other than those in the study (called **generalizability** or the extent to which the results apply to everyone with a particular disorder). If we control the total environment of the people who participate in the study so that only the independent variable changes, then the result is a situation that does not resemble the "real world." In their study on depression, Kendler and his associates limited the participants to women. One reason was to control for differences that might exist between men and women and their reasons for being depressed. While this limitation helps to eliminate any question about gender differences—thereby increasing internal validity—it also prevents the researchers from drawing conclusions about males, thereby decreasing external validity. As we just illustrated, internal and external validity are often inversely related, with greater internal validity resulting in poorer external validity. Researchers constantly try to balance these two concerns, and as we see later in this chapter, the best solution for achieving both may be to conduct several related studies.

Necessary, Sufficient, and Contributory Conditions

To be able to interpret the outcomes of research on abnormal behavior, we must first know something of the factors that can contribute to a disorder. Basic to this knowledge is an understanding of the concepts of necessary, sufficient, and contributory conditions. A **necessary condition** is something that must be present for something to occur. Water is a necessary condition for human life. Without water, people die. There are also necessary conditions in psychology. A necessary condition for schizophrenia may be a genetic predisposition. It is likely that some specific genetic pattern is, in part, responsible for the emergence of this disorder (Gottesman, 1991).

In contrast, a **sufficient condition** is one that, by itself, is responsible for some phenomenon. Although water is necessary for human life, it is not sufficient to sustain life. You will die within weeks if you ingest only water. Similarly, although being genetically predisposed to schizophrenia may be requisite for a person to display this disorder, a genetic predisposition alone does not appear to be sufficient to create it in someone. To illustrate the concept of sufficiency with a different disorder, Lyn Abramson, Gerry Metalsky, and Lauren Alloy (1989) have proposed that "hopelessness," an expectation of negative outcomes in important situations, is sufficient to cause the symptoms of one type of depression. In other words, a feeling of hopelessness alone is sometimes enough to produce this disorder. However, it is rare to find a sufficient condition for most psychological disorders because of the multiple influences responsible for abnormal behavior.

Finally, certain factors that are not necessary or sufficient to cause a disorder can contribute to it in some cases. The loss of a loved one will not necessarily cause clinical depression in someone, but it certainly can contribute to this disorder. The bereavement would therefore be considered a **contributory condition** to depression. Keep these distinctions in mind as we review the factors involved in the presence of psychological disorders.

Statistical Versus Clinical Significance

The move from a purely subjective study of human behavior to a more objective one has led to extraordinary advances in our understanding of abnormal behavior. Yet one aspect of this evolution has received considerable criticism: the use of statistical significance to determine the presence of effects in research.

The use of statistics in psychology is part of the field's history and evolution from a prescientific to a scientific discipline. *Statistics* is the branch of mathematics that deals with gathering, analyzing, and interpreting data from research. **Statistical significance** in psychological research typically means that the probability of obtaining the observed effect by chance is small. As an example, consider a group of older adults who have mental retardation and who also have self-injurious behavior—characterized by their hitting, slapping, or scratching themselves until they cause physical damage. Suppose they participate in a treatment program for their self-injurious behavior and are observed to hurt themselves less often than a similar group of adults who do not get the treatment. If a statistical test of these results indicates that this difference in behavior is expected to occur less than five times in every 100 experiments just by chance, then we can say that the difference is statistically significant. But is this really an important difference?

The previous example can illustrate the difficulty, which comes down to a difference between *statistical* and **clinical significance.** Suppose we were researching a new medical treatment for the self-injurious behaviors of the older adults just described. In our research study, we examined two groups—one group that received a new medication designed to reduce self-injury, and a second group that received a placebo medication. To learn whether the new drug affected the self-injury, we used a rating scale that allows clinicians to write down how frequently each person hits himself or herself. At the beginning of the study, all the study subjects were hitting themselves about 10 times a day on average. At the end of the study, we added all the scores from the rating scales and found that the group on medication received lower scores on the scale than the untreated group and that the results were statistically significant. Is this new treatment something we should recommend for all people who hit themselves?

Closer examination of the results leads to a concern about *the size of the effect.* Suppose when you look at the people who were rated as being improved you find that they still hit themselves about 6 times a day on average. Even though the frequency of hitting is lower, they are still hurting themselves. Some of these individuals will hit themselves just a few times and still produce serious cuts, bruises, and contusions. This result suggests that, even though your results were *statistically significant,* they may not have been *clinically significant.* In other words, your results may not have been important to the people who experience this self-hurting behavior. The distinction would be particu-

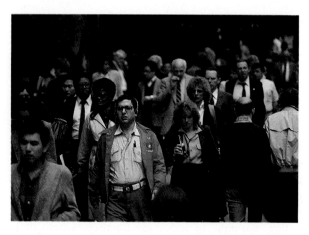

Studying people as part of a group sometimes masks important individual differences.

larly important if you had another treatment that might not reduce self-hits as much but would lead the person to hit himself or herself less intensely, causing less harm.

Fortunately, more attention is now being paid to the clinical significance of research results. This concern has led researchers to develop statistical methods that in some way address not just the fact that groups are different, but *how large these differences are* (called *effect size*) (for example, Sedlmeier & Gigerenzer, 1989). Although calculating the actual statistical measures involves fairly sophisticated procedures that are beyond the scope of this text, they basically take into account how much each treated and untreated person in a research study improves or worsens (Jacobson & Truax, 1991; Speer, 1992). In other words, instead of just looking at the results of the group as a whole, the procedures allow consideration of individual differences as well. Some researchers have also looked to more subjective judgments to determine whether truly important change has occurred as a result of treatments. The behavioral scientist Montrose Wolf (1978) has advocated the assessment of what he calls *social validity*. This measure involves obtaining input from the person being treated as well as significant others (for example, parents, spouse, friends) about the importance of the changes that have occurred. In the example above, we might ask employers and family members if they thought the medication led to truly important reductions in self-injurious behavior. If the effect of the treatment is large enough to impress those who are directly affected, then we can begin to say the treatment effect is clinically significant. Efforts to develop statistical measures of effect size and to assess subjective judgments of change will give us better information with which to judge the true results of our treatments.

The "Average" Client

Too often we look at the results from studies such as the one involving self-injurious behavior or the Kendler study on depression and make generalizations about the group, ignoring the individual differences. However, we know from our own lives that people are very different. Similarly, the individual experiences of psychological disorders can also be very different. Yet the practice of comparing group means can mask these differences. Kiesler (1966) has labeled the tendency to see all participants in these types of studies as being from one homogeneous group as the *patient uniformity myth*. Taking the results of our studies and comparing groups according to their mean scores ("Group A improved by 50% over Group B") will hide important differences in the individual reactions to our interventions.

This myth leads researchers to make broad and sometimes inaccurate generalizations about disorders and their treatments. It would not be surprising for a researcher studying the treatment of self-injurious behavior, as in the study we just described, to conclude that the drug used would be a good treatment for self-injury. Yet suppose we looked at the results of this study and found that, although some participants improved with treatment, others actually got worse. These differences would be averaged out in the analysis of the group, but for the person who was head banging more often with this new drug, it would make little difference that "on the average" people improved. Because people who display self-injurious behavior can differ in a number of ways, such as in age, cognitive abilities, gender, and history of treatment, a simple group comparison may be misleading. Practitioners who deal with people having all types of disorders understand the heterogeneity of their clients and therefore do not know whether treatments that are statistically significant will be effective for any individual client. As we discuss each disorder, we will return to this issue and attempts by researchers to address it.

Studying Individual Cases

Consider the following scenario: A psychologist thinks she has discovered a new psychological disorder. She has observed in her office several individuals who seem to show very similar characteristics. All of them are male adults who complain of a sleep disorder—specifically, falling asleep at work. Each of these men has obvious cognitive impairments (which could be determined from the initial interviews) and all appear to have very similar physical characteristics. In particular, all the men have significant hair loss and have a pear-shaped physique. Finally, their personality styles are also similar, being extremely "egocentric," or self-centered. Based on these preliminary observations, the psychologist has come up with a tentative name, the *Homer Simpson Disorder*. After careful consideration, she has decided to find out more about this condition and possible treatments. But how does the psychologist begin? What is the best way to proceed in investigating a relatively unknown disorder such as this one? One way is to study intensively one or more individuals who display the behavioral and physical patterns, a strategy otherwise known as the **case study method.** The case study method involves the extensive study of a person to provide a wide range of potentially important information about a particular disorder, its causes, and/or its treatment (Kazdin, 1981).

One way to describe the case study method is by noting what it is *not*. Specifically, this method does not use the scientific method. Few efforts are made to ensure internal validity and, typically, many confounding variables are present that can interfere with any conclusions the observer may want to make. Instead, the case study method relies on observations from a clinician to provide hints as to what might be different about a person or group of persons compared to people with other disorders, and compared to people with no psychological disorders. The clinician or researcher will usually include a detailed description of the person, with emphasis placed on collecting as much information as possible. Historically, a great deal of information comes from interviewing the person under study, including data on personal and family background, education, health, and work history as well as observations and insights by the person about the nature and causes of the problems being experienced.

Case studies have an important place in the history of psychology. Sigmund Freud developed psychoanalytic theory and the methods of psychoanalysis based on his observations of dozens of cases. Freud and Breuer's description of Anna O. (see Chapter 1) led to development of the clinical technique referred to as free association. More recently, the work of sex researchers Virginia Johnson and William Masters was based on many case studies and helped shed light on numerous myths regarding sexual behavior (Masters & Johnson, 1966). Joseph Wolpe based his work with systematic desensitization on over 200 cases in his landmark book *Psychotherapy by Reciprocal Inhibition* (1958). As our knowledge of psychological disorders grows, we have relied less and less on the case study method to guide our understanding of these conditions.

One difficulty with relying too heavily on individual cases to guide thinking is that sometimes coincidences can occur that do not relate to the condition under study. As a student, I learned firsthand the power of coincidence. I was in a large lab room working on the university computer system. The room held almost 100 terminals, and I was just learning how to use the keyboard. On the top righthand side was a rather ominous looking red button with nothing written on it. As I worked, the button seemed to call out to be pressed. During a lull in my work, I pressed the button, and at that moment, every terminal in the room went blank. Feeling panicky, I looked around the room to see if anyone knew I was the one who was to blame for this catastrophe. There was a great deal of exasperation and cursing, but it was not directed at me. For weeks thereafter I was convinced that I had knocked out the mainframe computer, even though the shutoff could not have been caused by the red button and was the result of some technical difficulty in the mainframe itself. Only after describing the incident to a good friend did I learn that I could not have caused the shutdown and that the red button had no purpose on my keyboard. The whole affair was instead a rather convincing coincidence.

Unfortunately, more meaningful coincidences in people's lives often lead to mistaken conclusions about what causes certain conditions and what treatment appears to be effective. Without the controls used in more experimental investigations, case studies can be misleading, and caution is required in interpreting observations of the study subjects.

In addition to the possibility that coincidence can influence the outcome in individual cases, there are other concerns with relying on this approach to studying abnormal behavior. Because a case study does not have the controls of an experimental study, the results may be unique to that particular person without our realizing it or may come about because of some special combination of factors that are not obvious. We are constantly exposed to instances of abnormal behavior through the media. The newspapers and television daily draw our attention to unusual behavior. The mass murderer Ted Bundy was executed in Florida for his crimes. Just before his death, he proclaimed that pornography was to blame for his violent and abhorrent behavior. The case of Jeffrey Dahmer, the man who killed and then mutilated and cannibalized his victims, is known throughout the world. Attempts have been made to piece together his childhood to discover the types of experiences that could possibly explain his bizarre behavior. Yet what conclusions should we draw from these accounts? Did Ted Bundy have valuable insight into his own behavior, or was he just attempting to gain attention from the world? Can childhood acquaintances and friends of the Dahmer family shed light on the developmental progression of this disturbed young man's behavior?

Without the types of experimental controls used in scientific investigations of abnormal behavior, we must be careful about concluding anything from such sensational portrayals. Researchers in cognitive psychology point out to us that the public as well as researchers themselves is often, unfortunately, more highly influenced in its opinions by dramatic accounts than by scientific evidence (Nisbett & Ross, 1980). The purpose of highlighting research issues in this book is to caution readers about our tendency to ignore these results. If we are to advance our understanding of the nature, cause, and treatment of abnormal behavior, we must guard against premature and inaccurate conclusions about the people who are affected by these disorders.

Research by Correlation

One of the most fundamental questions posed by scientists is whether two variables "go together." Any relationship between two variables is called a **correlation.** For example, is autism in a person related to damage that person sustained in the cerebellum? Are people with depression more likely to have negative attributions? Is the frequency of hallucinations higher among older people? These questions all center around determining how one variable (for example, number of hallucinations) is related to some other variable (for instance, age). Unlike experimental designs, correlational designs do not involve manipulating or changing anything. Researchers use these designs to study phenomena just as they occur. The result of a correlational study—whether variables occur together—is an important step in the ongoing search for knowledge about abnormal behavior.

One of the clichés of science is that a correlation does not imply causation. Just because two things occur together or are correlated does not mean that one caused the other. For example, the occurrence of marital problems in families is correlated with behavior problems in children (Emery, 1982; Reid & Crisafulli, 1990). If you conduct a correlational study in this area you will find that, in families with marital problems, you also tend to see children with behavior problems; in families with fewer marital problems, you are likely to find children with fewer behavior problems. Probably the most obvious conclusion from this kind of research is that having marital problems will cause children to misbehave. Right? If only it were as simple as that! The nature of the relationship between marital discord and childhood behavior problems can be explained in a number of ways. It may be that problems in a marriage cause disruptive behavior in the children. However, some evidence suggests that the opposite may be true as well: the disruptive behavior of children may cause marital problems (Rutter & Giller,

1984). In addition, recent evidence suggests genetic influences may play a role in both conduct disorders (Rutter et al., 1990) and marital discord (McGue & Lykken, 1992). In other words, the correlation between marital problems and childhood behavior problems may be caused by similar genetic endowments.

The above example points out the difficulties of trying to interpret the results of a correlation study. What we know from these studies is that variable "A" (for example, marital problems) is correlated with variable "B" (for instance, child behavior problems). We do not know from these studies whether A causes B (marital problems cause child problems), whether B causes A (child problems cause marital problems), or whether some third variable "C" causes both (genes influence both marital problems and child problems).

Another example suggests that allergies and depression may be related. Research in this area reveals a surprisingly high correlation between allergic reactions and depressive symptoms (Bell, Jasnoski, Kagan, & King, 1991). But what causes what? Does depression make people more likely to have allergies (A causes B)? Does the presence of allergies cause people to be depressed (B causes A)? Or does some common underlying biological factor serve to make people susceptible to both allergies and depression (C causes A and B)? At least one theory of this relationship points to the last explanation, with a complex neurochemical susceptibility resulting in a predisposition to both allergies and depression (C causes A and B) (Marshall, 1993).

The examples of the association between marital discord and child problems and the association between allergies and depression represent what is known as a **positive correlation.** This type of correlation means that great strength or quantity in one variable (for example, a great deal of marital distress) is associated with great strength or quantity in the other variable (for instance, more child disruptive behavior). At the same time, lower strength or quantity in one variable (such as less marital distress) is associated with lower strength or quantity in the other (for example, less disruptive behavior). For those of you who have trouble conceptualizing statistical concepts, you can think about this mathematical relationship in the same way you would a social relationship. If two people are getting along well, they will tend to go places together. This *positive* relationship means that "Where I go, you will go!" Your correlation (or **correlation coefficient**) would be represented as +1.00, with the plus sign meaning there is a positive relationship, and the 1.00 meaning it is a "perfect" relationship, whereby both people go everywhere together. Obviously, two people who like each other will not go everywhere together. The *strength* of this relationship is represented by the range between 0.00 and 1.00, with 0.00 meaning no relationship exists. The higher the number, the stronger the relationship, no matter whether the number is positive or negative (for example, a correlation of −.80 is "stronger" than a correlation of +.75). You would expect two strangers, for example, to have a relationship of 0.00 because their behavior is not related; they sometimes end up in the same place together, but this occurs rarely and randomly. What about two people who know each other but do not like each other? This *negative* relationship would be represented by a negative sign, with the range of −1.00 to 0.00. In this case, a strong negative relationship would be −1.00 which means "Anywhere you go, I won't be there!"

Using this analogy, you could say that allergies and depression have a relatively strong positive relationship (or positive correlation, represented by a number such as +.50). They tend to go together. On the other hand, there are other variables that are strangers. Schizophrenia and height are not related at all, so they don't go together, and probably would be represented by a number close to 0.00. If A and B have no correlation, then A and B have a "stranger" relationship, and their correlation coefficient would approximate 0.00. Other factors have negative relationships: As one increases, the other decreases. (See Figure 4.1 for an illustration of positive and negative correlations.) One example of this **negative correlation** was pointed out in Chapter 2 when we discussed social supports and illness. With more social supports present, it is *less* likely that a person will become ill. There is a relationship between social supports and illness—a negative one—and it could be represented by a number such as −.40. The next time someone wants to "break up" with you, ask him or her if the goal is to weaken the strength of your positive relationship to something like +.25 (friends), to become complete strangers at 0.00, or to have an intense negative relationship approximating −1.00 (enemies)?

A correlation allows us to see whether a relationship exists between two variables, but it does not allow us to draw conclusions about whether either variable *causes* these effects. This condition is referred to as a problem with **directionality.** In this case, it means that we do not know whether A causes B, B causes A, or a third variable C causes A and B. Therefore, even if we find an extremely strong relation-

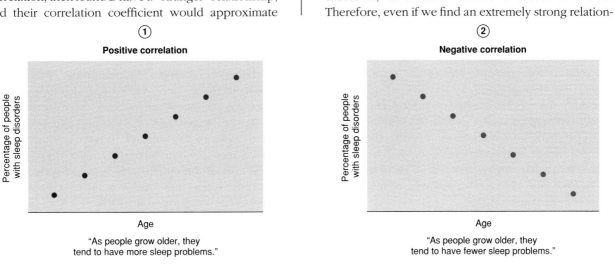

① **Positive correlation**

"As people grow older, they tend to have more sleep problems."

② **Negative correlation**

"As people grow older, they tend to have fewer sleep problems."

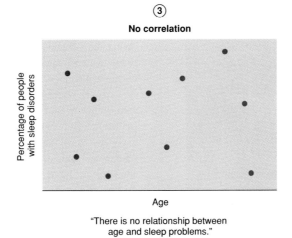

③ **No correlation**

"There is no relationship between age and sleep problems."

Figure 4.1   These three graphs represent hypothetical correlations between age and sleep problems.

ship between two variables (+.90), we still know nothing about the direction of causality.

Epidemiological Research

Scientists often think of themselves as detectives. Finding the "truth" by studying "clues" in a systematic way describes both detective work in the usual sense and scientific activity. One type of correlational research that is very much like the efforts of sleuths is called *epidemiology*. **Epidemiology** is the study of the incidence, distribution, and consequences of a particular problem or set of problems in one or more populations. The expectation of epidemiologists is that by tracking a disorder among many people, they will find clues to important information about why people might have this disorder. One of the strategies used by epidemiologists is to determine the **incidence** of a disorder—an estimate of the number of new cases during a specific period of time. As we will see in Chapter 12, the incidence or number of new cases of eighth graders using marijuana and cocaine is increasing. A second and related strategy involves determining the **prevalence** of a disorder, or the number of people with a disorder at any one time. The prevalence of alcohol dependency among Americans in 1990 was estimated at 10.5 million adults (U.S. Department of Health and Human Services, 1990). Epidemiologists also study the incidence and prevalence of disorders among different groups of people. For instance, data from epidemiological research indicate that the prevalence of alcohol dependency among African-Americans is lower than among whites, and Hispanics have the highest rates among all racial and ethnic groups (McCreery & Walker, 1993).

Although the primary goal of epidemiology is to determine the extent of medical problems, these

tools are also useful in the study of psychological disorders, as shown by this illustration from early in the century. In the early 1900s a number of Americans began displaying symptoms of a strange form of mental disorder. Its symptoms were similar to those of organic psychosis, a type of psychosis often brought on by the use of mind-altering drugs or great quantities of alcohol. Many patients would appear to be catatonic (immobile for long periods of time), or exhibit symptoms similar to those of paranoid schizophrenia. The people with this disorder were likely to be poor and African-American. The prevalence of the disorder among this population led to speculation about racial and class inferiority. However, by using the methods of epidemiological research, Joseph Goldberger found correlations between the incidence of the disorder and diet; he identified the cause of the disorder as a deficiency of the B vitamin niacin found among people with poor diets. The symptoms were successfully eliminated by niacin therapy and improved diets among the poor. A long-term, widespread benefit to many as a result of Goldberger's findings was the introduction of vitamin-enriched bread in the 1940s (Gottesman, 1991).

More recently, researchers have used epidemiological techniques to study the effects of stress on psychological disorders. In the spring of 1980, the Mount St. Helens volcano erupted, destroying much of the mountainside and creating extensive property damage and loss of life. This stressful event served as the focal point for research on its effects. Shore, Tatum, and Vollmer (1986) interviewed families who had lived in the area of the erupting volcano and were directly affected. When these subjects were compared to members of a comparable (control) community that was similar in demographics but had not experienced a similar traumatic event, the researchers found a significantly higher number of psychological disorders in the people who were exposed to high levels of stress caused by living near Mount St. Helens. This is a correlational study because the investigators did not manipulate the independent variable. In other words, they didn't set off the volcano! Despite its correlational nature, the study did show a relationship between amount of stress and psychological problems.

If you have followed the work on the AIDS virus, you have seen how epidemiologists study a problem. By tracking the incidence of this disease among several populations (gay men, intravenous drug users, spouses and children of infected individuals), researchers have been able to obtain important information about how the virus is passed from person to person. They inferred from the types of behaviors engaged in by these groups that the virus was likely spread by the transfer of bodily fluids through unprotected sex or by nonsterile needles. Epidemiological

The 1980 eruption of Mount St. Helens provided researchers with an opportunity to study how this stressful event affected the people living near it.

research, like other types of correlational research, can't tell us conclusively what causes a particular phenomenon. However, knowledge about the prevalence and course of psychological disorders is extremely valuable in adding to our understanding of these difficulties because it points researchers in the right direction to continue their investigation.

Research by Experiment

An **experiment** involves the manipulation of some variable—the *independent variable*—and the observation of its effects. We manipulate the independent variable to try to answer the question of casuality raised in the previous section. If we observe a correlation between social supports and psychological disorders, we can't conclude which of these factors influenced the other. We can, however, change the amount of social supports and see whether there is an accompanying change in the prevalence of psychological disorders—in other words, do an experiment.

What will this experiment tell us about the relationship between these two variables? If we increase social supports among people and find no change in the frequency of psychological disorders, it *may* mean that lack of social supports does not cause psychological problems. On the other hand, if we find that psychological disorders decrease in frequency with increased social support, we can be more confident that lack of supports does contribute to these disorders. However, because we are never 100% confident that our experiments are internally valid—there are no other possible explanations—we are cautious about the way we interpret these results. In the following section, we introduce a number of different ways researchers conduct experiments and consider how each one brings us closer to understanding abnormal behavior.

Group Experimental Designs

The correlation research we described involved using groups of people and then seeing how their behavior was related to certain variables (co-relational). With correlational research, the researcher observes these groups to see how different variables are associated. In group experimental designs, researchers are more active. They actually change an independent variable to see how the behavior of the people in the group is affected.

Suppose researchers want to examine insomnia among older adults. They might design an intervention to help reduce insomnia, a condition that occurs among all age groups but is particularly prevalent among older adults (Mellinger, Balter, & Uhlen-

huth, 1985). They treat 20 older adults for their sleep problems and follow them for 10 years to learn whether their sleep patterns improve. The experiment involves introducing (manipulating) an independent variable—in this case, the treatment. That is, they *introduce* a variable (treatment) that would not have occurred naturally (the older adults would not have been treated). They introduce this independent variable for each member of the group and then assess the members to learn whether their behavior changed as a function of what the researchers did. Introducing or withdrawing a variable in a way that would not have occurred naturally is also called *manipulating* a variable.

Unfortunately, the researchers find that a decade later, the adults that were treated for sleep problems still sleep about as long as they did 10 years earlier, and that they still, as a group, sleep less than eight hours per night. Is the treatment a failure? Maybe not. The question that can't be answered with this study is what would have happened to this group if they hadn't been treated for insomnia. Perhaps their sleep patterns would have been worse with no treatment. But we can't go back in time like Jimmy Stewart in "It's a Wonderful Life" or Michael J. Fox in "Back to the Future" to see what would have happened with no help, so how is it possible to find out?

Control Groups

One answer to the "what if" dilemma we just posed is to use a control group—a group of people who are similar to the experimental group in every way with the exception that the experimental group is exposed to the independent variable change while the control group is not. A control group would include a number of similar individuals who, in this case, would not receive the treatment, the independent variable. The researchers would also follow this group of people, assess them 10 years later, and look at their sleep patterns over this time. In doing so, they would likely observe that, without intervention, people tend to sleep fewer hours as they get older (Bootzin, Engle-Friedman, & Hazelwood, 1983). The control group, in other words, might sleep *significantly less* than the treated group, even though the treated group would sleep somewhat less now than 10 years earlier. Using the control group, the researchers would see that their treatment did help the subjects by keeping their sleep time from decreasing further.

Ideally, a control group is nearly identical to the subject group, similar on such things as age, gender, socioeconomic backgrounds, and the problems they are reporting. Furthermore, they are treated in exactly the same way as the experimental group except for the independent variable change. A researcher would do the same assessments before and after the independent variable manipulation (for example, a treatment) to people in both groups. Any differences between the groups after the change would, therefore, be attributable only to what was changed. Unfortunately, even if it were possible to find people so closely matched, it is often very difficult to treat people in the two groups in exactly the same way.

People who are in a treatment group often have the expectation that they will get better. This phenomenon is known as a **placebo effect**—where behavior changes as a result of a person's expectation of change rather than as a result of any manipulation by an experimenter. In other words, just *expecting* to get better may lead to improvements in some people. Conversely, people who are not in the treatment group may be disappointed that they are not receiving treatment. Depending on the type of disorder they are experiencing (for instance, depression), their disappointment may make them worse. This phenomenon would also make the treatment group look better by comparison.

One way researchers have addressed the expectation concern is through **placebo control groups.** The word *placebo* (which means "I shall please") has typically referred to the use of inactive medications such as sugar pills. This inactive medication is given to members of the control group to make them believe they are getting treatment rather than to treat any particular condition (Parloff, 1986). A placebo control in a medication study can be carried out with relative ease because it primarily requires the researcher to give people in the untreated group something that *looks like* the medication she is administering to the treatment group. In psychological treatments, however, devising something that people believe may help them but does not include the component the researcher believes is effective is not always as easy. Clients in these types of control groups are often given some *portion* of the therapy—for example, the same homework as the treated group—but not the portions the researchers believe are responsible for improvements.

It is important to note that you can look at the placebo effect as one portion of any treatment (Lambert, Shapiro, & Bergin, 1986). If you provide someone with a treatment and he or she improves, you would have to say that improvement was due to a combination of your treatment *plus* whatever benefits were gained by the client's *expectation* of improving (placebo effect). In fact, therapists want their clients to have some expectation that they will improve; this helps strengthen the treatment. However, when researchers are conducting an experiment to determine the portion of a particular treatment that is responsible for the observed changes, the placebo effect is a confound that can dilute the validity of the research. Thus, researchers use a placebo control group to help separate the results of expecting to improve from the results that are added from the treatment.

A variation on the placebo control group procedure is the **double-blind control.** As the name suggests, not only are the subjects or participants in the study "blind" or *unaware* of what group they are in or what treatment they are given (single blind), but so too are the researchers or therapists providing treatment (double blind). This type of control is used in research studies because it eliminates the possibility that an investigator might bias the outcome. For example, if a researcher were comparing two treatments and expected one treatment to be more effective than the other based on a theory of behavior, the researcher might "try harder" if the "preferred" treatment wasn't working as well as he expected. On the other hand, if the treatment that wasn't expected to work was not being successful, the researcher might not push as hard to see it succeed. A failure with this treatment was what was expected, so he may not persevere as he would with the preferred treatment. This behavior might not be deliberate, but it could happen. If, however, both the participants and the researchers/therapists are unaware of who is expected to improve, there is less chance that bias will affect the results.

A double-blind placebo control is not a perfect solution in all cases. If a researcher is using medication as a treatment, subjects may be able to tell whether they have or have not received active medication by the other physical reactions (side effects) they might experience. Even with psychological interventions, participants often know when they are or are not receiving a powerful treatment and may alter their expectations for improvement based on this knowledge.

Comparative Treatment Research

In addition to using no-treatment control groups to help evaluate treatment effects, some researchers want to compare different treatments. In this design, two or more comparable groups of people with a particular disorder are selected and the researcher gives a different treatment to each group. She can then assess how or if each treatment helped the people who received it. This approach is called **comparative treatment research** and allows direct comparison of treatments. In the sleep study we have been discussing, two groups of older adults could be selected, with one group given medication for insomnia and the other given a cognitive-behavioral intervention for their sleep problems. The results of the two groups could then be compared.

The treatment *process* and the treatment *outcome* are two important issues to be considered when different treatments are studied. *Treatment process* research focuses on the mechanisms responsible for behavior change. There is an old joke about someone going to a physician for a new miracle cure for the cold.

The physician prescribes the new drug, and then tells her patient that his cold will be gone in 7 to 10 days. As most of us know, colds typically improve in 7 to 10 days without "miracle drugs." The new drug probably adds nothing to the improvement observed in this patient's cold. When we test medical interventions, the "process" aspect of this work involves an evaluation of the biological mechanisms responsible for change. Does the medication lower serotonin levels, for example, and does this account for the changes we observe? Similarly, we look at psychological interventions and determine what is "causing" the observed changes in the people treated. This determination is important for several reasons. First, if we understand what the "active ingredients" of our treatment are, we can often eliminate aspects of treatment that are not important, thereby saving clients time and money. Additionally, knowing what is important about our interventions can help us create newer versions that are more powerful and may be more effective.

Treatment outcome research focuses on the results (positive and/or negative) of the treatment. In other words, does it work? Remember, treatment *process* involves finding out *why* or *how* your treatment works. In contrast, **treatment outcome** involves finding out *what* changes occur after treatment. You probably have guessed by now that even this seemingly simple task becomes more complicated the closer we look at it. Depending on the types of dependent variables you select to measure, when you assess them, and where you assess them, your view of "success" may vary considerably. For example, Greta Francis and Kathleen Hart (1992) recently described their work with depressed adolescents in an inpatient (hospital) setting. One of the treatment procedures they use includes "activity-increase" strategies. The goal is to help these adolescents become more involved in activities to help them have more access to positive experiences. Francis and Hart note that, although they observe improvements in depression when the adolescents are in their structured hospital environment, this improvement often disappears outside the hospital.

Does the use of activity-increase strategies result in positive treatment outcomes for depressed adolescents? Obviously, it depends on where you assess their depression. If you look at their outcomes in the hospital, you may see improvement. If you follow them home after being discharged, you might conclude that the treatment wasn't effective at all. Again, in evaluating whether a treatment is effective, researchers must decide carefully how to define success.

Randomization

Choosing people to be in experimental groups must be done carefully. Suppose a clinician is studying the effect of a new treatment on depression among women. She assigns women who come to her for treatment either to the treatment group or to a no-treatment control group. After treatment sessions are over, she finds that the women in the treatment group do improve, in comparison to the women in the control group. However, after the study is underway, she notices that the women in the treatment group are older and wealthier, on average, than the women in the control group. In talking to the women from both groups she learns that the older and/or wealthier women don't work outside their homes and are available for daytime treatment sessions while the younger women cannot leave their jobs to participate in day groups. The result is that the two groups are different in terms of age, income, and perhaps other important factors. Is this a problem? It is indeed, one that would cause people to question the study results. The researcher can't know whether the treatment group improved (a) because of the treatment, or (b) because the depression experienced by older and/or wealthier women is more likely to improve on its own. This confound (a difference in age and income as well as treatment between the groups) makes the study internally invalid.

To avoid the possible pitfalls of selecting groups that differ in some important way, researchers use *randomization*, or random assignment (Hsu, 1989). Researchers can assign participants to each group in an unbiased way with a variety of techniques such as using a random numbers table or flipping a coin. The goal of this process is to ensure that the people in each group do not differ in any *systematic* way—that the participants aren't different in a way that will somehow influence the results. Suppose the women in the depression treatment group described before were also more motivated to improve, and that's why they were willing to come in during the day for treatment. If this were so, the positive results might be related to how motivated the women are. By randomly assigning people to groups, researchers are better able to say that group selection wasn't based on some factor that will influence the outcomes.

Single-Case Experimental Designs

B. F. Skinner's innovations in scientific methodology were among his most important contributions to psychopathology. Skinner formalized the concept of **single-case experimental designs.** This method involves the systematic study of an individual under a variety of experimental conditions; the researcher manipulates an independent variable for a single individual in ways that reduce the likelihood of confounding explanations. Skinner thought it was much better to know a lot about the behavior of one individual than to make only a few observations of a large group, then present the "average" response. In psychopathology, we deal with the suffering of individual people, and this methodology has allowed us to make substantial advances in determining factors maintaining individual psychopathology (Barlow & Hersen, 1984). There are many examples of modern-day applications of Skinnerian methods throughout this book.

Like case studies, single-case experimental designs focus in detail on an individual rather than a group of people. Yet these designs differ from case studies by their use of various strategies to improve internal validity, thereby reducing the number of confounding variables. As we will see, these strategies have certain advantages as well as disadvantages with respect to the more traditional group designs we have been using as illustrations. It is important to note here that we use examples from treatment research to illustrate the single-case experimental designs. Yet like the other research strategies we will discuss, these designs can be used to explain why people engage in abnormal behavior as well as how to treat them.

Repeated Measurements

One of the more important strategies used in single-case experimental design is *repeated measurement*. Rather than measuring aspects of someone's behavior once before you change the independent variable and once afterward, single-subject designs measure the behaviors in which you are interested a number of different times. The researcher repeats these measurements over and over to learn how variable the behavior is (how much it changes day to day) and whether it shows any obvious trends (is it getting better or worse?). Suppose a young woman, Wendy, comes into the office complaining about feelings of anxiety. We ask her to rate her level of anxiety on a 10-point scale and find that she rates her present level of anxiety at about a 9 (with 10 being the worst). We then provide a treatment, and after several weeks of treatment Wendy rates her anxiety at 6. Can we say that she is now less anxious and that it was the treatment that reduced her anxiety? Not necessarily.

Suppose we had measured Wendy's anxiety each day for the weeks before her visit to the office (repeated measurement) and observed that her ratings were very different each day. On particularly good days, she rated her anxiety between 5 and 7. On bad days, it was up between 8 and 10. Suppose further that, even after treatment, her daily ratings continued to range from 5 to 10. In the first example, the rating of 9 that she gave prior to treatment and the 6 she described after treatment may only have been part of the daily variations she experienced normally. In fact, Wendy could just as easily have been having a good day and reported a 6 before treatment, and then had a bad day and reported a 9 after treatment, implying that the treatment made her worse!

Repeated measurement is a part of each single-subject experimental design, and is used to help the researcher determine not only how a person is doing before and after the intervention but also whether the trends suggest that the treatment accounted for the changes observed. Figure 4.2 illustrates Wendy's anxiety and the added information obtained by repeated measurement. The top graph shows Wendy's original before and after ratings of her anxiety. The middle graph shows that with daily ratings her reports are variable and that just by chance the previous measurement was probably very misleading. She had good and bad days both before and after the treatment, and, based on these ratings, she doesn't seem to have changed much.

Another possibility that would also have been obscured with just a before and after measurement is shown in the bottom graph—that the trend or direction of her anxiety was on its way down before the treatment. In other words, maybe she was getting better on her own, and, again, the treatment really didn't have much effect. Although the middle graph shows how the *variability* from day to day could be important in an interpretation of the effect of treatment, the bottom graph shows how the *trend* can also be important if the cause of any change is to be discovered. These graphs illustrate three parts of the repeated measurements that are important to examine: (a) the **level** or degree of difference in behavior with different interventions (shown on Wendy's top graph), (b) the **variability** or degree of change from day to day or week to week (shown in the middle graph), and (c) the **trend** or direction of change (shown in the bottom graph). Again, having only a before and after score does not necessarily show what is responsible for the changes in the patient.

Withdrawal Designs

One of the more common strategies used in single-subject research is called a **withdrawal design.** With this strategy, a researcher tries to determine whether the independent variable is responsible for changes in behavior by removing or withdrawing it and observing any behavior change in the patient. To go back to Wendy and her anxiety, the effect of the treatment could be tested by stopping treatment for a period of time to see whether her anxiety increased. A simple version of the withdrawal design would have three parts, starting with a period of time prior to treatment, called a **baseline.** This would be followed by the change in the independent variable—in this case, the beginning of treatment for Wendy's anxiety. In the last step, treatment would be stopped (the withdrawal or "return to baseline") and the researcher would assess whether Wendy's anxiety changed again as a function of this last step. If her anxiety lessened, in comparison to baseline, with the treatment, and then worsened again after treatment was withdrawn, the researcher

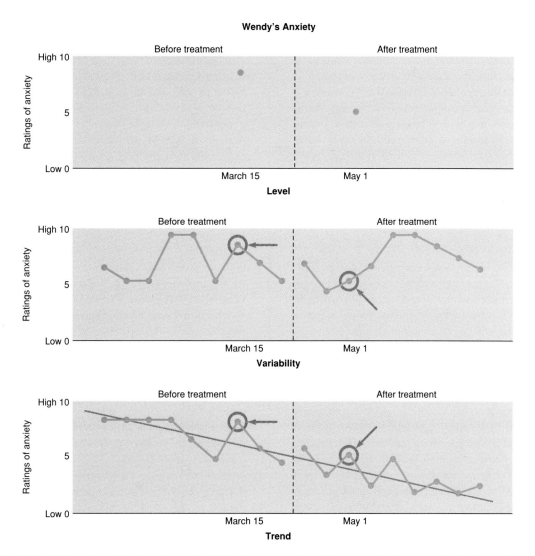

Figure 4.2 While graph 1 gives the impression that Wendy's anxiety level changed significantly, graphs 2 and 3 demonstrate how examining variability and trend can provide much more information about the true nature of the change.

could conclude that the treatment had reduced Wendy's anxiety.

How is this design different from a case study? One of the important differences is the manipulation or change in the treatment that is designed specifically to show whether treatment caused the changes in behavior. Although case studies often involve a treatment, they don't include any effort to try to learn whether the person would have improved without the treatment. By removing treatment in a withdrawal design, researchers get a better sense of whether the treatment itself and not something else is causing behavior change.

In spite of their advantages, withdrawal designs sometimes should not be used for several reasons. First, the design requires the researcher to remove what might be an effective treatment, and this decision is difficult to justify for ethical reasons. In Wendy's case, trying to prove that it was the treatment and not some other factor that caused the improvements in her anxiety may not be a sufficient reason to deliberately

make her anxious again. A withdrawal design is also unsuitable when the treatment can't be removed. Suppose the researcher's treatment for Wendy's anxiety involved asking her to visualize herself sitting on a beach on a tropical island, and then when he wanted to withdraw treatment he asked Wendy to stop thinking about the beach. It would be very difficult to stop her from imagining something once she has started. Similarly, some treatments involve teaching people skills, and it would be impossible to erase these learned skills from their minds. As part of the treatment for anxiety, the researcher could have taught Wendy how to be more skillful in social situations. How could he then tell Wendy that she had to revert to being socially unskilled? In light of these difficulties there is another single-case experimental design—the multiple baseline—that can address this limitation of the withdrawal design. We will discuss that shortly.

There are also several counterarguments supporting the use of withdrawal designs (Barlow & Hersen, 1984). Withdrawing treatment is routinely used when medications are involved. Called *drug holidays,* these are periods of time when the medication is withdrawn so clinicians can determine whether it is responsible for the treatment effects. This is done for a number of reasons. One reason is because any medication can have negative side effects, and avoiding unnecessary medication is preferred. At other times treatment withdrawal happens naturally. Finally, withdrawals do not have to be long periods of time that are harmful. A very brief withdrawal of the intervention may be relatively harmless but still give you a good idea about the role of the treatment.

Multiple Baselines

Another single-case experimental design strategy that is used frequently and that doesn't have some of the drawbacks of a withdrawal design is the **multiple baseline.** Rather than stopping the intervention to see whether it is effective, with a multiple baseline strategy the researcher starts treatment at different times across settings (for example, home versus school), behaviors (for instance, yelling at spouse, yelling at your boss), or people. This strategy could be used to look at the treatment for anxiety. After waiting a period of time and taking repeated measures of Wendy's anxiety both at her home and at her job (the baseline), the clinician could treat her first at home. Then, after the treatment begins to be effective for her at home, intervention could begin at work. If she improves at home after treatment, but improves at work only after treatment is used there, then we could conclude that the treatment was effective for Wendy's anxiety. This is an example of using a multiple baseline *across settings,* with the settings being home and work.

Is internal validity improved by using a multiple baseline? The answer is yes. Any time other explanations for the results can be ruled out, internal validity is improved. In Wendy's case, her anxiety improved only in those situations where it was treated. This rules out other competing explanations for her improvement—for example, winning the lottery. If she had won the lottery at the same time treatment had started and her anxiety improved in all situations, we couldn't conclude that her condition was affected by treatment.

It is also possible to conduct a multiple baseline *across behaviors.* Suppose a researcher wanted to assess the effectiveness of a treatment for children's problem behaviors. Treatment could begin on a child's crying, then later on a second problem the child has, such as fighting with her sister. If the treatment was effective in reducing crying, and only later after the second intervention was it effective for fighting, then the researcher could conclude that the treatment, not something else, accounted for the improvements.

Single-case experimental designs are criticized at times because they tend to involve only a small number of cases, leaving their external validity in doubt. In other words, we can't say that the results we saw with a *few* people would be the same *in general* for all people. However, although these are called *single*-case experimental designs, there are no rules about the number of cases presented in these studies. Researchers can and often do use these designs across several people, in part to address the issue of external validity. One of the authors recently studied the effectiveness of a treatment for the severe behavior problems of children with autism and other developmental disabilities (Durand & Carr, 1992). As part of the study, we taught these children to communicate instead of misbehave, a procedure known as *functional communication training* (we will discuss this in more detail in Chapter 16). We introduced this treatment to a group of six children using a multiple baseline. Our dependent variables were the incidence of the children's behavior problems as well as the use of their newly trained communication skills. As Figure 4.3 shows, only when we began treatment for each child did his behavior problems improve and did he begin to communicate with us verbally. Using this design we could rule out other explanations such as coincidence or some other change in the children's lives as causing the improvements in their behavior.

Among the advantages of the multiple baseline design over the withdrawal design in evaluating treatments is that it does not require treatment to be suspended. This characteristic is very valuable when withdrawing treatment would be difficult or impossible. Furthermore, the multiple baseline typically resembles the way treatment would naturally be implemented for people. Because a clinician can't help people with all their problems simultaneously, she can take repeated measures of the behaviors in which she is interested, and then observe when the behaviors change. If she sees predictable and orderly changes related to where and when the treatment is used, she can conclude that the treatment is causing the change. Again, in the example presented above, it is unlikely that we could provide treatment for each of these children at the same time. Therefore, the delay in delivering treatment was used to help us determine whether functional communication training was what was helping them.

Studying Genetics

We tend to think of genetics in terms of inheriting different things from our parents. "He's got his mother's eyes!" "She's thin just like her parents." "She's stubborn like her mother." Looking at genetics in this way often leads to a very simple view of how we become the

Figure 4.3 This figure shows how a multiple baseline design was used to illustrate that the treatment—functional communication training—was responsible for improvements in the children's behaviors. The green circles represent how often each child exhibited behavior problems (called *challenging behavior*), and the blue circles show how often they communicated without help from the teacher (referred to as *unprompted communication*) (adapted from Durand & Carr, 1992).

people we are. It suggests that the way we look, think, feel, and behave is predetermined. Yet, as we saw in Chapter 2, we now know there are always interactions between our genetic makeup and our experiences, and this interaction is what determines how we will develop. The goal of behavioral geneticists (people

who study the genetics of behavior) is to tease out the role of genetics in these interactions.

In studying abnormal behavior, genetic researchers examine both phenotypes and genotypes. **Phenotype** refers to the observable characteristics or behavior of the individual. **Genotype** is the individual's

OUR GENES: WHAT THE MAP SHOWS

A selection of the known locations of mutations uncovered by scientists

Muscular Dystrophy ●
(Duchenne and Becker types)
Progressive deterioration
of the muscles

Hemophilia ●
Blood defect
making it difficult
to control
hemorrhaging

Neurofibromatosis, Type 2 ●
Tumors of the auditory nerves and tissues
surrounding the brain

Down Syndrome ●
Congenital mental deficiency condition marked
three copies of chromosome 21

Amyotrophic Lateral Sclerosis* ●
(Lou Gehrig's Disease)
Fatal degenerative nerve ailment

ADA Deficiency ●
Severe susceptibility to infections.
First hereditary condition treated
by gene therapy

**Familial
Hypercholesterolemia** ●
Extremely high cholesterol

Myotonic Dystrophy ●
Frequent form of adult
muscular dystrophy

Amyloidosis ●
Accumulation in the
tissues of an insoluble
fibrillar protein

Breast Cancer* ●
5% to 10% of cases

Polycystic Kidney Disease ■
Cysts resulting in enlarged kedneys
and renal failure

**Tay-Sachs
Disease** ●
Fatal
hereditary
disorder
involving lipid
metabolism
often
occurring in
Ashkenazi
Jews and
French
Canadians

**Alzheimer's
Disease*** ■
Degenerative
nerve disease
marked by
premature
senility

FROM THE WHOLE TO THE (MICROSCOPIC) PARTS

The human body contains 100 trillion **cells**	There is a **nucleus** inside each human cell (except red blood cells)	Each nucleus contains 46 **chromosomes,** arranged in 23 pairs	One **chromosome** of every pair is from each parent	The chromosomes are filled with tightly coiled strands of **DNA**	**Genes** are segments of DNA that contain instructions to make proteins– the building blocks of life

Discoveries about the role of genetics in a variety of medical and mental disorders are being made daily (from *Time* Magazine, January 17, 1994).

WHEN CAN WE GET TESTED?
- DNA test currently available
- ■ Gene mapped but not yet isolated
- ◆ Diagnosis available through family-linkage study of DNA markers
- ○ DNA test under development

*One form of the disease

ALD ●
(adrenoleukodystrophy)
Nerve disease portrayed in
movie *Lorenzo's Oil*

Gaucher's Disease ●
A chronic enzyme
deficiency occurring
frequently among
Ashkenazi Jews

Familial Colon Cancer* ○
One in 200 people have this gene;
of those, 65% are likely to
develop the disease

Retinitis Pigmentosa ●
Progressive degeneration of the retina

Huntington's Disease ●
Neurodegenerative disorder tending to
strike people in their 40s and 50s

**Familial Polyposis
of the Colon** ●
Abnormal tissue growths
frequently leading to cancer

Hemochromatosis ◆
Abnormally high
absorption of iron from
the diet

Spinocerebellar Ataxia ●
Destroys nerves in the
brain and spinal cord,
resulting in loss of
muscle control

Cystic Fibrosis ●
Mucus fills up the
lungs, interfering with
breathing. One of the
most prevalent
genetic diseases
in the U.S.

Multiple Exostoses* ■
A disorder of cartilage
and bone

Malignant Melanoma ●
Tumors originating in the skin

Multiple Endocrine Neoplasia, Type 2 ○
Tumors in endocrine glands and other tissues

Sickle Cell Anemia ●
Chronic inherited anemia, primarily affecting blacks, in
which red blood cells sickle, or form crescents, plugging
arterioles and capillaries

Retinoblastoma ●
A relatively common tumor of
the eye, accounting for 2% of
childhood malignancies

PKU ●
(phenylketonuria)
An inborn error of metabolism
that frequently results in mental retardation

CHROMOSOME PAIRS

X Y
22 21 20 19 18 17 16 15 14 13 12 11 10 9 8 7 6 5 4 3 2 1

specific genetic makeup. To illustrate, a person with Down syndrome typically has some level of mental retardation and a variety of other physical characteristics such as "slanted" eyes and a thick tongue. These characteristics represent the phenotype. We know that Down syndrome is caused by an extra 21st chromosome, and this is the genotype.

To date, our knowledge of the phenotypes of different psychological disorders exceeds our knowledge of the specific genetic characteristics or genotypes, but that may soon change. Ever since the discovery of the now famous double helix, scientists have known that we would have to map the structure and location of every gene on all 46 chromosomes if we were ever to fully understand our genetic endowment. Beginning in 1990, scientists around the world, in a coordinated effort, began the **human genome project** (*genome* means all the genes of an organism). Using the latest advances in molecular biology, scientists working on this project will attempt to complete a comprehensive mapping of human genes in approximately 5 years. Although many scientists thought this was a fanciful goal, the work is progressing steadily. In 1992, for example, Mandel, Monaco, Nelson, Schlessinger, and Willard (1992) reported the results of a concerted international effort to map the 160 million base pairs on the X chromosome. Using a sophisticated technique that actually reproduces these base pairs and then puts them back together in the proper order, the geneticists have mapped about 40% of this chromosome. In the process, they have identified the location and structure of over 75 genes that contribute to certain inherited diseases. For example, the location of the damage that results in *fragile X mental retardation syndrome* (see Chapter 15) is on this chromosome, as is a gene for one form of muscular dystrophy. These are exciting findings and represent truly astounding progress in uncovering the nature of genetic endowment.

What follows is a brief review of four more traditional research strategies used by scientists to help them unravel the complex genetic questions they encounter as they study the interaction between environment and genetics in psychological disorders— family studies, adoption studies, twin studies, and genetic linkage analysis.

Family Studies

One way to examine the contribution of genetics to our behavior is to look at the presence of behavioral patterns or traits in families. In **family studies,** scientists simply examine the presence of a behavioral pattern or emotional trait in a family. The family member with the trait singled out for study is called the **proband,** and if there is a genetic influence, presumably this pattern or

trait should be present more often in first-degree relatives (parents, siblings, or offspring) of the person with the trait being studied than in more distant relatives. The presence of the trait in second-degree or more distant relatives, in turn, should be somewhat greater than the probability of the trait's appearing in the population as a whole. Think back to the example of Judy at the beginning of Chapter 1. Judy is the adolescent with blood-injury-injection phobia and the tendency to faint at the sight of blood. Remember that the family aggregation (the tendency of a trait to run in families) is as high as 60% for this disorder, meaning that 60% of the first-degree relatives of someone with blood-injury-injection phobia have the same reaction to at least *some* degree. This is one of the highest rates of familial aggregation for any psychological disorder we have studied.

But there is a difficulty with family studies. Families tend to live together, and there might be something in their environment that causes the high familial aggregation. For example, Mom might have developed a very bad reaction to blood as a young girl after witnessing a bloody accident. Every time she sees blood she has a very strong emotional reaction. Emotions are contagious. Chances are that all the young children watching Mom react this way would tend to react similarly and carry that tendency with them into adulthood, passing it on, in turn, to their children.

Adoption Studies

How do we separate environmental influences from genetic influences in families? One way is through **adoption studies.** In adoption studies, scientists find somebody with a particular behavioral pattern, or perhaps a psychological disorder, and attempt to locate that person's first-degree relatives, such as brothers and sisters, who were raised in different family settings. Suppose a young male has a disorder and scientists discover that his brother, for some reason, was adopted as a baby and brought up in a different home. The researchers would then attempt to find many case examples like this. If they can identify enough of these individuals (and they usually do after a lot of hard work) they can assess whether the brothers brought up in different families display the disorder to the same extent as the original subject. If the brothers raised with different families have the disorder more frequently than would be expected by chance, they can infer that genetic endowment contributes something to the disorder.

Twin Studies

Nature has presented behavioral geneticists with one elegant experiment that has allowed them their closest possible look at the role of genes in development:

Complex human behavior develops from a combination of biological and psychosocial influences. Although they are identical twins and were raised together, Paula Sossen (*right*), a graduate student at the University of Michigan, is heterosexual and Nina Sossen (*left*), who works in Madison, Wisconsin, is a lesbian.

identical, or monozygotic, twins. These twins not only look alike but they have exactly the same set of genes. Fraternal (or dizygotic) twins, on the other hand, coming from different eggs, share only about 50% of each other's genes, as do all first-degree relatives. The obvious scientific question then is whether identical twins share the same trait—say, fainting at the sight of blood—more than fraternal twins. Determining whether a trait is shared is easy with some physical traits such as height. As Plomin (1990) points out, correlations in height for both first-degree relatives and fraternal twins are 0.45. Correlations in height for identical twins are 0.90. These findings show that heritability of height is about 90%, leaving approximately 10% of the variance due to environmental factors. But remember the case of the child with psychosocial dwarfism we discussed in Chapter 2. This case reminds us that the 90% estimate is the *average* contribution. Given usual and customary types of environmental influences, if one identical twin was severely physically abused or selectively deprived of proper foods, he or she might be substantially different in height from the other twin.

Matt McGue, Roy Pickens, and Dace Svikis (1992) recently conducted a **twin study** among adults with alcohol dependency. They found that among male monozygotic (identical) twins, when one person had difficulties with alcohol, his twin was likely also to report problems with alcohol and drugs. This increased likelihood to report difficulties with alcohol and drugs was in contrast to their findings for male dizygotic (fraternal) twins, who were less likely to report these problems than identical twins. The twin

relationship, however, was not found among females in their study. In other words, among women, rates of alcohol and drug abuse did not differ for monozygotic or dizygotic twins. The researchers concluded that genetic factors were more important for explaining the alcohol problems seen in men than in women, although the exact reason for this difference is as yet unclear.

This way of studying genetics isn't perfect. You can assume that monozygotic twins have the same genetic makeup and that dizygotic twins do not. However, a complicating concern for these types of studies is whether monozygotic twins have the same experiences or environment as dizygotic twins. On the surface, you can probably think of examples of how identical twins are dressed alike and are even given similar names. Yet some people have pointed out that the twins themselves influence each other's behavior, and that in some cases, monozygotic twins may affect each other more than dizygotic twins (Carey, 1992).

One way to address this problem is by combining both the adoption study and twin study methods. If you can find identical twins, one of whom was adopted as an infant, then you can estimate quite precisely the role of genes versus the role of the environment. Such studies offer the best way to determine the contribution of genes compared to the environment (nature versus nurture) in the development of behavioral patterns. Finding the participants for these studies is difficult, but as we will see, such research has been done with some disorders.

Genetic Linkage Analysis

The results of a series of family, twin, and adoption studies may suggest that a particular disorder has a genetic component. Although these types of studies can suggest whether genes are involved in the etiology of a disorder, they can't provide the *location* of the implicated gene or genes. To locate a defective gene, scientists use **genetic linkage analysis.**

The basic principle behind genetic linkage analysis is very simple. When the occurrence of a disorder in a family is studied, other characteristics in the family that are inherited are assessed at the same time. These other characteristics—called **genetic markers**—are selected because we understand their genetic makeup well enough to know their exact location. If a match or "link" is discovered between the inheritance of the disorder and the inheritance of one of the genetic markers, the connection suggests that the genes for the disorder and the genetic marker are on the same chromosome and are close together. In a recent example, bipolar affective disorder (manic-depression) was studied among the members of a large Amish family (Egeland et al., 1987). Researchers found that two markers on chromosome 11, genes for insulin and a known cancer gene, were linked to the presence of mood disorder in this family, suggesting that a gene for bipolar affective disorder might be on chromosome 11. Unfortunately, although this study can be used as an example of a genetic linkage study, it can also be used to illustrate the danger of drawing premature conclusions from such research. This linkage study and a second study that purported to find a linkage between bipolar disorder and the X chromosome (Biron et al., 1987) have yet to be replicated. In other words, different researchers studying this disorder have not been able to show similar linkages in other families (Gottesman, 1991), a failure that casts doubt on the earlier conclusion that one gene is responsible for a disorder as complex as bipolar disorder. Be mindful of these limitations—even with an analysis technique as sophisticated as genetic linkage—the next time you read in a newspaper or hear on TV that a gene has been found to cause some disorder.

Studying Behavior over Time

Sometimes the question we want to ask is "How will a disorder or behavior pattern change (or remain the same) over time?" This question is important for several reasons. First, the answer will help us determine whether to treat a particular person for his or her problem. For example, should we begin an expensive and time-consuming treatment program for a young adult who is depressed over the loss of a grandparent?

You might not if you knew that, with normal social supports, this person's depression would likely diminish considerably over the next few months without treatment. On the other hand, if you had a good idea that this problem wasn't likely to go away on its own, you might want to begin treatment. As we will see below, we now know that aggression among very young children does not seem to go away easily and should be dealt with as early as possible.

It is also important to understand the developmental changes in abnormal behavior because sometimes these can provide insight into how problems are created or how they become more serious—a concept we refer to throughout this book called the *course* of a disorder. In the area of schizophrenia, for example, we will see how some researchers look at people who are at risk for developing this disorder by virtue of their family histories, and follow them through the entire risk period for this problem (18–45 years of age) (Sameroff & Seifer, 1990). The goal is to track these people and attempt to discover the factors (e.g., social status, family psychopathology) that predict who will ultimately manifest schizophrenia. This complex but fascinating research is described in Chapter 14.

Several research strategies have been used to examine psychopathology across time. These strategies are created by combining many of the individual and group research strategies we have already discussed, including the use of both correlational and experimental designs. We'll look here at two of the most frequently used of these strategies: cross-sectional and longitudinal designs.

Cross-Sectional Designs

One way to study how people and their problems change over time is to look at different people at different ages and compare them. This **cross-sectional design**—a variation of correlation research—allows researchers to see differences in the subjects' behaviors or attitudes at these different ages. They take a "cross-section" of a population across the different age groups and compare them on some characteristic. For example, if they were trying to understand the development of alcohol abuse and dependency, they could take groups of adolescents at 12, 15, and 17 years of age and assess their beliefs about alcohol use. In fact, Brown and Finn (1982) conducted such a comparison and made some interesting discoveries. They found that 36% of the 12-year-olds thought the primary purpose of drinking was to get drunk. This percentage increased to 64% with 15-year-olds, but dropped again to 42% for the 17-year-old students. The researchers also found that 28% of the 12-year-olds reported drinking with their friends at least sometimes, a rate that increased to 80% for the 15-year-olds and to 88% for the 17-year-olds.

Brown and Finn used this information to develop an explanation for teenage drinking, including the hypothesis that what underlies excessive drinking among teens is a deliberate attempt to get drunk rather than a mistake in judgment once they are under the influence of alcohol. In other words, teenagers do not, as a group, appear to drink too much because once they've had a drink or two they show poor judgment and drink excessively. Instead, their attitudes *before drinking* seem to influence how much they drink later.

The participants in each age group in research using cross-sectional designs are called **cohorts.** Using the example from the work of Brown and Finn, we described three cohorts: the 12-year-olds, the 15-year-olds, and the 17-year-olds. The members of each cohort share the commonalities of being the same age at the same time, and thus having all been exposed to similar cultural and historical experiences. At the same time, different cohorts not only differ from other cohorts in age but can also differ in their exposure to cultural and historical experiences. Looking at a group of 12-year-olds in the early 1990s, you would expect them to have received a great deal of education about drug and alcohol use ("Just Say No"), whereas the 17-year-olds may not have had similar experiences. Differences among the cohorts in their opinions about alcohol use may be related to their respective cognitive and emotional development at these different ages and/or their cumulative but dissimilar experiences. This **cohort effect,** or the confounding of age and experience, is a limitation of the cross-sectional design.

Researchers commonly rely on cross-sectional designs to study changes over time. One reason for this preference is that cross-sectional designs are relatively easy to use when compared to longitudinal designs (discussed next). Researchers don't have to wait for people to age to see how abnormal behavior changes across time. Additionally, some phenomena are less likely to be influenced by different cultural and historical experiences and are therefore less susceptible to cohort effects. For example, the study of the prevalence of Alzheimer's disease among people at ages 60 and 70—assumed to be strongly influenced by biology—would not likely be greatly affected by different experiences among the study subjects.

One question that is not answered by cross-sectional designs is how problems develop in individuals. For example, do children who refuse to go to school grow up to have anxiety disorders? A researcher cannot answer this question simply by comparing adults with anxiety problems and children who refuse to go to school. He could ask the adults to report whether they were anxious about going to school when they were children, but this **retrospective information** (looking back) is less than ideal. People are often not very accurate when they have to recall information from

Observing different people at different ages—called a *cross-sectional design*—provides researchers with a way of studying changes in behavior over time.

their past. To get a better picture of how individuals develop over the years, researchers use a second type of design to study change over time: longitudinal designs.

Longitudinal Designs

Rather than looking at different groups of people of differing ages, researchers may choose to follow one group over time and assess change in its members directly. **Longitudinal designs** have an advantage over cross-sectional designs because they do not suffer from cohort effect problems and they allow the researchers to assess changes in individuals (Figure 4.4 illustrates both the longitudinal and the cross-sectional designs). Illustrating this type of design, Susan Nolen-Hoeksema, Joan Girgus, and Martin Seligman (1992) conducted a 5-year longitudinal study on depression among children. These authors assessed depressive symptoms among 508 third-grade children through structured interviews conducted every 6 months over a 5-year period. In addition to measuring depressive symptoms such as feeling "sad" and troubles with eating and sleeping, the researchers also determined the number of negative events the children experienced, such as parents' divorcing, and also the children's "explanatory style" or their degree of expectation that bad things would happen. The study showed the importance of looking at disorders such as depression over time. The researchers found that negative events affected children more strongly when they were younger; as they grew up, their pessimism, along with actual negative events in their lives, predicted depression. In other words, younger children are almost exclusively influenced by the bad things that really happen to them, but as they grow older, their *thoughts*—that is, how they view negative events—

Longitudinal design

Group #1

Same people followed across time

Cross-sectional design

Group #1

Group #2

Group #3

People of different ages viewed at the same time

Figure 4.4 Two research designs

seem to play a greater role in whether they become depressed (see Chapter 7).

Imagine trying to conduct one of these major longitudinal studies. Not only must the researcher persevere over months and years but so must the people who participate in the study. They must remain willing to continue in the project, and the researcher must hope they will not move away, or worse, die! Longitudinal research is costly, time-consuming, and is

also subject to another potential pitfall: the distinct possibility that the research question will become irrelevant by the time the study is complete. Finally, longitudinal designs can suffer from a phenomenon similar to the cohort effect that can cloud cross-sectional designs. Known as a **cross-generational effect,** it involves trying to generalize the findings to groups who may have experiences as they develop that are very different from those of the study participants. For example, the drug use histories of people who were young adults in the 1960s and early 1970s will be vastly different from those of people who are born in the 1990s. What was true for the former group may not apply to the latter group.

Sometimes researchers combine longitudinal and cross-sectional designs to assess changes in psychopathology and to try to address the limitations of each of these approaches. This strategy is called the **sequential design** and involves repeated study of different cohorts over time. In a recent report, Julia Wallace and Michael O'Hara (1992) published their findings about depression among rural elderly adults. They used a combination of both a cross-sectional and a longitudinal design to learn whether and how depression among these older adults (65 years of age and older) changed over time. Their ambitious project involved conducting a structured interview for over 3,500 older residents of two counties in rural Iowa. Following the first interview, they compared the results among the adults from different age groups. The *cross-sectional* part of the study involved looking at depression among older adults at different ages, broken into the following age ranges: 65–69, 70–74, 75–79, 80–84, 85–89, and 90 and older (the cohorts). Later, Wallace and O'Hara went back to these adults to reinterview them for the *longitudinal* part of the study, conducting the follow-up interviews 3 and 6 years after the first ones. In this particular study, both parts of the sequential design produced similar findings: Depression seemed to increase as adults grew older, but the presence of social supports for these adults mitigated the increases. In other words, having more social supports seemed to help prevent some depression later in life.

Studying Behavior Across Cultures

Just as we can become narrowly focused when we study a disorder only among people at a certain age, we can also miss important aspects by studying people from only one culture. Studying the differences in behavior of people from different cultures can tell us a great deal about the origins and possible treatments of abnormal behaviors. Unfortunately, most of the research literature on psychopathology originates in Western cultures (Lambert et al., 1992). This ethnocentric view of psychopathology can limit our understanding of disorders in general and can also restrict the way we approach treatment. Re-

searchers in Malaysia have described a disorder they call *gila,* which, although having some of the features of schizophrenia, also differs in important ways (Resner & Hartog, 1970). Could we learn more about schizophrenia (and gila) by comparing these two disorders and the cultures in which they arose? There is an increasing awareness of the limited nature of our research in this area and a corresponding increase in cross-cultural research on psychopathology.

Many of the designs we have described are used and adapted for studying abnormal behavior across cultures. Some researchers in this area see the effects of different cultures in much the same way as we have been discussing different treatments (Malpass & Poortinga, 1986). In other words, the independent variable in their research is the effect of different cultures on behavior as opposed to, say, the effect of cognitive therapy versus simple exposure for the treatment of fears. The difference between looking at culture as a "treatment" and our typical design, however, is important. First, when researchers study the effects of cultures, they make no random assignment to groups. We discussed previously the importance of randomization in assigning people to groups to help eliminate possible confounding factors of which we may not be aware. In cross-cultural research, we can't randomly assign infants to different cultures and observe how they develop. People assign themselves to cultures based on a number of factors, including the culture in which their parents are raised and the employment/living opportunities available. People from varying cultures can differ in any number of important ways—their genetic backgrounds for one—that could explain variations in their behavior for reasons other than culture.

The characteristics of different cultures can also complicate efforts to study people from these groups. Symptoms of disorders or the description of these symptoms can be very dissimilar in different societies. People from Nigeria who are depressed complain of heaviness or heat in the head, crawling sensations in the head or legs, burning sensations in the body, and a feeling that the belly is bloated with water (Ebigno, 1982). In contrast, people in North America with depression report feeling worthless, being unable to start or finish anything, losing interest in usual activities, and thinking of suicide. Natives of China, on the other hand, do not report loss of the ability to experience pleasure, the helplessness or hopelessness, guilt, or suicidal thoughts seen in depressed people from North America (Kleinman, 1982). These few examples illustrate that trying to use one standard definition of depression across different cultures will

Differences within and across cultures can influence abnormal behavior. Studying these differences can give us a broader understanding of psychological disorders.

result in vastly different outcomes depending on how you define the disorder.

An additional complicating factor for research in cross-cultural psychopathology involves different tolerances or "thresholds" for abnormal behavior. If different cultures see the same behaviors in a very different light, researchers will have trouble comparing incidence and prevalence rates. Recent work by Lambert and colleagues (1992) with Jamaican and American adults suggests that Jamaican parents and teachers report fewer incidents of abnormal child behavior than do their American counterparts. Does the variation in such reports from one culture to another represent some biological or environmental difference in the children themselves, the effects of different thresholds of tolerance in the societies, or some combination of both? Understanding the attitudes and customs of each culture under study is an essential component of such research.

Finally, treatment research is also complicated when it is studied cross-culturally. Cultures adopt treatment models that reflect their own values. In Japan, psychiatric hospitalization is organized around a family model, with caretakers assuming parental roles. A family model was also common in psychiatric institutions in 19th-century North America until it was replaced with the medical model that is common today (Blue & Gaines, 1992; Dwyer, 1992). In Saudi Arabia, the custom of being veiled when outside the home

can prevent women from uncovering their faces in the presence of their therapists, complicating efforts to establish a trusting and intimate therapeutic client-therapist relationship (Dubovsky, 1983). In Islamic psychiatry, because medicine and religion are viewed as inseparable, medical and religious treatments are combined (Horikoshi, 1980). As you can see, something as basic as comparing the outcomes of a treatment is vastly more complex in a cross-cultural context when you must consider each culture's conception of the problem and how it should be addressed.

The Power of a Program of Research

Examining different research strategies independently, as we have done here, often gives the impression that some research approaches are "better" than others. It is important that you do not come away with that view of the practice of research. Depending on the type of question you are asking and the practical limitations inherent in the inquiry, any one of the types of research techniques described would be appropriate. In fact, important issues often get resolved, not by one perfectly designed study but rather by a *series* of studies examining different aspects of the problem. To show

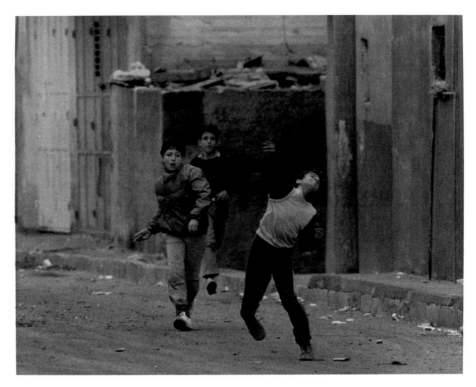

Palestinian children throwing stones at soldiers in the West Bank. Although unthinkable in most parts of the world, this behavior is almost commonplace in certain cultures—making a determination of what constitutes abnormal behavior extremely difficult.

how this is carried out in what is called a *program* of research, we will look at one of the more outstanding examples of this approach applied to studying the aggressive behavior of children, illustrated in the work of Gerald Patterson and his colleagues at the University of Oregon.

In some of the earliest research by this group, basic concerns such as why children are aggressive were the focus of the studies being conducted. As a start, the researchers did a series of *correlational studies* to determine what variables were associated with aggression in children. One study was conducted in a state institution for girls who had been admitted for various problem behaviors (Buehler, Patterson, & Furniss, 1966). Researchers in this study found that the "delinquent" behaviors of the girls—which included rule breaking, criticizing adults and adult rules, and behaving aggressively—were likely to be reinforced by the girls' peers. In other words, one reason they continued to be aggressive was that their peers encouraged it.

Using strategies from *epidemiology,* Patterson has also looked at the prevalence of aggression in children as a way to gain insight into this problem. In one example, he found that the likelihood of inappropriate behavior among children who are identified as

not having a disorder ranged from 41% to 11% with the mean being approximately 25% (Patterson, Cobb, & Ray, 1972). In other words, some level of aggression appears to be acceptable. Children are seen as "deviant" not when they display a behavior but when that behavior exceeds some acceptable level of frequency or intensity.

As you remember, interpreting the results from correlation studies can be difficult, especially if the intent is to determine causation. To answer this criticism, Patterson also conducted experimental studies. One strategy he used was a *single-case experimental design* (withdrawal design), in which he observed how a 5-year-old boy reacted to his mother's attempts to change his problem behavior (Patterson, 1982, p. 154). Patterson asked the boy's mother to restrain the child if he was aggressive but not to talk to him during this time (the "A" in an "ABA" withdrawal design). Patterson observed that the boy whined and complained when he was restrained. In the experimental condition (the "B" in an "ABA" design), Patterson asked the mother to talk with her son in a positive way when he complained. Later, Patterson had her again ignore her son's complaints. What was found was that the boy was more likely to complain when his mother talked with him about being restrained. One conclusion was

Gerald Patterson, who is at the University of Oregon, uses a variety of research strategies in his work with aggressive children. This program of research has provided valuable insight into why some children become aggressive and how to treat them.

that reinforcement from the mother encouraged the boy to try to escape the restraint by complaining. By observing both the boy's behavior (the dependent variable) and the mother's behavior (the independent variable), Patterson could make stronger conclusions about the role of the mother in influencing her son's behavior.

One of the questions about aggression in children concerns development. How does aggression change over time? To answer this question, Patterson has used *cross-sectional research* to observe how children at different ages differ in their aggression. In one study he found that the frequency or rate of aggression decreases as children get older (Patterson, 1982). It seems that children are aggressive less often as they get older, but their aggression may become more intense or destructive.

Using *treatment outcome research,* this group of researchers has also examined the effects of a treatment package on the aggressive behavior of children. Patterson and Fleischman (1979) introduced a behavioral treatment involving parent training (which we describe more fully in Chapter 13) and described the results of the treatment on the behavior of both parents and their children. The researchers found that they could reduce inappropriate child behavior *and* improve the parenting skills of the parents, and that these changes persisted a year after treatment.

This brief review does not do justice to the enormous and complex series of studies carried out at the University of Oregon on children with aggression. You should be aware, however, that research is conducted in stages, and that a complete picture of any behavior can be seen only after looking at it from many different perspectives. A program of research on a topic

can help researchers explore these various facets of abnormal behavior.

Replication

The motto of the State of Missouri is "Show Me." The motto of science could be "Show Me Again." Science in general, and behavioral science in particular, is never really convinced that something is "truth." People are very doubtful and skeptical when it comes to claims about causes or treatment outcomes. Replicating or duplicating findings gives researchers more confidence that what they are observing isn't some coincidence. We noted when we described the case study method that looking at the disorder in only one person, no matter how carefully we described and documented what we observed, prevented strong conclusions about what we saw.

The strength of conducting a program of research is in its ability to replicate findings in different ways to build confidence in the results. If you look back at the research strategies we have described, you will find that one of the most important aspects of each is *replication.* The single-subject experiments rely heavily on replication. The withdrawal design repeats the changes in the independent variable by first introducing the independent variable and then taking it away. The more times a researcher repeats this process (and the behavior he is studying changes as expected) the more confidence he can have that the independent variable caused the changes. Similarly, the multiple baseline design allows him to replicate the effect across people, behaviors, or settings.

The correlation and group experimental designs also incorporate aspects of replication. Correlation research uses observations from many people to demonstrate the association between variables. Group experimental designs repeat the outcomes with a number of people, since a certain number of people must be included in each group.

Research Ethics

A final issue, though not the least important, involves concerns about the ethics of doing research in the field of abnormal psychology. Some of these concerns were addressed briefly as we discussed individual research strategies. For example, one question that comes up frequently in treatment research is the appropriateness of a clinician's delaying treatment to people who need it, just to satisfy the requirements of an experimental design. In one single-case experimental design—the withdrawal design—we discussed how using this strategy can involve removing treatment for a period of

Children who participate in research require extra protection to ensure their psychological and physical safety.

time. Treatment is also withheld when placebo control groups are used in group experimental designs. When does a scientist's interest in preserving the internal validity of a study outweigh a client's right to treatment?

One answer to this question involves a concept referred to as **informed consent**—a research subject's approval to participate in a study following full disclosure of the nature of the research and the participant's role in this work. The concept of informed consent is actually derived from the war trials following World War II. Revelations that the Nazis had forced the participation of prisoners in "medical experiments" helped establish the informed consent guidelines that are still used today. In studies using some form of treatment delay or withdrawal, informed consent would include telling the subject about this manipulation, explaining why it will occur, describing the risks and benefits, and then obtaining his or her permission to proceed. In placebo control studies, subjects are told of the *possibility* that they may not receive an active treatment (all participants would be *blind* to or unaware of their group placement), but they are usually given the option of receiving treatment at a later time following the end of the study.

"True" informed consent can, at times, be elusive. The basic components of this concept involve competence, voluntarism, full information, and comprehension on the part of the subject (Imber et al., 1986). In other words, participants in research must be competent or capable of consenting to participation in the research, they must volunteer or not be coerced into participating, they must have all the information needed to make this decision, and they must understand what their participation will involve. In some circumstances these conditions are difficult to obtain. Children, for example, may not fully appreciate what will occur during the research. Similarly, individuals who may have cognitive impairments (such as people with mental retardation or some with schizophrenia) may have difficulty understanding their role in the research or their rights as subjects. In some settings—such as in institutions—there is concern that participants not be made to feel pressured or coerced into taking part in research.

Certain general protections can help assure that these concerns are properly addressed. First, research in university and medical settings must be approved by an institutional review board (more generally referred to as an IRB) (Ceci, Peters, & Plotkin, 1985). These committees are made up of university faculty as well as people from the community, and their purpose is to see that the rights of the people who will participate in the research are protected. The committee structure allows people other than the researcher to look at the research and try to determine whether sufficient care is being taken to protect the welfare and dignity of the participants.

To safeguard those who participate in psychological research and to clarify the responsibilities of researchers, the American Psychological Association has published *Ethical Principles of Psychologists,* which includes general guidelines for conducting research (American Psychological Association, 1992). In addition to the issue of informed consent, these principles also place on the investigator responsibility for the research participants' welfare. In other words, it is ultimately the researcher who must ensure that the welfare of the people in the research is given priority over any other consideration, such as experimental design. People in the research must be *protected from both physical and psychological harm.* Psychological harm (as opposed to actual physical harm) is difficult to define but its definition remains the responsibility of the investigator. Researchers *must hold in confidence* all information obtained from research participants. Participants have the right to concealment of their identity on all data collected and reported, either in writing or informally. Whenever deception is thought to be essential to the conduct of research, the investigator must satisfy a committee of peers that this judgment is correct. If deception or concealment is used, *participants must be debriefed*—that is, told, in language they can understand, the true purpose of the study and why it was necessary to deceive them.

In addition to the APA guidelines, the Society for Research in Child Development (1990) has endorsed ethical guidelines for research that address some of the issues unique to conducting research with children. For example, not only do these guidelines call for confidentiality, protection from harm, and debriefing, but they also specify that informed consent is necessary from children's caretakers and from the children themselves if they are age 7 and older. These guidelines specify that the research must be explained to children in language they can understand so that they can decide whether they wish to participate.

There are many other ethical issues that extend beyond protection of the participants, including how researchers deal with errors in their research, fraud in science, and the proper way to give credit to others. "Doing a study" involves much more than selecting the most appropriate design. Researchers must be knowledgeable and aware of a host of concerns that involve the rights of the people in the research itself as well as concerns about their own conduct.

Summary

- The research process involves establishing a hypothesis that is then tested. In abnormal psychology, research focuses on hypotheses meant to explain the nature, the causes, or the treatment of a disorder.

- The individual case study is a research method that can be used to study one or more individuals in depth. Though case studies have an important role in the theoretical development of psychology, they are not subject to experimental control and must necessarily be suspect in terms of both internal and external validity.

- Research by correlation can tell us whether a relationship exists between two variables, but it does not tell us if that relationship is a causal one. Epidemiological research is a type of correlational research that reveals the incidence, distribution, and consequences of a particular problem in one or more populations.

- Research by experiment can follow one of two designs: group or single case. In either design, a variable (or variables) is manipulated and the effects are observed in order to determine the nature of a causal relationship.

- Genetic research focuses on the role genetics may play in our behavior. Four research strategies that are used to do this include family studies, adoption studies, twin studies, and genetic linkage analysis.

- Research strategies to examine psychopathology across time include cross-sectional and longitudinal designs. Both designs focus on differences in behavior or attitudes at different ages, but the former does so by looking at *different* individuals at different ages while the latter looks at the *same* individuals at different ages.

- The clinical picture, causal factors, and treatment process and outcome can all be influenced by cultural factors.

- The findings of a research program gain in credibility the more they are replicated.

- Research ethics are important to the research process, and ethical guidelines are spelled out by many professional organizations in an effort to ensure the well-being of research subjects.

Key terms

adoption studies (138)

analog model (122)

baseline (132)

case study method (125)

clinical significance (123)

cohort (141)

cohort effect (141)

comparative treatment research (130)

confound (122)

contributory condition (123)

control group (122)

correlation (126)

correlation coefficient (126)

cross-generational effect (142)

cross-sectional design (141)

dependent variable (120)

directionality (127)

double-blind control (130)

epidemiology (128)

experiment (129)

external validity (120)

family studies (138)

generalizability (122)

genetic linkage analysis (140)

genetic markers (140)

genotype (135)

human genome project (138)

hypothesis (120)

incidence (128)

independent variable (120)

informed consent (147)

internal validity (120)

level (132)

longitudinal design (141)

multiple baseline (134)

necessary condition (123)

negative correlation (127)

phenotype (135)

placebo control group (130)

placebo effect (130)

positive correlation (126)

prevalence (128)

proband (138)

randomization (122)

research design (120)

retrospective information (141)

sequential design (143)

single-case experimental design (131)

statistical significance (123)

sufficient condition (123)

testability (121)

treatment outcome (131)

trend (132)

twin studies (139)

variability (132)

withdrawal design (132)

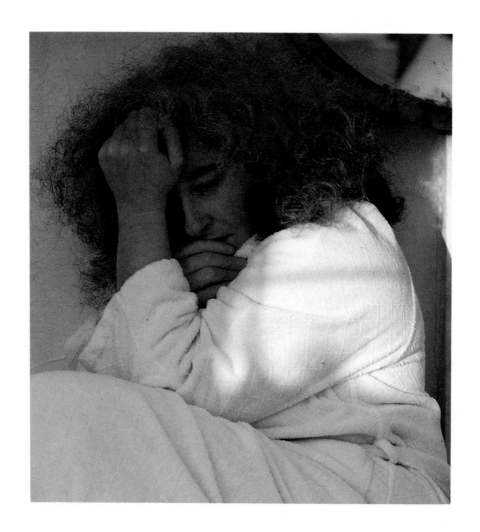

One thing is certain, that the problem of anxiety is a nodal point,
linking up all kinds of the most important questions; a riddle,
of which the solution must cast a flood of light upon our
whole mental life.

Sigmund Freud

The Standard Edition of the Complete
Psychological Works of Sigmund Freud

5

Anxiety Disorders

Anxiety is complex and mysterious, as suggested by Freud so many years ago. In some ways, the more we learn about it, the more baffling it seems. *Anxiety,* the term, designates a type of disorder in psychopathology, but it is much more than that. It is an emotion implicated so heavily across the full range of psychopathology that we begin the chapter by exploring its general nature, looking at both the biological and psychological processes associated with it. Following this, we consider the nature of *fear,* a somewhat different but clearly related emotion. Then we turn to the phenomenon of *panic* and suggest that it is really the basic emotion of fear occurring, perhaps, at an inappropriate time. With these important constructs clearly in mind, we turn to our chapter focus, an in-depth examination of each of the specific anxiety disorders.

Anxiety, Fear, and Panic

Anxiety

Have you ever experienced anxiety? A silly question, you might say, since most of us experience anxiety almost every day of our lives. Did you have a test in school today for which you weren't "perfectly" prepared? Did you have a date last weekend with somebody new and were you a little bit nervous about the impression you would make? And how about that job interview coming up? Even *thinking* about that might make you nervous. But have you ever stopped to think about the nature of your anxiety? What is it? What causes it?

Anxiety is a mood state characterized by marked negative affect and somatic symptoms of tension in which a person apprehensively anticipates future danger or misfortune (Barlow, 1988). This is also the DSM-IV definition (American Psychiatric Association, 1994). But it is important to note that anxiety is *very* hard to study. Anxiety in humans could refer to a subjective sense of unease, a set of behaviors (for example, looking worried and anxious, fidgeting), or a physiological response originating in the brain as reflected in elevated heart rate and muscle tension. Because anxiety is difficult to study in humans, much of the research on it has been carried out with animals. For example, we might teach laboratory rats that a light signals an impending shock. The animals certainly look and act "anxious" when the light comes on. They may fidget, tremble, and perhaps cower in a corner. Then, we might administer an anxiety-reducing drug to the animals and notice a reduction in their anxious behavior in the presence of the light. But is this experience the same as human anxiety? We don't know for sure, since research with animals may provide only general hints about the nature of anxiety in humans. For all these reasons, anxiety remains a mystery and we are only beginning our journey of discovery.

Anxiety is not very pleasant, so why do we have to experience it almost every time we do something important? A surprising answer is that anxiety is good for us, at least in moderate amounts. Psychologists have known for almost 90 years that you did better on that test the other day because you were a little bit anxious. You would not have done as well if you had had no anxiety at all. You were a little more charming and lively on that date last weekend because you were anxious. And you will be better prepared for that job interview coming up if you are anxious. This is because our physical and intellectual performance is driven and enhanced by the experience of anxiety. In 1908, Yerkes and Dodson demonstrated that this was true with laboratory animals, who performed somewhat better on a simple task if they were made "moderately anxious" by being threatened with mild levels of shock than if they were experiencing no anxiety at all. In fact, without anxiety very few of us would get much done.

The fundamental purpose of anxiety seems to be to help us plan for the future, taking into consideration everything that might go wrong so that we will be prepared for it. For this reason, the well-known early psychologist Howard Liddell (1949) called anxiety the "shadow of intelligence." He thought that the ability of the human race to plan in some detail for the future was connected to the experience of anxiety—specifically that gnawing feeling that things could go wrong and we had better be prepared for them. This is why anxiety is a future-oriented mood state. If you were to put this mood into words you might say, "Something might go wrong during that test/date/interview, and I'm not sure I can deal with it, but I've got to be ready to try." "Maybe I'd better study a little harder or do a little more research on that company before the interview."

But what happens when you have too much anxiety? With too much, you might actually fail the exam because you can't concentrate on the questions. All you can think about when you're too anxious is how terrible it would be if you failed. You might blow the interview for the same reason. On that date with a new person, you might spend the evening with perspiration running off your face, a sick feeling in your stomach, and the inability to think of even one reasonably interesting thing to say. As so often in life, too much of a good thing can be harmful, and there are very few things in life that can be more harmful than severe anxiety that is out of control.

What makes this situation even worse is that severe anxiety usually doesn't go away—that is, we don't seem to learn that there is really nothing to be anxious about. This unfortunate state of affairs has been called the neurotic paradox by Mowrer (1950), who said:

> [It is] the absolutely central problem in neurosis [an early name for anxiety-related states] and therapy. Most simply formulated, it is a paradox—the paradox of behavior which is at one and the same time self-perpetuating and self-defeating! . . . Common sense holds that a normal, sensible man, or even a beast to the limits of his intelligence, will weigh and balance the consequences of his acts: if the net effect is favorable, the action producing it will be perpetuated; and if the net effect is unfavorable, the action producing it will be inhibited, abandoned. In neurosis, however, one sees actions which have predominantly unfavorable consequences; yet they persist over a period of months, years, or a lifetime (p. 486).

We see examples of this irrationality all the time. John Madden, the well-known American sports announcer and former professional football coach, has written about his anxiety and used it as a source of humor in several television commercials. Despite his imposing size (6 feet 4 inches, 260 pounds), Madden has had to overcome the stigma, embarrassment, and effect of his anxiety on his everyday life, but he hasn't overcome the anxiety itself. Madden, who must announce a game in New York one Sunday and in Los Angeles the next Sunday, cannot fly across the country. For a long time he took trains to get around the country, but now he travels on a well-equipped bus that he purchased. He suffers from a phobia called *claustrophobia* (which we will discuss in this chapter). Madden and countless millions of other individuals suffering from anxiety-based disorders are well aware that there is little to be afraid of in the situations they find so difficult. In Mowrer's terms, Madden should have long since weighed the consequences of his acts and decided that, since flying is the safest way to travel, it would be in his best interest to fly in order to save himself time and help maintain his lucrative career. And yet he cannot abandon his self-defeating behavior. All the disorders discussed in this chapter are characterized by excessive anxiety, but this takes many different forms and is complicated further by the occurrence of panic attacks, as we will see shortly.

Fear

In Chapter 2 we discussed the emotion of **fear** as an immediate alarm reaction to present danger or life-threatening emergencies. This alarm reaction is called our "fight or flight" response because the massive response of our autonomic nervous system (increased heart rate, blood pressure, etc.) along with our subjec-

People with specific phobias often go to great lengths to avoid the feared object or situation. John Madden regularly travels across the country by bus because he is afraid of flying.

tive sense of terror motivates us to escape (flee) the danger quickly or, possibly, to attack (fight) a predator. This emergency response is one of our defensive reactions.

Emotion theorists commonly call this *emergency* or *defensive reaction* fear. Although not all emotion theorists agree, there is much evidence that this fear reaction differs both psychologically and biologically from anxiety. Anxiety, as noted above, is a future-oriented mood-state characterized by feelings that one cannot predict or control upcoming events. Fear, on the other hand, is a present-oriented emotional reaction to current danger characterized by strong escapist action tendencies and, most often, a surge in the sympathetic branch of the autonomic nervous system (Barlow, Brown, & Craske, in press). If someone experiencing fear put his feelings into words, he might say, "I've got to get out of here right now or I may not make it."

Fear and Panic

What happens if you experience the alarm response of fear when there is nothing to be afraid of—in other words, you have a false alarm? Consider the following example from the case of Gretchen, who appeared at one of our clinics.

I was 25 when I had my first attack. It was a few weeks after I'd come home from the hospital. I had had my appendix out. The surgery had gone

well, and I wasn't in any danger, which is why I don't understand what happened. But one night I went to sleep and I woke up a few hours later—I'm not sure how long—but I woke up with this vague feeling of apprehension. Mostly I remember how my heart started pounding. And my chest hurt; it felt like I was dying—that I was having a heart attack. And I felt kind of queer, as if I were detached from the experience. It seemed like my bedroom was covered with a haze. I ran to my sister's room, but I felt like I was a puppet or a robot who was under the control of somebody else while I was running. I think I scared her almost as much as I was frightened myself. She called an ambulance (Barlow, 1988).

Gretchen had experienced one type of panic attack.

The roots of the panic experience are deeply embedded in our cultural myths. The Greek god Pan, the god of nature, dwelled in the countryside presiding over rivers, woods, streams, and the various grazing animals. But Pan did not look like the typical god. He was very ugly and short, with legs resembling those of a goat. Unfortunately for those ancient Greeks who had to travel through the countryside, Pan had a habit of napping in a small cave or thicket near the road. If the traveling Greeks disturbed him, he would let out a bloodcurdling scream that was said to make one's hair stand on end. This scream was so overwhelmingly intense that many terrified travelers died when they heard it—frightened to death. This sudden overwhelming terror or fright came to be known as **panic.**

The term *panic* comes from the Greek god Pan, who terrified people with a bloodcurdling scream, sometimes scaring them to death.

Moving from myth to psychopathology, a **panic attack** is defined as an abrupt experience of intense fear or discomfort accompanied by a number of physical symptoms, most usually heart palpitations, chest pain, sensations of shortness of breath, and possibly dizzy feelings. The DSM-IV criteria for panic attack are presented in Table 5.1.

Three basic types of panic attacks have been identified. Some occur only in situations where you fully expect you are going to have them, even though, like John Madden, you know there is nothing to be afraid of. If you are afraid of high places or driving over long bridges to the point of having a phobia of these situations, then you might fully expect to have a panic attack in these situations, but not anywhere else. This attack would be an example of a *cued* or *situationally bound* panic attack. On the other hand, you might never know when you were going to have one of these attacks. This type of attack is described as an *unexpected* (*uncued*) panic attack. When experiencing one of these attacks, some individuals think (make the attribution) that they are dying, or going

crazy, as did Gretchen. A third type of panic attack, called *situationally predisposed*, is in between. For example, if you were in a large mall where it was *more likely* that you would have an attack because you had had one there before, but you didn't know whether it would happen today, the attack would be a situationally predisposed panic attack. The last two types—unexpected and situationally predisposed—play an important role in one of the anxiety disorders we will discuss: panic disorder. The first type, situationally bound, is more common in specific phobia or social phobia.

Think back now to the description of the emotion of fear. Remember that fear is an intense alarm accompanied by a surge in the autonomic nervous system that motivates us to flee or escape danger. Does Gretchen's panic attack sound like it could be the emotion of fear? A variety of evidence suggests that it is (Barlow, 1988, 1991), including similarities in reports of the experience of fear and panic, similar behavioral tendencies to escape, and similar underlying neurobiological processes.

"First time it happened to me, I was driving down the highway, and I had a kind of a knot in my chest. I felt like I had swallowed something and it got stuck, and it lasted pretty much overnight . . . I felt like I was having a heart attack . . . I assumed that's what was happening. I felt very panicky. A flushed feeling came over my whole body. I felt as though I was going to pass out . . ."

Recently we were able to record a panic attack in one of our clinics during a physiological assessment of a patient suffering from panic attacks. It occurred quite unexpectedly. The recordings capturing the physiological surge are shown in Figure 5.1. Notice the sudden doubling of heart rate from minute 11 through minute 13, accompanied by increases in muscle tension (frontalis EMG) and finger temperature. This massive autonomic surge had peaked and was on its way down within three minutes. The figure illustrates that fear and panic are very sudden experiences, as they must be if they are to mobilize us for instantaneous reaction to impending danger.

What Causes Anxiety and Panic?

You learned in Chapters 1 and 2 that there is no simple one-dimensional cause of excessive emotional reactions such as anxiety or panic. Causes come from multiple sources.

Genetic Contributions to Anxiety and Panic

Considering anxiety first, there is increasingly strong evidence that we inherit a tendency to be tense or uptight. We talked in Chapter 4 about how genetic investigators can breed dogs to be highly emotional. This emotionality seems very much like human anxi-

Table 5.1 Diagnostic Criteria for Panic Attack

The predominant complaint is a discrete period of intense fear or discomfort, in which at least four (or more) of the following symptoms developed abruptly and reached a peak within 10 minutes:

1. Palpitations, pounding heart, or accelerated heart rate
2. Sweating
3. Trembling or shaking
4. Sensations of shortness of breath or smothering
5. Feeling of choking
6. Chest pain or discomfort
7. Nausea or abdominal distress
8. Feeling dizzy, unsteady, lightheaded, or faint
9. Derealization (feelings of unreality) or depersonalization (being detached from oneself)
10. Fear of losing control or going crazy
11. Fear of dying
12. Paresthesias (numbness or tingling sensations)
13. Chills or hot flushes

Source: DSM-IV, APA, 1994.

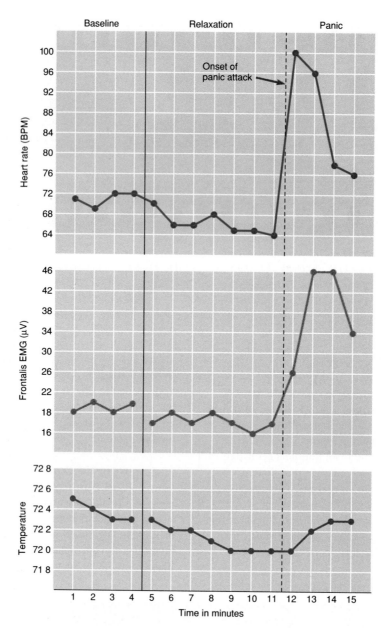

Figure 5.1 Physiological measurements during a panic attack (from Cohen, Barlow, & Blanchard, 1985)

ety, although as noted above, we can never draw any firm conclusions across species. The heritable component of emotionality has also been observed in humans through family studies and other methods (Eysenck, 1967; Lader & Wing, 1964; McGuffin & Reich, 1984). As with almost all psychological disorders, there does not seem to be any "single gene" that causes anxiety, unlike the ones that determine hair or eye color. Instead, there seem to be weak contributions from many genes, collectively making us vulnerable to anxiety. But a vulnerability is not anxiety itself. Rather, this genetic vulnerability sets the stage for us to become anxious if the right psychological and social factors line up.

Much as with anxiety, the tendency to panic seems to run in families and may have a genetic

component (Barlow, 1988). It is not clear whether the genetic contribution to panic is the same or different from the genetic contribution to anxiety; but similarly to the situation with anxiety, any genetic contribution to the experience of panic attacks, particularly when a person is under stress, would only create the condition for that person to experience panic rather than cause it directly.

Neurobiological Contributions to Anxiety and Panic

In the context of a genetic vulnerability, anxiety also seems to be associated with specific neurobiological processes (brain functions) that operate on specific related brain circuits. The neurotransmitter system most implicated in anxiety is the GABA-benzodiazepine system. Lower levels of this neurotransmitter are associated with higher levels of anxiety, although the relationship is not quite so direct. A variety of other neurotransmitter systems, including the noradrenergic and serotonergic systems, have also been implicated in anxiety. In fact, recent evidence from basic animal studies suggests that the serotonergic neurotransmitter system is particularly heavily involved in anxiety (Deakin & Graeff, 1991).

The area of the brain most often associated with anxiety is the limbic system (Gray, 1982; Gorman, Liebowitz, Fyer, & Stein, 1989). Remember that the limbic system acts as a "mediator" between the brain stem and the cortex. The more primitive brain stem monitors and senses changes in bodily functions. These potential danger signals are relayed to higher cortical processes through the limbic system. Jeffrey Gray, a prominent British neuropsychologist, has identified a brain circuit in the limbic system of animals that seems heavily involved in anxiety (Gray, 1982, 1985, in press). His research may have implications for the study of human anxiety. Specifically, Gray described a circuit leading from the septal and hippocampal area in the limbic system to the frontal cortex. The septal-hippocampal system is innervated by serotonergic circuits originating in the raphe nuclei and noradrenergic circuits originating in the locus ceruleus, both located in the brain stem. This brain system, which Gray calls the **behavioral inhibition system (BIS),** is activated by signs or signals of unexpected events arising from the brain stem, such as some major change in the functioning of our body that might signal danger. Danger signals also come down from the cortex to the septal-hippocampal system based on something we see that might be threatening. When the BIS is activated, by signals either arising from the brain stem or descending from the cortex, we tend to freeze (our behavior is inhibited), experience anxiety, and apprehensively evaluate the situation to see whether any danger is really present.

This brain circuit, the BIS, is distinct from a different circuit involved in panic (fear). Gray (1982, 1985) and Graeff (1987; Deakin & Graeff, 1991) have identified a brain circuit that Gray calls the **fight/flight system (FFS).** This circuit originates in the brain stem, perhaps in the raphe nucleus, and travels through several midbrain structures, including the amygdala, the ventromedial nucleus of the hypothalamus, and the central gray matter. When stimulated in animals, this circuit produces an immediate alarm and escape response that looks very much like panic in humans (Gray, 1991). Gray (1991) and Deaken and Graeff (1991) think this system is activated in part by deficiencies in serotonergic systems. Other theorists, such as Gorman et al. (1989), agree that brain circuits for

panic/fear begin in the brain stem and are primitive (alarms) but think that noradrenergic neurotransmitter pathways are more heavily involved. As Fowles (1992a, in press) points out, Gray's thinking is very close to a theory of anxiety and anxiety disorders proposed earlier (Barlow, 1988), although Gray emphasizes neurophysiological aspects of the two different types of experiences (anxiety and panic) while Barlow emphasizes clinical findings, among other differences.

Recently, findings have both confirmed and disconfirmed aspects of biological theories of the brain circuits involved in panic and anxiety described above (Nutt & Lawson, 1992; Gorman et al., 1990). For example, some of the evidence supporting the role of the limbic system in producing anxiety regarding future panic attacks was the result of brain imaging studies by Reiman et al. (1986) using PET scans (see Chapter 3). These researchers worked with two groups of patients: those who panicked during a test in which they were infused with lactate, a panic-provoking substance, and those who did not panic in response to lactate. Reiman and his associates discovered a difference between the two groups in patterns of blood flow in the limbic system. As noted in Chapter 3, increased blood flow is a sign of increased activity in that area of the brain known to be involved with anxiety. These findings attracted considerable attention from researchers in the late 1980s and early 1990s. However, a subsequent report by Drevets and colleagues indicated that the findings could be totally explained by the observation that patients were *clenching their teeth* very hard during the brain imaging procedures, which was causing different blood flow patterns (Drevets, Videen, MacLeod, Haller, & Raichle, 1992).

Brain imaging procedures will teach us much about psychopathology in years to come, but this is a good example of the blind alleys and false starts as well as the subsequent misleading results that occur any time we begin work with sophisticated new technology.

Psychological Contributions to Anxiety and Panic

A variety of theories exist on the nature of psychological causes of anxiety. We reviewed some of these theories in Chapter 2. For example, Freud saw anxiety as the psychic reaction to danger surrounding the reactivation of an infantile fear situation. Behaviorally oriented theorists view anxiety as a product of early classical conditioning or other forms of learning such as modeling (Bandura, 1986).

Evidence is accumulating (for example, Mineka, 1985a, 1985b; Barlow, 1988) to support an integrated model of psychological contributions to anxiety that involves a variety of factors. Basically, we may acquire in childhood a sense that events are not always in our control. This perception may range on a

Sue Mineka has developed important scientific evidence on psychological contributions to anxiety disorders.

continuum from feeling totally confident and in control in all aspects of our lives to feeling very uncertain about ourselves and having little confidence that we can deal with the upcoming events in our lives. The perception is most evident as a set of danger-laden beliefs. If you are anxious about schoolwork, you may think you're going to do poorly on the next exam and there is no way you can pass the course, even though all your grades up until now have been A's and B's. A general "sense of controllability" may be something we absorb early as a function of our upbringing and other environmental factors. It seems to be the primary psychological factor that makes us vulnerable to experiencing anxiety in later life when the right "trigger" occurs.

Most psychological accounts of the origins of panic attacks, on the other hand, invoke *conditioning* and *cognitive* explanations that are difficult to separate out. Thus, a strong fear response initially occurs during a period of extreme stress or perhaps as a result of some realistically dangerous situation in the environment (a true alarm). This emotional response then becomes *associated* with a variety of external and internal cues. In other words, these internal and external cues tend to provoke the fear response, along with cognitions or expectancies of danger, whether danger is present or not (Razran, 1961; Martin, 1983; Mineka, 1985a). Examples of external cues would be places or situations similar to the one where the initial panic attack occurred. Examples of internal cues would be increases in heart rate or respiration that were associated with the initial panic attack, even if these increases are due to perfectly normal circumstances, such as exercise. (Thus, if your heart is beating fast you are more likely to think of and, perhaps, experience a panic attack than if your heart is not beating fast.)

Social Contributions to Anxiety and Panic

The trigger that activates our biological and psychological vulnerabilities to experience anxiety seems to be stressful life events. Most of these are interpersonal in nature—marriage, divorce, difficulties with the boss at work, death of a loved one, and so on. Some might be physical such as an injury or illness. Social pressures to succeed at a given task, such as to achieve straight A's in all your courses, might also provide sufficient stress to trigger anxiety.

The same stressors seem capable of independently triggering physical reactions such as headaches or hypertension or more emotional reactions such as panic attacks (Barlow, 1988). The particular type of reaction we experience while under stress also seems to run in families. If you get headaches under stress, chances are other people in your family also get headaches. If you get panic attacks when stressed, that is probably the way at least some other members of your family react to stress (this finding also suggests a possible genetic contribution to panic). In some individuals, anxiety and panic occur together, which makes the development of an anxiety disorder more likely.

An Integrated Model of Anxiety and Panic

Putting these contributions together, we can see that you might inherit a tendency to be uptight or high strung. This would be a *biological vulnerability* to experience anxiety but would not be anxiety itself. You might also grow up with a sense that the world is not always a controllable place and that you might not be able to deal with things that go wrong. If this is a strong sense or perception, you have a *psychological vulnerability* to be anxious. Finally, you might have a lot of actual stress in your life, particularly from interpersonal stressors. A given stressor would then activate your biological tendencies to become very aroused as well as your psychological tendencies to feel that you might not be able to deal with the situation and control the stress. Once this anxiety starts, it tends to feed on itself so that it might not stop even if the particular life stressor has long since passed.

Anxiety can be very general. That is, you may focus your anxiety on many aspects of your life. But anxiety is more usually focused on one area, such as grades (if you're in college). It is this "focus" of anxiety, when it becomes severe, that determines the nature of a particular anxiety disorder.

Panic attacks or false alarms, on the other hand, also seem to be a characteristic response to stress that runs in families and may have a genetic component. These attacks in and of themselves are brief and relatively harmless but can become associated, through psychological processes, with any number of internal or external cues or situations that may then contribute to the formation of an anxiety disorder. Because an individual learns an association between the attack and internal or external cues (conditioning is one form of learning), the attacks are called *learned alarms*. Even if you have a realistic fear response to some dangerous situation (true alarm), your fear reaction can become associated with a variety of cues that may then trigger the attack in the future *in the absence* of any danger, making it a learned alarm also. Furthermore, anxiety and panic are closely related (Barlow, 1988) in that being anxious increases a person's likelihood of experiencing a panic attack. This relationship makes sense from an ethological point of view since sensing possible future threat or danger (anxiety) should prepare us to react instantaneously with an alarm response if the danger becomes imminent. Anxiety and panic need not occur together, but it makes sense that they often do.

Having briefly reviewed the nature of anxiety and panic we can now examine the anxiety disorders and the different relationships and roles of anxiety and panic in each of the disorders. We will begin with what some have called the "basic" anxiety disorder.

Generalized Anxiety Disorder

Clinical Description of Generalized Anxiety Disorder

Is somebody in your family a worrywart? Is somebody in your family perfectionistic? Perhaps it is you! As with many features found among the anxiety disorders, these are common traits. Most of us worry to some extent. We mentioned in the beginning of the chapter that worry has a very useful function. The process of worry helps us plan for the future, make sure that we're prepared for that test, or double check that we've thought of everything before we head home for the holidays. The worry process itself is not pleasant, but without it nothing would go very smoothly. But what if you worry about everything and earn the title "worrywart" from your family and friends? Furthermore, what if your worry is unproductive: No matter how much you worry, you can't seem to decide what to do about some upcoming problems or situations. And what if you *can't stop* worrying, even if you know the worrying is doing you no good and probably making everyone else around you miserable? It is these features that characterize the disorder we call **generalized anxiety disorder (GAD).** Consider the following case.

The Case of Irene

Irene was a 20-year-old college student, moderately attractive, with a very engaging personality but not many friends. She came to one of our clinics complaining of excessive anxiety and general difficulties in controlling her life. *Everything* was a catastrophe for Irene. Although she carried a 3.7 grade point average she was convinced that she was going to flunk every test she took. As a result of this belief, she would repeatedly threaten to drop courses after only several weeks of classes for fear that she would not be able to understand the material.

Her worrying caused her to drop out of the first college she attended after one month. She felt depressed for a while over her failure, then decided to take a couple of courses at a local junior college, believing she could handle the work there better than in the college she first attended. After achieving straight A's at the junior college for 2 years, she enrolled once again in a 4-year college as a junior. After a short time she began calling the clinic in a state of extreme agitation saying that she felt she had to drop this or that course because she couldn't handle it. With great difficulty her therapist and parents persuaded her to stay in the courses and also to seek further help. In any course Irene completed, she earned an A or, at worst, a B+. But she still worried with every upcoming test and every paper due that she would fall apart and be unable to understand and complete the work.

Irene did not devote all her attention to school. She was also concerned about relationships with her friends as well as a new boyfriend she had met. Every time she was with her boyfriend, she was afraid she was going to make a fool of herself and somehow turn him off. In fact, after each date she reported that the date went extremely well and that she had a good time, but she knew the next one would probably be a "disaster." As the relationship progressed to the point that some sexual contact seemed natural, she was worried sick that her inexperience would show through and that her boyfriend would consider her naive and stupid. Nevertheless, she reported enjoying the very beginnings of sexual contact and that he seemed to enjoy it also, but she was convinced that the next time they tried it some catastrophe would happen.

Irene was also concerned about her health. A routine physical checkup revealed that she had minor hypertension, probably associated with being somewhat overweight. She then attempted to greatly restrict her eating. She approached every meal as if death itself might result if she ate the wrong types or amounts of food. She became reluctant to check her blood pressure for fear that it would be very high. She was also reluctant to weigh herself for fear that she was not losing weight, something the doctor had suggested would be helpful. She began restricting her eating. As a result, she developed an occasional episode of binge eating, although these episodes were not frequent enough to warrant concern in their own right.

But these were only the beginnings of Irene's concerns. She also worried about her religion (was she religious enough, was she going to church often enough, was she doing the right thing?) and her relationships with her family, particularly her mother and her sister. Irene also had an occasional panic attack, but this was not a major issue to her. As soon as it passed she began focusing on the next possible catastrophe. In addition to high blood pressure, Irene complained of tension headaches and a "nervous stomach" with a lot of gas, occasional diarrhea, and some abdominal pain.

For Irene, life was nothing more than a series of impending catastrophes. No sooner would she survive one (and not only survive but usually excel in her performance) but another would loom large on the horizon. Her mother reported to us that she dreaded receiving a phone call from Irene, let alone a visit, because she knew there would be a crisis and that she would have to reassure her daughter and attempt to help her generate possible solutions. For the same rea-sons, Irene had very few friends. Even so, when she could leave her catastrophes aside for a period of time, she was really fun to be with.

Irene was suffering from generalized anxiety disorder. In many ways GAD is the "basic" anxiety disorder because every anxiety disorder considered in this chapter is characterized by intense generalized anxiety (Brown, Barlow, & Liebowitz, in press). Other anxiety disorders are complicated by panic attacks or other features that become the *focus* of the anxiety. In GAD the focus is more "generalized" on the events of everyday life. For that reason we are considering GAD first.

The DSM-IV criteria for generalized anxiety disorder are presented in Table 5.2. They specify that excessive anxiety and worry (apprehensive expectation) must be ongoing more days than not for at least 6 months. Furthermore, the individual must find it very difficult to turn off or control the worry process. This criterion is what distinguishes a pathological worry process from the normal kind of worrying that all of us do from time to time as we get ready for some upcoming event or challenge. Most of us will worry for a time, but we can set the problem aside to go on to another task. Even if the upcoming challenge is a big one, as soon as it is over the worry process will stop. For Irene, on the other hand, it would never stop. She would turn to the next crisis as soon as the last one was over.

Table 5.2   Diagnostic Criteria for Generalized Anxiety Disorder

A. Excessive anxiety and worry (apprehensive expectation), occurring more days than not for at least 6 months, about a number of events or activities (such as work or school performance).

B. The person finds it difficult to control the worry.

C. The anxiety and worry are associated with at least three (or more) of the following six symptoms (with at least some symptoms present for more days than not for the past 6 months) (*note:* only one item is required in children):

   1. Restlessness or feeling keyed up or on edge
   2. Being easily fatigued
   3. Difficulty concentrating or mind going blank
   4. Irritability
   5. Muscle tension
   6. Sleep disturbance (difficulty falling or staying asleep, or restless unsatisfying sleep)

D. The focus of the anxiety and worry is not confined to features of an Axis I disorder, that is, the anxiety or worry is not about having a panic attack (as in panic disorder), being embarrassed in public (as in social phobia), being contaminated (as in obsessive-compulsive disorder), being away from home or close relatives (as in separation anxiety disorder), gaining weight (as in anorexia nervosa), or having a serious illness (as in hypochondriasis), and is not part of posttraumatic stress disorder.

E. The anxiety, worry, or physical symptoms cause clinically significant distress or impairment in social, occupational, or other important areas of functioning.

F. Not due to the direct effects of a substance (e.g., drugs of abuse, medication) or a general medical condition (e.g., hyperthyroidism), and does not occur exclusively during a mood disorder, psychotic disorder, or a pervasive developmental disorder.

Source: DSM-IV, APA, 1994.

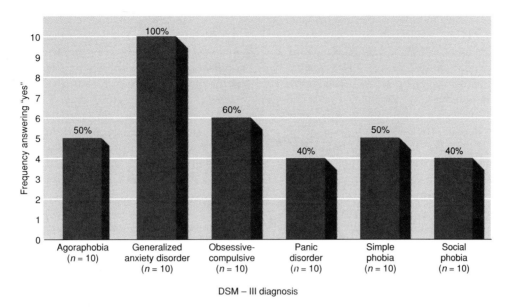

Figure 5.2 Clients' answers to interviewer's question, "Do you worry excessively about minor things?" (from Sanderson & Barlow, 1986, November)

The physical symptoms associated with generalized anxiety and GAD are somewhat different from those associated with panic attacks and panic disorder (covered shortly). Rather than autonomic arousal, presumably as a result of a sympathetic nervous system surge (for instance, heart rate increases and palpitations, perspiration, trembling, and so on), GAD is characterized by symptoms of muscle tension and agitation. This tension and "being on edge" is also associated with tiring easily, probably due to chronic excessive muscle tension, and some irritability and difficulty sleeping. Focusing attention on the task at hand becomes difficult as one's mind quickly switches from crisis to crisis.

What are the typical things that people with GAD worry about? They worry about minor, everyday life events for the most part. In fact, this characteristic distinguishes GAD from other anxiety disorders we will consider in this chapter. When asked, "Do you worry excessively about minor things?" 100% of individuals with GAD respond yes compared to approximately 50% of individuals with other anxiety disorder categories, as displayed in Figure 5.2. This difference is statistically significant. Of course, if major events come along, they quickly become the focus of anxiety and worry, too. Adults typically focus on possible misfortune to their children, family health, job responsibilities, or more minor things such as household chores or being on time for appointments. Children with GAD most often worry about academic, athletic, or social performance.

Statistics and Course for Generalized Anxiety Disorder

Although worry and physical tension are very common experiences for all of us, the kind of severe generalized

anxiety experienced by Irene is much more rare. Approximately 4% of the population would meet criteria for GAD during a given 6-month period (Blazer, Hughes, George, Swartz, & Boyer, 1991; Kessler et al., in press). This is still quite a large number, making GAD one of the most common anxiety disorders in the population, second only to specific and social phobia and, perhaps, panic disorder with agoraphobia. However, relatively few individuals with GAD seem to come for treatment compared to patients with panic disorder. Specialty anxiety clinics, such as ours in Albany, report that only approximately 10% of their patients meet criteria for GAD compared to between 30% to 50% for panic disorder.

In our clinic and in other anxiety disorder clinics, between 55% and 65% of individuals with GAD are female (Borkovec & Mathews, 1988; Sanderson, DiNardo, Rapee, & Barlow, 1990; DiNardo, 1991; Brown, Barlow, & Liebowitz, 1994). In epidemiological studies, which include people who do not necessarily seek out treatment, the sex ratio is approximately 67% female (Blazer, George, & Hughes, 1991).

Some people with GAD report an onset in early adulthood, usually in response to a life stress. Nevertheless, the majority of studies find that GAD is associated with an earlier and more gradual onset than most other anxiety disorders (Anderson, Noyes, & Crowe, 1984; Barlow, 1988; Sanderson & Barlow, 1990; Brown et al., 1994). Much like Irene, many of these people report feeling anxious and tense all their lives.

Anxiety in its various forms is very prevalent in the elderly. Himmelfarb and Murrell (1984) found that 17% of elderly men and 21.5% of elderly women surveyed in a community sample were found to have sufficiently severe anxiety symptoms to warrant treatment, although it is not clear that all of these individuals met criteria for GAD. We also know that the use of minor tranquilizers in the elderly is very high, ranging from 17% to 50% in one study (Salzman, 1991). It is not entirely clear why drugs are being prescribed with this frequency for the elderly. One possibility is that the drugs may not be entirely for anxiety. Prescriptions may be primarily for sleeping problems or other secondary effects of medical illnesses. In any case, benzodiazepines put the elderly at greater risks for falling down and breaking bones, particularly their hips. Major difficulties hampering investigation of anxiety in the elderly are the lack of good assessment instruments or treatment studies (Hersen & Van Hasselt, 1992; Hersen, Van Hasselt, & Goreczny, 1993), due in large part to what has been a lack of sufficient research interest in our elderly population (Sheikh, 1992).

Considering the studies reported by Judith Rodin and her colleagues, described in Chapter 2, it is possible that the elderly are particularly susceptible to developing anxiety over failing health or other life situations that begin to strip them of whatever remaining control they have over events in their lives. Their increasing lack of control of their lives, their failing health, and the gradual loss of meaningful functions may be a particularly unfortunate by-product of the way the elderly are treated in Western culture. If it were possible to reverse these trends, we might well reduce the frequent occurrence of anxiety as well as depression and early death in our elderly citizens.

Causes of Generalized Anxiety Disorder

What causes GAD? We have learned a great deal in the past several years. As with most anxiety disorders, there may be a genetic contribution to GAD. This conclusion is based on studies showing that GAD tends to run in families (Noyes, Clarkson, Crowe, Yates, & McChesney, 1987; Noyes et al., 1992). An important twin study has strengthened this suggestion. Kendler, Neale, Kessler, Heath, and Eaves (1992a) found that the risk of GAD was somewhat greater in monozygotic (identical) female twins than in dizygotic female twins when one twin already had GAD. However, these findings are only tentative (Swinson & Cox, 1993). For example, Kendler et al. (1992a) required a duration for GAD of only 1 month as specified in DSM-III instead of 6 months as required in DSM-III-R and DSM-IV. Other twin studies (for example, Torgersen, 1983) have not found a strong heritable factor in GAD. As noted at the beginning of this chapter, investigations of anxiety as a human trait show a clear heritable factor, and there is every reason to think that, when all the appropriate studies are done, GAD will be at least as strongly heritable as is the trait of anxiety (Barlow, 1988).

For a long time generalized anxiety disorder has posed a real puzzle to investigators. Although the definition of the disorder itself is relatively new, originating in 1980 with DSM-III, clinicians and psychopathologists were working with people with generalized anxiety long before diagnostic systems were developed. For years, clinicians thought that people who were generally anxious had simply not "focused" their anxiety on anything. Thus, their anxiety was described as "free floating." But now scientists have looked more closely and have discovered some very interesting differences.

The first hints of this difference were found in the physiological responsivity of individuals with GAD. Most people with anxiety disorders, and in particular those with panic disorder, evidence strong sympathetic arousal. That is, their bodies are aroused, their hearts beat fast, their blood is flowing rapidly, and they are ready for any threat or challenge. It is interesting that individuals with GAD do not show these characteristics as strongly as individuals with other anxiety disorders in which panic might play a more prominent role. In fact, several studies (Hoehn-Saric, McLeod, & Zimmerli, 1989; Borkovec & Hu, 1990) have found that individuals with GAD show *less responsiveness* on most physiological measures, such as heart rate, blood pressure, skin conductance, and respiration rate (Hoehn-Saric & Masek, 1981; Hoehn-Saric et al., 1989), than do individuals with other anxiety disorders. For this reason people with GAD have been called *autonomic restrictors*.

When individuals with GAD are compared to nonanxious normal subjects, the one physiological measure that consistently distinguishes the anxious group is muscle tension (Marten et al., in press). People with GAD are chronically tense. What could account for this? To understand this phenomenon we may have to know what's going on in the minds of people with GAD. With the new methods from cognitive science, we are now beginning to uncover the sometimes unconscious mental processes ongoing in GAD.

The evidence indicates that individuals with GAD are highly sensitive to threat in general, particularly if that threat has some personal relevance. If so, they will notice this threat much more quickly than other people. That is, they will allocate their attention much more readily to sources of threat than will people who are not anxious (Butler & Mathews, 1983; MacLeod, Mathews, & Tata, 1986; Mogg, Mathews, & Weinman, 1989). Furthermore, this tendency to be acutely aware of potential threat, particularly if it is personal, seems to be entirely automatic or *unconscious*. Using the Stroop color-naming task described in Chapter 2, MacLeod and Mathews (1991) presented threatening words on a screen for only *20 milliseconds* and *still* found that individuals with GAD were slower to name the colors of the words than were nonanxious individuals. Remember that in this task the words are presented very briefly in colored letters and subjects are asked to name the *color* rather than the *word*. The fact that the colors of threatening words were named more slowly suggests that the *words* were more relevant to people with GAD and interfered with their task of naming the color—even though the words *were not presented long enough* for the individuals to be conscious of them! Investigators using other paradigms have come to similar conclusions (Eysenck, 1992; Mathews, Richards, & Eysenck, 1989).

How do these mental processes link up with the tendency of individuals with GAD to be "autonomic restrictors"? Tom Borkovec and his colleagues have suggested some possible reasons. These researchers noticed that, although the peripheral autonomic arousal of individuals with GAD is restricted, the evidence showed marked *increases* in EEG beta activity, reflecting intense cognitive processing in the frontal lobes of their brains, particularly the left hemisphere. This finding suggests to Borkovec and Inz (1990) that people with GAD are engaging in frantic, intense thought processes or worry *without* accompanying images (which would be reflected by activity in the right hemisphere of the brain). Borkovec suggests that this process of worry may be exactly what is causing these individuals to be autonomic restrictors (Borkovec, Shadick, & Hopkins, 1991; Borkovec & Hu, 1990). That is, they are so busy thinking hard about the variety of problems upcoming that they don't have the attentional capacity left for the all-important process of *creating images* of the potential threat, images that would elicit more substantial negative affect and autonomic activity. In other words, they *avoid* all the negative affect associated with their threat words. But we know, from the point of view of therapy, that it is very important to "process" the images and negative affect associated with anxiety (Craske & Barlow, 1988). Since people with GAD do not seem to engage in this process, they may avoid much of the unpleasantness and pain associated with the negative affect and imagery, but they are never able to "work through" the problems that they face and arrive at solutions. Therefore they become *chronic worriers,* with accompanying autonomic inflexibility and quite severe muscle tension.

Thus, intense worrying for an individual with GAD may serve the same (maladaptive) purpose as avoidance does for people with phobias. It just puts off the process of facing the feared or anxiety-related situation so that his or her adaptive processes are never allowed to take over and deal effectively with it. This model is very current as it combines findings from cognitive science with accompanying biological data from both the central and peripheral nervous systems. Time will tell if the model is correct. In any case, it is

Tom Borkovec and his colleagues have presented a new theory of generalized anxiety disorder that suggests that individuals with this disorder engage in excessive worry in order to avoid images of deep-seated emotional threat. Borkovec has also developed some effective new psychosocial treatments for generalized anxiety disorder.

consistent with our view of anxiety as a future-oriented mood-state focusing on potential danger or threat as opposed to an emergency or alarm reaction to present danger. A model of generalized anxiety disorder is presented in Figure 5.3.

Treatment of Generalized Anxiety Disorder

There was a time in the 1970s when minor tranquilizers (benzodiazepines) were the most widely prescribed drugs in the United States (Solomon & Hart, 1978). In 1978 Greenblatt and Shader estimated that between 10% and 20% of adults in the Western world used prescription drugs, mostly benzodiazepines, on a regular basis for anxiety and tension. Obviously, given the enormous numbers of people involved, the majority of these people were not suffering from what we would now call GAD. But the impression remained that benzodiazepines were the treatment of choice for GAD. Based on the evidence we have, this seems to be a mistaken impression. Solomon and Hart, in 1978, reviewed 78 double-blind studies and concluded that although some rather small effects were present in some studies, the benzodiazepines were not demonstrated to be clinically more effective than placebo for the treatment of GAD. Any number of studies have been conducted since then and these conclusions have not changed (Barlow, 1988).

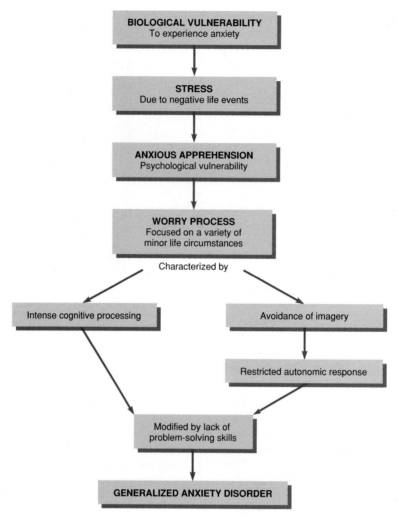

Figure 5.3 An integrative model of generalized anxiety disorder

At the present time most clinical investigators think these drugs may have some beneficial but relatively small effects in reducing anxiety over the short term (4 to 8 weeks), compared to placebo, but not over the long term. Furthermore, the benzodiazepines carry some risks. First, the benzodiazepines seem to create some problems with both cognitive and motor functioning (for instance, Petursson & Lader, 1981; Tyrer & Owen, 1984; O'Hanlon, Haak, Blaauw, & Riemersma, 1982; Hindmarch, 1986, 1990). Specifically, people don't seem to be as "alert" cognitively on the job or at school when they are taking the benzodiazepines. These drugs may impair a person's performance somewhat while he or she is driving, and they seem to be associated with a greater number of falls resulting in hip fractures in the elderly (Ray, Gurwitz, Decker, & Kennedy, 1992).

More important, benzodiazepines seem to produce both a psychological and physical dependence, making it very difficult for people to stop taking them (Rickels, Schweizer, Case, & Greenblatt, 1990;

Schweizer, Rickels, Case, & Greenblatt, 1990; Noyes, Garvey, Cook, & Suelzer, 1991). There is reasonably wide agreement that the optimal use of benzodiazepines is for the short-term relief of anxiety that may be associated with a temporary crisis or stressful event such as a family crisis. Under these circumstances a physician may prescribe a benzodiazepine until the crisis is resolved, but no more than several days or a week or two.

At the present, psychological treatments are not much better than treatment with benzodiazepines. You would think that by now we would have a successful psychotherapeutic treatment, considering the prevalence of this problem; however, one difficulty keeps occurring. Most treatments that we develop have some beneficial effect for a short time, but, until recently, few treatment approaches have proven to be more powerful than a "placebo" psychotherapy in which someone will simply talk to patients and reassure them without actively addressing her anxiety. As we learn more about generalized anxiety, we may find that helping people with this disorder to really focus on what is threatening to them in their lives will be useful. Specifically, since we now know that individuals with GAD seem to avoid "feelings" of anxiety and the negative affect associated with images, clinicians have designed treatments to help these people process the information at an emotional level, using images, so that they will experience anxious feelings. Recently, Borkovec and his colleagues constructed such a treatment and found it to be significantly better than a "placebo" psychological treatment, not only at posttreatment but at a 1-year follow-up (Borkovec & Costello, 1993). This may be the beginning of a new generation of effective psychological treatments for anxiety. In our clinic we have developed a cognitive behavioral treatment for GAD that attacks the worry process directly. Patients bring on the worry process during therapy sessions and confront anxiety-provoking images and worrisome thoughts head-on. With cognitive therapy and other coping techniques, the patient begins to counteract and control the worry process. Preliminary evidence shows that this treatment is also effective (Craske, Barlow, & O'Leary, 1992).

After trying a number of different drugs, Irene was treated with this approach and found herself much more able to cope with life. She completed college and graduate school and is engaged to be married. She is also successful in her career working as a counselor in a nursing home. But even now, Irene has trouble relaxing and stopping herself from worrying. She continues to experience mild to moderate anxiety, particularly when under stress, and continues to take minor tranquilizers on occasion as well as to use her psychological coping skills.

Panic Disorder with and without Agoraphobia

Did you ever have an eccentric aunt or other relative who never seemed to leave the house? When family reunions or visits occurred, they always had to be at her house. She would never go to anyone else's house. While this may not have happened in your family, many families have had this experience. Most would attribute their old aunt's behavior to being a little odd or perhaps just not being fond of travel. She would be very warm and friendly when people came to visit, so she was able to retain contact with the family.

In fact, your aunt, or your friend's aunt, may not be just odd or eccentric. She may suffer from a very debilitating anxiety disorder called **panic disorder with agoraphobia (PDA).** In this disorder, individuals experience severe unexpected panic attacks as described in the beginning of the chapter; at these times they may think they're dying or losing control. Since they never know when one of these attacks might happen, they experience **agoraphobia,** which is fear and avoidance of situations that they consider "unsafe" in the event they have a panic attack or paniclike symptoms. These would include situations from which it would be hard or embarrassing to escape or leave right away in case they needed to get to a hospital or home. In severe cases, people with PDA become totally unable to leave the house, sometimes for years on end, as illustrated in the next example.

The Case of Mrs. M.

Several years ago one of the authors was asked to make a house call to such a woman, Mrs. M. She was 67 years old and lived in a second-floor walk-up apartment in a lower-middle-class section of the city. Her adult daughter, one of her few remaining contacts with the world, had requested the evaluation with Mrs. M.'s consent. I rang the bell and the buzzer sounded signaling that I could open the door. I entered a narrow hallway; the entrance to the downstairs apartment was on the left and a stairwell was directly in front of me leading to the second-floor apartment. Mrs. M. was nowhere in sight. Knowing that she lived on the second floor, I walked up and knocked on the door at the top of the stairs. I heard Mrs. M. ask me to come in and I opened the door. She was sitting in her living room, and I could quickly see the layout of the rest of the apartment. The living room was in the front; in the back of the apartment, separated from the living room by a wall, was the kitchen, which led out onto a back porch. To the right of the stairs was the one bedroom, with a bathroom opening from it.

Mrs. M. was very friendly and glad to see me, offering me coffee and some cookies she had baked. I was the first person she had seen in 3 weeks. In fact, Mrs. M. had not set foot out of that apartment in 20 years, and she had suffered from panic disorder with agoraphobia for over 30 years.

As her story unfolded, she relayed vivid images of the tragedy of a life wasted. And yet, she continued to struggle in the face of her adversity and to make the best she could of her limited existence. Even areas in her apartment signaled the potential for terrifying panic attacks. She did not answer the door herself because she had not looked out in her hallway for the past 15 years. She reported that she could enter her kitchen and go into the areas containing her stove and refrigerator but that she had not been to the back of her kitchen overlooking the backyard or out on her back porch for the past 10 years. Thus,

Table 5.3 Diagnostic Criteria for Panic Disorder with Agoraphobia

A. Both 1 and 2:

1. Recurrent unexpected panic attacks are present.
2. At least one of the attacks has been followed by 1 month (or more) of one (or more) of the following: (a) persistent concern about having additional attacks, (b) worry about the implications of the attack or its consequences (e.g., losing control, having a heart attack, "going crazy"), or (c) a significant change in behavior related to the attacks.

B. The presence of agoraphobia in which the predominant complaint is anxiety about being in places or situations from which escape might be difficult or embarrassing, or in which help may not be available in the event of an unexpected or situationally predisposed panic attack or paniclike symptoms. Agoraphobic fears typically involve characteristic clusters of situations that include being outside the home alone; being in a crowd or standing in a line; being on a bridge; and traveling in a bus, train, or automobile.

C. The panic attacks are not due to the direct physiological effects of a substance (e.g., drug of abuse, medication) or a general medical condition (e.g., hyperthyroidism).

D. The panic attacks are not better accounted for by another mental disorder, such as social phobia (e.g., occurring on exposure to feared social situations), specific phobia (e.g., on exposure to a specific social situation), obsessive-compulsive disorder (e.g., on exposure to dirt, in someone with an obsession about contamination), posttraumatic stress disorder (e.g., in response to stimuli associated with a severe stressor), or separation anxiety disorder (e.g., in response to being away from home or close relatives).

Source: DSM-IV, APA, 1994.

her life for the last decade had revolved around her bedroom, her living room, and the front half of her kitchen. She relied on her adult daughter to bring in groceries and visit approximately once a week. Her only other visitor at that time was the parish priest, who would come to deliver communion every 2 to 3 weeks when he could. Her only remaining contact with the outside world was the television and the radio. Mrs. M. was nearing the end of a very difficult life; her husband, who had abused both alcohol and Mrs. M., had died 10 years previously of alcohol-related causes. Early in her very stressful marriage she had experienced her first terrifying panic attack and had gradually withdrawn from the world. As long as she stayed within the confines of her apartment, she was relatively free of panic. For this reason, and because in her mind there were few reasons left in her life to venture out, she declined treatment.

Clinical Description of Panic Disorder

The DSM-IV criteria for panic disorder with agoraphobia are presented in Table 5.3. At the beginning of the chapter we talked about the separate but related phenomena of anxiety and panic. In PDA, anxiety and panic come together, along with *phobic avoidance,* in an intricate relationship that can become as devastating as it was for Mrs. M. Many people have panic attacks but do not necessarily develop panic disorder. Similarly, many people experience anxiety and panic without developing agoraphobia. In those cases, the

disorder is called **panic disorder without agoraphobia (PD).**

To meet criteria for panic disorder (with or without agoraphobia) a person must experience one type of panic attack, an *unexpected* panic attack, *and* develop substantial anxiety or concern over the possibility of having another attack *or* about the implications of the attack or its consequences. In other words, he or she must think that each attack is a sign of impending death or incapacitation. A few individuals do not report that they are concerned about another attack but still change their behavior in a way that indicates the distress these panic attacks are causing them. They may avoid going to certain places or begin neglecting their duties around the house for fear that they might have an attack if they are too active. This is the reason for the added criterion in A2: "a significant change in behavior related to the attacks."

The Development of Agoraphobia

Many people with panic disorder develop the complication of agoraphobia, as did Mrs. M. The term *agoraphobia* was coined in 1871 by Westphal and, in the original Greek, refers to fear of the marketplace. This is a very appropriate term since the agora or Greek marketplace was a very busy, bustling area. One of the most stressful places for modern day agoraphobics is the shopping mall, the modern-day agora.

All the evidence now points to the conclusion that agoraphobic avoidance behavior is simply one associated feature of severe unexpected panic attacks. Simply put, if you have unexpected panic attacks, and are afraid you may have another one, you want to be in a safe place or at least with a safe person who knows what you are experiencing in the event another attack occurs. If you are in a safe place or with a safe person, then you can quickly get to a hospital or at least go into your bedroom and lie down (the home is usually a safe place). We know that anxiety is diminished for individuals with agoraphobia if they think the situation or person is "safe," even if there is nothing the safe person could really do if something bad did happen. If you are in a shopping mall or a crowded movie theater or church, not only is it more difficult to escape these situations but you are probably going to embarrass yourself if you try. For example, you may think you will have to climb over everyone in church to get out, or get up in the middle of the movie and run out, or worse, faint in the movie theater (individuals with agoraphobia seldom if ever do any of these things, particularly faint). For these reasons, when they do go to church, the movies, or similar places, agoraphobics always sit very near the door.

A list of typical situations commonly avoided by someone with agoraphobia is found in Table 5.4. Though agoraphobic behavior initially is closely tied to the occasions of panic, it can become relatively independent of panic attacks (Craske & Barlow, 1988; Craske, Rapee, & Barlow, 1988). In other words, an individual might not have a panic attack for years but still have strong agoraphobic avoidance, as was the case with Mrs. M. The explanation is that agoraphobic avoidance seems to be determined by the extent to

Michelle Craske demonstrated that agoraphobic avoidance is simply one way of coping with panic attacks. She also participated in developing, along with Ron Rapee, a new, effective psychosocial treatment for panic disorder.

which you *think or expect* you might have another attack rather than by how many attacks you actually have or how severe they are. Thus, agoraphobic avoidance is simply one way of coping with unexpected panic attacks.

Other methods of coping with panic attacks, in addition to agoraphobic avoidance, include resorting to the use (and eventually the abuse) of drugs and/or alcohol. Some individuals do not actually avoid agoraphobic situations but endure them with "intense dread." For example, people who simply must go to work each day or perhaps travel as a part of their job will suffer untold agonies of anxiety and panic simply to achieve their goals. Thus DSM-IV notes that agoraphobia may be characterized either by avoidance or by enduring the situations with marked distress.

One of the best examples of someone who "toughs it out" is the well-known weatherman on the "Today" show, Willard Scott. One day after doing the show successfully for years, he went on camera and suddenly felt his heart pounding and his chest getting tight and experienced the sheer terror of being totally unsure of what he was going to do or say next. He thought he was having a heart attack and was about to die right on camera. He reports that many times when he goes on camera he experiences these panic attacks, although most viewers would never know it. Somehow he makes it through. Although most individuals having

Table 5.4 Typical Situations Avoided by a Person with Agoraphobia

Shopping malls
Cars (as driver or passenger)
Buses
Trains
Subways
Wide streets
Tunnels
Restaurants
Theaters
Being far from home
Staying at home alone
Waiting in line
Supermarkets
Stores
Crowds
Planes
Elevators
Escalators

Source: Adapted from Barlow & Craske, 1994.

an attack think all the world sees their panic, only their families—and sometimes not even they—know that the person is having a panic attack.

Some patients with little or no agoraphobic avoidance (as well as most with severe agoraphobic avoidance) also display another cluster of avoidant behavior that we call *interoceptive avoidance* (Barlow, 1988; Barlow & Craske, 1989; Craske & Barlow, 1993). This cluster of avoidance behaviors involves removing yourself from situations or activities that might produce the physiological arousal that somehow resembles the beginnings of a panic attack. Some patients might avoid exercise because it produces increased cardiovascular activity or faster respiration, which reminds them of panic attacks. Other patients might avoid sauna baths or any rooms in which they might get hot and perspire. Psychopathologists are beginning to recognize that this cluster of avoidance behaviors is every bit as important as more classical agoraphobic avoidance. A list of situations or activities typically avoided within the interoceptive cluster is found in Table 5.5.

Table 5.5 Daily Activities within the Interoceptive Cluster Typically Avoided by People with Agoraphobia

Running up flights of stairs

Walking outside in intense heat

Hot, stuffy rooms

Hot, stuffy cars

Hot, stuffy stores or shopping malls

Walking outside in very cold weather

Aerobics

Lifting heavy objects

Dancing

Sexual relations

Watching horror movies

Eating heavy meals

Watching exciting movies or sports events

Getting involved in "heated" debates

Having showers with the doors and windows closed

Having a sauna

Hiking

Sports

Drinking coffee or any caffeinated beverages

Eating chocolate

Standing quickly from a sitting position

Getting angry

Source: Adapted from Barlow & Craske, 1994.

Statistics and Course for Panic Disorder with Agoraphobia

Panic disorder with or without agoraphobia is fairly common. Approximately 3.5% of the population meet the criteria for panic disorder at some point during their lives and another 5.3% would meet the criteria for agoraphobia (Kessler et al., in press). The rates of agoraphobia may be somewhat overestimated as a result of methodological difficulties in studies determining this rate, but the majority of people with panic disorder do have agoraphobic avoidance.

Onset of panic disorder most often occurs in early adult life—from mid-teens through about 40 years of age. The mean age of onset is between ages 25 and 29 (Ost, 1987). Prepubescent children have been known to experience unexpected panic attacks and occasionally panic disorder, although it is quite rare (Moreau & Weissman, 1992). Most initial unexpected panic attacks begin at or after puberty. In fact, puberty seems a better predictor of unexpected panic attacks than age since higher rates of panic attacks are found in more physically mature girls (Hayward et al., 1992). Furthermore, many prepubertal children are seen by general medical practitioners with symptoms of hyperventilation that may well be panic attacks. However, these children do not report fear of dying or losing control—perhaps because they are not at a stage of their cognitive development where they can make these attributions (Nelles & Barlow, 1988).

Important work on anxiety in the elderly has been carried out by Pat Wisocki and her colleagues (Wisocki, Handen, & Morse, 1986; Wisocki, 1988); they have discovered that health and vitality are the primary focus of anxiety in the elderly population, unlike younger adults or children. Lindesay (1991) studied 60 confirmed cases of phobic disorder in the elderly and found that they differed from younger adults in several ways. Specifically, the primary phobia evidenced in this group was agoraphobia. Furthermore, the agoraphobia had a late onset (after age 50) and was often related to a very stressful life event, most commonly an illness or injury.

A small number of people present to clinics with agoraphobic avoidance who do not technically meet criteria for panic attacks and panic disorder. These individuals are currently said to have *agoraphobia without history of panic disorder,* but we now know that in almost all instances they do experience paniclike attacks that occur unpredictably, making them afraid to venture far from a safe place. In a typical case of this sort, a woman in one of our clinics experienced dizziness and feelings in her stomach that made her think that she was about to have diarrhea all the time. Occasionally (but rarely), she would. Thus she avoided going anywhere that did not allow her ready access to a bathroom. Technically this was not

Pat Wisocki has made important discoveries about anxiety in the elderly that should assist the development of more effective treatments for this group of people.

a panic attack but it produced a very similar pattern of avoidance.

Seventy-five percent or more of those who suffer from agoraphobia are women (Myers et al., 1984; Thorpe & Burns, 1983; Barlow, 1988). For a long time we didn't know why, but now it seems that the most logical explanation is cultural: It is more culturally accepted for women to report fear and to act on this report by avoiding a large number of situations. Men, on the other hand, are expected to be stronger and braver and to "tough it out." In fact, the higher the severity of agoraphobic avoidance, the greater the proportion of women. For example, in our clinic, out of a group of patients suffering from panic disorder with mild agoraphobia, 72% were women; but if the agoraphobia was moderate, the percentage was 81%. Similarly, if agoraphobia was severe, the percentage was 89%.

What happens to men who have severe unexpected panic attacks? Are cultural influences so strong that most men are successful at simply enduring these? The answer seems to be no. A large proportion of males with unexpected panic attacks take another culturally acceptable route of dealing with their anxiety and panic. They consume large amounts of alcohol. The difficulty is that they become dependent on this alcohol, and often begin the long downward spiral into serious addiction. Thus, males may end up with an even more severe problem than panic disorder with agoraphobia. Because these men become so impaired by alcohol abuse, clinicians may not realize that they also have

PDA. Furthermore, even if they are successfully treated for their addiction, they still have their anxiety disorder that requires treatment (Mullaney & Trippett, 1979; Smail, Stockwell, Canter, & Hodgson, 1984; Chambless, Cherney, Caputo, & Rheinstein, 1987; Johannessen, Cowley, Walker, Jensen, & Parker, 1989).

Panic Disorder and Cultural Influences

Panic disorder and other anxiety disorders can be found throughout the world, although their expression may vary in different cultures and subcultures. Indeed, in Lesotho, Africa, the prevalence of panic disorder (and generalized anxiety disorder) was found to be equal to or greater than that found in North America (Hollifield, Katon, Spain, & Pule, 1990). In particular, somatic symptoms of anxiety may be emphasized in third world cultures. Feelings of dread or angst may not be part of the cultural idiom. In Chapter 2 we described a fright disorder called *susto* in Latin America. Another anxiety-related, culturally defined syndrome prominent among Hispanic-Americans, particularly those from the Caribbean, is referred to as *ataques de nervios*. The symptom picture of an ataque seems to be quite similar to panic attacks in North America, although such manifestations as shouting uncontrollably or bursting into tears may be associated more frequently with ataque than with panic.

Nocturnal Panic

Think back to the case of Gretchen, the woman who experienced a panic attack described on page 153. Notice anything unusual about her report of a panic attack? She was sound asleep when it happened! Approximately 40% of people with panic disorder have experienced these nocturnal panic attacks (Craske & Barlow, 1989). In fact, panic attacks occur more frequently between 1:30 A.M. and 3:30 A.M. than at any other time (Taylor et al., 1986). What's happening to these people? Are they having nightmares?

We now know a lot more about nocturnal attacks because we have studied these people in the sleep laboratory. This is a laboratory where patients come and spend a few nights sleeping while attached to an electroencephalograph (EEG) machine that monitors their brain waves (see Chapter 3). We all go through various stages of sleep each night and these stages are reflected by different patterns on the electroencephalogram. (Stages of sleep will be discussed more fully in Chapter 10.) We have learned that nocturnal panics occur during a specific stage of sleep. This stage, called delta wave or slow wave sleep, typically occurs several hours after we fall asleep and is the deepest stage of sleep. People with panic disorder often begin to panic when they start sinking into this deep stage of sleep, and then they awaken. Thus they wake up in the midst of a panic attack. Since there is no obvious reason for them to be anxious or panicky when they are sound asleep, most of these individuals report that they think they are dying.

What causes these attacks? Initially, we thought it might be nightmares, but nightmares and other dreamlike activity occur only during a stage of sleep characterized by rapid eye movement (REM sleep). This stage of sleep and the accompanying dreams typically occur much later in the sleep cycle. Therefore, these individuals are not dreaming of anything when they have nocturnal panics. This conclusion is consistent with reports of patients who say they cannot remember dreaming of anything. Sometimes therapists who are not aware of the stage of sleep associated with nocturnal panic attacks assume that the patients are "repressing" their dream material because it might relate to an early trauma too painful to be admitted to their consciousness. This is virtually impossible because nocturnal panic attacks do not occur during REM sleep, so there is no well-developed dream or nightmare activity going on when they happen. Thus, it is not possible for these patients to be dreaming anything.

Some therapists assume that the patients might have a breathing disorder called *sleep apnea*, where breathing is interrupted during sleep, making them feel like they're suffocating. This condition is often found in people who are substantially overweight. But in sleep apnea there is a repeated cycle of awakening and falling back to sleep that is not characteristic of nocturnal panics.

A related phenomenon occurring in children is called sleep terrors, which we will talk about in more detail in Chapter 10. Often children awake with sleep terrors and imagine that someone is chasing them around their room. It is common for them to scream and actually get out of bed as if something were after them. However, they *do not wake up,* and have no memory of the event in the morning. On the contrary, individuals experiencing nocturnal panic attacks do wake up and remember the event very clearly. It is interesting that sleep terrors occur at the same stage of sleep as nocturnal panics, suggesting that there may be a connection between them as yet unknown to us.

Finally, there is a fascinating condition called *isolated sleep paralysis* that seems culturally determined. Have you ever heard the expression "the witch is riding you"? If you're white, you probably haven't, but if you're African-American, chances are you at least know somebody who has had this frightening experience (Bell, Dixie-Bell, & Thompson, 1986).

Isolated sleep paralysis is a condition that occurs during the transitional state between sleep and waking. This can occur when a person is either falling asleep or waking up. During this period the individual

is unable to move and experiences a surge of terror that resembles a panic attack. Occasionally he or she might also experience vivid hallucinations. This event is interesting in that it rarely, if ever, occurs in Caucasians. In this country it is almost exclusively an experience of African-Americans. Since a high proportion of these individuals also suffer more traditional panic attacks, Bell et al. (1986) hypothesized that panic disorder in African-Americans may well be accompanied by the additional feature of isolated sleep paralysis. Even more interesting is that the disorder does not seem to occur in Nigerian blacks. In fact, the prevalence in Nigerian blacks is about the same as it is in American whites. The reasons for this absence are not clear, although all factors point to a cultural explanation.

But what about the phrase "the witch is riding you"? It turns out that this is a colloquial African-American expression referring to isolated sleep paralysis. This bit of knowledge is very important for clinicians who work with African-Americans. For years we thought the term was specific to this particular subculture. However, on a recent trip to Nova Scotia, a Canadian province with a strong Scottish tradition, one of the authors discovered a very interesting colloquialism that exists in rural areas to describe sudden attacks of fright or panic. In these areas people often use the phrase "I'm being ridden by the hag." *Hagge* is an ancient Scottish term referring to a female demon or a witch. It must be that somewhere, deep in the traditions of Scotland, a description of terror or panic similar to that of African-American cultures exists. Was there some connection between ancient Scotland and the forebears of African-Americans? It seems unlikely, but this is a vivid example of how expressions and manifestations of psychopathology can be dramatically similar from culture to culture.

Panic Disorder and Suicide

Based on epidemiological data, Weissman and her colleagues found that 20% of patients with panic disorder had made a suicide attempt, and they concluded that suicide attempts were associated with panic disorder. They also concluded that the risk of someone with panic disorder attempting suicide is comparable to that associated with individuals with major depression (Weissman, Klerman, Markowitz, & Ouellette, 1989; Johnson, Weissman, & Klerman, 1990). This finding is frightening since panic disorder is quite prevalent and clinicians have generally not been on the lookout for possible suicide attempts in patients with this disorder. The investigators also found that, even if patients with panic disorder did not have accompanying depression, they were still at risk for suicide.

Other researchers, however (Friedman, Jones, Chernen, & Barlow, 1992; Beck, Steer, Sanderson, & Skeie, 1991), examined hundreds of patients with panic disorder in outpatient clinics and did not find a suicide risk in those who had no additional disorders. They did find the risk of suicidal attempts and thoughts to be greater in patients with panic disorder who also had borderline personality disorder, in which suicidal attempts are a prominent characteristic.

Discrepant findings of this type are common in research in psychopathology and almost always force scientists to look closely at their methods and examine what might account for very different findings in two or more studies. When several possibilities are recognized, scientists then have some guidance in determining which possibility (or hypothesis) seems to account for the discrepancy. Thus does science advance.

What caused the discrepancy here? Among the several possibilities, the method of assessment and the type of interview used in the studies differed considerably. The epidemiological studies reported by Weissman et al. (1989) were conducted by lay interviewers who were not necessarily trained in determining suicidal risk. Also, the lay interviewers were interviewing a random sample of the population rather than a sample drawn from clinic patients. In addition, the lay interviewers did not necessarily identify other disorders individuals with panic disorder might have had in the past that could have accounted for suicidal ideation.

But there are other possibilities. The epidemiological study may have included individuals who not only were untreated for panic disorder but also were unaware of the possibility of treatment for this disorder. As a result, they might have become particularly hopeless and begun to think about suicide. All patients appearing at the outpatient clinics, on the other hand, were about to receive treatment and therefore had some hope of recovering. We must continue to conduct research that clarifies the true relationship between panic disorder and suicide.

Causes of Panic Disorder and Agoraphobia

It is not possible to understand the causes of panic disorder (with or without agoraphobia) without referring to the triad of contributing factors mentioned throughout this book: biological, psychological, and social. We have strong evidence indicating that agoraphobia develops after a person experiences unexpected panic attacks (or paniclike sensations); but whether agoraphobia develops after an unexpected attack and how severe it becomes seem to be socially and culturally determined, as noted above. The development of panic attacks and panic disorder, on the other hand, seems to be related most strongly to biological and psychological factors and their interaction.

At the beginning of the chapter we discussed how biological, psychological, and social factors may contribute to the development and maintenance of anxiety. We also examined factors contributing to the experience of an initial unexpected panic attack. Elsewhere we have suggested a model of the etiology of panic disorder that takes into consideration what we know about the development of anxiety and panic. That model is described in Figure 5.4.

As noted in the beginning of the chapter, we all inherit some vulnerability to experiencing stress. This vulnerability is a tendency to be neurobiologically overreactive to the stress of common life events. Thus, when confronted with anxiety-producing life events such as stress on the job or at school, death of a loved one, divorce, or even positive, happy life events that are nevertheless stressful, such as graduating from school and starting a new career, getting married, or changing jobs, some people are more likely than others to have an emergency alarm reaction (unexpected panic attack). (Remember that other people and their relatives might have headaches or high blood pressure in response to the same stressful life events.) These "false" alarms quickly become associated in an individual's mind with some external and internal cues that were present during the attack. The next time the person's heart rate increases during exercise, she might automatically think she is having a panic attack (conditioning). Harmless exercise would be an example of an internal cue or a conditioned stimulus (CS) for a panic attack. Being in a movie theater where the panic first occurred would be an example of an external cue that might become a CS for future panics. Since these alarms become associated with a number of different internal and external stimuli through a learning process, we call them "learned alarms."

But none of this would make much difference without the next step. The individuals then must develop *anxiety* over the possibility of having another panic attack. That is, they begin thinking that the physical sensations associated with the panic attack mean that something terrible is about to happen, such as death. This is what creates panic disorder. In other words, these people have a tendency to think that the worst is going to happen when they experience strong physical sensations. Thus, some of them focus their anxiety on the possibility of *future* panic attacks whereas other people experiencing these attacks do not. We know that approximately 8% to 12% of the population will have an occasional unexpected panic attack, often during a period of intense stress (Norton, Harrison, Hauch, & Rhodes, 1985; Salge, Beck, & Logan, 1988; Telch, Lucas, & Nelson, 1989). Most of these people do *not* develop anxiety over the next attack (Telch et al., 1989). Only 1% to 3% go on to develop anxiety over future panic attacks and thereby

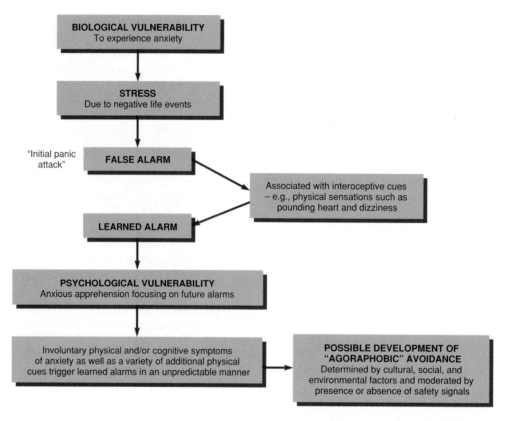

Figure 5.4 A model of the causes of panic disorder with or without agoraphobia (adapted from Barlow, 1988)

meet the criteria for panic disorder. What happens to those individuals who don't develop anxiety over another attack? They seem to attribute the attack to events of the moment, such as an argument with a friend, something they ate, or a "bad day," and go on with their lives, perhaps experiencing an occasional panic attack when they come under some stress again.

The influential cognitive theories of David Clark (Clark, 1986; 1988) explicate in more detail some of the cognitive processes that may be ongoing in panic disorder. Clark emphasizes the psychological vulnerability of people with this disorder to interpret normal physical sensations in a "catastrophic" way. In other words, we all typically experience rapid heartbeat after exercise. But if you have a psychological or cognitive vulnerability, you might interpret that rapid heartbeat as dangerous, provoking a surge of anxiety. This anxiety, in turn, produces more physical sensations because of the action of the sympathetic nervous system. But you perceive these additional physical sensations as even more dangerous, and a vicious cycle begins, producing a panic attack. Thus, Clark emphasizes the cognitive process in panic disorder as most important. Supporting this model, Ehlers and Breuer (1992) had panic disorder patients and several control groups without panic disorder try to

monitor their heart rates to estimate how fast their hearts were beating. The exercise demonstrated that patients with panic disorder seemed to be paying much closer attention to their internal somatic sensations such as heartbeats because they were much more *accurate* at estimating how fast their hearts were beating than were several groups of individuals without panic disorder. In other words, because they are anxious about bodily sensations to begin with—since these sensations might indicate an unexpected panic is about to occur—the patients are more *vigilant* for internal sensations, or more *interoceptively aware*. But this awareness helps maintain the vicious cycle because they quickly notice *any* somatic response and interpret it as dangerous. Some recent studies however, could not replicate this finding (Antony et al., 1993), so we need to study the phenomenon more closely.

One final hypothesis on the etiology of panic disorder and agoraphobia evolving from more psychodynamic conceptions suggested that early object loss and/or separation anxiety might predispose someone to develop panic disorder with agoraphobia as an adult. Object loss, or separation anxiety, refers to the substantial anxiety a child might experience on the threat of separation or actual separation from an important caregiver, such as a mother or father. Dependent

David Clark of Oxford University developed an important theory of the cause of panic disorder, emphasizing distorted cognitive processes. He also developed an effective psychosocial treatment for this common disorder.

Anke Ehlers, also of Oxford University, demonstrated that patients with panic disorder seem to attend more closely to their internal sensations than people without panic disorder. This may be one of the contributing causes of the disorder.

personality tendencies and a reliance on others often characterize someone with agoraphobia. These personality characteristics were hypothesized to be a possible reaction to early separation. Nevertheless, despite some intriguing early suggestions, there has been very little evidence that patients with panic disorder with agoraphobia experience separation anxiety in their childhood more frequently than individuals with other psychological disorders or, for that matter, normals based on direct comparison of early experience (Barlow, 1988; van der Molen, van den Hout, van Dieren, & Griez, 1989; Thyer, 1993). It is still possible, however, that the trauma of early separation might predispose someone to psychological disorders in general. Separation anxiety disorder is discussed below in the section on specific phobias.

Treatment of Panic Disorder with Agoraphobia

Drug Treatment

As noted in Chapter 1, research on the effectiveness of new treatments can be important in the study of psychopathology. Responses to certain specific treatments, whether drug or psychological, may reflect back on the causes of the disorder. For example, Donald Klein (1964), in some of his pioneering work, analyzed the effects of various drugs on panic and anxiety. He noticed that drugs affecting primarily the serotonergic and noradrenergic neurotransmitter systems, specifically a tricyclic antidepressant drug called imipramine, blocked panic attacks but did not seem to affect more generalized anxiety. Benzodiazepines, on the other hand, reduced anxiety but did not seem to block panic attacks. Thus, he separated panic from anxiety and developed his theory that panic was different from anxiety. This conclusion led to biological theories suggesting different locations in the brain for panic versus anxiety responses.

While subsequent studies strongly suggest that anxiety and panic may well be separate processes, the differential effects of the two classes of drugs have not been as strongly supported. It seems that some high-potency benzodiazepines are just as effective for panic disorder as are tricyclic antidepressants such as imipramine. In fact, a large number of drugs affecting either the noradrenergic, serotonergic, or benzodiazepine GABA neurotransmitter systems seem effective in treating panic disorder. Some drugs, however, do not seem to be effective. The class of drugs called beta blockers, often used to control blood pressure, have not proved effective in treating panic disorder.

Each class of drugs has advantages and disadvantages. *Imipramine,* one of the class of drugs called *tricyclic antidepressants,* produces strong side effects such as dizziness, dry mouth, and on occasion sexual dysfunction. For that reason many patients refuse to stay on it for very long. But if a person can become accustomed to the side effects or wait until they wear off, he will often find that the drug can reduce panic attacks and associated anxiety. On the other hand,

Don Klein, in some pioneering work, determined that panic disorder was a separate psychological disorder. He has contributed important theories on biological contributions to this and other disorders.

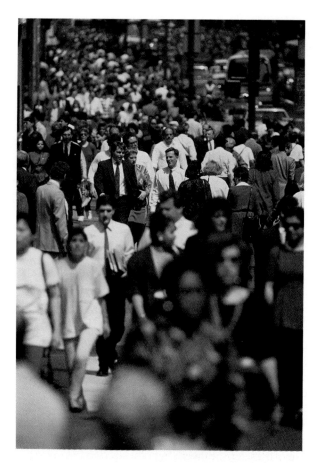

An effective psychosocial treatment for agoraphobia involves gradually exposing patients to crowded situations in which escape might be difficult in the event that they have a panic attack. This process allows them to "reality test" and learn, on an emotional level, that there is really nothing to fear in the phobic situation.

high-potency *benzodiazepines* such as *alprazolam* (known by the trade name Xanax) commonly used for panic disorder, are easy to begin taking, work very fast, but are hard to stop taking due to psychological and physical dependence and addiction. Also, all benzodiazepines adversely affect cognitive and motor functions to some degree. Therefore, people taking them in high doses often find their ability to drive a car or study to be somewhat reduced. Approximately 60% of patients with panic disorder will be free of panic as long as they stay on an effective drug (Ballenger et al., 1988; Klosko, Barlow, Tassinari, & Cerny, 1990), but relapse rates are high once the drug is stopped. Approximately 20% to 50% of patients will relapse after stopping tricyclic antidepressants (Telch, 1988; Telch, Tearnan, & Taylor, 1983). The relapse rate is closer to 90% for those who stop taking benzodiazepines (for example, Fyer et al., 1987).

Psychological Treatments

Psychological treatments have also proven quite effective for panic disorder. Originally, psychological treatments concentrated on reducing agoraphobic avoidance using strategies based on exposure to feared situations. The strategy of exposure-based treatments is to arrange conditions suitable for the patient to gradually face the feared situations. In this way, he or she can "reality test" and learn that there is really nothing to fear in the phobic situation. Of course, most patients with phobias are well aware of this rationally, but they must be convinced on an "emotional" level as

well while they are actually in the situation. Sometimes the therapist will accompany the patients on their exposure exercises. At other times, the therapist will simply help the patients structure their own exercises and provide them with a variety of psychological coping mechanisms to assist them in completing the exercises, which are typically arranged from least to most difficult. A sample of these can be found in Table 5.6. The therapist would identify situations relevant to the patient and then arrange the situations in order of difficulty.

Gradual exposure exercises accompanied by anxiety-reducing coping mechanisms, such as relaxation or breathing retraining, have proven effective in helping patients overcome agoraphobic behavior. As many as 70% of patients undergoing these treatments will be substantially improved as their anxiety and panic will be reduced and their agoraphobic avoidance greatly diminished. Very few, however, will be cured because many will still be experiencing

Table 5.6 Specification of Situation-Exposure Tasks (listed in order from least to most difficult)

Shopping in a crowded supermarket for 30 minutes alone.

Walking five blocks away from home alone.

Driving on a busy highway for five miles with spouse, and alone.

Eating in a restaurant, seated in the middle.

Watching a movie while seated in the middle of the row.

Source: Barlow & Craske, 1994.

some anxiety and panic attacks, albeit at a less severe level.

More recently, effective psychological treatments have been developed that treat panic attacks directly (Barlow & Craske, 1989; 1994; Klosko et al., 1990; Clark et al., in press). These treatments, called **panic control treatments (PCT),** concentrate on exposing patients with panic disorder to the cluster of interoceptive sensations that remind them of their panic attacks. Thus, the therapist will attempt to create "mini" panic attacks in the office by having the patients exercise to elevate their heart rates or perhaps spinning them in a chair to make them dizzy. A variety of exercises have been developed for this purpose (see Table 5.7). In addition to these exercises patients

receive cognitive therapy. In this therapy, basic attitudes and perceptions concerning the dangerousness of the feared but objectively harmless situations are identified and modified. As we learned above, many of these attitudes and perceptions are beyond the patient's awareness; that is, they are unconscious. Uncovering these cognitive processes requires a great deal of therapeutic skill. In addition to exposure to interoceptive sensations and cognitive therapy, patients are also taught relaxation or breathing retraining to help them cope with increases in anxiety and to reduce excess arousal.

These procedures are highly effective for panic disorder. Between 80% and 100% of patients undergoing the new, brief psychological treatments will be free of panic after approximately 12 weekly sessions. Data on the percentage of patients who are free of panic after 12 weeks of panic control treatment (PCT) are presented in Figure 5.5. In this study, PCT was compared to a successful drug treatment, alprazolam, as well as a placebo pill and a wait list control group who waited for 12 weeks without receiving any treatment (they were later treated). PCT was significantly more effective than placebo and wait list. Drug treatment was not significantly different from either PCT or placebo and occupied an intermediate position. Studies following up patients receiving the new psychological treatment (PCT) indicate that they do not relapse and stay better for at least 2 years (Craske, Brown, & Barlow, 1991). Remaining agoraphobic behavior can then be treated with more standard exposure exercises. Although these

Table 5.7 Exercises to Create the Sensation of Panic

1. Shake your head loosely from side to side for 30 seconds (to produce dizziness or disorientation).

2. Place your head between your legs for 30 seconds and then lift it quickly (to produce lightheadedness or blood rushing).

3. Take one step up, using stairs or a box or a footstool, and immediately step down. Do this repeatedly at a fast enough rate to notice your heart pumping quickly for 1 minute (to produce racing heart and shortness of breath).

4. Hold your breath for as long as you can or about 30–45 seconds (to produce chest tightness and smothering feelings).

5. Tense every part of your body for 1 minute without causing pain. Tense your arms, legs, stomach, back, shoulders, face—everything. Alternatively, try holding a push-up position for 1 minute or for as long as you can (to produce muscle tension, weakness, and trembling).

6. Spin in a chair for 1 minute. If you have a chair that spins, such as a desk chair, this is ideal. It's even better if someone is there to spin you around. Otherwise, stand up and turn around quickly to make yourself dizzy. Be near a soft chair or couch that you can sit in after 1 minute is up. This will produce dizziness and perhaps nausea as well.

7. Hyperventilate for 1 minute. Breathe deep and fast, using a lot of force. Sit down as you do this. This exercise might produce unreality, shortness of breath, tingling, cold or hot feelings, dizziness, or headache.

8. Breathe through a thin straw for 1 minute. Don't allow any air through your nose; hold your nostrils together (to produce feelings of restricted air flow or smothering).

9. Stare at a small spot on the wall or stare at yourself in the mirror for 2 minutes. Stare as hard as you can to produce feelings of unreality.

Source: Barlow & Craske, 1994.

Figure 5.5   Percentage of patients reporting zero panic attacks at post-treatment (from Klosko, Barlow, Tassinari, & Cerny, 1990)

treatments are quite effective, they are relatively new and not yet available to many individuals who suffer from panic disorder.

Specific Phobia

Remember Judy in Chapter 1? When she saw the film of the frog being dissected, Judy began having queasy feelings. Eventually she reached the point that she would faint if someone simply said "Cut it out." Earlier in this chapter you also read about John Madden and the difficulties he has with flying. Judy and John Madden have in common what we would call a specific phobia.

Clinical Description of Specific Phobia

A **specific phobia** is an unreasonable (irrational) fear of a specific object or situation that markedly interferes with an individual's ability to function. Prior to DSM-IV this category was called "simple" phobia to distinguish it from the more complex agoraphobia condition, but we now recognize that there is nothing simple about it. Many of you reading this chapter probably have some fears that may not be totally rational. That is, you might be afraid of something that is not dangerous, such as going to the dentist, or have a greatly exaggerated fear of something that is only mildly dangerous, such as driving a car or flying. For this reason, most people can identify to some extent with a phobia. Based on recent surveys, specific fears of a variety of objects or situations occur in a majority of the population (Myers et al., 1984). But the very commonality of fears, even severe

fears, often causes people to trivialize the psychological disorder known as a specific phobia. These phobias, in their severe form, can be extremely disabling, as we saw with Judy.

For people such as John Madden, on the other hand, phobias are a nuisance, sometimes an extremely inconvenient nuisance; but one can adapt to life with a phobia by simply working around it somehow. In upstate New York where we live and work, some people are afraid to drive in the snow in winter. We have had people come to one of our clinics who have been so severely phobic that, during snowy or icy conditions, they were ready to uproot, change their jobs and their lives, and move south. That would be one way of dealing with a phobia. We will discuss some other ways at the end of this chapter.

The DSM-IV criteria for specific phobia are listed in Table 5.8. The major characteristic held in common by Judy and John Madden, of course, is mentioned in criterion A of the table. They have marked and persistent fear cued or set off by a specific object or situation. Both also have recognized that their fear and anxiety is excessive or unreasonable. Finally, both went to considerable lengths to avoid situations where their phobic response might occur.

There the similarities end. In fact, there are as many phobias as there are objects and situations to fear. The variety of Greek and Latin names contrived to describe these fears or phobias stuns the imagination. Table 5.9 gives only the phobias beginning with the letter "a" from a long list compiled by Jack D. Maser from medical dictionaries and other diverse sources (Maser, 1985). Of course, this sort of list has little or no value for people studying psychopathology, but it does show the extent of the named phobias.

Table 5.8   Diagnostic Criteria for Specific Phobia

A. Marked and persistent fear that is excessive or unreasonable, cued by the presence or anticipation of a specific object or situation (e.g., flying, heights, animals, receiving an injection, seeing blood).

B. Exposure to the phobic stimulus almost invariably provokes an immediate anxiety response, which may take the form of a situationally bound or situationally predisposed panic attack. Note: in children, the anxiety may be expressed by crying, tantrums, freezing, or clinging.

C. The person recognizes that the fear is excessive or unreasonable. Note: In children, this feature may be absent.

D. The phobic situation(s) is avoided or else is endured with intense anxiety or distress.

E. The avoidance, anxious anticipation, or distress in the feared situations interferes significantly with the person's normal routine, occupational (or academic) functioning, or social activities or relationships, or there is marked distress about having the phobia.

F. In individuals under age 18, the duration is at least 6 months.

G. The anxiety, panic attacks, or phobic avoidance associated with the specific object or situation are not better accounted for by another mental disorder, such as obsessive-compulsive disorder (e.g., fear of dirt, in someone with an obsession about contamination), posttraumatic stress disorder (e.g., avoidance of stimuli associated with a severe stressor), separation anxiety disorder (e.g., avoidance of school), social phobia (e.g., avoidance of social situations because of fear of embarrassment), panic disorder with agoraphobia, or agoraphobia without history of panic disorder.

Specify type:
    Animal Type
    Natural Environment Type (e.g., heights, storms, and water)
    Blood-Injection-Injury Type
    Situational Type (e.g., planes, elevators, or enclosed places)
    Other Type (e.g., phobic avoidance of situations that may lead to choking, vomiting, or contracting an illness; or in children, avoidance of loud sounds or costumed characters)

Source: DSM-IV, APA, 1994.

Before the publication of DSM-IV in 1994, no meaningful grouping or classification of specific phobias existed. However, we have now learned what may seem obvious. The cases of Judy and John Madden represent types of a specific phobia that differ in some major ways from each other. Four major subtypes of specific phobia have now been identified. They include (a) animal type, (b) natural environment type (for instance, heights, storms, and water), (c) blood-injection-injury type, and (d) situational type (such as, planes, elevators, or enclosed places). A fifth category, "other," includes phobias that do not fit any of the four major subtypes (for instance, phobic avoidance of situations that may lead to choking, vomiting, or contracting an illness; or, in children, avoidance of loud sounds or costumed characters). Each is discussed briefly below.

Blood-Injection-Injury Phobia

How do these phobias differ from each other? We have already seen one major difference in the case of Judy. Rather than the usual fear response accompanied by a surge of activity in the sympathetic nervous system and increased heart rate and blood pressure, Judy actually experienced a marked drop in heart rate and blood pressure and experienced fainting as a consequence. Many people who suffer from phobias and experience a panic attack in their feared situation

report that they feel like they are going to faint, but they never do since their heart rate and blood pressure are actually increasing. Therefore, those with **blood-injection-injury phobias** almost always differ in their physiological reaction from people with other types of phobia (Öst, 1992). We also noted in Chapter 2 that blood-injection-injury phobia runs in families more strongly than any phobic disorder we know. This is probably because people with this phobia inherit a strong vasovagal response when they are confronted with blood, injury, or the possibility of an injection, any of which causes in them a drop in blood pressure and a tendency to faint. They then develop a phobia over the possibility of having this "fainting" response. The average age of onset for this phobia is approximately 9 years (Öst, 1989).

Situational Phobia

The phobias characterized by difficulties with public transportation or enclosed places are called **situational phobias.** Claustrophobia, a fear of small enclosed places, would be situational, as would a phobia of planes. Psychopathologists have noted that situational phobia is similar to panic disorder with agoraphobia (PDA) in a number of ways. One commonality between these two disorders is the age of the person at the onset of the disorder. Both situational phobia and PDA tend to emerge in an individual's early

Table 5.9 Phobias Beginning with "A"

Term	Fear of:
Acarophobia	Insects, mites
Achluophobia	Darkness, night
Acousticophobia	Sounds
Acrophobia	Heights
Aerophobia	Air currents, drafts, wind
Agoraphobia	Open spaces
Agyiophobia	Crossing the street
Aichmophobia	Sharp, pointed objects; knives; being touched by a finger
Ailurophobia	Cats
Algophobia	Pain
Amathophobia	Dust
Amychophobia	Laceration; being clawed, scratched
Androphobia	Men (and sex with men)
Anemophobia	Air currents, wind, drafts
Anginophobia	Angina pectoris
Anthropophobia	Human society
Antlophobia	Floods
Apeirophobia	Infinity
Aphephobia	Physical contact, being touched
Apiphobia	Bees, bee stings
Astraphobia	Thunderstorms, lightning
Ataxiophobia	Disorder
Atephobia	Ruin
Auroraphobia	Northern lights
Autophobia	Being alone; solitude; oneself; being egotistical

Source: Maser, 1985.

to mid-twenties. However, situational phobias are characterized by a "bimodal" peak, with a number of people also developing situational phobias at a much younger age (between 2 and 7 years old). The extent to which PDA and situational phobias run in families is also very similar (Curtis, Himle, Lewis, & Lee, 1989; Curtis, Hill, Lewis, 1990; Fyer et al., 1990; Craske, in press), with approximately 30% of first-degree relations having the same or a similar phobia.

The types of situations feared in the situational phobia subtype are very similar to agoraphobic situations in which people are afraid because they would have difficulty escaping if they had an unexpected panic attack. The difference between situational phobia and panic disorder with agoraphobia is that people with situational phobia never experience a panic attack outside the context of their phobic object or situation.

Therefore, they can "relax" when they don't have to confront their phobic situation. People with panic disorder, on the other hand, might experience an unexpected, uncued panic attack at any time.

Natural Environment Phobia

Sometimes, at a very young age, people develop fears of situations or events occurring in nature. These fears are called **natural environment phobias.** The major examples are heights, storms, and water. These fears also seem to cluster together (Craske, in press; Barlow, 1988): If you fear one situation or event, such as deep water, you are likely to fear another, such as storms. Many of these situations or experiences have some danger associated with them and, therefore, mild to moderate fear can be very adaptive. For example, one should be careful in a high place if not fully supported or while swimming in deep water. It is entirely possible that we are somewhat "prepared" to be afraid of these situations as we discussed in Chapter 2—that is, there is something in our genes that makes us very sensitive to these situations if any sign of danger is present. In any case, these phobias have a peak age of onset at about 7 years. They would not be phobias at all if they were only passing fears in children. They would have to be persistent and to interfere substantially with the person's functioning, leading her to avoid boat trips or summer vacations at the family cottage in the mountains where she might encounter a storm.

Animal Phobia

Fears of animals and insects are called **animal phobias.** Once again, these fears are common in a large number of people but become a phobia only if some severe interference with functioning is present. For example, we have seen cases in our clinic where people with fears of snakes or mice are unable to read magazines for fear of unexpectedly coming across a picture of one of these animals. There are many places that these people would be unable to go, even if they wanted to very badly, such as to the country to visit someone. The fear experienced by people with animal phobias is much different from someone's ordinary mild revulsion to a snake. The age of onset for these phobias, like that of the natural environment phobias, peaks at around 7 years (Öst, 1987; Barlow, 1988).

Other Phobias

Several additional types of phobias from the "other" category are described briefly here since they appear in considerable numbers and can cause substantial problems. If you are afraid of contracting a disease and go to excessive and irrational lengths to avoid getting that disease, it is possible that you have an *illness phobia.* In these cases, the individuals do *not* actually *believe* they have the disease but are afraid they might acquire it in any number of ways (Salkovskis, Warwick, & Clark, 1990). When this fear occurs in severe form it can be very incapacitating, since individuals with illness phobia may avoid all contact with people or places where they might "catch" something. Illness phobia has become more prevalent with the AIDS epidemic. People with this concern have no reason to believe they have AIDS, and they will test negatively for HIV, but they may avoid public restrooms, some restaurants, and any contact whatsoever with strangers for fear of contracting the disease. Illness phobia can also resemble other disorders, such as obsessive-compulsive disorder (see p. 195) or hypochondriasis (see Chapter 6), but is sufficiently different to be classified as a type of specific phobia. We will return to this issue when we discuss these two disorders.

Choking phobia is characterized by fear and avoidance of swallowing pills, foods, or fluids. This phobia can produce significant weight loss. Other names for choking phobia include "hypersensitive gag reflex" or "globus hystericus" (McNally, 1989). Phobias of choking and vomiting are relatively common and almost always have their origins in the traumatic experience of choking on a piece of food or hard candy. In some people the consequences of this experience are that they are unable to eat solid food and, in addition to weight loss, experience severe nutritional and dental problems. If the phobia is prolonged, the person is likely to experience deterioration in gum tissue and tooth structure from lack of use and, ultimately, tooth loss. These people often maintain themselves on liquid diets.

Separation Anxiety Disorder

In addition to childhood manifestations of all the anxiety disorders described in this chapter, there is one additional anxiety disorder unique to childhood. **Separation anxiety disorder** is characterized by a child's unrealistic and persistent worry that something will happen to his parents or other important people in his life, or that something will happen to the child himself that will separate him from his parents (for example, he will be lost, kidnapped, killed, or hurt in an accident). Because of these fears, the child often refuses to go to school or sometimes even to leave home, not because he is afraid of school but because he is afraid of separating from his parents or loved ones. These fears of separation can extend to refusals to sleep alone and may be characterized by nightmares involving possible separation as well as complaints of physical symptoms, distress, and anxiety.

Of course, all children experience separation anxiety to some extent; this fear usually decreases as the child grows older. Therefore, a clinician must judge

Tom Ollendick is a leading investigator into the nature and treatment of anxiety disorders in children.

whether the separation anxiety is greater than would be expected at that particular age (Ollendick & Huntzinger, 1990). It is also important to differentiate separation anxiety from school phobia. In school phobia, the fear is clearly focused on something in the school situation and the child can often leave the parents or other attachment figures to go elsewhere, such as to a friend's house to play. In separation anxiety, it is the act of separating from the parent or attachment figure that provokes anxiety and fear.

Francis, Last, and Strauss (1987) found that the prevalence of certain symptoms of the disorder varies as a function of age. For example, the most prominent symptom among the youngest children was worry about something happening to their parents or loved ones. Excessive distress on separation was most prominent in the middle group of children, while physical complaints on school days characterized separation anxiety in adolescents.

Last, Hersen, Kazdin, Finkelstein, and Strauss (1987) studied 91 children between 5 and 18 years of age in a child and adolescent anxiety disorders clinic. Children with this disorder tended to be white, prepubertal females (64%) from lower socioeconomic levels. Of course, these diagnoses were obtained in just one clinic and may not represent the characteristic child suffering from this disorder in other parts of the country.

Statistics and Course for Specific Phobia
Specific fears occur in a majority of people. The ones most commonly found in the population at large, categorized by Agras, Sylvester, and Oliveau (1969), are

Table 5.10 Prevalence and Standard Errors of Prevalence of Intense Fears and Phobia

Intense Fear	Prevalence per 1,000 Population	Sex Distribution	SE by Sex	Phobia	Prevalence per 1,000 Population*	Sex Distribution	SE by Sex
Snakes	253	M: 118 / F: 376	M: 34 / F: 48	Illness/injury	31 (42%)	M: 22 / F: 39	M: 15 / F: 20
Heights	120	M: 109 / F: 128	M: 33 / F: 36	Storms	13 (18%)	M: 0 / F: 24	M: 0 / F: 15
Flying	109	M: 70 / F: 144	M: 26 / F: 38	Animals	11 (14%)	M: 6 / F: 18	M: 8 / F: 13
Enclosures	50	M: 32 / F: 63	M: 18 / F: 25	Agoraphobia	6 (8%)	M: 7 / F: 6	M: 8 / F: 8
Illness	33	M: 31 / F: 35	M: 18 / F: 19	Death	5 (7%)	M: 4 / F: 6	M: 6 / F: 8
Death	33	M: 46 / F: 21	M: 21 / F: 15	Crowds	4 (5%)	M: 2 / F: 6	M: 5 / F: 7
Injury	23	M: 24 / F: 22	M: 15 / F: 15	Heights	4 (5%)	M: 7 / F: 0	M: 9 / F: 0
Storms	31	M: 9 / F: 48	M: 9 / F: 22				
Dentists	24	M: 22 / F: 26	M: 15 / F: 16				
Journeys alone	16	M: 0 / F: 31	M: 0 / F: 18				
Being alone	10	M: 5 / F: 13	M: 7 / F: 11				

*Percentages of the total of those with phobias are in parentheses.

Source: Adapted from Agras, Sylvester, & Oliveau, 1969.

presented in Table 5.10. Not surprisingly, fears of snakes and heights rank near the top. Notice also that the sex ratio among common fears is overwhelmingly female with a couple of exceptions. Most curious among these exceptions is fear of heights, for which the sex ratio is approximately equal.

Very few people reporting specific fears would qualify as having a phobia, but for approximately 11% of the population, these fears at some point during their lives are severe enough to be classified as "disorders" and earn the label phobia (Eaton, Dryman, & Weissman, 1991; Kessler et al., in press). This is a very high percentage, making it one of the most common psychological disorders in the population. And yet, even though phobias may interfere with an individual's functioning, only the most severe cases would actually come for treatment since they tend to work around their phobia; for example, someone with a fear of heights arranges her life so that she never has to be in a tall building or some other high place. Table 5.11 presents the distribution of the 68 patients who came to our Anxiety Disorders Clinic between March 17, 1988, and September 30, 1992, with a specific phobia as their primary problem; these are broken down by type of phobia. As you can see, people with situational phobias of such things as driving, flying, or small enclosed places most frequently come for treatment. However, there is reason to believe that people with blood-injury-injection phobias are quite prevalent in the population (Agras et al., 1969; Myers et al., 1984). These individuals might come for treatment if they knew good treatments were available.

Age of onset for various subtypes of phobia is provided in the description of each subtype. Once a phobia develops, it tends to last a lifetime (run a chronic course) (for instance, Agras, Chapin, & Oliveau, 1972; Barlow, 1988); thus, the issue of treatment, described shortly, becomes important.

While most anxiety disorders look pretty much the same in adults and children, clinicians must be very aware of the types of normal fears and anxieties experienced by children across the developmental span so as to distinguish these from specific phobias (King,

Table 5.11 Sixty-Eight Patients with Specific Phobia as the Primary Problem

Type of Phobia	Number
Animal	6
Natural environment	11
Blood and injury	3
Situational	29
Other	13
Not classified/unsure	6

Note: Patients were seen at the authors' Anxiety Disorders Clinic between March 17, 1988, and September 30, 1992.

Gullone, & Tonge, 1991; Morris & Kratochwill, 1983). Young infants, for example, show marked fear in the presence of loud noises and strangers. At 1 to 2 years of age, children quite normally are very anxious on separation from parents, but fears of animals and the dark also enter the picture. These fears may persist into the fourth or fifth year of life. At approximately age 3, fear of various monsters and other creatures may begin and last for several years. It is not until age 10 that children begin to develop evaluation fears as well as anxiety over their physical appearance. Generally, reports of fear decline with age, although performance-related fears, such as taking a test or talking in front of a large group of people, may increase with age. The prevalence of specific phobias seems to decline as one reaches old age (Blazer, George, & Hughes, 1991; Sheikh, 1992).

Cultural differences exist in the prevalence of specific phobias. African-Americans are three times more likely to report specific phobias than white Americans (Warheit, Holzer, & Arey, 1975; Brown, Eaton, & Sussman, 1990). It is possible that these phobias are related to the tendency for African-Americans to come from more socially disadvantaged and therefore realistically dangerous areas (Neal & Turner, 1991). Other suggestions are that excess stress present in these populations makes their members vulnerable to anxiety disorders in general and specific phobias in particular. The answers await further research.

A variant of phobia found in Chinese cultures is called *Pa-leng* and sometimes *frigo phobia* or "fear of the cold." Pa-leng can be understood only in the context of traditional ideas—in this case the traditional Chinese notions of yin and yang (Tan, 1980). Chinese medicine holds that there must be a balance of the yin and yang forces in the human body for health to be maintained. Yin represents the cold, dark, windy, energy-sapping aspects of life; yang refers to the bright, warm, energy-producing aspects of life. In Pa-leng, individuals present with a morbid fear of the cold. They ruminate over further loss of body heat, which may be a threat to life. People with Pa-leng may wear several layers of clothing even on a hot day. Complaints of belching and flatulence may reflect the presence of too much wind and therefore too much yin in the body.

Causes of Specific Phobia

For a long time we thought that most specific phobias began with some sort of unusual traumatic event. For example, if you were bitten by a dog you would develop a phobia of dogs. We now know this is not always the case (Öst, 1985; Barlow 1988). As described briefly in Chapter 1, "conditioning" experiences do not play a major role in the etiology of most phobias. This is not to say that traumatic conditioning experiences do not result in subsequent phobic behavior. Almost every person we see with a choking phobia has some kind of a choking experience in his background to which we can trace his phobic reactions. An individual with claustrophobia who recently came to our clinic reported a terrifying experience in which she was trapped in an elevator for an extraordinarily long period of time. These examples illustrate phobias acquired by *direct experience,* where one experiences real danger or pain resulting in an alarm response (a true alarm). This is one pathway to developing a phobia.

But in addition to direct experience with a traumatic situation, there are at least three other ways that one can develop a phobia: experiencing a *false* alarm (panic attack) in a specific situation, *observing* someone else experience severe fear (vicarious experience) or, under the right conditions, *being told* about some danger or other misinformation.

Remember our earlier discussion of unexpected panic attacks (false alarms)? We now know based on studies described below that many phobics do not necessarily experience real danger resulting in a true alarm at the beginning of their phobia. Many initially have an unexpected panic attack in a specific situation, related, perhaps, to some life stress they were experiencing at the time. A phobia of that situation may then develop. Munjack (1984) studied people with specific phobias of driving. He noted that about 50% of the people who could remember the beginning of their phobia experienced a true alarm due to a traumatic experience while driving, such as a car accident. The other half had had nothing terrible happen to them while they were driving, but they had experienced an unexpected panic attack accompanied by a feeling at that moment that they were going to lose control of the car and wipe out half the people on the highway. In fact, their driving was not impaired and their catastrophic thoughts were simply a part of their panic attack.

We can also learn fears vicariously. Seeing someone else have a traumatic experience or endure intense fear may be enough to instill a phobia in the watcher. Remember, we noted above that emotions are very contagious. If someone you are with is either happy or fearful, you will probably feel a tinge of happiness or fear also. Öst (1985) describes the development of a severe dental fear in this way. An adolescent boy was sitting in the waiting room at the school dentist's office partially observing, but fully hearing, his friend who was undergoing severe discomfort at the hands of the dentist. Evidently this discomfort resulted in sudden movement on the part of the dental patient. As a consequence, the drill partially punctured his cheek. The boy in the waiting room, upon overhearing this accident, bolted from the room and developed a severe and long-lasting fear of dental situations. Nothing happened to the "watcher" in this case but you can certainly understand how he developed his phobia. Susan Mineka and her colleagues in an elegant series of experiments have shown that monkeys can develop phobias by simply watching another monkey experience fear (Mineka, Davidson, Cook, & Keir, 1984).

Sometimes just being warned repeatedly about a potential danger is sufficient for someone to develop a phobia. Öst (1985) describes the case of a woman with an extremely severe snake phobia who had never encountered a snake in her life. Rather, she had been told repeatedly while growing up about the dangers of snakes in the high grass. She was encouraged to wear high rubber boots to guard against this imminent threat—and she did so, even when walking down the street. We call this mode of developing a phobia *information transmission.*

These experiences alone are not enough to create a phobia. As suggested at the beginning of this chapter, one must also develop *anxiety* over the possibility of experiencing another extremely traumatic event or another false alarm in that situation. Remember, when we are anxious, we are persistently anticipating that something terrible might happen, and we are likely to avoid the situation where that terrible thing might occur. If we don't develop anxiety, our fear reaction would presumably fall into a category of normal fears experienced by over half the population. This normal fear might cause some mild distress if we were directly confronted with the situation, but it is otherwise ignored and forgotten.

This point is best illustrated in a study by Peter DiNardo and his colleagues (1988). They studied a group of dog phobics as well as a matched group who did not have dog phobia. Similar to Munjack's (1984) driving phobics, about 50% of the group of dog phobics had experienced a frightening encounter with a dog, usually resulting in a bite. However, about 50% of another group of individuals who did *not* have dog phobia had also had a frightening encounter with a dog. Why hadn't they become dog phobics as well? The individuals who *did* acquire a dog phobia developed anxiety about another encounter with a dog while the group *without* the phobia did not.

In summary, several things have to occur for a person to develop a phobia. First, a traumatic conditioning experience often plays a role, although to experience a frightening event vicariously or even being told about it (information transmission) might be sufficient for some individuals. Second, we are more likely to develop fear if the initial experience involves a situation that is "prepared" in some way. That is, as mentioned in the beginning of this chapter, we seem to carry within us (inherit) a tendency to develop fear quickly in situations that have always been dangerous to the human race, such as being threatened by wild animals or trapped in small enclosed places.

But something more must take place. We also have to be susceptible to developing anxiety that the event will happen again. We have discussed the

Peter DiNardo and his colleagues made important discoveries about the causes of phobias by studying individuals with phobias of dogs, even dogs that appear calm and gentle.

biological and psychological reasons we develop anxiety and have seen that at least one phobia, blood-injection-injury phobia, is highly heritable (Öst, 1989). In examining first-degree relatives of 25 blood phobics at his center, Öst found that 64% of the patients had at least one relative with blood phobia. In addition to inheriting biological vulnerabilities to experience anxiety, the patients with blood phobia probably also inherit a strong vasovagal response that makes them susceptible to fainting. The fainting response alone would not be sufficient to ensure their development of a phobia, but combined with anxiety, they would have a strong vulnerability.

More recently, Fyer et al. (1990) demonstrated that approximately 31% of the first-degree relatives of people with specific phobias also had a phobia, compared with 11% of the first-degree relatives of normal controls. Because this was a family study, we do not know whether the tendency for phobias to run in families was due to genes or to modeling, but the finding is at least suggestive of a genetic contribution.

Finally, social and cultural factors are very strong determinants of who ultimately develops and reports a specific phobia. In most societies around the

world it is almost unacceptable for males to express fears and phobias. Thus, the overwhelming majority of specific phobias occur in women. What happens to the males? Very possibly they work hard to overcome their fears by repeatedly exposing themselves to their feared situations. Another possibility is that they simply endure their fears without telling anyone about them and without seeking any treatment. A diagram of the etiology of specific phobia that outlines the four pathways just described is presented in Figure 5.6.

Treatment of Specific Phobia

Although the development of phobias is relatively complex, the treatment is fairly straightforward. Almost everyone agrees that treating specific phobias requires structured and consistent exposure-based exercises. Nevertheless, when patients expose themselves gradually to what they fear, they must be under therapeutic supervision in most cases. Individuals with phobias attempting to carry out these exercises themselves often attempt to do too much too soon and end up escaping the situation, which may strengthen the phobia. In addition, if their fears center on having another

Figure 5.6   A model of the various ways a specific phobia may develop (from Barlow, 1988)

unexpected panic attack in this situation, we have recently determined that it is helpful to direct therapy at panic attacks in the manner described for panic disorder (Rygh & Barlow, 1986; Barlow, 1988). Finally, in cases of blood-injury-injection phobia where a severe drop in blood pressure resulting in fainting is a real possibility, graduated exposure-based exercises are still important, but they must be done in very specific ways. Individuals must *tense* various muscle groups during exposure exercises to keep their blood pressure sufficiently high to complete the practice (Öst & Sterner, 1987). It is interesting that when this is done, not only does the phobia disappear, but the tendency to experience the vasovagal response at the sight of blood also lessens considerably.

Social Phobia

Clinical Description of Social Phobia

Are you shy around people? If so, you have something in common with 20% to 50% of college students, depending on which survey you read. On the other hand, a much smaller number of people become so distressed around others that they suffer from a severe disorder we call **social phobia.** Consider the following case of a 13-year-old boy in junior high school.

The Case of Billy

Billy was the model boy at home. He did his homework, stayed out of trouble, did what his parents told him, and was generally quiet and reserved so that he didn't attract a lot of attention. However, when he got to junior high school, something his parents had noticed earlier became painfully evident. Billy had no friends. Not only did he have no friends, he seemed unwilling to attend any social activities or sporting events connected with his junior high school, even though his parents knew that most of the other kids in his class went to these events. When they decided it was time to check with the guidance counselor at the junior high school they found that she, in fact, had been about to call them. She reported that Billy was not socializing, he was not speaking up in class, and he would be sick to his stomach all day if he knew he was going to be called on. Furthermore, the teacher had difficulty getting anything more than a yes or no answer from him. More troublesome was the observation that Billy had begun skipping lunch. Recently he had been found hiding in a stall in the boy's restroom during lunch, something he said he had

been doing now for several months. After a subsequent referral to one of our clinics, we diagnosed Billy as having a severe case of social phobia, an irrational and extreme fear of social situations. In Billy's case, his phobia took the form of extreme shyness. He was afraid of being embarrassed or humiliated while in the presence of almost everyone except his parents.

But social phobia is more than exaggerated shyness (Schneier et al., in press), as illustrated in the following cases, which are representative of many appearing from time to time in the press.

In the second inning of this season's All-Star game, Los Angeles Dodger Second Baseman Steve Sax fielded an easy grounder, straightened up for the lob to first, and bounced the ball past First Baseman Al Oliver, who was less than 40 ft. away. It was a startling error even for an All-Star game studded with bush-league mishaps. But hard-core baseball fans knew it was one more manifestation of a leading mystery of the 1983 season: Sax, 23, last year's National League Rookie of the Year, cannot seem to make routine throws to first base. (Of his first 27 errors this season, 22 stem from bad throws.)

Sax is not alone. Over the years, a number of major league baseball players have developed odd mental blocks and sent psychologists scurrying for explanations. Among the most dramatic examples:

Mike Ivie, an outstanding catching prospect, was signed as a teenager by the San Diego Padres in 1970. In his first workout with the Padres, Ivie threw the ball too low to the pitcher and hit the screen used to protect pitchers during batting practice. A fellow catcher, Chris Cannizzaro, joked about it, and Ivie developed a block about throwing the ball back to the pitcher. Ivie switched to first base and, after a mediocre career with two other teams, is now a journeyman player for the Detroit Tigers.

Steve Blass, a World Series hero for the Pittsburgh Pirates in 1971 and an All-Star pitcher in 1972, mysteriously could not get the ball over the plate in 1973. As a result, he was out of baseball in 1974, at 32. Blass could throw with near-perfect control in practice, but apparently developed a phobia about facing hitters in a game. (Leo, 1983, p. 72)

Steve Sax obviously overcame his problem and went on to play for a number of major league teams. Many other athletes were not so fortunate. This type of problem is not limited to athletes but also occurs among well-known lecturers or performers. Carly

Some individuals with social phobia have no difficulty interacting with people but find it difficult to "perform" certain behaviors while other people are watching. This condition commonly occurs in athletes and entertainers—such as Steve Sax, Carly Simon, and Barbra Streisand—who must perform often, sometimes daily, in front of people.

Simon actually gave up performing for several years because of intolerable performance anxiety. The difficulties of a skilled athlete throwing a baseball to first base or a seasoned performer appearing on stage certainly do not correlate with the concept of "shyness" with which we are all familiar. In fact, many of these performers may well be among our more gregarious citizens. What holds these two seemingly different conditions together?

Billy, Steve Sax, and Carly Simon all experienced marked and persistent fear of one or more social or performance situations. In Billy's case, these situations were any in which he might have to interact with

people. For Steve Sax and Carly Simon, they were restricted to a specific behavior that they had to perform in public. Individuals with performance anxiety, such as Steve Sax and Carly Simon, usually have no difficulty interacting with people, but when they must do something *in front of* people, anxiety takes over and they focus on the possibility that they will screw up or embarrass themselves in some way. The most common type of performance phobia, to which most people can relate, is public speaking. This is the prototypical situation in which the individual would be subject to scrutiny by others while performing a specific task. Other types of situations also meet the criteria, such as eating in any public restaurant; writing one's signature in front of a bank clerk; or, primarily for males, urinating in a public restroom (called colloquially "bashful bladder"). Males with this problem must wait until a stall opens up, a difficult task at times. What is common about each of these examples is that the individual is required to *do* something while knowing that others will be watching and, to some extent, evaluating his behavior. It is truly a social phobia because these people report no difficulty whatsoever eating, writing, or urinating in private. Only when others are watching does the behavior deteriorate.

DSM-IV criteria for social phobia are presented in Table 5.12. Individuals who are extremely and painfully shy in almost all social situations would meet criteria for *social phobia generalized type*, which is a subtype of social phobia. Occasionally this subtype is called *social anxiety disorder* and is particularly prominent in children. In the child program in one of our clinics, 100% of children and adolescents with social phobia met criteria for generalized type (Albano et al., in press). Billy would also fit into this subtype (Schneier et al., in press).

Statistics and Course for Social Phobia

As many as 8% of the general population suffer from the disorder we call social phobia in a given 12-month period. These are substantial numbers (almost 20

million people in the United States alone, based on current population estimates) but far fewer than those who report they are shy. The sex ratio for social phobia breaks down to approximately 70% female and 30% male, based on a reanalysis of a very large epidemiological study (Schneier, Johnson, Hornig, Liebowitz, & Weissman, 1992). This distribution differs from the sex ratio of social phobics appearing at clinics, which is more nearly 50-50 (Barlow, 1988; Marks, 1985), suggesting that males may find this problem more incapacitating than other types of disorders and, therefore, seek help more frequently, perhaps because of career-related issues. Social phobia most often begins during the teenage years with a peak age of onset at about 15½ years. This is later than for specific phobias but earlier than for panic disorder. Social phobia also tends to be more prevalent in people who are younger (ages 18–29 years), less educated, single, and of lower socioeconomic class. The prevalence of social phobia declines slightly among the elderly (Blazer et al., 1991; Sheikh, 1992). Considering the difficulty meeting people presents to individuals with social phobia, it is not surprising that in the population of individuals with this disorder a greater percentage are single than is the case in the population at large.

In Japan the clinical presentation of what seems to be anxiety disorders is best summarized under the clinical label *shinkeishitsu*. One of the most common subcategories of shinkeishitsu is referred to as

Table 5.12   Diagnostic Criteria for Social Phobia

A. A marked and persistent fear of one or more social or performance situations in which the person is exposed to unfamiliar people or to possible scrutiny by others. The individual fears that he or she will act in a way (or show anxiety symptoms) that will be humiliating or embarrassing. Note: In children, there must be evidence of the capacity for age-appropriate social relationships with familiar people and the anxiety must occur in peer settings, not just in interactions with adults.

B. Exposure to the feared social situation almost invariably provokes anxiety, which may take the form of a situationally bound or situationally predisposed panic attack. Note: In children, the anxiety may be expressed by crying, tantrums, freezing, or shrinking from social situations with unfamiliar people.

C. The person recognizes that the fear is excessive or unreasonable. Note: In children, this feature may be absent.

D. The feared social or performance situations are avoided or are endured with intense anxiety or distress.

E. The avoidance, anxious anticipation, or distress in the feared social or performance situation(s) interferes significantly with the person's normal routine, occupational (academic) functioning, or social activities or relationships, or there is marked distress about having the phobia.

F. In individuals under age 18, duration is at least 6 months.

G. The fear or avoidance is not due to the direct physiological effects of a substance (e.g., a drug of abuse, medication) or a general medical condition, and is not better accounted for by another mental disorder (e.g., panic disorder with or without agoraphobia, separation anxiety disorder, body dysmorphic disorder, a pervasive developmental disorder, or schizoid personality disorder).

H. If a general medical condition or another mental disorder is present, the fear in criterion A is unrelated to it; e.g., the fear is not of stuttering, trembling in Parkinson's disease, or exhibiting abnormal eating behavior in anorexia nervosa or bulimia nervosa.

Specify if **Generalized**: if the fears include most social situations (also consider the additional diagnosis of avoidant personality disorder).

Source: DSM-IV, APA, 1994.

taijin kyōfushō (Kirmayer, 1991). This would be very close to social phobia in North America with some differences. People with this disorder in Japan have a strong fear of looking people in the eye and are afraid that some aspect of their personal presentation (for instance, blushing, stuttering, body odor, and so on) will appear reprehensible. Social phobias also seem to be more prevalent among blacks than whites (Brown & Eaton, 1986).

Causes of Social Phobia

Earlier we noted that we seem to be "prepared" in an evolutionary sense to fear certain wild animals or other dangerous situations in the natural environment. Similarly, it seems we are also "prepared" to fear angry, critical, or rejecting people (Öhman, 1986). In a series of studies Öhman and colleagues (for example, Öhman & Dimberg, 1978; Dimberg & Öhman, 1983) noted that we learn more quickly to fear angry faces than other facial expressions, and that this fear diminishes much more slowly than other types of learning. Why should we inherit a tendency to fear angry faces? Our ancestors probably tended to avoid hostile, angry, domineering people who might attack or kill them. Possibly, individuals with this tendency to avoid angry faces were more likely to survive and pass their genes down to us. Of course, this is just a theory.

Jerome Kagan and his colleagues (for example, Kagan, Reznick, & Snidman, 1988a; Kagan & Snidman, 1991) have demonstrated that some infants are born with a temperamental profile or trait of inhibition or shyness. This is evident when they are as young as 4 months of age. Four-month-old infants with this trait will become more agitated and cry more frequently when presented with toys or other normal stimuli than infants without this trait. Kagan et al. (1988a) also observed that these inhibited infants differ in *peripheral* physiological characteristics, such as heart rate increases or changes in skin conductance caused by arousal-related perspiration, that probably reflect differences in brain function. This trait seems to be inherited, but we do not know whether it differs fundamentally from a more general exaggerated responsivity to stress that seems to characterize the biological vulnerability to anxiety. Some evidence from researchers studying personality would suggest that anxiety and inhibition (or constraint, another word for inhibition) are two somewhat different traits (for instance, Tellegen, 1985). In any case, inhibition would relate more to the generalized type of social phobia than to discrete performance anxiety such as public speaking.

Putting this all together, a model of the etiology of social phobia would look somewhat like the models for the development of panic disorder and specific phobia already described. Three pathways to social phobia are possible in this model. First, one could inherit a biological vulnerability to develop anxiety and/or a biological tendency to be very socially inhibited. Middle to late adolescence is the period when social embarrassment and lack of social confidence is most common and experienced most intensely. Stressful life experiences of a social nature at this time may trigger the development of anxiety focused on social situations.

Second, when under stress, one might have an unexpected panic attack (false alarm) in a social situation and then develop anxiety over having additional false alarms (panic attacks) in the same or similar social situations. Third, someone might experience a real social trauma resulting in a true alarm. Anxiety would then develop (be conditioned) in the same or similar social situations. For example, one socially phobic client at our clinic reported that the onset of his social phobia dated to a time when he was making a presentation in front of a group of obviously critical supervisors who, he thought, were about to fire him. In fact, they did fire him. From that time on he had considerable difficulty making business presentations since anxiety and occasional "learned alarm" panic attacks would occur in the context of being critically evaluated and, perhaps, fired again, even if it were very unlikely. Traumatic social experiences may also extend back to difficult periods in childhood. Early adolescence—approximately ages 12 through 15 (junior high school in North America)—is a time when children may be brutally and traumatically taunted by members of their peer group attempting to assert their own dominance. But this taunting may produce anxiety and panic that is reproduced in future social situations.

Jerome Kagan has discovered that the trait of shyness or inhibition is evident as early as 4 months of age and is probably inherited.

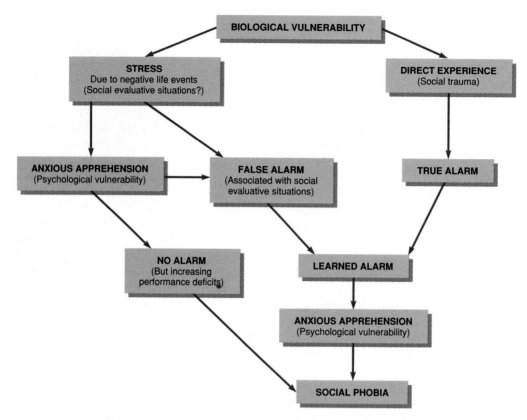

Figure 5.7 A model of the various ways a social phobia may develop (from Barlow, 1988)

A diagram of the etiology of social phobia is presented in Figure 5.7.

There is also evidence that at least some social phobics are predisposed to focus anxiety on events involving social evaluation when and if they occur. For example, Bruch, Heimberg, Berger, and Collins (1989) suggest that the parents of people with social phobia are significantly more socially fearful and concerned with evaluative opinions of others than are the parents of patients with panic disorder, and they pass this concern on to their children. Fyer, Mannuzza, Chapman, Liebowitz, and Klein (1993) reported that social phobia runs in families in that the relatives of people with this disorder had a significantly increased risk of developing it compared to the relatives of individuals without social phobia (16% vs. 5%). Thus, a combination of biological and psychological events may lead to the development of social phobia.

Treatment of Social Phobia

Effective treatments have been developed for social phobia only in the past several years (Butler, Cullington, Munby, Amies, & Gelder, 1984; Heimberg et al., 1990; Hope & Heimberg, in press). At our Center for Stress and Anxiety Disorders in Albany, Rick Heimberg and colleagues developed a program in which patients are treated in groups where they actually rehearse or role play their socially phobic situations in front of the group (Heimberg et al., 1990; Hope & Heimberg, in press). The other group members act as participants in the role-playing session. For example, if someone has extreme difficulty giving a speech, the rest of the participants will act as the audience. At the same time the therapist conducts rather intensive cognitive therapy aimed at uncovering and changing the automatic or unconscious perceptions of danger that the socially phobic client assumes to exist in the situation. These treatments have been proven highly effective compared to a credible psychotherapeutic control condition consisting of education about anxiety and social phobia and the provisions of social support for stressful life events. More important, a follow-up of 5 years indicates that the therapeutic gains are maintained (Heimberg, Salzman, Holt, & Blendell, 1993).

Effective drug treatments have now been discovered as well. For a time clinicians assumed that beta blockers were an effective treatment, particularly for performance anxiety, but the evidence does not seem to support that contention (Liebowitz et al., 1992). Most recently, tricyclic antidepressants and particularly monoamine oxidase (MAO) inhibitors have been found to be more effective than placebo in the treatment of severe social anxiety (Liebowitz et al., 1992), although relapse is common when drugs are stopped. Studies comparing MAO inhibitors to newly developed psychological treatments described earlier are now under way.

Posttraumatic Stress Disorder

Clinical Description of Posttraumatic Stress Disorder

In recent years we have heard a great deal about what happens to people who experience a traumatic event. Severe and long-lasting emotional disorders can occur after a variety of traumatic events. Perhaps the most impressive traumatic event is war, in recent times the Vietnam War, but emotional disorders also occur after physical assault (particularly rape), auto accidents, natural catastrophes (such as earthquakes or floods), or the sudden death of a loved one. The emotional disorder that arises after a trauma is known as **posttraumatic stress disorder (PTSD)**.

Table 5.13 presents the DSM-IV criteria for PTSD. Criterion A describes the setting event for PTSD as exposure to a traumatic event during which one feels fear, helplessness, or horror. Afterward, victims reexperience the event through memories or nightmares. Sometimes these memories come on very suddenly and the victims find themselves reliving the whole event. When this occurs it is called a *flashback*. Victims also avoid anything that reminds them of the trauma and display a characteristic restriction or numbing of their emotional responsiveness, sometimes being unable to remember certain aspects of the event. The restriction or "numbing" of emotional experiences seems to be a part of this avoidance and may be very disruptive to interpersonal relationships. It is possible that these victims are unconsciously attempting to avoid the experience of emotion itself, similarly to the behavior of people with panic disorder, since experiencing intense emotions could bring back memories of the trauma. Finally, victims typically are chronically overaroused, easily startled, and quick to anger.

The name for this disorder first appeared in 1980 with the publication of DSM-III (American Psychiatric Association, 1980), but it has a long history. The well-known British diarist Samuel Pepys witnessed the Great Fire of London in 1666, which resulted in substantial loss of life and property and threw the city into total chaos for a time. He captured the events in an account of the fire that is still read today. But Pepys did not escape the effects of the horrific event. Six months after it he wrote, "It is strange to think how to this very day I cannot sleep a night without great terrors of fire; and this very night could not sleep to almost 2 in the morning through thoughts of fire" (Daly, 1983, p. 66).

Richard Heimberg, working at the Center for Stress and Anxiety Disorders in Albany, has created an effective psychosocial treatment for social phobia.

The DSM-IV criteria show that difficulty sleeping and recurring intrusive dreams of the event are prominent features of PTSD. Pepys wrote about the guilt he experienced as a consequence of saving himself and his property while others died. He also experienced a sense of detachment and a numbing of his emotions concerning the fire, common experiences in posttraumatic stress disorder.

Consider the following case from one of our clinics.

The Case of the Joneses

Mrs. Betty Jones and her four children were on their way to visit a friend of Mrs. Jones who lived on a farm. Mr. Jones was working at the time. Jeff, the oldest child, was 8 years old. Jeff's three sisters, Marcie, Cathy, and Susan, were 6, 4, and 2 years of age. The family parked the car in the driveway, but to get to the front door of the house they had to cross a large front yard. Suddenly Jeff heard an animal growling somewhere near the house. Before he could warn the others, a large German Shepherd charged the family and leapt at Marcie, the 6-year-old girl, knocking her to the ground. The dog commenced a vicious attack tearing at Marcie's face. The family watched the attack helplessly, too stunned to move. After what seemed like an eternity, Jeff lunged at the dog and the dog moved away. The

Table 5.13   Diagnostic Criteria for Posttraumatic Stress Disorder

A. The person has been exposed to a traumatic event in which both of the following were present:

   1. The person experienced, witnessed, or was confronted with an event or events that involve actual or threatened death or serious injury, or a threat to the physical integrity of himself or herself or others
   2. The person's response involved intense fear, helplessness, or horror. Note: In children, it may be expressed instead by disorganized or agitated behavior

B. The traumatic event is persistently reexperienced in one (or more) of the following ways:

   1. Recurrent and intrusive distressing recollections of the event, including images, thoughts, or perceptions. Note: In young children, repetitive play may occur in which themes or aspects of the trauma are expressed
   2. Recurrent distressing dreams of the event. Note: In children, there may be frightening dreams without recognizable content
   3. Acting or feeling as if the traumatic event were recurring (includes a sense of reliving the experience, illusions, hallucinations, and dissociative flashback episodes, including those that occur on awakening or when intoxicated). Note: In young children, trauma-specific reenactment may occur
   4. Intense psychological distress at exposure to internal or external cues that symbolize or resemble an aspect of the traumatic event
   5. Physiologic reactivity on exposure to internal or external cues that symbolize or resemble an aspect of the traumatic event

C. Persistent avoidance of stimuli associated with the trauma and numbing of general responsiveness (not present before the trauma), as indicated by three (or more) of the following:

   1. Efforts to avoid thoughts, feelings, or conversations associated with the trauma
   2. Efforts to avoid activities, places, or people that arouse recollections of the trauma
   3. Inability to recall an important aspect of the trauma
   4. Markedly diminished interest or participation in significant activities
   5. Feeling of detachment or estrangement from others
   6. Restricted range of affect (e.g., unable to have loving feelings)
   7. Sense of a foreshortened future (e.g., does not expect to have a career, marriage, children, or a normal life span)

D. Persistent symptoms of increased arousal (not present before the trauma), as indicated by two (or more) of the following:

   1. Difficulty falling or staying asleep
   2. Irritability or outbursts of anger
   3. Difficulty concentrating
   4. Hypervigilance
   5. Exaggerated startle response

E. Duration of the disturbance (symptoms in B, C, and D) is more than one month.

F. The disturbance causes clinically significant distress or impairment in social, occupational, or other important areas of functioning.

Specify if:
   Acute: if duration of symptoms is less than 3 months
   Chronic: if duration of symptoms is 3 months or more

Specify if:
   With Delayed Onset: if onset of symptoms at least 6 months after the stressor

Source: DSM-IV, APA, 1994.

owner of the farm became aware of the attack and, in a state of panic, ran to a nearby house to get help. The mother immediately attended to Marcie and put pressure on her facial wounds in an attempt to stop the bleeding. Since the owner had neglected to retrieve the dog, the dog stood a short distance away, growling and barking at the frightened family for what seemed like a long time. Eventually the dog was restrained and Marcie was rushed to the hospital. At the hospital Marcie, who was hysterical at this point, had to be restrained on a papoose board so that emergency room physicians could stitch up the various lacerations on her face under local anesthesia.

This case was unusual because not only did Marcie develop PTSD, but so did her 8-year-old brother Jeff. In addition, Cathy (age 4) and Susan (age 2), although quite young, also evidenced some of the symptoms of the disorder. Specific symptoms that each of the children experienced are presented in Table 5.14 (Miller, Albano, & Barlow, 1992). As you can see from

Table 5.14 Symptoms of Posttraumatic Stress Disorder (PTSD) Evidenced by Marcie and Her Siblings

Symptoms	Jeff	Marcie	Cathy	Susan
Repetitive play—trauma themes		X	X	X
Nightmares	X	X	X	X
Reexperiencing		X		
Distress at exposure to similar stimuli	X	X	X	X
Avoidance of talk of trauma		X	X	
Avoidance of trauma recollections		X		
Regressive behavior	X	X		
Detachment	X	X		
Restricted affect	X	X		
Sleep disturbance	X	X	X	X
Anger outbursts	X	X		
Hypervigilance	X	X		
Startle response	X	X		
DSM-III-R PTSD diagnosis met	X	X		

Source: Miller, Albano, & Barlow, 1992.

the table, both Jeff and Marcie met criteria for (DSM-III-R) PTSD, and Cathy and Susan, while not quite meeting criteria, evidenced a substantial number of symptoms as did the mother. Jeff evidenced classic survivor guilt symptoms, reporting that he should have saved Marcie or at least put himself between Marcie and the dog. Both Jeff and Marcie "regressed" developmentally and began wetting the bed (nocturnal enuresis) and experiencing nightmares and separation fears. In addition Marcie, having been strapped to the papoose board, became very frightened of any medical procedures or even such routine daily events as having her nails trimmed or taking a bath. Furthermore, she refused to be tucked into bed, something she had enjoyed all her life, probably because it reminded her of the papoose board. Jeff started sucking his fingers, which he had not done for years. These behaviors, along with intense separation anxiety, are common, particularly in younger children (Eth, 1990). Cathy, the 4-year-old, evidenced considerable fear and avoidance when tested in our clinic but denied any problems what-

soever when she was interviewed by a child psychologist. Susan, the 2-year-old, also had some symptoms, as shown in Table 5.14, but was too young to talk about them. However, for several months following the trauma she would repeatedly say without any provocation, "Doggy bit sister." Memories of traumatic events can become embellished in children over the years. For example, some children incorporate into their traumatic memory a superhero coming to the rescue. These memories, while intense at times, are very malleable and subject to distortion.

As indicated in the criteria, PTSD is subdivided into *acute* and *chronic*. *Acute PTSD* can be diagnosed between 1 and 3 months after the event occurs. When PTSD continues longer than 3 months, it is considered chronic or long lasting because the evidence suggests that, if one is still experiencing severe symptoms of PTSD at 3 months, the disorder is likely to become chronic. *Chronic PTSD* is usually associated with more prominent avoidance symptoms and behaviors (Davidson et al., 1991), as well as the more frequent co-occurrence of additional diagnoses such as social phobia. Occasionally, individuals experiencing a trauma show few if any symptoms immediately following the trauma, but some time later, perhaps years afterward, they develop full-blown PTSD. This is called *delayed onset PTSD*. Why this happens in some individuals is not yet clear.

As noted above, PTSD cannot be diagnosed until 1 month has elapsed after the trauma. New to DSM-IV is a disorder called **acute stress disorder.** This is really PTSD occurring within the *first month* after the trauma, but it is given a different name to emphasize the very severe reaction that some people have immediately following a trauma. The reaction is characterized by PTSD-like symptoms but with more emphasis on severe dissociative symptoms. For example, symptoms of amnesia for all or part of the trauma, emotional numbing, and *derealization* are highlighted. Based on new studies, approximately 40% of individuals with acute stress disorder go on to develop PTSD. The decision was made to include acute stress disorder in DSM-IV because many people with very severe early reactions to trauma could not be diagnosed and, therefore, could not receive insurance coverage for immediate treatment for their condition.

Statistics and Course for Posttraumatic Stress Disorder

At first glance you would think that determining the prevalence rates for PTSD would be relatively straightforward: simply observe victims of a trauma and see how many are suffering from PTSD. But it is not that clear-cut. A number of studies have now demonstrated the remarkably *low* prevalence of PTSD in populations of trauma victims. Rachman (1978) studied the British citizenry who endured numerous life-threatening air raids during World War II. He concluded that "a great majority of people endured the air raids extraordinarily well, contrary to the universal expectation of mass panic. Exposure to repeated bombings did not produce a significant increase in psychiatric disorders. Although short lived fear reactions were common, surprisingly few persistent phobic reactions emerged" (Rachman, 1991, p. 162). Similar results have been observed after disastrous fires (Green, Grace, Lindy, Titchener, & Lindy, 1983).

Phillip Saigh (1984) made some interesting observations when he was teaching at the American University in Beirut, Lebanon, just before and during the Israeli invasion in the early 1980s. Saigh had been collecting questionnaires measuring anxiety among students at the American University just before the invasion. As the invasion began, half the students escaped to the surrounding mountains and were safe. The other half endured intense shelling and bombing for a period of time. Saigh continued administering the questionnaires and found a surprising result. There were no essential differences between the "safe" group in the mountains and the group in the city, although a few students in the city closely exposed to death and danger did develop emotional reactions that developed into PTSD.

On the other hand, some studies have found a very high incidence of PTSD after trauma. Kilpatrick et al. (1985) sampled more than 2,000 adult women who had personally experienced such trauma as rape, sexual molestation, robbery, and aggravated assault. Subjects were asked whether they had thought about suicide after the trauma, attempted suicide, or had a *nervous breakdown* (a lay term that has no meaning in

psychopathology but is commonly used to refer to a severe psychological upset). The authors also analyzed the results based on whether the attack was completed or attempted, as shown in Table 5.15. The crime with the most significant emotional impact was rape. Compared to 2.2% of nonvictims, 19.2% of rape victims had attempted suicide, and 44% reported suicidal ideation at some time following the rape.

What accounts for the discrepancies between the low rate of PTSD in citizens who endured bombing and shelling in London and Beirut and the relatively high rate in victims of crime? Investigators have now concluded that many of those experiencing air raids *may not have directly experienced the horrors of death, dying, and direct attack*. Bombs may have been falling at a distance, and they may not have witnessed death, near death, or injury. Direct experience with the trauma seems to be a necessary condition to develop this disorder (Barlow, 1988).

In the population at large, the lifetime prevalence of PTSD ranges from 1% to 2.6% depending on the survey (Helzer, Robins, & McEvoy, 1987). But the prevalence of PTSD always seems to be directly related to the intensity and severity of one's personal experience with a catastrophe or trauma.

But is this the whole story? It seems not. For we now know some individuals can experience the most horrifying trauma imaginable and emerge psychologically healthy. For other people, even relatively mild stressful events might be sufficient to produce a full-blown disorder. To understand how this can happen we must consider the etiology of PTSD.

Causes of Posttraumatic Stress Disorder

PTSD is the one disorder for which, it would seem, we know the etiology. After all, someone personally

Table 5.15   Proportion of Victimization Groups Experiencing Major Mental Health Problems

	Problem					
	Nervous Breakdown		Suicidal Ideation		Suicide Attempt	
Group	n	%	n	%	n	%
Attempted rape	7	9.0	23	29.5	7	8.9
Completed rape	16	16.3	44	44.0	19	19.2
Attempted molestation	2	5.4	12	32.4	3	8.1
Completed molestation	1	1.9	12	21.8	2	3.6
Attempted robbery	0	0.0	3	9.1	4	12.1
Completed robbery	5	7.8	7	10.8	2	3.1
Aggravated assault	1	2.1	7	14.9	2	4.3
Nonvictims	51	3.3	106	6.8	34	2.2

Source: Kilpatrick et al., 1985.

experiences a trauma and develops a disorder. However, whether one develops PTSD or not is a surprisingly complex issue involving biological, psychological, and social factors.

First, the intensity of the traumatic experience seems to be important. David Foy and his colleagues (Foy, Sipprelle, Rueger, & Carroll, 1984) concluded that the intensity of combat exposure in a group of Vietnam war veterans contributed to the etiology but did not account for all of it. If the combat exposure and trauma were severe, a high proportion of individuals developed PTSD; if the trauma was less severe, the proportion of people manifesting symptoms of the disorder was much lower. For example, approximately 67% of prisoners of war developed PTSD (Foy, Resnick, Sipprelle, & Carroll, 1987). This means that 33% of these prisoners who underwent long-term deprivation and torture *did not* develop the disorder. At lower levels of trauma, some people develop PTSD but most do not. What accounts for these differences?

As with other anxiety disorders, it seems that we bring our own biological and psychological vulnerability with us to these traumatic events. The greater the vulnerability, the more likely we are to develop PTSD. Davidson, Swartz, Storck, Krishnan, and Hammett (1985) and Foy et al. (1987) found that if anxiety runs in your family, you have a much greater chance of developing the disorder. We have seen, at the beginning of this chapter, that when anxiety runs in the family, this suggests there is a genetic contribution that creates a biological vulnerability for PTSD. More recently, True et al. (1993) reported that, given the same amount of combat exposure and one twin with PTSD, a monozygotic (identical) twin was more likely to develop PTSD than a dizygotic twin. The correlation of symptoms in identical twins was between .28 and .41 while for fraternal twins it was between .11 and .24, suggesting some genetic influence.

Also, there seems to be a psychological contribution based on early experiences with unpredictable or uncontrollable events. Foy et al. (1987) discovered that at very high levels of trauma, such as among prisoners of war, these vulnerabilities did not matter as much since most prisoners (67%) developed PTSD. However, at low levels of stress or trauma, the vulnerability that you bring to the experience matters a great deal in determining whether you will develop the disorder.

Finally, social and cultural factors play a major role in the development of PTSD (for example, Carroll, Rueger, Foy, & Donahoe, 1985). The results from a number of studies are very consistent in showing that, if you have a strong and supportive group of people around you (social support), it is much less likely that you will develop PTSD after a trauma. The broader and

deeper the network of social support, the less your chance of developing PTSD.

Why is this? As we saw in Chapter 2, we are all social animals and there is something about having a loving, caring group of people around us that directly affects our biological and psychological responses to stress. It is likely that one reason for the very high prevalence of PTSD in Vietnam veterans is the tragically low level of support they received from friends and colleagues when they returned from the war.

What are the neurobiological factors operating in PTSD? Recently, Dennis Charney and colleagues have suggested that PTSD involves a number of neurobiological systems (Charney, Deutch, Krystal, Southwick, & Davis, 1993; Southwick, Krystal, Johnson, & Charney, 1992). These investigators based their theorizing on work with animals, mostly rats, who were exposed to strong uncontrollable stress such as repeated shock. The effects of this uncontrollable stress on the neurobiological systems of the animals are presented in Table 5.16. Southwick et al. (1992) suggest that the simultaneous alterations of numerous brain neurochemical systems and structures probably represent adaptive responses to stress. Of course, work with animals is only suggestive of what happens with humans.

Earlier in the chapter we described a panic attack as an adaptive fear response occurring at an inappropriate time. It is not surprising that Southwick et al. (1992) trace a brain circuit for PTSD that is very similar to the brain circuit for panic attacks, originating in the locus coeruleus in the brain stem. We have speculated that the alarm reaction is much the same in both panic disorder and PTSD, but in panic disorder the alarm is false. In PTSD, the initial alarm is true in that a real danger is present (Jones & Barlow, 1990). If the alarm is severe enough, we may develop a conditioned or learned alarm reaction to stimuli that remind us of the trauma (for instance, being tucked into bed reminded Marcie of the papoose board). We may also develop anxiety about the possibility of having additional uncontrollable emotional experiences (such as flashbacks, which are common in PTSD). Whether or not we develop anxiety would depend in part on our vulnerabilities to do so. The etiology of PTSD, based on this model, is presented in Figure 5.8.

Treatment of Posttraumatic Stress Disorder

From the psychological point of view, most clinicians would agree on the necessity to reexpose the victim to the trauma in order to overcome the debilitating effects of PTSD; only then can patients face the trauma and begin to develop effective coping procedures so that

Table 5.16   Effects of Uncontrollable Stress on Neurobiological Systems of Rats

Neurochemical System	Functional Alteration Produced by Uncontrollable Stress	Acute Adaptive Behavioral Responses
Noradrenergic	Increased regional norepinephrine turnover in limbic and cortical areas Increased responsiveness of locus ceruleus neurons	Anxiety, fear, autonomic hyper-arousal, "fight" or "flight" readiness, encoding of traumatic memories, facilitation of sensory-motor responses
Dopaminergic	Increased dopamine release in frontal cortex and nucleus accumbens Activation of mesocortical dopamine neurons	Hypervigilance
Opiate	Increased endogenous opiate release in periaqueductal gray Decreased density of mu opiate receptors in cerebral cortex	Analgesia, emotional blunting, encoding of traumatic memories
Benzodiazepine	Decreased density of benzodiazepine receptors in hippocampus and cerebral cortex Reduced GABA*-dependent chloride flux	Fear, hyperarousal
Hypothalamic-pituitary-adrenal axis	Elevated glucocorticoid levels at the level of the hippocampus	Metabolic activation, learned behavioral responses

*GABA = gamma-aminobutyric acid.

Source: Southwick et al., 1991.

Figure 5.8   A model of the causes of posttraumatic stress disorder (from Barlow, 1988)

they can eventually tolerate the trauma. In psychoanalytic therapy, reliving the emotional trauma to relieve emotional suffering is called *catharsis*. The trick, of course, is arranging the reexposure so that it will be therapeutic rather than traumatic once again. Unlike specific phobias, traumatic events are difficult to recreate, and very few therapists would want to reenact them. Therefore, imaginal exposure, in which the contextual and emotional experiences of the trauma are worked through systematically, has been used for decades with trauma victims under a variety of names.

Another complication of treating trauma victims is that they often repress the images and memories of the traumatic event. They do this automatically or unconsciously in an attempt to avoid reliving the trauma. On occasion, with treatment, the memories come flooding back and the patient, in a very dramatic way, relives the episode. While this occurrence is very frightening to both the patient and the therapist, it is therapeutic if handled appropriately. Generally, reexposure to the trauma is best carried out in a very gradual fashion. Mardi Horowitz (1986, p. 125), a psychodynamic psychotherapist, recommends that if the patient is "frozen in (an) overcontrolled state of denial and numbness," it is all the more important that the therapeutic reliving be gradual.

In the case of Marcie, the young girl bitten by the dog, and her brother, both were treated simultaneously in one of our clinics. Since the primary difficulty was Marcie's reluctance to be seen by a doctor or to

Table 5.17 Fear and Avoidance Hierarchy for Marcie

	Pretreatment	Posttreatment
Being strapped on a papoose board	4	0
Having an electrocardiogram	4	0
Having a chest X-ray	4	0
Having M.D. listen to heart with stethoscope	3	0
Lying on examination table	3	0
Taking a bath after sustaining an accidentally inflicted cut	3	0
Allowing therapist to put Band-Aid on a cut	2	0
Letting therapist listen to heart with stethoscope	1	0
Having pulse taken	1	0
Allowing therapist to examine throat with tongue depressor	1	0
Having blood pressure taken	0	0
Giving doll an injection	0	0

Source: Miller, Albano, & Barlow, 1992.

undergo any physical examinations, a series of experiences was arranged from least to most intense. An example of a mildly anxiety-provoking procedure for Marcie was having her pulse taken. Other examples included lying on an examination table and taking a bath after having accidentally cut herself. The most intense item for her, as you can imagine, was being strapped on a papoose board. This hierarchy of items is presented in Table 5.17.

First, we had Marcie watch her brother go through these exercises. Her brother was not afraid of these particular procedures, although he had developed some fear about being strapped to a papoose board after hearing Marcie's terror at the thought of this procedure. After she watched her brother experience these situations with little or no fear, Marcie then tried each one in turn. The therapist took an instant photograph of her that she could keep after completing the procedure. Marcie also was asked to draw pictures of these situations. The therapist and all Marcie's family warmly congratulated her as she completed each exercise.

This type of real-life treatment was important for Marcie; because of her age, she was not adept at recreating memories of the traumatic medical procedures. Therefore, her treatment offered experiences designed to alter her current perceptions of these situations. Marcie's PTSD was successfully treated. Furthermore, her brother's guilt was greatly reduced as a function of helping in her treatment.

Some drug treatments have also been tried with PTSD but the investigation of effective ones is just beginning (Southwick, Krystal, & Charney, 1991). Preliminary experience suggests that some of the same drugs effective for anxiety disorders in general might be helpful with PTSD, perhaps because they relieve the severe anxiety and panic attacks (learned alarms) that are so prominent in this disorder.

Obsessive-Compulsive Disorder

Clinical Description of Obsessive-Compulsive Disorder

If a client with an anxiety disorder needs hospitalization, chances are the patient has **obsessive-compulsive disorder (OCD).** If a client is referred for psychosurgery because every psychological and pharmacological treatment has failed and her suffering is unbearable, chances are the patient has OCD. OCD is the devastating culmination of the anxiety disorders. It is not uncommon for someone with OCD to experience severe generalized anxiety, recurrent panic attacks, debilitating avoidance, and major depression, all occurring simultaneously in conjunction with his obsessive-compulsive symptoms. OCD is the disorder in which establishing even a foothold of control and predictability over the dangerous events in one's life seems so utterly hopeless that one resorts to magic and rituals.

But this is where OCD is different. In other anxiety disorders the dangerous event is usually an external object or situation, or at least a memory of one. In OCD the dangerous event is a thought, image, or impulse—but the client with OCD attempts to avoid these thoughts, images, or impulses as completely as someone with a snake phobia avoids snakes. The DSM-IV criteria for obsessive-compulsive disorder are presented in Table 5.18.

Has anyone ever told you not to think of pink elephants? If you really concentrate on not thinking of pink elephants, using every mental means possible, then you will realize how difficult it is to suppress a thought or image. Individuals with OCD fight this battle all day, every day, sometimes for most of their lives, usually failing miserably.

"I'm a little bit obsessive-compulsive. . . . It's a little difficult to deal with. The obsessive part—I'll get a thought in my head, and I can't put it out. It's just there all the time. I think about it when I go to bed, I think about it when I get up . . . I'm a 'checker'—I have to check things . . . I don't cook, but I have to check the stove every morning . . . not always really rational. . . . "

In Chapter 3 we discussed the case of Frank who experienced intrusive thoughts of epilepsy or seizures and would pray or shake his leg to try to rid himself of his thoughts. **Obsessions** are intrusive and mostly nonsensical thoughts, images, or urges (for instance, yelling in church) that the individual tries to resist or eliminate. **Compulsions** are thoughts or actions designed to suppress the thoughts and provide relief. Frank had both obsessions and compulsions but his disorder was mild compared to a case one of us saw several years ago.

The Case of Richard

Richard was a 19-year-old college freshman majoring in philosophy when he withdrew from school because of incapacitating ritualistic behavior. These rituals included excessive handwashing and showering; ceremonial rituals for dressing and studying; compulsive placements of any objects he handled; grotesque hissing, coughing, and head tossing while he was eating; and shuffling and wiping his feet while walking. Over the prior 2 years Richard's behavior had steadily deteriorated and finally he had isolated himself from his family and friends, refusing meals and neglecting his personal appearance. He had not cut his hair in 5 years nor had he shaved or trimmed his beard. Any time he walked anywhere he would take very small steps on his toes while continually looking back, checking and rechecking. On occasion he would run quickly in place. He had withdrawn his left arm completely from his shirt sleeve as if he were crippled and his shirt was a sling.

Before his hospital admission he had stopped all personal hygiene because the compulsive rituals that he had to carry out during washing or cleaning were so time-consuming that he could do nothing else. Almost continual showering became no showering. He stopped washing his hair, brushing his teeth, or changing his clothes. He left his room infrequently and, to avoid rituals associated with the toilet, had begun defecating on paper towels, urinating in paper cups, and storing the waste in a corner of the closet in his room. He stopped eating with his family and ate only late at night when others were asleep. To be able to eat he would have to exhale all air, making a lot of hissing noises, coughs, and hacks, and then fill his mouth with as much food as he could while no air was in his lungs. He had reached the point where all he would eat was a mixture of peanut butter, sugar, cocoa, milk, and mayonnaise. All other foods he considered contaminants.

Like everyone with OCD, Richard was experiencing intrusive and persistent thoughts and impulses. In Richard's case they revolved around sex, aggression, and religion. All his various behaviors were an attempt to suppress his sexual and aggressive thoughts or to ward off the disastrous consequences that he thought might ensue if he did not follow through with his rituals. Richard's compulsions comprised most of the repetitive behaviors and mental acts mentioned in the

Table 5.18 Diagnostic Criteria for Obsessive-Compulsive Disorder

A. Either obsessions or compulsions:

Obsessions as defined by 1, 2, 3, and 4:

1. Recurrent and persistent thoughts, impulses, or images that are experienced, at some time during the disturbance, as intrusive and inappropriate, and cause marked anxiety or distress
2. The thoughts, impulses, or images are not simply excessive worries about real-life problems
3. The person attempts to ignore or suppress such thoughts, impulses, or images, or to neutralize them with some other thought or action
4. The person recognizes that the obsessional thoughts, impulses, or images are a product of his or her own mind (not imposed from without as in thought insertion)

Compulsions as defined by 1 and 2:

1. Repetitive behaviors (e.g., handwashing, ordering, checking) or mental acts (e.g., praying, counting, repeating words silently) that the person feels driven to perform in response to an obsession, or according to rules that must be applied rigidly
2. The behaviors or mental acts are aimed at preventing or reducing distress or preventing some dreaded event or situation; however, these behaviors or mental acts either are not connected in a realistic way with what they are designed to neutralize or prevent, or are clearly excessive

B. At some point during the course of the disorder, the person has recognized that the obsessions or compulsions are excessive or unreasonable. Note: This does not apply to children.

C. The obsessions or compulsions cause marked distress, are time-consuming (take more than 1 hour a day), or significantly interfere with the person's normal routine, occupational (or academic) functioning, or usual social activities or relationships.

D. If another Axis I disorder is present, the content of the obsessions or compulsions is not restricted to it (e.g., preoccupation with food in the presence of an eating disorder; hair pulling in the presence of trichotillomania; concern with appearance in the presence of body dysmorphic disorder; preoccupation with drugs in the presence of a substance use disorder; preoccupation with having a serious illness in the presence of hypochondriasis; preoccupation with sexual urges or fantasies in the presence of a paraphilia; or guilty ruminations in the presence of major depressive disorder).

E. The disturbance is not due to the direct effects of a substance (e.g., drugs of abuse, medication) or a general medical condition.

Specify if: **With Poor Insight:** if, for most of the time during the current episode, the person does not recognize that the obsessions and compulsions are excessive or unreasonable

Source: DSM-IV, APA, 1994.

criteria. It is important to notice that compulsions can either be behavioral (handwashing, checking) or mental (thinking about certain words in a specific order, counting, praying, and so on) (Foa & Kozak, in press). The important thing is that the compulsions are designed to somehow reduce stress or prevent some dreaded event or situation from happening. Compulsions are often "magical" in that they frequently bear no logical relation to the obsession.

Obsessions

What are typical obsessions? Jenike, Baer, and Minichiello (1986) noted that the most frequent obsessions in a sample of 100 patients were contamination (55%), aggressive impulses (50%), sexual content (32%), somatic concerns (35%), and the need for symmetry (37%). Sixty percent of those sampled displayed multiple obsessions. The need for symmetry refers to keeping things in perfect order or doing something in a very specific way. Do you remember in your early years, walking down the sidewalk and being careful not to step on the cracks? You and your friends might have done this for a few minutes before tiring of

it. But what if you had to spend your whole life never stepping on a crack or driving a car across the lines in the road? Your life wouldn't be much fun. People who experience obsessive impulses may feel they are about to yell out a swear word while sitting quietly in church. One client we had, a young and attractive but very moral woman, was afraid to ride the bus for fear that, if a man sat down beside her, she would grab his crotch! In fact, this would be the last thing she would do, but the impulse was so horrifying that she made every attempt possible to suppress it or to avoid situations where the impulse might occur, such as riding the bus.

Compulsions

Most clients with OCD present with cleaning or washing rituals or checking rituals. There is an obvious difference between washing rituals and checking rituals. Individuals with washing rituals typically fear contact with objects or situations that may be contaminating. Washing or cleaning restores for them a sense of safety and control. Checking rituals, on the other hand, serve to prevent some future imagined disaster or catastrophe. Most checking rituals are logical, such as repeatedly checking the stove to see whether you turned it off, but in their severe form they can become illogical. For example, if Richard did not eat in a certain way he thought he might be possessed. If he didn't take small steps and look back, some disaster might happen to his family. There is no logical connection between these events, but without all the repetitive behavior involved in looking back and taking small steps he thought (obsessed) that something terrible might happen. Remember also that a mental act, such as counting, can be a compulsion. Many patients have both kinds of rituals as did Richard.

On rare occasions patients, particularly children, will present with few (if any) identifiable obsessions. We had a case of an 8-year-old child who felt compelled to undress for bed, put on his pajamas, and turn down the covers of his bed in a very time-consuming ritualistic fashion each night and then repeat each behavior 3 times. However, he could identify no particular reason why he was doing this. He simply had to do it.

Statistics and Course for Obsessive-Compulsive Disorder

The lifetime prevalence of OCD based on a large epidemiological study is 2.6% (Karno & Golding, 1991). This is a far greater prevalence than we had previously thought (for example, Coryell, 1981). But not all cases meeting criteria for OCD are as severe as that of Richard. We know with increasing certainty that obsessions and compulsions are on a continuum, as are most clinical features of anxiety disorders. Randy Frost and his colleagues found that between 10% and 15% of "normal" college students engaged in checking behavior substantial enough to score within the range of patients with OCD (Frost, Sher, & Geen, 1986).

It would be unusual for someone *not* to have an occasional intrusive or strange thought. Many people experience occasional bizarre, sexual, or aggressive thoughts, particularly if they are bored—for example, when sitting in class. But most individuals let these thoughts "go in one ear and out the other," so to speak. Certain individuals, however, become horrified at having these thoughts and consider them an alien, intrusive, evil force. As with other anxiety disorders, the majority of individuals with obsessive-compulsive disorder are female, but the ratio is not as large as for some other disorders. Rasmussen and Tsuang (1984, 1986) reported that 55% of 1,630 patients were female. The ECA epidemiology study noted 60% females in their sample of OCD (Karno & Golding, 1991). Average age of onset ranges from early adolescence to mid-twenties but typically peaks earlier in males than in females. The peak age of onset for males is from 13 to 15 years old while in females it is from 20 to 24 years old (Rasmussen

& Eisen, 1990). Once OCD develops, it tends to last and become chronic.

In Arabic countries, such as Saudi Arabia and Egypt, obsessive-compulsive disorder is easily recognizable, although cultural beliefs and concerns seem to influence the content of the obsessions and the nature of the compulsions. The theme of obsessions in these two countries is primarily related to religious practices, specifically the emphasis on cleanliness in the Moslem religion. Themes of contamination and dirt are also highly prevalent in India. Nevertheless, OCD looks remarkably similar across cultures. Insel (1984) reviewed studies from England, Hong Kong, India, Egypt, Japan, and Norway and found essentially similar types and proportions of obsessions and compulsions.

Causes of Obsessive-Compulsive Disorder

We noted above that many people experience intrusive, even horrific thoughts. Many people also occasionally engage in ritualistic behavior. The frequency of both intrusive, unpleasant thoughts and ritualistic behavior increases when we are in the midst of some stressful situation (Parkinson & Rachman, 1981a, 1981b). But very few of these individuals will go on to develop obsessive-compulsive disorder. Once again, as with panic disorder and posttraumatic stress disorder, simply experiencing intrusive thoughts is not sufficient. One must develop anxiety focused on the possibility of having additional intrusive thoughts.

The likelihood of having repetitive, intrusive, unacceptable thoughts may well be regulated by the hypothetical brain circuit for OCD described in Chapter 2. However, the propensity to develop anxiety over having additional thoughts may have the same biological and psychological precursors described for anxiety in general at the beginning of the chapter.

But why would clients with OCD focus their anxiety on the occasional intrusive thought rather than a panic attack or some other external situation? One hypothesis is that these individuals have had early experiences in their lives that taught them *some thoughts* are dangerous and unacceptable. They learn this through the same process of misinformation that convinced the person with snake phobia that snakes were dangerous and could be everywhere—even in the city. Clients with OCD equate thoughts with the specific actions or activity represented by the thoughts, a characteristic of some individuals with fundamentalist religious beliefs. One patient in our clinic believed that having a thought concerning abortion was the moral equivalent of having an abortion. Richard, the case presented earlier, finally admitted to having strong homosexual impulses that were unacceptable to him and to his father, who was a minister. That is, the impulses were just as sinful as actual homosexual acts. Many people who believe in the tenets of fundamental religions, whether Protestant, Catholic, Jewish, or Islamic, present with similar attitudes. The problem is that, if you hold this belief, you should try very hard to suppress the thought. But remember the pink elephant example? The more you try to suppress, the more difficult suppression becomes. Of course, the vast majority of individuals holding fundamental religious beliefs do not develop OCD. Once again, biological and psychological vulnerabilities must be present for this disorder to develop. Believing that some thoughts are "unacceptable" and therefore must be suppressed may put people at greater risk of OCD, an idea that has recently received some support (Parkinson & Rachman, 1981b; Salkovskis, 1985; Salkovskis & Campbell, 1994). A model of the etiology of obsessive compulsive disorder that is somewhat similar to other models of anxiety disorders is presented in Figure 5.9.

Treatment of Obsessive-Compulsive Disorder

Studies evaluating the effects of drugs for obsessive-compulsive disorder are showing some promise (Riggs & Foa, 1993). The most effective seem to be those that specifically target the serotonergic neurotransmitter system. Certain drugs that inhibit the reuptake of

Edna Foa has been instrumental in developing an effective psychosocial treatment for obsessive-compulsive disorder.

serotonin will have some therapeutic effect in up to 60% of patients with OCD. However, the average treatment gain is moderate at best (Greist, 1990) and relapse frequently occurs when the drug is discontinued (Pato, Zohar-Kadouch, Zohar, & Murphy, 1988).

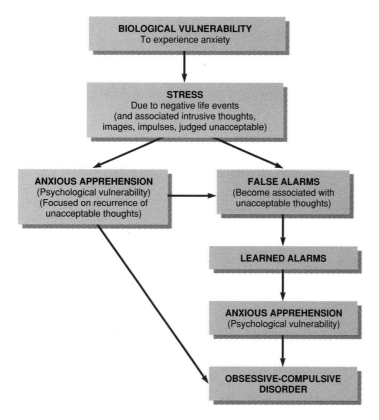

Figure 5.9   A model of the causes of obsessive-compulsive disorder (from Barlow, 1988)

Specific, highly structured psychological treatments fare somewhat better but they are not readily available. The most effective treatment approach is exposure and response prevention, a process whereby the rituals are actively prevented and the patient is systematically and gradually exposed to the feared thoughts or situations. In Richard's case, he would be systematically exposed to harmless objects or situations that he thought were contaminated, such as certain foods or household chemicals. At the same time his washing and checking rituals would be prevented. Usually this is done by simply working closely with patients to see that they do not wash or check. In severe cases, patients may be hospitalized and the handles removed from the bathroom sink for a period of time to help the patient refrain from repeated washing. However the rituals are prevented, the procedures seem to facilitate "reality testing" as the client soon learns, at an emotional level, that no harm will befall him or his loved ones whether he carries out the rituals or not. Studies are now under way examining the combined effects of medication and psychological treatments.

One of the more radical treatments for obsessive-compulsive disorder is psychosurgery. Psychosurgery is a misnomer that refers to neurosurgery for a psychological disorder. Jenike et al. (1991) recently reviewed the records of 33 patients with obsessive-compulsive disorder, most of whom were extremely severe cases who had failed to respond at all to either drug or psychological treatment. After a very specific surgical lesion to the cingulate bundle (cingulotomy), approximately 30% benefitted substantially. Considering that these patients seemed to have no hope whatsoever from existing treatments, surgery deserves consideration as a treatment of last resort.

Summary

- Anxiety disorders affect more people than any other psychological disorder.
- Anxiety is a future-oriented state in which a person focuses on the possibility of experiencing uncontrollable danger or misfortune.
- A panic attack represents the alarm response of real fear, but there is no actual danger.
- Panic attacks may be
  - unexpected (completely without warning).
  - situationally bound (always occurring in a specific situation).
  - situationally predisposed (likely but unpredictable in a specific situation).
- Panic and anxiety combine to create different anxiety disorders:
  - In generalized anxiety disorder, anxiety focuses on minor everyday events.
  - In panic disorder, anxiety focuses on the next panic attack.
  - In phobic disorders, the individual avoids situations that produce severe anxiety and/or panic.
  - Posttraumatic stress disorder focuses on avoiding thoughts or images of past traumatic experiences.
  - Obsessive-compulsive disorder focuses on avoiding frightening or repulsive intrusive thoughts or neutralizing these thoughts through the use of ritualistic behavior.
- Specific genetic vulnerabilities, as well as specific psychological vulnerabilities, seem to put individuals at risk for anxiety disorders.
- For an anxiety disorder to develop, biological and psychological tendencies must be activated by stressful life events.
- Psychosocial treatments are very effective for phobic and panic disorders and somewhat effective for posttraumatic stress, obsessive-compulsive disorders, and generalized anxiety disorders.
- Drug treatments are somewhat effective for social phobia, panic disorder, obsessive-compulsive disorder, and generalized anxiety disorder.

Key Terms

acute stress disorder (191)
agoraphobia (165)
animal phobia (178)
anxiety (151)
behavioral inhibition system
  (BIS) (157)
blood-injection-injury phobia (177)
compulsions (196)
fear (152)
fight/flight system (FFS) (157)
generalized anxiety disorder
  (GAD) (159)

natural environmental
  phobia (178)
obsessions (196)
obsessive-compulsive
  disorder (OCD) (195)
panic (153)
panic attack (154)
panic control treatments
  (PCT) (175)
panic disorder with agoraphobia
  (PDA) (165)

panic disorder without agoraphobia (PD) (166)
posttraumatic stress disorder
  (PTSD) (189)
separation anxiety disorder (179)
situational phobia (177)
social phobia (184)
specific phobia (176)

Disintegrated personality is no bizarre phenomenon,
but in its mild forms an almost every-day clinical affair.
Morton Prince
Hysteria from the Point of View of Dissociated Personality

6

Somatoform and Dissociative Disorders

Do you know somebody who's a hypochondriac? Most of us do. Maybe it's you! The popular image of a hypochondriac is someone who exaggerates the slightest physical symptom. Many of these people continually run to the doctor even though there is nothing really wrong with them. For many people with this trait, including, perhaps, some people you know, this is a harmless tendency that may even be worth some good-natured jokes. But for a few of these individuals, the preoccupation with their health or the appearance of their bodies becomes so great that it dominates their lives. The problems these people experience would fall under the general heading of **somatoform disorders:** *Soma* means body, and the problems preoccupying these people seem, initially, to be physical disorders. The disorders have one thing in common, however; examiners usually find no identifiable medical condition causing the physical complaints.

Have you ever felt "detached" from yourself or the setting where you were? ("This isn't really me" or "That doesn't really look like my hand" or "There's something unreal about this place.") In describing these experiences some people feel as if they are living in a dream. This happens to most people occasionally. These very mild sensations that many people experience from time to time represent slight alterations or detachments in consciousness or identity, which are known as *dissociative experiences* or *dissociation*. But there are a few people for whom these dissociative experiences are so intense and extreme that they lose their identity entirely and assume a new one, or they lose their memory or sense of reality and become unable to function. These individuals are suffering from one of several types of **dissociative disorders,** which we will discuss in the second half of this chapter.

These two sets of disorders are not necessarily closely related, although on occasion they share some common features, but they are very strongly linked historically. In prior diagnostic systems all disorders of these two types were categorized under one general heading, "hysterical neurosis." You may remember (from Chapter 1) that the term *hysteria* dates back to Hippocrates, and the Egyptians before him, and suggests that the cause of these disorders, many of which were originally thought to occur primarily in women, can be traced to a "wandering uterus." But the term *hysterical* came to refer more generally to physical symptoms without known organic cause, or to dramatic or "histrionic" behavior thought to be characteristic of women. The most specific historical usage of the term is found in the condition called *conversion hysteria*. Freud (1894) suggested that in this condition unexplained physical symptoms represented a *conversion* of unconscious emotional conflicts into a more acceptable form. The historical term *conversion* remains with us (without the theoretical implications); however, the prejudicial and stigmatizing term *hysterical* is no longer used.

The term *neurosis,* as defined in psychoanalytic theory, suggested a specific cause for certain disorders. Specifically, disorders called *neurotic* resulted from underlying unconscious conflicts, anxiety that resulted from those conflicts, and the implementation of ego defense mechanisms. *Neurosis* was also eliminated in 1980 from the diagnostic system because it was too vague, subsuming as it did almost all nonpsychotic disorders, and because it implied a specific but unproven cause for these disorders, based on psychoanalytic thinking.

Somatoform and dissociative disorders are rare and are not as well understood as many other disorders, but they have intrigued psychopathologists and the public for centuries. We will examine each in some depth in this chapter. A fuller understanding of these disorders will provide a rich perspective on the extent to which normal, everyday traits found in all of us can evolve into distorted, strange, and incapacitating disorders.

Somatoform Disorders

DSM-IV lists five basic somatoform disorders: hypochondriasis, somatization disorder, conversion disorder, pain disorder, and body dysmorphic disorder. In each of these disorders individuals are pathologically concerned with the appearance or functioning of their bodies, as we see in the following discussions.

Hypochondriasis

Clinical Description

Like many terms in psychopathology, **hypochondriasis** has ancient roots. To the Greeks, the hypochondria was the region below the ribs, and the organs in this region were responsible for changes in mental state. For example, ulcers and abdominal disorders were once part of the hypochondriacal syndrome. As the causes of ulcers and related disorders were discovered, physical complaints without a clear cause continued to be labeled "hypochondriasis" (Barsky, Wyshak, & Klerman, 1986). In hypochondriasis, a person develops severe anxiety that is focused on the possibility of having a serious disease. The possibility seems so real to the individual that no amount of reassurance, even from physicians, will help for long. Consider the following case.

The Case of Gail

Gail was married at 21 and looked forward to beginning a new life. She was one of many children growing up in a lower-middle-class household; she felt weak and somewhat neglected and suffered from low self-esteem. Her feelings were made worse by an older stepbrother who would berate and belittle her if he had been drinking. Her mother and stepfather refused to listen to or believe her complaints. But marriage was going to solve everything; she was finally someone special. Unfortunately, it didn't work out that way. During the first year of their marriage she discovered her husband was continuing to have an affair with an old girlfriend.

Three years after her wedding she came to one of our clinics complaining of anxiety and stress. At that time she was working part-time as a waitress and found her job extremely stressful. Although to the best of her knowledge her husband had stopped seeing his former girlfriend, she had trouble getting the thoughts and memories of the affair out of her mind.

Gail complained initially of anxiety and stress, but it soon became clear that her major concerns revolved around her health. Any time she experienced minor physical symptoms such as breathlessness or a headache, she became extremely frightened that the symptoms meant she had a serious illness. A headache indicated she might have a brain tumor. Breathlessness was an impending heart attack. Other physical sensations were quickly elaborated into the possibility of AIDS or cancer. Gail was afraid to go to sleep at night for fear that she would stop breathing. She avoided exercise and drinking and even laughing because the sensations upset her. Public restrooms and, on occasion, public telephones were sources of infection.

But the major source of uncontrollable anxiety and fear was the newspaper and television. Each time an article or show appeared on the "disease of the month" she found herself irresistibly drawn into it and intently noted symptoms that were a part of the disease. For days afterward she would become vigilant, looking for these symptoms in herself and others. She would even watch her dog closely to see whether he was coming down with the dreaded disease. Only with great effort could she dismiss these thoughts after several days. Hearing about a *real* illness in a friend or family member would incapacitate her for days at a time.

These fears developed during the first year of her marriage, around the time she discovered her husband was having an affair. At first, she spent a great deal of time and more money than they could afford going to doctors. Gradually over the years, she heard the same thing during each visit: "There's nothing wrong with you; you're perfectly healthy." Finally, she stopped going, as she became convinced that her concerns were excessive, but her fears did not go away and her life was miserable.

Gail's problems are fairly typical of someone experiencing hypochondriasis. The DSM-IV criteria for hypochondriasis are presented in Table 6.1. We have learned a great deal about hypochondriasis in just the past several years (although there is much we do not know). First, we have concluded that hypochondriasis is essentially an anxiety disorder (it is no accident that this is the first disorder to be presented following the chapter on anxiety disorders). Research has now indicated that hypochondriasis shares many features with the anxiety disorders, particularly panic disorder (Salkovskis, Warwick, & Clark, in press). Among these shared features are similar age of onset, personality characteristics, and patterns of familial aggregation (it runs in families in about the same way that anxiety disorders do). Indeed, the two disorders are frequently comorbid; that is, if individuals with a hypochondriacal disorder have additional diagnoses, these are most likely to be anxiety disorders (Adler, Côté, Barlow, & Hillhouse, submitted; Côté, O'Leary, Barlow, & Strain, in press).

If you look at the diagnostic criteria for hypochondriasis, you can easily see the reasons for the close relationship to the anxiety disorders. Hypochondriasis is characterized by anxiety or fear over the possibility that one has a serious disease. Therefore, the essential problem is anxiety, but its expression is different from that of the other anxiety disorders. In hypochondriasis, the individual is preoccupied with and misinterprets bodily symptoms as indicative of an illness or disease. Almost any physical sensation or symptom may become the basis for concern for individuals with hypochondriasis. Some individuals may focus on normal bodily functions such as heart rate or perspiration, others on very minor physical abnormalities such as a cough. Some individuals complain of very vague symptoms that are difficult to pin down, such as aches or fatigue.

Because a key feature of this disorder is concern or preoccupation with physical symptoms, individuals with hypochondriasis almost always go initially to family physicians. They come to the attention of mental health professionals only after family physicians have ruled out realistic medical conditions as a cause.

Another important feature of hypochondriasis is that reassurances from numerous doctors that all is well and the individual is healthy have, at best, only a short-term effect. It isn't long before patients like Gail are back in the office of another doctor on the assumption that the previous doctors have missed something.

In studying this feature for purposes of modifying the diagnostic criteria in DSM-IV, researchers confirmed a subtle but interesting distinction (Kellner, Hernandez, & Pathak, 1992; Salkovskis, Warwick, & Clark, in press; Côté et al., in press). Specifically, individuals who fear the possibility of *developing* a disease, and therefore avoid situations where they feel

Table 6.1 Diagnostic Criteria for Hypochondriasis

A. Preoccupation with fears of having, or the idea that one has, a serious disease based on the person's misinterpretation of bodily symptoms.

B. The preoccupation persists despite appropriate medical evaluation and reassurance.

C. The belief in Criterion A is not of delusional intensity (as in Delusional Disorder, Somatic Type) and is not restricted to a circumscribed concern about appearance (as in Body Dysmorphic Disorder).

D. The preoccupation causes clinically significant distress or impairment in social, occupational, or other important areas of functioning.

E. The duration of the disturbance is at least 6 months.

F. The preoccupation is not better accounted for by Generalized Anxiety Disorder, Obsessive-Compulsive Disorder, Panic Disorder, a Major Depressive Episode, Separation Anxiety, or another Somatoform Disorder.

Specify if:
   With Poor Insight: if, for most of the time during the current episode, the person does not recognize that the concern about having a serious illness is excessive or unreasonable

Source: DSM-IV, APA, 1994.

Paul Salkovskis has developed important evidence on the nature and treatment of hypochondriasis.

they might pick up the disease, are different from those individuals who currently are anxious over the possibility that they actually *have* the disease. Individuals who have marked fear of *developing* a disease are classified within the specific phobic disorders as having an *illness phobia* (see Chapter 5). On the other hand, individuals with a *conviction* that they currently *have* a disease based on consistently misinterpreting their own physical symptoms and sensations would be diagnosed with *hypochondriasis*. These two groups differ in several ways. Individuals with high disease conviction are more likely to misinterpret physical symptoms and display higher rates of checking behaviors and higher levels of trait anxiety than individuals with illness phobia (Côté et al., in press). Individuals with illness phobia, on the other hand, have an earlier age of onset than those with disease conviction. Based on these findings, *disease conviction* has become the core feature of hypochondriasis. Of course, some people may have both a disease conviction and a fear of developing additional diseases (Kellner, 1986).

If you have just read Chapter 5 on anxiety disorders, you may think that patients with panic disorder resemble patients with hypochondriasis. In panic disorder, patients also seem to misinterpret physical signs and symptoms as the beginning of the next panic attack. They perceive this attack may kill them. What are the differences between hypochondriasis and panic disorder? Salkovskis, Warwick, and Clark (in press) suggested that, while individuals with both disorders show characteristic concern with physical symptoms, patients with panic disorder typically fear *immediate* symptom-related catastrophes. Individuals with hypochondriacal concerns, on the other hand, focus on a more long-term process of illness and

disease (for example, cancer or AIDS). Hypochondriacal patients also continue to seek out the opinions of additional doctors in an attempt to rule out (or perhaps confirm) a disease process. Despite numerous visits confirming they are healthy, they remain unconvinced and unreassured. In contrast, panic patients continue to believe that their panic attacks might kill them, but they learn rather quickly to stop going to doctors and emergency rooms, where they are told again and again that nothing is wrong with them. Finally, the anxieties of individuals with panic disorder tend to focus on the specific set of 10 or 15 symptoms associated with a panic attack. Hypochondriacal concerns seem to range much wider. Nevertheless, there are probably more similarities than differences between these groups.

Minor, seemingly hypochondriacal, concerns are common in young children. A frequent complaint among children is abdominal aches and pains that do not seem to have a physical basis. In most cases these complaints represent passing responses to stress and do not develop into a full-blown chronic hypochondriacal syndrome.

Statistics and Course for Hypochondriasis

We know very little about the prevalence of hypochondriasis in the population. Based on early estimates, anywhere between 1% and 14% of medical patients end up with diagnoses of hypochondriasis, with this prevalence rising somewhat in elderly medical patients (Kellner, 1986). More recent estimates cite a range of 4% to 9% of patients in general medical practice (Barsky, Wyshak, Klerman, & Latham, 1990). Although historically considered one of the "hysterical" disorders unique to women, the sex ratio is actually 50–50 (Kellner, 1986; Kirmayer & Robbins, 1991). We also thought for a long time that hypochondriasis was more prevalent in elderly populations, but this does not seem to be true (Barsky, Frank, Cleary, Wyshak, & Klerman, 1991). In fact, hypochondriasis spreads itself fairly evenly across various phases of adulthood. Although older patients may receive a diagnosis of hypochondriasis more frequently, about the same *proportion* of patients in any age group seeing a physician for physical complaints meet criteria for hypochondriasis. Naturally, more elderly people go to see physicians, making the *absolute number* of patients in this age group somewhat higher than in the younger population. Hypochondriasis may also emerge at any time of life, with the peak age periods for onset of the disorder found in adolescence, middle age (40s and 50s), and after age 60 (Kellner, 1986).

Of course, hypochondriacal complaints might persist despite medical reassurance because they are reinforced by the larger community as "socially approved." A good example of this is seen in the case of mass hysteria described in Chapter 1 when everyone became sick at the same time, thinking the cause was the air in the buildings.

As with anxiety disorders, there are also some culture-specific syndromes that would seem to fit most comfortably with hypochondriasis. Among these is the disorder of *Koro* already described in Chapter 1. As you may remember, in this disorder there is a belief, accompanied by severe anxiety and sometimes panic, that the genitals are retracting into the abdomen. Most victims of this disorder are Chinese males; there are very few reports of the problem in Western cultures. Why would this occur in Chinese cultures? Rubin (1982) suggests that the answer may lie in the central importance of sexual functioning among Chinese males. He notes that typical precipitants for an attack of Koro are guilt over excessive masturbation, unsatisfactory intercourse with one's wife, or promiscuity. These kinds of events may set the stage or create a vulnerability for these men to focus their attention on their sexual organs. The self-focused attention could exacerbate anxiety and arousal, much as it does in the anxiety disorders, thereby setting off an "epidemic."

Another culture-specific disorder prevalent in India is an anxious concern about losing semen, something that obviously occurs during sexual activity. The disorder is called *dhat*. Dhat is associated with a vague mix of physical symptoms including dizziness, weakness, and fatigue. The mix of somatic symptoms is not so specific as in Koro. Rather, these low-grade depressive or anxious symptoms are simply attributed to a physical factor, such as semen loss, in certain parts of the Indian culture. Other specific culture-bound somatic symptoms would include hot sensations in the head or a sensation of something crawling in the head, specific to African patients (Ebigno, 1986), or a sensation of burning in the hands and feet in Pakistani or Indian patients (Kirmayer & Weiss, 1993).

Presentation of somatic symptoms may be among the more difficult manifestations of psychopathology with which to deal. First, the clinician must rule out a physical cause for the somatic complaints. This is usually done by a physician before he or she refers the patient to a mental health professional. Second, the mental health professional must determine the nature of the somatic complaints in order to know whether they are associated with a specific somatoform disorder or perhaps are part of some other psychopathological syndrome such as a panic attack. Third, the clinician must be acutely aware of the specific culture or subculture of the patient in order to understand the role that physical symptoms might play in that culture. Often this step requires consultation from professionals with expertise in cross-cultural presentations of psychopathology.

Causes of Hypochondriasis

There is wide agreement among investigators representing different points of view on psychopathological processes ongoing in hypochondriasis. Central to the development of hypochondriasis is a faulty interpretation of physical signs and sensations as evidence of physical illness. Therefore, almost every one agrees that hypochondriasis is basically a *disorder of cognition or perception* with strong emotional contributions (Kellner, 1985; Barsky & Wyshak, 1990; Clark & Salkovskis, 1992; Adler et al., submitted).

What seems to happen is that individuals with hypochondriasis experience normal physical sensations common to all of us as we go through a typical day in our lives. But these individuals quickly turn their attention to these sensations and begin focusing on them. Remember from Chapter 5 on anxiety disorders that the very *act* of focusing attention on yourself tends to increase arousal as well as make the physical sensations seem more intense than they actually are. If the individual also has a tendency to misinterpret these symptoms as indicative of a disease or physical illness, his anxiety will increase further. When anxiety increases, additional physical symptoms are produced. You can see how a vicious cycle can develop (Warwick & Salkovskis, 1990). A representation of this cycle is presented in Figure 6.1.

Recently, using some of the procedures from the field of cognitive science mentioned in Chapter 2, such as the Stroop test, Hitchcock and Mathews (1992) have confirmed that subjects with hypochondriacal concerns show enhanced perceptual sensitivity to illness cues. These individuals also tend to interpret ambiguous stimuli as threatening. Thus, they quickly become aware (and frightened) of any sign of possible illness or disease. A minor headache, for example, might be interpreted as a sure sign of a brain tumor. Once again, this vicious cycle is somewhat similar to what happens in panic disorder, as described in Chapter 5.

According to this model, when an individual with hypochondriasis experiences physical sensations, whether accurately or in a distorted way, these experiences become combined in the person's mind with a belief that the sensations are negative and/or dangerous, and a powerful pattern of anxiety, physical symptoms, and abnormal illness belief/behavior emerges. But what causes individuals to develop this pattern of somatic sensitivity and beliefs? Here the answers are uncertain. Once again, the solution is unlikely to be found in the context of biological or psychological factors in isolation. At the present time, there is every reason to believe that the fundamental causes of hypochondriasis may be similar to those implicated in the anxiety disorders. For example, there

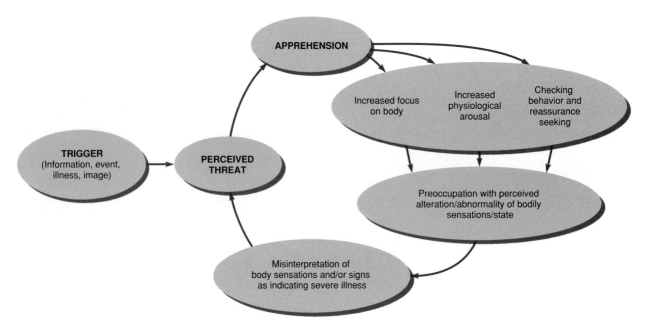

Figure 6.1 Integrative model of causes in hypochondriasis (based on Warwick & Salkovskis, 1990)

is some evidence that hypochondriasis runs in families (Kellner, 1985), suggesting a possible genetic contribution to the disorder. But this contribution may be very nonspecific, such as a tendency to be overly responsive to stress, and thus may be indistinguishable from the nonspecific genetic contribution to anxiety disorders. This hyperresponsivity would be combined with a tendency to view negative life events as unpredictable and uncontrollable and, therefore, something for which you would need to be on guard at all times. As described in Chapter 5, these factors would constitute the biological and psychological vulnerabilities to develop anxiety.

How does this anxiety become focused on physical sensations and illness? Once again, there is some evidence that the origin is in childhood. We know that children who display hypochondriacal concerns seem to report the same kinds of symptoms that other family members may have reported at one time—that is, the physical symptoms and diseases that concern adults with hypochondriasis resemble conditions that their parents experienced (Pilowsky, 1970; Kellner, 1985). It is therefore quite possible, as in panic disorder, that individuals who develop hypochondriasis *learn* to focus their anxiety on physical conditions and illness.

Three other factors seem to contribute to this etiological process (Kellner, 1985; Côté et al., in press). First, hypochondriasis seems to develop in the context of a stressful life event, as do many disorders, including anxiety disorders. The stressful life events often involve death or illness. In the case of Gail, her traumatic first year of marriage and her discovery of her husband's affair seemed to be associated with the beginning of

her disorder. Second, those who develop hypochondriasis tend to have had a disproportionate incidence of disease in their family when they were children. Thus, even if they did not develop hypochondriasis as children, they carry these negative childhood events very strongly in memory and the memories could easily become the focus of anxiety. Third, an important social and interpersonal influence may be operating. Since these individuals have often witnessed illness and come from families where this is a major issue, at least some of them seem to have learned that, when a person becomes ill, others pay him or her increased attention. To individuals for whom this expression of concern is important, the "benefits" of being sick might contribute to the development of the disorder. Being a "sick person" and thus receiving more attention and less responsibility is described as adopting a "sick role." These issues may play an even greater role in somatization disorder, described next.

Treatment for Hypochondriasis

Unfortunately, we know very little about treating hypochondriasis. There are almost no scientifically controlled studies evaluating the effects of treatment. Although attempts to uncover unconscious conflicts using psychodynamic psychotherapy seem to be common in clinical practice, results on the effectiveness of these treatment approaches have seldom been reported. In one study, Ladee (1966) noted that only 4 out of 23 patients seemed to derive some benefit.

As Kellner (1986) points out, most treatments attack the illness preoccupations or the anxiety directly, using cognitive and behavioral approaches, drugs commonly used for other anxiety disorders, or simply direct reassurance (Kellner, in press). Reassurance seems to be surprisingly effective, based on clinical reports—"surprisingly" because, by definition, patients with hypochondriasis are not supposed to benefit from reassurance about their health. However, reassurance is most usually provided only very briefly by family doctors who have little time to provide the type of support and reassurance that might be necessary. Psychologists and psychiatrists or other mental health professionals may well be able to provide reassurance in a more effective and sensitive manner, devote sufficient time to address all the concerns the patient may have, and attend to the "meaning" of the symptoms (for example, their relation to the patient's life stress). Participation in support groups may also give these people the reassurance they need. It is very likely we will see more research on the treatment of hypochondriasis in the future.

Somatization Disorder

Clinical Description

In 1859 Pierre Briquet, a French physician, described a very strange disorder in which patients would come to see him with a seemingly endless list of somatic complaints for which he could find no medical basis (American Psychiatric Association, 1980). But his findings would not deter these patients. They would be back again shortly thereafter with either the same complaints or a new list containing slight variations. For over 100 years this disorder bore his name, *Briquet's syndrome,* before being changed in 1980 to **somatization disorder.**

Consider the following case.

The Case of Linda

Linda, an intelligent woman in her 30s, who came to one of our clinics. Linda looked distressed and pained. As she sat down she noted that even coming into the office was very difficult for her as she was having trouble breathing and was experiencing considerable swelling in the joints of her legs and arms. She also pointed out that she was in some pain from chronic urinary tract infections and might have to leave at any moment to go to the restroom, but she reported that she was extremely happy that she had come in for the appointment. At least she was seeing someone who could help her with her considerable suffering. She said she knew we would have to go through a detailed initial interview, but she had something that might save some time. At this point she pulled out of her purse several sheets of paper and handed them over. One section, some five pages long, described contacts she had had with the health care system for *major difficulties only.* Times and dates, as well as potential diagnoses and days hospitalized were on this sheet. The second section, one and one-half single-spaced pages, consisted of a list of all the medications she had been on for her various physical complaints.

Linda was concerned about her symptoms. She felt that she had any one of a number of chronic infections that nobody could properly diagnose. She had begun to have these difficulties in her teenage years and would often seek out doctors and clergy with whom to share her symptoms and her fears. She was drawn to hospitals and medical clinics, and for this reason entered nursing school after high school. However, while in training in the hospital, she noticed her physical condition deteriorating rapidly as she seemed to "pick up" the diseases she was learning about and coming in contact with. After a series of stressful emotional events that resulted in her having to leave nursing school, she developed paralysis in her legs of unexplained origin and became unable to walk. At this point she was admitted to a psychiatric hospital for a year, where she regained her ability to walk. On discharge she obtained disability status, which freed her from the necessity of holding down a full-time job, and she began to volunteer at the local hospital. With her chronic but fluctuating incapacitation, there were some days that she could go in and some days she could not. At the present time, she was seeing seven different physicians, a family practitioner and six specialists, who were monitoring various aspects of her physical condition. She was also seeing two ministers for pastoral counseling.

Diagnostic criteria for somatization disorder are presented in Table 6.2. As you can see, Linda easily met and exceeded all these criteria. Do you notice anything different in the descriptions of Linda, who presented with somatization disorder, and Gail, who presented with hypochondriacal disorder? Of course Linda, with her multiple somatic complaints, was more severely impaired and also had suffered in the past from symptoms of paralysis, which we now call conversion symptoms (covered shortly). But the more telling difference was that Linda was *not so afraid* as Gail that she had a disease. Linda's concern focused on the symptoms themselves, not what the symptoms

Table 6.2   DSM-IV Criteria for Somatization Disorder

A. A history of many physical complaints beginning before age 30 that occur over a period of several years and result in treatment being sought or significant impairment in social, occupational, or other important areas of functioning.

B. Each of the following criteria must have been met, with individual symptoms occurring at any time during the course of disturbance.

1. *Four pain symptoms:* A history of pain related to at least four different sites or functions (such as head, abdomen, back, joints, extremities, chest, rectum, during sexual intercourse, during menstruation, or during urination)
2. *Two gastrointestinal symptoms:* A history of at least two gastrointestinal symptoms other than pain (such as nausea, diarrhea, bloating, vomiting other than during pregnancy, or intolerance of several different foods)
3. *One sexual symptom:* A history of at least one sexual or reproductive symptom other than pain (such as sexual indifference, erectile or ejaculatory dysfunction, irregular menses, excessive menstrual bleeding, vomiting throughout pregnancy)
4. *One pseudoneurologic symptom:* A history of at least one symptom or deficit suggesting a neurological disorder not limited to pain (conversion symptoms such as blindness, double vision, deafness, loss of touch or pain sensation, hallucinations, aphonia, impaired coordination or balance, paralysis or localized weakness, difficulty swallowing, difficulty breathing, urinary retention, seizures; dissociative symptoms such as amnesia; or loss of consciousness other than fainting)

Source: DSM-IV, APA, 1994.

might mean. Furthermore, Linda's life revolved around her symptoms. A very intelligent woman, she once said to one of us that her symptoms *were* her identity. Without her symptoms, she did not know who she was. By this she meant she would not know how to relate to people since all of her meaningful relationships, most of which were with health care professionals, revolved around discussions of her symptoms. Even the few friends she had who were not health care professionals were those who were able to relate to her through the veil of her symptoms. This would include clergy and other very sympathetic individuals who had the patience to "understand" her suffering.

Statistics and Course for Somatization Disorder

Somatization disorder is very rare. DSM-III-R criteria required 13 or more symptoms from a list of 35, making diagnosis of somatization disorder very difficult and tedious. Based on new research the criteria have been greatly simplified for DSM-IV with only eight symptoms required (Cloninger, in press). Using DSM-III-R definitions, between 0 and 0.7% of the population met criteria for somatization disorder (Swartz, Blazer, George, & Landerman, 1986; Escobar, Burnam, Karno, Forsythe, & Golding, 1987; Swartz, Blazer, George, & Landerman, 1988). However as Katon, Lin, Von Korff, Russo, Lipscomb, and Bush (1991) recently demonstrated, somatization disorder is really on a continuum: People with only a few somatic symptoms of unexplained origin also may experience sufficient distress and impairment of functioning to be considered to have a "disorder." This disorder has its own name, *undifferentiated somatoform disorder,* but it is really just somatization disorder with fewer than eight symptoms. Using between four and six symptoms as criteria,

Escobar and Canino (1989) found a prevalence of somatization disorder of 4.4% in one large city.

Linda developed her disorder during adolescence, apparently the typical age of onset. A number of studies have demonstrated that individuals with this disorder tend to be women, unmarried, and from lower socioeconomic groups (for example, Swartz et al., 1986). For instance, 68% of the patients in a large sample studied by Kirmayer and Robbins (1991) were female. In addition to a variety of somatic complaints, individuals with this disorder may also have accompanying psychological complaints, usually anxiety or mood disorders (Adler et al., submitted; Kirmayer & Robbins, 1991). Suicidal attempts that appear to be manipulative gestures rather than true death wishes are frequent. While symptoms may come and go, somatization disorder and the accompanying sick role behavior run a chronic course, often continuing into old age.

In other cultures, males present with somatic complaints at least as often and sometimes more often than females (Swartz, Landerman, George, Blazer, & Escobar, 1991). In Puerto Rico, for example, the sex ratio of individuals presenting with somatization disorder was approximately 50–50. Of course, one must be particularly careful to rule out medical causes of somatic complaints in third world countries. In many settings, parasitic and other infectious diseases are common as well as physical conditions associated with poor nutrition. These are not always easy to diagnose.

Causes of Somatization Disorder

Somatization disorder shares some features with hypochondriasis. First, those who develop somatization disorder have often witnessed illness or injury in their families while they were growing up. Therefore, they have seen the consequences of being sick or injured. But this is a minor factor at best, since countless families experience chronic illness or injuries without passing on the "sick role" to children in those families. Something else is making a strong contribution to this disorder. Furthermore somatization disorder "looks" very different from hypochondriasis.

Given the past difficulty in making this diagnosis, few studies have been done. Some early studies looking at possible genetic contributions to somatization disorder produced mixed results. For example, Torgersen (1986) conducted a sophisticated twin study and found no increased incidence of somatization disorder in monozygotic compared to dyzygotic pairs, but most studies find substantial evidence that this disorder runs in families and may have a heritable basis (Guze, Cloninger, Martin, & Clayton, 1986; Katon, 1993). A more startling finding has emerged from these studies, however. Somatization disorder is strongly linked in family and genetic studies to antisocial, or psychopathic, personality disorder, described in some detail in Chapter 13. The types of antisocial behavior characteristic of individuals with this disorder include vandalism, persistent lying, theft, irresponsibility with finances and at work, and outright physical aggression. Individuals with antisocial personality disorder seem insensitive to punishment or the negative consequences of their behavior. They seem to experience little anxiety or guilt over their aggression or criminal behavior and often act impulsively without considering or caring about the consequences of what they do.

While antisocial personality disorder (ASPD) occurs primarily in males and somatization disorder in females, they share a number of features. Both begin early in life, typically run a chronic course, predominate among lower socioeconomic classes, are difficult to treat, and are associated with marital discord, drug and alcohol abuse, and suicide attempts, among other complications (Lilienfeld, 1992; Cloninger, 1978; Goodwin & Guze, 1984). Once again, both family and adoption studies suggest that ASPD and somatization disorder tend to run in the same families and may well have a heritable component (for instance, Cadoret, 1978; Bohman, Cloninger, von Knorring, & Sigvardsson, 1984), although it is also possible that these behavioral patterns could be learned in a maladaptive family setting.

Yet the aggression, impulsiveness, and lack of emotion characteristic of antisocial personality disorder would seem, on the face of it, to be at the other end of the spectrum from somatization disorder. What could these two disorders possibly have in common? While we don't yet have the answers, Lilienfeld (1992) reviews a number of hypotheses that have been proposed. We will take a moment to look at some of them here because, taken together, they represent a fascinating example of integrative biopsychosocial thinking about psychopathology.

One model with some support suggests that somatization disorder and ASPD share a neurobiologically based disinhibition syndrome. How might this work? The well-known neuropsychologist Jeffrey Gray (1982, 1985) proposed three major functional systems: a behavioral inhibition system (BIS), a behavioral activation system (BAS), and a fight-flight system (FFS). As noted in Chapter 5, the BIS and the FFS may well play a prominent role in the expression of anxiety and panic. On the other hand, the BAS underlies, at least partly, impulsivity, thrill seeking, and excitability. A number of investigators (for example, Cloninger, 1987b; Gorenstein & Newman, 1980) have suggested that antisocial personality disorder and somatization disorder—as well as two other closely related disorders, substance abuse and attention deficit hyperactivity disorder in children—may have something in common (see Chapters 12 and 16). They propose that these disorders share a *weak* BIS that is incapable of exerting sufficient control over the BAS.

To review, the BIS basically ensures that we are very sensitive to threat or danger and avoid any situations or signals suggesting that threat or danger is imminent. The emotion that we feel when confronted with these signals of threat or danger is anxiety. Individuals with antisocial personality disorder don't seem to experience anxiety (although they may experience panic on occasion) (Fowles, in press). Instead, they are overly responsive to short-term rewards (impulsive), even if the pursuit of these rewards gets them in trouble. There is accumulating evidence that this impulsiveness is common in ASPD (for instance, Newman, Widom, & Nathan, 1985). How does this apply to people with somatization disorder? Many of the behaviors and traits associated with somatization disorder also seem to reflect short-term gain at the expense of long-term problems. The continual development of new somatic symptoms among these individuals gains them immediate sympathy and attention (for a while) but eventually social isolation (Goodwin & Guze, 1984). Other behaviors that would seem to indicate short-term gratification would be the novelty-seeking and provocative sexual behavior often present in these individuals (Kendall, Williams, & Agras, 1975).

The brain circuit mediating the BIS is relatively well established and was described in Chapter 5. It runs from the septal area through the hippocampus to the orbital frontal cortex. A variety of neurophysiological evidence suggests a dysfunction in this brain circuit not only in ASPD but also in somatization disorder, substance abuse, and perhaps, attention deficit hyperactivity disorder (Lilienfeld, 1992; Cloninger, 1987b).

Cathy Spatz Widom has suggested an important theory on the psychological causes of somatization disorder.

If individuals with ASPD and somatization disorder share the same underlying neurophysiological vulnerability, why does their behavior turn out so differently? The explanation is that social and cultural factors exert their strong effect. Both Cathy Spatz Widom (1984) and Robert Cloninger (1987b) have pointed out that the major difference between these two disorders is their degree of *dependency*. Aggression is a trait strongly associated with males, not only in humans but in most mammalian species including rodents (Gray & Buffery, 1971). Dependence and lack of aggression are strongly associated with females. Thus, both aggression and ASPD are strongly associated with males while dependence and somatization disorder are strongly associated with females. Gender roles are among the strongest components of our identity. It is very possible that gender socialization accounts almost entirely for the profound differences in the expression of the same biological vulnerability among men and women.

These theoretical models are still preliminary and require a great deal more data before we can have confidence in their validity. But these ideas are at the forefront of our knowledge of psychopathology and reflect the kinds of integrative approach to psychopathology described in Chapter 2 that will inevitably emerge as our knowledge increases.

To return to the case of Linda, were there any indications that these assumptions might apply to her or her family? Linda had a sister who, unlike Linda, had been married briefly and had two children before divorcing. She had been in therapy for the better part of her life. Occasionally Linda's sister would visit doctors

with various somatic complaints, but her primary difficulty was unexplained periods of recurring amnesia that might last several days; these spells were interspersed with blackout periods during which she would be rushed to the hospital.

What about signs of sexual impulsivity or ASPD in this family? The sister's older daughter, after a very stormy adolescence characterized by truancy and delinquency, was sentenced to a jail term for violations involving drugs and assault.

Over the years Linda had seen countless physicians, psychologists, and clergy for counseling and support. In the midst of one session with us, Linda noted that she had kept a list of the individuals with whom she had had sexual intercourse. The list numbered well over 20, with the majority of the sexual episodes occurring in the offices of mental health professionals or clergy!

For Linda this development in her relationship with caregivers was very important since, in the context of her disorder, it was the ultimate sign that the caregivers were concerned about her as a person and that she was important to them. But the relationships almost always ended tragically. Several of the caregivers' marriages disintegrated and at least one mental health professional committed suicide. Linda herself never was satisfied or fulfilled by the relationships but was greatly hurt when they inevitably ended.

The American Psychological Association has decreed that it is always unethical to have any sexual contact with a patient at any time during treatment. Over the years, violations of this ethical canon have nearly always resulted in tragic consequences.

Treatment for Somatization Disorder

Somatization disorder is exceedingly difficult to treat and there are no treatments with proven effectiveness that seem to "cure" the syndrome. In our clinic we have developed an approach that concentrates on providing reassurance, reducing stress associated with the disorder, and in particular, reducing the frequency of help-seeking behaviors. One of the most common patterns of help-seeking behavior is the person's tendency to visit numerous medical specialists depending on the particular symptom of the week. This pattern results in an extensive medical and physical workup with every visit to a new physician (or to a physician who has not been seen for a while). To control these visits a gatekeeper physician is assigned each patient to screen all physical complaints. Subsequent visits to specialists must be specifically authorized by this gatekeeper. In the context of a positive therapeutic relationship, most patients are amenable to this arrangement.

Additional therapeutic attention is directed at reducing any reinforcing or supportive consequences of relating to significant others on the basis of physical symptoms alone. To this end, more appropriate non-sex-role methods of interacting with others are encouraged and facilitated. Because Linda, like many patients with this disorder, had managed to become eligible for disability payments from the state, additional goals involved encouraging at least part-time employment with the ultimate goal of discontinuing disability.

Others who have worked extensively with these patients have enumerated similar therapeutic goals. For example, Smith, Monson, and Ray (1986) and Smith (1991) evaluated a similar procedure and found that, while it did not improve the patient's mental or physical health, it did substantially reduce the person's help-seeking behavior. This is an extremely important goal in this disorder since the cost in dollars—to the patient, to the medical system, and ultimately, to society—is enormous.

Conversion Disorder

Definition

Conversion disorders generally refer to physical malfunctioning, such as paralysis, blindness, or difficulty speaking (aphonia), without any physical or organic pathology that would account for the malfunction. Most conversion symptoms suggest some kind of neurological disease affecting sensory-motor systems, although conversion symptoms can mimic the full range of physical malfunctioning.

Conversion disorders provide us with some of the most intriguing, and in some cases astounding, examples of psychopathology that you will encounter in this book. What could possibly account for somebody going blind when their visual processes are perfectly normal, or experiencing paralysis of the arms or legs when there is no neurological damage? Consider the following case.

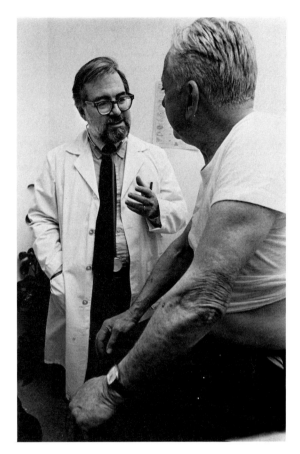

Family doctors play an important role in treating somatization disorder by preventing the patient from continually seeking out numerous medical specialists.

The Case of Judy

Judy sat on a chair in one of our offices with her legs under her, refusing to put her feet on the floor. Her mother sat close by ready to assist her if she needed to move or get up from her chair. Her mother had made the appointment and, with the help of a friend, had all but carried Judy into the office. Judy was a 20-year-old woman of borderline intelligence who was friendly and personable during the initial interview and readily answered all questions with a big smile. She was obviously enjoying the social interaction.

Judy had developed difficulty walking over a 5-year period. This difficulty began, according to Judy and her mother, when her right leg started "giving away" and she began falling. Gradually over time, this behavior worsened to the point that 6 months before her admission to the hospital she could move around only by crawling on the floor.

Physical examinations had revealed no physical causes for her difficulty in walking. In fact, Judy presented with a classic case of conversion disorder. Although she was not paralyzed, her specific symptoms included weakness in her legs and difficulty keeping her balance, with the result that she fell frequently. The name for this particular type of conversion symptom is *astasia-abasia*.

Judy lived with her mother, who ran a gift shop from the front of her house in their very small rural town. The town had been able to provide schooling for Judy through exceptional education programs until she was approximately 15; after this, no further programs were available. Judy began staying home. It was at this time that her walking deteriorated.

DSM-IV criteria for conversion disorder are presented in Table 6.3. Common types of conversion symptoms in addition to blindness and paralysis include aphonia, mentioned earlier, as well as mutism where the person is completely unable to speak. Some individuals also lose their sense of touch. Some have seizures, which can be psychological in origin since no significant EEG changes can be documented. Another relatively common reaction is the sensation of a lump in the throat that makes it difficult to swallow, eat, or sometimes talk. Another name for this symptom is *globus hystericus.*

The term *conversion* was popularized by Freud, who believed that the anxiety resulting from unconscious conflicts and needing to find expression somehow was "converted" into physical symptoms. This transforming allowed the individual to "get rid" of some of the anxiety without actually experiencing it. Much as in phobic disorders, the anxiety resulting from unconscious conflicts might be "displaced" onto another object. In fact, the term *conversion* did not originate with Freud but has been used off and on since the Middle Ages (Mace, 1992).

Differences among conversion reactions, physical disorders, malingering, and factitious disorders. Distinguishing among conversion reactions, real physical disorders, and outright **malingering** or faking is sometimes difficult. There are several factors that help in this differentiation. First, conversion reactions are often accompanied by the

same quality of indifference to the symptoms that is present in somatization disorder. This attitude has been referred to as *la belle indifférence* and is considered to be a hallmark of conversion reactions. Unfortunately, it is not a foolproof sign. A blasé attitude toward illness is sometimes displayed by people with physical disorders and some people with conversion symptoms become quite distressed.

Second, conversion symptoms are almost always precipitated by some marked stress. Ford (1985) noted that the incidence of marked stress preceding a conversion symptom occurred in 52% to 93% of the cases. Thus, if one cannot find a stressful event preceding the onset of the symptom, one might more carefully consider a true physical condition to account for the symptoms.

Finally, people with conversion symptoms can usually function normally, but they seem truly and honestly unaware of this ability or of the sensory input they are receiving. For example, individuals with the conversion symptom of blindness can usually make their way around and avoid objects in their visual field, but they can't tell you they saw the objects. Similarly, individuals with conversion symptoms of paralysis of the legs might suddenly get up and run down the hall in an emergency, and then be astounded afterward that they were able to accomplish this. Some similar type of unconscious process may be going on with many conversion symptoms. Once again, however, the person's *awareness* of the sensory and motor input is somehow disrupted. It is possible that some individuals experiencing miraculous cures during religious ceremonies may have been suffering from conversion reactions. While these factors may help in distinguishing between conversion and organically based physical disorders, clinicians often make mistakes. Fishbain and Goldberg (1991) describe three cases who subsequently were diagnosed with physical disorders, one of whom died. In one study 25% of patients diagnosed

Table 6.3   DSM-IV Criteria for Conversion Disorder

A. One or more symptoms or deficits affecting voluntary motor or sensory function that suggest a neurological or general medical condition.

B. Psychological factors are judged to be associated with the symptom or deficit because the initiation or exacerbation of the symptom or deficit is preceded by conflicts or other stressors.

C. The symptom or deficit is not intentionally produced or feigned (as in factitious disorder or malingering).

D. The symptom or deficit cannot, after appropriate investigation, be fully explained by a general medical condition, or by the direct effects of a substance, or as a culturally sanctioned behavior or experience.

E. The symptom or deficit causes clinically significant distress or impairment in social, occupational, or other important areas of functioning or warrants medical evaluation.

F. The symptom or deficit is not limited to pain or sexual dysfunction, does not occur exclusively during the course of somatization disorder, and is not better accounted for by another mental disorder.

Source: DSM-IV, APA, 1994.

with conversion reaction were later found to have physical disorders (Watson & Buranen, 1979).

Making the distinction between individuals who are truly experiencing conversion symptoms in a seemingly involuntary way and malingerers who happen to be very good at faking symptoms can also be very difficult. Once the latter are exposed, their motivation for malingering is clear; these individuals are either trying to get out of something, such as work or possibly legal difficulties, or they are attempting to gain something, such as a financial settlement. Malingerers are fully aware of what they are doing and are clearly attempting to manipulate the system to gain a desired end.

More puzzling is a set of conditions called *factitious disorders*, which fall somewhere between malingering and conversion disorders. With **factitious disorder,** the person's symptoms are also feigned and under voluntary control as with malingering, but there is *no good reason* for him or her to voluntarily produce the symptoms except, possibly, to assume the sick role and receive increased attention. Tragically, the person's realization of this disorder may extend to members of the family such as children. The person with the disorder purposely makes them sick, evidently for the attention and pity then given to the parent, who is causing the symptoms. When the individual is making someone else sick, such as a child, the condition is called factitious disorder by proxy (see Table 6.4).

Unconscious mental processes in conversion and related disorders. Unconscious cognitive processes seem to play a role in much of psychopathology, although not necessarily as Freud envisioned it, but nowhere is this phenomenon more readily and dramatically apparent than when we make the distinction between conversion disorders and re-lated conditions to set the stage for a discussion of unconscious processes. To take a closer look at the "unconscious" mental process in these conditions, we'll review briefly the case of Anna O. first mentioned in Chapter 2.

As you may remember, when Anna O. was 21 years old she was nursing her dying father. This was a very difficult time for her. She reported that after many days of sitting by her father, her mind wandered. Suddenly she found herself imagining (dreaming?) that a black snake was moving across the bed toward her father about to bite him. She tried to lift her right arm to grab the snake, but her arm had gone to sleep and she could not move it. Looking at her right arm and hand, she imagined that the fingers of her right hand had turned into little poisonous snakes. Horrified, all she could do was pray, and the only prayer that came to mind was an English language prayer (in Vienna, Anna O.'s native language was German). After this, she experienced paralysis in her right arm whenever something reminded her of this image or hallucination. The paralysis gradually extended to the right side of her body and, on occasion, to other parts of her body. She also experienced a number of other conversion symptoms such as deafness and, intriguingly, an inability to speak her native language, German, although she remained fluent in English.

Breuer's treatment of Anna O. involved recreating or reliving in imagination her traumatic experiences. The last experience she was able to recreate, in Breuer's office under a hypnotic state, was the memory of this horrific hallucination. As she recalled and processed these images, her paralysis left her and she regained her ability to speak German. Breuer called the therapeutic reexperiencing of emotionally traumatic events *catharsis* (meaning purging or releasing). Catharsis has proven to be an effective intervention with many emotional disorders, as noted in Chapter 5.

Table 6.4   DSM-IV Criteria for Factitious Disorders

A. Intentional production or feigning of physical or psychological signs or symptoms.

B. The motivation for the behavior is to assume the sick role.

C. External incentives for the behavior (such as economic gain, avoiding legal responsibility, or improving physical well-being, as in malingering) are absent.

Specify Type:
With Predominantly Psychological Signs and Symptoms if psychological signs and symptoms predominate in the clinical presentation.
With Predominantly Physical Signs and Symptoms if physical signs and symptoms predominate in the clinical presentation.
With Combined Psychological and Physical Signs and Symptoms if neither psychological nor physical signs and symptoms predominate in the clinical presentation.

Source: DSM-IV, APA, 1994.

Was Anna O.'s behavior really "unconscious," or did she realize at some level that she could move her arm and the rest of her body if she wanted to, and it simply served her purpose not to? This question has bedeviled psychopathologists down through the centuries. Now, new information reviewed in Chapter 2 on unconscious cognitive processes becomes important. There we learned that we are all capable of receiving and processing information in a number of sensory channels (for example, vision, hearing) without being "aware" of it. Remember the phenomenon of blind sight or unconscious vision mentioned in Chapter 2? Weiskrantz (1980) and others discovered that people with small, localized damage to certain parts of their brains could identify objects in their field of vision, but they had no "awareness" whatsoever that they could "see." Could this happen to people *without* brain damage? Consider the following case.

The Case of Celia

A 15-year-old teenage girl named Celia suddenly was unable to see. Shortly thereafter she regained some of her sight but her vision was so severely blurred that she could not read. When she was brought to a clinic for testing, psychologists arranged a series of sophisticated tests of her vision that did not require her to report when she could or could not "see." One of the tasks required her to examine three triangles displayed on three separate screens and press a button under the screen containing an upright triangle. Celia performed perfectly on this test without being aware that she could "see" anything (Grosz & Zimmerman, 1970). Was Celia faking? Evidently not, or she would have purposely done poorly.

Sackeim, Nordlie, and Gur (1979) evaluated this potential difference between a "real" unconscious process and faking by hypnotizing two subjects in the laboratory and giving each a suggestion of total blindness. One subject was also told that it was extremely important that she appear to everyone to be blind. The second subject, although provided with a hypnotic suggestion of blindness, was not given any further instructions. The first subject, evidently following instructions to try at all costs to appear blind, performed far below chance on a visual discrimination task similar to the upright triangle task mentioned above. On almost every trial she chose the wrong answer. The other subject with the hypnotic suggestion of blindness but no instructions to "appear" blind at all cost performed perfectly on the visual discrimination task—although, once again, she reported that she could not "see" anything.

How does this relate to identifying faking or malingering? In an earlier case Grosz and Zimmerman (1965) evaluated a male who seemed to have conversion symptoms of blindness. They discovered that he performed much more poorly than chance on a visual discrimination task. Subsequent information from other sources confirmed that he was almost certainly malingering.

To review these distinctions, someone who is *truly blind* would perform at a chance level on these visual discrimination tasks. People with conversion symptoms of blindness, on the other hand, can "see" objects in their visual field and therefore, would perform well on these tasks, but this experience is "detached" or dissociated from their awareness of sight. Malingerers and perhaps individuals with factitious disorders simply do everything possible to pretend they can't see.

Statistics and Course for Conversion Disorder

We have already seen that conversion disorder may occur in conjunction with other disorders, particularly somatization disorder as in the case of Linda. Linda's episode of paralysis passed after several months and did not return, although on occasion she would report "feeling as if" her paralysis were returning. Conversion disorders are relatively rare in mental health settings, but remember too that people who seek help for this condition are more likely to consult neurologists or other medical specialists. The prevalence estimates in neurological settings vary dramatically ranging from 1% to 30% (Trimbell, 1981; Marsden, 1986).

Much as with somatization disorder, conversion disorders are found primarily in women (Folks, Ford, & Regan, 1984) and typically develop during adolescence or slightly thereafter. However, these disorders may occur relatively frequently in males at times of extreme stress (Chodoff, 1974). Conversion reactions are not uncommon in soldiers exposed to combat conditions or military training (Mucha & Reinhardt, 1970). The symptoms often disappear after a time only to return later in the same or similar form when some new stressor occurs.

In other cultures, some conversion symptoms are very common aspects of religious or healing rituals. Conversion and dissociative symptoms (for instance, seizures, paralysis, trances) are commonly found in some rural fundamentalist religious groups in the United States (Griffith, English, & Mayfield, 1980).

Causes of Conversion Disorders

Freud stipulated four basic processes in the development of conversion disorder. First, the individual experiences some traumatic event—in Freud's view the emergence of some unacceptable, unconscious conflict. Second, since the conflict and the resulting anxiety are unacceptable, the person represses the conflict or makes it unconscious. Third, since the anxiety continues to increase and threatens to emerge into consciousness, the person somehow "converts" it into physical symptoms, thereby relieving the pressure of having to deal directly with the conflict. This reduction of anxiety is considered to be the *primary gain* or the primary reinforcing event that maintains the conversion symptom. Fourth, the individual begins to receive greatly increased attention and sympathy from loved ones and may also escape or avoid some difficult situation or task. Freud considered this attention or avoidance to be the *secondary gain* or the secondarily reinforcing set of events.

We believe Freud was basically correct on at least three counts and possibly a fourth, although firm evidence supporting any of these ideas is sparse and Freud's views were far more complex than represented here. What seems to happen is that individuals with conversion disorder experience a traumatic event in their lives that must be avoided or escaped at all costs. This might be combat, where death is imminent, or an impossible interpersonal conflict. Since simply "running away" is unacceptable in most cases, the socially acceptable alternative of "getting sick" is substituted; but getting sick "on purpose" is also unacceptable, so this motivation is detached or dissociated from the person's consciousness. Finally, since the avoidance or escape behavior (the conversion symptoms) is successful, to an extent, in avoiding or escaping the difficult or traumatic situation, the behavior tends to continue until the underlying problem or set of maintaining factors is resolved.

The one step in Freud's progression of events about which some questions remain is the issue of primary gain. The notion of primary gain accounts for the feature of *la belle indifférence* cited previously, where individuals seem not the least bit distressed about their symptoms, but formal tests of this feature provide little support for Freud's claim. For example, Lader and Sartorius (1968) compared patients with conversion disorder with control groups of anxious patients without conversion symptoms. Rather than showing less anxiety over their symptoms, the patients with conversion disorder evidenced equal or greater anxiety and physiological arousal than the other group. While it does seem clinically that these patients are relatively undisturbed by their symptoms, this impression may be more in the mind of the therapist than the patient.

Social and cultural influences also seem to contribute to conversion disorder. Conversion disorder, as with somatization disorder, tends to occur in less educated, lower socioeconomic groups where knowledge about disease and medical illness is not as well developed (Swartz, Blazer, Woodbury, George, & Landerman, 1986). Prior experience with real illness or physical difficulties, usually among other family members, tends to influence the later choice of specific conversion symptoms, since patients tend to "pick up" symptoms with which they are familiar (for example, Brady & Lind, 1961). Furthermore, there has been an overall decrease in the incidence of these disorders over the decades. The most likely explanation is that current-day knowledge would eliminate much of the "secondary gain" that seems so important in initiating and maintaining these disorders.

Finally, many conversion symptoms often seem to be part of a larger constellation of psychopathology. An example would be Linda, who had broad-ranging somatization disorder as well as a history of severe conversion symptoms resulting in her hospitalization. In similar cases, individuals may have a marked biological vulnerability to develop the disorder when under stress, with biological processes like those discussed in the context of somatization disorder. For countless other cases such as Judy's, however, biological contributory factors would seem to be less important. We will talk about Judy's treatment in the next section. There you will see that the extent of suffering present in her life and the successful resolution of this suffering brought about by her being unable to walk seem to point primarily to a psychological and social etiology.

Treatment of Conversion Disorder

We have few systematic controlled studies evaluating the effectiveness of treatment for conversion disorders, but these conditions are often treated in our clinics and elsewhere, and the treatment closely follows our thinking on the causes of the disorder described earlier. Since conversion disorder has much in common with somatization disorder, many of the treatment principles are similar.

Principal among these strategies is attending to the traumatic or stressful life event, if it is still present (either in real life or in memory), and removing, if possible, sources of "secondary gain." If conversion symptoms seem clearly identified with a traumatic event, as in the case of Anna O., therapeutic assistance in reexperiencing or "reliving" the event would seem to be a first step (catharsis).

More important, the therapist must work very hard, in collaboration with the patient and his or her family, to reduce any reinforcing or supportive consequences of the conversion symptoms (secondary gain). This is particularly apparent in the case of Judy. It seemed quite clear that Judy's mother found it much more "convenient" if Judy stayed pretty much in one place most of the day while her mother attended to the store in the front of the house. In Judy's case, immobility was strongly reinforced with motherly attention and concern. Any unnecessary mobility was punished.

Many times, removing the secondary gain is easier said than done. Judy was successfully treated in the clinic. Through intensive daily work with the clinic staff she was able to walk again. To accomplish this she had to practice walking every day with considerable support, attention, and praise from the staff. When her mother visited, the staff noticed that she would verbalize her pleasure with Judy's progress, but her facial expressions or "affect" would convey a different message. Since the mother lived a good distance from the clinic, she could not attend sessions but promised to carry out the program at home after Judy was discharged. She didn't, however. A follow-up contact 6 months after Judy was discharged revealed that she had totally relapsed and was once again spending almost all her time in a room in the back of her house while her mother attended to business out front.

Pain Disorder

A related somatoform disorder about which little is known is **pain disorder.** In pain disorder there may have been clear physical reasons for the pain, at least initially, but afterward psychological factors play a major role in maintaining the pain. The criteria for pain disorder are presented in Table 6.5. In the placement of this disorder in DSM-IV, serious consideration was given to removing it entirely from the somatoform disorders and putting it in a separate section. The reason was that a person rarely presents with localized pain as a major problem without some physical basis for that pain, such as an accident or illness. Therefore, it became very difficult to separate the cases where the causes were judged to be primarily psychological from the ones where the causes are primarily physical. Because this disorder fits most closely within the somatoform cluster (an individual presenting with physical symp-

toms judged to have strong psychological contributions), the decision was made to leave pain disorder in this section. Notice, however, that in the criteria the three subtypes of pain disorder run the gamut from pain judged to be due primarily to psychological factors to pain judged to be due primarily to a general medical condition.

An important feature of pain disorder is that, regardless of whether these causes are judged to be primarily psychological or medical, the pain is real and it hurts (King & Strain, 1991). Consider the following two cases.

The Case of the Medical Student

During her first clinical rotation in medicine, a 25-year-old, female, third-year medical student in excellent health was seen at her student health service for intermittent abdominal pain of several weeks' duration. The student denied any past history of similar pain. Physical examination revealed no physical problems, but during the examination she told the physician that she had recently separated from her husband. The student was referred to the health service psychiatrist. No other psychiatric problems were found, and she was taught relaxation techniques and provided with supportive therapy to help cope with her current stressful situation. The student's pain subsequently disappeared, and she successfully completed medical school.

The Case of the Woman with Cancer

A 56-year-old female with metastatic breast cancer complained of severe pain in her right

---

Table 6.5   DSM-IV Criteria for Pain Disorder

A. Pain in one or more anatomical sites is the predominant focus of the clinical presentation and is of sufficient severity to warrant clinical attention.

B. The pain causes clinically significant distress or impairment in social, occupational, or other important areas of functioning.

C. Psychological factors are judged to have an important role in the onset, severity, exacerbation, or maintenance of the pain.

D. The symptom or deficit is not intentionally produced or feigned (as in factitious disorder or malingering).

E. The pain is not better acounted for by a mood, anxiety, or psychotic disorder and does not meet criteria for dyspareunia.

Specify if:
   Acute (duration of less than 6 months)
   Chronic (duration of 6 months or more)

Source: DSM-IV, APA, 1994.

thigh for one month. She appeared to be coping appropriately with her disease. She obtained initial pain relief from a combination of drugs. The patient was subsequently treated with hypnotherapy and entered group therapy. These treatment modalities provided her with additional pain relief and enabled her to decrease her narcotic intake with no increase in pain.

In the case of the medical student, the causes were seen as purely psychological. In the case of the woman with cancer, the probable causes were related to the cancer. But we now know that pain, whatever its cause, has a strong psychological component. Once medical treatments for existing physical conditions have been completed and pain remains, or if pain seems clearly related to psychological factors, then psychological interventions are important. Due to the complexity of pain and the variety of narcotics and other pain-relieving medicines often prescribed for it, multidisciplinary pain clinics have been set up in most large hospitals. We will return to the subject of pain in Chapter 9 when we discuss health psychology and the contribution of psychological factors to physical disorders. There we will delve more deeply into types of pain disorders, the causes of pain, and its treatment.

Body Dysmorphic Disorder

And now for something completely different! Did you ever wish you could change some part of your appearance? Maybe your weight or the size of your nose or the way your ears stick out? Most people fantasize about improving some aspect of their physical appearance, but there are some relatively normal-looking people who imagine they are so ugly they are unable to interact with people or otherwise function normally for fear that people will laugh at their ugliness. This disorder, which is likely to seem very curious to you, is called **body dysmorphic disorder (BDD).** Central to this disorder is a preoccupation with some imagined defect in appearance in someone who otherwise looks reasonably normal. For this reason the disorder has been referred to as "imagined ugliness" (Phillips, 1991). Consider the following case from our files.

The Case of Jim

Jim was a young male in his mid-twenties with a suspected diagnosis of social phobia; he was referred to one of our clinics by another professional. Jim was a young rabbi who had just finished rabbinical school and had been offered a position at a synagogue in a nearby city. How-

ever, he found himself unable to accept this position because of his marked social difficulties. He reported that he found it very difficult to interact with people. Lately he had given up leaving his small apartment for fear of running into people he knew and being forced to stop and interact with them.

Jim was a good-looking young man of about average height, with dark hair and dark eyes. Although he was somewhat depressed during the interview, a mental status exam and a brief interview focusing on current functioning and past history did not reveal any remarkable problems. There was no sign of a psychotic process (Jim was not out of touch with reality). We then focused on the social difficulties Jim was having. We expected the usual kinds of social anxiety focused on interacting with people or "doing something" (performing) in front of them. But this was not Jim's concern. Rather, Jim was convinced that anyone who interacted with him, even his good friends, were staring at him and focusing on a part of his body that he found absolutely grotesque. He reported that strangers would never dare bring up the subject and that his friends felt too badly for him to mention it. Specifically, Jim thought his head was square. Much as with the beast in *Beauty and the Beast* who could not imagine people reacting to him with anything less than abhorrence, Jim could not imagine people getting past the fact that his head was square. In an attempt to hide his condition as well as he could, Jim had begun wearing soft floppy hats and was much more comfortable in winter when he could all but completely cover his head with a large stocking cap. To us, Jim looked perfectly normal.

Clinical Description of Body Dysmorphic Disorder

The DSM-IV criteria for body dysmorphic disorder are presented in Table 6.6. To give you a better idea of the types of concerns with which these people present to health professionals, the locations of imagined defects in 30 patients with the disorder are shown in Table 6.7.

Many of these people become fixated on mirrors. They find themselves looking in the mirror frequently, checking on their presumed ugly feature to see if any change has taken place. Others avoid mirrors to an almost phobic extent. Quite understandably, suicidal ideation, suicide attempts, and suicide are frequent consequences of this disorder (Phillips, 1991). Individuals with this problem have "ideas of reference."

Table 6.6   DSM-IV Criteria for Body Dysmorphic Disorder

A. Preoccupation with an imagined defect in appearance. If a slight physical anomaly is present, the person's concern is markedly excessive.

B. The preoccupation causes significant distress or impairment in social, occupational, or other important areas of functioning.

C. The preoccupation is not better accounted for by another mental disorder (e.g., dissatisfaction with body shape and size in anorexia nervosa).

Source: DSM-IV, APA, 1994.

Table 6.7   Location of Imagined Defects in 30 Patients with Body Dysmorphic Disorder*

Location	N	%
Hair†	19	63
Nose	15	50
Skin‡	15	50
Eyes	8	27
Head/face§	6	20
Overall body build/bone structure	6	20
Lips	5	17
Chin	5	17
Stomach/waist	5	17
Teeth	4	13
Legs/knees	4	13
Breasts/pectoral muscles	3	10
Ugly face (general)	3	10
Ears	2	7
Cheeks	2	7
Buttocks	2	7
Penis	2	7
Arms/wrists	2	7
Neck	1	3
Forehead	1	3
Facial muscles	1	3
Shoulders	1	3
Hips	1	3

*Total is greater than 100% because most patients had "defects" in more than one location.
†Involved head hair in 15 cases, beard growth in two cases, and other body hair in three cases.
‡Involved acne in seven cases, facial lines in three cases, and other skin concerns in seven cases.
§Involved concerns with shape in five cases and size in one case.

Source: Phillips et al., 1993.

Basically, such individuals have the notion that everything that goes on in their world somehow is related to or "refers" to them—in this case, the imagined defect. This disorder can cause considerable disruption in the patient's life. Many patients with severe cases become housebound for fear of "showing" themselves to other people.

If this disorder seems strange to you, you are not alone. For decades this condition, previously known as *dysmorphophobia* (literally, fear of ugliness), was thought by psychiatrists and psychologists in each instance to represent a psychotic delusional state in which the affected individuals were out of touch with reality because they were unable to realize, even for a fleeting moment, that their ideas were irrational. Whether this is the case is still debated.

In the context of obsessive-compulsive disorder discussed in Chapter 5, a similar issue arose as to whether patients really *believe* in their obsessions or realize that they are basically irrational. Within that disorder, a minority (approximately 10% or less) believed that their obsessional concerns about contaminating others or preventing catastrophes with their rituals were perfectly realistic and reasonable. This brought up the very major issue of what is "delusional" and what isn't. The same issue is even more pronounced in body dysmorphic disorder. For example, in the series of 30 cases examined by Phillips et al. (1993), 50% were absolutely convinced that their imagined bodily defect was realistic and a reasonable source of concern. Is this a delusion? Psychopathologists, including those on the DSM-IV Task Force, have wrestled long and hard with this issue. Their conclusion at this point is that there are no clear answers and more research is needed. For now, individuals with BDD and beliefs so firmly held that they could be called *delusional* will receive a second diagnosis of delusional disorder: somatic type (see Chapter 14).

Statistics and Course for Body Dysmorphic Disorder

The prevalence of this disorder is hard to estimate since by its very nature it tends to be secretive.

Michael Jackson (*left* "before"; *right* "after"). Many individuals, unhappy with their physical appearance, seek out surgery to alter the features they don't like. However, people with body dysmorphic disorder are seldom satisfied with the results of surgery.

However, the best estimates are that it is far more common than we had previously thought and that, once the disorder develops, it tends to run a lifelong course without some sort of treatment (Phillips, 1991). One of the patients with body dysmorphic disorder reported in Phillips et al. (1993) was 80 years old at the time she was examined and had suffered from her condition for 71 years, since the age of 9.

If you have friends in college who seem to have at least a mild version of this disorder, you're probably correct. A recent study suggested that as many as 70% of college students report at least some dissatisfaction with their bodies. Twenty-eight percent appear to meet all the criteria for the disorder (Fitts, Gibson, Redding, & Deiter, 1989). However, this study was done by questionnaire and may well have reflected a large percentage of students concerned simply with their body weight. In mental health clinics the disorder is also seen infrequently because most of these individuals seek out another type of health professional, the plastic surgeon (covered shortly).

BDD is not strongly associated with one sex or the other. Based on published reports, there are slightly more females than males with BDD in this country, but 62% of a large number of individuals with BDD in Japan were males. As you might suspect, very few people with this disorder get married. Age of onset ranges from early adolescence through the 20s, peaking at the age of 19. Most likely because this is a rather strange condition, individuals are somewhat reluctant to seek treatment. In many cases a relative will force the issue by demanding that the individual get help for the problem; this insistance may reflect the disruptiveness of the disorder for family members who must live with the person manifesting it.

Individuals with BDD are reacting to what they think is a horrible or grotesque facial or bodily feature. Thus, the psychopathology lies in their reacting to a perceived deformity that others cannot perceive. Of course, a "deformity" in one culture might be a sign of beauty in another culture. Social and cultural determinants of beauty and body image determine, in large part, what is "deformed." Nowhere is this more evident than in the very different cultural standards for body weight and shape. These cultural factors play a major role in eating disorders, as we will see in Chapter 8.

Over the centuries varying cultural norms have also dictated standards of desirability and beauty for other body parts and features. For example, in most cultures in the world it is desirable for a woman's skin to be lighter and more perfectly smooth than a man's skin (Liggett, 1974; Fallon, 1990). Over the centuries freckles have not been popular. In many cultures chemical solutions were devised for removing freckles. Unfortunately, these solutions removed more than the freckles. Whole layers of skin disappeared and the underlying flesh was severely damaged (Liggett, 1974).

Concerns with the width of the face, so common in BDD, can be culturally determined. Until very recently it was common practice in some areas of France, Africa, Greenland, and Peru to attempt to shape the head of newborn infants. This manipulation was done either by hand or by the use of very tight caps secured by strings. Sometimes the face was elongated; other times it was widened. Similarly, attempts were made to flatten noses of newborn infants, usually by hand (Liggett, 1974; Fallon, 1990).

Other more mutilating customs to enhance beauty in certain cultures are familiar to readers of the *National Geographic*. For example, in Uganda, it was common practice to insert a large disk or plate into the lower lip. In Australia and New Guinea, tribes knock out the two top front teeth of their adolescents to celebrate their reaching adulthood. In other tribes, holes are drilled through the six front teeth and star shaped plugs of brass are inserted. In addition, these teeth are filed to sharp points. In Burma, women start wearing brass neck rings from an early age, resulting in a lengthening of the neck. One woman's neck was measured to be nearly 16 inches long (Morris, 1985).

Finally, many are aware of the old practice in China of binding women's feet, often reducing the foot to one-third of its normal size. Women with bound feet were forced to walk in a way that was thought very seductive. As Brownmiller (1984) points out, the myth of an artificially small foot signifying extraordinary beauty and grace is still with us. Can you think of the fairy tale where a small foot becomes the identifying feature of the beautiful heroine? You're right; it is Cinderella.

In the context of BDD, what can we learn from these mutilating practices among cultures around the world? The practices of individuals with BDD seem remarkably strange because they go *against* current cultural practices that put less emphasis on altering facial features. Nevertheless, "aesthetic" plastic surgery, particularly for nose and lips, is still widely accepted and, since it is most often sought after by those with

wealth, carries a certain aura of status. In this light, BDD may not be so strange. As with most psychopathology, these attitudes and behavior may simply be an exaggeration of normal culturally sanctioned behavior.

Causes and Treatment for Body Dysmorphic Disorder

We know very little about the etiology or treatment of this curious disorder. We have almost no information on whether it runs in families, and therefore, may have a specific genetic contribution. Similarly, we do not have any meaningful information on biological or psychological predisposing factors or vulnerabilities that may lead to its development. Of course, psychoanalytic speculations are numerous but most center on the defensive mechanism of displacement—that is, the person has some underlying unconscious conflict that would be too anxiety-provoking to admit into consciousness, so he or she "displaces" it onto a body part.

What little evidence we do have on etiology comes from a very weak source: the pattern of co-morbidity of this disorder with other disorders. BDD is a somatoform disorder because the central feature is a psychological preoccupation with somatic issues. For example, in hypochondriasis the focus is on physical sensations. In BDD the focus is on actual physical appearance. We have already seen in this chapter that many of the somatoform disorders tend to co-occur. In Linda's case, described earlier, she presented with somatization disorder but also had a history of conversion disorder in her background. For some reason, BDD does not tend to co-occur with the other somatoform disorders, nor does it occur in family members of patients with other somatoform disorders.

There is another disorder, however, that frequently co-occurs with BDD and is also found among the family members of those who have BDD. This is obsessive-compulsive disorder (Tynes, White, & Steketee, 1990). Is BDD a variant of obsessive-compulsive disorder (OCD)? There are certainly a lot of similarities. The people you read about previously who have BDD complain of persistent intrusive and horrible thoughts (about their appearance), and they seem to engage in a lot of compulsive behaviors, such as repeatedly looking in mirrors to check their physical features. BDD and OCD also have, approximately, the same age of onset and run the same course. Perhaps most significantly, there is one, and only one, treatment with any evidence for effectiveness whatsoever for BDD. Drugs that block the reuptake of serotonin, such as clomipramine and fluoxetine, seem to provide relief to at least some of these patients. Intriguingly, these are the same drugs that seem to have the strongest effect in OCD. If BDD is a variant of obsessive-compulsive disorder, then we would know a lot more about some of the biological and psychological factors that might lead to its development. Furthermore, this connection would point to the possibility of successful psychological treatments such as exposure and response prevention, which is powerfully effective with many cases of OCD. But we need much more basic research before this link is established.

Another interesting lead on causes of BDD comes from cross-cultural explorations of disorders of this type. You may remember the Japanese variant of social phobia discussed in Chapter 5 that is called taijin kyōfushō. In that particular disorder it is not uncommon for individuals to believe they have the worst bad breath or body odor you could ever imagine, causing them to avoid social interactions. But they also have all the other characteristics of social phobia. In fact, patients who would be diagnosed BDD in our culture might simply be considered to have severe social phobia in Japan and Korea. Possibly, then, anxiety is fundamentally related to BDD, a connection that would give us hints on the nature of the disorder.

Plastic surgery.   Since the concerns within BDD involve mostly the face or head, it is not surprising that this disorder is big business for the plastic surgery profession—but it's bad business. These patients do not benefit from surgery and may return for additional surgery or, on occasion, file malpractice law suits. Even worse, a recent study found that preoccupations with imagined ugliness actually *increased* in people who sought out plastic surgery, dental work, or special skin treatments for their perceived problems (Phillips et al., 1993). Therefore, it becomes very important for plastic surgeons to attempt to screen out these patients, and many plastic surgeons do so by collaborating with medically trained psychologists (Pruzinsky, 1988). Some investigators estimate that as many as 2% of all patients requesting plastic surgery may be individuals with BDD (Andreasen & Bardach, 1977). Most commonly requested procedures are rhinoplasties (nose jobs), face lifts, eyebrow elevations, and surgery to alter the jaw line. The problem is, the surgery seldom produces the desired results. These individuals will return for additional surgery on the same defect, or will concentrate on some new defect. Hollander, Liebowitz, Winchel, Klumker, and Klein (1989) describe one patient who had four separate rhinoplasties, but then became concerned about his thinning hair and sloped shoulders. Andreasen and Bardach noted that some patients become "synthetic creations of artificial noses, breasts, ears, and hips." Phillips et al. (1993) report that, of 25 surgical or dental procedures performed, only 2 led to any relief. In more than 20 cases, the severity of the disorder and accompanying distress actually *increased* after surgery.

Dissociative Disorders

In the beginning of the chapter we mentioned dissociative experiences in which individuals feel detached from themselves or their surroundings almost as if they are living in a dream or living life in slow motion. Morton Prince, the founder of the *Journal of Abnormal Psychology,* noted over 90 years ago that many people experience something like dissociation occasionally (Prince, 1906–1907). This sensation is more likely to happen if you have experienced some extreme stress such as an accident. It might also happen if you're tired or if you're under some physical or mental stress from, say, staying up all night cramming for an exam. Because you thought you knew the cause, it may not have bothered you much (Dixon, 1963; Noyes, Hoenk, Kuperman, & Slymen, 1977). On the other hand, it could have been very, very frightening.

These experiences of unreality can be broken down into two types of feelings. During an episode of **depersonalization,** you experience an alteration in your perception so that you temporarily lose a sense of your own reality. During an episode of **derealization,** your sense of the "realness" of your external world is lost. Things may seem to change shape or size; people may seem dead or mechanical.

Symptoms of unreality are most prevalent in the **dissociative disorders** because depersonalization is, in a sense, a psychological mechanism whereby one "dissociates" from reality. In this way it is often a part of a much more serious set of conditions where reality, experience, and even one's identity disintegrate. What happens during these periods of "disintegration"? Consider for a minute how we usually function. As we go about our day-to-day lives, we ordinarily have an excellent sense of who we are (identity) as well as a general knowledge of the identity of other people with whom we interact, even if we don't know all their names. At the same time we have an awareness of events around us, including where we are and why we are there. Finally, except for occasional small lapses, our memories remain intact so that all events leading up to the current moment are clear in our minds.

But what happens if we lose our memory and can't remember why we are in a certain place or even who we are? What happens if we lose our sense that things are real, so that we are not "aware" of our surrounding as we usually are? Finally, what happens if we not only forget who we are but begin thinking that we are really somebody else—somebody who has a different personality, a different set of memories, and even a set of different physical reactions, such as allergies that are not really ours? All these examples are instances of disintegrated experience (Putnam, 1991; Spiegel & Cardena, 1991). In each case there are alterations in the relationship to the self, the world, or to memory processes.

In this section we will discuss a number of disorders in which some or all of these features are present. Since we know so little about these disorders, we will describe four of them—depersonalization disorder, dissociative amnesia, dissociative fugue, and dissociative trance disorder—very briefly before covering the fascinating condition of dissociative identity disorder in more detail. As you will see, the influence of social and cultural factors on psychopathology seems more clearly evident in dissociative disorders than in some other classes of psychopathology. As with most psychopathology, a basic emotional or behavioral pattern present to some degree across the human race and perhaps "normal" in some context (the tendency to dissociate) can become severely pathological in some individuals, resulting in distress and impairment for them. But the expression of the "pathology" does not stray far from socially and culturally sanctioned idioms.

Depersonalization Disorder

For a few people, feelings of being unreal or detached are so severe and frightening that they dominate the individuals' lives and prevent normal functioning. When this happens, clinicians may diagnose a very rare disorder called **depersonalization disorder.** Consider the following case from one of our clinics.

The Case of Bonnie

Bonnie, a dance teacher in her late 20s, was accompanied by her husband when she first visited the clinic and complained of "flipping out." When asked about "flipping out," she said, "It's the most scary thing in the world. It often happens when I'm teaching my modern dance class, I'll be up in front and I will feel 'focused on.' Then, as I'm demonstrating the steps, I just feel like it's not really me and that I don't really have control of my legs. Sometimes I feel like I'm standing in back of myself just watching. Also I get 'tunnel vision.' It seems like I can only see in a narrow space right in front of me and I just get totally separated from what's going on around me. Then I begin to panic and perspire and shake." It turns out that Bonnie's problems began after she smoked marijuana for the first time approximately 10 years previously. She had the same feeling at that time and found it very scary, but with the help of some friends, she got through it. Lately the feeling began recurring more frequently and more severely, particularly when she was teaching dance class.

Criteria for depersonalization disorder are presented in Table 6.8. We have already discussed some of these sensations and symptoms in the context of panic disorder in Chapter 5. You may remember that many people (approximately 50%) experience feelings of unreality in the course of an intense panic attack.

People undergoing intense stress or experiencing a traumatic event may also experience these symptoms. In fact, such experiences characterize the newly defined disorder, *acute stress disorder,* occurring immediately after a trauma as described in Chapter 5. Thus, feelings of depersonalization and derealization are part of several different disorders (Boon & Draijer, 1991). But when more severe experiences of depersonalization and derealization are the *major* problem, the individual would meet criteria for depersonalization disorder (Steinberg, 1991).

Dissociative Amnesia

Perhaps the easiest to understand of the more severe dissociative disorders is one called **dissociative amnesia.** There are several different patterns of dissocia-

Table 6.8 DSM-IV Criteria for Depersonalization Disorder

A. Persistent or recurrent experiences of feeling detached from, and as if one is an outside observer of, one's mental processes or body (e.g., feeling like one is in a dream).

B. During the depersonalization experience, reality testing remains intact.

C. The depersonalization causes clinically significant distress or impairment in social, occupational, or other important areas of functioning.

D. The depersonalization experience does not occur exclusively during the course of another mental disorder, such as schizophrenia, panic disorder, acute stress disorder, or another dissociative disorder, and is not due to the direct physiological effects of a substance (e.g., a drug of abuse, a medication) or a general medical condition (e.g., temporal lobe epilepsy).

Source: DSM-IV, APA, 1994.

tive amnesia. Some people are unable to remember anything, including who they are, and for this reason are said to suffer from **generalized amnesia.** Generalized amnesia may be lifelong or may extend from a period in the more recent past, such as 6 months or a year previously.

> ### The Case of the Woman Who Lost Her Memory
>
> Several years ago a woman in her early 50s brought her daughter to one of our clinics because of the girl's failure to attend school and other severely disruptive behavior. It turned out that the father in the family (who refused to come to the session) was very quarrelsome, a heavy drinker, and on occasion, abusive. The woman's son, now in his mid 20s, continued to live at home and was a burden on the family. Several times a week the whole family would erupt into a major battle complete with shouting, pushing, and shoving, as each accused and blamed the others for all their problems. It became clear that the mother, a very strong woman, was the peacemaker responsible for holding the family together. Approximately every 6 months, usually after a family battle, the mother would totally lose her memory (general amnesia) and the family would admit her to the hospital. After a few days away from the turmoil, the mother would regain her memory and come home, only to repeat the cycle in the coming months. Although we did not treat this family (they lived too far away), the situation resolved itself as the children moved away and the stress decreased.

Far more common is a more **localized amnesia,** a failure to recall specific events that occur during a specific period of time. Usually these are traumatic events. In fact, dissociative amnesia is very common during war (Loewenstein, 1991; Spiegel & Cardena, 1991).

Sackeim and Devanand (1991) describe the interesting case of a woman whose father had deserted her at an early age. She had also been forced to have an abortion at the age of 14. Years later, she came for treatment for frequent headaches. In therapy she would report these early events (for example, abortion) rather matter of factly; but under the influence of hypnosis, she would relive, with intense emotion, the early abortion and remember the fact that subsequently she was raped by the abortionist. She also would have images of her father attending a funeral for her aunt, one of the few times she ever saw him. Upon awakening from the hypnotic state she would have no memory whatsoever of *emotionally* reexperiencing these events, and she would wonder why she had been crying. In this case the woman did not have amnesia for the *events themselves* (the abortion and rape) but rather for her intense *emotional reactions to the events.* In most cases of dissociative amnesia, the forgetting is very selective for traumatic events or memories rather than generalized. Criteria for dissociative amnesia are presented in Table 6.9.

Dissociative Fugue

A related dissociative disorder is referred to as **dissociative fugue,** with *fugue* literally meaning "flight" (*fugitive* is from the same root). In these curious cases, not only is there memory loss but it revolves around a very specific incident—that is, the individual makes an unexpected trip (or trips). Mostly, these individuals just "take off," find themselves in some new place, not remembering why or how they got there. Most usually they are leaving behind some very difficult situation that they find intolerable. During these trips the individuals sometimes assume a new identity or at least become confused about their old identity. Consider the case of the "misbehaving sheriff."

Aktar and Brenner (1979) describe a 46-year-old sheriff who reported at least three episodes of dissociative fugue. On these three occasions he found himself as far as 200 miles from his home after suddenly

---

Table 6.9 DSM-IV Criteria for Dissociative Amnesia

A. The predominant disturbance is one or more episodes of inability to recall important personal information, usually of a traumatic or stressful nature, that is too extensive to be explained by ordinary forgetfulness.

B. The disturbance does not occur exclusively during the course of dissociative identity disorder, dissociative fugue, posttraumatic stress disorder, acute stress disorder, or somatization disorder and is not due to the direct physiological effects of a substance (e.g., a drug of abuse, a medication) or a neurological or other general medical condition (e.g., amnestic disorder due to head trauma).

C. The symptoms cause clinically significant distress or impairment in social, occupational, or other important areas of functioning.

Source: DSM-IV, APA, 1994.

Robert Clark was taken to a Yuma hospital after complaining of chest pains, but he awoke with no memory of anything that had ever happened to him. Clark apparently arrived by bus from St. Petersburg, Florida, and checked into a hospital there, but nothing else is known about him. The only things he carried were a small amount of money and four pictures that could be of his grandchildren. Other than memory loss, remaining cognitive function was intact, and there were no signs of organic impairment.

disappearing. When he "came to" he immediately called his wife but was never able to completely recall what he did when he was on these trips, some of which had lasted for several days. During treatment the individual remembered who he was on these trips. Despite his occupation as a sheriff, he became the

outlaw type he had always secretly admired. He adopted an alias, drank heavily, mingled with a rough crowd, and went to brothels and wild parties. Criteria for dissociative fugue are presented in Table 6.10.

Dissociative amnesia and fugue states usually do not appear until adolescence and more commonly come in adulthood. It is rare for these states to appear in an individual for the first time after he or she reaches the age of 50 (Sackeim & Devanand, 1991). However, once they appear, they may continue well into old age.

Usually, fugue states end rather abruptly, as did those of the misbehaving sheriff, and the individual returns home recalling most, if not all, of what happened. In this disorder, the disintegrated experience goes a step beyond memory loss and involves at least some disintegration of identity, if not the complete adoption of a new identity. We will return to this theme shortly in discussing a more extreme disorder, dissociative identity disorder, which is one of the most curious in all of psychopathology.

Dissociative Trance Disorder

Dissociative disorders differ in very important ways across cultures. In many areas of the world, dissociative phenomena may take the appearance of a trance or the experience of possession. The characteristics of these trance or possession states may be determined by the culture. The symptoms of the disorder include the usual sorts of dissociative symptoms such as sudden changes in personality, but the changes are attributed to possession by a spirit known to that particular culture. Often this spirit may demand presents or favors from the family and friends of the victim (given the cultural appropriateness of this kind of happening, the demands of the deity or spirit are usually met). Much like other dissociative states, this disorder seems to be more common in women and is often associated with some life stress or trauma. However, the stress or trauma, much as in dissociative amnesia and fugue states, is current rather than in the past.

Of course, these trance or possession states may be a common part of some traditional religious or

Table 6.10   DSM-IV Criteria for Dissociative Fugue

A. The predominant disturbance is sudden, unexpected travel away from home or one's customary place of work, with inability to recall one's past.

B. Confusion about personal identity or assumption of new identity (partial or complete).

C. The disturbance does not occur exclusively during the course of dissociative identity disorder and is not due to the direct physiological effects of a substance (e.g., a drug of abuse, a medication) or a general medical condition (e.g., temporal lobe epilepsy).

D. The symptoms cause clinically significant distress or impairment in social, occupational, or other important areas of functioning.

Source: DSM-IV, APA, 1994.

Table 6.11   DSM-IV Criteria for Trance and Possession Disorder

A. Either (1) or (2):

1. Trance, i.e., temporary marked alteration in the state of consciousness or loss of customary sense of personal identity without replacement by an alternate identity, associated with at least one of the following:
   (a) narrowing of awareness of immediate surroundings, or unusually narrow and selective focusing on environmental stimuli
   (b) stereotyped behaviors or movements that are experienced as being beyond one's control
2. Possession trance, a single or episodic alteration in the state of consciousness characterized by the replacement of customary sense of personal identity by a new identity. This is attributed to the influence of a spirit, power, deity, or other person, as evidenced by one (or more) of the following:
   (a) stereotyped and culturally determined behaviors or movements that are experienced as being controlled by the possessing agent
   (b) full or partial amnesia for the event

B. The trance or possession state is not accepted as a normal part of a collective cultural or religious practice.

C. The trance or possession state causes clinically significant distress or impairment in social, occupational, or other important areas of functioning.

D. The trance or possession trance state does not occur exclusively during the course of a Psychotic Disorder (including Mood Disorder With Psychotic Features and Brief Reactive Psychosis) or Dissociative Identity Disorder and is not due to the direct physiological effects of a substance or a general medical condition.

Source: DSM-IV, APA, 1994.

cultural practices and would not be considered abnormal in that context. Only if the trance or possession state is *undesirable* and considered *pathological* by members of that person's culture does it become a disorder. While trance and possession states are almost never seen in Western cultures, they are among the most common forms of dissociative disorders in other cultures. Therefore, a category to cover these states has been proposed for possible future editions of DSM. We include these criteria here because they illustrate the cultural relativity of some disorders. The criteria for this proposed category, **dissociative trance disorder,** are presented in Table 6.11.

Dissociative trance states commonly occur in India, Nigeria (where it is called *vinvuza*), Thailand (*phii pob*), and other Asian and African countries (Mezzich et al., 1992; Saxena & Prasad, 1989). In the United States, culturally accepted dissociation com-

In many cultures, it is normal or expected to experience dissociative symptoms by entering a trance state or by experiencing "possession."

monly occurs during religious ceremonies at African-American prayer meetings (Griffith et al., 1980), Native American rituals (Jilek, 1982) and Puerto Rican spiritist sessions (Comas-Diaz, 1981). Among Bahamians and Southern blacks, trance syndromes are often referred to colloquially as "falling out."

Another seemingly distinct dissociative disorder not found in Western cultures is called *amok* (as in running amok). This disorder has attracted some attention because individuals in this trancelike state often brutally assault and sometimes kill nearby persons or animals. If the person is not killed himself (the majority of people suffering from this disorder are males), he probably will not remember the episode. Running amok is only one of a number of "running" syndromes in which individuals enter a trancelike state and suddenly, imbued with a mysterious source of energy, run or flee for a long period of time. In most cultures, as with the majority of dissociative disorders, the prevalence of running disorders is somewhat greater in women (except for amok). Among native peoples of the Arctic, this disorder is termed *pivloktoq*. Among the Navajo tribe the disorder is referred to as *frenzy witchcraft*. These running disorders, despite their different culturally determined expression, would seem to meet criteria for dissociative fugue, with the possible exception of amok.

Dissociative Identity Disorder (Multiple Personality Disorder)

Clinical Description

In **dissociative identity disorder (DID)** one not only adopts a new identity but may also adopt as many as 100 new identities, all coexisting inside one body and mind. In some cases the identities are very complete, each with its own behavior, tone of voice, and physical gestures. In other cases only a few characteristics are distinct as the identities are only partially independent. Consider the following case, originally reported by Ludwig, Brandsma, Wilbur, Bendfeldt, and Jameson (1972).

The Case of Jonah

Jonah, a 27-year-old black male, was suffering from severe headaches. He reported that they were associated with unbearable pain and were lasting for longer and longer periods of time. Furthermore, he couldn't seem to remember things that happened while he had the headache except that sometimes a great deal of time had passed. Finally, when he could stand it no longer

after a particularly bad night, he arranged for admission to the local hospital. What really prompted Jonah to come to the hospital, however, was what other people told him he did while he had his severe headaches. For example, on the night before coming to the hospital he was told that he engaged in a violent fight with another man and attempted to stab him. Shortly thereafter he fled the scene and engaged in a high-speed chase while being shot at by the police. During a previous headache his wife told him he had chased her as well as his 3-year-old daughter out of the house, threatening them with a butcher knife. During his headaches, and while he was violent, he called himself Usoffa Abdulla, son of Omega. Among other incidents in his past for which he had no memory was an occasion when he attempted to drown a man in a river. The man survived and Jonah escaped by swimming a quarter of a mile upstream. He woke up the next morning in his own bed, soaking wet, with no memory of the incident.

During his hospitalization the staff was able to observe Jonah's behavior directly during these headaches as well as during other periods of which he had no memory. They noticed that he responded to different names at these times, acted differently, and generally seemed to be a totally different person. During this period they observed three separate identities or alters in addition to Jonah. **Alters** is the shorthand term for the different identities or personalities in DID. The first alter was Sammy. Sammy seemed rational, calm, and totally in control of the situation. The second alter was called King Young. King Young seemed to be in charge of all sexual activity and was particularly interested in having as many heterosexual interactions as possible. The third alter was the violent and dangerous Usoffa Abdulla.

As is characteristic of these cases, Jonah had no knowledge of the other three alters. Sammy, the detached rational alter, was most aware of the other personalities. King Young knew a little bit about the other alters but his knowledge was only indirect, as was the knowledge of Usoffa Abdulla.

Sammy first appeared when Jonah was approximately 6 years of age. Sammy came out immediately after Jonah witnessed his mother stabbing his father. When alone, Jonah's mother would dress him in girl's clothing on occasion. During one of these occasions and shortly after Sammy emerged, King Young appeared. When Jonah was 9 or 10 he was accosted and brutally

Table 6.12   DSM-IV Criteria for Dissociative Identity Disorder (Multiple Personality Disorder)

A. The presence of two or more distinct identities or personality states (each with its own relatively enduring pattern of perceiving, relating to, and thinking about the environment and self).

B. At least two of these identities or personality states recurrently take control of the person's behavior.

C. Inability to recall important personal information that is too extensive to be explained by ordinary forgetfulness.

D. The disturbance is not due to the direct physiological effects of a substance (e.g., blackouts on chaotic behavior during alcohol intoxication) or a general medical condition (e.g., complex partial seizures). Note: In children, the symptoms are not attributable to imaginary playmates or other fantasy play.

Source: DSM-IV, APA, 1994.

attacked by a group of white youths. At this point Usoffa Abdulla emerged, reporting that his sole reason for existence was to protect Jonah.

Diagnostic criteria for dissociative identity disorder are presented in Table 6.12. As you can see, amnesia is present, as it is in dissociative amnesia and dissociative fugue. But here identity has also fragmented. The number of "personalities" living inside one body is relatively unimportant, whether there are three, or four, or even 100 of them. Rather, the defining feature and the core of this disorder is that certain aspects of the person's identity become detached or dissociated. For this reason the name of the disorder was changed in DSM-IV to dissociative identity disorder from multiple personality disorder. This change was also made to get away from the notion that there are somehow multiple people living inside one body.

Characteristics.   Different identity fragments can present very differently. There is usually a "host" identity; this is the person who becomes the patient and asks for treatment. Host personalities are usually attempting to hold various fragments of identity together but end up being overwhelmed. The first personality to seek treatment is seldom the original personality of the person. Usually the host personality develops later (Putnam, 1992). Many patients have at least one impulsive alter, sometimes acting as a prostitute, to handle sexuality and generate income. In other cases all alters abstain from sex. It is not uncommon for individuals to have cross-gendered alters. For example, a small fragile woman might have a strong powerful male alter who serves as a protector. The transition from one personality to another is called a *switch.* Usually the switch is instantaneous (although when portrayed in movies or television it is often drawn out for dramatic effect). Physical transformations can take place during these switches. Posture, facial expressions, patterns of facial wrinkling, and

even physical disabilities may emerge during a switch. In one study, changes in handedness occurred in 37% of the cases (Putnam, Guroff, Silberman, Barban, & Post, 1986).

Real Identities or Fake Identities?

Are these fragmented identities "real" or is the individual just faking to avoid some responsibility or escape from some stress? Much as with conversion disorders, this question has been very difficult to answer for several reasons. First, evidence indicates that individuals with dissociative identity disorder (DID) are very suggestible (Bliss, 1984). It is possible that these identities are created by leading questions from therapists, either during psychotherapy or while the individuals are in a hypnotic state.

Also there is the notorious case of Kenneth Bianchi, the Hillside Strangler. During the late 1970s, Bianchi brutally raped and murdered 10 young women in the Los Angeles area and left their bodies naked and in full view on the sides of various hills. Thus he was called the "Hillside Strangler." Despite overwhelming evidence that Bianchi was the killer, he continued to claim his innocence. This denial prompted some professionals to think he might have DID. His lawyer brought in a clinical psychologist, who hypnotized him and asked whether there were another part of Ken to whom he could speak. Guess what? Somebody answered calling himself "Steve" and said that he did all the killing. Steve also said that Ken knew nothing about the murders. With this evidence, the lawyer entered a plea of not guilty by reason of insanity (multiple personality disorder).

The defense called on Martin Orne, a distinguished clinical psychologist *and* psychiatrist who is also one of the world's leading experts on hypnosis and dissociative disorders (Orne, Dinges, & Orne, 1984). Orne used procedures similar to those utilized in the context of conversion blindness described previously to determine whether Bianchi was simulating DID or if it was a "true" psychological disorder. For example, Orne suggested during an in-depth interview that a

Martin Orne is one of the leading experts in the world on hypnosis and dissociative disorders.

"true" multiple personality disorder had at least three personalities. Shortly thereafter, Bianchi produced a third personality. Orne also pointed out that there was no independent corroboration of the existence of different personalities before Bianchi's arrest. He established this by interviewing Bianchi's friends and relatives. Psychological tests also failed to show differences among the personalities; fragmented identities often score very differently on personality tests. It was also discovered that Bianchi had several textbooks on psychopathology in his room and therefore, presumably, knew a lot about the subject. Finally, Orne, an expert in hypnosis, concluded that Bianchi was responding more like someone simulating hypnosis than someone deeply hypnotized. Based on Orne's testimony, Bianchi was found guilty and sentenced to life in prison.

Some investigators have studied the ability of individuals to simulate or fake dissociative experiences. Spanos, Weeks, and Bertrand (1985) demonstrated in an experiment with college students that these students could simulate or fake an "alter" if it was suggested to them that this faking was plausible, as it was suggested to Bianchi during the interview. All students were told to play the role of an accused murderer claiming his innocence. Over 80% of the subjects who received *exactly the same interview* as Bianchi, word for word, adopted the strategy of simulating an alternate personality in order to avoid being convicted of murder. Groups that were given more vague instructions, without a direct suggestion that an alternate personality existed, were much less likely to use an alternate personality in their defense.

In an important experiment along the same lines Spanos, James, and de Groot (1990) compared subjects with *hypnotically induced amnesia* (considered to be similar to the type of amnesia present in dissociative disorders) and subjects who were instructed to *simulate* amnesia. While hypnotized (or instructed to simulate), all subjects were asked to memorize a list of words. Subjects were then presented the words along with a lot of words that were not in the original list. Subjects under hypnosis exhibited *above chance* levels of recognition of words that were on the original list. Simulators, on the other hand, evidenced *below chance* recognition for these same words. Below chance levels of recognition, of course, are more consistent with an instructed response to fake amnesia.

Objective tests suggest that most people with fragmented identities are not consciously and voluntarily simulating (Kluft, 1991). Condon, Ogston, and Pacoe (1969) examined a film of a patient, Chris Sizemore, who was the real-life subject for the book and movie, *The Three Faces of Eve*. They determined that one of the personalities (Eve Black) evidenced a transient microstrabismus (divergence in conjugant lateral movement of the eyes). This was not observed in the other personalities. These optical differences have been confirmed by Miller (1989), who demonstrated that DID subjects had 4.5 times the average number of changes in optical functioning in their alter identities, compared to control subjects who were simulating alter personalities. Again, Miller concludes that these optical changes, including measures of visual acuity, manifest refraction, and eye muscle balance, would be difficult to fake. Ludwig et al. (1972) found that the various identities present in Jonah evidenced different physiological responses to emotionally laden words. These responses included the galvanic skin response (GSR), a

Chris Sizemore, whose story was depicted in the book and movie *The Three Faces of Eve*, suffered from multiple personality disorder.

measure of otherwise imperceptible sweat gland activity, and electroencephalogram (EEG) pattern or brain waves.

Anna O. Revealed.

Remember the case of Anna O.? We return one more time to that very famous case that prompted some of the early insights concerning the unconscious and the development of psychoanalysis. Earlier in this chapter, we referred to Anna O.'s conversion symptoms, specifically paralysis in her right arm and anesthesia of her right side as well as loss of her ability to speak her native language, German (although she retained perfect command of English). As Anna confronted her traumatic memories of watching her father die while she nursed him, she increasingly recovered her physical abilities.

Anna O.'s real name was Bertha Pappenheim and, in fact, she was an extraordinary woman. What many people don't realize is that she was never completely cured by Breuer, who finally gave up on her in 1882. Over the next decade she was institutionalized several times with severe recurrences of her conversion symptoms. Thereafter, she began a slow recovery. She then went on to become a pioneering social worker and staunch crusader against the sexual abuse of women (Putnam, 1992). She devoted her life to freeing women who were trapped in prostitution and white slavery throughout Europe, Russia, and the Near East. She wrote a play about sadistic men who sexually exploit women. The purpose of this play was to illustrate the ongoing abuse of women. The title of the play was *Women's Rights*. At risk to her own life, she would enter brothels throughout Europe to liberate women from their captors. She founded a league of Jewish women in 1904 and a home for unwed mothers in 1907. Recognizing her extraordinary contributions as one of the first militant feminists, a commemorative stamp was later issued in her honor by the West German government (Sulloway, 1979).

Pappenheim's friends remarked that she seemed to lead a "double life." On the one hand, she was a radical feminist and reformer. On the other hand, she was the height of the cultural elite in *fin de siecle* Vienna. In fact, she was an integral part of high society in Vienna and was known as an author and collector of fine art.

Historical detective work tells us that Pappenheim's friends were correct (Putnam, 1992). In Breuer's notes it becomes clear that there were "two Anna O.'s" and that she suffered from dissociative identity disorder (DID). In one state of consciousness or personality, she was somewhat depressed and anxious but otherwise relatively normal. But in an instant she would turn dark and foreboding. It became increasingly clear to Breuer that during these times she was someone else. This someone else hallucinated and became verbally abu-

sive. And it was this "someone else," the second Anna O., who experienced conversion symptoms. The second Anna O. spoke only English or garbled mixtures of four or five languages. The first Anna O. spoke fluent French and Italian as well as her native German. Characteristically one personality had no memory of what happened when the other was "out." Almost anything might cause an instant switch in personalities—for example, the sight of an orange, which was Anna O.'s primary source of nourishment while she was nursing her dying father.

Although Anna O. integrated her life and made extraordinary contributions, do you think her friends were right that she was leading a "double life"? Which Anna O. was the crusading feminist? Which was the high society matron? Putnam (1992) reports that in 1936 Bertha Pappenheim died of cancer. "It is said that she left two wills, each written in a different hand" (p. 36).

Anna O.'s case is unusual in that it is not well known and there seem to be only two distinct personalities; typically there are more. (Anna O. also suffered from conversion disorder, as we saw earlier.)

Statistics and Course for Dissociative Identity Disorders

We described four identities for Jonah but the average number of alter personalities is closer to 15 (Ross, 1989; Sackeim & Devanand, 1991). Of people with DID, the ratio of females to males is as high as 9 to 1, although these data are based on accumulation of case studies rather than survey research. The onset is almost always in childhood, often as young as 4 years of age, although it is usually approximately 7 years before the disorder is recognized for what it is (Putnam et al., 1986). Once established, the disorder tends to last a lifetime in the absence of treatment. The form of the disorder does not seem to vary substantially over the person's life span, although there is some evidence that the frequency of "switching" decreases with age (Sakheim & Devanand, 1991). Different personalities may emerge over the years in response to new life situations, as was the case with Jonah. We don't know how prevalent the disorder is, although investigators now think it is more common than we previously estimated (Kluft, 1991).

A very large percentage of DID patients have additional psychological disorders at the same time, such as substance abuse, depression, somatization disorder, and borderline personality disorder as well as panic attacks and eating disorders (Ross et al., 1990). In some cases this high rate of co-occurring disorders, or comorbidity, may be present because certain disorders, such as borderline personality disorder, share many features with DID—for example, self-destructive, sometimes suicidal behavior and emotional instability. For the most part, however, the high frequency of additional disorders accompanying DID simply reflects the severity of the reaction of these deeply troubled individuals to what seems to be in almost all cases horrible child abuse. Interestingly, DID rarely occurs outside of Western cultures.

Causes of Dissociative Identity Disorder and Other Dissociative Disorders

It is informative to examine current thinking and evidence on causes of all dissociative disorders, as we do below, but our emphasis is on the etiology of DID. Life circumstances that set the stage for the development of DID seem quite clear in at least one respect. The history of almost every patient presenting with this disorder contains horrible, often unspeakable examples of child abuse. Consider the well-known case of Sybil. Some of you may have seen the full-length motion picture about Sybil starring Sally Field that was based on Sybil's biography (Schreiber, 1973). As a child, Sybil had the misfortune to grow up with a mother who had schizophrenia and a father who refused or was unable to intervene in the mother's brutality. Day after day throughout her childhood Sybil was sexually tortured and occasionally nearly murdered. Before Sybil was a year old her mother began tying her up in various ways and, on occasion, suspending her from the ceiling. Many mornings Sybil was placed on the kitchen table where her mother forcefully inserted various objects into her vagina. Sybil's mother reasoned, in her psychotic way, that she was preparing her daughter for adult sex. In fact, she was brutally tearing the child's vaginal canal in a way that was evident during adult gynecological exams. Sybil was also administered very strong laxatives but prohibited from using the bathroom. Because of the father's detachment and the otherwise normal appearance of this family, these activities continued without interruption throughout Sybil's childhood.

Imagine your reaction if your childhood was anything like this. What would you do? You're too young to run away. You're too young to call the authorities. Although the pain may be unbearable, you may not even realize at that very young age that it is unusual or wrong. But you can do one thing! You can escape into a fantasy world; you can be somebody else. If this escape blunts the physical and emotional pain just for a minute or makes the next hour bearable, chances are you'll escape again. Having succeeded once, your mind learns that there is no limit to the variety of identities that can be created just to suit the occasion. Fifteen? Twenty-five? A hundred? Such numbers have been recorded in some cases. You do whatever it takes to get through life.

How common is trauma in the background of these cases? Putnam et al. (1986) examined 100 cases and found 97% of the patients had experienced some significant trauma, usually sexual or physical abuse. Sixty-eight percent reported one specific type of sexual abuse: incest. Ross et al. (1990) reported that, of 97 cases they reviewed, 95% reported physical or sexual abuse. Unfortunately, the abuse is often as bizarre and sadistic as that experienced by Sybil. Some of these individuals have been buried alive. Before that, they were tortured with matches, steam irons, razor blades, or glass.

Not all of the trauma is from abuse. Putnam (1992) mentions the case of a young girl in a war zone who had seen both of her parents blown to bits in a mine field. Her heart-wrenching response was to attempt to piece the bodies back together, bit by bit.

Another background for some of these patients is a childhood filled with satanism and the ritual abuse that is part of satanic cults (Sakheim & Devine, 1992.) Killing and drinking the blood of others or sometimes individuals in your own family may be part of the required initiation in these cults. In one case, a young woman was forced to sacrifice her own baby on the altar of Satan. Most usually, the cult involves the whole of an otherwise unassuming and normal-appearing family.

These observations have led to wide-ranging agreement that the cause of DID is rooted in a natural tendency to escape or "dissociate" from the unremitting negative affect associated with severe abuse (Kluft, 1984, 1991). A lack of social support during or after the abuse also seems implicated in etiology. As with most psychopathology, the behavior and emotions that make up disorders seem rooted in otherwise normal tendencies present in all of us to some extent. As mentioned at the beginning of this section, it is quite common for otherwise normal individuals undergoing unusual stress to attempt to escape or dissociate from the emotional or physical pain in some way (Spiegel & Cardena, 1991). Noyes and Kletti (1977) surveyed over 100 survivors of various life-threatening situations (severe accidents, etc.) and found that most of these individuals had experienced some type of dissociation, such as feelings of unreality, a blunting of emotional and physical pain, and even detachment from their bodies. Dissociative amnesia and fugue states also seem clearly to be a reaction to severe life stress. But in these disorders the life stress or trauma seems to be in the present rather than the past, as was the case with the overwrought mother who suffered from dissociative amnesia (described earlier). Many of these patients are escaping from legal difficulties or severe stress at home or on the job (Sackeim & Devanand, 1991).

You may have noticed that DID seems very similar in its etiology to posttraumatic stress disorder

(PTSD). In both conditions we see strong emotional reactions to experiencing a severe trauma. But remember that not everyone experiencing a severe trauma goes on to experience posttraumatic stress disorder. To review, it seems that only those individuals who are vulnerable, both biologically and psychologically, to manifesting anxiety are at risk for developing this disorder at mild to moderate levels of trauma severity. However, as the severity of the trauma increases, a greater percentage of people develop PTSD as a consequence. But even after the most severe traumas, some people do not become victims of the disorder, suggesting that individual psychological and biological factors interact with the experience of trauma to produce PTSD.

There is a growing body of opinion that DID is a very extreme subtype of PTSD with a much greater emphasis on the process of dissociation than on symptoms of anxiety, although both are present in each disorder. We also must remember that we know relatively little about DID. Everything described above is really based on examining series of patients who have the disorder. In other words, our conclusions are based on retrospective case studies or correlations rather than the prospective examination of people who may have undergone the severe trauma that seems to lead to DID. Therefore, it is hard to say what psychological or biological factors might contribute to the development of this disorder, but there are some hints concerning individual differences that might play a role.

Suggestibility. One possibility may be a tendency for a person to be highly suggestible. Suggestibility is a personality trait that is distributed normally across the population, much like weight and height. That is, some people are much more suggestible than others; some people are relatively immune to suggestibility; and the majority fall in the midrange.

Did you ever have an imaginary childhood playmate? Many people did, and this is one index of an ability to lead a rich fantasy life, something that can be very helpful and adaptive. But it also seems to correlate with being suggestible or easily hypnotized (some people equate the terms *suggestibility* and *hypnotizability*). Being in a hypnotic trance is also very similar to "dissociating" (Bliss, 1986; Carlson & Putnam, 1989). In a hypnotic trance, people tend to become totally absorbed or focused on one aspect of their world (and become very vulnerable to suggestions by the hypnotist). There is also the phenomenon of self-hypnosis where individuals can dissociate from most of the world around them and "suggest" to themselves that, for example, they won't feel pain in one of their hands.

It is possible that people who tend to be more suggestible or hypnotizable are the ones who are able to use dissociation as a defense against extreme trauma. This explanation of the cause of dissociative disorder has been called the autohypnotic model (Putnam, 1991). As many as 50% of DID patients can clearly remember imaginary playmates in childhood (Ross et al., 1990). Whether these playmates were created before

In a hypnotic trance, people become very absorbed in certain aspects of their experience and are very suggestible.

or after their trauma is not entirely clear. When the trauma becomes unbearable, the person's very identity splits into multiple dissociative identities. Other people who are less suggestible may develop a severe post-traumatic stress reaction but not a dissociative reaction. Once again, these explanations are all very speculative because we have no controlled studies of this phenomenon.

Seizures and dissociative symptoms.

What about more biological factors? Much as with posttraumatic stress disorder, where the evidence is more solid, there is almost certainly a biological vulnerability of some sort to reacting in this particular way to trauma. However, there are other more interesting observations that may provide some hints about brain activity during dissociation. Individuals with certain neurological disorders, particularly seizure disorders, experience a lot of dissociative symptoms (Cardena, Lewis-Fernandez, Bear, Pakianathan, & Spiegel, in press). Devinsky, Feldman, Burrowes, and Bromfield (1989) reported that approximately 6% of patients with temporal lobe epilepsy (specifically, complex partial seizures) reported "out of body" experiences. Also, about 50% of another series of patients with temporal lobe epilepsy displayed some kinds of dissociative symptoms (Schenk & Bear, 1981). Some of these experiences include developing alternate identities or identity fragments. Could dissociative experiences be based on some kind of abnormal electrical activity of the brain? We haven't really studied DID patients closely enough to say yes or no, but if that is the case, we would have to assume that some specific brain circuits are involved in this experience.

Nevertheless, there are also clear differences between patients having dissociative experiences who have seizure disorders and those who don't. Ross et al. (1989) showed that these two groups differ substantially in the types of dissociative symptoms they typically have. Also, dissociative symptoms develop in adulthood and are not associated with trauma for the seizure patients, a clear contrast to the DID patients without seizure disorders. Nevertheless, this is an area for future study (Putnam, 1991).

Treatment for Dissociative Disorders

Individuals who experience an episode of dissociative amnesia or a fugue state usually get better on their own and go back to their homes or "remember" what they have forgotten. Their states seem so clearly related to current life stress that prevention of future episodes almost always involves therapeutic resolution of the stressful life situations, or possibly increasing the strength of their coping mechanisms. For those who cannot remember what happened during their amnesic or fugue states, therapy also focuses on uncovering this information, often with the help of friends or family who know what happened. Patients are then helped to confront the information and integrate it into their experience.

For DID, however, the process is not so easy. With the person's very identity shattered into many different elements, the process of reintegrating that personality might seem hopeless. Fortunately, that may not be the case. Although we have no controlled research on the effects of treatment, there are many documented successes of attempts to reintegrate identities during long-term psychotherapy (Putnam, 1989; Ross, 1989). Nevertheless, the prognosis for most people remains poor. Coon (1986) found that only 5 out of 20 patients were successful in treatment, meaning that they achieved a full integration of their identities.

The treatment strategies that therapists would utilize today are based on accumulated clinical wisdom as well as on procedures proven successful in the treatment of posttraumatic stress disorder (see Chapter 5). The fundamental goal of treatment is to confront and relive the early trauma in a way that the individual gains control over the horrible events, at least as they are continuing to occur in the patient's mind at the present time (Ross, 1989). In order to instill a sense of control, the therapist must skillfully, and very slowly, assist patients in visualizing and reliving aspects of their trauma. The goal is to make the trauma simply a terrible memory of a particularly bad period in their lives rather than a current event. Since much of this material is "unconscious," aspects of the experience are often not known to either the patient or therapist until they emerge during this process of reexperiencing. Hypnosis has often been used to access unconscious memories and bring into awareness various "alters." As the process of dissociation may be very similar to the process of hypnosis, the latter may be a particularly efficient way to access traumatic memories. Of course, there is as yet no evidence that hypnosis is a necessary part of treatment. We do know, however, that DID seems to run a chronic course and very seldom if ever improves spontaneously. This gives us some hints that treatments currently in use, primitive as they are, have some effectiveness.

It is also possible that reemerging memories of the trauma may trigger further dissociation. The therapist must be vigilant for these tendencies. Therapeutic relationships and a sense of trust are important in any psychotherapeutic context, but they are absolutely essential in the treatment of DID. Occasionally medication is employed as an adjunct to treatment, but there is little indication that medication adds much at the present time. What little clinical evidence there is indicates that antidepressant drugs might be helpful in some cases (Coon, 1986).

Summary

- In the somatoform disorders individuals are pathologically concerned with the appearance or functioning of their bodies and bring these concerns to the attention of health professionals who usually find no identifiable medical condition causing the physical complaints.

- There are several types of somatoform disorders. Hypochondriasis refers to a condition when individuals believe they currently have a serious disease and become very anxious over this possibility. Somatization disorder is characterized by a seemingly unceasing and wide-ranging pattern of physical complaints that dominates the individual's life and interpersonal relationships. Conversion disorder refers to physical malfunctioning, such as paralysis, without any physical problems that would account for the malfunction. In pain disorder, psychological factors are judged to play a major role in maintaining the pain. And in body dysmorphic disorder, a person who looks normal has a preoccupation with some imagined defect in appearance (imagined ugliness).

- Causes of somatoform disorders are not well understood, but at least some disorders, such as hypochondriasis and body dysmorphic disorder, seem to be very closely related to anxiety disorders.

- Treatment of somatoform disorders ranges from very basic techniques of reassurance and social support to those meant to reduce stress and remove any secondary gain for the behavior. Patients suffering from body dysmorphic disorder often turn to plastic surgery, which more often than not increases the individual's preoccupation and distress.

- Dissociative disorders are characterized by alterations in perceptions and/or a sense of detachment from one's own self, from one's world, or from memory processes. In these disorders an individual might lose portions of his or her memory or sense of reality. In the extreme, whole new identities may be formed as in dissociative identity disorder.

- The causes of dissociative disorders are not well understood but often seem related to traumatic events and the tendency to escape psychologically from the experience or memories of these traumatic events.

- Treatment of dissociative disorders focuses on reexperiencing these traumatic events in a controlled therapeutic manner in order to develop better coping skills. In the case of dissociative identity disorder, therapy is often long term and antidepressant drugs may occasionally be administered; particularly essential with this disorder is establishing a sense of trust between therapist and patient.

Key Terms

alters (228)
body dysmorphic disorder (BDD) (219)
conversion disorder (213)
depersonalization (223)
depersonalization disorder (224)
derealization (223)

dissociative amnesia (224)
dissociative disorders (203, 223)
dissociative fugue (225)
dissociative identity disorder (228)
dissociative trance disorder (DTD) (227)
factitious disorders (215)

generalized amnesia (225)
hypochondriasis (204)
localized amnesia (225)
malingering (214)
pain disorder (218)
somatization disorder (209)
somatoform disorders (203)

If there be a hell upon earth it is to be found in a melancholy man's heart.

Robert Burton
Anatomy of Melancholy

7
Mood Disorders

Think back over the last month of your life. It may seem like a normal month in most respects; you studied during the week, socialized on the weekend (and maybe during the week too), and thought about the future once in a while. Perhaps you were anticipating with some pleasure the next break from your courses, or seeing an old friend or a lover. But maybe sometime during the past month you also felt kind of down, or blue. Possibly that time is now as you contemplate finishing this chapter, along with all the other reading and work you have to do that should have been done last week. Or maybe you broke up with your boyfriend or girlfriend or, worse yet, somebody close to you died recently.

Think about your feelings during this period for a minute. How would you describe them? Were you sad? Perhaps you remember crying a little bit. Maybe you felt a little bit listless and you couldn't seem to get up the energy to go out with your friends. It may be that you feel this way once in a while for no good reason (that you can think of), and because of this, your friends think you're a bit moody.

If you are like most people, you know that your mood will pass. You will be back to your old self in a day or two. In fact, if you *never* got down or depressed, continually seeing only what was good in a situation, your friends might think that behavior was more remarkable than if you were depressed once in a while.

Feelings of depression (and joy) are universal, but the universality of these feelings makes it all the more difficult to understand disorders of mood, disorders that can become so incapacitating that taking one's own life in a violent and painful way seems to the sufferer far the better option than continuing to live. Consider the following case from one of our clinics.

The Case of Katie

Katie was an attractive but very shy young woman who came to our clinic in the company of her parents when she was approximately 16 years old. Katie had found it difficult to go to school for several years. In fact, she seldom interacted with anybody outside her family because of her considerable shyness and social anxiety. As going to school became more difficult and her social contacts decreased, her days became empty and dull. By the time she had reached age 16, the psychological problem blocking out the sun in her life was a deep, all-encompassing depression.

She described her condition as follows:

The experience of depression is like falling into a deep, dark hole that you cannot climb out of. You scream as you fall, but it seems like no one hears you. Some days you float upward without even trying; on other days you wish that you would hit bottom so that you would never fall again. Depression affects the way you interpret events. It influences the way you see yourself and the way you see other people. I remember looking in the mirror and thinking that I was the ugliest creature in the world. Later in life, when some of these ideas would come back, I learned to remind myself that I did not have those thoughts yesterday and chances were that I would not have them tomorrow or the next day. It is a little like waiting for a change in the weather.

But at 16 years, in the depths of her despair, Katie had no such perspective. At that time, it was not unusual for her to spend hours crying at the end of the day. She began drinking alcohol when she was 15, with the blessing of her parents, strangely enough, since the pills prescribed by her family doctor were not doing any good. Previous experience with a glass of wine around the dinner table suggested that alcohol had a temporary soothing effect on Katie and both she and her parents, in their desperation, were willing to try anything that might make her a more functional person. But it was not enough. She drank more and more often. She began drinking herself to sleep. She remembers it as a means of escaping what she felt about herself and her life: "I had very little hope of positive change. I do not think that anyone close to me was hopeful, either. I was angry, cynical, and in a great deal of emotional pain." Katie's life continued to spiral downward.

Several years previously, at the age of 13, Katie had thought about suicide as a solution to her unhappiness. She reported these thoughts to the psychologist she was seeing at the time in the presence of her parents. Her parents began crying, and the sight of their tears deeply affected Katie. From that point on she never shared her thoughts about suicide again, but they remained with her.

By the summer of her 16th year her preoccupations with her own death increased:

I think this was just exhaustion. I was tired of dealing with the anxiety and depression day in and day out. Soon I found myself trying to sever the few interpersonal connections that I did have, with my closest friends, with my mother, and my oldest brother. I was almost impossible to talk to. I was angry and frustrated all the time. One day I went over the edge. My mother and I had a disagreement about some unimportant little thing. I went to my bedroom where I kept a bottle of whisky or vodka or whatever I was drinking at the time. I drank as much as I could until I could pinch myself as hard as I could and feel nothing. Then I got out a very sharp knife that I had been saving and slashed my wrist deeply. I did not feel anything but the warmth of the blood running from my wrist.

The blood poured out onto the floor next to the bed that I was lying on. The sudden thought hit me that I had failed, that this was not enough to cause my death. I got up from the bed and began to laugh. I tried to stop the bleeding with some tissues. I stayed calm and frighteningly pleasant. I walked to the kitchen and called my mother. I cannot imagine how she felt when she saw my shirt and pants covered in blood. She was amazingly calm. She asked to see the cut and said that it was not going to stop bleeding on its own and that I needed to go to the doctor immediately. I remember as the doctor shot novocaine into the cut he remarked that I must have used an anesthetic before cutting myself. I never felt the shot or the stitches.

After that, thoughts of suicide became more frequent and much more real. My father asked me to promise that I would never do it again and I said I would not, but that promise meant nothing to me. I knew it was to ease his pains and fears and not mine, and my preoccupation with death continued.

We will return to Katie later in this chapter.

Think for a moment about your own experiences with depression. What are the major differentiating factors between your "normal" feelings and Katie's? Clearly, Katie's depression was outside the boundaries of normal experience. Her depression differed from normal feelings by virtue of its intensity and duration. In addition, her severe or "clinical" depression interfered substantially with her ability to function. Finally, there are a number of associated psychological and physical symptoms that accompany clinical depression over and above simply feeling "depressed." We will describe these in more detail below when we talk of diagnostic criteria for depression. However, much as with other emotional disorders, it is not yet entirely clear whether Katie's experience is simply a more severe variant of normal depression or if it represents something entirely different, an issue we will discuss again when we consider the nature of grief.

The Experience of Depression

Katie's experience may seem strange and bizarre to you if you have not had firsthand experience with the ravages of mood disorders, either in yourself or someone close to you, but these disorders are tragically common and affect people in all walks of life. Historians have made much of the severe depressions suffered by well-known public figures, including presidents. For example, Calvin Coolidge, the 30th president of the United States, does not generally receive high marks for his tenure as president. Most historians recount his presidency as characterized by an indifferent lack of leadership and his personal habits as lazy and taciturn to the point of being antisocial. His long naps and short workdays were often the object of ridicule. When he died several years after his term was over, the writer Dorothy Parker made the famous comment, "How could they tell?" (Gilbert, 1993). Most people attributed his behavior to Coolidge's Yankee traits of economy of word and behavior and relative indifference to strangers, but historians taking a closer look know better. Coolidge suffered from severe depression.

The first year of Coolidge's presidency, after he moved from the office of vice president on the death of Warren G. Harding, was characterized by vigorous and strong leadership on a number of fronts. But when

Calvin Coolidge, the 30th president of the United States, suffered from a severe and long-lasting depressive episode during the latter part of his presidency.

Abraham Lincoln, suffering from severe depression, did not even show up for his own wedding.

Coolidge had been in office only one year, during the summer of 1924, his 16-year-old son, Calvin, Jr., rubbed a blister on his foot while playing tennis on the south lawn of the White House, developed blood poisoning, and died. The president never recovered and later wrote, "When [Calvin Junior] went, the power and glory of the presidency went with him" (Gilbert, 1993). Historians note that Coolidge showed little interest in government and withdrew from interactions with Congress after the death of his son. His naps grew longer and more frequent, he developed a number of physical symptoms, and he all but stopped work. Coolidge's tragedy became a tragedy for the country because he did not seem to recover from his depression as most people do after a time, even without treatment.

In this respect, Coolidge differs from Abraham Lincoln, who also suffered severe bouts of depression but who seemed to have periods when his depression remitted, enabling him to function to the point that he is remembered as one of our greatest presidents. Nevertheless, on his wedding day, with his bride, Mary Todd, and the wedding party waiting for him, Lincoln, suffering from a severe depressive episode, never showed up! Only several days later, when his depression lifted, was he able to pull himself together sufficiently to get through the ceremony.

With an appreciation of the sometimes tragic consequences of mood disorders, it is important that we develop as full an understanding as possible of their nature. In the following sections we describe the various contributing emotional experiences and symptoms and how they can interrelate to produce specific mood disorders. We offer detailed descriptions of the variety of mood disorders, including an examination of the many criteria that define them, and describe their course. Then we discuss the relationship of anxiety and depression as well as the causes and treatment of mood disorders. Finally, we conclude with a discussion of suicide.

Mood Disorders: An Overview

In prior years, the disorders described in this chapter were categorized under several different general labels such as "depressive disorders" or "affective disorders." Beginning with DSM-III-R, these problems were grouped under the heading **mood disorders** since all the ones described in this section are characterized by gross deviations in mood.

There are two fundamental experiences that contribute, either singly or in combination, to all the specific mood disorders discussed below: depression and mania. We describe each one and then discuss how it contributes to the various mood disorders examined in the chapter. Afterward there is a brief description of additional defining criteria, such as temporal patterning of the mood states (for example, how often they recur) and additional features or symptoms that may accompany them, all of which help to define one or another specific mood disorder.

Depression

The most common (and most severe) experience of depression is called a **major depressive episode.** The criteria for a major depressive episode are presented in Table 7.1. Note that these criteria represent a quite severely depressed mood state that lasts at least 2

"I was having like a revelation, and the devil was saying something to me . . . go get her, she's trying to sleep with you . . . I hear lots of voices . . . [Jesus Christ] is my father . . . I feel like I'm being judged all time . . . I have a disease of the brain. There's something wrong with my brain."

Table 7.1   DSM-IV Criteria for Major Depressive Episode

A. Five (or more) of the following symptoms have been present during the same 2-week period and represent a change from previous functioning; at least one of the symptoms is either (1) depressed mood or (2) loss of interest or pleasure.

Note: Do not include symptoms that are clearly due to a general medical condition, or mood-incongruent delusions or hallucinations.

1. depressed mood most of the day, nearly every day, as indicated by either subjective report (e.g., feels sad or empty) or observation made by others (e.g., appears tearful). Note: In children and adolescents can be irritable mood.
2. markedly diminished interest or pleasure in all, or almost all, activities most of the day, nearly every day (as indicated by either subjective account or observation made by others)
3. significant weight loss when not dieting or weight gain (e.g., a change of more than 5% of body weight in a month), or decrease or increase in appetite nearly every day. Note: In children, consider failure to make expected weight gains.
4. insomnia or hypersomnia nearly every day
5. psychomotor agitation or retardation nearly every day (observable by others, not merely subjective feelings of restlessness or being slowed down)
6. fatigue or loss of energy nearly every day
7. feelings of worthlessness or excessive or inappropriate guilt (which may be delusional) nearly every day (not merely self-reproach or guilt about being sick)
8. diminished ability to think or concentrate, or indecisiveness, nearly every day (either by subjective account or as observed by others)
9. recurrent thoughts of death (not just fear of dying), recurrent suicidal ideation without a specific plan, or a suicide attempt or a specific plan for committing suicide

B. The symptoms do not meet criteria for a Mixed Episode.

C. The symptoms cause clinically significant distress or impairment in social, occupational, or other important areas of functioning.

D. The symptoms are not due to the direct physiological effects of a substance (e.g., a drug of abuse, a medication) or a general medical condition (e.g., hypothyroidism).

E. The symptoms are not better accounted for by Bereavement, i.e., after the loss of a loved one, and persist for longer than 2 months or are characterized by marked functional impairment, morbid preoccupation with worthlessness, suicidal ideation, psychotic symptoms, or psychomotor retardation.

Source: DSM-IV, APA, 1994.

weeks. Note also that there are many symptoms in addition to simply feeling depressed that a person must manifest to be given this diagnosis. These include cognitive symptoms such as feelings of worthlessness and indecisiveness, and disturbances in bodily activities such as changes in sleeping patterns, significant changes in appetite and weight, or a very notable loss of energy, to the point that even the slightest activity or movement requires an overwhelming effort. The episode is also, typically, accompanied by a marked loss of interest in things and an inability of the person to experience any pleasure whatsoever from events happening around her including interactions with family and friends, accomplishments at work or at school, and so on. The inability to experience pleasure is termed **anhedonia.** While all symptoms are important, recent evidence suggests that the bodily symptoms (sometimes called *vegetative* symptoms) are more central to this disorder (Buchwald & Rudick-Davis, 1993) as their presence is a strong indicator that a full major depressive episode is present. The average duration of an untreated major depressive episode is approximately 9 months.

Mania

The second fundamental experience contributing to mood disorders is a period of abnormally marked elation, joy, or euphoria referred to as **mania.** In a manic state, individuals experience extreme pleasure and joy from every activity; in fact, some patients compare their experience to a continuous sexual orgasm. They become extraordinarily active (hyperactive), requiring very little sleep. Individuals in a manic state develop grandiose plans with an accompanying attitude that they can accomplish anything whatsoever that they desire. Speech typically becomes very rapid and sometimes incoherent because the individual is attempting to express so many exciting ideas at once. This feature of speech is typically referred to as *flight of ideas.*

Criteria for a manic episode are presented in Table 7.2. Notice in these criteria that the required duration is only 1 week or less if the episode is severe enough to require hospitalization. Hospitalization could occur, for example, if the individual were engaging in self-destructive buying sprees during which he spent thousands of dollars that he did not have, thinking, perhaps, that he would make a mil-

Table 7.2   DSM-IV Criteria for Manic Episode

A. A distinct period of abnormally and persistently elevated, expansive, or irritable mood, lasting at least 1 week (or any duration if hospitalization is necessary).

B. During the period of mood disturbance, three (or more) of the following symptoms have persisted (four if the mood is only irritable) and have been present to a significant degree:

   1. inflated self-esteem or grandiosity
   2. decreased need for sleep (e.g., feels rested after only 3 hours of sleep)
   3. more talkative than usual or pressure to keep talking
   4. flight of ideas or subjective experience that thoughts are racing
   5. distractibility (i.e., attention too easily drawn to unimportant or irrelevant external stimuli)
   6. increase in goal-directed activity (either socially, at work or school, or sexually) or psychomotor agitation
   7. excessive involvement in pleasurable activities that have a high potential for painful consequences (e.g., engaging in unrestrained buying sprees, sexual indiscretions, or foolish business investments)

C. The symptoms do not meet criteria for a Mixed Episode.

D. The mood disturbance is sufficiently severe to cause marked impairment in occupational functioning or in usual social activities or relationships with others, or to necessitate hospitalization to prevent harm to self or others, or there are psychotic features.

E. The symptoms are not due to the direct physiological effects of a substance (e.g., a drug of abuse, a medication, or other treatment) or a general medical condition (e.g., hyperthyroidism).

Note: Manic-like episodes that are clearly caused by somatic antidepressant treatment (e.g., medication, electroconvulsive therapy, light therapy) should not count toward a diagnosis of Bipolar I Disorder.

Source: DSM-IV, APA, 1994.

[Blows bubble-gum bubble and pops it.] *"Whoo, whoo, whoo—on top of the world! . . . It's going to be one great day! . . . I'm incognito for the Lord God Almighty. I'm working for him, I have been for years. I'm a spy. My mission is to fight for the American way . . . the Statue of Liberty . . . I can bring up the wind, I can bring the rain, I can bring the sunshine, I can do lots of things . . . I love the outdoors . . . [laughs hysterically] . . ."*

lion dollars the next day so his spending did not make any difference. Notice also that being irritable is often part of a manic episode, either throughout or at some time during the episode, usually near the end. The average duration of an untreated manic episode is 6 months.

DSM-IV also defines a **hypomanic episode** that is identical to a manic episode in every way except that it is less severe and does not cause marked impairment in social or occupational functioning. (*Hypo*

means below, thus the episode is below the level of a manic episode.) A hypomanic episode, in and of itself, is not necessarily problematic, but it does contribute to the definition of several mood disorders as described next.

The Structure of Mood Disorders

If individuals experience only one of these moods (for example, either depression or mania), they are said to suffer from a *unipolar mood disorder*. Since the experience of manic symptoms alone is extremely rare, almost all individuals with unipolar mood disorders suffer from unipolar depression. If the individual alternates between experiences of depression and mania she is said to be suffering from a *bipolar mood disorder,* hence she experiences each "pole" of the depression/elation continuum. However, this is somewhat misleading since depression and elation may not be exactly opposite ends of the same mood state; in fact, they are often relatively independent (although related) in that an individual could experience elation but be somewhat depressed or anxious at the same time. When this combination occurs, the episode is referred to as **dysphoric manic** or **mixed episode** (McElroy et al., 1992).

Among individuals with mood disorders, these two experiences, depression and mania, may differ in terms of their severity, the frequency with which they tend to recur, or, occasionally, the presence of some additional accompanying symptoms. A very important feature of major depressive episodes is that they are *time limited*. By definition an episode must last at least 2 weeks, although an episode may last 6 months or more, with 9 months the average duration (Tollefson, 1993). Almost all major depressive episodes eventually remit on their own without treatment, although approximately 10% may last 2 years or longer. Manic episodes remit on their own without treatment after approximately 6 months. Thus, a very important consideration in mood disorders is the *temporal patterning* of these depressive or manic episodes. For example, do they tend to recur? If they do, does the patient fully recover between episodes? Do the depressive episodes alternate with manic or hypomanic episodes? All these different patterns come under the general heading in DSM-IV of *course modifiers* for mood disorders.

Course modifiers specify what has happened to the mood state in the past, in terms of recurrence of the episode, or a temporal association of the episode with other mood-related features, or perhaps the likelihood of the episode occurring at a certain time of the year, such as winter. Knowing past patterns helps us better predict the future of the disorder.

The importance of the temporal course of mood disorders makes the goals of treatment somewhat different than for other psychological disorders. Clinicians will want to do everything possible to relieve people like Katie from their *current* depressive episode. However, an equally important goal of treatment will be to prevent *future* episodes—in other words, to keep people like Katie better for a longer period of time. Studies are just beginning to appear evaluating the effectiveness of treatment based on this second goal (Frank et al., 1990).

It is also important to notice that depressive and manic episodes can look very different from individual to individual while still meeting the criteria for an episode. These extreme variations in mood can be very *heterogeneous*. Looking at the criteria for a major depressive episode in Table 7.1 you can see that either losing or gaining weight and either losing sleep (insomnia) or sleeping too much (hypersomnia) might contribute to the diagnosis of a major depressive episode. Similarly, for a manic episode, one individual may present with clear and extreme euphoria and elation accompanied by inflated self-esteem or grandiosity, while another may appear more irritable and present with accompanying flight of ideas. In reality, it is more common to see patients with a prototypical mix of these symptoms.

". . . I've been sad, depressed most of my life . . . I had a headache in high school for a year and a half . . . There have been different periods in my life when I wanted to end it all . . . I hate me, I really hate me. I hate the way I look, I hate the way I feel. I hate the way I talk to people . . . I do everything wrong . . . I feel really hopeless . . ."

In summary, as we discuss specific mood disorders you will see how the various mood states, sometimes with a somewhat different mix of symptoms, and the pattern in which they occur over time come together to form one mood disorder or another.

Clinical Descriptions of Mood Disorders

Depressive Disorders

The most straightforward mood disorder to recognize is one in which an individual suffers from a single major depressive episode. Criteria for **major depressive disorder, single episode** are presented in Table 7.3. Note that this disorder is defined by the absence of any manic or hypomanic episodes during the course of or before the disorder.

If two or more major depressive episodes have occurred and were separated by at least a 2-month period in which the individual was not depressed, **major depressive disorder, recurrent** is diagnosed. Otherwise, the criteria are the same as for major depressive disorder, single episode. Whether a major depressive episode recurs is very important in predicting the future course of the disorder as well as choosing appropriate treatments. If someone has *one recurrence* of a major depressive episode, the odds of his experiencing a *third* episode approach 80% (Angst, 1981). Therefore, it becomes very important to plan treatment in such a way as to maximize the probability of preventing a third episode. Individuals experiencing a recurrence of major depressive episodes also come from families in which a history of depression is more common, compared to individuals suffering single episodes. Approximately 50% of individuals experiencing major depressive disorder, single episode, will go on

to experience a second episode and meet criteria for major depressive disorder, recurrent.

Think back to the case of Katie. What diagnosis would you make? From the brief description, you can see that Katie was suffering at the time from severely depressed mood, feelings of worthlessness, difficulty concentrating, recurrent thoughts of death, sleep difficulties, and loss of energy. She clearly met the criteria for major depressive disorder. Furthermore, both from her own point of view and that of her parents, she would sink deeply into depression, almost as if falling into a hole, only to rise again unpredictably and unexpectedly before experiencing another unpredictable fall at some later time. Thus Katie met criteria for major depressive disorder, recurrent. Katie's depressive episodes were quite severe when they occurred, but they did not remain severe, since she tended to cycle in and out of them.

Another mood disorder shares many of the symptoms of major depressive disorder but differs in its course. In it the symptoms are somewhat milder but remain relatively unchanged over long periods of time, sometimes 20 or 30 years or more (Keller, Baker, & Russell, 1993; Rush, 1993). The name is **dysthymic disorder.**

Dysthymic disorder is defined as a persistently depressed mood present for at least 2 years. During these 2 years, patients cannot be without these symptoms for more than 2 months at a time. Criteria for dysthymic disorder are presented in Table 7.4. Note that the symptoms of dysthymic disorder differ from those constituting a major depressive episode only in severity and chronicity (the symptoms are milder but more chronic).

Double Depression

Recently, groups of individuals have been examined who suffer from both major depressive

---

Table 7.3   DSM-IV Diagnostic Criteria for Major Depressive Disorder, Single Episode

A. Presence of a single Major Depressive Episode

B. The Major Depressive Episode is not better accounted for by Schizoaffective Disorder and is not superimposed on Schizophrenia, Schizophreniform Disorder, Delusional Disorder, or Psychotic Disorder Not Otherwise Specified.

C. There has never been a Manic Episode, a Mixed Episode, or a Hypomanic Episode. **Note:** This exclusion does not apply if all of the manic-like, mixed-like, or hypomanic-like episodes are substance or treatment induced or are due to the direct physiological effects of a general medical condition.

Specify (for current or most recent episode):
Severity/Psychotic/Remission Specifiers
Chronic
With Catatonic Features
With Melancholic Features
With Atypical Features
With Postpartum Onset

Source: DSM-IV, APA, 1994.

Table 7.4   DSM-IV Diagnostic Criteria for Dysthymic Disorder

A. Depressed mood for most of the day, for more days than not, as indicated either by subjective account or observation by others, for at least 2 years. Note: In children and adolescents, mood can be irritable and duration must be at least 1 year.

B. Presence, while depressed, of two (or more) of the following:

   1. Poor appetite or overeating
   2. Insomnia or hypersomnia
   3. Low energy or fatigue
   4. Low self-esteem
   5. Poor concentration or difficulty making decisions
   6. Feelings of hopelessness

C. During the 2-year period (1 year for children or adolescents) of the disturbance, the person has never been without the symptoms in Criteria A and B for more than 2 months at a time.

D. No Major Depressive Episode has been present during the first 2 years of the disturbance (1 year for children and adolescents); i.e., the disturbance is not better accounted for by chronic Major Depressive Disorder, or Major Depressive Disorder, In Partial Remission.

   Note: There may have been a previous Major Depressive Episode provided there was a full remission (no significant signs or symptoms for 2 months) before development of the Dysthymic Disorder. In addition, after the initial 2 years (1 year in children or adolescents) of Dysthymic Disorder, there may be superimposed episodes of Major Depressive Disorder, in which case both diagnoses may be given when the criteria are met for a Major Depressive Episode.

E. There has never been a Manic Episode, a Mixed Episode, or a Hypomanic Episode, and criteria have never been met for Cyclothymic Disorder.

F. The disturbance does not occur exclusively during the course of a chronic Psychotic Disorder, such as Schizophrenia or Delusional Disorder.

G. The symptoms are not due to the direct physiological effects of a substance (e.g., a drug of abuse, a medication) or a general medical condition (e.g., hypothyroidism).

H. The symptoms cause clinically significant distress or impairment in social, occupational, or other important areas of functioning.

Specify if:
   Early Onset: if onset is before age 21 years
   Late Onset: if onset is age 21 years or older

Specify (for most recent 2 years of Dysthymic Disorder):
   With Atypical Features

Source: DSM-IV, APA, 1994.

episodes *and* dysthymic disorder. For these reasons, they are said to have **double depression.** Typically, these people develop dysthymic disorder, perhaps at an early age, and then some time later, have one or more major depressive episodes. It seems important to identify this particular patterning of depression since it is associated with more severe psychopathology and a more problematic future course of the disorder (Keller & Shapiro, 1982; Keller & Lavori, 1984; Klein, Taylor, Dickstein, & Harding, 1988). For example, Keller, Lavori, Endicott, Coryell, and Klerman (1983) found that 61% of patients suffering from double depression (dysthymic disorder with superimposed major depressive episodes) had not recovered from their underlying dysthymic disorder after 2 years of follow-up. The investigators also found that patients who had recovered from the superimposed major depressive episode experienced very high rates of relapse and recurrence. Consider the following case of a man who was admitted to one of our clinics.

The Case of Jack

Jack was a 49-year-old divorced white male with one child who lived with his mother. When he came in initially, he complained of experiencing chronic depression. He said that he finally realized he needed help. Jack reported that he had been a pessimist and a worrier for much if not all of his adult life. He noted that he consistently felt kind of down and depressed and did not find life to be much fun. He had difficulty making decisions, was generally pessimistic about the future, and thought very little of himself (poor self-esteem). During the past 20 years, the longest period he could remember in which his mood was "normal" or less depressed was about 4–5 days at a time.

Jack worked as a low-level clerk in a state agency. Despite his difficulties, he had managed to finish college and go on to obtain a master's degree in public administration. At that time time people told him his future was bright and that he would be highly valued in state government. Jack did not think so. Despite his postgraduate accomplishments, high marks in his courses, and approving comments from his professors, Jack took a job below his qualifications, thinking that he could always work his way up. He never did, and remained at the same desk for 20 years.

During this time, his wife, fed up with his continued pessimism, lack of self-confidence, and relative inability to enjoy day-to-day events in their marriage, became discouraged and divorced him. Jack continued working as a clerk but moved into his mother's house with his 10-year-old son so that his mother could help care for the son and share expenses.

About 5 years before coming to the clinic, Jack experienced a bout of depression worse than anything he had previously known. He went from lacking confidence in himself to feeling absolutely worthless. From his usual difficulty in making decisions he moved to total incapability to decide anything. He was exhausted all the time and felt as if large quantities of lead had been deposited in his arms and legs, making it difficult even to move. He became unable to complete projects or to meet deadlines. Seeing no hope he began to think of suicide. After tolerating subpar and listless performances for years from someone they had expected to rise through the ranks, Jack's employers finally fired him. After about 6 months, his major depressive episode resolved and he returned, once again, to his more chronic but milder state of depression. He could get out of bed and accomplish some things although he still doubted his own abilities. However, he was unable to obtain another job. After several years thinking that something might turn up, he realized that he was totally unable to solve his own difficulties and that his depression would certainly continue without help. After a thorough assessment, we determined that Jack suffered from a classic case of double depression.

Statistics and Course for Depressive Disorders

The mean age of onset for major depressive disorder is 27 years, but, as reflected in Table 7.5, the age of onset seems to be decreasing in recent years (Weissman, Bruce, Leaf, Florio, & Holzer, 1991). In addition, a frightening recent development is that the incidence of depression and one of its consequences,

suicide, seem to be steadily increasing (Cross-National Collaborative Group, 1992; Lewinsohn, Rohde, Seeley, & Fischer, 1993). In 1989, Myrna Weissman and her colleagues published a study surveying people in five different cities in the United States (Wickramaratne, Weissman, Leaf, & Holford, 1989; Klerman & Weissman, 1989). This survey revealed a greatly increased risk of developing depression in younger Americans. Among Americans born before 1905, only 1% had developed depression by age 75; of those born since 1955, 6% had become depressed by age 24.

A more recent study based on very similar surveys conducted in Puerto Rico, Canada, Italy, Germany, France, Taiwan, Lebanon, and New Zealand suggests that this trend toward developing depression at increasingly earlier ages is occurring worldwide (Cross-National Collaborative Group, 1992). Some of the data from the United States, Puerto Rico, Taiwan, and Beirut, Lebanon, four very different areas of the world, are depicted in Figure 7.1.

As noted above, the length of depressive episodes is variable, with some episodes lasting as little as 2 weeks; in more severe cases an episode might last for several years, with the average duration being approximately 9 months (Tollefson, 1993). Although 9 months is a long time to suffer with a severe depressive episode, evidence indicates that even in the most severe cases, the probability of remission of the episode approaches 90% (Thase, 1990). On occasion, however, episodes may not entirely clear up, leaving some residual symptoms. If this is the case, the likelihood of a subsequent episode is much higher. It is also likely that subsequent episodes will be associated with incomplete inter-episode recovery. This is important to know in terms of treatment planning, as treatment should be continued much longer in these cases.

Recent evidence also indicates that there are important subtypes of dysthymic disorder. The typical age of onset of dysthymic disorder has been estimated

Table 7.5   Mean Age of Onset and Duration of Major Depression by Current Age

	N	Mean Age of Onset (Years)	Mean Duration (Years)*
Total	914	26.5	8.7
Current age:			
18–29	264	18.1	4.9
30–44	369	26.2	7.8
45–64	184	34.9	13.8
65+	97	48.9	19.6

*Number of years between first and last reported episodes

Source: Adapted from Weissman et al., 1991.

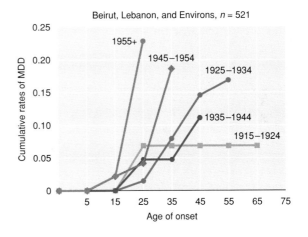

* Years indicate date of birth.

Figure 7.1   Cross-cultural data on the onset of major depressive disorder (adapted from Cross-National Collaborative Group, 1992).

to be a person's early 20s. Yet Klein et al. (1988) found that an *early onset* of the disorder (before 21 years of age and often much earlier) is associated with three characteristics: (a) greater chronicity (it lasts longer), (b) relatively poor prognosis in terms of response to treatment, and (c) a stronger likelihood of the disorder running in the family of the affected individual. Later in the chapter we will examine depression in children, but suffice it to say here that recent investigations have found a rather high prevalence of dysthymic disorder in children (Kovacs, Gatsonis, Paulauskas, & Richards, 1989).

Dysthymic disorder may last 20 or 30 years or more, although one preliminary study reported a median duration of approximately 5 years (Rounsaville, Sholomskas, & Prusoff, 1988). Barrett (1984) conducted a two-year naturalistic follow-up of individuals with dysthymic disorder and found that 63% of these individuals reported no improvement in their disorder during the follow-up period. In fact, the conditions of some of these people deteriorated over time. Johnson and Weissman (n.d.) found that between 48% and 59%

of a large group with dysthymic disorder suffered from the same or a different mood disorder 1 year later.

It is relatively common for major depressive episodes and dysthymic disorder to co-occur (double depression). Figure 7.2 shows the lifetime prevalence of major depressive disorder alone, dysthymic disorder alone, and the two together. Among those who have had dysthymia, 42% have also had a major depressive episode at some point in their lives. We will discuss the prevalence of all mood disorders in more detail below.

Bipolar Disorders

The key identifying feature of **bipolar disorders** is a tendency for manic episodes to alternate with major depressive episodes in an unending roller coaster from the peaks of elation to the depths of despair. Beyond that, bipolar disorders have many parallels with depressive disorders. For example, the manic episode, described in Table 7.2, could occur only once or it could recur. There is also a milder but more chronic version of bipolar disorder called **cyclothymic disorder,**

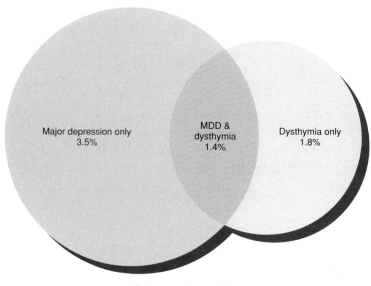

Lifetime rates in population

(Among those with major depression, 28% also have dysthymia.
Among those with dysthymia, 42% also have major depression.)

Figure 7.2   Comorbidity between major depressive disorder (MDD) and dysthymia (adapted from Weissman et al., 1991)

which has many parallels to dysthymic disorder. Consider the following case from one of our clinics.

The Case of Jane

Jane was the wife of a well-known and successful surgeon and the loving mother of three children. The family lived in a large old country house on the edge of town with plenty of room for the family and pets. Jane was now approaching 50 years of age and the older children had moved out, but the youngest son, Mike, was having substantial academic difficulties in school and also seemed very anxious. The reason for Jane's visit was to bring Mike to the clinic in an attempt to ascertain the cause of his difficulties.

As they entered the office I observed that Jane was a well-dressed, neat, vivacious, and personable woman with a bounce to her step. She immediately began talking about her wonderful and successful family before she and Mike even reached their seats. Mike, on the other hand, was tall and thin, very quiet and reserved. He seemed resigned, and perhaps relieved, that he was going to have to say very little during the session. By the time Jane reached her seat she had already pointed out the personal virtues of her husband as well as his material success and the brilliance and beauty of one of her older children, and was ready to proceed with a description of the second eldest child. But before this description was

complete, she noticed a book on anxiety disorders on the desk and, having read voraciously on the subject, began running through a litany of various anxiety-related problems that might be troubling Mike. In the meantime, Mike sat in the corner with a small smile on his lips that seemed to be masking considerable distress and uncertainty over what his mother might do next.

It became clear as the interview progressed that Mike was suffering from panic attacks. These attacks interfered with his concentration both in and out of school and he was failing all his courses. During the interview, it also became clear that Jane, herself, was in the midst of a hypomanic episode, as evidenced by her unbridled enthusiasm and grandiose perceptions of her family and their success, "pressured" speech that was very difficult to interrupt, and the report that she needed very little sleep these days. She was also easily distractible, as evidenced by the quick transition from conversations about her children to other topics. When asked about her own psychological state, Jane readily admitted that she was a manic depressive (the old name for bipolar disorder) and that she alternated rather rapidly between feeling on top of the world and feeling very depressed. She also noted that she was receiving medication for her condition.

Mike was treated intensively at the clinic for his panic disorder but little progress was noted.

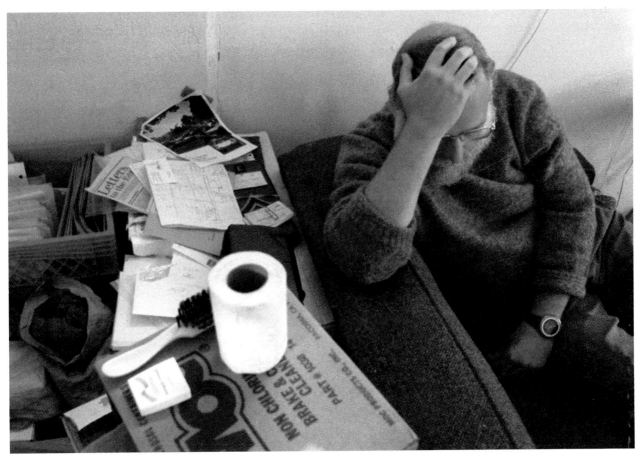

This dreary, crowded interior of Elliott's apartment "is not what I'm used to in life," he says after he returns from a hospitalization for bipolar disorder.

During treatment Mike reported that life was very difficult around the house when his mother was depressed. When asked about this, he revealed that his mother sometimes went to bed and might not get up for 3 weeks. During this time, she seemed to enter a depressive stupor, being essentially unable to move for days at a time. It was up to the children to care for their mother during these periods, including feeding her. Since the older children had left home, much of the burden fell on Mike. Clinically, these profound depressive episodes would remit after about 3 weeks and Jane would immediately enter another hypomanic episode that might last several months or more. During these hypomanic episodes Jane was, for the most part, funny and entertaining and a delight to be with if you could get a word in edgewise. Consultation with her therapist, an expert in the area, revealed that he had prescribed a number of medications but seemed unable to get her mood swings under control.

Jane suffered from **bipolar II disorder** in which major depressive episodes alternate with hypomanic episodes rather than full manic episodes. The criteria for bipolar II disorder are presented in Table 7.6. The criteria for **bipolar I disorder** are the same, except that the individual experiences a full manic episode. As in the criteria set for depressive disorder, for the episodes to be considered separate the person must experience a period of at least 2 months between them without any significant symptoms. Otherwise the condition is just a continuation of the same episode.

While Jane experienced hypomanic episodes, another case illustrates a full manic episode. This individual was first encountered as he was admitted to a hospital.

The Case of Billy

Before Billy reached the ward you could hear him laughing and carrying on in this deep voice sounding like he was having a wonderful time. As the nurse brought Billy down the hall to introduce him to the staff, Billy spied the Ping-

Table 7.6 DSM-IV Diagnostic Criteria for Bipolar II Disorder

A. Presence (or history) of one or more Major Depressive Episodes.

B. Presence (or history) of at least one Hypomanic Episode.

C. There has never been a Manic Episode or a Mixed Episode.

D. The mood symptoms in Criteria A and B are not better accounted for by Schizoaffective Disorder and are not super-imposed on Schizophrenia, Schizophreniform Disorder, Delusional Disorder, or Psychotic Disorder Not Otherwise Specified.

E. The symptoms cause clinically significant distress or impairment in social, occupational, or other important areas of functioning.

Specify current or most recent episode:
  Hypomanic: if currently (or most recently) in a Hypomanic Episode
  Depressed: if currently (or most recently) in a Major Depressive Episode

Specify (for current or most recent Major Depressive Episode only if it is the most recent type of mood episode):
  Severity/Psychotic/Remission Specifiers—Note: Fifth-digit codes specified cannot be used here because the code for Bipolar II Disorder already uses the fifth digit.
  Chronic
  With Catatonic Features
  With Melancholic Features
  With Atypical Features
  With Postpartum Onset

Specify:
  Longitudinal Course Specifiers (With and Without Interepisode Recovery)
  With Seasonal Pattern (applies only to the pattern of Major Depressive Episodes)
  With Rapid Cycling

Source: DSM-IV, APA, 1994.

Pong table on the unit. In a loud exuberant voice, he said, "Ping-Pong! I love Ping-Pong! I have only played twice but that is what I am going to do while I am here, I am going to become the world's greatest Ping-Pong player! And that table is gorgeous! I am going to start work on that table immediately and make it the finest Ping-Pong table in the world. I am going to sand it down, take it apart and rebuild it until it gleams and every angle is perfect!" Billy soon lost interest in the Ping-Pong table and went on to something else that totally absorbed his attention. In fact, the prior week Billy had emptied his bank account, taken his credit cards and those of his elderly parents with whom he was living, and bought every piece of fancy stereo equipment he could find. He thought that he would set up the best sound studio in the city and make millions of dollars, renting out the studio to people who would come from far and wide. It was this episode that had precipitated his admission to the hospital.

During manic or hypomanic phases, patients often deny that they have a problem, something that was characteristic of Billy. Even after spending inordinate amounts of money or making foolish business decisions, these individuals, particularly if they are suffering from a full manic episode, are so wrapped up in their enthusiasm and expansiveness that their behavior seems perfectly reasonable to them. A major problem with individuals suffering from this disorder is that the "high" during a manic state is so pleasurable that they will often stop taking their medication during periods of distress or discouragement, in an attempt to bring on a manic state once again.

Returning to the case of Jane, we continued to treat her son Mike for several months. We made very little progress before the school year ended. Since Mike was doing so poorly, the school administrators informed his parents that he would not be accepted the next year. Both Mike and his parents wisely decided it might be a good idea if he got away from the house and did something different for a while. Since Mike liked sports, he began working and living at a ski and tennis resort. Several months later his father called to tell us that his anxiety and panic had completely lifted now that he was away from home. The father thought the best thing was for Mike to continue living at the resort where he had also begun school again and was doing better academically. He now agreed with our previous assessment that Mike's attacks might be related to his relationship with his mother. Several years later we heard from the family once again. The previous year, coming out of the depths of a depressive stupor, Jane had killed herself.

Table 7.7   DSM-IV Criteria for Cyclothymic Disorder

A. For at least 2 years, the presence of numerous periods with hypomanic symptoms and numerous periods with depressive symptoms that do not meet criteria for a Major Depressive Episode. **Note:** In children and adolescents, the duration must be at least 1 year.

B. During the above 2-year period (1 year in children and adolescents), the person has not been without the symptoms in Criterion A for more than 2 months at a time.

C. No Major Depression Episode, Manic Episode, or Mixed Episode has been present during the first 2 years of the disturbance.

   Note: After the initial 2 years (1 year in children and adolescents) of Cyclothymic Disorder, there may be superimposed Manic or Mixed Episodes (in which case both Bipolar I Disorder and Cyclothymic Disorder may be diagnosed) or Major Depressive Episodes (in which case both Bipolar II Disorder and Cyclothymic Disorder may be diagnosed).

D. The symptoms in Criterion A are not better accounted for by Schizoaffective Disorder and are not superimposed on Schizophrenia, Schizophreniform Disorder, Delusional Disorder, or Psychotic Disorder Not Otherwise Specified.

E. The symptoms are not due to the direct physiological effects of a substance (e.g., a drug of abuse, a medication) or a general medical condition (e.g., hyperthyroidism).

F. The symptoms cause clinically significant distress or impairment in social, occupational, or other important areas of functioning.

Source: DSM-IV, APA, 1994.

Table 7.8   Mean Age of Onset and Duration of Bipolar Disorders by Current Age

	N	Mean Age of Onset (Years)	Mean Duration* (Years)
Bipolar Disorder I			
Total	156	18.0	13.4
Current age:†			
18–29	68	14.8	7.7
30–44	65	17.7	16.5
Bipolar Disorder II			
Total	99	21.7	9.4
Current age:†			
18–29	44	18.6	4.6
30–44	35	24.9	7.4

*Number of years between first and last reported episodes
†Too few cases over 45 to estimate their means

Source: Adapted from Weissman et al., 1991.

As with dysthymic disorder, *cyclothymic disorder* is a chronic condition characterized by alternating mood elevation and depression that does not reach the severity of manic or major depressive episodes. Individuals with cyclothymic disorder tend to be in one mood state or the other with relatively few periods of "neutral" (or euthymic) mood. Criteria for cyclothymic disorder are presented in Table 7.7. As with dysthymic disorder, cyclothymic disorder is, by definition, chronic.

This pattern must last for at least 2 years to meet criteria for the disorder (1 year for children and adolescents). Individuals with cyclothymic disorder alternate between the kinds of mild depressive symptoms experienced by Jack during his dysthymic states and the sorts of hypomanic episodes experienced by Jane. In neither case was the behavior severe enough to require hospitalization or immediate intervention. Much of the time, these individuals are just considered "moody." However, the chronically fluctuating mood states are, by definition, substantial enough to interfere with functioning, as was the dysthymic state in Jack's case. Furthermore, it is important to treat people with cyclothymia, since there is an increased risk that they will develop the more severe bipolar I or bipolar II disorder (Goodwin & Jamison, 1990; Depue et al., 1981; Akiskal, Khani, & Scott-Strauss, 1979).

Statistics and Course for Bipolar Disorders

The average age of onset for bipolar I disorder is 18 years of age, whereas for bipolar II disorder it is 22 years of age, although cases can begin in childhood (see Table 7.8). These ages are somewhat younger than the average age of onset for major depressive disorder and the condition may begin more acutely (suddenly) than major depressive disorder (Weissman et al., 1991; Winokur, Coryell, Endicott, & Akiskal, 1993). About one-third of the cases of bipolar disorder begin in adolescence (Taylor & Abrams, 1981) and the onset is often preceded by minor oscillations in mood or mild cyclothymic mood swings (Goodwin & Jamison, 1990). In only about 10% of cases, bipolar II disorder will progress to a full bipolar I syndrome (Depression Guideline Panel, 1993). It is relatively rare for bipolar disorder to begin after a person reaches the age of 40. Once it appears, the course is chronic—that is, the mood swings alternate with periods of well-being. Therapeutic goals usually involve managing the disorder with ongoing drug regimens that prevent recurrence of episodes. Suicide is an all-too-common consequence of bipolar disorder almost always occurring during depressive episodes. Estimates of suicide in bipolar disorder range from 9% to as high as 60%, with an average rate of 19% (Jamison, 1986).

In typical cases of cyclothymia the disorder is chronic and lasts a lifetime. In about one-third of the patients, cyclothymic mood swings will develop into a full-blown bipolar disorder (Waters, 1979). In one sample of cyclothymic patients, 60% of the cases were female and the age of onset was quite young, often during the teenage years or before, with some data suggesting the most common age of onset to be between 12 and 14 years (Depue et al., 1981). Most often these patients are not recognized as having a disorder but are thought to be high strung, explosive, moody, or hyperactive (Goodwin & Jamison, 1990). Subtypes of cyclothymia are based on the predominance of mild depressive symptoms (one subtype), the predominance of hypomanic symptoms (another subtype), or an equal distribution of both (a third subtype).

Additional Defining Criteria for Mood Disorders

Although the principal criteria for defining mood disorders are shown in the respective DSM Criteria tables, there are other patterns of symptoms called *specifiers* that may or may not accompany these disorders. In addition, mood disorders follow several different temporal patterns across the course of the disorder called *longitudinal course specifiers*. Mood disorders, the possible specifiers, and the projected course of the disorder combine in a variety of ways to create an overall structure of mood disorders shown in Figure 7.3.

Specifiers
Several patterns of additional features sometimes accompany the current or most recent major depressive or manic episodes and have implications for predicting course or response to treatment. These patterns of features are called **specifiers.** There are six basic specifiers: psychotic, chronic, melancholic, atypical, catatonic, and with postpartum onset.

Psychotic Symptoms
Some individuals in the midst of a major depressive or manic episode may experience *psychotic*

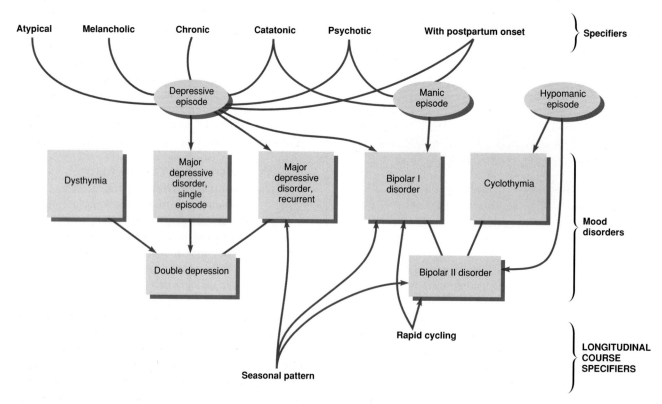

Figure 7.3 Mood disorders and their symptom feature modifiers and course specifiers

symptoms, specifically **hallucinations** (seeing or hearing things that aren't there) and **delusions** (strongly held but inaccurate beliefs). (The woman pictured in the photos on page 240 is experiencing delusions of this type.) These hallucinations and delusions may be either *mood congruent* or *mood incongruent.* Examples of mood congruent depressive delusions would be irrational beliefs by the patient that she is the most sinful, evil person in the world. A patient may also have delusions about her body, called *somatic delusions.* One example would be to believe that her body is rotting internally and that she is deteriorating into nothingness. Some individuals may also hear voices telling them how evil and sinful they are (*auditory hallucinations*). These hallucinations and delusions are called *mood congruent* because they seem directly related to depressed mood. On rare occasions depressed individuals might have other types of delusions or hallucinations, such as *delusions of grandeur* (for example, that they are supernatural beings or that someone is telling them they are supernatural beings) that do not seem consistent with the depressed mood. These are referred to as *mood incongruent* hallucinations or delusions. This condition is quite rare but signifies a very serious type of depressive episode that may progress to schizophrenia (see Chapter 14). On the other hand, delusions of grandeur accompanying a manic episode would be mood congruent (as is the case in the photo on page 242).

Psychotic depressive episodes (conditions in which psychotic symptoms accompany depressive episodes) are relatively rare, occurring in approximately 5% to 15% of identified cases of depression (Spiker et al., 1985; Thase, 1990; Depression Guideline Panel, 1993). The presence of psychotic features in general is associated with a somewhat poorer response to treatment (Glassman & Roose, 1981; Chan, Janicak, Davis, & Altman, 1987; Rush, 1993). This type of depression may respond better to a combination of drugs that treat *both* psychotic symptoms and depression than to a single treatment (Kocsis et al., 1990).

Chronic Specifier for a Major Depressive Episode

This specifier applies if full criteria for a major depressive episode have been met continuously for at least the past two years.

Melancholic (or Endogenous) Features and Chronicity

In addition to being classified by the presence or absence of psychotic symptoms, depressive episodes (but not manic episodes) can be subdivided by the nature of the presenting signs and symptoms. Depressive episodes associated with some of the more severe somatic symptoms (disturbances in bodily function or vegetative symptoms), such as early morning awakening, weight loss, loss of libido (sex drive) as well as anhedonia (partially diminished interest or pleasure in activities), are referred to as **melancholic depressive episodes.** An older name for this type of depression is **endogenous,** meaning that it might be more "internally" or biologically based (Keller, 1988; Zimmerman & Spitzer, 1989). Some studies suggest that this type of depression responds better to somatic treatments such as electroconvulsive therapy (ECT) or tricyclic antidepressant medication than do nonmelancholic depressive episodes, which may in turn respond better to psychological treatments (Crow et al., 1984; Simpson, Pi, Gross, Baron, & November, 1988; Robins, Block, & Peselow, 1990). Other studies, however, have not replicated these findings (for instance, Coryell & Turner, 1985; Paykel, Hollyman, Freeling, & Sedgwich, 1988; Norman, Miller, & Dow, 1988; Copolov et al., 1986). Melancholic episodes also occur more frequently in older people (Depression Guideline Panel, 1993). The concept of "melancholic" does seem to signify, at the very least, a more severe type of depressive episode. Whether this type represents anything more than a different point on a continuum of severity remains to be seen.

Atypical Features

A fourth type of specifier also modifying depressive episodes and dysthymia but not manic episodes has been referred to as **atypical features**, in which individuals consistently oversleep and overeat during their episodes and therefore gain weight (for example, Quitkin et al., 1988; Davidson, Miller, Turnbull, & Sullivan, 1982; Klein, 1989). These individuals also evidence considerable concurrent anxiety and are capable of reacting with interest or pleasure to *some* things that occur in their day-to-day lives, unlike most depressed individuals, who do not react with pleasure. It is possible that individuals with these atypical symptoms differ from depressed individuals without these symptoms in some important ways, such as response to treatment or age of onset (Quitkin et al., 1991; Pollitt & Young, 1971; Stewart, Rabkin, Quitkin, McGrath, & Klein, 1993). Another possibility, however, is that the symptoms simply represent an earlier stage of a depressive disorder that is characterized by slightly less severe symptoms and more anxiety (Rush, 1993; Casper et al., 1985; Himmelhoch & Thase, 1989).

Catatonic Features

A fifth specifier is the very rarely seen but very serious **catatonic depressive episode** (or **depressive stupor**). Rarely, this feature may accompany a manic episode. Most usually, this condition involves a total absence of movement (a stuporous state as in the case of Jane) or a state called **catalepsy,** in which the muscles are waxy and semirigid, so that the patient keeps his arms or legs in any position in which they are

Valerie Whiffen has studied postpartum depression and concluded that for most women symptoms are relatively minor and disappear rather quickly.

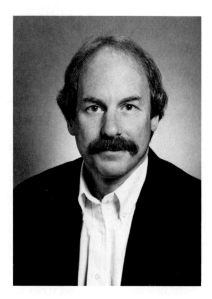

Ian Gotlib has made important contributions to research on the nature and treatment of mood disorders, including postpartum depression.

placed. Catalepsy is more commonly associated with schizophrenia. Catatonic symptoms may also involve excessive but random or purposeless movement.

These five specifiers may or may not be associated with the major depressive episodes or manic episodes that are part of the various mood disorders. For example, someone might have a major depressive episode with melancholia or without melancholia that is part of either a major depressive disorder or a bipolar I disorder.

Postpartum Onset Specifier

Clinical observations over the years suggest that the four-week period immediately following childbirth (*postpartum*) is a time of increased risk for unexpected episodes of depression or, on occasion, mania. Most people, including the new mothers themselves, have difficulty understanding the cause of these depressive episodes since they assume that this should be a joyous and happy occasion. Many new mothers overlook the extreme stressors and strains brought on by physical exhaustion, adjusting to new schedules and routines associated with nursing, and other changes that accompany motherhood.

However, upon careful examination, some researchers have concluded that the risks for developing mood disorders during this particular period of life might be overestimated (Whiffen, 1992). O'Hara et al. (1990) in one study found no differences in the rates of minor and major depression between a group of childbearing women, either during pregnancy or after delivery, and a well-matched control group. Also, a close examination of women who do become depressed during this period revealed no essential differ-

ences in the characteristics of the mood disorder compared to mood disorders occurring outside this period (Gotlib, Whiffen, Wallace, & Mount, 1991; Whiffen, 1992; Whiffen & Gotlib, 1993). In other words, postpartum depression does not seem to be a specific type of depression requiring a separate category in DSM-IV (Purdy & Frank, 1993). Minor adjustment reactions, sometimes called postpartum blues, typically last a few days and occur in 50% to 80% of women between 1 and 5 days after delivery. During this period, new mothers may become tearful and have some temporary mood swings, but these are really a normal response to the stresses of childbirth and disappear quickly (Kendell, 1985).

Valerie Whiffen (1992), in a comprehensive review, concludes that there probably is some increase of depressive symptoms in these women, compared to women not undergoing childbirth, but the symptoms are relatively minor and disappear quickly as the woman adjusts to her new role of motherhood. Obviously, this is a very major transition in life and one must have the coping skills and the interpersonal support to make it successfully. Not surprisingly, factors that *increase* stress during this period, such as difficulties with the baby's feeding or sleep schedules, also seem to increase depressive symptoms in mothers.

On the other hand, very severe manic or depressive episodes of a psychotic nature first occurring during this period, typically 2 to 3 days after delivery, may be the initial warning that a full-blown bipolar disorder is developing (Dean & Kendell, 1981). The incidence, however, is quite low, occurring with approximately 1 per 1,000 deliveries (for example, Meltzer & Kumar, 1985). If a new mother experiences one of these severe episodes postpartum, the chances are approximately 50% that she will experience another episode after the next birth (Davidson & Robertson, 1985; Depression Guideline Panel, 1993). Therefore, a severe postpartum episode helps to predict the future course of a mood disorder. Early recognition of severe postpartum episodes is important for another reason. In a few tragic cases, mothers in the midst of an episode will kill the newborn child (Purdy & Frank, 1993). The episode is specified as "postpartum onset" if it occurs within 4 weeks of birth.

Longitudinal Course Specifiers

We have already mentioned several important elements of the temporal patterning or course of mood disorders; these are called **longitudinal course specifiers.** We have noted, for example, that it is important to determine whether the individual has had major depressive episodes or mania in the past and, if so,

whether she has fully recovered between episodes. It is also important to determine whether the patient with a major depressive episode suffered from dysthymia before the episode (double depression), and whether the patient with bipolar disorder experienced previous cyclothymic disorder. This determination is important because antecedent dysthymia or cyclothymia also predicts a *decreasing* chance of full inter-episode recovery. Most likely, that patient will also require a longer and more intense course of treatment in an attempt to maintain a normal mood state for as long as possible after the patient recovers from the current episode (Rush, 1993).

Mood disorders can also be associated with two additional temporal patterns that are important to recognize. These temporal patterns may require different treatment strategies. Alternatively, they may suggest that the disorder will follow a different course in the future. These temporal patterns are *rapid cycling*, which applies only to bipolar I and bipolar II disorders,

LE DRAME DE SAINT-OUEN
UNE MÈRE QUI TUE SES ENFANTS

On rare occasions immediately after birth, new mothers experience a severe psychological disorder and, tragically, kill their newborn child.

and *seasonal patterning,* which applies to bipolar disorders and recurrent major depressive disorder and refers to episodes occurring during certain seasons of the year (for instance, winter depression).

Rapid Cycling Pattern

Some people with bipolar disorder may move very quickly in and out of depressive or manic episodes. If an individual with bipolar disorder experiences at least four manic or depressive episodes within a year, he is considered to be experiencing a *rapid cycling pattern.* It is important to recognize this pattern because it apparently represents a more severe variety of bipolar disorder and does not respond as well to standard drug treatments (for example, Dunner & Fieve, 1974). In addition, traditional antidepressant medication such as tricyclic antidepressants may actually *provoke* rapid cycling, making clinicians very wary of prescribing these drugs to this group of patients (Wehr & Goodwin, 1979). Some evidence exists that alternative drug treatment such as anticonvulsant drugs may be more effective with this severe group of patients (Post et al., 1989).

Approximately 20% of bipolar patients can be characterized as experiencing rapid cycling. As many as 90% of individuals with rapid cycling bipolar disorder are females, a higher rate than found in bipolar disorder without the rapid cycling characteristic (for example, Wehr, Sack, Rosenthal, & Cowdry, 1988). Unlike bipolar patients in general, the majority of individuals with rapid cycling begin their disorder with a depressive episode rather than a manic episode (McElroy & Keck, 1993). In most cases rapid cycling tends to increase in frequency over time and can reach very severe states in which patients may cycle continually from manic to depressive states without any break whatsoever.

Seasonal Pattern

A rather new and fascinating discovery is that some mood disorders seem tied to seasons of the year. The most usual pattern is a depressive episode beginning in the late fall and ending with the beginning of spring. This pattern can occur in both major depressive disorder and recurrent and bipolar disorder, where individuals will become depressed during the winter and sometimes manic during the summer.

This condition is called **seasonal affective disorder (SAD).** Although some studies have reported seasonal cycling of manic episodes, the overwhelming majority of seasonal mood disorders involve winter depression, which has been estimated to affect as many as 5% of the North American population (Lewy, 1993). Unlike more severe melancholic types of depression, people with winter depressions tend toward excessive sleep (rather than decreased sleep) and increased appetite and weight gain (rather than decreased appe-

tite and weight loss), symptoms shared with "atypical" depressive episodes. Although the symptoms of SAD seem a bit different from other major depressive episodes, family studies have not yet revealed any differential aggregation that would suggest winter depressions are really a separate type of depression (Allen, Lam, Remick, & Sadovnick, 1993).

Emerging evidence suggests that SAD may be related to daily/circadian and seasonal changes in the production of melatonin, a hormone secreted by the pineal gland. Exposure to light suppresses melatonin production. Therefore melatonin is produced only at night. Melatonin production also tends to increase in winter when there is less sunlight. One theory is that *increased* production of melatonin might trigger depression in vulnerable people (Goodwin & Jamison, 1990). We will return to this topic when we discuss biological contributions to depression shortly.

As you might expect, the prevalence of SAD is higher in northern than southern latitudes because there is less sunlight during the winter in northern latitudes. Studies have indicated less than 2% prevalence of SAD in Florida in contrast to nearly 10% prevalence in New Hampshire (Terman, 1988). These numbers include only those individuals meeting criteria for major depressive disorder. Many more people are troubled by more minor "winter blues" consisting of a few depressive symptoms that would not meet criteria for a disorder. A popular name for this type of reaction is "cabin fever." Seasonal affective disorder is also quite prevalent in Fairbanks, Alaska, where 9% of the population appears to meet criteria for the disorder and another 19% would have some seasonal symptoms of depression. Table 7.9 presents prevalence estimates at different locations in the United States for individuals meeting criteria for full disorder as well as those who do not meet the criteria but do have some symptoms (subsyndromal).

Some clinicians reasoned that exposure to bright light might slow melatonin production in individuals with SAD (Blehar & Rosenthal, 1989; Lewy, Kern, Rosenthal, & Wehr, 1982). In current treatment, most patients are exposed to two hours of very bright light (2500 lux) immediately on awakening. If the light exposure is effective, the patient begins to notice a lifting of mood within 3 to 4 days and a remission of winter depression in 1 to 2 weeks. Patients are also asked to avoid bright lights in the evening (from shopping malls, etc.) so as not to interfere with the effects of the morning treatments.

Because the treatment, called *phototherapy,* is so new, its effectiveness is not yet clear since no controlled studies have been conducted; also the mechanism of action or cause has not been established. Possibly factors other than changes in melatonin

Table 7.9 Summary of Prevalence Estimates of Seasonal Affective Disorder in Five Areas of the United States*

Site	Latitude	N	Seasonal Affective Disorder (%)	Subsyndromal Seasonal Affective Disorder (%)	Seasonal and/or Subsyndromal Seasonal Affective Disorder (%)
Fairbanks, Alaska (interview)	65° North	283	9.2	19.1	28.3
Nashua, N.H. (mail survey)	43° North	382	9.7	11.0	20.7
New York City (mail survey)	41° North	193	4.7	12.4	17.1
Montgomery County, Md.	39° North				
Mail survey		576	6.3	10.4	16.7
Telephone survey		383	4.3	13.5	17.8
Sarasota, Fla. (mail survey)	27° North	426	1.4	2.6	4.0

*According to random sampling and measures of seasonal affective disorder based on the Seasonal Pattern Assessment Questionnaire (6, 7, 10).

Source: Booker & Hellekson, 1992.

production are responsible for winter depression, or perhaps increases in melatonin are only one of many causal factors.

Additional Statistics and Course for Mood Disorders

The experience of mood disorders is devastating for many people, like Calvin Coolidge and Katie. Recently, several investigators (Mintz, Mintz, Aruda, & Hwang, 1992) discovered that 11% of a large group of depressed adults from around the country had become unemployed, and an additional 44% of this group evidenced absenteeism, decreased productivity at work, and marked interpersonal problems. Thus, 55% of these patients had either lost their jobs or were probably in some danger of being fired. In another study, declines in job status and income among individuals with mood disorders lasted up to 6 years, even among those who had *recovered* from their disorder (Coryell et al., 1993).

About 7.8% of the population have had a mood disorder at some point in their lives and 3.7% have experienced a disorder over the past year (Weissman et al., 1991). These rates do not vary much by ethnicity, but women are twice as likely to have mood disorders as men. Table 7.10 breaks down the lifetime prevalence by the four principal disorders among the mood disorders group. Notice here that the imbalance in prevalence between males and females is accounted for solely by major depressive disorder and dysthymia, since the bipolar disorders are distributed approximately equally across gender. It is interesting that the prevalence of major depressive disorder and dysthymia is significantly lower among blacks than among whites and Hispanics although, once again, no differences appear in bipolar

disorders. When one considers the chronicity and seriousness of mood disorders (Klerman & Weissman, 1992), these are very high numbers indeed, demonstrating a substantial impact not only on the affected individuals and their families but also on society.

There are many factors that can influence the course of mood disorders, several of which we will examine next. In addition to developmental and cultural considerations, we will look at the relationship between grief and depression.

The Experience of Grief: When Does It Change from Normal to Abnormal Depression?

At some point in your life, someone you love is going to die. Perhaps you have already experienced this loss. At the beginning of the chapter we asked if you had ever felt down or depressed. Almost everyone has. But if

Light therapy for seasonal affective disorder is becoming increasingly popular in Sweden, where the winters are long and dark.

Table 7.10   Lifetime Prevalence of Mood Disorder Subtypes by Age, Sex, and Ethnicity

| | Lifetime Prevalence in % | | | |
	Bipolar I	Bipolar II	Major Depression	Dysthymia
Total	0.8	0.5	4.9	3.2
Age:				
18–29	1.1	0.7	5.0	3.0
30–44	1.4	0.6	7.5	3.8
45–64	0.3	0.2	4.0	3.6
65+	0.1	0.1	1.4	1.7
Sex:				
Men	0.7	0.4	2.6	2.2
Women	0.9	0.5	7.0	4.1
Ethnicity:				
White	0.8	0.4	5.1	3.3
Black	1.0	0.6	3.1	2.5
Hispanic	0.7	0.5	4.4	4.0

Note: Significant variation within groups, adjusted for age, sex, or ethnicity.

Source: Adapted from Weissman et al., 1991.

someone you love has passed away, particularly if the death was unexpected and the person was a member of your immediate family, you may well have experienced most of the symptoms of a major depressive episode following your initial reaction to the trauma; these symptoms would be anxiety, emotional numbness, and denial. In fact, the frequency of severe depression following the death of a loved one is so high (approximately 62%) that mental health professionals do not consider it a disorder unless very severe symptoms, such as psychotic features or suicidal ideation, begin to appear or the symptoms last longer than 2 months (Jacobs, 1993). Some individuals experiencing grief might also require immediate treatment if they become so incapacitated by the symptoms (for example, severe weight loss, no energy whatsoever) that they cannot function.

It is important for us to confront death and to "work it through" or process it emotionally. Long ago, the world's major religions and cultures set up rituals such as funerals and burial ceremonies to help us work through our loss with the support and love of our relatives and friends. Usually the normal and natural grieving process resolves within the first several months, although some individuals may grieve for a year or longer (Jacobs, Hansen, Berkman, Kasl, & Ostfeld, 1989; Clayton & Darvish, 1979). It is also common for grieving people to experience increases in their grief at significant anniversaries, such as the birthday of the loved one, holidays, and other mean-ingful occasions, including the 1-year anniversary of the death. Mental health professionals might be concerned if someone did *not* grieve after a tragic death since this is our natural way of confronting and handling the trauma.

Sometimes grief lasts beyond 2 months or even 1 year, at which time mental health professionals begin to become concerned (Blanchard, Blanchard, & Becker, 1976). At this point the chance of someone's recovering from a severe grief reaction without treatment are considerably reduced and the "normal" process of grief can become a disorder (Jacobs, 1993). Many of the psychological and social factors that seem to contribute to the onset of mood disorders in general predict the development of a normal grief response into a full-blown mood disorder (Jacobs et al., 1989). This disorder has been called **pathological grief reaction** or **impacted grief reaction;** it occurs in approximately 20% of bereaved individuals (Jacobs, 1993). In these cases of long-lasting grief, the kinds of rituals intended to help us emotionally process the traumatic event of death were ineffective. As with victims suffering from posttraumatic stress of some kind, one therapeutic approach is to help the grieving individuals reexperience the trauma, in this case the death, under close therapeutic supervision. Usually this is accomplished by encouraging the grieving person to talk about the loved one, the death, and the meaning of the loss while experiencing the full range of emotions, until he or she can come to terms with the reality. This procedure allows the individual to process his or her negative emotions properly and begin to develop a sense of acceptance and coping with the trauma.

Mood Disorders in Children and Adolescents

You might assume that it takes some experience with life to get depressed. Maybe an accumulation of negative events or disappointments might bring one to take a more pessimistic view of the world, ultimately resulting in depression. Like many reasonable assumptions in psychopathology, this one is not uniformly true. We now have evidence that 3-month-old babies become depressed! These babies, who are infants of depressed mothers, display marked depressive behaviors (sad faces, slow movement, lack of responsiveness), even when interacting with a nondepressed adult (Field et al., 1988). Whether this behavior is due to some heritable tendency passed on from the mother, the result of early interaction patterns with a depressed mother, or a combination is not yet clear.

Most investigators agree that mood disorders in children are fundamentally similar to mood disorders in adults (Lewinsohn, Hops, Roberts, Seeley, & Andrews, 1993; Pataki & Carlson, 1990). Therefore, there

Table 7.11   Speculative Manifestations of Depressive Symptoms Through Childhood*

Adult Symptom	Childhood Symptom				
	0–36 Months	3–5 Years	6–8 Years	9–12 Years	13–18 Years
Dysphoric mood	Sad or expressionless face, gaze aversion, staring, irritability	Sad expression, somberness or labile mood, irritability	Prolonged unhappiness, somberness, irritability	Sad expression, apathy, irritability	Sad expression, apathy, irritability, increasing complaints of depression
Loss of interest or pleasure	No social play	Decreased socialization	Decreased socialization	Adult presentation	Adult presentation
Appetite or weight change	Feeding problems	Feeding problems	Adult presentation	Adult presentation	Adult presentation
Insomnia or hypersomnia	Sleep problems	Sleep problems	Sleep problems	Adult presentation	Adult presentation
Psychomotor agitation	Tantrums, irritability	Irritability, tantrums	Irritability, tantrums	Aggressive behavior	Aggressive behavior
Psychomotor retardation	Lethargy	Lethargy	Lethargy	Lethargy	Adult presentation
Loss of energy	Lethargy	Lethargy	Lethargy	Lethargy	Adult presentation
Feelings of worthlessness		Low self-esteem	Low self-esteem	Guilt, low self-esteem	Guilt
Diminished concentration			Poor school performance	Poor school performance	Poor school performance
Recurrent thoughts of death or suicide		Accident proneness	Accident proneness, morbid outlook	Adult presentation	Adult presentation
Anxiety	Separation/attachment problems	School phobia	Phobias, separation anxiety	Phobias, separation anxiety	Adult presentation
Somatic complaints		Present	Present	Present	Present

*From Weinberg et al. (1), Bemporad and Wilson (2), and Herzog and Rathbun (3).

Source: Carlson & Kashani, 1988.

are no "childhood" mood disorders in DSM-IV that are specific to a developmental stage, as is the case with anxiety disorders. However, it also seems clear that depression "looks" different as a function of age. In Table 7.11 Carlson and Kashani (1988) list the major symptoms of adult depression (from both major depressive disorder and dysthymia) and note how these symptoms might be altered as a function of age. For example, very young children up to 3 years of age might manifest depression by their facial expressions as well as their eating, sleeping, and play behavior. This manifestation would be quite different from that of children between the ages of 9 and 12, who would express their depression a bit more like adults. Data collected by Carlson and Kashani confirmed these differences.

Estimates on the prevalence of mood disorders in children and adolescents vary widely although more sophisticated studies are beginning to appear. The general conclusion is that depressive disorders occur *less frequently* in children than adults but that these numbers rise dramatically in adolescence, where, if anything, depression is *more frequent* than in adults (Kashani, Hoeper, Beck, & Corcoran, 1987; Lewinsohn et al., 1993; Peterson, Compas, Brooks-Gunn, Stemmler, & Grant, 1993). Furthermore, there is some evidence that, in young children, dysthymia is more prevalent than major depressive disorder, but that this ratio reverses in adolescence. Much like adults, adolescents experience major depressive disorder more frequently than dysthymia (Kashani et al., 1983; Kashani et al., 1987).

Bipolar disorder seems to be particularly rare in childhood although case studies of children as young as 4 years of age displaying bipolar symptoms have been reported (Poznanski, Israel, & Grossman, 1984). However, the prevalence of bipolar disorder rises substantially in adolescence, which is not surprising, since many adults with bipolar disorder report a first onset during the teen years (Keller & Wunder, 1990).

Depression and Aggression

One developmental difference between children and adolescents on the one hand and adults on the other is the tendency to become aggressive and even destructive during depressive episodes, behavior particularly prevalent in boys. For this reason, childhood depression is sometimes misdiagnosed as hyperactivity or, more commonly, conduct disorder in which aggression and even destructive behavior are common (see Chapter 16). Often conduct disorder and depression co-occur (Lewinsohn et al., 1993; Petersen et al., 1993; Sanders, Dadds, Johnston, & Cash, 1992). Puig-Antich (1982) found that one-third of prepubertal depressed boys met full criteria for a conduct disorder. In these boys the conduct disorder developed at approximately the same time as the depressive disorder and remitted with the resolution of the depression. Biederman et al. (1987) found that 32% of children with attention deficit disorder also met criteria for major depression. In any case, successful treatment of the underlying depression (or more naturalistic recovery from the depressive episode that runs its course) also brings a resolution of the associated problems in these specific cases. In bipolar disorder, adolescents may also become aggressive, impulsive, sexually provocative, and accident prone ("Manic States," 1979; Reiss, 1985; Keller & Wunder, 1990).

Whatever the presentation, mood disorders in children and adolescents are very serious because of their likely consequences. Rates of attempted suicide skyrocket during adolescence (Peterson et al., 1993; Pataki & Carlson, 1990; Keller & Wunder, 1990). Fleming, Boyle, and Offord (1993), in an important prospective study, followed 652 adolescents with either a major depressive disorder or a conduct disorder for 4 years. These adolescents, by and large, continued to suffer from serious psychopathology and experienced marked interference with their functioning over this period of time. Similar findings were reported by Garber, Weiss, and Shanley (1993).

Mood Disorders in the Elderly

Only recently have we begun to consider seriously the problem of depression in the elderly. Some studies estimate that between 18% and 20% of nursing home residents may experience major depressive episodes (Katz, Leshen, Kleban, & Jethanandani, 1989; Rock-

wood, Stolee, & Brahim, 1991). Particularly problematic are those mood disorders that seem to appear first late in life, after the age of 60, since these disorders are likely to be particularly chronic (Rapp, Parisi, & Wallace, 1991). Late onset depressions are also associated with marked sleep difficulties, hypochondriasis, and agitation. Much as with children, it can be difficult to diagnose depression in the elderly since the presentation of these mood disorders is often complicated by the presence of medical illnesses or symptoms of dementia (for example, Small, 1991; Blazer, 1989). This means that elderly people who become physically ill or display the beginning signs of dementia might become depressed about it, but the signs of depression would be attributed to the illness or dementia and missed.

Depression can also contribute to physical disease in the elderly. Researchers have found that increasing feelings of helplessness associated with the infirmities of older age, particularly in nursing homes, could lead to depression and early death (Grant, Patterson, & Yager, 1988; House, Landis, & Umberson, 1988). Similar findings along these lines suggest that elderly people who do develop a medical illness have longer hospital stays if they are also depressed, compared to those who are not depressed (Schubert, Burns, Paras, & Sioson, 1992; Agbayewa & Cossette, 1990).

An even more tragic finding is the evidence that symptoms of depression are increasing substantially in our growing elderly population. Wallace and O'Hara (1992) in a longitudinal study found elderly citizens becoming increasingly depressed over a 3-year-period. They suggest, with some evidence, that this trend is related to increasing illness and reduced social support. In other words, as our elderly become more frail and more alone, the psychological result is depression which, of course, increases the probability that they will become even more frail and have even less social support. This vicious cycle is deadly.

We also see the earlier imbalance in the sex ratio in depression disappearing in this age range. In early childhood, boys are more likely to be depressed than girls, but an overwhelming surge of depression in young adolescent girls produces an imbalance in the sex ratio that lasts until old age. After the age of 65, just as many women remain depressed, but increasing numbers of men also become depressed, thereby balancing out the sex ratio (Wallace & O'Hara, 1992). From the perspective of the life span, this represents the first time since early childhood that the sex ratio for depression becomes balanced.

Mood Disorders Across Cultures

When discussing anxiety disorders across cultures, we noted that there is a strong tendency for anxiety to be experienced in very physical or somatic ways in third world cultures. In other words, instead of talking about feeling frightened, panicky, or generally anxious about the future, many individuals in these cultures will talk about stomachaches, chest pains or heart distress, and headaches. Much the same tendency exists across cultures for mood disorders; this is not surprising given the close relationship of anxiety and depression. Feelings of "weakness" or "tiredness" might be more likely to characterize depression, particularly depression that is accompanied by mental or physical "slowing" or retardation. Some cultures have their own idioms for depression. For instance, the Hopi Indians may talk of being "heartbroken" (Manson & Good, 1993).

While somatic symptoms that characterize mood disorders seem to be roughly equivalent across cultures, there is difficulty in attempting to compare subjective feelings accompanying depressive disorders, which in our culture would be expressed as feelings of being "down," "depressed," or "dysphoric." The way members of a particular culture think of being depressed may be influenced by many of their own ideas about the individual and the role of the individual in the larger culture (Jenkins, Kleinman, & Good, 1990). For example, in more advanced Western societies that focus much more on the *individual* instead of the group, it is common to hear statements such as "I feel blue" or "I am depressed." However, in cultures where the individual is tightly integrated into the larger group, statements about depression may take a very different form. Rather than using an "I" pronoun, the individual might say "our life has lost its meaning" referring more to the function of the group in which the individual resides (Manson & Good, 1993).

Despite these cultural influences, there is general agreement that the best way to study the nature and prevalence of mood disorders or any psychological disorder in other cultures is first to determine their prevalence using standardized criteria (Neighbors, Jackson, Campbell, & Williams, 1989). DSM criteria along with semistructured interviews that operationalize these criteria are increasingly used. In this way the same questions are asked with some allowances for different words that might be specific to one subculture or another.

In the large epidemiological study mentioned earlier (see Figure 7.1), this procedure was followed; and Weissman et al. (1991) looked at the lifetime prevalence of mood disorders in African-American and Hispanic-American ethnic groups (see Table 7.10). Broken down by specific mood disorder, the figures are almost similar (although somewhat lower for blacks in major depressive disorder and dysthymia) indicating no particular difference in the prevalence of these disorders across subcultures. However, these figures were collected on a carefully constructed sample meant to represent the whole country.

In more specific locations, results can differ dramatically. Kinzie, Leung, Boehnlein, and Matsunaga (1992) used a structured interview to determine the percentage of adult members of an Indian village in the United States who met criteria for mood disorders. In this village, the lifetime prevalence for any mood disorder was 19.4% in men, 36.7% in women, and 28% overall. The prevalence of mood disorders in this Indian village is approximately four times as high as in the general population. Examined by disorder, almost all the increase is accounted for by greatly elevated rates of major depressive disorder. Findings in these Indian villages for substance abuse are very similar to the results for depression disorder (see Chapter 12). The appalling social and economic conditions present on many Indian reservations may well account for these rates as they fulfill all the requirements for the presence of chronic major life stress, which is so strongly related to the onset of mood disorders, particularly major depressive disorder.

Mood Disorders Among the Creative

Early in the history of the United States, Benjamin Rush, one of the signers of the U.S. Constitution and a father of American psychiatry, observed something very curious: "From a part of the brain preternaturally elevated, but not diseased, the mind sometimes discovers not only unusual strengths and acuteness, but certain talents it never exhibited before. Talents for eloquence, poetry, music and painting, and uncommon ingenuity in several of the mechanical arts, are often evolved in this state of madness" (Rush, 1812, p. 153).

This clinical observation has been made many times for thousands of years and applies not only to creativity but also to leadership, as we observed earlier in the chapter when discussing previous U.S. presidents. Is this simply a coincidence or is there truth in the old belief that genius is allied to madness? Several individuals including Kay Redfield Jamison and Nancy Andreasen have attempted to find out. The results are surprising. Table 7.12 lists a group of famous American poets, many of whom have been winners of the coveted Pulitzer Prize. As you can see, all almost certainly had bipolar disorder. Many committed suicide. Goodwin and Jamison (1990) point out that 36 American poets born in this century are represented in *The New Oxford Book of American Verse,* a collection reserved for the most distinguished poets in the country. The eight poets with bipolar disorder listed in Table 7.12 are among them. It is certainly striking that 20% of these 36 poets exhibited bipolar disorders, given the population prevalence of slightly less than 1%; but Goodwin and Jamison think that 20% is probably a conservative estimate. Unlike the eight poets in the table, the remaining poets have

Table 7.12   Partial Listing of Major 20th-Century American Poets, Born Between 1895 and 1935, with Documented Histories of Manic-Depressive Illness

Poet	Pulitzer Prize in Poetry	Treated for Major Depressive Illness	Treated for Mania	Committed Suicide
Hart Crane (1899–1932)		X	X	X
Theodore Roethke (1908–1963)	X	X	X	
Delmore Schwartz (1913–1966)		X	X	
John Berryman (1914–1972)	X	X	X	X
Randall Jarrell (1914–1965)		X	X	X
Robert Lowell (1917–1977)	X	X	X	
Anne Sexton (1928–1974)	X	X	X	X
Sylvia Plath* (1932–1963)	X	X		X

*Plath, although not treated for mania, was probably bipolar II.

Source: Goodwin & Jamison, 1990.

not been examined in sufficient detail to determine whether they also suffered from bipolar disorder. Andreasen (1987) reported results similar to those shown in Table 7.12 in a study of 30 creative writers. What could account for this? Many artists and writers, whether suspected of mood disorders or not, speak of periods of "inspiration." During these periods their thought processes quicken, their mood lifts, and they generate new associations among thoughts (Jamison, 1989). Perhaps there is something inherent in manic states that fosters creativity. On the other hand, it is possible that the genetic vulnerability to mood disorders is independently accompanied by a predisposition to creativity (Richards, Kinney, Lunde, Benet, & Merzel, 1988). In other words, the specific genetic patterns associated with bipolar disorder may also carry the spark of creativity.

These ideas are little more than speculations at present but it is possible that the study of creativity and leadership, so highly valued in all cultures in the world, will be enhanced by a deeper understanding of "madness" (Goodwin & Jamison, 1990; Prien et al., 1984).

The Relationship of Anxiety and Depression

One of the mysteries facing psychopathologists over the decades has been the substantial overlap that seems to exist between the emotional states of anxiety and depression. It is important that we understand the relation of anxiety to depression because some of the latest theories on the causes of depression are based, in part, on this research. A number of explanations for this distinction have appeared (for example, Kendall & Watson, 1989), but several theorists have now concluded that anxiety and depression are more alike than they are different. This may seem strange because anxiety and depression certainly *sound* like different mood states, and thinking of your own reactions, you probably feel different when you are anxious compared to when you are depressed. However, we now know that almost everyone who is depressed, particularly to the extent that they have a psychological disorder, is also anxious (Barlow, 1988; Di Nardo & Barlow, 1990; Sanderson, Di Nardo, Rapee, & Barlow, 1990), but not everyone who is anxious is depressed.

The evidence that anxiety and depression are closely related is relatively strong, based on neurobiological studies (Gray, 1985; Breier, Charney, & Heninger, 1985) and family studies of people with anxiety and depression (Puig-Antich & Rabinovich, 1986; Leckman, Weissman, Merikangas, Pauls, & Prusoff, 1983). If anxiety runs in a given family, depression is likely to run in the same family. In addition, as we will see, drug treatments that have been successful with anxiety disorders are often effective for depression. Investigators have compared popular rating scales or questionnaires for measuring either anxiety or depression and found that they are very highly correlated (Gotlib, 1984; Gotlib & Cane, 1989; Dobson, 1985). If you have a high score on a questionnaire measuring depression, you are likely to have a high score on another measuring anxiety.

Are there any important *differences* between the symptoms that people experience when they have anxiety and depression? New developments from a number of research centers suggest that there are. As we said, almost all depressed patients are anxious, but not all anxious patients are depressed. This means that there are certain core symptoms of depression that are *not* found in states of anxiety and, therefore, reflect what is "pure" about depression. These are best described as the inability to experience pleasure (*anhedonia*) and a depressive "slowing" where both motor and cognitive functions become extremely labored and effortful (Tellegen, 1985; Watson, Clark, & Carey, 1988; Watson & Kendall, 1989; Clark & Watson, 1991). Cognitive content (what one thinks about) also seems more negative in depressed individuals than in anxious individuals (Greenberg & Beck, 1989).

Recently, ongoing research in our own setting has also identified some symptoms that seem central to the emotions of anxiety and panic. In the case of panic, the symptoms reflect primarily autonomic activation (excessive physiological symptoms such as heart palpitations and dizziness). In more generalized anxiety, feelings of muscle tension and apprehension (excessive worrying about the future) seem to reflect the essence of anxiety (Zinbarg et al., 1994; Zinbarg & Barlow, in press). Many people with depression also have these anxious or panic symptoms. More important, we have identified a large number of symptoms that make up parts of the definition of *both* anxiety and depressive disorders. Since these symptoms are *not specific* to either anxiety or depression they are called symptoms of *negative affect* (Tellegen, 1985). In Chapter 4 we talked about the process of creating a new diagnosis of mixed anxiety/depression. We noted that people who met criteria for this new diagnosis presented with symptoms of negative affect *without* any specific symptoms of anxiety or depression. Identifying "pure" anxious or depressive symptoms as well as symptoms of negative affect that are common to both mood states was an important step in creating this diagnosis (Zinbarg et al, 1994). Other researchers have reported finding similar shared and discrete symptoms (for instance, Clark & Watson, 1991). The list of symptoms specific to anxiety, to depression, and to both states is presented in Table 7.13. Ultimately, research in this area may cause us to rethink our diagnostic criteria and combine anxiety and mood disorders into one larger category, but that decision is for the future.

Now think back for a minute to the case of Katie. You remember that Katie was severely depressed and clearly had experienced a major depressive episode along with serious suicidal ideation. A review of the list of depressive symptoms shows that Katie had all of them and met the criteria for major depressive disorder outlined in Table 7.1. However, remember that Katie was also anxious! Her difficulty began with severe anxiety, characterized by her dread of interacting with her classmates or teachers for fear of making a fool of herself. Finally, she became so anxious in the mornings that she stopped going to school. After seeing a doctor who recommended that she be "persuaded" to attend school, her parents became more firm. As Katie explained, however,

> I felt nauseated and sick each time that I went into the school building and so each day I was sent home. Uncomfortable physical experiences like sweaty palms, trembling, dizziness, and nausea accompanied my anxiety and fear. For me, being in a classroom, being in the school building, even the anticipation of being in school, triggered anxiety and illness. All of the sensations of anxiety draw your attention away from your surroundings and toward your own physical feelings. All of this would be bearable if it wasn't so extremely intense. I found myself battling the desire to escape and seek comfort. And, each escape brings with it a sense of failure and guilt.

Table 7.13 Symptoms Specific to Anxiety and to Depression as Well as Symptoms That Are Shared by Both States

Pure Anxiety Symptoms

Apprehension
Tension
Edginess
Trembling
Excessive worry
Nightmares

Pure Depression Symptoms

Helplessness
Depressed mood
Loss of interest
Lack of pleasure
Suicidal ideation
Diminished libido

Mixed Anxiety and Depression Symptoms (Negative Affect)

Anticipating the worst
Worry
Poor concentration
Irritability
Hypervigilance
Unsatisfying sleep
Crying
Guilt
Fatigue
Poor memory
Middle/late insomnia
Sense of worthlessness
Hopelessness
Early insomnia

Source: Adapted from Zinbarg et al., 1994.

I understood that my physical sensations were inappropriate for the situation but I couldn't control them. I blamed myself for my lack of control.

Katie's case is rather typical in that anxiety, which was quite severe in her case, eventually turned into depression. She never really lost her anxiety, she just became depressed, too. The finding that many episodes of depression seem to follow states of anxiety leads us to a discussion of causes of depression and other mood disorders.

Causes of Mood Disorders

Much of psychopathology, including mood disorders, seems subject to the principle of equifinality. We described equifinality in Chapter 2 as the same end product resulting from possibly different causes. Just as there may be many reasons for someone to have a fever, there may also be a number of reasons for someone to get depressed. For example, a depressive disorder, arising in the context of certain seasons of the year, such as winter, has a different precipitant than a severe depression following the sudden and unexpected death of a close family member, even though both depressive episodes might look quite similar.

Nevertheless, psychopathologists are beginning to identify biological, psychological, and social factors that seem strongly implicated in the etiology of mood disorders, whatever the precipitating factor. An integrative theory of the etiology of mood disorders would take into consideration the interaction of biological, psychological, and social dimensions, noting also the very strong relationship of anxiety and depression described above. Before describing an integrative approach, we will review evidence pertaining to each contributing factor separately.

Biological Dimensions: Familial and Genetic Influences

It is very difficult to do the necessary studies that would allow us to determine the genetic contribution to a particular disorder or class of disorders. We described in Chapter 4 the three major types of studies we can carry out with people to estimate this contribution. In the first of these strategies, called *family studies,* we look at the prevalence of a given disorder in the first-degree relatives of an individual known to have the disorder (the proband). If the disorder is more prevalent among first-degree relatives than in the population, there is some evidence that the disorder might be carried in that family's genes. The difficulty with this type of study, of

course, is that we cannot separate from true genetic contributions the effects of the common psychosocial environment experienced by family members living together. This problem is solved with *adoption studies* that let us look at the biological relatives of an individual with a given disorder who was adopted at an early age. If a genetic contribution exists, the adopted probands *with* the disorder should have more biological relatives with the same disorder than do the adopted probands *without* the disorder. Finally, nature allots us the elegant experiments involving twins. In *twin studies* we can examine the frequency with which identical twins (with their identical sets of genes) have the disorder, compared to fraternal twins who share only 50% of each other's genes (as do all first-degree relatives). If a genetic contribution exists, the disorder should be present in identical twins to a much greater extent than it is in fraternal twins.

Family Studies

In the heavily researched field of mood disorders, we have data from all three types of studies. Furthermore, we have enough studies utilizing at least one strategy, the family study strategy, to be able to arrive at some relatively firm conclusions. This is not an easy point to reach because these studies are very difficult to do. First, you must find an individual with the disorder (the *proband*) and administer a very careful, structured, diagnostic interview. Second, you must then locate all the family members you can find, some of whom may be living far away, and interview them at length to determine whether they manifest the psychological disorder in question (the *index disorder*) or related disorders. Small differences in the methodology of these studies can produce dramatically different results. Therefore, you cannot really be confident of the results until quite a large number are accumulated.

Table 7.14 summarizes the results of a large number of family studies. In these studies, the probands had either bipolar disorder or unipolar depression or no psychologic disorder (normal probands). The presence of either bipolar disorder or unipolar depression in the relatives of these probands is presented as "morbid risk."

Looking at the relatives of the normal probands first, you can see that the results approximate the prevalence of these disorders in the normal population. As expected, approximately 5% have a unipolar depressive disorder while slightly less than 1% have a bipolar disorder. The rate in relatives of the probands with mood disorders, however, is consistently about two to three times greater than the rate in the relatives of the normal control probands, although there is wide variability. This variability depends greatly on the types of methods used in the

Table 7.14   Affective Illness in First-Degree Relatives

	Relatives at Risk N Age-Corrected	Morbid Risk %	
		BP	UP
BP Probands			
Taylor et al., 1980	600	4.8	4.2
Baron et al., 1982	135	14.5	16.3
Gershon et al., 1982a	598	8.0	14.9
Coryell et al., 1984	389	7.0	22.4
Fieve et al., 1984	1,309	2.9	8.4
Tsuang et al., 1985	608	3.9	9.1
Angst, 1986b	1,441	5.6	6.2
Rice et al., 1987b	838*	10.6	24.3
UP Probands			
Taylor et al., 1980	121	4.1	8.3
Baron et al., 1981b	475	3.1	16.1
Baron et al., 1982	144	2.2	17.7
Gershon et al., 1982a	138	2.9	16.6
Coryell et al., 1984	572	2.8	29.4
Fieve et al., 1984	265	1.5	8.7
Weissman et al., 1984a	656	2.7	17.0
Tsuang et al., 1985	1,366	2.2	11.0
Angst, 1986b	1,300	1.7	6.4
Rice et al., 1987b	1,176*	5.4	28.6
Normal Probands			
Gershon et al., 1982a	217	0.5	5.8
Weissman et al., 1984a	442	1.8	5.6
Tsuang et al., 1985	1,140	0.2	4.8

Note: BP = Bipolar disorder; UP = Unipolar depression
*Interviewed only

Source: Adapted from Gershon, 1990.

studies. Note also that the most frequent mood disorder in the relatives of bipolar patients is *not* bipolar disorder but rather unipolar depression. In other words, having bipolar disorder is associated with a *general* risk of having another mood disorder but not a *specific* risk for bipolar disorder. For patients with unipolar depression, on the other hand, there is little or no chance that their relatives have bipolar disorder to a greater degree than found in the normal population. One possibility is that there may not be a *specific or separate* genetic contribution to bipolar disorder among the mood disorders. Rather, bipolar disorder may simply be a *more severe* manifestation of the underlying genetic vulnerability. This manifestation would be determined by other psychosocial or pathophysiological factors that would occur in addition to the genetic vulnerability, but this connection is not yet certain and investigators do not agree on whether unipolar and bipolar disorders are two disorders or one disorder on a continuum of severity (Blehar, Weissman, Gershon, & Hirschfeld, 1988).

Twin Studies

Twin studies are far more difficult to accomplish, but one fascinating study containing a sufficient number of twins to draw reasonable conclusions has been conducted. Figure 7.4 presents results from a twin study that compared the presence of mood disorders in identical and fraternal twins (Bertelsen, Harvald, & Hauge, 1977). As you can see, if one twin presents with a mood disorder, it is approximately three times more likely that an identical twin, compared to a fraternal twin, will have a mood disorder. The probability is particularly high for bipolar disorder. If one twin had a bipolar I disorder, 80% of the identical twins also had some mood disorder (although not necessarily bipolar disorder). These results are similar to those found in earlier twin studies (Nurnberger & Gershon, 1992), but later twin studies show a somewhat weaker rate of concordance (for instance, McGuffin & Katz, 1989).

Severity is also related to amount of concordance (the degree to which something is shared) in this study. For example, if one twin had severe depression (defined as three or more major depressive episodes), then 59% of the identical twins also presented with a mood disorder, compared with 30% of the fraternal twins. If the individual presented with fewer than three episodes, the concordance rate drops to 33% in identical twins and 14% in fraternal twins. This means

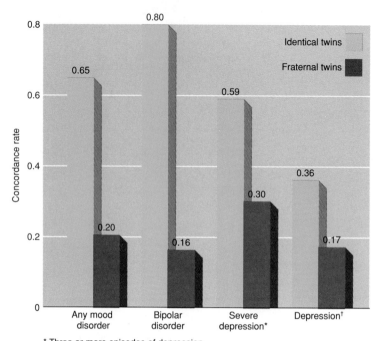

Figure 7.4   Mood disorders among twins (adapted from Bertelsen, Harvald, & Hauge, 1977). Graphically depicted data were derived from evaluation of 110 pairs of twins. Identical twins shared mood disorders, especially bipolar disorder, more frequently than fraternal twins.

that severe mood disorders may have a stronger genetic contribution than less severe disorders, a finding that holds true for most psychological disorders. It is important to note that bipolar disorder confers an increased risk of developing *some* mood disorder but not necessarily bipolar disorder. This conclusion supports findings noted above that bipolar disorder may simply be a more severe variant of mood disorders rather than a fundamentally different disorder. On the

other hand, of identical twins concordant for a mood disorder (both having a mood disorder), 80% are also concordant for polarity. In other words, if one identical twin is unipolar, there is an 80% chance the other twin will also be unipolar. This finding suggests that these disorders may be inherited separately and therefore be separate disorders after all (Nurnberger & Gershon, 1992). In any case, results from a large number of studies, presented in Table 7.14, suggest that the

Stealing a scene from the movie Taxi Driver, Elliott points an imaginary pistol, then turns it on himself and says, "You are looking at a man who can't take it anymore."

Bertelsen et al. (1977) study overestimates the genetic contribution somewhat, probably because of the different procedures used to define the patients or identify the mood disorder (for example, the diagnostic procedures may have varied). Nevertheless, it strongly reinforces the idea of a genetic vulnerability to mood disorders.

Adoption Studies

Finally, several adoption studies have appeared in the literature. It is interesting that one of the studies (Von Knorring, Cloninger, Bohman, & Sigvardsson, 1983) did *not* find that the *biological* relatives of the adopted probands had any greater risk of having a mood disorder than normal controls. But two additional studies (Mendlewicz & Rainer, 1977; Wender et al., 1986) reported a greater risk of mood disorder among the biological relatives of adoptees with a mood disorder.

Conclusions

While these findings do raise continuing questions about the psychosocial versus genetic contribution to mood disorders, the overwhelming body of evidence suggests that mood disorders are familial and almost certainly reflect an underlying genetic vulnerability. However, as with other psychological disorders, we have not yet found—and it seems unlikely that we will—any single "dominant" gene that is responsible for this disorder (Nurnberger & Gershon, 1992), although occasionally reports appear to the contrary. If you will, think back to Chapter 4, the section on genetic linkage analysis. This section notes the attention given several years ago to a study of Amish families in Pennsylvania who, because of their culture, are very homogeneous genetically (Egeland et al., 1987). The findings from this study pointed to a specific location on chromosome 11 that might be the site of a single gene associated with bipolar disorder. However, a reanalysis of the data several years later (Kelsoe et al., 1989) revealed that these results did not support the original findings. No later studies have had any success finding a specific gene associated with bipolar disorder (U.S. Congress, 1992). Thus, as with most psychological disorders, any genetic contribution appears to be the result of many genes, each contributing an additive effect.

Joint Heritability of Anxiety and Depression

Although most studies have looked at specific disorders in isolation, a growing trend is to examine the heritability of related groups of disorders. Evidence from many of these studies supports the supposition that there is a close relationship among depression, anxiety, and panic. For example, data from family studies indicate that the more signs and symptoms of anxiety and depression there are in a given patient, the greater will be the rate of anxiety or depression or both in first-degree relatives and children of these individuals (Leckman, Weissman, Merikangas, Pauls, & Prusoff, 1983; Weissman, 1985; Puig-Antich & Rabinovich, 1986; Kovacs et al., 1989; Hammen, Burge, Burney, & Adrian, 1990). In two important twin studies, Ken Kendler and his colleagues (Kendler, Heath, Martin, & Eaves, 1987; Kendler, Neale, Kessler, Heath, & Eaves, 1992b) also found that the same genetic factors contribute to both anxiety and depression. Social and psychological explanations seemed to account for the factors that differentiate anxiety from depression. These findings suggest, once again, that the biological vulnerability for mood disorders may not be specific to that disorder but may reflect a more general vulnerability for either anxiety or mood disorders. The specific form of the disorder would then be determined somewhat later by psychological, social, or additional biological factors (for instance, Weissman, 1985).

Biological Dimensions: Neurobiological Influences

Neurotransmitter Systems

Mood disorders have been the subject of more intense neurobiological investigations than almost any other area of psychopathology, with the possible exception of schizophrenia. New and exciting findings describing the relationship of specific neurotransmitters to mood disorders appear almost monthly and are punctuated by occasional reported "breakthroughs." In this difficult area, most breakthroughs prove to be illusory, but these false starts are valuable in providing us with an ever-deeper understanding of the enormous complexity of the neurobiological underpinnings of mood disorders.

We will start by reviewing briefly two theories that were very popular during the last decade but, as with most new ideas in this area, they have proven to be almost naively simplistic. Typically, these early theories would target a specific neurotransmitter system as causally related to mood disorders. The first of these theories was the **catecholamine hypothesis.** Joseph Schildkraut (1965), in a creative bit of theorizing, suggested that at least some forms of depression are associated with low levels of norepinephrine (one of the catecholamines). Conversely, he suggested that elation or mania was associated with an excess of this neurotransmitter, which is also called *noradrenalin.* This hypothesis, like many neurotransmitter-related theories, was developed after the researcher had observed an unexpected drug effect. Remember the snakeroot drug described in Chapter 1 (Rauwolfia serpentina or reserpine)? This drug seemed effective in alleviating schizophrenic symptoms, but it had an unfortunate side effect. Some people became very depressed. After noting that one of the effects of this drug was to reduce levels of norepinephrine, the catecholamine hypothesis was born. A second theory arising at about the same time was called the **indolamine hypothesis**, which suggested that low levels of serotonin (one of the indolamines) were associated with, and perhaps "caused," depression (Glassman & Platman, 1969).

In Chapter 2, we observed that we now know these neurotransmitter systems have many subtypes and interact in many complex ways with other neurotransmitters and neuromodulators (products of the endocrine system). For example, reserpine also affects dopamine, another of the catecholamines. Also, drugs that do *not* directly affect these neurotransmitter systems have antidepressant properties. Therefore, although successful treatments for depression do seem to have the effect of reducing levels of norepinephrine (Potter, 1984; Potter, Rudorfer, & Goodwin, 1987; Goodwin & Jamison, 1990), few researchers or clinicians now believe that single neurotransmitter systems are related in a specific and isolated manner to mood disorders.

A third, more modern approach takes into consideration advances in our knowledge of the neurotransmitters (for instance, Spoont, 1992). The **"permissive" hypothesis** (Goodwin & Jamison, 1990) implicates low levels of serotonin in the etiology of mood disorders but only through their interactions

Frederick Goodwin, a former Director of the National Institute of Mental Health, is a leading investigator in biological contributions to mood disorders.

with other neurotransmitter systems, including the norepinephrine and dopamine systems. Remember our discussion in Chapter 2, indicating the primary function of serotonin is apparently to modulate or to regulate many of our emotional reactions. For example, we are more impulsive, and our moods swing more widely, when our levels of serotonin are low. A reason for this variance may be that one of the functions of serotonin is to regulate other neurotransmitter systems such as systems involving norepinephrine and dopamine (Mandell & Knapp, 1979). When levels of serotonin are low, other neurotransmitters are "permitted" to range more widely, become dysregulated, and contribute to mood irregularities including depression. This theory is undoubtedly also overly simplistic, but it does represent current strategies in the study of the relationship of neurotransmitters to psychopathology. Current thinking is that the balance of the variety of neurotransmitters and their subtypes is more important than the absolute level of any one neurotransmitter.

In the context of this delicate balance there is increasing interest in the role of dopamine, particularly in relationship to manic episodes (Depue & Iacono, 1989). For example, the dopamine agonist L-dopa seems to produce hypomania in bipolar patients (for instance, Van Praag & Korf, 1975) along with other dopamine agonists (Silverstone, 1985). But, as with other research in this area, it has proven quite difficult to pin down any relationships with certainty.

The Endocrine System

Investigators became interested in the endocrine system when they noticed that patients with

Ken Kendler has made significant discoveries on genetic contributions to mood and anxiety disorders.

diseases affecting this system sometimes became depressed. Hypothyroidism, or Cushing's Disease, affecting the adrenal cortex, leads to excessive secretion of cortisol and, often, depression. Therefore, a **third early theory** strongly implicated the endocrine system, specifically high levels of cortisol, in producing depression.

In Chapter 2 we discussed the brain circuit called the HYPAC beginning in the hypothalamus and running through the pituitary gland, which is the master or coordinator of the endocrine system. One of the glands influenced by the pituitary is the cortical section of the adrenal gland. This gland produces the stress hormone, cortisol, which completes the HYPAC axis. Cortisol is called a *stress hormone* because we know it is elevated when we undergo stressful life events. We will discuss this system in some detail in Chapter 9. For now, it is enough to know that levels of cortisol are elevated in depressed patients, a finding that makes sense considering the relationship between depression and severe life stress (Gibbons, 1964; Gold, Goodwin, & Chrousos, 1988; Weller & Weller, 1988). This connection led to the development of what was thought to be a biological test for depression—the **dexamethasone suppression test (DST).** Dexamethasone is a glucocorticoid that suppresses cortisol secretion in normal subjects. However, when this substance was given to patients who were depressed, much *less* suppression was noticed or, if suppression did occur, it didn't last very long (Carroll, Martin, & Davies, 1968; Carroll et al., 1980). Approximately 50% of depressed patients would show this reduced suppression. The thinking was that in depressed patients, the adrenal cortex was secreting so much cortisol that the activity overwhelmed the suppressive effects of dexamethasone. This theory was heralded as very important since it suggested the beginnings of the first biological laboratory test for a psychological disorder. However, later research demonstrated that individuals with other disorders, particularly anxiety disorders, also demonstrate nonsuppression (Feinberg & Carroll, 1984; Goodwin & Jamison, 1990), casting doubt on the usefulness of this test to diagnose depression. Thus, much as with the catecholamine hypothesis, the role of cortisol in producing depression has proven overly simplistic.

Despite these developments, researchers remain very interested in the relationship of cortisol and depression, and recent research has taken some exciting new turns. Specifically, investigators have discovered that neurotransmitter activity in the hypothalamus regulates the release of hormones that have an effect on the brain as well as the HYPAC axis. Because they affect the brain, these hormones are called **neurohormones.** They are an increasingly important focus of study in psychopathology. By studying them we have learned that the release of

cortisol from the adrenal cortex is initiated in the central nervous system with the release of corticotropin releasing factor (CRF) from the hypothalamus. CRF, in turn, is a consequence of the activity of various neurotransmitter systems. CRF then makes its way down the HYPAC axis to the adrenal cortex. Charles Nemeroff and his colleagues (for example, Owens & Nemeroff, in press) point to a number of robust associations between CRF and depression suggesting a crucial role for this neurohormone in any biochemical explanations of depression. Of course, CRF activity could be a consequence of depression rather than a contributor to its cause. Also, there are literally thousands of neurohormones. Sorting out the relationship of these chemical agents to antecedent neurotransmitter systems (as well as determining their own independent effects on the central nervous system) is likely to be a very complex task indeed.

Sleep and Circadian Rhythms

On page 256 we discussed the interesting new findings on seasonal affective disorder (SAD), noting that one of the characteristic symptoms was an *increase* in time spent sleeping that accompanies winter depressions. But we have known for several years now that disturbances in sleep are a hallmark of most mood disorders. Many of the findings in this area have been discovered by David Kupfer and his colleagues (for example, Kupfer, Reynolds, Grochocinski, Ulrich, & McEachran, 1986). Furthermore, there is evidence that some specific sleep abnormalities occur *only in mood disorders,* unlike most other biological discoveries that seem to be found more generally across the full range of psychopathology.

Specifically, and most important, people who are depressed experience a significantly shorter period of time after falling asleep before beginning a period of rapid eye movement (REM) sleep. Basically, as you may remember from your introductory psychology or biology course, there are two major stages of sleep: REM sleep and non-REM sleep. When we first fall asleep we go through several substages of progressively deeper sleep where we achieve most of our rest. During these stages our body and brain effectively shut down. After a period of time, usually about 90 minutes, we enter REM sleep, when the brain comes alive, and we begin to dream. While we are dreaming, our eyes move rapidly back and forth under our eyelids, hence the name "rapid eye movement" sleep. As the night goes on, we tend to have increasing amounts of REM sleep. (We will discuss the process of sleep in more detail in Chapter 10, which deals with sleep disorders.)

In addition to beginning their REM sleep *much more quickly* than people who are not depressed, depressed patients experience REM activity that is much more intense. Also, the stages of deepest sleep don't occur until later and sometimes not at all. It seems that these sleep disturbances occur only *while* we are depressed and not at other times (Rush et al., 1986). It is not yet clear whether these sleep disturbances also characterize bipolar patients (Goodwin & Jamison, 1990).

Another interesting finding is that *depriving* patients of sleep, particularly during the second half of the night, causes temporary improvement in their depression (Wehr & Sack, 1988), although depression returns once the patients start sleeping again. In any case, since patterns of sleep represent one of our biological rhythms, there may be some relationship between seasonal affective disorder, sleep disturbances in depressed patients, and a more *general* disturbance in biological rhythms.

An additional interesting finding is that patients with bipolar disorder and their children (who are at risk for bipolar disorder) show *increased sensitivity to light* (for instance, Nurnberger et al., 1988). That is, these individuals will show greater suppression of melatonin when they are exposed to light at night. There is also evidence that extended bouts of insomnia trigger manic episodes (Wehr, Goodwin, Wirz-Justice, Breitmeier, & Craig, 1982). All these findings (and others) suggest that perhaps mood disorders are related to disruptions in our circadian (daily) rhythms. For example, sleep deprivation procedures may somehow temporarily readjust biological rhythms of depressed patients. Light therapy for seasonal affective disorder may have a similar effect.

Based on these findings, Goodwin and Jamison (1990) suggest that the specific genetic vulnerability connected with mood disorders may well be related to a serotonergic, mediated dysregulation in our circadian function. That is, low levels of serotonin somehow affect the regulation of our daily biological rhythms. Of course, many of the results cited above are very preliminary and this theory, although fascinating, is only speculative at this time.

Important research to come will look at the interaction between psychosocial factors and potentially important biological markers such as sleep characteristics. Monroe, Thase, and Simons (1992) recently reported that people with major depressive disorder who had experienced a major life stress just before their episode did *not* evidence reduced latency to REM sleep, but those *without* a precipitating life stress *did* have reduced REM latency values. This finding suggests that there may be subtypes of depression, at least in the early stages of the disorder, that are related to the experience of stressful life events. Individuals who had both severe life events *and* longer REM latency had the more severe disorders. This type of research is just the beginning of more integrated research strategies to come.

Psychological Dimensions

Context and Meaning of Stressful Life Events

One of the most striking contributions to the etiology of psychological disorders is found in the influence of stress and trauma. The importance of stressful life events is reflected throughout the broad field of psychopathology and is evident in the wide adoption of the diathesis-stress model of psychopathology described in Chapter 2 and found throughout this book. Basically, the diathesis describes our "vulnerabilities" such as genetic vulnerabilities just reviewed as well as (possibly) psychological vulnerabilities described below. But to activate this vulnerability (diathesis), we usually look to a traumatic or stressful life event.

It would seem that discovering stressful events in people's lives would be easy. It should be sufficient to ask people whether anything major had happened in their lives before they got depressed (or developed some other psychological disorder). When asked this question, most people do report experiencing some event, such as losing their job or getting divorced, or even a happy event such as having a child, or graduating from school and starting a new career. But, as with most issues in the study of psychopathology, discovering the significance of a major event is not simple. For that reason, most investigators studying the impact of life events have stopped simply asking patients whether something bad (or good) happened and have begun to look at the *context* of the event as well as the *meaning* that the event has for the individual.

For example, losing a job might be difficult for most people, but it is far more difficult for some people than for others. A few people might even see it as a blessing. If you were laid off from your job as a manager in a large corporation due to a restructuring, but your wife is the president of another corporation and makes more than enough money to support the two of you, it might not be so bad. Furthermore, if you are an aspiring writer or artist and have not had time to pursue your art, being jobless might be the opportunity you have been waiting for, particularly since your wife has been attempting for years to persuade you to devote yourself to your creative pursuits.

Now consider the same life event of losing your job if you are a single mother of two young children living from day to day and, due to a recent doctor's bill, you will have to make a choice between paying the electric bill or buying the food that you need for your children. The stressful life event is the same, losing your job, but the context is very different and transforms the significance of the event substantially. To complicate the scenario further, think for a minute about how the woman might react to losing her job.

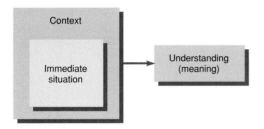

Figure 7.5 Context and meaning in life stress situations (from Brown, 1989)

One woman in this situation might well decide that she is a total failure and is unable to carry on and provide for her children. A second woman might decide that the job loss was not her fault at all and consider the situation an opportunity to take advantage of a job training program in which she was interested, resolving to scrape by somehow in the interim. Thus, not only is the *context* of the life event important, but the *meaning* of the event for the individual also has impact. This approach to studying life events was developed by George Brown and associates (Brown, 1989) in England and is represented in Figure 7.5.

This approach represents a considerable advance in studying life events, but it is difficult to carry out and the methodology is still evolving. American psychologists such as Scott Monroe (Monroe & Roberts, 1990) and others (Dohrenwend & Dohrenwend, 1981; Shrout et al., 1989) are in the forefront of developing some of these new methods. Another crucial issue is bias inherent in trying to remember events. If you ask

someone who is *currently depressed* what happened over 5 years ago when she first became depressed, you will probably get a different answer from one she would give if she were *not* currently depressed. This is because current moods such as depression distort our memories of past events. For this reason, many investigators have concluded that the only useful way to study stressful life events is to follow people *prospectively* so that you can determine more accurately the precise nature of the event and its relation to subsequent psychopathology.

In any case, in summarizing a large amount of research, it seems clear that stressful life events are strongly related to the onset of mood disorders. Using the approach mentioned above, where the *context* of events is measured and the impact of these events examined in a random sample of the population, a number of studies have found a marked relationship between severe, and in some cases traumatic, life events and the onset of depression (see Table 7.15). When groups of patients who are already depressed are compared with matched controls, similar findings emerge (for instance, Paykel et al., 1969). In addition, for people with recurrent depression, the clear occurrence of a severe life stress before or early in the latest episode predicts a much poorer response to treatment and a longer time before remission (Monroe, Kupfer, & Frank, 1992). Types of events most often implicated include family difficulties, job loss, or other major life changes. But, again, the context and meaning of the event are probably more important than the event itself.

Similar findings are available for the relationship of stressful episodes to the onset of manic episodes

David Kupfer and his colleagues have discovered sleep abnormalities in depressed individuals that may be important in understanding the biological causes of mood disorders.

Scott Monroe has developed important new methods for studying the contribution of stressful life events to the causes of mood disorders.

Table 7.15   Summary of Recent Studies of Life Events and Onset of Depression Among Psychiatric Patients

Source	Number of Subjects		Percentage with at Least One Event		Period Covered	Type of Event
	Patients	Comparison Group	Patients	Comparison Group		
Paykel et al. (1969): New Haven, CT, USA	185	185	44	17	6 months	"Undesirable"
Brown & Harris (1978): London	114	382	61	19	8 months	"Severe threat"*
Barrett (1979): Boston	130	—	58	—	6 months	"Undesirable"
Glassner, Haldipur, & Dessauersmith (1979): New York	25[†]	25	56	16	12 months	"Major role loss"
Fava, Munari, Pavan, & Kellner (1981): Padua, Italy	40	40	73	30	6 months	"Uncontrollable"
Benjaminsen (1981): Odense, Denmark	89	—	63	—	6 months	"Severe loss"
Vadher & Ndetei (1981): Nairobi, Kenya	30	40	67	8	12 months	"Severe threat"*
Murphy (1982): London	100[‡]	168	48	23	12 months	"Severe threat"*
Katschnig et al. (1981): Vienna	176[§]	—	42[§]	—	12 months	"Severe threat"*
Bebbington, Tennant, & Hurry (1981): London	45[**]	257	18	10	3 months	"Marked and moderate threat— independent"
Perris (1984): Sweden	38	—	62	—	12 months	"Exit event"

*Either independent or possibly independent events.
[†]Manic depressive, bipolar sample.
[‡]Elderly sample aged 65–87 years.
[§]Special analysis for this chapter.
[**]Includes some anxiety states.

Source: Brown, 1989.

although fewer studies are available and they are not as methodologically sophisticated (Ellicott, 1988; Goodwin & Jamison, 1990). However, there are several issues that may be relevant to the etiology of bipolar disorders in these studies. First, stressful life events seem to trigger early manic (and depressed) episodes in bipolar disorder, but as the disorder progresses these episodes seem to develop a life of their own. In other words, once the cycle begins there seems to be some psychological or pathophysiological process that takes over and ensures that the disorder will continue (for example, Post et al., 1989; Post, 1992). Second, some of the precipitants of manic episodes seem related to loss of sleep, as would occur after childbirth in the postpartum period (Goodwin & Jamison, 1990) or as a result of jet lag. Once again, this result may be related to disturbances in circadian rhythms. Finally, while almost all individuals who become depressed experience a sig-

nificant stressful life event, only a minority of people experiencing these life events become depressed. Although the data are not yet as precise as we would like, somewhere between 20% and 50% of individuals experiencing these severe events go on to become depressed. Thus, between 50% and 80% of individuals experiencing these events do *not* develop depression or, presumably, any other psychological disorder. Once again, these data strongly support the *interaction* of stressful life events with some kind of a vulnerability, either genetically based, psychological, or more likely, a combination.

Given a genetic vulnerability and a severe life event (the diathesis and the stress), what happens then? Research has isolated a number of psychological and biological processes that seem to occur. To illustrate one process, let's return to the case of Katie. Katie's "life event" was attending a new school.

I was a serious and sensitive 11-year-old at the edge of puberty, and at the edge of an adventure that many teens and pre-teens embark on—the transition from elementary to junior high school. A new school, new people, new responsibilities, new pressures. Academically, I was a good student up to this point but I didn't feel good about myself and generally lacked self-confidence.

Katie began to experience the severe anxiety reactions described above. Then she experienced another "life event." She became quite ill with a serious case of the flu. After getting over the flu and attempting to return to school, Katie discovered that her anxieties were worse than ever. More important, she began to feel she was losing control.

As I look back I can identify events that precipitated my anxieties and fears, but then everything seemed to happen suddenly and without cause. I was reacting emotionally and physically in a way that I didn't understand. I felt out of control of my emotions and body. Day after day I wished, as a child does, that whatever was happening to me would magically end. I wished that I would awake one day to find that I was the person I was several months before.

Katie's memory of a feeling of loss of control leads to a discussion of another important psychological factor in depression: learned helplessness.

Learned Helplessness

In Chapter 2 we discussed the phenomenon of learned helplessness. To review, Martin E. P. Seligman, working with animals such as dogs and rats, discovered that these animals have a very interesting emotional reaction to events over which they have no control. If rats are confronted with a situation in which they receive occasional shocks, they can function reasonably well if they learn that they can "cope" with the shocks by doing something to avoid them, such as pressing a lever. But if they learn that nothing they do helps them to cope with the shocks, eventually they become very helpless, give up, and manifest an animal equivalent of depression (Seligman, 1975).

Does this reaction happen with humans? Seligman suggests that it seems to, but only under one important condition. People will get anxious and depressed if they make an *attribution* that they have no control over the stress in their lives (Abramson,

Seligman, & Teasdale, 1978; Miller & Norman, 1979). These findings evolved into an important model of depression called the **learned helplessness theory of depression.** Often overlooked is Seligman's point that anxiety is the first response to a stressful situation. Anxiety may then be followed by depression, when marked hopelessness about coping with the difficult life events occurs (Barlow, 1988; Mineka & Kelly, 1989).

The depressive attributional style has three major characteristics. The attributions are (a) *internal* in that the individual attributes the cause of the negative events to their own failings ("it is all my fault"). The attributions are (b) *stable;* that is, even after one particular negative event passes, the attribution that "additional bad things will always be my fault" remains. Finally, the attributions are (c) *global* in that the attributions are not narrowly limited to one area of a person's life (such as, dating) but extend across a wide variety of issues.

Research is continuing on this interesting concept but you can see how it applies to Katie. At one point early in her difficulties attending school, she began to believe that events were totally out of her control and beyond her ability even to begin to cope. More important, in her eyes the bad situation was all her fault: "I blamed myself for my lack of control." A downward spiral into a major depressive episode followed.

But a major question remains. Is learned helplessness a *cause* of depression or a correlated side effect of becoming depressed? For it to be a *cause,* this attributional style would have to be shown to exist *before* the depressive episode. Some researchers have attempted to determine attributional styles in individuals who are not depressed and then follow them prospectively to see if they become depressed. Other researchers have attempted to look back in the lives of individuals currently depressed to find some evidence that negative attributional styles preceded their depression. The evidence from these studies is mixed. Some studies show that, under certain conditions, college students with negative attributional styles are somewhat more likely to become depressed than college students without these styles (Alloy, Clements, & Kolden, 1985; Metalsky, Halberstadt, & Abramson, 1987). However, results from these experiments did not always strongly support the theory. Other research suggests that the importance or *meaning* of the negative event is more crucial to the development of depression than the attributional style (Hammen, Ellicott, Gitlin, & Jamison, 1989; Brown, 1989). Working with patients, Hamilton and Abramson (1983) found that depressed patients displayed negative attributional styles while they were depressed. However, after the patients experienced successful treatment, these cognitive styles were no longer present, suggesting that this type of thinking might be a correlate rather than an enduring cause of depression (Lewinsohn, Steinmetz, Larson, & Franklin, 1981; Lewinsohn, Hoberman, & Rosenbaum, 1988; Barnett & Gotlib, 1988).

Results from a recent 5-year longitudinal study in children may shed some light on this issue. Nolen-Hoeksema, Girgus, and Seligman (1992) reported that negative attributional style did not predict later symptoms of depression in *young* children. Rather, stressful life events seemed to be the major precipitant of symptoms in these young children. However, as they *grew older,* they tended to develop more negative cognitive styles. These cognitive styles, to the extent that they existed, *did* tend to predict symptoms of depression in older children, when additional negative events occurred. Nolen-Hoeksema et al. speculate that meaningful negative events *early in childhood* may give rise to negative attributional styles in a developmental fashion, making these children more vulnerable to future depressive episodes when stressful events occur.

This thinking is very similar to the types of psychological vulnerabilities theorized to contribute to the development of anxiety disorders (Barlow, 1988). That is, if a person has a nonspecific genetic vulnerability to experience either anxiety or depression, stressful life events activate a psychological sense in that person that his life events are out of his control (Barlow, 1988). There is also recent evidence that these negative attributional styles are not specific to those with depression but characterize groups of anxiety patients as well (Heimberg, Klosko, Dodge, & Shadick, 1989). This finding may indicate that the cognitive vulnerability is no more specific for mood disorders than is the genetic vulnerability described previously.

Recently Abramson, Metalsky, and Alloy (1989) revised the learned helplessness theory to deemphasize specific attributions and highlight the development of a *sense of hopelessness* as a crucial cause of many forms of depression. Attributes would be important only to the extent that they contribute to a sense of hopelessness. This development fits well with recent thinking on crucial differences between anxiety and depression. In these similar emotional states, both anxious and depressed individuals develop a sense of helplessness and lack of control, but only in the midst of depression does one give up and become hopeless about ever regaining control (Alloy, Kelly, Mineka, & Clements, 1990; Barlow, 1991).

In summary, there is some evidence that a pessimistic style of attributing the causes of negative events to one's own character flaws results in a state of hopelessness. This pessimistic style may predate and therefore, in a sense, contribute to later anxious and/or depressive episodes when a person experiences negative or stressful events.

Dysfunctional Attitudes

In 1967 Aaron T. Beck (1967, 1976) suggested that depression may result from a tendency to interpret everyday events in a negative way. This tendency would be the opposite of the "rose-colored glasses" analogy in which someone sees the bright side of everything. According to Beck, people with depression make the worst of everything and conclude that the smallest setbacks are major catastrophes in their lives with which they cannot cope.

In his extensive clinical work, Beck observed that all his depressed patients had this style of thinking, and he began classifying the types of "cognitive errors" that characterized this style of thought. From a long list of cognitive errors he compiled, two representative examples are *arbitrary inference* and *overgeneralization.* Arbitrary inference describes a situation in which a depressed individual will draw a conclusion from a situation that emphasizes the negative rather than the positive. A high school teacher may assume he is a terrible instructor because two students in his class fell asleep. He fails to consider other reasons they might be sleeping (for example, up all night partying) and "infers" that his teaching style is at fault. To exemplify the second type of error, overgeneralization, your professor in English might make one critical remark on your paper. You then assume that she is going to fail you in the class despite a long string of very positive comments she made and good grades she awarded you on other papers. Thus, you would be overgeneralizing from one small remark. According to Beck, people who are depressed think like this all the time. In so doing they make cognitive errors in which they think negatively about *themselves,* their *immediate world,* and their *future.* These three areas combined are called the **(depressive) cognitive triad** (see Figure 7.6).

In addition, Beck theorized that after a series of negative events in childhood, depressed individuals may develop a deep-seated *negative schema. Schema* refers to an enduring and stable negative cognitive bias or belief system about some aspect of life (O'Hara, Rehm, & Campbell, 1982; Beck, Epstein, & Harrison, 1983; Barnett & Gotlib, 1990). In a "self-blame" schema, individuals feel responsible for every bad thing that happens. With a negative self-evaluation schema, individuals believe they can never do anything correctly.

In Beck's view these cognitive errors and schemas are very automatic. That is, they are not necessarily the person's conscious appraisal of the situation. Indeed, individuals might not even be aware

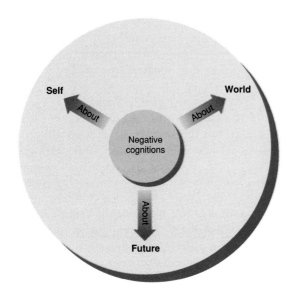

Figure 7.6 Beck's cognitive triad for depression

that they are thinking in this way or that it is illogical. Thus, given the existence of these schemas and the more specific cognitive errors that result from them, very minor negative events might lead to a major depressive episode.

A variety of evidence has accumulated in support of a cognitive theory of emotional disorders in general and depression in particular. For example, the thinking of individuals who are depressed is consistently more negative than that of nondepressed individuals (for instance, Hollon, Kendall, & Lumry, 1986). Depressed individuals think more negatively in each of the dimensions of the cognitive triad—about self, the world, and the future—than do nondepressed individuals (for example, Bradley & Mathews, 1988; Segal, Hood, Shaw, & Higgins, 1988). Also, depressive cognitions seem to emerge from distorted and probably automatic methods of processing information. Individuals are more likely to recall negative events when they are depressed compared to when they are not depressed or compared to nondepressed individuals (Clark & Teasdale, 1982; Lewinsohn & Rosenbaum, 1987).

Establishing the existence of negative schemas *prior* to the onset of depressive episodes, as would be required by the theory, has been more difficult (for instance, Lewinsohn et al., 1981; Barnett & Gotlib, 1990; Haaga, Dyck, & Ernst, 1991). Recently several studies have found that prior dysfunctional attitudes seem to predict *recurrence* of depression under some conditions (as opposed to initial onset) (Hammen, Ellicott, Gitlin, & Jamison, 1989; Segal, Shaw, & Vella, 1989). Also, there is some evidence that stress or a depressed mood activates negative thinking in some people but not others, suggesting that these

negative styles of thinking exist in some people but are latent until primed or activated (Miranda & Persons, 1988). More investigation is needed in this methodologically difficult area.

In any case, the implications of this theory are very important. By bringing these cognitive errors and the underlying schemas into awareness and correcting them, we can alleviate depression or other related emotional disorders. In developing ways to do this, Beck has become the father of cognitive therapy, one of the most important new therapeutic approaches to be developed in some time. Cognitive therapy is described below.

Although Seligman and Beck developed their theories independently, the basic premises overlap a great deal and are increasingly supported by evidence reviewed above. Considerable evidence exists that depression, of whatever type, is associated with pessimistic explanatory style and negative cognitions. Some evidence also exists that cognitive vulnerabilities are present in some people to process stressful life events in a very negative way, putting people at risk for developing depression. This becomes the major psychological vulnerability that, when combined with biological vulnerabilities described above, creates a slippery path to depression.

Social and Cultural Dimensions

Men, Marriage, Stress, and Depression: The Ultimate Life Stress?

Marital satisfaction and depression are strongly related (Beach, Sandeen, & O'Leary, 1990; Whiffen & Gotlib, 1989). Findings from a number of studies indicate that a marital disruption often precedes depression. Bruce and Kim (1992) collected data on 695 women and 530 men and then reinterviewed them up to 1 year later. During this period a number of participants separated from or divorced their spouses while the majority reported stable marriages. Approximately 21% of the women who reported a marital split during the study experienced severe depression, a rate three times higher than that for women who remained married. Nearly 17% of the men who reported a marital split developed severe depression, a rate *nine times* higher than that for men who remained married. However, when the researchers considered *only* those participants with *no history* of severe depression, 14% of the men who separated or divorced during the period experienced severe depression compared to approximately 5% of the women. In other words *only the men* faced a heightened risk of developing a mood disorder for the first time immediately following a marital split.

Is remaining married more important to men than to women? It would seem so.

Both Monroe, Bromet, Connell, and Steiner (1986) and O'Hara (1986) also implicated factors in the marital relationship as predicting the onset of depression at a later time. Important findings from the Monroe et al. (1986) study emphasize the necessity of separating *marital conflict* from *marital support*. In other words, it is possible, within the context of a marriage, that high marital conflict and strong marital social support may both be present at the same time or may both be absent. High conflict, low support, or both are particularly important in generating depression (Barnett & Gotlib, 1988).

Another finding receiving considerable support is the observation that the presence of depression, particularly continuing depression, may lead to substantial deterioration in marital relationships (Beach, Sandeen, & O'Leary, 1990; Coyne, 1976; Paykel & Weissman, 1973; Whiffen & Gotlib, 1989; Hokanson, Rubert, Welker, Hollander, & Hedeen, 1989). It is not hard to figure out why. Being around someone who is continually down, in a bad mood, and pessimistic gets pretty tiring after a while. Since emotions are contagious, you will probably begin to feel pretty bad also. These kinds of interactions precipitate arguments or, worse, make the spouse just want to leave (Biglan et al., 1985).

Thus, given the importance of a close intimate relationship in our lives, disruptions in this relationship can precipitate depression for the first time, lead to the recurrence of an existing mood disorder, and, because of the negative effect depression has on a relationship, create difficulties in regaining a supportive, satisfactory relationship after the depression lifts. These factors have caused Beach, Sandeen, and O'Leary (1990) to

suggest that therapists treat disturbed marital relationships at the same time as the mood disorder to ensure the highest level of success for the patient and the best chance of preventing future relapses.

Why Are Mood and Anxiety Disorders Most Common in Women?

Data on the prevalence of mood disorders indicate dramatic gender imbalances. Although bipolar disorder is evenly divided between men and women, almost 70% of the individuals with major depressive disorder and dysthymia are women (Weissman et al., 1991; Nolen-Hoeksema, 1987). Often overlooked is the similar ratio that exists for most anxiety disorders, particularly panic disorder and generalized anxiety disorder. Women represent an even greater proportion of specific phobias. What could account for this? One of the authors has theorized that gender differences in the development of emotional disorders are strongly influenced by perceptions of uncontrollability (Barlow, 1988). If you have a perception of mastery and control over your life and the difficult events that we all encounter, you might experience occasional stress but not the sense of helplessness that seems so central to the development of anxiety and mood disorders. The source of these differences may be found in our culture, specifically in the sex roles assigned to men and women in our society. Males in our society are strongly encouraged to be independent, masterful, and assertive. Females, on the other hand, are expected to be more passive and sensitive to other people and, perhaps, to rely on others more than males do. Although these stereotypes are changing, they still describe sex roles as they currently exist, to a large extent. But this culturally induced dependency and passivity may well put women at severe risk for

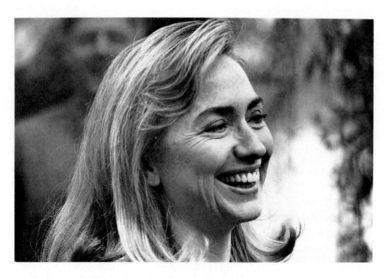

Modern women are conforming less to the old cultural stereotype requiring them to be more passive. Instead, expectations are increasing that women should be independent, masterful, and assertive.

Women seem to respond to negative emotions by ruminating and blaming themselves. Men, on the other hand, tend to ignore negative feelings and often become more active to distract themselves from how they feel.

emotional disorders by increasing their sense of uncontrollability and helplessness.

Constance Hammen and her colleagues (1985) think that the differential value women place in some areas of their lives, such as intimate relationships, may also put them at risk. For example, disruptions in these relationships, combined with an inability to cope with the disruptions, may be far more damaging to women than to men.

Another gender difference that may well be important has been suggested by Susan Nolen-Hoeksema (1987, 1990): In response to stress and feelings of depression, women tend to ruminate more about their situation and blame themselves for being depressed. Men, on the other hand, following common sexual stereotypes, tend to ignore their feelings and perhaps engage in some alternative activity to take their minds off them. This male behavior may be therapeutic, since "activating" people who are depressed (getting them busy doing something) is one common element of successful therapy for depression.

Finally, as Strickland (1992) points out, women *are* at a greater disadvantage in our society since they experience more discrimination, poverty, sexual harassment, and abuse than do men. They also earn less respect and accumulate less power than do men in our society. Three-quarters of the people living in poverty in this country are women and children. Women, particularly single mothers, have a difficult time entering the workplace. Therefore, the "meaning" of these stressful events relative to work disruptions may be more salient for women than for men.

Also interesting is the finding that married women employed full time outside the home report levels of depression no greater than those of men. However, single, divorced, and widowed women experience significantly more depression than men in these same categories (Weissman & Klerman, 1977).

This does *not* necessarily mean that women (or men) should go outside the home and work to avoid becoming depressed. Indeed, feelings of mastery, control, and value in the context of a strongly socially supported role of homemaker and parent in a man or woman should be associated with low rates of depression.

Finally, marked gender differences also exist for other disorders that may be related to gender role stereotypes but in the *opposite direction*. Specifically, disorders associated with aggressiveness, overactivity, and substance abuse occur far more frequently in men than in women (Barlow, 1988). Unraveling the reasons for gender imbalances across the full range of psychopathological disorders may prove important in discovering causes for them.

Social Support

In Chapter 2 we examined the powerful effect of social influences on our psychological and biological functioning. In fact, several examples of how social influences seem to contribute to death were described, such as the evil eye or lack of social support in old age. In general, the greater the number and frequency of your social relationships and contacts, the less likely you are to die (for instance, House et al., 1988). It is not surprising, then, that social factors influence whether we become depressed. We have already examined how the most important relationship of all in most people's lives, the marital relationship, may contribute to (or protect against) depression. But other relationships are also very important. The effects of these relationships can be summarized under the label *social support*. This is a very complex area of study that we are only beginning to understand (for example, Cohen & Wills, 1985). It is also fraught with methodological difficulties, such as most studies' reliance on self-report, which can be biased, rather than direct observation of the quality of social relationship (Dohrenwend, Dohrenwend, Dodson, & Shrout, 1984). But social support apparently contributes to our lives in a number of ways. When confronted with problems or adversity, we might go to our friends and relatives for advice on how best to cope with the situation. Even if the situation turns out badly, our friends and relatives will be there to support and reassure us. As the old saying goes, good friends double our joy and divide our grief.

In an early landmark study, Brown and Harris (1978) first suggested the important role of social support in the onset of depression. In a study of a large number of women who had experienced a serious life stress, they discovered that only 10% of the women who had a close friend in whom they could confide became depressed, compared to 37% of the women who did not have a supportive intimate relationship. More recent prospective studies have also confirmed the importance of social support (or lack of it) in predicting the onset of depressive symptoms at a later time (for instance, Cutrona, 1984; Lin & Ensel, 1984; Monroe, Imhoff, Wise, & Harris, 1983; Phifer & Murrell, 1986).

Other studies have established the importance of social support in speeding recovery from depressive episodes. McLeod, Kessler, and Landis (1992) discovered that, among people experiencing a major depressive episode, those who had the warm support of a spouse and fewer conflicts with their friends recovered significantly more quickly from their depressive disorder than those who did not. In addition, living in a family where there is a lot of nagging, criticism, and emotional outbursts (referred to collectively as *high expressed emotion*) increases the risk of relapse in people who have experienced major depressive episodes (Hooley, Orley, & Teasdale, 1986; Hooley & Teasdale, 1989). Recently Van Miller and his associates (Miller et al., 1992) followed a series of depressed patients for a year and found that those from dysfunctional families evidenced a significantly poorer course, in that they were more depressed and experienced lower levels of adjustment than patients from more supportive families. The researchers concluded that family functioning is a significant predictor of the course of depression. These findings and others on the importance of interpersonal relationships has led to an exciting new psychosocial therapeutic approach for emotional disorders called *interpersonal psychotherapy,* which we will discuss below.

Now let's return once again to Katie, whose depression and suicide attempt were described earlier in the chapter. In reflecting on her turbulent times and the days in her life when death seemed more rewarding than life, one thing sticks out clearly in her mind.

My parents are the true heroes of these early years. I will always admire their strength, their love, and their commitment. My father is a high school graduate and my mother has an eighth-grade education. They dealt with very complicated legal, medical and psychological issues. They had little support from friends or professionals, yet they continued to do what they believed best. In my eyes there is no greater demonstration of courage and love.

Katie's parents did not have the social support that might have helped them through these difficult years. But Katie did. What do you think happened to Katie? We will return to her case below.

An Integrative Theory of the Etiology of Mood Disorders

How do we put all this together? Basically, it seems that depression and anxiety may share a common, genetically determined biological vulnerability in many cases (Barlow, 1988, 1991). This vulnerability would be best described as an overactive neurobiological response to stressful life events. Once again, this vulnerability is simply a general tendency to develop depression (or anxiety) rather than a specific vulnerability for depression or anxiety itself.

A second important factor is the role of stressful life events. There is good evidence that these events precede the onset of depression in most cases. How do these two factors interact? The best current thinking is that stressful life events activate our stress hormones which, in turn, have wide-ranging effects on our neurotransmitter systems, particularly those involving serotonin and norepinephrine. There is also evidence that activation of these stress hormones over the long term may actually "turn on" certain genes producing long-term structural and chemical changes in the brain. For example, processes triggered by long-term stress may actually lead to atrophy of neurons in parts of the brain such as the hippocampus that contribute to the regulation of emotions. This kind of structural change might have ongoing implications for the regulation of neurotransmitter activity. The extended effects of stress may also disrupt the circadian rhythms in certain individuals, who then become susceptible to the recurrent cycling that seems so uniquely characteristic of the mood disorders (Post, 1992). What we have so far is a possible mechanism for the diathesis-stress model.

Those of us who develop mood disorders also possess a psychological vulnerability experienced as feelings of inadequacy for coping with the difficulties confronting us. As with anxiety, we may develop this sense of control in childhood. It may range on a continuum from feeling totally confident and in control to feeling that events are utterly beyond our ability to cope. When these vulnerabilities are triggered, it is the

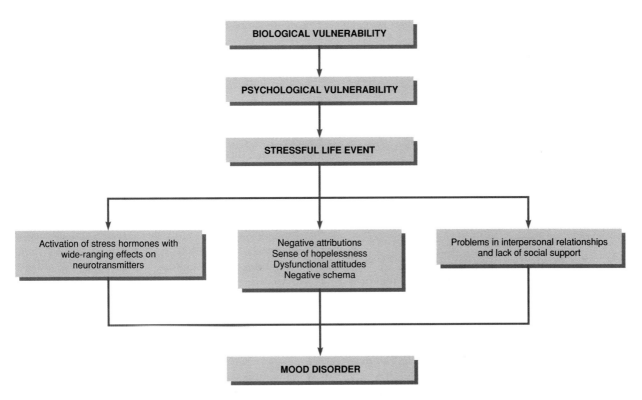

Figure 7.7 An integrative model of mood disorders

"giving up" process that is crucial to the development of depression (Alloy et al., 1990). A variety of evidence indicates that these attitudes and attributions correlate rather strongly with biochemical markers of stress and depression such as by-products of norepinephrine (for example, Samson, Mirin, Hauser, Fenton, & Schildkraut, 1992). There is also some evidence that early experience with stress, perhaps years before the onset of mood disorders, may create a more enduring cognitive vulnerability that enhances, and makes more severe, the biochemical and cognitive response to stress later in life (Nolen-Hoeksema et al., 1992).

Finally, it seems clear that social and cultural factors such as the number and quality of our interpersonal relationships or our gender (depending on the culture in which we are brought up) may "protect" us from the effects of stress and, ultimately, the development of mood disorders. Alternatively, these factors may at least ensure that we recover from these disorders more quickly.

In summary, we need biological, psychological, and social factors to account for the development of mood disorders, as depicted in Figure 7.7. This model does not account for the varied presentation of mood disorders, in terms of both severity and type (unipolar, bipolar, and so on). In other words, why would someone with an underlying genetic vulnerability who experiences a stressful life event develop a bipolar disorder as opposed to a unipolar disorder or, for that matter, an anxiety disorder? As with the anxiety disorders and other stress disorders, it is possible that specific psychosocial circumstances, such as early learning experiences, as well as perhaps other, more specific, genetic vulnerabilities and personality characteristics may interact to produce the richness of the expression of emotional disorders. Only time will tell.

Treatment

We have learned a great deal about the neurobiology of mood disorders during the past several years. Findings on the interplay of neurochemicals in the brain, while complex, are beginning to shed light on the nature of mood disorders. As we have noted, the principal effect of medications is to alter levels of these neurotransmitters and other related neurochemicals. Of course, medications are not the only way to change levels of neurotransmitters. Other biological treatments such as electroconvulsive therapy (ECT) also have dramatic effects on brain chemistry. A more interesting development, however, alluded to throughout this book, is that newer, more powerful, psychological treatments alter brain chemistry. We will review briefly the various treatments for mood disorders in this rapidly changing field, beginning with somatic (physical) treatments that are intended to alter biological components of depressive disorders. This will be followed by a discussion of effective psychological treatments for depressive disorders as well as newer strategies to prevent recurrence of depressive episodes. We will conclude by reviewing treatments available for bipolar disorders, before returning to the case of Katie and describing her outcome.

Somatic Treatments

We begin reviewing somatic treatments with a discussion of antidepressant medications. Then we examine of a more controversial treatment, electroconvulsive therapy, before discussing drug treatments for bipolar disorder.

Antidepressant Medications

There are basically three types of antidepressant medications in use today in the treatment of depressive disorders: *tricyclic antidepressants, monoamine oxidase (MAO) inhibitors,* and a new class of antidepressants, the *selective serotonergic reuptake inhibitors* (SSRIs). Most drugs are discovered by accident and the antidepressants are no exception. Tricyclic antidepressants (so called because the chemical structure of these drugs includes three rings) were developed in the 1950s. In one case, investigators were attempting to develop more effective drug treatments for schizophrenia. During testing, it seemed that one of these drugs, a tricyclic, displayed antidepressant properties (Kuhn, 1957).

Tricyclic antidepressants are perhaps the most widely used treatment for depression in the world today. There are many tricyclic antidepressants, but the best-known variants are probably *imipramine* (brand name Tofranil) and *amitriptyline* (brand name Elavil). These drugs work, at least partly, by blocking the reuptake of certain neurotransmitters at the synapse. This action allows the neurotransmitter to pool in the synapse and, as the theory goes, eventually results in a desensitization or "down-regulation" of the transmission of that particular neurotransmitter (so that less of the neurochemical is transmitted). Although this is a complex process not fully understood, you might think of what happens when your eyes are adjusting to a sudden light after being in the dark for a while. You can't see very well for a short time and it might hurt a little bit, but eventually your eyes adapt to the increased light and your vision is much improved. Similarly, when the neurotransmitter pools in the synapse you may actually feel worse for several days or weeks (more anxious and depressed) and thus it "hurts" a little bit until the adjustment takes place and you feel better.

Tricyclic antidepressants seem to have their greatest effect on the noradrenergic system by down-regulating norepinephrine, although other neurotransmitter systems are also affected. For this reason, anti-

depressants take a while to work, since the down-regulating process takes a while, often between 2 and 8 weeks. During this time, many patients feel a bit worse and develop a number of side effects such as blurred vision, dry mouth, constipation, difficulty urinating, drowsiness, weight gain (exceeding 13 lbs. on average), and, perhaps, sexual dysfunction. For this reason, as many as 30% to 40% of these patients may stop taking the drug, thinking tha t the cure is worse than the disease. Nevertheless, with careful management, many of the side effects disappear. Tricyclics alleviate depression in approximately 50% of patients who begin treatment compared to approximately 25% to 30% of patients taking placebo pills based on a summary analysis of over 100 studies (Depression Guideline Panel, 1993) (see Table 7.16). If dropouts are excluded and only those who complete treatment are counted, success rates increase to 65% to 70%. Another issue clinicians must consider with this drug is that it is *lethal* if taken in excessive doses; therefore, it must be prescribed *with great caution* to patients with any suicidal tendencies.

MAO inhibitors work very differently; as their name suggests, they block an enzyme (monoamine oxidase) that breaks down neurotransmitters such as norepinephrine and serotonin. The result is roughly equivalent to the effect of the tricyclics. Since they are not broken down, the neurotransmitters pool in the synapse, ultimately leading to a down-regulation or desensitization. MAO inhibitors seem to be approximately as effective or slightly more effective than the tricyclics, based on analyses of over 30 studies (see Table 7.16) (Depression Guideline Panel, 1993), with somewhat fewer side effects. But MAO inhibitors are used far less often because of two potentially serious consequences of taking the drug. Specifically, eating or drinking a number of foods or beverages containing tyramine, such as cheese, red wine, or beer, can lead to severe hypertensive episodes and, occasionally, death. In addition, many other medications that people take on a daily basis, such as cold medications sold over the counter in drugstores, become dangerous and even fatal in interaction with an MAO inhibitor. For this reason, MAO inhibitors are usually prescribed only when tricyclics are not effective. Recently, pharmaceutical companies have developed a new generation of more selective MAO inhibitors that are short acting and do not interact negatively with tyramine (Baldessarini, 1989). Testing is still continuing on these new drugs.

Another class of drugs, recently developed, seems to have a specific effect on the serotonergic system (although they affect other neurotransmitter systems to some extent). These drugs are called selective serotonergic reuptake inhibitors (SSRIs). Perhaps the best-known drug in this class is *fluoxetine* (brand name Prozac). As with many drugs, Prozac was initially hailed as a breakthrough drug; it even made the cover of *Newsweek* (March 26, 1990). Then reports began to appear that this drug might lead to suicidal preoccupation, paranoid reactions, and occasionally violence (for example, Mandalos & Szarek, 1990; Teicher, Glod, & Cole, 1990). Prozac then went from being a "wonder drug" in the eyes of the press to a potential menace to modern society. Of course, neither of these conclusions was true. More recent findings indicate that the risks of suicide with this drug are no greater than with any other antidepressant, and effectiveness is about the same (Fava & Rosenbaum, 1991). However, Prozac has its own set of side effects, the most prominent of which is agitation (difficulty sitting still, etc.) as well as insomnia, gastrointestinal upset, and lack of sexual desire. But these side effects, on the whole, seem to be somewhat less bothersome to most patients than the side effects associated with tricyclic antidepressants. The average effectiveness of all three classes of drugs relative to placebo (expressed as a percentage of the patients who begin treatment) is also presented in Table 7.16.

Current studies indicate that drug treatments effective with adults are *not* necessarily effective with children (Boulos et al., 1991; Geller et al., 1992; Ryan, 1992). Another difficulty is that sudden deaths of children below the age of 14 on tricyclic antidepressants have been reported, particularly during periods of exercise as might happen during routine school athletic competition (Tingelstad, 1991). The causes seem related to cardiac side effects.

Unlike children and adolescents, the elderly generally find traditional antidepressant drug treatments to be effective, but administering these treatments takes considerable skill since elderly people may suffer from a variety of side effects not experienced by younger adults. These can include memory impairment and a variety of physical side effects such as agitation (for instance, Marcopulos & Graves, 1990; Deptula & Pomara, 1990).

Clinicians and researchers have concluded in the last several years that recovery from depression, while important, may not be the *most* important therapeutic outcome (Frank et al., 1990; Prien & Kupfer, 1986). Eventually, the large majority of people recover from a major depressive episode, some rather quickly. A *more* important goal is often to delay, or even prevent entirely, the next depressive episode (Prien & Potter, 1993; Thase, 1990). The goal of delaying or preventing the next episode is particularly important for patients who have some remaining symptoms of depression and/or a past history of chronic depression or multiple depressive episodes. All these factors put people at risk for relapse. For this reason, it is now recommended that drug treatment go well beyond the termination of a depressive episode, continuing perhaps 6 to 12 months after the episode is over, or longer. Treatment would be followed by a gradual withdrawal of the drug over a period of weeks or months. We will return to the issue of strategies for *maintaining* therapeutic benefits below.

The development of antidepressant medications has relieved severe depression and undoubtedly prevented suicide in tens of thousands of patients around the world. One of the major advantages of this approach is that these medications are readily available. However, many individuals refuse, or are not eligible, to

Table 7.16 Efficacy of Various Antidepressant Drugs for Major Depressive Disorder

Drug	Drug Efficacy		Drug-Placebo	
	Inpt.	Outpt.	Inpt.	Outpt.
Tricyclics	50.0%	51.5%	25.1%	21.3%
SD	(6.5)	(5.2)	(11.5)	(3.9)
N	[33]	[102]	[8]	[46]
Monoamine oxidase inhibitors (MAOIs)	52.7%	57.4%	18.4%	30.9%
SD	(9.7)	(5.5)	(22.6)	(17.1)
N	[14]	[21]	[9]	[13]
Selective serotonin reuptake inhibitors (SSRIs)	54.0%	47.4%	25.5%	20.1%
SD	(10.1)	(12.5)	(21.7)	(7.8)
N	[8]	[39]	[2]	[23]

Note: The percentage shown in the *Drug Efficacy* column is the anticipated percentage of patients provided the treatment shown who will respond. The *Drug-Placebo* column shows the expected percentage difference in patients given a drug versus a placebo based on direct drug-placebo comparisons in trials that included at least these two cells. The numbers in parentheses are the standard deviations of the estimated percentage of responders. The bracketed numbers give the number of studies for which these estimates are calculated. *Inpt.* is inpatient. *Outpt.* is outpatient.

Source: Adapted from Depression Guideline Panel, 1993, April.

take these drugs. Some people are wary of the risk of long-term side effects. Women of childbearing age must protect themselves against the possibility of conceiving while on these medications as they can damage the fetus. In addition, 40% to 50% of patients do not respond to these drugs, and a substantial number of the remainder are left with residual symptoms.

Medications for Bipolar Disorder

A fourth type of antidepressant drug with seemingly equal effectiveness to those reviewed above is lithium. **Lithium** is a common salt widely available in the natural environment. It is found in our drinking water in amounts too small to have any effect. However, the side effects of therapeutic doses of lithium are potentially more serious than for other antidepressants. Dosage of the drug has to be very carefully regulated to prevent toxicity (poisoning) or thyroid problems, specifically lowered thyroid functioning, which might add to the patient's lack of energy associated with depression. Substantial weight gain is also common. Lithium, however, has one major advantage that distinguishes it from other antidepressants. It is often effective in treating and preventing manic episodes. Because tricyclic antidepressants must be used with great caution in the treatment of bipolar disorder—since these drugs in sufficient quantities can induce manic episodes, even in individuals without preexisting bipolar disorder (Goodwin & Jamison, 1990; Prien et al., 1984)—lithium is the treatment of choice for this disorder.

We are not sure how lithium works. It may reduce availability of the neurotransmitters dopamine and norepinephrine. But more important drug effects may occur among some of the neurohormones in the endocrine system, particularly those that influence the production and availability of sodium and potassium, electrolytes found in our body fluids (Goodwin & Jamison, 1990). Results indicate that 30% to 60% of bipolar patients will respond very well to lithium, 30% to 50% will evidence a partial response, and 10% to 20% will have a poor response (Show, 1985; Prien & Potter, 1993). Thus, while effective, lithium leaves many people with inadequate therapeutic benefit. However, for those patients who *do* respond, maintaining adequate doses of lithium is effective in preventing recurrence of episodes in approximately 66% of individuals (with 34% relapsing), based on 10 major double-blind studies comparing lithium to placebo. Relapse rates in the placebo group averaged a very high 81% over periods ranging from several months to several years (Goodwin & Jamison, 1990; Suppes, Baldessarini, Faedda, & Tohen, 1991).

There is another problem with lithium treatment of bipolar disorder. As noted above, people with manic episodes usually *like* the euphoric or high feeling the episode produces and they often stop taking the drug to maintain or regain that mood state. That is, they do not comply with the medication regimen. Since the evidence now clearly indicates that individuals who stop their lithium are at considerable risk for relapse, other methods, usually psychological in nature, must be employed in an attempt to increase compliance with lithium administration. Failing that, the experience of three or four manic episodes that result in severe negative consequences to the patient and his or her interpersonal relationships (for instance, extraordinarily high credit card bills) may well be sufficient to motivate compliance in the future. For almost anyone with recurrent manic episodes, long-term maintenance on lithium is recommended to prevent relapse. For individuals for whom lithium is ineffective, antiseizure drugs such as carbamazepine have recently proven effective in some cases (Prien & Gelenberg, 1989).

Electroconvulsive Therapy

For those not responding to medication (or for extremely severe cases), clinicians sometimes consider a more dramatic treatment, **electroconvulsive therapy (ECT).** ECT is the most controversial treatment for psychological disorders, next to psychosurgery. In Chapter 1 we reviewed the beginnings of ECT in the early part of this century. There have been many unfortunate abuses of it along the way, but ECT is considerably changed today. It now offers a safe and reasonably effective treatment for *very severe* depression that has not responded to other treatments (Crowe, 1984; Black, Winokur, & Nasrallah, 1987; Klerman, 1988).

Electroconvulsive therapy seems to be an effective treatment for very severe depression but is most often used only as a last resort.

In current administrations, the patient is anesthetized to reduce his or her discomfort and muscle-relaxing drugs are administered to prevent bone breakage from convulsions. Electric shock is administered directly through the brain for less than a second, leading to a series of brief convulsions. These convulsions typically last for several minutes. In current practice, treatments are administered once every other day for a total of 6 to 10 treatments (or perhaps fewer if the patient's mood returns to normal). Side effects are surprisingly few and are limited generally to some short-term memory loss and confusion. These effects seem to disappear after a week or two, although some patients may have long-term memory problems. For severely depressed inpatients with psychotic features, controlled studies (including some in which the control group undergoes a "sham" ECT procedure in which they don't actually receive shocks) indicate that 50% to 70% of those *not responding* to medication will benefit, although continued treatment with medication or psychotherapy is then necessary since the relapse rate approaches 60% (Brandon et al., 1984; Prudic, Sackeim, & Devanand, 1990; Depression Guideline Panel, 1993). For psychotically depressed and acutely suicidal inpatients, it may not be in the patient's best interest to wait 3 to 6 weeks to determine whether a drug or psychological treatment is working. To treat this dangerously severe disorder as soon as possible, ECT may be appropriate.

We do not really know why ECT works. Obviously, repeated seizure activity induces massive functional and perhaps structural changes in the brain, some of which seems to be therapeutic. Because of the controversial nature of this treatment, its usage declined considerably during the 1970s and 1980s. In view of our broad ignorance of how it works, ECT is unlikely to become widely available again any time soon (American Psychological Association, 1990).

Psychosocial Treatments

Effective psychosocial treatments are now available for depressive disorders. While a number of treatments have been developed, two major approaches suggest the most effectiveness at this time. The first approach is cognitive-behavioral; Aaron T. Beck, the founder of **cognitive therapy,** is the principal individual associated with this approach. A second approach, called *interpersonal psychotherapy,* was developed by Myrna Weissman and Gerald Klerman.

Cognitive Therapy

Beck's cognitive therapy grew directly out of his observations of the role of deep-seated negative thinking in generating depression (Beck, 1967, 1976; Beck & Young, 1985; Young, Beck, & Weinberger, 1993). In this treatment clients are taught to examine carefully the types of thinking processes they engage in while they are depressed and to recognize "depressive" errors in thinking when these occur. This task is not always easy for clients because many of these thoughts are very automatic and may be beyond the client's awareness. Negative thinking just seems natural to them. Clients are then informed of how these errors in thinking can directly cause their depression and that treatment will involve correcting these cognitive errors and substituting alternative less depressing and (perhaps) more realistic thoughts and appraisals. Later in

Myrna Weissman along with her husband, Gerald Klerman, developed interpersonal psychotherapy, a psychosocial treatment that has been proven effective with mood and other disorders.

therapy, underlying negative cognitive schemas (characteristic ways of viewing the world) that give rise to specific cognitive errors are targeted in treatment, not only in the office but also as part of the client's day-to-day life. Throughout the treatment, the therapist purposefully takes a Socratic approach to therapy, making it clear that the therapist and the client are working together as a team to uncover the faulty thinking patterns and the underlying schemas from which they are generated. Therapists must be skillful and highly trained to carry out this part of treatment. An example of an actual interaction, where Dr. Beck is working with a client to identify automatic depressive thoughts and their meaning, is presented in the following case.

First Session

Irene was treated initially by the second author (Beck). Since an intake interview had already been completed by another therapist, Beck did not spend time reviewing symptoms in detail or taking a history. The session began with Irene describing the "sad states" she was having. Beck almost immediately started to elicit her automatic thoughts during these periods:

Therapist: What kind of thoughts were you having during these 4 days when you said your thoughts kept coming over and over again?

Patient: Well, they were just—mostly, "Why is this happening again"—because, you know, this isn't the first time he's been out of work. You know, "What am I going to do"—like I have all different thoughts. They are all in different things like being mad at him, being mad at myself for being in this position all the time. Like I want to leave him or if I could do anything to make him straighten out and not depend so much on him. There's a lot of thoughts in there.

T: Now can we go back a little bit to the sad states that you have. Do you still have that sad state?

P: Yeah.

T: You have it right now?

P: Yeah, sort of. They were sad thoughts about—I don't know—I get bad thoughts, like a lot of what I'm thinking is bad things. Like not—there is like, ah, it isn't going to get any better, it will stay that way. I don't know. Lots of things go wrong, you know, that's how I think.

T: So one of the thoughts is that it's not going to get any better?

P: Yeah.

T: And sometimes you believe that completely?

P: Yeah, I believe it, sometimes.

T: Right now do you believe it?

P: I believe—yeah, yeah.

T: Right now you believe that things are not going to get better?

P: Well, there is a glimmer of hope but it's mostly . . .

T: What do you kind of look forward to in terms of your own life from here on?

P: Well, what I look foward to—I can tell you but I don't want to tell you (*Giggles.*) Um, I don't see too much.

T: You don't want to tell me?

P: No, I'll tell you but it's not sweet and great what I think. I just see me continuing on the way I am, the way I don't want to be, like not doing anything, just being there, like sort of with no use, that like my husband will still be there and he will, you know, he'll go in and out of drugs or whatever he is going to do, and I'll just still be there, just in the same place.

By inquiring about Irene's automatic thoughts, the therapist began to understand her perspective—that she would go on forever, trapped, with her husband in and out of drug centers. This illustrates the hopelessness about the future that is characteristic of most depressed patients. A second advantage to this line of inquiry is that the therapist introduced Irene to the idea of looking at her own thoughts, which is central to cognitive therapy. (Young, Beck, & Weinberger, 1993, pp. 34–35)

Between sessions, clients carefully *monitor and log* their thought processes, particularly in various situations where they might feel depressed. They also attempt to change their behavior by carrying out specific activities assigned as homework. Some of these activities might involve specific tasks in which clients can "test" their faulty thinking. For example, a client who has to participate in an upcoming meeting might think, "If I go to that meeting, I'll just make a fool of myself and all my colleagues will think I'm stupid." The therapist might instruct the client to go to the meeting, predicting ahead of time the reaction of her colleagues, and then seeing what really happens. This part of treatment is called *hypothesis testing* because the client makes a hypothesis about what's going to happen (usually a depressing outcome) and then, most often, discovers that it is

Peter Lewinsohn has developed an effective psychsocial treatment for depression that focuses on reactivating patients and enriching their lives.

Lynn Rehm has developed an effective psychosocial treatment for depression that focuses on increasing one's self-control over moods and daily activities.

incorrect. ("My colleagues congratulated me on my presentation.")

The therapist typically schedules other activities as well in order to "reactivate" a depressed patient who has stopped engaging in most activities to help her put some fun back into her life. Along similar lines, other investigators have shown that exercise alone can improve self-concept and lift depression in clinically depressed women (Doyne et al., 1987; Ossip-Klein et al., 1989). Cognitive therapy typically takes from 10 to 20 sessions, scheduled weekly.

Two related cognitive-behavioral approaches to depression were developed by Peter Lewinsohn and his colleagues (for example, Lewinsohn & Clarke, 1984) and Lynn Rehm and his colleagues (for instance, Rehm, Kaslow, & Rabin, 1987). Initially, Lewinsohn focused on *reactivating* depressed patients, countering their depressed mood by bringing them in contact with various kinds of reinforcing events in their lives. For example, individuals might be assigned a task of going to a social event they used to enjoy with their friends. As such, this treatment concentrated on behavioral change. During the past several years, however, this successful program has introduced cognitive procedures as well and is now similar to the program developed by Beck. Similarly, Rehm emphasized behavioral change associated with increasing one's self-control over moods and daily activities, an approach that also involves targeting cognitive components.

Interpersonal Psychotherapy

The evidence reviewed above shows that major disruptions in our interpersonal relationships, including marital distress, form one important category of life stress that can trigger mood disorders (Barnett & Gotlib, 1988; Coyne, 1976). In addition, people with few, if any, important social relationships in their lives seem at risk for the development of mood disorders. **Interpersonal psychotherapy (IPT)** (Klerman, Weissman, & Rounsaville, 1984) focuses on resolving interpersonal problems and stresses in existing relationships and/or building the skills to form important new interpersonal relationships.

As with cognitive-behavioral approaches, interpersonal psychotherapy is highly structured and seldom takes longer than 15 to 20 sessions, usually scheduled once a week. After identifying life stressors that seem to precipitate the depression, the therapist and patient work collaboratively on the patient's current interpersonal problems. Typically, these include one or more of *four* interpersonal issues: *dealing with interpersonal role disputes* such as marital conflict; *adjusting to the loss of a relationship* such as grief over the death of a loved one; or *acquiring new relationships* such as getting married or establishing relationships with people in a new job. The fourth area is *identifying and correcting deficits in social skills* that might make it hard for the person to initiate or maintain important intimate relations. To take one common focus, interpersonal dispute, the therapist's first job is to identify and define the interpersonal dispute (Weissman, in press). One example would be a wife who expects her spouse to take care of her financially but has had to take an outside job to help meet the bills. The husband, on the other hand, might have the expectation that the wife would share equally in generating income. If this type of dispute seems to be associated with the onset of the depressive symptoms and to result in a continuing series of arguments and disagreements without resolution, it would become the focus for IPT.

Neil Jacobson, one of the pioneers in developing couples' therapy, has recently applied it with success to women who are depressed.

Dan O'Leary has developed important new procedures for treating depressed individuals in a marital context.

After helping the patient to identify the dispute, the job of the therapist is to help bring the dispute to a resolution. First, the therapist will help the patient determine the stage of the dispute. For example, (a) are both marital partners aware that it *is* a dispute and are they trying to renegotiate it (Negotiation Stage)? (b) Is the dispute at an impasse? Often disputes of this nature smolder beneath the surface and result in low-level resentment, but no attempts are made to resolve the dispute (Impasse Stage). (c) Are some attempts ongoing to resolve the dispute? This would occur if the dispute was so bad that the partners were taking some action such as divorce or separation (Resolution Stage). The therapist's job will vary depending on the stage of the dispute, but in all cases he or she will work with the patient to define the dispute clearly for both parties and develop specific strategies for resolving the dispute. Along similar lines, Daniel O'Leary, Steve Beach, and their colleagues as well as Neil Jacobson and his colleagues have modified marital therapy to make it applicable to the large numbers of individuals they see, particularly women, who are in the midst of a very dysfunctional marriage (as is the case for as many as 50% of all depressed patients) (Beach, Sandeen, & O'Leary, 1990; O'Leary & Beach, 1990; Jacobson, Dobson, Fruzetti, Schmaling, & Salusky, 1991; Jacobson, Fruzzetti, Dobson, Whisman, & Hops, 1993).

Cognitive-behavioral and interpersonal approaches have proven to be effective in treating depression. Recent studies that have compared cognitive therapy and IPT to use of tricyclic antidepressants as well as other control conditions have found that both psychosocial approaches and tricyclic antidepressants are equally effective, and all treatments are more effective than placebo conditions or other appropriate control conditions for both major depressive disorder and dysthymia (Beck, Hollon, Young, Bedrosian, & Budenz, 1985; Covi & Lipman, 1987; Murphy, Simons, Wetzel, & Lustman, 1984; Hollon et al., 1992; Weissman et al., 1979). This result would indicate, depending on how "success" is defined, that approximately 50% to 70% of people benefit from these treatments to some significant extent, compared to approximately 30% in placebo or control conditions.

One recently completed study sponsored by the NIMH and carried out in three different clinics in North America is the largest study reported to date (Elkin et al., 1989). The results indicate no essential differences in effectiveness among interpersonal psychotherapy, cognitive therapy, and tricyclic antidepressants when all patients who were treated were considered. There are some hints in this study that medication was more effective than cognitive therapy if the patients were *severely* depressed. But this finding seemed to be true at only one of the three clinics and very possibly was related to less skillful cognitive therapists administering the treatment at that site (Hollon, 1993; Hollon & Beck, in press). Furthermore, other similar studies have not found a difference in treatment effectiveness based on severity of depression (Hollon et al., 1992; McLean & Taylor, 1992). In any case, when patients who *had* recovered were followed up for 18 months, the results were very disappointing (Shea et al., 1992). Of all patients entering treatment, only 30% receiving cognitive therapy remained well compared to 26% receiving IPT, 19% in the tricyclic drug group, and 20% in the placebo group. These results were not significantly different. Shea et al. concluded that treatments were just not delivered long enough (or well enough) to effect meaningful change.

In view of the seriousness of mood disorders in childhood and adolescence, speculation is beginning on how we might prevent the occurrence of these disorders in these age groups (Munoz, 1993). Most of this work focuses on instilling adequate social and problem-solving skills in children to prevent the kinds of social stress that so often seem to be associated with depression. In fact, Sanders et al. (1992) and Dadds, Sanders, Morrison, and Rebgetz (1992) determined that disordered communication and problem-solving skills, particularly within the family, were characteristic of depressed children and a natural target for treatment.

The results of psychosocial treatment with children and teens approximates initial rates of effectiveness with adults. Particularly important in this regard is the work of Peter Lewinsohn (Lewinsohn, Clarke, Hops, & Andrews, 1990), who found cognitive-behavioral treatment significantly more effective than no treatment with depressed adolescents. However, since these results are from only one study, more attention must be devoted to the development and evaluation of effective treatments with depressed adolescents. We know much less about the effects of psychosocial treatments with the elderly although a few preliminary case studies and reports indicate some promise (for example, Goddard & Carstensen, 1986).

Combined Medication and Psychosocial Treatments

A few studies have looked at the very important question of combining psychosocial treatments with medication to treat depression (for instance, Teasdale, Fennell, Hibbert, & Amies, 1984; Beck et al., 1985; Miller, Norman, Keitner, Bishop, & Down, 1989; Hollon et al., 1992). Hollon et al. (1992) assigned depressed patients to one of three treatment groups: cognitive therapy, tricyclic antidepressant drug treatment, or a combination. Results in Table 7.17 for people who completed treatment indicate no statistically significant differences among the treatment conditions, although a *trend* was apparent for superiority of the combined group. Fifty-three percent of the medication group, 50% of the cognitive therapy group, and 75% of the combined group had recovered at the end of therapy, figures that suggest the combined group seem to be doing better; but the results could have been due to chance and, therefore, were not statistically significant. If one includes the *total number of people* who otherwise qualified for treatment but refused the treatment they were offered or stopped participating in treatment for one reason or another, the rates drop to 33%, 32%, and 52%, respectively.

As you can see, we have a long way to go to improve our treatments for depression. The results thus far do not suggest strongly that there is any *immediate* advantage of combined treatments compared to separate administration of drugs or psychosocial treatment. However, the treatments clearly operate in different ways. Medication, when it works, does so more quickly than do the psychosocial treatments, while psychosocial treatments have the advantage of increasing the patient's social functioning over the long term (particularly in the case of IPT) and also protecting against relapse or recurrence (particularly cognitive therapy). Combining treatments, therefore, might take advantage of the more rapid action of drugs combined with the apparent ability of psychosocial treatments to protect against recurrence or relapse, thereby allowing discontinuation of the medications. These possibilities would have to be verified by carefully done research.

Preventing Relapse: Maintenance Treatment

Given the high rate of recurrence in depression, it is not surprising that well over 50% of patients on antidepressant medication relapse if their medication is stopped within 4 months after their depressive episode remits (Hollon, Shelton, & Loosen, 1991; Thase, 1990). Therefore, one important question has to do with **maintenance treatment,** the ability of various treatments to *prevent* relapse or recurrence over the long term.

In a number of studies, cognitive therapy reduced rates of subsequent relapse in depressed patients by over 50% when compared to groups treated with antidepressant medication (for example, Kovacs, Rush, Beck, & Hollon, 1981; Simons, Murphy, Levine, & Wetzel, 1986; Evans et al., 1992). In one study, Thase et al. (1992) found that only 32% of a group of 48 patients relapsed during the first year after receiving cognitive-behavioral therapy. Slower response to cognitive-behavioral treatment predicted higher rates of relapse.

Table 7.17 Patients Recovered at Termination of Treatment

| | No. (%) of Patients | | |
Score	Drug (pooled)	Cognitive	Combined
Completers Only (N = 64)			
N	32	16	16
BDI ≤9	18 (56)	10 (62)	11 (69)
HRSD ≤6	17 (53)	8 (50)	12 (75)
All Patients Assigned (N = 107)			
N	57	25	25
BDI ≤9	23 (40)	11 (44)	12 (48)
HRSD ≤6	19 (33)	8 (32)	13 (52)

*BDI indicates Beck Depression Inventory; HRSD, Hamilton Rating Scale for Depression.

Source: Hollon et al., 1992.

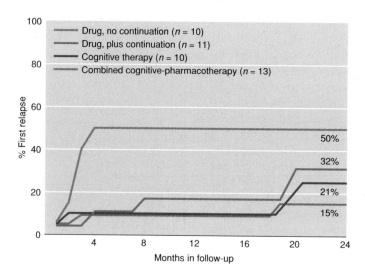

Figure 7.8 Data on relapse after treatment for depression (from Evans et al., 1992).

Thase et al. recommend longer-term cognitive-behavioral therapy for those patients at risk of relapsing to ensure that those who respond more slowly receive sufficient therapy to recover completely.

In another important study comparing cognitive therapy to continuing treatment with tricyclic antidepressants (Evans et al., 1992), cognitive therapy prevented subsequent relapse to the same extent as did continuing medication over a 2-year period. Data on relapse presented in Figure 7.8 show that 50% of a group whose medication was stopped relapsed during this period, compared to 32% of a group whose medication was continued at least 1 year. For those receiving cognitive therapy, relapse rates were only 21% for the group receiving cognitive therapy alone and 15% for those receiving cognitive therapy combined with medication. It is interesting that the cognitive therapy was *not* continued beyond the initial 12-week period in this study.

Ellen Frank and her colleagues have pioneered the use of psychosocial treatments to prevent the recurrence of episodes of mood disorders.

Ellen Frank and her colleagues (1990) found that IPT also significantly reduced the risk for recurrence among recovered depressed outpatients who, based on past history, were at substantial risk for relapse. These patients had been treated initially with a combination of tricyclic antidepressant medication and IPT. However, if patients were *maintained* on full therapeutic dosages of tricyclic medication across the 3-year period of study, their rate of relapse or recurrence was even lower than that of patients continuing to receive IPT. Specifically, 46% of a group of patients who were better after initial treatment (with medication and IPT) and were maintained on therapeutic doses of the drug for the 3-year period remained better (among those who didn't, some dropped out while others had recurrences). This figure compares to 31% receiving monthly sessions of IPT alone across the 3 years, and 9% of patients receiving placebo for 3 years. Combining drug and IPT did not significantly improve the result. More recently, Kupfer et al. (1992) substituted placebo tablets after 3 years with 50% of the people who had *done well* on drugs but left the other half of the group on medication. After 2 more years (for a total of 5 years) 82% of those who stayed on drugs were still better, compared to only 33% who were switched to placebo. These findings provide strong support for continuing drug treatment in *severe* patients who are at high risk for relapse and who have had an initial successful response to antidepressant medication.

Frank, Kupfer, Wagner, McEachran, and Cornes (1991) in a further analysis examined tape recordings of the IPT sessions to determine whether the manner in which treatment was delivered was important. They discovered that, when this therapy was delivered in a manner that was rated by experts as being qualitatively better, the average number of months that patients stayed better (did not relapse) was twice as long as the overall average (2 years instead of 1 year) and four times as long as for those patients receiving lower-quality therapy (2 years instead of 6 months).

In summary, both brief psychosocial treatments and continuing medication *may* be effective in preventing relapse and recurrence, pending further study. If this proves to be true, psychosocial treatments may be a desirable initial strategy so that people can avoid the various medical risks associated with long-term use of medication and/or, in the case of women of childbearing age, feel free to conceive children. But continuing full therapeutic dosages of medication also looks very promising if psychosocial strategies are ineffective.

Treatments for Depression: Conclusion

As is no doubt obvious from our discussion, psychosocial and drug treatments for mood disorders have wide-ranging effects that are not limited to either the psychological or the biological realm. That is, psychosocial treatments affect biological aspects of disorders, and drug treatments affect psychological components. For this reason, the multidimensional integrative model of mood disorders can be of value when one studies the effects of treatment. Consistent with this model, there is evidence that psychological treatments alter neurochemical correlates of depression. McKnight, Nelson-Gray, and Barnhill (1992) treated groups of patients with major depressive disorder using either cognitive therapy or tricyclic medication. They found that an abnormal pretreatment response to the dexamethasone suppression test (DST) (suggesting high rates of secretion of cortisol) did *not* predict which treatment would be more effective. Furthermore, cognitive therapy and the tricyclic antidepressant both produced a normalization of posttreatment DST responses.

It is also possible that identifying specific subtypes of mood disorders may predict which treatments would be more effective. We have already mentioned the preliminary evidence suggesting that very severe major depressive disorders might respond somewhat better to medication than cognitive therapy, although most studies do not find this to be the case. Also noted was the clinical recommendation that acutely suicidal depressed patients with psychotic features should be hospitalized and, perhaps, administered ECT.

More interesting, theoretically, is a finding that patients with higher levels of a metabolite (by-product) of norepinephrine, specifically, *3-methoxy-4-hydroxyphenylglycol* (MHPG) *do not* respond as well to tricyclic antidepressants as do those with lower levels of MHPG (Garvey, Hollon, De Rubeis, & Evans, 1990a, 1990b; Mooney, Schatzberg, Cole, & Samson, 1991). Why might this be important? Samson et al. (1992) reported that levels of MHPG correlate with measures of learned helplessness or hopelessness. (The higher the level of MHPG, the higher was the subject's score on a measure

of learned helplessness.) It is possible, therefore, that cognitive therapy, which presumably directly addresses cognitive aspects of learned helplessness and hopelessness, might be more effective with this type of depression than medication. This assumption remains to be demonstrated, but it provides an illustration of another strategy in attempts to discover meaningful subtypes of depression.

Psychosocial Treatments for Bipolar Disorder

Although medication, particularly lithium, is the treatment of choice for bipolar disorder, most clinicians emphasize the need for psychosocial intervention to better manage the interpersonal and practical problems that emerge during the course of the disorder (for example, marital and job difficulties as a result of having the disorder). Until recently the principal objective of psychosocial intervention was to increase compliance with medication regimens such as lithium (Cochran, 1984). We noted above that the "pleasures" of a manic state make refusal to take lithium one of the major therapeutic obstacles in the treatment of this disorder. Deliberate cessation of drugs between episodes or skipping medication dosages during an episode will undermine treatment. Therefore, a careful integration of psychosocial treatment with lithium treatment is very important if treatment is to be ultimately successful (Goodwin & Jamison, 1990).

There are some reports of the administration of psychosocial treatments in the *absence* of medications. This might be done, for example, with women with bipolar disorder who wish to become pregnant without assuming risks to the fetus associated with taking medication. Although some reports of success using cognitive therapy to treat manic states have appeared (for example, Chor, Mercier, & Halper, 1988), no systematic efforts have been made to determine the effectiveness of these procedures.

More important, reports are beginning to appear suggesting a significant advantage to adding focused psychosocial treatment to a drug treatment regimen. For instance, Miller and his colleagues, in a small pilot study, added family therapy to a drug regimen and reported a significant increase in the percentage of patients with bipolar disorder fully recovering (56%) compared to the percentage of those who fully recovered after drug treatment alone (20%) (see Figure 7.9). During a 2-year follow-up, patients receiving psychosocial treatment experienced less than half the recidivism compared to drug treatment alone (Miller, Keitner, Epstein, Bishop, & Ryan, 1991). David Miklowitz and his colleagues have also found that interpersonal conflict in the family is associated with relapse in bipolar disorder and that psychosocial treatment directed at family conflict prevents relapse

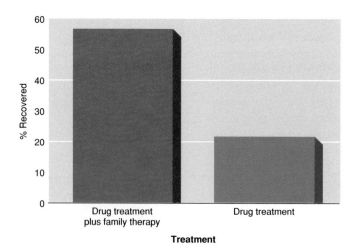

Figure 7.9   Percentage of patients with bipolar disorder recovered after standard drug treatment or drug treatment plus family therapy (adapted from Miller et al., 1991)

based on preliminary studies (Miklowitz & Goldstein, 1990; Miklowitz, Simoneau, Sachs-Ericsson, Warner, & Suddath, in press). More advanced studies on the effects of psychosocial treatments with bipolar disorder are continuing.

The Case of Katie: Outcome

Let us now return to Katie, who, you will remember, had made a serious suicide attempt in the midst of a major depressive episode.

The Case of Katie

As with the overwhelming majority of people with serious psychological disorders, Katie had never received an adequate course of treatment, although she was evaluated from time to time by various mental health professionals. She lived in a rural area where competent professional help was not readily available. Her life ebbed and flowed around her struggle to subdue her anxiety and depression. When she could manage her emotions sufficiently, she would take an occasional course in the external study program at her high school. Gradually, she discovered that she was fascinated by learning. She enrolled in a local community college at the age of 19 and did extremely well, despite the fact that she had not progressed beyond her freshman year at the local high school. She began to attend college more steadily and earned a high school equivalency degree. She also began working in a local factory. But she continued to drink heavily and to take valium; on occasion, her anxiety and depression would return and disrupt her life.

Finally, she left home, began attending college full time, and met a boy. She fell in love, but the romance was one-sided. Ultimately she was rejected.

One night after a phone conversation with him, I nearly drank myself to death. I lived in a single room alone in the dorm. I drank as much vodka as quickly as I could. I fell asleep. When I awoke I was covered in vomit and couldn't recall falling asleep or being sick. I was drunk for much of the next day. When I awoke the following morning, I realized I could have killed myself by choking on my own vomit. More importantly, I wasn't sure if I fully wanted to die. That was the last of my drinking.

Katie decided to make some changes in her life. Taking advantage of what she had learned in the little treatment she had received, she began looking at life and herself differently. Instead of dwelling on how inadequate and evil she was, she began to notice some of her own strengths, "but I now realized that I needed to accept myself as is, and work with any stumbling blocks that I faced. I needed to get myself through the world as happily and as comfortably as I could. I had a right to that." Other lessons learned in treatment now became valuable, and Katie learned to become more aware of some of her mood swings:

I learned to objectify periods of depression as (simply) periods of 'feeling.' They are a part of who I am, but not the whole. I recognize when I feel that way, and I check my perceptions with someone that I trust when I feel uncertain of them. I try to hold on to the belief that these periods are only temporary.

Katie developed other strategies for coping successfully with life.

I try to stay focused on my goals and what is important to me. I have learned that if one strategy to achieve some goal doesn't work there are other strategies that probably will. My endurance is one of my blessings. Patience, dedication, and discipline are also important. None of the changes that I have been through occurred instantly or automatically. Most of what I have achieved has required time, effort, and persistence.

Katie developed a dream that maybe if she worked hard enough she could help other people who had problems similar to her own. Katie pursued that dream and shortly will earn her Ph.D. in psychology.

Katie is a remarkable person who illustrates some of the great strengths of human character. Very few people suffering from severe psychological disorders, particularly mood disorders, are able to pull themselves together on a relatively permanent basis as did Katie. Some day, psychologists hope to learn more about what it is in people like Katie that helps them to overcome emotional disorders and achieve their goals. When we learn more about these remarkable strengths we may be able to develop better treatments and,

perhaps, prevent emotional disorders from occurring in the first place.

Suicide

Who Kill Themselves?

Most days we are confronted with news about the war on cancer or the frantic race to find a cure for AIDS. We also hear never-ending admonitions to change our diet and exercise habits to prevent death by heart disease. But there is one cause of death that ranks right up there with the most frightening and dangerous medical conditions. This is the inexplicable decision, by over 30,000 people a year in the United States alone, to kill themselves. This statistic makes suicide the eighth leading cause of death in the United States and most epidemiologists agree that this is almost certainly an underestimate. The actual number of suicides may be two to three times higher. Many of these unreported suicides occur in the form of single car accidents where people purposefully drive into a bridge or off a cliff (Blumenthal, 1990).

It is also interesting to note that suicide is overwhelmingly a Caucasian phenomenon. Most minority groups, including African-Americans and Hispanics, seldom resort to this violent alternative, as is evident in Figure 7.10. On the other hand, as you might expect from information provided above on the incidence of depression in Native Americans, rates of suicide in these groups are extremely high, although there is great variability across tribes. In some tribes

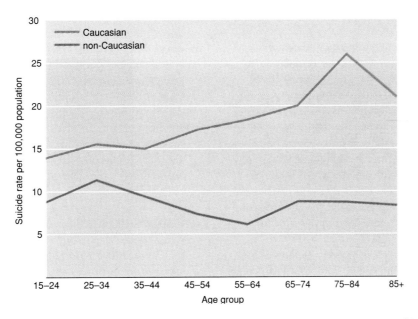

Figure 7.10   United States suicide rates for Caucasians and non-Caucasians by age group, sexes combined (data from the National Center for Health Statistics, Vital Statistics of the United States, 1987) (from Buda & Tsuang, 1990)

Figure 7.11   Suicide rates per 100,000 in population for total population and for 15–19-year-olds (data for the years 1966–1988 from *Vital Statistics of the United States: Volume II. Mortality—Part A*. National Center for Health Statistics, 1968–1991, Washington, DC: U.S. Government Printing Office. In the public domain) (from Buda & Tsuang, 1990)

such as the Apache, the rates are nearly four times the national average (Berlin, 1987).

Even more frightening is the dramatic *increase* in death by suicide in recent years. Tragically, this increase is most evident among adolescents. Figure 7.11 presents suicide rates for the population as a whole, as well as the rates for teenagers aged 15–19 years. As you can see, between 1960 and 1988 the rate of suicide in adolescents increased from 3.6 to 11.3 per 100,000 population. This is an increase of 200% compared with a general population increase of 17%. In this age group, suicide is the *third* leading cause of death. Note also the dramatic increase in suicide rates occurring among the elderly. This rise has been connected to the growing incidence of medical illness in our oldest citizens as well as their increasing loss of social support. As we have noted, a strong relationship exists between feelings of illness and infirmity, hopelessness, and depression. Suicide attempts are not restricted to adolescents and adults. Rosenthal and Rosenthal (1984) described 16 children 2½ to 5 years of age who had attempted suicide at least once, often injuring themselves severely.

In both adolescents and the population as a whole, males are four to five times more likely to *commit* suicide than females. This startling fact seems to be related in part to gender differences in the types of suicide *attempts*. Males generally choose far more violent methods such as guns and hanging when they attempt suicide. Females, on the other hand, tend to rely on less violent options such as drug overdose (Buda & Tsuang, 1990). The suicide rate for young men in the United States is now the highest in the world, surpassing rates in even Japan and Sweden, countries long known for high rates of suicide (Blumenthal, 1990).

In addition to successfully completed suicides, there are two other important indices of suicidal behavior: **suicidal attempts** (that are not successful) and serious thoughts about suicide referred to as **suicidal ideation.** Although males successfully *complete* suicide more often than females, the reverse is true

for suicide attempts. Females *attempt* suicide at least three times as often as do males (Berman & Jobes, 1991). This high incidence may be related to the fact that more women are depressed than men, and we know that depression is strongly related to suicide attempts (Frances, Franklin, & Flavin, 1986). Some estimates place the ratio of attempted to completed suicides at 50:1 or higher (Garland & Zigler, 1993). In addition, results from a recent study (Kovacs, Goldston, & Gatsonis, 1993) suggested that the ratio of *thoughts* about suicide in a group of adolescents to *attempts* at suicide is between 3:1 and 6:1. In other words, between 16% and 30% of adolescents in this study who had *thought* about killing themselves actually *attempted* it. Thoughts in this context does not refer to a fleeting philosophical type of consideration but rather to a serious contemplation of the act. Nevertheless, the first step down the dangerous road to suicide is thinking about it.

In a recent study among college students (where the rate of suicide is only about half that of the normal population) approximately 25% had thought about suicide during the past 12 months (Meehan, Lamb, Saltzman, & O'Carroll, 1992; Schwartz & Whitaker, 1990). Only a minority of these college students with thoughts of suicide (perhaps around 15%) will attempt to kill themselves, and of those, only a few will succeed (Kovacs et al., 1993). Nevertheless, given the enormity of the problem, these thoughts about suicide are taken very seriously by mental health professionals.

Causes of Suicide: Past Conceptions

What causes a person to commit suicide? The great sociologist Emile Durkheim (1951) categorized suicide into a number of types based on the social or cultural conditions in which they occurred. One type is "formalized" suicides that were approved and even expected by some cultures, such as the ancient custom of *hara-kiri* in Japan, in which an individual who brought dishonor to himself or his family would be expected to impale himself on a sword. Durkheim referred to this as *altruistic suicide*. Durkheim also recognized disintegrating social supports as an important context for suicide; he called this *egoistic suicide*. Many of our elderly citizens who kill themselves after losing touch with their friends or family would fit into this category. Magne-Ingvar, Ojehagen, and Traskman-Bendz (1992) found that only 13% of 75 individuals who had made a serious suicide attempt had an adequate social network of friends and relationships. *Anomic suicides* might occur with marked disruptions in one's life such as the sudden loss of a high-prestige job. *Anomic* refers to a sense of being lost and confused. Finally, *fatalistic suicides* refer to those committed as a result of a loss of control over one's destiny. Some of the suicides occurring during the recent tragedy in Waco, Texas, might be an example of this type since the lives of those people were largely in the hands of David Koresh. Durkheim's work was important in alerting us to the social contribution to suicide.

Freud (1957/1917) originated the psychological idea, in the context of psychoanalytic thinking, that suicide (and depression to some extent) represented unconscious hostility or anger directed *inward* to the self rather than *outward* to the person or situation causing the anger. Indeed, suicide often does seem to be an angry act where the victim, through a suicide note, is "punishing" someone who may have rejected him or caused some other personal hurt. Current thinking on the causes of depression considers social and psychological factors but also highlights the potential importance of biological contributions considered more fully below.

Risk Factors for Suicide

The study of risk factors for suicide has been pioneered by the important work of Edward Shneidman (Shneidman, Farberow, & Litman, 1970; Shneidman, 1989). Risk factors are those conditions and events that make one more vulnerable to the possibility of committing suicide. Among the methods Shneidman and others have used to study risk factors is a method called the **psychological autopsy.** In this method, psychological profiles of the individual committing suicide are reconstructed based on extensive interviews with friends and family members who are likely to know what the individual was thinking and doing just before his or her death. Utilizing these and other methods, a number of risk factors for suicide have been identified.

Family History

If a family member has committed suicide, there is an increased risk that someone else in the family, such as a son or daughter, will also commit suicide (Kety, 1990). This may not be surprising since so many people who kill themselves are depressed and we know that depression runs in families. Nevertheless, the question remains: Are these individuals who kill themselves simply adopting a solution to their problem that they witnessed one of their family members use, or is something inherited, such as a trait of impulsivity, that accounts for the increases in suicidal behavior in families? The possibility that something is inherited is supported by several adoption studies. In these studies there was an increased rate of suicide in the biological relatives of individuals who were adopted and had committed suicide compared to a control group of adoptees who had not committed suicide (Schulsinger, Kety, & Rosenthal, 1979; Wender et al., 1986). This finding suggests that there is *some* biological (genetic) contribution to the tendency to commit suicide, even if it is a relatively small one.

Neurobiology

A variety of evidence suggests that low levels of serotonin may be associated with suicide as well as violent suicide attempts (Asberg, Nordstrom, & Traskman-Bendz, 1986; Winchel, Stanley, & Stanley, 1990). As we have noted, extremely low levels of serotonin are associated with impulsivity, instability, and the tendency to overreact to situations (Spoont, 1992). It is very possible, then, that low levels of serotonin may contribute to creating a vulnerability to act impulsively. This may include killing oneself, which is sometimes a very impulsive act.

Existing Psychological Disorders

Over 90% of individuals who kill themselves suffer from an existing psychological disorder of some kind (Garland & Zigler, 1993; Brent & Kolko, 1990; Black & Winokur, 1990). Suicide is often associated with mood disorders, and for good reason. As many as 60% of suicides are associated with an existing mood disorder (Frances et al., 1986) and as many as 75% of adolescent suicides were found to have an existing mood disorder (Brent & Kolko, 1990). Lewinsohn, Rohde, and Seeley (1993) concluded that suicidal behavior is in large part an expression of severe depression in adolescents. But there are many people with mood disorders who do not attempt suicide and, conversely, many people attempting suicide do not have an existing mood disorder. Therefore, depression and suicide, while very strongly related, are still independent events. Looking more closely at the relationship of mood disorder and suicide, some investigators have isolated a specific component of depression, hopelessness, as strongly predicting suicide (Kazdin, 1983; Beck, Steer, Kovacs, & Garrison, 1985; Beck, 1986) .

Some teenagers, after learning of the suicide of one of their friends, may attempt suicide themselves.

Alcohol use and abuse is associated with approximately 25% to 50% of suicides (for example, Frances et al., 1986). Brent et al. (1988) found that approximately one-third of adolescents who commit suicide were intoxicated at the time of their death, and that many more might have been under the influence of drugs. Combinations of disorders, such as substance abuse and mood disorders in adults or mood disorders and conduct disorder in children and adolescents, seem to create a stronger vulnerability than any one disorder alone.

Another strong risk factor for suicide is the presence of past suicide attempts. Any time there is a past suicide attempt in an individual's history, the mental health professional must take this very seriously.

A disorder characterized more by impulsivity than depression is borderline personality disorder (see Chapter 13). Frances and Blumenthal (1989) suggest that these individuals, known for making manipulative and impulsive suicidal gestures without necessarily wanting to destroy themselves, sometimes kill themselves by mistake in as many as 10% of the cases.

Therefore, it is incorrect to assume that suicide occurs primarily in people who are disappointed in love or life but are otherwise perfectly healthy. In fact, suicide is often associated with severe psychological disorders, most often depression.

Is Suicide Contagious?

An all-too-common occurrence is the death of a high-school student by suicide or the appearance in the newspaper of the suicide of a well-known celebrity or sports figure. Most people react to these accounts with sadness and perhaps curiosity (why did he kill himself?). However, for a short period of time, a number of people may react in a much more violent way. They may attempt suicide themselves, often copying some of the methods they may have just read or heard about. Gould (1990) reported an increase in suicides in the community for a 9-day period after wide publicity of a suicide appearing in a newspaper or on television. Clusters of suicides (several individuals following the lead of one individual) seem to occur predominantly among teenagers, with as many as 1% to 5% of all teenage suicides reflecting "copycat" or imitation suicides (Gould, 1990).

Why would anyone want to "copy" a suicide? First, suicides are often romanticized in the media. This means that an attractive young person under unbearable pressure in her life kills herself and in so doing becomes something of a martyr to her friends by getting even with the (adult) world for putting her in such a difficult situation. Also, media accounts often describe in detail the methods used in the suicide thereby providing a guide to the potential victim who may not have known how to do it. Little is said in the media about the paralysis, brain damage, or other, tragic consequences of the incomplete or failed suicide, or the fact that the suicide is almost always associated with a severe psychological disorder. More important, even less is said about the futility of this method of solving one's problems (O'Carroll, 1990; Gould, 1990). To

Susan Blumenthal and her colleagues have developed some important models on the causes of suicidal behavior.

prevent these tragic occurrences it is important that the media not inadvertently glorify suicides in any way, and mental health professionals must intervene immediately in schools and other locations with friends of adolescent suicide victims who might be depressed or otherwise vulnerable to the contagion of suicide.

Stressful Life Events

Perhaps the most important risk factor for suicide is the occurrence of a severe stressful event that is experienced as a shameful or humiliating experience. Events such as a failure (real or imagined) in school or at work, an unexpected arrest, or rejection by a loved one are often implicated in suicide (Brent et al., 1988; Shaffer, Garland, Gould, Fisher, & Trautmen, 1988; Blumenthal, 1990). Given preexisting biological and psychological vulnerabilities—including psychological disorders, traits of "impulsiveness," or lack of social support—this type of stressful event can often put a person over the edge. An integrated model of the causes of suicidal behavior is presented in Figure 7.12.

Recognizing and Treating People at Risk for Suicide

Despite the identification of important risk factors for suicide, predicting suicide is still an uncertain business. Individuals with very few of the factors mentioned

above may unexpectedly kill themselves, and many with seemingly insurmountable stress and illness in their lives and little social support or guidance somehow survive and go on to overcome their difficulties.

Mental health professionals are very thoroughly trained in assessing for possible suicidal ideation that might lead to attempted suicide. Many people who are not mental health professionals might be reluctant to ask about thoughts of suicide for fear of putting the idea in the individual's head. However, we know that it is far more important to check for these "secrets" since the risk of putting an idea about suicide in someone's head is very small and the risk of leaving such an idea undiscovered is enormous. Therefore, if there is any indication whatsoever that these thoughts might exist, the mental health professional will inquire about suicidal ideation ("Has there been any time recently when you've had some thoughts about hurting yourself or possibly killing yourself?").

The mental health professional will also check for possible humiliating events that may have occurred and determine whether a number of factors are present that might indicate a high probability of suicide. For example, if the person is thinking of suicide, does he have a detailed plan or is it just some vague thought? If a detailed plan is discovered involving a specific time, place, and method, the risk is higher. Does the detailed plan include putting all of his affairs in order, giving away his possessions, and other final acts? If so, the risk

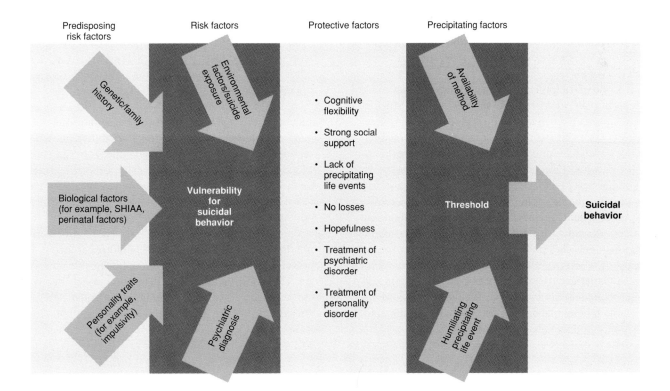

Figure 7.12   Threshold model for suicidal behavior (from Blumenthal & Kupfer, 1988)

is higher. What specific method is the person considering? Generally, the more lethal and violent the method, the greater the risk that it will be used (guns, hanging, poison, and so on). Does the person really understand what will happen if he attempts suicide? Many people have only a vague idea of the effects of certain pills on which they might overdose. Finally, has he taken any precautions against being discovered? If so, the risk is higher.

After ascertaining whether any risk is present, clinicians will routinely attempt to get the individual to agree to or even sign a no-suicide "contract." Usually this contract will include a promise by the individual not to do anything remotely connected with suicide without contacting the mental health professional first. If the person at risk will not agree to the contract (or the clinician has serious doubts about the patient's sincerity) and the suicidal risk is judged to be very high, then immediate hospitalization is indicated, even if it is against the will of the patient. Whether the person is hospitalized or not, treatment aimed at resolving underlying stressors in his life and treating existing psychological disorders should be initiated immediately.

In view of the public health consequences of suicide a number of programs to reduce the rates of suicide have been implemented. Some of these include curriculum-based programs using teams of professionals who go into schools or other organizations to teach about suicide and provide individuals with information on handling life stress. Unfortunately, most research indicates that these programs are not effective in preventing suicide (Shaffer, Garland, Vieland, Underwood, & Busner, 1991; Garland and Zigler, 1993).

More helpful are programs targeted to individuals at risk. Adolescents in schools where a suicide has occurred are one population at risk. The Centers for Disease Control (1988) have recommended making services available immediately to friends and relatives of the victims. One of the more important steps is limiting access to lethal weapons for anyone at risk for suicide. In an important study, Brent et al. (1989), following a suicide in a high school, identified 16 students strongly at risk for suicide and referred them for treatment. Telephone hotlines and other crisis intervention services also seem to be useful. Nevertheless, as Garland and Zigler point out, it is important that these volunteer telephone crisis hotlines be backed up by competent mental health professionals who are able to identify potentially serious risks.

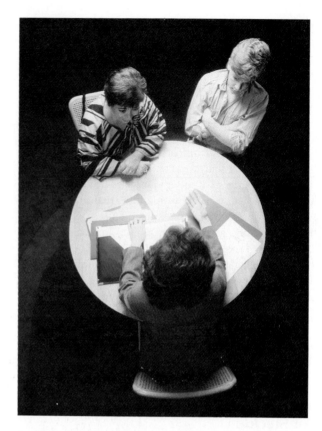

Teens and other individuals often require psychological treatment after a traumatic experience such as the death of a friend. Sometimes this treatment is delivered individually. Other times, parents become involved.

Specific treatments for people at risk have also been developed. For example, Salkovskis, Atha, and Storer (1990) identified 20 patients at high risk for repeated suicide attempts and treated them with a cognitive-behavioral problem-solving approach. Results indicated that those treated were significantly less likely to attempt suicide in the 6 months following treatment. Marsha Linehan and her colleagues (Linehan & Kehrer, 1993) have developed an important treatment for the type of impulsive suicidal behavior associated with borderline personality disorder. This new treatment approach is described in Chapter 13.

With the increased rate of suicide, particularly in adolescents, the tragic and paradoxical event is receiving increased scrutiny from public health authorities. The quest will go on to determine more effective and efficient ways of preventing the most serious consequence of any psychological disorder, the taking of one's own life.

Summary

- Mood disorders are among the most common psychological disorders, and the risk of developing mood disorders is increasing, particularly in younger generations around the world.

- Two fundamental experiences can contribute either singly or in combination to all the specific mood disorders: depression and mania. If an individual suffers only from episodes of depression, he or she is said to have a *unipolar* disorder. If the individual alternates between experiences of depression and mania, he or she has a *bipolar* disorder.

- Severe periods of depression (major depressive episodes) are time limited, whereas in another form of depression (dysthymic disorder), the symptoms are somewhat milder but remain relatively unchanged over long periods of time.

- Patterns of additional features sometimes accompanying mood disorders, called *specifiers or symptom feature modifiers*, have implications for predicting course or patient response to treatment, as does the temporal patterning or course of mood disorders.

- The causes of mood disorders lie in a complex interaction of biological, psychological, and social factors.

- A variety of treatments, both biological and psychological, have proven effectiveness for the mood disorders, at least in the short term. However, relapse and recurrence of mood disorders is common in the long term.

- Suicide is often associated with mood disorders but can occur in their absence. In any case, the incidence of suicide has been increasing in recent years, particularly among adolescents, where suicide is the third leading cause of death.

Key Terms

anhedonia (241)
atypical features (253)
bipolar disorders (247)
bipolar I disorder (249)
bipolar II disorder (249)
catalepsy (253)
catatonic depressive episode (depressive stupor) (253)
catecholamine hypothesis (267)
cognitive therapy (283)
cyclothymic disorder (247)
delusions (253)
depressive cognitive triad (274)
dexamethasone suppression test (DST) (269)
double depression (245)
dysthymic disorder (244)
dysphoric manic / mixed episode (243)

electroconvulsive therapy (ECT) (282)
endogenous (253)
hallucinations (253)
hypomanic episode (241)
indolamine hypothesis (268)
interpersonal psychotherapy (IPT) (285)
learned helplessness theory of depression (273)
lithium (282)
longitudinal course specifiers (255)
maintenance treatment (287)
major depressive episode (240)
major depressive disorder, recurrent (244)
major depressive disorder, single episode (244)

mania (241)
melancholic (endogenous) depressive episode (253)
mood disorders (240)
neurohormones (269)
pathological grief reaction (impacted grief reaction) (258)
"permissive" hypothesis (268)
psychological autopsy (293)
psychotic depressive episode (252)
seasonal affective disorder (SAD) (256)
specifiers (252)
suicidal attempts (292)
suicidal ideation (292)
third early theory (269)

They are as sick that surfeit with too much,
as they that starve with nothing.
Shakespeare
The Merchant of Venice,
Act I, sc. 2, 1. 6

8

Eating Disorders

An epidemic of which many of us are not aware is in our midst in the Western world. This epidemic seems to have begun sometime in the 1950s or early 1960s and has spread insidiously over the ensuing decades. The disorders that are increasing so dangerously are eating disorders, specifically, anorexia nervosa and bulimia nervosa. **Anorexia nervosa** refers to a person's refusal to eat anything except minimal amounts of food, with the result that body weight sometimes drops to dangerously low levels. In **bulimia nervosa,** attempts to restrict food intake result in out-of-control eating episodes, or **binges,** often followed by self-induced vomiting, excessive use of laxatives, or other attempts to "purge" (get rid of) the food just eaten. Both of these related disorders are associated with one overriding characteristic: an overwhelming, all-encompassing drive to be thin. When people with anorexia nervosa are followed over a sufficient period of time, the results show that up to 20% of them will die as a result of their disorder (for example, Ratnasuriya, Eisler, Szmuhter, & Russell, 1991; Theander, 1985). As many as half these deaths will be suicides (Agras, 1987).

That this epidemic is widespread is reflected in a growing number of studies from different locations in the Western world. In Switzerland from 1956 to 1958, the number of new cases of anorexia nervosa under treatment among females between the ages of 12 and 25 was 3.98 per 100,000. This figure increased to 16.76 per 100,000 during the 1973–1975 period, a fourfold increase (Willi & Grossman, 1983). Similar results were found by Jones, Fox, Babigan, and Hutton (1980) in the state of New York for the same time period and by Lucas, Beard, O'Fallon, and Kurlan (1991) over a 50-year period in Minnesota.

Even more dramatic evidence of the current epidemic is present for bulimia nervosa. Figure 8.1 shows the rates of referral for patients with bulimia to a major eating disorder center in Canada (Garner & Fairburn, 1988). At this center between 1975 and 1986, the referral rates for anorexia rose slowly, but there was a dramatic and remarkable increase in the rates of referral for bulimia—from virtually none to over 140. Similar findings have been reported from other parts of the world (Lacey, 1992; Hay & Hall, 1991). Recent studies estimate a sixfold increase in death rates in this group compared to the normal population (Patton, 1988; Crisp, Callender, Halek, & Hsu, 1992). Because of this rapid increase in numbers of cases and because we now know more about eating disorders, they are included for the first time as a separate group of disorders in DSM-IV.

This epidemic would be puzzling enough if it were occurring across the population as a whole. What

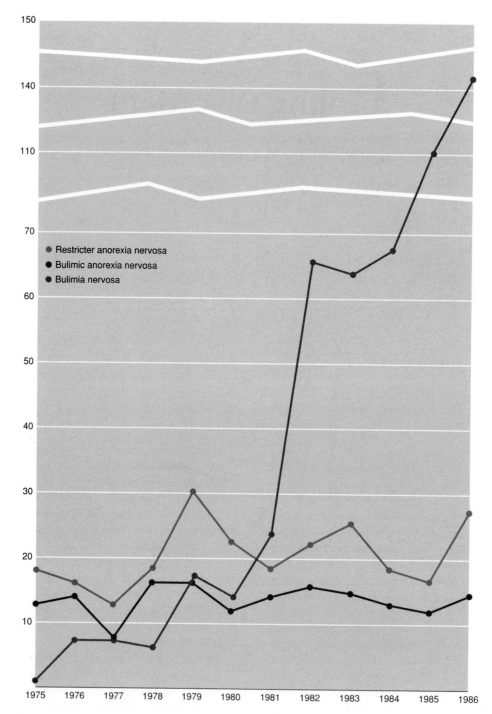

Figure 8.1   Rates of referral for eating disorders (from Garner & Fairburn, 1988)

makes it more intriguing is that anorexia and bulimia are highly culturally specific; that is, they occur in only one type of culture. In previous chapters we have examined culturally specific variants of anxiety disorders or dissociative disorders that are found only in third world cultures. For anorexia and bulimia the situation is quite different. These serious disorders are not found in developing countries, where access to sufficient food is so often a daily struggle. Only in

Western culture, where food is plentiful, is this epidemic so rampant.

Not everyone in the Western world is at risk. In fact, the disorder is localized in a relatively small segment of the population. Over 90% of the cases of severe eating disorders are found in young, white females of upper socioeconomic status who are living in a competitive environment. Perhaps the most visible example of someone who meets these criteria is

Diana, Princess of Wales, who recently recounted her 7-year battle with bulimia (Morton, 1992). Aboard the royal yacht Britannia on her honeymoon, she reported binging and vomiting four or more times a day.

The very specificity of these disorders—not only in terms of culture but also in the context of sex, age, and social class—is unparalleled among the psychological disorders studied in this book and makes the search for causes all the more interesting. In these disorders, unlike almost any other, the strongest contribution to etiology seems to come from sociocultural rather than psychological or biological factors.

In this chapter we look in some detail at the clinical features of bulimia nervosa and anorexia nervosa, including a discussion of both developmental and cultural considerations. We examine briefly some other eating disorders more commonly occurring in infancy or among people with mental retardation. This is followed with an examination of some of the quickly accumulating information on causes and treatment; here again, much of our attention is focused on sociocultural factors.

Bulimia Nervosa

Bulimia nervosa is a disorder of which you are likely to have some personal knowledge, from your own experience or that of a friend or perhaps a friend of a friend. It is one of the most common psychological disorders encountered on college campuses. Consider the following case.

The Case of Phoebe

Phoebe was an all-American girl. She was popular, attractive, intelligent, and talented, and by the time she was a senior in high school, she had accomplished a great deal. She was a class officer throughout high school and was elected homecoming princess her sophomore year and junior prom queen her junior year. She dated the captain of the football team and socialized with the "in" crowd. Phoebe had many talents, among them a beautiful singing voice and marked ability in ballet. Each year at Christmas time her ballet company danced the *Nutcracker Suite,* and Phoebe attracted much attention with her poised and confident performance in one of the lead roles. Phoebe maintained an A-minus average and also played on several of the school athletic teams. She was headed for a top ranked university and was considered a model student by many

people in the town, who hoped that their younger daughters would turn out as well.

But Phoebe had a secret. In fact, it was more than a secret. Almost every waking moment of her days she was haunted by thoughts that she was fat and ugly. Every single bite of food that she put in her mouth was, in her mind, another step down the slow but inexorable path that would lead to the end of her success and her popularity.

As early as age 11, Phoebe was concerned about her weight. Ever the perfectionist, she began regulating her eating in junior high school. She would skip breakfast (over the protestations of her mother), eat a small bowl of pretzels at noon, and allow herself one-half of whatever she was served for dinner. One day in her freshman year at high school, after a particularly strenuous workout following several days when she had eaten very little, Phoebe and her friends came home to have a snack. They split a coffee roll three ways, and then watched television for a while before the friends left. But Phoebe could

Many well-known young females, such as Princess Diana, have suffered from eating disorders.

not get the coffee roll off her mind. Its taste and texture seemed like the most delicious food she had ever eaten in her life. As soon as her friends were gone she finished off the whole box of rolls at once. Deep inside, Phoebe felt that this was the worst thing she had ever done. She felt weak, worthless, and ugly. She thought that if somehow she could get rid of those coffee rolls her problems would be solved. She tried sticking her fingers down her throat, having heard that this might make you vomit, but it only hurt and did not work.

Throughout high school Phoebe struggled to restrict her eating only to occasional binges on junk food. Sometimes she would try sticking her fingers down her throat (she even tried a tooth-brush once) but this tactic continued to be unsuccessful. During her sophomore year in high school, Phoebe reached her full adult height of 5′2″, with a weight of 110 pounds; she continued to fluctuate between 105 and 110 pounds throughout high school. By the time she was a senior, Phoebe's waking hours were almost totally centered on what she would eat and when she would eat it. She used every bit of her willpower to attempt to restrict her eating but occasionally she would fail. One day during the fall of her senior year, she came home after school and, while she was alone in front of the TV, she ate two big boxes of candy. Depressed, guilty, and absolutely desperate, she went to the bath-room and stuck her fingers further down her throat than she had ever before dared. She vomited. And she kept vomiting. Although physi-cally exhausted to the point that she had to lie down for half an hour, Phoebe had never in her life felt such an overwhelming sense of relief from the anxiety, guilt, and tension that always accom-panied her binges. The thought occurred to her that she had actually gotten to eat all that candy and now her stomach was empty. It was the perfect solution to her problems.

From that point on she learned very quickly what foods she could eat that she could then easily vomit. And she always drank lots of water. She began to restrict her eating even more. She would eat almost nothing until after school, but then the results of her dreaming and scheming and planning all morning would be realized. Although the food sometimes varied, the routine would not. She might stop at Dunkin' Donuts and pick up a dozen doughnuts. She would then stop at the bakery and buy a box of cookies. When she got home she might make a bowl of popcorn.

And then she would eat and eat, in an episode of *binge eating* in which she would force down the doughnuts, cookies, and popcorn in a short period of time until her stomach would actually hurt from the amount of food forced into it so quickly. Finally, with a mixture of revulsion and relief, she would *purge*—that is, she would force herself to vomit the food she had eaten. When she was done she would step on the scale to make sure she had not gained any weight and then collapse into her bed, falling sound asleep for about half an hour.

This routine went on for about 6 months until April of Phoebe's senior year in high school. At this point Phoebe had lost much of her energy and her school work was deteriorating. Her teachers noticed this and also noticed that, physically, she looked bad. She was continually tired, her skin began breaking out, and her face began to puff up, particularly around her mouth. The teachers suspected that she might have an eating problem. At this time her mother, who was ordinarily not home in the afternoon, heard her vomiting in the bathroom one day and became suspicious. Shortly thereafter, following a particu-larly horrendous binge, Phoebe attempted to vomit and nothing happened. Her gag reflex was gone. She then had to lie down in bed and tolerate the intense pain and discomfort of her binge; she ended up crying hysterically for over an hour.

When her mother and teachers confronted her she was relieved that her problem was finally out in the open. In an effort to prevent her from having the opportunity to binge and purge, her mother rearranged her schedule to be home in the afternoon when Phoebe got home from school; in general, her parents minimized the occasions Phoebe was left alone, particularly after eating. It worked, for about a month. Mortally afraid of gaining weight and losing her popularity, she resumed her pattern, but she was now much better at hiding it. For 6 months Phoebe would binge and purge approximately 15 times a week.

After going away to college that fall, things became more difficult. Now she had a roommate to contend with and she was more determined than ever to keep her problem a secret. Although the student health service at her college put on workshops and seminars on eating disorders for the freshman women, Phoebe knew that she could not break her cycle without the risk of gaining weight. To avoid the communal bath-room she found herself running off to a deserted place behind a nearby building to vomit. Social life at college often revolved around drinking beer and eating fattening foods, so she began vomiting more often. Despite her efforts she gained 10 pounds and now weighed 120 pounds. Many other freshman women also gained weight, a common occurrence among freshmen; but her mother noticed it and commented without thinking one day that Phoebe seemed to be putting on weight. This remark was devastating to Phoebe.

Her secret continued for another year. But during the beginning of her sophomore year in college her world fell apart. One night, after a party where Phoebe drank a lot of beer, she and her friends went to Kentucky Fried Chicken. Although Phoebe did not truly "binge" because she was with her friends, she did eat a lot of fried chicken, the most forbidden food on her list. Her guilt, anxiety, and tension increased to new heights. Her stomach was throbbing with pain, but when she tried to vomit, once again her gag reflex seemed to be gone. Breaking into hysterics, she called her boyfriend and told him she was ready to kill herself. Her loud sobbing and crying attracted the attention of her friends in her dormitory, who came in and attempted to comfort her. She confessed her problem to them. She also called her parents. At this point, Phoebe realized that her life was totally out of control and that she needed professional help.

We'll return to Phoebe later in this chapter.

Clinical Description of Bulimia Nervosa

The DSM-IV diagnostic criteria for bulimia nervosa are presented in Table 8.1. The hallmark of the disorder is binge eating. For the committee establishing the DSM-IV criteria for bulimia nervosa, one of the bigger challenges was arriving at a quantitative determination of what constituted a minimum amount of food that must be eaten to qualify for a *binge* (Beglin & Fairburn, 1992). In one study designed to address this question, Rosen, Leitenberg, Fisher, and Khazam (1986) had 20 bulimic patients self-monitor their food intake over the course of a week. In terms of content, what these patients reported as "binges" consisted of significantly more "junk" food and significantly fewer fruits and vegetables. The researchers found that in 27% of the binge-eating episodes patients consumed more than 2,000 calories while 33% involved 600 or fewer calories; in the average binge-eating episode, patients consumed 1,459 calories, as opposed to 321 calories for non–binge-eating episodes. Clearly, actual episodes of binge eating vary significantly in terms of calorie intake. Because of this broad variation, the DSM-IV committee decided to follow the definition of binge eating given in *The Eating Disorder Examination* (Fairburn & Cooper, in press), a highly respected, structured interview for eating disorders. In this assessment instrument, a binge is defined as "a larger amount of food than most people would eat under the circumstances." Though seemingly open-ended, this definition works quite well since patients with bulimia readily identify with this description of their binge-eating behavior.

Just as important as the *amount* of food eaten is the fact that the eating is *out of control* (Fairburn,

Table 8.1   DSM-IV Criteria for Bulimia Nervosa

A. Recurrent episodes of binge eating. An episode of binge eating is characterized by both of the following:

1. Eating, in a discrete period of time (e.g., within any 2-hour period), an amount of food that is definitely larger than most people would eat during a similar period of time and under similar circumstances
2. A sense of lack of control over eating during the episode (e.g., a feeling that one cannot stop eating or control what or how much one is eating)

B. Recurrent inappropriate compensatory behavior in order to prevent weight gain, such as self-induced vomiting; misuse of laxatives, diuretics or other medications; fasting; or excessive exercise.

C. The binge eating and inappropriate compensatory behaviors both occur, on average, at least twice a week for 3 months.

D. Self-evaluation is unduly influenced by body shape and weight.

E. The disturbance does not occur exclusively during episodes of anorexia nervosa.

Specify type:
   Purging Type: During the current episode of bulimia nervosa, the person has regularly engaged in self-induced vomiting or the misuse of laxatives, diuretics, or enemas
   Nonpurging Type: During the current episode of bulimia nervosa, the person has used other inappropriate compensatory behaviors, such as fasting or exercise, but has not regularly engaged in self-induced vomiting or the misuse of laxatives, diuretics, or enemas

Source: DSM-IV, APA, 1994.

Cooper, & Cooper, 1986). This criterion has now been incorporated as an integral part of the definition of binge eating. Both criteria, binge eating and lack of control, characterized Phoebe. She binged on large amounts of food on a regular basis, despite all attempts to resist or control her binging.

Another important part of the criteria concerns *attempts* by the individual *to compensate* somehow for the binge eating and potential weight gain. By far the largest and most distinct group of patients with bulimia use **purging techniques.** These techniques include vomiting immediately after eating, as in the case of Phoebe, or the use of laxatives or other similar medications. Some individuals use both methods. A number of patients with bulimia do not engage in these types of purging behaviors. Rather, they attempt to compensate in other ways. Some may exercise excessively, although rigorous exercising is more usually a characteristic of anorexia nervosa, which we will discuss later. Others may fast for long periods of time between binges. For this reason bulimia nervosa is subtyped in DSM-IV into *purging* type and *nonpurging* type with nonpurging referring to those who fast only, in combination perhaps with exercise. Approximately two-thirds of bulimics are purgers; the remaining one-third are nonpurgers. McCann, Rossiter, King, and Agras (1991) and Willmuth, Leitenberg, Rosen, and Cado (1988) have compared purging versus nonpurging bulimics. In both studies, purging bulimics evidence more severe psychopathology than nonpurging bulimics, including more frequent binge episodes, higher lifetime prevalence of major depression and panic disorder (the occurrence of major depression or panic disorder at some point in their lives), and higher scores on measures of disordered eating attitudes and behaviors.

The DSM-IV committee devising the criteria also specified a frequency of binge eating of at least twice a week for 3 months; but they were not entirely satisfied with this stipulation since some individuals who would otherwise meet the criteria for bulimia nervosa might not binge at this frequency. However, the committee was unable to come up with a more satisfactory alternative.

Researchers have compiled some interesting data on techniques of purging (Mitchell & Pyle, 1988; Pyle, Neuman, Halvorson, & Mitchell, 1991). Among bulimic purgers, approximately 70% to 90% practice self-induced vomiting on a regular basis, with most of those who vomit doing so at least once a day. Between 15% and 16% use—and by this we mean abuse—laxatives, with 20% of this group using them on a daily basis; approximately 33% use diuretics at least occasionally. Diuretics are drugs that result in removal of fluids from the body through greatly increased frequency of urination. Seven percent use enemas. Sixty-five percent of individuals with bulimia engage in a practice that has not been well studied: chewing and spitting out food without swallowing it to prevent weight gain. It is important to note that purging is not a particularly efficient method of reducing caloric intake. Vomiting will result in a reduction of approximately 50% of the calories that were consumed immediately before vomiting (Kaye, Weltzin, Hsu, McConaha, & Bolton, 1993), while laxatives and related procedures have very little effect, acting, as they do, so long after the binge.

One of the more important additions to the DSM-IV criteria is the specification of a psychological characteristic clearly present in Phoebe. Despite her accomplishments and success, she felt that her continuing popularity and self-esteem would be determined, to a large extent, by her weight and the shape of her body. Garfinkel (in press) noted that, out of 107 women seeking treatment for bulimia nervosa, only 3% did not evidence this type of attitude.

Chronic bulimia with accompanying purging has a number of medical consequences. One consequence is salivary gland enlargement, which gives the face a chubby appearance. This was very noticeable with Phoebe. Repeated vomiting also may erode the dental enamel on the inner surface of the front teeth. More important, continued vomiting may upset the chemical balance of bodily fluids including sodium and potassium levels or the acid balance of fluids. This condition, called an *electrolyte imbalance,* can result in serious medical complications if unattended. Normalization of eating habits will quickly reverse any imbalance. Finally, some bulimics develop marked callouses on their fingers or the backs of their hands caused by friction from contact with the teeth and throat as a consequence of repeatedly sticking their hands down their throats to stimulate the gag reflex.

Anorexia Nervosa

The overwhelming majority of individuals with bulimia are within 10% of their normal weight, as was evident in the case of Phoebe (Hsu, 1990). Individuals with anorexia nervosa (literally and incorrectly meaning a "nervous loss of appetite") differ in one important way from individuals with bulimia. They are successful at losing weight—so successful that they put their lives in considerable danger. Consider the following case of a young woman who came to one of our clinics.

The Case of Julie

Julie was 17 years old when she first came for help. If you looked hard enough past her sunken eyes and pale complexion you could see that she was once an attractive young girl. But at present, it looked like she had just been liberated from a concentration camp. Eighteen months before coming to our clinic, she had been overweight, weighing 140 pounds at 5'1". Her mother, a well-meaning but overbearing and demanding woman, nagged Julie relentlessly about her appearance. Her friends were kinder but no less relentless. Julie, who had never had a date, was told by a friend that she was really cute and would have no trouble at all getting dates if she lost some weight. So she did! After many previous unsuccessful attempts she was determined to succeed this time.

After several weeks of a strict diet she noticed the weight beginning to come off. She experienced a feeling of control and mastery that she had never known before. It wasn't long before she was drawing positive comments, not only from her friends but from her mother. Julie began to feel good about herself. The difficulty was that she was losing weight too fast. She stopped menstruating. But now nothing could stop her diet because Julie was finally in control. By the time she reached our clinic she weighed 75 pounds but, as with most individuals like her, she thought she looked fine and, perhaps, could even stand to lose a bit more weight. Her parents had just begun to worry about her. In fact, Julie did not initially seek out treatment for her eating behavior. Rather, she had developed a numbness in her left lower leg and a left foot drop that the neurologist determined was caused by peritoneal nerve paralysis believed to be related to her inadequate nutrition. The neurologist referred her to our clinic.

Like most people with anorexia Julie verbalized that she thought she probably should put on a little weight, but she didn't mean it. Basically, she thought she looked fine but reported that she had "lost all taste for food," a report that may not have been true since most people with anorexia crave food at least some of the time, but control their cravings. Nevertheless, she was participating in most of her usual activities and was continuing to do extremely well in school and in her extracurricular pursuits. Her parents were happy to buy her most of the workout videotapes available and she began doing one every day, and then two. When her parents suggested she was really doing enough, perhaps too much, she began exercising at times of day when no one was around. After every meal she would do a workout tape until, in her mind, she must have burned up all the calories she had just taken in.

Clinical Description of Anorexia Nervosa

DSM-IV criteria for anorexia nervosa are presented in Table 8.2. Bulimia nervosa is by far the more common condition but there is a great deal of overlap between bulimia and anorexia. For example, many bulimics have a history of anorexia; that is, they were at one time successful in reducing their body weight below desirable levels (Mitchell & Pyle, 1988).

Although decreased body weight is the most notable feature of anorexia nervosa, it is not the "core"

Table 8.2   DSM-IV Criteria for Anorexia Nervosa

A. Refusal to maintain body weight at or above a minimally normal weight for age and height (e.g., weight loss leading to maintenance of body weight less than 85% of that expected; or failure to make expected weight gain during period of growth, leading to body weight less than 85% of that expected).

B. Intense fear of gaining weight or becoming fat, even though underweight.

C. Disturbance in the way in which one's body weight or shape is experienced; undue influence of body weight or shape on self-evaluation, or denial of the seriousness of the current low body weight.

D. In post-menarchal females, amenorrhea, that is, the absence of at least three consecutive menstrual cycles. (A woman is considered to have amenorrhea if her periods occur only following hormone, e.g., estrogen, administration.)

Specify type:
   Restricting type: During the episode of anorexia nervosa, the person does not regularly engage in binge eating or purging behavior (i.e., self-induced vomiting or the misuse of laxatives or diuretics).
   Binge-eating/purging type: During the episode of anorexia nervosa, the person has regularly engaged in binge eating or purging behavior (i.e., self-induced vomiting or the misuse of laxatives or diuretics).

Source: DSM-IV, APA, 1994.

Although they are at different stages of the disorder, both women shown here suffer from anorexia nervosa.

of the disorder. Many individuals might evidence decreased body weight, usually due to some medical condition, but in anorexia there is an intense fear of obesity and a relentless pursuit of thinness (Garfinkel & Garner, 1982; Bruch, 1986; Hsu, 1990; Schlundt & Johnson, 1990). As with Julie, the disorder most commonly begins in an adolescent who is overweight or perceives herself as overweight. She will then start a diet that escalates into an obsessive preoccupation with being thin. Severe, almost punishing, exercise is also a common part of the condition, as it was with Julie. Dramatic weight loss may be achieved through severe caloric restriction or through a combination of caloric restriction and the use of purging behaviors. DSM-IV specifies two subtypes of anorexia nervosa, based on the method used to limit caloric intake: in the *restricting type,* individuals diet to limit calorie intake; in the *binge-eating/purging type,* they rely on purging to limit calorie intake. Unlike individuals with bulimia, the binge-eating/purging anorexic will binge on relatively small amounts of food and purge the food more consistently, in some cases after each time she eats. Approximately half the individuals meeting criteria for anorexia engage in binge eating and purging behavior (Agras, 1987; Garfinkel, Moldofsky, & Garner, 1979).

Binge/purge anorexics seem to engage in more impulsive behavior such as stealing, alcohol and drug use, and self-mutilation, and their moods are more variable (labile), compared to patients who do not binge/purge. In this way individuals with binge/purge anorexia resemble normal-weight bulimics more than they resemble restricting anorexics. Individuals who binge and purge, whether they suffer from anorexia or

not, are also more likely to have been obese as children and to have a history of obesity in their families (Garner, Garfinkel, & O'Shaughnessy, 1985). Nevertheless, anorexia, like bulimia, is characterized by a morbid fear in the individual of gaining weight and losing control over eating. The major difference seems to be whether the individual is successful at losing weight using one or another of the strategies mentioned above (Anderson, 1983).

A young girl with anorexia is never satisfied with her weight loss. Staying the same weight from one day to the next or gaining any weight at all is likely to cause her intense panic, anxiety, and depression. Only continued weight loss every day for weeks on end is satisfactory. Although DSM-IV criteria specify body weight 15% below that expected, individuals with anorexia usually weigh less than this by the time they come for treatment. Their average is approximately 25% to 30% below their expected weight (Hsu, 1990).

Another key criterion of anorexia, as was clear in the case of Julie, is a marked disturbance in body image. When Julie looked at herself in the mirror she saw something very different from what her parents or friends saw. Her parents saw an emaciated, sickly, tiny young girl in the throes of semistarvation. Julie, on the other hand, saw a young girl who needed to lose at least a few pounds from some parts of her body. For Julie, her face and buttocks were the problems. In other young girls it might be other parts of the body such as the arms or the legs.

After seeing numerous doctors, people like Julie become good at mouthing what others expect to hear. Therefore they may report that they are underweight and need to gain a few pounds—but they don't believe it. Scratch the surface and they will tell you that there is a fat little girl in the mirror. For this reason individuals with anorexia seldom seek treatment. Usually it is pressure from somebody in the family that brings them for an initial visit to the doctor, as was the case with Julie (Agras, 1987; Sibley & Blinder, 1988).

Some anorexic individuals, perhaps as a demonstration of absolute control over their eating, show increased interest in cooking and food. Some have become expert chefs, preparing all the food for the family. Others hoard food in their rooms, looking at it from time to time. We will review some research below that seems to explain the *cause* of these bizarre patterns.

The most common medical complication of anorexia nervosa is cessation of menstruation. This is a defining feature of the disorder that serves as an objective physical index of the degree of food restriction. In fact, studies have now demonstrated that there is a strong correlation between ovulation and resulting menstruation and weight (Pirke, Schweiger, & Fichter, 1987). The overwhelming evidence indicates that endocrinological difficulties are a consequence of the semistarvation rather than a cause, however. Other medical signs and symptoms of anorexia include dry skin, brittle hair or nails, and sensitivity to or intolerance of cold temperatures. Also it is relatively common to see growth of downy hair on the limbs and sides of the person's face.

Additional Eating Disorders

There are several additional eating disorders that deserve some mention. Before continuing with a deeper discussion of bulimia and anorexia, we will describe these briefly.

Binge-Eating Disorder

Recent research has focused on a group of individuals who experience marked distress due to binge eating but do *not* engage in extreme compensatory behaviors and therefore cannot be diagnosed with bulimia (Spitzer et al., 1991). These individuals have been characterized as having what might become a new disorder, called **binge-eating disorder (BED).** This condition is currently being studied intensively to determine whether it can be considered a disorder and be accorded full status as a diagnostic category.

Many individuals meeting preliminary criteria for this disorder are found in weight-control programs. For example, among obese individuals attending hospital-affiliated weight-loss programs, 30% could be characterized as obese binge eaters based on results from questionnaires administered to these groups (Spitzer et al., 1992). Among obese individuals engaged in less intensive weight-control programs such as self-directed diets or Weight Watchers, 11.3% could be characterized as having BED, but among those attending Overeaters Anonymous, 71% met criteria. In surveys of the population at large, 19% could be classified as obese, with 2% of the population meeting criteria for BED. On the other hand, more thoroughly done epidemiological surveys are now beginning to appear; conducted by skilled interviewers, these studies suggest that the above figures, all based on questionnaires alone, may be overestimates and that BED may not be as common as it first appeared (Fairburn, Beglin, & Davies, 1992).

People with this condition seem to differ in a variety of ways from individuals with other eating disorders or from obese people who don't binge. For example, the gender difference is not as dramatic in BED as in other eating disorders, with the female-to-male ratio at 3:1 in the weight-control samples and approximately 2:1 in the community surveys (Bruce & Agras, 1992). It also seems that individuals suffering from BED are older on average than individuals with anorexia or bulimia (Arnow, Kenardy, & Agras, 1992; Schwalberg, Barlow, Alger, & Howard, 1992).

In addition, individuals with BED show an increased frequency of additional psychological disorders and more psychopathology in general, compared to obese people who don't binge. Marcus et al. (1990) reported significant rates of mood and anxiety disorders as well as psychosexual dysfunction among obese binge eaters. Schwalberg et al. (1992) also reported roughly equal rates of anxiety and mood disorders

Among obese individuals attending weight-loss programs, as many as 30% may meet criteria for binge-eating disorder.

among normal-weight bulimics and obese binge eaters. Other studies have found similar results (Marcus, Smith, Santelli, & Kaye, 1992; Kirkley, Kolotkin, Hernandez, & Gallagher, 1992).

For all these reasons BED has found its way into the appendix of DSM-IV as a potential new disorder requiring further study. Many individuals feel that far too little is known about individuals with this condition to warrant creating a new disorder, even one that is placed only in the appendix. To date most studies of BED have relied on self-report questionnaires rather than direct observation and interviews, as noted above. In addition, the criteria for the disorder, as formulated in the appendix of DSM-IV, have not yet been carefully evaluated to determine their reliability and validity. Nevertheless, this category is likely to generate a considerable amount of research in the years to come (Fairburn, Hay, & Welch, in press; Fairburn & Wilson, in press).

The last two eating disorders differ from those covered thus far in that they are often associated with mental retardation and involve some rather bizarre eating patterns. However, they share with other eating disorders the consequence of a substantially increased risk of illness or death for the person manifesting them if they are not treated.

Rumination Disorder

Rumination involves regurgitating and then reswallowing partially digested food. The term comes from a description of a quite normal process in animals (chewing the cud). **Rumination disorder** is present when this process interferes with appropriate nutritional intake or weight gain. Consider the following case seen in one of our settings.

The Case of Sandra

Sandra was born in September to an economically marginal, rural family after an unplanned, uncomplicated pregnancy. She was delivered at home by a nurse-midwife and weighed eight pounds. The next day she was admitted to the University Hospital for feeding difficulties associated with a cleft palate and lip. These difficulties were rectified with gastric tube feedings, and Sandra was discharged to her aunt nine days after admission. During the next four months, weight gain was below average, although neither mother nor aunt reported any further feeding difficulties. There were, however, indications of neglect, and Sandra was cared for during this period by a number of different individuals, including neighborhood children.

Sandra was admitted to the University Hospital for the second time in February of the following year, at the age of about 6 months, by her aunt because of a failure to gain weight associated with rumination. On examination, she was emaciated and unresponsive to her environment. There was very little grasping of objects, no smiling, no babbling, no gross movements, and some crying. She was primarily lethargic and lay passively in her crib. Exhaustive medical examinations and laboratory analyses revealed no organic cause for her difficulties. Her weight, however, was falling rapidly and was below her birth weight and below the third percentile for infant girls. Malnutrition and dehydration were pressing problems, and death, resulting from possible complications, was a distinct possibility.

Feeding consisted of a commercially prepared formula every four hours. Immediately after each feeding, ruminative behavior would begin. Sandra would open her mouth, elevate and fold her tongue, and then vigorously thrust her tongue forward and backward. Within a few seconds milk would appear at the back of her mouth and then slowly flow out. This behavior would continue for about 20 to 40 minutes until she apparently lost all of the milk she had previously consumed. No crying or evidence of pain and discomfort was observed by nurses during this behavior. Rumination could be interrupted by touches, pokes, or mild slaps, but would resume immediately. (Sajwaj, Libet, & Agras, 1974, p. 558)

Rumination occurs among children, particularly infants, and is classified as a disorder of infancy, childhood, or adolescence in DSM-IV. Approximately 10% of adults who have mental retardation also evidence this behavior. Little is known about this disorder, but many investigators believe that the causes can be found in a combination of biological and psychological variables (Blinder, Goodman, & Goldstein, 1988). Blinder et al. believe that infants with this disorder may have a predisposition or a tendency to gastroesophageal reflux, which puts the infant at risk. This term refers to a tendency for the esophagus to regurgitate some food. In some cases this disorder may be related to physical abnormalities involving eating. One recent study found that a majority of mentally retarded people with chronic rumination also had abnormalities of chewing and swallowing that may have contributed to their eating problems (Rogers, Stratton, Victor, Kennedy, & Andres, 1992). Intervention with this population might involve efforts to help them chew and swallow their food more effectively and thoroughly (for example, Rast, Johnston, Lubin, & Ellinger-Allen, 1988).

Whatever the biological predispositions, all investigators agree that psychological factors are at work, but there is little agreement on the nature of the psychological factors. Some evidence indicates that rumination is associated with depression; infants and children with the disorder seem to be depressed, and depression in the parents, particularly the mother, seems to be common (Blinder et al., 1988). Others have suggested that rumination seems to come and go as a function of environmental stress and that it possibly attracts a lot of attention from the parents when it does occur, a result that may reinforce the behavior.

In any case, direct behavioral treatment of rumination seems to be successful based on single-case studies. In the case of Sandra described above, small amounts of lemon juice were squirted into her mouth by a nurse at the very beginning of her tongue movements. After several days all rumination stopped and 1 year later Sandra was developing normally. Considering the mortality rate for infants with this disorder, which approaches 25%, these quick and effective treatments can be lifesaving.

Rumination can also occur in individuals with bulimia. Fairburn and Cooper (1984) reported 7 such cases out of 35 patients with bulimia. These individuals would regurgitate small quantities of food shortly after eating and "chew" on it. Sometimes they would do this for several hours. Most described the process as soothing, and four reported that the taste of food was improved by a period of "marination" in the stomach. Successful treatment for bulimia also eliminated rumination in these patients, a finding reported in other studies as well (Murray, Keele, & McCarver, 1976; Singh, Manning, & Angell, 1982).

Pica

Pica is a disorder, commonly occurring in infants or among people with mental retardation or dementia, that is characterized by the repeated eating of non-nutritive substances. Individuals with pica disorder typically eat paint, plaster, string, hair, or cloth. Older children may eat animal droppings, sand, insects, leaves, or pebbles. The majority of cases involve individuals with severe or profound intellectual disabilities (Singh & Winton, 1984; Bell & Stein, 1992). Consider the case of Mike.

The Case of Mike

Mike was a 17-year-old young man who lived in an institution for people who like himself had mental retardation. This was before the current practice of placing people such as Mike in their own communities. One of the authors worked with Mike a number of years ago in this institution on a variety of behavior problems, the most serious of which was his habit of eating anything available. If left alone for any period of time, he would secretly pick up small pieces of paper, string, or cardboard and eat them. Unfortunately, his appetite often went beyond these relatively harmless objects to more dangerous things. Once, when he was in the hospital for an appendectomy, an X-ray of his stomach revealed paper clips, thumb tacks, and what appeared to be a metal spring.

The people who worked with Mike made every effort to lock up any objects that might be dangerous for him to eat. However, despite his mental retardation, Mike was ingenious at getting inedible objects to ingest. One day when I was showing a group of people around the bedroom where Mike and his roommate lived, someone asked to see the closets. As I opened the large door to Mike's closet, it fell off its hinges and crashed to the floor. When we looked more closely, we saw that the wood around the hinges had been, bit by bit, chipped away. Mike had eaten large parts of his closet door!

Pica poses serious health problems such as lead poisoning and roundworm infection; sometimes surgery is required to remove ingested objects (for instance, Foxx & Martin, 1975). Occasionally, eating non-nutritive substances is culturally determined. For example, among certain black cultures in Africa and during the early history of the United States, pregnant women ate clay to facilitate childbearing (Cooper, 1957). For this reason, culturally approved pica is not considered a disorder.

Causes of pica (other than cultural) are largely unknown, although it is thought that certain mineral deficiencies may, on occasion, result in this behavior. Some studies have reported that patients with iron-deficiency anemia stop their pica after treatment with iron (for example, Gutelius, Millicin, & Layman, 1963). However, even in those individuals with demonstrated iron-deficiency anemia, psychosocial factors such as stress seem important as a contribution to the behavior (Blinder et al., 1988). Most often these psychological factors are associated with substantial neglect or abuse of the patient (Singhi, Singhi, & Adwani, 1981). In addition, pica also seems in some cases to be maintained by reinforcing consequences such as taste or other forms of sensory reinforcement, although this is hard to conceptualize for people without the disorder.

You might appreciate pica better by understanding the places in which these people live. Because many of the people who eat inedibles spent considerable time in institutions, pica may develop as a habit that reduces the boredom that so often afflicts people in these settings.

Some operant conditioning procedures have been used with cases of pica, primarily the systematic reinforcement of appropriate eating and mild punishment or withholding of reinforcement when pica occurs (Foxx & Martin, 1975). Still, this disorder does not yet have an accepted treatment (Bell & Stein, 1992).

Finally, in Chapter 2 we mentioned *feeding disorder of infancy or early childhood*, also referred to as "failure to thrive," in which failure to eat adequately results in insufficient weight gain. Working with or changing caregivers almost always rectifies the situation. This condition accounts for up to 5% of all admissions to pediatric units.

Statistics and Course for Eating Disorders

Bulimia nervosa was recognized as a distinct psychological disorder only in the 1970s (Boskind-Lodahl, 1976; Russell, 1979). Therefore, information on prevalence has been developed quite recently.

We have already noted that the overwhelming majority (90% to 95%) of individuals with bulimia are women. They are most usually white and middle to upper-middle class. Among the 5% to 10% of cases who are male, no important descriptive differences are apparent. Because of the overwhelming preponderance of women with this disorder, most of the examples in the remainder of this chapter will concern women. Age of onset is typically between 16 and 19 years of age (Mitchell & Pyle, 1988), although early signs of impending bulimic behavior can occur much earlier, as was the case with Phoebe. Schlundt and Johnson (1990), summarizing a large number of surveys, suggest that between 6% and 8% of young women, especially on college campuses, meet criteria for bulimia nervosa. Gross and Rosen (1988) reported that as many as 9% of high school girls would meet criteria for the disorder although a smaller percentage (approximately 2%) were utilizing purging techniques at that age. The overwhelming majority of individuals with bulimia who seek treatment come from the purging subtype.

A somewhat different view of the prevalence of bulimia comes from studies examining the population as a whole rather than surveying specific groups of adolescents. In one of the better studies, sampling almost 800 individuals (Bushnell, Wells, Hornblow, Oakley-Browne, & Joyce, 1990), the lifetime prevalence of bulimia nervosa among women aged 18–44 years was 1.6%. However, the rate was substantially higher among younger women. For instance, among women aged 18–24 the prevalence was 4.5%. Among women aged 25–44 the prevalence was 2%, but it was only 0.4% among women aged 45–64 years.

Perhaps the most important study of prevalence was reported by Kendler, et al., (1991). In this study 2,163 twins were interviewed and the lifetime prevalence of bulimia nervosa was found to be 2.8%, increasing to 5.3% with inclusion of marked bulimic symptoms that did not meet full criteria for the disorder. Once again, when broken down by age the prevalence was much greater in younger women. As is evident in Figure 8.2, for people born from 1960 onward the risk was much higher than for people born between 1950 and 1959 or before 1950. Nevertheless, as pointed out by Fairburn and his colleagues (Fairburn & Beglin, 1990; Fairburn, Hay, & Welch, in press), these figures are probably underestimates since many individuals with eating disorders refuse to participate in studies of these conditions. Therefore, the percentages described above are only from those individuals who consented to participate in the survey.

As with bulimia, 90% to 95% of individuals with anorexia are female, with age of onset also in adolescence, usually beginning around the age of 13 (Herzog, 1988). Studies cited in the beginning of this chapter noted the increase in rates of anorexia, particularly in the 1960s and 1970s. As mentioned above, bulimia was defined as a separate disorder only in the late 1970s. Considerable overlap in symptoms makes it difficult to ascertain relative prevalence rates for the two disorders, but data in Figure 8.1 suggest that bulimia is more common than anorexia.

Cross-Cultural Considerations

We have already discussed the highly culturally specific nature of anorexia and bulimia within Western cultures. In addition, a particularly striking finding is the development of these disorders in immigrants who have recently moved to Western countries (Nasser, 1988). One of the more interesting studies is Nasser's (1986) survey of 50 Egyptian females in London universities compared to 60 Egyptian females at Cairo universities. There were no instances of eating disorders in Cairo, but 12% of the Egyptian women in England had developed an eating disorder. Among most North American minority populations including blacks, Hispanics, and American Indians, the incidence of anorexia is low. When it does occur, however, it is more often found in higher social classes and among minorities who have become more acculturated to the majority

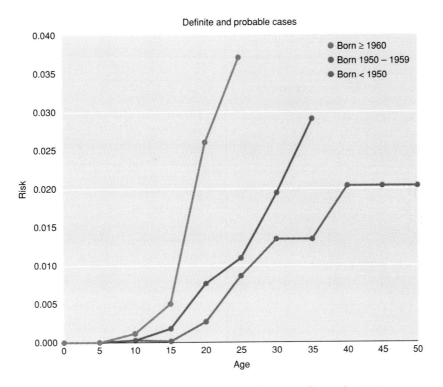

Definite and probable cases

● Born ≥ 1960
● Born 1950 – 1959
● Born < 1950

Figure 8.2   Lifetime cumulative risk for bulimia among female twins (from Kendler et al., 1991)

class (for example, Anderson & Hay, 1985; Smith & Krejci, 1991; Raich et al., 1992).

A relatively high incidence of purging behavior seems to exist in some of these minority groups. In most cases the purging seems to be associated with obesity. Rosen et al. (1988) found widespread use of purging and other eating-disorder-related behaviors in a group of Chippewa Indian women. Among this group, 74% had dieted and 55% had used deleterious weight-loss techniques such as fasting or purging; 12% had vomited and 6% reported the use of laxatives or diuretics.

The only significant culturally determined difference in criteria for eating disorders discovered thus far has been reported by Lee et al. (1991) in traditional Chinese cultures. In this culture, being slightly overweight is highly valued. Ideals of beauty are focused on the face rather than the body. Therefore, in this group, acne was most often reported as a precipitant for anorexia nervosa rather than a fear of being fat, and body image disturbance is rare (Lee, Hsu, & Wing, 1992). These patients said they refused to eat because of feelings of fullness or pain, although it is possible that they related food intake to their skin conditions. Beyond that, they met all other criteria for anorexia.

In Japan the prevalence of anorexia nervosa among Japanese teenage girls is approximately 10% of the rate in North America although it is rising. The need to be thin or the fear of becoming overweight does not seem to be as important in Japanese culture as it is in North American culture, although body image distor-

tion and denial that a problem exists are clearly present in those patients with the disorder (Ritenbaugh, Shisstak, Teufel, Leonard-Green, & Prince, 1993).

In conclusion, anorexia and bulimia are relatively homogeneous and overwhelmingly associated with Western cultures. However, they do occur in some non-Western cultures, where they present slightly differently. In addition, the frequency and pattern of occurrence of eating disorders in minority Western cultures differs somewhat from the norm, particularly as one moves further away from middle- and upper-middle-class socioeconomic groups.

Life-Span Development Considerations

It is very clear that anorexia and bulimia are strongly related to developmental considerations since the overwhelming majority of these cases begin in adolescence. As pointed out by Striegal-Moore, Silberstein, and Rodin (1986), differential patterns of physical development in the sexes interact with cultural demands to set the occasion for eating disorders. After puberty, girls gain weight primarily in the form of fat tissue while boys develop more muscle and lean tissue. As the ideal look for men is tall and muscular whereas the currently "in vogue" look for women is thin and prepubertal, physical development brings boys closer to the male ideal and girls further away from the female ideal.

Occasionally one sees cases of eating disorders, particularly anorexia nervosa, in very young children before the age of 11 years. Gislason (1988) described some differences between child and adolescent anorexics. In those rare cases where young children do develop anorexia, they are very likely to restrict fluid intake as well as food intake, perhaps not knowing the difference. Of course, this is particularly dangerous. Concerns about being fat were less common in these children but many of them had experienced severe stress such as death, parental divorce, or the birth of a sibling.

There is also some documentation of both bulimia and anorexia in later years, particularly after the age of 55 years. Hsu and Zimmer (1988) reported that most of these cases were individuals who had had an eating disorder for decades with very little change in their behavior. However, in a few cases the onset did not occur until later years. It is not yet clear what factors would account for this.

The Causes of Eating Disorders

As with all disorders discussed in this book, biological, psychological, and social factors each make a contribution to the development of these serious eating disorders, but the evidence has become increasingly clear that the most dramatic and clear-cut contributing factor is social. As such, we will look at this contribution first.

Social Dimensions

Sociocultural Factors

Remember that anorexia and bulimia are among the most highly culturally specific psychological disorders yet discovered. What is it about Western culture that drives so many young women into a punishing and life-threatening condition of semistarvation or dangerously frequent purging? The answer seems to be that, for many young women, looking good is more important than being healthy. In fact, for young white females in middle- to upper-class competitive environments, one's self-worth, happiness, and success are determined to a large extent by body measurements and percentage of body fat, factors that, in reality, have little or no correlation with personal happiness and success in the long run. The cultural imperative for thinness directly results in the first dangerous step down the slippery slope to anorexia and bulimia: dieting.

What makes Western society's emphasis on thinness in women even more puzzling is that ideas about desirable body sizes change much like fashion styles in clothes, albeit not as quickly. Several groups of investigators have documented this phenomenon in some interesting ways. Garner, Garfinkel, Schwartz, and Thompson (1980) collected data from *Playboy Magazine* centerfolds as well as Miss America Pageants from 1959 to 1978. They found that over the years, both *Playboy* centerfolds and Miss America contestants had become thinner, with the percentage of weight for a given age and height decreasing significantly since 1960. Also, bust and hip measurements became smaller,

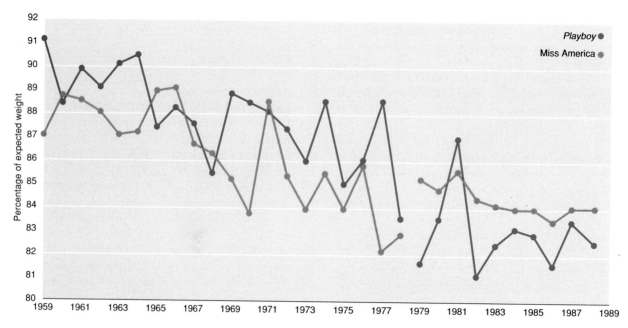

Figure 8.3 Average percentage of expected weight of *Playboy* centerfolds and Miss America contestants, 1959–1978 (from Wiseman et al., 1992)

although waists became somewhat larger, suggesting a change in what is considered desirable in the *shape* of one's body in addition to weight. The preferred shape that emerged during the sixties and seventies was a more thin, tubular shape (Agras & Kirkley, 1986). More recently, Wiseman, Gray, Mosimann, and Ahrens (1992) updated these data covering the years 1979 to 1988 to see if any changes had occurred. They reported that Miss America contestants continued to decrease their expected weight significantly while *Playboy* centerfolds remained at a relatively low level of body weight. In fact, 69% of the *Playboy* centerfolds and 60% of the Miss America contestants had weights 15% or more *below* their expected weights for their age and height. Being this much underweight actually meets one of the criteria for anorexia. Data from both of these studies are presented in Figure 8.3. Just as important, Wiseman et al. (1992) investigated diet and exercise articles in six women's magazines from 1959 to 1988. They found a significant increase in both diet and exercise articles, with writings on exercise increasing dramatically over the past 8 years, even surpassing the number on diet (see Figure 8.4).

Pictures of Marilyn Monroe, the popular movie star of the 1950s, reflect standards of beauty at that time. Marilyn Monroe in turn represents a much thinner standard than some of the beauties depicted in famous Renaissance paintings several hundred years ago. Paintings by Rubens and Botticelli depicted women who were gorgeous by the standards of the time but would be quite overweight by today's norms (Brownell, 1991).

If standards of beauty emphasizing thinness had increased steadily over the centuries, this would be a source of substantial concern for future generations; but this has not been the case. During the 1920s the ideal female body shape was similar to the ideal today (Agras & Kirkley, 1986); however, there was a critical difference between the two time periods. In the 1920s this shape was achieved through fashion (for instance, binding of the breasts) without dependence on dieting. In fact, no diet articles appeared in the magazines sampled in the 1920s whereas the number of diet articles has increased substantially in more recent years, resulting in what Brownell and Rodin (in press) have called "the dieting maelstrom," in which health professionals, the media, and a powerful diet and food industry all have a stake.

The problem with today's standards is that they are increasingly difficult to achieve. Surveys indicate that the average American woman between 17 and 24 years of age has become five to six pounds heavier over the last 20 years (Bureau of the Census, 1983). Some of this change may be due to improved nutrition or health habits since it is generally true that the human species has increased in height and weight over the centuries. It is also possible that a somewhat less active life-style in recent decades accounts for the change.

Whatever the cause, this collision between our culture and our physiology (Brownell, 1991) has had some very negative effects, one of which is that women are no longer satisfied with their body image. A second clear effect is the dramatic increase, especially among women, in dieting and exercise to achieve what may be an impossible goal. Dwyer, Feldman, Seltzer, and Mayer reported in 1969 that over 80% of female high school seniors wished to lose weight and 30% were dieting.

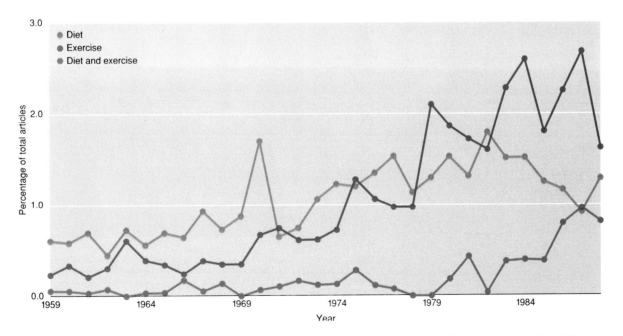

Figure 8.4 Number of articles as a percentage of total articles in six women's magazines (from Wiseman et al., 1992)

Standards of beauty regarding body shape may change dramatically over time, as is evident in these photos from different periods. (*top left*) This painting by Renoir illustrates that in the 19th century large women were considered the ideal. (*top right*) Marilyn Monroe was considered the sex symbol of the 1950s. (*bottom left*) During the 1920s, women achieved the "thin" look through clothing styles. (*bottom right*) Today's models continually struggle to meet unrealistic standards, sometimes using unhealthy means to appear as thin as possible.

Among their male counterparts, less than 20% wished to lose weight and 6% were dieting. More recently Hunnicut and Newman (1993) surveyed a national sample of 3,632 eighth and tenth grade students and found that 60.6% of females and 28.4% of males were actually dieting.

Fallon and Rozin (1985), studying male and female undergraduates, found that males rated their current body size, their ideal body size, and the body size they figured would be most attractive to the opposite sex as approximately equal; indeed, males rated their ideal body weight as *heavier* than the weight females thought most attractive (see Figure 8.5). Women, however, rated their current figure as much *heavier* than the most attractive, which in turn was rated as as heavier than the ideal. In addition, females' judgment of an ideal female body weight was *less* than the weight males thought most attractive. It is this conflict between reality and the current fashion in body size that seems most closely related to the epidemic of eating disorders.

The efforts of some people to maintain a thin and athletic shape are almost superhuman. Miss America contestants work out an average of 14 hours per week, with some exercising 35 hours per week (Trebbe, 1979). The abhorrence of fat, however, can have tragic consequences. Remember the case of failure to thrive or psychosocial dwarfism mentioned in Chapter 2? In these cases, the individual's growth was severely stunted because of inadequate nutrition in the

Kelly Brownell has documented the collision between culture and physiology, resulting in overwhelming pressures to be thinner than we should be in many cases.

context of severely abusive or neglectful parenting. Recently, a number of young infants of affluent parents have showed up at hospitals with the same syndrome, but in these cases, the parents were not trying to abuse their children. In fact, in each case, these parents had put their young, healthy, but somewhat chubby infants on diets in the hope of preventing obesity in them at a

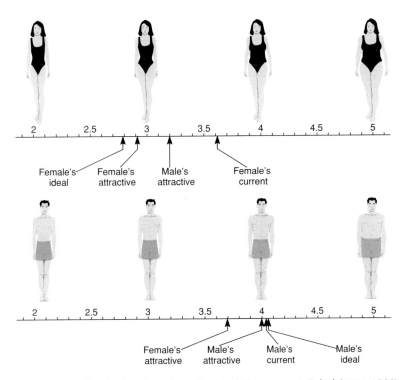

Figure 8.5 Male and female ratings of body size (based on Stunkard, Sorensen, & Schulsinger, 1980)

later date (Pugliese, Weyman-Daun, Moses, & Lifshitz, 1987).

Of course, most people who diet don't develop eating disorders, but Patton, Johnson-Sabine, Wood, Mann, and Wakeling (1990) determined in a prospective study that adolescent girls who were dieting were eight times more likely to develop an eating disorder 1 year later than those who weren't dieting. More recently, Telch and Agras (1993) noted marked increases in binging during and after rigorous dieting in 201 obese women. It is not yet entirely clear why dieting leads to binging in some, but not all, people (Polivy & Herman, 1993), but the relationship is strong.

This conflict would be bad enough if body size were infinitely malleable, but it is not. Increasing evidence indicates a strong genetic contribution to our body size—that is, some of us are born to be heavier, or shaped differently from others. While all of us can be physically fit, not all, and in fact very few, can achieve the kinds of fitness and body size so highly valued today. It is biologically impossible (Brownell, 1991). Nevertheless, many young women in our society fight biology tooth and nail to the point of starvation or dangerous purging in an unceasing attempt to reach that ideal. In adolescence, cultural standards, often experienced as peer pressure, have a much stronger influence than reason and fact.

Dietary Restraint and Eating Disorders

What is the effect of continual and rigorous dieting? During World War II, Keys and his colleagues (Keys, Brozek, Henschel, Michelson, & Taylor, 1950) conducted a semistarvation experiment involving 36 conscientious objectors who volunteered for the study as an alternative to military service. These healthy men were placed on diets for 6 months that consisted of about half their former full intake. This period was followed by a 3-month rehabilitation phase over which the men were gradually re-fed. During the diet the subjects lost an average of 25% of their body weight. The results of this diet were carefully documented, particularly the psychological effects.

First, the investigators found that the subjects became preoccupied with food and eating. Conversations, reading, and daydreams revolved around food. Many began to collect recipes and to hoard food-related items. Some men never lost their obsession with food.

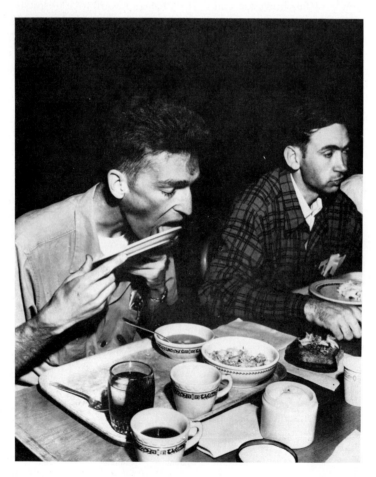

One of the subjects in the study done by Keys and colleagues is shown licking his plate during a meal.

Remember the bizarre behavior often found in individuals with anorexia who become "chefs" for their families and hoard food. Could this be an effect of dieting or starvation alone? Data from this experiment would indicate that it is.

If cultural pressures to diet and be thin are as important as they seem to be in triggering eating disorders, then one would expect an increase in eating disorders where these pressures are particularly severe—and this is just what seems to happen in one group of young girls under extraordinary pressures to be thin: ballet dancers. In an important study, Szmukler, Eisler, Gillis, and Haywood (1985) examined 100 adolescent female ballet students in London. Fully 7% were diagnosed with anorexia nervosa, and an additional 3% were borderline cases. Another 20% had previously lost a significant amount of weight, and 30% were clearly afraid of becoming fat, although they were actually below normal weight (Garner & Garfinkel, 1985). All these figures are much higher than one would expect to find in the population as a whole. In another study, Garner, Garfinkel, Rockert, and Olmsted (1987) followed a group of 11- to 14-year-old female students in ballet school. Their conservative estimate was that at least 25% of these girls developed eating disorders over the 2 years of the study.

What exactly goes on in ballet classes that has such a devastating effect on young girls? Phoebe remembered very clearly her early years in ballet. One of her first memories, at age 11, was of the older girls talking incessantly about their weight. Phoebe performed very well in ballet and looked forward to the occasional but rare compliment from her ballet mistress. In fact, comments from the ballet mistress to the class seemed to concern weight more than dance technique. Remarks such as "You'd dance better if you lost weight" were common. If one little girl would manage to lose a few pounds through heroic dieting the instructor would not fail to point it out: "You've done well working on your weight; the rest of you better follow this example." One day without warning the instructor said to Phoebe, "You need to lose five pounds before the next class." At that time Phoebe was 5'2" and weighed 98 pounds. The next class was two days away. It was after one of these admonitions and several days of restrictive eating that Phoebe experienced her first uncontrollable binge.

Early in high school, Phoebe gave up the rigors of ballet to pursue a variety of additional interests. She did not soon forget the glory of her starring roles at a young age, nor did she forget many of the steps. She would still dance from time to time when she heard the music, and also retained the grace of movement that the best dancers effortlessly display. But, in college, as she stuck her head in the toilet bowl, vomiting her guts out for perhaps the third time that day, she realized that

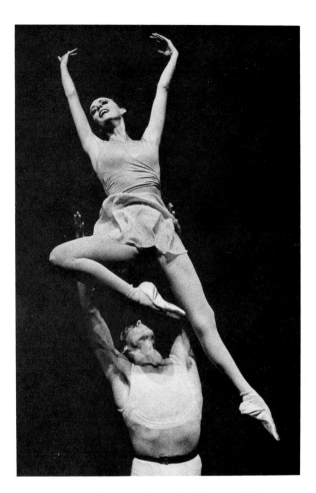

Ballet dancers often experience significant social pressure to be thin.

there was one lesson she had learned in ballet class more deeply and thoroughly than any other—the life or death importance of being thin at all costs.

Family Influences

Much has also been made of the possible significance of family interaction patterns in cases of eating disorders. Given that the large majority of these parents are middle- and upper-middle-class, high-achieving families, a number of investigators (for example, Minuchin, Rosman, & Baker, 1978; Humphrey, 1986, 1988, 1989; Bruch, 1985) have looked for typical patterns of interaction. The "typical" anorexic family seems to be successful, hard-driving, concerned about external appearances including physical appearance, and eager to maintain harmony. To accomplish these goals family members often deny or ignore conflicts or negative feelings and tend to attribute their problems to other people at the expense of open communication (Hsu, 1990).

Recently, Pike and Rodin (1991) confirmed the existence of differences in family interactions among the families of young girls with disordered eating versus

Ally Sheedy, a famous young actress, suffered from bulimia.

control families. Basically, mothers of girls with disordered eating seemed to act as "society's messenger" in that they wanted their daughters to be thin, were very likely to be dieting themselves, and, generally, were a lot more "perfectionistic" in that they were less satisfied with their family and its cohesion than were control mothers. Of course, to confirm the possible causal contribution of this characteristic the observations would have to be documented in mothers of daughters who later went on to develop eating disorders (prospective studies).

Whatever the preexisting relationships, after the onset of an eating disorder, particularly anorexia, family relationships can deteriorate quickly. Nothing is more frustrating than watching your daughter starve herself in front of your eyes at a dinner table where food is plentiful. Educated and knowledgeable parents including psychologists and psychiatrists with a full understanding of the disorder at hand have reported, in moments of extreme frustration, resorting to physical violence (for instance, hitting or slapping) in a vain attempt to get their daughters to put some food, however little, in their mouths. The guilt and anguish

experienced by these parents often exceeds the levels of anxiety and depression present in the children with the disorder.

Biological Dimensions

Obviously, biological processes are quite active in the regulation of eating and eating disorders. There is reasonably good agreement at this time, however, that neurobiological factors do not play a substantial role in *precipitating* eating disorders, although some of these processes may well contribute to the *maintenance* of the disorder once it begins. Of course, these conclusions could change as our understanding of eating disorders advances.

Genetic Factors

As with most psychological disorders, eating disorders run in families and seem to have a genetic component. Although the studies completed thus far are only preliminary, they suggest that relatives of patients with eating disorders are four to five times more likely than the general population to develop an eating disorder themselves (for instance, Hudson, Pope, Jonas, & Yurgelun-Todd, 1983; Strober & Humphrey, 1987). Several twin studies (albeit with relatively few sets of twins) have also reported concordance rates for monozygotic twins running between 30% and 50%, whereas the rates for dizygotic twins are typically 10% or less (Garfinkel & Garner, 1982; Holland, Hall, Murray, Russell, & Crisp, 1984; Hsu, Chesler, & Santhouse, 1990).

The most important twin study thus far in terms of numbers of twins and the use of state-of-the-art structured interviews has been reported by Kendler et al. (1991). In this study 2,163 female twins were interviewed to ascertain the prevalence of bulimia. Twenty-three percent of monozygotic twins both had bulimia, as compared to 9% of dizygotic twins. Since no adoption studies have yet been reported, strong sociocultural influences cannot be ruled out in the Kendler study. But results from this study, if replicated, would certainly *suggest* a genetic contribution to bulimia. However, once again, there is no clear agreement on just *what* is inherited. Hsu (1990) speculates that nonspecific personality traits such as emotional instability and, perhaps, poor impulse control might be what is inherited. In other words, one might inherit a tendency to be "emotionally" responsive to stressful life events that might have as one consequence impulsive eating as an attempt to relieve stress and anxiety. This might be a biological vulnerability that then would interact with social and psychological factors to produce an eating disorder. As such, this biological vulnerability might be similar to that for anxiety disorders described in Chapter 5.

Neurobiological Factors

A substantial body of evidence points to the hypothalamus as playing an important role in regulating our eating and weight. Therefore, it is quite reasonable that investigators would look to the hypothalamus to determine whether something is dysfunctional when eating disorders occur.

Generally, the hypothalamus hosts a number of crosscurrents of the major neurotransmitter systems. Early research centered on noradrenergic action in the hypothalamus (for example, Liebowitz, 1983). Indeed, there is some evidence that norepinephrine may affect eating behavior in various ways. For example, norepinephrine seems to decrease eating if present in some sites of the hypothalamus but increase eating if present in other sites (Schlundt & Johnson, 1990). However, changes in norepinephrine levels may be a *result* of the eating disorder rather than a cause. Similarly, there is some evidence that increased levels of dopamine in the hypothalamus decrease eating (Hsu, 1990), but as yet there is little or no evidence that dopamine is related in any way to eating disorders (Fava, Copeland, Schweiger, & Herzog, 1989).

Somewhat more evidence exists for the role of serotonin in eating disorders. A characteristic of some individuals with eating disorders is "carbohydrate craving." Carbohydrate craving seems to be one possible consequence of low levels of brain serotonin (Wurtman, 1984). Conversely, eating large quantities of carbohydrates (that is, starchy foods) seems to increase brain serotonin and may, via this mechanism, improve mood. Thus, it is possible that individuals with eating disorders evolve into a vicious cycle of cyclical mood states as a function of alternate food restriction and binges, particularly if these binges involve carbohydrates. However, other evidence exists that does not support the "serotonin hypothesis." For example, when the eating behavior of bulimics has been carefully observed, patients do not seem to binge preferentially on carbohydrates that would raise brain serotonin levels. Rather, they binge on a variety of foods. Furthermore, as we shall see, drugs that specifically raise brain serotonin levels do not seem to be any more effective than other types of drugs in the treatment of eating disorders.

Finally, endogenous opioid peptides (EOPs) also seem related to food intake. *Endogenous* means that these opioids reside naturally in our bodies (Reid, 1985; Liebowitz, 1985). Specifically, EOPs are released in response to starvation and may possibly be one of the body's ways of motivating us to eat. EOPs seem particularly involved in preference for sweet-tasting foods and seem to play an important role in contributing to the pleasure of eating in general. The opiate systems also help to decrease pain. Some researchers have speculated (for instance, Liebowitz, 1985; Marrazzi & Luby, 1986) that individuals with eating disorders become "addicted" to the release of these opiates in their bodies during dietary restriction and, thus, they maintain their cycles of starvation, alternating with binging, since these cycles continually stimulate the production of the opiates. However, as Wilson (1991) points out, there is very little evidence for an addiction model of bulimia nervosa.

If investigators do determine a strong association between certain neurobiological functions in the brain and eating disorders, the question of cause or effect still remains. At present, the consensus is that some neurobiological and endocrinological abnormalities do exist in eating disorders but they are a *result* of semistarvation or a binge/purge cycle, rather than a cause.

Psychological Dimensions

Clinical observations indicate that many young women with eating disorders evidence a marked lack of self-esteem or a diminished sense of personal control and confidence in their own abilities and talents (Bruch, 1973, 1985). In one recent study Striegal-Moore, Silberstein, and Rodin (1993) compared 222 women without eating disorders to 34 women with bulimia and to another 33 women who were not bulimic but were at risk for the disorder because they displayed many of the same attitudes toward eating and body shape as evidenced by the bulimic women. All groups were administered a series of questionnaires concerned with social anxiety and perception of self. Results indicated that women with eating disorders were intensely preoccupied with how they appeared to others. They also perceived themselves as frauds in that they considered false any impressions they gave of being adequate, self-sufficient, or worthwhile. In this sense they felt like imposters in their social groups. These women also experienced heightened levels of social anxiety. Striegal-Moore et al. (1993) suggest that these social self-deficits are likely to increase as a consequence of having an eating disorder, further isolating the woman from her social world.

Specific distortions in perception of body shape also seem to change frequently depending on day-to-day experience. McKenzie, Williamson, and Cubic (1993) compared 18 women with bulimia to 18 women without eating disorders. Consistent with previous studies the bulimic women judged their body size to be larger than same-sized controls and their ideal weight to be less than the controls'. All subjects then ate a candy bar and soft drink designed to arouse concerns about eating. After the snack, women with bulimia judged that their body size had increased whereas judgments of body size in normals were unaffected by the snack. Thus, rather minor events related to eating

Harold Leitenberg has studied the nature and treatment of purging among bulimics.

Judith Rodin and her colleagues have made important discoveries on the social influences on individuals with eating disorders.

may activate fear of gaining weight, further distortions in body image, and corrective schemes such as purging.

Other researchers have emphasized the dramatic increases in anxiety among individuals with bulimia that becomes focused on eating. Rosen and Leitenberg (1985) observed substantial anxiety before and during snacks among individuals with bulimia and theorized that purging *relieves* the built-up anxiety. They suggested that this state of relief strongly reinforces the purging, since we tend to repeat behavior that gives us relief from anxiety or pleasure. This result seemed to be true for Phoebe and, as noted earlier, anxiety focused on weight gain is a defining feature of anorexia and bulimia. However, other evidence suggests that in the treatment of bulimia, while reducing the anxiety associated with eating is important, it is less important than countering the person's tendencies to overly restrict her food intake and her associated negative attitudes about body image that lead to binging and purging (for example, Agras, Schneider, Arnow, Raeburn, & Telch, 1989; Fairburn et al., 1992). These findings, however, may not contradict a role for anxiety in the development and maintenance of bulimia.

An Integrative Model of Eating Disorders

Putting together what we know about eating disorders, it is important to remember, once again, that no one factor seems sufficient to cause these disorders (see Figure 8.6). Based on the few studies that have been carried out, particularly the twin study by Kendler et al. (1991), it does seem that a tendency, or at least a vulnerability, to develop eating disorders is inherited. But just

what is inherited is not clear. As noted previously, this vulnerability may be a very generalized trait such as emotional instability or responsiveness to stress associated with impulsive eating, which may, in fact, be similar or identical to the biological vulnerability that appears to be important among people who develop anxiety or mood disorders. Other reasons to think that individuals with eating disorders might share some of the same biological vulnerabilities (such as being highly responsive to stressful life events) found in individuals with anxiety disorders include the high rates of anxiety disorders in individuals with eating disorders. Anxiety disorders are also found at a high frequency in the families of individuals with eating disorders (Pope & Hudson, 1984; Schwalberg et al., 1992). These findings indicate that anxiety and eating disorders are closely associated. In addition, as we will see, drug and psychosocial treatments with proven effectiveness for anxiety disorders are also the treatments of choice for eating disorders. Indeed, one could conceptualize eating disorders as anxiety disorders with excessive anxiety focused exclusively on becoming overweight, as suggested in the definition of these disorders.

In any case, it seems clear that social and cultural pressures to be thin provide the trigger that motivates a marked and significant restriction of eating, usually through severe dieting. Remember, however, that many people go on strict diets, including many adolescent females, but only a small minority develop eating disorders, so severe dieting alone does not account for the disorder. It also seems important to note that something about the family interactions occurring in high-income, high-achieving families may well contribute to this disorder. The emphasis on looking your

Inherited vulnerability

BIOLOGICAL
Unstable or excessive neurobiological
response to stress associated with impulsive eating

PSYCHOLOGICAL
Anxiety focused on appearance
and presentation to others
Distorted body image

SOCIAL
Cultural pressures to be thin
Family interactions/pressures
re: social presentation

**Restriction
of eating**

ANOREXIA

Binge   or   Continued
restriction

Purge

Reduced anxiety

Excessive weight loss

BULIMIA

Binge eating

Purge

Reduced anxiety

Retain weight

Figure 8.6 An integrative causal model of eating disorders

best and on high achievement in everything you attempt, as well as other aspects of social presentation, may well set the stage for the very strong attitudes that develop in young women with eating disorders concerning the overriding contribution of physical appearance to their overall popularity and success. Finally, there is the question of why a small minority of individuals with eating disorders seem able to control their intake successfully, resulting in substantial weight loss (anorexic restricters), while the majority are unsuccessful and compensate by entering a cycle of binging and purging. These different end points in eating disorders may be determined by biology or physiology, such as a genetically determined disposition to be somewhat thinner to begin with. On the other hand, perhaps preexisting personality characteristics, such as

Many young women today assume that physical appearance is the key factor in their popularity and success.

a tendency to be overcontrolling, are important determinants of whether one develops anorexia versus bulimia.

In view of the recency of the epidemic of eating disorders, particularly bulimia, investigators are only beginning to examine carefully the role of the biological, psychological, and social dimensions of these disorders to determine who is truly at risk for developing these severe and health-threatening conditions. Ultimately, increases in knowledge will help us prevent their occurrence. In the meantime, other groups of investigators have been working hard at developing treatments for these disorders.

Treatment of Eating Disorders

Only in the decade of the 1980s have treatments been developed for bulimia. Treatments of one form or another for anorexia have been around much longer but were not well developed. Based on rapidly accumulating evidence, it now seems that we have at least one, possibly two, effective psychosocial treatments for these eating disorders, particularly bulimia nervosa. Certain drugs may also be effective for bulimia although the evidence is not so strong.

Drug Treatments

The drugs generally considered the most effective for bulimia are the same antidepressant medications proven effective for mood disorders and anxiety disorders (Wilson, 1993; Fairburn, Agras, & Wilson, 1992; Craighead & Agras, 1991).

Effectiveness of treatment for bulimia nervosa is usually measured by reductions in the frequency of binge eating as well as the number of patients (usually expressed as a percentage) who stop binge eating and purging altogether, at least for a period of time. Assuming these patients did not relapse at a later point in time, they would be considered cured.

In a large, well-controlled study assessing the effects of tricyclic antidepressant drugs, Walsh, Hadigan, Devlin, Gladis, and Roose (1991) determined that the average *reduction* in binge eating and purging was 47% in a group of 80 patients, with a "remission" rate (complete cessation of binging and purging) of 12%. Earlier studies with fewer subjects found somewhat better results with tricyclics (Craighead & Agras, 1991; Pope, Hudson, Jonas, & Yurgelun-Todd, 1983; Barlow, Blouin, Blouin, & Perez, 1988). In another well-conducted study evaluating 382 patients on a different antidepressive drug (fluoxetine, or Prozac) that acts more specifically on the serotonergic neurotransmitter system (described in Chapter 2), the average decline in

Tim Walsh has made significant scientific contributions regarding the nature and treatment of eating disorders.

frequency of binge eating for the group on the highest dosage of the drug was 65%, with 27% of the patients in remission at the end of treatment (Walsh, 1991). These findings are similar to results recently reported from a large but short-term study also using Prozac (Fluoxetine Bulimia Nervosa Collaborative Study Group, 1992).

Walsh and his colleagues (1991) also looked at the long-term maintenance of treatment with tricyclic antidepressants. Patients in their study who had reduced their binge eating by at least 50% were continued on the drug. However, only 41% (29 of 71) met the criteria of reducing their binge eating by 50%. Of these 29, 8 declined to continue with treatment. Of the remaining 21 patients, only 11 completed a 16-week maintenance period during which they continued to take the drug. The others dropped out or discontinued, mostly because of side effects of the drug, such as agitation. Although more effective than placebo in the short term, the available evidence suggests that, pending further evaluation, antidepressant drugs do not have substantial long-lasting effects on bulimia nervosa.

At present, drug treatments have not been found to be effective in the treatment of anorexia nervosa (for example, Halmi, Eckert, LaDu, & Cohen, 1986; Agras, 1987).

Psychosocial Treatments

Psychosocial treatments, until recently, were directed at underlying feelings of low self-esteem and difficulties in developing one's own individual identity. Disordered patterns of family interaction and communication were also targeted for treatment. However, these treatments alone have not had the effectiveness that clinicians

Christopher Fairburn developed an effective psychosocial treatment for bulimia nervosa.

Stewart Agras has made many important contributions to our understanding of eating disorders.

hoped they might (for instance, Minuchin et al., 1978; Russell, Szmukler, Dare, & Eisler, 1987). In more recent years, short-term cognitive-behavioral treatments have been developed that target problem eating behavior—including binge eating and purging (or restricting)—and associated attitudes about the overriding importance and significance of body weight and shape.

Bulimia Nervosa

In this cognitive-behavioral treatment approach, pioneered by Christopher Fairburn (1985), the first stage is providing the patient a thorough education regarding the physical consequences of binge eating and purging as well as the ineffectiveness of vomiting and laxative abuse as a means of weight control. The adverse effects of dieting are also described and a plan is developed to facilitate a pattern of regular eating behavior. Specifically, patients are scheduled to eat small, manageable amounts of food five or six times per day with no more than a 3-hour interval between any planned meals and snacks. Usually patients are cooperative in attempting this strategy, although on occasion the support of parents or friends is sought to facilitate their compliance. Introducing this eating pattern eliminates the alternating periods of overeating and dietary restriction that are hallmarks of the disorder. Later stages of treatment focus on altering dysfunctional thoughts and attitudes regarding body shape, weight, and eating by the use of cognitive therapy. Coping strategies for resisting binge eating and purging are also developed, including arranging activities so that the individual will not spend time alone after eating during the early stages of treatment (Wilson & Pike, in press; Fairburn, Marcus, & Wilson, in press).

This approach has been evaluated in a number of studies. Craighead and Agras (1991) summarized 10

studies using this general approach and report a mean reduction in purging of 79%, with 57% of the patients having eliminated binging and purging altogether (Mitchell et al., 1990; Fairburn et al., 1991; Agras et al., 1992). Thackwray, Smith, Bodfish, and Meyers (1993) also found cognitive-behavioral therapy significantly better than a credible comparison treatment.

Furthermore, these results seem to last. In one of the most carefully conducted studies to date, Fairburn, Jones, Peveler, Hope, and O'Connor (1993) evaluated three different treatments: cognitive-behavioral therapy (CBT); behavior therapy alone (BT), which consisted of only the part of CBT concerned with changing eating habits without any attention to attitudes about weight and shape; and interpersonal psychotherapy (IPT) (described in Chapter 7). For patients receiving CBT, both binge eating and purging declined by over 90% at a 1-year follow-up. In addition, 36% of the patients had ceased all binge eating and purging, with the others continuing to have occasional episodes 1 year following treatment. Patients' attitudes toward their body shape and weight also improved. These results were significantly better than the results from BT. Even more interesting was the finding that IPT did as well as CBT at the 1-year follow-up, although CBT was more effective than IPT (and BT) at the assessment that occurred immediately after treatment was completed. This result indicates that IPT "caught up" with CBT in terms of effectiveness by the end of the 1-year follow-up. This is particularly interesting since IPT does not concentrate directly on disordered eating patterns or dysfunctional attitudes about eating but rather on improving interpersonal functioning, a focus that may, in turn, promote changes in eating habits and attitudes. Both treatments were more effective than BT. These results are presented in Figure 8.7. A more recent study

Figure 8.7 Effectiveness of treatments for bulimia: Proportions of patients (N = 75) receiving cognitive-behavior therapy (CBT), behavior therapy (BT), or interpersonal psychotherapy (IPT) who no longer purged or had bulimic episodes (objective or subjective) (from Fairburn et al., 1993)

by Wilfley et al. (1993) also found that IPT and CBT were equally effective. Clearly, we need to understand much more about how to make these treatments more effective and to determine precisely why they are effective before we can begin to deal successfully with the growing number of eating disorders we are now facing.

During her sophomore year in college, Phoebe contacted one of the authors and entered the short-term therapeutic program outlined above. She made good progress during the first several months and worked carefully on eating regularly and gaining control over her eating. She also made sure that she was with somebody during her high-risk times and planned alternative activities that would reduce her temptation to purge if she felt she had eaten too much at a restaurant or drunk too much beer at a party. During the first 2 months she had three slips; Phoebe and her therapist would discuss what led to her temporary relapse at the next session. Much to Phoebe's surprise, she did not gain any weight on this program even though she did not increase her exercise because of a lack of time. Nevertheless, she found that she still was preoccupied with food, was concerned about her weight and appearance, and had strong urges to vomit if she thought she had overeaten the slightest amount.

During the 9 months following treatment she reported that her urges seemed to decrease somewhat although she had one major slip after eating a big pizza and drinking a lot of beer. She reported that she became thoroughly disgusted with herself and was quite careful to return to her program for several days following this episode. Two years after finishing treatment, Phoebe was interviewed and reported that all thoughts and urges to vomit had disappeared, a report confirmed by her parents. All that remained of her problem were some very bad but increasingly vague and distant memories.

Existing short-term treatments for eating disorders, while clearly effective, are no panacea. As noted above, only 36% of the patients had ceased all binge eating and purging at a 1-year follow-up in the Fairburn et al. study. Many of them may have been like Phoebe, who had only an occasional episode and will go on to complete remission in the future. Others may relapse.

Table 8.3 Strategies to Attain Weight Gain

1. Weight restoration occurs in conjunction with other treatments, such as individual and family therapy, so that the patient does not feel that eating and weight gain are the only goals of treatment.

2. The patient trusts the treatment team and believes that she will not be allowed to become overweight.

3. The patient's fear of loss of control is contained; this may be accomplished by having her eat frequent, smaller meals (e.g., four to six times per day, with 400 to 500 calories per meal) so as to produce a gradual but steady weight gain (e.g., an average of 0.2 kg/day).

4. A member of the nursing staff is present during mealtimes to encourage the patient to eat and to discuss her fears and anxiety about eating and weight gain.

5. Gradual weight gain rather than the amount of food eaten is regularly monitored, and the result is made known to the patient; thus the patient should be weighed at regular intervals, and she should know whether she has gained or lost weight.

6. Some negative and positive reinforcements exist, such as the use of graduated level of activity and bedrest, whether or not these reinforcements are formally conceptualized as behavior modification techniques, so that the patient may thereby learn that she can control not only her behavior but also the consequence of her behavior.

7. The patient's self-defeating behavior, such as surreptitious vomiting or purging, is confronted and controlled.

8. The dysfunctional conflict between the patient and the family about eating and food is not reenacted in the hospital; or if the pattern is to be reenacted in a therapeutic lunch session, the purpose is clearly defined.

Source: Hsu, 1990.

"Basically . . . I don't want to eat because it seems like, as soon as I eat, I just gain weight, get fat . . . There are some times when I can't stop it, I just have to, and then, once I eat, there is a strong urge to either purge or take a strong laxative . . . It never stops . . . It becomes very obsessive, where you're getting on the scales ten times a day . . . I weigh 96 pounds now . . ."

More important, some people do not benefit at all from short-term cognitive-behavioral treatments. There is evidence that combining drugs with psychosocial treatments might "boost" the overall outcome at least in the short term (Agras et al., 1992). Also, studies show that some of these people might benefit from more interpersonal psychotherapeutic methods (Fairburn et al., 1993; Klerman, Weissman, Rounsaville, & Chevron, 1984).

Results from a recent survey by Fairburn, however, are discouraging. Fairburn and his colleagues identified a large number of individuals with bulimia through surveying general practitioners in England (Fairburn, Beglin, & Davies, 1992). Despite the existence of a National Health Service in England where treatment is free, only 12% of individuals identified with bulimia were receiving any treatment at all, let alone a treatment with proven effectiveness. Since the more severe forms of bulimia do not improve without treatment and tend to run a long-term chronic course, these results are very discouraging indeed.

Smith, Marcus, and Kaye (1992) have adapted cognitive-behavioral treatments for bulimia to obese binge eaters, and the preliminary results look very promising. In their study the frequency of binge eating was reduced by an average of 81%, with 50% of the subjects totally abstinent from binging by the end of treatment. This is a particularly important finding, if replicated, since obese individuals who binge typically fail to adhere to less rigorous diets and other weight-loss procedures (Marcus, Wing, & Hopkins, 1988; Telch, Agras, & Rossiter, 1988; Marcus et al., 1990). However, patients' weight neither decreased nor increased in these studies.

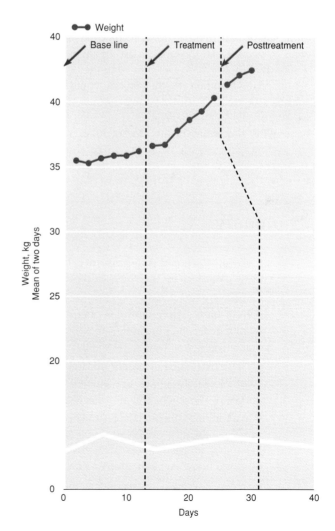

Figure 8.8 Julie's weight gain during hospital stay (from Agras et al., 1974)

Anorexia Nervosa

In anorexia, of course, the most important initial goal is the restoration of the patient's weight to a point that is at least within the low-normal range (American Psychiatric Association, 1993). Some guidelines exist for this initial phase of treating anorexia. For example, if body weight has fallen below 70% of the average, or if weight has been lost very rapidly, inpatient treatment to restore weight would be recommended (American Psychiatric Association, 1993; Casper, 1982). The reason for this is that the person could experience severe medical complications, particularly acute cardiac failure, if weight restoration is not begun immediately. If the patient's weight loss has been more gradual and seems to have stabilized, weight restoration can be accomplished on an outpatient basis.

Restoring weight in anorexia is probably the easiest part of treatment. The experience of clinicians treating these patients in different contexts, as reported in a variety of studies, is that at least 85% of the patients will be able to gain weight in these settings. The weight gain is often as much as a half-pound to a pound a day until weight is within the normal range. Typical strategies to accomplish this goal in an inpatient unit are outlined in Table 8.3. In fact, knowing they can leave the hospital when their weight gain is adequate is often sufficient to motivate these young women to put on weight initially (Agras, Barlow, Chapin, Abel, & Leitenberg, 1974). Returning to the case of Julie, a chart of her weight gain, which occurred while she was in

the hospital for a period of 6 weeks, is shown in Figure 8.8.

Then the difficult part comes. As Hsu (1988) and others have demonstrated, gaining weight is a poor predictor of long-term outcome in anorexia. Without attention to the patient's dysfunctional attitudes about body shape, she will almost always relapse. For restricting anorexics, the focus of treatment must shift to their marked anxiety over becoming obese and losing control of eating as well as their undue emphasis on thinness as a determinant of self-worth, happiness, and success. In this regard, effective treatments for restricting anorexics are similar to those for patients with bulimia nervosa *without* the addition of procedures directed at eliminating the binge/purge cycle so central to bulimia nervosa.

In addition, every effort is made to include the family in the treatment of anorexia to accomplish two goals. First, all the negative and dysfunctional communication surrounding food and eating needs to be eliminated and meals made more structured and reinforcing. Second, attitudes toward body shape and body image distortion are discussed at some length in family sessions so that the results of attempts through cognitive therapy to change underlying attitudes toward eating can be reinforced. Unless the therapist attends to these attitudes, individuals with anorexia are likely to face a lifetime battle of preoccupation with weight and body shape, struggling to maintain marginal weight and social adjustment, and subject to repeated hospitalization.

Summary

- The prevalence of eating disorders has increased rapidly over the last half of this century. As a result, these disorders are included for the first time as a separate group of disorders in DSM-IV.

- There are two major eating disorders. The first is bulimia nervosa, in which dieting results in out-of-control binge-eating episodes often followed by attempts to "purge" (get rid of) the food through vomiting or other means. The second is anorexia nervosa, in which food intake is cut down dramatically, resulting in substantial weight loss and sometimes dangerously low body weight.

- These two eating disorders are largely confined to young, middle- to upper-class women in Western cultures who are pursuing a culturally mandated thin body shape that is biologically inappropriate, making it extremely difficult to achieve.

- In addition to the pursuit of a thin body shape, a sociocultural dimension, other causal factors include possible biological and genetic vulnerabilities, as suggested by the fact that this disorder tends to run in families, and psychological factors of low self-esteem, social anxiety including fears of rejection, and distorted body image in which relatively normal-weight individuals view themselves as fat and ugly.

- Several psychosocial treatments, including cognitive-behavioral approaches combined with family therapy and interpersonal psychotherapy, are effective in alleviating eating disorders. Drug treatments seem less effective at the current time. Without treatment, these eating disorders run a chronic course and can, on occasion, result in death.

Key Terms

anorexia nervosa (299)

binge (299)

binge-eating disorder (BED) (307)

bulimia nervosa (299)

pica (309)

purging techniques (304)

rumination disorder (308)

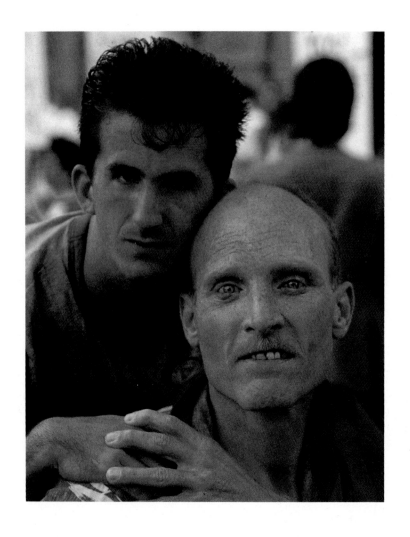

*Chillingworth scrutinized his patient carefully . . . He deemed it
essential . . . to know the man before attempting to do him good.
Wherever there is a heart and an intellect, the diseases
of the physical frame are tinged with the peculiarities of these.
In Arthur Dimmesdale, thought and imagination were so active,
and sensibility so intense that the bodily infirmity would be likely
to have its groundwork there. . . . Few secrets can escape
an investigator, who has the opportunity and license
to undertake such a quest, and skill to follow it up.
A man burdened with a secret should especially avoid
the intimacy of his physician.*
Nathaniel Hawthorne
The Scarlet Letter

9

Physical Disorders and Health Psychology

In 1979 the U.S. Surgeon General pointed out that "at the beginning of this century, the leading causes of death were influenza, pneumonia, diphtheria, tuberculosis, and gastrointestinal infections. Since then, the yearly death rate from these diseases per one hundred thousand people has been reduced from 580 to 30!" a decrease of nearly 95% (U.S. Surgeon General, 1979). This reduction represents a revolution in public health that has been due in large part to the elimination of many infectious diseases. But the enormous success of our health care system in reducing mortality from disease has unveiled another more complex and difficult problem. At present, some of the major *contributing factors* to illness and death in this country are *psychological and behavioral*. Consider one example: the relationship between genital herpes and stress.

There's a chance that one of your friends has *genital herpes*. It is also probable that this friend hasn't told you about it. It's not difficult to understand why. Genital herpes is caused by the Herpes Simplex Virus II. It is an incurable sexually transmitted disease. Recent estimates indicate that 30 million or more Americans—between 10% and 15% of the entire population—have been infected with this virus (Johnson et al., 1989). Since this disease is concentrated in young adults, the percentage in that group would be much higher.

The virus remains dormant but is reactivated periodically. Most times when it recurs, the infected individuals may experience a number of symptoms including pain, itching, vaginal or urethral discharge, and most commonly, ulcerative lesions (open sores) in the genital area. Lesions recur on the average approximately 4 times each year but the recurrences can be much more frequent. Reasons for recurrence are not entirely clear, but there is increasing evidence that stress plays a role (for example, Juels-Jensen, 1973; Glaser, Kiecolt-Glaser, Speicher, & Holliday, 1985; Stout & Bloom, 1986) and that the relationship between stress and genital herpes is mediated by the suppressive effects of stress on the immune system (Kemeny, Cohen, Zegans, & Conant, 1989).

Now there is evidence that stress-control procedures, and particularly relaxation, may decrease the frequency of occurrence of genital herpes as well as the duration of each episode. Burnette, Koehn, Kenyon-Jump, Hutton, and Stark (1991) treated 8 people with genital herpes (7 women and 1 man) using a single-case, multiple baseline, across-subjects design (see Chapter 4). In this design, treatment is introduced at a different time for each subject. If changes in the disorder do not occur *until* treatment is introduced, we can have some confidence that the change is being caused by the treatment and not some other factor, such as attention from the therapist. Data from 5 individuals who evidenced some response to treatment are presented in Figure 9.1. These data reflect the number of days per week that each person would have

a recurrence of genital herpes. On the horizontal line is the average number of recurrences during each phase (before and after treatment). Note the response of Subject #7. During some weeks she would have out-

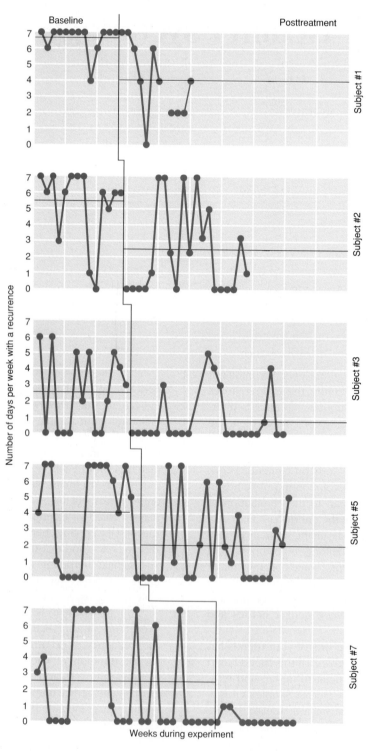

Figure 9.1 Measures of genital herpes outbreaks. The graphs show before- and after-treatment measures of genital herpes outbreaks for 5 subjects who received stress reduction treatment. The horizontal broken lines—representing the average number of outbreaks during baseline and posttreatment periods—show that these subjects experienced a significant decrease in outbreaks after treatment (adapted from Burnette et al., 1991).

breaks almost every day, but after stress reduction treatment her outbreaks were almost eliminated. Subjects 1 and 2 each had multiple lesions (open sores) in 6 and 4 different sites, respectively. After treatment both subjects had only 2 active lesion sites and lesions were occurring significantly less frequently in these specific sites, although it is important to note that they were still recurring.

Three additional subjects in this study did not respond in a clinically significant way. At least 1 reported not practicing relaxation, which might have accounted for the lack of progress; the other two, evidently, just did not benefit. While these data are only preliminary, the findings strongly suggest a relationship between psychological factors and viral infections.

In Chapter 2 we detailed the profound effects of psychological and social factors on brain structure and function. Psychological and social factors seem to influence neurotransmitter activity, the secretion of neuromodulators in the endocrine system, and, at a more fundamental level, gene expression. In other chapters in this book we have looked more specifically at the complex interplay of biological, psychological, and social factors in the production and maintenance of psychological disorders. With this background it will come as no surprise that psychological and social factors play a major role in the development and maintenance of a number of additional disorders, including endocrinological disorders such as diabetes and disorders of the immune system. The difference about these and other disorders to be discussed in this chapter is that they are clearly *physical disorders*. They have known (or strongly inferred) physical causes and, for the most part, observable physical pathology (for example, genital herpes, damaged heart muscle, malignant tumors, measurable hypertension). Contrast this with the somatoform disorders discussed in Chapter 6 such as conversion disorders where clients *complain* of physical damage or disease (for instance, paralysis) but evidence no physical pathology. In DSM-IV physical disorders such as hypertension and diabetes are coded separately on Axis III. However, there is a provision for recognizing specific psychological factors that may be affecting physical disorders or diseases. This grouping of factors is termed *psychological factors affecting medical condition*.

In previous decades the study of psychological and social factors affecting physical disorders was distinct and somewhat separate from the remainder of psychopathology. Early on it was called *psychosomatic medicine* (Alexander, 1950), which meant that in these physical disorders, *psychological* factors were affecting *somatic* (physical) function. *Psychophysiological disorders* was another label used to communicate a similar idea. These labels are less often used today because they have been misleading. The difficulty is that using

these labels for some disorders—those with a more obvious physical component—but not for others resulted in a tendency of some to think that those other disorders—typically the standard psychological (translate "mental") disorders such as mood and anxiety disorders—did not have a strong biological (somatic or physiological) component. As we now know, this is not a viable assumption. In fact, drawing a firm line between the *causes* of "mental" disorders and "physical" disorders is not at all supported by current evidence. Biological, psychological, and social factors are implicated in the cause and maintenance of each type of disorder.

The contribution of psychosocial factors to the etiology and treatment of physical disorders is being studied in several areas. Some of the discoveries are among the more exciting findings in all of psychology and biology. For example, in Chapter 2 we described briefly the specific and harmful influences of anger on heart function. The tentative conclusion from that research (Ironson et al., 1992) was that when a person is angry, the pumping efficiency of his heart is reduced, putting him at risk for dangerous disturbances of heart rhythms (arrhythmia). We also discussed recent studies by Antoni et al. (1991) demonstrating that reducing stress seems to *increase* immune system functioning in patients carrying the HIV virus who have not yet developed AIDS. Therefore, stress reduction may delay the onset of the disease itself. Remember also the tragic description in Chapter 2 of the physical and mental deterioration and, sometimes, death that occurs in elderly people who are removed from social networks of family and friends (Broadhead, Kaplan, & James, 1983; Grant, Patterson, & Yager, 1988).

The shift from a focus on infectious disease to psychological factors contributing to illness and disease has been called the second revolution in public health. Efforts along these lines are continuing and will be described in this chapter. To consummate this revolution, two closely related fields of study have come into existence. The first has come to be called **behavioral medicine** (Agras, 1982; Meyers, 1991). Very simply, behavioral medicine involves the application of knowledge derived from behavioral science to the prevention, diagnosis, and treatment of medical problems. This is largely an interdisciplinary field where psychologists, physicians, and other health professionals work closely together to investigate the contributions of behavioral science to physical problems and to develop new treatments and preventive strategies for these problems based on psychological knowledge (Schwartz & Weiss, 1978).

A second field of study, is referred to as **health psychology.** Usually considered a subfield of behavioral medicine, health psychology is not interdisciplinary but is rather the study of psychological factors

This boy's mother died of AIDS, and his father suffers from the disease. If the child develops AIDS, psychological and social factors may play an important role in determining the course of the disorder. The boy is being held by a health care worker.

important in the promotion and maintenance of health, including the analysis and improvement of the health care system and health policy formation within the discipline of psychology (Feuerstein et al., 1986; Stone, 1987).

The Relation of Psychological and Social Factors to Physical Health

Psychological and social factors influence health and physical problems in *two* distinct ways. First, these factors might affect a person's basic biological processes that lead to illness and disease. Second, long-standing patterns of behavior or life-styles may put people at risk for the development of certain physical disorders. Sometimes both of these avenues may contribute to the etiology or maintenance of disease.

Consider the manner in which both types of influences are operative in the tragic example of AIDS. We have already mentioned that alleviating psychological stress in AIDS patients might facilitate their immune system functioning, thereby prolonging their lives. Since AIDS is a disease of the immune system and since stress seems to directly affect the functioning of the immune system at a biological level, then, stress may contribute to the deadly progression of AIDS—a conclusion that is pending confirmation from additional studies. This is an example of how psychological factors may directly influence biological processes.

We also know that a variety of things we may choose to *do* (behavior or life-styles) put us at risk for

AIDS. For example, having unprotected sex or sharing "dirty" needles (for those addicted to drugs) may contribute directly to the acquisition of the AIDS virus. There is no medical cure for AIDS at this time. Because of this fact, large-scale behavior modification to *prevent acquisition* of the disease (facilitating safe sex, and so on) is the only weapon currently available to us from a public health point of view in the life and death battle society is waging against AIDS.

Other behavioral patterns and life-styles also contribute to disease. Fully 50% of deaths from the 10 leading causes of death in the United States can be traced to behaviors common to certain life-styles (Centers for Disease Control, 1980; Miller. 1987). A Surgeon General report (U.S. Department of Health and Human Services, 1982) estimates that smoking causes one-third of all cancers. Behavioral patterns subsumed under unhealthy life-styles, in addition to smoking, include poor eating habits, lack of exercise, and behaviors involving injury control (not wearing seat belts, and so on). These behaviors are grouped under the label *life-style* because they are, for the most part, enduring behavioral habits forming an integral part of a person's daily pattern of living (Faden, 1987; Oyama & Andrasik, 1992). We will return to life-styles in the closing pages of this chapter when we look at efforts to modify them and promote health.

In the remainder of this chapter we discuss both avenues in which psychological and social factors affect physical disorders and disease in the context of a number of specific disorders. We address in particular AIDS, rheumatoid arthritis, cancer, cardiovascular disease, chronic pain, chronic headaches, and an interesting new disorder, chronic fatigue syndrome. First, we discuss in some depth how psychological and social factors contribute to physical disorder directly through their effect on basic biological processes, concentrating on some fascinating new work on the nature and consequence of stress on our bodies. We also examine newly developed psychosocial treatments for physical disorders as well as more broad-based treatments for stress and pain reduction. Next, toward the end of the chapter, we describe work on changing behavioral habits and life-styles that put people at risk for disease.

Psychological and Social Factors Affecting Biological Processes in Physical Disorders and Disease

We have much to learn about the specific manner in which psychological factors affect physical disorders and disease. Available evidence suggests that the same

Certain behaviors, such as engaging in unprotected sex or sharing hypodermic needles, put one at risk for acquiring the AIDS virus.

kinds of causal factors active in psychological disorders—that is, social, psychological, and biological—play a role in some physical disorders.

We have already alluded to the important contributions of *social factors* to physical health and well-being. Indeed, the degree of social "connectedness" may literally be a matter of life and death in our elderly population. Social factors also play a major role in some physical disorders, but the function of social support may differ from disorder to disorder. For example, social support seems to help individuals suffering from chronic pain (due to various lower-back,

abdominal, or chest conditions) return to work earlier and rely less on medications (Jamison & Virts, 1990). On the other hand, pain patients involved in highly satisfying marital relationships report *more* pain and display more pain-related behavior, perhaps because there is someone to listen and sympathize (Kerns, Haythornwaite, Southwick, & Giller, 1990). We will return to the interesting subject of chronic pain below. Additionally, too much social support, perhaps better described as *overinvolvement,* may do more harm than good (Coyne, Wortman, & Lehman, 1988). This would happen if the individual giving the support was

Some behavioral habits, such as smoking, drinking excessive amounts of alcohol, failing to exercise, and eating unhealthy foods, are known to contribute to a number of serious health problems.

A sense of helplessness and a passive coping style are thought to contribute negatively to the course of physical disorders.

smothering, overly critical in the manner in which she or he provided the support, or generally pushed too hard for change.

Psychological factors also seem to contribute substantially to physical disorders. In previous chapters we discussed psychological vulnerabilities that, when activated by stressful life events, lead to psychological disorders. In Chapter 2, and subsequent chapters describing specific psychological disorders, we discussed several potential psychological vulnerabilities such as "learned helplessness" (Seligman, 1975), "dysfunctional attitudes" (Beck, 1976; Beck & Young, 1985), or perceptions of control over negative life events (Barlow, 1988). Evidence reviewed in the anxiety and mood disorders chapters suggest that these psychological vulnerabilities may be acquired early in childhood and make individuals more "vulnerable" to the development of psychological disorders during times of stress. It is possible that the same process is ongoing in physical disorders. That is, preexisting positive or negative attitudes may well affect how a person copes with physical disorders and disease; these factors, in turn, may influence the course of the disorder and/or the speed of recovery.

Psychological vulnerabilities may manifest themselves in different coping styles. A leading authority in this area has been Richard Lazarus (for example, Lazarus & Folkman, 1984) who suggests that the way one copes with a physical disorder affects its course and outcome. In addition, some investigators (for instance, Peterson, Seligman, & Vaillant, 1988; Burns & Seligman, 1989) have found that helpless and pessimistic cognitive styles in a person's early adulthood seem to predict poor physical health for him or her in later years. On the other hand, optimistic cognitive styles seem to influence physical health in a positive way. For example, evidence exists that a person's tendency to be optimistic—to have what is termed *dispositional optimism*—leads to his or her more rapid recovery from surgery and better adjustment after surgery (Scheier & Carver, 1987; Scheier et al., 1989). Finally, we have already alluded to the strong relationship between hostile emotions such as anger and cardiovascular disease. But the factor attracting the most attention in terms of contributions to physical disorders and disease is the role of stress, particularly the neurobiological components of the stress response.

The Nature of Stress

In 1936 a young scientist in Montreal named Hans Selye noticed that when he injected one group of rats with a certain chemical extract, they developed ulcers and other physiological problems including atrophy of immune system tissues. But Selye also was studying a control group of rats who were receiving a daily saline (salty water) injection that should not have had any effect. Selye was surprised, to say the least, to discover that his control rats developed *the same* physical problems.

Selye did not ignore this unexpected finding. Rather, he pursued it and discovered that the daily injections themselves seemed to be the culprit rather than the substance being injected. Furthermore, many different types of environmental changes produced these results. Borrowing a term from engineering, he decided that the cause of this nonspecific reaction was **stress.** As so often happens in science, this accidental or "serendipitous" observation was the beginning of a new area of study: *stress physiology* (Selye, 1936).

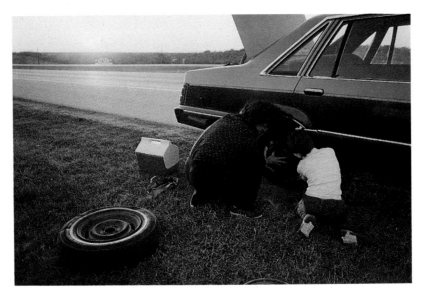

A sense of control and an optimistic coping style are thought to have a positive effect on the course of physical disorders.

Selye theorized that the body went through several stages or phases in response to *sustained* stress. During the first phase he noted a type of *alarm* response described earlier in reaction to immediate danger or threat. With continuing stress he observed that we seem to pass into a stage of *resistance* in which we mobilize various coping mechanisms to respond to the stress. Finally, if the stress is too intense or lasts too long, we may enter a stage of *exhaustion* in which our bodies suffer permanent damage or we may die (Selye, 1936, 1950). Selye referred to this process as the **general adaptation syndrome (GAS).**

The word *stress* has come to mean many things in modern-day life. In engineering, stress could be thought of as the strain that a bridge undergoes if a heavy truck drives on it. In this sense stress is the *response* of the bridge to the truck's weight. But stress is also a *stimulus*. The truck is a "stressor" for the bridge, just as being fired from a job or having to take a difficult final exam is a stimulus or stressor for a person. These varied ways of using the term *stress* make for some confusion, but in this chapter we will concentrate on stress as the physiological response of the individual to a stressor.

The Physiology of Stress

In Chapter 2 we described the basis of many of the physiological effects of the earlier stages of stress, noting in particular the activating effect of stress on the sympathetic nervous system (Baum, Davidson, Singer, & Street, 1987). You will remember that this part of the nervous system mobilizes our resources during times of threat or danger by activating internal organs such as the heart and blood vessels to prepare the body for immediate action such as fight or flight. These changes

increase our strength and mental activity (Munck, Guyre, & Holbrook, 1984; De Kloet, Rosenfeld, Van Eekelen, Sutanto, & Levine, 1988).

We also noted in Chapter 2 that the activity of the endocrine system increases when we are stressed, primarily through activation of the HYPAC axis. Although a variety of neurotransmitters (such as norepinephrine) begin flowing in the nervous system when we are stressed, much attention has also been focused on the endocrine system's **neuromodulators,** or **neuropeptides,** hormones secreted by the glands directly into the bloodstream (Krishnan, Doraiswamy, Venkataraman, Reed, & Richie, 1991). In many ways these neuromodulating hormones act very much like neurotransmitters in that they carry the brain's messages to various parts of the body. In Chapter 7 on mood

In 1936 Hans Selye suggested that stress contributes to the development of certain physical problems.

The human experience of stress can be compared to that of a bridge bearing the heavy weight of a truck.

disorders we discussed some exciting new research on one of these neuromodulators called the *corticotropin releasing factor (CRF)*. CRF is secreted by the hypothalamus and stimulates the pituitary gland. Farther down the chain of the HYPAC axis, the pituitary gland (along with the autonomic nervous system) activates the adrenal gland which secretes, among other things, **corticosteroids** such as cortisol (see Chapter 2). Be-

According to Selye, our first reaction to stress is often an alarm response.

cause of their very close relationship to the stress response these corticosteroids, and other related hormones, have become known as the *stress hormones*.

To complete your envisioning of the circuit, remember that the HYPAC axis is closely related to the limbic system of the brain. The hypothalamus, at the very top of the brain stem, in the diencephalon, is located right next to the limbic system, which is sandwiched between the brain stem and the forebrain. Part of the limbic system is the hippocampus, which seems to control much of our system of emotional memories. We will see in this chapter that the hippocampus is also very responsive to corticosteroids. When stimulated by these hormones during HYPAC axis activity the hippocampus helps to *turn off* our body's stress response. This action completes a feedback loop between the limbic system and the various parts of the HYPAC axis.

This feedback loop may be important for a number of reasons. Sapolsky and his colleagues (for instance, Sapolsky & Meaney, 1986) working with primates have shown that increased levels of corticosteroids in response to chronic stress may cause the death of nerve cells in the hippocampus. If hippocampal activity is compromised (due to premature cell death) there is excessive secretion of corticosteroids and, over time, a decreased ability to turn off the stress response. This inability leads to further aging of the hippocampus. These findings indicate that chronic stress, leading to chronic secretion of corticosteroids, may have long-lasting effects on physical function including brain damage. Such cell death may, in turn, lead to deficits in problem-solving abilities among the aged, and ultimately, dementia. This physiological process may also affect our susceptibility to, or recovery from, infectious disease in other pathophysiological systems.

Psychological and Social Contributions to the Stress Response

It is important to note that the physiological (stress) response does not occur in a vacuum. Consistent with the interaction of biological, psychological, and social factors as articulated throughout this book, stress physiology is profoundly influenced by psychological and social factors. This link has been demonstrated in an unexpected area of study by Robert M. Sapolsky who is studying baboons living freely in a national reserve in Kenya, He is studying baboons because their primary sources of stress, like those of humans in modern society, are psychological rather than physical.

As with many species, baboons arrange themselves in a social hierarchy with dominant members at the top and more submissive members at the bottom. And life is tough at the bottom! The lives of subordinate animals are made difficult (Sapolsky calls it "stressful") by continual attack and "bullying" from the dominant animals. Specifically, subordinate animals have less access to food, preferred resting places, and sexual partners.

Particularly interesting are Sapolsky's findings on levels of cortisol in these animals as a function of their social rank in a dominance hierarchy. Remember from our description of the HYPAC axis that the secretion of cortisol from the adrenal glands is the final step in a "cascade" of hormone secretion that begins with the limbic system in the brain during periods of stress. The secretion of cortisol contributes to our

Baboons who are at the bottom of their social hierarchy experience stress because they have less access to food, preferred resting places, and sexual partners.

Baboons who are at the top of the social hierarchy have a sense of predictability and controllability in their lives. This helps them cope with problems as they arise and promotes better physical health.

arousal and mobilization in the short run, but if produced chronically (as when an organism is chronically stressed), it can have damaging effects on physiology, specifically causing damage to the hippocampus. In addition, muscles atrophy, fertility is affected due to declines in levels of testosterone, hypertension develops in the cardiovascular system, and the immune response is impaired. Sapolsky (1990) discovered that dominant males in the baboon hierarchy ordinarily had *lower* resting levels of cortisol than subordinate males. But when some "emergency" occurred, levels of cortisol rose more quickly in the dominant males than in the subordinate males.

Sapolsky and his colleagues searched out the causes of these differences by working backward up the HYPAC axis. They found that the most likely explanation was an excess secretion of corticotropin-releasing factor (CRF) by the hypothalamus in subordinate animals combined with a diminished sensitivity of the pituitary gland (which is stimulated by CRF). Therefore, subordinate animals, unlike dominant animals, are continually secreting the hormone cortisol, probably

because their lives are so stressful. In addition, they have a HYPAC system that is less sensitive to the effects of cortisol, making the system less efficient in "turning off" the stress response.

Sapolsky also discovered that subordinate males have fewer circulating lymphocytes (white blood cells) compared to dominant males, signaling immune system suppression. In addition, subordinate males evidence less circulating HDL (high density lipoprotein) cholesterol which puts them at higher risk for atherosclerosis and coronary heart disease, a subject we will discuss below.

What is it about being "on top" or dominant that leads to these positive effects? Sapolsky concluded that it is primarily the psychological benefits of having a sense of *predictability and controllability* that comes from being at the top of a dominant social hierarchy. Parts of the data that support his conclusion are based on his observations of the baboons during years in which a number of males were sitting at the top of the hierarchy with no clear "winner." Although these males dominated the rest of the animals in the group, they were continually attacking and stressing each other. Under these conditions they displayed hormonal profiles more like those seen in subordinate males than in dominant males. Thus, dominance combined with stability led to the optimal stress hormone profiles. But the most important factor in regulating stress physiology seems to be a sense of control (Sapolsky & Ray, 1989). Specifically, those animals who are in control of social situations and are able to cope with any tension that arises can go a long way toward blunting the long-term effects of stress. "Personality characteristics" in baboons that reflect a sense of control are shown in Figure 9.2. Dominant males with these characteristics have lower basal levels of cortisol than dominant males without the characteristics.

The Relationship of Stress, Anxiety, Depression, and Excitement

If you have read the earlier chapters on anxiety, mood, and related psychological disorders, you might conclude, correctly, that stressful life events combined with psychological vulnerabilities such as an inadequate sense of control seem to play a role in both psychological and physical disorders. Is there any relationship between emotional disorders and the physical disorders currently under discussion? The answer seems to be that there is a very strong relationship. In a very important study, George Vaillant (1979) studied over 200 Harvard University sophomore men between 1942 and 1944 who were, at that time, mentally and physically healthy. He followed these men closely for over 30 years. He found that among those who developed psychological disorders such as depression or anxiety disorders, or who were highly stressed

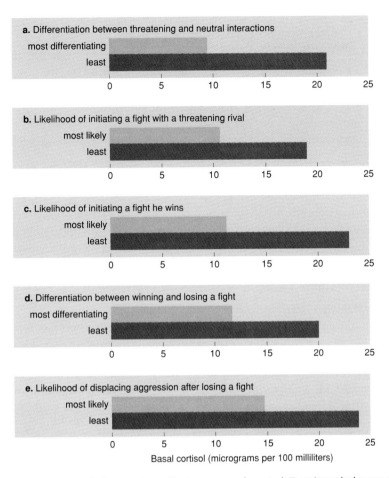

Figure 9.2   Personality characteristics in baboons that reflect a sense of control. Dominant baboons with certain personality traits (orange) have lower base levels of cortisol than do other dominant males (maroon), which suggests that attitude is a more important mediator of physiology than is rank alone. Dominant males who can distinguish between the threatening and neutral actions of a rival have cortisol levels that are about half as high as those of other dominant males (a). Similarly, low cortisol levels are found in males who start a fight with a threatening rival instead of waiting to be attacked (b); who know which fights to pick, and so are likely to win fights they initiate (c); who distinguish between having won and lost a fight (d); or who, when they do lose, take out their frustration on subordinates (e) (from Sapolsky & Ray, 1989).

during their lives, a significantly higher proportion later became chronically ill or died, compared to those men who remained well adjusted and without psychological disorders. This finding suggests that the same types of stress-related psychological factors that contribute to psychological disorders may also contribute to the later development of physical disorders. The study also suggests that the concepts of stress, anxiety, and depression are closely related.

Can you tell the difference between feeling stressed, feeling anxious, feeling depressed, or, perhaps, feeling excited? You might say "No problem," but in fact, these four feeling states have a lot in common. The particular "feeling" that you experience may depend on your sense of control at the moment or how well you think you can cope with the threat or challenge you are facing (Barlow, 1988; Barlow & Rapee, 1991). This continuum of feelings extends from excitement to stress to anxiety to depression as shown in Figure 9.3.

Terry Anderson, one of the political prisoners held in Beirut, may have experienced a variety of emotions from anxiety to depression, depending on his ability to cope.

Figure 9.3   Responses to threats and challenges. Our feelings range along a continuum from depression to anxiety to stress to excitement, depending in part on our sense of control and ability to cope (after Barlow & Rapee, 1991).

Sometimes you might experience more than one of these feelings at the same time, such as excitement and stress or stress and anxiety. But it is unlikely that you will experience feelings at either end of the continuum such as excitement and depression at the same time.

Consider how you feel when you are excited. You might experience a rapid heartbeat, sudden burst of energy, or a jumpy stomach. But if you're really well prepared for the challenge—for example, if you're an athlete, really "up" for the game and confident in your abilities, or a musician, sure you are going to give an outstanding performance—these feelings of excitement can actually be pleasurable.

At other times when you are facing a challenging task, you may feel that you could handle it if you only had the time or help you need, but because you don't have these resources, you may feel pressured. In response, you may work harder in an attempt to do better and be perfect, even though you think you will be all right in the end. If you begin feeling too much pressure, you may become tense and irritable, develop a headache, or get an upset stomach. This would be the *feeling* of being stressed.

On the other hand, if something really threatening is about to happen and you believe there is little you can do about it, your feelings may turn into anxiety. The threatening situation, as mentioned in Chapter 5, could include anything from a physical attack to making a fool of yourself in front of someone. You may be unable to get this upcoming event out of your mind as your body prepares for this challenge and so you worry about it over and over. Your sense of control in this situation is considerably less than if you were stressed. In some cases, there may not be any difficult situation out there at all. Sometimes we are just "anxious" for no good reason (except that we feel certain aspects of our lives are out of control). Finally, individuals who continually perceive life as threatening and dangerous may begin to lose hope about ever controlling these threats and slip into a state of depression. These people seem to give up hope that they will ever be able to change anything and even give up trying to cope.

Therefore, based on our knowledge at the current time, the underlying physiology of these emotional states is relatively similar. For this reason we have made repeated references to the activation of specific neurotransmitters and neuromodulators in chapters on anxiety, depression, and, in this chapter, stress-related physical disorders. But psychological factors, specifically a sense of control or a perception of one's ability to cope with stress or challenges—called **self-efficacy** by Bandura (1986)—seem to differ and thus lead to a different experience of feelings.

Having explored the nature of the stress response from biological, psychological, and social perspectives, we now turn to the effects of psychological and social factors on specific physical disorders. We first examine disorders related to the immune system, after a brief review of how this system works.

The Immune System

Have you had a cold at some point during the past several months? How did you pick it up? Did you spend the day with someone else who had a cold? Did someone sneeze in your face while you were sitting in class? Exposure to cold viruses is a necessary factor in your developing a cold, but the level of stress you are experiencing at the time seems to play a major role in whether exposure to a cold virus results in your developing a cold. Sheldon Cohen and his associates (Cohen, Tyrrell, & Smith, 1991, 1993) exposed volunteer subjects to a specific dosage of a cold virus and followed the subjects very closely to see who got sick. They found that the chance a subject would get sick was directly related to how much stress that person had experienced during the past year. The Cohen study is one of the first well-controlled studies to demonstrate that stress actually *increases* the risk of infection.

Think back to your last exam. Did you (or your roommate) get a cold? One stressor that has been shown to produce increased infections, particularly upper respiratory tract infections, is exam periods (Glaser et al., 1987; Glaser et al., 1990). Therefore, if you are susceptible to colds, one solution would be to

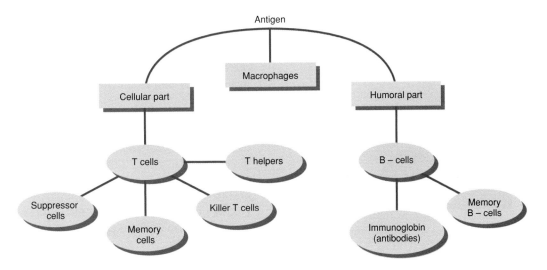

Figure 9.4 An overview of the immune system

skip final exams! A better solution would probably be to learn how to control your stress before and during exams. Almost certainly the effect of stress on susceptibility to infections is mediated through the **immune system,** whose purpose is to protect the body from any foreign materials that may enter it. To understand how this protection occurs, one must understand how the immune system works (see Figure 9.4).

The immune system identifies and eliminates foreign materials (called **antigens**) in the body. These antigens could be any one of a number of substances, most usually bacteria, viruses, or parasites. But the immune system may also target the body's own cells that have become aberrant or damaged in some way, perhaps because they have changed radically as part of a malignant tumor. Since donated organs are foreign, the immune system will also attack these organs after surgical transplant; consequently, in a successful organ transplant program, it is necessary to suppress the immune system temporarily after surgery.

The immune system has two main parts: the *humoral* and the *cellular.* Specific types of cells function as agents of both main parts of our immune system. White blood cells, called *leukocytes,* do most of the work.

There are several different types of leukocytes. *Macrophages* are one type. They might be considered one of the body's first lines of defense; they surround identifiable antigens and destroy them. They also signal helper T Cells (see below) about the presence of antigens in the body. Lymphocytes are another type and consist of two groups, one of which is called *B cells.* B cells operate within the humoral part of the immune system, releasing molecules that circulate in blood and other bodily fluids seeking out antigens with the purpose of neutralizing them. The B cells accomplish this by identifying the antigens and producing highly

specific molecules called immunoglobulins that act as *antibodies.* These antibodies *combine* with the antigens to neutralize them. After the antigens are encountered and neutralized, another subgroup of B cells, called *memory B cells,* are created so that the next time that antigen is encountered, the response of the immune system will be even faster. This action accounts for the success of inoculations you may have received for mumps or measles as a child. An inoculation actually contains small amounts of the organism, but not enough to make you sick. Your immune system then "remembers" this organism and prevents you from coming down with the full disease at a later time.

The second group of lymphocytes, called *T cells,* or *Killer T cells,* operate in the cellular branch of the immune system. These cells don't produce antibodies. Instead one subgroup of T cells targets viral infections and cancerous processes within the cells by directly destroying the antigens (Borysenko, 1987; Roitt, 1988; O'Leary, 1990). As is the case with B cells, after this process is complete, *memory T cells* are created to speed future responses to the same antigen. Other subgroups of T cells help regulate the immune system. For example, the cells in one subgroup (*T4 cells*) are called *helper T cells.* They *enhance* the immune system response by signaling B cells to produce antibodies and telling other T cells to destroy the antigen. Another subgroup of T cells, *Suppressor T cells, suppress* the immune response. For example, these T cells suppress the production of antibodies by B cells when they are no longer needed.

Ordinarily we should have twice as many T4 (helper) cells as Suppressor T cells. With too many T4 cells, however, the immune system is overly reactive and may attack the body's normal tissue rather than antigens. When this happens we have what is called an **autoimmune disease.** One example is rheumatoid

Robert Ader showed, through a conditioning process, that the immune system is responsive to environmental cues.

arthritis (described shortly). With too many Suppressor T cells, the body is subject to invasion by a number of antigens. The human immunodeficiency virus (HIV) directly attacks the T-helper cells, lymphocytes that have a key role in both humoral and cellular immunity, thereby severely weakening the immune system and causing AIDS.

Until the mid 1970s, most scientists believed that the brain and the immune system operated independently of each other. However, in 1974 Robert Ader and his colleagues (Ader & Cohen, 1975, 1993) made a startling discovery. Working with a classical conditioning paradigm, they gave sugar-flavored water to rats together with an injection of a drug that suppresses the immune system. Ader and Cohen then demonstrated that giving the same rats the sweet-tasting water *alone* produced similar changes in the immune system *without* injections of the drug. In other words, the rats had "learned" (through classical conditioning) to respond to the water with a suppression of their immune systems.

We now know that there are many connections between the nervous system and the immune system. For example, nerve endings exist in many of the tissues that are implicated in the immune system such as the thymus, the lymph nodes, and bone marrow. These findings have generated a new field known as **psychoneuroimmunology** or **PNI** (Ader & Cohen, 1993). This long word simply implies that the object of study in this field is *psycho*logical influences on the *neuro*logical responding implicated in our *immune* response.

The Immune System and Physical Disorders

Over 50 years of research dating back to the original reports of Hans Selye (1936) has demonstrated the detrimental effects of stress on immune system func-

tioning (for example, Borysenko & Borysenko, 1982; Levy & Wise, 1987; Zakowski, Hall, & Baum, 1992). It now also seems clear that humans show increased rates of infectious diseases when they are under stress; these include colds, herpes, and mononucleosis (for instance, Vander Plate, Aral, & Magder, 1988). Direct evidence links a number of stressful situations, in addition to stressful exam periods, to lowered immune system functioning. These stressful situations include marital discord or relationship difficulties (Kiecolt-Glaser et al., 1987), job loss (Arnetz et al., 1987), and death of a loved one (Irwin, Daniels, Smith, Bloom, & Weiner, 1987). Furthermore, these stressful events impact the immune system very rapidly. Some studies in laboratories have demonstrated weakened immune system response in a subject within 2 hours of his or her being stressed in some way (Weisse, Pato, McAllister, Littman, & Breier, 1990; Kiecolt-Glaser & Glaser, 1992; Zakowski, McAllister, Deal, & Baum, in press). It is therefore possible that stress leads directly to physical illness, although this last link has not been firmly established.

We have already noted that emotional disorders seem to make us more susceptible to developing physical disorders (Vaillant, 1979). We had assumed this was due to the effect of emotional disorders on the immune system. Now direct evidence exists suggesting that depression lowers immune system functioning (Weisse, 1992; Herbert & Cohen, 1993), particularly in the aged (Schleifer, Keller, Bond, Cohen, & Stein, 1989; Herbert & Cohen, 1993). Carol Silvia Weisse (1992) suggests that the level of depression (and perhaps the underlying sense of uncontrollability that accompanies most depressions) is a more potent factor in lowering immune system functioning than are specific stressful life events, such as job loss. For humans, similar to Sapolsky's baboons, the ability to retain a sense of control over events in our lives may be one of the most

Janet Kiecolt-Glaser has examined the effect of psychosocial interventions designed to bolster the response of the immune system in patients with physical disorders.

This African woman is tending to her husband, who is dying of AIDS. Caring for a sick family member can be chronically stressful.

important psychological factors contributing to whether we stay healthy.

Most studies concerning stress and the immune system have examined a sudden or acute stressor. But *chronic stress* may be more problematic for those who perceive the stress as "uncontrollable" and beyond their coping abilities since the effects are, by definition, longer lasting. In the 1970s, the nuclear power plant at Three Mile Island near Harrisburg, Pennsylvania, exploded. Many residents feared that any exposure to radiation they might have sustained during this episode would lead to cancer or other illnesses at a later time. These residents lived with this fear for years. More than 6 years after the explosion, some individuals who had been in the area during the crisis still had lowered immune system functioning (McKinnon, Weisse, Reynolds, Bowles, & Baum, 1989). A similar finding has been reported for individuals with the responsibility of caring for chronically ill family members, such as Alzheimer patients (Kiecolt-Glaser & Glaser, 1987). In this section we discuss psychosocial contributions to the biology of three diseases strongly related to immune system functioning: AIDS, rheumatoid arthritis, and cancer.

AIDS

The ravages of the AIDS epidemic have made this disease the number one priority of our public health system. In the absence of a cure or more effective prevention, the world can expect 20 million new cases by the year 2000 (Merson, cited in Cohen, 1993).

Once one becomes infected with HIV, the course of the disease is quite variable. After a period that can last from several months to several years with no symptoms, patients may begin developing some minor health problems such as weight loss, fever, and night sweats. These symptoms make up the condition known as **AIDS-related complex (ARC).** A diagnosis of AIDS itself is not made until one of several serious diseases appears, such as pneumonia, cancer, dementia, or a wasting syndrome in which the body literally withers away. The median time from initial infection to the development of full-blown AIDS has been estimated to range from 7.3 to 10 years (Moss & Bacchetti, 1989). After a diagnosis of AIDS has been made, the survival time also varies a great deal. Although the majority of people with AIDS die within 1 year, as many as 15% or more survive 5 years or longer (Rothenberg et al., 1987; Kertzner & Gorman, 1992). Since this is a relatively new disease with a very long latency to development, we are still learning about length of survival as well as the factors, including possible psychological factors, that increase survival. Recently, investigators have identified a group of people who have been exposed repeatedly to the AIDS virus but have not contracted the disease. One major difference in these people is that their immune systems, particularly the cellular branch, seem very robust and strong (Ezzel, 1993). Therefore, any efforts to boost the immune system may contribute to the prevention of AIDS.

Can psychological factors affect the progression of AIDS? In Chapter 2 (p. 60) and above, we mentioned briefly the study by Antoni et al. (1991) demonstrating the seemingly beneficial effect of stress-reduction procedures on immune system functioning in patients who were informed that they had AIDS. Regular exercise is known to have stress-reducing effects, possibly because exercise reduces some of the physical consequences of stress and provides a physical outlet for stress-related tension. An aerobic exercise program thus affords an effective coping procedure and gives individuals an enhanced sense of control. In a study conducted by La Perriere, Antoni, Schneiderman, Ironson, and Klimas (1990), exercise alone enhanced both mood and immune system functioning in patients recently diagnosed with AIDS, compared to patients who did not engage in regular exercise. In more advanced AIDS patients, an exercise program has also been shown to counteract the "wasting" syndrome that is so often a part of the progression of AIDS (Spence, Galantino, Mossberg, & Zimmerman, 1990). Of course, it is too early to tell whether these results will be strong enough or persistent enough to translate into increased survival time for AIDS patients. It is also important to

note that some earlier studies utilizing stress-reduction procedures with AIDS patients found no effect on the immune system (for example, Coates, McKusick, Kuno, & Stites, 1989).

In another preliminary study O'Leary, Temoshok, Jenkins, and Sweet (1989) found that individuals with AIDS who evidenced increased activity in the autonomic nervous system when reliving emotional events, survived longer after being diagnosed with the disease. Indicators of immune functioning were also higher. The authors suggest that autonomic arousal in these individuals might signify that they were coping with the disease more actively, possibly reflecting a greater sense of control over the disease process. However, these results are preliminary and have yet to be replicated.

If stress and related variables do have a clinically significant impact on immune response in AIDS patients, then it is possible that psychosocial interventions designed to bolster immune system responding might increase their survival rates and, in the most optimistic scenario, prevent the slow deterioration of the immune system (Kiecolt-Glaser & Glaser, 1992). These interventions would be particularly important for women and minorities who are often faced with a greater number of stressors in their environment and possess fewer resources with which to cope (Schneiderman et al., 1992).

We are a long way from making such a determination at this time, however. We do not yet know whether psychosocial procedures increase survival; if they do, it would be very difficult to determine whether the effects are mediated in large part by changes in the immune system. Other effects of psychosocial procedures discussed below, including

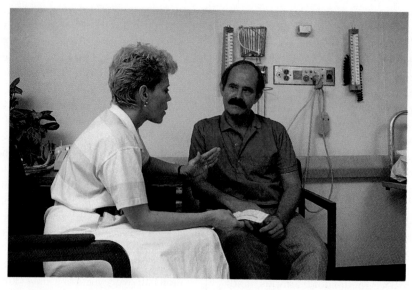

Reducing stress and providing social support may have a positive effect on the course of the AIDS virus.

increased compliance with medical treatments or avoidance of sexually transmitted diseases, may do more to prevent the onset of the disease than psychosocial mediated alterations in the immune system (Kertzner & Gorman, 1992). In addition, if stress-reduction procedures do affect the disease process directly, perhaps through the immune system, it is not clear why these interventions are effective. Among the possible mechanisms, stress-reduction procedures may help instill in the patient a greater sense of control, decrease his or her hopelessness, build active coping responses, change negative cognitions, help him or her use social support networks more effectively, or some combination of all the above. We don't know the answer, but few areas of study in behavioral medicine and health psychology are more urgent.

Rheumatoid Arthritis

Rheumatoid arthritis, a painful degenerative disease that results in stiffness, swelling, and even destruction of the joints, affects from 1% to 4% of the population (Lawrence et al., 1989; O'Leary, 1990). Prevalence is three times greater in women than in men. In this disease the immune system basically attacks itself, possibly because of inadequate functioning of the Suppressor T cell system (T8 cells).

Young (1992) notes that one of the more important preliminary findings is that psychosocial intervention may directly affect the disease process in arthritis. A number of studies have reported results indicating reductions in pain and increased functioning in patients with rheumatoid arthritis after they have received cognitive-behavioral interventions (Bradley et al., 1987; O'Leary, Shoor, Lorig, & Holman, 1988; Appelbaum, Blanchard, Hickling, & Alfonso, 1988; Young, 1992). In the O'Leary study, one group of patients suffering from rheumatoid arthritis received instruction in cognitive-behavioral stress management. A second group received a therapeutic self-help book explaining how to cope better with the disease. The stress-reduction treatment was significantly more successful in reducing patients' pain and disability, and in increasing their joint function (as judged by physicians specializing in rheumatoid arthritis who did not know which treatment the subjects had received). Subjects in the study who improved substantially, in the sense that they could cope with the disease and its consequences, also demonstrated increased numbers of Suppressor T cells, which may be related to improved functioning of the joints.

Cancer

Among the more mind-boggling developments in the study of illness and disease is the discovery that the development and course of different varieties of **cancer** are also subject to psychosocial influences. This

Stress influences the course of rheumatoid arthritis, a degenerative disease that affects the joints.

has resulted in a new field of study called **psychoncology** (Andersen, 1992; Antoni & Goodkin, in press). Oncology refers to the study of cancer. What kinds of effects could psychosocial procedures have on this often fatal disease? David Spiegel, a psychiatrist at Stanford University, and his colleagues (1989) studied 86 women with advanced breast cancer that had already metastasized (spread) to other areas of their bodies and was expected to kill them within 2 years. Clearly, the prognosis was very poor indeed. While Spiegel and his colleagues had little hope of affecting the disease itself, they thought that by treating these people in group psychotherapy at least they could relieve some of the anxiety, depression, and pain that accompanies the process of dying from a fatal disease.

All patients had routine medical care for their cancer. In addition, 50 patients (out of the 86) met with their therapist for psychotherapy once a week in small groups. Therapy consisted of a number of components including discussions among the women of how to cope with cancer and a sharing of their feelings about the illness and its effect on their lives. The therapist also taught the women pain-control strategies, specifically

Breast cancer cell

self-hypnosis, but his major function was to keep the individuals in the group focused on their condition so as to facilitate grieving and other "emotional processing" of their difficult situation. You may remember from Chapter 5 that facing up to and reliving traumatic experiences with the help of a therapist is one of the major treatment modalities for posttraumatic stress disorder. At no time were patients led to believe that participation in the therapy would affect the course of their cancer or the length of their survival. In fact, Spiegel did not believe at the time that psychosocial factors could affect the disease process and thought that this study might *disprove* it!

But survival time for the treatment group was significantly longer when compared to the control group who did not receive group therapy but otherwise

David Spiegel found that psychosocial intervention helped to prolong the lives of women with advanced breast cancer.

benefited from the best care available. In fact, the group receiving therapy lived twice as long on average (approximately 3 years) as did the controls (approximately 18 months). Four years after the study began, one-third of the therapy patients were still alive while all the patients receiving the best medical care available *without* therapy had died. The differences are displayed in Figure 9.5. Of course, these findings do not mean that psychosocial interventions "cured" this advanced cancer. At 10 years, only 3 patients in the therapy group still survived.

Since the groups were very well matched on every other conceivable factor that might have produced differences in survival, what could account for these impressive results? We don't know for sure. Social support may have played a role. The group therapy experience, particularly for individuals suffering from the same disorder or disease, can facilitate a powerful bonding with other members of the group who are sharing your pain and suffering in a way that no one else can really understand. In fact, other studies have shown that cancer patients who are married survive longer than those patients who are not married (Goodwin, Hunt, Key, & Samet, 1987) (although in the Spiegel et al. study, an approximately equal number were married in each group). Involvement in the group may also have facilitated patients' compliance with the medical treatment to a greater degree, or perhaps reduced their depression. More likely, in view of our discussion of the immune system, patients receiving therapy may have developed a better sense of control over their pain and the consequences of the disease in their lives, thereby strengthening their immune systems. It is not possible to determine which of these possibilities, if any, were responsible for the dramatic differences, but ongoing studies are attempting to find out.

Supporting these findings, Fawzy and his colleagues studied 56 cancer patients with malignant melanoma (skin cancer) who, unlike the patients in the Spiegel et al. study, had a reasonably good prognosis at the start of the study. Thirty-eight of these patients received 6 weekly 1½ hour treatment sessions delivered in small groups; here the individuals were taught relaxation techniques, stress-management procedures, and more generally how to cope with illness-related problems. Six months after treatment, immune functioning was higher in the group receiving treatment than in a control group receiving usual and customary medical care (Fawzy, Cousins et al., 1990; Fawzy, Kemeny et al., 1990). More important, at a 5- to 6-year follow-up, control patients tended to have more recurrences of the cancer and were significantly more likely to die. Ten control patients had died compared to only 3 in the treatment group, replicating the findings of Spiegel et al. (1989) (Fawzy et al., 1993).

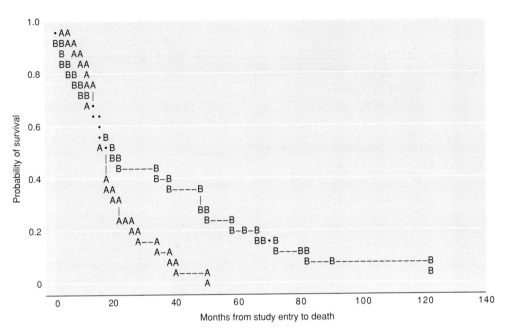

Figure 9.5 Survival time for women with advanced breast cancer. In a study of women being treated for advanced breast cancer, researchers found that women in a treatment group (N = 50) who received psychosocial intervention survived significantly longer than did women who were in a control group (N = 36) with no psychosocial treatment (adapted from Spiegel et al., 1989).

There is even some preliminary evidence that psychological factors may contribute not only to the *course* of cancer but also to the *development* of cancer and other diseases (for example, Stam & Steggles, 1987). Perceptions of a lack of control, inadequate coping responses, overwhelmingly stressful life events, or the use of inappropriate coping responses such as denial may all contribute to the development of cancer (Antoni & Goodkin, in press; Schneiderman et al., 1992). However, most studies on which these conclusions are based involve examining scores of subjects on psychological tests retrospectively and correlating these scores with the onset of cancer in these individuals. Much stronger evidence will be required to demonstrate that psychological factors may contribute to the cause of cancer.

Psychological factors are implicated in other aspects of the progression of cancer and its treatment. In Chapter 2 we mentioned the problem facing all persons undergoing chemotherapy—the negative side effects of nausea and vomiting. These reactions are so powerful that they become "conditioned" or learned so that they occur at times other than treatment. For some patients, the conditioned nausea and vomiting can become associated with a wide variety of stimuli that happen to resemble people or things present during the chemotherapy, such as nurses' uniforms or even the sight of the hospital itself. The problem with this reaction is that it can become so severe that many people will refuse the chemotherapy treatments altogether, thinking the cure worse than the disease. Others

stop eating because of the nausea, or generally just feel miserable. These reactions usually develop gradually, starting after the fourth or fifth treatment and escalate in severity. Somewhere between 18% and 50% of patients experience conditioned nausea (Morrow & Dobkin, 1988). Morrow (1986) reported 23% of 1,480 patients suffered from these reactions. Psychological treatments focusing on relaxation and a gradual exposure to the cues triggering the conditioned nausea reactions can diminish or eliminate the response. This treatment effect facilitates compliance with chemotherapy and generally improves a patient's overall physical and mental health (Redd, Andreason, & Minagawa, 1982; Morrow, 1986; Burish, Carey, Krozely, & Greco, 1987; Carey & Burish, 1988).

Psychological factors are also very prominent in treatment and recovery from cancer in children. To take one example, many different types of cancer require invasive and painful medical procedures; the pain and suffering associated with some of these procedures can be very difficult to bear, not only for the children but also for parents and health care providers. Two of these procedures involve inserting a large needle into the lower body to obtain samples of either bone marrow from the hip bone or cerebral spinal fluid from the spinal column, respectively. Samples are then examined for malignant cells (Hubert, Jay, Saltoun, & Hayes, 1988). In order to complete these procedures children, who usually struggle and cry hysterically, must be physically restrained. Not only does their behavior interfere with successful completion of the procedure, but the stress and anxiety associated with repeated procedures of this type may have their own detrimental effect on the disease process. Psychological procedures designed to reduce pain and stress in these children include breathing exercises, watching films of exactly what is going to happen in order to take the uncertainty out of the procedure, and rehearsal of the procedure with toy dolls, all of which make the interventions much more tolerable and therefore more successful for these young patients (Jay, Elliott, Ozolins, Olson, & Pruitt, 1985; McGrath & DeVeber, 1986; Hubert et al., 1988). Much of this work is based on the pioneering efforts of Barbara Melamed and her colleagues, who demonstrated the importance of incorporating psychological procedures into children's medical care, particularly children about to undergo surgery (for example, Melamed & Siegel, 1975). In any case, pediatric psychologists (psychologists specializing in children's medical care) are making more routine use of these procedures.

Cardiovascular Disease

The *cardiovascular system* comprises the heart, blood vessels, and complex control mechanisms for regulating their function. The purpose of this system generally is to move blood among various tissues and organs in order to keep us alive and to meet the various demands placed on us during emergencies or challenges. In emergencies, the blood carries vital substances such as oxygen and nutrients to areas of the body that may

need a bit of extra energy or correction of a temporary metabolic imbalance. As you will recall, our alarm or fight/flight response, which occurs when we are badly frightened, causes massive redistribution of blood in the system to allow our bodies to respond immediately to the threat, demonstrating that the cardiovascular system is very responsive to psychosocial influences.

Many things can go wrong with the cardiovascular system, leading to **cardiovascular disease.** Many individuals, particularly older individuals, suffer **strokes,** also called *cerebral vascular accidents (CVA),* which are temporary blockages of blood vessels leading to the brain or a rupture of blood vessels in the brain resulting in temporary, or possibly permanent, brain damage and loss of functioning. Some people also lose circulation to peripheral parts of their bodies such as their fingers and toes (a condition referred to as *Raynaud's disease*). Individuals with this particular cardiovascular disease suffer some pain and continual sensations of cold in their hands and feet. However, the two cardiovascular problems receiving the most attention these days are hypertension and coronary heart disease, and we will look at both. First, let's consider a case.

The Case of John

John is a 55-year-old business executive, married with two teenage children. For the majority of his adult life, John has smoked about a pack of cigarettes each day. Although he

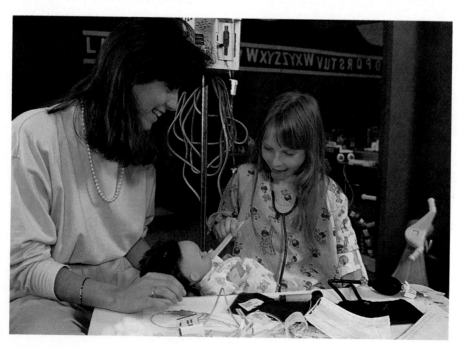

Psychological preparation, such as rehearsing surgical procedures with a doll, reduces suffering and facilitates recovery from surgery in children.

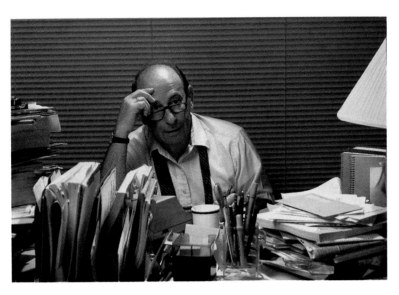

Some behaviors that are part of a stressful life-style can be risk factors for cardiovascular disease.

maintains a busy and active daily schedule, John is mildly obese, partly from eating out with business partners and colleagues on a regular basis. He is currently taking several high-blood pressure medications, and has done so since age 42. John's doctor has warned him over and over again to cut down on his smoking and to exercise more frequently, especially since John's father died of a heart attack. Although John experiences episodes of chest pain, he continues his busy and stressful life-style. It has been difficult for John to slow down as his business has been doing extremely well over the last 10 years.

Moreover, John believes that life is too short, that there is no time to slow down. He spends relatively little time with his family since he works late most evenings. Even when he's at home, John typically works into the night. It is very difficult for him to relax; he feels a constant urgency to get as many things done as possible and prefers to work on several tasks simultaneously. For instance, John will often proofread a document, engage in a phone conversation, and eat lunch all at the same time. He attributes much of the success of his business to his working style. Despite his success, John is not well liked among his peers. His co-workers and employees often find him to be overbearing, easily frustrated and, at times, even hostile. His subordinates, in particular, claim he is overly impatient and critical of their performance.

Do you think John has a problem? Today most people would recognize the collection of behaviors and attitudes descriptive of John's case as not only making his life unpleasant but also as possibly being lethal. It seems that at least some of these behaviors and attitudes operate directly on the cardiovascular system and may result in hypertension and coronary heart disease.

Hypertension

Hypertension, or high blood pressure, is a major risk factor not only for stroke and heart disease but also for kidney disease. This makes hypertension an extremely serious medical condition. Blood pressure increases when the blood vessels leading to organs and other more peripheral areas of the body constrict, forcing more and more blood to muscles located in more central parts of the body. Since so many blood vessels have constricted (become narrower), the heart muscles must work much harder to force the blood to all parts of the body, which causes the increased pressure. These factors produce wear and tear on the ever-shrinking blood vessels, leading to some forms of cardiovascular disease. A small percentage of cases of hypertension can be traced to specific physical abnormalities such as kidney disease or tumors on the adrenal glands (Papillo & Shapiro, 1990); but the overwhelming majority have no specific verifiable physical cause. These cases are referred to as **essential hypertension.**

Blood pressure is considered high (and is defined as such by the World Health Organization) if it exceeds 160 over 95 (Papillo & Shapiro, 1990), although measures of 140/90 or above are borderline and cause for concern. The first value is called the *systolic blood pressure* and refers to pressure during the time when the heart is actually working (by pumping blood). The second value is the *diastolic blood pressure* or pressure between beats when the heart is at rest. The elevations in diastolic pressure seem to be more worrisome in terms of risk of disease.

As many as 18% of adults between the ages of 25 and 74 suffer from essential hypertension (Roberts & Rowland, 1981)—extraordinary numbers when you consider that hypertension, contributing to as many fatal diseases as it does, has been called the "silent killer." These numbers are much higher than for any single psychological disorder. Even more striking is the fact that blacks are approximately *twice* as likely to develop hypertension than whites (Anderson & Jackson, 1987). The rate of hypertension is approximately 18 per 100 for white males ages 25 to 74 compared to approximately 35 per 100 for black males in the same age range. For females, the figures are approximately 15 per 100 for whites compared to 30 per 100 for blacks (Roberts & Rowland, 1981). More important, blacks who have developed hypertension have hypertensive vascular diseases at a rate 5 to 10 times greater than whites. This makes hypertension, in the eyes of some, the principal disorder of concern among our black population. Recently Saab et al. (1992) has demonstrated that during laboratory stress tests, blacks *without* high blood pressure show greater vascular responsiveness, including heightened blood pressure. Thus, blacks in general may be at greater risk to develop hypertension.

What causes essential hypertension? By now you will not be surprised to learn that there are biological, psychological, and social contributions to the development of this potentially deadly condition.

It has long been clear that hypertension runs in families and very likely is subject to marked genetic influences (Papillo & Shapiro, 1990). We also know that, when stressed in the laboratory, even individuals with *normal* blood pressure will show greater reactivity in their blood pressure reactions if their parents have high blood pressure, compared to individuals with normal blood pressure whose parents also had normal blood pressure (Fredrikson & Matthews, 1990). In other words, it doesn't take much to activate an inherited vulnerability to be hypertensive. In fact, the offspring of hypertensives are at twice the risk of developing hypertension compared to children of parents with normal blood pressure (Kaplan, 1980). Elevated blood pressure is evident even during the first few weeks of life in new babies of hypertensive parents (Turk, Meichenbaum, & Genest, 1987).

Studies examining neurobiological causes of hypertension have centered on two factors that are very central to the regulation of blood pressure: autonomic nervous system activity and mechanisms regulating sodium operating through the kidneys. When the sympathetic branch of our autonomic nervous system becomes active, one of the consequences is the constriction of blood vessels thereby producing greater resistance against circulation. As a result, blood pressure is elevated (Guyton, 1981). Since the sympathetic nervous system is very responsive to stress, many investigators have long assumed that stress is a major contributor to essential hypertension.

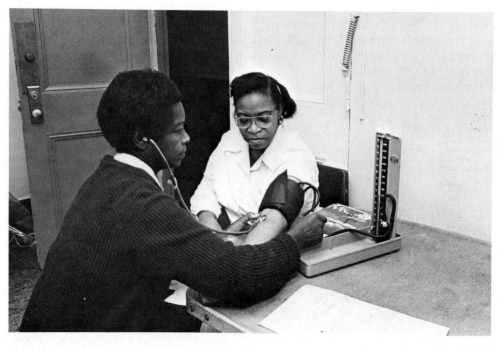

A disproportionately high number of African-Americans suffer from hypertension.

Sodium and water regulation, one of the functions of the kidneys, is also highly important in regulating blood pressure. Retaining too much salt increases blood volume and heightens blood pressure. This is one reason that people with hypertension are often told to change their diet by greatly restricting their intake of salt.

Psychological factors such as personality, coping style, and, as noted above, level of stress, have been used to explain individual differences in blood pressure. For example, both anger and hostility have been associated with increases in blood pressure in the laboratory setting (Houston, 1988; Armstead, Lawler, Gorden, Cross, & Gibbons, 1989; King, Taylor, Albright, & Haskell, 1990; Jamner, Shapiro, Goldstein, & Hug, 1991). The notion of hostility or repressed hostility as a personality factor predicting hypertension (and other cardiovascular problems) can be traced back to Alexander (1939) who suggested, even at that time, that an inability to express anger could result in hypertension and other cardiovascular problems. What may be more important in long-term effects on cardiovascular functioning is not whether anger is suppressed but rather how frequently anger and hostility are experienced (Ironson et al., 1992).

Does this sound familiar? Let's return to the case of John for a moment. John clearly suffered from hypertension. Do you detect any anger or hostility in John's case study? John's hypertension may well be related to his stressful life-style, frustration levels, and hostility.

Coronary Heart Disease

It may not surprise you that psychological and social factors contribute to high blood pressure, but what about heart attacks? Can changes in behavior and attitudes prevent heart attacks? The answers are still not entirely clear, but increasing evidence indicates that psychological and social factors are implicated in coronary heart disease. Why is this important? Because heart disease is the number one cause of death, at least in Western cultures.

Coronary heart disease (CHD) refers, quite simply, to a blockage of varying severity of the arteries supplying blood to the heart muscle. Another name for the heart muscle is the *myocardium*. A number of terms are used to describe heart disease. Chest pain resulting from partial obstruction of the arteries is called *angina pectoris* or, usually, just *angina*. *Atherosclerosis* is the process in which a fatty substance or plaque builds up inside the arteries causing an obstruction. *Ischemia* is the name for deficiency of blood to a body part caused by the narrowing of the arteries that occurs when too much plaque builds up. And *myocardial infarction,* or *heart attack,* refers to the death of heart tissue supplied by a specific artery when it becomes completely

clogged with plaque. Arteries can constrict or become blocked for a variety of reasons other than plaque. For example, a blood clot might lodge in the artery.

It seems clear that we inherit a vulnerability to experience CHD (as well as many other physical disorders) and that other factors such as diet and exercise and cultural factors make very important contributions to our cardiovascular status (Thoresen & Powell, 1992). But in this section our focus is on psychological factors.

What sort of psychological factors contribute to coronary heart disease? Many factors put people at risk for heart disease, such as smoking, lack of exercise, obesity, hypertension, and diets containing animal fats that might result in high levels of blood cholesterol. Many of these factors are behaviors that can be modified to minimize risk for heart disease. Later in the chapter we discuss modifying behaviors and life-styles to promote health, but it will come as no surprise by now that the effects of stress are heavily implicated in coronary heart disease.

Nancy Frasure-Smith (1991) studied 461 men who were in the hospital after experiencing an acute myocardial infarction (heart attack) and followed their progress for 5 years. Psychological stress was measured in this group on the basis of symptoms of stress on a clinical rating scale obtained during periodic telephone interviews. Approximately half the men received stress-reduction treatments whenever they reported high levels of stress during the 5-year period. Control patients received routine medical care. Men in both groups modified their risk factors for heart disease by improving their diet or increasing their exercise to approximately the same extent.

For those patients who experienced high stress some time after their discharge from the hospital, approximately three times as many in the control group died compared to those in the stress-reduction group. In addition, men in the control group were at greater risk of another heart attack over the same period compared to men in the treatment group. It is interesting that among those individuals in either group who *did not* experience high levels of stress, the stress-reduction program was of little benefit, as might be expected. The data for deaths in both groups are displayed in Figure 9.6. These results replicate and extend an earlier study by Friedman et al. (1984).

These data certainly suggest that psychological factors are implicated directly in the process of heart disease. Other studies have reported similar findings. For example, Ahern et al. (1990) reported that patients with *arrhythmias* (irregular heart beats) experiencing depressive symptoms while in the hospital after a heart attack were more likely to die during a one-year follow-up period than those without depressive symptoms. In a later and different study, Frasure-Smith,

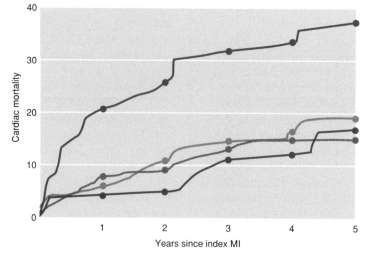

Figure 9.6   Cardiac mortality. For patients in low-stress situations, stress-reduction training seems to make little difference in cardiac deaths; however, for patients in high-stress situations, cardiac mortality was dramatically reduced for those who received stress-reduction training (adapted from Frasure-Smith, 1991).

Lesperance, and Talajic (1993) found that in the first 6 months following a heart attack, individuals suffering from major depression experience three to four times the death rate of nondepressed individuals with the same degree of heart damage. Earlier, we pointed out the very close relationship between depression, anxiety, and stress as negative emotional states.

Although the physiological mechanism is not clear, the variety of evidence indicates that ischemia, even if "silent" (no discernible symptoms experienced by the patient), is highly correlated with stress and anxiety (Freeman, Nixon, Sallabank, & Reaveley, 1987; Rozanski et al., 1988). Since ischemia, depending on its severity, may lead to arrhythmias and/or heart attacks, it would be logical to assume that those patients most susceptible to stress as well as those patients who respond to stress with marked constriction of their arteries, would be most at risk for heart attacks. More recent studies have also suggested that *healthy* men experiencing stress are more likely to experience coronary heart disease at a later time than low stress groups (Rosengren, Tibblin, & Wilhelmsen, 1991). For individuals such as these, stress reduction procedures may prove to be an important preventive technique.

The Type A behavior pattern.   Most of the studies described above have concerned people who have already had a heart attack. Can we identify, before an attack, people who are experiencing a great deal of stress that might make them susceptible to their

first heart attack? The answer seems to be yes, but it is a more complex answer than we first thought.

Clinical investigators reported several decades ago that certain groups of people, when they are in stressful situations, engage in a cluster of behaviors that seems to put them at considerable risk for coronary heart disease. These behaviors include excessive competitive drive, a sense of always being pressured for time, impatience, incredible amounts of energy that may show up in accelerated speech and motor activity, and angry outbursts. This set of behaviors came to be called the **Type A behavior pattern** and was first identified by two cardiologists, Meyer Friedman and Ray Rosenman (Friedman & Rosenman, 1959, 1974). The **Type B behavior pattern,** on the other hand, also put forth by these clinicians, describes the person who basically does not have Type A attributes. In other words the Type B individual is more relaxed, less concerned about deadlines, and seldom feels the pressure or, perhaps, the excitement of challenges or overriding ambition.

The concept of the Type A personality or behavior pattern has become widely accepted in our hard-driving, goal-oriented, culture. Indeed, some early studies supported the concept of Type A behavior as putting people at risk for coronary heart disease (Friedman & Rosenman, 1974). But the most convincing evidence came from two large prospective studies following literally thousands of patients over a long period of time to determine the relationship of their behavioral patterns to heart disease. The first study was the Western Collaborative Group Study (WCGS). In this project 3,154 healthy men, aged 39–59, were interviewed at the beginning of the study to determine their typical behavioral patterns. They were then followed for 8 ½ years. The basic finding was that those men displaying a Type A behavior pattern at the beginning of the study were at least twice as likely to develop coronary heart disease as the men with a Type B behavior pattern. When the investigators analyzed the data for the younger men in the study (aged 39–49) the results were even more striking, with coronary heart disease developing approximately six times more frequently in the Type A group than in the Type B group (Rosenman et al., 1975). Other investigators looking at the same data set reached similar conclusions (Jenkins, Zyzanski, & Rosenman, 1976; Brand, 1978).

A second major study is the Framingham Heart Study that has been ongoing for over 40 years (Haynes, Feinleib, & Kannel, 1980). This study has taught us much of what we know about the development and course of coronary heart disease. In this study 1,674 healthy males *and females* were categorized by Type A or Type B behavior pattern and followed for 8 years. Once again, both men and women with a Type A pattern were over twice as likely to develop coronary heart disease than their Type B counterparts (in men the risk was nearly three times as great). But in this study, in the male group, the results were evident only in those individuals in higher-status white collar occupations and were not evident in those individuals with blue collar socioeconomic status and occupations. For women the results were strongest for those with a low level of education (Eaker, Pinsky, & Castelli, 1992).

Other population-based essentially replicated these results for (French-Belgian Collaborative Group, 1982; Kittel, Kornitzer, & Dramaix, 1983). It is interesting one large study of Japanese men conducted in Hawaii *did not* replicate these findings (Cohen & Reed, 1985). In fact, the prevalence of Type A behavior among Japanese men is very low compared to males in the United States (18.7% compared to approximately 50%). Similarly, the prevalence of CHD is equally low (Japanese men 4%, American men in the Framingham study 13%) (Haynes & Matthews, 1988). Clearly, sociocultural differences make an important contribution.

Despite the positive results, at least from Western cultures, the Type A concept has proven much more complex and elusive than scientists had hoped. First, it is very difficult to determine whether someone is a Type A from structured interviews, questionnaires, or other measures of this construct. The measures often do not agree with one another. One reason for the disagreement is that many people have *some* of the characteristics of Type A but not all of them, while others present with a mixture of Type A and Type B.

One of the assumptions underlying this early work is the long-since discarded notion that we can divide the world into two types of people. As a result of this realization, any number of studies conducted in more recent years have not necessarily supported the relationship of Type A behavior to coronary heart disease. Some subsequent studies simply showed no relationship between Type A and coronary heart disease. Others actually showed a negative relationship, with Type Bs more at risk under some circumstances (Matthews & Haynes, 1986; Dembroski & Costa, 1987;

Both Type A behavior and coronary heart disease seem to be culturally determined.

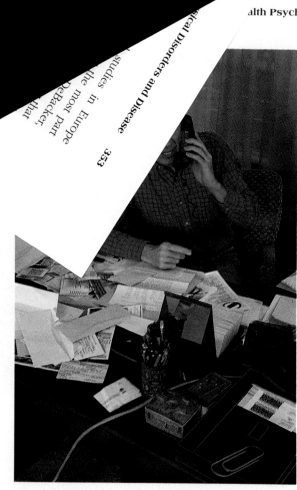

A pattern of hostile outbursts while under stress puts individuals at risk for cardiovascular disease.

Ragland & Brand, 1988; Hollis, Connett, Stevens, & Greenlick, 1990).

The role of chronic negative emotions. At this point investigators in the area decided that something might be wrong with the Type A construct itself (Matthews, 1988; Rodin & Salovey, 1989). A general consensus developed that some specific behaviors and emotions representative of the Type A personality might be very important in the development of coronary heart disease, but not all of them. Among these, the primary factor that seems to be responsible for much of the relationship is anger, which will come as no surprise to you if you read the study in Chapter 2 of this book. As you will remember, Ironson and her colleagues (1992) instructed individuals with heart disease to imagine situations or events in their own lives that made them angry compared to imagining other situations, such as exercise, that also increased heart rate. They found that the emotion of anger actually impaired the pumping efficiency of the heart, putting these individuals at risk for dangerous disturbances in heart rhythm (arrhythmias). This study confirms, at least for now, earlier findings relating the frequent experi-

ence of the emotion of anger to later coronary heart disease (Dembroski, MacDougall, Costa, & Grandits, 1989; Houston, Chesney, Black, Cates, & Hecker, 1992; Smith, 1992).

In conclusion, is Type A irrelevant to the development of heart disease? Most investigators would conclude that some components of the Type A construct are important determinants of CHD, with a chronically high level of negative affect, such as anger, one of the prime candidates (Thoresen & Powell, 1992). Recall again the case of John who had all the Type A behaviors but also had frequent angry outbursts. But what about people experiencing other closely related varieties of negative affect on a chronic basis? Look back to Figure 9.3 and notice the very close relationship between stress, anxiety, and depression. There is some evidence that the physiological components of these emotions and their effects on the cardiovascular system may be identical, or at least very similar. We also know that the emotion of anger so commonly associated with stress is very closely related to the emotion of fear as evidenced in the fight/flight syndrome. Fight is the typical behavioral action tendency associated with anger while flight or escape is associated with fear. But our bodily alarm response, activated by some immediate danger or threat, is associated with both emotions. Some investigators, after reviewing the literature, have concluded that anxiety and depression play as important a role as anger in the development of CHD (Booth-Kewley & Friedman, 1987; Barlow, 1988). Thus, it may be that the experience, on a chronic basis, of the negative emotions of stress (anger), anxiety (fear), and depression (ongoing) and the neurobiological activation that accompanies these emotions provides the most important psychosocial contribution to CHD and perhaps other physical disorders as well. On the other hand, in the Ironson et al. (1992) study, when subjects were asked to imagine being in situations producing performance anxiety (having to give a speech or take a difficult test), these experiences *did not* have the same effect on their hearts as the emotion of anger—at least, not in those individuals with existing CHD. We still have much to learn about these relationships.

Chronic Pain

The experience of pain is not, by definition, a physical disorder, yet pain is the fundamental experience for most of us that signals the presence of injuries, illness, or disease. The importance of pain in our lives cannot be underestimated. Without low levels of pain providing us feedback on the functioning of the body and its various systems, we might incur substantially more injuries. For example, you might lean on the edge of a hot stove a lot longer. You might not roll over while sleeping or shift your posture while sitting, thereby affecting your circulation in a way that might be physically harmful. Reactions to this kind of low-level pain are mostly automatic; that is, we are not aware of the discomfort. When pain crosses the threshold of awareness, a threshold that varies a great deal from individual to individual, pain forces us to take action. If we are unable to remediate the source of the pain ourselves or we are not sure of its cause, we most likely seek medical help. And Americans seek help for pain in droves, spending at least 100 billion dollars annually on over-the-counter pain medication to reduce temporary pain from headaches, colds, or other minor disorders. Twenty million tons of aspirin are consumed each year by headache sufferers alone (Taylor, 1991).

But the more substantial interest in the experience of pain is centered on those individuals whose pain is *chronic* as opposed to acute or episodic. There are basically two kinds of clinical pain: acute and chronic. *Acute pain* typically follows an injury, as when you break your arm or wound yourself in some way. Acute pain disappears once the injury heals or is effectively treated, often within a month (Philips & Grant, 1991). **Chronic pain,** on the other hand, may begin with an acute episode but *does not decrease* over time, even when the injury has healed or effective treatments have been administered. Typically, chronic pain involves pain in the muscles, joints, or tendons, particularly the lower back or any joints that are inflamed. Other types of chronic pain include vascular pain due to enlarged blood vessels as is the case with many headaches, or pain caused by the slow degeneration of tissue as in some terminal diseases, or the growth of cancerous tumors that impinge on pain receptors (Melzack & Wall, 1982; Taylor, 1991). In this country alone, estimates of the number of people suffering from chronic pain have reached 65 million (Taylor, 1991), yet most researchers now agree that the cause of chronic pain and the resulting enormous drain on our health care system *is substantially psychological and social.*

To have a better understanding of the experience of pain, we need to divide this experience into components. Clinicians and researchers in the area generally make a clear distinction between the subjective experience termed *pain* as reflected in reports of the patient and the overt manifestations of this private and conscious experience termed *pain behaviors.* Pain behaviors would include changing one's posture or the way one walks, continually complaining about pain to others with accompanying facial expressions that communicate "I'm in pain," and, most important, avoiding various activities, particularly those involving work or leisure. Finally, an emotional component of pain called "suffering" sometimes accompanies pain and sometimes does not (Fordyce, 1988; Liebeskind, 1991). DSM-IV diagnostic criteria for pain disorder are found in

Table 6.5 (p. 218). Because of the importance of these factors, we will review psychological and social contributions to pain before discussing biological contributions and how all these factors interact to produce pain.

Psychological and Social Aspects of Pain

In mild forms, chronic pain can be an annoyance that eventually wears you down and takes the pleasure out of life. In more severe forms, chronic pain may cause you to lose your job, withdraw from your family, give up anything fun in your life, and focus your entire existence around seeking relief from pain. What is interesting for our purposes is that the *severity* of chronic pain does not seem to predict one's *reaction* to it, such as level of distress or disability. Some individuals experience pain frequently and intensely and yet continue to work productively, rarely seek out medical services, and lead reasonably normal lives. Other individuals essentially become invalids. These differences appear to be due primarily to psychological factors (Turk, Meichenbaum, & Genest, 1983; Jensen, Turner, Romano, & Karoly, 1991; Keefe, Dunsmore, &

Some people cope extremely well with chronic pain and go on to extraordinary achievements.

Burnett, 1992). What are the psychological factors? It will come as no surprise that these factors are the same ones implicated in the stress response and other negative emotional states, such as anxiety and depression, described in Chapters 5 and 7. Specifically, the determining factor seems to be the individual's general sense of control over the situation as reflected in attitudes that he or she can deal with the pain and its consequences in an effective and meaningful way. When this sense of control is combined with a generally optimistic outlook about the future, the individual will experience substantially less distress and disability (Bandura, O'Leary, Taylor, Gauthier, & Gossard, 1987; Jensen, Karoly, & Hager, 1987; Bandura, Cioffi, Taylor, & Brouillard, 1988; Flor & Turk, 1988; Jensen et al., 1991; Keefe et al., 1992). These psychological factors also are associated with more active attempts to cope with the pain, such as exercise or other regimens, as opposed to passive suffering from the pain (Lazarus & Folkman, 1984; Brown & Nicassio, 1987).

To take one example, Philips and Grant (1991) studied 117 patients who suffered from back and neck pain following an injury of some type. Almost all patients expected to recover very quickly, but fully 40% of them still reported substantial pain at 6 months, thereby qualifying for "chronic pain" status. Of the 60% who reported no pain at the 6-month point, most had been pain free since approximately 1 month after the accident. Furthermore, Philips and Grant report that the relationship between the experience of pain and subsequent disability *was not* strongly related to the intensity of the pain. Rather, other factors seemed to influence the occurrence of disability such as personality and socioeconomic differences as well as whether the individual had decided to initiate a lawsuit concerning the injury.

That the experience of pain can be largely disconnected from disease or injury is perhaps best exemplified by *phantom limb pain*. In this not uncommon condition, individuals who have had an arm or leg surgically removed for various reasons continue to feel excruciating pain in the arm or leg that is no longer there. Furthermore, they can describe in exquisite detail the location of the pain in the phantom limb and the type of pain experienced, such as a dull ache versus a sharp cutting type of pain. The fact that they are fully aware that the limb is amputated does nothing to relieve the pain. Recent evidence suggests that some changes in the sensory cortex of the brain may also contribute to this phenomenon (Ramachandran, 1993).

Generally, if someone thinks the experience of pain is disastrous, uncontrollable, or reflective of personal failure in some way, he or she will experience more intense pain and greater psychological distress than those who do not feel this way about pain (Gil,

Williams, Keefe, & Beckham, 1990). Thus, treatment programs for chronic pain, discussed below, concentrate on these psychological factors.

Other examples of psychological influences on the experience of pain are encountered every day. Despite significant tissue damage, athletes frequently continue to perform and report relatively little pain. In one important study, 65% of war veterans wounded in combat reported feeling no pain. Presumably, attentional processes were focused externally on what they had to do to survive rather than internally on the experience of pain (Melzack & Wall, 1982).

In addition to psychological factors, such as the amount of perceived control over the sources of pain, active coping styles, and focus of attention, *social factors* also influence the experience of pain. Fordyce (1976, 1988) has studied the importance of social forms of pain behavior such as verbal complaints, facial expressions, and obvious limps or other signs of pain that may come under the control of strong social contingencies. For some individuals, these social behaviors change the way people react to them. Family members who were formerly critical and demanding may become caring and sympathetic (Kerns et al., 1991). This phenomenon is referred to as "operant" control of pain behavior, since the behavior, including reports of pain, clearly seem under the control of social consequences. But these consequences have an uncertain relation to the amount of pain actually experienced.

On the other hand, a strong network of social support may also *reduce* pain, although the data are only correlational at present. Jamison and Virts (1990) studied 521 chronic pain patients (with back, abdominal, and chest conditions) and discovered that those individuals lacking in general social support from their families reported more pain sites and showed more pain behavior, such as staying in bed. The patients also exhibited more emotional distress *without* rating their pain as any more intense than those subjects with strong socially supportive families. The subjects with strong social support returned to work earlier, showed less reliance on medications, and increased their activity levels more quickly than those with weaker social supports.

While these results may seem contradictory to studies on the operant control of pain, it is possible that different mechanisms are at work. General social support may reduce stress associated with the pain and injury, allowing individuals to use more adaptive coping procedures and develop more control over their lives. However, specifically reinforcing certain pain behaviors, particularly in the absence of social supports, may powerfully increase pain behavior. These are very complex issues that have not yet been entirely sorted out.

Social and familial support are important in reducing pain and stress.

Gate Control Theory of Pain

In any case, no one today would think that pain is entirely psychological, just as no one would think that it is entirely physical. One theory of pain, the *gate control theory* (Melzack & Wall, 1965, 1982), accommodates both psychological and physical factors. According to this theory, nerve impulses from painful stimuli, occurring somewhere in our body, make their way to the spinal column which controls the flow of pain stimulation to the brain. An area called the *dorsal horns of the spinal column* acts as a "gate" and may open and transmit sensations of pain if the stimulation received is sufficiently intense. Specific nerve fibers referred to as *small fibers* (A-delta and C fibers) as well as *large fibers* (A-beta fibers) determine the pattern as well as the intensity of the stimulation. Small fibers tend to open the gate thereby increasing the transmission of painful stimuli, whereas large fibers tend to close the gate.

Most important for our purpose is that the brain sends signals back down the spinal cord that may affect this gating mechanism. For example, if one is experiencing negative emotions such as fear or anxiety, the experience of pain may be more intense since the basic message from the brain is to be vigilant for possible danger or threat. On the other hand, if one is experiencing more positive emotions or is totally absorbed in some other activity (such as an athlete intent on finishing a long grueling race), the brain will send down an inhibitory signal thus closing the gate. While many think that the gate control theory is overly simplistic (for example, Nathan, 1976; Liebeskind, 1991), the basic elements of the theory, particularly as the theory describes the complex interaction of psychological and biological factors in the experience of pain, have held up.

Endogenous Opioids

The neurochemical means by which the brain inhibits pain was discovered only recently but it was a very important discovery. It seems that we all have within us naturally occurring or **endogenous opioids.** Drugs such as heroin and morphine are manufactured from opioid substances. It now turns out that there are substances like these within the body that act very much like neurotransmitters. The brain uses these endogenous opioids, called *endorphins* or *enkephalins,* to shut down pain, even in the presence of marked tissue damage or injury. Since endogenous opioids are distributed widely throughout the body, they may be implicated in a variety of psychopathological states. We have already seen in Chapter 8 how endogenous opioids may contribute to eating disorders. A more common occurrence that many of you may have experienced is the "runners' high" that at some point is related to the release of endogenous opioids after intense (and sometimes painful) physical activity.

In one important experiment that lends further support to the multidimensional theme of this book, Bandura et al. (1987) found that those individuals with a greater sense of self-efficacy and control had a higher tolerance for pain, and they actually increased their production of endogenous opioids when they were confronted with a painful stimulus, compared to individuals with low self-efficacy.

Effective coping and a sense of control reduce pain and stress during traumatic situations.

Gender Differences in Pain

Most studies, both with animals and humans, have been conducted on males to avoid the complications of hormonal variation. But men and women seem to experience different types of pain. For example, in addition to labor pains of childbirth, women suffer more frequently than men from migraine headaches and arthritis. Men, on the other hand, may experience more cardiac pain and backache.

It now seems that both males and females may have systems that are based on endogenous opioids, although the system in males may be more powerful. But males and females seem to have additional pain-regulating mechanisms that may be separate. The neurochemistry of the additional female system may be based on an estrogen-dependent neuronal system (Mogil, Sternberg, Kest, Marek, & Liebeskind, 1993). The investigators speculate that this additional pain-regulating pathway in women may have evolved in females to cope with pain associated with reproductive activity such as childbirth. Also, this pathway seems to be redundant—that is, it is an "extra" pathway in females that, if taken away by removing hormones, has no implications for the remaining pathways, which continue to work as well. One implication of this finding is that males and females may benefit from different kinds of drugs, different kinds of psychosocial interventions, or unique combinations of these treatments to best manage and control pain.

Chronic Headaches

There is one type of pain with which almost everyone can identify: a headache. But headaches are very private and, seemingly, very complex events. In fact, individu-

als suffering from them report a wide variety of phenomena associated with their headaches. They may describe different locations in the head that seem to be the source of the pain. Their descriptions vary in intensity, frequency, and duration. Many different symptoms have been reported to precede, accompany, or follow headaches. For example, some individuals at various times may experience dizziness, acute sensitivity to light or sounds, nausea, or a variety of other sensations before, during, or after their headaches.

Because of this great variability, investigators have attempted to classify headaches into types. The International Headache Society divides headaches into 13 major types, of which two are predominant: **tension** and **migraine** (HCC, 1988). To give you just a taste of the complexity of headache classification, major types as well as the subcategories of the tension and migraine categories are listed in Table 9.1.

Approximately 10% to 15% of migraine headaches involve what is called an *aura,* most usually consisting of visual disturbances (seeing a flash of light) or sensations of unreality. The remainder of migraines occur without aura. These headaches typically come on relatively suddenly (several minutes to, occasionally, as long as an hour) and involve pulsing and throbbing sensations, which can become extremely severe and typically occur in one side of the head (unilateral). As the attack progresses, the pain becomes more steady and the pulsating subsides. Conversely, tension headaches are more often characterized by a dull ache that may be present on both sides of the head (bilateral) but usually begin in the frontal or occipital (back) areas of the head.

Another subtype of headache that is important to note is termed *analgesic rebound headache.* Many

Table 9.1 The Headache Classification System of the International Headache Society

1. Migraine
   1.1 Migraine without aura
   1.2 Migraine with aura
       1.2.1 Migraine with typical aura
       1.2.2 Migraine with prolonged aura
       1.2.3 Familial hemiplegic migraine
       1.2.4 Basilar migraine
       1.2.5 Migraine aura without headache
       1.2.6 Migraine with acute onset aura
   1.3 Ophthalmoplegic migraine
   1.4 Retinal migraine
   1.5 Childhood periodic syndromes that may be precursors to or associated with migraine
       1.5.1 Benign paroxysmal vertigo of childhood
       1.5.2 Alternating hemiplegia of childhood
   1.6 Complications of migraine
       1.6.1 Status migrainosus
       1.6.2 Migrainous infarction
   1.7 Migrainous disorder not fulfilling above criteria

2. Tension-type headache
   2.1 Episodic tension-type headache
       2.1.1 Episodic tension-type headache associated with disorder of pericranial muscles
       2.1.2 Episodic tension-type headache unassociated with disorder of pericranial muscles
   2.2 Chronic tension-type headache
       2.2.1 Chronic tension-type headache associated with disorder of pericranial muscles
       2.2.2 Chronic tension-type headache unassociated with disorder of pericranial muscles
   2.3 Headache of the tension-type not fulfilling above criteria

3. Cluster headache and chronic paroxysmal hemicrania

4. Miscellaneous headaches unassociated with structural lesion

5. Headache associated with head trauma

6. Headache associated with vascular disorders

7. Headache associated with nonvascular intracranial disorder

8. Headache associated with substances or their withdrawal

9. Headache associated with noncephalic infection

10. Headache associated with metabolic disorder

11. Headache or facial pain associated with disorder of cranium, neck, eyes, ears, nose, sinuses, teeth, mouth, or other facial or cranial structures

12. Cranial neuralgias, nerve trunk pain, and deafferentation pain

13. Headache not classifiable

Note: Subcategories are not shown for categories 3–13.

Source: HCC, 1988.

individuals relying on pain-reducing medications, including aspirin, may find that several hours after the medication wears off, they experience a headache more severe than they had ever experienced prior to taking the medications. This "rebound" phenomenon may last several weeks (Kudrow, 1982; Michultka, Blanchard, Appelbaum, Jaccard, & Dentinger, 1989).

Generally, researchers in this field find evidence to support the two global headache categories, migraine and tension headache, but find that it is more difficult to subdivide headaches further since the reports from patients are not as clear-cut and discrete as the categories would imply (Arena, Blanchard, Andrasik, & Dudek, 1982; Mindell & Andrasik, 1987). Some investigators have argued that one should not rely too much even on the broad categories of tension and migraine since many individuals have both types of headaches. These investigators also argue that the setting events for the headaches (for instance, where were you when the headache occurred, were you under stress, what seemed to trigger the headache?) and the consequences of the headache (how do you cope with the headaches, how do other people react?) are much more important in planning appropriate treatments than is dividing headache experiences into ever-more discrete categories (for example, Martin, 1993).

In any case, headaches are a common problem. Reported prevalence rates generally range from 66% to 83% in developed countries (Martin, 1993). Somewhere between 10% and 50% of headache sufferers experience pain to a sufficient degree that they will consult their doctor in an attempt to obtain relief. Presumably, the majority resort to over-the-counter medication if they take any action at all.

Headaches are also common in children; some as young as 18 months old have been diagnosed with this complaint (Selby & Lance, 1960). Another study of 7-year-old children found that almost 38% experienced headaches before starting school (Sillanpaa, 1976). The prevalence seems to increase through childhood and adolescence. In one well-done longitudinal study, 73 children with migraine headaches—some as young as 7 years old—were followed until all were over 30 years of age. Sixty percent still had migraines at age 30, although approximately 22% of these individuals had experienced at least a 2-year headache-free period during that time. Thus, 40% of childhood migraine sufferers had "outgrown" their headaches (Bille, 1981). Generally, headaches are more common in women than men (approximately 75% of women experience headaches versus 60% of men) but do not relate to social class, education, or type of employment. For more severe headaches, the female-male ratio is as high as 4:1.

In the extreme, headaches can be very disabling. Consider the following case.

The Case of Sandy

Sandy is a 39-year-old elementary school teacher. She is single and lives alone in a major urban center. Sandy maintains a very hectic schedule. In addition to teaching classes and coaching the girls' softball team at school, she is president of the homeowners' board for her condominium complex, organizes regular church events, and sings in her church choir. Sandy's busy life-style is complicated by the fact that she suffers from tension headaches almost every other day. Approximately half the headaches are relieved relatively quickly by over-the-counter medications; however, some of the headaches last up to 3 or 4 hours. Sandy has learned to tolerate these headaches, and she usually continues her activities despite the dull nagging pain.

On the other hand, the migraine headaches she experiences are virtually disabling. The migraines were particularly severe when Sandy was in her late 20s. At that time, she tried many different approaches, including chiropractic massages, diets, herbal medicines, and eventually strong headache medications. Eventually, the migraines subsided, occurring only once every 3 to 4 months, but they became progressively more frequent and severe over the last year, occurring once per week on average. As a result, Sandy has had to cancel several major obligations in recent months. Of course, she regrets having to postpone meetings and other responsibilities, and feels much pressure to make up for lost time afterward. Indeed, the pressure seems to build constantly since the migraines seem to be taking up more and more of her time. Sandy feels as if the headache pain is controlling her life. She feels worn down and unable to cope with the throbbing pain and nausea associated with the migraines. All she can do at these times is to lie down.

Sandy is generally apprehensive about the recurrence of migraines. Just recently, she has become rather sad and lonely, particularly when she is lying at home alone trying to "ride out" a migraine. In general, it has been harder for her to keep up with her usual pace of activities. She feels drained, has lost her appetite, is not sleeping as well, and sometimes even cries. In addition, she has become very sensitive to bright lights, loud noises, or any source of stimulation that she feels might trigger a migraine. She sees herself as suffering alone like this for the rest of her life.

Causes of Headaches

Traditionally investigators have thought that migraine headaches are caused by a two-stage process. First, the cranial arteries severely constrict, a condition that is associated with the "aura" phase and some of the sensory disturbances. This is followed by a rebound phenomenon when the cranial arteries dilate, leading to severe head pain. However, recent evidence indicates that the origins of migraine headaches are not so simple because a number of physiological factors, such as muscle tension and elevated respiration rate, may contribute to them (Saper, 1989; Martin, 1993).

Conversely, tension headaches for many years were thought to be very clearly associated with the contraction of muscles in the face and neck. Unfortunately for the theory, most studies that have directly examined muscle tension in individuals suffering from tension headaches compared to control subjects have found little evidence for increased muscle tension as the cause of these headaches (Flor & Turk, 1989; Hatch, Prihoda, Moore, & Cyr-Provost, 1991; Martin, 1993), although some studies have found severity of reported pain to correlate with increased muscle tension (Ahles & Martin, 1989), or that muscle tension is present in tension headache sufferers when measured in a different way (Hudzinski & Lawrence, 1988).

More recent research, however, does seem to suggest that some changes in vascular activity are associated with headaches, particularly in response to stress. That is, individuals suffering from migraine headaches seem to experience more marked or exaggerated vascular activity when confronted with physical or psychological stress compared to individuals without headaches (for example, McCaffrey, Goetsch, Robinson, & Isaac, 1986; Martin, 1993). Also Lehrer and Murphy (1991) exposed tension headache sufferers to a series of psychological stressors (having them imagine a stressful situation or do arithmetic very quickly in their heads) as well as physical pain (tying tourniquets around their arms). They found that compared to control subjects, the headache patients showed higher heart rates and evidence of more prolonged constriction of the veins in the hands and earlobes; they also rated the tourniquet as more painful than did control subjects. The researchers concluded that headache patients were more emotionally and autonomically hyperreactive to pain and psychological stress than were control subjects.

The more puzzling finding is that individuals suffering primarily from tension headaches *do not seem to differ* from individuals with migraine headaches in terms of vascular functioning, nor do these groups differ on any other psychophysiological or muscle tension variable either in response to stress or at rest (Andrasik, Blanchard, Arena, Saunders, & Barron, 1982; Nicholson, Blanchard, & Appelbaum, 1990; Martin, Marie, & Nathan, 1992). Thus, it seems that individuals suffering from both types of headaches may suffer from some blood flow abnormalities, particularly in response to stress. It is also possible that pain thresholds in the region of the head are somewhat lower for headache sufferers.

Part of the difficulty is the complexity of doing precise psychophysiological measurement of vascular changes or muscle tension. As this field advances, it may be that we will discover that more substantial differences do exist between types of headaches as it seems they must. Nevertheless, at the present time the precise physiological and psychological underpinnings of different types of headaches are a mystery.

Chronic Fatigue Syndrome

In the middle of the last century a veritable epidemic arose in which patients experienced a lack of energy, marked fatigue, a variety of aches and pains, and, on occasion, low-grade fever. No physical pathology could be discovered and George Beard (1869) labeled the condition *neurasthenia* or, literally, lack of nerve strength (Morey & Kurtz, 1989; Abbey & Garfinkel, 1991). This disorder disappeared in the early part of the 20th century in Western cultures but remains the most prevalent form of psychopathology in China (Good & Kleinman, 1985; Kleinman, 1986). In the last century the disease was attributed to the demands of the time, including a preoccupation with material success, a strong emphasis on hard work, and the changing role of women.

More recently, another condition has made an appearance and seems to be spreading rapidly throughout the Western world. This disorder has been referred to as **chronic fatigue syndrome (CFS)** and, until recently, was attributed to viral infection, specifically the Epstein-Barr virus (Straus et al., 1985), immune system dysfunction (Straus, 1988), or exposure to toxins. Evidence as yet has failed to support any of these hypothetical physical causes. In fact, the symptoms of CFS, listed in Table 9.2, are almost identical to cases of neurasthenia in the last century.

We don't know what causes CFS, although we do know that people presenting with this constellation of symptoms undergo considerable suffering and often must give up promising, lucrative careers. As Abbey and Garfinkel (1991) point out, both neurasthenia in the last century and CFS in the present have been attributed to the greatly increased stress of the times, the changing role of women, and the stress-producing rapid dissemination of new technology and information. Both of these disorders are also more common in women.

It is possible, of course, that a virus or a specific immune system dysfunction will be found to account

Table 9.2 Symptoms of Chronic Fatigue Syndrome

Incapacitating exhaustion or fatigue (the fatigue produced by low levels of exertion)

Marked reduction in activity

Muscle and joint pain and weakness

Low-grade fever

Recurrent sore throats

Swollen or tender lymph nodes

Headaches, dizziness, and lightheadedness

Irritability, depression, and anxiety

Source: Adapted from Abbey & Garfinkel, 1991.

for CFS. Another possibility suggested by Abbey and Garfinkel (1991) is that the condition represents a rather nonspecific response to stress. In any case, there is now some preliminary evidence for the success of a *psychosocial treatment* for chronic fatigue syndrome. Michael Sharpe in Oxford has developed a cognitive-behavioral program for chronic fatigue syndrome sufferers that includes procedures to increase their activity and regulate periods of rest. This treatment also includes relaxation, breathing exercises, and general stress-reduction procedures, interventions we will describe more fully in the next section (Sharpe, 1992, 1993). Pharmacological treatment has not proven to be effective (Sharpe, 1992).

Psychosocial Treatment of Physical Disorders

Recent experiments suggest that pain is not only bad for you but that it may kill you. John Liebeskind and his colleagues (Page, Ben-Eliyahu, Yirmiya, & Liebeskind, 1993) have now demonstrated in rats that post-surgical pain doubles the rate at which a certain type of cancer metastasizes (spreads) to the lungs. Specifically, rats undergoing abdominal surgery *without* morphine developed double the number of lung metastases compared to rats who underwent exactly the same surgery with morphine. In fact, the rats undergoing surgery *with the pain-killing drug* had even lower rates of metastases than rats that had no surgery whatsoever.

It is possible that the source of this effect is the interaction of pain with the immune system. Specifically, it seems that pain may reduce the number of natural killer (NK cells) in the immune system, perhaps because of the general stress reaction associated with the pain. Thus, if someone is in *extreme* pain, the stress associated with this pain may enhance the disease process or injury that is causing the pain in the first place, completing a vicious circle.

If this finding is also found to apply to humans, it is important because the general consensus is that humans are very reluctant to use pain-killing medication in chronic diseases such as cancer. Some estimates suggest that fewer than half of all cancer patients in the United States receive sufficient pain relief. Adequate pain-management procedures, either drug or psychological, may be an essential part of the management of chronic disease.

A variety of specific psychosocial treatments have been developed for physical disorders and pain. Among these are biofeedback, relaxation procedures, and hypnosis. But because of the overriding role of stress in the etiology and maintenance of many physical disorders, comprehensive stress-management programs are increasingly finding their way into medical centers where these physical disorders are treated. We will first review, briefly, some more specific psychosocial approaches to physical disorders before describing a typical comprehensive stress management program.

Biofeedback

Biofeedback refers, literally, to a process by which we make patients aware of specific bodily processes or physiological functions which, ordinarily, they would not notice consciously. Examples would be heart rate, blood pressure, muscle tension in specific areas of the body, EEG rhythms (brain waves), or patterns of blood

Noted biofeedback expert, Frank Andrasik, administers treatment to a young woman.

flow in various parts of the body. This is the first step; but the second step is more remarkable.

Until about 30 years ago, few people would have thought there was any reason to make individuals more aware of these physiological processes since we would be unable to control them in any case. But in the 1960s, Neal Miller reported that animals could *learn to directly control* many of these responses (such as heart rate and blood pressure). Miller demonstrated this phenomenon by using a variation of operant conditioning procedures in which the animals were reinforced for either increases or decreases in these responses (Miller, 1969). Although it subsequently proved difficult to replicate these findings with animals, by this time clinicians had already applied the procedures with some success to humans suffering from various physical disorders or stress-related conditions, such as hypertension and headache.

To do this, clinicians use physiological monitoring equipment to make the physiological response, such as heart rate, visible or audible to the patient. The patient then works with the therapist to learn to control the response, usually by increasing or decreasing it. Typically, when the patient is successful, he receives some type of signal. For example, if the patient is successful in lowering his blood pressure by a certain amount, the pressure reading will be visible on a gauge and a tone will sound.

It wasn't long before researchers discovered that humans could discriminate changes in autonomic nervous system activity with a high degree of accuracy (Blanchard & Epstein, 1977). The question then became this: Why are people ordinarily so poor at discriminating their internal states? Zillmann (1983) suggests that our abilities have always been highly developed in this regard, but that we have simply lost our power to utilize these skills through lack of practice. Shapiro (1974) suggested a good reason for this. Specifically, it might have been very adaptive, in an evolutionary sense, to turn our attention away from precisely monitoring our internal responses. He proposes that humans functioning in past millennia as hunter-gatherers, or today in the home or the office, would be far less effective and efficient if they were continually distracted by a welter of internal stimuli to which they fully attended. In other words, to focus successfully on the task at hand and to accomplish anything, they may have found it necessary over the centuries purposefully to *ignore* their internal functioning and leave that to the more automatic and less aware parts of the brain. Of course, there are many times when internal sensations take control of our consciousness and make us fully aware of our needs. Consider for example, the compelling sensations that arise on the need to void urine or the insistence of hunger pangs. In any case, it does seem that individuals, through precise feedback, can learn to control these responses although the mechanisms by which they do so are as yet not clearly known.

To take the example of tension headaches, the goal of biofeedback procedures has been to reduce tension in the muscles of the head and scalp, thereby relieving the headaches. Indeed, early experiments conducted by pioneers in the area, such as Ed Blanchard and Frank Andrasik, found that biofeedback of muscle tension in this area *was* successful in reducing headaches (Holroyd, Andrasik, & Noble, 1980), although no more successful than deep muscle relaxation procedures (Blanchard, Andrasik, Ahles, Teders, & O'Keefe, 1980; Blanchard & Andrasik, 1982; Holroyd & Penzien, 1986). Based on these results, there is some thought that biofeedback might be achieving its effects with tension headaches by simply teaching people to relax. However, even this conclusion seems to run counter to evidence reviewed above—that muscle tension might play little or no role in the genesis of "tension" headaches. Indeed, Frank Andrasik, Ken Holroyd, and their colleagues conducted a very clever experiment to demonstrate this point in a dramatic way.

Andrasik and Holroyd (1980) divided patients with tension headaches into three biofeedback conditions. All were hooked up to a machine monitoring muscle tension (EMG) on their foreheads. All were told they were learning to *reduce* tension in their foreheads and would receive a signal when they were successful. But only one group of subjects actually received the signal when their muscle tension was reduced. For a second group of subjects, the biofeedback signal indicating success appeared only when their muscle tension remained stable, while for a third group, the signal was administered only if they *increased* their muscle tension. Remember, all three groups thought that when they received the signal they were being successful at lowering the muscle tension and therefore helping their headaches.

The results indicated that *all groups improved significantly* and equally on measures of headaches, suggesting that changes in muscle tension had *little to do* with improvement in headaches. These results are shown in Figure 9.7. Holroyd et al. (1984), replicating this experiment, found the important element was that patients developed an *illusion* that they were being successful in controlling their headache. This illusion of success, which presumably enhanced their sense of self-efficacy, seemed to lead directly to reductions in pain. Thus, the success of biofeedback, at least for headaches, may depend on the extent to which the procedures instill in the patient a *sense of control over the pain*. How do you think this relates to the study of stress in baboons described in the beginning of the chapter?

The varied findings shown in Figure 9.7 do not mean that biofeedback doesn't work. In fact, Blanchard

Edward Blanchard has been one of the pioneers in developing and testing biofeedback procedures for a variety of conditions.

et al. (1982) demonstrated that biofeedback training could lead to significant reductions *over and above* the effects of relaxation in certain patients who failed to respond to relaxation training. Rather than directly affecting muscle tension, biofeedback in these particular patients may have induced in them a feeling of self-efficacy and control.

Whatever the mechanism, biofeedback and relaxation are effective treatments when compared to, for example, placebo medication interventions. Several reviews have found that 38% to 63% of patients undergoing relaxation and/or biofeedback achieve significant reductions in headache activities in comparison to approximately 35% receiving placebo medication (Blanchard et al., 1980; Holroyd & Penzien, 1986; Blanchard, 1992). Furthermore, the effects of biofeedback and relaxation seem to be long lasting. Generally, any success achieved during treatment for headache pain is maintained at a one-year follow-up, although the gains may deteriorate slightly thereafter (Blanchard, 1987). On the other hand, Lisspers and Öst (1990) found that patients with migraine headaches treated with different forms of biofeedback and relaxation training maintained their gains as long as 6 years after treatment ended. At that time, between 48% and 60% of the subjects continued to report significant reductions in headaches compared to a period of time before treatment. Unfortunately, as Blanchard et al. (1989) demonstrated in a trial with people suffering from essential hypertension, it is not clear in advance who will respond to biofeedback and who will not.

Relaxation and Meditation

Various types of relaxation and meditation procedures have also been used, either alone or in combination with other procedures, to treat physical disorder and

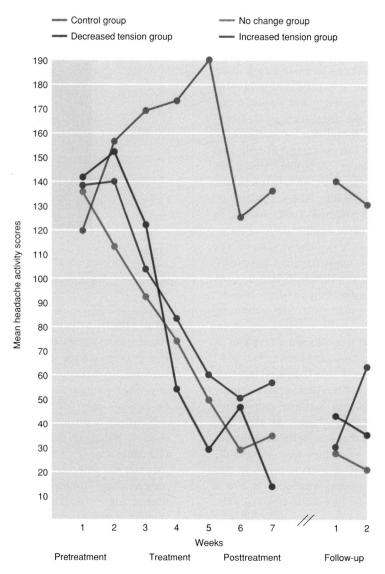

Figure 9.7 Tension headaches and biofeedback. Though all subjects thought they were receiving biofeedback for reducing muscle tension, they actually received feedback for three different conditions. It is interesting that all groups significantly decreased their headaches, no matter their muscle tension (adapted from Andrasik & Holroyd, 1980).

pain patients. *Progressive muscle relaxation* was a technique devised by Edwin Jacobson in 1938. The purpose of this set of exercises is to teach individuals to become acutely aware of any tension in their bodies and to counteract this tension by relaxing specific muscle groups. In Jacobson's original conception, learning the art of relaxation was a structured procedure that took months or even years to master. In most clinics today, however, the procedure is taught in a much briefer period of time, usually a matter of weeks, and is very seldom used as the sole treatment (Bernstein & Borkovec, 1973).

A variant of relaxation training is called *autogenic relaxation training*. In this procedure, patients focus their attention on blood flow and on different muscle groups that might be tense; they suggest to

themselves that they are becoming more relaxed and warm.

A number of procedures focus attention very specifically on either some part of the body or perhaps a single thought or image. This attentional focus is often accompanied by more regular and slowed breathing. *Transcendental meditation* (TM) is a form of this basic process. In TM, attention is focused solely on repeating a specific syllable softly (the mantra).

Herbert Benson stripped TM of what he considered its nonessentials and developed a brief procedure he calls the **relaxation response.** Basically this procedure requires a person to repeat silently a sound (or mantra) to minimize distracting thoughts, and to develop the ability to close the mind to other intruding thoughts. While Benson suggested focusing on the word *one,* any word or phrase would do. Individuals who practice this meditational procedure for 10 or 20 minutes a day report feeling more calm or relaxed throughout the day. These brief, simple procedures can be very powerful in actually reducing the flow of certain neurotransmitters and stress hormones, possibly mediated by an increased sense of control and mastery (Benson, 1975, 1984).

Much as with headaches and hypertension, relaxation has generally positive effects on acute and chronic pain, although the results are relatively modest (Taylor, 1991). Nonetheless, relaxation and meditation almost always form part of a more comprehensive pain management program.

Comprehensive Stress- and Pain-Reduction Programs

Most comprehensive psychological treatment programs now include relaxation or related techniques combined with the acquisition of new and more effective coping procedures. All are designed to instill a greater sense of control and to reduce negative emotions associated with the stressful or pain-related experience.

We will look in some detail at a stress-management program developed in one of our own clinics (Barlow & Rapee, 1991). In this program, individuals learn a variety of stress-management procedures presented to them in a workbook. First, they learn to monitor their stress very closely and attempt to identify the stressful events in their daily life.

Samples of a stressful events record and a daily stress record are found in Figure 9.8. Note how clients in this program are taught to be very specific about recording the periods during the day when they are experiencing stress, the intensity of the stress, and what seems to trigger the stress. They also note their responses in terms of somatic symptoms and thoughts when they are stressed. All this monitoring becomes important in carrying through with the program. But monitoring can be very helpful in itself as it shows clients precise patterns and causes of stress and assists them in learning what changes to make in their lives to better cope with stress.

After learning to monitor stress, clients are taught deep muscle relaxation; this involves first tensing these muscles to identify the location of the different muscle groups. Instructions for tensing specific muscle groups are included in Table 9.3. After learning the location of muscle groups, clients are systematically taught to relax these muscle groups beyond the point of inactivity. That is, they are taught to actively "let go" of the muscle so that no tension remains in it.

Meditation and relaxation procedures can be valuable in reducing stress.

Appraisals and attitudes are an important part of stress, and working with a therapist or counselor, clients are taught how they tend to exaggerate the negative impact of events in their day-to-day lives. In the program, the therapist and client work together using *cognitive therapy* to develop more realistic appraisals and attitudes, as exemplified in the case of Sally.

The Case of Sally

Sally is a 45-year-old real estate agent.

Sally: My mother is always calling just when I'm in the middle of doing something important and it makes me so angry, I find that I get short with her.

Therapist: Let's try and look at what you just said in a more realistic way. When you say that she *always* calls in the middle of something, it implies 100% of the time. Is that true? How

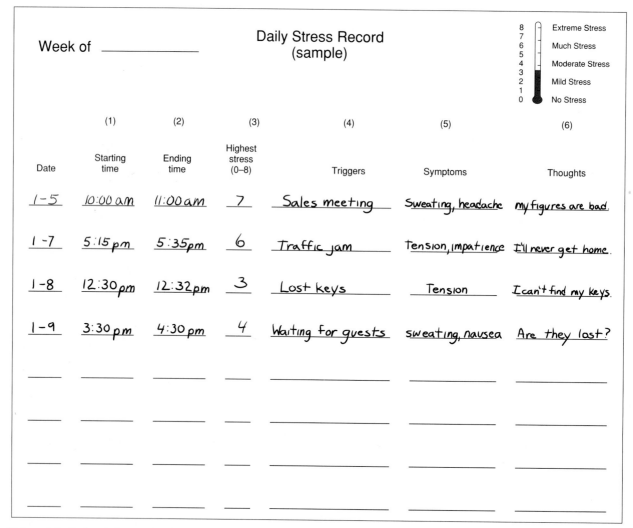

Figure 9.8   Methods for monitoring stress (from Barlow & Rapee, 1991)

likely is it really that she will call when you are doing something important?

Sally: Well, I suppose that when I think back over the last 10 times she's called, most of the times I was just watching TV or reading. There was once when I was making dinner and it burned because she interrupted me. Another time, I was busy with some work I had brought home from the office and she called. I guess that makes it 20% of the time.

Therapist: OK, great; now let's go a bit further. So what if she calls at an inconvenient time?

Sally: Well, I know that one of my first thoughts is that she doesn't think anything I do is important. But before you say anything, I know that is a major overestimation since she obviously doesn't know what I'm doing when she calls. However, I suppose I also think that it's a major

interruption and inconvenience to have to stop at that point.

Therapist: Go on. What is the chance that it is a *major* inconvenience?

Sally: When I was doing my work, I forgot what I was up to and it took me 10 minutes to work it out again. I guess that's not so bad; it's only 10 minutes. And when the dinner burned, it was really not too bad, just a little burned. Part of that was my fault anyway, because I could have turned the stove down before I went to the phone.

Therapist: So, it sounds like quite a small chance that it would be a major inconvenience, even if your mother does interrupt you. **Sally:** True. And I know what you are going to say next. Even if it is a major inconvenience, it's not the end of the world. I have handled plenty of bigger problems than this at work.

Daily Stress Record
(sample)

Week of _January 5_

Date	Average stress	Highest stress	Most stressful event of the day
1-5	2	2	
1-6	4	6	Argument with wife. Late for work.
1-7	3	6	Johnny sick at school.
1-8	4	5	Doctor's report. Lost file at work.
1-9	4	4	
1-10	5	8	Parking ticket.
1-11	3	4	Bought expensive gift.

Figure 9.8 *(continued)*

Table 9.3   Suggestions for Tensing Muscles

12 Muscle Groups

Lower arm	Make fist, palm down, and pull wrist toward upper arm.
Upper arm	Tense biceps, with arms by side, pull upper arm toward side without touching. (Try not to tense the lower arm while doing this; let the lower arm hang loosely.)
Lower leg and foot	Point toes upward to knees.
Thighs	Push feet hard against floor.
Abdomen	Pull in stomach toward back.
Chest and breathing	Take a deep breath and hold it about 10 seconds, then release.
Shoulders and lower neck	Shrug shoulders, bring shoulders up until they almost touch ears.
Back of neck	Put head back and press against back of chair.
Lips	Press lips together; don't clench teeth or jaw.
Eyes	Close eyes tightly but don't close too hard (be careful if you have contacts).
Lower forehead	Pull eyebrows down (try to get them to meet).
Upper forehead	Raise eyebrows and wrinkle your forehead.

Source: Barlow & Rapee, 1991.

Individuals work hard in this program on identifying unrealistic negative thoughts and developing new appraisals and attitudes on the spot when negative thoughts occur. This reassessing is often the most difficult part of the program. After the session above, Sally began using what she had learned in cognitive therapy to reappraise stressful situations.

Finally, clients going through stress reduction develop new coping strategies for dealing with events in their lives such as time management and assertiveness training. During time-management training, patients are taught among other things to prioritize their activities and pay less attention to nonessential duties. During assertiveness training, they rehearse standing up

368 Chapter 9 Physical Disorders and Health Psychology

for themselves in an appropriate way (as was done for Sally later in the program). Clients also learn other coping procedures to manage the everyday problems that arise in their lives.

A number of studies have evaluated some version of this stress-reduction program with individuals suffering from pain, stress, or more usually some combination. The results suggest that the program is generally more effective than applying individual components alone, such as relaxation or biofeedback. This conclusion seems to be true for chronic pain (Keefe, Crisson, Urban, & Williams, 1990; Keefe et al., 1992), tension headaches (Murphy, Lehrer, & Jurish, 1990; Blanchard et al., 1990), hypertension (Ward, Swan, & Chesney, 1987), and cancer pain (Fawzy, Cousins et al., 1990).

One of the more successful comprehensive treatments for chronic pain has been originated by Clare Philips (Philips, 1987a, 1987b). This program contains many of the same components found in general stress-reduction programs such as relaxation and cognitive therapy focused on developing new approaches and attitudes toward pain. After a 9-week treatment program for chronic pain, 12.6% of the treatment group were entirely free of pain, 41.8% were much improved, and 38% were improved. Only 8% were in need of further treatment. Also, pain intensity gradually decreased over the 12-month follow-up.

Drugs and Stress-Reduction Programs

We have already noted the enormous reliance among the population on over-the-counter analgesic medication for pain, particularly headaches. There is now some evidence that *chronic* reliance on these types of medications lessens the efficacy of comprehensive programs in the treatment of headache. Michultka et al. (1989) compared high analgesic users to low analgesic users matched in terms of age, duration of headache activity, and response to comprehensive treatment. Only 29% of high users versus 55% of low users achieved at least a 50% reduction in headache activity. In addition, Holroyd, Nash, Pingel, Cordingley, and Jerome (1991) compared a comprehensive cognitive-behavioral treatment to an antidepressant drug, amitriptyrine, in the treatment of tension headache. The comprehensive psychological treatment produced at least a 50% reduction in headache activity in 56% of the patients versus 27% taking the drug. It is important that psychological treatment also seems to reduce drug consumption in a fairly consistent manner (Radnitz, Appelbaum, Blanchard, Elliott, & Andrasik, 1988). Additionally, such treatments reduce the amounts of medications required to control severe hypertension.

The Advantages and Disadvantages of Denial as a Means of Coping with Chronic Illness

Throughout this chapter and indeed throughout the book, we have pointed out evidence on the importance of confronting and working through one's feelings, particularly following stressful or traumatic events. Mental health professionals dating back to Freud have long recognized the importance of reliving or processing intense emotional experiences in order to put the experiences behind you and/or to develop better and more positive coping responses. For example, individuals undergoing coronary artery bypass surgery who were generally more optimistic prior to surgery recovered from the surgery more quickly, returned to normal activities subsequent to discharge more rapidly, and evidenced a stronger quality of life 6 months after surgery than did those individuals who were not optimistic (Scheier et al., 1989). Scheier et al. also discovered that people who are mostly optimistic were less likely to use denial as a means of coping with a severe stressor such as surgery. To this end most mental health professionals would work to eliminate avoidance or denial of these events. Denial has many negative effects. For example, individuals who deny or avoid severe pain connected with a disease process may not notice variations in their symptoms that might be meaningful when reported to health professionals. In addition, these individuals may typically avoid seeking treatment. If they are denying or minimizing their difficulties, they may not follow through with treatment regimens or rehabilitation programs.

But is denial always harmful? The well-known health psychologist, Shelley Taylor (1991), points out that denial may not always be bad. Most individuals who are functioning well typically may deny the implications of a potentially serious condition, at least initially. A common reaction is to think and say that what they have is not serious, and even if it is, it will go away very quickly. Most people with serious diseases react this way, including those with cancer (Meyerowitz, 1983) and coronary heart disease (Krantz & Deckel, 1983). But several groups of investigators (for example, Hackett & Cassem, 1973; Meyerowitz, 1983) have found that during that extremely stressful period when a person is first diagnosed with a serious and perhaps chronic disease, denial of the implications (and avoidance of the inevitable emotional reactions of anxiety and depression that accompany the notification) may help the patient get through this period more easily. He or she is then more capable of developing coping responses at a later time. In one study, high initial denial resulted in less time in the intensive care section of the hospital (Levine et al., 1988), although after discharge, the same patients were not as good at doing what they had to do to enhance their rehabilitation. Other studies show lower levels of corticosteroids and other stress-related responses among deniers during the most stressful phase of the illness (Katz, Weiner, Gallagher, & Hellman, 1970).

Thus, the value of denial as a coping mechanism may depend more on timing than anything else. In the long run though, all the evidence indicates that, at some point in time, individuals must face their situations, process their emotions, and come to terms with what is happening in their lives.

Modifying Behaviors and Life-Styles to Promote Health

In 1991 the director of the National Institutes of Health said, "Our research is teaching us that many common diseases can be prevented and others can be postponed or controlled simply by making possible life style changes" (U.S. Department of Health and Human Services, 1991). Unhealthy eating habits, lack of exercise, and smoking are three of the most common examples that put us at risk in the long term for a number of physical disorders. A listing of high-risk behaviors or conditions is found in Table 9.4.

Many of these behaviors contribute to diseases and physical disorders that are among the leading causes of death. These would include not only coronary heart disease and cancer, described above, but also accidents of various kinds (related to consumption of alcohol and the nonuse of safety restraints), cirrhosis of the liver (related to excessive consumption of alcohol) and a variety of respiratory diseases including influenza and pneumonia, directly related to smoking and stress (Sexton, 1979). Considerable work is ongoing in developing effective behavior modification procedures for each of these high-risk areas, including diet modification, increasing adherence to drug and medical treatment programs, and developing optimal exercise programs. Here we review briefly two crucial areas of interest—injury control and the prevention of AIDS—and then look at two major community interventions.

Injury Control
Injuries are the leading cause of death for persons from ages 1 to 45. Furthermore, the loss of productivity to the individual and society from injuries is far greater than from the other three leading causes of death: heart disease, cancer, and stroke (Rice & MacKenzie, 1989). For this reason our government has become very interested in methods for reducing injury. Spielberger and Frank (1992) point out that psychological variables are crucial in mediating virtually all factors

Table 9.4 Areas for Health-Risk Behavior Modification

Smoking

Hyperlipidemia

High blood pressure

Dietary habits related to disease

High sodium; low calcium, magnesium, potassium—high blood pressure

High fat—cardiovascular disease and cancer of the prostate, breast, colon, and pancreas

High simple carbohydrates—diabetes mellitus

Low fiber—diabetes mellitus, digestive diseases, cardiovascular disease, colon cancer

Low intake of Vitamins A and C—cancer

Sedentary life-style

Obesity

Substance abuse (alcohol and drug)

Nonuse of seatbelts

High-risk sexual behavior

Nonadherence to recommended immunization and screening procedures

High stress levels and Type A personality

High-risk situations for childhood accidents, neglect, and abuse

Poor dental hygiene/infrequent care

Sun exposure

Poor-quality relationships/supports

Occupational risks

Source: Johns et al., 1987.

leading to injury. The psychological contributors have been understudied until recently. However, they are now beginning to receive attention, a good example being the work of Lizette Peterson and her colleagues (for instance, Peterson & Roberts, 1992). Peterson is particularly interested in preventing accidents in children. Injuries kill more children than the next six causes of death combined (Dershewitz & Williamson, 1977) and yet most individuals, including parents, don't think too much about preventing injuries, even in their own children. Most often they consider injuries to be due to fate and, therefore, out of their hands (Peterson, Farmer, & Kashani, 1990; Peterson & Roberts, 1992). A variety of programs with proven effectiveness, however, exist for preventing injuries in children. For example, children have been systematically and successfully taught to escape fires (Jones & Haney, 1984), identify and report emergencies (Jones & Kazdin, 1980), safely cross streets (Yeaton & Bailey, 1978), ride bicycles safely, and deal with

Lizette Peterson originated some important behavior-change procedures to prevent injuries in children.

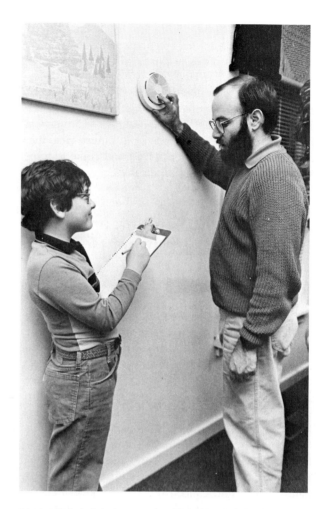

Appropriate training can reduce injuries and death in children.

injuries such as serious cuts (Peterson & Thiele, 1988). In many of these programs the participating children maintained the safety skills they had learned for months after the intervention—as long as assessments were continued, in most cases. Since there is little evidence that repeated warnings are effective in preventing injuries, more programmatic efforts to change behavior would seem to be very important, and yet such effective programs are almost nonexistent in most communities.

AIDS

In 1981, 189 cases of AIDS were reported in the United States, 77% of which were in New York and California. By 1992, the number of AIDS cases in the United States was approximately 235,000 and the cumulative number of deaths was 158,000 (Chesney, 1993). But this is only the beginning. Estimates place the number of Americans currently infected with HIV at 1.5 million, and the World Health Organization projects the number of infected individuals by the year 2000 to increase worldwide to between 30 and 40 million (Mann, 1991). There is no vaccine for the disease. Changing high-risk behavior is the only effective prevention strategy.

We discussed possible psychosocial contributions to the development of AIDS mediated by immune system functioning. It is possible that powerful stress-reduction procedures and other psychosocial interventions may prove to be an effective treatment for individuals already infected with the AIDS virus. These procedures might delay and possibly even prevent the onset of the disease and, in general, bolster the person's immune system. However, this outcome remains to be demonstrated.

A far more effective intervention would be to prevent infection with the AIDS virus to begin with. At the present time, in the absence of *any* treatments with proven effectiveness, either drug or psychosocial, prevention through behavior change is the only measure available to combat this modern-day plague (Kelly & Murphy, 1992).

Some countries take more draconian measures to alter behavior implicated in HIV transmission. Cuba, for example, has an ongoing program to test its entire population for HIV antibodies. People found to be infected with HIV are isolated from any interpersonal contact with individuals free of the virus to prevent the spread of the disease (Coates, 1990). Those measures would not be permissible or desirable in a democracy for more than a short period of time, particularly since the problem is not the presence of someone infected with HIV but rather the specific behaviors that person engages in.

One of the most successful behavior change programs ever conducted to combat the transmission of

HIV has been carried out in San Francisco during the past several years. Comprehensive programs like this are particularly important since testing alone and learning whether one is HIV positive or HIV negative does little to change behavior (for example, Landis, Earp, & Koch, 1992). Table 9.5 shows the specific behaviors that were targeted and the methods used to achieve behavior change in various groups in San

Table 9.5   The San Francisco Model: Coordinated Community-Level Program to Reduce New HIV Infection

Information	Motivation	Skills	Norms	Policy/legislation
Intervention: Media				
Educate about how HIV is and is not transmitted	Provide examples of different kinds of individuals who have become HIV infected	Model how to clean needles and use condoms and spermicides Model skills for safer sex/needle negotiation	Publicize the low prevalence of high-risk behaviors Publicize public desirability of safer sex classes and condom advertisements	Generate concern and action about policy
Health Care Establishments and Providers				
Provide educational materials and classes about HIV transmission	Ask all patients about risk factors for HIV transmission Advise high-risk patients to be tested for HIV antibodies	Provide classes and videos to demonstrate safe sex skills	Advise patients about prevalent community norms	Advocate policies and laws that will prevent spread of HIV
Schools				
Materials about HIV transmission and prevention	Models of teens who became infected with HIV	Classes and models for safe sex/drug injection skills	Create a climate of acceptance for HIV infected students and teachers Publicize student perceptions about desirability of safe sex	Mobilize students and faculty to work to allow sex education to take place in the schools Condom machines in bathrooms
Worksites				
Materials and videos about HIV transmission and prevention	Examples of co-workers who became infected with HIV	Classes and models for safe sex/drug injection skills	Create a climate of acceptance for HIV infected persons	Policy: Allow HIV infected persons to work Condom machines in bathrooms
STD, Family Planning, and Drug Abuse Treatment Centers				
Materials and video models about HIV transmission	Detailed assessment of HIV risk Advise about testing for antibodies to HIV	Classes and videos for safer sex/drug injection skills Instruction and rehearsal of safer sex/drug injection skills during medical and counseling encounters		Mobilize clients to request additional treatment slots and facilities Advocate beneficial laws and policies
Community Organizations (Churches, Clubs)				
Guest speakers, materials, videos available	Examples of HIV infected individuals similar to club/organization membership	Classes and videos for AIDS risk-reduction skills		Advocate policy changes and laws suggesting AIDS risk reduction
Antibody Testing Centers				
Materials and instruction about HIV transmission	Detailed assessment of risk for HIV infection		Classes and videos for AIDS risk-reduction skills	Advocate confidentiality and nondiscrimination

Note: HIV = human immunodeficiency virus; STD = sexually transmitted disease.

Source: Coates, 1990.

Francisco in that community's successful model. Prior to the introduction of this program, frequent unprotected sex was reported by 37.4% of one sample and 33.9% of another sample of gay men in the city (Stall, McKusick, Wiley, Coates, & Ostrow, 1986). At a follow-up point in 1988 the incidence had dropped to 1.7% and 4.2%, respectively, in the same two samples (Ekstrand & Coates, 1990). These changes did not occur in comparable groups where a program of this type had not been instituted. Careful evaluation of smaller groups or individuals at risk demonstrates that high-risk sexual practices among these individuals are reduced substantially by a comprehensive program of cognitive-behavioral self-management training and the development of an effective social support network, compared to control subjects who do not receive the program (Kelly, St. Lawrence, Hood, & Brasfield, 1989).

Analysis of factors that predict the adoption of safe sex practices indicates consistently that high self-efficacy and perceived control over one's own sexual behavior are very strong determinants of successful risk reduction (Aspinwall, Kemeny, Taylor, Schneider, & Dudley, 1991; O'Leary, 1992). Thus, treatment programs should focus on instilling in participants a sense of control and self-efficacy over their own sexual practices.

It is crucial that these programs be extended to minorities and women since these groups frequently do not perceive themselves to be at risk. Their lack of perception can probably be traced to media coverage, most of which has focused on gay white males (Mays & Cochran, 1988). Indeed, most research on the epidemiology and natural history of AIDS has largely ignored the disease in women (Ickovics & Rodin, 1992). And

yet, as demonstrated in Table 9.6, the number of female cases as a percentage of all cases is steadily rising. In 1992 women accounted for 14% of AIDS cases and the proportion continues to grow rapidly. A report from the Centers for Disease Control and Prevention indicates that women are contracting AIDS four times as fast as men. Furthermore, the highest age of risk for women is in late adolescence between ages 15 and 25. This contrasts with the peak risk for men, which occurs during the late 20s and early 30s. In fact, women between the ages of 15 and 25 make up about 70% of the 3,000 women per day who become infected with AIDS and the 500 women per day who die of AIDS, according to a recent report from the United Nations Development Program. The primary mode of transmission in women is now heterosexual interactions rather than intravenous drug use. Particularly tragic is the fact that 67% of all women with AIDS are black or Hispanic, and most are socially disadvantaged and poor (Centers for Disease Control, 1991). The incidence is particularly high among prostitutes and among those carrying sexually transmitted diseases, possibly because features of various sexually transmitted diseases, such as open genital sores, facilitate transmission of the disease. Even more tragically, women die significantly sooner than men after developing AIDS (Friedland, Saltzman, Vilene, Freeman, Schrager, & Klein, 1991).

In view of the very different circumstances in which women put themselves at risk for HIV infection—for example, the economic reasons some of these women engage in high-risk behaviors (for instance, prostitution)—effective behavior change programs for them must be very different from the ones developed for men. And yet we have barely begun to attend to this pressing need.

Table 9.6   Number of AIDS Cases Reported Between 1981 and 1991 by Sex, and Percentage of Female Cases in Total

Sex	Year(s)										
	1981–1982	1983	1984	1985	1986	1987	1988	1989	1990	1991*	Total†
Female	48	155	293	530	923	1,690	3,281	3,639	4,890	5,246	20,739
Male	795	2,065	4,253	7,580	11,987	19,333	28,320	30,946	37,667	35,884	178,678
Percentage of female cases in total	5.7	7.0	6.4	6.5	7.1	8.0	10.4	10.5	11.5	12.8	10.4

Notes: Data accumulated from Centers for Disease Control HIV/AIDS Surveillance Report for each calendar year, Atlanta, GA. A new definition of AIDS was instituted in 1987.
*New cases through November 30, 1991.
†A slight discrepancy exists between the cumulative total as reported by the CDC and the sum of figures given in each of the annual surveillance reports.

Source: Ickovics & Rodin, 1992.

Community Interventions

There is increasing evidence that some of the most effective interventions to change behavior and prevent disease occur at the level of the community rather than the individual, and therefore fall directly within the purview of our national public health policy. We will look at two examples.

Smoking in China

In China, smoking is a major health-related behavioral risk factor. Despite efforts of the Chinese government to reduce smoking behavior in its citizens, China is reported to have one of the most tobacco-addicted populations in the world. Approximately 250 million individuals in China are habitual smokers, 90% of them male. This number equals the entire population of the United States—men, women, and children. In an attempt to reach these individuals, Chinese health professionals took advantage of the strong family ties in China and decided to persuade the *children* of these smokers to attempt to intervene with their fathers. In 1989 they developed an antismoking campaign in 23 primary schools in Hangzhou Province. These children took home antismoking literature and questionnaires to almost 10,000 fathers to fill out and return. The children then wrote their fathers letters, asking them to quit smoking, and they submitted monthly reports on their fathers' smoking habits to the schools. Approximately 9 months later the results were assessed. Indeed, the intervention by the children had had some effect. Almost 12% of the fathers in the intervention group had quit smoking for at least 6 months. By contrast, in a control group of another 10,000 males, the quit rate was only 0.2% ("Somber News," 1993).

Stanford Three Community Study

One of the best-known and most successful efforts to reduce risk factors for disease in the community is known as the *Stanford Three Community Study* (Meyer, Nash, McAlister, Maccoby, & Farquhar, 1980). Rather than assemble three groups of people, these investigators studied three entire communities in northern California that were reasonably alike in size and type of residents between 1972 and 1975. The target was reduction of risk factors for coronary heart disease (CHD). The risk-reducing behaviors introduced included reductions in smoking and high blood pressure, dietary changes, and weight reduction. In the first community, Tracy, no interventions were conducted, but detailed information was collected from a random sample of adults to assess any increases in their knowledge of risk factors as well as any changes in risk factors over time. In addition, these participants also received a medical examination assessing cardiovascular factors. The residents of the community of Gilroy and part of Watsonville were subjected to a media blitz

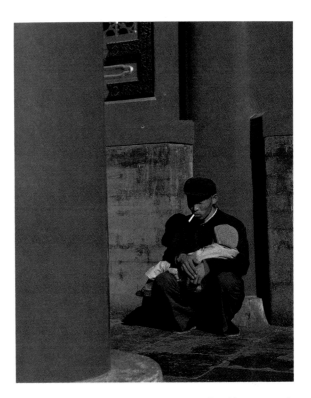

The prevalence of smoking is a serious health concern in China.

educating them on the dangers of behavioral risk factors for CHD and the importance of, as well as helpful hints for, reducing these factors. Most residents of the third community, Watsonville, not only received the media blitz but also had a face-to-face intervention in which behavioral counselors worked with the townspeople judged to be at particularly high risk for CHD. Subjects in all three communities were surveyed once a year for a three-year period following the intervention.

Results reflected in Figure 9.9 indicate that the interventions were markedly successful at reducing risk factors for coronary heart disease in these communities. Furthermore, for the residents of Watsonville who also received individual counseling, risk factors were substantially lower than for people in Tracy, or even in Gilroy and the part of Watsonville who received only the media blitz, and their knowledge of risk factors was substantially higher.

Interventions such as the Stanford study cost money, although in many communities the media are willing to donate time to such a worthy effort. The results from this study show that mounting an effort like this is worthwhile to the community; it is also valuable to public health officials since many lives almost certainly will be saved, and disability days will be decreased in a way that will more than cover the original cost of the program.

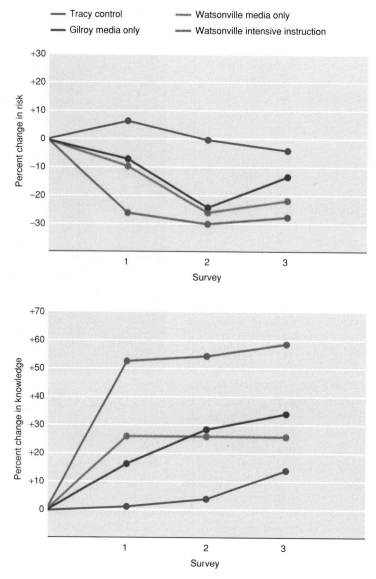

Figure 9.9   Results of the Stanford Three Community Study (from Meyer et al., 1980)

Summary

• Psychological and social factors play a major role in the development and maintenance of a number of physical disorders. These factors influence health and physical problems in two distinct ways.

• First, psychological and social factors may contribute directly to illness and disease. One way this occurs is through the psychological effects of stress on the immune system and other physical functions. Other diseases that may be related in part to the effects of stress on the immune system include AIDS, rheumatoid arthritis, and cancer.

• Second, long-standing patterns of behavior or life-style may put people at risk for developing certain physical disorders. As examples, unhealthy sexual practices can lead to AIDS and other sexually transmitted diseases. Unhealthy behavioral patterns, such as poor eating habits or lack of exercise, may contribute to coronary heart disease.

• Fully 50% of deaths from the 10 leading causes of death in the United States can be traced to behaviors that are a part of certain life-styles.

• Psychological and social factors also contribute in a fairly substantial manner to the chronic pain many people experience.

• A variety of psychosocial treatments have been developed with the goal of either treating or preventing physical disorders. Among these are biofeedback, relaxation, and comprehensive stress- and pain-reduction programs.

• Other interventions aim to modify behaviors and life-styles such as unsafe sexual practices, smoking, or unhealthy dietary habits to prevent the onset of disease.

Key Terms

AIDS-related complex (ARC) (343)
antigens (341)
autoimmune disease (341)
behavioral medicine (331)
biofeedback (362)
cancer (345)
cardiovascular disease (348)
chronic fatigue syndrome (CFS) (361)
chronic pain (355)
coronary heart disease (351)
corticosteroids (336)

endogenous opioids (357)
essential hypertension (349)
general adaptation syndrome (GAS) (335)
health psychology (331)
hypertension (349)
immune system (341)
migraine [headaches] (358)
neuromodulators (neuropeptides) (335)
psychoncology (345)

psychoneuroimmunology (PNI) (342)
relaxation response (364)
rheumatoid arthritis (345)
self-efficacy (340)
stress (334)
strokes (cerebral vascular accidents, CVA) (348)
tension [headaches] (358)
Type A behavior pattern (352)
Type B behavior pattern (352)

O sleep! O gentle sleep!
Nature's soft nurse, how have I frightened thee,
That thou no more wilt weigh my eyelids down
And steep my senses in forgetfulness?
William Shakespeare
Henry IV, Part III, i, 5

10
Sleep Disorders

Many of us who read about the 1989 *Exxon Valdez* oil spill assume that it was caused by the alcohol problems of the captain. In actuality, the disaster may have occurred because the ship's third mate—who was in charge at the time—was suffering from severe fatigue due to lack of sleep. His exhaustion has been credited with causing the mistakes that led to the grounding of the oil tanker (Holden, 1993).

We spend about one-third of our lives asleep. That means most of us sleep nearly 3,000 hours *a year.* A question that arises frequently is, What is a "normal" amount of sleep? Most of us think that 8 hours of sleep out of a 24-hour period is ideal, but this varies considerably from person to person. For some people, 5 to 6 hours per night is enough for them to feel fully rested; others may need as much as 9 hours. Our sleep needs also change as we age (see Figure 10.1). Infants sleep as much as 16½ hours per day, while college-age students average 7 to 8 hours per day. When people pass the age of 50, their total hours of sleep per day can drop to below 6 hours.

For many of us, our sleeping hours energize us, both mentally and physically. However, you or someone you know probably has a problem sleeping. Most of us know what it's like to have a bad night's sleep. The next day we're a little tired and groggy, and as the day wears on, we may become irritable. Imagine

if you can that this is a chronic problem for you, and it has been years since you've had a good night's sleep. Your relationships suffer, your schoolwork is more difficult, and your efficiency and productivity at work are negatively affected. It is possible that lack of sleep would also affect you physically. People who do not get enough sleep often report more health problems and more frequent hospitalizations than those who sleep normally (Morin, 1993). Sleep problems in the United States are estimated to cost about $50 billion per year in lost worker productivity, absenteeism, and related outcomes (Holden, 1993).

The pervasiveness of sleep problems in our society has attracted both public and scientific attention. A casual inspection of a local bookstore will uncover numerous popular books on such topics as dreams and their meaning along with ways to help you or your child sleep better. At the same time, research on the topic of sleep and its disorders has blossomed in recent years, and we now have a greater understanding of the causes of many of the sleep problems and how to treat them. This chapter describes this recent work, as we highlight some of the more common sleep problems.

Here you might ask yourself how sleep disorders fit into a textbook on abnormal psychology. The different variations of disturbed sleep, such as being unable to fall asleep at night, not getting sufficient rest

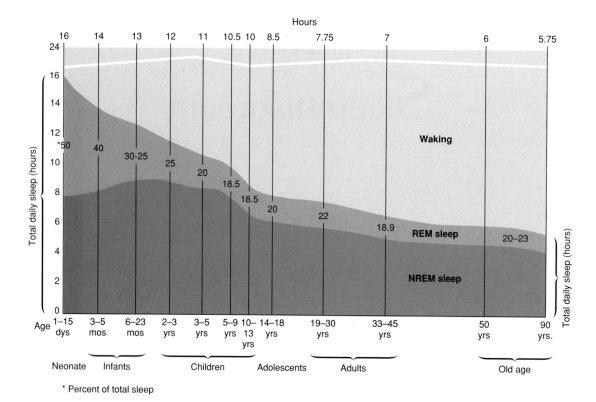

Figure 10.1   Sleep across the life span: Graph showing changes with age in total amounts of NREM sleep and REM sleep as well as percentage of REM sleep. Note the sharp diminution of REM sleep in the early years. REM sleep falls from 8 hours at birth to less than 1 hour in old age. The amount of NREM sleep remains more constant, falling from 8 hours to 5 hours (from Roffwarg, Muzio, & Dement, 1966).

even with a full night's sleep, or walking and talking during sleep, clearly have physiological bases and therefore could be considered purely medical concerns. However, just as we saw in Chapter 9 when we reviewed physical disorders, all the sleep problems interact in important ways with psychological factors.

Sleep and its deviations have been influential in the development of modern-day concepts of abnormal psychology. Early therapies such as *moral treatment*—used in the 19th century for people with severe mental illness—relied to a degree on having the patient get adequate amounts of sleep as part of the therapy (Armstrong, 1993). Sigmund Freud placed a great deal of emphasis on dreams and would ask his patients to write down and later discuss their dreams with him to help both Freud and the patients better understand their emotional lives (Anch, Browman, Mitler, & Walsh, 1988). Early work with sleep deprivation (preventing people from sleeping for prolonged periods of time) showed that chronic lack of sleep had profound effects on some people. One of the early studies in this area looked at the effects of keeping 350 volunteers awake for 112 hours (Tyler, 1955). Seven of these volunteers engaged in bizarre, psychotic-like behavior. Subsequent research suggested that interfering with the sleep of people with preexisting psycho-

logical problems can create these disturbing results (Brauchi & West, 1959).

Sleep disorders in and of themselves can result in the "harmful distress" that is characteristic of the other disorders we consider in this text. Contemporary clinicians now recognize the importance of sleep and its disorders in understanding other psychological problems. A number of the disorders covered in this book are frequently associated with sleep complaints, including schizophrenia, major depression, bipolar disorder, and anxiety-related disorders. Your first impression may be to think of a sleep problem as the *outcome* or the result of having a psychological disorder such as anxiety or depression. For example, how many of you have been anxious about some future event (for example, an upcoming exam) and have not been able to fall asleep? However, the nature of the relationship between sleep disturbances and our mental health is more complex. Sleep problems may themselves be the cause of difficulties people experience in everyday life (Balter & Bauer, 1975), or they may result from some disturbance common to both sleep problems and other psychological disorders. For example, in Chapter 5 we discussed how the *locus ceruleus,* which is in the brain stem and is innervated by noradrenergic circuits, was involved with the experience of anxiety. We also know that this region of the brain is involved with our dream sleep (otherwise called REM or rapid eye movement sleep) (Ware, 1988). This shared neurobiological connection suggests that anxiety and sleep may be interrelated in important ways, although the exact nature of the relationship is still unknown to us.

Similarly, recent work with depressed individuals suggests that REM sleep (rapid eye movement sleep) may also be related to this disorder. In an intriguing recent study, researchers have found that cognitive-behavior therapy resulted not only in improvement in depressed symptoms among a group of depressed men but also in more normalized REM sleep patterns (Nofzinger et al., 1994). Furthermore, depriving people of sleep has been shown to have temporary antidepressant effects in a portion of people with depression (Hillman, Kripke, & Gillin, 1990). Although we do not fully understand the interaction of psychological disorders and the mechanisms involved with sleep, accumulating research points to the importance of understanding sleep if we are to help complete the broader picture of abnormal behavior.

Overview of Sleep

Our bodies go through regular cycles throughout the day; at certain times we are very active and alert while at other times we are more tranquil and serene. During sleep the brain is not "shut off" but is instead going through much the same type of cyclical process the body does when we are awake. This cycle of sleep is divided into two broad categories: **rapid eye movement** or **REM sleep** (what we commonly refer to as dream sleep), and **non-rapid eye movement** or **NREM** (pronounced non-REM) **sleep** (Hauri, 1982). Our brain cycles through these stages of sleep throughout the night in a pattern that is similar across all human beings.

The NREM sleep is usually divided into four stages (referred to as stages 1–4), and these stages are based on different brain wave patterns seen during different points in NREM sleep (see Figure 10.2). The brain wave patterns are measured using an electroencephalogram or EEG. The stages of sleep roughly correspond to how deeply we sleep. For example, stage 1 represents "light" sleep, stage 2 would be a "deeper" sleep, and stages 3 and 4 represent the "deepest" levels of sleep. Stage 1 sleep is a transitional stage between sleep and wakefulness (if you remember, this is where Tinkerbell told Peter Pan she would wait for him!). People tend to feel that they are awake during this time, although their thoughts begin to drift; in research when volunteers had their eyes taped open, they couldn't recall pictures presented to them while they were in this

sleep stage (Rechtschaffen & Foulkes, 1965). As the brain runs through its cycle and shifts back from the deeper stages of sleep into the light sleep of stage 1, we also go through what is called "partial arousals" or "partial wakenings" (Anch, Browman, Mitler, & Walsh, 1988). If you've ever slept next to someone who, in the middle of the night, sat up, looked around, maybe even said something, and then went back to sleep, but did not remember the event the next morning, you have witnessed a partial wakening. In other words, we all wake up briefly several times each night, but we tend to go right back to sleep and not remember these episodes the next day.

Stage 2 is the first true sleep state and includes two characteristic brain wave patterns called *sleep spindles* and *K-complexes*. Because they are very similar, stages 3 and 4 sleep are often considered together by researchers, who refer to them collectively as *slow wave* or *delta sleep* (for the type of brain wave pattern), or *deep sleep*. It is very difficult to wake someone from this stage of sleep; even if you are successful, it can take some time before the person is fully alert. We begin sleep in NREM sleep and progress through stages 1 through 4. A complete "cycle" of the four stages of NREM sleep takes about 90 minutes in adults and about 60 minutes in infants (Hauri, 1982) (see Figure 10.3).

A number of sleep disorders occur primarily during NREM sleep, including sleepwalking, sleep terrors (a disorder characterized by extreme emotional distress while sleeping but not occurring during dream or REM sleep), and sleep bruxism (grinding the teeth during sleep) (Giles & Buysse, 1993). The purpose of NREM sleep is still unknown, although some preliminary research indicates that one function may be related to the immune system—possibly signaling the rebuilding of this system (Blakeslee, 1993; Palmblad, Petrini, Wasserman, & Akerstedt, 1979). If this supposition is found to be true, it may explain why people who get little sleep and therefore do not revitalize their immune systems seem to be more susceptible to illness.

Following this progression of sleep stages (from stages 1 to 4), we then move into rapid eye movement or REM sleep. Most of you also know that this is the period of time when we dream. If you wake someone during REM sleep, about 80% of the time the person will report very vivid dreams (Snyder, 1971). Our eyes move rapidly during this time, yet the body is "atonic" or does not move. If you look at a person's closed eyelids while he or she is in REM sleep, you will see the eyelids move because of the movement of the eyes under them. Rapid eye movement can be measured more formally by use of an *electrooculograph* (EOG), which can detect the activity of the muscles that are responsible for eye movement. REM sleep is often char-

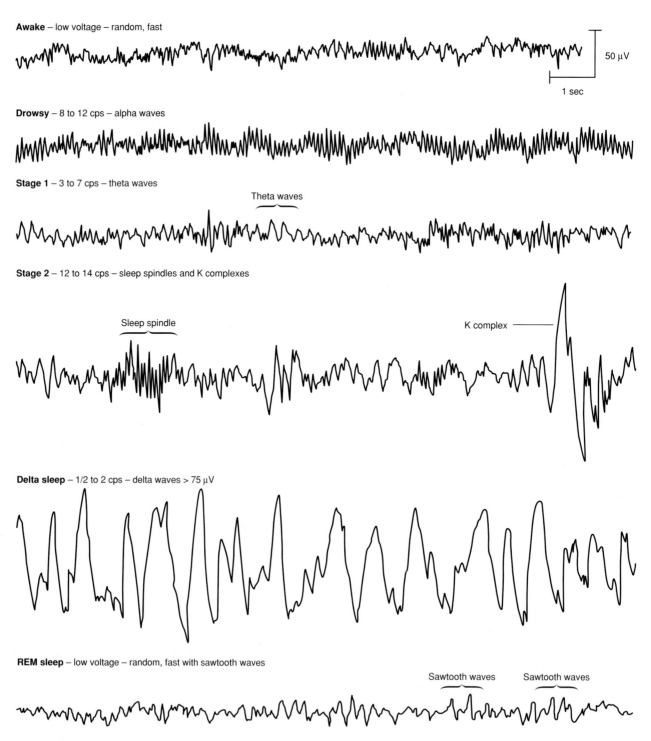

Figure 10.2   EEG's of sleep stages (from Hauri, 1982)

acterized as a time when the brain is active but the body is not; in contrast, NREM sleep is a time during sleep when the brain is relatively inactive but the body is not. We progress through NREM and REM stages of sleep several times throughout the night (Carskadon & Dement, 1989).

Depriving people of REM sleep—which is done by monitoring their brain waves while they are asleep and then waking them as they enter REM—gives us some insight into its importance to us. When people are deprived of REM sleep they will tend to compensate (Dement, 1960). After several nights of not going through REM sleep, people will attempt to enter this sleep stage more frequently and more quickly on successive nights, and they will "rebound" by having more REM sleep across the next few nights.

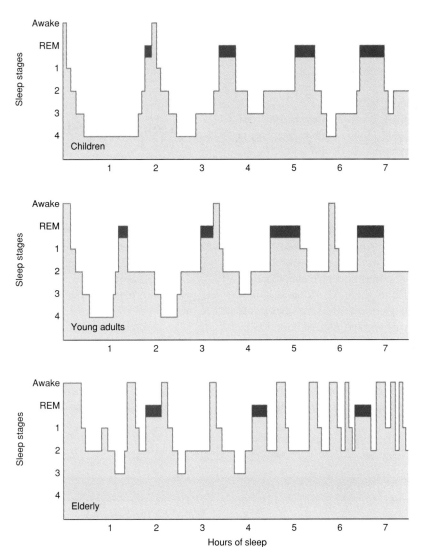

Figure 10.3 Sleep cycles. A representative night for a child, a young adult, and an elderly person. The occurrence of each sleep stage varies throughout the night. The difference in stage 4 sleep across the three age groups is most dramatic (from Kales & Kales, 1974).

There is some evidence that REM sleep is involved with memory in helping us consolidate newly learned information (Smith & Lapp, 1991). One implication of this research is that it may be important to get a good night's sleep after studying in order to remember the material for an exam! Although we don't yet fully understand the function of REM sleep—what purpose it serves for our physical and mental well-being—it is generally thought to serve some restorative function for the brain.

Some sleep disturbances occur primarily during REM sleep. As you might expect, nightmares are reported when people are in this sleep stage. Another predominantly REM sleep phenomenon is called *sleep paralysis;* in this state, people are unable to move their arms or legs and often experience brief but intense fear. A number of other disorders occur during either NREM

or REM sleep, and include urination while sleeping (called *sleep enuresis*), snoring, and talking in your sleep.

Classifying Sleep Problems

Throughout this textbook, we have used the American Psychiatric Association's *Diagnostic and Statistical Manual* (DSM-IV) as a guide for discussing the disorders. Table 10.1 lists the DSM-IV sleep disorders, divided into **dyssomnias** and **parasomnias.** Dyssomnias are sleep problems that involve difficulties in getting enough sleep, problems with sleeping when you want to—not being able to fall asleep until 2 A.M. when you have a 9 A.M. class—and complaints about the quality of sleep, such as not feeling refreshed even though you have slept the whole night. The second group of sleep disorders—the parasomnias—are characterized by abnormal behavioral or physiological events that occur during sleep, such as nightmares and sleepwalking (see Table 10.1).

Not until DSM-III-R was published in 1987 did the manual provide a separate section for sleep disorders (Buysse, Reynolds, & Kupfer, 1993). In DSM-IV the number of sleep disorders has been expanded to include narcolepsy (sleep attacks throughout the day) and breathing-related sleep disorder (sleepiness attributed to disrupted sleep caused by breathing difficulties during sleep). However, there are many sleep disorders—more than are in DSM-IV and more than we can describe in this book—and there is also a separate and more comprehensive classification system that is used to identify them. This system, called the *International Classification of Sleep Disorders* (ICSD) (American Sleep Disorders Association, 1990), lists over 80 individual sleep disorders and was developed by the American Sleep Disorders Association in conjunction with the European Sleep Research Society, the Japanese Society of Sleep Research, and the Latin American Sleep Society. Readers interested in learning more about the range of problems surrounding sleep may want to refer to this resource. Here we limit our discussion primarily to the sleep problems outlined in the DSM-IV.

Assessing Sleep Problems

How do you determine whether you have a sleep problem, and if so, what that problem might be? Usually, people tell their doctor if they are not sleeping well; the physician will typically make a diagnosis and prescribe a treatment based on the patient's verbal report. Unfortunately, people are often unaware of important facts about their own sleep habits. They may thus provide misinformation about the problem, which can lead to improper diagnosis and inappropriate treatment.

Determining the nature and cause of many sleep disorders often requires identifying a number of factors. The best and most complete picture of your sleep habits can be determined only by a **polysomnographic (PSG) evaluation.** This is a type of testing in which the patient spends one or more nights sleeping

Table 10.1 DSM-IV Sleep Disorders

	Sleep Disorder	Description
Dyssomnias	(Disturbances in the amount, timing, or quality of sleep.)	
	Primary Insomnia	Difficulty initiating or maintaining sleep, or sleep that is not restorative (person not feeling rested even after normal amounts of sleep).
	Primary Hypersomnia	Complaint of excessive sleepiness that is displayed as either prolonged sleep episodes or daytime sleep episodes.
	Narcolepsy	Irresistible attacks of refreshing sleep occurring daily, accompanied by episodes of brief loss of muscle tone (cataplexy).
	Breathing-Related Sleep Disorder	Sleep disruption leading to excessive sleepiness or insomnia that is caused by sleep-related breathing difficulties.
	Circadian Rhythm Sleep Disorder (Sleep-Wake Schedule Disorder)	Persistent or recurrent sleep disruption leading to excessive sleepiness or insomnia that is due to a mismatch between the sleep-wake schedule required by a person's environment and his or her circadian sleep-wake pattern.
Parasomnias	(Disturbances in arousal and sleep stage transition that intrude into the sleep process.)	
	Nightmare Disorder (Dream Anxiety Disorder)	Repeated awakenings with detailed recall of extended and extremely frightening dreams, usually involving threats to survival, security, or self-esteem. The awakenings generally occur during the second half of the sleep period.
	Sleep Terror Disorder	Recurrent episodes of abrupt awakening from sleep, usually occurring during the first third of the major sleep episode and beginning with a panicky scream.
	Sleepwalking Disorder	Repeated episodes of arising from bed during sleep and walking about, usually occurring during the first third of the major sleep episode.

Source: DSM-IV, APA, 1994.

A man participates in an overnight polysomnographic evaluation of his sleep.

in a "sleep laboratory" while being monitored on a number of measures, including respiration and oxygen desaturation (a measure of airflow); leg movements; brain wave activity, measured by an *electroencephalograph* (EEG); eye movements, measured by an *electrooculograph* (EOG); muscle movements, measured by an *electromyograph* (EMG); and heart activity, measured by an *electrocardiogram*. In addition, the individual's daytime behavior and typical sleep patterns are noted—for example, whether he or she uses drugs or alcohol, is experiencing anxiety over work or other interpersonal problems, takes afternoon naps, or has a psychological disorder.

Collecting all these data can be both timely and costly, but it is important to ensure an accurate diagnosis and treatment plan. With advances in electronic technologies, a new version of PSG evaluation is on the rise. It involves what is called *ambulatory polysomnography* because it is portable and allows patients to do the necessary data collection in their own homes (McCall, Edinger, & Erwin, 1989). The data can then be analyzed by a computer and evaluated by a sleep disorder professional. This new methodology has several advantages. It may help reduce the high cost of sleep lab evaluations, and, more important, the data collected may more accurately represent the individual's normal sleep patterns because it is recorded while

he is in his familiar sleep environment. A drawback is that without a technician on the scene, if any of the equipment is improperly attached or operating, the data will be inaccurate and the procedure will have to be repeated. Also, the technician can control extraneous variables in a laboratory setting more readily than in a home setting. Nonetheless, this may be a situation where the benefits of the natural environment—and more natural sleep—outweigh the control of the laboratory.

In addition to all the data gained from a polysomnograph, clinicians and researchers find it helpful to know the individual's **total sleep time (TST),** the total number of hours she sleeps each day. It is also informative to know the individual's **sleep efficiency (SE),** the *percentage* of time she actually sleeps as opposed to being in bed, either trying to sleep or sleeping. Sleep efficiency is calculated by dividing the amount of time sleeping by the amount of time in bed. A SE of 100% would mean that you fall asleep as soon as your head hits the pillow and do not have times during the night when you lie awake in bed. In contrast, a SE of 50% would mean that half the time you spend in bed you are trying to fall asleep—that is, half the time you are awake. These ways of looking at sleep (TST and SE) help the clinician determine objectively how well you sleep.

How do you determine how "sleepy" a person is? One frequently used test of sleepiness was developed by Mary Carskadon and William Dement and is called the *Multiple Sleep Latency Test* (MSLT) (Carskadon & Dement, 1982). This test involves scheduling naps for the people being assessed and seeing how long it takes them to fall asleep. These naps are usually at

The technology for conducting a polysomnographic analysis now provides the possibility of using portable equipment, making unnecessary an overnight stay in a sleep laboratory.

9:30 A.M., 11:30 A.M., 1:30 P.M., 3:30 P.M., and 5:30 P.M., and the person is monitored in a laboratory bedroom. The time between "lights out" and when you fall asleep is measured for each nap. A mean MSLT time of about 10 to 15 minutes is considered average for adults; much shorter times—less than 6–7 minutes—may be considered problematic.

One way to determine whether a person has a problem with sleep is to observe his behavior when he is awake (also referred to as daytime *sequelae*). For example, if it takes you 90 minutes to fall asleep at night, but this occurrence doesn't bother you, and you feel rested during the day, then you would not have a problem. On the other hand, if your friend also takes 90 minutes to fall asleep, but finds this delay in going to sleep to be anxiety provoking and feels fatigued during the day, then it might be considered a sleep problem for her. As you can see, whether a person's sleep habits are considered a problem is to some degree a subjective decision and is dependent in part on how the person perceives and reacts to the situation.

Dyssomnias

Primary Insomnia

Insomnia is one of the most frequently expressed concerns of people who have sleep disorders. You may picture someone who has insomnia as being awake all the time and never sleeping. However, it isn't possible to go completely without sleep. For example, if someone does not sleep for more than about 40 hours, he will begin having brief periods (several seconds or longer) of sleep called **microsleeps** (Anch, Browman, Mitler, & Walsh, 1988). Despite the common use of the term *insomnia* to mean "not sleeping," it actually involves a number of complaints. People are considered to have insomnia if they have trouble falling asleep at night (difficulty initiating sleep), if they wake up frequently during the night or wake up too early and can't go back to sleep (difficulty maintaining sleep), or even if they are sleeping a reasonable number of hours but still feel that they are not rested during the day (nonrestorative sleep).

Consider the following case.

The Case of Kathryn

Kathryn was a 73-year-old woman who reported having difficulty with her sleep for the past 19 years. Her problems seem to have originated around the time her husband died. This traumatic event seriously disrupted her sleep to the point that she could not fall asleep each night until she had lain in bed for several hours, and she would awaken a number of times each night. She slept an average of 4–5 hours per night. It is not surprising that she was chronically tired throughout the day and complained that her fatigue interfered with her friendships. She no longer enjoyed activities like going to the movies or concerts with her friends because she would fall asleep and this was very embarrassing to her.

Kathryn had used nonprescription "sleeping pills" on and off over the years during times when she needed to feel rested. At other times, she would just lie in her bed listening to the radio. She thought that she probably "nodded off" occasionally but would wake up periodically throughout the night. When her sleep problems first started, she recognized her distress over her husband's death as probably being to blame. As the years passed, she assumed her lack of sleep was normal for a person her age and that her fatigue was also part of the aging process. However, the last few months had been particularly difficult for her when she began to realize that she wasn't playing with her grandchildren and wasn't leaving her house because she was too tired. On the advice of a friend, she decided to get some help.

We will return to Kathryn's case and how we treated her sleep problems later in this chapter.

Clinical Description

The DSM-IV diagnostic criteria for insomnia are listed in Table 10.2. DSM-IV refers to this problem as **primary insomnia**—using the term *primary* to indicate that the complaint of sleep problems is not related to other medical or psychiatric problems. For example, if a person were suffering from severe pain and couldn't sleep, the sleep problem would be "secondary" or resulting from the pain and not a separate and distinct problem. The difficulty with looking at sleep disorders as "primary" can be seen in our previous discussion of the overlap between sleep problems and other psychological disorders such as anxiety and depression. Because these problems are so interrelated—for example, when not sleeping makes you anxious, being anxious further interrupts your sleep, which makes you more anxious, and so on—it is uncommon to find a person with just a "simple" sleep disorder and no other related problems.

Kathryn's case is typical for people who experience insomnia. She had trouble both initiating sleep (falling asleep at night) and maintaining sleep (sleeping through the night without interruption).

Table 10.2   DSM-IV Criteria for Pimary Insomnia

A. The predominant complaint is difficulty initiating or maintaining sleep, or nonrestorative sleep, for at least 1 month.

B. The sleep disturbance (or associated daytime fatigue) causes clinically significant distress or impairment in social, occupational, or other important areas of functioning.

C. The sleep disturbance does not occur exclusively during the course of Narcolepsy, Breathing-Related Sleep Disorder, Circadian Rhythm Sleep Disorder, or a Parasomnia.

D. The disturbance does not occur exclusively during the course of another mental disorder (e.g., Major Depressive Disorder, Generalized Anxiety Disorder, a delirium).

E. The disturbance is not due to the direct physiological effects of a substance (e.g, a drug of abuse, a medication) or a general medical condition.

Source: DSM-IV, APA, 1994.

Other people will sleep through an entire night but still feel as if they've been up for hours. As a result of their disturbed sleep, people with this disorder often feel tired and drained throughout the day, having difficulty concentrating for any length of time. Although most of these people can carry out necessary day-to-day activities, their problems with attention and concentration can result in serious consequences, such as debilitating accidents when they attempt to do things such as drive long distances (e.g., bus drivers) or handle dangerous material (e.g., electricians). Kathryn, for example, wouldn't drive her car on the highway because she was fearful of falling asleep at the wheel. Students with insomnia may do poorly in school because of difficulty concentrating.

Statistics and Course for Insomnia

Problems of insomnia are the most common of sleep problems. Almost a third of the general population will report some symptoms of insomnia during any given year, and 17% indicate that their problems with sleeping are "severe" (Gillin, 1993). In a recent study, 31% of the people who expressed concern about their sleeping problems continued to experience these difficulties a year later (Ford & Kamerow, 1989), a result showing that many sleep problems do not just "go away"; they may become chronic. In fact, insomnia appears to be one of the most frequently reported health complaints made to physicians, second only to pain (Morin, 1993).

A number of psychological disorders are associated with problems of insomnia (Benca, Obermeyer, Thisted, & Gillin, 1992). Total sleep time (the amount of time spent sleeping) is often decreased among people with depression, substance use disorders, anxiety disorders, and dementia of the Alzheimer's type. The interrelationship between alcohol use and sleep disorders can be particularly troubling. Alcohol is one of the most common methods people use to initiate sleep (Gillin, 1993). In small amounts it will induce sleep, but it will also interrupt ongoing sleep. Interrupted sleep will cause drowsiness, often leading to repeated alcohol use and an obviously vicious cycle.

Women report problems with insomnia twice as often as do men. Does this mean that men sleep better than women? Not necessarily. Our impression of how well or poorly we sleep often does not match more objective measures. Some people complain of insomnia, but assessment of their actual sleep indicates that they are sleeping a normal amount of time, a condition that is referred to as **sleep state misperception (SSM).** Other people underestimate their sleeping difficulties. Researchers studying older adults who do not report sleep problems have found among this group of supposedly good sleepers that the men were more likely to experience obstructed breathing during sleep (called *sleep apnea*) and periodic jerky movements of the arms and legs (referred to as *nocturnal myoclonus*) (Reynolds et al., 1985). These sleep problems can be serious, yet none of the men were aware of them. Remember, insomnia (or other sleep problems) is generally considered a problem only *if you experience discomfort about it*. This means that women are more frequently diagnosed as having insomnia because of their more frequent reports of the problem, not necessarily because their sleep is more disrupted than that of men. Women may be more aware of their sleep patterns or may be more comfortable acknowledging and seeking help for their sleeping difficulties compared to men.

Just as normal sleep needs differ with age, the frequency of complaints of insomnia also differ among people of different ages. With children the "difficulty initiating sleep" usually takes the form of bedtime tantrums or complaints of not wanting to go to bed. Many children who wake up in the middle of the night experience crying and distress. Estimates of insomnia among young children range from 25% to over 40% of all children (Mindell, 1993). This percentage goes down in adolescence and early adulthood but rises to more than 25% again for people over the age of 65 (Mellinger, Balter, & Uhlenhuth, 1985). This increase in reports of sleeping problems among older people makes sense if you remember that the number of hours we sleep decreases as we age. It is not uncommon for someone over 65 to sleep fewer than 6 hours and wake up several times each night.

Causes of Insomnia

Insomnia often occurs along with many medical and psychological disorders. For example, people in pain or physical discomfort, those who have decreased amounts of physical activity during the day, and those with respiratory problems will often report problems sleeping. The temperature of our bodies may contribute to insomnia (Monk & Moline, 1989). Our bodies have their own biological rhythms, sometimes called "biological clocks," that regulate various bodily changes and thus affect our behavior throughout the day. This regulatory activity, the "clock," is located in the suprachiasmatic nucleus found in the hypothalamus. One of the factors that appears to be regulated by this clock is internal body temperature. The body temperature is lowest in the early morning hours, begins to rise just before we wake, declines slightly in mid-afternoon, is highest in the early evening, and begins to decline again at around 11:00 P.M. This temperature cycle corresponds to wakefulness. When body temperature is low, as in the early morning hours and in mid-afternoon, we tend to be drowsy. On the other hand, when body temperature is higher, as in the early evening, we tend to be more alert. So if you tend to get sleepy during your early afternoon class, it is probably *not* because it comes right after lunch, and it *may* not be because the professor is boring; instead, it probably is more directly related to the drop in your body temperature at this time.

Some people with insomnia may have problems with their "biological clock" and its control of temperature. People who can't fall asleep at night may have a delayed temperature rhythm: their body temperature doesn't drop and they don't become drowsy until later at night (Morris, Lack, & Dawson, 1990). As a group, people with insomnia also seem to have higher body temperatures than people who are good sleepers, and their body temperatures seem to vary less. In other words, their temperatures may not rise and fall as much as those of people who sleep well, and this lack of fluctuation may interfere with their sleeping (Monk & Moline, 1989).

Among the other factors that can cause problems with sleeping are the effects of drug use (as we discussed is the case of alcohol) and a variety of environmental influences such as changes in light, noise, or temperature. People admitted to hospitals often have difficulty sleeping because the noises and routines differ from those at home. Other sleep disorders, such as sleep apnea (a disorder that involves obstructed nighttime breathing) or restless leg syndrome (excessive "jerky" leg movements while sleeping), can cause people to have interrupted sleep and may seem similar to insomnia.

Finally, various psychological stresses can also disrupt your sleep (Morin, 1993). Poll your friends around finals time to see how many of them are having trouble falling asleep or are not sleeping through the night. The stress that you experience during times such as final exams may interfere with your sleep, at least temporarily. Gross and Borkovec (1982), for example, found that if good sleepers were told that they would have to present a speech the next day, they took longer to fall asleep than did control subjects.

Research on the beliefs of people with insomnia shows that they may have unrealistic expectations about how much sleep they need (for example, "I need a full 8 hours of sleep to be completely rested") and may also be unrealistic about how disruptive disturbed sleep will be (for instance, "I won't be able to think or do my job if I only sleep for 5 hours") (Morin, Stone, Trinkle, Mercer, & Remsberg, in press). These studies point to the role of cognition in insomnia, indicating that our thoughts alone may disrupt our sleep.

Can you learn to be a poor sleeper? It is generally accepted that people can begin to associate bedtime, their bedroom, and even their bed with the frustration and anxiety that go with not being able to sleep. Eventually, the arrival of bedtime itself may cause anxiety (Bootzin & Nicassio, 1978). For children, interactions surrounding sleep may contribute to their sleep problems. For example, a recent study found that children of parents who were present when the child fell asleep were more likely to wake during the night (Adair, Bauchner, Philipp, Levenson, & Zuckerman, 1991). In these cases, researchers think that some children learn to fall asleep only with a parent present; if they wake up at night alone, they are frightened and their sleep is disrupted. Despite the widespread acceptance of the role of learning in insomnia—which, as we'll see, includes its integration into many treatment strategies—there is relatively little research on this phenomenon. This may be due in part to the difficulty of conducting this type of research, which would involve going into the homes and bedrooms of the subjects.

Research on cultural influences has focused primarily on the sleep problems of children. The predominant culture in the United States appears to expect infants to sleep on their own, in a separate bed and, if available, in a separate room. However, other cultures as diverse as those from rural Guatemala to urban Japan expect the young child to spend the first few years of life in the same room and sometimes the same bed as the mother (Morelli, Rogoff, Oppenheim, & Goldsmith, 1992). As a result, families in these cultures infrequently report bedtime problems. In a recent study, for example, researchers questioned 14 mothers from a Mayan village and 18 middle-class mothers from the United States, each of whom had a young child (Morelli, Rogoff, Oppenheim, & Goldsmith, 1992). In contrast to the U.S. mothers, the Mayan mothers had their infants and toddlers sleep with them for several years. They reported that this sleeping arrangement helped them to create a close bond with their children and usually resulted in few bedtime problems. Similarly, a recent study in Korea found that 98% of Korean mothers had their infants sleep with them (Lee, 1992). The study also found that out of 218 mothers questioned, only one said she ignored the cries of her child. This is in stark contrast to parents in the United States, where most pediatricians recommend that parents ignore the cries of their infants at night (Ferber, 1985). One view of this type of research is that sleep problems can be negatively impacted by cultural demands, as in the United States. Unmet sleep demands can serve as an additional stress that will negatively affect the ultimate sleep outcome of children (Durand, Mindell, Mapstone, & Gernert-Dott, in press).

It is clear from our discussion of assessment issues that biology—the physiological mechanisms that underlie sleep problems—interacts with cognitive, behavioral, and even cultural dimensions to create the "sleep problem" that is presented to the clinician. This multidimensional view of sleep problems has several assumptions. The first is that at some level, *both biological and nonbiological factors will be present* in most cases of sleep problems. We saw that body temperature may make someone vulnerable to disturbed sleep. In addition, someone who awakens frequently throughout the night may have a disruption in her sleep cycles that makes her likely to have full instead of partial waking during the night.

A second assumption is that these multiple factors are *reciprocally related*. One example of this reciprocal relationship can be seen in the study we just described on parental presence at bedtime. Adair and colleagues observed that parents were more likely to be present at the bedtime of children who had frequent night waking (Adair et al., 1991). However, they also noted that child temperament or personality may have played a role in this relationship. It was found that children with more difficult temperaments were more likely to have their parents present at bedtime—

Different cultures often have varying views of the way children should sleep at night. At left we see a Brazilian indian family. The infants sleep in bed with their parents for several years before sleeping alone. At right we see an American child alone in his bed. These differing expectations will affect whether or not a child's disrupted sleep will be considered a problem.

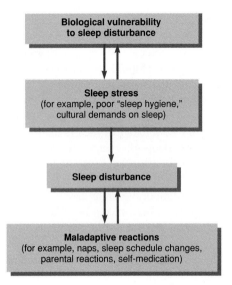

Figure 10.4 Integrative-multidimensional model of sleep disturbance

presumably to attend to sleep initiation difficulties. One explanation of these findings is that parental presence at bedtime *does* influence night waking, but that this will more likely occur among infants with difficult temperaments. In other words, sleep difficulties, parental reaction to these difficulties, and personality characteristics of the child (e.g., difficult temperament) interact in a reciprocal manner to produce and maintain these sleep problems.

People may be biologically vulnerable to having disturbed sleep patterns. This vulnerability differs from person to person and can range from mild to more severe disturbances. For example, a person may be easily aroused at night, more commonly known as being a "light sleeper." Or he may have a family history of insomnia, narcolepsy, or obstructed breathing. All these factors can make a person vulnerable to sleeping problems. These influences have been referred to by others as *predisposing conditions* (Spielman & Glovinsky, 1991); they may not, by themselves, always cause sleep problems, but they may combine with other factors to interfere with sleep (see Figure 10.4).

Interacting with this biological vulnerability is the occurrence of *sleep stress* (Durand, Mindell, Mapstone, & Gernert-Dott, in press). Sleep stress includes a number of events that can negatively impact sleep. For example, poor "sleep hygiene" habits (for example, having too much caffeine before bedtime) can interfere with the initiation of sleep (Hauri, 1991). It is important to point out that biological vulnerability and sleep stress reciprocally influence each other (as can be seen in the double arrows in the integrative model of sleep disturbance in Figure 10.4). Although it may be most intuitive to think of biological factors as coming first, extrinsic influences such as poor sleep hygiene also impact the physiology of sleep. One of the most striking

examples of this phenomenon is "jet lag," in which a person's sleep patterns are disrupted, sometimes seriously, when he or she flies across several different time zones. Among children, sleep stress such as vacations (where sleep schedules are significantly modified) or visits from relatives can serve to disturb previously normal sleep habits.

The combination of biological vulnerability and sleep stress may create one or more sleep disturbances. Whether these disturbances continue or become more severe may depend on how they are managed. For example, many people will react to disrupted sleep by taking over-the-counter sleeping pills. Unfortunately, most people are not aware of the "rebound effect" that occurs after they stop taking these medications. Once these medications are stopped, many people will reexperience disrupted sleep, which is caused by the withdrawal of the medication. This "rebound" leads people to think they still have a sleep problem, readminister the medicine, and go through the cycle over and over again. In other words, taking sleep aids can be a perpetuating factor in sleep problems.

Other ways you react to poor sleep can also prolong these problems. It seems reasonable if a person

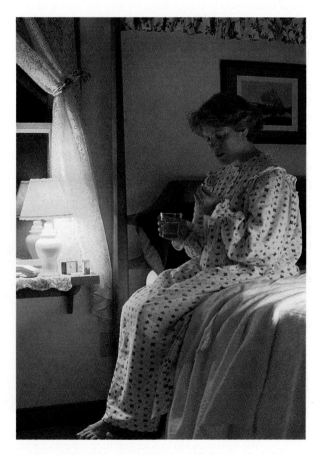

Medication is a commonly used solution for sleep disturbances, despite the difficulties associated with its long-term use.

Boston firefighter resting between calls. A combination of lifestyle stressors and biological vulnerabilities results in disturbed sleep.

hasn't had enough sleep that he or she make up for this loss by taking naps during the day. Unfortunately, the naps may make the person feel rested that day, but they will also disrupt his or her sleep the next night. Anxious thoughts can help to extend this problem. Lying in bed worrying about school, family problems, or even not being able to sleep will interfere with your sleep (Morin, 1993). For children, the behavior of their parents can also help to maintain these problems. Giving children a great deal of positive attention at night when they wake up can cause these children to wake up during the night more often (Durand & Mindell, 1990). Such maladaptive reactions, when combined with a biological predisposition to have sleep problems and sleep stress (for example, disrupted sleep schedule), may explain why people have continuing problems with their sleep.

Primary Hypersomnia

If *insomnia* involves not getting enough sleep (the root *in* meaning lacking or without), **hypersomnia** is a problem of sleeping too much (*hyper* meaning in great amount or abnormal excess). Despite getting a full night's sleep each evening, many people find themselves falling asleep several times each day. Consider the following case.

The Case of Ann

Ann was a college student who came to our office during office hours to discuss her progress in class. We discussed the last exam and several questions that she got wrong, and as she was about to leave she said that she never fell asleep during my class. This seemed like faint praise, but I thanked her for the feedback. "No," she said, "you don't understand. I usually fall asleep in *all* of my classes, but not in yours." Again, I didn't quite understand what she was trying to tell me, and joked that she must be more careful picking out her professors. She laughed. "That's probably true. But I also have this problem with sleeping too much."

As we discussed her sleeping problem (this time, a little more seriously), Ann told me that excessive sleeping had been a problem for her since her teenage years. If she were in situations that were monotonous or boring, or if she couldn't be active, she would find herself falling asleep. This could happen several times a day, depending on what she was doing. Recently, large lecture classes had become a problem for her unless the lecturer was particularly interesting or animated. Watching television and driving long distances along highways were also problematic.

Ann reported that her father had a similar problem with falling asleep, but that his problem was more severe. He had recently been diagnosed with *narcolepsy* (a sleep problem we will describe next that can result in sudden and irresistible sleep attacks, along with disturbing sleep events such as brief paralysis and hallucinations) and was now being seen at a sleep clinic to help him deal with the problem. Both she and her brother had been diagnosed with hypersomnia. Ann had been prescribed Ritalin (a stimulant medication) about 4 years ago, and said that it was

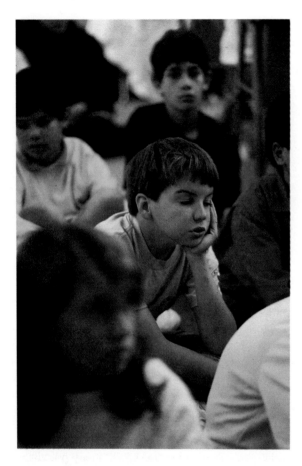

Excessive sleepiness can seriously disrupt the affected person's life.

only somewhat effective in keeping her awake during the day. She said the drug helped to reduce the attacks but did not eliminate them altogether.

When I asked her how she coped with falling asleep all the time, she became a bit embarrassed. "I think of things," she said finally. I asked her what she meant. "Well, I can pretty much control it if I keep my mind busy. I think of exciting things." I waited, and she continued. "I usually fantasize about sex. I can tell if I'm about to fall asleep, and if I think about sex, for some reason I don't tend to sleep. It seems to work for me." She went on to say that imagining any exciting experiences she'd had (for example, winning an award in high school) would help her if she started to feel that she was falling asleep.

The DSM-IV diagnostic criteria for hypersomnia listed in Table 10.3 include not only the excessive sleepiness that Ann described but also the subjective impression of this problem. If you remember when we discussed insomnia, we mentioned that whether it is a problem depends on how it affects each person individually. In Ann's case, she found her disorder very disruptive because it interfered with her driving and paying attention in class. Ann's hypersomnia caused her to be less successful academically and also upset her personally, both of which are defining features of this disorder. She would sleep approximately 8 hours each night, so her daytime sleepiness couldn't be attributed to a lack of sleep. When people with hypersomnia are given the Multiple Sleep Latency Test (MSLT) we described in the assessment section of this chapter, they usually fall asleep in less than 6 minutes, as opposed to people without the disorder who average 10 minutes or more (Gillin, 1993). In other words, people with this sleep disorder require much less time to fall asleep,

Table 10.3   DSM-IV Criteria for Primary Hypersomnia

A. The predominant complaint is excessive sleepiness for at least 1 month (or less if recurrent) as evidenced by either prolonged sleep episodes or daytime sleep episodes that occur almost daily.

B. The excessive sleepiness causes clinically significant distress or impairment in social, occupational, or other important areas of functioning.

C. The excessive sleepiness is not better accounted for by insomnia and does not occur exclusively during the course of another Sleep Disorder (e.g., Narcolepsy, Breathing-Related Sleep Disorder, Circadian Rhythm Sleep Disorder, or a Parasomnia) and cannot be accounted for by an inadequate amount of sleep.

D. The disturbance does not occur exclusively during the course of another mental disorder.

E. The disturbance is not due to the direct physiological effects of a substance (e.g., a drug of abuse, a medication) or a general medical condition.

Specify if:
Recurrent: if there are periods of excessive sleepiness that last at least 3 days occurring several times a year for at least 2 years.

Source: DSM-IV, APA, 1994.

even if they have had a full night's sleep; therefore, they are considered sleepier than those without the disorder.

Several factors can cause excessive sleepiness but would not be considered hypersomnia. For example, people with insomnia (who get inadequate amounts of sleep) often report being tired during the day. In contrast, people with hypersomnia will sleep through the night and appear rested upon awakening, but still complain of being excessively tired throughout the day. Another sleep problem that can cause the same excessive sleepiness seen in hypersomnia is a breathing-related sleep disorder called *sleep apnea*. People with this problem have difficulty breathing at night. They often snore loudly, have pauses when they breathe, and will wake up in the morning with a drymouth and a headache. When trying to identify someone with hypersomnia, you need to rule out insomnia, sleep apnea, or other reasons for why they may be sleepy during the day (Gillin, 1993).

We are just beginning to understand the nature of hypersomnia, so to date there is relatively little research on its causes. Genetic influences seem to be involved in a portion of cases, with 39% of people having hypersomnia also having a family history of the disorder (Parkes & Block, 1989). An excess of serotonin has been implicated as one influence, although researchers generally believe that there are several biological causes for hypersomnia (Anch, Browman, Mitler, & Walsh, 1988). For example, the infectious disease mononucleosis has been found in about one-sixth of the patients with hypersomnia (Guilleminault & Mondini, 1986).

Narcolepsy

Ann described her father as having a different form of the sleeping problem she and her brother shared, a disorder called **narcolepsy.** In addition to the daytime sleepiness seen in people with hypersomnia, people with narcolepsy also experience **cataplexy,** or a sudden loss of muscle tone. This loss of muscle tone happens while the person is awake and can range from a feeling of slight weakness in the facial muscles to a complete collapse to the floor. Cataplexy can last from several seconds to several minutes; it is usually preceded by some strong emotion such as anger or happiness. Imagine that you have narcolepsy: in the middle of cheering for your favorite team, you might suddenly fall asleep; or while having an argument with a friend you might collapse to the floor in a sound sleep. You can imagine how disruptive this type of disorder can be! The variations in sleep latency or sleepiness results between people with and without narcolepsy are shown in Figure 10.5.

Cataplexy appears to result from the onset of REM sleep. Instead of falling asleep and going through

Figure 10.5 Mean sleep latencies for narcoleptics and normals (from Mitler, 1982)

the four NREM stages before reaching REM sleep, people with narcolepsy will periodically throughout the day progress right to this dream sleep stage almost directly from the state of being awake. Recall that we described REM sleep as a stage when the brain was active but the body wasn't. One of the outcomes of REM sleep is the inhibition of input to the muscles, and this seems to be the process that leads to cataplexy.

Two other characteristics distinguish people who have narcolepsy (American Sleep Disorders Association, 1990). They commonly report **sleep paralysis,** a brief period of time on awakening when they can't move or speak. This experience is often reported as frightening to those going through it. The last characteristic of narcolepsy is **hypnagogic hallucinations,** vivid experiences that begin at the start of sleep and are said to be unbelievably realistic because they include not only visual aspects but also touch, hearing, and even the sensation of body movement. Examples of hypnagogic hallucinations, which like sleep paralysis can be quite terrifying, include the experience of being caught in a fire or flying through the air.

Sleep paralysis and hypnagogic hallucinations may serve a role in explaining a most unusual phenomenon—UFO experiences. Each year numerous people report sighting unidentified flying objects—UFOs—and some even tell of visiting with inhabitants of other planets (Sheaffer, 1986). Recently, a group of scientists examined people who had had such experiences, separating them into those who had nonintense experiences (seeing only lights and shapes in the sky) and those with intense experiences (seeing and communicating with aliens) (Spanos, Cross, Dickson, & DuBreuil, 1993). They found that a majority of the reported UFO incidents occurred at night, and that 60% of the intense UFO stories were associated with sleep episodes. Specifically, the reports of these intense accounts were often described in ways that resembled accounts of people experiencing a frightening episode

Table 10.4 DSM-IV Criteria for Narcolepsy

A. Irresistible attacks of refreshing sleep that occur daily over at least 3 months.

B. The presence of one or both of the following:
   1. Cataplexy (i.e., brief episodes of sudden bilateral loss of muscle tone, most often in association with intense emotion)
   2. Recurrent intrusions of elements of rapid eye movement (REM) sleep into the transition between sleep and wakefulness, as manifested by either hypnopompic or hypnagogic hallucinations or sleep paralysis at the beginning or end of sleep episodes

C. The disturbance is not due to the direct physiological effects of a substance (e.g., a drug of abuse, a medication) or another general medical condition.

Source: DSM-IV, APA, 1994.

of sleep paralysis and hypnagogic hallucination, as illustrated by the following account.

> I was lying in bed facing the wall, and suddenly my heart started to race. I could feel the presence of three entities standing beside me. I was unable to move my body but could move my eyes. One of the entities, a male, was laughing at me, not verbally but with his mind. He made me feel stupid. He told me telepathically, "Don't you know by now that you can't do anything unless we let you?" (Spanos, Cross, Dickson, & DuBreuil, 1993, p. 627)

The realistic and frightening stories of people who have had UFO sightings may not be the products of an active imagination or the results of a hoax, but at least in some cases they may be a disturbance of sleep. Sleep paralysis and hypnagogic hallucinations do occur in a portion of people without narcolepsy, a phenomenon that may help explain why not everyone with these "otherworldly" experiences has narcolepsy.

The DSM-IV criteria for narcolepsy appear in Table 10.4. Narcolepsy is relatively rare, occurring in 0.03% to 0.16% of the population, with the numbers approximately equal among males and females. Although some cases have been reported in young children, the problems associated with narcolepsy usually are first seen during the teenage years. Excessive sleepiness usually occurs first, with cataplexy appearing either at the same time or with a delay of up to 30 years. Fortunately, the cataplexy, hypnagogic hallucinations, and sleep paralysis often decrease in frequency over time, although the sleepiness during the day does not seem to go away as people get older.

Blood tests of people with narcolepsy almost always show the presence of human leukocyte antigen DR2, otherwise called HLA-DR2. This is a factor in white blood cells that stimulates the production of antibodies that protect us from certain microorganisms. HLA-DR2 probably doesn't itself indicate narcolepsy, but it may indicate a genetic predisposition in an individual to develop the disorder.

Specific genetic models of narcolepsy are just now being studied, primarily with animals. We know that many animals share the same types of sleep experiences as humans. It makes sense, then, that some animals also have the same problems sleeping that we do. In fact, the study of the sleep of animals has historically been invaluable to understanding our own sleep disorders. For example, veterinarians discovered sleep apnea (interrupted breathing) and treated this problem in English bulldogs back in the 1920s before it was even identified as a problem in humans. More recently, scientists have been looking to animals to understand narcolepsy.

Finding an animal model of narcolepsy seems to have happened quite by accident (Carskadon, 1992). When Dr. William Dement, a noted expert in sleep research, gave a lecture to the American Academy

Dr. William C. Dement, pioneering sleep researcher and director of the Sleep Disorders Center at Stanford University

A Doberman pinscher experiencing an episode of narcolepsy

of Neurology in Boston, one of the people in the audience was a veterinarian who, at the time, was treating a miniature poodle named Monique. It seems that Monique had the same symptoms of narcolepsy being described by Dr. Dement in his human patients. Because of Dement's great interest in comparing Monique's problem with those in humans, she was flown to California to his sleep laboratory at Stanford University. It was there he discovered that the dog had a disorder identical to narcolepsy in humans.

As a result of this encounter, researchers have since been able to identify that Doberman pinschers and Labrador retrievers also inherit this disorder. At least in these dogs, narcolepsy seems to be associated with a cluster of genes on chromosome number 6, and it may be an autosomal recessive trait. Advances in understanding the etiology and treatment of disorders such as narcolepsy can be credited to the help of "man's best friend."

Breathing-Related Sleep Disorders

For some people, sleepiness during the day or disrupted sleep at night has a physical origin—namely, problems with breathing while asleep. DSM-IV diagnostic criteria for **breathing-related sleep disorders** are listed in Table 10.5. Because their breathing is interrupted during their sleep, these people experience numerous brief arousals throughout the night and do not feel rested even after 8 or 9 hours "asleep" (Bootzin, Manber, Perlis, Salvio, & Wyatt, 1993). For all of us, the muscles of our upper airway relax when we sleep, constricting this passageway somewhat and making breathing a little more difficult. Unfortunately for some,

breathing is constricted a great deal, and these people may have very labored breathing while they sleep (*hypoventilation*), or in the extreme, they may have short periods (10–30 seconds) when they stop breathing altogether, called **sleep apnea.** Often the person affected is only minimally aware of his or her breathing difficulties and doesn't attribute his sleep problems to his breathing. However, a bed partner will usually be aware of his loud snoring (which is one sign of this problem) or will have witnessed the episodes of interrupted breathing, a frightening experience to observe. Other signs indicating that a person's breathing difficulties may be responsible for his disturbed sleep are heavy sweating during the night, morning headaches, and episodes when he falls asleep during the day (called *sleep attacks*) but has no feeling of being rested after these episodes (Hauri, 1982).

It is important to distinguish three types of apnea because they can have different causes, daytime complaints, and treatment. They are *obstructive, central,* and *mixed sleep apnea*. Obstructive sleep apnea (OSA) occurs when a person's air flow stops despite the continued activity of the respiratory system. For some people the airway is too narrow; for others some abnormality or damage obstructs or interferes with the ongoing effort to breathe. One hundred percent of a group of people with OSA also reported snoring at night (Guilleminault, 1989). Obesity is sometimes associated with this problem, as is increasing age. Sleep apnea is more often found among males and is thought to occur in 1% to 2% of the population (American Sleep Disorders Association, 1990). The second type of apnea—central sleep apnea—involves the complete cessation of respiratory activity for brief periods of time and is often associated with certain central nervous

Table 10.5   DSM-IV Criteria for Breathing-Related Sleep Disorder

A. Sleep disruption, leading to excessive sleepiness or insomnia, that is judged to be due to a sleep-related breathing condition (e.g., obstructive or central sleep apnea syndrome or central alveolar hypoventilation syndrome).

B. The disruption is not better accounted for by another mental disorder and is not due to the direct physiological effects of a substance (e.g., a drug of abuse, a medication) or another general medical condition (other than a breathing-related disorder).

Source: DSM–IV, APA, 1994.

system disorders such as cerebral vascular disease, head trauma, and degenerative disorders (Wooten, 1990). Unlike people with obstructive sleep apnea, those with central sleep apnea will wake up frequently during the night, but they tend not to report excessive daytime sleepiness and often are not aware that they have a serious breathing problem. Because of the lack of daytime symptoms, people tend not to seek treatment for this problem, so we know relatively little about its prevalence or course. The final breathing disorder— mixed sleep apnea—refers to a combination of both obstructive and central sleep apneas. All these breathing difficulties interrupt sleep and result in symptoms similar to those of insomnia.

Circadian Rhythm Sleep Disorders

"Spring ahead; fall back." This is the mnemonic device people in most of the United States use to remind themselves to turn the clocks ahead 1 hour in the spring, and back again 1 hour in the fall. Most of us consider the shift to daylight saving time a minor inconvenience (although getting worse with so many electronic watches and clocks to change!) and are thus surprised to see how disruptive this time change can be. For at least a day or two we may be sleepy during the day and have difficulty falling asleep at night, almost as if we were "jet lagged." The reason for this disruption is not just because we gain or lose 1 hour of sleep—our bodies adjust to this fairly easily. The difficulty has to do with how our biological clocks adjust to this change in time. Convention says to go to sleep at this new time while our bodies are saying something different. If the struggle continues for any length of time, with a mismatch between what your body tells you and what is expected in society as far as sleep is concerned, you may have what is called a **circadian rhythm sleep disorder.** This disorder is characterized by disturbed sleep (either insomnia or excessive sleepiness during the day) brought on by the body's inability to synchronize its sleep patterns with the current patterns of day and night.

In the 1960s, German and French scientists identified several bodily rhythms that seem to persist without cues from the environment or society, rhythms that are controlled by our own bodies (Aschoff & Wever, 1962; Siffre, 1964). Because these rhythms don't exactly match the 24-hour day we use, they are called circadian (from *circa* meaning about and *dian* meaning day). If our circadian rhythms don't match the 24-hour day, why doesn't our sleep get completely confused over time?

Fortunately, our bodies have a mechanism that lets us get "in synch" with the outside world. We mentioned before that our biological clock is found in a region of the brain called the suprachiasmatic nucleus in the hypothalamus. Connected to the suprachiasmatic nucleus is a pathway that comes from our eyes. The light we see in the morning and the decreasing light at night help signal the brain to reset the biological clock each day according to these changes. The light-dark cycle, because it helps cue our circadian system, is called a *Zeitgeber* (a German word meaning "time giver"). Unfortunately, some people have trouble sleeping when they want to because of problems with their circadian rhythms. Sometimes the problems have causes outside the person (for example, crossing several time zones in a short amount of time), or causes that are internal and related to the person's circadian rhythm.

The DSM-IV diagnostic criteria for circadian rhythm sleep disorder are presented in Table 10.6. As you can see, not being synchronized with the normal wake and sleep cycles causes people to have interruptions when they do try to sleep, and to be tired during the day. There are several different types of circadian rhythm sleep disorders. For example, *jet lag type* is, as its name implies, caused by rapidly crossing multiple time zones. People who are "jet-lagged" usually report difficulty going to sleep at the proper time, as well as feeling fatigued during the day. It is interesting to note that there is some indication that older people, introverts (loners), and early risers (morning people) are more likely to be negatively affected by these time zone changes (Gillin, 1993). *Shift work type* consists of sleep problems associated with work schedules. Many people such as hospital employees, police, or emergency personnel must work at night or work irregular hours; as a result they may have problems sleeping or experience excessive sleepiness during waking hours. Unfortunately, the problems of working (and thus staying awake) at unusual times can go beyond sleep and can include gastrointestinal symptoms, increased potential for alcohol abuse, low worker morale, and the disruption of family and social life. About 36% of working men and 26% of working women in the United States work at times other than the typical "9 to 5" and are therefore at risk for having this sleep problem (Czeisler & Allan, 1989).

In contrast with jet lag and shift work sleep-related problems, which have external causes such as long-distance travel and job selection, several circadian rhythm sleep disorders seem to arise from within the person experiencing the problems. Extreme "night owls," or people who stay up late and sleep late, may have a problem known as *delayed sleep phase type*. Falling asleep is "delayed" or later, compared to normal bedtime. At the other end of the extreme, people with an *advanced sleep phase type* of circadian rhythm disorder are "early to bed and early to rise." Here, sleep is "advanced" or earlier, in relation to normal bedtime. DSM-IV does not include advanced sleep phase as a type of circadian rhythm sleep disorder, in part because of our general lack of knowledge about it.

A more disruptive circadian rhythm sleep disorder (and one also not yet included in the DSM-IV) is the *non-24-hour sleep-wake syndrome*. Here, instead of your biological clock being reset each day to a 24-hour period, it runs independent of the environment cues on a schedule more like 25 hours. This means that each day, people with this disorder have their sleep-wake cycle off by 1 to 2 hours. So on Monday, a person with this problem might fall asleep at 11 P.M., on Tuesday at midnight, and by Sunday he or she would be

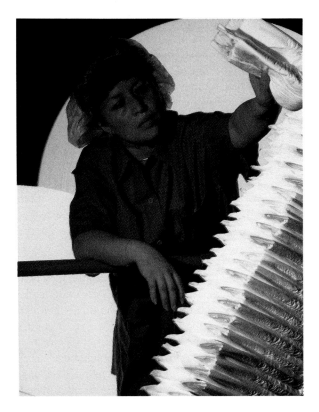

Shifting work schedules can disrupt sleep patterns and cause people to be excessively tired throughout the day.

falling asleep at 5 or 6 A.M. You can imagine how disturbing this would be.

Research on why our sleep rhythms may become disrupted is advancing at a great pace, and we are now beginning to understand the circadian rhythm process. One of the internal processes that

Table 10.6   DSM-IV Criteria for Circadian Rhythm Sleep Disorder (Sleep-Wake Schedule Disorder)

A. A persistent or recurrent pattern of sleep disruption leading to excessive sleepiness or insomnia that is due to a mismatch between the sleep-wake schedule required by a person's environment and his or her circadian sleep-wake pattern.

B. The sleep disturbance causes clinically significant distress or impairment in social, occupational, or other important areas of functioning.

C. The disturbance does not occur exclusively during the course of another Sleep Disorder or other mental disorder.

D. The disturbance is not due to the direct physiological effects of a substance (e.g., a drug of abuse, a medication) or a general medical condition.

Specify type:
Delayed Sleep Phase Type: a persistent pattern of late sleep onset and late awakening times, with an inability to fall asleep and awaken at a desired earlier time
Jet Lag Type: sleepiness and alertness that occur at an inappropriate time of day relative to local time, occurring after repeated travel across more than one time zone
Shift Work Type: insomnia during major sleep period or excessive sleepiness during major awake period associated with night shift work or frequently changing shift work
Unspecified Type

Source: DSM-IV, APA, 1994.

scientists believe contribute to the setting of our biological clock, and therefore tell us when to sleep, involves the hormone *melatonin*. This hormone is produced by the pineal gland found in the center of the brain. Melatonin (which shouldn't be confused with melanin, the chemical that determines our skin color) has been nicknamed the "Dracula hormone" because its production is stimulated by darkness and ceases in daylight. When our eyes detect it is nighttime because of the reduction of sunlight, this information is passed on to the pineal gland, which in turn begins producing melatonin. Researchers believe that both light and melatonin help set the biological clock (see Figure 10.6).

People who study sleep are interested in melatonin because it helps to explain the sleep mechanism in our bodies. In addition, this hormone may help us treat some of the sleep problems people experience. For example, one group of people who do not get help from daylight to properly set their biological clocks are those who are totally blind. People without sight are a sort of natural circadian rhythm experiment because, as you would expect, without cues from the sun their clocks continually run out of phase, resulting in a chronic form of jet lag. Researchers have discovered that they can reset the circadian rhythms of people with blindness by giving them melatonin (Sack & Lewy, 1993). The melatonin tells their brains it is nighttime even when their eyes cannot. In the future, melatonin may be used as a treatment for people who experience severe jet lag and other sleep problems associated with circadian rhythm disruption.

Treatment for Dyssomnias

The normal progression of sleep arrives like nightfall. Just as the approaching darkness is almost imperceptible, sleep sneaks up and overtakes us without our fully being aware of its presence. When this normal process is disturbed, when we can't fall asleep or we awaken frequently, or when our sleep does not restore our energy and vitality, then we need help. A number of biological and psychological interventions have been designed and evaluated to help people regain the benefits of normal sleep.

Biological Treatment

Perhaps the most common treatment for insomnia is medical. Researchers have estimated that during any given year, 2.7% of men and 5.5% of women in the general population use prescription drugs for sleep problems, and 3.0% of men and 3.1% of women use over-the-counter medications (Mellinger et al., 1985). People who complain of insomnia to a medical professional will most likely be prescribed one of several *benzodiazepine* medications. These include short-acting drugs such as *triazolam* (Halcion) and long-acting drugs such as *flurazepam* (Dalmane). Short-acting drugs (those that cause drowsiness for only a short amount of time) are preferred because the

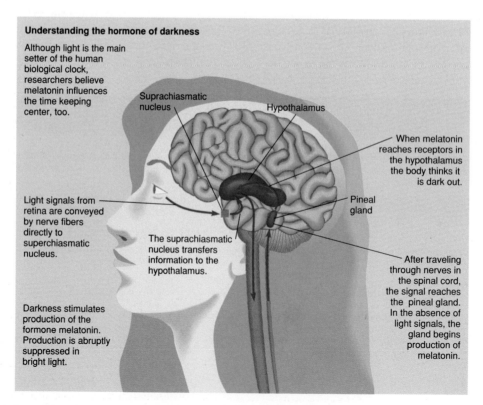

Figure 10.6   Understanding the hormone of darkness (from *New York Times*, 1992, November 3)

longer-acting drugs sometimes do not stop working by morning, and people report more daytime sleepiness. The longer acting benzodiazepines are sometimes preferred when negative effects such as daytime anxiety are observed in people taking the short-acting drugs (Gillin, 1993). People over the age of 65 tend to be the most likely group to use medication to help them with their sleep, although people of all ages, including young children (Mindell, 1993), have been prescribed these medications for insomnia.

There are several drawbacks to the use of medication to treat insomnia. First, benzodiazepine medications can cause excessive sleepiness. Second, individuals taking these drugs can easily become dependent on them, and they can rather easily misuse them, knowingly or unknowingly (see Chapter 12, "Substance-Related Disorders," for a full discussion of these concerns). Third, these medications are meant for short-term treatment and are not recommended for use longer than 4 weeks. Longer use than this can cause dependence and the phenomenon known as **rebound insomnia** or a withdrawal experience that causes worse sleep problems after the medication is stopped, even if it is used for only a few days. Therefore, while taking medications may be helpful for sleep problems that will correct themselves in a short period of time (for example, insomnia due to anxiety related to hospitalization), they are not meant to be used for long-term, chronic problems.

Treatment for hypersomnia and narcolepsy has primarily been medical. To help people with their sleepiness, physicians usually prescribe a stimulant such as *methylphenidate* (otherwise called Ritalin, the medication Ann was taking) or *amphetamine* (Gillin, 1993). These help them stay awake during the day. The problem with cataplexy, or loss of muscle tone, is usually addressed with antidepressant medication. This medication isn't used because people with narcolepsy are depressed but because one of its effects is to suppress REM (or dream) sleep. Cataplexy seems to be related to the sudden onset of REM sleep, and therefore the antidepressant medication can be helpful in reducing these attacks.

Treatment for the breathing-related sleep disorders focuses on helping the person breathe better during sleep. For some, this can involve a recommendation for weight loss. Breathing can be impaired in some people who are obese because the neck's soft tissue compresses the airways. Unfortunately, as we have seen in the chapter on eating disorders, voluntary weight loss is rarely successful in the long term; as a result, this treatment has not proven to be very successful for breathing-related sleep disorders (Guilleminault & Dement, 1988).

With mild or moderate cases of obstructive sleep apnea, the treatment recommended usually involves either the use of medication or a mechanical device that improves breathing. Medications used with individuals suffering from this disorder include those that help stimulate respiration (for example, *medroxyprogesterone*) or the *tricyclic antidepressants*. The antidepressants are thought to act on the locus ceruleus, which affects REM sleep. These drugs seem to reduce the amount of muscle tone loss usually seen during REM sleep, which means that the respiratory muscles do not relax as much as usual at this time, thereby improving the person's breathing (Guilleminault & Dement, 1988). Certain mechanical devices have also been used to reposition either the tongue or the jaw during sleep to help improve breathing, but people tend to resist using these types of devices because of discomfort. A final option for more severe cases of breathing problems involves surgery to help remove blockages in parts of the airways found in some of these patients.

Short-term use of sleeping pills is often a person's first reaction to the insomnia problems associated with circadian rhythm sleep disorders. However, because these medications cannot be used for more than several weeks and because of the rebound effects that can cause more sleep problems, using medication as a primary treatment isn't usually recommended (Czeisler & Allan, 1989). Instead, other ways of getting people back in step with their sleep rhythms are usually tried.

One general principle for treating circadian rhythm disorders is that "phase delays" (moving the bedtime later) are easier than "phase advances" (moving bedtime earlier). In other words, it is easier to stay up several hours later than usual than to force yourself to go to sleep several hours earlier. For shift workers, scheduling their shift changes in a clockwise direction (going from day to evening schedule) seems to help them adjust better. People can readjust their sleep patterns better by using phase delays to get back on schedule. For example, you would have the person delay bedtime several hours each night, until bedtime began to approximate the desired time (see Figure 10.7). This approach is called *chronotherapy* (*chrono* meaning time) and has proven helpful for some people with circadian rhythm disorders (Czeisler et al., 1981). A drawback of this approach is that it requires the person to sleep during the day for several days, something obviously difficult for people with regularly scheduled responsibilities.

Another recent effort to help people with these sleep problems involves using *bright light* to "trick" the brain into readjusting the biological clock. Remember that we said light cues the brain to reset the biological clock on a daily basis. In Chapter 7, we described light therapy for *seasonal affective disorder* (a form of depression that may be related to the decreased amount of light in northern climates during the winter months). Recent research indicates that using very bright light may help people with circadian rhythm sleep problems

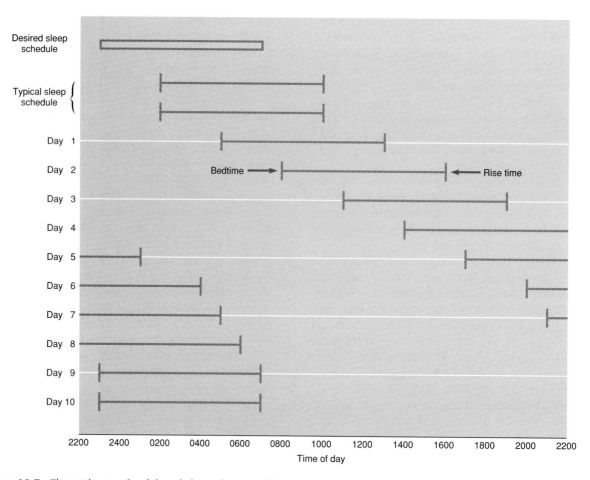

Figure 10.7   Chronotherapy for delayed sleep phase syndrome. In this example, a patient cannot fall asleep until 2:00 A.M. and has difficulty getting up before 10:00 A.M. The patient would prefer to sleep from 11:00 P.M. until 7:00 A.M. On days 1–6 of the schedule the patient retires and gets up 3 hours later each day. On days 7–9 the bedtime schedule is delayed 1 hour each day. By day 9 the schedule coincides with the desired sleep schedule which was determined prior to the start of chronotherapy (adapted from Czeisler et al., 1981).

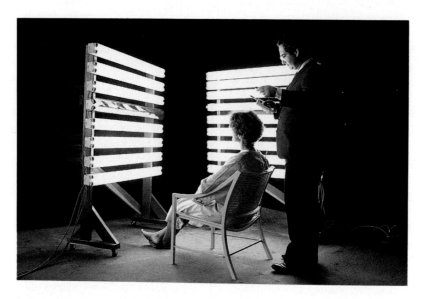

Bright light therapy can help people with circadian-rhythm sleep disorders readjust their sleep patterns.

readjust their sleep patterns (Czeisler et al., 1986). People typically sit in front of a bank of fluorescent lamps and are exposed to light greater than 2,500 lux, an amount significantly different from normal indoor light (250 lux). Several hours of exposure to this bright light have been used to successfully reset the circadian rhythms of a number of individuals (Czeisler & Allan, 1989). Although this type of treatment is still new and relatively untested, it provides some hope for people with these sleep problems.

Psychological Treatments

As you can imagine, the limitations of using only a drug approach to helping people sleep better has led others to look to psychological treatments. Table 10.7 lists and briefly describes some of the psychological approaches used to treat insomnia. The different treatments are aimed at helping people with different aspects of their problems. For example, the relaxation spasm treatments focus on reducing the physical tension that seems to prevent some people from falling asleep at night. Other people report that their thoughts of work, relationships, or other anxiety-producing situations prevent them from sleeping or wake them up in the middle of the night. To address this problem, cognitive treatments are used to help them deal with and reduce anxiety-producing thoughts at bedtime (see Table 10.7).

Research on the different psychological treatments for insomnia shows that some may be more effective than others. For adult sleep problems, more research has been conducted with the use of *stimulus control* on sleep problems. Although not a cure for insomnia, instructing people to use their bedroom only for sleeping and for sex, and *not* for work or other possibly anxiety-provoking activities (for example, watching the news on television), can help many with their sleeping difficulties. On the other hand, using *progressive relaxation* or *sleep hygiene* alone may not be as effective as stimulus control alone for some people (Lacks & Morin, 1992). Research that specifically "matches" treatment to symptom is still not common. We need more studies that match the particular complaint of an individual to the treatment. People who are anxious at bedtime might do better with cognitive interventions. In comparison, people with poor sleep habits might benefit more from the sleep hygiene approaches (see Table 10.8). Individual treatments may be more successful if they are properly designed to fit each individual's sleep needs.

If you remember Kathryn, her sleep problems were addressed using several of the techniques de-

Table 10.7 Psychological Treatments for Insomnia

Sleep Treatment	Description
Cognitive	This approach focuses on changing the sleeper's unrealistic expectations and beliefs about sleep ("I must have 8 hours of sleep each night"; "If I get less than 8 hours of sleep it will make me ill"). Therapist attempts to alter beliefs and attitudes about sleeping by providing information on topics such as normal amounts of sleep and a person's ability to compensate for lost sleep.
Cognitive relaxation	Because some people become anxious when they have difficulty sleeping, this approach uses meditation or imagery to help with relaxation at bedtime or after a night waking.
Graduated extinction	Used for children who have tantrums at bedtime or wake up crying at night, this treatment instructs the parent to check on the child after progressively longer periods of time, until the child falls asleep on his or her own.
Paradoxical intention	This technique involves instructing individuals in the opposite behavior from the desired outcome. Telling poor sleepers to lie in bed and try to stay awake as long as they can is used to try to relieve the performance anxiety surrounding efforts to try to fall asleep.
Progressive relaxation	This technique involves relaxing the muscles of your body in an effort to introduce drowsiness.
Scheduled awakening	Used for children who wake frequently during the night, this treatment involves waking the child approximately 60 minutes before he or she usually awakens at night. This helps teach children to fall back asleep on their own while they are aroused from a deeper stage of sleep.
Sleep hygiene	Some people's daily habits can interfere with their nighttime sleeping. This approach involves instructing the sleeper about the negative effects on their sleep of using caffeine, nicotine, alcohol, exercise too close to bedtime, certain foods, and medications.
Sleep restriction	This consists of limiting a person's time in bed to the actual amount slept. The restriction helps the sleeper associate time in bed only with sleeping, and not with tossing and turning trying to fall asleep.
Stimulus control	This approach includes instructions to go to bed only when sleepy, use the bedroom only for sleep and sex (not for reading, TV watching, or eating), get out of bed when unable to fall asleep, get out of bed in the morning at the same time each day regardless of the amount of time you sleep.

Table 10.8   Recommendations for Good Sleep Hygiene

Caffeine	Because caffeine is a stimulant, avoid consuming foods with caffeine (e.g., coffee, soda) during the 4–6 hours prior to bedtime.
Nicotine	Nicotine can also act as a stimulant, and its use should be avoided in the hours (4–6) prior to sleep.
Alcohol	Alcohol may cause drowsiness and help initiate sleep, but it will also disrupt sleep during the night. Limit its use in the evening prior to bedtime.
Snacks	Because hunger will disturb sleep, a light snack before bedtime may help. Eating too much late in the evening can disturb sleep.
Exercise	Exercise during the day may improve sleep, but vigorous exercise too close to bedtime (3–4 hours before) may make initiation of sleep difficult.
Sleep patterns	Select a regular bedtime and time to awaken. This may help strengthen circadian rhythms.
Sleep environment	Avoid trying to sleep in environments that are too noisy, those with too much light, or those with extremes of temperature (too hot or too cold).

Source: Adapted from Hauri, 1982, & Morin, 1993.

scribed. She was instructed to limit her time in bed to about 4 hours sleep time (*sleep restriction*), or about the amount of time she actually slept each night. This was later lengthened as she began to sleep through the night. Kathryn was also asked not to listen to the radio while in bed, and to get out of bed if she couldn't fall asleep (stimulus control). Finally, therapy involved confronting her unrealistic expectations about how much sleep was enough for a person of her age (cognitive therapy). Within about 3 weeks of treatment Kathryn was sleeping longer (6–7 hours per night as opposed to 4–5 hours previously) and had fewer interruptions in her sleep. Also, she reported feeling more refreshed in the morning and having more energy during the day. Kathryn's results mirror those of a recent study that found this combination of treatments to be effective in older adults with insomnia (Morin, Kowatch, Barry, & Walton, 1993).

For young children, using some of the cognitive treatments may not be possible. Instead, treatment often includes setting up bedtime routines such as a bath, followed by a parent's reading a story to help children go to sleep at night. Graduated extinction (described in Table 10.7) has been used with some success for bedtime problems as well as waking up at night (Durand & Mindell, 1990).

Integrating both medical and behavioral treatments seems especially important for insomnia. Recent research suggests that short-term use of medication in combination with the types of interventions we have been discussing may prove to be a quick and lasting treatment for insomnia (Milby et al., 1993; Morin & Azrin, 1988).

Psychological treatment research for the other dyssomnias is virtually nonexistent. For the most part, help in the form of counseling or support groups to assist in managing the psychological and social effects of having disturbed sleep has been of value, especially for people who suffer from feelings of low self-esteem and depression (Bootzin et al., 1993).

Parasomnias

Have you ever been told that you walk in your sleep? Talk in your sleep? Have you ever had troublesome nightmares? Do you grind your teeth in your sleep? If you answered yes to one or more of these questions (and it's likely that you did), you have experienced sleep problems that are included within the category of **parasomnia.** Parasomnias are abnormal events—such as nightmares or sleepwalking—that occur either during sleep or during that twilight time between being asleep and being awake. They are not problems with sleep itself, but rather they are events that intrude on your sleep. Some of the problems that are associated with parasomnia are not unusual if they happen while you are awake (walking to the kitchen to look into the refrigerator) but can be distressing if they take place while you are sleeping.

Parasomnias are of two types: those that occur during rapid eye movement (REM) sleep, and those that occur during non-rapid eye movement sleep (NREM). As you might have guessed, nightmares occur during REM or dream sleep. However, the time during sleep when other sleep problems come up may not be so obvious. For example, sleepwalking occurs in NREM sleep, suggesting that you are *not* dreaming during this time. We will discuss a few of the parasomnias and the research into these fascinating and sometimes disturbing sleep events.

Table 10.9 lists several common parasomnias that occur during REM and NREM sleep, along with their

Table 10.9   Common Parasomnias

Disorder	Prevalence	Sex Ratio (Female to Male)	Age of Onset	Course
Parasomnias in REM Sleep				
Nightmares	20%: children 5–10%: adults	1:1 children 2:1–4:1 adults	3–6 yrs.	Can persist into adulthood Decrease over decades
Sleep paralysis	Once 40–50% >1: 3–6%	1:1 except familial (F > M)	Young adults	Usually isolated unless familial (then chronic)
Impaired sleep-related penile erections	10% Increase with age	Males only	>45 yrs.	Increases with age. Seldom improves without treatment
Parasomnias in NREM Sleep				
Sleepwalking	1–15%: children <1%: adults	1:1	4–8 yrs.	Disappears with adolescence
Sleep terrors	5%: children <1%: adults	F < M–children 1:1–adults	4–12 yrs. 20–30 yrs.	Disappears with adolescence
Confusional arousals	Common: children Rare: adults	1:1	<5 yrs.	Decrease with age
Sleep starts	60%–70%	1:1	Any age	Benign

Source: Adapted from Buysse, Reynolds, & Kupfer, 1993.

prevalence rates, sex ratio, age of onset, and course. Perhaps the most common of these is **nightmares,** which involve frightening and anxiety-provoking dreams and which we discuss in more detail below. **Sleep paralysis** was described as part of the disorder of narcolepsy and involves the loss of muscle control for a short period of time at the beginning or end of sleep. As we mentioned in Chapter 5, sleep paralysis is sometimes mistaken for nocturnal panic attacks.

Sleep terrors, which we describe more fully later, on the surface resemble nightmares but occur during NREM sleep and have very distinct differences. **Confusional arousals,** sometimes called sleep drunkenness, include confusion following awakening from sleep. This confusion makes the person look bewildered; it can involve slow speech and movement and actions such as picking up the phone as if it has just rung. These episodes can last for several minutes and sometimes go on for hours. Although confusional arousals occur mostly among children, the use of certain medications or the presence of circadian rhythm sleep disorders can also cause this problem in adults.

If you've ever seen someone jerk his or her legs just as sleep was coming on, then you have witnessed what is called **sleep starts.** Sleep starts involve brief contractions of the legs, and sometimes the rest of the body, just as sleep is initiated. Although sleep starts occur in almost everyone, they can be disruptive if they continually wake you and cause

insomnia. We turn now to a brief review of three of the parasomnias outlined in DSM-IV.

Nightmare Disorder

We have all, from time to time, had a dream that was frightening or distressful. You dream that someone is about to kill you, or you are running away from some threat but can't run fast enough, or you missed an important final exam. These dreams are so frightening that you awaken feeling very upset and can usually remember at least part of the dream. DSM-IV diagnostic criteria for nightmare disorder are listed in Table 10.10. To qualify as a nightmare disorder, according to DSM-IV criteria, these experiences must be so distressful that they impair a person's ability to carry on normal activities. Often, recurring nightmares will lead to disruption of sleep—either by causing people to be fearful of sleep or because of the interruptions during sleep—and will present as insomnia. As you can see in Table 10.9, nightmares are common among children, occurring in about 20%, but they decrease in frequency as we get older to about 5% to 10% of adults. Fortunately, for most people these experiences are infrequent and short-lived. However, persistent nightmares can be very troublesome for some people.

You would expect that because nightmares are so common, a great deal of research would have focused on their causes and treatment. Unfortunately,

Table 10.10   DSM-IV Criteria for Nightmare Disorder

A. Repeated awakenings from the major sleep period or naps with detailed recall of extended and extremely frightening dreams, usually involving threats to survival, security, or self-esteem. The awakenings generally occur during the second half of the sleep period.

B. On awakening from the frightening dreams, the person rapidly becomes oriented and alert (in contrast to the confusion and disorientation seen in Sleep Terror Disorder and some forms of epilepsy).

C. The dream experience, or the sleep disturbance resulting from the awakening, causes significant distress or impairment in social, occupational, or other important areas of functioning.

D. The nightmares do not occur exclusively during the course of another mental disorder (e.g., a delirium, Posttraumatic Stress Disorder) and are not due to the direct physiological effects of a substance (e.g., a drug of abuse, a medication) or a general medical condition.

Source: DSM-IV, APA, 1994.

we still know little about why people have nightmares and about how to treat them. In one recent study, researchers examined the nightmares experienced by college students following the 1989 San Francisco earthquake (Wood, Bootzin, Rosenhan, Nolen-Hoeksema, & Jourden, 1992). On October 17, 1989, an earthquake measuring 7.1 on the Richter scale jolted the San Francisco Bay area. This frightening phenomenon

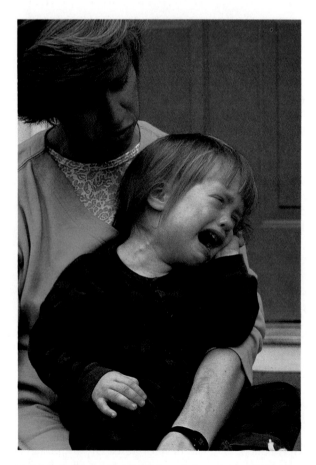

Nightmares, a common childhood sleep disorder, can be distressing for both the child and the parent.

provided researchers with a traumatic event. They reasoned that if traumatic stressors trigger nightmares, then people who experienced the earthquake (in this case, college students at Stanford University and San Jose State University, both near the earthquake epicenter) should have more nightmares than people who were not in the San Francisco area at the time (a control group of students at the University of Arizona).

One of the findings of this research probably would not surprise you. Approximately 40% of those college students who were near the area affected by the earthquake did report nightmares as compared to only 5% of the students in Arizona who did not directly experience the earthquake. However, in a less obvious finding, the nightmares described by the California students were not reported to be more intense or frightening than those of the students in Arizona. In other words, although a traumatic event may trigger *more* nightmares, these nightmares may not necessarily be more traumatic.

We are not surprised to learn that external stressors like earthquakes can cause unpleasant sleep disruptions such as nightmares; but it is disconcerting to suspect that internal stressors can also have negative effects. These stressors occur during the REM sleep that produces dreams and nightmares.

REM sleep is a very active time for our bodies. Heart rate and blood pressure rise during this time to levels that are similar to the levels when we are awake. And recently it has been found that our sympathetic nervous system, which we learned in Chapter 2 is responsible for mobilizing the body during stressful or dangerous times, increases to twice its normal state in REM sleep (Somers, 1993). This finding of overactivation of the sympathetic nervous system has led some researchers to believe that the changes occurring in our bodies during REM sleep can contribute to heart attacks.

Physicians have for some time observed that painful angina attacks, which are caused by a lack of oxygen to the heart, can occur during sleep. The observation that heart attacks are more common in the morning also fits with this theory because we tend to dream more just before we wake up in the morning. All of these elements suggest that when the sympathetic nervous system is highly active, during dreams and nightmares, this is a potentially dangerous time for our hearts. Although we can't stop dreaming, this information can help us to begin to understand what triggers heart attacks, and possibly how to prevent them.

Little research, however, has been aimed at treatment of nightmares. Because nightmares are related to REM sleep, medication such as antidepressants that suppress REM sleep are sometimes prescribed. In addition, relaxation training has also been reported to reduce nightmares in some people (Karacan, 1988). Still, systematic research on reducing nightmares is yet to be done.

Sleep Terror Disorder

Imagine being fast asleep during a quiet evening and then being suddenly wakened by the blood-curdling screams of your 3-year-old son. The screaming and crying continue as you race to his room, all the while trying to picture what unspeakable horror could be causing his distress. You enter the room and pick him up to comfort him. Your relief that nothing seems to be wrong quickly changes to concern when he struggles to get away from you and acts as if *you* are now the problem. The few minutes that go by seem like hours, as you try unsuccessfully to comfort or even wake him, until he finally falls back to sleep. The next morning your son seems perfectly normal and rested, and unaware that anything unusual happened the night before.

This scenario describes several nights one of the authors went through with his own son, who was experiencing what are called *sleep terrors,* a form of parasomnia that is often mistaken for a nightmare.

Called *incubus* in adults, and *pavor nocturnus* in children, these events can be extremely disturbing, especially for an observer. The DSM-IV criteria for sleep terror disorder are listed in Table 10.11. The child usually begins these attacks with a piercing scream; she appears to be extremely upset, is often sweating, and frequently has a rapid heartbeat. Sleep terrors resemble nightmares because the child (it most often occurs among young children) cries and appears frightened. However, sleep terrors occur during NREM sleep and therefore are not frightening dreams. In addition, during sleep terrors, children cannot be easily waked and comforted, as is possible when a child has a nightmare. In the case of sleep terrors, children do not remember the incident, despite its often dramatic effect on the observer.

About 5% of otherwise healthy young children have sleep terrors at some point, and a small percentage of adults also experience this disorder. Fortunately, sleep terrors decrease in frequency over time and are usually gone by the time the child is a teenager.

We know relatively little about sleep terrors although several theories of their cause have been proposed (Mindell, 1993). Psychological influences were proposed at one time, but research now suggests that they may not be an important consideration (Kales, Kales, et al., 1980). Biological theories have implicated enlarged adenoids in children as well as an immature central nervous system as the cause of this problem, although there is very little evidence to support or discount these ideas (Karacan, 1988). We do know that members of the same family tend to have this disorder, so there may be a genetic component, but none has yet been found.

Treatment for sleep terrors usually begins with a recommendation to wait them out to see if they disappear on their own. When the problem is frequent or continues to occur over a long period of time, sometimes medication such as antidepressants (imipramine) or benzodiazepines is recommended, although their

Table 10.11 DSM-IV Criteria for Sleep Terror Disorder

A. Recurrent episodes of abrupt awakening from sleep, usually occurring during the first third of the major sleep episode and beginning with a panicky scream.

B. Intense fear and signs of autonomic arousal, such as tachycardia, rapid breathing, and sweating, during each episode.

C. Relative unresponsiveness to efforts of others to comfort the person during the episode.

D. No detailed dream is recalled and there is amnesia for the episode.

E. The episodes cause clinically significant distress or impairment in social, occupational, or other important areas of functioning.

F. The disturbance is not due to the direct physiological effects of a substance (e.g., a drug of abuse, a medication) or a general medical condition.

Source: DSM-IV, APA, 1994.

Table 10.12   DSM-IV Criteria for Sleepwalking Disorder

A. Repeated episodes of rising from bed during sleep and walking about, usually occurring during the first third of the major sleep episode.

B. While sleepwalking, the person has a blank, staring face, is relatively unresponsive to the efforts of others to communicate with him or her, and can be awakened only with great difficulty.

C. On awakening (either from the sleepwalking episode or the next morning), the person has amnesia for the episode.

D. Within several minutes after awakening from the sleepwalking episode, there is no impairment of mental activity or behavior (although there may initially be a short period of confusion or disorientation).

E. The sleepwalking causes clinically significant distress or impairment in social, occupational, or other important areas of functioning.

F. The disturbance is not due to the direct physiological effects of a substance (e.g., a drug of abuse, a medication) or a general medical condition.

Source: DSM-IV, APA, 1994.

effectiveness has not yet been clearly demonstrated (Mindell, 1993). To date, there is not much evidence for a good and lasting treatment of sleep terrors.

Sleepwalking Disorder

It might surprise you to learn that **sleepwalking** occurs during NREM sleep. This means that when people walk in their sleep (also called **somnambulism**), they are probably not acting out a dream. This parasomnia will typically occur during the first few hours of sleep and happens while a person is in the deep stages of sleep—stages 3 and 4. The DSM-IV criteria for sleepwalking (see Table 10.12) require that the person leave the bed during the episode, although less active episodes can involve small motor behaviors such as sitting up in bed and picking at the blanket or making gestures with the arms. Because sleepwalking occurs during the deepest stages of sleep, waking someone during an episode of sleepwalking is difficult; if the person is wakened, he or she typically will not remember what has happened.

Sleepwalking is primarily a problem during childhood, although a small proportion of people continue to sleepwalk as adults. A relatively large number of children—from 15% to 30%—have at least one episode of sleepwalking, with about 2% of children reported to have multiple incidents (Thorpy & Glovinsky, 1987). For the most part, the course of sleepwalking is short, and few people over the age of 15 continue to exhibit this parasomnia. Thus, it is less common

among adults, with a prevalence less than 1% (Bootzin et al., 1993). However, when it does occur among adults, sleepwalking is more often associated with other psychological disorders. One study found that almost three-quarters of a sample of adults who frequently walked in their sleep had psychiatric diagnoses (Kales, Soldatos, Cadwell, et al., 1980).

One of the myths about this disorder is that wakening a sleepwalker is dangerous to that person. Sleepwalkers are difficult to waken—because of the stage of sleep they are in—and will be confused if wakened, but they will suffer no harmful consequences. A second myth is that the sleepwalker will never do anything harmful during one of these episodes. People who sleepwalk seem generally aware of their surroundings and tend to avoid harming themselves. However, there are occasional reports of people harming themselves or others during sleepwalking. In one recent incident, a 35-year-old man who was sleepwalking was reported to have stabbed another man (Ovuga, 1992). We do not yet have a clear understanding as to why some people sleepwalk, although factors such as extreme fatigue, being previously sleep deprived, the use of sedative or hypnotic drugs (drugs to help you fall asleep), or stress have been implicated (Anch, Browman, Mitler, & Walsh, 1988). There also seems to be a genetic component to sleepwalking, with a higher incidence observed among identical twins and within families (Kales, Soldatos, Bixler, et al., 1980).

Summary

- Sleep disorders are highly prevalent in the general population.

- There are two types of sleep disorders: dyssomnias (which are disturbances of sleep) and parasomnias (which are abnormal events such as nightmares and sleepwalking that occur during sleep).

- The most common sleep disorder—insomnia—involves the inability to initiate sleep, problems maintaining sleep, or failure to feel refreshed after a full night's sleep.

- Sleep disruptions can have biological, cognitive, psychological, and even cultural influences.

- Benzodiazepine medications have been helpful for short-term treatment of many of the dyssomnias, although long-term treatment should include psychological interventions such as stimulus control and sleep hygiene.

- Parasomnias such as nightmares occur during REM (or dream) sleep, and sleep terrors and sleepwalking during NREM sleep.

Key Terms

breathing-related sleep disorders (393)
cataplexy (391)
circadian rhythm sleep disorders (394)
confusional arousals (401)
dyssomnias (381)
hypersomnia (389)
hypnagogic hallucinations (391)
microsleeps (384)
narcolepsy (391)

nightmares (401)
non-rapid eye movement (NREM) sleep (379)
parasomnias (381, 400)
polysomnographic (PSG) evaluation (382)
primary insomnia (384)
rapid eye movement (REM) sleep (379)
rebound insomnia (397)
sleep apnea (393)

sleep efficiency (SE) (383)
sleep paralysis (391, 401)
sleep starts (401)
sleep state misperception (SSM) (385)
sleep terrors (401)
somnambulism (sleepwalking) (404)
total sleep time (TST) (383)

Man, dominated by drives, has no power over himself. . . .
We are in bondage in proportion
as we are dominated by drives.
Benedict de Spinoza
"Ethics," in Philosophy
of Benedict de Spinoza

11

Sexual and Gender Identity Disorders

On the face of it, the study of sexual arousal and behavior as well as gender identity should be straightforward. There are only two sexes, each sex has the same basic anatomy and identity, and, in most species, the principal purpose of sex is propagation of the species. Therefore, it should be an easy matter to describe what is "normal" and what could go wrong along the way, making it a topic for this book.

But it isn't! We're not even sure what is "normal" in our own country. In 1989 and 1991 the Congress of the United States voted not to fund research designed to survey sexual practices in certain segments of our population and the reasons people engage in certain sexual practices. They did this for fear that the questions in the survey might offend some people or even put ideas in people's heads. The result of this lack of funding has been that crucial information is not now available to public health officials. An example is the frequency of sexual practices that may put certain groups, such as adolescents, at risk for serious diseases—for instance, AIDS. We know that type of sexual contact (vaginal, anal, or oral) and number of sex partners are risk factors for the acquisition of sexually transmitted diseases including AIDS. But we don't know who is engaging in this behavior or why. Therefore, it has been difficult if not impossible to design effective programs to limit the spread of communicable diseases, lower the number of unwanted pregnancies, and reduce other consequences

of sexual behaviors that people seldom consider at the time of sexual contact.

There are some indications that federal funding of research on current sexual practices will soon resume; but it will take some time before we can "catch up" to the data base that has been lost to us. In the meantime, some studies are beginning to appear on what is normal in North America as we approach the year 2000. In this chapter we first review what is considered normal sexual behavior before discussing what can go wrong (disorders). Then we look at three kinds of disorders and their treatment. The first is *gender identity disorder*, wherein a person is dissatisfied with his or her own gender identity or sense of being a male or female. The second is *sexual dysfunction*, in which people find it difficult to function adequately during sexual relations. Last is *paraphilia*, in which one is attracted to inappropriate people, such as children, or objects, such as articles of clothing. Paraphilia is the new term for sexual deviation.

What Is "Normal" in Our Culture and Other Cultures?

You have all read magazine surveys reporting sensational information on sexual practices. Recently one magazine reported that men can reach orgasm 15 or more times a day (very rare) and that women fantasize about being raped (even rarer). Almost none of these magazine surveys is dependable or reliable; they are just meant to sell magazines. To determine the prevalence of sexual practices in a scientific and accurate manner requires carefully planned surveys that randomly sample the population. In a recent well-done survey, Billy, Tanfer, Grady, and Klepinger (1993) reported data from 3,321 men between the ages of 20 and 39. The participants were interviewed, a more reliable method than simply having respondents fill out a questionnaire about their sexual practices, and the responses were analyzed in detail. The main purpose of this survey was to ascertain risk factors for sexually transmitted diseases and AIDS. Some of the data are presented in Figure 11.1.

Results indicate that virtually all men in the study are sexually experienced and that vaginal intercourse is a nearly universal experience among them,

even those who have never been married. Three-fourths of the men have also engaged in oral sex but only one-fifth have ever engaged in anal sex, a particularly high-risk behavior for AIDS transmission, and half the latter group had not engaged in anal sex in the past year and a half. Slightly more troublesome is the finding that 23.3% of these males have had sex with 20 or more partners during their lives, another high-risk behavior. On the other hand, over 70% has had no more than one sexual partner during the past 1½ years and fewer than 10% had had 4 or more partners during that same period.

Even more surprising is the finding from this study that the overwhelming majority of the men had engaged exclusively in **heterosexual** *activity* (sex with the opposite sex). Only 2.3% of the men in this study had engaged in **homosexual** *activity* (sex with the same sex), with only 1.1% engaging in exclusively homosexual activity. These results require some rethinking of our past suppositions, because for over 40

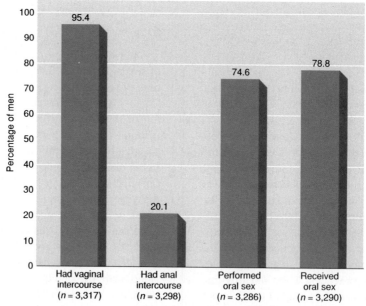

Percentage of men, ages 20–39, who have ever had vaginal intercourse, had anal intercourse, performed oral sex, or received oral sex

Percentage of men, ages 20–39, who engaged in vaginal intercourse with either 1–3 partners or 20 or more partners

Figure 11.1   Results of a survey of male sexual practices (data from Billy et al., 1993)

years sex researchers and public health officials have relied on the last really comprehensive survey of sexual behaviors and attitudes performed by one of the pioneer investigators into sexual behavior, Alfred Kinsey. Kinsey and his colleagues (Kinsey, Pomeroy, & Martin, 1948; Kinsey, Pomeroy, Martin, & Gebhard, 1953) reported the figure for any same-gender sexual activity to be closer to 10%. Since sampling procedures were not nearly so sophisticated in Kinsey's day as now, his data are presumed to be inaccurate, particularly in light of the additional surveys reported below.

Two other recent studies—one from Britain (Johnson, Wadsworth, Wellings, Bradshaw, & Field, 1992) and one from France (Spira et al., 1992)—also surveyed sexual behavior and practices among more than 20,000 men *and women* in each country. These studies produced results surprisingly similar to those reported for American men. More than 70% of the respondents from all age groups in the British and French studies also reported only one (or no) sexual partner during the past year (see Figure 11.2). Women were somewhat more likely than males to have had fewer than two partners. Also similar to the American study, only 4.1% of French males and 3.6% of British males reported ever having had a male sexual partner. Almost certainly the percentage of males engaging exclusively in homosexual behavior would be considerably lower. The consistency of these data across three different countries suggests strongly that these results represent something close to the norm.

Nevertheless, the types of sexual risks taken by college students and young adults remain alarmingly high despite the AIDS epidemic and publicity surrounding it as well as the recent increase in other sexually transmitted diseases such as genital herpes and chlamydia, a sexually transmitted bacterial infection resulting in a variety of genital symptoms such as burning, itching, and pain. DeBuono, Zinner, Daamen, and McCormack (1990) surveyed college women in 1975, in 1986, and again in 1989. They found very little change over these years in the number of *male sexual partners,* the frequency of *oral sex,* or the frequency of *anal intercourse.* These results are presented in Table 11.1. Regular condom use during sexual intercourse increased somewhat from 12% in 1975 to 41% in 1989. This is an improvement, but over half the college-age women who were sexually active were still practicing unprotected sex.

Although both males and females tend toward a monogamous (one partner) pattern of sexual relationships, gender differences in sexual behavior do exist and some of them are quite dramatic. One common finding among sexual surveys is that a much higher percentage of males than females report that they masturbate, or self-stimulate to orgasm (Oliver & Hyde, 1993). When Leitenberg, Detzer, and Srebnik

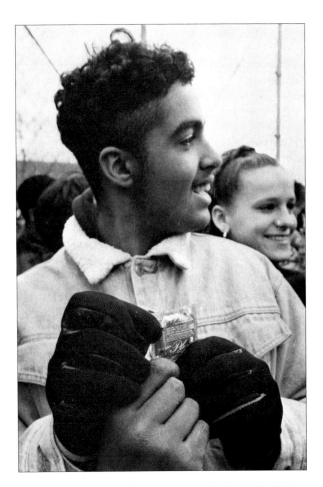

In New York City, condoms are being distributed in high schools to prevent the spread of sexually transmitted diseases.

(1993) surveyed 280 university students regarding masturbatory practices, they found that this discrepancy between males and females was still evident despite attempts during the past 25 years to encourage women to take more responsibility for their own sexuality and to engage in more sexual self-exploration. Specifically, 81% of males versus only 45% of females reported ever masturbating. More detailed data are presented in Table 11.2.

Among those who did masturbate, the frequency of masturbation was about three times greater for males than for females throughout adolescence as well as currently. Masturbation was not related in any way to later sexual functioning. That is, whether individuals masturbated or not during adolescence had no influence on whether they had experienced intercourse, the frequency of intercourse, the number of partners, or other factors reflecting sexual adjustment. Thus, it would seem that masturbation is neither beneficial nor harmful to later sexual adjustment.

Why do women masturbate less frequently than men? This finding puzzles sex researchers, par-

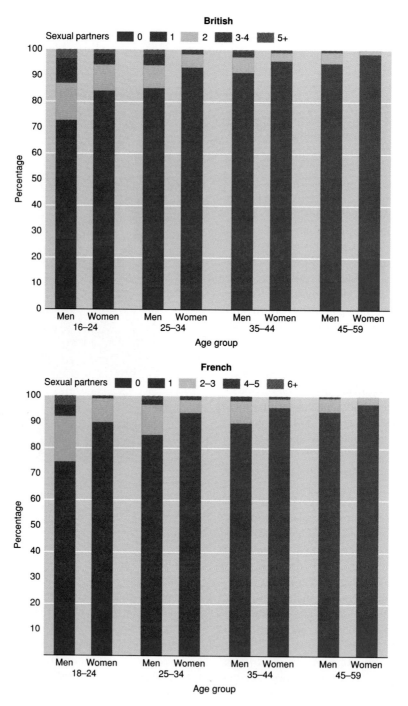

Figure 11.2 Sexual behavior and practices. The graphs show the number of sexual partners in a large sample of British and French men and women over the year previous to each subject's participation in a survey (from Taylor, 1993).

ticularly when other long-standing gender differences in sexual behavior, such as the probability of engaging in premarital intercourse, have virtually disappeared in recent years (Clement, 1990). One traditional view accounting for differences in masturbatory behavior is that women have been taught to associate sex with romance and emotional intimacy whereas men are more interested in physical gratification. But this explanation seems unlikely since the discrepancy in

masturbatory behavior continues despite the decrease in gender-specific attitudes toward sexuality. A more likely reason is anatomical. Because of the nature of the erectile response in males and the relative ease for them in providing sufficient stimulation to reach orgasm, masturbation may simply be more convenient for males than for females. This may explain why gender differences in masturbation are also evident in primates and other animals further down the phylogenetic scale

Table 11.1 Percentages of College Women Who Participated in Various Sexual Activities in 1975, 1986, and 1989

No. of Male Sexual Partners Ever	1975 (n = 486)	1986 (n = 161)	1989 (n = 132)
0	12.1	13.0	12.9
1	25.1	24.8	12.1
2–5	40.5	42.2	52.3
≥ 6	22.2	19.9	21.2
No answer	0	0	1.5
Fellatio (female oral contact with male genitals):			
Never	17.9	16.8	12.9
Occasionally	47.3	45.3	43.9
Regularly	32.5	33.5	42.4
No answer	2.3	4.3	0.8
Cunnilingus (male oral contact with female genitals):			
Never	33.1	34.8	33.3
Occasionally	38.9	37.3	36.4
Regularly	24.3	23.6	28.8
No answer	3.7	4.3	1.5
Anal intercourse:			
Never	87.4	89.4	90.2
Occasionally	9.7	7.5	8.3
Regularly	0.6	0	0.8
No answer	2.3	3.1	0.8

Frequency of condom use during sexual intercourse in college women in 1975, 1986, and 1989.

	% of Women		
	1975 (n = 427)	1986 (n = 140)	1989 (n = 113)
Frequency			
Always or almost always	12	21	41
Seldom or never	87	71	58
Uncertain	1	8	1

Source: DeBuono et al., 1990.

Table 11.2 Sex Differences in Masturbation

	% Who Had Masturbated		
	Men	Women	p
Preadolescence	30.3	22.8	ns
During age 13	45.5	25.1	< 0.01
During age 14	59.2	25.7	< 0.01
During age 15	67.3	29.8	< 0.01
Past year	73.5	34.3	< 0.01
Past month	61.2	26.9	< 0.01

Note: Percentages of men and women who reported ever having masturbated during preadolescence and/or early adolescence and during the past year and past month.

Source: Adapted from Leitenberg, Detzer, & Srebnik, 1993.

(Ford & Beach, 1951). In any case, incidence of masturbation continues to be the largest gender difference in sexuality.

Another continuing gender difference is reflected in attitudes toward *casual* premarital sex, with males expressing a far more permissive attitude than females, although this gap is becoming much smaller as the years pass. On the other hand, results from a large number of studies suggest that *no* gender differences are apparent at the current time in attitudes about homosexuality, the experience of sexual satisfaction (important for both), or attitudes toward masturbation (it's generally acceptable). Small to moderate gender differences were evident in attitudes toward premarital intercourse when the couple was engaged or in a committed relationship (with males more approving than females); the same held for attitudes toward extramarital sex. Consistent with the British and French studies mentioned above, the number of sexual partners and the frequency of intercourse were slightly greater for males, and males were slightly younger at age of first sexual intercourse. Examining trends from the 1960s to the 1980s, we see that almost all existing gender differences became smaller over time, especially in regard to attitudes toward premarital sex.

Nevertheless, differences still exist in attitudes toward sexuality between men and women even if they are decreasing. Recently, Hatfield, Sprecher, Pillemer, Greenberger, and others (1988) assessed young, unmarried women (undergraduates in college) as well as a sample of newly married couples (age 17 to 46 years) to determine what parts of the sexual relationship contributed most substantially to their sexual satisfaction. Consistently with long-standing gender differences, women desired more activities that demonstrated love and intimacy during sex while men were more interested in activities that focused on the arousal aspects of

Havelock Ellis was an influential early scholar of human sexuality.

sexual activity. While these attitudes may not correlate perfectly with what actually happens (behavior) during sexual relations, they probably represent something basically different in the way men and women approach sexual relations.

What happened to the sexual revolution? Where are the effects of the "anything goes" attitude toward sexual expression and fulfillment that supposedly began in the 1960s and 1970s? Clearly there has been some change. The "double standard" has disappeared somewhat in that women no longer feel constrained by a stricter and more conservative standard of sexual conduct imposed by society. The sexes are definitely drawing together in their attitudes and behavior. Regardless, the overwhelming majority of individuals engage in traditional heterosexual, vaginal intercourse in the context of a relationship with one partner. Based on these data, the sexual revolution may be largely a creation of the media, focusing as it does on extreme or sensational cases.

On the other hand, what is normal as we approach the year 2000 clearly has changed from times past. Not too long ago masturbation was widely condemned and said to cause such disorders as failing eyesight, digestive disorders, and insanity (Gagnon, 1977; Caird & Wincze, 1977). Today masturbation is actually part of a number of sex therapy approaches and, therefore, is "prescribed" by doctors. In early writings, eliminating or suppressing such sexual activity and arousal was seen as virtuous and conducive to full spiritual development. Today the absence of sexual desire is officially designated a clinical disorder. Of course, we had no scientific sexual surveys in earlier days so it is not clear what effect these early prohibitions had on people's behavior.

Attitudes toward specific sexual practices *within* a heterosexual relationship have also changed. The most influential early scholars of sexuality had very narrow views of what was normal. Both Richard von Krafft-Ebing in *Psychopathia Sexualis* (1886) and Havelock Ellis in *Studies in the Psychology of Sex* (1906) condemned masturbation and homosexuality and implied that the only legitimate road to orgasm was vaginal intercourse (coitus). Sigmund Freud held a similar point of view (1905/1962). As late as 1968, DSM-II noted that individuals whose sexual interests were "directed primarily toward objects other than people of the opposite sex or toward sexual acts not usually associated with coitus are classified as suffering from sexual disorders."

What is normal in the year 2000 in Western countries may not necessarily be normal in other parts of the world. The Sambia tribe in New Guinea believes that semen is an essential substance for growth and development in young boys of the tribe. They also believe that semen is *not* produced naturally—that is, the body is incapable of producing it spontaneously. Therefore, all young boys in the tribe, beginning at approximately age 7, become semen recipients by engaging exclusively in homosexual oral sex with teenage boys. Only oral sexual practices are permitted; masturbation is forbidden and totally absent. Early in adolescence the boys switch roles and become semen providers to younger boys. Heterosexual relations, and even contact with the opposite sex, are prohibited until the boys become teenagers. Late in adolescence the boys are expected to marry and begin exclusive heterosexual activity. And they do, with no exceptions (Herdt, 1987; Herdt & Stoller, 1989). On the other hand, the Munda tribe of Northeast India also requires adolescents and children to live together. But in this tribe both male and female children live in the same setting and the sexual activity, consisting mostly of petting and mutual masturbation, is all heterosexual (Bancroft, 1989).

Even within Western cultures there are some variations. Schwartz (1993) surveyed attitudes surrounding the first premarital experience of sexual intercourse in nearly 200 female undergraduates from the United States and compared them to a similar sample in Sweden, where attitudes toward sexuality are somewhat more permissive. The average age at the time of first coitus for the woman and the age of her partner are presented in Table 11.3. Also presented is the age at which the women thought it would be socially acceptable in their culture for them to have sexual intercourse. Perceived ages acceptable for both men and women were significantly younger in Sweden but few other differences existed, with one striking exception: 73.7% of Swedish women used some form of contraception during their first sexual intercourse compared to only 56.7% of American women, a significant difference.

In approximately half of more than 100 societies surveyed worldwide, premarital sexual behavior is culturally accepted and encouraged. But in the remaining half, premarital sex is unacceptable and discouraged (Broude & Greene, 1980; Bancroft, 1989).

Thus, what is normal sexual behavior in one culture is not necessarily normal in another, and the wide range of sexual expression must be considered in determining the existence of sexual disorders. In Chapter 1 we discussed the problems and pitfalls of defining a disorder. The difficulty posed in Chapter 1 was this: When does a behavior somewhat different from the norm become a disorder? The current approach is to be quite tolerant of a variety of sexual expressions, even if they are unusual, unless and until the sexual behavior becomes associated with a substantial impairment in functioning. Within this context there are three kinds of sexual behavior disorders: *gender identity disorders, sexual dysfunctions,* and *paraphilias.* The first category, **gender identity disorders,** refers to psychological dissatisfaction with one's biological sex. As such, gender identity disorder is not specifically a sexual disorder but rather a disturbance in the sense of one's identity as a male or a female. But this disorder is often grouped with sexual disorders, as it is in DSM-IV.

Turning to sexual disorders, individuals with **sexual dysfunction** find it difficult to function adequately while having sex. For example, they may be unable to become sexually aroused or to achieve orgasm. **Paraphilia** is the relatively new term for sexual deviation and describes a series of disorders in which sexual arousal occurs in a relatively exclusive manner in the context of inappropriate objects or individuals. *Philia* refers to a strong attraction or liking and *para* refers to a specific object or direction for the attraction that is abnormal. Thus, **pedophilia** technically means strong sexual attraction or liking (*philia*) toward children (*ped* being the Latin root word for children). People with paraphilias have very intense patterns of sexual arousal and fantasies toward individuals, objects, or activities that are inappropriate in some way. Thus, they may be aroused by sexual activity with a child or by inflicting pain on others. These paraphilic arousal patterns tend to be focused rather narrowly, often precluding mutually consenting adult patterns, even if desired. In the remainder of this chapter we will review

Table 11.3 Group Differences Between U.S. and Swedish Female Undergraduates Regarding Premarital Sex

Variable	U.S. Mean/(SD)	Sweden Mean/(SD)
Age at first coitus	16.97 (1.83)	16.80 (1.92)
Age of first coital partner	18.77 (2.88)	19.10 (2.96)
Perceived age of social acceptance for *females* to engage in premarital coitus	18.76 (2.57)	15.88 (1.43)
Perceived age of social acceptance for *males* to engage in premarital coitus	16.33 (2.13)	15.58 (1.20)

Source: Schwartz, 1993.

these three types of disorders. But before we turn to that discussion we'll look briefly at three topics relevant to normal sexuality—the stages of sexual arousal and activity, sexuality across the life span, and the development of sexual orientation—that will provide an important perspective when we examine the disorders.

The Stages of Sexuality

Until relatively recently, we knew little about physiological responding in healthy well-functioning adults. William Masters and Virginia Johnson made enormous strides in deepening our understanding of this process in their laboratory in St. Louis during the 1950s and 1960s. Their 1966 book, *Human Sexual Response,* summarized thousands of hours of very carefully done but controversial research during which they used physiological measures to actually monitor adult volunteers engaging in sexual activity. Based on this work they discovered that well-functioning adults proceed through four distinct stages during sexual activity: (a) excitement or arousal, (b) plateau, (c) orgasm, and (d) resolution. Subsequent to these findings, sex researchers such as Kaplan (1979) specified another stage prior to the excitement or arousal phase referred to as the "desire phase," which describes the person's interest in and readiness for sexual activity.

Masters and Johnson and others working in this area described in great detail the physiological changes occurring in the genitals and other locations in the body during each of these five stages. In the *desire phase* sexual urges occur, perhaps after the individual sees an attractive person or in reaction to some cue that makes him or her think of sex. Sexual fantasies may also occur in the absence of any sexual cues. That is, you may find yourself daydreaming about sex. The *arousal stage* is associated with a subjective sense of sexual pleasure and clear physiological signs of sexual arousal including penile tumescence in males (increased flow of blood into the penis); in women, blood pools in the pelvic area (vasocongestion) leading to vaginal lubrication along with breast tumescence (erect nipples). The *orgasm phase* is associated with feelings of the inevitability of ejaculation in men and contractions of the walls of the lower third of the vagina in women. After orgasm, women can respond again immediately and therefore experience multiple orgasms. Men, on the other hand, enter a refractory period during which erections are not possible for a period of time.

The *plateau phase* simply refers to a brief period of time before orgasm, and the *resolution phase* describes the decrease in arousal occurring after orgasm, particularly in men. Dysfunctions are not associated with either of these last two phases, and they will not be mentioned further.

Sexuality in the Elderly

The primary focus of a developmental view of sexual dysfunction concerns sexuality in the elderly. Despite many misconceptions about sexuality in this group, it is clear that healthy sexuality can continue well into old

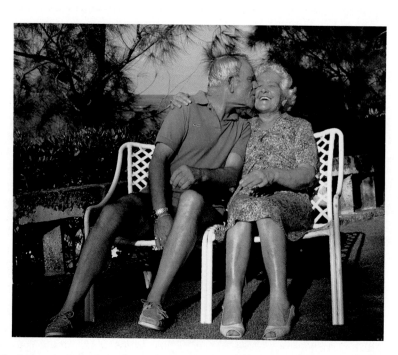

Sexuality is often a continuing part of a loving relationship for older couples.

Table 11.4   Sexual Activity of Elderly Married Respondents Classified by Age and Sex

Age, y	Males			Females		
	Yes	%	Total	Yes	%	Total
60–64	83	87.4	95	57	64.0	89
65–69	64	79.0	81	49	63.6	77
70–74	18	58.1	31	13	43.3	30
75–79	13	50.0	26	9	36.0	25
80+	4	28.6	14	1	25.0	4
Total	182	73.7	247	129	57.3	225

Source: Diokno, Brown, & Herzog, 1990.

age, even past the age of 80 for some people. Table 11.4 presents the percentage of married individuals in a community sample who were sexually active and continuing to have sexual intercourse by age group (Diokno, Brown, & Herzog, 1990). Notable is that 50% of males aged 75 to 79 and 36% of females in the same age range remained sexually active. Reasons for the discrepancy between men and women are not clear, although one possibility is that many women are married to an older spouse who falls in a somewhat older age bracket in this survey. The sample of individuals over the age of 80 is too small to allow meaningful conclusions, although many remained sexually active. On the other hand, it is evident that males have an increasingly difficult time as they age in achieving or maintaining an erection (see Table 11.5). Decreases in sexual activity are correlated, for the most part, with decreases in general mobility as well as various disease processes.

These data reflect fairly accurately the results from other surveys in the elderly (for example, Kellett, 1991; Bancroft, 1989). Masters and Johnson (1966) have provided physiological documentation of the tendency for the speed and intensity of various vasocongestive re-

sponses to be reduced as one ages. In aging women the most notable and important change is a reduction in vaginal lubrication. Aging males take longer to develop an erection and they require more direct erectile stimulation.

The Development of Sexual Orientation

A number of reports are appearing of late suggesting that homosexuality runs in families (Bailey & Benishay, 1993), is more common among monozygotic twins than among dizygotic twins or natural siblings (Bailey & Pillard, 1991; Bailey, Pillard, Neale, & Agyei, 1993; Whitnam, Diamond, & Martin, 1993), and is associated with differential exposure to hormones early in life, perhaps before birth in the uterus (Gladue, Green, & Hellman, 1984; Ehrhardt et al., 1985), and that the actual structure of the brain in individuals with homosexual patterns of arousal might be different from the brain structure of those with heterosexual patterns of arousal (LeVay, 1991; Allen & Gorski, 1992). A report has now appeared identifying the specific location of a possible gene (or genes) for homosexuality located on the X chromosome (Hamer, Hu, Magnuson, Hu, & Pattatucci, 1993). In the two very well-done twin studies (Bailey & Pillard, 1991; Bailey et al., 1993), homosexual orientation was shared in approximately 50% of monozygotic twins compared with 16% to 22% of dizygotic twins. Approximately the same or a slightly lower percentage of nontwin brothers or sisters were homosexual.

The principal conclusion drawn by the media is that sexual orientation has a biological cause. Gay rights activists are decidedly split on the significance of these findings. Some are pleased with the "biological cause" interpretation, noting that the public can no longer assume that homosexuals have made some sort of a morally depraved choice of "deviant" arousal patterns. Other gay rights activists, however, note how quickly the public and media have pounced on the notion that there is something "biologically wrong"

Table 11.5   Difficulty for Elderly Married Men in Getting or Maintaining Erection

Age	n	%	Total
60–64	27	28.7	94
65–69	27	34.6	78
70–74	14	46.7	30
75–79	15	62.5	24
80+	9	64.3	14
Total	92	38.3	240

Source: Diokno, Brown, & Herzog, 1990.

John Bancroft, one of the leading sexuality researchers in the world, was one of the first to describe in some detail the interaction of biological and psychological determinants of sexual behavior.

with individuals with homosexual arousal patterns, the assumption being that this biological abnormality could be detected, using sophisticated tests, in the fetus and prevented some day, perhaps through genetic engineering.

Do the arguments over biological causes sound familiar? Think back to studies described in Chapter 2 that attempted to link complex behavior to particular genes. In almost every case these studies

Michael Bailey and his colleagues have carried out some pioneering studies on genetic contributions to sexual orientation.

could not be replicated and investigators fell back on a model in which genetic contributions to behavioral traits (and psychological disorders) come from many genes, each making a relatively small contribution to the creation of a *vulnerability*. This biological vulnerability then interacts with various environmental conditions, personality traits, and other contributors in a complex way to determine behavioral patterns. We also discussed gene-environment interactions in which certain learning experiences and environmental events may affect brain structure and function and genetic expression.

Theoretical models outlining these complex gene-environment interactions for sexual orientation are beginning to appear (Byne & Parsons, 1993). For example, Byne and Parsons (1993) propose that a person inherits particular personality traits, which then influence the manner in which he or she responds as sexual orientation and other personality characteristics unfold environmentally. This view implies that there might be many pathways to the development of heterosexuality or homosexuality, and that no one factor, biological or psychological, can predict the outcome with any degree of strength (Bancroft, 1994).

Almost certainly, in our view, scientists will pin down biological contributions to the formation of sexual orientation, both heterosexual and homosexual. And just as certainly, the environment and experience will be found to play very powerful roles in determining whether these potential patterns of sexual arousal develop. Most likely, the size of the biological contribution to sexual orientation will be in the same range as it is for other personality traits such as shyness or activity levels. Careful scientists working in the genetics of sexual orientation, such as Michael Bailey at Northwestern University, are among the first to underscore the important contributions of environment and experience in the complex interactions with inherited biological vulnerabilities.

Of course, one of the more intriguing findings from the twin studies of Bailey and his colleagues is that approximately 50% of the monozygotic twins with *exactly* the *same genetic structure* as well as the *same environment* (growing up in the same house) *did not* share the same sexual orientation (Bailey & Pillard, 1991). But the media, most likely, will continue to favor simple, one-dimensional explanations such as claims that homosexuality is caused by a gene, or heterosexuality is caused by healthy early developmental experiences. Although we could be wrong, neither explanation is likely to be proven correct.

With that brief coverage of some points critical to our understanding of human sexuality, we turn now to gender identity disorders.

Gender Identity Disorders

What is it that makes you think you are a man? Or a woman? Clearly, it's more than your sexual arousal patterns or your anatomy. It's also more than the reactions and expectations you get from your family and society at large. The essence of your masculinity and femininity is a deep-seated personal sense called gender identity. Gender identity disorder is present when a person's gender identity is not consistent with his or her biological sex. People with this disorder feel trapped in a body of the wrong sex. Consider the following case, who presented to our sexuality clinic.

The Case of Joe

Joe was a 17-year-old male and the last of five children. He was a keen disappointment to his mother since she desired a girl. Nevertheless he became her favorite child. His father worked long hours and had little contact with the boy.

For as long as Joe could remember he had thought of himself as a girl. He began cross-dressing spontaneously (dressing in girls clothes totally of his own accord) before he was 5 years old and continued into junior high school. During this period his mother reported that he developed an interest in cooking, knitting, crocheting, and embroidering, skills he acquired by reading an encyclopedia. His older brother often scorned him for his distaste of "masculine" activities such as hunting. Joe reported associating mostly with girls during this period, although he remembered being strongly attracted to a "boyfriend" in the first grade. In his sexual fantasies, which developed at about 12 years of age, he pictured himself as a female having intercourse with a male. His extremely effeminate behavior made him the object of scorn and ridicule when he entered high school at age 15. Usually passive and unassertive, he ran away from home at this time and attempted suicide. Unable to continue in high school he

Table 11.6 DSM-IV Criteria for Gender Identity Disorders

A. A strong and persistent cross-gender identification (not merely a desire for any perceived cultural advantages of being the other sex).
   In children, the disturbance is manifested by four (or more) of the following:

1. Repeatedly stated desire to be, or insistence that he or she is, the other sex
2. In boys, preference for cross-dressing or simulating female attire; in girls, insistence on wearing only stereotypical masculine clothing
3. Strong and persistent preferences for cross-sex roles in make-believe play or persistent fantasies of being the other sex
4. Intense desire to participate in the stereotypical games and pastimes of the other sex
5. Strong preference for playmates of the other sex

   In adolescents and adults, the disturbance is manifested by symptoms such as a stated desire to be the other sex, frequent passing as the other sex, desire to live or be treated as the other sex, or the conviction that he or she has the typical feelings and reactions of the other sex.

B. Persistent discomfort with his or her sex or sense of inappropriateness in the gender role of that sex.
   In children, the disturbance is manifested by any of the following: in boys, assertion that his penis or testes are disgusting or will disappear or assertion that it would be better not to have a penis, or aversion toward rough-and-tumble play and rejection of male stereotypical toys, games, and activities; in girls, rejection of urinating in a sitting position, assertion that she has or will grow a penis, or assertion that she does not want to grow breasts or menstruate, or marked aversion toward normative feminine clothing.
   In adolescents and adults, the disturbance is manifested by symptoms such as preoccupation with getting rid of primary and secondary sex characteristics (e.g., request for hormones, surgery, or other procedures to physically alter sexual characteristics to simulate the other sex) or belief that he or she was born the wrong sex.

C. The disturbance is not concurrent with a physical intersex condition.

D. The disturbance causes clinically significant distress or impairment in social, occupational, or other important areas of functioning.

Code based on current age:
   302.6   Gender Identity Disorder in Children
   302.85 Gender Identity Disorder in Adolescents or Adults

Specify if (for sexually mature individuals):
   Sexually Attracted to Males
   Sexually Attracted to Females
   Sexually Attracted to Both
   Sexually Attracted to Neither

Source: DSM-IV, APA, 1994.

In some cultures, including some native American cultures, males assuming feminine roles are accorded high social status.

began attending secretarial school, where he was the only boy in his class. During his first interview with a therapist he reported that "I am a woman trapped in a man's body and I would like to have surgery to become a woman."

DSM-IV diagnostic criteria for gender identity disorder are presented in Table 11.6. Gender identity disorder (or *transsexualism* as it used to be called) must be distinguished from *transvestic fetishism,* a paraphilic disorder discussed later, in which individuals, usually males, are sexually aroused by wearing articles of clothing of the opposite sex. In these cases an occasional preference for the female role (on the part of the male) is present. However, the primary purpose of cross-dressing is sexual gratification. In the case of gender identity disorder, the primary goal is not sexual but rather the desire to live one's whole life in a manner consistent with that of the underlying and opposite gender.

Gender identity disorder must also be distinguished from *intersex individuals (hermaphrodites),* who are actually born with ambiguous genitalia asso-

ciated with documented hormonal or other physical abnormalities and, depending on their particular mix of characteristics, are "assigned" to a specific sex at birth. Sometimes these individuals require surgery as well as hormonal treatments to more completely alter their sexual anatomy. Individuals with gender identity disorder, on the other hand, have *no* demonstrated physical abnormalities.

Finally, gender identity disorder must be distinguished from the homosexual arousal patterns of a male who behaves on occasion in an effeminate manner. Such an individual does not feel like a woman trapped in a man's body nor does he have any desire to be a woman.

Note also, as the DSM-IV criteria do, that gender identity is *independent* of sexual arousal patterns. For example, a male-to-female transsexual (a male with a feminine gender identity) may be sexually attracted to females, which, technically, makes his arousal homosexual. Recently Eli Coleman and his associates (Coleman, Bockting, & Gooren, 1993) reported on nine female-to-male cases who were sexually attracted to men. Thus, they were heterosexual women before surgery but became gay men after surgery.

Gender identity disorder is relatively rare. The estimated incidence based on studies in Sweden and Australia is 1 in 37,000 in Sweden and 1 in 24,000 in Australia for biological males compared to 1 in 103,000 and 1 in 150,000 in these two countries for biological females (Ross, Walinder, Lundstrom, & Thuwe, 1981).

Individuals with mistaken gender identity in other cultures are often accorded the status of "shaman" or "seer" and are consulted for advice. In these other cultures the individual is almost always a male adopting a female role (for example, Coleman, Colgan, & Gooren, 1992). Stoller (1976) reports on two contemporary feminized Native American males who are not only accepted but esteemed by their tribes for their expertise in the various healing rituals. Contrary to the respect accorded these individuals in other cultures, social tolerance for them is relatively low in Western cultures, where they are the objects of curiosity at best and derision at worst.

Causes of Gender Identity Disorders

Research has yet to uncover any biological contributions to the development of gender identity disorder, although it seems likely that some biological predisposition will ultimately be discovered. As with sexual orientation, some early research suggests that exposure to specific hormones (such as slightly higher levels of testosterone or estrogen) at certain critical periods of development of the fetus in utero might "masculinize" a female fetus or "feminize" a male fetus (for instance,

Imperato-McGinley, Peterson, Gautier, & Sturla, 1979; Gladue et al., 1984). These variations in hormonal levels could occur naturally or because of specific medication that a prospective mother would be taking for other reasons. This explanation seemed likely when first offered because lower animals such as rodents are masculinized or feminized by these influences but subsequent research has not supported these findings (Bancroft, 1994; Ehrhardt & Meyer-Bahlburg, 1981). Scientists have yet to establish a link between prenatal hormonal influence and later gender identity, although it is still possible that a link exists.

Psychologically, it seems that an individual's gender identity develops when he or she is somewhere between 18 months and 3 years of age (Money & Ehrhardt, 1972; Ehrhardt & Meyer-Bahlburg, 1981). Before that time, it is possible to "reassign" the sex of an infant if necessary. One interesting case illustrating this developmental phenomenon was reported several years ago by Green and Money (1969), who described the following sequence of events.

A set of male identical twins was born into a well-adjusted family. Several weeks later when time came for the circumcision an unfortunate accident occurred. Although routine circumcision was uneventful for one of the boys, the physician's hand slipped as the procedure was carried out with the second boy, cutting off the penis flush with the abdominal wall. After working through their hostility to the physician, the parents, who consulted specialists in children with intersexual problems, were faced with a choice. These specialists pointed out to the parents that the easiest solution might be to reassign the child as a girl, a possibility to which the parents agreed. At the age of several months, the young child began to be raised as a girl, with the parents purchasing a new wardrobe and treating the child in every way possible as a baby girl.

These twins were followed through childhood and, upon reaching puberty, the young girl was given hormonal replacement therapy. By all measures this particular twin grew up to be a psychologically normal young woman.

What makes this case particularly interesting is that genetically the twins were identical. Therefore, this "experiment in nature" suggests that gender identity is something one *learns* at a very young age. But if a person learns "normal" gender identity then it would seem possible to learn mistaken gender identity. The difficulty is that we don't know exactly what influences during the critical period of 18 months to 3 years are most important in the formation of gender identity.

Richard Green, one of the pioneering researchers in this area, has made a study of feminine boys and masculine girls, what makes them that way, and what happens to them (Green, 1987). In the case of most young boys, he discovered that, when they spontaneously display feminine interests and behaviors, these behaviors are typically discouraged by most families. However, in the "feminine" boys these behaviors are not discouraged and are sometimes encouraged, as seemed to be the case with Joe. Other factors, such as excessive maternal attention and physical contact on the part of the mother, *may* also play some role, as well as a lack of male playmates during early years of socialization. These are just some of the factors identified by Green as characteristic of more effeminate boys. Remember that as yet undiscovered biological factors may also contribute to the spontaneous display of cross-gender behaviors and interests. However, in following up these boys (in a study not yet complete), Green has discovered that very few seem to develop the wrong gender identity, although he is not sure how many do so since follow-ups are continuing. The most likely outcome is the development of homosexual preferences, but even this particular sexual arousal pattern seems to occur exclusively in only approximately 40% of the boys. Another 32% show some degree of *bisexuality,* or sexual preferences for both their own sex and the opposite sex. Looking at it from the other side, 60% of these "effeminate" boys were functioning heterosexually. Thus it is safe to say that the causes of mistaken gender identity are still something of a mystery.

Treatment of Gender Identity Disorders

Treatment is available for gender identity disorder in a few selected specialty clinics around the world, although much controversy surrounds approaches to treatment. Presently the most common treatment is surgery to physically alter a person's anatomy to be consistent with gender identity. This surgical procedure is called **sex reassignment surgery.** Recently, psychosocial treatments to directly alter mistaken gender identity have been attempted in a few cases.

Sex Reassignment Surgery

To qualify for surgery at a reputable clinic, individuals must live in the opposite sex role for 18 months to 2 years so they can be sure they want to be a person of that sex. They also must be stable psychologically, financially, and socially. For male-to-female candidates, male genitals are removed and a vagina is constructed. Hormones are administered to promote gynecomastia (the growth of breasts) and the development of other secondary sex characteristics. Facial hair is typically removed through electrolysis.

For female-to-male transsexuals, an artificial penis is typically constructed through plastic surgery by removing sections of skin and muscle from elsewhere in the body, such as the thigh. Breasts are surgically

George Jorgenson was one of the first individuals to undergo sex reassignment surgery; he later became Christine Jorgenson.

Renee Richards, a well-known physician with gender identity disorder, played competitive tennis both before surgery (when her name was Richard Raskin) and after sex-reassignment surgery as a woman, pictured above.

removed. Genital surgery is a more difficult and cumbersome operation in biological females.

While early reports on sex reassignment surgery were encouraging, more recent follow-up reports are somewhat more sobering (Bockting & Coleman, 1992). At least one study (Meyer & Reter, 1979) found no differences in satisfaction between transsexuals who had had surgery and those who had not, but there were some methodological problems with this study. More recent estimates (Abramowitz, 1986; Kuiper & Cohen-Kettenis, 1988; Bancroft, 1989; Green & Fleming, 1990; Blanchard & Steiner, 1992) indicate predominantly successful adjustment (approximately 75% improved) among those who could be reached for follow-ups, with female-to-male conversions adjusting better than male-to-female conversions (Abramowitz, 1986). However, many people were lost to follow-up. Approximately 7% of the cases undergoing sex reassignment procedures later regret surgery (Lundstrom, Pauly, & Walinder, 1984; Bancroft, 1989). This result, of course, is unfortunate since the surgery is irreversible. Nevertheless, surgery has made life worth living for some individuals suffering the effects of existing in what they consider to be the wrong body.

Psychosocial Treatment

In some clinics, therapists attempt to change gender identity directly before considering surgery. This is not possible with most adult clients with gender identity disorders since the majority cannot conceive of changing their basic gender identity. However, some individuals, usually because they are in great psychological distress or because surgery is unavailable, request psychosocial treatment prior to embarking on a treatment course leading to surgery. The first successful effort to change gender identity was reported from our sexuality clinic (Barlow, Reynolds, & Agras, 1973). This was the case of Joe reported earlier. Joe was extremely depressed and suicidal, and since surgery was not possible at his age without parental consent, which was not forthcoming, he agreed to a course of psychosocial treatment.

In Joe's life, his greatest difficulty was the ridicule and scorn heaped on him for his extremely effeminate motor behavior and gestures. We developed a behavioral rating scale for gender-specific motor behavior (Barlow et al., 1979; Beck & Barlow, 1984) to help Joe identify the precise ways in which he was sitting, standing, and walking that were typically masculine or feminine. Through behavioral rehearsal and modeling, we taught him to act in a more typically masculine manner when he so chose. Very quickly he reported enormous satisfaction in avoiding the ridicule to which he had been subjected by simply choosing to behave differently in some situations. What followed was more extensive role playing and rehearsal for social skills as he was taught to make better eye contact and converse with others more positively and confidently. After this phase of therapy he was better adjusted but still felt himself to be a woman and was strongly sexually aroused to males.

During the next phase, a female therapist worked directly on his fantasies in an intense, almost hypnotic way by encouraging him to imagine himself in sexual situations with a woman and to generate more characteristically masculine fantasies as he went about his day-to-day business. After several months of intensive training, Joe's gender identity began to change, slowly at first, then more rapidly. At the end of this phase, much to his delight, he reported that he now felt like a 17-year-old boy in addition to behaving like one, although he was still sexually attracted to males.

Since he expressed a strong desire to become sexually attracted to females, procedures were implemented to alter his patterns of sexual arousal, and at a 5-year follow-up Joe had made a very successful adjustment.

Two additional cases were treated in a similar fashion (Barlow, Abel, & Blanchard, 1979) and also resulted in a change in gender identity. These two individuals, who were somewhat older than Joe, wished to retain their homosexual arousal patterns, and they were assisted in adjusting to a more standard homosexual life-style without the burden of mistaken gender identity.

Sexual Dysfunctions: Clinical Descriptions

Before describing sexual dysfunctions, we should note that the variety of problems that arise in the context of sexual interactions may occur in both heterosexual and homosexual relationships. Inability to become aroused, reach orgasm, or achieve an erection all seem to be as common in homosexual as in heterosexual relationships, but we discuss these problems for the most part here in the context of heterosexual relationships, which are the majority of cases we see in one of our clinics. Three stages of sexuality—desire, arousal, and orgasm—are each associated with specific sexual dysfunctions. In other words, a sexual dysfunction is an impairment in one of these stages. In addition, pain can become associated with sexual functioning, leading to additional sexual dysfunctions. We first describe each of the major sexual disorders, and then discuss general causes of sexual dysfunction as well as available treatments.

Categories of sexual dysfunction are presented in Table 11.7. As you can see, both males and females can experience parallel versions of most disorders, but the disorders take on specific forms determined by anatomy and other gender-specific characteristics. However, two disorders are sex specific. Premature ejaculation, obviously, occurs only in males, and vaginismus, or painful contractions of the vagina during attempted intercourse, appears only in females. All sexual dysfunctions are further specified as (a) due to psychological factors or (b) due to psychological factors combined with a general medical condition. The latter specification occurs when there is some demonstrable vascular, hormonal, or associated physical condition that would be known to *contribute* to the sexual dysfunction.

Sexual Desire Disorders

Hypoactive Sexual Desire Disorder

In **hypoactive sexual desire disorder** the person seems to have no interest in any type of sexual activity. How would you define low sexual desire? You might determine it by frequency of sexual activity—say, less than twice a month for a married couple. Or you might consider asking someone if he or she ever *thinks* about sex or has sexual fantasies. But what about the individual who has sex twice a week but really doesn't want to and "thinks" about sex only because "his wife is on his case to live up to his end of the marriage and have sex more often." This individual might, in fact, have no desire whatsoever despite having frequent sex. For these reasons, it is very difficult to assess low sexual desire; in these cases a great deal of clinical judgment is required (Friedman & Hogan, 1985; Leiblum & Rosen, 1988). Consider the following cases from our sexuality clinic.

The Case of Judy and Ira

The contact was initiated by Judy, a married woman in her late 20s who, when she reached one of our clinic staff on the phone, reported that she thought her husband, Ira, was having an affair and that she was very upset about it. The reason for her assumptions? He had demonstrated no interest whatsoever in sex during the past 3 years and they had not had sex at all for 9 months. Judy reported, however, that Ira was prepared to come in to the clinic. When he was interviewed, it became clear that Ira was not having an affair. In fact, he did not masturbate and hardly ever thought about sex. He noted that he loved his wife very much but that he had not been concerned about the issue until now, since he had too many other things to think about in his life and he thought that eventually they would get back to having sex. He now realized that his wife was quite distressed about the lack of sexual activity, particularly since they were thinking about having children.

Although Ira did not have extensive sexual experience, he had engaged in several very erotic relationships before his marriage, relationships of which Judy was aware. During a separate interview, Ira confided that during his premarital affairs he would get a "hard on" just thinking about his lovers, each of whom was quite promiscuous. His wife, on the other hand, was a pillar of the community and very unlike these women, although attractive. Since he did not become aroused thinking about his wife, he did not initiate sex.

	Sexual dysfunction	
Type of disorder	Men	Women
Desire	Hypoactive sexual desire disorder	Hypoactive sexual desire disorder
	Sexual aversion disorder	Sexual aversion disorder
Arousal	Male erectile disorder	Female sexual arousal disorder
Orgasm	Inhibited male orgasm	Inhibited female orgasm
	Premature ejaculation	
Pain	Dyspareunia	Dyspareunia
		Vaginismus

Table 11.7 Categories of Sexual Dysfunction Among Men and Women

Source: Wincze & Carey, 1991.

The Case of Mr. & Mrs. C.

Mrs. C. was a 31-year-old, very successful businesswoman who was married to a 32-year-old lawyer. They had two children ages 2 and 5 and had been married 8 years when they entered therapy. The presenting problem was Mrs. C.'s lack of sexual desire. Mr. and Mrs. C. were interviewed separately during the initial assessment and both professed attraction and love for their partner.

Mrs. C. reported that she could enjoy sex once she got involved and almost always was orgasmic. The problem was her total lack of desire to get involved in sex. She avoided her husband's sexual advances and looked on his affection and romanticism with great skepticism and usually with anger and tears.

Mrs. C. was raised in an upper-middle-class family that was supportive and loving. However, from age 6 to age 12 she was repeatedly cajoled and pressured into sexual activity by a male cousin who was 5 years her senior. This sexual activity was always initiated by her cousin and always against her will. She did not tell her parents because she felt guilty since her cousin did not use physical force to make her comply. It appeared that any romanticism on Mr. C.'s part triggered thoughts of abuse by her cousin. The treatment of Mr. and Mrs. C. will be discussed later in the chapter.

DSM-IV diagnostic criteria for hypoactive sexual desire disorder are presented in Table 11.8. Problems of this disorder in the past presented more often as marital rather than sexual difficulties. With the recognition of hypoactive sexual desire as a distinct disorder, however, there has been an increase in the number of couples presenting to sex therapy clinics with one of the partners reporting this problem (Leiblum & Rosen, 1988). Best estimates suggest that something over 50% of patients coming to sexuality clinics for help complain of hypoactive sexual desire, and almost 55% of these patients are males (LoPiccolo & Friedman, 1988; Kaplan, 1979). Although no community studies have been reported recently, earlier community studies (for example, Frank, Anderson, & Rubinstein, 1978) suggested that approximately 25% of individuals might be characterized as experiencing hypoactive sexual desire. Schreiner-Engel and Schiavi (1986) noted that the patients they have studied with hypoactive sexual desire rarely have sexual fantasies, seldom masturbate (with 35% of the women and 52% of the men not masturbating at all and most of the rest reporting masturbation no more than once a month), and attempt intercourse once a month or less.

Sexual Aversion Disorder

On a continuum with hypoactive sexual desire disorder is **sexual aversion disorder.** In these cases individuals not only have no interest in sex, but even the thought of sex or a brief touch, such as someone's taking the person's hand to assist him or her in getting

Table 11.8 DSM-IV Criteria for Hypoactive Sexual Desire Disorder

A. Persistently or recurrently deficient (or absent) sexual fantasies and desire for sexual activity. The judgment of deficiency or absence is made by the clinician, taking into account factors that affect sexual functioning, such as age and the context of the person's life.

B. The disturbance causes marked distress or interpersonal difficulty.

C. The sexual dysfunction is not better accounted for by another Axis I disorder (except another Sexual Dysfunction) and is not due exclusively to the direct physiological effects of a substance (e.g., a drug of abuse, a medication) or a general medical condition.

Specify type:
   Lifelong Type
   Acquired Type

Specify type:
   Generalized Type
   Situational Type

Specify:
   Due to Psychological Factors
   Due to Combined Factors

Source: DSM-IV, APA, 1994.

out of a car, may evoke fear, panic, or disgust (Kaplan, 1987). In some cases of sexual aversion disorder, the principal problem might actually be panic disorder (see Chapter 5) when the fear or alarm response has become associated with the physical sensations of sex. In other cases, sexual acts and fantasies may trigger traumatic images or memories in a manner similar to but perhaps not as severe as those experienced by individuals who would meet criteria for posttraumatic stress disorder (see Chapter 5). Consider the following case from one of our clinics.

The Case of Lisa

Lisa was a 36-year-old female, married for 3 years, and currently a full-time student working on an associate degree. She had been married previously. Lisa reported that sexual problems had begun 9 months earlier. She complained of difficulty lubricating during intercourse and of having "anxiety attacks" during sex. She had not attempted intercourse in 2 months and had tried only intermittently during the past 9 months. Other than sexual difficulties, Lisa had a loving and close relationship with her husband. She could not remember precisely what happened 9 months ago except that she was under a great deal of stress and experienced an anxiety attack during sex. Even having her husband touch her was becoming increasingly difficult since she was afraid it might bring on the scary feelings again. Her primary fear was of having a heart attack and dying during sex.

DSM-IV diagnostic criteria for sexual aversion disorder are presented in Table 11.9. Among male patients presenting to our sexuality clinic 10% experienced panic attacks during attempted sexual activity. Kaplan (1987) reports that 25% of 106 patients presenting with sexual aversion disorder also met criteria for panic disorder. In these cases, treating the panic may be a necessary first step.

Sexual Arousal Disorders

Disorders of arousal refer to **male erectile disorder** and **female sexual arousal disorder.** The problem here is not desire. Many individuals with arousal disorders have frequent sexual urges and fantasies and a strong desire to have sex. Their problem is difficulty becoming aroused—that is, a male has difficulty achieving and/or maintaining an erection and a female often cannot achieve or maintain adequate lubrication. Consider the following case of male erectile disorder seen at one of our clinics.

The Case of Bill

Bill was a 58-year-old white male referred to our clinic by his urologist. He was a retired accountant who had been married to his 57-year-old wife, a retired nutritionist, for 29 years. They had no children. For the past several years Bill had been experiencing difficulties obtaining and maintaining an erection. During an interview, he reported what seemed to be a rather rigid routine of sexual behavior the couple had developed to

---

Table 11.9   DSM-IV Criteria for Sexual Aversion Disorder

A. Persistent or recurrent extreme aversion to, and avoidance of, all (or almost all) genital sexual contact with a sexual partner.

B. The disturbance causes marked distress or interpersonal difficulty.

C. The sexual dysfunction is not better accounted for by another Axis I disorder (except another Sexual Dysfunction).

Specify type:
  Lifelong Type
  Acquired Type

Specify type:
  Generalized Type
  Situational Type

Specify:
  Due to Psychological Factors
  Due to Combined Factors

Source: DSM-IV, APA, 1994.

deal with the problem. The couple scheduled sex every Sunday morning. However, before attempting sex Bill had a number of chores that he had to complete, such as letting the dog out, washing up, shaving, and so on. The couple's current behavior consisted of mutual hand stimulation. Bill was "not allowed" to attempt insertion until after his wife had climaxed. Bill's wife was adamant that she was not going to change her sexual behavior, or "become a whore" as she described it. This included her refusal to try K-Y jelly as a lubricant due to her postmenopausal status and a reported decrease in lubrication. She described their sexual behavior as "lesbian sex." Both Bill and his wife stated that, although they had had marital problems over the years, they had always maintained a good sexual relationship until the onset of the current problem and that the sexual relationship had kept them together during their earlier difficulties.

Useful information was obtained from the two when they were assessed alone. The client described masturbating the Saturday evening before sexual relations in an attempt to control his erections the following morning. He stated that his wife was unaware of this behavior. In addition, he quickly and easily achieved a full erection when viewing erotica in the privacy of the sexuality clinic laboratory (surprising the assessor). When interviewed alone, Bill's wife described being very angry at her husband for an affair that he had had 20 years earlier.

At the final session, three specific recommendations were made: for Bill to cease masturbating the evening before sex, for the couple to use a lubricant, and for them to delay the morning routine until after they had had sexual relations. The couple called back 1 month later to report that their sexual activity was much improved.

DSM-IV diagnostic criteria for male erectile disorder and female arousal disorder are presented in Table 11.10. The old and somewhat pejorative terms for these conditions are *impotence* and *frigidity,* but these terms are imprecise and do not specify the specific phase of the sexual response where the problems are localized. Arousal disorders can be either *lifelong* or *acquired.* Lifelong refers to a chronic condition that is present during a person's entire sexual life, while acquired arousal disorder begins at a specific time before which sexual activity was relatively normal. In addition, arousal disorders can either be *generalized,* in which case they occur every time the individual attempts sex, or they can be *situational,* occurring only with some partners or at certain times, but not with other partners or at other times.

Of the two disorders, the male typically perceives his problem as more impairing. Inability to achieve an erection makes intercourse difficult or impossible (depending on how much of an erection the male can achieve). On the other hand, women who are unable to achieve vaginal lubrication may be able to compensate for this problem by using a vaginal lubricant (Schover & Jensen, 1988). In women, decreases in arousal and vaginal lubrication may occur at any time but, as in men, they tend to increase with age (Morokoff, 1993). In addition, until recently, some women have not been as concerned about experiencing intense pleasure during sex as long as they could carry on with sexual intercourse sufficiently to consummate the act. As noted above, these attitudes have changed in recent years (Wincze & Carey, 1991; Morokoff, 1993).

It is unusual for a male to be completely unable to achieve an erection. More typical is the situation like Bill's, where full erections might be possible during masturbation and partial erections during attempted intercourse, with insufficient rigidity to allow penetration.

Before we describe the prevalence of arousal disorders and other sexual dysfunctions, it is important to note an important study by Ellen Frank and her colleagues, who carefully interviewed 100 well-educated, happily married couples who were *not* seeking treatment (Frank et al., 1978). Over 80% of these couples reported that their marital and sexual relations were happy and satisfying. Nevertheless, a surprising finding from this study was that 40% of the men reported occasional erectile and ejaculatory difficulties. Similarly, 63% of the women reported occasional dysfunctions of arousal or orgasm. But the crucial finding was that these dysfunctions *did not detract* from the respondents' overall sexual satisfaction. This study underlines that sexual satisfaction and occasional sexual dysfunction are not mutually exclusive categories. In the context of a healthy, loving, and full relationship, occasional or partial sexual dysfunctions can easily be accommodated.

The finding of a discordance or split between sexual satisfaction and sexual functioning has been replicated several times, most recently in a study of male alcoholics by Bansal, Wincze, Nirenberg, Liepman, and Engle-Friedman (1990). Thus, only a small percentage of individuals with some sexual dysfunction actually come for treatment. While the reasons have not been studied with any thoroughness, most likely the severity or the interpersonal context of the dysfunction may have more to do with who seeks treatment than the fact of the dysfunction itself.

Table 11.10   DSM-IV Criteria for Sexual Arousal Disorders

Female

A. Persistent or recurrent inability to attain, or to maintain until completion of the sexual activity, an adequate lubrication-swelling response of sexual excitement.

B. The disturbance causes marked distress or interpersonal difficulty.

C. The sexual dysfunction is not better accounted for by another Axis I disorder (except another Sexual Dysfunction) and is not due exclusively to the direct physiological effects of a substance (e.g., a drug of abuse, a medication) or a general medical condition.

Specify type:
  Lifelong Type
  Acquired Type

Specify type:
  Generalized Type
  Situational Type

Specify:
  Due to Psychological Factors
  Due to Combined Factors

Male

A. Persistent or recurrent inability to attain, or to maintain until completion of the sexual activity, an adequate erection.

B. The disturbance causes marked distress or interpersonal difficulty.

C. The erectile dysfunction is not better accounted for by another Axis I disorder (other than a Sexual Dysfunction) and is not due exclusively to the direct physiological effects of a substance (e.g., a drug of abuse, a medication) or a general medical condition.

Specify type:
  Lifelong Type
  Acquired Type

Specify type:
  Generalized Type
  Situational Type

Specify:
  Due to Psychological Factors
  Due to Combined Factors

Source: DSM-IV, APA, 1994.

The prevalence of erectile dysfunction is startlingly high. Spector and Carey (1990), reviewing a large number of studies conclude that between 4% and 9% of adult males experience erectile difficulties that are impairing. Bancroft estimates the percentage to be between 8% and 10% of the general male population, with the majority of cases involving men over the age of 50 (Bancroft, 1989). But male erectile disorder is easily the most common problem for which males seek help, accounting for 50% or more of the males referred to specialists for sexual problems (for instance, Renshaw, 1988; Masters & Johnson, 1970). The prevalence of female arousal disorders is somewhat more difficult to estimate since many females still do not consider this problem to be a disorder. In community studies, disorders of arousal in females have been estimated to occur in 11% (Levine & Yost, 1976) to 48% of the population (Frank et al., 1978). Since disorders of desire, arousal, and orgasm often blend into one another, it is difficult to estimate precisely the number

of women with a specific arousal disorder who present to sex clinics (Wincze & Carey, 1991).

Orgasm Disorders

Inhibited Orgasm

Inhibited orgasm, an inability to achieve an orgasm despite adequate sexual desire and arousal, is a disorder commonly seen in women requesting treatment (Stock, 1993) but relatively rarely seen in men. Consider the following case from one of our clinics.

The Case of Greta and Bill

Greta and Bill, a very attractive couple, came together to the first interview and entered the office clearly showing affection for each other. They had been married for 5 years, and were in their late 20s. When asked about the problems that had brought them to the office, Greta quickly reported that she didn't think she had ever had an orgasm—"didn't think" because she wasn't really sure what an orgasm was! She loved Bill very much and on occasion would initiate lovemaking, although these initiations had decreased substantially in frequency over the past several years.

Greta was a school teacher and Bill was an engineer with a local manufacturing firm. Bill added that he certainly didn't think Greta was reaching orgasm. In any case, he reported, they were clearly going in "different directions" sexually, since Greta was less and less interested. She had progressed from initiating sex occasionally early in their marriage to almost never doing so, except for an occasional spurt every 6 months or so, when she would initiate 2 or 3 times in a week. But Greta noted that it was the physical closeness she wanted most during these times rather than sexual pleasure. Further inquiry revealed that she was, in fact, becoming sexually aroused on occasion but had never in her life reached orgasm, even during several attempts at masturbation occurring mostly before her marriage. Both individuals reported that the sexual problem was a concern to them because everything else about their marriage was very positive.

Greta reported that she was brought up in a strict but loving and supportive Catholic family that more or less ignored sexuality. The parents were always very careful not to display their affections in front of Greta and, one time during childhood when her mother caught Greta touching her genital area, she was cautioned rather severely to avoid that kind of activity. We will discuss Greta and Bill's treatment in the section on treatment below.

An inability to reach orgasm is the most common complaint among women seeking therapy for sexual problems. In community samples, estimates from a number of studies suggest that 5% to 10% of females may experience female orgasmic disorder in which they *never or almost never* reach orgasm (Wincze & Carey, 1991). This distinction is important because only approximately 50% of women experience reasonably regular orgasms during sexual intercourse (LoPiccolo & Stock, 1987). The remaining women do not achieve orgasm with every sexual encounter, unlike males, who tend to experience orgasm more consistently during sex. Thus, the "never or almost never" inquiry becomes important, along with the establish-

ment of distress on the part of the couple in determining the presence of orgasmic dysfunction. Surprisingly, community samples also suggest that somewhere between 1% and 10% of males have delayed or absent orgasms during sexual interactions, although, as noted above, males seldom seek treatment for this condition. It is quite possible that some of these males reach climax through alternative forms of stimulation and that the male's delayed orgasm is accommodated by the couple in many cases.

The DSM-IV diagnostic criteria for **female orgasmic disorder,** described above, and **male orgasmic disorder** are presented in Table 11.11. Some males with this disorder report that they are unable to ejaculate with their partners even though they can obtain an erection and ejaculate during masturbation. The most usual pattern is one in which ejaculation is delayed, referred to most commonly as *retarded ejaculation* in sexuality clinics. Occasionally males suffer from *retrograde ejaculation,* in which ejaculatory fluids travel backward into the bladder rather than forward. This phenomenon is almost always due to the effects of certain drugs or a coexisting medical condition and should not be confused with male orgasmic disorder.

Premature Ejaculation

A far more common disorder of orgasm experienced by males is **premature ejaculation,** which refers to ejaculation occurring well before the partner wishes it to. The DSM-IV diagnostic criteria are presented in Table 11.12. A rather typical case presented to one of our clinics several years ago.

The Case of Gary

Gary, a 31-year-old salesman, reported engaging in sexual activity with his wife 3 or 4 times a month. He noted that he would have liked to have had sex more frequently but could not because of his very busy schedule, as he was working approximately 80 hours a week. He noted that his primary difficulty was controlling the timing of his ejaculation. Approximately 70% to 80% of the time he attempted sex, he would penetrate his wife's vagina and ejaculate a few seconds later. This had been a continual pattern since he met his wife approximately 13 years earlier. Experience with other women prior to his wife, although limited, was not characterized by premature ejaculation. In an attempt to control his tendency to ejaculate very quickly, Gary would distract himself by thinking of nonsexual things (scores of ball games or work-related issues) and

Table 11.11   DSM-IV Criteria for Orgasmic Disorder

Female

A. Persistent or recurrent delay in, or absence of, orgasm following a normal sexual excitement phase. Women exhibit wide variability in the type or intensity of stimulation that triggers orgasm. The diagnosis of Female Orgasmic Disorder should be based on the clinician's judgment that the woman's orgasmic capacity is less than would be reasonable for her age, sexual experience, and the adequacy of sexual stimulation she receives.

B. The disturbance causes marked distress or interpersonal difficulty.

C. The orgasmic dysfunction is not better accounted for by another Axis I disorder (except another Sexual Dysfunction) and is not due exclusively to the direct physiological effects of a substance (e.g., a drug of abuse, a medication) or a general medical condition.

Specify type:
  Lifelong Type
  Acquired Type

Specify type:
  Generalized Type
  Situational Type

Specify:
  Due to Psychological Factors
  Due to Combined Factors

Male

A. Persistent or recurrent delay in, or absence of, orgasm following a normal sexual excitement phase during sexual activity that the clinician, taking into account the person's age, judges to be adequate in focus, intensity, and duration.

B. The disturbance causes marked distress or interpersonal difficulty.

C. The orgasmic dysfunction is not better accounted for by another Axis I disorder (except another Sexual Dysfunction) and is not due exclusively to the direct physiological effects of a substance (e.g., a drug of abuse, a medication) or a general medical condition.

Specify type:
  Lifelong Type
  Acquired Type

Specify type:
  Generalized Type
  Situational Type

Specify:
  Due to Psychological Factors
  Due to Combined Factors

Source: DSM-IV, APA, 1994.

on occasion would attempt sex soon after a previous attempt since he seemed not to climax as quickly under these circumstances. Gary reported masturbating very seldom (3–4 times a year at most). When he did masturbate, he usually attempted to reach orgasm quickly, a pattern he had begun in his teens to avoid being caught by a family member.

One of his greatest concerns was that he was not pleasing his wife and under no circumstances did he want her told that he was seeking treatment. Further inquiry revealed that he made many extravagant purchases at the request of his wife, even though it strained their finances, since he wished to please her. He felt that, had they met

recently, his wife probably would not even accept a date with him since he had lost much of his hair and she had lost weight, making her much more attractive than she used to be. Treatment for Gary and his wife is described shortly.

Frequency of premature ejaculation seems to be quite high, with a prevalence of 36% to 38% in community samples (Spector & Carey, 1990). This difficulty is also a presenting complaint in as many as 60% of men entering at least one sex therapy clinic (Malatesta & Adams, 1984). Many of these men also present with erectile dysfunction as the major problem.

A major difficulty here is defining "premature." Definitions of what is an adequate length of time before

Table 11.12   DSM-IV Criteria for Premature Ejaculation

A. Persistent or recurrent ejaculation with minimal sexual stimulation before, on, or shortly after penetration and before the person wishes it. The clinician must take into account factors that affect duration of the excitement phase, such as age, novelty of the sexual partner or situation, and recent frequency of sexual activity.

B. The disturbance causes marked distress or interpersonal difficulty.

C. The premature ejaculation is not due exclusively to the direct effects of a substance (e.g., withdrawal from opioids).

Specify type:
   Lifelong Type
   Acquired Type

Specify type:
   Generalized Type
   Situational Type

Specify:
   Due to Psychological Factors
   Due to Combined Factors

Source: DSM-IV, APA, 1994.

ejaculation vary widely from individual to individual based on hearsay, personal preferences, or other such guides. Some small surveys indicate that individuals complaining of premature ejaculation typically climax no more than 1 or 2 minutes after penetration, compared with 7 to 10 minutes in individuals without this complaint (Strassberg, Kelly, Carroll, & Kircher, 1987). A perception of lack of control over orgasm, however, may be the more important psychological determinant of this complaint.

Although occasional early ejaculation is perfectly normal, more serious and consistent premature ejaculation appears to occur primarily in young men, particularly inexperienced ones. The prevalence of this problem appears to decline with age (Masters & Johnson, 1970). The contrast in ages between males with erectile disorder and those complaining of premature ejaculation is striking and is presented in Figure 11.3. One possibility is that many cases of premature

ejaculation evolve into cases of erectile dysfunction in later years.

Sexual Pain Disorders

In the **sexual pain disorders,** marked pain is associated with sexual intercourse. Two subtypes have been identified: dyspareunia and vaginismus. For some males and females, sexual desire is present, and arousal and orgasm are easily attained, but the pain of intercourse is so severe that sexual behavior is disrupted. This disorder is named **dyspareunia** which, in its original Greek, means "unhappily mated as bedfellows" (Wincze & Carey, 1991). Obviously this is not a very accurate or descriptive name, but it has been used for decades and has become accepted. The DSM-IV diagnostic criteria for dyspareunia are presented in Table 11.13; as indicated, the identification of a physical cause for the pain would rule out this

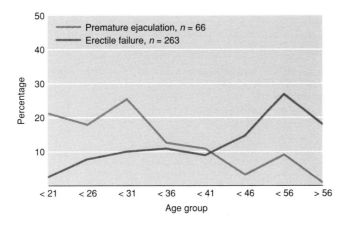

Figure 11.3   Age distribution of men presenting with erectile failure and premature ejaculation. The prevalence of premature ejaculation decreases with age, while the prevalence of erectile failure increases (from Warner et al., 1987).

diagnosis. Thus, dyspareunia is diagnosed only if all medical reasons for pain are ruled out. This can be a very tricky assessment to make. Several years ago a patient presented to our sexuality clinic reporting sharp pains in his head that resembled a description of a migraine headache; they began during ejaculation and would then last for several minutes. This male, in his 50s at the time, reported a healthy sexual relationship with his wife until he had a severe fall approximately 2 years earlier. The fall left him partially disabled and with a severe limp. His pain during ejaculation developed shortly thereafter. Extensive medical examination from a number of specialists could reveal no physical reason whatsoever for the pain. Thus, he met the criteria for dyspareunia, and psychosocial interventions were administered—in this case, with no benefit. In subsequent sexual relations he would engage in manual stimulation of his wife and, occasionally, intercourse but he would avoid ejaculation.

This condition is rarely seen in clinics, with estimates ranging from 1% to 5% in males (Bancroft, 1989; Spector & Carey, 1990; Wincze & Carey, 1991) a more substantial 11% of females report pain or discomfort in intercourse (Bancroft, 1989). Community samples provide estimates ranging from 8% (Schover, 1981) to 33.5% (Glatt, Zinner, & McCormack, 1990). Glatt et al. report that many women experience pain occasionally, but the pain either resolves or is not sufficient to motivate them to seek treatment.

More common than dyspareunia is **vaginismus.** In this condition, occurring in women, the pelvic muscles located in the outer third of the vagina undergo involuntary spasms when intercourse is attempted. The DSM-IV diagnostic criteria for vaginismus are presented in Table 11.13. The spasm reaction of vaginismus may occur during any attempted penetration, including a gynecological exam or insertion of a tampon (Beck, 1993). Women report sensations of "ripping, burning, or

Table 11.13 DSM-IV Criteria for Sexual Pain Disorders

Dyspareunia

A. Recurrent or persistent genital pain associated with sexual intercourse in either a male or a female.

B. The disturbance causes marked distress or interpersonal difficulty.

C. The disturbance is not caused exclusively by Vaginismus or lack of lubrication, is not better accounted for by another Axis I disorder (except another Sexual Dysfunction), and is not due exclusively to the direct physiological effects of a substance (e.g., a drug of abuse, a medication) or a general medical condition.

Specify type:
  Lifelong Type
  Acquired Type

Specify type:
  Generalized Type
  Situational Type

Specify:
  Due to Psychological Factors
  Due to Combined Factors

Vaginismus

A. Recurrent or persistent involuntary spasm of the musculature of the outer third of the vagina that interferes with sexual intercourse.

B. The disturbance causes marked distress or interpersonal difficulty.

C. The disturbance is not better accounted for by another Axis I disorder (e.g., Somatization Disorder) and is not due exclusively to the direct physiological effects of a general medical condition.

Specify type:
  Lifelong Type
  Acquired Type

Specify type:
  Generalized Type
  Situational Type

Specify:
  Due to Psychological Factors
  Due to Combined Factors

Source: DSM-IV, APA, 1994.

tearing during attempted intercourse" (Beck, 1993, p. 384). Consider the following case.

The Case of Jill

Jill was referred to our clinic by another therapist because she had not consummated her marriage of 1 year. At 23 years of age, she was an attractive and loving wife who managed a motel while her husband worked as an accountant in the city. Despite numerous attempts in a variety of different positions to engage in intercourse, Jill's severe vaginal spasms prevented penetration of any kind. Jill also noted that she was unable to use tampons. With great reluctance, she submitted to gynecological exams at infrequent intervals. Sexual behavior with her husband consisted of mutual masturbation or, on occasion, Jill would have her husband rub his penis against her breasts to the point of ejaculation. She refused to engage in oral sex.

Jill, a very anxious young woman, came from a family in which sexual matters were seldom discussed and sexual contact between the parents had ceased some years before. Although she enjoyed petting, Jill's general attitude was that sexual intercourse was disgusting. Furthermore, she expressed some fears of becoming pregnant despite taking adequate contraceptive measures. She also thought that she would perform poorly when she did engage in intercourse, therefore embarrassing herself with her new husband.

Although we have no data on the prevalence of vaginismus in community samples, best estimates are that well over 5% of women coming for treatment to a sex therapy clinic in North America and 10% to 15% coming to a British sex therapy clinic experience vaginismus (Bancroft, 1989; Beck, 1993). The prevalence of this condition in cultures with more conservative views of sexuality, such as Ireland, may be much higher—as high as 42% to 55% in at least two clinic samples (O'Sullivan, 1979; Barnes, Bowman, & Cullen, 1984). Of course, results from this one clinic may not be applicable even to other clinics, let alone the population of Ireland.

Assessing Sexual Behavior

Before discussing the causes and treatment of sexual dysfunctions, we next describe briefly the state-of-the-art procedures for assessing sexual responsivity in general and sexual dysfunctions in particular. We dis-

cuss assessment before the causes of sexual dysfunction because it is important for you to be aware of several assessment devices and procedures that are frequently employed in research on causes of sexual dysfunction.

Given the very private and sensitive nature of this subject, sexual functioning and sexual problems are among the most difficult topics for many people to discuss, even with experienced health professionals in the privacy of an office. One of the authors, an experienced sex researcher and therapist, saw a young male patient weekly for almost 3 months, working with him on a number of interpersonal problem areas. Only after that amount of time did the patient feel comfortable enough to talk about the primary reason he came to therapy in the first place—a sexual problem!

There are three major aspects to the assessment of sexual behavior: (a) interviewing, usually accompanied by a number of relevant questionnaires; (b) a thorough medical evaluation, in view of the variety of medical conditions that can contribute to sexual problems; and (c) psychophysiological assessment, to measure more directly the physiological aspects of sexual arousal.

Interviewing

All clinicians conducting interviews for sexual problems should be aware of several useful assumptions that have been detailed by John Wincze and Michael Carey, two of the leading sex therapists and researchers in the country (Wincze & Carey, 1991). For example, when interviewing for sexual problems, clinicians must demonstrate to the patient through their actions and interviewing style that they are perfectly comfortable talking about these issues. Since many patients will not

Michael Carey and John Wincze have developed new treatment approaches for individuals with sexual dysfunction.

know the various clinical terms used to describe the sexual response cycle or various aspects of sexual behavior, clinicians must always be prepared to talk about these problems in the vernacular of the patients, realizing also that terms used to describe sexual interactions will vary from place to place.

Examples of issues addressed in a semistructured interview used in our own sexuality clinic include the following.

1. How would you describe your current interest in sex?
2. Do you avoid engaging in sexual behavior with your/a partner?
3. Do you have sexual fantasies?
4. How often do you currently masturbate?
5. How frequently do you engage in sexual intercourse?
6. How often do you engage in mutual caressing or "cuddling" without intercourse?
7. Have you ever been sexually abused, raped, or had a very negative experience associated with sex?
8. Do you have problems attaining/getting an erection? or, Do you have problems achieving or maintaining lubrication of your vagina?
9. Do you ever have problems reaching orgasm during sex?
10. Do you ever experience pain associated with sexual activity?

A clinician would be very sensitive about presenting these questions in a manner that would put the patient at ease. During an interview lasting approximately 2 hours, the clinician would also cover nonsexual relationship issues and physical health, and would screen for the presence of additional psychological disorders. When possible, the partner is interviewed concurrently.

Since patients may write information on questionnaires that they are not ready to talk about to another person, a variety of questionnaires detailing a person's sexual activity and attitudes toward sexuality are typically administered in a human sexuality clinic. Among these are the Sexual Interaction Inventory compiled by LoPiccolo and Steger (1974), which surveys in some detail the frequency with which the individual engages in various sexual behaviors.

Medical Examination

Any human sexuality clinic will routinely inquire about medical conditions that impact sexual functioning. A variety of drugs including drugs commonly prescribed for hypertension or for anxiety and depression may often disrupt sexual arousal and functioning, as described below. If a patient has had recent surgery or

has concurrent medical conditions, all these must be evaluated for their impact on his or her sexual functioning. Many times the surgeon or treating physician will not have informed the patient of possible side effects of the treatment or drug on his or her sexual functioning. Similarly, the patient may not have told the physician that a medical procedure or drug has affected the patient's sexual functioning. Most males with specific sexual dysfunctions such as erectile disorder will have already visited a urologist—a physician specializing in disorders of the genitals, bladder, and associated structures—before coming to a sexuality clinic. Similarly, many females will already have visited a gynecologist. These specialists may check levels of sexual hormones necessary for adequate sexual functioning and, in the case of males, evaluate vascular functioning necessary for an erectile response.

Psychophysiological Assessment

Many specialty sexuality clinics assess the ability of individuals to become sexually aroused under a variety of conditions by using newly developed psychophysiological measures while the patient is either awake or asleep. In males, penile erection is measured directly using, for example, a **penile strain gauge** developed in our sexuality clinic (Barlow, Becker, Leitenberg, & Agras, 1970). As the penis expands, the strain gauge picks up the changes and records them on a polygraph. It is interesting that subjects are often not aware of these more objective measures of their arousal, and this awareness differs as a function of the type of problem they have (see below).

The comparable device for women is called a **vaginal photoplethysmograph,** developed by James Geer and his associates (Geer, Morokoff, & Greenwood, 1974). This device, which is smaller than a tampon, is inserted by the woman into her vagina. A light source at the tip of the instrument and two light-sensitive photoreceptors on the sides of the instrument measure the amount of light reflected back from the vaginal walls. Since blood flows to the vaginal walls during arousal, the amount of light passing through them decreases with increasing arousal. Ray Rosen and Gayle Beck (Rosen & Beck, 1988; Beck, Sakheim, & Barlow, 1983) have described in great detail the rapidly increasing sophistication of these measures.

Typically in our clinic, individuals undergoing physiological assessment view an erotic videotape for 2 to 5 minutes or, on occasion, listen to an audiotape depicting erotic material. The patient's sexual responsivity during this time is assessed psychophysiologically. Patients also report subjectively on the amount of sexual arousal they experience. This assessment allows the clinician to observe carefully the conditions under which arousal is possible for the patient. For example, many individuals with psychologically based sexual dysfunctions may achieve strong arousal in a laboratory but be unable to become aroused with a partner (Sakheim, Barlow, Abrahamson, & Beck, 1987).

In males, erections also occur while they are asleep, specifically during REM sleep in physically healthy individuals. For this reason, psychophysiological measurement of *nocturnal penile tumescence* (NPT) was used frequently in the past as an indication of a male's ability to obtain normal erectile response. If he could attain normal erections while he was asleep, the reasoning went, this would suggest that the causes of his sexual dysfunction were psychological. In recent years a new device called the *Rigiscan* (Bradley, Timm, Gallagher, & Johnson, 1985; Ackerman et al., 1991) has been increasingly used for measurement of NPT since it measures rigidity as well as expansion. However, because of the expense and inconvenience of observing patients in a sleep lab where they must spend two or three nights, this diagnostic procedure is not widely used.

A cheaper way to monitor nocturnal erections is for the clinician to provide a simple "snap gauge" that the patient fastens around his penis each night before he goes to sleep at home. The patient then checks in the morning to see if the snap gauge has come undone. If it has, it suggests that he has had a nocturnal penile erection. But this is a crude and often inaccurate screening device that should never supplant medical and psychological evaluation (Mohr & Beutler, 1990; Meisler & Carey, 1990). Finally, we now know that lack of NPT could also be due to psychological problems, such as depression, or to a variety of medical difficulties that have nothing to do with physiological problems preventing erections.

Causes of Sexual Dysfunction

The individual sexual dysfunctions described previously seldom present in isolation. Usually a patient will be referred to a sexuality clinic complaining of a wide assortment of sexual problems, although one may be primary or of most concern in his or her mind (Segraves & Segraves, 1991; Krause et al., 1991). One 45-year-old male recently referred to our sexuality clinic was free of problems until 10 years before his visit, when he was under a great deal of stress at work and was preparing to take a major career-related licensing examination. At that time he began experiencing erectile dysfunction about 50% of the time, a condition that progressed to approximately 80% of the time in subsequent years. In

Ray Rosen and Gayle Beck have both carried out pioneering research on the psychophysiological measurement of sexual arousal.

addition, he reported that at that time he had no control over his ejaculation when he attempted sexual intercourse, often ejaculating prior to penetration with only a semi-erect penis. Over the past 5 years he had lost most interest in sex and was coming to treatment only at his wife's insistence. Thus, this individual suffered simultaneously from erectile dysfunction, premature ejaculation, and low sexual desire, a not uncommon presentation. Because of the frequency of such combinations we will present an integrated view of the causes of sexual dysfunction, reviewing briefly the biological, psychological, and social contributions. Where indicated, we also mention specific causal factors thought to be associated exclusively and specifically with one or another of the dysfunctions.

Biological Contributions

A number of physical and medical conditions contribute to sexual dysfunction. While this is not surprising, the fact that most patients and even many health professionals seem unaware of these circumstances is unfortunate.

For years endocrine deficiencies were thought to be a major contributor to specific sexual dysfunctions, particularly arousal difficulties and hypoactive sexual desire in both males and females. However, there is very little support for this notion (Bancroft, 1989; Bansal et al., 1990; Wincze & Carey, 1991). Abnormal levels of testosterone, the primary male sex hormone, and estrogen, the primary female sex hormone, can be associated with some sexual dysfunctions such as hypoactive sexual desire, but it is very unusual to find that hormonal variations contribute in a major way to sexual dysfunctions (LoPiccolo & Friedman, 1988; Schover & Jensen, 1988).

On the other hand, neurological diseases or other diseases that affect the nervous system, such as diabetes and kidney disease, may directly interfere with a person's sexual functioning by reducing sensitivity in the genital area. These diseases are a common cause of erectile dysfunction in males (Schover & Jensen, 1988).

Chronic illness can also affect sexual functioning in an *indirect* way. For example, it is not uncommon for individuals who have had heart attacks to be wary of the physical exercise involved in sexual activity to the point that they become preoccupied by these concerns. They often become unable to achieve arousal despite being assured by their physicians that it is safe for them to engage in sexual activity (Cooper, 1988).

There is growing evidence that several physical factors previously thought to contribute to sexual dysfunction are not related to it. For example, it was widely believed in the 1970s that if a woman strengthened the pubococcygeus muscle that surrounds the vagina she could overcome female orgasmic disorder; such strengthening was also thought to enhance orgasms in functional women (Stock, 1993). To strengthen this muscle women were often taught to do a series of movements called *Kegel exercises*. However, Chambless et al. (1984) determined that there was no relationship between pubococcygeus strength and sexual functioning.

Three additional biological contributors to sexual dysfunction—prescription medication, alcohol and drug abuse, and vascular disease—are examined next.

Prescription Medications

One of the major physical causes of sexual dysfunction is medication. Antihypertensive medications, specifically the class of drugs known as beta blockers including propranolol, may contribute to sexual dysfunction. Tricyclic antidepressant medications and other antidepressant and anti-anxiety drugs may also interfere with sexual desire and arousal in both men and women (Segraves, 1988). A number of these drugs, particularly the psychoactive drugs, may dampen sexual desire and arousal by altering levels of certain subtypes of the neurotransmitter serotonin in the brain (Spoont, 1992). Remember that in Chapter 2 we discussed the effects of serotonin. As an example, Zajecka, Fawcett, Schaff, Jeffriess, and Guy (1991) reported that Prozac, a serotonin reuptake inhibitor, has been associated with a number of cases of sexual dysfunction. On the other hand, drugs such as the beta blockers do not act directly on the serotonergic system and yet may also interfere with sexual arousal and desire, although Wincze and Bansal (1993), in a well-controlled study, did not find any effects on sexual functioning caused by the beta blocker propananol.

Alcohol and Drug Abuse

Some people are aware that alcohol suppresses sexual arousal, but they may not know that most other drugs of abuse such as cocaine and heroin also suppress sexual arousal and result in widespread sexual dysfunction in frequent users and abusers, both male and female. Cocores, Miller, Pottash, and Gold (1988) and Macdonald, Waldorf, Reinarman, and Murphy (1988) reported that over 60% of a large number of cocaine users had a sexual dysfunction. In the Cocores study, some of the patients also abused alcohol.

Among other people, there is a misconception that alcohol facilitates sexual arousal and behavior. What actually happens is that alcohol at low and moderate levels reduces people's social inhibitions and makes them feel more like having sex (and perhaps more like requesting it) (Crowe & George, 1989). In fact, people's expectation that their sexual arousal will increase when they drink alcohol may have more effect than any disinhibition that does occur because of the effects of the alcohol itself, at least at low doses (Wilson, 1977; Roehrich & Kinder, 1991). Physically, alcohol is a central nervous system *suppressant*. For males to achieve erection and females to achieve lubrication is much more difficult when the central nervous system is suppressed (Schiavi, 1990). This dual effect of alcohol (social disinhibition and physical suppression) has been recognized since the time of Shakespeare:

> [I]t provokes the desire, but it takes away the performance; therefore much drink may be said to be an equivocator with lechery: it makes him and it mars him; it sets him on and it takes him off; it persuades him and disheartens him; makes him stand to and not stand to; in conclusion, equivocates him in a sleep, and giving him the lie, leaves him. (*Macbeth,* II, iii, 29)

Chronic alcohol abuse may cause a person to have permanent neurological damage and may virtually eliminate his or her sexual response cycle. Such abuse may lead to liver and testicular damage resulting in decreased testosterone levels and concomitant decreases in sexual desire and arousal. Chronic alcoholism can also cause fertility problems in both males and females. Fahrner (1987) examined the prevalence of sexual dysfunction among males addicted to alcohol and found that 75% had erectile dysfunction, low sexual desire, and premature or delayed ejaculation.

Many people report enhanced sexual pleasure with cocaine or marijuana. While little is known about the effects of marijuana across the wide range of use, it is unlikely that any pleasure enhancement is due to chemical effects. Rather, in those individuals who report some enhancement of sexual pleasure (and many don't), the effect may be psychological in that their attention is focused more completely and fully on sensory stimulation (Buffum, 1982), a factor that seems to be an important part of healthy sexual functioning. If so, this enhancement of imagery and attentional focus can be achieved using nondrug procedures such as meditation training, in which a person practices concentrating on something with as few distractions as possible.

Vascular Problems

A major contributor to arousal disorders, particularly erectile problems in males, is vascular disease. The two principal vascular problems that may contribute to dysfunction are arterial insufficiency and venous leakage. With arterial insufficiency (constricted arteries), it is difficult for blood to reach the penis. In venous leakage, once blood reaches the penis, the veins may "leak," causing blood to flow out too quickly for an erection to be maintained (Wincze & Carey, 1991).

Psychological Contributions

Until recently, most sex researchers and therapists thought the principal cause of sexual dysfunctions was anxiety. Pioneers such as Masters and Johnson (1970) speculated that anxiety plays a central role in the etiology and maintenance of sexual dysfunctions. Referring to male erectile dysfunction, Masters and Johnson pointed out, "The prevalent roadblock is one of fear. Fear can prevent erections just as fear can increase the respiratory rate or lead to diarrhea and vomiting" (p. 196). These researchers popularized the term *spectatoring*, wherein someone with a sexual dysfunction will detach himself from the sexual experience as if he were an uninvolved observer. The famous sex therapist, Helen Singer Kaplan (1979), stated that "the sexual dysfunctions . . . are caused by a single factor called anxiety" (p. 24). Kaplan identified sources of anxiety as the fear of failure during sex, an excessive need to please one's partner, and demands by the partner that one perform sexually.

Several years ago, while evaluating the role of anxiety and sexual functioning in our laboratory, we discovered a surprising and unexpected effect. Specifically, anxiety *increases* sexual arousal in certain circumstances. Based on pioneering work by John Wincze and associates (Hoon, Wincze, & Hoon, 1977), we designed an experiment in which young, sexually functional males viewed erotic films under three different conditions. In one condition we attempted to replicate the kinds of performance anxiety that males might experience during a sexual interaction. Prior to viewing an erotic film, all subjects were exposed to a harmless but somewhat painful electric shock to the forearm. During one condition subjects were told to relax and enjoy the film and that there was no chance of shock. This served as a control condition. In the second condition, subjects were told that there was a 60% chance that they would receive the shock at some

time while they were watching the erotic film no matter what they did (noncontingent shock threat). In the third condition, most closely parallelling the types of performance anxiety that some individuals might experience, subjects were told that there was a 60% chance that they would receive a shock if they *did not achieve the average level of erection achieved by the previous subjects* (contingent shock threat). In fact, no shocks were delivered during the viewing of the erotic films in any of the conditions, although subjects really believed that they might be administered.

The results, presented in Figure 11.4, indicate that the noncontingent shock threat condition *increased* sexual arousal compared with the no-shock threat control condition. However, in an even more surprising development, the contingent shock threat condition (when subjects were told there was a 60% chance they would be shocked if they did not achieve adequate arousal) increased their sexual responding *even more significantly* than the no-shock threat control condition. Similar results were reported by Hoon, Wincze, and Hoon (1977) and Palace and Gorzalka (1990), who developed slightly different experimental paradigms for women, using the vaginal photoplethysmograph.

These counterintuitive findings actually have some parallels outside the laboratory in real life. In one unusual and startling report, Sarrel and Masters (1982) described the ability of men to perform sexually under threat of physical harm. These men, the victims of gang rape by women, reported later that they had been able to achieve erections and successfully engage in intercourse repeatedly despite being under constant physical threat with knives and other weapons if they failed. Certainly they experienced extreme levels of anxiety, and yet they reported that their sexual performance was not affected.

If anxiety does not necessarily decrease sexual arousal and performance, what does interfere with them? Building on the work of Geer and Fuhr (1976) we conducted a series of experiments demonstrating that *distraction* interferes with the process of sexual arousal. In one experiment subjects were asked to listen to a narrative through earphones while they watched an erotic film. They were also told that they would later have to report on the narrative to make sure they were listening. Sexually functional males demonstrated significantly less arousal based on penile strain gauge measurements when they were distracted by the narrative than when they were not distracted (Abrahamson, Barlow, Sakheim, Beck, & Athanasiou, 1985). To anyone who has tried to concentrate on baseball scores or some other nonsexual event to reduce unwanted arousal, this result will come as no surprise.

Males with sexual dysfunctions, specifically erectile dysfunction, in whom physical disease pro-

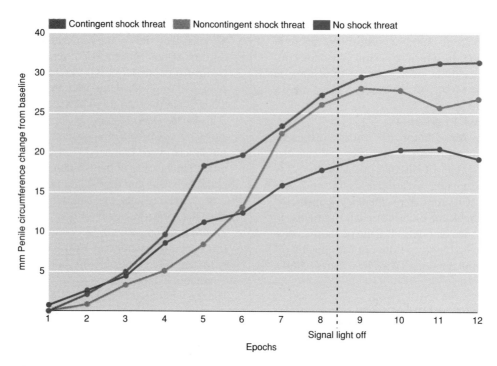

Figure 11.4 Performance anxiety and sexual arousal in males. Shown here are the average changes in male sexual arousal (penile circumference change) during each of three conditions (from Barlow, Sakheim, & Beck, 1983). (*Note:* An epoch is a period of 10 seconds.)

cesses had been ruled out, reacted somewhat differently from functional males to both shock threat and distraction conditions (for instance, Beck, Barlow, Sakheim, & Abrahamson, 1984, 1987; Abrahamson et al., 1985). Specifically, anxiety induced by shock threat (you'll be shocked if you don't get aroused) *did* seem to reduce sexual arousal in males who were dysfunctional. Remember that the reverse was true for the normally functioning males. On the other hand, the kind of neutral distracting conditions present in the Abrahamson et al. (1985) experiment *did not* reduce arousal in those males who were dysfunctional. This discovery was puzzling.

"In the process of becoming aroused, all of a sudden it would be over. And I didn't understand that at all. So then everything is coupled with a bunch of depressing thoughts, like the fear of failure. And so I begin to say, is this happening to me because I'm afraid I'm going to fail, and I don't want to be embarassed by that? It's really very difficult to deal with emotionally . . . The worse I feel about myself, the slower I am sexually, and sometimes I describe it as the fear of losing masculinity."

One other finding from a different experiment revealed that patients with erectile dysfunction consistently *underreport* their actual levels of arousal. That is, at the same level of erectile response (as measured by the penile strain gauge), men who are dysfunctional will report far less sexual arousal than will sexually functional males (Sakheim et al., 1987). This result seems to be true for dysfunctional women as well (Morokoff & Heiman, 1980).

In summary, normally functioning males show increased sexual arousal during "performance demand" conditions, are distracted by nonsexual stimuli, and have a pretty good idea of how aroused they are. On the other hand, males with sexual problems such as erectile dysfunction show decreased arousal during performance demand, are *not* distracted by nonsexual stimuli, and *do not* have a good idea about how aroused they are. This process seems to apply to most sexual dysfunctions, which, you will remember, tend to occur together, but it is particularly applicable to sexual arousal disorders.

How do we interpret this complex series of experiments to account for sexual dysfunction from a psychological perspective? Basically, we have to break the concept of "performance anxiety" into several components. One component is arousal; another is cognitive processes.

When confronted with a sexual situation, such as the possibility of having sexual relations, individuals who are dysfunctional tend to "think the worst" and find the situation to be relatively negative and unpleasant. As far as possible, they will avoid becoming aware of any sexual cues (and therefore will not be aware of how aroused they are physically, thus underreporting their arousal). They also may begin distracting themselves by thinking negative thoughts, such as "I'm going to make a fool of myself; I'll never be able to get aroused; she (or he) will think I'm stupid." We know that as arousal increases a person's attention becomes focused more intently and consistently. But if the person is focusing intently and consistently on negative thoughts, as seems to be true of individuals who have difficulty with sexual functioning, he or she will find it impossible to become sexually aroused because of the preoccupation with negative thoughts.

People with normal sexual functioning, on the other hand, react to a sexual situation very positively. They focus their attention on the erotic cues and do not become distracted. When they become aroused, they find their attention focused even more strongly on the sexual and erotic cues, allowing them to become more and more sexually aroused. The model presented in Figure 11.5 illustrates both functional and dysfunctional sexual arousal (Barlow, 1986, 1988; Cranston-Cuebas & Barlow, 1990).

This series of experiments demonstrates that sexual arousal is strongly determined by psychological factors, particularly cognitive factors. These cognitive factors are powerful enough to actually determine whether blood flows to the appropriate areas of the body, such as the genitals, an observation demonstrating once again the strong interaction of psychological and biological factors in most of our functioning.

With premature ejaculation, another of the dysfunctions we have discussed, we know little about the psychological factors associated with it. We do know that it is a condition more prevalent in young men, and that excessive physiological arousal in the sympathetic nervous system may lead to rapid ejaculation. These observations suggest that some men may have a naturally lower threshold for ejaculation, requiring less stimulation and arousal to ejaculate. Unfortunately, a psychological factor, anxiety, also increases sympathetic arousal. Thus, when a man becomes anxiously aroused about ejaculating too quickly, his concern only makes the problem worse. We will return to the role of anxiety in sexual dysfunctions later.

Social and Cultural Contributions

The model of sexual dysfunction displayed in Figure 11.5 helps to explain why some individuals may be dysfunctional *at the present time* but not how they *became* that way in the first place. While we do not know for sure why some people develop this problem, many individuals may have learned early that sexuality can be negative and somewhat threatening, and they develop sexual responses to reflect this belief. Donn Byrne and his colleagues call this cognitive set or disposition *erotophobia*. They have demonstrated that erotophobia, presumably learned early in childhood from families, religious authorities, or others, seems to predict sexual difficulties later in life (Byrne & Schulte, 1990). Thus, for some individuals, sexual cues become associated early with negative affect. In other cases, both males and females may experience specific negative or traumatic events after a period of relatively well-adjusted sexuality. These negative events might include sudden failure to become aroused one night or actual sexual trauma such as rape. We have already spoken about the potentially tragic effects on sexual functioning caused by early sexual abuse (page 423). These stressful or negative events may initiate negative affect, in which individuals experience a loss of control over their sexual response cycle, throwing them into the kind of dysfunctional pattern depicted in Figure 11.5. Recall the case of the individual who experienced erectile failure during a particularly stressful time at work but retained his sexual dysfunction long after the stressful situation had ended.

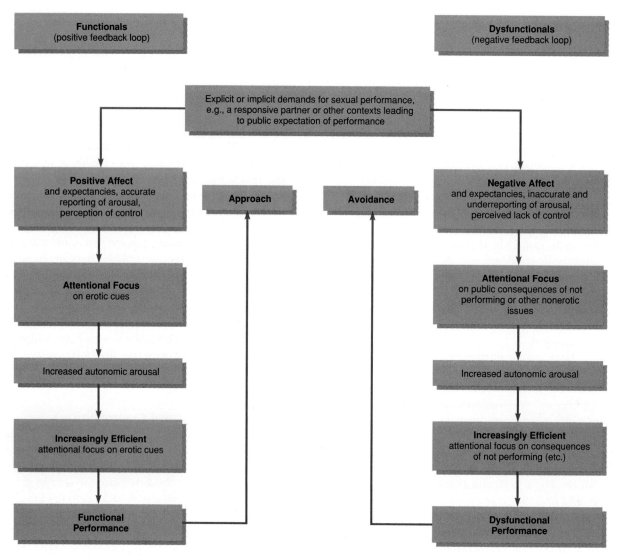

Figure 11.5 A model of functional and dysfunctional sexual arousal (adapted from Barlow, 1986)

In addition to generally negative attitudes or experiences associated with sexual interactions, a number of other factors may contribute to sexual dysfunction. Among these, the most common is a marked deterioration in close interpersonal relationships. It is difficult to have a satisfactory relationship in the context of growing dislike for one's partner. Occasionally, the partner may no longer be sexually attractive after, for example, gaining 50 pounds or otherwise deteriorating physically. Kelly, Strassberg, and Kircher (1990) compared 24 orgasmic and 10 anorgasmic women on a variety of variables. The anorgasmic women, in addition to displaying more negative attitudes toward masturbation, greater sex guilt, and greater endorsement of sex myths, specifically reported discomfort in communicating with their partner about sexual activities that might increase their arousal or lead to orgasm, such as direct clitoral stimula-

tion. Poor sexual skills might also lead to frequent sexual failure and, ultimately, lack of desire.

Thus social and cultural factors seem to affect later sexual functioning. John Gagnon has studied this phenomenon and constructed an important theory of sexual functioning called *script theory* of sexual functioning. According to this theory, we all operate according to scripts that reflect social and cultural expectations and guide our behavior (Gagnon, 1990). Discovering these scripts, both in individuals and across cultures, will tell us much about sexual functioning. For example, if one learns that sexuality is potentially dangerous, dirty, or forbidden, he or she will be more vulnerable to developing sexual dysfunction later on in life. This pattern is most evident in the studies of cultures with very restrictive attitudes toward sex. For example, vaginismus is relatively rare in North America but is the most common cause of unconsummated marriages in Ireland (O'Sullivan, 1979; Barnes, 1981). Even in our own culture certain socially communicated expectations and attitudes may stay with us despite our relatively enlightened and permissive attitude toward sex. Zilbergeld (1992), one of the foremost authorities on male sexuality, has elaborated a number of myths about sex held by many males, and Heiman and Lo-Piccolo (1988) have done the same for females. These myths are listed in Table 11.14. Baker and DeSilva (1988) converted an earlier version of Zilbergeld's male myths into a questionnaire and presented it to groups of sexually functional and dysfunctional men. They found that men with dysfunctions showed significantly greater belief in the myths than did men who were functioning sexually. These myths are explored further in the discussion of treatment on the next page.

The Interaction of Psychological and Physical Factors

Having reviewed the various causes of sexual dysfunction, we must now say that seldom is any sexual dysfunction exclusively associated with either psycho-logical or physical causes. More often a subtle combination of factors is present. To take a typical example, a young man, vulnerable to developing some anxiety and holding to a certain number of sexual myths (the social contribution), may experience erectile failure unexpectedly after using drugs or alcohol, as many men do (the biological contribution). This individual will anticipate the next sexual encounter with anxiety, wondering if the failure might happen again. This combination of experience and apprehension activates the psychological sequence depicted in Figure 11.5, regardless of whether he's had a few drinks or not.

In summary, a person's socially transmitted negative attitudes about sex may interact with his or her relationship difficulties and predispositions to develop performance anxiety and, ultimately, lead to sexual dysfunction. From a psychological point of view, we don't know why some individuals develop one dysfunction and not another, although it is common for several dysfunctions to occur in the same patient. Very possibly, an individual's specific biological predispositions may interact with psychological factors to produce a specific sexual dysfunction.

Table 11.14 Myths of Sexuality

Heiman and LoPiccolo's Myths of Female Sexuality*	Zilbergeld's Myths of Male Sexuality†
1. Sex is only for women under 30.	1. We're liberated folks who are very comfortable with sex.
2. Normal women have an orgasm every time they have sex.	2. A real man isn't into sissy stuff like feelings and communicating.
3. All women can have multiple orgasms.	3. All touching is sexual or should lead to sex.
4. Pregnancy and delivery reduce women's sexual responsiveness.	4. A man is always interested in and always ready for sex.
5. A woman's sex life ends with menopause.	5. A real man performs in sex.
6. There are different kinds of orgasm related to a woman's personality. Vaginal orgasms are more feminine and mature than clitoral orgasms.	6. Sex is centered on a hard penis and what's done with it.
7. A sexually responsive woman can always be turned on by her partner.	7. Sex equals intercourse.
8. Nice women aren't aroused by erotic books or films.	8. A man should be able to make the earth move for his partner, or at the very least knock her socks off.
9. You are frigid if you don't like the more exotic forms of sex.	9. Good sex requires orgasm.
10. If you can't have an orgasm quickly and easily, there's something wrong with you.	10. Men don't have to listen to women in sex.
11. Feminine women don't initiate sex or become wild and unrestrained during sex.	11. Good sex is spontaneous, with no planning and no talking.
12. Double jeopardy: You're frigid if you don't have sexual fantasies and wanton if you do.	12. Real men don't have sex problems.
13. Contraception is a woman's responsibility, and she's just making up excuses if she says contraceptive issues are inhibiting her sexually.	

*Source: Heiman & LoPiccolo, 1988.
†Source: Zilbergeld, 1992.

Treatment of Sexual Dysfunction

Unlike other disorders discussed in this book, there is one surprisingly simple treatment that is effective for a large number of individuals who experience sexual dysfunction: education. Ignorance of the most basic aspects of the sexual response cycle and sexual intercourse may often lead to long-lasting dysfunctions. Consider the case of Carl, who recently came to our sexuality clinic.

The Case of Carl

Carl was a 55-year-old white male referred to our sexuality clinic by his urologist for difficulty maintaining an erection. Although he had never been married, he was at present involved in an intimate relationship with a 50-year-old woman. This was only his second sexual relationship. He was reluctant to ask his partner to come to the clinic because of his own embarrassment in discussing sexual issues.

A careful interview revealed that Carl was engaging in sex twice a week but requests by the clinician for a step-by-step description of his sexual activities revealed a very unusual pattern. Carl would immediately proceed to intercourse and skip foreplay! Unfortunately, since his partner was not aroused and lubricated, he would be unable to penetrate her. His valiant efforts would on occasion result in painful abrasions for both of them. Two sessions of extensive sex education, including very specific step-by-step instructions for carrying out foreplay, provided Carl with a whole new outlook on sex. For the first time in his life he had successful, satisfying intercourse, much to the delight of both him and his partner.

In the case of hypoactive sexual desire disorder, one common presentation is a marked difference in desire *within* a couple that leads to one partner's being labeled as having low desire. For example, if one partner is quite happy with sexual relations once a week but the other partner desires sex every day, the latter partner may accuse the former of having low desire and, unfortunately, the former partner might agree.

The Case of Nick

In one of our clinics, Nick, a male in his early 40s, came in and reported that he was very depressed. What had been a close, loving marriage had deteriorated badly to the point that he and his wife had recently separated, much to the displeasure of their three children. Subsequent interviewing revealed that Nick and his wife Susan were accustomed to having sexual relations daily and, on occasion, twice a day. As Nick got older, he found this more and more difficult to do and began to dread sexual encounters. His wife, Susan, interpreted this behavior as a waning of his affections for her and even suspected that he might be having an affair. Several sessions of basic education on sexual functioning in aging males and a facilitation of communication concerning their feelings for each other solved most of their problems.

Of course, it's not always this easy to resolve difficulties, but for people with more complex sexual dysfunctions, treatments are now available, both psychosocial and biological (medical). We will look first at psychosocial treatments since they represent the more widely used and less intrusive methods of treatment; then we'll examine several medical procedures that are available though more intrusive.

Psychosocial Treatments

Among the many advances in our knowledge of sexual behavior in recent years, none was more dramatic than the publication in 1970 by William Masters and Virginia Johnson of *Human Sexual Inadequacy*. The procedures outlined in this book literally revolutionized sex therapy by providing a brief, direct, and successful therapeutic program for sexual dysfunctions. Underscoring once again the common basis of most sexual dysfunctions, the same or a very similar approach to therapy is taken with all patients, male and female, with some slight variations depending on the specific sexual problem (for instance, premature ejaculation, orgasmic disorder, and so on).

This program utilizes an intensive approach involving both a male and a female therapist to facilitate communication on the part of the dysfunctional couple. (Masters and Johnson were the original male and female therapists.) Therapy is conducted intensively, with daily visits, over a 2-week period.

The actual therapeutic program is quite straightforward. In addition to providing basic information and education about sexual functioning, altering deep-seated myths, and increasing communication, the clinicians' primary goal in sex therapy is to eliminate psychologically based performance anxiety (refer back to Figure 11.5). To accomplish this, Masters and Johnson introduced procedures called *sensate focus*

Therapists usually treat sexual dysfunctions in one partner by seeing the couple together.

and *nondemand pleasuring*. In this exercise couples are instructed to refrain from intercourse or genital caressing and simply to explore and enjoy each other's body through touching, kissing, hugging, massaging, or other similar kinds of behavior. In the first phase, breasts and genitals are excluded from these exercises. This phase is called nongenital pleasuring. After successfully accomplishing this phase, the couple moves to genital pleasuring with the ban on orgasm and intercourse continuing, and clear instructions to the male that achieving an erection is not the goal of these exercises.

At this stage arousal should be reestablished and the couple should be ready to begin intercourse. So as not to proceed too quickly, this behavior is also broken down into stages. For example, a couple might be instructed to attempt *the beginnings* of penetration. That is, the depth of penetration and the amount of time is only very gradually built up with both genital and nongenital pleasuring continuing. Eventually, full intercourse and thrusting is accomplished.

After this 2-week intensive program, recovery was reported by Masters and Johnson for the vast majority of over 790 sexually dysfunctional patients, with some differences in the rate of recovery depending on the disorder. Close to 100% of individuals with premature ejaculation recovered, whereas the rate for more difficult cases of lifelong generalized erectile dysfunction was closer to 60%.

Based on the pioneering work of Masters and Johnson, specialty sexuality clinics were established around the country to administer these new treatment techniques. Subsequent research revealed

that many of the structural aspects of the Masters and Johnson program did not seem to be necessary. For example, one therapist seems to be as effective as two therapists (LoPiccolo, Heiman, Hogan, & Roberts, 1985) and seeing patients once a week seems to be as effective as seeing them every day (Heiman & LoPiccolo, 1983).

Sex therapists have expanded on and modified these procedures over the years to take advantage of recent advances in knowledge (for example, Wincze & Carey, 1991). More recent results with sex therapy for erectile dysfunction indicate that as many as 70% of the cases show a positive treatment outcome (Hawton, Catalan, & Fagg, 1992). For better treatment of *specific* sexual dysfunctions, sex therapists integrate different procedures into the context of general sex therapy as described previously. For example, to treat premature ejaculation, most sex therapists use a procedure developed by Semans (1956), sometimes called the "squeeze" technique. In this procedure the penis is stimulated, usually by the woman, to nearly full erection. At this point the woman firmly squeezes the penis near the top where the head of the penis joins the shaft. This type of stimulation quickly reduces arousal. These steps are repeated and eventually the penis is inserted in the vagina briefly without thrusting. If arousal proceeds too quickly, the penis is removed and the squeeze technique employed again. In this way the male develops a sense of control over arousal and ejaculation.

Gary, the 31-year-old salesman, was treated in this way and his wife was very cooperative during these procedures. Brief marital therapy in the context of this couple's treatment also persuaded Gary that his insecurity over his perception that his wife no longer found him attractive was unfounded. After treatment, he reduced his work hours somewhat and both marital and sexual relations of the couple improved.

Lifelong female orgasmic disorder may be treated with explicit training in masturbatory procedures. For example, Greta, described earlier, was still unable to achieve orgasm with manual stimulation by her husband Bill, even after proceeding through the basic steps of sex therapy. At this point, following certain standardized treatment programs for this problem (for instance, Heiman & LoPiccolo, 1988), Greta and Bill purchased a vibrator. As part of this program, Greta was taught to "let go" of any inhibitions by talking out loud about how she felt during sexual arousal and even shouting or screaming if she wanted to. In the context of appropriate genital pleasuring and disinhibition exercises, the vibrator brought on Greta's first orgasm. With practice and good communication, the couple eventually learned how to bring on Greta's orgasm without the vibrator. Although Bill was delighted with her progress, as was Greta, Bill was concerned that Greta was now screaming so loudly during orgasm he was afraid she would attract the attention of the neighbors. They had also planned a vacation at a lake, but were concerned about whether the cabin had electricity to power the vibrator in case they needed it!

To treat vaginismus, the woman and, eventually, the man gradually insert larger and larger dilators at the woman's own pace. After the woman (and then the man) can insert the largest dilator, she begins gradually inserting his penis. These exercises are carried out in the context of genital and nongenital pleasuring so as to retain arousal. Of course, close attention must be accorded to any increased fear and anxiety that may be associated with this process since it may on occasion trigger memories of early sexual abuse that may have contributed to the onset of the condition. These procedures are highly successful, with a large majority of women overcoming vaginismus in a relatively short period of time (Beck, 1993).

A variety of treatment procedures have also been developed for low sexual desire (for instance, LoPiccolo & Friedman, 1988; Wincze & Carey, 1991). At the heart of these are the standard reeducation and communication phases of traditional sex therapy with, possibly, the addition of masturbatory training and exposure to erotic material. Of course, each case may require individual strategies. Remember Mrs. C., who was sexually abused by her cousin? Therapy involved helping the couple to understand the impact of the repeated, unwanted sexual experiences in Mrs. C.'s past and to approach sex so that Mrs. C. was much more comfortable with foreplay. She gradually lost the idea

that once sex was started she had no control. She and her husband worked on starting and stopping sexual encounters. Cognitive restructuring was used to help Mrs. C. interpret her husband's romanticism in a positive rather than a skeptical light.

Medical Treatments

Several medical approaches have been developed in recent years to treat sexual dysfunction, almost all focusing on male erectile disorder. A variety of pharmacological and surgical techniques have been attempted for male erectile dysfunction but here we focus on the three most popular procedures at the present time.

Vasoactive Therapy: Papaverine

Some urologists teach patients to inject the vasodilating drug, *papaverine*, directly into the penis when they want to have sexual intercourse. Papaverine works by dilating the blood vessels, allowing blood to flow to the penis and thereby producing an erection within 15 minutes. Erections can last from 1 to 4 hours (Althof et al., 1987). This procedure can be unpleasant, however, if not painful; as a result, a substantial number of men refuse to use it. In one study 35% of the participants dropped out within 6 months (Althof et al., 1987). In another study, Lakin, Montague, Vanderbrug Medendorp, Tesar, and Schover (1990) reported that 50 of 100 patients discontinued using papaverine for various reasons. In a third study, Gilbert and Gingell (1991) noted that, of 194 men offered treatment with papaverine, 95 declined. Eighty were reported to benefit from treatment. Surprisingly, of those men who declined, 65.3% had previously benefited from a treatment trial of papaverine. Therefore, Gilbert and Gingell concluded that the primary reason for the limited success of papaverine was neither inefficacy nor unpleasant side effects. The overwhelming majority of men declined treatment because either they or their partners felt the method was too intrusive or aversive to be used as a long-term treatment method. This conclusion is supported by the finding that, among the men who declined treatment, 83.3% did so because they objected to the use of needles. Major side effects include bruising and the development of fibrosis or nodules in the penis with repeated injections (Gregoire, 1992). Although some patients have found the procedure very helpful, at present it needs more study.

Surgery: Penile Implants and Vascular Procedures

Although surgical insertion of *penile* prostheses or *implants* has been attempted for almost 100 years, only recently have procedures been developed that are good enough to approximate normal sexual functioning. One procedure involves implantation of

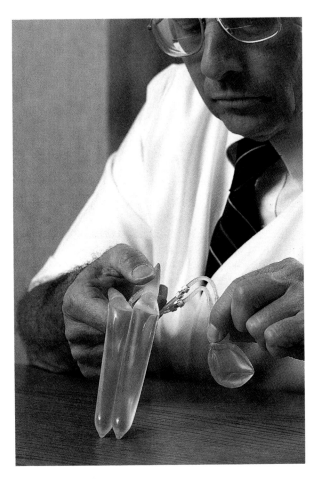

This inflatable penile implant is one of many devices currently in use for males with inadequate sexual functioning.

a semirigid silicone rod that can be maneuvered by the male (bent) into correct position for intercourse (and maneuvered out of the way at other times). Another, more popular, device is an inflatable cylinder. The male squeezes a small pump that has been surgically implanted into the scrotum, forcing fluid into the cylinder and thus producing an erection. The newest model of penile prosthetic devices is a self-contained inflatable rod with the pumping device located within the rod itself. This is more convenient than having the pumping mechanism outside the rod. However, surgical implants fall short of restoring presurgical sexual functioning or satisfaction in most patients (Steege, Stout, & Carson, 1986; Gregoire, 1992). More recently, vascular surgery to correct arterial or venous malfunctions has been attempted (for example, Bennett, 1988). Although the initial results are often successful, follow-up evaluations reveal a high failure rate.

Surgery is a rather drastic procedure but can be very useful for some individuals, particularly those with clear neurological or vascular pathology. Nevertheless, these procedures should be integrated with a comprehensive educational and sex therapy program to ensure maximum benefit.

Vacuum Device Therapy

Another approach is *vacuum device therapy*. For this technique, a new device has been developed that works by creating a vacuum in a cylinder placed over the penis. The creation of the vacuum draws blood into the penis, which is then trapped by placing a specially designed ring around the base of the penis. Although rather awkward to use, many males report satisfaction with this device, particularly if psychosocial sex therapy is ineffective (Nadig, Ware, & Blumoff, 1986; Witherington, 1988). The procedure is also less intrusive than surgery or injections.

Summary

Treatment programs, both psychosocial and medical, offer hope to most individuals suffering from sexual dysfunctions. Unfortunately, these programs are not readily available in many locations since few health and mental health professionals possess the necessary expertise to apply them. Psychosocial treatment of sexual arousal disorders requires further improvement, and treatments for low sexual desire are largely untested. New developments in medical approaches are appearing yearly, but most are still intrusive and clumsy.

Unfortunately, most health professionals tend to ignore the issue of sexuality in the aging. Along with the usual emphasis on communication, education, and sensate focus, use of appropriate lubricants for women and a discussion of methods to maximize the erectile response in men should be a part of any sexual counseling in older couples. More important, even with reduced physical capabilities, continued sexuality, not necessarily including intercourse, should be a very enjoyable and important part of an aging couple's relationship. Further research and development in the treatment of sexual dysfunction must address all these issues.

Paraphilia: Clinical Descriptions

If you are like most people reading this book, when you become sexually aroused, your interest is directed to other physically mature adults (or late adolescents), all of whom are capable of freely offering their consent to your interest. But what if you are sexually attracted to something or somebody other than another mature person? What if you are attracted to a vacuum cleaner?

(Yes, it does happen!) Or your only means of obtaining sexual satisfaction is to brutally murder somebody? These patterns of sexual arousal and countless others too numerous to describe in this chapter exist in a large number of individuals, causing untold human suffering for the individual and, if their behavior involves other people, for their victims. As noted in the beginning of the chapter, these disorders of sexual arousal are called **paraphilias.**

Over the years, one of the authors has assessed and treated a large number of these individuals, ranging from the slightly eccentric and sometimes pitiful case to some of the most dangerous killer-rapists encountered anywhere. We begin here by describing briefly the major types of paraphilia, using in all instances cases from our own files. Much as with sexual dysfunctions, it is unusual to see an individual with just one paraphilic pattern of sexual arousal. Many of our cases may present with two, three, or more patterns, although one pattern of arousal is usually dominant (Brownell, Hayes, & Barlow, 1977; Abel et al., 1987; Abel et al., 1988).

Although paraphilias are not widely prevalent and estimates of their frequency are hard to come by, some disorders, such as transvestic fetishism, seem

Women's shoes are a frequent fetishistic object.

relatively common (Bancroft, 1989). It is interesting that one seldom sees a case of paraphilia in a female. One exception would be the occasional female heavily involved in sadomasochism, such as a case described below; but even these cases are relatively rare. In addition, women on occasion sexually abuse children, usually while babysitting, but this seems to occur much less frequently than with males, a topic we touch on when we discuss causes of paraphilia.

Fetishism

Fetishism refers to a person's sexual attraction to nonliving objects. There are almost as many different types of fetishes as there are objects, although women's undergarments are a very popular item, as noted in the DSM-IV diagnostic criteria presented in Table 11.15. In one instance brought to our attention, there was a period of several months in which bras hung out on the clothesline in the backyard of one woman would disappear. The women in the neighborhood soon began talking to each other and discovered that these articles were being taken from every clothesline for blocks around. A police stakeout caught the perpetrator who, it was determined, had a strong fetish for women's bras. News stories during the past several years have reported that a male former employee of the celebrity Marla Maples was recorded during video surveillance stealing her shoes. It was learned that he had stolen hundreds of pairs and confessed to a severe fetish.

A slightly more complex case involved an 18-year-old boy referred to our clinic for "attacking" women. Interviews with the boy and others involved in the incidents revealed that his "attack" was limited to approaching a strange woman on the street and briefly stroking her hair before walking off. This development was relatively recent in a young man who was actually reasonably good-looking, socially skilled, and had had a number of dates. On each date he would manage to find himself alone with the woman and proceed to stroke her hair. He reported that most of his dates seemed to actually enjoy this and the stroking would often lead to some sexual activity. He would perform reasonably well as long as he could continue holding and stroking his date's hair during sexual activities. His mother reported discovering a hoard of some 50 to 60 women's wigs in his room that he would stroke while masturbating.

These cases illustrate what is unique about a fetish. Fetishistic arousal can be associated with two different classes of objects or activities: (a) an inanimate object; or (b) a source of specific tactile stimulation, such as rubber, particularly clothing made out of rubber. Shiny black plastic may also be used (Bancroft, 1989). Most, if not all, of the person's sexual fantasies, urges, and desires revolve around this nonliving object. A third

Table 11.15 **DSM-IV Criteria for Fetishism**
A. Over a period of at least 6 months, recurrent, intense sexually arousing fantasies, sexual urges, or behaviors involving the use of nonliving objects (e.g., female undergarments).
B. The fantasies, sexual urges, or behaviors cause clinically significant distress or impairment in social, occupational, or other important areas of functioning.
C. The fetish objects are not limited to articles of female clothing used in cross-dressing (as in Transvestic Fetishism) or devices designed for the purpose of tactile genital stimulation (e.g., a vibrator).

Source: DSM-IV, APA, 1994.

source of attraction can be a part of the body, such as the foot, buttocks, or hair (sometimes called *partialism*), but this attraction is no longer technically classified as a fetish since separating partialism from more normal patterns of arousal is often difficult.

Additionally, it is relatively common in emergency rooms for a urologist to be called to surgically remove long thin objects, such as pencils or the side of an eyeglass frame, from the urethra running through the penis. Individuals who insert such objects think that partially blocking the urethra in this way can increase the intensity of ejaculation during masturbation. However, if the entire object slips into the penis, major medical intervention is required.

Voyeurism and Exhibitionism

Voyeurism refers to the practice of observing an unsuspecting individual undressing or naked in order to experience sexual arousal. **Exhibitionism,** on the other hand, refers to sexual arousal and gratification associated with exposing one's genitals to unsuspecting strangers. Consider the following case.

The Case of Robert

Robert, a 31-year-old married blue collar worker, reported that he first started "peeping" into windows when he was aged 14. He would ride around the neighborhood on his bike at night, and when he spotted a female through a window, he would stop and stare. During one of these episodes he felt the first pangs of sexual arousal. Eventually he began masturbating during these episodes, thereby exposing his genitals, although out of sight. When he became old enough to drive a car, he would drive around until he spotted some prepubescent girls, park his car near them, unzip his fly, and then call the girls over. He would then attempt to carry on a nonsexual conversation. Later he would, on occasion, be able to talk some young girls into mutual masturbation and fellatio. Although he

was arrested several times, paradoxically the threat of arrest *increased* his arousal (Barlow & Wincze, 1980).

Remember the experiment we described previously in which anxiety actually *increases* arousal under some circumstances? (See Figure 11.4.) This seems to happen in paraphilias also. For example, many voyeurs just don't get the same satisfaction from attending readily available strip shows at a local bar. DSM-IV diagnostic criteria for voyeurism and exhibitionism are presented in Table 11.16. Although these paraphilias may occur separately, it is not unusual to find them co-occurring.

Exhibitionism is not always associated with a lower-class, marginally employed male continually in trouble with the law, as in the following case.

The Case of the Lawyer

Several years ago a distinguished lawyer appeared at our sexuality clinic and reported that he needed help and that his career was on the line. As a bright, intelligent, good-looking single man, he noted, without bragging, that he could have sex with any number of beautiful women he would meet in the course of his law practice.

However, the only way he could become aroused was to leave his office at some point during the day, go down to the bus stop, ride the bus around the city until a reasonably attractive young woman got on the bus, expose himself just before the next stop, and then run off the bus, often with people chasing after him. To achieve maximal arousal, the bus could not be full nor could it be empty; there had to be just a few people sitting on the bus, and the woman getting on the bus had to be the right age. Sometimes hours would pass before these circumstances lined up correctly. The lawyer observed that if

Table 11.16   DSM-IV Criteria for Voyeurism and Exhibitionism

Voyeurism

A. Over a period of at least 6 months, recurrent, intense sexually arousing fantasies, sexual urges, or behaviors involving the act of observing an unsuspecting person who is naked, in the process of disrobing, or engaging in sexual activity.

B. The fantasies, sexual urges, or behaviors cause clinically significant distress or impairment in social, occupational, or other important areas of functioning.

Exhibitionism

A. Over a period of at least 6 months, recurrent, intense sexually arousing fantasies, sexual urges, or behaviors involving the exposure of one's genitals to an unsuspecting stranger.

B. The fantasies, sexual urges, or behaviors cause clinically significant distress or impairment in social, occupational, or other important areas of functioning.

Source: DSM-IV, APA, 1994.

he was not fired for being caught exhibiting himself, he would be fired for all the time he was missing from work. On several occasions, he had requested one of his girlfriends to role play sitting on a bus while she was in his apartment. During these role plays he would attempt to expose himself, but he could not achieve sexual arousal and gratification since the activity just wasn't exciting.

Note again that the element of risk or thrill seems to be an important part of exhibitionism.

Transvestic Fetishism

In **transvestic fetishism,** sexual arousal is strongly associated with the act of dressing in clothes of the opposite sex, or cross-dressing. DSM-IV criteria for transvestic fetishism are included in Table 11.17. Consider the following case from our sexuality clinic.

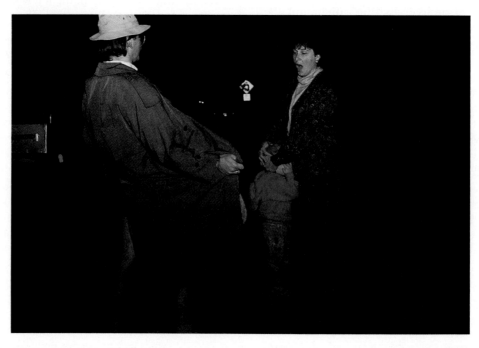

Individuals with exhibitionistic arousal patterns become aroused by shocking victims by unexpectedly exposing their genitals. These same individuals may not become aroused if the viewing of the individual's genitals is expected or occurs in an appropriate situation.

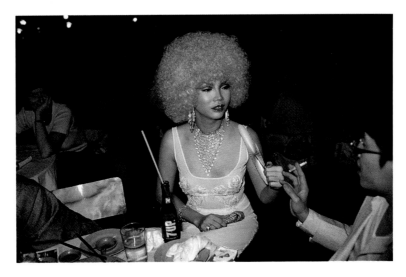

Some males with the condition of transvestic fetishism experience intense sexual arousal at the thought of cross-dressing or while cross-dressed.

The Case of Mr. M.

Mr. M. was a 31-year-old married policeman who came to our clinic seeking treatment for uncontrollable urges to dress in women's clothing and appear in public. He had been doing this for 16 years and had been discharged from the Marine Corps for cross-dressing. Since then, he had risked public disclosure on several occasions. Mr. M.'s wife had threatened to divorce him because of the cross-dressing, and yet she frequently purchased women's clothing for him and was "compassionate" while he was cross-dressed.

Note that Mr. M. was a member of the Marine Corps before joining the police force. It is very common for males who are strongly inclined to dress in female clothes for sexual reasons to attempt to compensate for this by associating themselves with "macho" organizations. Some of our patients with this condition have had prior associations with various paramilitary organizations. On the other hand, most individuals with this disorder do not seem to display any of these "compensatory" behaviors, as shown in the following case also from our clinic.

The Case of Jack

Jack, a good-looking, well-groomed, 35-year-old father of three, appeared at our clinic and announced he had reached the end of his rope. Unless we were able to help him, his only solution was to kill himself. Jack had irresistible longings to dress like a woman. As much as he struggled, he could not control his overwhelming urges to put on women's clothes and imagine that he was living the life of a woman. Jack had a very interesting view of a woman's life. He reported that "women have it made. Women get taken care of." In his mind, women had few of the onerous burdens borne by men. Men had to fight and

Table 11.17   DSM-IV Criteria for Transvestic Fetishism

A. Over a period of at least 6 months, in a heterosexual male, recurrent, intense sexually arousing fantasies, sexual urges, or behaviors involving cross-dressing.

B. The fantasies, sexual urges, or behaviors cause clinically significant distress or impairment in social, occupational, or other important areas of functioning.

Specify if:
   With Gender Dysphoria: if the person has persistent discomfort with gender role or identity

Source: DSM-IV, APA, 1994.

struggle in the world to bring home a paycheck to support the family and otherwise assume major responsibilities. Women, on the other hand, could sit back and receive love and attention and enjoy life. Jack realized, rationally, that particularly in the present day and age, this was not an entirely accurate view of the world. Nevertheless, it was the image in his head and he wanted nothing more than to dress like a woman.

Jack would eagerly anticipate periods of time, particularly on weekends, when his wife would leave the house for an extended period of shopping or visiting. At this point he would rush into the bedroom and grab his well-hidden cache of female clothes and makeup. He would then dress to the hilt, complete with cosmetics and perfume, and mostly just relax around the house watching television. He reported that an overwhelming feeling of relaxation would come over him during these times and that the weight of the world would be lifted off his shoulders. If he found himself alone for the weekend, he would remain dressed like a woman for the entire period of time, occasionally venturing out in his yard, thinking that the neighbors (who were some distance away) would assume that he was his wife. Near the end of his allotted time for cross-dressing, Jack would masturbate.

Jack continued like this for several years until he discovered that he achieved a greater sense of relaxation and satisfaction if he shaved his body hair so that, while feeling his skin, the image of a woman was more real. But his shaved skin was very hard to explain to his wife on her return. Shortly after he began shaving his body, his wife discovered his clothes and, following an enormously emotional confrontation, withdrew from him entirely and insisted he get help.

Although Jack found his uncontrollable urges repulsive, he was perfectly happy with his relationship with his wife and with his male gender identity. His fondest wish, sexually, was that she would accept his appearance and dress so that they could have sexual relations while he assumed the role of a woman. He reported no homosexual inclinations or attractions nor had he ever had sex with anyone but his wife.

In fact, the wives of many individuals who cross-dress *have* accepted their husband's behavior and can be quite supportive since this is something private between them that goes on only in their own bedrooms. Other individuals, either married or single, are more open and join cross-dressing clubs that meet periodically or subscribe to newsletters devoted to this topic.

Sexual Sadism and Sexual Masochism

Both **sexual sadism** and **sexual masochism** are associated with either inflicting pain or humiliation (sadism) or being made to suffer pain or humiliation (masochism). Although Mr. M., the married policeman described above who cross-dressed, was extremely concerned about this behavior, he also reported another problem that he found disturbing. To maximize his sexual pleasure during intercourse with his wife, he would tie her to the bed, handcuff her, and have her wear an animal leash with a collar. On occasion he would also tie himself with ropes, chains, handcuffs, and wires, all while he was cross-dressed.

Mr. M. was concerned that he was going to injure himself seriously. As a member of the police force, he had heard of a number of cases and had even investigated one himself where an individual was found very tightly and completely bound up in harnesses, handcuffs, and ropes. By the time the police arrived, the person was dead. What seems to happen in many of these cases is that something goes wrong and the individual accidentally hangs himself.

Mr. M. presented with three different patterns of deviant arousal: sexual masochism, sexual sadism, and transvestic fetishism. As noted above, it is not uncommon for individuals to present with multiple paraphilias. The DSM-IV diagnostic criteria for sexual sadism and masochism are presented in Table 11.18.

Jeffrey Dahmer obtained sexual gratification from mutilating his victims, a form of sexual sadism.

Acting out fantasies of domination or submission are often a part of sexual sadism and sexual masochism.

It may seem paradoxical that one has to either inflict pain or receive pain to become sexually aroused, but these types of cases are not uncommon. On many occasions the patterns are quite mild and harmless in and of themselves, but they can become dangerous and costly. Recently a local politician who was older and quite obese came to our clinic and reported a mildly sadistic pattern of sexual arousal in which he would "spank" his gay lover while he masturbated (sometimes with the help of his gay lover). The difficulty was that this man's gay lovers were all male prostitutes, and he was vulnerable to blackmail for this illicit activity. One night early in treatment, one of the authors received an emergency phone call at home that the worst had happened. The politician had been called with a blackmail threat. Rather than acquiesce, he was encouraged to go to the police who, much to his surprise, were able to

keep the events pretty much under wraps, saving his career. Although he stopped seeing male prostitutes, he then became associated with an extensive sadomasochistic telephone club. Late at night he would call various numbers provided by the club, listen to various people describing sadomasochistic scenarios, and masturbate. This might go on for hours with repeated masturbatory activity. While the telephoning was relatively harmless to him personally, it began to be quite expensive in telephone bills, again threatening his family, this time with financial difficulties.

Sadistic Rape

The act of rape is one of the most devastating assaults one person can make on another, short of murder. But rape is not classified as a paraphilia because most instances of rape are better characterized as an assault

Table 11.18 DSM-IV Criteria for Sexual Sadism and Sexual Masochism

Sexual Sadism

A. Over a period of at least 6 months, recurrent, intense sexually arousing fantasies, sexual urges, or behaviors involving acts (real, not simulated) in which the psychological or physical suffering (including humiliation) of the victim is sexually exciting to the person.

B. The fantasies, sexual urges, or behaviors cause clinically significant distress or impairment in social, occupational, or other important areas of functioning.

Sexual Masochism

A. Over a period of at least 6 months, recurrent, intense sexually arousing fantasies, sexual urges, or behaviors involving the act (real, not simulated) of being humiliated, beaten, bound, or otherwise made to suffer.

B. The fantasies, sexual urges, or behaviors cause clinically significant distress or impairment in social, occupational, or other important areas of functioning.

Source: DSM-IV, APA, 1994.

by a male (or, quite rarely, a female), whose patterns of sexual arousal could not be characterized as paraphilic. For example, many individuals prone to committing rape meet criteria for antisocial personality disorder (see Chapter 13). These individuals also engage in a variety of antisocial and aggressive acts. In fact, many rapes could be described as opportunistic, in that an aggressive or antisocial individual took advantage of a situation where he came across an unsuspecting woman who was vulnerable. These unplanned acts may often occur during robberies or other criminal events. Knight and Prentky (1990) also describe rapes that are motivated by anger and vin-

dictiveness against specific women. In these cases the rape may have been planned in advance.

Several years ago we determined in our sexuality clinic that certain rapists do, in fact, fit definitions of paraphilia closely and could probably better be described as *sadists*. Using the audiotape method of assessment and penile plethysmograph measures described earlier, we constructed audiotapes describing (a) mutually enjoyable sexual intercourse and (b) sexual intercourse involving force on the part of the male (rape). Each tape was played twice for selected listeners. Differences between a group of rapists and a group of nonrapists are presented in Figure 11.6 (Abel,

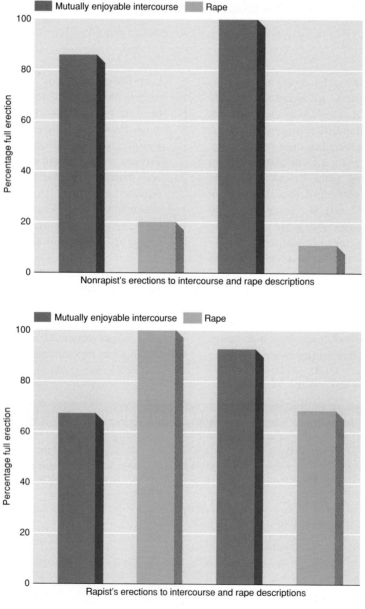

Figure 11.6 Erectile arousal differences between rapists and nonrapists. Nonrapists became aroused to descriptions of mutually enjoyable intercourse but not to descriptions of rape; rapists, on the other hand, experienced significant arousal to both types of descriptions (from Abel et al., 1977).

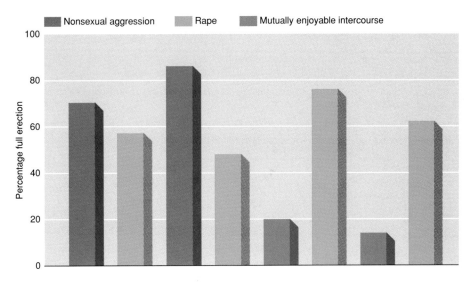

Figure 11.7 One sadist's erections on listening to audiotapes of nonsexual aggression, rape, and intercourse descriptions (from Abel et al., 1977).

Barlow, Blanchard, & Guild, 1977). As you can see, the nonrapists became sexually aroused to descriptions of mutually consenting intercourse, but not to descriptions involving force. Rapists, however, became aroused to both types of descriptions.

We also noticed, among the rapists we were evaluating, a subgroup who seemed to be particularly aroused by force and acts of cruelty involved in the rape. To assess this reaction more completely we put together a third audiotape consisting of aggression and assault *without* any sexual content. A number of individuals displayed strong sexual arousal to nonsexual aggressive themes as well as rape, and little or no arousal to mutually enjoyable intercourse, as depicted by the data from one individual in Figure 11.7. In fact, this man was among the most brutal rapists we have ever encountered. He had raped, by his own report, well over 100 times and his last victim spent 2 weeks in the hospital recovering from various injuries. This rapist typically would bite his victim's breasts, burn her with cigarettes, beat her with belts and switches, and pull out her pubic hair while shoving objects in her vagina. Although there was some evidence that he had killed at least three of his victims, the evidence was not sufficient to convict him. Nevertheless, he was convicted of multiple assaults and rapes and was on his way to spending the rest of his life in a closely guarded area of the maximum security state prison. It is interesting that he himself was eager to get there, realizing that his behavior was hopelessly out of control. Before going he reported that all his waking hours were spent ruminating uncontrollably on sadistic fantasies. He knew he was going to spend the rest of his life in prison, probably in solitary confinement, but wondered if there was something we could do in the way of treatment that would relieve him of this continual preoccupation. By

any definition, this individual met criteria for sexual sadism.

Pedophilia and Incest

Perhaps the most tragic deviant pattern of arousal is a sexual attraction to children (or very young adolescents), called **pedophilia.** The DSM-IV diagnostic criteria for pedophilia are presented in Table 11.19. Note that individuals with this pattern of arousal may be attracted to male children, to female children, or to both. If the children are members of the person's family, such as a daughter or son, the pedophilia is referred to more specifically as **incest.** While pedophilia and incest have much in common, victims of pedophilia tend to be younger children while victims of incest tend to be daughters who are beginning to mature physically, as in the case of Tony below. Marshall, Barbaree, and Christophe (1986) demonstrated by using penile strain gauge measures that incestuous males are, in general, more aroused to adult women than are males with pedophilia, whose arousal pattern may be exclusively focused on children. Thus, incestuous relations may have more to do with availability and other interpersonal issues ongoing in the family than pedophilia, as in the following case from our files.

The Case of Tony

Tony, a 52-year-old married television repairman, who came in very depressed, noted that approximately 10 years previously he had begun sexual activity, consisting primarily of light kissing and some fondling, with his daughter, who

Table 11.19 DSM-IV Criteria for Pedophilia

A. Over a period of at least 6 months, recurrent, intense sexually arousing fantasies, sexual urges, or behaviors involving sexual activity with a prepubescent child or children (generally age 13 years or younger).

B. The fantasies, sexual urges, or behaviors cause clinically significant distress or impairment in social, occupational, or other important areas of functioning.

C. The person is at least age 16 years and at least 5 years older than the child or children in Criterion A.

Note: Do not include an individual in late adolescence involved in an ongoing sexual relationship with a 12- or 13-year-old.

Specify if:
  Sexually Attracted to Males
  Sexually Attracted to Females
  Sexually Attracted to Both

Specify if:
  Limited to Incest

Specify type:
  Exclusive Type (attracted only to children)
  Nonexclusive Type

Source: DSM-IV, APA, 1994.

was 12 years old at the time. Gradually this behavior escalated to heavy petting and finally mutual masturbation, which continued until his daughter was 17 years old. When his daughter was 16 years old, his wife learned about the ongoing incestuous relationship. She separated from and eventually divorced her husband, with the oldest daughter staying with her mother. Soon after this Tony remarried. After a 5-year separation from his daughter and just before his initial visit to our clinic, Tony had occasion to visit his daughter, then 22 years old, who was living alone in a different city. A second visit, shortly after the first, led to a recurrence of the incestuous behavior. At this point Tony became extremely depressed and told his new wife the whole story. She initiated contact with our clinic with his full cooperation, while his daughter sought treatment in her own city.

We will return to the case of Tony later but there are several features worth noting. First, Tony loved his daughter very much and was bitterly disappointed and depressed over his behavior. On occasion the child molester will be abusive and aggressive, sometimes killing his victims. In many of these cases the disorder is really both sexual sadism and pedophilia. But most child molesters are *not* physically abusive. Very rarely is a child actually physically forced or injured. From the perspective of the child molester, no harm is done to the child because there is no physical force or threats. In fact, child molesters will often rationalize their behavior as "loving" the child or

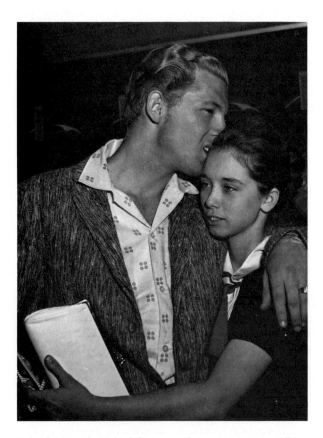

Individuals with pedophilic arousal patterns are sexually attracted to children, generally aged 13 or younger. Jerry Lee Lewis, the famous rock singer from the 1950s, at one point married a 13-year-old girl.

teaching the child useful lessons about sexuality. The child molester almost never considers the psychological damage he or she is causing the victim, and yet these interactions often undermine a child's trust and ability

Physiological assessment of pedophilic arousal patterns assists in diagnosing pedophilia and monitoring its course during treatment.

to share intimacy. A child molester rarely can gauge the "power" that he or she holds over a child. Children may participate in the molestation without seeming to protest, yet they may be frightened and unwilling without expressing it. Often children feel responsible for the abuse because of the lack of outward force or threat used by the adult abuser, and only when the abused children are adults are they able to understand that they were powerless and not responsible for what happened.

Miscellaneous Paraphilias

While there are numerous paraphilias, several of the more common additional ones are listed as paraphilias not otherwise specified in Table 11.20. *Telephone scatologia* refers to a person's compulsively making obscene phone calls, usually while he or she is masturbating. It has much in common with exhibitionism. You may have recently read about a major university president who was arrested after numerous obscene phone calls were traced to his presidential office, usually during the evening. Although it is not listed in Table 11.20, *frotteurism* is a paraphilia that you may have been the victim of if you were in a

large city, most typically on a crowded subway or bus (We mean really crowded, with people packed in like sardines). In this situation women have been known to experience more than the usual jostling and pushing from behind. What they discover, much to their horror, is that some male, with a frotteuristic arousal pattern, is rubbing against them until he is stimulated to the point of ejaculation. Since the victims are in a situation where they cannot escape easily, the frotteuristic act is usually successful.

Causes of Paraphilia

The traditional approach to ascertaining possible causes of psychopathology is to look deep into the histories of individuals presenting with the specific problem, in an attempt to find clues to the cause of the behavior. As described in some detail in Chapter 4, this method is fraught with difficulties and has not proved particularly useful. Clinicians and investigators tend to find what they are looking for in the case histories of their patients. Therefore, this strategy is no substitute for the types of scientific inquiries described in Chapter 4.

Table 11.20   DSM-IV Criteria for Paraphilia Not Otherwise Specified

This category is included for coding paraphilias that do not meet the criteria for any of the specific categories. Examples include, but are not limited to, telephone scatologia (obscene phone calls), necrophilia (corpses), partialism (exclusive focus on part of body), zoophilia (animals), coprophilia (feces), klismaphilia (enemas), and urophilia (urine).

Source: DSM-IV, APA, 1994.

However, the close examination of case histories will often provide hypotheses that can then be tested using controlled scientific observations. To illustrate, we can look at the cases of Robert and Tony described earlier to see if there are any clues in their histories.

The Case of Robert

Robert, who had sought help for exhibitionism, was raised by a very stern authoritarian father and a passive mother in a small Texas town. His father, who was a firm believer in old-time religion, often preached the evils of sexual intercourse to his family. Robert learned little about sex from his father except that it was bad. For this reason Robert seemed to suppress any emerging heterosexual urges and fantasies and as an adolescent he felt very uneasy around females his own age. By accident, he discovered other sources of sexual gratification that were more private as he would spot attractive females through the window. This discovery resulted in his first masturbatory experience.

Robert didn't seem to mind being arrested in those early days. In fact, he reported in retrospect that being arrested was not so bad because it disgraced his father and therefore was the only way he had of "getting back at him." In fact, the courts treated him lightly (which is not unusual) and his father was publicly humiliated, forcing the family to move away from their small Texas town (Barlow & Wincze, 1980).

The Case of Tony

Tony, who had sought help because of an incestuous relationship with his daughter, reported an early sexual history that contained a number of interesting events. Although he was brought up in a reasonably loving and outwardly normal Catholic family, he had an uncle who did not fit the family pattern. Between the ages of 9 and 10 years Tony was encouraged by his uncle to observe a game of strip poker which the uncle was playing with a neighbor's wife. During this period he also observed his uncle fondling a waitress at a drive-in restaurant and shortly thereafter was instructed by his uncle to fondle his

Crowded subway cars are a frequent setting for frotteuristic activity, in which an individual stimulates himself during forced close contact with other passengers.

young female cousin. Thus, he had an early model for mutual fondling and masturbation and obtained some pleasure from interacting in this way with young girls. When Tony was approximately 13 years old, he engaged in mutual manipulation with a sister and her girlfriend, which he remembers as pleasurable. Later when Tony was 18, a brother-in-law brought him to a prostitute, with whom he first experienced sexual intercourse. He remembered this visit as unsatisfactory since, on that and subsequent visits to prostitutes, he ejaculated prematurely—a sharp contrast to his early experience with young girls. Other experiences with adult women were also unsatisfactory. When he joined the service and was sent overseas, he remembers seeking out young prostitutes, often as young as 12 years of age.

A Model of Paraphilia

These cases point out that the development of deviant patterns of sexual arousal often occurs in the context of other sexual and social difficulties and deficiencies. Undesired sexual arousal may or may not be associated with *deficiencies in levels of "desired" arousal with consensual adults.* This was certainly true for both Tony and Robert, whose sexual development with adults was incomplete. Individuals with deviant arousal may also have *deficiencies in consensual adult social skills,* that is, they may lack the social skills necessary for meeting, dating, and relating to persons of the opposite sex (or the same sex if adult homosexual relations are the desired arousal pattern). In many cases when one is unable to develop adequate relationships with the appropriate people for sexual purposes, this seems to be associated with developing inappropriate sexual outlets (Barlow & Wincze, 1980).

On the other hand, many people with deficiencies in adult sexual and social skills do *not* develop deviant patterns of arousal. Something else seems to happen, and *early experience* seems to play a role. Surprisingly, and often tragically, this "something else" may be quite accidental. Tony's early sexual experiences just happened to be the same experiences he found sexually arousing later in life. Robert's first erotic experience was "peeping." The case of transvestic fetishism noted above included a wife who seemed to encourage the behavior. It is *very* common in cases of transvestic fetishism to find a mother, aunt, or sister who dressed the patient in girl's clothing when he was a young boy. Sometimes this is because the mother really wanted a girl. Other times it is simply for the adult's own amusement.

But many of us have these types of early experiences and do not develop deviant sexual arousal. Another important contributing factor seems to be the nature of the person's early sexual fantasies. For example, Rachman and Hodgson (1968; Bancroft, 1974) demonstrated that sexual arousal could become associated with a neutral object—a boot, for example—if the boot was repeatedly presented while the individual was sexually aroused. One of the most powerful engines for the development of unwanted arousal may be *early sexual fantasies that are repeatedly reinforced through the very strong sexual pleasure associated with masturbation.* Before a pedophile or sadist ever acts on his behavior, he may fantasize about it thousands of times, and these fantasies are gradually strengthened over the years through masturbatory activity. Expressed as a clinical or operant conditioning paradigm, this would be another example of a learning process in which a behavior (sexual arousal to a specific object or activity) is repeatedly reinforced through association with a pleasurable consequence (orgasm). This mechanism may partially explain why paraphilias are almost exclusively male disorders. In other words, the basic differences in frequency of masturbation between men and women that exist across cultures may contribute to the differential development of paraphilias. On the other hand, some women masturbate and some of them do so quite frequently, so one would think that at least occasionally a woman would present with a paraphilic arousal pattern if this mechanism were contributory. On rare occasions, cases of women with paraphilia do turn up. For example, Robert Stoller (1982) describes three cases of transvestic fetishism in women.

However, if early experiences contribute strongly to later sexual arousal patterns, then what about the Sambia tribe mentioned at the beginning of the chapter? Males in that tribe practice exclusive homosexual behavior during childhood and early adolescence and yet are exclusively heterosexual as adults. Of course, in these primitive tribes, the social demands or "scripts" for sexual interactions are much stronger and more rigid than in our culture and thus may override the effects of these early experiences (Baldwin & Baldwin, 1989).

In addition, therapists and sex researchers working with paraphilics have observed what seems to be an incredibly strong sex drive in these individuals. It is not uncommon for some paraphilics to masturbate three or four times a day. In one case seen in our clinic, the individual, a sadistic rapist, masturbated approximately every half hour all day long, just as soon as it was physiologically possible. We have speculated elsewhere that this increase in fantasy and sexual activity may be related to obsessional processes found in obsessive-compulsive disorder (Barlow, 1988). In

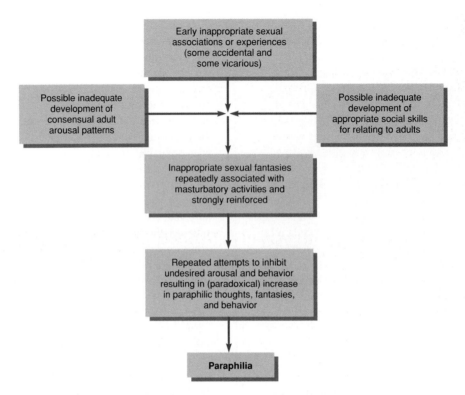

Figure 11.8   A model of the development of paraphilia

both instances, the individual is *unable to suppress the thought processes or fantasies;* that is, the very act of trying to suppress unwanted emotionally charged thoughts and fantasies seems to have the paradoxical effect of *increasing* their frequency and intensity (see Chapter 5). This psychological factor, rather than biological variables as commonly presumed, may account for the uncontrollably intense and frequent sexual activity in paraphilias.

   You may recognize this process as ongoing in other disorders also, such as eating disorders and addictions. Specifically, attempts to control thoughts or to restrict strong drives such as hunger or addictive cravings paradoxically result in uncontrollable *increases* in undesired behaviors and thoughts. Scientists studying psychopathology are becoming more interested in the phenomenon of weak inhibitory control across these disorders, reflecting, possibly, a weak biologically based behavioral inhibition system (BIS) in the brain (Fowles, in press). You will remember from Chapter 5 that the BIS is a brain circuit associated with anxiety and inhibition.

   The model shown in Figure 11.8 incorporates the factors that are thought to contribute to the development of paraphilia. Nevertheless, all speculations on the origins of paraphilias, including the hypotheses mentioned previously, have little scientific support at this time. For example, this model includes no biological dimensions. Excess arousal in paraphilics could be biologically based. Before we can make

any steadfast conclusions here, more research will be needed.

Assessment and Treatment of Paraphilia

Assessment

In recent years we have developed more sophisticated methods for assessing specific patterns of sexual arousal. This is important in paraphilia because we have come across cases where even the individual presenting with the problem was not fully aware of what was arousing to him. Sound strange? It is, but it happens. In one case in our clinic, an individual came in complaining of uncontrollable arousal to open-toed white sandals worn by women. He noted that he would be irresistibly drawn to any woman wearing open-toed white sandals and would follow her for miles. These urges occupied much of his summer. Subsequent assessment, using procedures described below, revealed that the sandal itself had *no erotic value* for this individual. Rather, he had a strong sexual attraction to women's feet, particularly women's feet moving in a certain way. He was as surprised by this discovery as we were.

   To make this determination we used the psychophysiological assessment procedures described on page 432. To do so, we first construct audiotapes (tapes 1, 2, and 3) based on the patient's description of

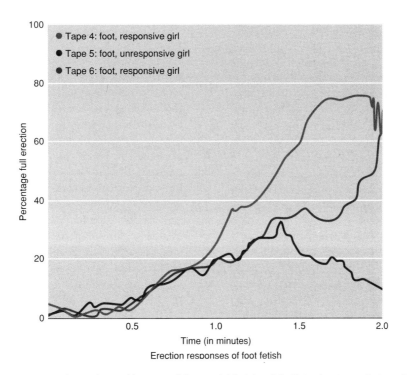

Erection responses of foot fetish

Figure 11.9 Erection responses of a patient with a possible sandal fetish while listening to audiotaped narratives (from Abel et al., 1975).

what is erotic. By closely examining subtle erectile changes in the patient as he listens to various portions of the narrative on the audiotape, we can determine the parts of the narrative that are most erotic to him. New audiotapes are then constructed expanding on the erotic parts of the material (tapes 4, 5, and 6) (Abel, Blanchard, Barlow, & Mavissakalian, 1975; Abel, Levis,

& Clancy, 1970). Responses to successively constructed audiotapes for the case of the foot fetish described above are presented in Figure 11.9. Although sexual offenders may, on occasion, attempt to control and therefore misrepresent their arousal on these tests, especially if some legal contingency is possible, methods have been devised to maximize the validity of the assessments (Harris, Rice, Quinsey, Chaplin, & Earls, 1992), which, in any case, are always supplemented by other information collected during assessment.

Using the model of paraphilia described above, we assess each patient not only for the presence of deviant arousal but also for levels of appropriate arousal to adults, for social skills, and for the ability to form relationships. Returning to the case of Tony, no problems with social skills were present since he was 52 years old, reasonably happily married, and generally compatible with his second wife. His major difficulty was his continuing strong incestuous attraction to his daughter. On the other hand, he reported that he loved his daughter very much and strongly desired to interact in a normal fatherly way with her.

Psychosocial Treatment

A number of treatment procedures exist for decreasing unwanted arousal. Most are behavior therapy procedures directed at changing the associations and context of the unwanted erotic patterns from arousing and pleasurable to neutral. One procedure, carried out entirely in the imagination of the patient, is called **covert sensitization,** first described by Joseph Cautela (1967; Barlow, 1993). In this procedure strong sexually arousing images are associated with the very consequences of the behavior that bring the patient to treatment in the first place. The notion here is that these arousal patterns are undesirable to the patient because of their long-term consequences, but the immediate pleasure and strong reinforcement they provide more than overcome any thoughts of possible harm or danger that might arise in the future. This model also applies to much addictive behavior that is unwanted but uncontrollable, as well as to bulimia.

In imagination, these harmful or dangerous consequences can be associated quite directly with the unwanted behavior and arousal in a very powerful and emotionally meaningful way. In the case of Tony, one of the most powerful negative aspects of his behavior was his embarrassment over the thought of being discovered by his current wife, other family members, or most important, the family priest. Therefore a scene was conducted depicting this arrangement:

The Case of Tony

You are alone with your daughter in your trailer. You get the feeling that you want to caress your daughter's breasts. So you put your arm around her, insert your hand in her blouse, and begin to caress her breasts. Unexpectedly the door to the trailer opens and in walks your wife with Father X [the family priest]. Your daughter immediately jumps up and runs out the door. Your wife follows her. You are left alone with Father X. He is looking at you as if to ask for some explanation of what he has just seen. Seconds pass, but it seems like hours. You think of what Father X must be thinking as he stands there staring at you. You are very embarrassed and want to say something, but you can't seem to find the right words. You realize that Father X can no longer respect you as he once did. Father X finally says, "I don't understand this; this is not like you." You both begin to cry. You realize that you may have lost the love and respect of both Father X and your wife, which are very important to you. Father X asks, "Do you realize what this has done to your daughter?" You think about this and you hear your daughter crying; she is hysterical. You feel like you want to run, but you can't. You are miserable and disgusted with yourself. You don't know if you will ever regain the love and respect of your wife and Father X. (adapted from Harbert et al., 1974, p. 82)

After 6 or 8 sessions in which the therapist portrays the scenes in a dramatic way for the patient to recreate in his imagination, the patient is then instructed to practice these scenes on a daily basis until all his arousal disappears.

Results of treatment from Tony's case are presented in Figure 11.10. *Card-sort scores* refer to a measure of how much Tony desired having sexual interactions with his daughter versus having nonsexual fatherly interactions with her. His incestuous arousal was largely eliminated after 3 to 4 weeks, but the treatment did not affect his desire to interact with his daughter in a more healthy manner. These results were confirmed by psychophysiological measurement of his arousal response.

A return of some arousal at a 3-month follow-up prompted us to ask Tony if anything unusual was happening in his life at that time. He confessed that his current marriage had taken a turn for the worse and that sexual relations with his wife had all but ceased. A period of marital therapy then restored the therapeutic gains (see Figure 11.10). Several years later, after his daughter's therapist decided she was ready, father and (adult) daughter resumed a nonsexual relationship, something they both desired.

Tony had two major areas in his life needing treatment. Deviant (incestuous) sexual arousal and marital problems. Most individuals with paraphilic arousal patterns need a great deal of attention to their family functioning or the interpersonal systems in

Figure 11.10 Ratings of Tony's incestuous urges (deviant) and desire for normal interactions with daughter (nondeviant) during covert sensitization treatment (from Harbert et al., 1974)

which they operate (Lanyon, 1986; Marshall, Eccles, & Barbaree, 1991). In addition, many of them require intervention to help strengthen more appropriate, desirable patterns of arousal. One method of accomplishing this is called **orgasmic reconditioning.** In this procedure patients are instructed to masturbate to their usual fantasies but to substitute more desirable ones just before ejaculation. With repeated practice, subjects should be able to insert the desired fantasy earlier in the masturbatory process and still retain their arousal. This technique, first described by Gerald Davison (1968), has been used with some success in a variety of different settings (Brownell, Hayes, & Barlow, 1977).

Finally, as with most strongly pleasurable but undesirable behaviors, including addiction, care must be taken in treatment to provide the patient with coping skills to prevent slips or relapses. Treatment procedures created for addictions and termed **relapse prevention** (Laws, 1989) do just that. In these procedures patients are taught to recognize the early signs of temptation to engage in the undesired sexual behavior and to institute a variety of self-control procedures before their arousal and urges become too strong.

Contrary to what you may think, the success of treatment using a rich array of the procedures described above is surprisingly high. Barry Maletzky, a psychiatrist at the University of Oregon Medical School, and his staff report on the treatment of some 5,000 sexual offenders of various types using a variety of procedures such as those described previously in a program that covers 3 to 4 months. This program takes place in a clinic devoted exclusively to this type of treatment. The numbers of people successfully treated are presented in parentheses after each category in Table 11.21 (Maletzky, 1991).

These are truly astounding numbers. What makes this series even more impressive is that Maletzky

collected objective physiological outcome measures on almost every case in addition to reports of progress from the patients. He also obtained corroborating information from families and legal authorities in many cases. These cases were collected in a large clinic for sexual offenders over a period of as long as 17 years. In his follow-up of these patients Maletzky defined a treatment success as somebody who had (a) completed all treatment sessions, (b) demonstrated no deviant sexual arousal on plethysmograph testing at any annual follow-up testing session, (c) reported no deviant arousal or behavior at any time since treatment ended, and (d) had no legal record of any charges of deviant

Table 11.21 Percentage of Offenders Satisfying Criteria for Successful Treatment Outcome (N = 5,000)	
Diagnostic Category	*Percentage Successful at Time of Last Follow-Up*
Heterosexual pedophilia (N = 2,865)	94.7
Homosexual pedophilia (N = 855)	86.4
Heterosexual and homosexual pedophilia combined (N = 112)	75.7
Other multiple paraphilias (N = 54)	71.7
Exhibitionism (N = 770)	93.1
Rape (N = 145)	73.5
Public masturbation (N = 75)	91.1
Voyeurism (N = 70)	88.1
Frotteurism (N = 60)	80.6
Transvestism (N = 60)	91.7
Fetishism (N = 30)	88.8
Obscene telephone callers (N = 25)	100.0
Sadomasochism (N = 25)	80.0
Zoophilia (N = 20)	100.0

Source: Maletzky, 1991.

sexual activity, even if unsubstantiated. He defined a treatment failure as anyone who was not a treatment success. In other words, any offender who did not complete treatment for any reason was counted as a failure even though some of the offenders may well have benefited from the partial treatment and gone on to recover.

Although these results are extremely good, Maletzky points out that men who rape have the lowest success rate among all offenders with a *single* diagnosis. Also, individuals who have multiple paraphilias have the lowest success rate of any group.

Maletzky also examined factors associated with failure. Among the strongest predictors of a person's failure was a history of unstable social relationships, an unstable employment history, strong denial that the problem exists, a history of multiple victims, and a situation in which the offender is continuing to live with a victim (as might be typical in cases of incest).

Other groups utilizing similar treatment procedures have achieved comparable success rates (Abel, 1989). Marshall, Jones, Ward, Johnston, and Barbaree (1991) reviewed a number of studies and also concluded that such treatments have high success rates, although they were somewhat more pessimistic about the outcome with rapists. Nevertheless, with exhibitionists they have reported recidivism rates similar to those of Maletzky (Marshall et al., 1991). A similar program for sexual offenders in Vermont, run by William D. Pithers, revealed that only 6% of 473 sexual offenders, mostly child molesters and rapists, had reoffended at followups up to 8 years later (Pithers, 1991). Finally, Judith Becker has developed a program for adolescent sexual offenders in an inner city setting (for example, Becker, 1990) utilizing procedures described previously. Preliminary results indicate that 10% of those who completed treatment had recommitted sex crimes. If these results hold up, the findings will be important because many of these adolescent offenders carry the AIDS virus and literally are putting their victims' lives in danger when they offend. These results are also important

because the recidivism rate of sexual offenders without treatment is very high (for instance, Hanson, Steffy, & Gauthier, 1993), just as it is for all pleasurable but undesirable behavior such as substance abuse (see Chapter 12).

Drug Treatments

Certain drugs are sometimes used to treat paraphilics. The most popular drug is an anti-androgen drug called *medroxy progesterone acetate* (depoprovera is the injectable form of the drug). This drug eliminates an individual's sexual desire and fantasy by reducing his testosterone levels dramatically, but fantasies and arousal return as soon as the drug is removed. This is the "chemical castration" treatment you may have read about in the news. This drug may be useful for dangerous sexual offenders who do not respond to alternative treatments, but in the Maletzky series mentioned above, it was necessary to administer the drug to only 8 out of approximately 5,000 patients.

Summary

Based on evidence from a number of clinics, the psychosocial treatment of paraphilia is surprisingly effective. Success rates ranging from 70% to 100% with follow-ups of over 10 years in some cases would seem to make this one of the more treatable psychological disorders reviewed in this book. However, most of the results are from a small number of clinical research centers and it is not yet clear if the results would be as good in other clinics and offices. In any case, much as with the treatment of sexual dysfunctions, these psychosocial approaches to paraphilia are not readily available. Only in specialized treatment centers does the expertise exist to carry out these treatment programs. In the meantime, the outlook for most individuals with this disorder is bleak since paraphilias run a very chronic course and recurrence is common.

Summary

- Patterns of sexual behavior vary widely across different cultures around the world. Therefore, it is difficult to ascertain what is "normal."

- Although most individuals around the world, particularly in Western cultures, practice safe sex, approximately 20% of individuals who have been surveyed engage in sex with numerous partners that potentially puts them at risk for sexually transmitted diseases such as AIDS. Recent surveys also suggest that as many as 60% of American college females practice unsafe sex by not using appropriate prophylactic measures.

- Three different types of disorders are associated with sexual functioning and gender identity: gender identity disorders, sexual dysfunctions, and paraphilias.

- Gender identity disorder refers to a dissatisfaction with one's biological sex and the sense that one is the opposite gender (for instance, a woman trapped in a man's body). A person develops gender identity between 18 months and 3 years of age, and it seems that both appropriate gender identity and mistaken gender identity are learned. Treatment includes both psychosocial approaches, which have been attempted only on a few cases thus far, and sex reassignment surgery.

- Sexual dysfunction refers to a series of disorders in which people find it difficult to function adequately during sexual relations.

- Specific sexual dysfunctions include disorders of sexual desire, in which interest in sexual relations is extremely low or nonexistent; disorders of sexual arousal, in which achieving or maintaining adequate penile erection or vaginal lubrication is problematic; orgasmic disorders, in which orgasm occurs too quickly or not at all; and sexual pain disorders, in which unbearable pain is associated with sexual relations.

- The causes of sexual dysfunction are associated with the development of socially transmitted negative attitudes about sex, which interact with current relationship difficulties, and the occurrence of anxiety focused on sexual activity.

- Psychosocial treatment of sexual dysfunctions is generally successful but not readily available. In recent years various medical approaches such as penile implants have become available. These treatments focus mostly on male erectile dysfunction and offer promise but currently are intrusive and clumsy.

- Paraphilia refers to sexual attractions to inappropriate people, such as children, or to inappropriate objects, such as articles of clothing.

- The development of paraphilia is associated with deficiencies in consensual adult sexual arousal, deficiencies in consensual adult social skills, deviant sexual fantasies that may develop before or during puberty, and attempts by the individual to suppress thoughts associated with these arousal patterns.

- Psychosocial treatments of paraphilia seem highly successful but are available only in specialized clinics.

Key Terms

O God, that men should put an enemy in their mouths
to steal away their brains! That we should, with joy, pleasance,
revel and applause, transform ourselves into beasts!
William Shakespeare
Othello, Act ii, sc. 3, 1. 291

12

Substance-Related Disorders

What if we told you that researchers had identified a group of psychological disorders that cost U.S. citizens hundreds of billions of dollars each year, that kill 500,000 Americans annually, and that are implicated in the causes of street crime, homelessness, and gang violence? Would you be surprised? Would you be even more surprised to learn that most Americans have behaved in ways characteristic of these disorders at some point in their lives? You shouldn't. Smoking cigarettes, drinking alcohol, and using illegal drugs all make up part of this group of disorders—and as such are responsible for astronomical financial costs and the tragic waste of hundreds of thousands of human lives each year. This chapter will explore that group of disorders, **substance-related disorders,** which covers the range of problems associated with using and abusing drugs such as alcohol, cocaine, and heroin as well as a variety of other substances people take to alter the way they think, feel, and behave. These disorders represent a problem that has cursed us for millenia and that continues to affect how each of us lives, works, and plays.

The cost in lives, money, and emotional turmoil has made the issue of drug abuse a major concern in the United States and worldwide. Many presidential administrations in this country have declared various "wars on drugs," but the problem re-

mains. In 1992 the Roman Catholic church issued a new universal catechism, officially declaring that drug abuse and drunk driving were sins (Riding, 1992). Still, too often we hear stories of destruction and death due to drug abuse; in November 1993 on the same day an autopsy revealed that the young actor River Phoenix had consumed lethal quantities of cocaine and heroin just before his death, singer Michael Jackson admitted to being addicted to painkillers. Stories such as these are not limited to the rich and famous; they reach into every corner of our society.

Fortunately, drug use in the United States has declined in recent years. A survey over a 20-year period of time found that drug use among college students rose from 1969 to 1978 but had declined substantially by 1989 (Pope, Ionescu-Pioggia, Aizley, & Varma, 1990). Weekly use of marijuana was reported by 16% of students in 1969 and increased to 26% of students in 1978, but declined to only 6% in 1989. Similar findings were observed for drugs such as LSD, amphetamines, and heroin. Cocaine use was relatively low in 1969; approximately 5% of students reported having tried it at least once. This number increased substantially to over 30% in 1978 but had dropped to about 20% in 1989. The use of alcohol remained relatively unchanged over these years, with about 40% of students reporting they drink at least once per week. These findings of reduced

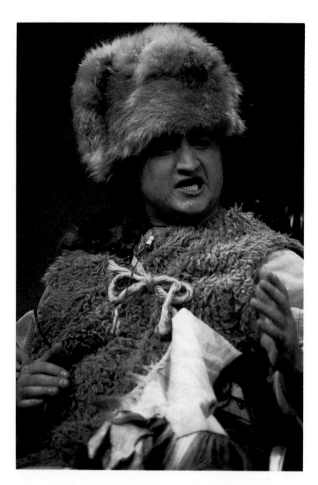

Comedian John Belushi is only one of many celebrities to have been dependent on drugs. Belushi died as a result of his abuse of a combination of cocaine and heroin.

drug use are encouraging; nonetheless, the numbers suggest that a significant number of people continue to use illicit drugs on a regular basis. Consider the case of Danny, who illustrates the disturbing but common practice of **polysubstance use,** the use of multiple substances. This is an issue we will cover in more detail later in the chapter.

The Case of Danny

At the age of 35, Danny was in jail, awaiting trial on charges that he broke into a gas station and stole money. How did he end up in jail? Danny's story illustrates the lifelong pattern of behavior that characterizes many people who are affected by substance-related disorders. Danny grew up in suburban America, the youngest of three children. He was well liked in school and was an average student academically. Like many of his friends, he tried smoking cigarettes in his early teens and drank beer with his friends at night behind his high school. Unlike most of his friends, however, Danny would almost always drink until he was obviously drunk; he also experimented with many other drugs, including cocaine, heroin, "speed" (amphetamines), and "downers" (barbiturates).

After high school, Danny attended a local community college for one semester, but he dropped out after failing most of his courses. His dismal performance in school seemed to be related to his missing most classes rather than to his ability to learn and understand the material. He had difficulty getting up for classes after partying most of the night, which he was doing with increasing frequency. His moods were also very variable, and he was often unpleasant to be around. Danny's family knew he occasionally drank too much, but they didn't know (or didn't want to know) about his other drug use. He had for years forbidden anyone to go into his room, following an incident when his mother found little packets of white powder (probably cocaine) in his sock drawer. He said he was keeping them for a friend and that he would return the packets immediately. He was furious that his family might suspect him of using drugs. Money would sometimes be missing from the house, and once some stereo equipment "disappeared," but if anyone in his family suspected Danny they would never admit it.

After high school, Danny held a series of low-paying jobs, and when he was working his family reassured themselves that he was "back on track" and things would be fine. Unfortunately, he rarely held a job for more than a few months. The money he earned had a magical way of turning into drugs, and he was typically fired for poor job attendance and performance. Because he continued to live at home, Danny could survive with these frequent periods of unemployment.

When he was in his late 20s he seemed to have a personal revelation. He announced that he needed help for his drug use and planned to admit himself into an alcohol rehabilitation center; he still would not admit to using other drugs. His family's joy and relief was overwhelming, and no one questioned his request for several thousand dollars to help pay for the private program he said he wanted to attend. Danny disappeared for several weeks, presumably in the rehabilitation program. However, a call from the local police station introduced a bit of reality into this fantasy: Danny had been found quite high, living in an abandoned building. As was the case with many of these "incidents," we never learned all the details, but it appears that he spent his family's money on drugs and had a 3-week drug orgy with some friends.

His deception and the financial burden he placed on them greatly strained his relationship with his family. He was allowed to continue living at home, but they excluded him from their emotional lives. This combination of unfortunate events seemed to "straighten out" Danny, and he obtained and held a job at a local gas station for almost 2 years. He became friendly with the station's owner and his son, and they frequently went hunting together during the season. However, once again, and without any obvious warning, Danny lapsed. As we mentioned at the beginning of this case, Danny was arrested for robbing a gas station, the very place that had kept him employed for many months.

Why did Danny become dependent on drugs when many of his friends and siblings did not? Why did he steal from his family and friends? What ultimately happened to him? We will return to Danny's frustrating story and its outcome as we look at the causes and treatment of substance-related disorders later in this chapter.

Perspectives on Substance-Related Disorders

Although each of the different drugs described in this chapter has its own unique effects, there are also similarities in the way they are used and how their abuse is treated. Because of these commonalities, we first look at some concepts that apply to substance-related disorders in general, noting important terminology and addressing several diagnostic issues.

Substance Use, Intoxication, Abuse, and Dependence

Can you use drugs and not abuse them? Can you abuse drugs and not become addicted to or dependent on them? To answer these important questions, we first need to outline what we mean by *substance use, substance intoxication, substance abuse,* and *dependence.* The term *substance* is used to refer to chemicals that people ingest in some way in order to alter their mood or behavior. Although your first thoughts might be of drugs such as cocaine and heroin, this definition also includes more commonplace and legal drugs such as alcohol, the nicotine found in cigarettes, and the caffeine in coffee, soft drinks, and chocolate. As we will see, these "safe" drugs also affect our mood and behavior; they can be addicting, and they account for more health problems and mortality than all the illegal drugs combined. You could make a good argument for directing the "war on drugs" to cigarette smoking (nicotine use), in addition to the use of such drugs as marijuana, cocaine, or heroin, based on its addictive properties and negative health consequences alone.

To begin to understand substance-related disorders, we must first know what it means to ingest **psychoactive substances**—substances that alter mood and/or behavior—to become intoxicated or "high," to abuse these substances, and to become dependent or "addicted" to them.

Substance Use

Substance use implies the ingestion of psychoactive substances in moderate amounts that do not significantly interfere with a person's social, educational, or occupational functioning. Most of you reading this chapter probably use some sort of psychoactive substance on occasion. Having a cup of coffee in the morning to wake up or smoking a cigarette and having a drink with a friend to relax would all be included as substance use, along with occasional use of illegal drugs such as marijuana, cocaine, amphetamines, or barbiturates.

Substance Intoxication

Our physiological reaction to ingesting these substances—sometimes called drunkenness or getting high—is referred to as **substance intoxication.** For a person to become intoxicated will depend on the drug he or she takes, how much of the drug is ingested, and the person's individual biological reaction. For many of the substances we discuss here, intoxication is experienced as impaired judgment, mood changes, and lowered motor ability (for example, problems walking or talking). The DSM-IV criteria for substance intoxication are listed in Table 12.1.

Substance Abuse

Defining **substance abuse** by how much of a substance is ingested is problematic. For example, is drinking two glasses of wine in an hour abuse? Three glasses? Six? Is taking one injection of heroin considered abuse? DSM-IV addresses the concept of substance abuse by defining it by how significantly the use of these substances interferes with a person's life. Using substances to the point that they disrupt your education, job, or relationships with others would be considered abuse. DSM-IV has specific criteria that define its concept of substance abuse; these are listed in Table 12.2.

Table 12.1   DSM-IV Criteria for Substance Intoxication

A. The development of a reversible substance-specific syndrome due to recent ingestion of (or exposure to) a substance. *Note:* Different substances may produce similar or identical syndromes.

B. Clinically significant maladaptive behavioral or psychological changes that are due to the effect of the substance on the central nervous system (e.g., belligerence, mood lability, cognitive impairment, impaired judgment, impaired social or occupational functioning) and develop during or shortly after use of the substance.

C. The symptoms are not due to a general medical condition and are not better accounted for by another mental disorder.

Source: DSM-IV, APA, 1994.

Table 12.2   DSM-IV Criteria for Substance Abuse

A. A maladaptive pattern of substance use leading to clinically significant impairment or distress, as manifested by one (or more) of the following, during the same 12-month period:

1. Recurrent substance use resulting in a failure to fulfill major role obligations at work, school, or home (e.g., repeated absences or poor work performance related to substance use; substance-related absences, suspensions, or expulsions from school; neglect of children or household)
2. Recurrent substance use in situations in which it is physically hazardous (e.g., driving an automobile or operating a machine when impaired by substance use)
3. Recurrent substance-related legal problems (e.g., arrests for substance-related disorderly conduct)
4. Continued substance use despite having persistent or recurrent social or interpersonal problems caused or exacerbated by the effects of the substance (e.g., arguments with spouse about consequences of intoxication, physical fights)

B. The symptoms have never met the criteria for Substance Dependence for this class of substance.

Source: DSM-IV, APA, 1994.

As you can see, Danny met several of these criteria. His inability to complete a semester of community college was directly a result of his drug use (criterion A-1). Danny would often drive while drunk or when he was under the influence of other drugs (A-2), and he had already been arrested twice because of his drug use (A-3). In fact, Danny's use of multiple substances was so relentless and pervasive that he would probably be considered drug dependent, a concept that indicates a more severe form of the disorder.

Substance Dependence

Being dependent on drugs is usually described in our everyday language as being "addicted." Although we use the term *addiction* repeatedly in our routine descriptions of people who seem to be enslaved by drugs, there is some disagreement about how to define addiction or **substance dependence** (Johnson & McCown, 1993). In one definition of substance dependence, the person has become physiologically dependent on the drug or drugs, requires greater and greater amounts of the drug to experience the same effect (**tolerance**), and will respond physically in a negative way when the substance is no longer taken (**withdrawal**) (Kalant, 1989). These concepts of *tolerance*

and *withdrawal* are physiological reactions by our bodies to the chemicals being ingested. How many of you have experienced headaches when you didn't get your morning coffee? If this has happened to you, you were probably going through caffeine withdrawal. In a more extreme example, withdrawal from alcohol can cause *alcohol withdrawal delirium* (or *delirium tremens*—the "DTs"), in which a person can experience frightening hallucinations and body tremors. In general, withdrawal from many substances can bring on chills, fever, diarrhea, nausea and vomiting, and body aches and pains. This reaction to the cessation of drug taking is a physiological response, one that can be observed in laboratory animals under the same conditions (Goode, 1993). However, not all substances are physiologically addicting in this way. For example, you do not go through these severe physical withdrawal symptoms when you stop taking drugs such as LSD or marijuana. Withdrawal from cocaine produces its own pattern and includes anxiety, lack of motivation, and boredom (Gawin, 1991). We return to this difference in the ways drugs act on our bodies when we examine the causes of abuse and dependence later in the chapter.

Another view of substance dependence uses the "drug-seeking behaviors" themselves as a measure of a person's dependence on a drug or drugs. In other

Table 12.3 DSM-IV Criteria for Substance Dependence

A maladaptive pattern of substance use, leading to clinically significant impairment or distress, as manifested by three (or more) of the following, occurring at any time in the same 12-month period:

1. Tolerance, as defined by either of the following:
   a. a need for markedly increased amounts of the substance to achieve intoxication or desired effect
   b. markedly diminished effect with continued use of the same amount of the substance
2. Withdrawal, as manifested by either of the following:
   a. the characteristic withdrawal syndrome for the substance (refer to Criteria A and B of the criteria sets for Withdrawal from the specific substances)
   b. the same (or a closely related) substance is taken to relieve or avoid withdrawal symptoms
3. The substance is often taken in larger amounts or over a longer period than was intended
4. There is a persistent desire or unsuccessful efforts to cut down or control substance use
5. A great deal of time is spent in activities necessary to obtain the substance (e.g., visiting multiple doctors or driving long distances), use the substance (e.g., chain-smoking), or recover from its effects
6. Important social, occupational, or recreational activities are given up or reduced because of substance use
7. The substance use is continued despite knowledge of having a persistent or recurrent physical or psychological problem that is likely to have been caused or exacerbated by the substance (e.g., current cocaine use despite recognition of cocaine-induced depression, or continued drinking despite recognition that an ulcer was made worse by alcohol consumption)

Specify if:
   With Physiological Dependence: evidence of tolerance or withdrawal (i.e., either Item 1 or 2 is present)
   Without Physiological Dependence: no evidence of tolerance or withdrawal (i.e., neither Item 1 nor 2 is present)

Source: DSM-IV, APA, 1994.

words, repeated use of a drug, a desperate need to ingest more of the substance (for example, stealing to get money to buy drugs, a willingness to stand outside in the cold to smoke a cigarette), and the likelihood that you will resume using it after a period of abstinence define how dependent you are on the drug. This reaction is different from the physiological responses to drugs we described before, and is sometimes referred to as *psychological dependence.* The DSM-IV definition of substance dependence, shown in Table 12.3, combines the physiological aspects of tolerance and withdrawal with the behavioral and psychological aspects.

This definition of dependence must be seen as a "work in progress." By these criteria, many people could be seen as dependent on such activities as sex, work, or even eating chocolate. Figure 12.1 shows the results of applying the DSM-IV definition of dependence to a variety of other daily activities including substance use (Franklin, 1990). Can you see your own behavior in this list? Obviously, what most people would consider "serious addiction" or dependence on drugs is qualitatively different from a dependence on shopping or television. The physiological and behavioral patterns may need to be further refined to help us separate the truly serious phenomenon of substance dependence from less debilitating "addictions."

Let's go back to the questions that started this section: "Can you use drugs and not abuse them?" "Can you abuse drugs and not become addicted to or dependent on them?" The answer to the first question is yes. Obviously, there are people who drink wine or beer on a pretty regular basis without drinking to excess. Even though it is not so commonly believed, some people use drugs such as heroin, cocaine, or "crack" (a form of cocaine) on an occasional basis (for instance, several times a year) without abusing them (Goldman & Rather, 1993). The disturbing aspect, obviously, is that we do not know ahead of time who might be more susceptible to losing control and abusing these drugs, and who is likely to become dependent with even a passing use of a substance.

What may be counterintuitive to you is that dependence may be present without abuse. For example, cancer patients who take morphine for pain may become dependent on the drug (that is, build up a tolerance, and go through withdrawal if it is stopped) without abusing it (Barnes, 1988). Later in this chapter we discuss biological and psychosocial theories of the causes for substance-related disorders and why people may have individualized reactions to these substances.

Expert professionals in the substance-use field were asked about the relative "addictiveness" of various drugs (Franklin, 1990). The survey results are shown in Figure 12.2. You may be surprised to see nicotine placed just ahead of methamphetamine and crack cocaine as the most addictive of drugs. Although this is only a subjective rating by these experts, it shows that our society sanctions or proscribes drugs based on factors other than their addictiveness.

Crack, a highly addictive form of cocaine, is usually sold in small amounts that are easily affordable to young children.

It's not always easy to tell if your child is using drugs. Changes in behavior, loss of appetite, lack of interest in favorite activities, depression or hostility may indicate drug use.

A crack 'rush' can be felt in as little as ten seconds, but crack's negative effects can last for years.

Abuse of prescription drugs can lead to a host of dangerous psychological and physiological

LSD hallucinations, commonly referred to as 'tripping,' can range from disorientation or disassociation from reality to extreme psychosis. Delayed effects, or 'flashbacks,' can occur when use has ceased.

Possession of common items such as eye droppers, film canisters, or butane lighters may signal a child is using drugs.

Many convenience stores carry cigarette papers which can be used for rolling 'joints,' while other types of drug paraphernalia are readily available in record stores and 'head' shops.

Doctors will tell you that cocaine use can ulcerate the mucous membrane of the nose. Translation: Cocaine will eat away your nose.

Heroin produces a euphoric feeling, followed by drowsiness, nausea and vomiting. Tolerance to the drug builds quickly, requiring an addict to use increasing amounts of the drug to get 'high.' An overdose may result, causing convulsions, coma or death.

Introduce your nine year old to drugs.

Nine years old isn't too young for kids to learn about drugs. The question is, who will teach them? Show your kids this ad. Tell them about the dangers. Let them see what drugs and drug paraphernalia look like. Because if you don't, someone else will. **Partnership for a Drug-Free America**

If you would like to get a copy of the free booklet "Growing Up Drug Free: A Parent's Guide To Prevention," just call 1-800-624-0100. In the Washington, D.C. area, call 202-785-1161.

side effects, even death.

Powdered heroin is melted in aluminum foil, a spoon or the bottom of a soda can, so that it can be injected directly into the bloodstream. And because users often share needles, they also share deadly diseases such as hepatitis and AIDS.

Often referred to as 'magic' mushrooms or 'shrooms,' psilocybin's hallucinogenic effects are similar to that of LSD.

Sold in tablet form or soaked into small bits of blotter paper or sugar cubes, LSD's small size packs a big wallop to the body's central nervous system.

With devices like this 'bong' or waterpipe, users often inhale marijuana smoke deeply and hold it in their lungs as long as possible for maximum effect. Which makes it even more damaging to the lungs and pulmonary system.

Marijuana has many names, such as 'reefer,' 'pot,' 'dope,' 'herb' or 'weed.' It has also been called the 'gateway' to harder drugs, as users are at a substantially higher risk of going on to use cocaine and other illegal drugs.

Cocaine use increases the heart rate and elevates blood pressure, which can cause cardiac arrest or respiratory failure.

Marijuana can impair or reduce short-term memory, comprehension, concentration, and coordination. It may also produce paranoia and dependence.

ACCORDING TO THE STANDARD psychiatric definition, any drug user who passes three of the nine tests below is hooked. Several researchers were asked to apply the tests not only to drugs but also to other substances and activities–chocolate, sex, shopping. Their responses show it's possible to become addicted to all sorts of things. For example, serious runners could pass three of the tests by spending more time running than originally intended, covering increasing distances, and experiencing withdrawal symptoms (a devoted runner forced to stop because of an injury, say, might become anxious and irritable). Of course, that sort of dependency isn't necessarily destructive. Conversely, a drug that fails the addictiveness test–LSD, for instance—may be harmful just the same. That so many things are potentially addictive suggests the addiction's cause is not confined to the substance or activity–our culture may play a large role, too.

	Nicotine	Alcohol	Caffeine	Cocaine	Crack	Heroin	Ice*	LSD	Marijuana	PCP	Valium, Xanax, etc.†	Steroids	Chocolate	Running	Gambling	Shopping	Sex	Work	Driving	Television	Mountain climbing
TAKES substance or does activity more than originally intended	✓	✓	✓	✓	✓	✓	✓		✓	✓	✓	✓	✓	✓	✓	✓	✓	✓		✓	✓
WANTS to cut back or has tried to cut back but failed	✓	✓	✓	✓	✓	✓	✓		✓	✓	✓	✓	✓	✓	✓	✓	✓	✓		✓	✓
SPENDS lots of time trying to get substance or set up activity, taking substance or doing activity, or recovering	✓	✓		✓	✓	✓	✓	✓	✓	✓				✓	✓	✓	✓			✓	✓
IS OFTEN intoxicated or suffers withdrawal symptoms when expected to fulfill obligations at work, school, or home		✓		✓	✓	✓	✓		✓	✓	✓										
CURTAILS or gives up important social, occupational, or recreational activities because of substance or activity		✓		✓	✓	✓	✓		✓	✓				✓	✓	✓	✓	✓		✓	✓
USES substance or does activity despite persistent social, psychological, or physical problems caused by substance or activity	✓	✓	✓	✓	✓	✓	✓	✓	✓	✓	✓	✓	✓	✓	✓	✓	✓	✓		✓	✓
NEEDS more and more of substance or activity to achieve the same effect (tolerance)	✓	✓	✓	✓	✓	✓	✓				✓										
SUFFERS characteristic withdrawal symptoms when activity or substance is discontinued (cravings, anxiety, depression, jitters)	✓	✓	✓	✓	✓	✓	✓				✓		✓	✓	✓	✓	✓	✓		✓	✓
TAKES substance or does activity to relieve or avoid withdrawal symptoms	✓	✓	✓	✓	✓	✓	✓				✓										

* Methamphetamine smoked
† Benzodiazepines

Research by Valerie Fahey

Figure 12.1   Ice, LSD, chocolate, TV: Is everything addictive (from Franklin, 1990)?

Diagnostic Issues

In early editions of the DSM, alcoholism and drug abuse weren't considered disorders in and of themselves. Instead, they were put under the category *sociopathic personality disturbances* (a forerunner of the current "antisocial personality disorder," which we'll discuss in Chapter 13), a sign that substance use was thought of as a symptom of other problems. In fact, substance use was seen as a sign of "moral weakness," with little recognition of the influence of genetics or biology in its origin or maintenance. Since the introduction of DSM-III in 1980, this disorder has been placed in a separate

TO RANK today's commonly used drugs by their addictiveness, experts were asked to consider two questions: How easy is it to get hooked on these substances and how hard is it to stop using them? Although a person's vulnerability to a drug also depends on individual traits—physiology, psychology, and social and economic pressures—these rankings reflect only the addictive potential inherent in the drug. The numbers below are relative rankings, based on the experts' scores for each substance.

```
        10  20  30  40  50  60  70  80  90  100
Nicotine
████████████████████████████████████████████

Ice, glass (methamphetamine smoked)
████████████████████████████████████████████

Crack
████████████████████████████████████████████

Crystal meth (methamphetamine injected)
████████████████████████████████████████

Valium (diazepam)
████████████████████████████████████

Quaalude (methaqualone)
██████████████████████████████████

Seconal (secobarbital)
██████████████████████████████████

Alcohol
██████████████████████████████████

Heroin
████████████████████████████████

Crank (amphetamine taken nasally)
████████████████████████████████

Cocaine
██████████████████████████████████████

Caffeine
██████████████████████████████████

PCP (phencyclidine)
██████████████████████████

Marijuana
████████████████

Ecstasy (MDMA)
██████████████

Psilocybin mushrooms
████████████

LSD
██████████

Mescaline
██████████
```

Research by John Hastings

Figure 12.2 Easy to get hooked on, hard to get off (from Franklin, 1990)

category, acknowledging the complex biological and psychological nature of the problem.

The DSM-IV term *substance-related disorders* shows that people can receive several subtypes of diagnoses for each of the drugs or substances. Specifically, for most of the substances, a person—where

appropriate—receives a diagnosis of dependence, abuse, intoxication, and/or withdrawal.

This distinction helps to clarify the nature of the problem and to focus treatment on those aspects of the substance-related disorder in need of attention. In Danny's case, he received the diagnosis *cocaine dependence* because of the tolerance he showed for the drug, his use of larger amounts than he intended, his unsuccessful attempts to stop using it, and the activities he gave up to use cocaine. This pattern of use and dependence was more pervasive than just cocaine abuse, and his diagnosis provided a clear picture of his need for help.

In the case of substance-related disorders, the presence of symptoms of other disorders can complicate the picture significantly. For example, are some individuals depressed and as a result do they drink alcohol to excess, or does drinking and its consequences (for example, loss of friends, job) make them depressed? Some researchers have estimated, for example, that, just among people with alcohol disorders, more than half have an additional psychiatric diagnosis such as antisocial personality disorder, schizophrenia, and bipolar disorder (Regier et al., 1990).

There are at least three reasons why substance use might occur concurrently with other disorders (Schuckit, 1993).

1. Substance-related disorders and such disorders as anxiety and the mood disorders are all highly prevalent in our society and occur together so often just by chance.

2. Drug intoxication and withdrawal can cause symptoms of anxiety, depression, and psychosis.

3. Several of the other disorders such as schizophrenia and antisocial personality disorder have a high likelihood of a secondary problem of substance use.

Because substance-related disorders can be so complicated, the DSM-IV tries to define when a symptom is a result of substance use and when it is not. Basically, if people experience symptoms such as those seen in schizophrenia or in extreme states of anxiety, either while they are intoxicated or within 6 weeks after their withdrawal from drugs, these aren't considered to be signs of a separate psychiatric disorder. So, for example, individuals who show signs of severe depression just after they have stopped taking heavy doses of stimulants would *not* be considered to have a major mood disorder. However, individuals who are severely depressed before using stimulants or those whose symptoms persist more than 6 weeks after they stop using these drugs might be considered to have a separate disorder (Schuckit, 1993).

With this discussion of abuse and dependence as a background, we now turn to the individual substances themselves, their effects on our brains and our bodies, and how they are used in our society.

We have grouped the substances into four categories depending on their effect on behavior.

1. **Depressants**—These substances result in behavioral sedation, and include alcohol (ethyl alcohol) and the sedative, hypnotic, and anxiolytic drugs in the families of barbiturates (for example, Seconal) and benzodiazepines (for instance, Valium, Halcion).

2. **Stimulants**—These substances cause us to be more active and alert, and can elevate our mood. Included in this group are amphetamines, cocaine, nicotine, and caffeine.

3. **Opiates**—The major effect of these substances is to temporarily produce analgesia (reduce pain) and euphoria. Heroin, opium, codeine, and morphine are included in this group.

4. **Hallucinogens**—These substances can produce delusions, paranoia, hallucinations, and altered sensory perception. Marijuana and LSD are included here.

Following this discussion, we next examine the causes of substance use, abuse, and dependence, and the efforts to help people cope with or overcome their involvement with drugs. We review the causes and the treatments of these disorders together because there are many commonalities among the different substances in the way they affect us and in the way they are treated.

Depressants

The depressants are substances that primarily *decrease* central nervous system activity. Their principal effect is to reduce our levels of physiological arousal and help us relax. Included in this group are alcohol and the sedative, hypnotic, and anxiolytic drugs such as those prescribed for insomnia (which we discussed in Chapter 10). These substances are among those most likely to produce symptoms of physical dependence, tolerance, and withdrawal. We first look at the most commonly used of these substances—alcohol—and the **alcohol use disorders** that can result.

Alcohol Use Disorders

We saw that Danny's substance abuse began with his drinking beer with friends—a "rite of passage" for many contemporary teenagers. However, alcohol use has been prevalent throughout the ages, with reports that alcoholic beverages were manufactured and used thousands of years ago. For hundreds of years, people in Europe drank large amounts of beer, wine, and hard liquor. When the Europeans came to North America in the early 1600s, they brought their considerable appetite for alcohol with them. In the United States during the early 1800s, consumption of alcohol (mostly whiskey) was over seven gallons per year for every person older than 15. This rate is about three times the current use of alcohol in this country (Rorabaugh, 1991).

When certain yeasts react with sugar and water, *fermentation* takes place, and one by-product of this process is *alcohol* (ethyl alcohol). Our history demonstrates that we have been very creative about fermenting alcohol from just about any fruit or vegetable, in part because many foods contain sugar. The alcoholic drinks produced throughout time include mead from honey, sake from rice, wine from palm, mezcal and Central American pulque from agave and cactus, liquor from maple syrup, liquor from South American jungle fruits, wine from grapes, and beer from grains (Lazare, 1989).

Table 12.4   DSM-IV Criteria for Alcohol Intoxication

A. Recent ingestion of alcohol.

B. Clinically significant maladaptive behavioral or psychological changes (e.g., inappropriate sexual or aggressive behavior, mood lability, impaired judgment, impaired social or occupational functioning) that developed during, or shortly after, alcohol use.

C. One or more of the following signs, developing during, or shortly after, alcohol use:

 1. Slurred speech
 2. Incoordination
 3. Unsteady gait
 4. Nystagmus
 5. Impairment in attention or memory
 6. Stupor or coma

D. The symptoms are not due to a general medical condition and are not better accounted for by another mental disorder.

Source: DSM-IV, APA, 1994.

Clinical Description

Even though alcohol is a depressant, the initial effect of ingesting it is an apparent stimulation. (The DSM-IV diagnostic criteria for alcohol intoxication are listed in Table 12.4.) We generally experience a feeling of well-being, we become more outgoing, and our inhibitions are reduced. This reaction occurs because what is initially depressed or slowed down are the inhibitory centers in our brain. With continued drinking, however, alcohol begins to depress more areas of the brain and it starts to interfere with our ability to function properly. Our motor coordination is impaired (staggering, slurred speech), our reaction time is slowed, we become confused, and our ability to make judgments is reduced. Even vision and hearing can be negatively affected, all of which help to explain why driving while intoxicated is so dangerous.

Alcohol and Its Effects

Alcohol affects many parts of the body. Its passage through the various systems is shown in Figure 12.3. After it is ingested, it passes through the esophagus (1) and into the stomach (2), where small amounts are absorbed. From there the vast majority of it continues to travel to the small intestine (3), where it is easily absorbed into the bloodstream. The circulatory system distributes the alcohol throughout the body, where it has contact with many organs, including the heart (4).

Figure 12.3   The path traveled by alcohol throughout the body (see text for complete description)

Some of the alcohol makes its way to the lungs, where it vaporizes and is exhaled. This phenomenon is the basis for police use of the *breathalyzer test* to measure someone's level of intoxication. As alcohol passes through the liver (5) it is broken down or metabolized into carbon dioxide and water by enzymes (Gordis, 1991). An average-size person is able to metabolize about 7 to 10 grams of alcohol per hour, an amount comparable to about one glass of beer or 1 ounce of 90-proof spirits (Nathan, 1993).

For most of the substances we describe in this chapter, such as marijuana, the opiates, and tranquilizers, we know that they interact with specific receptors in the brain cells. Alcohol's effects, however, are much more complex. Alcohol tends to influence a number of different neuroreceptor systems, and therefore it is more difficult to study. For example, one system that seems to be particularly sensitive to alcohol is the gamma-aminobutyric acid **(GABA) system**, which we discussed in Chapter 2 and Chapter 5. GABA, as you will recall, is an inhibitory neurotransmitter. This means that its major role is to interfere with the firing of the neuron it attaches to. When GABA attaches to its receptor, chloride ions enter the cell and make the cell less sensitive to the effects of other neurotransmitters (Gordis, 1991). Alcohol seems to reinforce the movement of these chloride ions; as a result, the neurons have difficulty firing. In other words, just as alcohol seems to "loosen our tongues" and make us more sociable, it facilitates the movement of these chloride ions; this action creates difficulty for these neurons in communicating with others. Because this system seems to act on our feelings of anxiety, alcohol's anti-anxiety properties may result from its interaction with the GABA system.

Another system currently under study for its role in the effects of alcohol is the *glutamate system*. In contrast to the GABA system, the glutamate system is an excitatory neurotransmitter system that helps the neurons to fire. This system is suspected to involve learning and memory, and it may be the avenue through which

alcohol affects our cognitive abilities. A third major system—the *serotonin system*—also appears to be sensitive to alcohol. This neurotransmitter system affects our mood, sleep, and eating behavior and is thought to be influential in the cravings alcoholics have for alcohol (Gordis, 1991). Realizing that alcohol affects so many brain chemical systems, we should not be surprised that it has such widespread and complex effects.

The long-term effects of heavy drinking are often severe. Withdrawal from chronic alcohol use typically includes hand tremors and, within several hours, symptoms such as nausea or vomiting, anxiety, transient hallucinations, agitation, and insomnia. At its most extreme, withdrawal can lead to alcohol **withdrawal delirium** (or **delirium tremens**—the **DTs**); this condition can produce frightening hallucinations and body tremors. The devastating experience of delirium tremens can be reduced with adequate medical treatment (McCreery & Walker, 1993).

Because alcohol travels throughout the body in the bloodstream, it has contact with virtually every important organ. Whether it will cause damage seems related to a person's genetic vulnerability, the frequency of his or her drinking, the length of drinking binges, the blood alcohol levels attained during the drinking periods, and whether the body is given time to recover from these binges (Gordis, 1991). Some of the consequences of long-term excessive drinking include liver disease, pancreatitis, cardiovascular disorders, and damage to the brain. The possible damage that extensive drinking can cause to a person's liver and brain is shown in Figures 12.4 and 12.5.

Part of the folklore concerning alcohol and its use is that it permanently kills brain cells (neurons). As we see below, this may not be true. Some of the evidence for brain damage comes from the experiences of people who are alcohol dependent. They may experience blackouts, seizures, and hallucinations, all signs of brain damage. Also affected are memory and the ability to perform certain tasks. More seriously, two types of

Figure 12.4 A healthy liver (*left*) and a cirrhotic liver (*right*) (from Gordis, 1991)

Figure 12.5 Brain images of males with a history of light and very heavy alcohol consumption (from Gordis, 1991)

organic brain syndromes may result from long-term and heavy alcohol use: dementia and Wernicke's disease. *Dementia,* which we discuss more fully in Chapter 15, involves the general loss of intellectual abilities. As in the present case, dementia can be a direct result of neurotoxicity or "poisoning" of the brain by excessive amounts of alcohol (Nathan, 1993). *Wernicke's disease* results in confusion, loss of muscle coordination, and unintelligible speech (Gordis, 1991). This disorder is believed to occur because of a deficiency of thiamine—a vitamin that is metabolized poorly by heavy drinkers.

In spite of such damaging results, a new study suggests that not all the effects of heavy drinking on the brain are permanent. Recently, researchers in Denmark have made an important discovery concerning the effect of alcohol (Jensen & Pakkenberg, 1993). By painstakingly counting the neurons in the brains of deceased alcoholics and nonalcoholics, they've found that chronic alcohol use *may not* permanently damage the neurons in the cortex (the outer area of the brain). Instead, the damage may be occurring to the connections between the neurons, which may be able to regrow or regenerate themselves (Jensen & Pakkenberg, 1993). This finding suggests that improvement in a heavy drinker's cognitive ability may be possible if the person successfully stops drinking.

The effects of alcohol abuse can stretch beyond the health and well-being of just the person drinking. Because alcohol enters the bloodstream it can affect a developing fetus. Although the effects of alcohol were suspected for years to impact negatively on prenatal development, only recently has this been studied in earnest. First described in France only a short time ago (Jones & Smith, 1973; Lemoine, Harousseau, Borteyru, & Menuet, 1968), **fetal alcohol syndrome (FAS)** is now generally recognized as a combination of problems that can occur in a child whose mother drank while she was pregnant. These include cognitive deficits, behavior problems, and learning difficulties (Phelps & Grabowski, 1992). Children born with fetal alcohol syndrome often have characteristic facial features.

It is interesting that not all women who drink during pregnancy are at equal risk for having children with this syndrome. In other words, if two women drink the same amount during the same period in pregnancy, they may have different chances of bearing a child with FAS. In particular, women of certain racial groups, including African-Americans and the Apache and Ute Indian tribes of the American Southwest, appear to be at greater risk for having children with FAS (Gordis, 1991; May & Hymbaugh, 1983). One reason for this difference may be in the ways people break down alcohol. We metabolize alcohol with the help of an enzyme called *alcohol dehydrogenase* (ADH) (Gordis, 1991). Three different forms of this enzyme have been identified (called beta 1, beta 2, and beta 3 ADH); one form (beta 3 ADH) has been found much more frequently among the African-American population. Initial work has also shown that beta 3 ADH may be more prevalent among children with fetal alcohol syndrome. What these two findings suggest is that, in addition to the drinking habits of the mother, the

Characteristics of children with fetal alcohol syndrome include skin folds at the corner of the eye, low nasal bridge, short nose, groove between nose and upper lip, small head circumference, small eye opening, small midface, and thin upper lip.

likelihood that a child will have FAS may also depend on the genes of both parents—in this case, whether there is a genetic vulnerability to have certain enzymes. Children from certain racial groups may be more susceptible to fetal alcohol syndrome. If this research is confirmed, it may give us a way of identifying parents who might put their children at risk for this disorder.

Positive effects of alcohol. We have spent a considerable amount of time discussing the negative effects of alcohol use, but what about the positive aspects of moderate drinking? Because it is a central nervous system depressant, moderate amounts of alcohol can relax an individual and reduce his or her inhibitions. Whether you react positively or negatively to drinking alcohol will depend not only on the physiological effect of the alcohol itself but also on your expectations, or what you expect will happen. There may also be direct health benefits from moderate levels of drinking. Research has suggested that moderate alcohol consumption may help prevent heart attacks by

as much as 50% (Gaziano et al., 1993). This protective aspect of alcohol may come about by raising levels of high-density lipoprotein cholesterol (HDL). HDL, or the "good cholesterol," seems to cleanse the blood vessels of fatty buildups. An alternative view held by some researchers is that the benefits do not come from alcohol itself but from specific compounds (called phenolic compounds) found in one type of alcohol—wine (Kinsella, Frankel, German, & Kanner, 1993). This finding is said to explain why the French, who are known for eating high-fat foods such as cheese and cream sauces, have lower than average risks of coronary heart disease. Although physicians do not yet recommend drinking to people who currently abstain from alcohol, it does seem that having one drink per day (perhaps wine) may raise your HDL levels by about 15%, thereby helping to protect you from coronary heart disease.

Statistics on Alcohol Use

Because alcohol is legal in this country, we know more about its use than about most of the other psychoactive substances we discuss in this chapter (with the possible exception of nicotine and caffeine, also legal here). For example, despite this country's history of heavy alcohol use, we know that the trend has been headed downward over the past 20 years (U.S. Department of Health and Human Services, 1990). Although this decline in the use of alcohol may represent a temporary pattern, it is paralleled in many other countries of the world (Horgan, Sparrow, & Brazeau, 1986). Figure 12.6 shows the change in alcohol consumption for 25 countries between 1979 and 1984. In many of the major industrialized countries, alcohol use has declined. This pattern of reduced consumption may be due in part to the public's increased awareness of the health risks associated with alcohol use and abuse. A change in demographics may also account for some of this decline. The proportion of the population over the age of 60 has increased, and the use of alcohol among people in this age group is historically low (U.S. Department of Health and Human Services, 1990).

In the United States, the type of beverage that accounts for the reduction in alcohol use is spirits or "hard liquor." Its use dropped to 0.83 gallons per capita in 1987, the lowest level of use since 1958 (U.S. Department of Health and Human Services, 1990) (see Figure 12.7). Increasing concerns about the effects of alcohol on health may account for the reduction in the use of spirits.

Men are more likely than women to drink alcohol and are also more likely to drink heavily (U.S. Department of Health and Human Services, 1990). In one large survey among college-age men and women, about 42% of respondents said they "went on a binge"

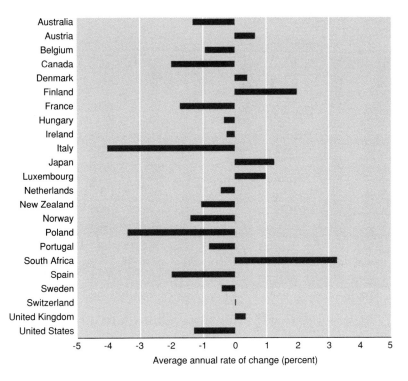

Figure 12.6 Average annual rate of change (percent) in per capita alcohol consumption for 25 countries, 1979–1984 (from Brazeau & Burr, 1992)

of heavy drinking once in the preceding 2 weeks, drinking five or more drinks (Presley & Meilman, 1992). Men, however, were more likely to report having had several binges in the 2-week period. The same survey found that students with a grade-point average of "A" drank no more than three drinks per week, while "D" and "F" students averaged 11 alcoholic drinks per week (Presley & Meilman, 1992). Overall, these data point to the popularity and pervasiveness of drinking in our society—which leads to the next section: research on problem drinking. Here we attempt to estimate the prevalence of alcohol abuse and dependence.

Statistics on Alcohol Abuse and Dependence

Our everyday experience tells us that not everyone who drinks becomes dependent on or abuses alcohol. However, researchers estimate that about 10% of Americans experience some level of problem with drinking alcohol, with about 10.5 million adults thought to be alcohol dependent (McCreery & Walker, 1993). As we mentioned before, men tend to drink more heavily than women and also to have a higher rate of alcohol problems. Males seem to be most vulnerable to having problems with drinking when they are between the ages of 18 and 29. Approximately 14% report symptoms of dependence during this period, and 20% report some

negative drinking-related consequences (U.S. Department of Health and Human Services, 1990). This number decreases with age to about 5% reporting dependence and 7% reporting drinking-related consequences by age 60 and older. The picture for women is not so clear-cut. The number of women reporting symptoms of dependence stays at a low and stable rate of about 5% to 6% through age 49, and then decreases to around 1%. Drinking-related consequences start out higher at around 12%, but they quickly decline until they are almost nonexistent after age 60. In short, among the general population, young (18–29), single males are most likely to be heavy drinkers and to have alcohol use problems (U.S. Department of Health and Human Services, 1990).

This picture of a heavy drinking, young, single male doesn't fit with your stereotype of a "skid row drunk," does it? It is true, however, that homelessness is associated with alcohol use and dependence. Unlike the general population, the homeless experience their highest level of alcohol abuse and dependence during the middle years of life, with estimates ranging from 20% to 45%. Over their lifetime, some 63% of this group will at some point experience problems with drinking (U.S. Department of Health and Human Services, 1990). Some may continue to drink through mid-life to help cope with the frustration and desperation of being

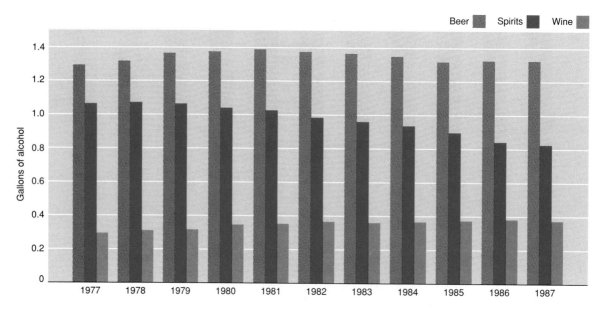

Figure 12.7 Apparent U.S. per capita consumption of beer, spirits, and wine, 1977–1987 (from National Institute on Drug Abuse, 1991)

homeless. It is probably also true that, for some, their homelessness is in part a consequence of their drinking or a combination of substance abuse and other mental health problems.

There are clear differences in drinking habits among the major racial groups in the United States. For example, African-Americans, Hispanics, and Asian-Americans have the highest rates of abstinence from drinking. African-Americans and Asian-Americans also have low rates of heavy drinking. The low rates for Asian-Americans may be partially due to a physiological response to alcohol called the "skin-flushing response," a negative reaction experienced by some in this group (a more detailed explanation of this response is provided later in the chapter when we describe the causes of substance abuse). Whites in America have high rates of driving while drinking. Native Americans are highly variable in their drinking

Binge drinking is commonly observed among college-age males and may represent the beginning of a life-long pattern of problem drinking for some.

habits but have high mortality rates as a result of alcohol-related conditions (U.S. Department of Health and Human Services, 1990).

Outside the United States rates of alcohol abuse and dependence vary widely. Compared to the U.S. average of 10%, the prevalence of alcohol dependence in Peru is about 35%; in the Korean population it is approximately 22%; it is about 3.5% in Taipei and as low as 0.45% among the people in Shanghai (Helzer & Canino, 1992; Yamamoto, Silva, Sasao, Wang, & Nguyen, 1993). These cultural differences can be accounted for by different attitudes toward drinking, accessibility of alcohol, physiological reactions, and family norms and patterns. For example, the high drinking rates in Korea have been blamed on the expectation in that culture that men drink heavily on some social occasions (Lee, 1992). In this case, it seems that the negative effect of the "flushing response" we mentioned before is outweighed by the cultural expectations for heavy drinking among Korean males.

Course of Alcohol Abuse and Dependence

If you remember the case of Danny, you recall that he seemed to go through periods of heavy alcohol and drug use, but he also had times when he was relatively "straight" or unaffected by drugs. Similarly, many people who abuse or are dependent on alcohol fluctuate among periods of time when they are drinking heavily, times when they can control their drinking and can drink "socially" without negative effects, and still other times when they are abstinent and do not drink at all (Schuckit, Smith, Anthenelli, & Irwin, 1993; Vaillant, 1983). It seems that about 20% of people with severe alcohol dependence go through spontaneous remission and do not reexperience problems with drinking (Ludwig, 1985; Vaillant, 1983).

An early notion of alcohol use and dependence was that, once problems arose with drinking, these problems would continue to become worse and follow a predictable downward pattern if the person kept drinking (Sobell & Sobell, 1993). In other words, like a *disease* that isn't treated properly, alcoholism will get progressively worse if left unchecked. First championed by Jellinek several decades ago, this view of alcohol abuse and dependence continues to influence the way people view and treat this disorder (Jellinek, 1946, 1952, 1960). Unfortunately, Jellinek based his model of the progression of alcohol use on a now famous, but faulty study (Jellinek, 1946), which we will briefly review.

In 1945, the newly formed self-help organization Alcoholics Anonymous (AA) sent out some 1,600 surveys to its members asking them about symptoms related to drinking, such as feelings of guilt or remorse,

and rationalizations about their actions, and when these reactions first occurred to them. In other words, they were given a list of problems and asked to think back and report if and when they had happened. Only 98 of the almost 1,600 surveys were returned, however. As you know, such a small response could cause serious problems in interpreting these data. Obviously, this group of 98 may be very different from the group as a whole, so their answers may not represent what happens to the "typical" person with alcohol problems. Also, because the responses were retrospective (participants were recalling past events), the information they reported may not be correct. Despite this and other problems, Jellinek agreed to analyze the data taken from participants of the AA survey and developed a four-stage model for the progression of alcoholism based on this limited information (Jellinek, 1952). According to his model, these individuals go through a *prealcoholic stage* (drinking occasionally with few serious consequences), a *prodromal stage* (drinking heavily but with few outward signs of a problem), a *crucial stage* (a loss of control of drinking, with occasional "benders" or binges of heavy drinking), and a *chronic stage* (where the primary activities during the day surround getting and drinking alcohol). A number of attempts by other researchers to confirm this progression of stages has not been successful (Schuckit, Smith, Anthenelli, & Irwin, 1993).

It appears instead that the course of alcohol *dependence* may be progressive for most people, although the course of alcohol *abuse* may be more variable. For example, a recent study followed 636 males who were inpatients in an alcohol rehabilitation center (Schuckit, Smith, Anthenelli, & Irwin, 1993). Among these chronically alcohol-dependent men, a general progression of alcohol-related life problems did emerge, although not the specific pattern proposed by Jellinek. Three-quarters of the men reported moderate consequences of their drinking—for example, demotions at work—in their 20s. During their 30s, the men reported more serious problems such as regular blackouts and signs of alcohol withdrawal. By their late 30s and early 40s, these men demonstrated long-term serious consequences of their drinking, which included hallucinations, withdrawal convulsions, and hepatitis/pancreatitis. This study suggests that, among people with chronic alcohol abuse and dependence, a pattern of increasingly severe consequences of drinking is common. This progressive pattern is not inevitable for everyone who abuses alcohol, although we do not as yet understand what distinguishes those who do and those who do not display this negative progression (Sobell & Sobell, 1993).

Finally, statistics frequently link the use of alcohol with violent behavior. Numerous studies have

Heavy drinking can impair a person's judgment and can increase the risk of acting violently.

found that people who commit violent acts such as murder, rape, and assault are often intoxicated at the time of the crime (U.S. Department of Health and Human Services, 1990). We hope that you are skeptical of this type of correlation. Just because they occur together does not mean that drinking alcohol will necessarily make you violent. Laboratory studies show that drinking alcohol does make subjects more aggressive (Bushman, 1993). However, whether a person will act aggressively outside the research laboratory probably involves a number of interrelated factors such as the quantity and timing of alcohol consumed, the person's history of violence, his or her expectations about drinking, and what happens to the individual while intoxicated. Alcohol does not *cause* aggression. More likely, it may reduce the fear associated with being punished, and it may impair a person's ability to think through the consequences of acting impulsively. Combined with the right circumstances, these impairments of rational thinking may increase the risk that a person will behave aggressively (Pihl, Peterson, & Lau, 1993).

Sedative, Hypnotic, or Anxiolytic Substance Use Disorders

Joined with alcohol under the general group of "depressants" are **sedative, hypnotic,** and **anxiolytic**

drugs, so named because they have a calming (sedative), sleep-inducing (hypnotic), and anxiety-reducing (anxiolytic) effect. These drugs include the barbiturates and the benzodiazepines. **Barbiturates** (which include Amytal, Seconal, and Nembutal) are a family of sedative drugs first synthesized in Germany in 1882 (McKim, 1991). They were prescribed to help people sleep and replaced such drugs as alcohol and opiates (for example, opium), which were then used as sleeping aids. These drugs were widely prescribed by physicians in the 1930s before their addictive properties were fully understood. By the 1950s they were among the drugs most abused by adults in the United States (Abadinsky, 1993).

The **benzodiazepines** (which today include Valium, Xanax, and Halcion) have been used since the 1960s primarily to reduce anxiety. These drugs were originally touted as a miracle cure for living with the anxieties resulting from our highly pressured and technological society. Although in 1980 the Food and Drug Administration ruled that they were not appropriate for reducing the tension and anxiety resulting from everyday stresses and strains, 3.7 billion doses of benzodiazepines are estimated to be consumed by Americans each year (Shabecoff, 1987). In general, benzodiazepines are considered much safer than barbiturates, with less risk of abuse and dependence (Warneke, 1991).

Clinical Description

At low doses, barbiturates relax the muscles and can produce a mild feeling of well-being. However, larger doses can have results similar to those of drinking alcohol heavily; a person's speech can slur and he or she may have problems walking, concentrating, and working. At extremely high doses the diaphragm muscles can relax so much as to cause death by suffocation. In fact, taking overdoses of barbiturates is a common form of committing suicide.

Like the barbiturates, benzodiazepines are used to calm an individual and induce sleep. In addition, drugs in this class are prescribed as muscle relaxants and anticonvulsants—or antiseizure medications (Warneke, 1991). People who use them for other than medical reasons first report feeling a pleasant "high" and a reduction of inhibition, similar to the results of drinking alcohol. However, with continued use, tolerance and dependence can develop. When they try to stop taking the drug, users experience withdrawal symptoms like those of alcohol (anxiety, insomnia, tremors, and delirium).

The DSM-IV criteria for sedative, hypnotic, and anxiolytic drug use disorders are listed in Table 12.5; they do not differ substantially from the criteria found under alcohol use disorders. Included in the definition

Table 12.5 DSM-IV Criteria for Sedative, Hypnotic, or Anxiolytic Intoxication

A. Recent use of a sedative, hypnotic, or anxiolytic drug.

B. Clinically significant maladaptive behavioral or psychological changes (e.g., inappropriate sexual or aggressive behavior, mood lability, impaired judgment, impaired social or occupational functioning) that developed during, or shortly after, sedative, hypnotic, or anxiolytic use.

C. One or more of the following signs, developing during, or shortly after, sedative, hypnotic, or anxiolytic use:

1. Slurred speech
2. Incoordination
3. Unsteady gait
4. Hystagmus
5. Impairment in attention or memory
6. Stupor or coma

D. The symptoms are not due to a general medical condition and are not better accounted for by another mental disorder.

Source: DSM-IV, APA, 1994.

of both disorders are maladaptive behavioral changes such as inappropriate sexual or aggressive behavior, variable moods, impaired judgment, and impaired social or occupational functioning. Also included would be slurred speech, motor coordination problems, and unsteady gait.

Similarly to alcohol, the sedative, hypnotic, and anxiolytic drugs affect the brain by impacting the GABA neurotransmitter system (McKim, 1991). Alcohol and the sedative, hypnotic, and anxiolytic drugs affect the GABA system using slightly different mechanisms; as a result, when people combine alcohol with any of these drugs, there can be synergistic effects (Fils-Aime, 1993). In other words, if you have a drink after taking a benzodiazepine or barbiturate, the total effects can increase to dangerous levels. One theory about actress Marilyn Monroe's death in 1962 is that she combined alcohol and too many barbiturates and unintentionally killed herself.

Statistics and Course for Sedative, Hypnotic, or Anxiolytic Substance Use Disorders

The use of barbiturates has declined while the use of benzodiazepines has increased since 1960 (Warneke, 1991). Recent surveys to learn the extent of benzodiazepine use annually, other than for sleep or different medical uses, estimate that approximately 11.1% of Americans use them, 7.4% of the Dutch, and 17% of Belgians, with females being twice as likely to report their use as males (Warneke, 1991). The prescription by physicians of barbiturates has decreased over the years in favor of the benzodiazepines because the latter provide similar beneficial effects with fewer of the harmful effects of barbiturates such as their greater potential for abuse and fatal overdose. Benzodiazepines may be less likely to be misused because they

have an upper limit of effectiveness—in other words, there is a point at which taking more of the drug has no additional effect (McKim, 1991). This characteristic of benzodiazepines is one factor that may help to explain why people are less likely to abuse these drugs.

Stimulants

Of all the psychoactive drugs used in this country, the most commonly consumed fall under the class called *stimulants.* Included in this group are caffeine (found in coffee, chocolate, and many soft drinks), nicotine (in tobacco products such as cigarettes), amphetamines, and cocaine. You probably used one of these stimulants—caffeine—when you got up this morning. In contrast to the depressant drugs, stimulants—as their name suggests—make you more alert and energetic. We will describe several of these stimulants along with their effects on behavior, mood, and cognition.

Amphetamine Use Disorders

At low doses, amphetamines can induce feelings of elation and vigor, and can reduce fatigue. You literally feel "up." Unfortunately, after a period of time of feeling elated, the opposite effect can result and you feel depressed or come back down and "crash." In sufficient quantities these stimulants can lead to **amphetamine use disorders.**

Amphetamines are manufactured in the laboratory; they were first synthesized in the 1930s to be used as a treatment for asthma and as a nasal decongestant. Because amphetamines also reduce your desire to eat, they are used by some people to lose weight. In 1987 Kitty Dukakis, wife of Michael

Actress Marilyn Monroe on the set of her last film, *The Misfits*. During its filming she at one point had to be hospitalized after collapsing from a sleeping pill overdose. In 1962, shortly after the release of the film, she died from an overdose of barbiturates.

Dukakis, who was then governor of Massachusetts, revealed that she had been addicted for 26 years to the amphetamines that were originally prescribed for weight control. Others, such as long-haul truck drivers, pilots, and some college students trying to "pull all-nighters" to study for exams, use amphetamines to get that extra energy boost and stay awake. Their ability to keep people alert accounts for the use of amphetamines by people with *narcolepsy,* a sleep disorder characterized by excessive sleepiness. Some of these drugs (for example, Ritalin, Cylert) are even used for children with problems with hyperactivity and attention, a disorder called *attention deficit disorder,* which we'll discuss in Chapter 16.

DSM-IV diagnostic criteria for amphetamine intoxication are listed in Table 12.6. The danger from this and the other drugs we discuss is the negative effects they have on us. As you can see from the DSM-IV criteria for amphetamine intoxication, continued use of these drugs can cause such negative changes in behavior as social withdrawal, anxiety, and anger along with the physical effects of hot and cold spells, nausea, and vomiting. More severe intoxication or "overdose" can cause hallucinations, panic, agitation, and paranoid delusions (Stein & Ellinwood, 1993). Tolerance to this drug builds quickly and makes

it doubly dangerous. Withdrawal from the drug often results in apathy, prolonged periods of sleep, irritability, and depression.

Periodically, certain "designer drugs" erupt in local mini-epidemics. For example, an amphetamine called methylene-dioxymethamphetamine (MDMA) was first synthesized in 1898 in Germany and used as an appetite suppressant. Recreational use of this drug, now commonly called "Ecstasy," has risen in the late 1980s (O'Hagan, 1992). Its effects are best described in one user's own words: " just like speed but without the comedown, and [makes] you feel warm and trippy like acid, but without the possibility of a major freak-out" (O'Hagan, 1992, p. 10). Another purified and crystallized form of amphetamine, called "ice," is ingested through smoking. This drug causes marked aggressive tendencies and stays in the system longer than cocaine, making it particularly dangerous (Stein & Ellinwood, 1993). Unfortunately, however enjoyable these drugs may be in the short term, the potential for users to develop dependence on and tolerance for these new versions of amphetamines is extremely high, placing people at great risk for experiencing long-term difficulties.

Amphetamines work to stimulate the central nervous system by enhancing the activity of two

The Complexities of Mental Illness

Our discussing each of the disorders in this book in separate chapters may lead the reader to the impression that psychological disorders are disconnected entities. Our language often reinforces this tendency to keep things in nice, neat, and separate "boxes." People talk of "alcoholics," "schizophrenics," "depressives," or "psychopaths." However, rarely are things so simple. Textbook cases are just that: examples used in books like this to simplify what can be very puzzling problems. It may be useful to step back from our job of trying to simplify and for a moment introduce you to an example of a more complex situation. An excellent illustration of the complicated and personal nature of mental illness is a recent book by William Styron, the Pulitzer Prize winning author of such novels as *The Confessions of Nat Turner* and *Sophie's Choice*. In *Darkness Visible* (1990), Styron describes his private battle with severe depression. Trying to understand the origins of his depression, he describes his use of alcohol and sedative, hypnotic, and anxiolytic medications.

When I reflected on this curious alteration of my consciousness—and I was baffled enough from time to time to do so—I assumed that it all had to do somehow with my enforced withdrawal from alcohol. And, of course, to a certain extent this was true. But it is my conviction now that alcohol played a perverse trick on me when we said farewell to each other: although, as everyone should know, it is a major depressant, it had never truly depressed me during my drinking career, acting instead as a shield against anxiety. Suddenly vanished, the great ally which for so long had kept my demons at bay was no longer there to prevent those demons from beginning to swarm through the subconscious, and I was emotionally naked, vulnerable as I had never been before. Doubtless depression had hovered near me for years, waiting to swoop down. (Styron, 1990, pp. 42–43)

According to Styron, his 40-year abuse of alcohol served to delay the onset of his depression. It "kept the demons at bay" throughout most of hislife, but they came rushing in once the alcohol

was gone. But it wasn't just alcohol that complicated the picture. He describes the insomnia that accompanied his depression and how attempts to deal with this sleeplessness may have further exacerbated his depression.

A final cautionary word, however, should be added concerning Halcion. I'm convinced that this tranquilizer is responsible for at least exaggerating to an intolerable point the suicidal ideas that had possessed me before entering the hospital. The empirical evidence that persuades me of this evolves from a conversation I had with a staff psychiatrist only hours after going into the institution. When he asked me what I was taking for sleep, and the dosage, I told him .75 mg of Halcion; at this his face became somber, and he remarked emphatically that this was three times the normally prescribed hypnotic dose, and an amount especially contraindicated for someone my age. (pp. 70–71)

* * *

Much evidence has accumulated recently that indicts Halcion (whose chemical name is triazolam) as a causative factor in producing suicidal obsession and other aberrations of thought in susceptible individuals. (p. 70)

* * *

In my case Halcion, of course, was not an independent villain—I was headed for the abyss—but I believe that without it I might not have been brought so low. (p. 72)

Is William Styron an "alcoholic"? Is he a "drug addict" or a "depressive"? As you can see, these labels do little to help us understand the complex interrelationships between our experiences and our biology, and how they combine to create the problems described in this book. Just as in the case of Danny, whom we introduced at the beginning of this chapter, the reasons behind William Styron's use of certain substances are entwined in his unique combination of personal circumstances—a situation that describes everyone who experiences a psychological disorder.

---

neurotransmitters: norepinephrine and dopamine. More specifically, amphetamines seem both to help the release of these neurochemicals and to block their reuptake, thereby making more of these chemicals

available throughout the system (Stein & Ellinwood, 1993). The effects of too much amphetamine—and therefore too much dopamine and norepinephrine—can include hallucinations and delusions. As we will

William Styron, the Pulitzer Prize winning author, wrote poignantly about the effects of Halcion on his depression and suicidal thoughts.

discuss in Chapter 14, this effect has stimulated theories on the causes of schizophrenia, which can also include hallucinations and delusions.

Cocaine Use Disorders

The use and misuse of drugs, such as those leading to **cocaine use disorders,** wax and wane according to societal fashion, moods, and sanctions (Uddo, Malow, & Sutker, 1993). Cocaine replaced amphetamines as the

stimulant of choice in the 1970s (Stein & Ellinwood, 1993). *Coca* is a flowering bush indigenous to South America that produces the leaves from which cocaine is derived. A young Sigmund Freud wrote of cocaine's magical properties in his essay "On Coca" (1885/1974):

> I have tested [the] effect of coca, which wards off hunger, sleep, and fatigue and steels one to intellectual effort, some dozen times on myself (p. 60).

People have chewed coca leaves for centuries to get relief from hunger and fatigue (Musto, 1992). America's first introduction to cocaine came in the late 19th century; it was widely used from then until the 1920s. As an illustration of its availability, in 1885, Parke, Davis & Co. in the United States was manufacturing coca and cocaine for consumption in 15 different forms, including coca-leaf cigarettes and cigars, inhalants, and crystals. For people who couldn't afford these products, a cheaper way to get cocaine was in Coca-Cola, which had a small but noticeable amount of the drug as late as 1900 (Musto, 1992).

Clinical Description

DSM-IV diagnostic criteria for cocaine intoxication are listed in Table 12.7. Like the amphetamines, in small amounts cocaine increases alertness, produces a feeling of euphoria, increases blood pressure and pulse, and causes insomnia and loss of appetite. Remember that Danny would snort cocaine (inhale it) to "party" through the night with his friends. He later described the drug as making him feel powerful, invincible—the only time he really felt self-confident. The effects of the drug are short-lived; for Danny they

---

Table 12.6   DSM-IV Criteria for Amphetamine (or Related Substance) Intoxication

A. Use of amphetamine or a related substance (e.g., methylphenidate).

B. Clinically significant maladaptive behavioral or psychological changes (e.g., euphoria or affective blunting; changes in sociability; hypervigilance; interpersonal sensitivity, anxiety, tension, or anger; stereotyped behaviors; impaired judgment or impaired social or occupational functioning) that developed during, or shortly after, use of amphetamine or a related substance.

C. Two (or more) of the following, developing during, or shortly after, use of amphetamine or a related substance:

1. Tachycardia or bradycardia
2. Pupillary dilation
3. Elevated or lowered blood pressure
4. Perspiration or chills
5. Nausea or vomiting
6. Evidence of weight loss
7. Psychomotor agitation or retardation
8. Muscular weakness, respiratory depression, chest pain, or cardiac arrhythmias
9. Confusion, seizures, dyskinesias, dystonias, or coma

D. The symptoms are not due to a general medical condition and are not better accounted for by another mental disorder.

Specify if:
  With perceptual disturbances

Source: DSM-IV, APA, 1994.

Table 12.7 DSM-IV Criteria for Cocaine Intoxication

A. Recent use of cocaine.

B. Clinically significant maladaptive behavioral or psychological changes (e.g., euphoria or affective blunting; changes in sociability; hypervigilance; interpersonal sensitivity; anxiety, tension, or anger; stereotyped behaviors; impaired judgment or impaired social or occupational functioning) that developed during, or shortly after, use of cocaine.

C. Two (or more) of the following, developing during, or shortly after, cocaine use:

1. Tachycardia or bradycardia
2. Pupillary dilation
3. Elevated or lowered blood pressure
4. Perspiration or chills
5. Nausea or vomiting
6. Evidence of weight loss
7. Psychomotor agitation or retardation
8. Muscular weakness, respiratory depression, chest pain, or cardiac arrhythmias
9. Confusion, seizures, dyskinesias, dystonias, or coma

D. The symptoms are not due to a general medical condition and are not better accounted for by another mental disorder.

Specify if:
  With perceptual disturbances

Source: DSM-IV, APA, 1994.

lasted less than an hour, and he had to inhale cocaine repeatedly to keep himself up. During these cocaine "binges" he would often become paranoid, experiencing exaggerated fears that he would be caught or that someone would steal his cocaine. Such paranoia is common among cocaine abusers, occurring in approximately two-thirds or more of these individuals (Satel, 1992). Cocaine also makes the heart beat more rapidly and irregularly, and its use can cause fatal consequences depending on a person's physical condition and the amount of the drug ingested. It is now believed that the outstanding college basketball player Len Bias died from cardiac irregularities after using only a moderate amount of cocaine.

We saw that alcohol use by pregnant women can cause damage to the developing fetus. It has also been suspected that the use of cocaine and especially crack cocaine by pregnant women *may* also adversely affect their babies. Nationally, some estimates suggest that as many as 250,000 children may have been exposed to cocaine prenatally (Phibbs, Bateman, & Schwartz, 1991). Nicknamed *crack babies,* these infants at birth appear to be more irritable than normal babies, have long bouts of high-pitched crying, and were thought to have permanent brain damage, all of which was initially attributed to the mother's cocaine use. However, a closer look at these children suggests that we may have been too quick to assign blame exclusively to cocaine. Recent work suggests that many children born to mothers who have used cocaine during pregnancy may have decreased birth weight but show no evidence of problems with cognitive or motor skills at birth or 1 month later (Woods, Eyler, Behnke, & Conlon, 1992). The problem with evaluating most

children born to mothers who have used cocaine is that these mothers almost always use other substances such as alcohol and nicotine in addition to the cocaine. Many of these children are also being raised in disrupted home environments, further complicating the picture. It may be that signs of damage once attributed only to cocaine are the result of the mother's use of a combination of drugs and/or inadequate parenting. Continuing research should help us better understand cocaine's negative effects on children. One recent study suggests that prenatal cocaine exposure may affect the fetus's "biological clock"—the suprachiasmatic nucleus (Weaver, Rivkees, & Reppert, 1992). In effect, repeated cocaine use by the mother may cause a reaction similar to "jet lag" in the fetus that may contribute to some of the observations of irritability and other problems experienced by the newborn.

Statistics and Course for Cocaine Use Disorders

Cocaine use across most age groups has decreased over the past decade, with approximately 2.5% of people reporting their use of the drug in 1979, and less than 1.0% reporting its use in 1991 (National Institute on Drug Abuse, 1991). Approximately 17% of cocaine users have also used crack cocaine (a crystallized form of cocaine that is smoked) (Closser, 1992). In 1991, one estimate was that about 0.2% of Americans had tried crack cocaine, with an increasing proportion of the abusers seeking treatment being young, unemployed adults living in urban areas (Closser, 1992). Use of cocaine by high school seniors seems to have been at its highest level in 1985 and has been decreasing since that time, with 3.4% of seniors in 1988 saying that they

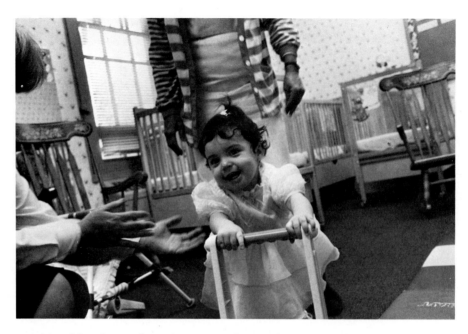

A little girl born to a mother addicted to crack cocaine. Research is just beginning to determine the effects of this drug on children born to dependent mothers.

had used cocaine in the past month (Stein & Ellinwood, 1993).

Because cocaine is in the same group of stimulants as amphetamines, it has similar effects on the brain. The "up" feeling you get from using this drug seems to come primarily from the drug's effect on the dopamine system of the brain, making more of this neurochemical available. If you look at Figure 12.8 you will see how this action takes place. Cocaine enters the bloodstream and is carried to the brain. There the cocaine molecules act to block the reuptake of dopamine. As we have described before, neurotransmitters such as dopamine are released at the synapse, stimulate the next neuron, and then are recycled back to the original neuron. Cocaine seems to bind to the places where the dopamine neurotransmitters would reenter their "home" neuron, blocking their reentry into the neuron. Because some of the dopamine cannot be taken in by the neuron, it continues to be present in the synapse, causing repeated stimulation of the next neuron. This repeated stimulation of the dopamine neurons in the "pleasure pathway" (the site in our brains that seems to be involved in our experience of pleasure) causes the "high" associated with cocaine use.

As late as the 1980s, many felt that cocaine was a wonder drug that produced feelings of euphoria without being addictive (Gawin & Kleber, 1992). Such a conservative source as the *Comprehensive Textbook of Psychiatry* in 1980 indicated that, "taken no more than two or three times per week, cocaine creates no serious problems" (Grinspoon & Bakalar, 1980). Just imagine—a drug that could give you extra energy, that could help you think clearly and more creatively and

could help you accomplish more throughout the day, all without any negative side effects! In our highly complex and competitive technological society, this would seem like a dream come true. But as you have probably realized by now, these temporary benefits come with a cost. We now know that cocaine fooled us. Unlike many of the other substances we have examined, cocaine dependence comes on slowly. Dependence often does not become apparent until 2 to 5 years after use begins (Gawin & Kleber, 1992). Few negative effects are noted at first; however, with continued use, sleep becomes disrupted, tolerance increases causing a need for higher doses, and the cocaine user gradually becomes socially isolated.

Again, Danny's case illustrates this pattern. He was a "social" cocaine user for a number of years, using it only with friends on an occasional basis. However, over the years, his use increased and he had more frequent episodes of excessive use or "binges." With the increased binges, he would find himself craving the drug more and more between the binges. After the binges, Danny would "crash" and sleep. What is deceptive for Danny and other cocaine abusers is that they go through a withdrawal phase that isn't like that of drugs such as alcohol. Instead of having symptoms such as rapid heart beat, tremors, or nausea, withdrawal from cocaine involves pronounced feelings of apathy and boredom. Think for a minute how dangerous this type of withdrawal is. You're bored with life and find little pleasure from the everyday activities of work or relationships. There is, however, one thing that can "bring you back to life"—cocaine. As you can imagine, a particularly vicious cycle develops

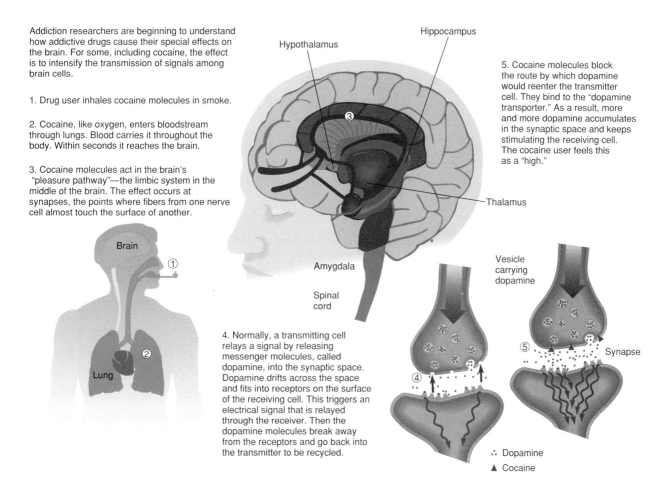

Addiction researchers are beginning to understand how addictive drugs cause their special effects on the brain. For some, including cocaine, the effect is to intensify the transmission of signals among brain cells.

1. Drug user inhales cocaine molecules in smoke.

2. Cocaine, like oxygen, enters bloodstream through lungs. Blood carries it throughout the body. Within seconds it reaches the brain.

3. Cocaine molecules act in the brain's "pleasure pathway"—the limbic system in the middle of the brain. The effect occurs at synapses, the points where fibers from one nerve cell almost touch the surface of another.

5. Cocaine molecules block the route by which dopamine would reenter the transmitter cell. They bind to the "dopamine transporter." As a result, more and more dopamine accumulates in the synaptic space and keeps stimulating the receiving cell. The cocaine user feels this as a "high."

4. Normally, a transmitting cell relays a signal by releasing messenger molecules, called dopamine, into the synaptic space. Dopamine drifts across the space and fits into receptors on the surface of the receiving cell. This triggers an electrical signal that is relayed through the receiver. Then the dopamine molecules break away from the receptors and go back into the transmitter to be recycled.

Figure 12.8 Anatomy of a high (from *The Washington Post*)

(cocaine abuse—apathy—cocaine abuse). It was this atypical withdrawal pattern that misled people into believing that cocaine was not "addicting." We now know that cocaine abusers go through patterns of tolerance and withdrawal comparable to those experienced by users of other psychoactive drugs (Gawin & Kleber, 1992).

Nicotine Use Disorders

When you think of "addicts," what image comes to mind? Do you see dirty and disheveled people huddled on an old mattress in an abandoned building, waiting for the next fix? Do you, instead, picture business people huddled outside a city building on a rainy afternoon furtively smoking cigarettes? Of course, both these images would be correct because the nicotine in cigarettes is a psychoactive substance that produces patterns of dependence, tolerance, and withdrawal—**nicotine use disorders**—comparable to the other drugs we have so far discussed. It was back in 1942 that the Scottish physician Lennox Johnson "shot up" the nicotine found in cigarettes and found after 80 injections that he liked it more than cigarettes and felt

deprived without it (Kanigel, 1988). He discovered that this colorless, oily liquid found in tobacco—called nicotine after Jean Nicot who introduced tobacco to the French court in the 16th century—was what gave smoking its pleasurable qualities.

Tobacco is indigenous to North America, and native Americans first cultivated and smoked the leaves of the tobacco plant centuries ago. Today, although the number continues to decline, almost a quarter of all Americans smoke. Unfortunately, we have not seen a decline in smoking among teenagers, and 17% of all high school seniors report that they smoke daily (U.S. Department of Health and Human Services, 1989); overall, approximately 2.2 million teenagers between the ages of 12 and 17 smoke.

DSM-IV does not describe an intoxication pattern for nicotine. Rather, it provides a description of the withdrawal from nicotine, which is listed in Table 12.8. Nicotine in small doses stimulates the central nervous system; it can also relieve stress and improve mood (U.S. Department of Health and Human Services, 1988). But it can cause high blood pressure and increase the risk of heart disease and cancer (McKim, 1991). Higher doses of the drug can

The addictive properties of nicotine drive people from their smoke-free offices.

blur your vision, cause confusion, lead to convulsions, and sometimes even cause death. Once they are dependent on nicotine, smokers also go through characteristic withdrawal symptoms when they stop smoking; these include irritability, anxiety, difficulty concentrating, hunger, and restlessness (Hughes, Gust, Skoog, Keenan, & Fenwick, 1991). And if you doubt the addictive power of nicotine, consider that the rate of relapse among people trying to give up drugs is comparable among those using alcohol, heroin, and cigarettes (see Figure 12.9).

When a person smokes a cigarette, he or she inhales nicotine into the lungs, where it enters the bloodstream. Only 7–19 seconds after a person inhales the smoke, the nicotine reaches the brain (Benowitz, 1992). Nicotine appears to stimulate recep-

tors specific to this chemical—*nicotinic receptors*—in the midbrain reticular formation and the limbic system, the site of the "pleasure pathway" we mentioned before with other substances (Knott, 1988). Smokers actually "dose" themselves throughout the day, in an effort to keep nicotine at a steady level in their bloodstream (10 to 50 nanograms per milliliter) (see Figure 12.10) (Dalack, Glassman, & Covey, 1993).

Despite the overwhelming evidence that nicotine is addictive and that smoking carries serious health risks, one group steadfastly refuses to accept these facts: the tobacco industry. These businesses earn billions of dollars each year on the sale of cigarettes, cigars, and related products. A glimpse into their position was recently provided by testimony from tobacco industry executives involved in a class-action lawsuit filed by

Table 12.8   DSM-IV Criteria for Nicotine Withdrawal

A. Daily use of nicotine for at least several weeks.

B. Abrupt cessation of nicotine use, or reduction in the amount of nicotine used, followed within 24 hours by four (or more) of the following signs:

  1. Dysphoric or depressed mood
  2. Insomnia
  3. Irritability, frustration, or anger
  4. Anxiety
  5. Difficulty concentrating
  6. Restlessness
  7. Decreased heart rate
  8. Increased appetite or weight gain

C. The symptoms in Criterion B cause clinically significant distress or impairment in social, occupational, or other important areas of functioning.

D. The symptoms are not due to a general medical condition and are not better accounted for by another mental disorder.

Source: DSM-IV, APA, 1994.

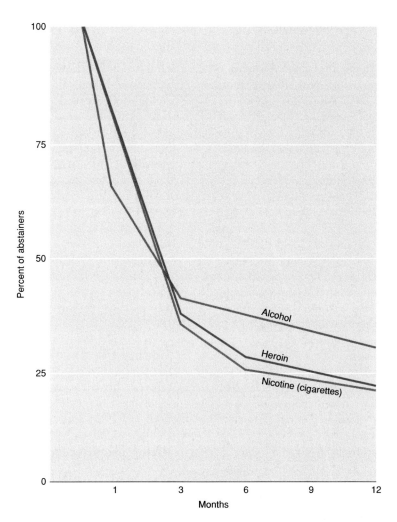

Figure 12.9 Relapse rates for nicotine compared to alcohol and heroin. Smokers trying to give up cigarettes backslide about as frequently as alcoholics and heroin addicts trying to give up their favorite drugs (adapted from Kanigel, 1988).

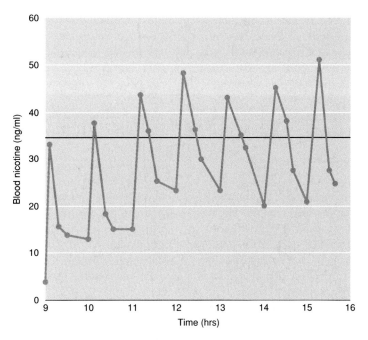

Figure 12.10 Smoking patterns and nicotine levels. This subject, who smoked one cigarette an hour, illustrates how smokers manipulate their smoking pattern, inhaling more or less deeply or more or less often, to get the desired blood levels of nicotine—on average 35 nanograms per milliliter (adapted from Kanigel, 1988).

flight attendants. The flight attendants contend that they were harmed by inflight smoking. What follows are excerpts from the executives' responses to attorney Stanley Rosenblatt's questions (Janofsky, 1993).

> **Mr. Rosenblatt:** Does cigarette smoking cause cancer?
>
> **Mr. Campbell** (president and chief executive, Philip Morris U.S.A.): To my knowledge, it's not been proven that cigarette smoking causes cancer.
>
> **Mr. Rosenblatt:** What do you base that on?
>
> **Mr. Campbell:** I base that on the fact that traditionally, there is, you know, in scientific terms, there are hurdles related to causation, and at this time there is no evidence that— they have not been able to reproduce cancer in animals from cigarette smoking.
>
> **Mr. Rosenblatt** (*to Bennett Lebow of Liggett and Meyers*): Is it fair to say, then, that since you're satisfied that you have a legal right to sell cigarettes, you have never really explored or studied the issue of whether or not cigarettes cause disease?
>
> **Mr. Lebow:** That is absolutely correct.
>
> **Mr. Rosenblatt:** If I asked you, does smoking cause lung cancer . . .
>
> **Mr. Lebow:** I don't know.
>
> **Mr. Rosenblatt:** O.K., and you really don't care because you are selling a legal product?
>
> **Mr. Lebow:** Correct.

Smoking and signs of negative affect such as depression, anxiety, and anger have for some time been linked together (Hall, Muñoz, Reus, & Sees, 1993). For example, many people who quit smoking but later go back to smoking report that feelings of depression or anxiety were responsible for the relapse (Marlatt & Gordon, 1980). This finding suggests that some people return to using cigarettes to help improve their mood. Cigarette smoking may help some people relieve feelings of anxiety and depression.

More recently, however, two studies have examined the complex relationship between cigarette smoking and negative affect. In one study, for example, severe depression was found to occur significantly more often among people with nicotine dependence (Breslau, Kilbey, & Andreski, 1993). This was true whether they continued smoking or tried to quit during the study period. In other words, people dependent on nicotine may be more likely than others to be depressed, whether they are trying to quit or they are not. A second, related study attempted to further explore this relationship between depression and smoking. Kenneth Kendler, whose large-scale twin study of depression among women we discussed in Chapter 4,

found that among identical twins there was a relationship between smoking and depression only if both pairs of identical twins had a history of depression or smoking (Kendler et al., 1993). In other words, if only one of the pair had a history of depression—and the other didn't—then there was no relationship between depression and smoking. What does this mean? It suggests that in some women there may be a genetic vulnerability that, combined with personal experiences, may lead to both depression and smoking. The implication is that some people may inherit a factor that makes them vulnerable to *both* depression and cigarette smoking—rather than suggesting that depression causes smoking or smoking causes depression. We discuss evidence for the genetics of smoking when we cover the causes of substance abuse later in this chapter.

Caffeine Use Disorders

The final stimulant we discuss is also the most common of the psychoactive substances, used regularly by 90% of all Americans (Goldstein, 1994). Called the "gentle stimulant" because it is thought to be the least harmful of all the addictive drugs, caffeine can still lead to **caffeine use disorders.** This drug is found in tea, coffee, many of the cola drinks sold today, and in cocoa products.

The DSM-IV criteria for caffeine intoxication are listed in Table 12.9. As most of you have experienced firsthand, caffeine in small doses can elevate your mood and decrease fatigue. Taken in larger doses, it makes you feel "jittery" and can cause insomnia. Because caffeine takes a relatively long time to leave our bodies (it has a blood "half-life" of about 6 hours), sleep can be disturbed if the caffeine is ingested in the hours close to bedtime (Bootzin, Manber, Perlis, Salvio, & Wyatt, 1993). As with the other psychoactive drugs, people react variously to caffeine, with some individuals being very sensitive to it and others able to consume relatively large amounts with little effect on them. Recent research suggests that moderate use of caffeine (a cup of coffee per day) by pregnant women does not harm the developing fetus (Mills et al., 1993).

Similarly to the other substances discussed here, regular caffeine use can result in tolerance and dependence on the drug. Those of you who have experienced headaches, drowsiness, and a generally unpleasant mood when denied your morning coffee have gone through withdrawal symptoms characteristic of this drug (Silverman, Evans, Strain, & Griffiths, 1992). Caffeine's effect on the brain seems to involve the neurotransmitter *adenosine*. Caffeine seems to block the reuptake of this transmitter by occupying its place at the adenosine receptors (Snyder, 1984). However, we do not yet know the role of adenosine in the way the brain functions, nor do we know whether this inter-

Table 12.9   DSM-IV Criteria for Caffeine Intoxication

A. Recent consumption of caffeine, usually in excess of 250 mg (e.g., more than 2–3 cups of brewed coffee).

B. Five (or more) of the following signs, developing during, or shortly after, caffeine use:

  1. Restlessness
  2. Nervousness
  3. Excitement
  4. Insomnia
  5. Flushed face
  6. Diuresis
  7. Gastrointestinal disturbance
  8. Muscle twitching
  9. Rambling flow of thought and speech
  10. Tachycardia or cardiac arrhythmia
  11. Periods of inexhaustibility
  12. Psychomotor agitation

C. The symptoms in Criterion B cause clinically significant distress or impairment in social, occupational, or other important areas of functioning.

D. The symptoms are not due to a general medical condition and are not better accounted for by another mental disorder (e.g., Anxiety Disorder).

Source: DSM-IV, APA, 1994.

ruption of the adenosine system is responsible for the feelings of elation and increased energy that come with caffeine use.

Opioid Use Disorders

The word *opiate* has been used to refer to the naturally occurring chemicals in the poppy that have a *narcotic* effect (they relieve pain and induce sleep). In some circumstances they can cause **opioid use disorders.** The broader term *opioids* is used to refer to the family of substances that include these opiates as well as synthetic variations created by chemists (for example, methadone, pethidine) and the similar-acting substances that occur naturally in the brain (for instance, enkephalins, beta-endorphins, and dynorphins) (Jaffe, 1991). Those of you who remember the movie *The Wizard of Oz* will also remember the scene when the Wicked Witch of the West puts Dorothy, Toto, and their companions to sleep by having them walk through a field of poppies. This literary allusion is a reference to the chemicals in poppies that in various forms include the opiates *opium, morphine, codeine,* and *heroin.*

The DSM-IV diagnostic criteria for opioid intoxication are listed in Table 12.10. Just as the poppies lulled the Tin Man, the Scarecrow, Dorothy, the Cowardly Lion, and Toto, these opiates bring on a feeling of euphoria, followed by drowsiness and

Table 12.10   DSM-IV Criteria for Opioid Intoxication

A. Recent use of an opioid.

B. Clinically significant maladaptive behavioral or psychological changes (e.g., initial euphoria followed by apathy, dysphoria, psychomotor agitation or retardation, impaired judgment, or impaired social or occupational functioning) that developed during, or shortly after, opioid use.

C. Pupillary constriction (or pupillary dilation due to anoxia from severe overdose) and one (or more) of the following signs, developing during, or shortly after, opioid use:

  1. Drowsiness or coma
  2. Slurred speech
  3. Impairment in attention or memory

D. The symptoms are not due to a general medical condition and are not better accounted for by another mental disorder.

Specify if:
  With Perceptual Disturbances

Source: DSM-IV, APA, 1994.

slowed breathing. At higher doses, this slowed breathing is more pronounced and can lead to death if respiration is completely depressed. These drugs are also *analgesics,* or substances that help relieve pain. People are sometimes given morphine before and after surgery because it will both calm them and help block the sensation of pain.

Withdrawal from opioids can be an extremely unpleasant experience. Efforts to avoid the unpleasant withdrawal symptoms partially account for why people continue to use these drugs despite their obvious desire to stop. However, the withdrawal symptoms following the cessation of barbiturate use or alcohol use can be more severe. The perception among many people that withdrawal from opioids can be life-threatening stems from the experiences of heroin addicts in the 1920s and 1930s. These users had access to cheaper and purer forms of the drug than are available today and withdrawal from these had more serious side effects than withdrawal from the weaker versions currently in use (McKim, 1991). Even so, people who cease or reduce their opioid use begin to experience symptoms within 6 to 12 hours; these include excessive yawning, nausea and vomiting, chills, muscle aches, diarrhea, and insomnia—often resulting in disruption in important areas of functioning such as work, school, or social relationships. The symptoms can persist for 1 to 3 days, and the process is completed in about a week.

Because of the clandestine nature of opiate use, estimates of the exact number of people who use, abuse, or are dependent on these drugs are difficult to come by, but one estimate is about one million people in the United States (Goldstein, 1994). We noted before that drug use seems to follow trends. Opiate use, and in particular heroin, was more popular in the early to mid 1970s, and has more recently been replaced by cocaine and its derivatives as the drug of choice (Uddo, Malow, & Sutker, 1993). Unfortunately, there is some indication that opiate use may be making a comeback, with a steady increase in abuse of "speedballs," a dangerous combination of both heroin and cocaine (Pollack, Brotman, & Rosenbaum, 1989). The concern for people who use opiates extends beyond the drugs' addictive qualities and the threat of overdose. Because most people who use these drugs inject them intravenously, they are at increased risk for HIV infection, and therefore AIDS.

The life of an addict dependent on opiates is bleak. Recently, results were published from a 24-year follow-up study conducted on over 500 addicts in California (Hser, Anglin, & Powers, 1993). Figure 12.11 illustrates the history of their addiction. At the follow-up in 1985–1986, 27.7% of these individuals had died, although the mean age at death was only about 40 years. Almost half the deaths were the results of homicide, suicide, or accident, and about a third were

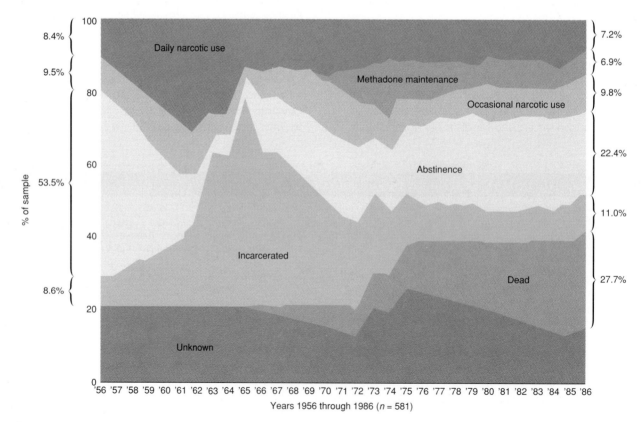

Figure 12.11 The natural history of narcotics addiction (from Hser et al., 1993)

from drug overdose. There is a fairly stable pattern of daily narcotic use in about 7%–8% of the group.

The "high" or "rush" experienced by users of this family of drugs comes from activation of the body's natural opioid system. In other words, the brain already has its own opioids—called enkephalins and endorphins—that provide narcotic effects (Barinaga, 1992). Ingesting heroin, opium, morphine, or other opiates activates this existing system. The discovery of this natural opioid system was a major breakthrough in the field of psychopharmacology: Not only does it allow us to study the effects of these addicting drugs on the brain, but it has led to important discoveries that may help us treat people dependent on these drugs.

Hallucinogen Use Disorder

The substances we have examined up to this point primarily affect people by making them feel "up" as in the case of the stimulants such as cocaine, caffeine, and nicotine, or "down" as with the depressants, which include alcohol and the barbiturates. Next we will explore the substances that can lead to **hallucinogen use disorder.** They essentially change the way the user perceives the world. Sight, sound, feelings, and even smell are distorted, sometimes in dramatic ways, when a person is under the influence of drugs such as marijuana and LSD.

Marijuana

Marijuana was the drug of choice in the 1960s and early 1970s. Although it has decreased in popularity, it continues to be the most routinely used of the illegal substances, with 66.5 million Americans reporting they

have tried marijuana and 5.5 million saying they smoke it at least once each week (Roffman & Stephens, 1993). Marijuana is the name given to the dried parts of the **cannabis** or hemp plant, its full scientific name being *cannabis sativa.* The cannabis plant grows wild throughout the tropical and temperate regions of the world, which accounts for one of its nicknames— "weed."

> Three men, so the story goes, arrived one night at the closed gates of a Persian city. One was intoxicated by alcohol, another was under the spell of opium, and the third was steeped in marihuana (hashish, as it was then called).
>
> The first blustered: "Let's break the gates down."
>
> "Nay," yawned the opium eater, "let us rest until morning, when we may enter through the wide-flung portals."
>
> "Do as you like," was the announcement of the marihuana addict. "But I shall stroll in through the keyhole!" (Rowell & Rowell, 1939)

As demonstrated by this parable, people who smoke marijuana often experience alterations in their perception of the world.

The DSM-IV diagnostic criteria for cannabis intoxication are listed in Table 12.11. Reactions to marijuana usually include mood swings—with otherwise normal experiences seeming to be extremely funny, or with the person entering a dreamlike state where time seems to stand still. Individuals often report heightened sensory experiences such as seeing vivid colors or appreciating the subtleties of music. Perhaps more than any of the other drugs, however, marijuana can produce very different reactions in people. It is not uncommon for someone to report having no reaction to his or her first use of the drug; it also appears that people can "turn off" the high of the drug if they are

Table 12.11   DSM-IV Criteria for Cannabis Intoxication

A. Recent use of cannabis.

B. Clinically significant maladaptive behavioral or psychological changes (e.g., impaired motor coordination, euphoria, anxiety, sensation of slowed time, impaired judgment, social withdrawal) that developed during, or shortly after, cannabis use.

C. Two (or more) of the following signs, developing within 2 hours of cannabis use:

1. Conjunctival injection
2. Increased appetite
3. Dry mouth
4. Tachycardia

D. The symptoms are not due to a general medical condition and are not better accounted for by another mental disorder.

Specify if:
With Perceptual Disturbances

Source: DSM-IV, APA, 1994.

sufficiently motivated (McKim, 1991). The feelings of well-being produced by small doses can change to paranoia, hallucinations, and dizziness when larger doses are used. Research on people who identify themselves as frequent marijuana users suggests that impairment of memory, concentration, motivation, self-esteem, relationships with others, and employment are common negative outcomes of long-term use (Haas & Hendin, 1987; Roffman & Barnhart, 1987). The impairment in motivation—an apathy or unwillingness to carry out long-term plans—has sometimes been called *amotivational syndrome,* although how prevalent this problem is remains controversial (McKim, 1991).

The evidence for users' tolerance of marijuana is contradictory. Among chronic and heavy users of the drug, there are reports of tolerance, especially to the euphoric "high" that often accompanies drug use (Johnson, 1991); users are unable to reach the levels of pleasure they had experienced earlier. However, there is also evidence of "reverse tolerance," when regular users report experiencing more of the pleasurable aspects of the drug after repeated use. The major signs of withdrawal seen with other drugs do not usually occur with marijuana. Chronic users who stop taking the drug will report a period of irritability, restlessness, appetite loss, nausea, and difficulty sleeping (Johnson, 1991); but there is no evidence that people go through the craving and psychological dependence characteristic of other substances.

Some controversy surrounds the use of marijuana for medicinal purposes. The popular media frequently present stories of individuals who illegally use marijuana to help ward off the nausea associated with chemotherapy or to ease the symptoms of other illnesses such as glaucoma. For a time, the Food and Drug Administration (FDA) allowed the "compassionate use" of marijuana among terminally ill patients, but in 1992 it banned the practice even under these circumstances.

Efforts continue, however, to determine whether marijuana has a place in medical treatment. In 1993 the FDA approved a study comparing the medicinal benefits of marijuana and Marinol, a synthetic, pill form of the main psychoactive chemical in marijuana (THC). Some users report that swallowing a pill is not as effective as smoking marijuana cigarettes (Stone, 1994). There is not currently a great deal of evidence that smoking marijuana produces relief beyond that of a placebo, but even this level of relief may be beneficial for some people. There is evidence, however, that marijuana smoke may contain as many carcinogens as tobacco smoke. Obviously this potential health risk should be weighed against the benefits of using marijuana under certain circumstances, such as with

cancer patients. The results of the FDA-approved study should help to clarify these important issues.

Most users of marijuana inhale the drug by smoking the dried leaves in marijuana cigarettes; others use preparations such as hashish, which is the dried resin from the top of the female plant. Marijuana includes over 80 varieties of substances called *cannabinoids*—the family of chemicals believed to be involved in its ability to alter mood and behavior. The most common of these chemicals includes the *tetrahydrocannabinols,* otherwise referred to as THC. One of the most exciting findings in the area of marijuana research has only recently appeared; it seems that the brain makes its own version of THC, as it makes its own opiates. This neurochemical is called *anandamide* after the Sanskrit word *ananda,* which means bliss (Fackelmann, 1993). Because this work is so new, scientists are only now beginning to explore how this neurochemical affects the brain and how it might affect our behavior.

LSD and Other Hallucinogens

On one ordinary Monday afternoon in April 1943, Albert Hoffmann, a scientist at a large Swiss chemical company, was preparing to test a newly synthesized compound on himself. He had been studying derivatives of ergot, a fungus that grows on diseased kernels of grain, and had an intuition that he had missed something important in the 25th compound of the lysergic acid series. Taking what he thought was an infinitesimally small amount of this drug—referred to in his notes as LSD-25—he waited to see what subtle changes might come over him as a result. Thirty minutes later he reported no change; but some 40 minutes after taking the drug he began to feel dizzy and had a noticeable desire to laugh. He decided to ride his bicycle home, and on the way began to hallucinate that the buildings he was passing were moving and melting. By the time he arrived home, he was terrified that he was losing his mind. Albert Hoffmann was experiencing the first recorded "trip" on LSD (Stevens, 1987).

LSD (d-lysergic acid diethylamide) is the most common of the hallucinogenic drugs. It is produced synthetically in laboratories, although naturally occurring derivatives of this grain fungus (ergot) have been found historically. In Europe during the Middle Ages, an outbreak of illnesses occurred as a result of people's eating grain that was infected with the fungus. One version of this illness—later called *ergotism—resulted in constriction of blood flow to the arms or legs and eventually gangrene and the loss of limbs. Another type of illness resulted in convulsions, delirium, and hallucinations. Years later, scientists connected ergot with the illnesses and began studying versions of this* fungus for possible benefits. This is the type of work Albert Hoffmann was engaged in when he discovered LSD's hallucinogenic properties. LSD remained primarily in the laboratory until the 1960s, when it began being produced illegally for recreational use. The mind-altering effects of this drug meshed well with the effort to reject the established culture and the search for enlightenment that characterized the mood and behavior of many people during that decade. Timothy Leary, at the time a Harvard research professor, first used LSD in 1961 and immediately began a movement to have every child and adult try the drug and "turn on, tune in, and drop out." A number of other hallucinogens exist, some occurring naturally in a variety of plants. These hallucinogens include *psilocybin* (found in certain species of mushrooms), *lysergic acid amide* (found in the seeds of the morning glory plant), *dimethyltryptamine* (DMT) (found in the bark of the Virola tree which grows in South and Central America), *mescaline* (found in the peyote cactus plant), and *phencyclidine* (PCP) (processed synthetically).

The DSM-IV diagnostic criteria for hallucinogen intoxication are listed in Table 12.12. Those who have used hallucinogens and have written about their effects describe a variety of experiences. The sensory distortions reported by Hoffmann are characteristic of reactions to these drugs. People tell of watching intently as a friend's ear grows and bends in beautiful spirals or looking at the bark of a tree and seeing little civilizations living there. These people will tell you that they usually know what they are seeing isn't real, but that nevertheless it looks as real as anything they have ever seen. But many also recount more intense experiences beyond just having hallucinations. The emotional content of these encounters can sometimes take on religious proportions.

A person quickly develops tolerance to a number of the hallucinogens, including LSD, psilocybin, and mescaline (McKim, 1991). If taken repeatedly over a period of days, these drugs completely lose their effectiveness. However, one's sensitivity does return after about a week of abstinence. For most of the hallucinogens, no withdrawal symptoms are reported. Even so, a number of concerns have surfaced over their use. One is the possibility of psychotic reactions among users. Stories in the popular press of people jumping out of windows believing they could fly or stepping out into moving traffic under the mistaken idea that they couldn't be hurt have provided for sensational reading, but there is little evidence that using the hallucinogens produces any increased risk over that of being drunk or under the influence of any other drug. People do report having "bad trips"; these usually involve frightening episodes such as watching the clouds overhead turn into threatening monsters or experiencing deep feelings of paranoia. Usually someone having a bad trip can be "talked down" by supportive people who provide constant reassurance that what the user is experiencing is the temporary effect of the drug he or she took, and that the effects of the hallucinogen should wear off after a few hours.

To date, we still do not fully understand how LSD and the other hallucinogens affect the brain. Most of these drugs bear some resemblance to neurotransmitters that naturally occur in the brain. For example, LSD, psilocybin, lysergic acid amide, and DMT (dimethyltryptamine) are chemically similar to the neurotransmitter serotonin; mescaline resembles norepi-

Table 12.12 DSM-IV Criteria for Hallucinogen Intoxication

A. Recent use of a hallucinogen.

B. Clinically significant maladaptive behavioral or psychological changes (e.g., marked anxiety or depression, ideas of reference, fear of losing one's mind, paranoid ideation, impaired judgment, or impaired social or occupational functioning) that developed during, or shortly after, hallucinogen use.

C. Perceptual changes occurring in a state of full wakefulness and alertness (e.g., subjective intensification of perceptions, depersonalization, derealization, illusions, hallucinations, synesthesia) that developed during, or shortly after, hallucinogen use.

D. Two (or more) of the following signs developing during, or shortly after, hallucinogen use:

   1. Pupillary dilation
   2. Tachycardia
   3. Sweating
   4. Palpitations
   5. Blurring of vision
   6. Tremors
   7. Incoordination

E. The symptoms are not due to a general medical condition and are not better accounted for by another mental disorder.

Source: DSM-IV, APA, 1994.

nephrine; and a number of other hallucinogens that we have not discussed are similar to acetylcholine. However, the mechanisms responsible for the hallucinations and other perceptual changes people experience from using the hallucinogens remain unknown.

Causes of Substance-Related Disorders

We have described a number of psychoactive drugs currently in use throughout the world today. Their effects on mood, perception, and behavior have caused people to continue their use despite the obvious negative consequences of abuse and dependence. In the case of Danny, we saw that, despite his clear potential as an individual, he continued to use drugs to his detriment. We next turn our attention to the various factors that help explain why people like Danny persist in the use of drugs in spite of the sometimes fatal outcomes they produce. Drug abuse and dependence, once thought to be the result of "moral weakness," appear to be influenced by a combination of biological and psychosocial factors.

Several basic questions concerning substance-related disorders are explored next. For example, why do some people use these drugs and not abuse or become dependent on them, while others do? Why do some people stop using these drugs or use them in

moderate amounts after being dependent on them, while others show a lifelong pattern of dependence despite their efforts to stop? These questions continue to occupy the time and effort of numerous researchers throughout the world, and we next turn our attention to this important work.

Biological Dimensions: Familial and Genetic Influences

In 1994, Mickey Mantle—the famed baseball player of the New York Yankees—experienced the most tragic event that can befall a parent: the death of his child. His son died while living in a rehabilitation center getting help for his addiction to drugs. Mickey Mantle himself had just recently finished a stay at the Betty Ford Clinic for his own, multi-year addiction to alcohol. Did his son inherit a vulnerability to become addicted to drugs from his father? Did he pick up Mickey's habits from living with him over the years? Is it just a case of a tragic coincidence that both father and son were dependent on drugs?

Students often misinterpret what is meant by a genetic vulnerability to having a certain disorder. They assume that the disorder is inevitable—in other words, they believe that the person *will* display the symptoms of this problem if their genetics dictate it. However, especially in the case of substance abuse, even if a given person inherits a vulnerability, abuse and dependence are not inevitable. First, the drug has to be available. The

Famed baseball player Mickey Mantle with his son Mickey Jr., both of whom suffered from drug addictions. Mickey Jr. later died as a result of complications due to his addiction.

connection between availability and abuse is the rationale for outlawing many drugs; if you can't get it, you can't become addicted. When the People's Republic of China was established in the late 1940s, that government was successful in virtually eliminating access to opium, thus effecting significant reductions in abuse of and dependence on it. Second, the genetically vulnerable person must choose to use the drug, and many choose not to, even avoiding those drugs that are legal and readily available (for example, alcohol). If you never drink, you can't become addicted to alcohol. People who have parents with serious addictions often choose never to use certain drugs, even on a one-time basis, because of the fear that they too will develop a dependency on drugs. Third, even if people try certain drugs, a genetic vulnerability does not automatically lead to dependence. These issues become important when we discuss the genetics of substance abuse and dependence.

A great deal of research with animals points to the importance of genetic influences in explaining substance abuse (Crabbe, McSwigan, & Belknap, 1985; Horowitz & Dudek, 1983). In work with humans, a handful of twin and adoption studies suggest that certain people may be vulnerable to drug abuse by virtue of their genetics (Cadoret, O'Gorman, Troughton, & Heywood, 1987). A recent twin study of smoking found a moderate genetic influence among male smokers (Carmelli, Swan, Robinette, & Fabsitz, 1992). However, the majority of genetic data on substance abuse comes from research on alcoholism. This is partly because alcohol use is legal (as opposed to use of such drugs as heroin, cocaine, marijuana, or the hallucinogens), and a great many people are dependent on this drug. Among men, both twin and adoption studies have suggested that genetic factors play a role in alcoholism (Bohman, Sigvardsson, & Cloninger, 1981; Cloninger, Bohman, & Sigvardsson, 1981; Cook & Gurling, 1991; Goodwin, 1979). The research on women, however, has sometimes been contradictory. Several studies have suggested that genetics is relatively unimportant to alcoholism among women (for instance, McGue, Pickens, & Svikis, 1992), while others suggest that the disorder may be inherited in some form (for example, Pickens et al., 1991).

To try to resolve the discrepancies in the research on the genetics of alcoholism among women, Kenneth Kendler and his fellow researchers surveyed a large number of women who were twins—a total of 1033 twin pairs—about their drinking habits (Kendler, Heath, Neale, Kessler, & Eaves, 1992). These researchers looked at a much larger sample of twins than had been examined in any previous studies, and also had the advantage of surveying women from the general population rather than those who were staying in psychiatric facilities or who were seeking treatment for

their alcohol problems. By looking only at women who have alcohol problems, previous researchers may have examined an unrepresentative group of women. In this study Kendler found that, like the men studied in previous research on genetics, women also seem to inherit a vulnerability to alcoholism (see Table 12.13). Kendler wisely used several definitions of alcoholism in this study—ranging from just problem drinking to alcoholism with both tolerance and dependence—and still found that the range of influence that could be explained by genetics was comparable to that of alcoholism among men regardless of the definition used (Kendler et al., 1992).

An interesting question remains: Why did Kendler's study find a strong relationship between genetics and substance abuse among women while other studies have not? Although we have already mentioned some of the methodological differences in these studies (size of the sample of twins, the nature of the study population), another explanation may shed some light on the complex interrelationship between genetic influences and psychosocial influences in the cause of substance abuse. The women in Kendler's study tended to be younger than the women in previous studies. Kendler believes that, as societal attitudes about drinking among women have become more permissive over the years, more women drink, and therefore more women are exposed to their genetic vulnerabilities to alcohol dependence. Because drinking had been more strongly discouraged among women in the past, the absence of women with drinking problems may have been related to their lack of access to alcohol rather than their lack of a genetic vulnerability. As our society has become more egalitarian in its attitudes toward women, a negative side effect may be the increased expression of genetic vulnerabilities to substance abuse.

The rapid advance of knowledge about the influence of genetic vulnerability has led to exciting

Table 12.13 Alcohol Problems Among Female Twin Pairs

Definition of Alcoholism	Concordance, MZ Twins	Concordance, DZ Twins
Narrow	26.2%	11.9%
Intermediate	31.6%	24.4%
Broad	46.9%	31.5%

Note: Narrow = Only alcoholism with dependence-tolerance.
Intermediate = Alcoholism with or without dependence-tolerance (the DSM-III-R definition of alcohol dependence).
Broad = Alcoholism with or without dependence-tolerance or problem drinking.

Source: Adapted from Kendler et al., 1992.

new findings about the relationship of inherited vulnerability to substance abuse. In 1990, a study was published suggesting that alcoholism may be related to a particular gene present on chromosome 11 (Blum et al., 1990). This gene (also referred to as DRD2) involves the neurotransmitter dopamine and appears to regulate the sensitivity of certain receptor sites (D_2 receptors) to this neurotransmitter. Blum and colleagues found that about two-thirds of the alcoholics they examined carried the DRD2 gene while only about one-fifth of the nonalcoholics did. Several studies have since replicated parts of this finding (Cloninger, 1991). Does this mean that the DRD2 gene causes people to be alcoholic? Not exactly. The research suggests that the DRD2 gene interacts with other factors to affect our susceptibility to alcoholism. In other words, just having the DRD2 gene is not sufficient by itself to cause someone to become alcoholic (note that one-fifth of Blum's nonalcoholics also had this gene), and *not* having the gene is no guarantee that you are protected from having problems with drinking (one-third of Blum's alcoholics did not have the DRD2 gene). As we will see later in this chapter, the dopamine system is involved with the ability of drugs to provide us with pleasurable experiences or to block unpleasant ones, and the DRD2 gene may influence this system to increase the positive quality of these experiences. This hypothesis seems to be supported by recent evidence that abuse of drugs in addition to alcohol among polysubstance abusers (people who regularly abuse two or more drugs) is also affected by the DRD2 gene (Smith et al., 1992).

One genetic factor that appears to be involved in alcoholism involves the body's ability to metabolize alcohol. We previously described how the liver produces an enzyme (called aldehyde dehydrogenase) that breaks down a by-product of alcohol, a chemical called acetaldehyde. If acetaldehyde is not broken down and is allowed to build up in a person's body, the person becomes very ill. Efforts to get people to stop drinking by giving them drugs such as Antabuse (the trade name for the drug disulfiram) accomplish their aim by chemically preventing the breakdown of acetaldehyde and making people feel sick when they drink. In one particular group of people—those of Asian descent—the enzyme responsible for breaking down acetaldehyde seems to be absent naturally. It appears that the gene that produces this enzyme is altered or mutated in many Asians, and they therefore have difficulty metabolizing alcohol (Goedde & Agarwal, 1987; Yoshida, Huang, & Ikawa, 1984). The result is a physiological response, known as the alcohol-flush syndrome or skin-flushing response, characterized by reddening and warmth on the face, dizziness, and nausea; it is experienced by 30% to 50% of Asian individuals and is thought to contribute partially to the

relatively low rates of alcohol use among people from this group (Newlin, 1989).

The genetic research to date tells us that substance abuse is affected by our genes. However, just as we have seen with all the disorders described in this book, no one gene causes people to abuse or become dependent on psychoactive substances. Research on the DRD2 gene, the different types of alcohol abuse patterns, and the gene responsible for making aldehyde dehydrogenase suggests that genetic factors may affect how people experience certain drugs, which in turn may partly determine who will or will not abuse these drugs.

Biological Dimensions: Neurobiological Influences

We turn now to the neurobiological factors that affect drug use—such as the influence of the dopamine system—and how these systems contribute to substance use and abuse. For the most part, the pleasurable experience reported by people who use psychoactive substances (an experience that is different for the different drugs) seems to play an important role in explaining why people continue to use them. In behavioral terms, people are *positively reinforced* for using drugs because of these pleasurable consequences. But what mechanism is responsible for these experiences? A series of complex but fascinating studies points to evidence that our brain appears to have a natural reward center or "pleasure pathway" that mediates our experience of reward. And although we have reviewed the effects of the different drugs and how they interact with different neurotransmitter systems, all the abused substances seem to have an effect on this internal reward center. In other words, what these drugs may have in common is their ability to activate this reward center and provide the user with a pleasurable experience, at least for a time.

The story of the pleasure center in the brain begins over 40 years ago with the work of James Olds, who studied the effects of electrical stimulation of rat brains (Olds, 1956; Olds & Milner, 1954). Olds found that, if certain areas of the brain were stimulated with very small amounts of electricity, rats behaved as if they had received something very pleasant, such as food. The exact location of this area in the brain in humans is still subject to debate, although it is believed to include the *dopaminergic system* along with *opioid-releasing neurons*. Many of the neurons in this system begin in the midbrain region, in an area called the *ventral tegmental area,* and then work their way forward through the *nucleus accumbens* and on to the *frontal cortex* (Korenman & Barchas, 1993). This is the area of the brain thought to be involved with our experience of reward.

How do different drugs, many of which affect completely different neurotransmitter systems, all converge in this one area to activate the pleasure pathway, which is primarily made up of dopamine-sensitive neurons? Researchers are only now beginning to sort out the answers to this question, but some surprising findings have emerged in recent years. For example, we know that drugs such as amphetamine and cocaine act directly on the dopamine system, causing more of this neurochemical to be available. Taking these drugs seems to activate the reward center directly by activating dopamine. The other drugs, however, appear to affect this system in more roundabout and intricate ways. For example, the neurons in one portion of the pleasure pathway—the ventral tegmental area—are held back from firing continuously by GABA neurons. If you remember, the GABA system is an inhibitory neurotransmitter system that functions to block other neurons from sending information. One thing that keeps us from being on an unending "high" is the presence of these GABA neurons, acting as the "brain police" or superegos of the reward neurotransmitter system. One group of drugs that seems to inhibit GABA release is the opiates (opium, morphine, heroin). The opiates, then, inhibit GABA, which in turn stops the GABA neurons from inhibiting dopamine, allowing more dopamine to be available in the reward center. The drugs that have been shown in some way to stimulate the reward center directly or indirectly include not only amphetamine, cocaine, and the opiates, but also nicotine and alcohol (Goldstein, 1994; Koob, 1992).

This complicated picture is far from complete. There may be other pleasure pathways operating in the brain (Wise, 1988). The coming years should yield even more interesting insights into the interaction of drugs of abuse and the brain. One of the areas that awaits explanation is the way drugs not only provide pleasurable experiences (the positive reinforcement process we just discussed) but also how these substances help to remove unpleasant experiences such as pain, feelings of illness, or anxiety (negative reinforcement). An everyday example of a negative reinforcer would be aspirin. Our reason for taking aspirin is not because it makes us feel good; we take it because it stops us from feeling bad. In much the same way, another property of the psychoactive drugs is that they stop people from feeling bad, an effect that is as powerful as making people feel good.

Related to this concept of negative reinforcement is the anxiolytic effect that several drugs have. This is the ability to reduce anxiety, a property discussed briefly in the section on the sedative, hypnotic, and anxiolytic drugs. Alcohol too has an anxiolytic effect. The neurobiology of how these drugs reduce anxiety seems to involve the septal/hippocampal system in the

James Olds studied the effects of electrical stimulation of rat brains.

brain (Gray, 1987). This area of the brain includes a large number of GABA sensitive neurons; certain drugs may reduce anxiety by enhancing the activity of GABA in this region, thereby inhibiting the brain's normal reaction (anxiety/fear) to anxiety-producing situations (Pihl, Peterson, & Lau, 1993).

Researchers have identified individual differences in the way people respond to at least one of the abused substances—alcohol. Understanding these response differences is important because they may help explain why some people continue to use drugs until they acquire a dependency on them while others stop before this happens. Newlin and Thomson (1990) reviewed numerous studies comparing individuals with and without a family history of alcoholism. They concluded that, compared to the sons of nonalcoholics, the sons of alcoholics may be more sensitive to alcohol when it is first ingested, and then become less sensitive to its effects as the hours pass after drinking. This finding is significant because the euphoric effects of alcohol occur just after drinking, but the experience after several hours is often feelings of sadness and depression. People who are at risk for developing alcoholism (in this case, the sons of alcoholics) may be better able to appreciate the initial "highs" of drinking and be less sensitive to the "lows" that come later, making them ideal candidates for continued drinking. In support of this observation, a recent study followed the sons of alcoholics and sons of nonalcoholics for 10 years and found that those men who tended to be less sensitive to alcohol also tended to drink more heavily and more often (Schuckit, 1994).

One line of research examining the neurobiology of alcoholism involves studying the brain wave patterns of people who are at risk for developing alcoholism. In this research, the sons of people with alcohol problems are recruited to participate, because of their increased likelihood of having alcohol problems compared with people in the general population. Subjects in these studies are asked to sit quietly in a room and listen for a particular tone. When they hear the tone, they are to signal the researcher. During this time, their brain waves are monitored and a particular pattern emerges called the *P300 amplitude.* At approximately 300 milliseconds (which is the origin of the "P300" designation) after the tone is presented, a characteristic "spike" in brain waves occurs that indicates the brain's processing of this information. In general, researchers find that this spike is lower among males with a family history of alcoholism (Polich, Pollock, & Bloom, 1994).

Is this brain wave difference somehow connected to the reasons people later develop a dependence on alcohol, or is it just a "marker" or sign that these individuals have in common but one that is otherwise not related to their drinking? One piece of evidence that argues against the P300 difference as a marker for alcoholism is that individuals with a variety of other psychological disorders—for example, schizophrenia, depression—also show lower P300 amplitude compared to control subjects (Polich, Pollock, & Bloom, 1994). It is not yet clear whether or how the P300 amplitude is related to alcoholism, although researchers continue trying to understand this interesting but puzzling phenomenon.

Psychological Dimensions

Positive Reinforcement

We have shown that the different substances people use to alter their mood and behavior have different effects. The "high" from heroin differs substantially from the experience of smoking a cigarette, which in turn differs from the results of taking amphetamines or LSD. Despite these differences, it is important to point out the similarities in the way people react to most of these substances. We have already mentioned the evidence for viewing these drugs as positive reinforcers. In other words, the feelings that result from using them are all pleasurable in some way, and people will continue to readminister the drugs to recapture this experience. Research shows quite clearly that many of the drugs used and abused by humans also seem to be pleasurable to animals (Young & Herling, 1986). Laboratory animals will self-administer—work to have the drug injected into their bodies—drugs such as cocaine, amphetamines, opiates, sedatives, and alcohol, a result demonstrating that even without social and cultural influences these drugs are pleasurable.

Human research also indicates that to some extent all the psychoactive drugs provide a pleasurable experience (Goldstein, 1994). People are often very inventive in how they administer these drugs in order to maximize their euphoric effects. For example, individuals dependent on heroin will sometimes combine their dose with benzodiazepines (for instance, Valium) to intensify their pleasure (American Psychiatric Association, 1990). Users of cocaine will often heat the drug and inhale the fumes—a process known as "freebasing"—or use the highly concentrated form known as "crack" to obtain a more rapid and intense experience. These activities tend to increase as the person's tolerance of the drug increases and more of the substances are needed to produce the "high" that is the hallmark of drug use.

Negative Reinforcement

Most research has looked at how drugs help reduce unpleasant feelings through negative reinforcement. Many people probably initiate and continue drug use to escape from the unpleasant experiences of their lives. In addition to the initial pleasant feelings that accompany the use of some substances, many drugs provide people escape from physical pain (for example, opiates), from thinking about stresses in their lives (for instance, alcohol), and from feelings of panic and anxiety (for example, benzodiazepines). This phenomenon has been explored under a number of different names, including *tension reduction, negative affect,* and *self-medication,* each of which has a somewhat different focus (Cappell & Greeley, 1987).

Basic to many views of abuse and dependence is the premise that substance use becomes a way for users to cope with the unpleasant feelings that go along with life circumstances (Cooper, Russell, & George, 1988). One tragic example of this phenomenon can be seen in the drug experiences of soldiers who were in Vietnam. A significant number of these mostly young men became addicted to heroin while in that country, because of their exposure to the drug and because of the extreme stress associated with the fighting. It is interesting that only 12% of these soldiers were still using heroin within 3 years of their return to the United States (Robins, Helzer, & Davis, 1975), a fact suggesting that, once the stressors were removed, they no longer needed the drug to relieve their pain. While they may have become dependent on heroin under the extreme stress of war, once this stress was gone, their need for a drug was reduced and many of them successfully stopped taking heroin. This observation again points to the important role played by each aspect of abuse and dependence—biological, psychological, social, and cultural—in determining who will and who will not have difficulties with these substances.

A recent study has examined the development of substance use among adolescents as a way to reduce stress (Chassin, Pillow, Curran, Molina, & Barrera, 1993). These researchers compared one group of adolescents, who had at least one biological parent with an addiction to alcohol, with a second group of adolescents whose parents did not have drinking problems. The average age of the adolescents in these two groups was 12.7 years. The researchers found that just having a parent with alcohol dependency was a major factor in predicting which of the adolescents would use alcohol and other drugs. However, they also found that children who reported negative affect, such as feeling lonely, crying a lot, or being tense, were more likely than others to use drugs. The researchers were further able to determine that these adolescents tended to use drugs as a way to cope with their unpleasant feelings. Although this study needs to be replicated by other researchers, it suggests that one contributing factor to children's drug use is their desire to escape from the unpleasantness of their lives. It also suggests that, to prevent people from using drugs, we may need to address influences such as stress and anxiety, a strategy that we will discuss in our section on treatment.

One type of response experienced by many people who use psychoactive substances is the "crash" after a period of being "high." These negative experiences are characteristic of most of the substances we have reviewed and are the withdrawal symptoms described in the beginning of this chapter. If people reliably "crash" after a period of time, why don't they just stop taking these drugs? One explanation is given by Solomon and Corbit in an interesting integration of both the positive and negative reinforcement processes (Solomon & Corbit, 1974; Solomon, 1980). Called the *opponent-process theory,* this account suggests that when a person experiences an increase in positive feelings, it will be followed by an increase in negative feelings a short time afterward. Similarly, if a person has an increase in negative feelings, it will be followed by a period of time with positive feelings. Athletes often report a period of feeling depressed after finally attaining a long-sought goal. In the case of the psychoactive substances, this describes the "high" individuals initially experience and the "crash" that follows. The opponent-process theory claims that this mechanism is strengthened with use and weakened by disuse. So, after a person takes a drug for a period of time, he or she will need more to achieve the same results (tolerance). At the same time, the negative feelings that result following drug use tend to intensify. For many people, this is the point at which the motivation for drug taking shifts from a desire for the euphoric high to a need to alleviate the increasingly unpleasant negative feelings that follow drug use.

Unfortunately, the best remedy for these unpleasant feelings is more of the same drug. People with a "hangover" after drinking too much alcohol are often given this advice—humorously referred to as having the "hair of the dog that bit you." There is a sad irony here. The very drug that can make you feel so bad is also the one thing that can take away your pain. You can see why people can become enslaved by this insidious process.

Researchers have also addressed people's continued drug use by looking at substance abuse as a way users self-medicate for other problems. If people have difficulties with anxiety, for example, they may be attracted to barbiturates or alcohol because of the drugs' anxiety-reducing qualities. In one illustrative study, researchers found that they were successful in treating a small group of cocaine addicts who had attention deficit disorder (a disorder that makes it difficult for people to concentrate and focus their attention for extended periods of time) with methylphenidate (Ritalin) (Khantzian, Gawin, Kleber, & Riordan, 1984). They hypothesized that these individuals used cocaine to help focus their attention. Once their ability to concentrate improved with the methylphenidate, the users stopped ingesting cocaine. Taken together, this research is just beginning to outline the complex interplay among the stressors in our lives, negative feelings, the presence of other psychological disorders, and the negative reactions to the drugs themselves as causative factors in psychoactive drug use.

Cognitive Factors

What people expect to experience when they use drugs will also influence how they react to them. If a person expects to be less inhibited when she drinks alcohol, she will act less inhibited whether she actually drinks alcohol or a placebo that she thinks is alcohol (Cooper, Russell, Skinner, Frone, & Mudar, 1992; Wilson, 1987). This observation about the influence of cognition or thoughts about drug use has been labeled an *expectancy effect* and has received considerable research attention.

These expectancies seem to develop before people actually use drugs, perhaps as a result of being exposed to parents' and peers' drug use, advertising, or other media figures who model drug use (Miller, Smith, & Goldman, 1990). In one study, a large group of seventh and eighth graders were given questionnaires that focused on their expectations about drinking. The researchers reexamined the students 1 year later to see how their expectancies predicted their later drinking (Christiansen, Smith, Roehling, & Goldman, 1989). One surprising finding was the marked increase in drinking among the students only 1 year later. When researchers first questioned them, about 10% of the students reported getting drunk 2–4 times per year. This number had risen to 25% of the students by the time they were requestioned the next year. The researchers also found that the students' expectations of drinking did predict who would later have problems drinking. Students who thought that drinking would improve their social behavior as well as their cognitive and motor abilities (despite all evidence to the contrary) were more likely to have problems drinking 1 year later. These results suggest that one factor influencing why children begin drinking may be their belief that drinking will have positive effects on them.

Expectations about drug use appear to change as people have more experience with drugs, although the expectations appear similar whether the drug is alcohol, nicotine (Brandon & Baker, 1992), marijuana, or cocaine (Schafer & Brown, 1991). One theory about why drug abusers *relapse* (fail in their efforts to abstain from using drugs and go back to their use) suggests that the users' expectations about the positive effects of the drug—called "urges"—are in part responsible (Baker, Morse, & Sherman, 1987; Tiffany, 1990). If you've ever tried to give up ice cream, and then found yourself compelled to have some, you have some limited idea of what it might be like to have a craving or urge for a drug. These urges seem to be triggered by factors such as the availability of the drug, coming in contact with things that have been associated with drug taking (for example, sitting in a bar), or having a small dose of the drug; any one may motivate the person to "fall off the wagon" and reabuse drugs (Goldman & Rather, 1993).

One factor studied so far only in people who drink alcohol is a cognitive phenomenon called *alcohol myopia*. This condition has been defined as "a state of shortsightedness in which superficially understood, immediate aspects of experience have a disproportionate influence on behavior and emotion" (Steele & Josephs, 1990, p. 923). Picture someone who is drunk, carefully and methodically placing one foot in front of the other as he walks so as not to fall, walking straight into the path of an oncoming truck. Although alcohol myopia may not be useful in explaining why people drink in the first place, it may help us understand why people continue to drink despite knowing that excess drinking can have severe negative consequences. People who are under the influence of alcohol may not be able to evaluate properly the risks involved in their continued drinking.

Social Dimensions

Previously we pointed out the importance of exposure to psychoactive substances as a necessary prerequisite to their use and possible abuse. You could probably list a number of ways people are exposed to these substances—through friends, through the media, and

so on. One recent study has looked at how early in their social development very young children might be introduced to drugs (Noll, Zucker, & Greenberg, 1990). Children between the ages of 3 and 6 were given a smelling task at their school. They were told to close their eyes and try to tell just by smelling what was in a jar. Nine different substances were presented to them; apple juice, Playdoh, popcorn, coffee, perfume, beer, whiskey, wine, and cigarettes. Of the older children in this group, more than half could already recognize either beer, wine, or whiskey, while 20% of the youngest children were able to identify alcohol. The importance of this study is its suggestion that many children are exposed to alcohol as preschoolers; because the children in this study were able to identify the substances by smell, it seems that they learn about alcohol at home rather than just from television.

Another influence from the home seems to lead to exposure to drugs *indirectly*. Research among children suggests that drug-addicted parents spend less time monitoring their children than do parents without drug problems (Dishion, Patterson, & Reid, 1988), and a recent study found that an important contribution to early adolescent substance use was this lack of parental monitoring (Chassin, Pillow, Curran, Molina, & Barrera, 1993). When parents did not appropriately supervise their children, the children developed friendships with peers who supported drug use. Not only do children observe and become influenced by drug use at home; use of drugs by parents may lead to their children's being exposed to peers who use drugs as well. There seems to be a self-perpetuating pattern associated with drug use that extends beyond just the genetic influences we discussed previously.

How does our society view people who are dependent on drugs? This issue is of tremendous importance because it will affect efforts to legislate the sale, manufacture, possession, and use of these substances. It will also dictate how these drug-dependent individuals are treated in our society. Two views of substance abuse and dependence characterize contemporary thought—*moral weakness* and the *disease model* of dependence. The moral weakness view sees drug use as a failure on the part of these people to control themselves in the face of temptation. Drug users lack the "character" or "moral fiber" to resist the lure of drugs. We saw earlier, for example, that the Catholic Church recently made drug abuse an official sin—an indication of its disdain of this behavior. The disease model, on the other hand, assumes that drug dependency is caused by an underlying physiological disorder. Just as having diabetes or asthma can't be blamed on the afflicted individuals, neither should drug dependency. In a sense, the disease model is less judgmental than the moral view. Alcoholics Anonymous and similar organizations see drug dependency as a disease—one that you have for a lifetime and over which you have no control (Marlatt, 1985).

This distinction marks the clear difference between a psychosocial (moral weakness) versus a biological (disease) view of substance-related disorders. Obviously, neither of these views alone does justice to the complex interrelationship between the psychosocial and biological influences that affect these disorders. The disease model does not involve blaming people for the problem. A societal view of drug use as moral weakness tends to punish those afflicted with the disorder, while a disease model tends to seek treatment for the problem, which is presumed to be medical. On the other hand, people can certainly have an impact on the outcome of their treatment for drug abuse and dependence, and messages that this disorder is "out of their control" can at times be counterproductive. A more comprehensive view of substance-related disorders—which includes both psychosocial and biological influences—will be needed if this important societal concern is to be addressed adequately.

Cultural Dimensions

When you examine a behavior across different cultures, it is necessary to reexamine what is considered abnormal behavior (Matsumoto, 1994). In the area of substance abuse, each culture has its own preferences for psychoactive drugs as well as its own proscriptions for substances it finds unacceptable. Keep in mind that these cultural norms, in addition to defining what is or is not acceptable, will affect the rates of substance abuse and dependence in important ways. As an example, certain cultures including that of Korea expect their members to engage in heavy use of particular drugs such as alcohol on certain social occasions (Lee, 1992). As we have seen before, exposure to these substances—in addition to the social expectations and pressure for heavy and frequent use—may facilitate their abuse, and this may explain the high abuse rates in countries like Korea. On the other hand, poor economic conditions in certain parts of the world may limit the availability of drugs, which appears in part to account for the relatively low prevalence of substance abuse in Mexico and Brazil (de Almeidia-Filho, Santana, Pinto, & de Carvalho-Neto, 1991; Ortiz & Medicna-Mora, 1988).

Cultural factors will not only influence the rates of substance abuse but can also affect the manifestation of this abuse. Research from both Poland and Finland indicates that alcohol consumption in those countries is relatively low, yet conflicts related to drinking and arrests for drunkenness in Poland and Finland are high compared to those in a country like the Netherlands, which has about the same rate of alcohol consumption (Osterberg, 1986). If you remember our

discussion of expectancies, it may provide some insight into how the same amount of drinking can have different behavioral outcomes. Possibly expectancies about the effects of alcohol use differ across cultures (for example, "Drinking makes me more aggressive" versus "Drinking makes me more withdrawn"); these differing expectancies could partially account for the variations in the consequences of drinking in countries such as Poland, Finland, and the Netherlands. Whether substance use is considered a "harmful dysfunction" often depends on how the people in each cultural group respond to this use.

As yet we do not know whether biological differences across cultures contribute to the varying use and abuse rates. Looking ahead to what we may find through future research, it is important for us to consider that biological differences may interact with cultural norms in a complex way. For example, it seems logical that cultural norms may be created over time as a consequence of biological difference. Certain cultures may adapt their drug use (for instance, condoning substance use only in "safe" social surroundings) based on their own idiosyncratic reactions to these drugs (for example, a tendency to react aggressively). On the other hand, for other disorders we have seen how behavior can also affect biology, and we may discover that the norms established by a society affect the biology of the people living in that group. Research on the cultural influences of substance abuse is in its infancy, but it may hold great promise for helping to unravel the mysteries of this disorder.

An Integrative Model of Substance-Related Disorders

Any explanation of substance use, abuse, and dependence must account for one of the basic issues raised earlier in this chapter: "Why do some people use, but not abuse or become dependent on drugs?" Figure 12.12 illustrates one view of how the multiple influences we have discussed may come together to account for this process. Exposure or access to the drug is a necessary but obviously not sufficient condition for drug abuse or dependence. This exposure can come from many influences, including the media, parents, peers, and indirectly from a lack of supervision. Whether people use a drug will depend also on social and cultural expectations about its use, with certain practices encouraging substance use and other practices discouraging its use—such as making laws against possession or sale of the drug.

The path from drug use to abuse and dependence is more complicated (see Figure 12.12). As with many of the disorders we have discussed, the presence

Figure 12.12   An integrative model of substance-related disorders

of major stressors seems to increase the risk of abuse and dependence on psychoactive substances. Here genetic influences appear to play a part, and these may be of several different types. For example, some individuals may inherit a greater sensitivity to the effects of certain drugs; others may inherit an ability to metabolize substances more quickly, thereby being able to tolerate higher—and more dangerous—levels of drugs. Some may display other psychiatric conditions that indirectly put them at risk for substance abuse. For example, individuals with antisocial personality disorder—a disorder characterized by the frequent violation of social norms—are thought to have lower rates of arousal than others, and this may account for the increased prevalence of substance abuse among this group (see Chapter 13). Still others with mood disorders or anxiety disorders may self-medicate, or use drugs to relieve the negative symptoms that characterize their disorder, a practice that may account for the high rates of substance abuse among these individuals.

The concept of equifinality (the notion that a particular disorder may arise from multiple and different paths) seems particularly appropriate here. It is clear that abuse of and dependence on any of the substances cannot be predicted from one factor, be it genetic, neurobiological, psychological, or cultural. We saw, for example, that *some* people with the DRD2 gene—the gene common to many people with substance abuse problems—do not go on to substance abuse. Many other individuals who experience the most crushing of life's stressors, such as living in abject poverty or being the target of bigotry and violence, seem to cope without resorting to drug use. There appear to be different pathways to drug abuse, and we are only now beginning to identify the basic outlines of these trails toward drug dependence.

Once a drug is used repeatedly, the brain's reaction in the areas of biology and cognition conspire to contribute to dependence. Continual use of most drugs causes tolerance, which then requires the user to ingest more of the drug to produce the same effect.

Also, conditioning develops around drug use. Associating pleasurable experiences with certain settings will later cause urges to develop in people, even if the drugs themselves are not available.

This obviously complex picture still does not do justice to the intricacies of the lives of the individuals who ultimately develop substance-related disorders. Each person has his or her own story, and his or her own path to abuse and dependence. We have only begun to scratch the surface on the commonalities of this vexing problem. We need to understand a great deal more about how all the factors interact to produce this disorder.

Treatment of Substance-Related Disorders

When we left Danny, he was in jail, awaiting the legal outcome of his arrest for robbery. At this point in his life Danny needed more than legal help; he needed to rid himself of his addiction to a number of drugs, including alcohol and cocaine. And the first step in his recovery had to come from him. Danny needed to admit he needed help, that he did indeed have a problem with drugs, and that he needed others to help him overcome this chronic dependency. This factor—having the motivation to work on a drug problem—appears to be essential in the treatment of substance abuse (Miller, 1985). A therapist cannot help someone who doesn't want to change, and this can be a problem in treating substance abuse just as it is for people with disorders such as anorexia nervosa and antisocial personality disorder. Fortunately (and at last), Danny's arrest seemed to shock him into realizing how serious his problems had become, and he was now ready to confront them head-on.

Treating people who have substance-related disorders is a difficult task. Perhaps because of the many ways people can come to use these drugs and because of the combination of influences that sometimes work together to keep them "hooked," the outlook for those who are dependent on drugs is often not very positive. We will see in the case of heroin dependence, for example, that a best-case scenario is often just trading one addiction (heroin) for another (methadone). And even for those people who successfully cease taking drugs, the urges and cravings to resume their drug use may last a lifetime.

Treatment for Danny and for others with substance-related disorders focuses on several areas. In certain cases the treatment is designed to help them through the withdrawal process; typically, the ultimate goal is abstinence. In other situations the goal is to get people to maintain a certain level of drug use without escalating its intake, and sometimes it is geared toward preventing people from being exposed to drugs. Because the causes of substance abuse cut across just about all the influences we have discussed in this book, it should not be surprising that treating people who abuse and are dependent on these substances is not a simple matter of finding just the right drug or the best way to change thoughts or behavior.

We discuss here the treatment of substance-related disorders as a group. We do so because of the commonalities that exist in these treatments. For example, many of the programs that treat people for dependence on a variety of substances attempt to teach users skills to cope with the stressors in their lives. Other, biological research also has a common theme and has looked at how to mask the effects of the substances being ingested. At the same time, there are obvious differences among these substances, and we discuss these differences as they arise.

Biological Treatments

Agonist Substitution

Our increased knowledge about the workings of the psychoactive drugs on the brain has led researchers to explore ways to change the way these drugs are experienced by people dependent on them. One method is called **agonist substitution,** and it involves providing the person with another drug that has a chemical makeup similar to the addictive drug (therefore the name *agonist*). *Methadone* is an opiate agonist and is often given as a substitute to people addicted to heroin. Methadone is a synthetic narcotic that was developed in Germany during World War II when morphine was not available; it was originally called *adolphine* after Adolph Hitler (Bellis, 1981). Although it does not give the user the quick high of heroin, methadone does initially provide the same analgesic (pain reducing) and sedative effects. With increased use, however, users develop a tolerance for methadone and it loses its analgesic and sedative qualities. Because heroin and methadone are *cross-tolerant,* acting on the same neurotransmitter receptors, the effect on a heroin addict of taking methadone is to become addicted to methadone in place of heroin. Research on the use of methadone as a treatment for heroin addiction suggests that, when addicts combine its use with regular counseling, many reduce their use of heroin and engage in less criminal activity (Ball & Ross, 1991). All the news is not good, however. A proportion of people under methadone treatment continue to abuse other substances such as cocaine (Condelli, Fairbank, Dennis, & Rachal, 1991) and benzodiazepines (Iguchi et al., 1990). The results from research in this area suggest that some

A heroin addict receives methadone mixed with orange juice at a clinic in Brooklyn, New York.

people benefit significantly from using methadone as a substitute for heroin, but they may have to use methadone for the rest of their lives.

Addiction to cigarette smoking has also been addressed through a substitution process in the form of *nicotine gum* and the *nicotine patch*. Nicotine is provided to smokers by prescription in a form (by mouth for the gum and through the skin with the patch) that lacks the carcinogens included in cigarette smoke; the dose is later tapered off to lessen withdrawal from the drug. In general, nicotine gum has been successful in helping people stop smoking, although its effects are best when it is combined with supportive psychological therapy (Cepeda-Benito, 1993; Hughes, 1993). Problems with nicotine gum treatment include the need to teach people how to use it properly, and the fact that about 20% of people who successfully quit smoking with it become dependent on the gum itself (Hughes et al., 1991). Possibly because the nicotine patch, unlike the gum, requires less effort and provides a steadier nicotine replacement, it may be somewhat more effective in helping people quit smoking (Hughes, 1993). For both these treatments, however, if they are used without a more comprehensive psychological treatment program (see below), a substantial number of smokers relapse after the gum or patch is stopped (Cepeda-Benito, 1993).

A teenager uses a nicotine patch to help curb her urge to smoke.

Antagonist Treatment

We described how many of the psychoactive drugs achieve their euphoric effects through their interaction with the neurotransmitter systems in the brain. What would happen if the effects of these drugs were blocked so that they no longer produced the pleasant results? Would people stop using the blocked drugs? **Antagonist drugs** block or counteract the effects of psychoactive drugs, and a variety of drugs that seem to cancel out the effects of opiates have been used with people dependent on a variety of substances. The most commonly used of the opiate-antagonist drugs—*naltrexone*—has been used with only limited success (Goldstein, 1994). If it is given to a person who is dependent on opiates, it produces immediate withdrawal symptoms, an extremely unpleasant effect. A person must be withdrawn from the opiate completely before starting naltrexone, and because it removes the euphoric effects of the opiates, the user must be highly motivated to continue treatment.

Naltrexone has also been evaluated as a treatment for people dependent on alcohol. Joseph Volpicelli and his colleagues at the University of Pennsylvania in Philadelphia studied 70 men who had an average of 20 years of heavy alcohol use (Volpicelli, Alterman, Hayashida, & O'Brien, 1992). Each man was required to attend group therapy sessions, individual counseling, and sessions focusing on health and exercise. In addition, half the men were given naltrexone and the other half received a placebo pill. After three months, about one-quarter of the men in the naltrexone group had returned to drinking heavily, while one-half of the group receiving the placebo had relapsed. These results have been replicated by other investigators and suggest that naltrexone may add to an overall treatment approach that includes therapy (O'Malley et al., 1992). Overall, naltrexone is not the "magic bullet" that some had hoped would essentially shut off the addict's response to psychoactive drugs and put an end to dependence. It does appear to help some drug abusers handle the withdrawal symptoms and the craving that accompanies attempts to abstain from drug use, and therefore antagonists may serve as a useful addition to other therapeutic efforts.

Aversive Treatments

In addition to looking for ways to block the euphoric effects of psychoactive drugs, workers in this area have tried to use drugs that make the ingestion of the abused substances extremely unpleasant. The expectation is that by associating the drug with feelings of illness, the person would avoid using the drug. The most commonly known of these attempts is with the drug *disulfiram*—otherwise known as *Antabuse*—which is used with people who are alcohol dependent. This drug prevents the breakdown of acetaldehyde, a by-product of alcohol, and the buildup of acetaldehyde causes feelings of illness. More specifically, if people drink after taking Antabuse, they will experience nausea, vomiting, and elevated heart rate and respiration. Under ideal situations, the person takes Antabuse each morning, before the desire to drink prevents him from doing so (Nathan, 1993). Unfortunately, noncompliance is a major concern with the use of this drug, and avoiding Antabuse for a few days is sufficient for a person to be able to resume drinking.

Efforts to make smoking aversive have included the use of a chemical called *silver nitrate*. Used in lozenges or gum, this chemical combines with the saliva of a smoker to produce a bad taste in the mouth. Research on its effectiveness in reducing cigarette smoking, however, has not shown it to be particularly effective (Jensen, Schmidt, Pedersen, & Dahl, 1991). Both Antabuse for alcohol abuse and silver nitrate for cigarette smoking have generally been less than successful as treatment strategies on their own, primarily because they require that people be extremely motivated to continue taking these drugs outside the supervision of a mental health professional (Leccese, 1991).

Other Biological Treatments

Medication is frequently prescribed to help people deal with the often very disturbing symptoms of withdrawal from drugs. A drug that is typically used to treat hypertension, called *clonidine,* has been used for people withdrawing from opiates. Because the withdrawal from certain prescribed medications such as the sedatives can cause cardiac arrest or seizures, people are gradually tapered off these drugs to minimize dangerous reactions to their removal. In addition, sedative drugs (benzodiazepines) are often prescribed to help minimize discomfort for people withdrawing from other drugs such as alcohol (McCreery & Walker, 1993).

One of the few controlled studies of the use of medication to treat cocaine abuse was conducted only recently (Gawin et al., 1989). This study found that the drug *desipramine,* one of the antidepressant drugs, was effective in increasing abstinence rates among cocaine users, compared to lithium or a placebo. However, 41% of those receiving the medication were unable to achieve even a month of continuous cocaine abstinence, suggesting that it may not be helpful for a large subgroup of users.

A recently developed enzyme may hold some promise for the treatment of people addicted to cocaine. Although not yet used on humans, this enzyme seems to cut cocaine molecules into two parts, neither of which has any narcotic effect (Landry, Zhao, Yang, Glickman, & Georgiadis, 1993). Because it breaks down the cocaine so fast, it would make the brain immune to the effects of cocaine. We do not know whether the enzyme will eventually be helpful to people addicted to cocaine, but it offers some hope that we may soon be able to "immunize" people against the euphoric effects of such drugs.

Psychosocial Treatments

Most of the biological approaches aimed at treating substance abuse showed some promise in aiding people who were trying to eliminate their drug habit. However, none of these treatments alone was successful for most people. Most of the research indicates a need for some level of social support or therapeutic intervention. Because so many people need help to overcome their abuse and dependence on drugs, a number of models and programs have been developed to help them. Unfortunately, in no other area of psychology have unvalidated and untested methods of treatment been so widely accepted. A reminder: Just because a program has not been subject to the scrutiny of research does not mean it doesn't work, but the sheer numbers of people receiving services of unknown value is cause for concern. Below we review several therapeutic approaches that have been evaluated and discuss what we know about the best methods for treating drug disorders.

Inpatient Hospital Treatment

The establishment of specialized facilities to care for people with substance abuse problems dates back to 1935 with the first federal narcotic "farm" built in Lexington, Kentucky. Now mostly privately run, facilities such as these are designed to help people get through the initial withdrawal period and to provide supportive therapy to help them go back to their communities (Morgan, 1981). Inpatient care can be extremely expensive; the cost of a course of treatment often exceeds $15,000 (Miller & Hester, 1986). The question arises, then, as to how effective this type of care is compared to outpatient therapy that can cost 90% less. Research on the comparative effectiveness of treatments for alcohol abuse suggests that there may be no difference in the outcomes for alcoholic patients between intensive residential setting programs and quality outpatient care (Miller & Hester, 1986). Although some people with alcohol dependency problems do improve in these inpatient settings, they may not need this expensive in-hospital care.

Alcoholics Anonymous and Its Variations

Without question, the most popular model for the treatment of substance abuse is a variation of the 12-step program first developed by Alcoholics Anonymous. Established in 1935 by two professionals (William "Bill W." Wilson and Robert "Dr. Bob" Holbrook Smith) who were also alcoholics, its foundation rests on the notion that alcoholism is a disease and that alcoholics must acknowledge their addiction to alcohol and its destructive power over them. The addiction is seen as more powerful than any individual, and therefore they must look to a Higher Power to help them overcome their shortcomings. Central to its design was its independence from the established medical community and a separation from the stigmatization that surrounded alcoholism at the time (Denzin, 1987; Robertson, 1988). An important component of Alcoholics Anonymous appears to be the social support it provides through its meetings.

In 60 years Alcoholics Anonymous (AA) has expanded to include over 20,000 groups holding more than 25,000 meetings each week all over the world (Nathan, 1993). In a recent survey, over 3% of the adult population in the United States reported that they had at one time attended an AA meeting (Room, 1993). The Twelve Steps of AA form the basis of their philosophy (see Table 12.14). In them you can see the reliance on prayer and a belief in God.

Reaction to AA and other similar organizations, like Cocaine Anonymous and Narcotics Anonymous, and the use of the 12-step treatment approach for other drugs (Miller, Gold, & Pottash, 1989) is rarely neutral. Many people credit this approach to treatment with saving their lives, while others have found its reliance on spirituality and its adoption of a disease model—assuming alcoholics can't help themselves—to foster dependency and have objected to its approach. Because of the nature of this organization—participants attend meetings anonymously and only when they feel the need to—conducting systematic research on its effectiveness has been unusually difficult (Miller & McCrady, 1993). There have been numerous attempts, however, to evaluate AA's effect on alcoholism, and just

recently this work has been compiled and analyzed (Emrick, Tonigan, Montgomery, & Little, 1993). Although there are not enough data to show what percentage of people abstain from using alcohol as a result of participating in AA, Emrick and his colleagues found that the research that does exist suggests that those people who have increased participation in AA activities and follow its guidelines more carefully are more likely to have a positive outcome. On the other hand, a very large number of people who initially contact AA for their drinking problems seem to drop out, with 50% dropping out after 4 months, and 75% after 12 months (Alcoholics Anonymous, 1990). AA is clearly an effective treatment for *some* people with alcohol dependency. We do not yet know, however, who is likely to succeed and who is likely to fail in AA. Because so many drop out of this program, evidently other treatments are needed for the large numbers of people who do not respond to AA's approach.

Controlled Use

One of the tenets of Alcoholics Anonymous is total abstinence; recovered alcoholics who have just one sip of alcohol are believed to be "out of control" until they again achieve abstinence. However, some researchers question this assumption and believe that at least a portion of abusers of several substances (notably alcohol and nicotine) may be capable of becoming "social users" without going on to abuse these drugs. The evidence for this lies in the fact that, among cigarette smokers, some people smoke only occasionally; they are thought to react differently to nicotine than do heavy users (Goldstein, 1994).

In the alcoholism treatment field, the notion of teaching people **controlled drinking** is extremely controversial, in part because of a study showing partial success in teaching severe abusers to continue to drink

Table 12.14   Twelve Suggested Steps of Alcoholics Anonymous

1. We admitted we were powerless over alcohol—that our lives had become unmanageable.
2. Came to believe that a power greater than ourselves could restore us to sanity.
3. Made a decision to turn our will and our lives over to the care of God *as we understood Him.*
4. Made a searching and fearless moral inventory of ourselves.
5. Admitted to God, to ourselves, and to another human being the exact nature of our wrongs.
6. Were entirely ready to have God remove all these defects of character.
7. Humbly asked Him to remove our shortcomings.
8. Made a list of all persons we had harmed, and became willing to make amends to them all.
9. Made direct amends to such people wherever possible, except when to do so would injure them or others.
10. Continued to take personal inventory and, when we were wrong, promptly admitted it.
11. Sought through prayer and meditation to improve our conscious contact with God *as we understood Him,* praying only for knowledge of His will for us and the power to carry that out.
12. Having had a spiritual awakening as the result of these steps, we tried to carry this message to alcoholics and to practice these principles in all our affairs.

Source: Alcoholics Anonymous World Services, Inc.

in a limited way (Sobell & Sobell, 1978). In this study, the subjects were 40 male alcoholics who were at the time in an alcoholism treatment program at a state hospital and were thought to have a good prognosis. The men were assigned either to a program that taught them how to drink in moderation (experimental group) or to a group that was abstinence oriented (control group). The researchers, Mark and Linda Sobell, followed this group of men for over 2 years and maintained contact with 98% of them. During the second year after treatment, those who participated in the controlled drinking group were functioning well for 85% of the days, while the abstinence group were reported to be doing well for only 42% of the days. Although the two groups differed significantly, some of the men in both groups suffered serious relapses and required rehospitalization; some were incarcerated during this time. The results of this study suggested that controlled drinking may be a viable alternative to abstinence for some alcohol abusers, although it clearly wasn't a "cure."

The controversy over this study began with a paper published in the prestigious journal *Science* (Pendery, Maltzman, & West, 1982). The authors reported that they had contacted the men in the Sobell study after 10 years (the original study was initiated in the early 1970s) and found that only one of the men in the controlled drinking group continued to maintain a pattern of controlled drinking. Although this reevaluation made headlines and was the subject of a segment on the *60 Minutes* television show, it had a number of flaws (Marlatt, Larimer, Baer, & Quigley, 1993). Most serious of the problems with this study was the lack of data on the abstinence group over the same 10-year follow-up period. Because no treatment study on substance abuse pretends to help everyone who participates, control groups are added to compare progress. In this case, there is obviously a need to know how well the controlled drinking group fared *compared to the abstinence group*. This comparison was not done.

Despite these problems, the controversy over the Sobell study had a chilling effect on the treatment of alcohol abuse with controlled drinking in the United States. In contrast, controlled drinking is widely accepted as a treatment for alcoholism in the United Kingdom (Rosenberg, 1993). Despite opposition to its use, research on this treatment approach has been conducted in the ensuing years (Marlatt, Larimer, Baer, & Quigley, 1993). Among the research that has looked at controlled drinking as an option, the results seem to show that this treatment is at least as effective as abstinence approaches, but that neither treatment is successful for 70%–80% of patients over the long term—a rather bleak outlook for people with alcohol dependence problems.

Components of Psychological Treatments

Most comprehensive treatment programs aimed at helping people with substance abuse and dependency problems include a number of different elements or components thought to boost the effectiveness of their "treatment package." As we saw in the review of biological treatments, adding psychologically based therapy appears to increase the effectiveness of these treatments. One component that is sometimes added to them is a form of *aversion therapy*. Using a conditioning model, substance use is paired with something extremely unpleasant such as a brief electric shock or feelings of nausea. For example, a person might be asked to have a drink of alcohol, and when the glass reaches his lips, he receives a painful shock. The goal is to counteract the positive associations with substance use with these new negative associations. The negative associations can also be made by imagining unpleasant scenes (having a person picture herself beginning to "snort" cocaine but being interrupted with visions of herself becoming violently ill) in a technique called *covert sensitization* (Cautela, 1966).

One component that seems to be a valuable part of therapy for substance use is *contingency management*. Here, the clinician and client together select the behaviors that the client needs to change and the reinforcers—things like money or small retail items (for example, CDs)—that will be his or her rewards for reaching certain goals. In a recent study of cocaine abusers, contingency management was instituted and clients could receive things like lottery tickets for having cocaine-negative urine specimens (Higgins et al., 1993). This study found greater abstinence rates among cocaine-dependent users with the contingency management approach and other skills training than among users in a more traditional counseling program that included a 12-step approach to treatment.

Another strategy that is a package of treatments in and of itself is called the *community reinforcement approach* (Sisson & Azrin, 1989). In this approach, in keeping with the multiple influences that affect substance use, several different facets of the drug problem are addressed. First, a spouse, friend, or relative who is not a substance user is recruited to participate in relationship therapy in order to help the abuser improve his or her relationships with important other people. Second, clients are taught how to identify their own antecedents and consequences that influence their drug taking. For example, if cocaine use is likely to occur with certain friends, the client is taught to recognize this relationship and is encouraged to try to avoid these associations. Third, clients are given assistance in the areas of employment, education, finances, or other social service needs that may help reduce their stress. Fourth, new recreational options are provided to help the person replace substance use with new activities. These different components help identify and correct aspects of the person's life that might contribute to his or her substance use, or interfere with his or her efforts to abstain. Preliminary use of the community reinforcement approach with alcohol and cocaine abusers appears encouraging, although more research is needed to assess its long-term effectiveness.

Because people present such different challenges to substance abuse treatment, a "shotgun-like" effort is often useful to cover the range of problems influencing their substance use. It is unlikely that any single approach will be effective for all people and all substances. Treatment should be individualized to "fit" the needs of each person. In one example of this individualized approach, a study recently reported on the treatment of smokers who had a history of major depressive disorder (Hall, Muñoz, & Reus, 1994). The researchers creatively combined education on smoking cessation, use of nicotine gum, and cognitive-behavioral intervention for the users' mood disorder; they found that the addition of the mood disorder treatment increased participants' rates of abstinence. By individually determining and treating in an integrated fashion the factors that support a person's substance abuse, clinicians may help improve the success rates of the treatment approaches we have just discussed.

Relapse Prevention

A somewhat different approach to the treatment of people with substance-related disorders is to address the problem of relapse directly. Marlatt and Gordon's (1985) **relapse prevention** treatment model looks at the learned aspects of dependence and sees

G. Alan Marlatt, Ph.D., a renowned alcohol researcher, is Director of the Addictive Behaviors Research Center at the University of Washington.

relapse as a failure of a person's cognitive and behavioral coping skills. Therapy involves helping users remove any ambivalence about stopping their drug use by examining their beliefs about the positive aspects of the drug (for example, "There's nothing like a cocaine high") and confronting the negative consequences of its use (for instance, "I fight with my wife when I'm high"). High-risk situations are identified (for example, "having extra money in my pocket") and strategies are developed to deal with the potentially problematic situations as well as the craving that will arise from abstinence. Incidents of relapse—when people reuse the substance they are trying to abstain from—are dealt with as occurrences from which the person can recover. In other words, instead of looking on these episodes as overwhelming and inevitably leading to more drug use, people in treatment are encouraged to see them as episodes brought on by some temporary stress or situation that can be changed. Research on the use of this technique suggests that it may be useful in treating marijuana dependence (Stephens, Roffman, & Simpson, 1994), smoking (Gruder et al., 1993), cocaine abuse (Carroll, 1992), and alcohol dependence (Baer et al., 1992).

Sociocultural Intervention

It seems particularly appropriate that we end this chapter by looking at the potential of sociocultural intervention for substance-related disorders. We noted in the beginning of the chapter that the rates of substance use and abuse across most of the psychoactive drugs are declining in the United States. Although treatment efforts of the kind we have just discussed have improved in recent years, the decline in use is probably not directly attributable to the use of these techniques. It seems plausible—although we certainly cannot say conclusively—that the major influence on this reduced use of drugs is primarily cultural. Over the past 25 years or so, we have gone from a "turn on, tune in, drop out," "if it feels good, do it," and "I get by with a little help from my friends" society to one that champions statements like "Just say no to drugs." The social unacceptability of drinking, smoking, and other drug use is probably responsible for this change. The sociocultural influence on cigarette smoking, for example, is readily apparent in the following description from one former smoker:

> I began smoking (in Boy Scouts!) at age 11. By the time I was a college freshman, freed from the restrictions of school and home, my smoking had increased to a pack a day. The seminal Surgeon General's Report *Smoking and Health* was issued that year (1964), but I didn't notice. The warnings that began appearing on cigarette packs a couple of years later were also easy to ignore, since I had grown up knowing that

"When I drink, I don't care about anything, as long as I'm drinking. Nothing bothers me. The world doesn't bother me. So when I'm not drinking, the problems come back, so you drink again. The problems will always be there. You just don't realize it while you're drinking. That's why people tend to drink a lot."

smoking was unhealthy. As a graduate student and young professor I often smoked while leading class discussions, as had some of my favorite teachers. That ended in 1980, when an undergraduate student, no doubt empowered by the anti-smoking movement, asked me to stop because smoke bothered him. A few years later there were hardly any social situations left in which it was acceptable to smoke. Even my home was no longer a refuge, since my children were pestering me to quit. And so I did. Now my status as former smoker puts me in company with fully half of all those who have ever smoked regularly and are alive today. For many of us the deteriorating social environment for smoking made it easier to quit. (Cook, 1993, p. 1750)

Implementing these types of interventions is obviously beyond the scope of one research investigator or even a consortium of researchers collaborating across many sites. It requires intervention on a societal level with the cooperation of governmental, educational, and even religious institutions. At this time, it looks as though these efforts will not only continue but thrive. This type of prevention may be more effective than any treatment-oriented approach we can ever envision.

Summary

- Substance-related disorders in DSM-IV are divided into the depressants (for example, alcohol, barbiturates, and benzodiazepines), the stimulants (for instance, amphetamine, cocaine, nicotine, and caffeine), the opiates (for example, heroin, codeine, and morphine), and the hallucinogens (for instance, marijuana and LSD).

- Specific diagnoses are further categorized as *substance dependence, substance abuse, substance intoxication,* and *substance withdrawal.*

- Drug use has declined in recent times, although it continues to cost billions of dollars and seriously impairs the lives of millions of people each year.

- Depressants are a group of drugs that primarily *decrease* central nervous system activity. The primary effect is to reduce our levels of physiological arousal and help us relax. Included in this group are alcohol and the sedative, hypnotic, and anxiolytic drugs such as those prescribed for insomnia.

• Stimulants are the most commonly consumed psychoactive drugs and include caffeine (found in coffee, chocolate, and many soft drinks), nicotine (in tobacco products such as cigarettes), amphetamines, and cocaine. In contrast to the depressant drugs, stimulants work to make you more alert and energetic.

• Opiates include drugs such as *opium, morphine, codeine,* and *heroin;* they have a *narcotic* effect—relieving pain and inducing sleep. The broader term *opioids* is used to refer to the family of substances that include these opiates as well as synthetic variations created by chemists (for example, methadone, pethidine) and the similarly acting substances that occur naturally in our brains (for instance, enkephalins, beta-endorphins, and dynorphins).

• Hallucinogens essentially change the way the user perceives the world. Sight, sound, feelings, and even smell are distorted, sometimes in dramatic ways, when under the influence of drugs such as marijuana and LSD.

• Most of the drugs seem to produce positive effects by acting directly or indirectly on the dopaminergic mesolimbic system (the "pleasure pathway"). In addition, psychosocial factors such as expectations, stress, and cultural practices interact with the biological influences to influence drug use.

• The treatment of substance dependence is successful only with a minority of those affected, and the best results seem to be a product of the motivation of the drug user and a combination of biological and psychosocial treatments.

• Programs aimed at prevention of drug use may hold the greatest chance of having a significant effect on the drug problem.

Key Terms

agonist substitution (505)
alcohol use disorders (472)
amphetamine use disorder (481)
antagonist drugs (506)
barbiturates (480)
benzodiazepines (480)
caffeine use disorders (490)
cocaine use disorders (484)
controlled drinking (508)
depressants (472)
fetal alcohol syndrome (FAS) (475)
GABA system (474)

hallucinogens (472)
hallucinogen use disorder (493)
LSD (d-lysergic acid diethylamide)
    (494)
marijuana (cannabis) (493)
nicotine use disorders (487)
opiates (472)
opioid use disorders (491)
polysubstance use (464)
psychoactive substances (465)
relapse prevention (510)

sedative, hypnotic, or anxiolytic
    drugs (480)
stimulants (472)
substance abuse (465)
substance dependence (466)
substance intoxication (465)
substance-related disorders (463)
tolerance (466)
withdrawal (466)
withdrawal delirium (delirium
    tremens/DTs) (474)

Lord deliver me from myself.
Sir Thomas Browne
Religio Medici, Pt. ii, sec. 10

13
Personality Disorders

Personality disorders are "enduring patterns of perceiving, relating to, and thinking about the environment and oneself" that "are exhibited in a wide range of important social and personal contexts," and "are inflexible and maladaptive, and cause either significant functional impairment or subjective distress" (DSM-IV, p. 630). Now that you have taken out your yellow marker and highlighted this definition of personality disorders, what does it mean?

We all have an idea about what a person's "personality" is. It's made up of the ways a person *behaves* and *thinks* that characterize him or her. "Michael tends to be shy." "Mindy likes to be very dramatic." "Juan is always suspicious of others." "Annette is very outgoing." "Bruce seems to be very sensitive and gets upset very easily over minor things." "Sean has the personality of an eggplant!" We tend to "type" people for behaving in a certain way across many situations. For example, like Michael, many of us are shy among people we don't know; but we wouldn't be shy around our friends. A shy person would be shy even among people he has known for some time. His "shyness" would seem to be part of the way he behaves in most situations. From time to time, we have all probably behaved in ways noted above ("dramatic," "suspicious," "outgoing," "easily upset"). However, we usually consider a way of behaving as being part of a

person's personality only if it cuts across many times and places. In this chapter we look at these characteristic ways of behaving as they relate specifically to personality disorders. First we examine in some detail how we conceptualize personality disorders and the issues related to their prevalence. Then we review each of the personality disorders in turn.

Conceptualizing Personality Disorders

What if a person's characteristic ways of thinking and behaving cause the person or his or her loved ones significant distress? What if he or she can't change this way of relating to the world and it makes him or her unhappy? In this case, we might consider the person to have a "personality disorder." The definition at the beginning of the chapter notes that these personality characteristics are inflexible and maladaptive, and cause either significant functional impairment or subjective distress. Unlike many of the other disorders we have already discussed, personality disorders are considered chronic problems that do not come and go during different times in a person's life. On the contrary, personality disorders are believed to originate in childhood and to continue throughout adulthood. These chronic problems, because they involve a person's personality, pervade every aspect of a person's life. If a man is overly suspicious, for example (a sign of a possible paranoid personality disorder), this trait will affect almost everything he does, including his employment (he may have to change jobs frequently if he believes co-workers conspire against him), his relationships (he may not be able to sustain a lasting relationship if he can't trust a girlfriend), and even where he lives (he may have to move often if he suspects his landlord is out to get him).

DSM-IV notes that the results of having this disorder *may* distress the person affected. However, individuals with personality disorders may feel no subjective distress; indeed, the distress may be felt by others because of the actions of individuals with personality disorder. This is particularly common with antisocial personality disorder when the individual shows a blatant disregard for the rights of others, yet exhibits no remorse (Hare, 1993). In certain cases, a judgment has to be made by someone other than the person with the personality disorder. This individual must decide whether the disorder is causing significant functional impairment because the affected person often cannot make such a judgment.

DSM-IV lists 10 specific personality disorders and several others that are being studied for future consideration. We review all of these in this chapter. Unfortunately, as we will see later, people who have personality disorders along with other psychological problems tend to do poorly in treatment. Data from a recent study showed that people who were depressed had a worse outcome in treatment if they also had a diagnosis of a personality disorder (Shea et al., 1990).

The majority of the disorders we discuss in this book are included in Axis I of the DSM-IV. The Axis I disorders are considered the standard and traditional disorders, ones that justify separate classification. The personality disorders are included in a separate axis of DSM-IV, Axis II. These disorders are separated because they differ from the ones in Axis I. The traits characterizing them are more ingrained and inflexible in the people who exhibit these disorders. The disorders also seem less likely to be successfully modified.

Having personality disorders on a separate axis also forces the clinician to consider whether each person assessed has a personality disorder. In the axis system of classification, a patient could receive a diagnosis on only Axis I or only Axis II, or he or she could receive diagnoses on both axes. Having a diagnosis on both Axis I and Axis II would indicate that a person has both a current disorder that is negatively affecting him or her (Axis I) and a more chronic problem (for instance, personality disorder). As you will see, it is not so unusual to have diagnoses on both axes.

You may be surprised to learn that the category of personality disorders is also one of the more controversial ones. What seems at first to be a simple category involves a number of unresolved issues that we will discuss before describing the specific disorders themselves. Examining the difficulties with personality disorders can help us understand this group of disorders as well as the others we describe in this book.

Categorical Versus Dimensional Models

At some level, we all can relate to many of the personality disorders described in this chapter. Most of us, at times, have been suspicious of others and a little paranoid, or have been overly dramatic, or too self-involved, or have avoided being with other people. Fortunately, these characteristics have not lasted for too long or been overly intense, and they haven't significantly impaired how we live and work. People with personality disorders, however, display these problem characteristics over extended periods of time and in many situations, causing great emotional pain for themselves and/or for those around them. Their difficulty, then, can be seen as one of *degree* rather than *kind*. In other words, the problems experienced by people with personality disorders may just be more extreme examples of the problems many of us experience on a temporary basis, such as being shy or suspicious.

The distinction between problems of *degree* versus problems of *kind* is usually described in terms of *dimensions* versus *categories*. The issue that continues to be debated in the field is whether personality disorders are just extreme versions of otherwise normal personality variations ("dimensions") or ways of relating that are different from psychologically healthy behavior ("categories") (Gunderson, 1992; Livesley, Schroeder, Jackson, & Jang, 1994). We can see the difference between dimensions and categories in everyday life. For example, we tend to look at gender categorically. Our society views us as being in one category or the other—as "male" or "female." Yet we could also look at these characteristics along dimensions. For example, we know that "maleness" and "femaleness" are in part determined by hormones (testosterone and estrogen being the major hormones influencing gender). We could identify people along testosterone and/or estrogen dimensions and rate them on a continuum of "maleness" and "femaleness" rather than in the absolute categories of "male" or "female." We also often label people's size categorically as "tall," "medium," or "short." But height too can be viewed dimensionally, in inches or centimeters.

Most people in the field also see personality disorders as extremes on one or more personality *dimensions*. Yet because of the way people receive diagnoses with the DSM, the personality disorders—and most of the other disorders—end up being viewed in *categories,* or in different and distinct divisions or groups. For example, either you have *antisocial personality disorder* or you don't. The DSM doesn't rate how obsessive or compulsive you are; if you meet the criteria, you are labeled as having *obsessive-compulsive personality disorder.* In this categorical system, you have two choices—either you do ("yes") or you do not ("no") have a disorder. There is no in-between when it comes to personality disorders.

There are advantages to using categorical models of behavior, the most important being their ease of use. With only two choices available ("yes" or "no"), a clinician's job is simplified. With this simplicity, however, also come problems. One is that the mere act of using categories leads clinicians to "reify" the categories. That is, they start to view these disorders as real "things," comparable to the realness of an infection or a broken arm. Some argue that personality disorders are not things that exist but are points at which society decides that a particular way of relating to the world has become a problem. There is an important but as yet unresolved issue that we return to again: *Are personality disorders just an extreme variant of normal personality, or do they represent distinctly different disorders?*

Personality Disorder Clusters

A number of researchers are convinced that many or all of the personality disorders represent extremes on one or more personality dimensions. Consequently, a number of these researchers have proposed that the personality disorders section either be replaced or at least supplemented by a dimensional model (Widiger, 1991; Widiger & Frances, 1985). In such a system, individuals would not be given categorical diagnoses only but would also be rated on a series of personality dimensions. Widiger (1991) believes that such a system would have at least three advantages over a purely categorical system: (a) It would retain more information about each individual, (b) it would be more flexible because it would permit both categorical and dimensional differentiations among individuals, and (c) it would avoid the often arbitrary decisions involved in deciding whether a person should be assigned to a diagnostic category.

Unfortunately, there is no general consensus about what these basic personality dimensions might be. As a result, there are several contenders for this alternate dimensional system of rating (Eysenck & Eysenck, 1975; Tellegen, 1978; Watson, Clark, & Harkness, 1994). Among the different systems proposed, the most widely accepted is taken from work on normal personality and is called the *five factor model* or the

"Big Five" (Costa & McCrae, 1990; Goldberg, 1993; Tupes & Christal, 1992). This work suggests that people can be rated on a series of personality dimensions, and that the combination of five components of personality can describe why people are so different. The five factors or dimensions in this model are *extraversion* (talkative, assertive, and active versus silent, passive, and reserved), *agreeableness* (kind, trusting, and warm versus hostile, selfish, and mistrustful), *conscientiousness* (organized, thorough, and reliable versus careless, negligent, and unreliable), *emotional stability* (even-tempered versus nervous, moody, and temperamental), and *openness to experience* (imaginative, curious, and creative versus shallow and imperceptive) (Goldberg, 1993).

On each of these five dimensions, you can rate yourself high, low, or somewhere in-between. A number of researchers are now trying to determine whether people with personality disorders can also be rated in a meaningful way along these dimensions and whether using such a system will help us better understand these disorders (Clark, 1993; Schroeder, Wormworth, & Livesley, 1993). Again, the major obstacle to the acceptance of a dimensional approach to personality disorders has been the lack of consensus regarding the most appropriate framework to adopt (Widiger, 1991). Because of this lack of agreement, the DSM-IV continues to use categories for these disorders.

DSM-IV divides the personality disorders into three groups or "clusters"; this will continue until there is a strong scientific basis for grouping personality disorders together in a particular way (see Table 13.1). The cluster division of the disorders is based on resemblance. Cluster A is called the "odd" or "eccentric" cluster; it includes paranoid, schizoid, and schizotypal personality disorders. Cluster B is known as the "dramatic," "emotional," or "erratic" cluster; it consists of antisocial, borderline, histrionic, and narcissistic personality disorders. Cluster C is called the "anxious" or "fearful" cluster; it includes avoidant, dependent, and obsessive-compulsive personality disorders. We follow this order in our review of each of the disorders.

Statistics and Course for Personality Disorders

We depart in this chapter from our usual format of discussing the statistics and course for the disorders after their clinical description. Instead, in the case of the personality disorders it may be more helpful to the reader to get an overview of this information before examining each of these individually in detail. We first look at the statistics on the personality disorders, followed by

Table 13.1 DSM-IV Personality Disorders

Personality Disorder	Description
Cluster A—Odd or Eccentric Disorders	
Paranoid personality disorder	A pervasive distrust and suspiciousness of others such that their motives are interpreted as malevolent.
Schizoid personality disorder	A pervasive pattern of detachment from social relationships and a restricted range of expression of emotions in interpersonal settings.
Schizotypal personality disorder	A pervasive pattern of social and interpersonal deficits marked by acute discomfort with and reduced capacity for close relationships as well as by cognitive or perceptual distortions and eccentricities of behavior.
Cluster B—Dramatic, Emotional, or Erratic Disorders	
Antisocial personality disorder	A pervasive pattern of disregard for and violation of the rights of others.
Borderline personality disorder	A pervasive pattern of instability of interpersonal relationships, self-image, affects, and control over impulses.
Histrionic personality disorder	A pervasive pattern of excessive emotionality and attention seeking.
Narcissistic personality disorder	A pervasive pattern of grandiosity (in fantasy or behavior), need for admiration, and lack of empathy.
Cluster C—Anxious or Fearful Disorders	
Avoidant personality disorder	A pervasive pattern of social inhibition, feelings of inadequacy, and hypersensitivity to negative evaluation.
Dependent personality disorder	A pervasive and excessive need to be taken care of, which leads to submissive and clinging behavior and fears of separation.
Obsessive-compulsive personality disorder	A pervasive pattern of preoccupation with orderliness, perfectionism, and mental and interpersonal control, at the expense of flexibility, openness, and efficiency.

Source: Adapted from DSM-IV, APA, 1994.

discussions of gender differences, their developmental course, and comorbidity issues.

Personality disorders are fairly common, and are found in 10% to 13% of the general population (Weissman, 1993). As you can see from Table 13.2, several of the individual personality disorders are relatively rare. In particular, schizoid, narcissistic, and avoidant personality disorders are all found in fewer than 1% of the general population. In addition, some of the personality disorders are found differentially among males and females. Borderline personality disorder, for example, is relatively rare among men (Widiger & Weissman, 1991), while antisocial personality disorder is infrequently observed among women (Sutker, Bugg, & West, 1993). The rest of the disorders, including paranoid, schizotypal, histrionic, dependent, and obsessive-compulsive personality disorders, are found in 1% to 4% of the general population.

Developmental Course

Unlike some of the disorders we have so far discussed, personality disorders are thought to originate in childhood and continue into the adult years. These ways of behaving are believed to be so ingrained that it is difficult to pinpoint an onset for personality disorders;

rather, the particular maladaptive personality characteristics develop over time into the maladaptive behavior patterns that create distress for the person affected and draw the attention of others. One theme that will repeat itself as we discuss a number of these personality disorders is a relative lack of information regarding important features, such as their developmental course. Table 13.2 shows the gaps in our knowledge concerning the course of about half these disorders. One reason for this dearth of research is that many individuals with personality disorders do not seek treatment in the early developmental phases of their disorder. Only after years of distress do many of these people or their families seek assistance from mental health professionals. Because they do not identify themselves as having a problem early in this process, it is difficult to study people with personality disorders from the beginning signs of a problem to its later stages.

A handful of research studies have helped us to understand the development of several of the personality disorders. People diagnosed with borderline personality disorder are characterized by their volatile and unstable relationships; they tend to have persistent problems in early adulthood, with frequent hospitalizations, unstable personal relationships, and severe problems with depression and suicidal gestures.

Table 13.2 Statistics and Course for Personality Disorders

Disorder	Prevalence	Gender Differences	Course
Paranoid personality disorder	.5% to 2.5% (Bernstein, Useda, & Siever, 1993)	More common in males (O'Brien, Trestman, & Siever, 1993)	Insufficent information
Schizoid personality disorder	Less than 1% in United States, Canada, New Zealand, Taiwan (Weissman, 1993)	More common in males (O'Brien, Trestman, & Siever, 1993)	Insufficient information
Schizotypal personality disorder	3% to 5% (Weissman, 1993)	More common in males (Kotsaftis & Neale, 1993)	Chronic; some go on to develop schizophrenia
Antisocial personality disorder	3% in males; less than 1% in females (Sutker et al., 1993)	More common in males (Dulit et al., 1993)	Dissipates after age 40 (Hare, McPherson, & Forth, 1988)
Borderline personality disorder	1% to 3% (Widiger & Weissman, 1991)	Females make up 75% of cases (Dulit, Marin, & Frances, 1993)	Symptoms gradually improve if individuals survive into their 30s (Dulit et al., 1993). Approximately 6% die by suicide (Perry, 1993).
Histrionic personality disorder	2% (Nestadt et al., 1990)	Equal numbers of males and females (Nestadt et al., 1990)	Chronic
Narcissistic personality disorder	Less than 1% (Zimmerman & Coryell, 1990)	More prevalent among men	May improve over time (Cooper & Ronningstam, 1992; Gunderson, Ronningstam, & Smith, 1991)
Avoidant personality disorder	Less than 1% (Reich, Yates, & Nduaguba, 1989; Zimmerman & Coryell, 1990)	Equal numbers of males and females (Millon, 1986)	Insufficient information
Dependent personality disorder	2% (Zimmerman & Coryell, 1989)	May be equal numbers of males and females (Reich, 1987)	Insufficient information
Obsessive-compulsive personality disorder	4% (Weissman, 1993)	More common in males (Stone, 1993)	Insufficient information

Approximately 6% succeed in their suicidal attempts (Perry, 1993; Stone, 1989). On the bright side, their symptoms gradually improve if they survive into their 30s (Dulit, Marin, & Frances, 1993), although elderly individuals may experience difficulty formulating future plans and may be disruptive in nursing homes (Rosowsky & Gurian, 1992). Individuals with antisocial personality disorder display a characteristic disregard for the rights and feelings of others; they tend to continue their destructive behaviors of lying and manipulation through adulthood. Fortunately, some of these people tend to "burn out" after the age of about 40 and engage in fewer criminal activities (Hare, McPherson, & Forth, 1988). As a group, however, people with personality disorders continue to display their characteristic problems, as shown when researchers follow their progress over several years. This pessimistic prognosis appears to hold even when significant efforts are made to treat these individuals over the intervening years (Perry, 1993).

Gender Differences

With one exception, all the personality disorders are either more commonly observed in males or are equally prevalent among males and females (see Table 13.2). Borderline personality disorder is the anomaly; it tends to be diagnosed more frequently among females, who make up about 75% of the identified cases (Dulit et al., 1993). Historically, several of the other personality disorders—histrionic and dependent personality disorders—have also been identified by clinicians as occurring more often in women (Dulit et al., 1993; Stone, 1993). However, recent studies of their prevalence in the general population seem to contradict this observation. The surprising finding from this research is that there may be equal numbers of males and females with histrionic and dependent personality disorders (Lilienfeld, VanValkenburg, Larntz, & Akiskal, 1986; Nestadt et al., 1990; Reich, 1987). If this observation of equal prevalence rates for these disorders holds up in future studies, why have these personality disorders been predominantly diagnosed among females in general clinical practice and in other studies (Dulit et al., 1993)?

Do these disparities indicate differences between men and women in certain basic genetic and/or sociocultural experience, or do they represent biases in the definitions of the disorders or the clinicians who diagnose people? Take, for example, a recent study by Maureen Ford and Thomas Widiger (1989), who sent out fictitious case histories to clinical psychologists and asked them to make a diagnosis. One case described a person with *antisocial personality disorder,* which is characterized by irresponsible and reckless behavior and is usually diagnosed in males; the other case described a person with *histrionic personality disorder,* which is characterized by excessive emotionality and attention seeking and is more often diagnosed in females. Some versions of each case were said to describe a man and other versions were said to describe a woman, although everything else about the cases themselves were the same. The graph in Figure 13.1 shows that when the antisocial personality disorder case was labeled as being a man, most psychologists gave the correct diagnosis. However, when the same case was labeled as describing a female, most psychologists diagnosed the case as a histrionic personality disorder rather than the antisocial personality disorder. In the case of histrionic personality disorder, being labeled a woman increased the chances of that diagnosis being used. Ford and Widiger concluded that the psychologists were incorrectly diagnosing more women as having histrionic personality disorder (Ford & Widiger, 1989).

This gender difference in prevalence has also been criticized by other authors (for example, Kaplan, 1983) on the grounds that histrionic personality disorder, like several of the other personality disorders, is biased against females. As Kaplan (1983) points out, many of the features of histrionic personality disorder, such as overdramatization, vanity, seductiveness, and overconcern with physical appearance, are characteristic of Western society's view of a "stereotypical female." This disorder may simply represent the embodiment of the individual possessing extremely "feminine" traits (Chodoff, 1982); branding such an individual as mentally ill, according to Kaplan, reflects society's inherent bias against females. Interestingly, the "macho" personality (Mosher & Sirkin, 1984), the individual possessing stereotypically masculine traits, is nowhere to be found in the DSM.

The issue of gender bias in diagnosing personality disorder remains highly controversial. It is important to remember, however, that just because certain disorders are observed more in men or women doesn't necessarily indicate bias (Lilienfeld et al., 1986); but when it is present, bias can come from different aspects of the diagnostic process. Widiger and Spitzer (1991) point out that the criteria for the disorder may themselves be gender biased (referred to as *criterion gender bias*), or the assessment measures and the way they are used could be biased (called *assessment gender bias*). Research efforts will undoubtedly continue as we try to make the diagnosis of personality disorders more accurate with respect to gender.

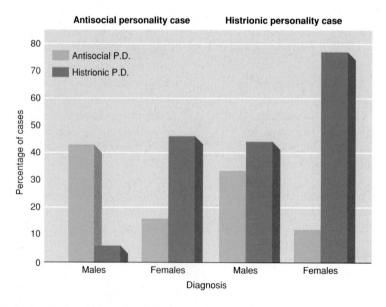

Figure 13.1 Gender bias in diagnosing personality disorders. Data are shown for the percentage of cases clinicians rated as antisocial personality disorder or histrionic personality disorder, depending on whether the case was described as a male or a female (from Ford & Widiger, 1989).

Comorbidity

Looking at Table 13.2 a reader might be tempted to add up the prevalence rates across the personality disorders and conclude that somewhere between 20% and 30% of all people have a personality disorder. In fact, the percentage of people in the general population with a personality disorder is estimated to fall between 10% and 13% (Weissman, 1993). What accounts for this discrepancy? One of the major concerns with the personality disorders is that people tend to be diagnosed with more than one. The term *comorbidity* has historically been used in medicine to describe the condition in which a person has multiple diseases (Caron & Rutter, 1991). There is a fair amount of disagreement about whether the term should be used with psychological disorders because of problems regarding the overlap of the different disorders (for example, Nurnberg et al., 1991). In just one example, Morey (1988) conducted a study of 291 persons who received a diagnosis of personality disorder and found considerable overlap with these diagnoses (see Table 13.3). In the left column of Table 13.3 you see the diagnosis they received, and you see the percentage of people who would also meet the criteria for another disorder. In other words, if a person is identified with one particular personality disorder such as borderline personality disorder, he or she is likely to fit the definition of another one of these supposedly different personality disorders. In general, about half the people diagnosed with any one of the personality disorders will meet the criteria for at least one additional personality disorder (Grove & Tellegen, 1991).

Does this finding mean that people tend to have more than one type of personality disorder? Does it mean that how we define these disorders is inaccurate and we need to improve our definitions so they do not overlap? Or did we divide up these disorders in the wrong way to begin with, and do we need to rethink these different categories? These questions about comorbidity are just a few of the important issues facing researchers who study personality disorders.

Specific Personality Disorders

We turn now to a review of the personality disorders that are currently in DSM-IV—10 in all. Then we will look briefly at a few personality disorder categories that are being considered for inclusion.

Paranoid Personality Disorder

Although it is probably very adaptive to be a little wary of other people and their motives, being too distrustful can interfere with your making friends, working with others, and in general, getting through the daily interactions everyone needs to function well in today's society. People with **paranoid personality disorder** are excessively mistrustful and suspicious of other people, without any justification. They tend not to confide in others and expect other people to do them harm. Consider the following case taken from the Quality Assurance Project (1990), a commission studying psychological disorders under the auspices of the

Table 13.3 Diagnostic Overlap of Personality Disorders

Percentage of People Qualifying for Other Personality Disorder Diagnoses

Diagnosis	Para-noid	Schizoid	Schizo-typal	Anti-social	Border-line	Histri-onic	Narcis-sistic	Avoidant	Depen-dent	Obsessive-compulsive
Paranoid		23.4	25.0	7.8	48.4	28.1	35.9	48.4	29.7	7.8
Schizoid	46.9		37.5	3.1	18.8	9.4	28.1	53.1	18.8	15.6
Schizotypal	59.3	44.4		3.7	33.3	18.5	33.3	59.3	29.6	11.1
Antisocial	27.8	5.6	5.6		44.4	33.3	55.6	16.7	11.1	0.0
Borderline	32.0	6.2	9.3	8.2		36.1	30.9	36.1	34.0	2.1
Histrionic	28.6	4.8	7.9	9.5	55.6		54.0	31.7	30.2	4.8
Narcissistic	35.9	14.1	14.1	15.6	46.9	53.1		35.9	26.6	10.9
Avoidant	39.2	21.5	20.3	3.8	44.3	25.3	29.1		40.5	16.5
Dependent	29.2	9.2	12.3	3.1	50.8	29.2	26.2	49.2		9.2
Obsessive-compulsive	21.7	21.7	13.0	0.0	8.7	13.0	30.4	56.5	26.1	

Source: Adapted from Morey, 1988.

Royal Australian and New Zealand College of Psychiatrists.

The Case of Mr. P.

Mr. P. was a 41-year-old man with paranoid personality disorder, who had been seen repeatedly over an 8 year period. Mr. P. grew up in a family with a psychotic father, and at high school was noted to be suspicious, a troublemaker, and a fighter. He enlisted and went to Vietnam where his suspiciousness and attacks on Vietnamese civilians caused him to be reprimanded. Returning to Australia he remained unsettled, moving from job to job because co-workers used to "gang up on me." He came to attention because he was imprisoned for assault on a girl who had rejected his advances. [It was] reported that although Mr. P. has continued to work he has remained arrogant, suspicious, and very difficult to help apart from the rare occasion when he would accept help for feelings of depression. (pp. 341–342)

Clinical Description

The DSM-IV diagnostic criteria for paranoid personality disorder are presented in Table 13.4. As we saw with Mr. P., the defining characteristic of people with paranoid personality disorder is a pervasive distrust, and importantly, without justification. Certainly there may be times when people are being deceitful and are "out to get you"; however, people with paranoid personality disorder are suspicious in situations where most other people would agree that their suspicions are unfounded. Because of this suspiciousness, even events that have nothing to do with them are interpret-

ed as attacks. These people would view a neighbor's barking dog as an attempt to annoy them. A delayed airline flight would be a personal affront. Unfortunately, this mistrust often extends to people close to them, such as relatives or friends, and makes maintaining meaningful relationships with others very difficult. Imagine what a lonely existence this must be! Their suspiciousness and mistrust can show itself in a number of ways. People with paranoid personality disorder may be argumentative, may complain, or may be quiet but obviously hostile toward others. They will often appear tense and "ready to pounce" if slighted by someone.

Causes of Paranoid Personality Disorder

Evidence for biological contributions to paranoid personality disorder is limited. Some work in this area suggests that paranoid personality disorder may be slightly more common among the relatives of people who have schizophrenia, although the association does not seem to be a strong one (Coryell & Zimmerman, 1989; Kendler & Gruenberg, 1982). In other words, relatives of individuals with schizophrenia *may be* more likely to have paranoid personality disorder than people who do not have a relative with schizophrenia. As we will see with the other odd or eccentric personality disorders grouped together under Cluster A (that is, schizoid and schizotypal as well as paranoid personality disorders), there seems to be some relationship between them and schizophrenia although the exact nature of their relationship is not yet clear (Siever, 1992).

Psychological contributions to this disorder are even less certain, although there are some interesting speculations. Some psychologists point directly to the cognitions or thoughts of people with paranoid personality disorder as a way of explaining their behavior. One

Table 13.4   Diagnostic Criteria for Paranoid Personality Disorder

A. A pervasive distrust and suspiciousness of others such that their motives are interpreted as malevolent, beginning by early adulthood and present in a variety of contexts, as indicated by four (or more) of the following:

1. Suspects, without sufficient basis, that others are exploiting, harming, or deceiving him or her
2. Is preoccupied with unjustified doubts about the loyalty or trustworthiness of friends or associates
3. Is reluctant to confide in others because of unwarranted fear that the information will be used maliciously against him or her
4. Reads hidden demeaning or threatening meanings into benign remarks or events
5. Persistently bears grudges, i.e., is unforgiving of insults, injuries, or slights
6. Perceives attacks on his or her character or reputation that are not apparent to others and is quick to react angrily or to counterattack
7. Has recurrent suspicions, without justification, regarding fidelity of spouse or sexual partner

B. Does not occur exclusively during the course of Schizophrenia, a Mood Disorder with Psychotic Features, or another Psychotic Disorder and is not due to the direct physiological effects of a general medical condition.

Note: If criteria are met prior to the onset of Schizophrenia, add "Premorbid," e.g., "Paranoid Personality Disorder (Premorbid)."

Source: DSM-IV, APA, 1994.

view is that people with this disorder have the following basic mistaken assumptions about others: "People are malevolent and deceptive," "They'll attack you if they get the chance," and "You can be OK only if you stay on your toes" (Freeman, Pretzer, Fleming, & Simon, 1990). This is a maladaptive way to view the world, yet it seems to pervade every aspect of the lives of these individuals. We don't know how they develop these perceptions but there is some speculation that the roots are in the early upbringing of the affected individuals. Their parents are thought to teach them to be careful about making mistakes and to impress on them that they are different from other people (Turkat & Maisto, 1985). This vigilance causes them to see signs that other people are being deceptive and malicious toward them (Beck & Freeman, 1990). These views can arise because people are not always benevolent and sincere, and because our interactions are sometimes ambiguous enough to make other people's intentions unclear. Looking too closely at what other people say and do can sometimes cause you to misinterpret their actions.

Cultural factors have also been implicated in paranoid personality disorder. Certain groups of people such as prisoners, refugees, people with hearing impairments, and the elderly are thought to be particularly susceptible to this disorder because of their unique experiences (Christenson & Blazer, 1984; O'Brien et al., 1993). Imagine how you might view other people if you were a refugee from another country who had difficulty with the language and the customs of your new culture. Such innocuous things as other people laughing or talking quietly might be interpreted as somehow directed at you. The late musician Jim Morrison of the Doors wrote of this phenomenon in his song "When You're Strange" (The Doors, 1967):

> People are strange,
> When you're a stranger,
> Faces look ugly,
> When you're alone.

Our previous discussion of cognitive factors points out how someone could misinterpret ambiguous situations and see them as malevolent. Thus, cognitive and cultural factors may interact to help produce the suspiciousness observed in some people with paranoid personality disorder.

Treatment of Paranoid Personality Disorder

People who have paranoid personality disorder tend to be mistrustful of everyone, including mental health professionals. As a result, they are much less likely to seek out professional help when they need it and will also have difficulty developing the types of trusting relationships necessary for successful therapy (Quality Assurance Project, 1990). When they do seek therapy, the trigger is usually some crisis in their lives or other problems they experience, such as anxiety or depression, and not necessarily their personality disorder.

In keeping with what we have observed about these individuals, therapists try to provide an atmosphere in therapy conducive to development of a sense of trust (Freeman, Pretzer, Fleming, & Simon, 1990). They often use cognitive therapy to try to counter the person's mistaken assumptions about others. In other words, they focus the therapy on changing the per-

A man with a hearing impairment. Sometimes not being able to hear clearly can incorrectly lead to paranoid beliefs that others are talking about you behind your back.

son's beliefs that all people are malevolent and that most people cannot be trusted. Be forewarned, however, that to date there are no clear-cut demonstrations that *any* form of treatment can significantly improve the lives of people with paranoid personality disorder. In fact, a recent survey of mental health professionals indicated that only 11% of therapists who would treat someone with paranoid personality disorder thought that these individuals would continue in therapy long enough to be helped (Quality Assurance Project, 1990).

Schizoid Personality Disorder

Do you know someone who is a "loner"? Someone who would choose a solitary walk in the woods over an invitation to a party? A person who comes to class alone, sits alone, and leaves alone? Now, magnify this seeming preference for isolation from others many times over and you can begin to grasp the impact of having **schizoid personality disorder.** People with this personality disorder show a pattern of detachment from social relationships and a very limited range of emotions in interpersonal situations. They seem "aloof," "cold," and "indifferent" to other people. The term *schizoid* is a relatively old one, having been used by Bleuler in 1924 to describe people who have a tendency to turn inward and away from the outside world. These people were said to lack emotional expressiveness and pursued vague interests. Consider the following case.

The Case of Mr. Z.

A 39-year-old scientist referred after his return from a tour of duty in Antarctica where he had stopped cooperating with others, had withdrawn to his room and begun drinking on his own. Mr. Z. was orphaned at 4 years, raised by an aunt until 9, and subsequently looked after by an aloof housekeeper. At university he excelled at physics, but chess was his only contact with others. Throughout his subsequent life he made no close friends and engaged primarily in solitary activities. Until the tour of duty in Antarctica he had been quite successful in his research work in physics. He was now, some months after his return, drinking at least a bottle of Schnapps each day and his work had continued to deteriorate. He presented as self-contained, unobtrusive, and was difficult to engage effectively. He was at a loss to explain his colleagues' anger at his aloofness in Antarctica and appeared indifferent to their opinion of him. He did not appear to require any interpersonal relations although he did complain of some tedium in his life and at one point during the interview became sad, expressing longing to see his uncle in Germany, his only living relation. (Quality Assurance Project, 1990, p. 346)

Clinical Description

The DSM-IV diagnostic criteria for schizoid personality disorder are presented in Table 13.5. Individuals with this disorder *seem* neither to desire nor enjoy close relationships with others, including romantic or sexual relationships. Perhaps as a result of this apparent disinterest in others, they appear cold and unconnected to others and do not seem affected by praise or criticism. In Mr. Z.'s case, he seemed disinterested in his co-workers' annoyance with him. One of the changes in DSM-IV from previous versions is a recognition that, although these individuals may appear on the outside to be disinterested in social relationships, at least some people with schizoid personality disorder

---

Table 13.5   Diagnostic Criteria for Schizoid Personality Disorder

A. A pervasive pattern of detachment from social relationships and a restricted range of expression of emotions in interpersonal settings, beginning by early adulthood and present in a variety of contexts, as indicated by four (or more) of the following:

1. Neither desires nor enjoys close relationships, including being part of a family
2. Almost always chooses solitary activities
3. Has little, if any, interest in having sexual experiences with another person
4. Takes pleasure in few, if any, activities
5. Lacks close friends or confidants other than first-degree relatives
6. Appears indifferent to the praise or criticism of others
7. Shows emotional coldness, detachment, or flattened affectivity

B. Does not occur exclusively during the course of Schizophrenia, a Mood Disorder with Psychotic Features, another Psychotic Disorder, or a Pervasive Developmental Disorder and is not due to the direct physiological effects of a general medical condition.

Note: If criteria are met prior to the onset of Schizophrenia, add "Premorbid," e.g., "Schizoid Personality Disorder (Premorbid)."

Source: DSM-IV, APA, 1994.

are sensitive to the opinions of others but are unwilling or unable to express this emotion. For them, social isolation may be an extremely painful personal experience.

People with schizoid personality disorder have social deficiencies, similar to those of people with paranoid personality disorder, although their social deficits are more extreme in nature. As Beck and Freeman (1990) put it, these people "consider themselves to be observers rather than participants in the world around them" (p. 125). They differ from those with the other two disorders in Cluster A (paranoid and schizotypal personality disorders) because they do not seem to have the very unusual thought processes that characterize those disorders (Kalus, Bernstein, & Siever, 1993) (see Table 13.6). For example, people with paranoid and schizotypal personality disorders (but not people with schizoid personality disorder) often have *ideas of reference*—mistaken beliefs that meaningless events relate just to them. In contrast, those with schizoid personality disorder share the social isolation, poor rapport, and constricted affect (showing neither positive nor negative emotion) seen in people with paranoid personality disorder. We see later in Chapter 14 that this distinction between psychoticlike symptoms is an important one for understanding people with schizophrenia, with some of these individuals showing the "positive" symptoms—or actively unusual behaviors such as ideas of reference—and others having only the "negative" symptoms—or the more passive manifestations of social isolation or poor rapport with others.

Causes and Treatment of Schizoid Personality Disorder

What we know about people who have schizoid personality disorder remains incomplete. Research on the genetic, neurobiological, and psychosocial contributions to this disorder remains to be con-

ducted (Siever, 1992). It is interesting to note, however, that the preference by people with this disorder for social isolation resembles aspects of another disorder: autism. As we discuss more fully in Chapter 16, autistic disorder is characterized by a pervasive impairment in social interaction. Those with autism either ignore people or respond to them unemotionally. Although they have significant difficulties with language—which is not a problem among those with schizoid personality disorder—their shared indifference to interactions with others is strikingly similar to this trait in schizoid personality disorder. Research over the past several decades has pointed to the role of biological influences in the cause of autism, and it is possible that some similar biological dysfunction in combination with early learning or early problems with interpersonal relationships will help explain the social deficits that define schizoid personality disorder.

In treating people with schizoid personality disorder, therapists often begin by encouraging them to develop an interest in social relationships, initially by pointing out the value in these. The person with the disorder may even need to be taught the different emotions felt by others to help him or her learn empathy (Beck & Freeman, 1990). Because their social skills were never established or atrophied through lack of use, people with schizoid personality disorder often receive social skills training. The therapist acts out the role of a friend or a significant other, in a technique known as *role playing*, and helps the patient learn the skills necessary to establish and keep social relationships (Beck & Freeman, 1990).

Unfortunately, a recent survey illustrates the pessimistic view of the treatment prospects for people with schizoid personality disorder as assessed by the mental health profession. The Quality Assurance Project (1990), under the direction of the Royal Australian and New Zealand College of Psychiatrists, sent out and received responses from 360 mental health professionals about the case of Mr. Z., which we described at the beginning of this discussion of schizoid personality disorder. Seventy-five percent reported that they saw individuals like Mr. Z. in their practices about twice a year. Almost half of them either felt they couldn't provide therapy to such people or believed they were untreatable. The other half, who thought they could treat them, believed that any therapy would be complicated because the patients probably wouldn't follow treatment recommendations. One of the more "optimistic" replies by a psychiatrist to this survey still rings of pessimism:

> This man [Mr. Z.] has a severe personality disorder and the issues are: Does he want help and is he able to persist in seeking it despite difficulties in himself and the difficulties of treatment; will he

Table 13.6 Grouping Schema for Cluster A Disorders

	Psychoticlike Symptoms	
Cluster A Personality Disorder	*"Positive" (e.g., ideas of reference, magical thinking, and perceptual distortions)*	*"Negative" (e.g., social isolation, poor rapport, and constricted affect)*
Paranoid	Yes	Yes
Schizoid	No	Yes
Schizotypal	Yes	No

Source: Adapted from Siever, 1992.

Specific Personality Disorders **525**

be able to develop trust and decrease intellectual-distancing defences; can the therapist understand and soothe him rather than have him continue to use work and alcohol; and it will take 12 months before it is clear if supportive psychotherapy will help him. (p. 346)

Schizotypal Personality Disorder

People with **schizotypal personality disorder** are typically socially isolated, like those with schizoid personality disorder. In addition, however, individuals with schizotypal personality disorder also behave in ways that would seem unusual to many of us. Also, they tend to be suspicious and to have odd beliefs about the world (Kotsaftis & Neale, 1993). Consider the following case.

The Case of Mr. S.

Mr. S. was a 35-year-old chronically unemployed man who had been referred by a physician because of a vitamin deficiency. This was thought to have eventuated because Mr S. avoided any foods that "could have been contaminated by machine." He had begun to develop alternative ideas about diet in his twenties, and soon left his family and began to study an eastern religion. "It opened my third eye, corruption is all about," he said.

He now lived by himself on a small farm, attempting to grow his own food, bartering for items he could not grow himself. He spent his days and evenings researching the origins and

mechanisms of food contamination and, because of this knowledge, had developed a small band who followed his ideas. He had never married and maintained little contact with his family: "I've never been close to my father. I'm a vegetarian."

He said he intended to do a herbalism course to improve his diet before returning to his life on the farm. He had refused medication from the physician and became uneasy when the facts of his deficiency were discussed with him. (Quality Assurance Project, 1990, p. 344)

Clinical Description

The DSM-IV diagnostic criteria are presented in Table 13.7. People who are given a diagnosis of schizotypal personality disorder are often considered "odd" or "bizarre" based on the way they relate to other people, the way they think and behave, and even the way they dress. They are described as having *ideas of reference,* a descriptive term that means they create misconceptions about insignificant events, thinking that somehow these meaningless events relate to them. For example, they may have a sense that somehow everyone on a passing city bus is talking about them, yet they may be able to acknowledge that this is unlikely. Again, as we will see in Chapter 14, some people with schizophrenia also have ideas of reference, but they are usually not able to "test reality" or see the illogic of these ideas like those with schizotypal personality disorder.

Individuals with schizotypal personality disorder also have odd beliefs or "magical thinking,"

Table 13.7   Diagnostic Criteria for Schizotypal Personality Disorder

A. A pervasive pattern of social and interpersonal deficits marked by acute discomfort with, and reduced capacity for, close relationships as well as by cognitive or perceptual distortions and eccentricities of behavior, beginning by early adulthood and present in a variety of contexts, as indicated by five (or more) of the following:

1. Ideas of reference (excluding delusions of reference)
2. Odd beliefs or magical thinking that influences behavior and is inconsistent with subcultural norms (e.g., superstitiousness, belief in clairvoyance, telepathy, or "sixth sense"; in children and adolescents, bizarre fantasies or preoccupations)
3. Unusual perceptual experiences, including bodily illusions
4. Odd thinking and speech (e.g., vague, circumstantial, metaphorical, overelaborate, or stereotyped)
5. Suspiciousness or paranoid ideation
6. Inappropriate or constricted affect
7. Behavior or appearance that is odd, eccentric, or peculiar
8. Lack of close friends or confidants other than first-degree relatives
9. Excessive social anxiety that does not diminish with familiarity and tends to be associated with paranoid fears rather than negative judgments about self

B. Does not occur exclusively during the course of Schizophrenia, a Mood Disorder with Psychotic Features, another Psychotic Disorder, or a Pervasive Developmental Disorder.

Note: If criteria are met prior to the onset of Schizophrenia, add "Premorbid," e.g., "Schizotypal Personality Disorder (Premorbid)."

Source: DSM-IV, APA, 1994.

believing, for example, that they are clairvoyant or telepathic. In addition, they report having unusual perceptual experiences, including *illusions* such as feeling as if another person is in the room when they are alone. Again, you should notice the subtle but important difference between feeling *as if* someone else is in the room, and the more extreme perceptual distortion found among people with schizophrenia who might report that there *is* someone else in the room when there isn't. Only a small proportion of individuals with schizotypal personality disorder go on to develop schizophrenia (Wolff, Townshed, McGuire, & Weeks, 1991). Unlike people who may just have unusual interests or beliefs, those with schizotypal personality disorder also tend to be suspicious and have paranoid thoughts, will appear to express little emotion, and may dress or behave in unusual ways (for example, wear many layers of clothing in the summertime, mumble to themselves) (Siever, Bernstein, & Silverman, 1991).

Causes of Schizotypal Personality Disorder

Historically, the word *schizotype* was used to describe people who were predisposed later to develop schizophrenia (Meehl, 1962; Rado, 1962). Schizotypal personality disorder is viewed by some to be one phenotype of a schizophrenia genotype. If you think back to our discussion of genetics, you will recall that a phenotype is one way a person's genetics is expressed. In other words, your *genotype* is the gene or genes that, in this example, make up a particular disorder. However, depending on a variety of other influences, the way you "turn out" or your *phenotype* may vary from other people with a similar genetic makeup. In this case, some people are thought to have "schizophrenia genes" (the genotype), yet because of the relative lack of biological (for instance, prenatal illnesses) or environmental (for example, poverty) stresses, some of these people with schizophrenia genes will have a less severe disorder in the form of schizotypal personality disorder (the phenotype).

The idea that there is a relationship between schizotypal personality disorder and schizophrenia arises in part from the way people with these two disorders behave. Many of the descriptions of schizotypal personality disorder, including ideas of reference, illusions, and paranoid thinking, are described as similar but "milder" forms of the behaviors observed among people with schizophrenia. Research on the genetics of these two disorders also seems to support a relationship. Family, twin, and adoption studies have shown an increased prevalence of schizotypal personality disorder among relatives of people with schizophrenia who do not also have schizophrenia themselves (Dahl, 1993; Torgersen, Onstad, Skre, Edvardsen, & Kringlen, 1993). However, these studies also tell us that there is a great

deal of room for the environment to influence schizotypal personality disorder. It may be that a subgroup of people with schizotypal personality disorder is related to people with schizophrenia.

Treatment of Schizotypal Personality Disorder

There are some estimates that between 30% and 50% of the people with this disorder who enter a clinical setting for help also meet the criteria for major depressive disorder. Treatment for them will obviously involve some of the medical and psychological treatments we outlined for depression (Goldberg, Schultz, Resnick, Hamer, & Schultz, 1987).

Controlled studies of attempts to treat groups of people who have schizotypal personality disorder are few, and unfortunately, the results of these treatment efforts are modest at best. One general approach has been to teach these individuals social skills to help them reduce their isolation from and suspicion of others (Bellack & Hersen, 1985; O'Brien et al., 1993). A rather unusual tactic used by some therapists has been not to encourage major changes in these individuals at all; instead, the goal is to try to help the person accept and adjust to his or her solitary life-style (Stone, 1983).

Because schizotypal personality disorder is thought to be related to schizophrenia, and because many of the problems manifested in this disorder resemble the problems experienced by people with schizophrenia, it is not surprising that medical treatment has been similar to that used with people who have schizophrenia. In one study, a common drug used with schizophrenia—haloperidol—was given to a group of 17 people with schizotypal personality disorder (Hymowitz, Frances, Jacobsberg, et al., 1986). The use of the drug led to some improvements in the group, especially with their ideas of reference, odd communication, and social isolation. Unfortunately, because of the negative side effects of the medication—for example, feelings of drowsiness—many stopped taking their medication and dropped out of the study. About half the subjects in this study persevered through treatment but showed only mild improvement.

Further research on the treatment of people with this disorder is important for a variety of reasons. First, they tend not to improve over time. Second, there is some evidence that a portion of them will go on to develop the more severe characteristics of schizophrenia.

Antisocial Personality Disorder

People with **antisocial personality disorder** have a history of failing to comply with social norms. They perform actions most of us would find unacceptable, such as stealing from friends and family. They also tend to be irresponsible, impulsive, and deceitful. Dr. Robert Hare describes these individuals as

> social predators who charm, manipulate, and ruthlessly plow their way through life, leaving a broad trail of broken hearts, shattered expectations, and empty wallets. Completely lacking in conscience and in feelings for others, they selfishly take what they want and do as they please, violating social norms and expectations without the slightest sense of guilt or regret. (Hare, 1993, p. xi)

Just who are these people with antisocial personality disorder? Consider the following case.

The Case of Ryan

One of the authors first met Ryan on his 17th birthday. Unfortunately, he was "celebrating" this event in a psychiatric hospital. He was there because he had been truant from school for several months and had gotten into some trouble; the local judge who was hearing his case in court had recommended psychiatric evaluation one more time. Ryan had been hospitalized six previous times, all for problems related to drug use and to not attending school. He was a "veteran" of the system and already knew most of the staff. I interviewed him to try to assess why he was admitted this time, and to decide how to proceed with his treatment for the next few months.

My first impression of Ryan was that he was cooperative and pleasant to talk to. For example, he pointed out the tattoo of his initials and a skull on his arm that he had made himself. He said that it was a "stupid" thing to do, and that he now regretted it. In fact, he told me that he regretted many of the things that he had done and was looking forward to moving on with his life. I would later find out that this was one of the many "hollow" regrets he would express; he was never truly remorseful for anything he had done.

My second interview, several days later, was quite different. In those 48 hours, Ryan had done a number of things to illustrate why he needed a great deal of help. The most serious incident involved a 15-year-old girl named Ann who was attending class with Ryan in the hospital school. Ryan had told her that he was going to get himself discharged and sent to prison, the same prison Ann's father was now in. While in prison, Ryan told her he was going to rape her father. Ryan's threat caused Ann a great deal of emotional pain and upset her so that she hit her teacher and several of the staff. When I spoke to

Ryan about this, he smiled slightly and said he was bored and that it was fun to upset Ann. When I asked whether it bothered him that his behavior might prevent her from leaving the hospital sooner, he looked puzzled and said, "Why should it bother *me*? She's the one who will have to stay in this hell hole!"

We also spoke about the other incident that had brought him to the hospital this time. Just prior to his admittance, there was an incident in his town involving the murder of a teenager. A group of teens would go to the local cemetery at night, perform satanic rituals, and do drugs, and a young man was apparently stabbed to death over a drug purchase during one of these "parties." Ryan was part of this group, although not the one who stabbed the boy. He told me how they would occasionally dig up graves to get skulls for their parties; not because they really believed in the devil, but just because it was fun and it scared the younger kids in his crowd. When I asked him if this ever bothered him, he said no. I continued, "What if this were the grave of someone you knew, a relative or a friend? Would it bother you that strangers were digging up the remains?" He shook his head, "They're *dead*, man; they don't care. Why should I?"

We also discussed his drug use. He told me he loved PCP, angel dust, and that he would rather be "dusted" than anything else. He would routinely make a 2-hour trip to New York City to buy drugs in a particularly dangerous neighborhood. He denied that he was ever nervous going into these areas. This wasn't machismo; he really seemed unconcerned and bored with the question.

During his stay at the hospital, Ryan made little progress. I discussed his future with his parents in family therapy sessions with Ryan and we talked about his pattern of supposedly showing regret and remorse, which was routinely followed by his stealing money from his parents and going back onto the street. In fact, most of our discussions centered on trying to give his parents the courage to say no to him and not to believe his lies. One memorable session illustrates Ryan's power over his parents.

On that evening, after many sessions discussing these issues, Ryan began to say that he had seen the "error of his ways" and that he felt bad that he had hurt his parents. If they would only take him home this one last time, he would be able to be the son that he should have been all these years. His speech was so moving that both his parents were in tears and looked at me gratefully as if to thank me for curing their son. When he finished talking, I smiled at him and applauded, telling him that was the best performance I had ever seen. His parents turned to me in anger. Ryan paused for a second, then he too smiled and said, "It was worth a shot!" Ryan's parents were astounded that he had once again tricked them into believing him; he hadn't meant a word of what he had just said.

Ryan was eventually discharged from the hospital to a drug rehabilitation program. Within 4 weeks, he had convinced his parents to have him discharged to be at home with them, and within 2 days, he had stolen all the cash they had in the house and disappeared, apparently back to his friends and to drugs. This pattern has continued over the years as Ryan has turned into an adult. Later, when he was in his 20s, he was diagnosed as having antisocial personality disorder after one of his many arrests for theft. His parents never summoned the courage to turn him out and refuse him money, and he continues to con them into providing him with a means of buying more drugs.

Clinical Description

The diagnostic criteria for antisocial personality disorder are in Table 13.8. Like Ryan, individuals with this disorder tend to have long histories of violating the rights of others. They are often described as being aggressive because they take what they want, indifferent to the concerns of other people. Lying and cheating seem to be second nature to them, and often they appear unable to tell the difference between the truth and the lies they make up to further their own goals. They show no remorse or concern over the sometimes devastating effects of their actions. Ryan felt no sympathy for the families affected by his grave digging, he had no feelings for the pain he caused his parents, nor did he care about the effect of his lie on Ann, who was always nice to him. Also, as we saw in Ryan's case, substance abuse is often found among such individuals, occurring in 83% of people with antisocial personality disorder (Dulit et al., 1993; Smith & Newman, 1990).

People with antisocial personality disorder have been given a number of names over the years. Phillipe Pinel (1801/1962) identified what he called *manie sans délire* (mania without delirium) to describe people with unusual emotional responses, impulsive rages, but with no deficits in reasoning ability (Sutker et al., 1993). Other labels have included "moral insanity," "egopathy," "sociopathy," and "psychopathy." A great deal has been written about the labels used to describe these individuals; we will focus on the two that have figured most prominently in psychological research: **psychopathy** and DSM-IV's *antisocial personality disorder*. As you will see, there are important differences between the two.

Hervey Cleckley (1941, 1982), a psychiatrist who spent much of his career working with these individuals, identified the "psychopathic personality" by a constellation of 16 major characteristics, most of which are personality traits. These characteristics are sometimes referred to as the "Cleckley criteria" and include

superficial charm and good intelligence; absence of delusions and other signs of irrational thinking; absence of "nervousness" and other psycho-

Table 13.8 Diagnostic Criteria for Antisocial Personality Disorder

A. There is a pervasive pattern of disregard for and violation of the rights of others occurring since age 15 years, as indicated by three (or more) of the following:

1. Failure to conform to social norms with respect to lawful behaviors as indicated by repeatedly performing acts that are grounds for arrest
2. Deceitfulness, as indicated by repeated lying, use of aliases, or conning others for personal profit or pleasure
3. Impulsivity or failure to plan ahead
4. Irritability and aggressiveness, as indicated by repeated physical fights or assaults
5. Reckless disregard for safety of self or others
6. Consistent irresponsibility, as indicated by repeated failure to sustain consistent work behavior or honor financial obligations
7. Lack of remorse, as indicated by being indifferent to or rationalizing having hurt, mistreated, or stolen from another

B. The individual is at least age 18 years.

C. There is evidence of Conduct Disorder with onset before age 15 years.

D. The occurrence of antisocial behavior is not exclusively during the course of Schizophrenia or a Manic Episode.

Source: DSM-IV, APA, 1994.

neurotic manifestations; unreliability; untruthfulness and insincerity; lack of remorse or shame; inadequately motivated antisocial behavior; poor judgment and failure to learn by experience; pathologic egocentricity and incapacity for love; general poverty in major affective reactions; specific loss of insight; unresponsiveness in general interpersonal relations; fantastic and uninviting behavior, with drink and without; suicide rarely carried out; sex life impersonal, trivial, and poorly integrated; failure to follow any life plan. (Cleckley, 1982, p. 204)

More recently, Robert Hare and his colleagues, building on the descriptive work of Cleckley, have researched the nature of psychopathy (for example, Hare, 1970; Harpur, Hare, & Hakstian, 1989) and developed a checklist that serves as an assessment tool for identifying people with psychopathy [see Table 13.9 for the criteria Hare (1991) includes in his Revised Psychopathy Checklist-PCL-R]. With some training, clinicians are able to gather information from interviews with a person, along with material from significant others or institutional files (for example, prison records), and assign the person scores on this 20-item checklist, with high scores indicating psychopathy (Hare, 1991).

In contrast to the DSM-IV criteria for antisocial personality, which focus almost entirely on observable *behaviors* (for instance, "impulsively and repeatedly changes employment, residence or sexual partners"), the Cleckley/Hare criteria focus primarily on underlying *personality traits* (for instance, being self-centered, manipulative). DSM-IV and previous versions chose to use only observable behaviors so that clinicians could

Table 13.9 Psychopathy Checklist— Revised	
Item	
1.	Glibness/superficial charm
2.	Grandiose sense of self-worth
3.	Proneness to boredom/need for stimulation
4.	Pathological lying
5.	Conning/manipulative
6.	Lack of remorse
7.	Shallow affect
8.	Lack of empathy
9.	Parasitic life style
10.	Poor behavioral controls
11.	Promiscuous sexual behavior
12.	Early behavior problems
13.	Lack of realistic long-term plans
14.	Impulsivity
15.	Irresponsibility
16.	Failure to accept responsibility for actions
17.	Many marital relationships
18.	Juvenile delinquency
19.	Poor risk for conditional release
20.	Criminal versatility

Source: Hare, 1991.

reliably agree on a diagnosis of antisocial personality disorder. The framers of the criteria felt that trying to assess a personality trait—for example, whether someone was manipulative—would be more difficult than determining whether the person engaged in certain behaviors, such as being involved in repeated fights.

Although Cleckley did not deny that many psychopaths are at greatly elevated risk for criminal and antisocial behaviors, he did emphasize that some psychopaths have few or no legal or interpersonal difficulties. In other words, some psychopaths are not criminals (they do not get caught breaking the law), and some do not engage in the fighting and aggression identified among the DSM-IV criteria as characteristics of antisocial personality disorder. Although the relationship between psychopathic personality and antisocial personality disorder is uncertain, the two syndromes clearly do not overlap perfectly (Figure 13.2) (Hare, 1983). Figure 13.2 may help to illustrate the overlap and lack of overlap among the concepts of *psychopathy* as described by Cleckley and Hare, *antisocial personality disorder* as outlined in DSM-IV, and *criminality,* which includes all people who get into trouble with the law.

Dr. Robert Hare, Professor of Psychology at the University of British Columbia, has extensively studied people with psychopathic personalities.

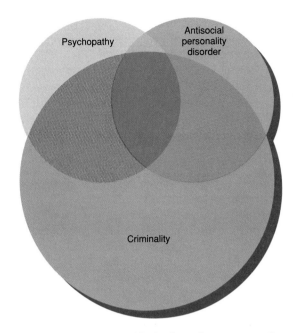

Figure 13.2 Overlap and lack of overlap among antisocial personality disorder, psychopathy, and criminality.

One group that may be included under the category antisocial personality disorder but *not* psychopathy may be individuals called *dyssocial psychopaths* (McNeil, 1970), or individuals whose antisocial behavior is thought to be primarily attributable to allegiance to a culturally deviant subgroup. Many former "gang delinquents" may fall into this category, as may some members of the Cosa Nostra and ghetto guerrillas in South Africa. Unlike Cleckley psychopaths, dyssocial psychopaths are presumed to have the capacity for guilt and loyalty toward other subgroup members.

As you can see in the diagram, not everyone who has psychopathy or antisocial personality disorder has contact with the legal system. This is shown in the section of the circles for these disorders that do not overlap with criminality. Who are these people? Separating many in this group from those who get into trouble with the law may be IQ. In a prospective, longitudinal study, White, Moffit, and Silva (1989) recently followed almost 1,000 children beginning at age 5 to see what would predict antisocial behavior at age 15. They found that among the children who, at age 5, were determined to be at "high risk" for later delinquent behavior, 16% did indeed have some run-in with the law, while 84% did not by the age of 15. What distinguished these two groups? In general, the at-risk children with lower IQs tended to get into trouble with the law. This observation suggests that having a higher IQ may help protect some people from going on to develop more serious problems, or may at least prevent them from getting caught when they do break the law!

Some psychopaths function quite successfully in certain segments of society (for example, politics, business, entertainment). Because of the difficulty in identifying these people, such "successful" or "subclinical" psychopaths (those who meet some but not all the criteria for psychopathy) have been the focus of little research. In a clever exception, Widom (1977) recruited a sample of subclinical psychopaths in the community. She did so by newspaper advertisements, placed in underground newspapers, which contained many of the major personality characteristics of psychopathy. For example, one of the advertisements read:

> "Wanted: charming, aggressive, carefree people who are impulsively irresponsible but are good at handling people and at looking after number one."

Widom found that her sample appeared to possess many of the same characteristics as imprisoned psychopaths; for example, a large percentage of them received low scores on questionnaire measures of empathy and socialization (such as, the extent to which individuals have internalized social norms) and had high rates of parental psychopathology, including alcoholism. Moreover, many of these individuals had stable occupations and had managed to stay out of prison. Widom's study, although lacking a control group, shows that at least some individuals with psychopathic personality traits avoid repeated contact with the legal system and may even function successfully in society.

Identifying people who are psychopaths among the criminal population seems to have important implications for predicting their future criminal behavior. One study found that criminals who scored high on Hare's Psychopathy Checklist (PCL-R) put in less effort and showed fewer improvements in a therapy program than did criminals who were not psychopaths (Ogloff, Wong, & Greenwood, 1990). Other studies have shown that psychopaths are more likely than nonpsychopathic criminals to repeat their criminal offenses—in particular, those offenses that are violent and/or sexual in nature (Rice, Harris, & Quinsey, 1990).

As we review the research on antisocial personality disorder, we should note that the people included in the research may be members of only one of the three groups we just described. For example, research on genetics in this area is usually conducted with people who are criminals because they and their families are easier to identify (through contacts with the legal system) than are members of the other groups. As you now know, the criminal group may include people other than those with antisocial personality disorder or psychopathy. Keep this in mind as you read on.

Before we move into a discussion of causal factors, it is important to note the developmental nature of antisocial behavior. When children engage in behaviors that violate societal norms, DSM-IV provides a separate diagnosis: *conduct disorder*. Many children with conduct disorder will become juvenile offenders (Eppright, Kashani, Robison, & Reid, 1993). And just as we saw with antisocial personality disorder in adults, children with conduct disorder tend to become involved with drugs (Van Kammen, Loeber, & Southamer-Loeber, 1991). Remember that when he was a youth, Ryan fit into this category. More important, the lifelong pattern of antisocial behavior experienced by this group is evident in the fact that young children who display antisocial behavior will likely continue to show these behaviors as they grow older (Charlebois, LeBlanc, Gagnon, Larivée, & Tremblay, 1993; Loeber, 1982). Data from long-term follow-up research indicate that many

adults who engage in the antisocial behaviors characteristic of antisocial personality disorder or psychopathy had conduct disorder as children (Robins, 1978). The DSM-IV diagnostic criteria for conduct disorder are listed in Table 13.10.

How similar are the criteria for this disorder and those for antisocial personality disorder? For the most part, the behaviors that make up the DSM-IV criteria for conduct disorder are very similar. In many cases, the types of norm violations that an adult would engage in—irresponsibility regarding work or family—appear as younger versions in conduct disorder: truant from school, running away from home. One of the major differences is the lack of remorse, which is included under antisocial personality disorder but is not present in the conduct disorder criteria.

Table 13.10 Diagnostic Criteria for Conduct Disorder

A. A repetitive and persistent pattern of behavior in which the basic rights of others or major age-appropriate societal norms or rules are violated, as manifested by the presence of three (or more) of the following criteria in the past 12 months, with at least one criterion present in the past 6 months:

Aggression to people and animals

1. Often bullies, threatens, or intimidates others
2. Often initiates physical fights
3. Has used a weapon that can cause serious physical harm to others (e.g., a bat, brick, broken bottle, knife, gun)
4. Has been physically cruel to people
5. Has been physically cruel to animals
6. Has stolen while confronting a victim (e.g., mugging, purse snatching, extortion, armed robbery)
7. Has forced someone into sexual activity

Destruction of property

8. Has deliberately engaged in fire setting with the intention of causing serious damage
9. Has deliberately destroyed others' property (other than by fire setting)

Deceitfulness or theft

10. Has broken into someone else's house, building, or car
11. Often lies to obtain goods or favors or to avoid obligations (i.e., "cons" others)
12. Has stolen items of nontrivial value without confronting a victim (e.g., shoplifting, but without breaking and entering; forgery)

Serious violations of rules

13. Often stays out at night despite parental prohibitions, beginning before age 13 years
14. Has run away from home overnight at least twice while living in parental or parental surrogate home (or once without returning for a lengthy period)
15. Is often truant from school, beginning before age 13 years

B. The disturbance in behavior causes clinically significant impairment in social, academic, or occupational functioning.

C. If the individual is age 18 years or older, criteria are not met for Antisocial Personality Disorder.

Specify type based on age at onset:
   Childhood-Onset Type: onset of at least one criterion characteristic of Conduct Disorder prior to age 10 years
   Adolescent-Onset Type: absence of any criteria characteristic of Conduct Disorder prior to age 10 years

Specify severity:
   Mild: few if any conduct problems in excess of those required to make the diagnosis and conduct problems cause only minor harm to others
   Moderate: number of conduct problems and effect on others intermediate between "mild" and "severe"
   Severe: many conduct problems in excess of those required to make the diagnosis or conduct problems cause considerable harm to others

Source: DSM-IV, APA, 1994.

"I have hatred inside me. I don't care how much I be somebody . . . The more I hear somebody, the more anger I get inside me . . . I used drugs when I was . . . probably 9 or 10 years old . . . smoked marijuana . . . First time I drank some alcohol I think I was probably about 3 years old . . . I assaulted a woman . . . I had so much anger . . . I was just like a bomb . . . it's just ticking, and it's just a matter of seconds before this bomb blows up, and you're trying to get out of there . . . and the way I'm going, that bomb was going to blow up in me. I wouldn't be able to get away from it . . . going to be a lot of people hurt . . . I'm not going out without taking somebody with me . . ."

Causes of Antisocial Personality Disorder

Obviously there is a tremendous amount of interest in studying this group of individuals who, collectively, cause a great deal of harm to society. As a result, research has continued in this general area for a number of years, and we know a great deal more about antisocial personality disorder than we do about the other personality disorders discussed in this chapter.

Biological dimensions: Genetic influences. Family, twin, and adoption studies all suggest a genetic influence on both antisocial personality disorder and criminality (DiLalla & Gottesman, 1991). For example, Crowe (1974) examined adopted-away children of mothers who were felons and compared them with adopted-away children of normal mothers. All these offspring were separated from their mothers after their first several months of life, minimizing the possibility that environmental factors from their biological families could have been responsible for the results. Crowe found that the adopted-away offspring of felons had significantly higher rates of arrests, conviction, and antisocial personality than did the adopted-away offspring of normal mothers. This finding suggests that at least some genetic influence on criminality and antisocial behavior exists.

However, Crowe also found something else quite interesting: The adopted children of felons who themselves later became criminals had spent more time in interim orphanages than did either the adopted children of felons who did not become criminals or the adopted children of normal mothers. As Crowe points out, this finding suggests as well a likely *gene-environment interaction;* in other words, genetic factors may play an important role *only* in the presence of certain environmental influences (or alternatively, certain environmental influences play an important role only in the presence of certain genetic predispositions). Genetic factors may present a vulnerability toward criminality, but actual development of criminality may require environmental factors, such as a deficit in early, high-quality contact with parents or parent-surrogates (in the orphanages).

More recently, Mednick, Gabrielli, and Hutchings (1987) have conducted a large-scale adoption study of criminality in Denmark. They compared the criminal convictions of 14,427 adoptees with the criminal convictions of both their biological and adoptive parents. The researchers found a correlation between adoptees and their biological parents for criminal convictions, although for nonviolent crimes only. In contrast, they did not find a significant correlation between adoptees and adoptive parents for criminal convictions of any kind. These findings build on those of Crowe, adding to the evidence that there is a genetic component among perpetrators of at least some forms of criminality—in this case, nonviolent crime.

Data from twin studies generally support those of the adoption studies. In a review of the major twin studies of criminality, Eysenck and Eysenck (1978) found that the average concordance rate for criminality among identical or monozygotic (MZ) twins was 55%, whereas this rate among fraternal or dizygotic (DZ) twins was only 13%.

It is important to remember several limitations when you interpret findings on the genetics of criminality. First, "criminality" is an extremely heterogeneous category, including people with and without antisocial personality disorder and psychopathy. The genetic influence on criminality may apply to several or to only one subtype of criminality. Second, as is apparent from the twin studies, it is clear that environmental factors play a substantial role in many, if not all, cases of criminality. In the studies reviewed by Eysenck and Eysenck (1978), for example, the concordance rate of criminality among identical twins was 55%, much below the 100% rate if criminality were explainable entirely by genetic factors. Therefore, environmental factors must play a key role in the development of criminality. Third and finally, there is some suggestion (from the study by Crowe, for example) that the interaction between genes and environment may be important in the genesis of criminality. Genetic factors may play a substantial role in the cause of criminal behavior only in the presence of certain environmental factors.

Biological dimensions: Neurobiological influences. A great deal of research has focused on neurobiological influences that may distinguish people with antisocial personality disorder from others. One thing seems clear: General brain damage does not seem to explain why people become psychopathic or criminal. Criminals and psychopaths appear to score as well on neuropsychological tests as do the rest of us (Hart, Forth, & Hare, 1990). However, these tests are designed to detect physical damage in the brain and will not pick up subtler changes in brain chemistry or structure that could affect behavior. Two major theories of the etiology of psychopathy and antisocial personality disorder involve less severe structural damage and have attracted a great deal of attention over the years: (a) the *underarousal hypothesis* and (b) the *fearlessness hypothesis*. We will discuss both.

According to the underarousal hypothesis, psychopaths are said to have abnormally low levels of *cortical arousal* (Quay, 1965); in other words, they experience abnormally low levels of arousal in the cerebral cortex that forms the outer surface of the brain. There appears to be an inverted U-shaped relation between arousal, on the one hand, and performance, on the other. This relation, often referred to as the *Yerkes-Dodson curve,* suggests that people with *either* very high or very low levels of arousal will tend to experience negative affect and perform poorly in many situations, whereas individuals

with intermediate levels of arousal will tend to be relatively content and perform satisfactorily in most situations.

According to the underarousal hypothesis, the abnormally low levels of cortical arousal characteristic of psychopaths are the primary cause of their antisocial and risk-taking behaviors. Psychopaths may engage in stimulation-seeking behaviors, including violating the law, in order to boost their levels of arousal to more optimal levels. This would mean that Ryan lied to Ann, took drugs, and dug up graves to give himself the same level of arousal we might get from talking on the phone with a good friend or watching television. The risk taking of the psychopath represents an understandable effort to reduce the boredom and negative affect often associated with chronically low arousal.

The evidence for the underarousal hypothesis comes from several researchers who have examined childhood and adolescent psychophysiological predictors of adult antisocial behavior and criminality. Raine, Venables, and Williams (1990), for example, assessed a sample of 15-year-olds on a variety of autonomic and central nervous system variables. They found that future criminals had lower skin conductance activity, lower heart rate during rest periods, and more slow-frequency brain wave activity. Because each of these findings is indicative of low arousal, the results support the underarousal hypothesis of psychopathy and suggest that underarousal, when combined with as yet unidentified environmental factors, may be a risk factor for at least some forms of criminality.

Another finding that is related to the functioning of the brain in people with psychopathy involves evidence that many psychopaths have excessive *theta waves* when they are awake. Low-frequency theta waves are found in brain wave measures of children and largely disappear in adulthood; their specific purpose is as yet unknown. This finding has generated another theory related to arousal levels that is sometimes referred to as the *cortical immaturity hypothesis* of psychopathy (Hare, 1970). According to this hypothesis, the cerebral cortex of psychopaths is at a more primitive stage of development than that of other individuals. The cortical immaturity hypothesis may help to explain why the behavior of psychopaths is often childlike and impulsive; their cerebral cortices, which play such a key role in the inhibition and control of impulses, may be insufficiently developed.

One must not draw conclusions that are too general here, because the data on theta waves are open to an alternative and perhaps simpler explanation. Theta waves have also been found to reflect states such as drowsiness or boredom. Psychopaths' higher levels of theta waves may simply reflect their relative absence of concern regarding being hooked up to psychophysi-

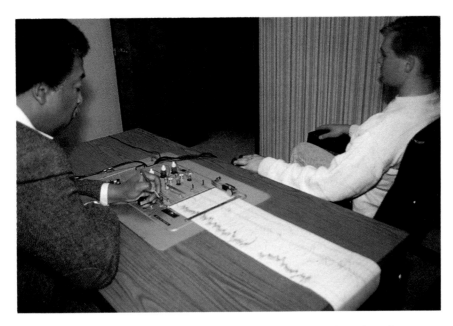

Young man being evaluated using a polygraph machine. Psychopaths may react differently to these types of assessments than people who do not have psychopathy.

ological equipment! Picture yourself having your brain waves measured. You are seated next to an intimidating machine, the polygraph, affixed with a number of electrodes, and attached to a large number of wires. How will you react? As a nonpsychopath, you will probably experience anxiety and apprehension. In contrast, a psychopath, who is low in anxiety, will probably be bored, apathetic, and unresponsive. The excessive theta waves of psychopaths may simply reflect their relative absence of anxiety.

According to the second major hypothesis of the cause of psychopathy, the *fearlessness* hypothesis, psychopaths possess a higher threshold for experiencing fear than most other individuals (Lykken, 1957, 1982). In other words, things that greatly frighten the rest of us have little or no effect on the psychopath. Remember that Ryan said he was unafraid of going alone to dangerous neighborhoods to buy drugs. According to proponents of this hypothesis, the fearlessness of the psychopath gives rise to all the other major features of the syndrome.

Early evidence for the fearlessness hypothesis came from a series of studies by Lykken (1957) using prison inmates. In the first study, Lykken developed a questionnaire—later termed the Activity Preference Questionnaire—consisting of a number of items, each of which had two options. The subject's task was to select the one he or she would prefer to engage in. There was one catch, however: both options referred to activities that virtually all individuals would find unpleasant and prefer not to do. Lykken's test can essentially be thought of as a "lesser of two evils" questionnaire. In each case, one option was unpleas-

ant primarily because it was boring or demanding (for example, "standing in a long line for something," "shoveling the walks after a snowstorm") whereas the other option was unpleasant primarily because it was frightening or embarrassing (for instance, "being given an electric shock as part of a medical experiment," "belching in church during a prayer"). Lykken thought that if the fearlessness hypothesis were correct psychopaths would choose the more frightening option more often than did nonpsychopaths, because the psychopaths would be less distressed by potentially frightening activities. Indeed, this is precisely what happened.

In a second study, Lykken constructed a classical conditioning task involving painful electric shock. In this study, his primary dependent measure was galvanic skin response (GSR). The GSR is a reaction

Dr. David Lykken conducted early research on the nature of psychopathy.

marked by an increase in palmar sweating and is typically interpreted as a sign of autonomic arousal. Lykken repeatedly paired a tone, which was the conditioned stimulus, with electric shock to the subjects' fingertips, which was the unconditioned stimulus. Following this, he presented subjects with the tone (conditioned stimulus) alone on multiple occasions. Nonpsychopaths showed a predictable and understandable pattern: They exhibited marked GSRs to the tones presented alone, demonstrating classical conditioning to these tones. In other words, when they heard the tone, their palms began to sweat, signaling that they expected the shock to come next. Moreover, their GSRs were quite slow to extinguish. In contrast, psychopaths showed a striking pattern: In most cases, they exhibited very weak GSRs to the tones alone, and their GSRs tended to extinguish rapidly.

This study by Lykken has important implications. It suggests that psychopaths may have difficulty associating certain cues or signals with impending punishment or danger. Much of the way in which children are socialized to inhibit their behavior is by means of such cues or signals. Parents do not punish their children directly on every occasion for harmful or inappropriate behavior, but instead rely frequently on cues such as "No" or even a threatening stare to inhibit inappropriate behavior. Largely because of classical conditioning, such cues tend to be quite effective with most children and act as substitutes for direct punishment. But if these cues have little or no impact on the prepsychopathic child, he or she will probably not acquire a well-developed capacity for impulse control.

In his third and final study, Lykken developed a task he termed the *mental maze*. In this task, subjects were required to learn a complex sequence of 20 lever presses as efficiently and accurately as possible; there were four levers to choose from in each case. For each of the 20 lever presses, there were three possible outcomes. First, if the subject chose the correct lever, a green light came on, and a counter on the machine would advance, signaling to the subject that he or she had selected the correct option. But if the subject chose one of the three incorrect levers, one of two things occurred. For two of the three levers, a red light would come on and the counter would not advance, signaling to the subject that he or she had selected the incorrect option. But for one of the levers, in addition to the red light coming on and the counter not advancing, the subject received a painful electric shock. Note that Lykken actually embedded two tasks in one. The first task, which Lykken called the *manifest* task, was the task the subject was informed of—namely, to learn the sequence of 20 lever presses with as few errors as possible. The manifest task can be thought of as a "control" task. The second task, which Lykken called the *latent* task, was actually the task the experimenter

was more interested in, although the subject was never explicitly informed of it. The latent task was the extent to which the subject learned to avoid shock.

Lykken's findings were dramatic: On the manifest task there were no differences between psychopaths and nonpsychopaths, indicating that psychopaths do not have a learning deficit per se. On the latent task, however, the psychopaths did much more poorly than nonpsychopaths, indicating that they have difficulty *learning to avoid punishment*. This finding is consistent with both clinical observations (for example, Cleckley, 1982) that psychopaths frequently make the same mistakes over and over again, and with data suggesting that psychopathy is one of the best predictors of recidivism among criminals (Guze, 1976). The difficulty that psychopaths experience in learning to avoid punishment supports the fearlessness hypothesis, because this difficulty may stem from a lack of sufficient anticipatory anxiety. If people are not afraid of the consequences of punishment, they will be unlikely to go out of their way to avoid it.

Recent theories have tried to tie together our current understanding about the workings of the brain and clinical observations about the unusual behavior of people with antisocial personality disorder (especially those with psychopathy). Several theorists have applied Jeffrey Gray's (1987) model of brain functioning to this population (Fowles, 1988; Quay, 1993). According to Gray, there are three major brain systems that influence learning and emotional behavior: the behavioral inhibition system (BIS), the reward system (REW), and the fight/flight system (F/F). Box 13.1 illustrates the possible role of the fight/flight system in psychopathic behavior. The behavioral inhibition system and reward system seem to be important as well in psychopathy. The BIS is responsible for our ability to stop or slow down when we are faced with impending punishment, nonreward, or novel situations, leading us to feel anxiety and frustration. The BIS is thought to be located in the septohippocampal system and involves the noradrenergic and serotonergic neurotransmitter systems. The reward system is responsible for our approach behaviors—in particular, our approach to positive rewards—and is associated with feelings of hope and relief. This system probably involves the dopaminergic system in the mesolimbic area of the brain—the system we previously noted as the "pleasure pathway" for its role in substance use and abuse (Chapter 12).

If you think about the behavior of psychopaths, the possible malfunctioning of these systems seems clear; there may be an imbalance between the BIS and REW with the result that the fear and anxiety produced by the BIS is less apparent in these individuals, and the positive feeling associated with REW is more prominent (Fowles, 1988; Quay, 1993). Theorists

Box 13.1   Is There an "Aggression" Gene?

Researchers in the Netherlands are cautiously optimistic over their discovery that a gene mutation found in a large Dutch family may cause aggression (Brunner et al., 1993). This study is important because it may tell us more about how genes affect our behavior.

Hans G. Brunner and his colleagues at the university hospital in Nijmegen have tracked the males of one Dutch family since 1978. Some of the men in this family are prone to particularly violent outbursts. One of the men raped his sister, two other family members were arsonists, and still another tried to run over his boss after being told his work wasn't good enough. All the men in the family who have these violent outbursts also have mild levels of mental retardation. None of the women in the family appear to be affected; they neither have these outbursts nor do they exhibit the mental retardation seen in some of the men.

The evidence for a genetic explanation of these outbursts is impressive. You may already have guessed the first piece of information: The condition occurs only in the males. This observation tells geneticists that the gene is probably on the X chromosome. Because men have only one X chromosome, any "bad" or mutated gene will show up. On the other hand, because women have two X chromosomes, they will tend to have a "good" or normal gene to balance out the bad one.

To further narrow down the location of the mutated gene, Brunner and his colleagues conducted a linkage study. If you remember these from Chapter 4, such studies try to identify "marker genes" that are inherited along with the gene you are trying to locate. Because we already know where the marker genes are, we can get a good idea about the approximate location of the mutated gene.

From the linkage study and from biochemical analyses, Brunner and his fellow researchers believe the gene defect in these males involves the gene responsible for producing monoamine oxidase A or MAOA. MAOA is an enzyme that helps break down neurotransmitters, specifically those neurotransmitters that are involved in our "fight or flight" responses to threats and other stresses, including serotonin, dopamine, and noradrenaline. If the MAOA enzyme isn't working properly, the fight or flight neurotransmitters may build up and the people affected will have trouble handling stressful situations. For example, the two arsonists in the Dutch family set fires following the deaths of close relatives. Put simply, these individuals may be more likely to exhibit the fight (react aggressively) reaction than the flight (avoid or leave) reaction in situations that are anger producing, frightening, or frustrating. A subsequent study by this group confirms that only in the affected males is there a deficiency in MAOA (Brunner, Nelen, Breakefield, Ropers, & van Oost, 1993).

What we have is a possible genetic vulnerability to react violently to stressful situations. This vulnerability, in combination with certain stresses, may result in aggression. It is important to realize that this genetic defect, to date, has been found only in this one family. It is unlikely that all or even most aggressive behavior will be traced to this cause. Finally, social, economic, and cultural factors will determine the type and severity of stresses experienced by such people. What this research suggests, however, is that just the right (or wrong!) combination of genetic, neurobiological, and psychosocial contributions have come together in this one Dutch family to create devastating outcomes.

have proposed that this type of neurobiological dysfunction may explain why psychopaths don't feel anxiety about committing the antisocial acts that characterize antisocial personality disorder.

Psychological and social dimensions.

What goes through the mind of a psychopath? Cognitive researchers are trying to discover whether the way psychopaths think can help explain their disturbing behavior. In one of several studies of how psychopaths process reward and punishment, Newman, Patterson, and Kosson (1987) set up a card-playing task on a computer, and provided five cent rewards and fines for correct and incorrect answers to psychopathic and

nonpsychopathic criminal offenders. The game was constructed so that at first they were rewarded about 90% of the time and fined only about 10% of the time. Gradually, the odds of winning changed until the probability of getting a reward was 0%. The researchers observed that despite feedback that reward was no longer forthcoming, the psychopaths continued to play and lose. As a result of this and other studies, they hypothesized that once psychopaths set their sights on a reward goal, they are less likely than nonpsychopaths to be deterred from that goal despite signs that the goal is no longer achievable (Newman & Wallace, 1993). Again, considering the types of reckless and daring activities of some psychopaths—robbing banks without a mask and getting caught immediately—failure to shift attention away from some now unattainable goal seems to fit with the overall picture of a psychopath.

Remember our discussion of programs of research in Chapter 4 and recall the series of studies by Gerald Patterson on aggressive children. Studying these children is important for understanding antisocial personality disorder because they may represent early versions of the people with antisocial personality disorder or psychopathy that we have been discussing (Robins, 1978). Patterson's influential work suggests that aggressive children may continue to act aggressively, and may escalate their aggression, in part as a result of their interactions with their parents (Patterson, 1982). He has found that parents of these children often "give in" to the problems displayed by their children. For example, a mother asks her son to make his bed, and he refuses. Upset by his disobedience, the mother yells at the boy. He in turns yells back and becomes abusive toward the mother. At some point this interchange becomes so aversive for the mother that she stops fighting with her son and walks away, thereby ending the fight but also letting her son not make his bed. Giving in to these problems results in short-term gains for both the mother (calm is restored in the house) and the child (he gets what he wants), but it results in continuing problems. The child has learned to continue fighting and not give up, and the mother learns that the only way to "win" these fights is to give up her demands. This "coercive family process" is coupled with other factors, such as parents' inept monitoring of their child's activities and less parental involvement, to help maintain the aggressive behaviors of these children (Patterson, DeBaryshe, & Ramsey, 1989; Sansbury & Wahler, 1992).

Although little is known regarding which environmental factors play a *direct* role in the cause of antisocial personality disorder and psychopathy (as opposed to childhood conduct disorders), evidence from adoption studies strongly suggests that shared environmental factors—factors that tend to make family members more similar to each other—play an important role in the etiology of criminality and perhaps antisocial personality disorder. For example, in the adoption study by Sigvardsson, Cloninger, Bohman, and von-Knorring (1982), low social status of the adoptive parents increased the risk of nonviolent criminality among females. As we saw with children having conduct disorders, other researchers have reported that individuals with antisocial personality disorder come from homes with inconsistent parental discipline (for example, Robins, 1966). It is not known for certain, however, whether inconsistent discipline directly causes children to develop antisocial personality disorder; it is conceivable, for example, that parents have a genetic vulnerability to antisocial personality disorder

that they pass on to their children but that also causes them to be inadequate parents.

Developmental influences. Many children who exhibit antisocial behaviors will continue these behaviors as they grow older. The form they take changes as the children move into adulthood, going from truancy and stealing from friends to extortion, assaults, armed robbery, or other crimes. Fortunately, clinical lore, as well as scattered empirical reports (Robins, 1966), suggest that many psychopaths burn out over time, particularly around the age of 40, as rates of antisocial behavior begin to decline rather markedly around this age. Hare, McPherson, and Forth (1988) have recently provided empirical support for the existence of this burn out phenomenon. They examined the conviction rates of both male psychopaths and male nonpsychopaths who had been incarcerated for a variety of crimes. The researchers found that between the ages of 16 and 45 (the age range examined in their study), the conviction rates of nonpsychopaths remained relatively constant. In contrast, the conviction rates of psychopaths remained relatively constant up until about 40, at which time they decreased markedly (see Figure 13.3). These results support the claim that psychopaths' rates of antisocial behavior often decline around middle age, although they leave unanswered the question of why this should be so.

An Integrative Model of Antisocial Personality Disorder

How can we put all this information together to get a better understanding of people with antisocial personality disorder? It is important for us to remember that the research in each different area is sometimes carried out with people labeled as having antisocial personality disorder, sometimes with people labeled as being psychopathic, and sometimes with criminals. Whatever the label or grouping, it appears that people with this disorder have a genetic vulnerability that somehow leads to the antisocial behaviors and personality traits we have described. Perhaps this vulnerability leads them to be underaroused and/or fearless. The genetic inheritance might be the propensity for weak inhibition systems (BIS) and overactive reward systems (REW), a condition that could partially account for the differences in cognitive set we saw in the research by Newman and his colleagues (Newman & Wallace, 1993). The weak BIS and strong REW could make it difficult for psychopaths to stop reaching for unattainable goals, thus making them act in impulsive ways.

In a family that may already be under stress because of divorce or substance abuse (Hetherington, Stanley-Hagan, & Anderson, 1989; Patterson, DeBaryshe, & Ramsey, 1989), an interaction style may occur

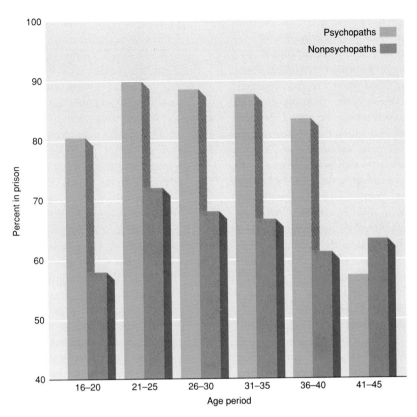

Figure 13.3 Lifetime course of criminal behavior in psychopaths and nonpsychopaths (based on Hare, McPherson, & Forth, 1988)

that actually encourages antisocial behavior on the part of the child. As the child ages, his or her antisocial and impulsive behavior pushes away other children who might be good role models and leaves him or her with others who encourage antisocial behavior (Vuchinich, Bank, & Patterson, 1992). These antisocial behaviors may also contribute to the child's dropping out of school and later to a poor occupational history in adulthood, which help channel the individual into increasingly frustrating life circumstances that further incite him or her to acts against society (Caspi, Elder, & Bem 1987).

The model sketched out here is, admittedly, an abbreviated picture of a complex scenario. The important element is that in this integrative model of antisocial behavior, biological, psychological, and cultural factors combine in intricate ways to create someone like Ryan.

Treatment of Antisocial Personality Disorder

One of the major problems with treating people in this group is shared by a number of the personality disorders: These individuals rarely identify themselves as needing treatment. Because they do not recognize their need for any assistance and because they can be very manipulative even with their therapists, most clinicians have a pessimistic view about the

outcome of treatment for adults who have antisocial personality disorder—and with good reason; there are few documented success stories on the treatment of these individuals. In general, therapists typically defer to incarcerating these people in prison as a deterrent to their committing future antisocial acts. Because of this treatment history, clinicians encourage identification of high-risk individuals as children so treatment of them can be attempted before they become adults (Patterson, 1982).

The most common treatment strategy for children who are at risk for later developing antisocial behavior involves parent training (Patterson, 1986; Sanders, 1992). These programs teach parents to recognize behavior problems early and instruct them on how to use praise and privileges to reduce problem behavior and to encourage more prosocial behaviors. Treatment studies typically show that these types of programs can be effective in significantly improving the behaviors of many children who display antisocial behaviors (Fleischman, 1981; Patterson, Chamberlain, & Reid, 1982). A number of factors, however, put families at risk for either not succeeding in this type of treatment or for dropping out early from treatment; these include cases with a high degree of family dysfunction, socioeconomic disadvantage, high family stress, mother's history of antisocial behavior, and severe conduct disorder on the part of the child (Dumas & Wahler, 1983; Kazdin, Mazurick, & Bass, 1993).

In a recent development, some programs have begun to address these problems even earlier, in an attempt to *prevent* problems from arising. Typically preschool programs, they combine attempts to teach parents good parenting skills with provision of a variety of social supports for families with social and economic disadvantages (Zigler, Taussig, & Black, 1992). It is too soon to assess the success of such programs in preventing the types of adult antisocial behaviors typically observed among people with this personality disorder. However, given the pessimism over the treatment of adults, prevention of antisocial behavior disorders may be the best approach to this problem currently available.

Borderline Personality Disorder

People with **borderline personality disorder** lead tumultuous lives. They lack stability in their moods and in their relationships with other people, and usually they have a very poor self-image. These people often feel empty inside and are at great risk from dying by their own hands. Consider the following case.

The Case of Claire

I have known Claire for over 25 years and have watched her through the good but mostly bad times of her often shaky and erratic life as a person with *borderline personality disorder*. Claire and I went to school together from the eighth grade through high school, and we've kept in touch periodically throughout the years. My first memory of her was of her hair. When we would walk together to school each morning as part of a group, I noticed that occasionally her hair was cut short and rather unevenly. She told me that, when things were not going well, she would cut her own hair severely, and that this activity helped to "fill the void." I later found out that the long sleeves she usually wore hid the scars and cuts on her arms that she had made herself.

Claire was the first of our friends to smoke. What was unusual about her smoking and her later drug use was not that they occurred (this was in the 1960s when "If it feels good, do it!" was more popular than "Just say no!") or that they happened early; the unusual aspect was that she didn't seem to use them to get attention, like others of our peers. Claire was also one of the first of our friends to have divorced parents, and both her parents seemed to have abandoned her

emotionally. She later told me that her father was an alcoholic and that he had regularly beaten her and her mother. She also did poorly academically and had a very low self-image. She would frequently say she was stupid and ugly, yet she was obviously neither of those.

Throughout her school years, Claire would "leave town" periodically, without any explanation. I learned many years later that during these times she was in psychiatric facilities to help with her depression and suicidal behaviors. She would often threaten to kill herself, although we didn't know at the time the seriousness of such threats.

In our later teenage years, we all drifted apart from Claire. She became more and more unpredictable, sometimes berating us for some perceived slight ("You're walking too fast. You don't want to be seen with me!"), and at other times being desperate to be around other people so as not to feel abandoned. We were obviously confused by her behavior toward us. With some people, these emotional outbursts can tend to bring you closer together. Unfortunately for Claire, these incidents and her overall demeanor made us feel that we didn't know her at all. As we all grew older, the "void" she described in herself became overwhelming and eventually shut us all out.

From time to time, I have gotten information about Claire and her progress. She married twice, both times very passionate but stormy relationships interrupted by her hospitalizations. She said that she had once tried to stab her first husband during a particularly violent rage, but fortunately she was unsuccessful. She tried a number of drugs over the years, but mainly used alcohol to "deaden the pain." Now, in her mid-30s, she says that things have "calmed down" some. Although she says she is rarely happy, she does feel a little better about herself and is doing well as a travel agent. She is seeing someone again but is reluctant to become very involved because of her personal history with men. She was ultimately diagnosed as being depressed and having borderline personality disorder.

Clinical Description

The DSM-IV diagnostic criteria for borderline personality disorder are listed in Table 13.11. This is one of the more common of the personality disorders; in psychiatric settings, individuals with borderline personality disorder make up approximately 15% of the population and about 50% of the people in

Table 13.11   Diagnostic Criteria for Borderline Personality Disorder

A pervasive pattern of instability of interpersonal relationships, self-image, and affects, and marked impulsivity beginning by early adulthood and present in a variety of contexts, as indicated by five (or more) of the following:

1. Frantic efforts to avoid real or imagined abandonment. **Note:** Do not include suicidal or self-mutilating behavior covered in Criterion 5.
2. A pattern of unstable and intense interpersonal relationships characterized by alternating between extremes of idealization and devaluation
3. Identity disturbance: markedly and persistently unstable self-image or sense of self
4. Impulsivity in at least two areas that are potentially self-damaging (e.g., spending, sex, substance abuse, reckless driving, binge eating). **Note:** Do not include suicidal or self-mutilating behavior covered in Criterion 5.
5. Recurrent suicidal behavior, gestures, or threats, or self-mutilating behavior
6. Affective instability due to a marked reactivity of mood (e.g., intense episodic dysphoria, irritability, or anxiety usually lasting a few hours and only rarely more than a few days)
7. Chronic feelings of emptiness
8. Inappropriate, intense anger or difficulty controlling anger (e.g., frequent displays of temper, constant anger, recurrent physical fights)
9. Transient, stress-related paranoid ideation or severe dissociative symptoms

Source: DSM-IV, APA, 1994.

these settings who have personality disorders have borderline personality disorder (Widiger & Weissman, 1991). Claire's unfortunate life is illustrative of the instability characteristic of people with borderline personality disorder. They tend to have very intense but turbulent relationships with other people, at once fearing abandonment and at other times sarcastic and lacking control over their emotions. Just as we saw with Claire, these individuals frequently engage in suicidal and/or self-mutilative behaviors, cutting their arms or wrists or sometimes burning or punching themselves. Claire would sometimes use her cigarette to burn her palm or forearm, and once carved her initials in her arm. A significant proportion of these individuals succeed in their suicidal attempts (Widiger & Trull, 1993).

People with this personality disorder are sometimes described as very intense, going from anger to deep depression in a short time. They also are characterized by impulsivity, which can be expressed in drug abuse or self-mutilation. Claire's "void" or a feeling of emptiness also seems common; these people are sometimes described as being chronically bored. The mood disorders that we discussed in Chapter 7 are commonly found among people with this personality disorder, with 24% to 74% having major depression, and 4% to 20% having bipolar disorder (Widiger & Rogers, 1989). In addition, eating disorders, particularly bulimia (see Chapter 8), are also common in these individuals, with almost 25% of bulimics also having borderline personality disorder (Levin & Hyler, 1986). And, as we saw with Claire, substance abuse is common, with up to 67% of the people with this disorder also receiving a diagnosis of at least one substance use disorder (Dulit et al., 1993). As we mentioned earlier in this chapter, suicide is common among people with this disorder, with approximately 6% successfully committing suicide

(Stone, 1989). Similiar to antisocial personality disorder, people with borderline personality disorder seem to improve when they reach their 30s and 40s, although they may continue to have difficulties into old age (Rosowsky & Gurian, 1992).

Causes of Borderline Personality Disorder

The results from almost 20 family studies suggest that borderline personality disorder is more prevalent in families with the disorder, and it is somehow linked with mood disorders (for example, Baron, Gruen, Asnis, & Lord, 1985; Links, Steiner, & Huxley, 1988; Zanarini, Gunderson, Marino, Schwartz, & Frankenburg, 1988). Just as schizotypal personality disorder seems to share a familial association with schizophrenia, borderline personality disorder may have a similar connection to mood disorders (Widiger & Trull, 1993). Although this personality disorder may involve some traits that are inherited (for instance, impulsivity), there appears to be a great deal of room for environmental influences to determine how these individuals fare in the world.

One psychosocial influence that has received a great deal of attention is the possible contribution to this disorder of early trauma, especially sexual and physical abuse. Several studies have shown that people with this disorder are more likely to report abuse than are individuals with other psychiatric conditions (for example, Goldman, D'Angelo, DeMaso, & Mezzacappa, 1992; Ogata et al., 1990). Wagner and Linehan (1994) found that, among women with a history of both borderline personality disorder and parasuicidal behavior (which includes both serious and more minor attempts to commit suicide), 76% reported some type of childhood sexual abuse. In addition, those women with a history of early sexual abuse engaged in more serious attempts to commit suicide. Although we obviously do not know whether such abuse causes later borderline personality disorder (the data here are based on recollection and a correlation between the two phenomena), abuse may be a predisposing factor in at least some cases. If childhood abuse does lead to most cases of borderline personality disorder, this connection may help to explain why women are diagnosed with this disorder more often than men. Girls are two to three times more likely to be sexually abused than boys and thus may be more frequently exposed to the conditions leading to this personality disorder (Herman, Perry, & van der Kolk, 1989).

Building on the possible link to abuse, Gunderson and Sabo (1993) have recently argued that borderline personality disorder is similar to posttraumatic stress disorder (PTSD); they see many resemblances in the borderline personality behavior pattern to behavior patterns of individuals with PTSD. Similarly, Herman, Perry, and van der Kolk (1989) have drawn parallels between the symptoms of people with borderline personality disorder and those of people with PTSD; for example, both syndromes are frequently marked by difficulties in the regulation of mood, impulse control, and interpersonal relationships. These observations all seem to support the hypothesis that borderline personality disorder may be caused by early trauma.

Borderline personality disorder has been observed among people who go through rapid cultural changes. The problems of identity, emptiness, fears of abandonment, and low anxiety threshold have been found in child and adult immigrants (Laxenaire, Ganne-Vevonec, & Streiff, 1982; Skhiri, Annabi, Bi, & Allani, 1982). These observations suggest that early trauma may, in some individuals, lead to the types of behaviors seen among people with borderline personality disorder.

Remember, however, that a history of childhood trauma, including sexual and physical abuse, occurs in a number of other disorders such as somatoform disorder (Chapter 6), panic disorder (Chapter 5), and multiple personality disorder (Chapter 6). In addition, roughly 20% to 40% of individuals with borderline personality disorder have no apparent history of such abuse (Gunderson & Sabo, 1993). Although childhood sexual and physical abuse seems to play some role in the etiology of borderline personality disorder, neither appears to be necessary or sufficient to produce the syndrome.

Treatment of Borderline Personality Disorder

In contrast to the research on the nature of borderline personality disorder, relatively few studies have been done to examine the effects of treatment on people with this disorder. Psychoanalytic treatment is

often used with this group, but there are few or no adequately controlled studies. Many people with borderline personality disorder appear to respond positively to a variety of medications, including tricyclic antidepressants (Soloff et al., 1989; Stone, 1986), minor tranquilizers (Gardner & Cowdry, 1986), and lithium (Links, Steiner, Boiago, & Irwin, 1990). However, people with borderline personality disorder often have problems with drug abuse, compliance with treatment, and suicide attempts, and these conditions complicate efforts to provide successful treatments.

Research on psychological treatment is limited. In one exception, Linehan (1987) described her approach to treating people with this personality disorder; she called it *dialectical behavior therapy (DBT)*. This therapy involves helping the individuals cope with the stressors in their lives that seem to trigger suicidal behaviors. Weekly individual sessions are conducted to provide support and teach patients how to identify and regulate their emotions. In addition, they receive treatment similar to that used for people with posttraumatic stress disorder, where prior traumatic events are reexperienced to help extinguish the fear associated with them (see Chapter 5). Preliminary results suggest that this treatment approach may help reduce suicide attempts, dropouts from treatment, and hospitalizations (Linehan, Armstrong, Suarez, Allmon, & Heard, 1991; Linehan, Heard, & Armstrong, 1992). A recent follow-up of 39 women who received either dialectic behavior therapy (DBT) or general therapeutic support (called "treatment-as-usual") for 1 year showed that, during the first 6 months of follow-up, the women in the DBT group had less suicidal behavior, less anger, and better social adjustment (Linehan & Kehrer, 1993). This type of treatment appears to hold some promise for people with borderline personality disorder.

Histrionic Personality Disorder

Individuals with **histrionic personality disorder** tend to be overly dramatic and often appear almost to be acting, which is why the term *histrionic*, meaning theatrical in manner, is used. Consider the following case.

The Case of Pat

When we first met, Pat seemed to radiate a certain enjoyment of life. She was single, in her mid-30s, and had recently gone back to school for her master's degree. She often dressed in a very flamboyant manner that made her stand out from the rest of her co-workers. During the day she worked as a teacher for children with disabilities, and when she wasn't in class she was often out late on a date. When I first spoke with her, she enthusiastically told me how impressed she was with my work in the field of developmental disabilities and that she had been extremely successful in using some of my techniques with her students. She was clearly overdoing the praise, but who wouldn't appreciate such flattering comments?

Because some of our research was being done with children in her classroom, I had frequent meetings with Pat. Over a period of weeks, however, our interactions grew strained. She frequently complained of different illnesses and injuries (for instance, falling in the parking lot, twisting her neck looking out a window) that interfered with her duties in the classroom. She was very disorganized, often leaving to the very last minute tasks that required considerable planning. Pat made promises to other people that were impossible to keep but that seemed to be aimed at winning their approval. When she couldn't keep the promise she had made, she would usually make up a story that was designed to elicit sympathy and compassion. For example, she promised the mother of one of her students that she would put on a "massive and unique" birthday party for her daughter, but seemed to have completely forgotten about her promise until the mother showed up with cake and juice. Upon seeing her, Pat flew into a rage and blamed the principal for keeping her late after school, although there was no truth to this accusation.

Pat often interrupted meetings about research to talk about her latest boyfriend. The boyfriends changed almost weekly, but her enthusiasm ("Like no other man I have ever met!") and optimism about the future ("He's the guy I want to spend the rest of my life with!") remained high for each of them. Wedding plans were seriously discussed with almost every one, despite the brief time they had together. Pat was very ingratiating, especially to the other male teachers, who would often "bail her out" of trouble she would get into because of her disorganization.

When it became clear that she would probably not be able to keep her teaching job due to her poor performance, she managed to manipulate several of the male teachers and the assistant principal into recommending her for a new job in a nearby school district. A year later she was still employed at the new school, but had been moved twice to different classrooms. According to other teachers she worked with, Pat continued to lack close interpersonal relationships with significant others, although she herself described the person she was with currently as "deeply involved." After a rather long period of depression, Pat sought help from a psychologist, who, along with her depression, diagnosed her as having histrionic personality disorder.

Like other people with this personality disorder, Pat engaged in excessive displays of emotion that primarily served to keep her at the center of attention. Through their dress, mannerisms, and speech, people with this disorder often act in very dramatic ways. Pat promised a "massive and unique" party for one of her students. She was very self-centered, yet on the surface seemed to be very interested in others.

The DSM-IV diagnostic criteria for histrionic personality disorder are in Table 13.12. People with histrionic personality disorder are inclined to express their emotions in an exaggerated fashion; for example, they may hug individuals they have just met or cry uncontrollably following a sad movie. They also tend to be vain and self-centered, and to be uncomfortable in settings in which they are not in the limelight. These

---

Table 13.12 Diagnostic Criteria for Histrionic Personality Disorder

A pervasive pattern of excessive emotionality and attention seeking, beginning by early adulthood and present in a variety of contexts, as indicated by five (or more) of the following:

1. Is uncomfortable in situations in which he or she is not the center of attention
2. Interaction with others is often characterized by inappropriate sexually seductive or provocative behavior
3. Displays rapidly shifting and shallow expression of emotions
4. Consistently uses physical appearance to draw attention to self
5. Has a style of speech that is excessively impressionistic and lacking in detail
6. Shows self-dramatization, theatricality, and exaggerated expression of emotion
7. Is suggestible, i.e., easily influenced by others or circumstances
8. Considers relationships to be more intimate than they actually are

Source: DSM-IV, APA, 1994.

individuals are often seductive in both their appearance and behavior, and they are typically very concerned about their looks. Pat, for example, would spend a great deal of money on unusual jewelry and be sure to point it out to anyone who would listen. In addition, they seek reassurance and approval constantly and may become upset or angry when others do not attend to them or praise them. People with histrionic personality disorder also tend to be impulsive and have great difficulty delaying gratification.

Individuals with histrionic personality disorder often possess an impressionistic cognitive style (Shapiro, 1965) characterized by a tendency to view situations in very global, black-and-white terms. In addition to this way of thinking, they often talk in a way that is vague, lacking in detail, and characterized by hyperbole (Pfohl, 1991). For example, when Pat was asked about a date she had had the night before, she might say it was "way cool" but be unable to provide any more detailed information.

Causes of Histrionic Personality Disorder

Despite the long history of attention to this concept, very little research has been done on the causes or treatment of histrionic personality disorder. The origins of *hysteria* lie with the ancient Greek philosophers who believed that many unexplainable problems of women were caused by the uterus (*hystera*) migrating within the body (Abse, 1987). As we have seen, however, histrionic personality disorder is also observed among men.

One hypothesis concerning this disorder involves its possible relationship with another personality disorder—antisocial personality disorder. There is evidence that histrionic personality and antisocial personality are associated within individuals much more often than expected by chance. Lilienfeld and his colleagues (1986), for example, found that roughly two-thirds of people with histrionic personality also met criteria for antisocial personality disorder.

The evidence for this association has led to the suggestion (for example, Cloninger, 1978; Lilienfeld, 1992) that histrionic personality and antisocial personality may represent sex-typed alternative expressions of the same underlying condition. That is, females with this underlying condition, which has yet to be identified, may be predisposed to exhibit a predominantly histrionic pattern, whereas males with this underlying condition may be predisposed to exhibit a predominantly antisocial pattern.

Treatment of Histrionic Personality Disorder

Although a great deal has been written about ways of helping people with this disorder, there is very little research that can demonstrate that they work

(Dulit et al., 1993). Some therapists have tried to modify the attention-getting behavior exhibited by these individuals. Kass, Silvers, and Abrams (1972) worked with five women, four of whom had been admitted to the hospital due to suicide attempts and all of whom were later diagnosed with histrionic personality disorder. As part of the therapy the women were given rewards for appropriate interactions and were fined for inappropriate, attention-getting behavior. The therapists noted improvement after an 18-month follow-up, but they did not collect scientific data to confirm this observation.

A large part of therapy for these individuals usually involves a focus on their problematic interpersonal relationships. They often manipulate others through emotional crises, using charm, sex, and seductiveness, or complaining (Beck & Freeman, 1990). People with histrionic personality disorder often need to be shown how the short-term gains derived from this interactional style result in long-term costs, and they need to be taught more appropriate ways of negotiating their wants and needs.

Narcissistic Personality Disorder

We all know people who think highly of themselves—perhaps beyond their real abilities. These people consider themselves special and somehow different from others and deserving of special treatment. **Narcissistic personality disorder** describes this tendency taken to its extreme. The name for this disorder was borrowed from Greek mythology. Narcissus was a youth who was said to have spurned the love of Echo, so enamored was he of his own beauty. He spent his days pining away, admiring his own image reflected in a pool of water. Psychoanalysts, including Sigmund Freud, used the term *narcissistic* to describe people who show an exaggerated sense of self-importance and a preoccupation with receiving the attention of others (Cooper & Ronningstam, 1992). Consider the following case.

The Case of David

David was an attorney in his early 40s when he sought treatment for depressed mood. David appeared to be an outgoing man who paid meticulous attention to his appearance. He made a point of asking for the therapist's admiration of his new designer suit, his winter tan, and his new foreign convertible. He also asked the therapist what kind of car he drove and how many VIP clients he dealt with. David wanted to make sure that he was dealing with someone who was the best in the business. David spoke of being an "ace" student and a "super" athlete, but could not provide any details that would validate a superior performance in these areas.

During law school, David became a workaholic, fueled by fantasies of brilliant work and international recognition. He spent minimal time with his wife, and after their son was born, even less time with either of them. He waited until he felt reasonably secure in his first job so that he could let go of her financial support, and then he sought a divorce.

After his divorce, David decided that he was totally free to just please himself. He loved spending all his money on himself, and he lavishly decorated his condominium and bought an attention-getting wardrobe. He constantly sought the companionship of different, attractive women.

David felt better when someone flattered him; when he was in a group social situation where he could easily grab the center of attention; and when he could fantasize about obtaining a high-level position, being honored for his great talent, or just being fabulously wealthy. (Beck & Freeman, 1990, pp. 245–246)

Clinical Description

The DSM-IV diagnostic criteria for narcissistic personality disorder are listed in Table 13.13. People with this disorder have an unreasonable sense of self-importance and are so preoccupied with themselves that they lack sensitivity and compassion for other people. They aren't comfortable unless someone is admiring them. Their exaggerated feelings and fantasies of greatness or "grandiosity" create in these people a number of negative attributes. They require and expect a great deal of special attention from other people—the best table in the restaurant, the illegal parking space in front of the movie theater. They also tend to use or exploit other people for their own interests and show little empathy for others. When confronted with other successful people, they can be extremely envious and arrogant.

Causes and Treatment of Narcissistic Personality Disorder

Children start out in life being narcissistic—self-centered and demanding. However, part of our socialization process involves teaching children empathy and altruism. Some writers, including Kohut (1971, 1977), believe that narcissistic personality disorder arises largely from a profound failure of empathic "mirroring" on the part of parents very early in a child's development. As a consequence of these empathic failures, the child remains fixated at a self-centered, "grandiose" stage of development. In addition, the child (and later the adult) becomes involved in an essentially endless (and fruitless) search for the "ideal" person who will meet their unfulfilled empathic needs.

In a sociological view of narcissistic personality disorder, Christopher Lasch (1978) wrote in his popular book *The Culture of Narcissism* that this personality disorder is increasing in prevalence in most Western societies, primarily as a consequence of large-scale social changes such as greater emphasis on short-term hedonism, individualism, competitiveness, and success. According to Lasch, the "me generation" has produced more than its share of individuals with narcissistic personality disorder. Indeed, there are reports that narcissistic personality disorder is increasing in prevalence (Cooper & Ronningstam, 1992). However, this rise may be a consequence of increased interest in, and research on, this disorder.

Treatment research on people with narcissistic personality disorder is extremely limited in both number of studies and in reports of success (Turkat & Maisto, 1985). When therapy is attempted with these individuals it often focuses on their distorted view of

Table 13.13 Diagnostic Criteria for Narcissistic Personality Disorder

A pervasive pattern of grandiosity (in fantasy or behavior), need for admiration, and lack of empathy, beginning by early adulthood and present in a variety of contexts, as indicated by five (or more) of the following:

1. Has a grandiose sense of self-importance (e.g., exaggerates achievements and talents, expects to be recognized as superior without commensurate achievements)
2. Is preoccupied with fantasies of unlimited success, power, brilliance, beauty, or ideal love
3. Believes that he or she is "special" and unique and can only be understood by, or should associate with, other special or high-status people (or institutions)
4. Requires excessive admiration
5. Has a sense of entitlement, i.e., unreasonable expectations of especially favorable treatment or automatic compliance with his or her expectations
6. Is interpersonally exploitative, i.e., takes advantage of others to achieve his or her own ends
7. Lacks empathy: is unwilling to recognize or identify with the feelings and needs of others
8. Is often envious of others or believes that others are envious of him or her
9. Shows arrogant, haughty behaviors or attitudes

Source: DSM-IV, APA, 1994.

themselves (their grandiosity), their hypersensitivity to evaluation, and their lack of empathy toward others (Beck & Freeman, 1990). Cognitive therapy aims at replacing their grandiose fantasies with a focus on the day-to-day pleasurable experiences that are truly attainable. Coping strategies such as relaxation training are used to help them face and accept criticism by others. In addition, helping them focus on the feelings of others is also a goal. Because narcissistic personality disorder is frequently accompanied by depressed mood and individuals with this disorder appear to be prone to severe depressive episodes, particularly in middle age, treatment is often initiated for the depression. However, it is impossible to draw any conclusions about the impact such a treatment focus may have on the actual narcissistic personality disorder.

Avoidant Personality Disorder

As the name suggests, people with **avoidant personality disorder** are extremely sensitive to the opinion of others and therefore avoid social relationships. Don't confuse this disorder with just being "shy," however. Individuals with avoidant personality disorder actively avoid close relationships. They have extremely low self-esteem. This poor opinion of themselves, coupled with a fear of being rejected, causes them to reject the attention others crave. Consider the following case.

The Case of Jane

Jane was raised by an alcoholic mother who had borderline personality disorder and who abused her verbally and physically. As a child she made sense of her mother's abusive treatment by believing that she (Jane) must be an intrinsically unworthy person to be treated so badly. As an adult in her late 20s, Jane still expected to be rejected when others found out that she was inherently unworthy and bad.

Jane was highly self-critical and predicted that she would not be accepted. She thought that people would not like her, that they would see she was a loser, and that she would not have anything to say. She became upset if she perceived that someone in even the most fleeting encounter was reacting negatively or neutrally. If a newspaper vendor failed to smile at her, or a sales clerk was slightly curt, Jane automatically thought it must be because she (Jane) was somehow unworthy or unlikable. She then felt quite sad. Even when she was receiving positive-feedback from a friend, she discounted it. As a result, Jane had few friends and certainly no close ones. (Beck & Freeman, 1990, p. 263)

The DSM-IV diagnostic criteria for avoidant personality disorder are listed in Table 13.14. Theodore Millon (1981), who initially proposed this diagnosis, notes that it was important to distinguish between individuals who are asocial because they are apathetic, affectively flat, and relatively uninterested in interpersonal relationships (comparable to what DSM-IV terms *schizoid* personality disorder) and individuals who are asocial because they are interpersonally anxious and fearful of rejection. It is the latter who would fit the criteria of avoidant personality disorder.

Causes of Avoidant Personality Disorder

A number of theories have been proposed that integrate biological and psychosocial influences as the cause of avoidant personality disorder. Millon (1981), for example, suggests that individuals with this disorder may be born with a difficult "temperament" or personality characteristics. As a result, their parents may reject them, or at least not provide them with enough early, uncritical love. This rejection, in turn, may lead them to

Table 13.14   Diagnostic Criteria for Avoidant Personality Disorder

A pervasive pattern of social inhibition, feelings of inadequacy, and hypersensitivity to negative evaluation, beginning by early adulthood and present in a variety of contexts, as indicated by four (or more) of the following:

1. Avoids occupational activities that involve significant interpersonal contact, because of fears of criticism, disapproval, or rejection
2. Is unwilling to get involved with people unless certain of being liked
3. Shows restraint within intimate relationships because of the fear of being shamed or ridiculed
4. Is preoccupied with being criticized or rejected in social situations
5. Is inhibited in new interpersonal situations because of feelings of inadequacy
6. Views self as socially inept, personally unappealing, or inferior to others
7. Is unusually reluctant to take personal risks or to engage in any new activities because they may prove embarrassing

Source: DSM-IV, APA, 1994.

feel socially alienated and to have low self-esteem, conditions that persist into adulthood. Some limited support does exist for psychosocial influences. Stravynski, Elie, and Franche (1989) questioned a group of people with avoidant personality disorder and a group of control subjects who had no personality disorder about their treatment by their parents when they were children. The authors of this study found that those with the personality disorder remembered their parents as more rejecting, more guilt engendering, and less affectionate than the control group.

Some caution is in order in interpreting the results of this study. You probably noticed that this is a *retrospective study,* meaning it relies on the subjects' memory for a report of what has happened before. The differences in the reports by these two groups could be a consequence of differences in their ability to remember their childhood rather than actual differences in the way they were treated. Also, it could be that people with avoidant personality disorder are more sensitive to the way they are treated by others, and therefore their memory of how they were treated is different from their actual treatment. The findings from this study are intriguing, nonetheless, and should be followed up as a possible contributor to our understanding of this disorder.

Treatment of Avoidant Personality Disorder

In contrast to what has been the case for most of the other personality disorders, a number of well-controlled studies exist on the approaches to therapy for people with avoidant personality disorder. Behavioral intervention techniques for anxiety and social skills problems have had some success with these individuals (Alden, 1989; Alden & Capreol, 1993; Renneberg, Goldstein, Phillips, & Chambless, 1990; Stravynski, Lesage, Marcouiller, & Elie, 1989). Because the problems experienced by people with avoidant personality disorder resemble those of people with social phobia, many of the same treatments are used for both groups. A number of these were discussed in Chapter 5.

As an example of treatment, Renneberg et al. (1990) identified areas that caused anxiety in a group of 17 people with this personality disorder, including a fear of rejection, a fear of criticism, and anxiety concerning their appearance. In groups of five or six patients, they used *systematic desensitization*—which involves relaxation in the presence of feared situations (for example, "You speak to a group of people at work, and you realize that your voice is not powerful enough. Your voice is childish")—and *behavioral rehearsal*—acting out situations that cause the patients to be anxious—to help reduce the anxiety. They found that, as a group, these people improved in such areas as fear of negative evaluation and social avoidance and distress. The

improvements tended to be modest for the people in the treatment groups, although, given the usually poor outcomes found among people with personality disorders, even this moderate improvement is encouraging.

Dependent Personality Disorder

We all know what it means to be "dependent" on another person. For the individuals with **dependent personality disorder,** however, this reliance on others extends to making everyday decisions as well as important life decisions, and it results in an unreasonable fear of being abandoned. Consider the following case.

The Case of Karen

Karen was a 45-year-old married woman who was referred for treatment by her physician for problems with panic attacks. During the evaluation, she appeared to be very worried, sensitive, and naive. She was easily overcome with emotion and cried on and off throughout the session. She was self-critical at every opportunity throughout the evaluation. For example, when asked how she got along with other people, she reported that "others think I'm dumb and inadequate," although she could give no evidence as to what made her think that. She reported that she didn't like school because "I was dumb," and that she always felt that she was not good enough.

Karen described staying in her first marriage for 10 years, even though "it was hell." Her husband had affairs with many other women and was verbally abusive. She tried to leave him many times, but gave in to his repeated requests to return. She was finally able to divorce him, and shortly afterwards she met and married her current husband, whom she described as kind, sensitive, and supportive. Karen stated that she preferred to have others make important decisions, and agreed with other people in order to avoid conflict. She worried about being left alone without anyone to take care of her, and reported feeling lost without other people's reassurance. She also reported that her feelings were easily hurt, so she worked hard not to do anything that might lead to criticism. (Beck & Freeman, 1990, pp. 288–289)

Clinical Description

The DSM-IV diagnostic criteria for dependent personality disorder are listed in Table 13.15. Individuals with dependent personality disorder sometimes

Table 13.15 Diagnostic Criteria for Dependent Personality Disorder

A pervasive and excessive need to be taken care of that leads to submissive and clinging behavior and fears of separation, beginning by early adulthood and present in a variety of contexts, as indicated by five (or more) of the following:

1. Has difficulty making everyday decisions without an excessive amount of advice and reassurance from others
2. Needs others to assume responsibility for most major areas of his or her life
3. Has difficulty expressing disagreement with others because of fear of loss of support or approval. Note: Do not include realistic fears of retribution.
4. Has difficulty initiating projects or doing things on his or her own (because of a lack of self-confidence in judgment or abilities rather than a lack of motivation or energy)
5. Goes to excessive lengths to obtain nurturance and support from others, to the point of volunteering to do things that are unpleasant
6. Feels uncomfortable or helpless when alone because of exaggerated fears of being unable to care for himsef or herself
7. Urgently seeks another relationship as a source of care and support when a close relationship ends
8. Is unrealistically preoccupied with fears of being left to take care of himself or herself

Source: DSM-IV, APA, 1994.

agree with other people despite their belief in their own but different opinion, due to a fear of being rejected. Submissiveness, timidity, and passivity are important characteristics. In some ways, individuals with this disorder are similar to those with *avoidant personality disorder* because of their feelings of inadequacy, their sensitivity to criticism, and their need for reassurance from others. However, although people with avoidant personality disorder respond to these feelings by avoiding social relationships, those with dependent personality disorder respond by clinging to these relationships (Hirschfeld, Shea, & Weise, 1991).

Causes and Treatment of Dependent Personality Disorder

We are all born dependent on other people. We require the help of our parents for things such as food, protection from the environment, and nurturance. Part of the socialization process involves helping us live more independent lives (Bornstein, 1992). It is thought that disruptions in this development, such as the death of a parent at an early age or neglect or rejection by caretakers, could cause people to grow up always afraid that they will be abandoned (Stone, 1993). This view comes from work in child development on "attachment" or how children learn to bond with their parents or other important people in their lives (Bowlby, 1977). If these early experiences are disrupted, individuals may be constantly anxious that they will lose people close to them.

The treatment literature for this disorder is mostly descriptive; very little research exists to show whether a particular treatment is effective in improving the lives of these individuals. On the surface, because

Box 13.2 Should There Be a Diagnosis of "Independent" Personality Disorder?

We have pointed out previously in this chapter issues surrounding the possibility of sexism in several of the personality disorders. Marcie Kaplan (1983) has been one of the critics of these disorders, and facetiously uses a new but fictitious diagnosis to illustrate her case. Should there be a new personality disorder with the following criteria? What do you think the sex ratio would be for this disorder? Do you know anyone who fits this description, and in whom it results in significant functional impairment or subjective distress?

Diagnostic Criteria for "Independent" Personality Disorder (Kaplan, 1983)

A. Puts work (career) above relationships with loved ones (e.g., travels a lot on business, works late at night and on weekends).

B. Is reluctant to take into account others' needs when making decisions, especially concerning the individual's career or use of leisure time, e.g., expects spouse and children to relocate to another city because of individual's career plans.
C. Passively allows others to assume responsibility for major areas of social life because of inability to express necessary emotion (e.g., lets spouse assume most child-care responsibilities).

of their attentiveness and eagerness to give responsibility for their problems to the therapist, people with dependent personality disorder can appear to be ideal patients in therapy. However, their submissiveness negates one of the major goals of therapy, which is to make the person more independent and responsible for his or her own progress. Therapy therefore progresses gradually, with the therapist trying to have the patient develop confidence in his or her ability to make decisions independently (Beck & Freeman, 1990). There is a particular need for care that the patient with dependent personality disorder does not come to be overly dependent on the therapist.

Obsessive-Compulsive Personality Disorder

People who have **obsessive-compulsive personality disorder** are characterized by a fixation on things being done "the right way." Although many might envy their persistence and dedication, this preoccupation with details prevents them from actually completing much of anything. Consider the following case.

The Case of Daniel

Each day at exactly 8 A.M., Daniel would arrive at his office at the university, where he was a graduate student in psychology. On his way into the office, he would always stop at the 7-11 for coffee and a copy of the *New York Times*. From 8 to 9:15 A.M. he would drink his coffee and read the *Times*. At 9:15 he would organize the files that held the hundreds of papers related to his doctoral dissertation, now several years overdue. At 10 A.M. until lunch he would read one of

these papers and highlight relevant passages. At noon, he would take the paper bag that held his lunch (always a peanut butter and jelly sandwich with an apple) and go to the cafeteria to purchase a soda and eat by himself. From 1 P.M. until 5 P.M. he would have meetings, organize his desk, make lists of things to do, and enter the references he had into a new database program on his computer.

At home, he would have dinner with his wife, then excuse himself to work on his dissertation. He would routinely work until after 11 P.M., although much of the time was spent trying out new features of his home computer. Daniel was no closer to completing his dissertation than he had been four and a half years ago. His wife was threatening to leave him because he was equally as rigid about everything at home and she didn't want to remain in this "limbo" with Daniel in school forever. He eventually sought help from a therapist for the anxiety he was feeling over his deteriorating relationship with his wife, and was diagnosed as having obsessive-compulsive personality disorder.

Clinical Description

The DSM-IV diagnostic criteria for obsessive-compulsive personality disorder are listed in Table 13.16. Like many with this personality disorder, Daniel is very work-oriented and spends little time going to movies, parties, or anything that isn't related to psychology. And because of their general rigidity, these people tend to have poor interpersonal relationships. As you saw with Daniel, his wife was becoming

Table 13.16 Diagnostic Criteria for Obsessive-Compulsive Personality Disorder

A pervasive pattern of preoccupation with orderliness, perfectionism, and mental and interpersonal control, at the expense of flexibility, openness, and efficiency, beginning by early adulthood and present in a variety of contexts, as indicated by four (or more) of the following:

1. Is preoccupied with details, rules, lists, order, organization, or schedules to the extent that the major point of the activity is lost
2. Shows perfectionism that interferes with task completion (e.g., is unable to complete a project because his or her own overly strict standards are not met)
3. Is excessively devoted to work and productivity to the exclusion of leisure activities and friendships (not accounted for by obvious economic necessity)
4. Is overconscientious, scrupulous, and inflexible about matters of morality, ethics, or values (not accounted for by cultural or religious identification)
5. Is unable to discard worn-out or worthless objects even when they have no sentimental value
6. Is reluctant to delegate tasks or to work with others unless they submit to exactly his or her way of doing things
7. Adopts a miserly spending style toward both self and others; money is viewed as something to be hoarded for future catastrophes
8. Shows rigidity and stubbornness

Source: DSM-IV, APA, 1994.

increasingly frustrated trying to support him, and seriously considered divorce.

This personality disorder seems to be only distantly related to *obsessive-compulsive disorder,* one of the anxiety disorders we described in Chapter 5. People like Daniel tend not to have the obsessive thoughts and the compulsive behaviors (for example, checking the door 15 times to see that it is locked) seen in the like-named obsessive-compulsive disorder (OCD). Although people with OCD will sometimes show characteristics of this personality disorder, they also show the characteristics of a number of the other personality disorders as well (for example, avoidant, histrionic, dependent) (Stone, 1993).

Causes and Treatment of Obsessive-Compulsive Personality Disorder

There seems to be a contributing role for genetics in this disorder, although the contribution seems to be weak (McKeon & Murray, 1987; Stone, 1993). Some people may be predisposed to favor structure in their lives, but for this predisposition to reach the level it did in Daniel may require parental reinforcement of conformity and neatness.

We do not have much information on the successful treatment of individuals with this disorder. Therapy often proceeds by attacking the fears that seem to underlie the need for orderliness. Often these individuals are anxious that what they do will be inadequate, so they procrastinate and excessively ruminate about the important and the not-so-important things in their lives. Therapists will help the individual relax, or will use distraction techniques to redirect his or her compulsive thoughts.

Personality Disorders Under Study

We started this chapter by noting difficulties that remain with the categories of personality disorders—for example, much overlap exists among the different categories, suggesting that there may be other ways to divide up these pervasive difficulties of character. It shouldn't surprise you to learn that other personality disorders have been proposed over the years for inclusion in the DSM. For example, DSM-III-R included two additional disorders for possible inclusion: a *sadistic personality disorder,* which included people who receive pleasure by inflicting pain on others, and a *self-defeating personality disorder,* which included people who are overly passive and accept the pain and suffering imposed by others. However, there were few studies to support the existence of these disorders, so they have not been included in the DSM-IV (Pfohl, 1993). Two new categories of personality disorder are under study in DSM-IV. One of these—*depressive personality disorder*—includes personality traits dominated by self-criticism, dejection, a judgmental stance toward others, and a tendency to feelings of guilt. A second category—*negativistic personality disorder*—is characterized by a "passive-aggressive" attitude, where people adopt a negativistic attitude to resist routine demands and expectations. This category is an expansion of a previous DSM-III-R category, *passive-aggressive personality disorder.* Neither of these new categories has had enough research attention to warrant inclusion as additional personality disorders in the DSM.

Summary

- The personality disorders represent long-standing and ingrained ways of thinking, feeling, and behaving that can cause a person and/or other people significant distress. Because people may display two or more of these maladaptive ways of interacting with the world, considerable disagreement remains over the way the personality disorders are categorized.

- DSM-IV includes 10 personality disorders that are divided into three "clusters": Cluster A includes the "odd or eccentric" disorders of paranoid, schizoid, and schizotypal personality disorders; Cluster B includes the "dramatic, emotional, or erratic" disorders of antisocial, borderline, histrionic, and narcissistic personality disorders; Cluster C includes the "anxious or fearful" disorders of avoidant, dependent, and obsessive-compulsive personality disorders.

- People with paranoid personality disorder are excessively mistrustful and suspicious of other people, without any justification. They tend not to confide in others and expect other people to do them harm.

- People with schizoid personality disorder show a pattern of detachment from social relationships and a very limited range of emotions in interpersonal situations. They seem "aloof," "cold," and "indifferent" to other people.

- People with schizotypal personality disorder are typically socially isolated and behave in ways that would seem unusual to many of us. Additionally, they tend to be suspicious and have odd beliefs about the world.

- People with antisocial personality disorder have a history of failing to comply with social norms. They perform actions most of us would find unacceptable—such as stealing from friends and family. They also tend to be irresponsible, impulsive, and deceitful.

- In contrast to the DSM-IV criteria for antisocial personality, which focuses almost entirely on observable behaviors (for example, impulsively and repeatedly changing employment, residence, or sexual partners), the related concept of psychopathy focuses primarily on underlying personality traits (for instance, self-centeredness, manipulativeness).

- People with borderline personality disorder lack stability in their moods and in their relationships with other people, and usually have a very poor self-image. These individuals often feel empty inside and are at great risk from dying by their own hand.

- Individuals with histrionic personality disorder tend to be overly dramatic and often appear almost to be acting, which is why the term *histrionic,* meaning theatrical in manner, is used.

- People who display narcissistic personality disorder think highly of themselves—beyond their real abilities. These people consider themselves special and somehow different from others and deserving of special treatment.

- People with avoidant personality disorder are extremely sensitive to the opinion of others and therefore avoid social relationships. They have extremely low self-esteem; this poor opinion of themselves, coupled with a fear of being rejected, causes them to reject the attention others crave.

- Individuals with dependent personality disorder rely on others to the extent that they let them make everyday decisions as well as important life decisions; this results in an unreasonable fear of being abandoned.

- People who have obsessive-compulsive personality disorder are characterized by a fixation on things being done "the right way." This preoccupation with the details prevents them from actually completing much of anything.

- Personality disorders are important for the clinician to consider because they may interfere with efforts to treat more specific problems such as anxiety, depression, or substance abuse. Unfortunately, the presence of one or more of these personality disorders is associated with a poor treatment outcome and a generally negative prognosis.

Key Terms

antisocial personality disorder (527)
avoidant personality disorder (546)
borderline personality disorder (540)
dependent personality disorder (547)

histrionic personality disorder (542)
narcissistic personality disorder (544)
obsessive-compulsive personality disorder (549)
paranoid personality disorder (521)

personality disorders (515)
psychopathy (529)
schizoid personality disorder (524)
schizotypal personality disorder (526)

"I started to withdraw socially. For example, I would go to the unfinished basement, set up an old 12-inch black and white TV, and watch game shows or movies. While watching TV, I thought I had mental telepathy. I started destroying objects and erupted into heated arguments with almost anyone who crossed my path. I felt there was no way out, no sense of escape both mentally and physically."

J. A. DeMann

"First Person Account: The Evolution of a Person with Schizophrenia"

14

Schizophrenia and Other Psychotic Disorders

A middle-aged man walks the streets of New York City with aluminum foil on the inside of his hat so that the Martians can't read his mind. A young woman sits in her college classroom and hears the voice of God telling her that she is a vile and disgusting person. You try to strike up a conversation with the supermarket bagger, but he stares at you vacantly and will say only one or two words in a flat, toneless voice. Each of these people may have the rather startling disorder known as **schizophrenia**, which is characterized by a broad spectrum of cognitive and emotional dysfunctions including delusions and hallucinations, disorganized speech and behavior, and inappropriate emotions.

Schizophrenia is a complex syndrome that inevitably has a devastating effect on the lives of the person affected and on his or her family. This disorder can disrupt a person's perception of the world, the way he or she thinks, speaks, and moves, and almost every aspect of daily functioning. And despite important advances in treatment, for someone to make a complete recovery from schizophrenia is rare. Obviously, this catastrophic disorder can take a tremendous emotional toll on everyone involved. In addition to the emotional costs of this disorder, its financial costs are considerable, estimated nationally to exceed the amount spent on the treatment of people with cancer (National Foundation for Brain Research, 1992). Because it is so widespread,

affecting approximately one out of every hundred persons at some point in their lives, and because its consequences are so severe, research on understanding its causes and treatment has understandably proliferated over the years. Given the great deal of attention schizophrenia has received, you would think that the question, "What is schizophrenia?" would by now be easily answered. It is not.

In this chapter we explore this intriguing disorder and examine the history of efforts to determine whether schizophrenia is in fact one distinct disorder or a combination of disorders. The search is complicated by the presence of subtypes of schizophrenia—different presentations and combinations of symptoms such as hallucinations, delusions, and disorders of speech, emotion, and socialization. After discussing the characteristics of people with schizophrenia, we describe some of the research that has delved into the nature of the disorder to try to uncover its causes and its treatment.

Perspectives on the Concept of Schizophrenia

It can be helpful to look at the concept of schizophrenia as it has evolved over the years. This history is unparalleled among that of other disorders outlined in this book. Knowing something about it may assist you in realizing the multifaceted nature of the disorder itself and the corresponding complexity of both understanding and treating this perplexing problem.

In *Observations on Madness and Melancholy,* published in 1809, John Haslam eloquently portrayed what he called "a form of insanity." The following quotation illustrates some of the symptoms that resemble our modern-day conception of schizophrenia, although it does not capture all the problems we now consider characteristic of this disorder.

> The attack is almost imperceptible; some months usually elapse before it becomes the subject of particular notice; and fond relatives are frequently deceived by the hope that it is only an abatement of excessive vivacity, conducting to a prudent reserve, and steadiness of character. A degree of apparent thoughtfulness and inactivity precede, together with a diminution of the ordinary curiosity, concerning that which is passing before them; and they therefore neglect those objects and pursuits which formerly proved courses of delight and instruction. The sensibility appears to be considerably blunted: they do not bear the same affection towards their parents and relations: they become unfeeling to kindness, and careless of reproof. . . . I have painfully witnessed this hopeless and degrading change,

which in a short time has transformed the most promising and vigorous intellect into a slavering and bloated idiot. (Haslam, 1809, pp. 64–67)

At approximately the same time Haslam wrote his description in England, the French physician Philippe Pinel wrote about the cases he was seeing that also resembled people whom we would describe as having schizophrenia (Pinel, 1801, 1809). Some 50 years later another physician, Benedict Morel, used the French term *démence* (loss of mind) *précoce* (early, premature), which is *dementia praecox* in Latin, to describe the disorder's frequent onset in adolescence.

Toward the end of the 19th century, the German psychiatrist Emil Kraepelin built on the writings of Haslam, Pinel, and Morel (among others) to give us what stands today as the most enduring description and categorization of this disorder. Two of his accomplishments are especially important. First, Kraepelin (1899) brought together several concepts of insanity that prior to his influence were usually viewed as separate and distinct disorders. He saw these concepts—**catatonia** (alternating immobility and excited agitation), **hebephrenia** (silly and immature emotionality), and **paranoia** (delusions of grandeur or persecution)—as sharing similar underlying features and included them under the Latin term *dementia praecox*. Although the clinical manifestation might differ from person to person, Kraepelin believed that at the heart of each person's disorder was an onset early in life that ultimately developed into "mental weakness."

In a second important contribution, Kraepelin (1898) distinguished dementia praecox from manic-depressive illness (bipolar disorder). He wrote that, for people with dementia praecox, an early age of onset and a poor outcome were characteristic; in contrast, he did not see these patterns as essential to manic depression (Peters, 1991). Kraepelin also noted the numerous symptoms that occurred in people with dementia praecox, including hallucinations, delusions, negativism, and stereotyped behavior.

A second major figure in the history of schizophrenia was Eugen Bleuler (1908), a contemporary of Kraepelin and a Swiss psychiatrist, who introduced the term *schizophrenia*. His use of this term was significant because it signaled his departure from Kraepelin on what he thought was the "core" problem plaguing individuals with the disorder. Schizophrenia, which comes from the combination of the Greek words for split (*skhizein*) mind (*phren*), signified Bleuler's belief that underlying all the unusual behaviors shown by people with this disorder was an **associative splitting** of the basic functions of personality. The concept of associative splitting or "breaking of associative threads" referred to destruction of the forces that connect one function to the next. Furthermore, these

Eugen Bleuler (1857–1939) was a Swiss psychiatrist who first introduced the term *schizophrenia* and who made pioneering contributions to the field.

individuals had a difficult time keeping a consistent train of thought, and Bleuler believed that it was this problem that was characteristic of all persons with this disorder and led to the many and diverse symptoms they displayed. Whereas Kraepelin focused on the early onset and poor outcomes of these people, Bleuler highlighted what he believed to be the underlying problem common to each person with schizophrenia. Unfortunately, this concept of "split mind" has led to the common but erroneous use of the term schizophrenia to mean split or multiple personality. For a summary of the early contributors to the concept of schizophrenia, see Table 14.1.

Efforts to Identify Symptoms

It is not easy to point to one thing that makes a person "schizophrenic." Reading about the different disorders in this book, you can usually find a behavior, a way of thinking, or an emotion that defines or is characteristic of that particular disorder. For example, depression always includes feelings of sadness, and panic disorder is always accompanied by intense feelings of anxiety. Yet, surprisingly, this isn't the case for schizophrenia. The concept of schizophrenia is actually made up of a number of behaviors or symptoms that aren't necessarily shared by all the people with this diagnosis. Kraepelin described this situation when he outlined his view of *dementia praecox* in the late 1800s.

> The complexity of the conditions which we observe in the domain of dementia praecox is very great, so that their inner connection is at first recognizable only by their occurring one after the other in the course of the same disease. In any case certain fundamental disturbances, even though they cannot for the most part be regarded as characteristic, yet return frequently in the same form, but in the most diverse combinations. (Kraepelin, 1919, p. 5)

The heterogeneity of this disorder was also highlighted by Bleuler in the title of his 1911 book, *Dementia Praecox or the Group of Schizophrenias,* with the phrase "group of schizophrenias" emphasizing the complexity of the disorder. The varied nature of schizophrenia is something we will come back to throughout this chapter. Individuals who have schizophrenia have different symptoms, and it seems clear that we will ultimately find that the causes for their disorder vary as well.

Despite these complexities, workers in the field have identified symptoms that seem to group together to make up the disorder of schizophrenia. Later we describe these very dramatic symptoms—such as seeing or hearing things that others do not (hallucinations) or having beliefs that are unrealistic and bizarre and not shared by others in the same culture (delusions). But first, consider the following cases of individuals the authors have worked with over the years and who display these types of unusual behaviors.

The Case of David

David was 25 years old the first time I met him; he had been living in a psychiatric hospital for about 3 years before that. He was a little overweight and of average height; he typically dressed in a T-shirt and jeans and tended to be active. I first encountered him while I was talking to another man who lived on the same floor. David interrupted us by pulling on my shoulder. "My uncle Bill is a good man. He treats me well." Not wanting to be impolite, I told him, "I'm sure he is. Maybe after I've finished talking to Michael here, we can talk about your uncle." David persisted, "He can kill fish with a knife. Things can get awfully sharp in your mind, when you go down the river. I could kill you with my bare

Table 14.1 Early Figures in the History of Schizophrenia

Historical Figure	Date of Contribution	Contribution
John Haslam (1764–1844)	1809	Superintendent of a British hospital—in his book, *Observations on Madness and Melancholy,* outlined a description of the symptoms of schizophrenia.
Philippe Pinel (1745–1826)	1801/1809	French physician—described cases of schizophrenia.
Benedict Morel (1809–1873)	1852	Physician at a French institution—used the term *démence précoce* (in Latin, *dementia praecox*), meaning early or premature (*précoce*) loss of mind (*démence*) to describe schizophrenia.
Emil Kraepelin (1856–1926)	1898/1899	German psychiatrist—unified the distinct categories (hebephrenic, catatonic, and paranoid) under the name *dementia praecox.*
Eugen Bleuler (1857–1939)	1908	Swiss psychiatrist—introduced the term *schizophrenia,* meaning splitting of the mind.

hands—taking things into my own hands. . . . I know you know!" He was now speaking very quickly, and had gained emotionality along with speed as he spoke. I talked to him quietly until he calmed down for the moment; later I looked into David's file for some information about his background.

David was brought up on a farm by his aunt Katie and uncle Bill. His father's identity is unknown and his mother had mental retardation and couldn't care for him as a child. David too was diagnosed as having mental retardation, although his functioning was only mildly impaired, and he attended school through high school. It was in high school, the year David's uncle Bill died, that his teachers first reported unusual behavior. David would occasionally talk to his deceased uncle Bill in class. Later, he became increasingly agitated and verbally aggressive toward others. He was at this time diagnosed as having schizophrenia. He managed to graduate from high school but never obtained a job after that; he lived at home with his aunt for several years. Although his aunt really wanted him to stay with her at home, his threatening behavior escalated to the point that she requested he be seen at the local psychiatric hospital.

I spoke with David again and had a chance to ask him a few questions. "Why are you here in the hospital, David?" "I really don't want to be here," he told me. "I've got other things to do. The time is right, and you know when opportunity knocks . . . " He continued talking for a few minutes until I interrupted him. "I was sorry to hear that your uncle Bill died a few years ago. How are you feeling about him these days?" "Yes, he died. He was sick and now he's gone. He likes to fish with me, down at the river. He's going to take me hunting. I have guns. I can shoot you and you'd be dead in a minute."

David's conversational speech resembled a ball rolling down a rocky hill. Like an accelerating object, his speech gained momentum the longer he went on, and as if bouncing off obstacles, the topics almost always went in unpredictable directions. Often, if he continued for too long, he would become agitated and speak of harming others. At another time, David also told me that he heard his uncle's voice and that it spoke to him repeatedly. David said that other voices spoke to him, but he couldn't identify them and couldn't tell me what they said. We will return to David's case later in this chapter when we discuss causes and treatments for schizophrenia.

The Case of Arthur

We first had contact with the 22-year-old Arthur at an outpatient clinic that was part of a psychiatric hospital. Arthur's family had brought him there because they were extremely concerned and upset by his unusual behavior, and they were desperately seeking help for him. They said that he was "sick" and "talking like a crazy man," and they were afraid he might harm himself.

Arthur had a normal childhood in a middle-class suburban neighborhood. His mother reported that her's was a happy marriage that lasted until her husband's death several years earlier. Arthur was an average student throughout school and had completed an associate's degree in junior college. His family seemed to think he was disappointed that he didn't continue on in college to receive his bachelor's degree. Arthur had worked in a series of temporary jobs but his mother reported that he seemed satisfied with what he was doing. He lived and worked in a major city, some 15 minutes away from his mother and his married brother and sister.

About 3 weeks before he came to the clinic, Arthur's family said that he had started speaking strangely. He had been laid off from his job a few days before due to cutbacks and hadn't communicated with any of his family members for several days. When they next spoke with him, his behavior startled them. Although he had always been idealistic and anxious to help other people, he began talking about his blueprint to save all the starving children in the world with his "secret plan." At first they thought this was just an example of his sarcastic wit, but his demeanor changed to one of extreme concern, and he began speaking nonstop about these plans. He also began carrying several spiral notebooks that he claimed outlined his scheme for helping these children and said that he would reveal them only at the right time to the right person. Suspecting that he might be taking drugs and that this could explain the sudden and dramatic change in his behavior, his family searched his apartment. Although they didn't find any evidence of drug use, they did find his checkbook and noticed a number of strange entries. Over the previous several weeks, his handwriting had begun to deteriorate, and he had started writing notes instead of the usual check information ("Start to begin now" "This is important!" "They must be saved"). Family members also found unusual writings in several of his most prized books, a particularly alarming development given his reverence for these books.

As the days went on, Arthur began to show dramatic changes in emotion, often crying and acting very apprehensive. He stopped wearing socks and underwear, and despite the extremely cold weather, wouldn't wear a jacket when he went outdoors. He had moved into his mother's apartment at the family's insistence, wouldn't sleep much at night, and kept the family up until the early morning. His mother told me that it was like being in a living nightmare. Each morning she would wake up with a knot in her stomach, not wanting to get out of bed because she felt so helpless to do anything to rescue Arthur from his obvious distress.

His family's sense of alarm grew as he began to reveal more details of his "plan." He said that he was going to the German embassy because they were the only ones who would listen to him. He said he would climb the fence at night when everyone was asleep and present his plan to the German ambassador. Fearing that Arthur would be hurt trying to enter the embassy grounds, they contacted a local psychiatric hospital, described Arthur's condition, and asked that he be admitted. Much to their surprise and disappointment, they were told that Arthur could come in himself, but that the family couldn't bring him in involuntarily unless he was in danger of doing harm to himself or others. Even if they thought Arthur might be harmed, this wasn't sufficient reason to admit him involuntarily.

His family finally talked Arthur into speaking with the staff at an outpatient clinic. In our interview together, it was clear that he was delusional—firmly believing in his ability to help all starving children. After some cajoling, I finally convinced him to let me see his "plan." In his books were written random thoughts (for example, "The poor, starving souls" "The moon is the only place") and drawings of rocket ships. It seems that parts of his plan involved building a rocket ship that would go to the moon where he would create a community for all malnourished children, a place where they could live and be helped. After a few brief comments on his plan, I began to ask him about his health. "You look tired; are you getting enough sleep?" "Sleep isn't really needed," he noted. "My plans will take me through, and then they can all rest." "Your family is worried about you," I said. "Do you understand their concern?" "It's important for all concerned to get together, to join together," he replied. With

that, he got up and walked out of the room. He continued walking, out of the building, saying to his family that he would be right back. After 5 minutes they went to look for him, but he had disappeared. He was missing for 2 days, causing his family a great deal of concern about his health and safety. In an almost miraculous sequence of events, they found him walking the streets of their city. He acted as if nothing had happened. Gone were his notebooks and the talk of his secret plan.

What caused Arthur to act so differently? Was it being fired from his job? Was it the death of his father? Was it a genetic predisposition to have schizophrenia or one of the other disorders that "kicked in" during this time of stress? Unfortunately, we will never know exactly what happened to Arthur to make him behave so bizarrely and then recover so quickly and completely. However, the research on schizophrenia and the other psychotic disorders that we discuss next may shed some light on this disorder and potentially help other Arthurs and their families.

Clinical Description of Schizophrenia

The cases of David and Arthur are examples of the range of problems experienced by persons with schizophrenia and other psychotic disorders. The term **psychotic** has been used to characterize many unusual behaviors, although in its strictest sense it usually involves delusions (which involve irrational beliefs) and/or hallucinations (experiencing things through the senses in the absence of any external events—such as hearing voices). Schizophrenia is just one of the disorders that involve psychotic behavior; other forms are described in more detail later. Because it is the most common of these psychotic disorders, we first describe schizophrenia.

The features of schizophrenia can involve the whole spectrum of functions we rely on to get us through the day. Processes disrupted by schizophrenia include those that involve thought, our perception of the world, our emotions, and even how we move. Before we describe the symptoms of schizophrenia, it is important to caution you to look carefully at the specific characteristics of people exhibiting these behaviors. One reason for this warning is that we are constantly barraged with mistaken images of people with schizophrenia. Headlines such as "Ex-Mental Patient Kills Family," although common, falsely portray everyone with schizophrenia as a dangerous murderer.

Popular books also contribute to this misinformation. Mark Vonnegut—son of author Kurt Vonnegut—in his book *The Eden Express* describes what he calls his entry into schizophrenia, although the phases of depression and manic behavior suggest instead that he had bipolar affective disorder. The major character of the book *I Never Promised You a Rose Garden* is often thought to have schizophrenia, although her dramatic periods of blindness, deafness, and hallucinations are more characteristic of somatization disorder. As we illustrated before with the mistaken use of the word *schizophrenia* to mean "split personality," the popular press often misrepresents abnormal psychology, oftentimes to the detriment of people who experience these debilitating disorders.

The DSM-IV diagnostic criteria for schizophrenia are listed in Table 14.2 and offer a much more scientific account of this disorder. DSM-IV has a multiple-part process for determining whether someone does or does not have schizophrenia. Below we discuss several of these parts, including the *symptoms* the person experiences during the disorder (called *active phase symptoms*), the course of the disorder, and the subtypes of schizophrenia that are currently used to classify different forms of the condition.

Workers in this field typically distinguish between what are called *positive* and *negative* symptoms of schizophrenia. Positive symptoms refer to more active manifestations of abnormal behavior, or an excess or distortion of normal behavior; these include delusions, hallucinations, and disorganized speech (Fowles, 1992). Negative symptoms involve deficits in normal behavior on such dimensions as affect, speech, and motivation (Carpenter, 1994). A diagnosis of schizophrenia requires that two or more of these positive and/or negative symptoms are present for at least 1 month. A great deal of research has examined the

Table 14.2   DSM-IV Diagnostic Criteria for Schizophrenia

A. *Characteristic symptoms:* Two (or more) of the following, each present for a significant portion of time during a 1-month period (or less if successfully treated):

1. Delusions
2. Hallucinations
3. Disorganized speech (e.g., frequent derailment or incoherence)
4. Grossly disorganized or catatonic behavior
5. Negative symptoms, i.e., affective flattening, alogia, or avolition

Note: Only one Criterion A symptom is required if delusions are bizarre, or hallucinations consist of a voice keeping up a running commentary on the person's behavior or thoughts or two or more voices conversing with each other.

B. *Social/occupational dysfunction:* For a significant portion of the time since the onset of the disturbance, one or more major areas of functioning such as work, interpersonal relations, or self-care are markedly below the level achieved prior to the onset (or when the onset is in childhood or adolescence, failure to achieve expected level of interpersonal, academic, or occupational achievement).

C. *Duration:* Continuous signs of the disturbance persist for at least 6 months. This 6-month period must include at least 1 month of symptoms (or less if successfully treated) that meet Criterion A (i.e., active-phase symptoms) and may include periods of prodromal or residual symptoms. During these prodromal or residual periods, the signs of the disturbance may be manifested by only negative symptoms or two or more symptoms listed in Criterion A present in an attenuated form (e.g., odd beliefs, unusual perceptual experiences).

D. *Schizoaffective and mood disorder exclusion:* Schizoaffective Disorder and Mood Disorder with Psychotic Features have been ruled out because either (1) no Major Depressive, Manic, or Mixed Episodes have occurred concurrently with the active-phase symptoms; or (2) if mood episodes have occurred during active-phase symptoms, their total duration has been brief relative to the duration of the active and residual periods.

E. *Substance/general medical condition exclusion:* The disturbance is not due to the direct physiological effects of a substance (e.g., a drug of abuse, a medication) or a general medical condition.

F. *Relationship to a pervasive developmental disorder:* If there is a history of Autistic Disorder or another Pervasive Developmental Disorder, the additional diagnosis of Schizophrenia is made only if prominent delusions or hallucinations are also present for at least a month (or less if successfully treated).

Classification of longitudinal course (can be applied only after at least 1 year has elapsed since the initial onset of active-phase symptoms):
Episodic with Interepisode Residual Symptoms (episodes are defined by the reemergence of prominent psychotic symptoms); *also specify if:* with Prominent Negative Symptoms
Episodic with No Interepisode Residual Symptoms
Continuous (prominent psychotic symptoms are present throughout the period of observation); *also specify if:* with Prominent Negative Symptoms
Single Episode in Partial Remission; *also specify if:* with Prominent Negative Symptoms
Single Episode in Full Remission
Other or Unspecified Pattern

Source: DSM-IV, APA, 1994.

different symptoms of schizophrenia, each of which is described here in some detail.

Delusions

A belief that would be seen by most members of a society as a misrepresentation of reality is called a *disorder of thought content,* or a **delusion.** Because of its importance in schizophrenia, delusion has been called "the basic characteristic of madness" (Jaspers, 1963). If, for example, you believe that squirrels really are aliens sent to earth on a reconnaissance mission, this belief would be considered a delusion. The media often portray people with schizophrenia as having *delusions of grandeur,* or a belief that they are especially famous or important people (such as Napoleon or Jesus Christ). Recall how Arthur believed that he had a plan to end starvation for all the world's children. This too would be considered a delusion of grandeur.

A common delusion held by people with schizophrenia is the belief that others are "out to get them." Called *delusions of persecution,* these beliefs can be most disturbing. One of us worked with a woman who was a world-class cyclist and on her way to making the Olympic team. Tragically, however, her belief that other competitors were determined to sabotage her efforts forced her to stop riding for years. She believed, for instance, that opponents would spray her bicycle with chemicals that were designed to take her strength away. She also thought that they would conspire to put small pebbles in the road that _____ ____ ride over, thereby slowing her down. All _____ ____ great deal of anxiety in her, a_____ near her bicycle for some tim_____

Recently, a man _____ schizophrenia poignantly _____ with delusional thoughts (_____ from his writings follows.

I am 35 years old. _____
Many psychologist_____
me this over the ye_____
point where I actu_____
to believe that I a_____
intensity of my b_____
My delusional sy_____
am *not* schizop_____
psychic, that I_____
anyone who is—_____
Mentally focuse_____
on Earth? I don't know. _____ _____
these possibilities and more, but presently I believe that people can "read my mind" only if they are in my immediate vicinity.

I've had many different "crazy" thoughts over the years . . . , but my main delusion of grandeur—psychic phenomena—and my main delusion of persecution have remained

constant. These delusions are supported by hallucinations so vivid that I usually cannot distinguish them from reality except by telling myself that none of this is real, that what the people I love and trust the most are telling me is true, that I am extraordinary only in that I am schizophrenic, and that anything I think regarding the supernatural is the result of a disease.

I am now about to enter the job market for the first time since I was discharged from the Navy. I don't know if I will succeed in holding down gainful employment, but I feel I am ready. I go out among people almost every day and, although I still feel "stared at" and occasionally talked about, I do not believe, even if I am psychic, that I am an agent of God. This can change from day to day, but generally speaking I mainly believe that I am suffering from a mental disorder. (Bowden, 1993, pp. 165–167)

An intriguing view of delusions is that they may serve a purpose for people with schizophrenia who are otherwise quite upset by the changes taking place within themselves. For example, Roberts (1991) recently studied 17 people who had quite elaborate delusions about themselves and the world, and compared them to a matched group of people who previously had delusions but were now improving. The "deluded" individuals expressed a much stronger sense of purpose and meaning in life *and less depression,* all of which seemed related to their delusional belief systems. Compare this with the opposite situation we discussed in the mood disorders chapter where we found that people who were depressed seemed "sadder ___ ____" (see Chapter 7). That delusions may serve an _____ n for delusional individuals is at present _____ vith little support, but it may help us _____ s phenomenon and the reactions to it _____ hose experiencing the delusion.

_____ions

_____ r think someone called your name, only _____ hat no one was there? Did you ever think _____ ething move by you, yet nothing did? We _____ eting moments when we think we see or _____ hing that isn't there. However, for many _____ h schizophrenia, these perceptions seem _____ d occur on a regular basis. The experience _____ events without any input from the sur- _____ environment is called an **hallucination.** _____ ions can involve any of the senses, although hearing things that aren't there, or *auditory hallucination,* is the most common form experienced by people with schizophrenia.

David had frequent auditory hallucinations, usually of his uncle's voice. Although many times David would tell us he heard a voice and he could tell it was his uncle Bill, he said he couldn't understand what his uncle was saying. On other occasions, the voice was clearer. "He told me to turn off the TV. He said, 'It's too damn loud, turn it down, turn it down.' Other times he talks about fishing. 'Good day for fishing. Got to go fishing.'" You could tell when David was hearing voices. He was usually unoccupied, and he would be sitting and smiling as if listening to the person next to him, but no one was there. This behavior is consistent with research on hallucinations, which suggests that people tend to experience hallucinations more frequently when they are unoccupied or restricted from sensory input (for example, Margo, Hemsley, & Slade, 1981).

Exciting new research on hallucinations uses sophisticated brain-imaging techniques to try to localize these phenomena in the brain. By studying cerebral blood flow using single photon emission computed tomography (SPECT), researchers in London have made a surprising discovery (McGuire, Shah, & Murray, 1993). They studied men with schizophrenia who also had auditory hallucinations. The researchers used the brain-imaging technique while these men were experiencing hallucinations and later while they were not. The researchers found that the part of the brain most active during hallucinations was the area called *Broca's area* (see Figure 14.1). This observation is surprising because Broca's area is known to be involved in speech production. If hallucinations involve understanding the "speech" of others, you might expect more activity in the area of the brain that involves language comprehension, an area called *Wernicke's area*. However, this study supports an earlier finding by a different group of researchers who also found that Broca's area was active during hallucinations and that Wernicke's area was less

active at this time (Cleghorn et al., 1992). This observation of brain activity during hallucinations supports a theory that people who are hallucinating are in fact not hearing the voices of others, but instead are listening to their own thoughts or their own voices and cannot recognize the difference.

Disorganized Speech

Trying to have a conversation with someone who has schizophrenia can be a particularly frustrating experience. If you are trying to understand what is bothering or upsetting this person, trying to elicit relevant information is especially difficult. For one thing, people with schizophrenia often lack *insight* or an awareness that they have a problem. In addition, they experience what Bleuler called associative splitting and what Paul Meehl calls *cognitive slippage* (Bleuler, 1908; Meehl, 1962). These phrases help describe the problems people with schizophrenia have with their speech, sometimes jumping from topic to topic and at other times talking illogically. DSM-IV has used the term **disorganized speech** to describe these problems with communication. Let's go back to our conversation with David to illustrate disorganized speech.

> **VMD:** Why are you here in the hospital, David?
> **David:** I really don't want to be here. I've got other things to do. The time is right, and you know when opportunity knocks . . .

David didn't really answer the question he was asked. This type of response is referred to as *tangentiality*—that is, not answering specific questions but going off instead on a tangent (Andreasen, 1979). He also quickly moved the topic of conversation to unrelated areas. This behavior has variously been called *loose association* or *derailment* and refers to moving abruptly between unrelated ideas (Cutting, 1985).

> **VMD:** I was sorry to hear that your uncle Bill died a few years ago. How are you feeling about him these days?
> **David:** Yes, he died. He was sick, and now he's gone. He likes to fish with me, down at the river. He's going to take me hunting. I have guns. I can shoot you and you'd be dead in a minute.

Again, he didn't answer my question. I could not be sure whether the problem was with his understanding the question or whether it was difficult for him to talk about his uncle. You can see how people might spend a great deal of time trying to "interpret" all the hidden meanings behind this type of conversation. Unfortunately, however, such analyses have yet to provide us with useful information about the nature of schizophrenia or its treatment.

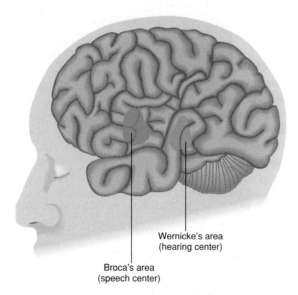

Wernicke's area
(hearing center)

Broca's area
(speech center)

Figure 14.1   Looking for voices in the brain

Grossly Disorganized or Catatonic Behavior

People with schizophrenia engage in a number of other "active" behaviors that might be considered positive symptoms. For example, **catatonia** is one of the most curious of the symptoms present in some individuals with schizophrenia; it involves a spectrum of motor dysfunctions from wild agitation to immobility. On the active side of the continuum, some individuals will pace excitely or move their fingers or arms in stereotyped ways. At the other end of this extreme, people adopt unusual postures and will hold them as if they were fearful of something terrible happening if they move (**catatonic immobility**). This manifestation can also involve **waxy flexibility,** or the tendency to keep their bodies and limbs in the same position when they are moved by someone else.

Occasionally, people with schizophrenia display **inappropriate affect,** laughing or crying at improper times. Sometimes they engage in bizarre behaviors such as hoarding objects or acting in unusual ways in public.

Negative Symptoms

In contrast to the active presentations that characterize the positive symptoms of schizophrenia, the negative symptoms usually refer to the absence or insufficiency of normal behavior, and include emotional and social withdrawal, blunted affect, apathy, and poverty of thought or speech (Carpenter, 1992).

Flat Affect

Imagine that people wore masks at all times. You could communicate with them but you wouldn't be able to see their emotional reactions. Approximately two-thirds of the people with schizophrenia exhibit what is called **flat affect** (World Health Organization, 1973). They are similar to people wearing masks because they do not show emotions when you would normally expect an emotional response. These people may stare at you with vacant eyes, speak in a flat and toneless manner, and seem not to be affected by things going on around them. However, although they do not seem to react openly to emotional situations, it appears that they may indeed be responding on the inside.

Howard Berenbaum and Thomas Oltmanns (1992) recently compared people with and without flat or "blunted" affect. These two groups, who also had schizophrenia, were shown clips from films (for instance, *Chinatown, Marathon Man, Bill Cosby: Himself*) selected to create emotional reactions in the viewer. Berenbaum and Oltmanns found that the people with flat affect showed little change in facial expression (smiles, frowns), although, when asked, they reported experiencing the appropriate emotions. The authors concluded that the flat affect in schizophrenia may represent the person's difficulty with expressing emotion and not an inability to feel the emotion.

The expression of affect—or the lack of this expression—may have important implications for the development of schizophrenia. Elaine Walker and her colleagues, in a creative research study, recently examined the facial expressions of children who later developed schizophrenia and compared them with the expressiveness of their brothers and sisters who did not develop the disorder (Walker, Grimes, Davis, & Smith, 1993). They identified people who already showed signs of schizophrenia, and looked at home movies taken by their families when they were children. From these childhood home movies, the researchers were able to show that children who later went on to develop schizophrenia typically displayed less positive and more negative affect than their siblings. This research suggests that emotional expression may be one way to distinguish between children who do and those who do not go on to display the more dramatic symptoms of schizophrenia.

Avolition

Derived from the prefix *a* meaning "without," and *volition,* which means "an act of willing, choosing, or deciding," **avolition** is an inability to initiate and persist in many important activities. Also referred to as apathy, people with this symptom show little interest in even the most basic day-to-day activities, including personal hygiene.

Alogia

Alogia refers to the relative absence in either the amount or the content of speech. The word derives from the combination of *a* (without) and *logic* (reasoning). A person with alogia may respond to questions with very brief replies that have little content, and may appear disinterested in the conversation. For example, if they are asked "Do you have any children?" most parents might reply, "Yes, a boy and a girl. My son is 6 and my daughter is 12." Someone with alogia might have the following exchange regarding the same question:

> **Interviewer:** Do you have any children?
> **Client:** Yes.
> **Interviewer:** How many children do you have?
> **Client:** Two.
> **Interviewer:** How old are they?
> **Client:** Six and twelve.

This deficiency in communication by some people with schizophrenia is believed to reflect a negative thought disorder rather than an inadequacy in communication skills per se. Sometimes alogia takes the form of delayed comments or slow response to questions. Trying to talk with individuals who manifest this symptom can be extremely frustrating, making you feel as if you are "pulling teeth" to get them to respond.

A related symptom is called **anhedonia,** which derives from the word *hedonic,* pertaining to pleasure. It refers to the presumed lack of pleasure experienced by some people with schizophrenia. Similar to people with some of the mood disorders, individuals with anhedonia report a loss of enjoyment for activities that would typically be considered pleasurable, including eating, social interactions, and sexual relations.

Again, to receive a diagnosis of schizophrenia, a person must display two or more of these symptoms for a major portion of at least 1 month. Depending on the combination of symptoms displayed, two people could receive the same diagnosis but look very different. One individual could have marked hallucinations and delusions while a second person with the same diagnosis could primarily display disorganized speech and some of the negative symptoms. Because of treatment implications, it is important to differentiate individuals based on their varying presentations of symptoms. We next examine these attempts at differentiation.

Schizophrenia Subtypes

As we noted earlier, the search for subtypes of schizophrenia has a history predating Kraepelin's description of the concept of schizophrenia. A persistent division has been the identification of *catatonic* (alternate immobility and excited agitation), *hebephrenic* (disorganization; silly and immature emotionality), and *paranoid* (delusions of grandeur or persecution) subtypes. Research on these subtypes suggests the usefulness of dividing schizophrenia in this manner because of the identifiable differences among these conditions (Andreasen & Flaum, 1990). For example, individuals with the hebephrenic subtype seem to have a more pessimistic outcome than people with the other sub-

types. Also, individuals with the catatonic subtype seem to have a distinctive course and treatment response. Because of the potential usefulness of these subtypes, DSM-IV has integrated all of them in its revised classification system for schizophrenia.

Paranoid Type

People with the **paranoid type of schizophrenia** stand out because of their delusions or hallucinations; at the same time, their cognitive skills and affect are relatively intact. They generally do not have disorganized speech or flat affect, and they typically have a better prognosis than people with other forms of schizophrenia. The delusions and hallucinations usually have a theme, such as persecution by others or being someone important. The DSM-IV criteria for inclusion in this subtype are listed in Table 14.3.

Disorganized Type

In contrast with the paranoid type of schizophrenia, people with the **disorganized type of schizophrenia** tend to show marked disruption in their speech (disorganized speech) and behavior (disorganized behavior); they also show the flat affect discussed previously or inappropriate affect such as laughing in a silly way at the wrong times. In these individuals, if delusions or hallucinations are manifested they tend not to be organized around a central theme, as in the paranoid type, but instead seem to be more fragmented and not tied together. This subtype was previously called *hebephrenic*. Individuals with this diagnosis tend to show signs of difficulty early; their problems are often chronic, lacking the remissions (improvement of symptoms) that characterize other forms of the disorder (McGlashan & Fenton, 1991). The DSM-IV criteria for inclusion in this subtype are listed in Table 14.4.

Catatonic Type

We previously described several of the characteristics of people with the **catatonic type of schizophrenia,** including the unusual motor responses of remaining in fixed positions (waxy flexibility), engaging in excessive activity, and being opposi-

Table 14.3   DSM-IV Diagnostic Criteria for Paranoid Type

A type of Schizophrenia in which the following criteria are met:

A. Preoccupation with one or more delusions or frequent auditory hallucinations.

B. None of the following is prominent: disorganized speech, disorganized or catatonic behavior, or flat or inappropriate affect.

Source: DSM-IV, APA, 1994.

Table 14.4 DSM-IV Diagnostic Criteria for Disorganized Type

A type of Schizophrenia in which the following criteria are met:

A. All the following are prominent:

  1. Disorganized speech
  2. Disorganized behavior
  3. Flat or inappropriate affect

B. The criteria are not met for Catatonic Type.

Source: DSM-IV, APA, 1994.

Table 14.5 DSM-IV Diagnostic Criteria for Catatonic Type

A type of Schizophrenia in which the clinical picture is dominated by at least two of the following:

1. Motoric immobility as evidenced by catalepsy (including waxy flexibility) or stupor

2. Excessive motor activity (that is apparently purposeless and not influenced by external stimuli)

3. Extreme negativism (an apparently motiveless resistance to all instructions or maintenance of a rigid posture against attempts to be moved) or mutism

4. Peculiarities of voluntary movement as evidenced by posturing (voluntary assumption of inappropriate or bizarre postures), stereotyped movements, prominent mannerisms, or prominent grimacing

5. Echolalia or echopraxia

Source: DSM-IV, APA, 1994.

tional by remaining rigid. In addition, these individuals sometimes display odd mannerisms with their bodies and faces, including grimacing. They often repeat or mimic the words of others (echolalia) or the movements of others (echopraxia). This cluster of behaviors is relatively rare and there is some debate about whether it should remain as a separate subtype of schizophrenia (McGlashan & Fenton, 1991). Its infrequency may be due partly to the success of neuroleptic medications in the treatment of people with this form of schizophrenia. The criteria for this subtype, which has been retained in DSM-IV, are listed in Table 14.5.

Undifferentiated Type

Some people do not fit neatly into these subtypes; they would be classified as having an **undifferentiated type of schizophrenia.** People who have the major symptoms of schizophrenia but who do not meet the criteria for paranoid, disorganized, or catatonic types of schizophrenia would be given this diagnosis.

Residual Type

Some people who have had at least one episode of schizophrenia but who no longer manifest the major symptoms of the disorder would be diagnosed as having the **residual type of schizophrenia.**

Although they may not suffer from bizarre delusions or hallucinations, they still display some "residual" or "leftover" symptoms, such as some of the negative beliefs, or they continue to have unusual ideas that are not fully delusional. These manifestations can include social withdrawal, bizarre thoughts, inactivity, and flat affect. All the versions of the DSM (from DSM-I through DSM-IV) have included a residual type of schizophrenia to describe the condition of individuals who continue to have less severe problems associated with an episode of schizophrenia. The DSM-IV criteria for this type are listed in Table 14.6.

Research on these subtypes suggests that the paranoid type may have a stronger familial link than the others; also, people with the paranoid type may function better before their experience of schizophrenia and may be more likely to do better after episodes of schizophrenia than people diagnosed with other types of this disorder (McGlashan & Fenton, 1991). More work is needed at this point to tell us whether dividing schizophrenia into these five subtypes is useful in understanding and treating people with the disorder. In addition to schizophrenia, several other disorders are also characterized by "psychotic" behaviors such as hallucinations and delusions, but they do not manifest in the same way as schizophrenia. They are mentioned briefly in the next section to distinguish them from schizophrenia, after which we describe that disorder in greater detail.

Table 14.6   DSM-IV Diagnostic Criteria for Residual Type

A type of Schizophrenia in which the following criteria are met:

A. Absence of prominent delusions, hallucinations, disorganized speech, and grossly disorganized or catatonic behavior.

B. There is continuing evidence of the disturbance, as indicated by the presence of negative symptoms or two or more symptoms listed in Criterion A for Schizophrenia, present in an attenuated form (e.g., odd beliefs, unusual perceptual experiences).

Source: DSM-IV, APA, 1994.

Other Psychotic Disorders

Also related but not included in this section is **schizotypal personality disorder,** which was discussed in Chapter 13. As you may recall, the characteristics of this disorder are similar to those experienced by people with schizophrenia, only in a less severe form. There is also some evidence that schizophrenia and schizotypal personality disorder may be genetically related and may be part of a "schizophrenia spectrum."

Schizophreniform Disorder

Some people experience the symptoms of schizophrenia, but for only a few months. These symptoms disappear as quickly as they come—sometimes as the result of successful treatment, but often for reasons unknown—and the person can usually resume his or her life as before. Such symptoms would be classified under the label **schizophreniform disorder.** There are relatively few studies on this disorder; therefore, data on important aspects of it are sparse. It appears, however, that the lifetime prevalence is approximately 0.2% (American Psychiatric Association, DSM-IV, 1994). The diagnostic criteria for schizophreniform disorder are listed in Table 14.7.

Schizoaffective Disorder

Historically, people who had symptoms of schizophrenia and who also exhibited the characteristics of mood disorders (for example, depression, bipolar affective disorder) were lumped together under the category of schizophrenia (Siris, 1993). This mixed bag of problems, which for some time posed an enigma for professionals in the field, is now diagnosed as **schizoaffective disorder.** The prognosis for people with this disorder is similar to the prognosis for those with schizophrenia—that is, these individuals tend not to get better on their own and are likely to continue experiencing major life difficulties for many years (Tsuang & Coryell, 1993). The DSM-IV criteria for schizoaffective disorder are listed in Table 14.8.

Delusional Disorder

The major feature of **delusional disorder** is a persistent *delusion,* or belief that is contrary to reality, in the absence of the other characteristics of schizophrenia. An example of delusional disorder would be a woman who believes that co-workers are tormenting her—putting poison in her food and spraying her apartment with harmful gases—without any evidence for her belief. This disorder is characterized by a persistent delusion that is not the result of an organic factor such

Table 14.7   DSM-IV Diagnostic Criteria for Schizophreniform Disorder

A. Criteria A, D, and E of Schizophrenia are met.

B. An episode of the disorder (including prodromal, active, and residual phases) lasts at least 1 month but less than 6 months. (When the diagnosis must be made without waiting for recovery, it should be qualified as "Provisional.")

Specify if:
Without Good Prognostic Features
With Good Prognostic Features: as evidenced by two (or more) of the following:

1. Onset of prominent psychotic symptoms within 4 weeks of the first noticeable change in usual behavior or functioning
2. Confusion or perplexity at the height of the psychotic episode
3. Good premorbid social and occupational functioning
4. Absence of blunted or flat affect

Source: DSM-IV, APA, 1994.

Table 14.8   DSM-IV Diagnostic Criteria for Schizoaffective Disorder

A. An uninterrupted period of illness during which, at some time, there is either a Major Depressive Episode, a Manic Episode, or a Mixed Episode concurrent with symptoms that meet Criterion A for Schizophrenia.

   Note: The Major Depressive Episode must include Criterion A1: depressed mood.

B. During the same period of illness, there have been delusions or hallucinations for at least 2 weeks in the absence of prominent mood symptoms.

C. Symptoms that meet criteria for a mood episode are present for a substantial portion of the total duration of the active and residual periods of the illness.

D. The disturbance is not due to the direct physiological effects of a substance (e.g., a drug of abuse, a medication) or a general medical condition.

Specify type:
   Bipolar Type: if the disturbance includes a Manic or a Mixed Episode (or a Manic or a Mixed Episode and Major Depressive Episodes)
   Depressive Type: if the disturbance only includes Major Depressive Episodes

Source: DSM-IV, APA, 1994.

as brain seizures or any severe psychotic disorder. Individuals with these delusions tend not to have most of the other problems associated with schizophrenia. For example, they do not have the flat affect or anhedonia or the other negative symptoms of schizophrenia; but importantly, they may become socially isolated because of their suspicion of others. Their delusions will often be long-standing, sometimes persisting over several years (Breier, 1993). The DSM-IV criteria for delusional disorder are listed in Table 14.9.

Delusions are beliefs that are not generally held by other members of the society. DSM-IV divides the different types of delusions into the following subtypes: erotomanic, grandiose, jealous, persecutory, and somatic (see Table 14.9). These delusions differ from the more bizarre types often found in people with schizophrenia because in delusional disorder *the imagined events could be happening but aren't* (for example, mistakenly believing you are being followed by another person); in schizophrenia, on the other hand, *the imagined events aren't possible* (for example, believing that you broadcast your thoughts by your brainwaves alone to other people around the world).

Delusional disorder seems to be relatively rare, affecting 24 to 30 people out of every 100,000 in the general population. Among those people with identified psychological disorders, between 1% and 4% are thought to have delusional disorder (Kendler, 1982). Researchers can't be confident about these percentages because they feel sure that an unknown number of these individuals do not have contact with the mental health system.

The onset of this disorder is relatively late compared to other disorders, with the average age of first admission to a psychiatric facility falling between 40 and 49 years of age (Kendler, 1982). However, because these individuals may not seek help earlier, and because many people with this disorder can lead relatively normal lives, this later age of admission for treatment may not represent the beginning of the delusions but rather the point at which the symptoms become most disruptive. There seem to be more females than males with this disorder (55% and 45%, respectively, of the affected population).

Homeless man suffering from paranoid schizophrenia. His auditory hallucinations and persecutory delusions continue to interfere with efforts to assist him.

Table 14.9 DSM-IV Diagnostic Criteria for Delusional Disorder

A. Nonbizarre delusions (i.e., involving situations that occur in real life, such as being followed, poisoned, infected, loved at a distance, or deceived by spouse or lover, or having a disease) of at least 1 month's duration.

B. Criterion A for Schizophrenia has never been met. **Note:** Tactile and olfactory hallucinations may be present in Delusional Disorder if they are related to the delusional theme.

C. Apart from the impact of the delusion(s) or its ramifications, functioning is not markedly impaired and behavior is not obviously odd or bizarre.

D. If mood episodes have occurred concurrently with delusions, their total duration has been brief relative to the duration of the delusional periods.

E. The disturbance is not due to the direct physiological effects of a substance (e.g., a drug of abuse, a medication) or a general medical condition.

Specify type (the following types are assigned based on the predominant delusional theme):
Erotomanic Type: delusions that another person, usually of higher status, is in love with the individual
Grandiose Type: delusions of inflated worth, power, knowledge, identity, or special relationship to a deity or famous person
Jealous Type: delusions that the individual's sexual partner is unfaithful
Persecutory Type: delusions that the person (or someone to whom the person is close) is being malevolently treated in some way
Somatic Type: delusions that the person has some physical defect or general medical condition
Mixed Type: delusions characteristic of more than one of the above types but no one theme predominates
Unspecified Type

Source: DSM-IV, APA, 1994.

In a longitudinal study, Opjordsmoen (1989) followed 53 persons with delusional disorder for an average of 30 years and found that they tended to fare better in life than people with schizophrenia, but not as well as those with other psychotic disorders such as schizoaffective disorder. About 80% of the 53 individuals had been married at some time, and half were employed, demonstrating their ability to function relatively well despite their delusions.

We know relatively little about either the biological or psychosocial influences on delusional disorder (Breier, 1993). Research on families suggests that the characteristics of suspiciousness, jealousy, and secretiveness may occur more often among the relatives of people with delusional disorder than among the population at large, suggesting that some aspect of this disorder may be inherited (Winokur, 1985).

A number of other disorders can cause delusions and their presence should be ruled out before considering someone as having delusional disorder. For example, substance abuse with amphetamines, alcohol, and cocaine can cause symptoms of this disorder. In addition, brain tumors, Huntington's disease, and Alzheimer's disease can also produce similar symptoms (Breier, 1993).

Brief Psychotic Disorder

Recall the puzzling case of Arthur, who suddenly experienced the delusion that he could "save the world" and who had intense emotional swings that lasted for only a few days. He would receive the DSM-IV diagnosis of **brief psychotic disorder,** indicating the presence of one or more "positive" symptoms such as delusions, hallucinations, or disorganized speech or behavior over the course of less than a month. Individuals like Arthur regain their previous ability to function well in day-to-day activities. Often this disorder is precipitated by extremely stressful situations. The DSM-IV criteria for brief psychotic disorder are listed in Table 14.10.

Shared Psychotic Disorder (Folie à Deux)

Although relatively little is known about **shared psychotic disorder (folie à deux),** it is the name given to the condition in which an individual develops delusions simply as a result of a close relationship with a delusional individual. The content and nature of the delusion depends on the delusion of the partner and can range from the relatively bizarre, such as believing that enemies are sending harmful gamma rays through your house, to the less bizarre, such as believing that you are about to receive a major promotion despite evidence to the contrary. The DSM-IV criteria for shared psychotic disorder are listed in Table 14.11.

People with other psychotic disorders display many of the characteristics of schizophrenia. It is important to remember, however, that there are also significant differences in these disorders, and we next return to schizophrenia to examine the nature of this important disorder and how researchers have attempted to understand and treat people who have it.

Table 14.10   DSM-IV Diagnostic Criteria for Brief Psychotic Disorder

A. Presence of one (or more) of the following symptoms:

1. Delusions
2. Hallucinations
3. Disorganized speech (e.g., frequent derailment or incoherence)
4. Grossly disorganized or catatonic behavior

Note: Do not include a symptom if it is a culturally sanctioned response pattern.

B. Duration of an episode of the disturbance is at least 1 day but less than 1 month, with eventual full return to premorbid level of functioning.

C. The disturbance is not better accounted for by a Mood Disorder with Psychotic Features, Schizoaffective Disorder, or Schizophrenia and is not due to the direct physiological effects of a substance (e.g., a drug of abuse, a medication) or a general medical condition.

Specify if:
With Marked Stressor(s) (brief reactive psychosis): if symptoms occur shortly after and apparently in response to events that, singly or together, would be markedly stressful to almost anyone in similar circumstances in the person's culture
Without Marked Stressor(s): if psychotic symptoms do *not* occur shortly after, or are not apparently in response to events that, singly or together, would be markedly stressful to almost anyone in similar circumstances in the person's culture
With Postpartum Onset: if onset within 4 weeks postpartum

Source: DSM-IV, APA, 1994.

Statistics and Course for Schizophrenia

Schizophrenia is a disorder that sometimes defies our desire for simplicity. We have seen how very different presentations of symptoms can be displayed by individuals who would all be considered as having this disorder; the symptoms appear in some people slowly over time while in others they can come on suddenly. For most, however, there are some commonalities. Schizophrenia is generally chronic, and people with the disorder will have a very difficult time functioning in society. This is especially true with regard to their ability to relate socially with others; they tend not to establish or maintain significant social relationships, and therefore many of them never marry or have children. When delusions are present, they tend to be bizarre. In other words, unlike the delusions of people with other psychotic disorders, the delusions of people with schizophrenia are likely to be outside the realm of possibility. Finally, even when individuals with schizophrenia improve with treatment, they will likely continue to experience difficulties throughout their lives.

Worldwide, the prevalence rate of schizophrenia is estimated at 0.2% to 2% in the general population (American Psychiatric Association, DSM-IV, 1994). In the United States alone, approximately 4.5 million people are believed to have the active symptoms of the disorder at any given time (Carson & Sanislow, 1993). The life expectancy of a person with schizophrenia is slightly less than average, partly due to the higher rate of suicide among people with this disorder (Potkin, Albers, & Richmond, 1993).

Given the large number of surveys of people with schizophrenia, you may be surprised to learn that there is some disagreement about how prevalent the disorder is among males and females. The common belief has been that schizophrenia affects an equivalent number of men and women in a lifetime. However, recent reports indicate that the disorder may actually occur more frequently among men (Iacono & Beiser, 1992).

Although there is still disagreement about the distribution of schizophrenia across men and women,

Table 14.11   DSM-IV Diagnostic Criteria for Shared Psychotic Disorder

A. A delusion develops in an individual in the context of a close relationship with another person(s), who has an already-established delusion.

B. The delusion is similar in content to that of the person who already has the established delusion.

C. The disturbance is not better accounted for by another Psychotic Disorder (e.g., Schizophrenia) or a Mood Disorder with Psychotic Features and is not due to the direct physiological effects of a substance (e.g., a drug of abuse, a medication) or a general medical condition.

Source: DSM-IV, APA, 1994.

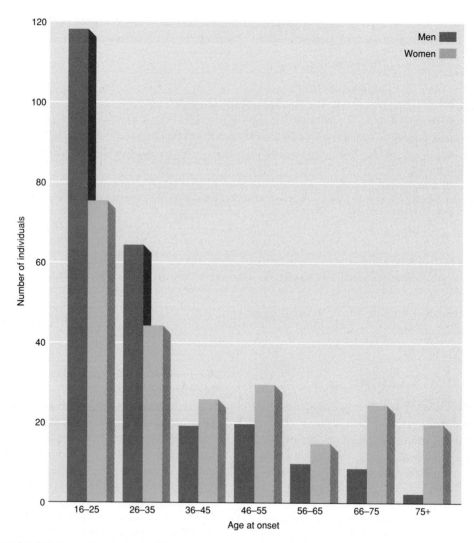

Figure 14.2 Gender differences in onset of schizophrenia (from Howard et al., 1993)

there is agreement about the clear difference between the sexes in the onset of this disorder. As you can see in Figure 14.2, the onset of schizophrenia among a group of 470 patients is highest in early adulthood (ages 16–25) (Howard, Castle, Wessely, & Murray, 1993). For men, the onset trails off as they age but can still first occur after the age of 75. The onset for women is lower than for men until age 36, when the relative risk for onset switches, with more women than men being affected. This higher incidence among women continues, with a relatively large number of women first experiencing schizophrenia in older adulthood.

Variations in Onset and Duration

As we have just seen, subtypes (for example, catatonia, hebephrenia, and paranoia) have existed for as long as the concept of schizophrenia itself. One grouping that focused on onset of the disorder and that received considerable attention for a time was the *process* and *reactive* distinction (Carson & Sanislow, 1993). Table 14.12 illustrates how these subtypes differed across four characteristics. **Process schizophrenia,** which is similar to Kraepelin's description of dementia praecox, was

Characteristic	Process	Reactive
Onset	Slow	Abrupt
Precipitating stress	Absent	Present
Social functioning	Inadequate social skills	Adequate social skills
Emotional expression	Flat, blunted	Volatile, intense

thought to come on slowly, without any obvious stressful event to bring it on, leaving a person basically withdrawn and showing little emotion. In contrast, **reactive schizophrenia** (as the name suggests) was thought to be primarily a reaction to some extremely stressful set of situations that came on suddenly and produced behavior that was highly social, volatile, and intense. Process schizophrenia was believed to be physiologically based and to have a poor prognosis, while reactive schizophrenia was brought on by stress and was thought to have a good outcome.

Despite the simplicity that this process-reactive distinction seems to bring to the concept of schizophrenia, many people do not fall neatly into these categories. There is also another problem: Over time, some people with "reactive" schizophrenia take on many of the characteristics of those with "process" schizophrenia. In fact, the changing nature of schizophrenia—the common observation that people have different forms of the disorder at different times in their lives—continues to perplex workers in this field and defies efforts to categorize people with the disorder. Because of these limitations, the process-reactive distinction for schizophrenia is no longer accepted by most workers in this field. A similar division, **poor premorbid** versus **good premorbid,** which refers to the social functioning of the person just before the major symptoms of schizophrenia are observed, was also adopted for a time, but it too has been abandoned as a useful distinction.

A more recent approach that relies on the types of symptoms displayed by people with schizophrenia, along with a number of other factors, is currently being studied as an alternate classification system. Introduced in the mid-1970s by Strauss, Carpenter, and Bartko (1974), this view of schizophrenia emphasizes the "positive" and "negative" symptoms mentioned earlier. Timothy Crow elaborated on this view and suggests that schizophrenia can be dichotomized into Type I and Type II forms of the disorder (Crow, 1980, 1985). These "types" are based on a variety of characteristics, including the symptoms displayed by people with schizophrenia, their response to neuroleptic medications, their outcome, and the presence or absence of intellectual impairment. Type I is associated with the **positive symptoms** such as hallucinations and delusions, a good response to medication, an optimistic prognosis, and the absence of intellectual impairment. In contrast, Type II includes people with the **negative symptoms** of flat affect and poverty of speech, who show a poor response to medication, a pessimistic prognosis, and intellectual impairments. Although not without its critics (Andreasen & Carpenter, 1993), Crow's model has influenced current thinking regarding the nature of schizophrenia.

Developmental Considerations

An increasing amount of attention is being paid to the developmental course of schizophrenia (Walker, 1991). Researchers are interested in how this disorder develops because the study of its course may shed some light on the cause or causes of the disorder. Research suggests that children who later develop schizophrenia show some abnormal signs prior to displaying the symptoms characteristic of the disorder (Fish, 1987). These children may show abnormal emotional reactions such as less positive and more negative affect than their unaffected siblings (Walker, Grimes, Davis, & Smith, 1993). Remember that the age of onset varies for schizophrenia but is generally seen in early adulthood. Why does the disorder show itself only later in life, when the factors causing it are present very early on?

One answer may be that brain damage very early in the developmental period is responsible for causing later schizophrenia (Weinberger, 1987). However, instead of resulting in a progressive deterioration or worsening of the brain's ability to function, the damage may lie dormant and not be noticeable until later in development when the signs of schizophrenia first appear. How then could prenatal or perinatal brain damage cause a disorder to manifest itself in a person's teens or twenties? One piece of supporting evidence comes from an animal study showing that damage to a certain part of the rat brain (the hippocampus) manifests itself only when the rat matures (Lipska, Jaskiw, & Weinberger, 1993). A recent study with humans found that people with schizophrenia who demonstrated *more* early signs of abnormality at birth and during early childhood tended to fare *better* than people who had fewer early signs of difficulty (Torrey, Bowler, Taylor, & Gottesman, 1994). One interpretation of these results is that the earlier the damage, the more time the brain has to compensate for this damage, resulting in milder symptoms.

Finally, looking at schizophrenia across the entire life span may also shed some light on the development of the disorder (Belitsky & McGlashan, 1993). In one of only a handful of studies that have followed people with schizophrenia into late life, researchers tracked 52 people over a 40-year period (Winokur, Pfohl, & Tsuang, 1987). Their general finding was that these older adults tended to display fewer of the "positive" symptoms, such as delusions and hallucinations, and more of the "negative" symptoms, such as speech and cognitive difficulties. In other words, people with schizophrenia appear not to continue to deteriorate over time but in some ways may show improvement as they enter later adulthood.

A final consideration in discussing the course of schizophrenia is the relapse rate. Unfortunately, a

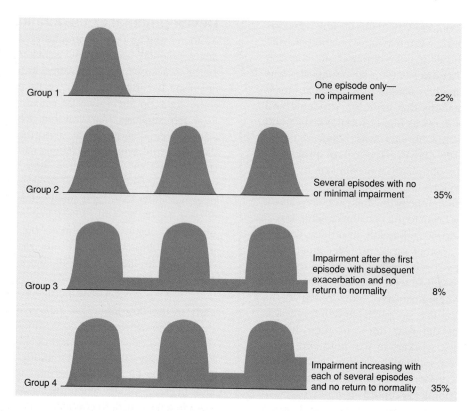

Figure 14.3 The natural history of schizophrenia: a five-year follow-up (from Shepherd et al., 1989)

great many people who experience an episode of schizophrenia and then improve will later reexperience the symptoms of the disorder. Figure 14.3 illustrates the data from one study that show the course of schizophrenia among four prototypical groups (Zubin, Steinhauer, & Condray, 1992). As you can see, about 22% of the group had one episode of schizophrenia, improved, and had no lasting impairment. However, the remaining 78% experienced several episodes of schizophrenia, with differing degrees of impairment between these episodes. These relapses have become an important focus in the field of schizophrenia; we will return to this phenomenon when we discuss the causes and the treatment of the disorder.

Cultural Factors

Because of the complexity of the concept of schizophrenia, the diagnosis or label of schizophrenia itself can be controversial. Some have argued that *schizophrenia* per se does not really exist and is instead a culturally created label for people who behave in ways that are outside the norm (for instance, Laing, 1967; Sarbin & Mancuso, 1980; Szasz, 1961). Although it is certainly provocative to consider that schizophrenia exists only in the minds of mental health professionals, this extreme view flies in the face of experience with this disorder. On a personal level, both of us have had

a great deal of contact not only with people who have this disorder but also with their families and friends, and the tremendous amount of emotional pain that can result when someone has schizophrenia certainly lends considerable credence to its existence. In addition, extremely diverse cultures across the world describe people with the symptoms of schizophrenia, supporting the notion that it is a reality for many people worldwide.

Although the general concept of schizophrenia seems universal, the specific symptoms do seem to vary from culture to culture. For example, there is a high prevalence of visual hallucinations among people with schizophrenia who live in Mexico and Kenya (Krassoievitch, Perez-Rincon, & Suarez, 1982; Ndetei & Singh, 1983). Hallucinations of all types seem to be more prevalent among people from African, West Indian, and Asian cultures (Ndetei & Vadher, 1984). These differences may be due to cultural variations or to biological influences that are more or less prevalent in these cultures (for example, immunizations for influenza-type infections). We cannot yet explain the sources of these differences in symptoms.

In the United States, proportionately more African-Americans receive the diagnosis of schizophrenia than do whites (Lindsey & Paul, 1989). Research from both England and the United States suggests that people from devalued and ethnic minority groups (Afro-Caribbean in England, and African-Americans and Puerto Ricans in the United States) may be the subject of bias and stereotyping when it comes to this diagnosis (Jones & Gray, 1986; Lewis, Croft-Jeffreys, & Anthony, 1990). In other words, they may be more likely to receive a diagnosis of schizophrenia than persons who are not members of a minority group. The higher rate of schizophrenia, therefore, appears to be due to *misdiagnosis* rather than to any real difference in the prevalence of this disorder in different cultures.

Causes of Schizophrenia

The multiple layers of explanation that are needed to decipher what makes us behave the way we do are never in greater evidence than for the present disorder—schizophrenia. As we survey the work of the many people who study this disorder, we will examine many state-of-the-art techniques for studying both biological and psychosocial influences. It may be slow going at times, but the perspective it will provide about schizophrenia and causality should bring new insight to your understanding of psychopathology.

Biological Dimensions: Genetic Influences in Schizophrenia

We could argue that no other area of abnormal psychology so clearly illustrates the enormous complexity yet also the intriguing mystery of genetic influences on behavior as does the phenomenon of schizophrenia. Apart from the concern that schizophrenia may not be one "thing" but rather several different disorders, we can safely make one generalization: *Genes are responsible for making some individuals vulnerable to schizophrenia.* To examine the evidence of genetic vulnerability we will look at a range of research findings from family, twin, adoptee, offspring of twins, and linkage studies. We conclude with a discussion of the compelling reasons that no one gene is responsible for schizophrenia and that the genetic component of the disorder is based on multiple genes that come together to make people vulnerable to it. Readers who want a more in-depth but highly readable discussion of this research should refer to *Schizophrenia Genesis: The Origins of Madness* by Irving Gottesman (1991).

Family Studies

We begin our genetic journey with a discussion of the family studies of schizophrenia. One of the early contributors to this field was Franz Kallmann who, in 1938, published a major study on the families of

Irving Gottesman, a psychologist at Washington University, has made significant contributions to modern-day understanding of schizophrenia.

people with schizophrenia (Kallmann, 1938). Kallmann examined the family members of over 1,000 persons diagnosed with schizophrenia in a Berlin psychiatric hospital. Several of his observations about these families continue to guide present-day research on schizophrenia. Kallmann showed that the *severity* of the parent's disorder influenced the likelihood of the child's having schizophrenia. The more severe the parent's form of schizophrenia, the more likely were the children to develop the disorder. Another observation was important: All *forms of schizophrenia* (for instance, catatonic, paranoid) were seen within the families. In other words, it does not appear that you inherit a predisposition for, say, *paranoid* schizophrenia. Instead, you may inherit a general predisposition for schizophrenia that may be the same or different from that of your parent.

Gottesman (1991) has recently summarized the data from about 40 studies of schizophrenia, shown in Figure 14.4. The most striking feature of this graph is the orderly demonstration that the risk of having schizophrenia varies according to how many genes an individual shares with someone who has the disorder. For example, you have the greatest chance (approximately 48%) of having schizophrenia if you have an identical (monozygotic) twin who has schizophrenia, a person who shares 100% of your genetic information. Your risk drops to about 17% if you have a fraternal (dizygotic) twin, a person who on the average shares about 50% of your genetic information. And having *any* relative with schizophrenia makes you more likely to have the disorder than someone in the general popu-

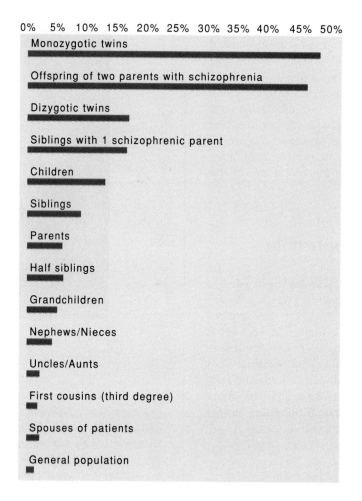

Figure 14.4 Risk of developing schizophrenia (based on Gottesman, 1991)

lation without such a relative (about 1%). Obviously, the other part of this equation that is not answered by family studies is the role of environmental influences. Because family studies can't separate from the genetic influence the impact of the family's environment on the disorder, we look to twin and adoption studies to help us evaluate the role of shared experiences in the cause of schizophrenia.

Twin Studies

Remember that identical twins share 100% of their genes and 100% of their environment (if they are raised together) while fraternal twins share only about 50% of their genes and 100% of their environment. If the environment is solely responsible for schizophrenia, we would expect little difference between identical and fraternal twins with regard to this disorder. On the other hand, if the disorder was unaffected by environmental influences and was caused only by genetic factors, then both identical twins would always have schizophrenia and the fraternal twins would both have the disorder (be *concordant*) about 50% of the time. Research from twin studies on schizophrenia indicates that the "truth"

is somewhere in the middle (Carson & Sanislow, 1993; Fowles, 1992; Gottesman, McGuffin, & Farmer, 1987; Kendler & Diehl, 1993).

In a recent Norwegian study, the concordance rate for identical twins was 48.4% while the concordance rate for fraternal twins was only 3.6% (Onstad, Skre, Torgersen, & Kringlen, 1991). Referring to Figure 14.4, you see that this percentage resembles Gottesman's summary of the concordance rates of 48% and 17%, respectively—a finding suggesting that the shared genes of the identical twins may account for their higher rates of schizophrenia.

In one of the most fascinating of "nature's experiments," a set of quadruplets (four identical siblings), all of whom have schizophrenia, has been studied extensively. Nicknamed the "Genain" quadruplets (from the Greek, meaning "dreadful gene"), these women have been followed by David Rosenthal and his colleagues at the National Institute of Mental Health for a number of years (Rosenthal, 1963). In a sense, the women represent the complex interaction between genetics and the environment on schizophrenia. All four shared the same genetic predisposition for schizo-

The Genain quadruplets (shown here at age 4 and later at 60 years), four women who share the same genes, all have schizophrenia but have exhibited the disorder in different ways over the years.

phrenia, and all were brought up in a particularly dysfunctional household; yet their symptoms and diagnoses, the time of onset for schizophrenia, the course of the disorder, and ultimately their outcomes differed significantly.

The case of the Genain quadruplets touches on an important aspect of studying genetic influences on behavior—*unshared environments* (Plomin, 1990). We tend to think of siblings, and especially identical twins (or quadruplets, in this case), as being brought up in a parallel manner. The impression is that "good" parents expose all their children to favorable environments, and "bad" parents provide unstable experiences for their children. However, even identical siblings can have very different prenatal and family experiences and therefore be exposed to varying degrees of biological and environmental stress. For example, one of the Genain sisters (Hester) was described by her disturbed parents as a habitual masturbator, and she had more problems socially as she grew up. Hester was the first to experience the severe symptoms of schizophrenia (at age 18) while her sister Myra was not hospitalized until 6 years later. This very unusual case illustrates that even siblings who are very close in every aspect of their lives can still have considerably different experiences physically and socially as they grow up, conditions that may contribute to vastly different outcomes.

Adoption Studies

Several adoption studies have separated the roles of the environment and genetics as they affect schizophrenia. These studies often span many years;

because people can show the first signs of schizophrenia in middle age, researchers need to be sure that all the offspring have a chance to develop the disorder before drawing conclusions. Many of the schizophrenia studies are conducted in Europe, primarily because of the extensive and comprehensive records that are kept in countries where socialized medicine is practiced.

Figure 14.5 illustrates the two primary strategies for studying the effects of adoption on children: the *adoptees' study method* and the *adoptees' relatives method* (Tienari, 1992). The largest and most recent adoption study is currently being conducted in Finland (Tienari, 1991) and is an example of the adoptees' study method outlined in Figure 14.5. From a sample of almost 20,000 women with schizophrenia, the researchers found 164 mothers who gave up children for adoption. To date, 155 offspring of mothers with schizophrenia and 185 children of control mothers (those without schizophrenia) have been studied. As of 1991, 16 children with schizophrenia and other psychotic disorders (for example, schizophrenia, delusional disorder, schizophreniform disorder) who had mothers with schizophrenia have been identified (1/155 = 10.3%) and only 2 children with schizophrenia and other psychotic disorders who came from the non-schizophrenic mothers have been found (2/185 = 1.1%). Even when raised in a home other than that of their biological parents, children of parents with schizophrenia have a much higher chance of themselves having the disorder.

The second strategy—the adoptees' relatives method—is exemplified in a study by a team of re-

Adoption Strategy	First Find	Then	Look For and Evaluate
Adoptees' study method	Birth parents, one of whom has schizophrenia	→	Their offspring, adopted into another family
Adoptees' relatives method	Grown-up adoptees with schizophrenia	→	Their biological and adoptive families

Figure 14.5 Two adoption research strategies that can be applied to the study of schizophrenia (adapted from Tienari, 1992)

searchers from the United States and Denmark. This team searched the national register of Denmark for people with schizophrenia who had been given up for adoption (Kety, Rosenthal, Wender, Schulsinger, & Jacobsen, 1978; Lowing, Mirsky, & Pereira, 1983; Rosenthal et al., 1968). They then examined these adoptees and compared them to adoptees without schizophrenia. Although this study has been analyzed in a number of different ways, the general conclusion is that children of people with schizophrenia who are adopted into families without schizophrenia still have a higher than average rate of having schizophrenia themselves. In other words, something other than living in the home of a person with schizophrenia must account for this disorder.

The Offspring of Twins

The evidence from the twin and adoption studies strongly suggests a genetic component for schizophrenia; but what about the children who develop schizophrenia even though their parents do not have the disorder? For example, the Tienari (1991) study we just discussed found that 1.1% of the children with nonschizophrenic parents developed schizophrenia. Does this mean that you can develop schizophrenia without "schizophrenic genes?" Or are some people "carriers," having the genes for schizophrenia but for some reason not showing the disorder themselves? An important clue to this question comes

from research on the children of twins with schizophrenia.

In a study begun in 1971 by Margit Fischer and later continued by Irving Gottesman and Aksel Bertelsen, 21 identical twin pairs and 41 fraternal twin pairs with a history of schizophrenia were identified along with their children (Fischer, 1971; Gottesman & Bertelsen, 1989). These researchers wanted to determine the *relative* likelihood that a child would have schizophrenia if his or her parent also had schizophrenia, or if the parent's twin had schizophrenia but the parent did not. Figure 14.6 illustrates the findings from this study, showing the likelihood of a child's having schizophrenia given the status of his or her parent. For example, if your parent is an identical (monozygotic) twin with schizophrenia, you have about a 17% chance of having the disorder yourself. Even if you are the child of an unaffected identical twin (no schizophrenia) whose co-twin has the disorder, you are just as likely to have schizophrenia as a child of the twin who does have schizophrenia.

On the other hand, look at the risks if you are the child of a fraternal (dizygotic) twin. If your parent is one of the pair who has schizophrenia, you too have about a 17% chance of having schizophrenia. However, if your parent does not have schizophrenia but your parent's fraternal twin does, your risk is less—about 2%. The only way to explain this finding is through genetics. These data clearly indicate that

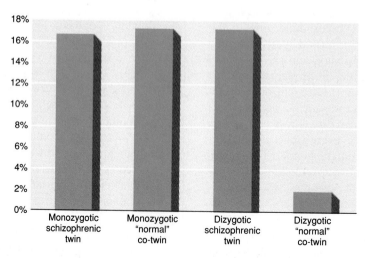

Figure 14.6 Risk for schizophrenia among children of twins

you can have the genes that predispose you to schizophrenia, not show the disorder yourself, but still pass on the genes to your children. In other words, you can be a "carrier" for schizophrenia. These data represent some of the strongest evidence yet that people are genetically vulnerable to schizophrenia. Remember, however, that there is *only* a 17% chance even if your parent has this disorder, meaning that other factors besides genetics come into play in determining who will have this disorder.

Linkage Studies

If genes are involved in schizophrenia, where are they? A report made several years ago brought the astonishing news that a gene responsible for the disorder was found on the fifth chromosome (Bassett, 1989; McGillivray, Bassett, Langlois, Pantzar, & Wood, 1990). A young man and his uncle were identified as both having schizophrenia as well as the same unusual facial features. An analysis conducted on their chromosomes showed that they both had the same anomaly involving the fifth chromosome, suggesting that both their facial features and their schizophrenia were due to their unusual fifth chromosome. As startling as the news that the location of the "schizophrenia gene" was found was how rapidly this finding was refuted by other studies. Within 3 years, more than 10 linkage studies were conducted showing little evidence for a schizophrenia gene located on the fifth chromosome (Kendler & Diehl, 1993).

Recall from Chapter 4 that linkage studies rely on traits such as blood types (whose exact location on the chromosome is already known) that are inherited in families along with the disorder you are looking for—in this case, schizophrenia. Because we know the location of the genes for these traits (called *marker genes*), we can make a rough guess about the location of the disorder genes that are inherited along with the marker genes. To date, research has looked at several sites for genes that may be responsible for schizophrenia. For example, because there is some evidence that siblings who have schizophrenia tend to be of the same gender (Crow, 1988), researchers have examined the X and Y chromosomes (our sex chromosomes) for evidence of a gene for schizophrenia. Just as we saw for chromosome 5, there was initial evidence for schizophrenia being found on the sex chromosomes (d'Amato et al., 1992); however, this finding could not be replicated (Asherson et al., 1992).

One line of this genetic linkage research relates to a topic we discuss shortly: neurobiological influences in schizophrenia. One long-standing theory about the cause of schizophrenia is that it involves the neurotransmitter *dopamine*. Because of this interest in dopamine, researchers have understandably been interested in the genes responsible for dopamine func-

tioning and their relationship to schizophrenia. Instead of looking for a "schizophrenia gene" or genes, this research seeks the location of these dopamine genes and attempts to determine whether they are related to schizophrenia. Linkage studies have sought to establish a link between dopamine sites (referred to as D_1, D_2, D_3, and D_4 loci) and the presence of schizophrenia, although to date the evidence has not been strong (Byerly et al., 1991; Su et al., 1993).

Evidence for Multiple Genes

Because identical twins can be discordant for schizophrenia (only one of the twins having the disorder) despite having identical genetic material, something about their different environments must contribute to their ultimate outcomes. However, the observation that both the affected and unaffected twin have the same likelihood of passing on schizophrenia to their children seems to be overwhelming evidence that there is a genetic component to schizophrenia. It would appear then that some people are genetically vulnerable to developing schizophrenia. However, researchers using sophisticated genetic techniques have not yet been able to find the site for the genes responsible for schizophrenia.

One reason may be that schizophrenia is a *polygenic abnormality* (Fowles, 1992; Gottesman, 1991; Gottesman & Shields, 1982). The schizophrenia we see in most people with the disorder is probably caused by several (*poly*) genes (*genic*) located at different sites throughout our chromosomes. This explanation would help to account for researchers' difficulty in finding one site for the gene. It also helps to clarify why there can be gradations of severity in people with the disorder (from mild to severe), and why the risk of having schizophrenia increases with the number of affected relatives in the family. It is likely that this polygenic model is not unique to schizophrenia and that many of the disorders people experience are caused by more than one gene.

Biological Dimensions: Neurobiological Influences in Schizophrenia

A parent of someone with schizophrenia recently wrote of the cause of this disorder:

> Many of us who have a son, daughter, or other relative with schizophrenia have observed so great a change in the person's behavior with the onset of the psychosis that we know intuitively that the cause had to be something basic, such as an alteration of the brain's functioning. (Johnson, 1989, p. 553)

The belief that schizophrenia somehow involves a malfunctioning brain goes back as far as the writings of Emil Kraepelin (1856–1926). It is therefore not surprising that a great deal of research has focused on the brain as the place to find the cause of schizophrenia. Before we discuss some of this work, however, be forewarned: Trying to study abnormalities in the brain as clues to the cause of schizophrenia carries with it all the classic problems of doing correlational research that were discussed in Chapter 4. For example, if a person has schizophrenia and too much of a brain chemical (neurotransmitter), (a) does too much brain chemical cause schizophrenia, (b) does schizophrenia create too much of this chemical, or (c) does something else cause both the schizophrenia and the chemical imbalance? Keep this caveat in mind as you review the following research.

The Role of Dopamine

One of the most enduring theories of the cause of schizophrenia involves the neurotransmitter *dopamine* (Davis, Kahn, Ko, & Davidson, 1991). Before we discuss the research on dopamine and schizophrenia, however, we first need to review briefly how neurotransmitters such as dopamine operate in the brain and how neuroleptic medications affect this operation. In Chapter 2 we discussed the sensitivity of specific neurons to certain neurotransmitters such as dopamine, and described their clustering as pathways throughout the brain. The top of Figure 14.7 shows two of these neurons and the important synaptic gap that separates them. Neurotransmitters are released from the storage vessels (synaptic vesicles) at the end of the axon, cross the gap, and are taken up by receptors in the dendrite

of the next axon. The chemical "messages" are transported in this way from neuron to neuron in pathways throughout the brain.

This process can be influenced in a number of ways, and the rest of Figure 14.7 illustrates some of them. The chemical messages can be increased by *agonistic agents* or can be decreased by *antagonistic agents*. You should recognize the word *antagonistic* as meaning hostile or unfriendly; in some way this is the effect of antagonistic agents on this chemical messenger service. *Antagonistic effects* include interfering with the release of the neurotransmitters, blocking the uptake at the level of the dendrite, and causing leaks that reduce the amount of neurotransmitter that is ultimately released, all of which will slow down or stop messages from being transmitted. On the other hand, *agonistic effects* assist with this transfer, and in extreme, can produce too much neurotransmitter activity. This can occur through the increased production of the neurotransmitter, the increased release, and the facilitation of more receptors at the dendrites.

The effectiveness of antipsychotic medications, their side effects, and a variety of other observations point to the possibility that somehow the dopamine system is too active in persons with schizophrenia. The simplified picture portrayed in Figure 14.7, however, does not show that there are actually different receptor sites and that the same chemical, such as dopamine, can produce different results depending on which of those sites it affects. In schizophrenia, attention has focused on four dopamine sites simply referred to as D_1, D_2, D_3, and D_4 loci. We will see that

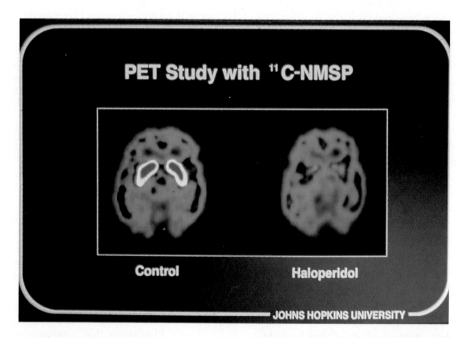

PET images of the brain of a never-medicated individual with schizophrenia both before (*left*) and after (*right*) the administration of the neuroleptic haloperidol. The red and yellow colored areas show activity of the D_2 receptors, indicating that haloperidol resulted in reduced dopamine acitivity.

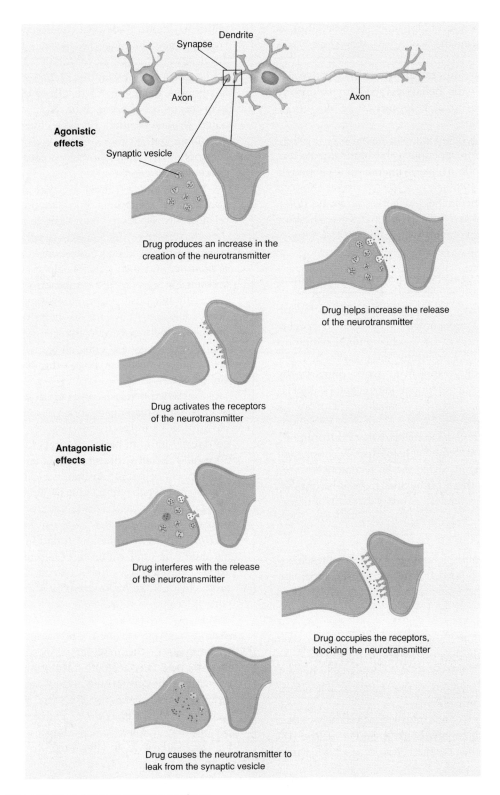

Figure 14.7 The effects of drugs in neurotransmitters

the site called D_2 is of particular interest to researchers in this field.

In a story that resembles some mystery novels, several pieces of "circumstantial evidence" point to excessive activity of the dopamine system as possibly causing the symptoms of schizophrenia. The following are four of these clues to the role of dopamine:

1. Antipsychotic drugs (called *neuroleptics*) that are often effective in treating people with schizophrenia, are dopamine antagonists and partially

block the brain's use of dopamine (Creese, Burt, & Snyder, 1976; Seeman, Lee, Chau Wong, & Wong, 1976).

2. These drugs can also produce negative side effects similar to the behaviors seen in Parkinson's disease, a disorder that is known to be due to insufficient dopamine.

3. The drug L-dopa, which is a dopamine agonist and is used to treat people with Parkinson's disease, produces schizophrenia-like symptoms in some people (Davidson et al., 1987).

4. Amphetamines, which also activate dopamine, can make psychotic symptoms worse in some people with schizophrenia (van Kammen, Docherty, & Bunney, 1982).

In other words, when certain drugs are administered that are known to increase dopamine (agonists), there is an increase in schizophrenia-like behavior; when drugs that are known to decrease dopamine activity (antagonists) are used, schizophrenic symptoms tend to be reduced. Specifically, the neuroleptic drugs (antagonistic agents) appear to work primarily by blocking one group of dopamine receptors: the D_2 receptors (Bates, Gingrich, Senogles, Falardeau, & Caron, 1991; Carlsson, 1978). All these observations together led researchers to theorize that schizophrenia in some people was attributable to excessive dopamine activity, especially involving the D_2 receptors.

Despite these observations, some recent evidence seems to contradict the theory that schizophrenia is related to excess dopamine (Carson & Sanislow, 1993; Davis et al., 1991):

1. A significant number of people with schizophrenia are not helped by the use of the dopamine antagonists.

2. Although the neuroleptics act to block the reception of dopamine quite quickly, the affected symptoms are reduced only after several days or weeks, much more slowly than one would expect.

3. These drugs are also only partially helpful for the negative symptoms (for instance, flat affect, anhedonia) of schizophrenia.

4. There is conflicting evidence about whether people with schizophrenia have more of the D_2 receptors than other people (Crow et al., 1981; Farde et al., 1990).

5. Genetic linkage studies are inconclusive about the connection between schizophrenia and the gene region for D_2 receptors (Su et al., 1993).

In addition to these concerns, there has been recent evidence of a "double-edged sword" with respect to schizophrenia. A relatively new medication—*clozapine*—has been found to be effective with many of the people who have not been helped

with the more traditional neuroleptic medications (Kane, Honigfeld, Singer, & Meltzer, 1988). That's the good news. The bad news for the dopamine theory is that clozapine is by far one of the weakest dopamine antagonists, being much less able to block the D_2 sites than the others (Creese, Burt, & Snyder, 1976). How could this medication be less efficient at blocking dopamine but be more effective as a treatment for schizophrenia if schizophrenia is caused by excessive dopamine activity?

The answer may be that dopamine is involved in the symptoms of schizophrenia but that the relationship is more complicated than we once thought (Potter & Manji, 1993). Several recent studies suggest that two neurotransmitters, *serotonin* and *dopamine,* and their relationship to each other may account for some of the symptoms of schizophrenia, especially the positive symptoms (such as, hallucinations, delusions). To try to describe the complex interaction between these two neurotransmitters and the daunting task of disentangling their effects, we will use a rather unusual analogy—the mail system in the United States.

When neuroscientists try to study the amount of a neurotransmitter in the brain of a living person they have to do so indirectly. Because they can't ethically go directly into the brains of individuals who are still alive and healthy, these researchers look for the by-products of neurotransmitters—called *metabolites.* For dopamine, the researchers measure the amount of *homovanillic acid (HVA)* and for serotonin they measure the metabolite *5-hydroxyindoleacetic acid (5-HIAA),* both of which are found in the cerebrospinal fluid (the fluid within the brain and spinal cord). To use our analogy, that's like trying to guess the productivity of the mail system by rummaging through garbage cans of customers and looking for empty envelopes and packages. As you can imagine, estimating mail effectiveness and production from the by-products of the mail (envelopes and packaging) may not be a very accurate form of measurement. For example, although the U.S. Postal Service might stop delivery of the mail briefly, this wouldn't necessarily stop the production of garbage because some people may hold on to envelopes and packages to be disposed of at a later time. In a similar way, there are "pools" of neurotransmitters at the nerve endings. Therefore, even though the production of dopamine or serotonin was interrupted, you might see no decrease in the amounts of HVA and 5-HIAA in cerebrospinal fluid because of these extra reserves.

Also, the amounts of dopamine and serotonin being made are not independent of each other. For example, let's compare the U.S. Postal Service (dopamine) and Federal Express (serotonin). A major snowstorm might slow down or temporarily stop both the postal service and Federal Express from delivering some mail. In fact, you could complicate the system even further by supposing that an interruption in the U.S. mail could affect the communication ability of Federal Express because of its reliance on the U.S. Postal Service. Like it or not, what one does affects the other. In a similar way, dopamine and serotonin interact with each other and can be affected by mixed antagonists, drugs that affect both neurotransmitters (snowstorm). Again, trying to learn whether the dopamine system is overactive in people with schizophrenia by studying the HVA metabolite is comparable to looking through other people's garbage cans for mail-related trash. Production of the metabolite is certainly related, but it can't give you a completely accurate measure of dopamine production.

Two recent studies suggest that estimating the dopamine–serotonin relationship rather than looking at the levels of dopamine alone may better explain the effects of neuroleptic drugs (Hsiao et al., 1993; Kahn et al., 1993). This dopamine–serotonin interaction receives additional support from research on clozapine, which seems to be more effective with difficult cases of schizophrenia but does not block dopamine as effectively as other neuroleptic medications (Breier et al., 1994). Clozapine is also a serotonin antagonist, so it actually blocks both dopamine and serotonin (Lee & Tang, 1984; Peroutka & Snyder, 1980). The success of this drug may relate to its ability to affect both dopamine and serotonin in just the right combination. Clozapine may be like the snowstorm—affecting several systems at the same time.

The type of sophisticated research described in Box 14.1 allows us to further refine our understanding of the complex relationship between the neurotransmitter systems and schizophrenia. Our incomplete and complicated view of the role of neurotransmitters in schizophrenia may be clarified by improvements in our ability to monitor neurotransmitters directly rather than rely on measuring their by-products. New technologies such as in vivo brain receptor imaging and metabolic brain activity mapping involving positron emission tomography should help us advance our understanding of the interaction of these brain chemicals and possibly help us group people with schizophrenia into more meaningful subtypes (Potter & Manji, 1993).

The Role of Brain Structure

Evidence for neurological damage in people with schizophrenia comes from a number of observations. There is convincing evidence that children who are at risk for schizophrenia (children with a parent who has the disorder) tend to show subtle but observable neurological problems such as abnormal reflexes and problems with attention (Fish, 1977; Hans & Marcus, 1991). In addition, these difficulties seem to persist, with adults who have schizophrenia showing deficits in their ability to perform certain tasks and to attend during reaction time exercises (Cleghorn & Albert, 1990). These types of findings suggest that specific brain damage or dysfunction may cause or accompany schizophrenia.

Timothy Crow, who has been a major force in subdividing people with schizophrenia into those with "positive" and those with "negative" symptoms, has hypothesized separate neurobiological influences on these two groups (Crow, 1980, 1985). He sees the positive symptoms of schizophrenia such as hallucinations and delusions as coming primarily from excessive dopamine activity. The research suggests that this may be too simple an explanation for the behavior of people with schizophrenia. At the same time, Crow suggests that those with predominantly "negative" symptoms such as flat affect and anhedonia may behave in that way because of structural abnormalities in the brain such as enlarged ventricle size. This too may be an oversimplification of the research, but it gives us a starting point for examining current thinking in this area.

One of the most reliable observations about the brain in people with schizophrenia involves the size of the ventricles. As early as 1927 measurements were made of the size of these liquid-filled cavities in the brains of people with schizophrenia and showed enlargement of the lateral ventricles (the cavities in the brain; see Figure 14.8) in some but not all of these individuals (Jacobi & Winkler, 1927). With the introduction of more sophisticated techniques for observing the brain, almost 50 studies have been conducted on ventricle size, with the large majority showing abnormally large lateral ventricles in people with schizophrenia (Pahl, Swayze, & Andreasen, 1990). The size of the ventricles alone may not be a problem, but in these cases the dilation or enlargement of the ventricles indicates that the parts of the brain adjacent to the ventricles have atrophied or have not developed fully. In other words, damage to parts of the brain next to the ventricles may have caused the ventricles to become larger.

Ventricle size enlargement is not seen in all people who have schizophrenia. Several factors seem to be associated with this neurological finding. For example, larger ventricle size is observed more often in men than in women (Andreasen et al., 1990). Also, the older you are and the longer you have had this disorder, the larger the ventricle size seems to be.

In a recent study of ventricle size, researchers investigated the possible interaction between genes and the physical environment (Suddath, Christison, Torrey, Casanova, & Weinberger, 1990). They found 15 pairs of

Box 14.1   The Complexities of Research on Neurotransmitter Interactions

Researchers have come a long way in a short time toward gaining a more in-depth understanding of the chemistry of schizophrenia. Although we still have many questions, the research technology is becoming quite advanced; it is informative to look behind the scenes of one of these studies to see what is involved. Recently, at the Bronx Veterans Affairs Hospital, researchers recruited 19 male inpatients who had a diagnosis of schizophrenia to participate in a study (Kahn et al., 1993). The inpatients agreed to take a neuroleptic medication called Haldol (haloperidol) to learn whether it could help them. At the same time, the researchers wanted to study the way the medication was working in the men's brains to affect their dopamine and serotonin levels.

The subjects were selected for the study if they had had schizophrenia for at least 5 years and had not had any illegal drug or alcohol involvement for at least 6 months. The researchers also controlled the patients' diets and had them fast for approximately 12 hours before sampling their cerebrospinal fluid. This extraordinary concern about diet was to ensure that their levels of HVA (a metabolite of dopamine) and 5-HIAA (a metabolite of serotonin) would not be affected by their eating more or less of certain foods.

After this period of being drug-free and fasting, all the patients had a lumbar puncture. This is the procedure for extracting a sample of cerebrospinal fluid, which was used to measure HVA and 5-HIAA levels. Measurement of these levels gave researchers the baseline measure of the two metabolites that they would use later to compare with the metabolite levels after the patients had received neuroleptic medication. At this time, and again after they had been given the medication, the patients' schizophrenic symptoms were assessed with a rating scale called the *Brief Psychiatric Rating Scale*. The researchers wanted to learn whether the medication changed the metabolite levels and whether the change predicted who would improve and who would not.

Within 2 weeks of these assessments (during which time they received no neuroleptic medication), the patients were given the medication Haldol; 5 weeks later they again had a lumbar puncture and were assessed with the rating scale. Their cerebrospinal fluid was analyzed to assess HVA and 5-HIAA levels by use of a machine called a high-performance liquid chromograph, a device that uses light to identify certain chemicals.

Their results showed that the drug Haldol did affect the metabolites, increasing HVA concentrations in the cerebrospinal fluid. This indicates that dopamine was being produced but was blocked by the Haldol from going to the receptors—sort of like your blocking your mailbox, causing the mail carrier to throw your mail directly into the garbage! However, the researchers found improvements in schizophrenic symptoms only in those patients who had a higher ratio between their HVA and 5-HIAA—meaning more HVA *relative* to the amount of 5-HIAA. This finding suggests that blocking dopamine alone may not cause reductions in these symptoms. Rather, you may need to block dopamine *and* serotonin, but *you may need to block more dopamine than serotonin*. Although this study does not answer all our questions about neurotransmitters and schizophrenia, its description should give you an idea of how difficult, but ultimately rewarding (many of the patients improved!), research can be in this highly technical area of schizophrenia.

---

identical twins who were discordant for schizophrenia, meaning that only one of each pair had the disorder. Using the brain-imaging technique of magnetic resonance imaging (MRI), they showed that the ventricles of most of the affected twins were enlarged and that the anterior hippocampus was reduced, in comparison to the unaffected twin.

The results of this twin study return us to the concept of *unshared environments*, which we raised in the section on genetics (Plomin, 1990). Even though the twins are identical genetically, they can experience a number of differences in their environments, even before they are born. For instance, in the intrauterine environment twins need to compete for nutrients from their mother, and they may not be equally successful. In addition, birth complications such as the loss of oxygen (anoxia) could affect only one of the twins (Carson & Sanislow, 1993). In fact, obstetrical complications such as these do appear often among the twins with schizophrenia in discordant identical twin pairs, and among the more severely affected of the twins if they both have schizophrenia (McNeil, 1987). Different

Brain image of twins, one with and one without schizophrenia. The arrows point to the ventricles, which are normal in the unaffected twin and enlarged in the schizophrenic twin.

experiences among twins who are already predisposed to a disorder such as schizophrenia could result in damage to the brain that could cause the types of symptoms we see in some people with schizophrenia.

The frontal lobes of the brain have also been of interest to people looking for structural problems associated with schizophrenia (Gur & Pearlson, 1993). The basic finding is that this area of the brain may be less active in people with schizophrenia compared to people without the disorder, a phenomenon known as *hypofrontality* (*hypo* meaning less active or deficient). Research by Weinberger and other scientists at the National Institute of Mental Health further refined this observation, suggesting that deficient activity in a particular area of the frontal lobes, called the dorsolateral prefrontal cortex (DLPFC), may be responsible for

Right ventricle

Left ventricle

Third ventricle

Fourth ventricle

Spinal canal

Figure 14.8 Location of the cerebrospinal fluid in the human brain. This extracellular fluid surrounds and cushions the brain and spinal cord. It also fills the four interconnected cavities (cerebral ventricles) within the brain and the central canal of the spinal cord.

Nancy Andreasen of the University of Iowa has made numerous contributions that have furthered our understanding of the nature of schizophrenia.

this condition (Berman & Weinberger, 1990; Weinberger, Berman, & Chase, 1988). When people with and without schizophrenia are given tasks that involve this area of the frontal lobes (the DLPFC), less activity (measured by cerebral blood flow) is recorded in the brains of people with schizophrenia. Researchers measured DLPFC activity among the 15 twin pairs discussed in the previous section on ventricle size and found that all the twins with schizophrenia showed reduced brain activity compared to the healthy twin (Weinberger, Berman, Suddath, & Torrey, 1992). Hypofrontality also seems to be associated with the negative symptoms of schizophrenia (Andreasen et al., 1992; Wolkin et al., 1992).

Kenneth Davis and his colleagues have integrated this research on structural problems in the brain with the research on neurotransmitters (Davis, Kahn, Ko, & Davidson, 1991). They note that the prefrontal area of the brain that seems to be less active among many people with schizophrenia is also one site of a major dopamine pathway that is thought to be involved in schizophrenia. They hypothesize that the inactivity here causes other points on this dopamine pathway that are located deeper in the brain (the mesolimbic area) to become more active. They suggest that the relative inactivity causes the negative symptoms of schizophrenia, and that the excessive activity deeper in the brain accounts for the positive symptoms. If this change in activity at different sites happened over the course of a number of years, it would help explain why some people have both positive and negative symptoms at different points in their lives. The researchers' idea is currently just a theory, but it can be tested and may help

us put together in a meaningful way these seemingly very different observations about the neurobiology of people with schizophrenia.

The Role of Viral Infection

A curious fact about schizophrenia is that, according to some authors, no adequate descriptions of people having this disorder appear earlier than 1800 or thereabout (for example, Gottesman, 1991). If you look at historic records or read ancient literature, you can find descriptions of such disorders as mental retardation, mania, depression, and senile dementia. Even William Shakespeare, who in his many writings describes most human foibles, makes no mention of anything that resembles our current notion of schizophrenia. There is a puzzling absence of any mention of such an obvious aberration of behavior.

One intriguing hypothesis used to explain the omission is that schizophrenia really is a recent phenomenon, appearing in the past 200 years, and like AIDS, it may involve the spread of some newly introduced virus (Gottesman, 1991). In other words, there may be a "schizo-virus" that could explain some of the cases of this debilitating disorder (Torrey, 1988). Although there is some disagreement about the lack of historical description of schizophrenia, we have evidence that a virus-like disease may account for some cases of the disorder (Kirch, 1993). Some indirect support for a virus-like cause of schizophrenia comes from observing a higher prevalence of schizophrenia among men living in urban areas (Lewis, David, Andreasson, & Allbeck, 1992), implying that these men are more likely to be exposed to infectious agents than their peers in less-populated areas.

Several studies have shown that schizophrenia may be more prevalent in individuals who experienced prenatal exposure to epidemics of influenza. For example, Sarnoff Mednick and his colleagues followed a large number of people after a severe Type A2 influenza epidemic in Helsinki, Finland, and found that persons whose mothers were exposed to influenza during the second trimester of pregnancy were much more likely to have schizophrenia than were others (Cannon, Barr, & Mednick, 1991). This observation has been documented by some researchers (for instance, O'Callaghan, Sham, Takei, Glover, & Murray, 1991) but not by others (for example, Torrey, Rawlings, & Waldman, 1988).

There has recently been more direct evidence of a link between schizophrenia and influenza from research being conducted on the brains of deceased people with this disorder. One group of researchers has found, deep in the brains of people with schizophrenia, a certain type of brain cell containing an enzyme called nicotinamide-adenide dinucleotide phosphate-diaphorase (NADPH-d, for short) (Akbarian, Bunney et al., 1993; Akbarian, Vinuela et al., 1993). Normally, cells containing NADPH-d migrate from inner portions of the brain to the cortex in mid-pregnancy. The observation that the cells have not made this migration among people with schizophrenia suggests a problem during this phase of fetal development, perhaps the presence of some disease state. Another group of researchers studying a different type of brain cell found similar developmental problems in the brains of people with schizophrenia (Scheibel & Conrad, 1993). They note that influenza is one of the few viruses known to have the ability to disrupt this developmental migration on the part of neurons.

The evidence for problems of development during the second trimester in the pregnancies of women who later have children with schizophrenia has led to interest in other signs of this fault in fetal development. Among the types of cells that migrate to the cortex of the brain during this period are the fingertip dermal cells, which are responsible for the number of "fingerprint" ridges on fingertips. Although there is no such thing as an abnormal number of ridges on the fingertips, identical twins generally have the same number. However, if there was some interruption in fetal development that resulted in schizophrenia during the second trimester (the time when the viral theory suggests that a virus may have its effect), it would also affect the fingertip dermal cells. Recently, researchers examined the ridge count of identical twins who were discordant for schizophrenia and compared them with identical twins without schizophrenia (Bracha, Torrey, Gottesman, Bigelow, & Cunniff, 1992). They found that the number of ridges on the fingertips of the twins without schizophrenia differed very little from each other; however, they differed a great deal among about one-third of the twins who were discordant for schizophrenia. This study suggests that ridge count may be a marker of early brain damage during pregnancy. Although there is no characteristic "fingerprint" for schizophrenia, this sign may add to our understanding of the second-trimester conditions that can result in the stress needed to trigger the genetic predisposition for schizophrenia.

Taken together, these observations—that virus-like diseases may cause damage to the fetal brain, which later may cause the symptoms of schizophrenia—are similar to the circumstantial evidence we explored with the excessive dopamine hypothesis. They are interesting to consider, and they may help explain why *some* people with schizophrenia behave they way they do. However, we need to have more direct evidence that something like influenza does affect fetal brains in this way, and that this damage causes the behaviors that characterize people with schizophrenia. There is not yet enough evidence to show convincingly that there is a "schizo-virus."

Marsha, the mother of a schizophrenic son, struggles with the consequences of his illness. "I've been depressed and getting migraines," she says. "I think I'm losing it."

The Search for Markers

Recall from the genetic linkage studies that one way to conduct genetic research is to identify markers that are inherited along with a disorder in some families. If a certain blood type is common to family members who also have schizophrenia, for example, and we know where the gene for this blood type is located, we can guess that a gene influencing schizophrenia might be nearby. In a similar way, researchers have examined people who have schizophrenia, looking for common traits other than the symptoms of the disorder itself. If some people have the positive symptoms of schizophrenia, others have the negative symptoms, and still others have a mixture of these symptoms, yet they all have a particular problem completing a certain task, this skill deficit would be very useful for identifying what else these people may have in common. The earlier discussion of fingertip ridge counts is an example of a possible marker for schizophrenia.

Several of these potential markers for schizophrenia have been studied over the years. One of the more highly researched of these signs is called *smooth-pursuit eye movement* or *eye-tracking*. Keeping your head still and trying to follow a moving pendulum, you must be able to track it, back and forth, with your eyes. This ability to track objects smoothly across the visual field seems to be deficient in many people who also have schizophrenia (Clementz & Sweeney, 1990; Holzman & Levy, 1977; Iacono, 1988); it does not appear to be the result of drug treatment or institutionalization (Lieberman et al., 1993). It also seems to be a problem for relatives of these people (Kuechenmeister, Linton, Mueller, & White, 1977) and is observed more frequently among people with schizophrenia than in others who do not have the disorder (Clementz & Sweeney, 1990). Finally, recent genetic research suggests that deficient eye-tracking may be the result of a single gene defect that is inherited along with the gene or genes involved in schizophrenia (Grove, Clementz, Iacono, & Katsanis, 1992). When all these observations are combined, they suggest that an eye-tracking deficit may be a marker for schizophrenia that could be used to study the nature of this disorder further.

Psychological and Social Contributions to Schizophrenia

We know that with identical twins, who share 100% of their genetic information, one may develop schizophrenia while the other may not. This phenomenon suggests that something is involved in schizophrenia in addition to genes. We know that early brain trauma, perhaps resulting from obstetrical complications or a second trimester virus-like attack, is being examined as a type of possible early physical stress that may contribute to schizophrenia. All these observations show clearly that schizophrenia does not fall neatly into one or even a few simple "causal packages." For instance, not all people with schizophrenia have enlarged ventricles, nor do they all have a hypofrontality or excessive activity in their dopamine systems. To complicate the causal picture further, psychological and social factors may play a role. We next look at research that has examined possible influences of psychosocial factors, such as emotional stressors or family interaction patterns, on *initiating* the symptoms of schizophrenia, and how those factors may cause people to *relapse* or worsen after a period of improvement in their symptoms.

High-Risk Research

In our discussion of genetics, we noted that approximately 13% of the children born to parents who have schizophrenia are likely themselves to develop the disorder. These high-risk children have been the focus of several studies, both *prospective* (studying people before and during some event or events of interest that are expected to occur, for example, certain stressors) and *longitudinal* (studying people over long periods of time).

A classic "at-risk" study was initiated in the 1960s by Sarnoff Mednick and Fini Schulsinger in Denmark (Mednick & Schulsinger, 1965, 1968). They identified 207 Danish children of mothers who had severe cases of schizophrenia and 104 control children born to mothers who had no history of the disorder. The average age of these children was about 15 at the time they were first identified, and the researchers followed them for 10 more years to determine which ones later developed schizophrenia and whether any factors had

predicted who would and would not develop this disorder. Mednick and Schulsinger found that several factors seemed to predict the onset of schizophrenia. One of these factors—*pregnancy and delivery-related complications*—we have already discussed as early biological stressors. Another influence—*instability of early family rearing environment*—suggests that environmental influences may also trigger the onset of schizophrenia (Cannon, Barr, & Mednick, 1991). Poor parenting may place additional strain on a vulnerable person already at risk for schizophrenia. We must wait until these at-risk children enter middle age, the time when we will know the eventual outcomes for all of these people, before we can draw strong conclusions from these studies.

The Role of Stress

An important issue is to learn how much and what kind of stress is needed to move a person from having a predisposition for schizophrenia to having the disorder itself. Think back to the two cases we presented at the beginning of this chapter. Did you notice any precipitating events? For Arthur, his father had died several years earlier and he was laid off from his job right around the time his symptoms first appeared. For David, his uncle had died the same year he began acting strangely. Were these just coincidences, or did these stressful events contribute to the men's later problems?

Researchers have studied the effects of a variety of stressors on schizophrenia. Dohrenwend and Egri (1981), for instance, observed that otherwise healthy people who engage in combat during a war (an extremely stressful life event) often display temporary symptoms that resemble those of schizophrenia. In an early study, Brown and Birley (1968; Birley & Brown, 1970) studied people whose onset of schizophrenia could be narrowed down to a certain week. They found that these individuals tended to have a high number of stressful life events in the 3 weeks just before they started showing signs of the disorder. Recently, a large-scale study sponsored by the World Health Organization also looked at the role of life events in the onset of schizophrenia (Day et al., 1987). This cross-national study confirmed the findings of Brown and Birley across eight different centers.

One of the potential problems with studies such as those by Brown and Birley and the World Health Organization is the retrospective nature of the research. Each relies on after-the-fact reports, collected after the person showed signs of schizophrenia. One always wonders whether such reports have been biased in some way and whether they could be misleading us about the role of stressful life events in schizophrenia

(Hirsch, Cramer, & Bowen, 1992). A partial reply to these concerns is found in a recent study that used a *prospective* approach to examine the impact of stress on relapse.

Ventura, Nuechterlein, Lukoff, and Hardesty (1989) identified 30 people who had had recent onsets of schizophrenia and followed them for a 1-year period. The researchers interviewed the subjects every 2 weeks to learn whether they had experienced any stressful life events or whether their schizophrenia symptoms had changed. During the 1-year assessment period, 11 of the 30 people had a significant relapse in that their symptoms returned or worsened. Notice that, unlike the previous studies, this research examines the factors that predict the recurrence of schizophrenic symptoms after a period of improvement. Like Brown and Birley, these researchers found that the people who relapsed experienced an increase in stressful life events in the month before their relapse. An important finding is that, although the people who relapsed experienced more stressful events *as a group* just before their relapse, this wasn't true for all the people who relapsed. In fact, 55% of those who relapsed *did not* have a major life event during the month before their relapse. Other factors must account for the return of symptoms among these people.

The Role of the Family in Relapse

There has been a great deal of research on how interactions within the family can affect people who have schizophrenia. For example, the term **schizophrenogenic mother** was used for a time to describe a parent whose cold, dominant, and rejecting nature was thought to cause schizophrenia in her children (Fromm-Reichmann, 1948). In addition, the term **double bind** was used to portray a type of communication style that produced conflicting messages, which, in turn, caused schizophrenia to develop (Bateson, 1959). Here, the parent presumably communicates messages that have two conflicting meanings (for example, a mother responding coolly to her child's embrace, but saying, "Don't you love me anymore?" when the child withdraws). The belief that this double-bind communication pattern or an overall schizophrenogenic style of relating is the cause of schizophrenia does not have much support in the research literature today. Unfortunately, these types of theories have been—and in some cases continue to be—destructive, producing guilt in parents who believe that their early mistakes caused devastating consequences for their children.

Recent work has focused more on how family interactions contribute, not to the cause of schizophrenia itself but instead to relapse after initial symptoms are observed. One area of research has focused on a particular emotional communication style of these families and is referred to as **expressed emotion (EE).** This concept originated in the work of George W. Brown and his colleagues in London. These researchers followed a sample of people who had been discharged from the hospital after an episode of schizophrenic symptoms and found that former patients who had limited contact with their relatives did better than the patients who spent longer periods of time with their families (Brown, 1959). When the researchers conducted additional research to try to learn why this phenomenon existed, they found that, if the level of *criticism* (expressing disapproval), *hostility* (expressing animosity), and *emotional overinvolvement* (being intrusive) expressed by the families was high, patients tended to relapse (Brown, Monck, Carstairs, & Wing, 1962).

Since that initial research, others such as researcher Jill Hooley (1985) have found that ratings of high expressed emotion in a family are a good predictor of relapse among people with chronic schizophrenia. In fact, if you have schizophrenia and live in a family with high expressed emotion, you are 3.7 times more likely to relapse than if you lived in a family with low expressed emotion (Kavanagh, 1992; Parker & Hadzi-Pavlovic, 1990). To show how families of people with schizophrenia might communicate expressed emotion, below are examples of interviews taken from families with high and low ratings of expressed emotion (Hooley, 1985).

HIGH EXPRESSED EMOTION

I always say, "why don't you pick up a book, do a crossword or something like that to keep your mind off it." That's even too much trouble.

Jill Hooley of Harvard University is a noted researcher of expressed emotion in schizophrenic families.

I've tried to jolly him out of it and pestered him into doing things. Maybe I've overdone it, I don't know.

I know it's better for her to be on her own, to get away from me and try to do things on her own.
Whatever she does suits me.
I just tend to let it go because I know that when she wants to speak she will speak. (from Hooley, 1985, pp. 148–149)

The literature on expressed emotion is valuable for our understanding of why people have recurrences of the symptoms of schizophrenia. It may also show us how to treat people with this disorder so that they do not continue to experience psychotic episodes (Mueser et al., 1993).

An interesting issue that arises when you study family influences, such as expressed emotion, is whether this is a phenomenon unique to our culture or one found in other cultures as well. Looking at expressed emotion across different cultures may help us learn whether it is a *cause* of schizophrenia. Remember that schizophrenia is observed worldwide and at about the same rate—with a prevalence of about 1% in the general population. If a factor like high expressed emotion in families is a causal agent, we should see the same rates in families across cultures. In fact, rates of high expressed emotion do differ across cultures, as you can see in Figure 14.9. These data come from a recent analysis of the concept of expressed emotion across several studies from India, Mexico, Great Britain, and the United States (Jenkins & Karno, 1992). The differences suggest that there are cultural variations in how families react to someone with schizophrenia, and that these reactions do not cause someone to have the disorder. However, it seems clear that living in more critical and hostile cultures may provide additional stressors that can in turn lead to more relapses.

Treatment of Schizophrenia

If you remember our descriptions of Arthur and David, you will recall their families' concern for them. Arthur's mother spoke of the "living nightmare" and David's aunt expressed concern for both her safety and David's. There is little doubt that there was a desperate desire on the family's part to help, but what do you do for someone who has delusions, hears his dead uncle's voice, or can't communicate complete thoughts? This search for help has taken many paths, sometimes down some very disturbing roads. For example, the picture on the next page depicts the primitive surgery conducted in the 1500s to remove the "stone of madness," which was thought to cause disturbed behavior. As barbaric as this may seem today, it is not much different from the prefrontal lobotomies performed on people with schizophrenia as late as the 1950s. This surgical procedure severed the part of the brain connecting the frontal lobes to the lower portion of the brain, a technique that sometimes "calmed" the patient but also caused cognitive and emotional deficits. Even today, some societies use crude surgical procedures for schizophrenia. In Kenya, for instance, Kisii tribal doctors listen to their patients to find out where the noises in their heads (hallucinations) are coming from, then proceed to get them drunk, cut out a piece of scalp, and scrape the skull in the area of the "voices" (Mustafa, 1990).

Our concern here is with more contemporary approaches to treating people with this devastating disorder. Treatment typically begins with a neuroleptic drug. These medications have been in-

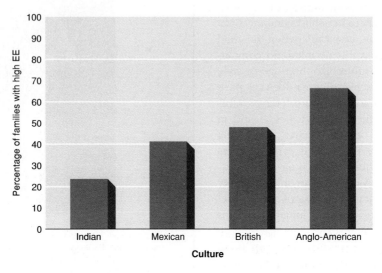

Figure 14.9 Cultural differences in expressed emotion (EE)

An early depiction (circa 1500) of psychosurgery—removing part of the brain to treat mental illness

valuable in reducing the symptoms of schizophrenia for many people. They are typically used in combination with a variety of psychosocial treatments to assist in reducing relapse, to improve skills deficits, and to improve compliance for taking the medications (Liberman, Kopelowicz, & Young, 1994). Evidence for the effectiveness of these treatments is discussed next.

Biological Interventions

Researchers have thought for over a hundred years that schizophrenia would require some form of biological intervention. Emil Kraepelin, who so eloquently described dementia praecox in the late 19th century, saw the disorder as a brain disease. Lacking a biological treatment, he routinely recommended that the physician use "good patience, kindly disposition, and self-control" to calm excited patients (Nagel, 1991). This approach was seen as only a temporary way of helping the person through disturbing times and was not thought to be a treatment for schizophrenia per se.

During the 1930s, several novel biological treatments were attempted to treat this "brain disorder." One approach used massive doses of insulin—the drug used to treat diabetes—to induce comas deliberately in people suffering from schizophrenia. Called *insulin coma therapy*, this procedure was thought for a time to be a helpful treatment, but closer examination showed that it carried great risk of serious illness and death. During this time *psychosurgery*, including prefrontal lobotomies, was introduced; and in the late 1930s, *electroconvulsive therapy* (ECT) was even advanced as a treatment for schizophrenia. As with other early, drastic treatments, initial enthusiasm for ECT faded as its effects were found not to be beneficial for most people with schizophrenia. As we described in Chapter 7, ECT is currently used only for people who experience very severe episodes of depression.

A breakthrough in the treatment of schizophrenia came during the 1950s with the introduction of several drugs that relieved the symptoms of this disorder for many people (Potkin, Albers, & Richmond, 1993). Called *neuroleptics* (meaning "taking hold of the nerves") these medications provided the first real hope that help was available for people with schizophrenia. When they are effective, the drugs help people think more clearly, and they reduce or eliminate the hallucinations and delusions that are common. They work by affecting the "positive" symptoms (for example, delusions, hallucinations, agitation) and

Josh is frustrated after being admitted to the hospital for a psychotic episode. "It feels bad, but not as bad as the drugs," he says, referring to antipsychotic medications.

Table 14.13   Neuroleptic Drugs

Class	Example	Trade Name
Phenothiazine	Chlorpromazine	Thorazine
	Thioridazine	Mellaril
	Fluphenazine	Prolixin
	Perphenazine	Trilafon
	Trifluoperazine	Stelazine
Thioxanthenes	Thiothixene	Navane
Butyrophenones	Haloperidol	Haldol
	Pimozide	Orap
Benzamides	Clozapine	Clozaril
Dibenzo-diazepine	Loxapine	Loxitane
Dihydro-indolones	Molindone	Moban

Recall from our discussion of the dopamine theory of schizophrenia that the neuroleptics are dopamine antagonists. One of their major actions in the brain is to interfere with the dopamine neurotransmitter system. However, they can affect other neurotransmitter systems such as the serotonergic system. We are just beginning to understand the mechanisms by which these drugs effect improvements in schizophrenic symptoms.

In general, each of the drugs is effective with some people and not with others. Clinicians often must go through a "trial and error" process to find the medication that works best for each patient; and some individuals do not benefit significantly from any of these drugs. Until lately, many people were not helped by the neuroleptic drugs. However, a number of people who were not helped by the more traditional neuroleptic medications have responded well to the recently discovered *clozapine*. First marketed in 1990, clozapine is now used widely for previously unresponsive patients (Kane & Marder, 1993).

Despite the optimism generated by the effectiveness of neuroleptic medication, it works only when it is taken properly, and many people with schizophrenia do not regularly and routinely take their medication.

not the "negative" ones, such as the social deficits experienced by some people with schizophrenia. Table 14.13 shows the six classes of these drugs (based on their chemical structure) and the trade names of several examples (Potkin, Albers, & Richmond, 1993).

"It's no fun being fried on meds," he says. "It's like a coffeepot boiling over." This is Josh, an individual that has been diagnosed as schizophrenic, and as schizo-affective most recently.

Remember the case of David and the Haldol that was helpful in reducing his hallucinations. He would frequently "cheek" the pills, holding them in his mouth until he was alone, then he would spit them out. Approximately 7% of the people prescribed neuroleptic medication refuse to take it at all (Hoge et al., 1990). Research on the prevalence of occasional noncompliance suggests that a majority of people with schizophrenia stop taking their medication from time to time. A recent follow-up study, for example, found that, over a 2-year period of time, three out of four patients studied refused to take their neuroleptic medication for at least 1 week (Weiden et al., 1991).

A number of factors seem to be related to patients' noncompliance with a medication regimen, including negative doctor–patient relationships, cost of the medication, and poor social support (Weiden et al., 1991). Not surprisingly, a major factor in patient refusal seems to be the negative side effects that come with use of the drugs. Neuroleptic medication use can produce a number of unwanted physical symptoms such as grogginess, blurred vision, and dryness of the mouth. Because these medications affect neurotransmitter systems, more serious side effects—called *extrapyramidal symptoms*—can result. These changes resemble the motor difficulties experienced by people with Parkinson's disease and are sometimes referred to as parkinsonian symptoms. One of the most common of the negative side effects is called *akinesia* and includes an expressionless face, slow motor activity, and monotonous speech (Blanchard & Neale, 1992). Another extrapyramidal symptom is *tardive dyskinesia*, which involves involuntary movements of the tongue, face, mouth, or jaw, and can include protrusions of the tongue, puffing of cheeks, puckering of the mouth, and chewing movements. Tardive dyskinesia seems to result from long-term use of high doses of neuroleptic medication, is often irreversible, and may occur in as many as 20% of people who remain on these medications over long periods of time (Morgenstern & Glazer, 1993). Obviously, these are very serious negative side effects that have justifiably concerned people who otherwise benefit from these drugs.

To learn what patients themselves say about these medications, Windgassen (1992) questioned 61 people who had had recent onsets of schizophrenia. About half reported that the feeling of sedation or "grogginess" was an unpleasant effect of taking these medications. They made statements such as, "I always have to fight to keep my eyes open," "I felt as though I was on drugs . . . drowsy, and yet really wound up" (p. 407). Other complaints included deterioration in patients' ability to think or concentrate (18%), problems with salivation (16%), and blurred vision (16%). Although a third of the patients questioned felt that the medications were beneficial, about 25% had a negative attitude toward the drugs. A significant proportion of people who could benefit from neuroleptic medications find them unacceptable as a treatment, and this aversion may explain the relatively high rates of refusal and noncompliance.

Recently, researchers have taken on this concern as a major treatment issue in schizophrenia, realizing that these medications can't be successful if they aren't taken regularly. Clinicians hoped that the introduction of clozapine—which produces fewer negative side effects—would allay some of these legitimate concerns. However, even clozapine produces some undesirable effects, and its use must be monitored closely to avoid rare but potentially life-threatening effects of the drug (Idanpaan-Heikkila, Alhava, Olkinuora, & Palva, 1977). One advance researchers hoped would improve compliance rates was the introduction of injectable medications. Instead of taking neuroleptics by mouth, patients can inject newer versions of these medications and their effectiveness can last for several weeks. Unfortunately, noncompliance also occurs among people who take neuroleptics in this way, primarily because they do not return to the hospital or clinic for repeated doses (Weiden et al., 1991). Psychosocial interventions are now being used not only to treat schizophrenia but also to increase medication-taking compliance by helping patients communicate better with professionals about their concerns over side effects.

Psychosocial Interventions

Historically, a number of psychosocial approaches have been tried as a treatment for schizophrenia, born of the belief that the disorder results from a person's problems in adapting to the world, brought on by early experiences (Nagel, 1991). Many therapists thought that, if these individuals could be helped to

Marsha is excited after her son is returned to her home from a stay in the psychiatric hospital. "Now," she says, "the real struggle begins."

achieve insight into the presumed role of their early experiences in their current problems, they could be safely led to deal with the realities of their existing situation. Although a number of clinicians, including those following a psychodynamic or psychoanalytic approach to therapy, continue to use this type of treatment, research suggests that these efforts at best may not be beneficial and at worst may be harmful (Mueser & Berenbaum, 1990).

Today, few believe that psychological factors *cause* people to have schizophrenia and that traditional psychotherapeutic approaches such as insight will *cure* them of this disorder. We will see, however, that there is some role for psychological approaches in the treatment of schizophrenia. The outcome of many such efforts has been a realization that schizophrenia may not be treatable with nonbiological approaches alone (Bellack & Mueser, 1993). At the same time, we have seen that, despite the great promise of drug treatment for people with this disorder, the problems with negative symptoms, medication taking, and relapse

suggest that drugs alone may not be effective with many people who have schizophrenia. As with a number of the disorders outlined in this text, recent work in the area of psychosocial intervention has suggested the value of a combined approach using both treatments (Bachrach, 1992).

Until relatively recently, most people with severe and chronic cases of schizophrenia have been treated in hospital settings. During the 19th century, this type of inpatient care involved "moral treatment," a strategy that emphasized helping these people improve in areas such as socialization, assisting them to establish routines for self-control, and showing them the value of work and religion (Armstrong, 1993). Various types of such inpatient and supportive "milieu" treatment have been promoted and favored over the years, but with one important exception, none seems to have been helpful to people with schizophrenia (Tucker, Ferrell, & Price, 1984).

The exception to this disappointing history of hospital treatment came in the 1970s with the pioneer-

Because of the tensions between them, this mother and son decide that they should not continue living in the same house.

ing work of Gordon Paul and Robert Lentz at a mental health center in Illinois (Paul & Lentz, 1977). These researchers, who borrowed some of the behavioral approaches used by others in the field such as Ted Ayllon and Nate Azrin (Ayllon & Azrin, 1968), designed an environment for inpatients that encouraged appropriate socialization, participation in group sessions, and more self-care (for instance, bed making) while it discouraged violent outbursts. They did this by setting up an elaborate **token economy,** in which the residents could earn access to meals and small luxuries by behaving appropriately. A patient could, for example, buy cigarettes with the tokens earned for keeping his room neat. On the other hand, a patient would be fined (lose tokens) for being disruptive or otherwise acting inappropriately. This incentive system was combined with a full schedule of activities during the day. Paul and Lentz compared the effectiveness of this application of behavioral (or *social learning*) principles to more traditional inpatient environments. In general, they found that patients who went through their program did better than others on social, self-care, and vocational skills, and more of the people in their treatment environment were able to be discharged from the hospital. This study was one of the first to show that, despite the debilitating effects of schizophrenia, people affected by this disorder can learn and can be motivated to perform some of the skills they need to live more independently.

Over the past 40 years, starting in 1955, many efforts have combined to halt the routine institutionalization of people with schizophrenia in the United States (Talbott, 1990). This trend has occurred in part because of court rulings that limit involuntary hospitalization (as we saw in Arthur's case) and in part because of the relative success in using neuroleptic medication. The bad news is that policies of deinstitutionalization have often been ill conceived and have led to large numbers of homeless persons who have schizophrenia and other serious psychological disorders. The good news is that more attention has been focused on supporting these people in their communities, among their friends and families. The trend is away from creating better hospital environments and toward the perhaps more difficult task of addressing the complex problems faced by these people in the less-predictable and insecure world that we live in each day. To date, these positive efforts represent only a small fraction of what is needed to support the growing number of homeless individuals with mental disorders.

One of the more insidious effects of schizophrenia is its negative impact on a person's ability to relate to other people. While not as dramatic as hallucinations and delusions, this problem with socialization can be the most visible impairment displayed by

A new drug, clozapine, has put Michael into "a mellow mood," he says. "My biggest fear is falling back into the mental frame of mind I was in and having my family notice it and take advantage of me in some way."

people with schizophrenia and can prevent them from getting and keeping jobs and making friends. To address this problem, clinicians have attempted to re-teach social skills such as basic conversation skills, assertiveness, and relationship skills to those who have schizophrenia (Bellack & Mueser, 1993).

Therapists break these complex social skills into their component parts, then model the behaviors, and have the individuals role play their parts and ultimately practice their new skills in the "real world," all the while receiving feedback and encouragement for signs of progress. This isn't as easy as it sounds. For example, how would you teach someone to make a friend? Many skills are needed, such as maintaining eye contact when you talk to someone and providing the prospective friend with some (but not too much!) positive feedback on his or her own behavior ("I really enjoy talking to you"). These individual skills are practiced and then combined until they are used in a natural way (Liberman, DeRisi, & Mueser, 1989). The results of this type of research suggest that basic skills can be taught to people with schizophrenia. However, there is some disagreement about how ultimately successful the treatment is (Bellack & Mueser, 1992; Hogarty et al., 1992). The problem is that the positive results of social skills training often fade in the months following the termination of the training. The challenge with teaching social skills, as with all therapies, is to maintain the effects over a long period of time.

To address some of the obstacles to this much-desired maintenance of treatment effects, some workers are taking a more comprehensive approach to helping people with schizophrenia cope more successfully outside the hospital environment. The Independent Living Skills Program at UCLA, as one example, focuses on helping people take charge of their own care by such

"If anyone gets into the house, they said I'd get shot . . . [Therapist: Who said?] That's the eagle . . . The eagle works through General Motors. They have something to do with my General Motors check I get every month . . . when you do the 25 of the clock, it means that you leave the house 25 after 1 to mail letters so that they can check on you . . . and they know where you're at. That's the eagle . . . If you don't do something they tell you to do, Jesus makes the shotgun sound, and then . . . not to answer the phone or the doorbell . . . because you'd get the shot [by the] eagle."

Table 14.14   Independent Living Skills Program at UCLA

Module	Skill Areas	Learning Objectives
Symptom management	Identifying warning signs of relapse	To identify personal warning signs To monitor personal warning signs with assistance from other people
	Managing warning signs	To obtain assistance from health care providers in differentiating personal warning signs from persistent symptoms, medication side effects, and variations in mood; to develop an emergency plan for responding to warning signs
	Coping with persistent symptoms	To recognize and monitor persistent personal symptoms; to obtain assistance from health care providers in differentiating persistent symptoms from warning signs, medication side effects, and variations in mood; to use specific techniques for coping with persistent symptoms To monitor persistent symptoms daily
	Avoiding alcohol and street drugs	To identify the adverse effects of alcohol and illicit drugs and the benefits of avoiding them; to refuse offers of alcohol and street drugs; to know how to resist using these substances in coping with anxiety, low self-esteem, or depression; to discuss openly use of alcohol and drugs with health care providers
Medication management	Obtaining information about antipsychotic medication	To understand how these drugs work, why maintenance drug therapy is used, and the benefits of taking medication
	Knowing correct self-administration and evaluation	To follow the appropriate procedures for taking medication; to evaluate responses to medication daily
	Identifying side effects of medication	To know the specific side effects that sometimes result from taking medication and what to do when these problems occur
	Negotiating medication issues with health care providers	To practice ways of obtaining assistance when problems occur with medication

Source: Eckman et al., 1992.

things as identifying warning signs that a relapse may be coming on and learning ways to manage their medication (see Table 14.14) (Eckman et al., 1992). There is some preliminary evidence that this type of training may help prevent relapses among people with schizophrenia, although longer-term outcome research is needed to see how long these effects last.

In our description of the psychosocial influences on schizophrenia we reviewed some of the work linking the social and emotional environment of the person's home and family—such as family members who are overly critical or hostile, engaging in what is called expressed emotion—to the recurrence of schizophrenic episodes (Hooley, 1985). A logical question that follows asks whether families could be helped by learning to reduce their level of expressed emotion, and whether this would result in fewer relapses and better overall functioning for people with schizophrenia. Several studies have addressed these issues in a variety of ways (Hogarty et al., 1986; Hogarty et al., 1991; Falloon et al., 1985). For one, behavioral family therapy has been used with the families of persons with schizophrenia to teach them the skills necessary to be more supportive (Mueser, Liberman, & Glynn, 1990).

In contrast to a "traditional therapy" session, behavioral family therapy more closely resembles classroom education (Falloon et al., 1985). Family members are given information about the disorder and its treatment, such as sessions debunking the myth that families cause schizophrenia and practical information about neuroleptic medications and their side effects. They are also helped with communication skills so they can become more empathic listeners, and they learn more constructive ways of expressing negative feelings to replace the harsh criticism that characterizes some family interactions. In addition, they learn problem-solving skills to help them resolve problems and conflicts that arise. Like the research on social skills

training, outcome research suggests that the effects are significant for the first year, but that the results are less robust 2 years after intervention (Hogarty et al., 1991). This type of therapy, therefore, must be ongoing for patients and their families to continue to benefit from it.

Taken together, the research on individual social skills training and family intervention suggests that they may be helpful additions to biological treatment for schizophrenia. Significant relapses may be avoided or delayed with these psychosocial interventions. Figure 14.10 illustrates the studies reviewed by one group (Falloon, Brooker, & Graham-Hole, 1992) showing that these treatments reduce the number of relapses among persons receiving drug therapy in comparison with simple social support or educational efforts.

The locus where treatment of people with schizophrenia takes place has expanded over the years from locked wards in large mental hospitals to their families' homes to their local communities. In addition, the delivery of services has also expanded to include self-advocacy and self-help groups. Former patients have organized programs such as Fountain House in New York City to provide mutual support (Beard, Propst, & Malamud, 1982). These types of psychosocial clubs have differing models, but all are "person centered" and focus on obtaining positive experiences through employment opportunities, friendship, and empowerment. In just one example, 25,000 New Yorkers over the past 20 years have participated in "Clubhouses" sponsored by the New York Association of Psychiatric Rehabilitation Services. Some research indicates that participation in these psychosocial clubs may help reduce relapses (Beard, Malamud, & Rossman, 1978), but it is also possible that those who participate may be a special group of individuals. Therefore, it is difficult to interpret these improvements (Mueser, Liberman, & Glynn, 1990).

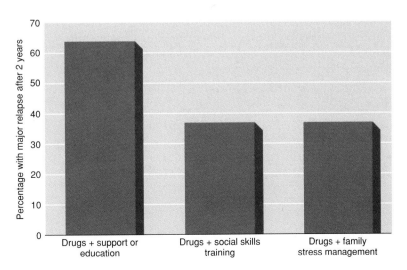

Figure 14.10 Studies on treatment of schizophrenia from 1980 to 1992 (from Falloon, Brooker, & Graham-Hole, 1992)

Treatment and its delivery for people with schizophrenia differ across cultures. In China, the most frequently used treatment for this disorder is neuroleptic medication, although 7% to 9% of patients also receive traditional herbal medicine and acupuncture (Mingdao & Zhenyi, 1990). For both financial and cultural reasons, more people in China are treated outside the hospital than is the case in Western societies. In many countries in Africa, people with schizophrenia are kept in prisons, primarily because of the lack of adequate alternatives (Mustafa, 1990). In general, the movement away from housing people in large institutional settings to community care is ongoing in most Western countries.

Summary

- Schizophrenia is characterized by a broad spectrum of cognitive and emotional dysfunctions that include symptoms of delusions and hallucinations, disorganized speech and behavior, and inappropriate emotions.

- The symptoms of schizophrenia can be divided into "positive" and "negative" symptoms. Positive symptoms refer to more active manifestations of abnormal behavior, or an excess or distortion of normal behavior, and include delusions, hallucinations, and disorganized speech. Negative symptoms involve deficits in normal behavior on such dimensions as affect, speech, and motivation.

- DSM-IV divides schizophrenia into five subtypes. People with the *paranoid type of schizophrenia* have prominent delusions or hallucinations; at the same time, their cognitive skills and affect are relatively intact. People with the *disorganized type of schizophrenia* tend to show marked disruption in their speech (disorganized speech) and behavior (disorganized behavior); they also show flat or inappropriate affect. People with the *catatonic type of schizophrenia* have unusual motor responses such as remaining in fixed positions (waxy flexibility), excessive activity, and being oppositional by remaining rigid. In addition, they will display odd mannerisms with their bodies and faces, including grimacing. Some people do not fit neatly into these subtypes, and these individuals would be classified as having an *undifferentiated type of schizophrenia*. Some people who have had at least one episode of schizophrenia, but who no longer have the major symptoms of the disorder, would be diagnosed as having the *residual type of schizophrenia*.

- Several other disorders are characterized by "psychotic" behaviors such as hallucinations and delusions; these include *schizophreniform disorder* (which includes people who experience the symptoms of schizophrenia for less than 6 months), *schizoaffective disorder* (which includes people who have symptoms of schizophrenia and who also exhibit the characteristics of mood disorders such as depression and bipolar affective disorder), *delusional disorder* (which includes people with a persistent delusion or belief that is contrary to reality, in the absence of the other characteristics of schizophrenia), *brief psychotic disorder* (which includes people with one or more "positive" symptoms such as delusions, hallucinations, or disorganized speech or behavior over the course of less than a month), and *shared psychotic disorder* (which includes individuals who develop delusions simply as a result of a close relationship with a delusional individual).

- A number of causative factors have been implicated for schizophrenia, including genetic influences, neurotransmitter imbalances, structural damage to the brain such as that caused by a viral infection, and psychological stressors.

- Relapse appears to be influenced by hostile and critical family environments characterized by *high expressed emotion*.

- Treatment typically involves the use of neuroleptic drugs, usually administered in combination with a variety of psychosocial treatments to assist in reducing relapse, to improve skills deficits, and to improve compliance in taking the medications. Effectiveness of these treatments is limited, as schizophrenia is typically a chronic disorder.

Key Terms

alogia (561)

anhedonia (562)

associative splitting (554)

avolition (561)

brief psychotic disorder (566)

catatonia (554, 561)

catatonic immobility (561)

catatonic type of schizophrenia (562)

delusion (559)

delusional disorder (564)

disorganized speech (560)

disorganized type of schizophrenia (562)

double bind (585)

expressed emotion (EE) (585)

flat affect (561)

good premorbid (569)

hallucination (559)

hebephrenia (554)

inappropriate affect (561)

negative symptoms (569)

paranoia (554)

paranoid type of schizophrenia (562)

poor premorbid (569)

positive symptoms (569)

process schizophrenia (568)

psychotic (557)

reactive schizophrenia (569)

residual type of schizophrenia (563)

schizoaffective disorder (564)

schizophrenia (553)

schizophreniform disorder (564)

schizophrenogenic mother (585)

schizotypal personality disorder (564)

shared psychotic disorder (folie à deux) (566)

token economy (591)

undifferentiated type of schizophrenia (563)

waxy flexibility (561)

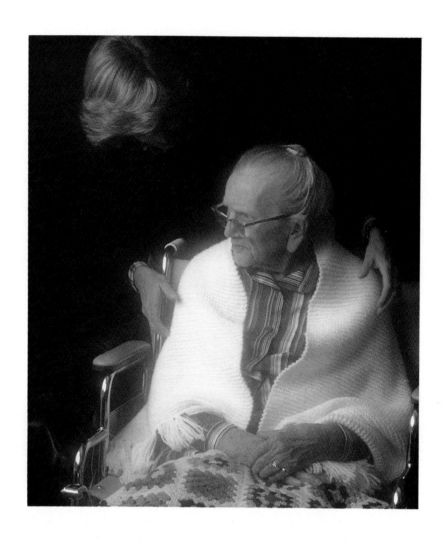

As I watched her at play . . . it came to me that this child
would pass through life as the angels live in Heaven.
The difficulties of existence would never be hers.
Pearl Buck
On her daughter, who had mental retardation
The Child Who Never Grew

15

Mental Retardation and the Cognitive Disorders

Consider the cases of the following two individuals—Brian, who was born in 1955, and his niece Marie, who was born 30 years later (Kirk, 1993).

Brian and Marie both have mental retardation caused by a chromosomal disorder, once referred to as mongoloidism but now called *Down syndrome*. The way they were treated—Brian being sent to an institution immediately after birth and Marie staying at home receiving support in the community—had less to do with their diagnoses or even their ability levels than with public attitudes toward children with mental retardation then and now. A dramatic change has occurred during the four decades since Brian's birth.

Research on the brain and its role in psychopathology has increased in recent years, and we have chronicled many of the latest advances throughout the chapters of this book. All the disorders we have reviewed are in some way influenced by the brain. We have seen, for example, how relatively subtle changes in neurotransmitter systems can have significant effects on a person's mood, cognition, and behavior. Unfortunately, the brain is sometimes affected profoundly, and when this happens, drastic changes occur. This chapter reviews disorders that affect cognitive processes such as learning, memory, and consciousness. We begin with a discussion of disorders that occur early in development: *mental retardation,* which involves significant deficits in cognitive abilities, and *learning disorders,* which are characterized by one or more difficulties in areas such as reading and writing. The next chapter (Chapter 16) outlines specific disorders of development such as *autism,* which is characterized by significant deficits in social and language development. In the second half of this chapter, we describe several organic (brain) disorders that typically but not always emerge later in life: *delirium,* characterized by disorientation and difficulties in thinking and sustaining attention; *dementia,* identified by a combination of progressive and usually irreversible difficulties such as impaired judgment, memory, and abstract reasoning ability; and *amnestic disorders,* involving impairments in memory.

Mental Retardation

Mental retardation is a disorder that is present from childhood and is evident in significantly below-average

intellectual and adaptive functioning. People with mental retardation experience difficulties with day-to-day activities, although the degree of difficulty they face is a product of both the severity of their cognitive deficits and the type and amount of assistance they receive. Throughout history, perhaps more than any other group of people we have studied to this point, people with mental retardation have received treatment that can best be described as shameful (Scheerenberger, 1983). Although there are notable exceptions, societies throughout the ages have devalued individuals who have intellectual abilities deemed less than adequate.

The field of mental retardation has undergone dramatic and fundamental changes over the last decade. Our conception of what it means to have mental retardation, its definition, and the way people with this disorder are treated and cared for have all been scrutinized, debated, and fought over by a variety of concerned groups. Here we describe the disorder in the context of these very important changes and attempt to reflect the status of people who have mental retardation as well as our current understanding of how best to understand the causes of the disorder and its treatment.

The manifestations of mental retardation appear in a greater variety than probably any other disorder we examine in this textbook. Some individuals function quite well and independently in our complex society—one example being the actor Chris Burke, who starred in the television series "Life Goes On." Others with mental retardation have significant cognitive and physical impairments and require considerable assistance to carry on day-to-day activities. Consider the case of James.

The bedroom of the Illinois Asylum for Feeble-Minded Children around 1880. Today efforts are underway to support keeping children with mental retardation in their homes and in their communities.

The Case of James

We first saw James when his mother contacted us because he was being disruptive at school and at work. James was 17 and attended the local high school. He had Down syndrome and was described as being very likable and, at times, mischievous. He enjoyed skiing, bike riding, and all the other activities common among teenage boys. In fact, his desire to participate in them was a source of some conflict between him and his mother: He wanted to take the driver's education course at school—which his mother felt would set him up for failure—and he had a girlfriend whom he wanted to date—a prospect that also caused his mother concern.

The school administrators complained because he wasn't participating in activities such as physical education, and at the work site that was part of his school program he was often sullen, sometimes lashing out at the supervisors. They were considering moving him to a program with more supervision and less independence.

James was the youngest of three children. His mother became pregnant with him when she was in her 40s, not planning for a child at her age but eagerly anticipating his birth nonetheless. It was apparent at birth that James had Down syndrome, initially because of the characteristic facial features and later through formal assessment. He was born with a congenital heart defect—a hole in his heart—that required several surgical operations, and he today wears a pacemaker. Doctors at the time—he was born in the mid-1970s—tried to be supportive, and suggested that his mother might want to consider placing him with a local agency that would care for him. His mother recalls that, although she was in shock after the birth, she quickly felt the same love and affection for the infant that she did for her other two children. She decided he would come home and be part of the family.

Because James's mother was a single parent—his father left the family shortly after his birth—and had continuing financial difficulties, the family moved frequently during his youth. They experienced striking differences in the way each community they lived in responded to James and his mental retardation. During his school years, some school districts immediately placed him in classes with other children his age and provided his teachers with additional assistance and consultation to help them adapt to James's needs. Others just as quickly recommended placements that were separate from the regular classroom. Sometimes the school district had a

Actor Chris Burke of the television show "Life Goes On." Chris has Down syndrome, yet has been able to successfully pursue an acting career.

special classroom in the local school for children who, like James, had mental retardation. Other districts had programs in specific schools, sometimes in other towns, and James would at times have to travel an hour to and from school each day to get to these programs. Every time he was assessed in a new school, the evaluation was similar to earlier ones. He would receive scores on his IQ tests in the range of 40 to 50, which placed him in a moderate range of mental retardation. Each school gave him the same diagnosis—Down syndrome with moderate mental retardation. At each school, the teachers and other professionals were competent and caring individuals who wanted the best for James and his mother. Yet what differed was their attitude toward children like James. Some believed that James needed a separate place where he would learn skills, in a program with specialized staff. Others felt they could provide a comparable education for children like James in a regular classroom, and that an added benefit would be for him to have peers without disabilities to model.

In his high school placement, James had several academic classes in a separate classroom just for children with learning problems, but he would participate in some classes such as gym with students who did not have mental retardation. His current difficulties in gym—not participating—and at the work site—being oppositional—were jeopardizing his placement in both programs. When I spoke with James's mother, she expressed frustration that the work program was "beneath him" and that he was asked to do boring, repetitive work such as folding paper. James expressed a similar frustration, saying that they treated him like a baby. He could communicate fairly well when he wanted to, although he sometimes would get confused about what he wanted to say and it was difficult to understand everything he was trying to articulate. On observing him at school and at work, and after speaking with his teachers, we realized that a common paradox had developed. The teachers would give James work to accomplish and he would resist if he thought it was too easy. His teachers interpreted his resistance to mean that the work was too hard for him and they would give him even simpler tasks. He would resist or protest more vigorously, and they would respond with even more supervision and structure.

Later, when we discuss treatment, we will return to James to show how we intervened at school and work to help him progress and become more independent.

Clinical Description

People with mental retardation display a broad range of abilities and personalities. Individuals like James, who have mild or moderate impairments, can, with proper preparation, carry out most of the day-to-day activities expected of any of us. Many of these individuals can learn to use mass transportation, purchase groceries at a store, or hold a variety of jobs. Others, who have more severe impairments, will need more assistance to care for themselves. They may need help to eat, bathe, and dress themselves, although with the proper training and support, they can achieve a degree of independence. These individuals experience impairments that cut across most areas of functioning. Language and communication skills are often the most obvious difficulties. James was only mildly impaired in this area, needing help with articulation. In contrast, people with more severe forms of mental retardation may never learn to use speech as a form of communication and will need alternative strategies such as sign language or special communication devices to express even their most basic needs. Because many of their cognitive processes are adversely affected, individuals with mental retardation have difficulty learning. However, the level of difficulty varies depending on how extensive the person's cognitive disability is. The DSM-IV diagnostic criteria for mental retardation are listed in Table 15.1.

Before examining the specific criteria for mental retardation, the reader should note that—like the personality disorders we described in Chapter 13—mental retardation is included on Axis II of DSM-IV. Remember that separating disorders by axes serves two purposes: first, to indicate that Axis II disorders tend to be more chronic and less amenable to treatment, and second, to remind clinicians to consider whether these disorders are present and if they are affecting some Axis

Table 15.1 DSM-IV Diagnostic Criteria for Mental Retardation

A. Significantly subaverage intellectual functioning: an IQ of approximately 70 or below on an individually administered IQ test (for infants, a clinical judgment of significantly subaverage intellectual functioning).

B. Concurrent deficits or impairments in present adaptive functioning (i.e., the person's effectiveness in meeting the standards expected for his or her age by his or her cultural group) in at least two of the following areas: communication, self-care, home living, social/interpersonal skills, use of community resources, self-direction, functional academic skills, work, leisure, health, and safety.

C. The onset is before age 18 years.

Code based on degree of severity reflecting level of intellectual impairment:
Mild Mental Retardation: IQ level 50–55 to approximately 70
Moderate Mental Retardation: IQ level 35–40 to 50–55
Severe Mental Retardation: IQ level 20–25 to 35–40
Profound Mental Retardation: IQ level below 20 or 25
Mental Retardation, Severity Unspecified: when there is strong presumption of Mental Retardation but the person's intelligence is untestable by standard tests

Source: DSM-IV, APA, 1994.

This young girl cannot speak but is learning to communicate with others by means of an eye-gaze board—pointing to or simply looking at the picture that conveys her message.

I disorder. People can have a diagnosis on both Axis I (for instance, generalized anxiety disorder) and Axis II (for example, mild mental retardation).

The DSM-IV criteria for mental retardation are grouped into three parts. First, a person must have "significantly subaverage intellectual functioning," a determination made with one of several IQ tests (described in more detail in Chapter 3) with the cutoff score set by DSM-IV at approximately 70 or below. This score represents a number that is two standard deviations below the average score of 100 (one standard deviation here is 15 points) (Morgenstern & Klass, 1991). Roughly 2% to 3% of the population would score at 70 or below on these tests. Recently, the American Association on Mental Retardation—which has its own, very similar definition of mental retardation—somewhat ambiguously listed the cutoff score as approximately 70 to 75 or below (Luckasson et al., 1992). The difference between a cutoff of 70 and one of 75 is significant: Raising the score to 75 increases from about 3% to about 6% the proportion of people who potentially have mental retardation. This number would go up because approximately 3% of the population score between 70 (the DSM-IV cutoff score) and 75 (the AAMR cutoff score). Use of the higher score has caused some concern because of the number and ethnicity of the people it would affect. If this portion of the population is included under the definition of mental retardation, the number of people eligible for certain services would increase drastically and the number of minority children in this grouping could expand disproportionately (MacMillan, Gresham, & Siperstein, 1993; Reschly & Ward, 1991).

This concern is lessened somewhat by the second criterion of both the DSM-IV and AAMR definitions for mental retardation, which calls for "concurrent deficits or impairments in adaptive functioning." In other words, scoring "approximately 70 or below" on an IQ test is not sufficient for a diagnosis of mental retardation; one must also have significant difficulty in at least two of the following areas: communication, self-care, home living, social/interpersonal skills, use of community resources, self-direction, functional academic skills, work, leisure, health, and safety. To illustrate, while James had many strengths, such as his ability to communicate and his social/interpersonal skills (he had several good friends), he was not as proficient as other teenagers at caring for himself in areas such as home living, health, and safety, or in academic areas. This aspect of the definition is important because it excludes people who can function quite well in society but for various reasons do poorly on IQ tests. For instance, someone whose primary language is not English may do poorly on an IQ test but may still be able to function at a level comparable to his or her peers. This person would not be considered to have mental retardation even if he or she scored below 70 on the IQ test.

A number of assessment devices can be used to determine how well a person handles activities involved in daily living; these include the AAMD Adaptive Behavior Scales (ABS) (Nihira, Foster, Shellhaas, & Leland, 1974), the revised Vineland Adaptive Behavior Scales (Sparrow, Balla, & Cichetti, 1984), and the Scales of Independent Behavior (Bruininks, Woodcock, Weatherman, & Hill, 1984). Examples of questions

Table 15.2   Sample Questions from the AAMD Adaptive Behavior Scales

[1] *Use of Table Utensils* (Circle only *ONE*)

Uses knife and fork correctly and neatly	6
Uses table knife for cutting or spreading	5
Feeds self with spoon and fork—neatly	4
Feeds self with spoon and fork—considerable spilling	3
Feeds self with spoon—neatly	2
Feeds self with spoon—considerable spilling	1
Feeds self with fingers or must be fed	0

[19] *Public Transportation*
     (Check *ALL* statements which apply)

Rides on train, long-distance bus or plane independently	_____
Rides in taxi independently	_____
Rides subway or city bus for unfamiliar journeys independently	_____
Rides subway or city bus for familiar journeys independently	_____
None of the above	_____

Source: From the AAMD Adaptive Behavior Scale.

on one of these assessment instruments are shown in Table 15.2.

These assessment devices fail to address several problems. First, the types of assessment measures used are not appropriate for infants, and yet it is important to assess very young children for mental retardation (MacMillan, Gresham, & Siperstein, 1993). Second, whether someone can perform the types of adaptive skills examined by these devices is a function not only of ability but also of the kinds of experiences the person has had (Evans, 1991). For example, whether someone can "prepare a snack" will in part depend on whether he or she has been taught this skill and has had opportunities to practice it. If the person being assessed has not had experience with this particular skill, clinicians and assessors must make educated guesses regarding his or her potential for learning and performing it. Clearly, such guesses lack reliability, making some diagnoses of mental retardation problematic.

The final criterion for mental retardation is the age of onset. The characteristic below-average intellectual and adaptive abilities must be evident before the person is 18. This age cutoff is designed to identify individuals who manifest such deficits during the developmental period, the time when the brain is developing and therefore when any problems should become evident. The age criterion rules out the

diagnosis of mental retardation for people who, as adults, may suffer from brain trauma or forms of dementia that impair their abilities. The age of 18 is somewhat arbitrary and signifies the age at which most children leave the public school system and the time when our society considers a person an adult. Relative to age, note that the prevalence rates for mental retardation differ across ages. In general, the number of people identified as having mental retardation increases with age until about 20 years, and then declines somewhat (McLaren & Bryson, 1987). It appears that, during the school years, a significant number of children are identified as having mental retardation— usually the less severe forms of this disorder—who would otherwise go undetected. As these children leave school, their adaptive skills have often reached such a level that they no longer differ significantly from their peers; they can function adequately in the community and therefore no longer warrant a diagnosis of mental retardation.

The imprecise nature of the definition of mental retardation points up an important issue: Mental retardation, perhaps more than any of the other disorders, is defined by our society. The cutoff score of 70 or 75 needed on IQ tests is based on a statistical concept (two or more standard deviations from the mean) and not on qualities inherent in people who supposedly have mental retardation. We will see that there is little disagreement about the diagnosis of mental retardation for people with the most severe disabilities; however, the majority of people diagnosed with the disorder fall in the mild range of cognitive impairment. These individuals still need a level of support and assistance, but it is important to remember that the criteria for placing on someone the label of "mental retardation" are based partially on a somewhat arbitrary cutoff score for IQ that can (and does) change with changing expectations of our society.

People with mental retardation differ significantly in their degree of disability. Almost all classification systems have differentiated these individuals based on their level of ability or on the etiology of the mental retardation (Hodapp & Dykens, 1994). Traditionally, as is still evident in the DSM-IV, classification systems have identified four levels of mental retardation: *mild,* which is identified by an IQ score in the range of 50–55 up to 70; *moderate,* considered to be 35–40 up to 50–55; *severe,* ranging from 20–25 up to 35–40; and *profound,* which would include people with IQ scores below 20–25. It is difficult to categorize each of these levels of mental retardation based on the "average" individual achievements by people at each level. Someone with severe or profound mental retardation will tend to have extremely limited formal communication skills (such as, no spoken speech or only one or two words) and may require a great deal

Table 15.3 American Association on Mental Retardation's Definitions of Needed Supports

Intermittent

Support on an "as needed" basis. Episodic in nature, with person not always needing the support(s) required during life-span transitions (e.g., job loss or an acute medical crisis). Intermittent support may be high or low intensity when provided.

Limited

Support characterized by consistency over time; time-limited but not intermittent. This level may require fewer staff members and less cost than more intense levels of support (e.g., time-limited employment training or support during the school-to-adult transition period).

Extensive

Support characterized by regular involvement (e.g., daily) in at least some environments (such as work or home) and not time-limited (e.g., long-term support and long-term home living support).

Pervasive

Support characterized by constancy and high intensity; provided across environments; potentially life-sustaining in nature. Pervasive support typically involves more staff members and intrusiveness than does extensive or time-limited support.

Source: Luckasson et al., 1992.

of—or even total—assistance to dress, bathe, or eat. Yet the range of skills of people with these diagnoses can vary considerably, depending on their training and the availability of other supports. Similarly, people with mild or moderate mental retardation—like James— should be able to live independently or with minimal supervision; again, however, their achievement of this end will depend in part on their education and the community support available to them.

Perhaps the most controversial change in the AAMR definition of mental retardation is its description of different levels of this disorder. The AAMR criteria identify the differences among people with this disorder based on the level of support or assistance they need—*intermittent, limited, extensive,* or *pervasive* (Luckasson et al., 1992). Definitions of these "needed supports" levels are presented in Table 15.3. You may recognize parallels between this system and the DSM-IV levels of mental retardation, including the use of four categories. Thus, someone who needs only intermittent support is similar to a person labeled by DSM-IV as having mild mental retardation. Similarly, the categories of needing limited, extensive, or pervasive support may be analogous to the levels of moderate, severe, and profound mental retardation. The difference is that the AAMR system identifies the role of "needed supports" in determining the level of functioning of these individuals, while DSM-IV implies that the ability of the person is the sole determining factor.

This is an important difference in categorizing people with mental retardation. The AAMR system focuses on specific areas of assistance that the person needs, and these can then be translated into individual training goals. Instead of a DSM-IV diagnosis of "moderate mental retardation," James might receive the

following AAMR diagnosis: "a person with mental retardation who needs limited supports in home living, health and safety, and in academic skills." The AAMR definition is more descriptive of the types of support James—or others—require, and it highlights the need to identify what assistance is available to a person when considering his or her abilities and potential. However, at this writing, the AAMR "needed supports" system of categorizing individuals with mental retardation has not been assessed empirically to determine whether it has greater value than more traditional systems.

An additional method of classification has been used in the educational system to identify the abilities of students with mental retardation. It relies on three categories: *educable mental retardation* (based on an IQ of 50 to approximately 70–75), *trainable mental retardation* (IQ of 30 to 50), and *severe mental retardation* (IQ below 30) (Cipani, 1991). The assumption of this system was that students with educable mental retardation—comparable to mild mental retardation—could learn basic academic skills; students with trainable mental retardation—comparable to moderate mental retardation—could not master academic skills but could learn rudimentary vocational skills; and students with severe mental retardation—comparable to severe and profound mental retardation—would not benefit from academic or vocational instruction. Built into this categorization system is the negative and automatic assumption that certain individuals cannot benefit from certain types of training. This system and the potentially stigmatizing and limiting DSM-IV categories (mild, moderate, severe, and profound mental retardation) were the impetus for the AAMR categorization of needed supports. Current trends have moved away from the educational system of classification because it inappropriately creates negative expectations by teachers for their students. Most workers continue to use the DSM-IV system; we have yet to see whether the AAMR categories will be widely adopted.

Statistics and Course for Mental Retardation

Prevalence rates for mild mental retardation (IQ from 50 to 70) are about 3 to 4 per 1,000 people, with a comparable combined prevalence for those with moderate, severe, and profound mental retardation (IQ below 50)—a total of 6 to 8 per 1,000, or less than 1% of the population (McLaren & Bryson, 1987). Recall that, with a cutoff IQ score of 70, about 3% of the population is estimated to fall below that score. Why then are so few individuals identified as having mental retardation?

One explanation may relate to the concept of adaptive behavior described earlier. Especially for people on the higher end of the IQ spectrum, their ability to function adequately in society may preclude their being identified as having mental retardation. In Sweden, for example, the prevalence rate of mild mental retardation is much lower than in the United States, in part because of the practice in Sweden of not putting these individuals in special placements such as large institutions (Sonnander, Emanuelsson, & Kebbon, 1993). Because people with mental retardation in Sweden are not automatically separated from others in the general population, they may not be officially labeled.

Another explanation may be that individuals with low IQ scores also tend to have multiple physical ailments, which can seriously shorten their life expectancy (Eyman, Call, & White, 1991). The mortality rate for people with severe mental retardation is 4.1 times that of the general population (Kastner, Nathanson, & Friedman, 1993). Thus, these and other factors may be responsible for the lower than expected rate of mental retardation reported in epidemiological studies.

The course of mental retardation is chronic, meaning that people do not "recover" from this condition. However, the prognosis for people with this disorder varies considerably. If given appropriate training and support, individuals with less severe forms can be expected to live relatively independent and productive lives. People with more severe impairments require greater levels of assistance to participate in activities such as work and community life. Mental retardation is observed more often among males, with a male-to-female ratio of about 1.6 to 1 (Laxova, Ridler, & Bowen-Bravery, 1977). Most of this difference may be present only among people with mild mental retardation, with no gender differences found in people with more severe forms of this disorder (Richardson, Katz, & Koller, 1986).

Causes of Mental Retardation

There are literally hundreds of different known causes of mental retardation. Causal factors can include environmental influences (for example, deprivation, abuse, and neglect) as well as genetic, chromosomal, prenatal (for instance, exposure to disease or drugs while still in the womb), perinatal (such as difficulties during labor and delivery), and postnatal (for example, infections, head injury) influences. We mentioned in Chapter 12 that drug use, especially heavy use of alcohol among pregnant woman, can produce a disorder in their children called *fetal alcohol syndrome,* a condition that can lead to severe learning disabilities. Other prenatal factors that can produce mental retardation include the pregnant woman's exposure to disease, chemicals, and poor nutrition. In addition, birth injury from a lack of oxygen (anoxia) as well as insults during the developmental period such as malnutrition and head injuries can also lead to severe cognitive impairments. Despite the rather large number of known causes of mental retardation, one fact must be kept in mind: Nearly 70–75% of cases either cannot be attributed to any known cause or are thought to be the result of social and environmental influences (Zigler & Hodapp, 1986). Most of the affected individuals have mild mental retardation and are sometimes referred to as having *cultural/familial* mental retardation, discussed in more detail later.

Before we describe the causes of mental retardation, remember that the criteria for who does and who does not have mental retardation have changed periodically and that the cutoffs for performance on IQ tests and for adaptive behavior skills remain arbitrary. You might argue that *everyone* has some degree of cognitive impairment and/or difficulty with certain aspects of adaptive behavior, and that we differ from each other in terms of degree rather than kind. In other words, just like other disorders that can be viewed dimensionally—for instance, the personality disorders—mental retardation can be considered on a dimension of intellectual and adaptive abilities. We all may have some level of "mental retardation." This assessment is consistent with a polygenic view of IQ, which would classify low IQ in mental retardation not as a disorder but as a normal variation. This perspective is especially relevant in our discussion of certain individuals with mild mental retardation; they may simply represent the lower end of the normal distribution of IQ in the general population.

We start this section by reviewing some of the more prevalent biological causes of mental retardation. Genetic and chromosomal influences are reviewed separately because of the important advances being made in these fields related to mental retardation. Following this discussion, we turn to cultural/familial influences.

Biological Dimensions: Genetic Influences

Most researchers believe that people with mental retardation probably are influenced by multiple gene disorders in addition to environmental influences (Abuelo, 1991). However, a portion of the people with more severe mental retardation have identifiable single-gene disorders, consisting of *dominant* (involving a gene that expresses itself when paired with a normal gene), *recessive* (involving a gene that expresses itself only when paired with another copy of itself), and *X-linked* (involving a gene that is present on the X or sex chromosome) gene disorders.

Only a few dominant genes result in mental retardation. This is probably the result of natural selection: Those who carry a dominant gene that results in mental retardation do, of course, express the characteristics of the gene, but statistics show that individuals with mental retardation are less likely to have children and thus less likely to pass the gene to offspring. Therefore this gene becomes less likely to continue being present in the population. However, some people with mental retardation—especially those with mild mental retardation—do marry and have children, thus passing on their genes. One example of a dominant gene disorder for mental retardation is *tuberous sclerosis,* a relatively rare disorder occurring in 1 out of approximately every 30,000 births. Estimates are that about 60% of the people with this disorder have mental retardation (Vinken & Bruyn, 1972) and most have seizures—uncontrolled electrical discharges in the brain—and characteristic bumps in their skin that during adolescence resemble acne.

The next time you drink a diet soda, notice the warning, "Phenylketonurics: Contains Phenylalanine." This is a caution for people with the recessive disorder called *phenylketonuria* or *PKU*. PKU affects 1 out of every 14,000 newborns and is characterized by the inability to break down a chemical in our diets called phenylalanine. Until the mid 1960s, the majority of people with this disorder would develop mental retardation, seizures, and behavior problems, resulting from the buildup of high levels of this chemical. However, at that time researchers discovered a screening technique that identifies the existence of PKU; this testing is now done on infants routinely at birth, and any individuals identified with PKU can be successfully treated with a specialized diet that avoids the chemical phenylalanine. This is a rare example of the successful *prevention* of one form of mental retardation.

Ironically, the success of the early identification and treatment of people with PKU over the last three decades has some worried that an outbreak of PKU-related mental retardation will recur. The special diet for people with PKU is necessary to prevent symptoms only until the person reaches age 6 or 7. At this point people tend to become lax and eat a regular diet; fortunately, with no harmful consequences for themselves. Because maternal PKU—if untreated—can harm the developing fetus (Lenke & Levy, 1980), there is concern now that women with PKU—who are at or

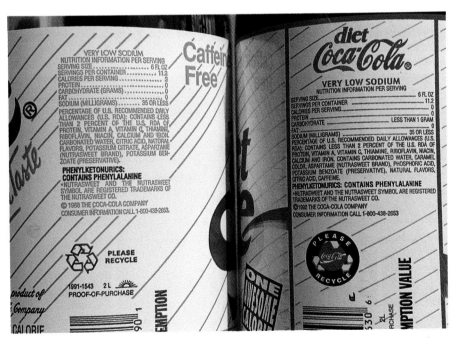

People with phenylketonuria can prevent brain damage by avoiding foods with phenylalanine.

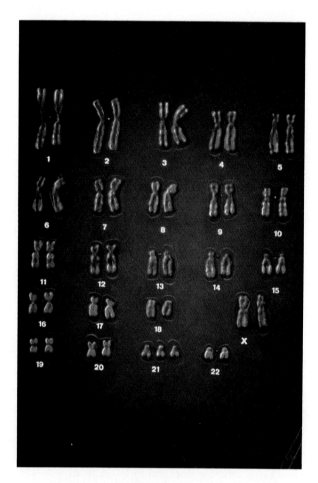

The chromosomes of a person with Down syndrome. Note the three sets of number 21 chromosomes. Can you tell the gender of this person?

approaching childbearing age—may inadvertently (by not sticking to their diets) harm their children before birth, causing a return to PKU-related mental retardation. Many physicians are now recommending dietary restriction through the childbearing period—thus the warnings on products with phenylalanine (Abuelo, 1991).

An example of an X-linked disorder is *Lesch-Nyhan syndrome,* which is characterized by mental retardation, signs of cerebral palsy (spasticity or tightening of the muscles), and self-injurious behavior including finger and lip biting (Nyhan, 1978). This genetic disorder affects only males because the gene responsible is a recessive gene; when it is on the X chromosome in males, it does not have a normal gene to balance it out because males do not have a second X chromosome. Women with this gene are carriers and do not show any of the symptoms.

As our ability to detect genetic defects improves with advancing gene technology, more disorders are expected to be identified genetically. The hope is that this increase in our knowledge will be accom-

panied by improvements in our ability to treat or, as in the case of PKU, prevent mental retardation and other negative outcomes of these disorders.

Biological Dimensions: Chromosomal Influences

It was only about 40 years ago that the number of chromosomes—46—was correctly identified in human cells (Tjio & Levan, 1956). Three years later, researchers found that people with Down syndrome—the disorder James displayed—had an additional small chromosome (Lejeune, Gauthier, & Turpin, 1959). Since that time, a number of other chromosomal aberrations have been identified that result in mental retardation. We will describe two of these disorders—Down syndrome and fragile X syndrome—in some detail, but there are hundreds of ways in which abnormalities among the chromosomes can lead to mental retardation.

Down syndrome is the most common chromosomal cause of mental retardation and was first identified by the British physician Langdon Down in 1866. Down had tried to develop a classification system for people with mental retardation based on their resemblance to people of other races, and described individuals with this disorder as "mongoloid" because of similarities with people from Mongolia (Scheerenberger, 1983). The term *mongoloidism* was used for some time, but has been replaced with the modern-day term **Down syndrome.** We now know that this disorder is caused by the presence of an extra 21st chromosome and is therefore sometimes referred to as trisomy 21. For reasons not completely understood, during cell division, two of the 21st chromosomes "stick together"—a condition called *nondisjunction*—and create one cell with only one copy, which is nonviable and dies, and one cell with three copies, which continues to divide to create a person with Down syndrome.

People with Down syndrome have characteristic facial features including folds in the corners of their eyes, an upward slant to the eyes, a flat nose, and a small mouth with a flat roof that makes the tongue protrude somewhat. They also tend to have congenital heart malformations, as did James. Finally, people with Down syndrome are at increased risk for dementia of the Alzheimer's type, a degenerative brain disorder that causes impairments in memory and other cognitive disorders. The increased risk of this disorder among people with Down syndrome occurs at an earlier than usual age for these individuals (sometimes in their early 20s) and has led to the finding that at least one form of Alzheimer's disease is attributable to a gene on the 21st chromosome.

The incidence of children born with Down syndrome has been tied to maternal age: As the age of the mother increases, so does her chance of having a child with this disorder (Figure 15.1). A woman at age 20 has a 1 in 2,000 chance of having a child with Down syndrome; at the age of 35 this risk increases to 1 in 500, and at the age of 45 it increases again to 1 in 18 births (Evans & Hammerton, 1985; Hook, 1982). Despite these numbers, many more children with Down syndrome are born to younger mothers because as women get older they tend to have fewer children in general. The reason for the rise in incidence with maternal age is not clear. Some suggest that, because a woman's ova or eggs are all produced in youth, the older ones may be more likely to have been exposed to toxins, radiation, and other harmful substances over longer periods of time. This exposure may interfere with the normal meiosis or division of the chromosomes, causing an extra 21st chromosome (Pueschel & Goldstein, 1991). Others believe that the hormonal changes that occur in women as they age are responsible for this error in cell division (Crowley, Hayden, & Gulati, 1982).

For some time it has been possible to detect the presence of Down syndrome through **amniocentesis,** a procedure that involves removing a sample of the fluid surrounding the fetus in the amniotic sac. Testing of this fluid can alert parents as to the status of the developing fetus with regard to Down syndrome and a number of other disorders. How the parents decide to use the information they get from amniocentesis depends on a number of factors, including whether they plan to abort the fetus if it has a chromosomal abnormality. To complicate this decision, amniocentesis can determine whether the child will have Down syndrome, but it cannot indicate the degree of disability the child will ultimately experience. People with Down syndrome can have a range of abilities, from mild to severe mental retardation, but where a child will fall on

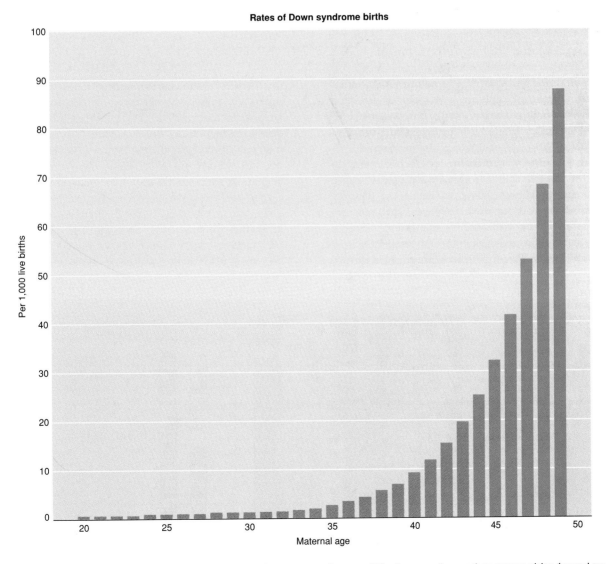

Figure 15.1   The increasing likelihood that a child with Down syndrome will be born as the mother grows older (based on data from Hook, 1982)

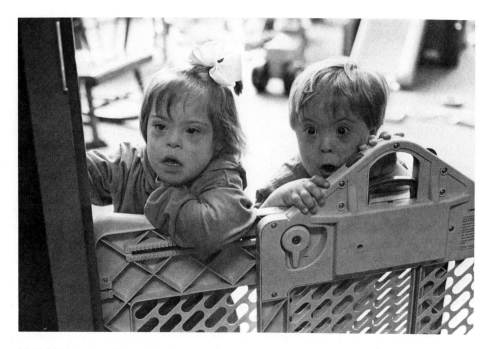

Two preschoolers who have Down syndrome. People with this disorder have characteristic facial features including folds in the corner of the eyes, upward slant to the eyes, flat nose, and small mouth.

this continuum cannot be determined from an amniocentesis. Our technology can make possible detection of Down syndrome before birth; how we use this technology is determined by our values and those of our society.

Fragile X syndrome is second only to Down syndrome as a chromosomally related cause of mental retardation (Dykens, Leckman, Paul, & Watson, 1988). As its name suggests, this disorder is caused by an abnormality on the X chromosome, a mutation that makes the tip of the chromosome look as though it were hanging from a thread,

thus giving it the appearance of being fragile (see photo of fragile X chromosome below) (Sutherland & Richards, 1994). As with Lesch-Nyhan syndrome, which also involves the X chromosome, fragile X primarily affects males because they do not have a second X chromosome with a normal gene to balance out this mutation. Unlike Lesch-Nyhan carriers, however, women who are carriers of fragile X syndrome commonly display mild to severe learning disabilities (Smith, 1993). Men with this disorder display moderate to severe levels of mental retardation and also have higher rates of hyperactivity, short

The ends of the X chromosomes appear "pinched" among those with fragile X syndrome.

attention spans, gaze avoidance, and perseverative speech. In addition, physical characteristics such as large ears and testicles as well as large head circumference are also common. Estimates are that 1 of every 2,000 males is born with fragile X syndrome (Dykens, Leckman, Paul, & Watson, 1988).

In addition to the extra 21st chromosome found in Down syndrome and the abnormality of the X chromosome found in fragile X syndrome, there are numerous chromosomal aberrations that bring on mental retardation. With the sex chromosomes alone there are disorders that involve one X and no second sex chromosome or XO—called Turner's syndrome—XYY syndrome, XXY or Klinefelter's syndrome, XXYY, XXXY, XXXX, XXXXY, and XXXXX or penta-X syndromes (Luckasson et al., 1992). In **Turner's syndrome** (XO), a second X chromosome is missing in women; in addition to mental retardation, these individuals often have immature genitalia as well as cardiovascular problems and urinary tract anomalies (Pueschel & Thuline, 1991). **Klinefelter's syndrome** (XXY) is a disorder among males. Because of their extra X chromosome, they tend to have small genitals and little facial or pubic hair; also they will be infertile. About 20% of children with this disorder will have mental retardation.

Psychological and Social Dimensions

One form of mental retardation, referred to as **cultural/familial retardation,** is the presumed cause of up to 75% of the cases of mental retardation and is perhaps the least understood of them all (Scott & Carran, 1987). Individuals with cultural/familial retardation tend to score in the mild mental retardation range on IQ tests and have relatively good adaptive skills (Zigler & Cascione, 1984). Their mental retardation is thought to result from a combination of both psychosocial and biological influences, although the exact nature of these influences—the specific mechanisms that lead to this type of mental retardation—are not understood at this time. Some of the cultural influences that may contribute to this condition include abuse and neglect as well as social deprivation.

It is sometimes useful to consider people with mental retardation as being in two distinct groups: those with cultural/familial retardation, whom we have been discussing, and those with "organic" forms of mental retardation, whom we described in the sections under biological dimensions. People in the latter group have more severe forms of mental retardation that are usually traceable to known causes such as fragile X syndrome. Figure 15.2 shows that the cultural/familial group is composed primarily of individuals who represent the expected lower end of the IQ continuum, whereas those who make up the organic group are people for whom genetic, chromosomal, and other factors affect intellectual performance. You see that the organic group increases the number of people at the lower end of the IQ continuum so that it exceeds the expected rate from a normal distribution (Zigler & Hodapp, 1986).

Two views of cultural/familial retardation have been articulated in an attempt to further our understanding of this phenomenon. In the *difference* view-

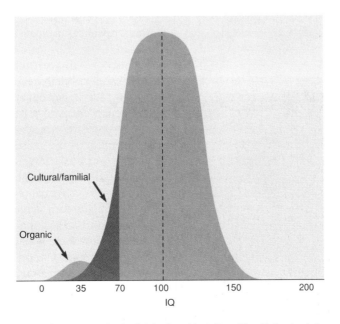

Figure 15.2   The actual distribution of IQ scores for individuals with cultural/familial retardation and organic retardation. Note that the cultural/familial group represents the normal expected lower end of the continuum while the organic group is a separate and overlapping group (adapted from Zigler & Hodapp, 1986).

point, those with cultural/familial retardation are believed to have a subset of deficits, such as attentional (Fisher & Zeaman, 1973) or memory problems (Ellis, 1970), that represents a limited portion of the larger set of deficiencies experienced by people with more severe forms of mental retardation. In other words, these individuals *differ* from people without mental retardation based on this specific damage, and they are similar to people with more severe retardation. In contrast, the *developmental* view sees the mild mental retardation of people with cultural/familial retardation as simply a difference in the rate and ultimate ceiling of an otherwise normal developmental sequence (Zigler & Balla, 1982). Put another way, as children, these individuals go through the same developmental stages as people without mental retardation, but they do so at a slower pace and do not attain all the skills they probably would have developed in a richer environment (Zigler & Stevenson, 1993). Support is mixed for both these views of the nature of cultural/familial retardation. Recent research suggests that, at least for some tasks, people with mild mental retardation may do

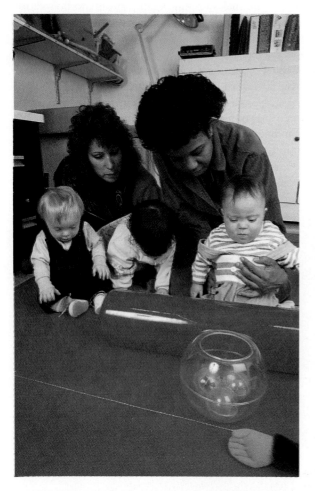

Early intervention can prove very successful for children with mental retardation. Here members of a pediatric rehabilitation team help toddlers with motor skills.

significantly worse than people who are matched with them based on their mental age—younger individuals who perform at a similar level on IQ tests (Weiss, Weisz, & Bromfield, 1986). This means that, for some skills, people with mild mental retardation may in fact differ from people without mental retardation in a way that is not explained just by a developmental delay. Given the many ways such retardation could be caused, it should not be surprising to find that people with mild mental retardation would differ from people without mental retardation, and in fact would differ among themselves. There is still much that is not understood about people with cultural/familial retardation, and future work may reveal important subgroups among them.

Treatment of Mental Retardation

Generally, the treatment of individuals with mental retardation involves attempts to teach them the skills they need to become more productive and independent in society. For individuals with mild mental retardation, intervention often involves education of the type we describe next for people with learning disorders. Specific learning deficits are identified and remediated to help the student improve his or her skills in academic areas such as reading and writing. At the same time, however, these individuals often need additional support to live in the community. For people with more severe disabilities, the general goals are the same; however, the level of assistance they need to achieve these goals is frequently more extensive. Remember that the expectation for everyone with mental retardation is that he or she will in some way participate in community life, attend school and later hold a job, and have the opportunity for meaningful social relationships. Advances in electronic and educational technologies in recent years have made this a realistic goal even for people with severe and profound mental retardation. We next briefly review some of these efforts.

We begin our discussion with the youngest children, those whose later lives may be substantially affected by early educational and medical efforts. Early intervention has been used to target and assist children who, because of inadequate environments, are at risk for developing cultural/familial retardation (Ramey & Ramey, 1992). The national Head Start program is one such effort at early intervention; it combines educational with medical and social supports for these children and their families. One project identified a group of children and provided them with an intensive preschool program along with medical and nutritional supports. This intervention began shortly after birth and continued until the children began formal education in kindergarten (Martin, Ramey, & Ramey, 1990). The authors found that, for all but one of the children in a control group who received medical and nutritional support but not the intensive educational experiences,

With the proper supports, people with mental retardation can lead productive and fulfilling lives.

each had IQ scores below 85 at age 3 while children in the experimental group all tested above 85 by 3 years of age. Obviously, such findings are important because they show the potential for creating a lasting impact on the lives of these children and their families. Other prevention strategies include genetic counseling services, prenatal care, the use of screening such as amniocentesis, and drug prevention and treatment programs for women of childbearing age (Crocker, 1992).

Treatment for the skills needed by people with mental retardation relies on the many behavioral innovations first introduced in the early 1960s to teach some of the basic self-care skills such as dressing, bathing, feeding, and toileting to persons with even the most severe disabilities (Reid, Wilson, & Faw, 1991). The approach for teaching these skills follows the same general pattern. The skill is broken into its component parts—a procedure called a *task analysis*—and the person is taught each part in succession until he or she

Many schools now include students with disabilities in classes with their peers, providing the extra help they may need right in their classroom.

can perform the whole skill. Performance on each of the steps is encouraged by praise and by providing access to objects or activities the person desires (reinforcers). Success in teaching these skills is usually measured by the level of independence the person can attain in using them. Typically, most individuals, regardless of their disability, can be taught to perform some portion of these skills.

Communication training is an important priority for people with mental retardation. Having a way to make their needs and wants known is essential for personal satisfaction and for participating in most social activities. We tend to take our own communication skills for granted, rarely being fully aware of our amazing ability to communicate complex information and to carry on a conversation with others. The goals of this type of training will differ depending on the existing skills of the individual. For people with mild levels of mental retardation, the skills needed may be relatively minor (for instance, improving articulation) to more extensive (for instance, organizing a conversation) (Abbeduto & Rosenberg, 1992). For some, like James, communication skills are adequate for day-to-day needs.

For individuals with the most severe disabilities, this type of training can be particularly challenging as they may have multiple physical and/or cognitive deficits that make spoken communication difficult or impossible (Warren & Reichle, 1992). Creative researchers, however, have used alternative systems that may be easier for these individuals to learn, including the sign language used primarily by people with hearing disabilities as well as *augmentative communication strategies*. Augmentative strategies can include the use of picture books, with the person taught to make a request by pointing to a picture—for instance, pointing to a picture of a cup to request a drink (Reichle, Mirenda, Locke, Piche, & Johnston, 1992). Also available are a variety of computer-assisted devices; these can be programmed so that the individual presses a button thereby producing complete spoken sentences (for example, "Would you come here? I need your help"). People with very limited skills can be taught to use these devices to communicate, helping them reduce the frustration of not being able to relate their feelings and experiences to other people (Durand, 1993).

Concern is often expressed by parents, teachers, and employers that some people with mental retardation can be physically or verbally aggressive or may hurt themselves. Considerable debate has ensued over the proper way to reduce these behavior problems, with the most heated discussions involving whether to use painful punishers (Repp & Singh, 1990). There are alternatives to punishment that may be

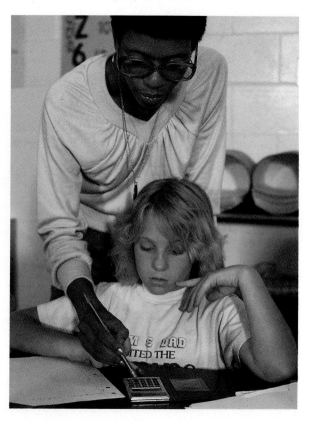

Some children who excel in other areas may display significant deficits in math and may need remedial help.

equally effective in reducing behavior problems such as aggression and self-injury (Durand, 1990). Some of these strategies involve teaching people how to communicate to others their need or desire for the things, such as attention, that they seem to be getting with their problem behaviors—a strategy we discussed in Chapter 4. To date, however, no treatment or treatment package has proven to be successful in all cases, although important advances are being made in significantly reducing even severe behavior problems for some people.

In addition to ensuring that people with mental retardation are taught specific skills such as communication, socialization, or basic self-care, those concerned with this group also focus on the important task of supporting these individuals in their communities. "Supported employment" involves supporting an individual's efforts to find and satisfactorily participate in a competitive job (Bellamy, Rhodes, Mank, & Albin, 1988). Research has shown that not only can these efforts be successful in placing people with mental retardation in meaningful jobs but that, despite the costs associated with supported employment, it can ultimately be cost effective. One study found that, for every dollar invested in supported employment, $2.21 was returned in taxes (McCaughrin, 1988). The benefits to those people who achieve the satisfaction of being a productive part of society are incalculable.

There is general agreement about *what* should be taught to people with mental retardation. The controversy in recent years has been over *where* this teaching should take place. Should people with mental retardation—especially those with more severe forms—be taught in specially designed and separate classrooms or sheltered workshops, or should they attend their neighborhood public schools and work at local businesses? More and more, the teaching strategies to help these students learn are being applied in regular classrooms with their nondisabled peers and in preparing them to work at jobs in the community (Meyer, Peck, & Brown, 1991). There is at present no cure for mental retardation, but the current prevention and treatment efforts suggest that meaningful changes can have a positive effect on the lives of these people.

An extremely controversial issue surrounding people with Down syndrome is the use of plastic surgery to change their characteristic facial features (Katz & Kravetz, 1989). Over the past 20 years, this surgery has been performed—primarily in Germany, Australia, Israel, and Canada—with the expectation that, if these individuals are made to look less like people with Down syndrome, they will not experience the social stereotyping and discrimination often directed at people with mental retardation. Opponents argue that the risks of such surgery cannot be ignored, and by emphasizing looks, clinicians who recommend

surgery are engaging in "facial prejudice" (Dodd & Leahy, 1989). A review of the research on the effects of this surgery suggests that parents of children with Down syndrome are often pleased with the results; however, more objective measures about the surgery's effects on the child and the reactions of others suggest that it may not produce significant changes (Katz & Kravetz, 1989). Such surgery may not be a panacea eliminating all the negative effects that can accompany having a disorder such as Down syndrome.

Learning Disorders

Academic achievement is highly regarded in our society. We often compare the performance of school children in our own culture with that of children from other cultures as a sign that the nation is succeeding or failing as a potential world leader and economic force. On a personal level, parents often invest a great deal of time and emotional energy to assure their child's academic success. Therefore, it can be extremely upsetting when a child who has no obvious intellectual deficits does not achieve as expected in school. In this section we describe **learning disorders** in *reading, mathematics,* and *written expression*—all characterized by performance that is substantially below what would be expected given the person's age, IQ, and education. Consider the following case.

The Case of Alice

Alice was a 20-year-old college student who sought help because of her difficulty in several of her classes at the university. She reported that she had enjoyed school and had been a good student up until about the sixth grade, when her grades suffered significantly. Her teacher informed her parents that she "wasn't working up to her potential" and that she needed to be better motivated. Alice had always worked hard in school but promised to try harder. However, with each report card, her mediocre grades made her feel worse about herself. She managed to graduate from high school, but by that time she felt she was "stupid" and not as bright as her friends.

She enrolled in the local community college and again found herself struggling with the work. Over the years, she had learned several tricks that seemed to help her study and at least get passing grades. Alice would read aloud the material from her textbooks to herself; she had earlier discovered that she could recall this material much better than if she just read silently to herself. In fact, reading silently, she could barely remember any of the details just minutes later.

After her sophomore year, Alice transferred to the university, which she found even more demanding and where she began to fail most of her classes. After our first meeting, I suggested that she receive a formal assessment that was available through the university to identify what might be giving her difficulty. As suspected, Alice had a learning disability. She had received a score on an IQ test that placed her slightly above average but was assessed to have significant difficulties with reading. Specifically, her reading comprehension was poor, and she could not remember most of the content of what she read. We recommended that she continue with the "trick" she had stumbled onto by herself of reading aloud because her comprehension for things she heard was adequate. In addition, Alice was taught how to analyze what she was reading—that is, how to outline and take notes; she was even encouraged to audiotape her lectures and play them back to herself as she drove around in her car. Although Alice did not become an "A" student, she was able to graduate from the university and now works with young children who themselves have learning disabilities.

Clinical Description of Learning Disorders

Alice would be diagnosed according to DSM-IV criteria as having a **reading disorder,** which is defined as a significant discrepancy between a person's reading achievement and what would be expected for someone of the same age. More specifically, the criteria require that the person read at a level significantly below that

of a typical person of the same age and cognitive ability (as measured on an IQ test) and similar educational background. In addition, this disability cannot be caused by a sensory difficulty such as trouble with sight or hearing. Similarly, DSM-IV defines a **mathematics disorder** as achievement below expected performance in mathematics, and a **disorder of written expression** as achievement below expected performance in writing. In each of these disorders, the difficulties are sufficient to interfere with the person's academic achievement and to disrupt his or her daily activities. The DSM-IV criteria for these learning disorders are listed in Table 15.4.

Statistics and Course for Learning Disorders

Because definitions of learning disorders vary considerably, the incidence and prevalence of these disorders are difficult to estimate. Very conservatively, there is a 1% to 3% incidence of learning disorders in the United States (Reeve & Kauffman, 1988). Among school-aged children the prevalence rate is estimated at 10% to 15% (Heaton, 1988). Boys are more often identified as having a learning disorder than are girls, and the ratio probably falls between 2:1 and 6:1 boys to girls (Rubin & Balow, 1971). Having a learning disorder can lead to a number of different outcomes for an individual, depending in part on the extent of the disability as well as the level of support available. A recent study found that about 32% of students with learning disabilities dropped out of school (Wagner, 1990). In addition, employment rates for students with learning disorders tend to be discouragingly low, ranging from 60% to 70% (Shapiro & Lentz, 1991). In part, the low figure may be due to the students' low expectations; one study reported that only 50% of students with learning disabilities leaving school had postgraduation plans (Shapiro & Lentz, 1991). Some individuals with

Table 15.4   DSM-IV Diagnostic Criteria for Learning Disorders* for Reading Disorder (Developmental Reading Disorder), Mathematics Disorder (Developmental Arithmetic Disorder), and Disorder of Written Expression (Developmental Expressive Writing Disorder)

A. (Reading achievement)
(Mathematical ability)
(Writing skill), as measured by individually administered standardized tests, is substantially below that expected given the person's chronological age, measured intelligence, and age-appropriate education.

B. The disturbance in Criterion A significantly interferes with academic achievement or activities of daily living that require (reading skills) (mathematical ability) (composition of written texts).

C. If a sensory deficit is present, the learning difficulties are in excess of those usually associated with it.

*The three separate learning disorders are combined here because the basic criteria are identical with the exception of the specific ability that is affected.

Source: Adapted from DSM-IV, APA, 1994.

learning disorders succeed in attaining their education and/or career goals; however, this appears to be more difficult for people with severe learning disorders (Spreen, 1988).

Interviews with adults who have learning disabilities reveal that their school experiences are generally negative, and the effects may last beyond graduation. One man who did not have special assistance during school reports:

> I faked my way through school because I was very bright. I resent most that no one picked up my weaknesses. Essentially I judge myself on my failures. . . . [I] have always had low self-esteem. In hindsight I feel that I had low self-esteem in college. . . . I was afraid to know myself. A blow to my self-esteem when I was in school was that I could not write a poem or a story. . . . I could not write with a pen or pencil. The computer has changed my life. I do everything on my computer. It acts as my memory. I use it to structure my life and for all of my writing since my handwriting and written expression has always been so poor. (Polloway, Schewel, & Patton, 1992, p. 521)

Causes of Learning Disorders

Despite the relatively high prevalence of learning disorders in the general population, research on the causes of these problems is comparatively sparse. Theories about etiology include genetic, neurobiological, and environmental factors as contributing to learning disorders. As an example, disorders of reading may have a genetic basis; the parents and siblings of people with reading disorders are more likely to display these disorders than are the relatives of people without reading problems (Reeve & Kauffman, 1988). Pennington and Smith (1988) have reported several studies supporting the notion that some aspect of this disorder is inherited, although the exact mechanism may differ across families.

Various forms of subtle brain damage have also been thought to be responsible for learning disabilities; some of the earliest theories about these problems involve a neurological explanation (Hinshelwood, 1896). Recent research suggests that there may be structural as well as functional differences in the brains of people with learning disabilities although the differences are not always consistent across individuals (Hynd & Semrud-Clikeman, 1989). This lack of consistency is not surprising, given that people with learning disorders display very different types of cognitive problems and therefore probably represent a number of etiological subgroups.

We saw that Alice persisted in the face of the obstacles caused by her learning disorder as well as by the reactions of teachers and others. What helped her to continue toward her goal when others instead choose to drop out of school? Psychological and motivational factors that have been reinforced by others seem to play an important role in the eventual outcome of people with learning disorders. Factors such as socioeconomic status, cultural expectations, parental interactions and expectations, and child management practices seem to combine with existing neurological deficits and the types of support provided in the school to determine outcome (Taylor, 1988).

Treatment for Learning Disorders

Like mental retardation, learning disorders require primarily educational intervention. Biological treatment is typically restricted to those individuals who may also have attention deficit disorder, a problem involving impulsivity and the inability to sustain attention; it can be helped with certain stimulant medications such as Ritalin. Educational efforts can be broadly categorized into (a) efforts to remediate directly the underlying basic *processing* of problems experienced by students—for instance, by teaching them visual and auditory perception skills; (b) efforts to improve the *cognitive* skills of the students through general instruction in listening, comprehension, and memory; and (c) targeting the *behavioral* skills needed to compensate for specific problems the student may have with reading, mathematics, or written expression—such as those we discussed in the case of Alice (Reeve & Kauffman, 1988). Considerable research supports the usefulness of teaching the behavioral skills necessary to improve academic skills, although the prospects of long-term success for any of these approaches awaits further study.

Cognitive Disorders

In contrast with mental retardation and the learning disorders that are believed to be present from the time of birth, the cognitive disorders primarily (but not exclusively) develop much later in life. They involve a significant deficit in cognition or memory that differs from typical functioning. In this section we review three classes of cognitive disorders: *delirium* (an often temporary condition that is displayed as confusion and disorientation), *dementia* (a progressive and degenerative condition marked by gradual deterioration of a broad range of cognitive abilities), and *amnestic disorders* (a dysfunction in memory due to a medical condition or the use of a drug, medication, or toxin).

The use by DSM-IV of the title "cognitive disorders" represents a shift in the way these disorders are viewed in relation to the other disorders included in this diagnostic system (Tucker, Popkin, Caine, Folstein, & Grant, 1990). Previous editions of the DSM grouped them under the heading of "organic mental disorders." This category also included additional organic disorders believed to be caused by known or suspected brain involvement, namely, organic mood, anxiety, personality, hallucinosis, and delusional disorders. The word *organic* was used to indicate that brain damage or dysfunction was believed to be involved in the cause of these disorders. Although brain dysfunction is still thought to be the primary cause of these disorders, realization is growing that some dysfunction in the brain is involved in most of the disorders described in DSM-IV (Tucker, 1993). We have repeatedly pointed to the complex relationship between the brain and psychosocial influences in the cause of many, if not all, of the disorders covered in this text. Few people would disagree, for example, that disorders such as schizophrenia also involve some damage to the brain. One could argue, then, that most disorders are in one sense "organic." This fundamental shift in the way the disorders are viewed had an immediate impact on the category of disorders. Obviously, the term *organic mental disorders* would now cover so many of the disorders as to make that distinction relatively meaningless. One outcome of the shift was that the traditional organic disorders—delirium, dementia, and amnestic disorders—were kept together while the others—organic mood, anxiety, personality, hallucinosis, and delusional disorders—were placed within the categories that shared their symptoms (such as, anxiety disorders or mood disorders).

Once the term *organic* was dropped from the name of this category, attention moved to developing an alternative name under which to group delirium, dementia, and amnestic disorders. The term *cognitive disorders* was chosen to signify that their predominant feature is the impairment of cognitive abilities such as memory, attention, perception, and thinking. Other disorders such as schizophrenia or depression also involve cognitive impairment, although problems with cognitive functioning are not believed to be the primary characteristics of these disorders (Tucker et al., 1990). Problems still exist with this term, however. Other disorders such as mental retardation and learning disorders also have cognitive impairment as a predominant characteristic. Possibly forthcoming research will provide a more useful way to distinguish these disorders.

We opened the section by pointing out that the cognitive disorders more often manifest themselves in older adults. Figure 15.3 illustrates the incidence of several different disorders in people of varying ages. Most of the disorders such as schizophrenia, alcoholism, and the personality disorders tend to appear first in adolescence or early adulthood. In contrast, the cognitive disorders (which are given the older label of "brain syndromes" in this figure) generally first appear in the patient's 50s or 60s and accelerate after the age of 70.

As our population continues to live longer, these disorders have increased in prevalence and have become a major concern for mental health professionals.

As with other disorders, it may be useful to discuss why conditions such as cognitive disorders are included in a textbook on abnormal psychology. Because their origins are so clearly based in organic causes, one could argue for considering cognitive disorders as purely medical concerns. We will see, however, that the consequences of the cognitive disorders often include profound changes in a person's behavior and personality. Especially among those with dementia, feelings of intense anxiety and/or depression are common. In addition, feelings of paranoia are frequently reported by these people, as are more overt expressions such as extreme agitation or aggression. At the same time, families and friends can be profoundly affected by these changes. Imagine having to watch as a loved one is transformed into a different person, often one who no longer remembers who you are or your history together. The emotional distress caused by the cognitive disorders goes beyond the person affected and extends to his or her family and friends as well. The changes in cognitive ability, behavior, and personality along with the effects on others make cognitive disorders an important topic of concern for mental health professionals.

Delirium

The disorder known as **delirium** is characterized by a reduced clarity of consciousness and cognition, and develops over the course of several hours or days. Delirium is one of the first mental disorders to be recounted in history; descriptions of people with these symptoms are found in writings over 2,500 years old (Lipowski, 1990). People with delirium are unable to think and reason clearly and they lose contact with what is going on around them. Consider the following case.

The Case of Mr. J.

An older gentleman—Mr. J.—was brought into the hospital emergency room. He didn't know his own name and at times he didn't seem to recognize his daughter, who had brought him to the hospital. Mr. J. appeared confused, disoriented, and a little agitated. He had difficulty speaking clearly or focusing his attention to answer even the most basic questions. Mr. J.'s daughter reported that he had begun acting this way the night before, had been awake most of the time since then, was frightened, and seemed even more confused today. She told the nurse that this behavior was not normal for him and she was worried that he was becoming senile. She mentioned that his doctor had just changed his medication for hypertension and wondered whether the new medication could be causing his distress. Mr. J. was ultimately diagnosed as having substance-induced delirium (a reaction to his new hypertension medication) and improved significantly over the course of the next 2 days, once the medication was stopped. This scenario is played out on a daily basis in most major metropolitan hospital emergency rooms.

Clinical Description of Delirium

The DSM-IV diagnostic criteria for delirium are listed in Table 15.5. People with delirium appear confused, disoriented, and out of touch with their surroundings. They have trouble focusing on even the simplest tasks. These individuals also show marked changes in other cognitive functions such as memory and language. Mr. J. was having trouble speaking; he was not only confused but was also having difficulty remembering basic facts such as his own name. As we saw with Mr. J., the characteristic confusion and disorientation do not come on gradually, over a long

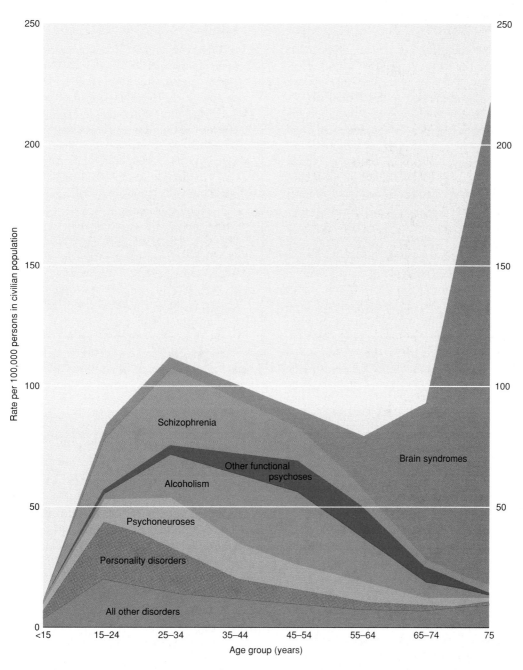

Figure 15.3 Rates for first admission to state and county mental hospitals in the United States in 1965, specific for age and mental disorder (from Kramer, 1969)

Table 15.5   DSM-IV Diagnostic Criteria for Delirium Due to . . . [*Indicate the General Medical Condition*]

A. Disturbance of consciousness (i.e., reduced clarity of awareness of the environment) with reduced ability to focus, sustain, or shift attention.

B. A change in cognition (such as memory deficit, disorientation, language disturbance) or the development of a perceptual disturbance that is not better accounted for by a preexisting, established, or evolving dementia.

C. The disturbance develops over a short period of time (usually hours to days) and tends to fluctuate during the course of the day.

D. There is evidence from the history, physical examination, or laboratory findings that the disturbance is caused by the direct physiological consequences of a general medical condition.

Source: DSM-IV, APA, 1994.

period of time. Instead, they can develop over hours or days.

Statistics and Course for Delirium

Delirium is common among people who come into acute care facilities, such as emergency rooms, and is estimated to be present in as many as 10% to 15% of the persons who seek treatment at these sites (Katz, 1993). It is even more prevalent among older adults, people going through medical procedures, cancer patients, and people with acquired immunodeficiency syndrome (AIDS) (Adams, 1988; Fernandez, Levy, & Mansell, 1989).

Estimates of the number of people who experience this disorder are lacking. This may be due in part to the transient nature of delirium. Because this disorder can occur and then resolve itself so quickly—sometimes within hours or days—it is difficult for researchers to study. In fact, the course of delirium is an important characteristic of this disorder. Again, as we saw with Mr. J., the symptoms of the disorder usually develop over a relatively short period of time, typically over several hours or days (Katz, 1993). Delirium also tends to improve in a short period, with full recovery expected in most cases after several weeks. A minority of individuals will continue to experience problems on and off, or will lapse into a coma or die.

Causes of Delirium

Delirium often signals the presence of a medical condition that is causing brain dysfunction. Many medical conditions have been linked to the onset of delirium including intoxication by drugs and poisons; withdrawal from drugs such as alcohol and the sedative, hypnotic, and anxiolytic drugs; infections; head injury; and various other types of brain trauma (Lipowski, 1990). DSM-IV recognizes several causes of delirium in its subtypes of this disorder. Table 15.5 lists the criteria for one subtype, *delirium due to a general medical condition*. Other subtypes include the diagnosis received by Mr. J.—*substance-induced delirium*—as well as *delirium due to multiple etiologies* and *delirium not*

otherwise specified. The last two categories indicate the often complex nature of delirium. Especially among the elderly population, the combination of medical illnesses and medications being used will typically make a determination of the cause extremely difficult if not impossible (Francis, Martin, & Kapoor, 1990). This disorder also is experienced by children who have high fevers or who are taking certain medications and is often mistaken for noncompliance. Delirium often occurs during the course of other cognitive disorders such as dementia; as many as 44% of people with dementia experience at least one episode of delirium (Purdie, Hareginan, & Rosen, 1981). Because many of the medical conditions are potentially treatable, delirium can often be reversed in a relatively short amount of time.

Not all persons who experience these medical conditions have episodes of delirium; other factors can facilitate the occurrence of delirium as a consequence of the primary condition. Age, for one, is an important factor; the incidence of delirium increases significantly in older adults, making them more susceptible to developing delirium when they experience mild infections or medication changes (Lipowski, 1983). Other factors such as sleep deprivation, immobility, and excessive stress can also contribute to its onset (Wolanin & Phillips, 1981).

Treatment for Delirium

As implied by the previous discussion, the first treatment approach usually involves exploring the medical problem or problems that precipitated the delirium. Delirium brought on by withdrawal from alcohol or other drugs is usually treated with benzodiazepines, calming and sleep-inducing medications (Katz, 1993). Other medical concerns related to the delirium, such as infections, brain injury, or tumors, are cared for by the necessary and appropriate medical intervention.

In addition to medical attention for the person with delirium, psychosocial interventions may also be beneficial (Richeimer, 1987). The goal of nonmedical treatment is to reassure the person to help him or her deal with the accompanying problems of agitation, anxiety, and psychotic-like symptoms such as halluci-nations. If the person is staying in the hospital, he or she may be comforted by familiar and personal belongings such as family photographs. Also, including the patient in all treatment decisions helps him or her retain a sense of control (Katz, 1993). This type of psychosocial treatment can aid the person in managing this disrup-tive period until the medical causes can be identified and addressed.

Dementia

Few prospects are more frightening than the fear that you will one day not recognize those you love, that you will not be able to perform the most basic of tasks such as finding your way home after driving only a few blocks, and worse yet, that you will be acutely aware of this failure of your mind. **Dementia** is a cognitive disorder that makes these fears real—a gradual dete-rioration of brain functioning that affects judgment, memory, language, and other advanced cognitive processes. Dementia is the consequence of several medical conditions or the abuse of certain substances such as alcohol that cause these negative changes in cognitive abilities. Some of these conditions—for in-stance, infection or depression—can cause dementia, although it is often reversible through treatment of the primary condition. Other forms of the disorder are at present irreversible, as is the case for Alzheimer's disease. Although delirium and dementia can occur together, dementia has a gradual and usually slow progression as opposed to delirium's acute onset; people with dementia are not disoriented or confused in its early stages, unlike people with delirium. Like delirium, however, the causes of dementia are many and include a variety of insults to the brain such as the infectious diseases of syphilis and HIV, severe head injury, the introduction of certain toxic or poisonous substances, and diseases such as Parkinson's, Hunting-ton's, and Alzheimer's—the latter being the most common cause of dementia. Consider the following case of a woman who, in a rare personal account, poignantly writes of her own experiences with this disorder (McGowin, 1993).

The Case of Diana

At the age of 45, Diana Friel McGowin was a successful legal assistant, wife, and mother; but she was beginning to experience "lapses." She writes about these developing problems just before a party she was planning for her family.

Nervously, I checked off the table appoint-ments on a list retrieved from my jumpsuit pocket. Such a list had never been necessary

before, but lately I noticed frequent little episodes of confusion and memory lapses.

I had decided to "cheat" on this family buffet and have the meal prepared on a carry-out basis. Cooking was also becoming increasingly difficult, due to what my children and my husband Jack teasingly referred to as my "absentmindedness." (pp. 1–2)

Along with her memory difficulties, Diana recalled other problems that began at this time. Several times she experienced brief dizzy spells and wrote of her family's growing awareness of additional symptoms:

Shaun walked past me on his way to the kitchen, and paused. "Mom, what's up? You look ragged," he commented sleepily. "Late night last night, plenty of excitement, and then up early to get your father off to work," I answered. Shaun laughed disconcertingly. I glanced up at him ruefully. "What is so funny?" I demanded. "You, Mom! You are talking as though you are drunk or something! You must really be tired!" (pp. 4–5)

In the early stages of this disorder, Diana tended to explain these changes in herself as having temporary causes such as tension at work. However, the extent of her dysfunction continued to widen, and she was confronted with more frightening experiences. In one episode, she

Diana Friel McGowin, who has Alzheimer's disease and who authored the book *Living in the Labyrinth: A Personal Journey Through the Maze of Alzheimer's.*

describes her memory and cognitive problems during an attempt to drive home from a short trip in the car.

> Suddenly, I was aware of car horns blowing. Glancing around, nothing was familiar. I was stopped at an intersection and the traffic light was green. Cars honked impatiently, so I pulled straight ahead, trying to get my bearings. I could not read the street sign, but there was another sign ahead; perhaps it would shed some light on my location.
>
> A few yards ahead, there was a park ranger building. Trembling, I wiped my eyes, and breathing deeply, tried to calm myself. Finally, feeling ready to speak, I started the car again and approached the ranger station. The guard smiled and inquired how he could assist me. "I appear to be lost," I began, making a great effort to keep my voice level, despite my emotional state. "Where do you need to go?" the guard asked politely. A cold chill enveloped me as I realized I could not remember the name of my street. Tears began to flow down my cheeks. I did not know where I wanted to go. (pp. 7–8)

Diana's difficulties continued. She sometimes had trouble remembering the names of her children, and once ran into her nephew but astounded him when she didn't recognize him. If she left her home, she would almost invariably get lost. She learned to introduce herself as a tourist from out of town, because people would give her better directions to get to her destination. She described feeling as if there "was less of me every day than there was the day before."

During initial medical examinations, she didn't recall any family history of this type of problem. However, a look through some of her late mother's belongings revealed the possibility that she was not the first in her family to experience these symptoms.

> Then I noticed the maps. After mother's death I had found mysterious hand drawn maps and bits of directions scribbled on note papers all over her home. They were in her purses, in bureau drawers, in the desks, seemingly everywhere. Too distraught at the time to figure out their purpose, I simply packed them all away with other articles in the box.
>
> Now I smoothed out each map and scrawled note, and placed them side by side. They covered the bedroom floor. There were maps to every place my mother went about town, even to my home and my brother's home. As I deciphered each note and map, I

began recollecting my mother's other eccentric habits. She would not drive out of her neighborhood. She would not drive at night. She was teased by both myself and my brother about "memory goofs" and would become irate with both of her children over their loving teasing.

> Then with a chill, I recalled one day when I approached my mother to tell her something, and she did not recognize me. (p. 52)

After several evaluations—which included an MRI showing some damage in several parts of her brain—Diana's neurologist concluded that she had dementia. The cause could be a stroke she had experienced several years before. The stroke had caused damage to several small areas of her brain because of breakdowns or blockages in several of the brain's blood vessels. The dementia could also be the result of Alzheimer's disease, or he believed, it could be both. As of this writing, Diana Friel McGowin is still alive, but her condition will continue to worsen, and eventually she will probably die from complications of her disorder.

Clinical Description and Statistics

Dementia—as in the case of Diana Friel McGowin—involves a gradual and progressive deterioration of brain functioning. Depending on the individual and the cause of the disorder, the progression of symptoms may be somewhat different, although all aspects of cognitive functioning are eventually affected by dementia. In its initial stages, memory impairment typically involves a failure in the ability to register ongoing events. In other words, these individuals will remember how to talk and may remember events from many years ago but may have trouble remembering what happened in the past hour. For example, Diana could still operate a stove, but couldn't remember whether she had turned it on or off.

Visuospatial skills are impaired among people with dementia—such as Diana's inability to find her way home. *Agnosia*—or the inability to recognize and name objects—is one of the most familiar symptoms. *Facial agnosia,* which is the inability to recognize even familiar faces, is a variation of this impairment that can be extremely distressing to family members. Early on, Diana failed to recognize her nephew, and more and more had difficulty recognizing co-workers with whom she had worked on a daily basis for a number of years. A general deterioration of intellectual function occurs as a result of problems with memory, planning, and abstract reasoning.

Perhaps as a result of both brain deterioration and an awareness of this decline in functioning, emotional changes are often noted in people with dementia. Common among these individuals are delusions (irrational beliefs), depression, agitation, aggression, and apathy (Sultzer, Levin, Mahler, High, & Cummings, 1993). Again, it is difficult to establish the cause-and-effect relationship. We don't know how much of this change is due to progressive brain deterioration directly and how much is a result of frustration and discouragement, inevitable accompaniments to the loss of the ability to carry on activities of daily living and the isolation caused by "losing" loved ones from memory failure. Cognitive functioning continues to deteriorate until the person requires almost total support to carry out day-to-day activities. Ultimately, death occurs as the result of inactivity combined with the onset of other illnesses such as pneumonia.

Dementia can occur at almost any age, although the likelihood of experiencing this disorder is highest in older adults. Numerous studies have estimated the prevalence of dementia. In one large, representative study, researchers found that its prevalence was a little over 1% in people between the ages of 65 and 74; this rate increased to almost 4% in those aged 75 to 84, and to more than 10% in people 85 and older (see Figure 15.4) (George, Landoman, Blazer, & Anthony, 1991). The actual rate may be considerably higher, however, especially among older adults. Some researchers have estimated that as many as 47% of adults over the age of 85 may have dementia of the Alzheimer's type (Evans et al., 1989). The discrepancy in estimates may result from the difficulty in identifying people with dementia, especially in its early stages.

An additional problem with identifying the prevalence figures for dementia is that survival rates will alter the outcomes. For this reason, incidence studies—which deal with the number of new cases in a year—may be the most reliable method for assessing the frequency of dementia, especially among the elderly. In a recent study, the annual incidence rates for dementia were 2.3% for people 75–79 years of age, 4.6% for people 80–84 years of age, and 8.5% for those 85 and older (Paykel et al., 1994). The research showed that the rate for new cases doubled every 5 years. In addition, the rate for dementia was comparable for men and women and was equivalent across educational level and social class. Other studies, on the other hand, often find small increases of dementia among women (for example, Rorsman, Hagnell, & Lanke, 1986), although this result may be due partially to the tendency for women to live longer. Together, these results suggest that dementia is a relatively common disorder among older adults, with the chances of developing it increasing rapidly over the age of 75. Keep in mind, however, that approximately 85% of all individuals over the age of 65 are not cognitively impaired; cognitive disorders are not the inevitable consequence of aging (see Figure 15.4).

The statistics we just described cover dementia arising from a variety of etiologies. DSM-IV groups the types of dementias according to presumed cause, but determining the cause of dementia is an inexact procedure. Sometimes, as with dementia of the Alzheimer's type, clinicians rely on ruling out alternative explanations—identifying all the things that are *not* the cause—rather than precisely determining the origin of the disorder. With that in mind, five classes of dementia based on etiology are identified: *dementia of the Alzheimer's type* (dementia as the result of Alzheimer's disease), *vascular dementia, dementia due to other general medical conditions, substance-induced persisting dementia,* and *dementia due to multiple etiologies,* with a sixth—*dementia not otherwise specified*—included when a determination of etiology cannot be made. We describe each of these variations, with an emphasis on dementia of the Alzheimer's type, given its prevalence (almost half of those with dementia exhibit this type) and the relatively large amount of research conducted on its etiology and treatment.

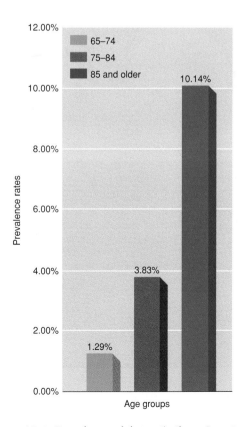

Figure 15.4 Prevalence of dementia (from George, Landoman, Blazer, & Anthony, 1991)

Dementia of the Alzheimer's Type: Description and Statistics

The German psychiatrist Alois Alzheimer first described the disorder that bears his name in 1906. He wrote of a 51-year-old woman who had a "strange disease of the cerebral cortex" that manifested itself as a progressive memory impairment and other behavioral and cognitive problems including suspiciousness (Bogerts, 1993; Loebel, Dager, & Kitchell, 1993). He called this disorder an "atypical form of senile dementia," although thereafter it was referred to as **Alzheimer's disease.** The predominant cognitive deficit displayed by individuals with Alzheimer's disease is the impairment of their memory. Specifically, their inability to integrate new information results in their failure to learn new associations. These individuals forget important events and lose objects (for instance, car keys). Their interest in activities other than routine ones also begins to narrow. It is difficult, however, to determine how much of this social isolation is the direct result of the

Alois Alzheimer (1864–1915), the German psychiatrist and neuropathologist who first described the disorder that bears his name

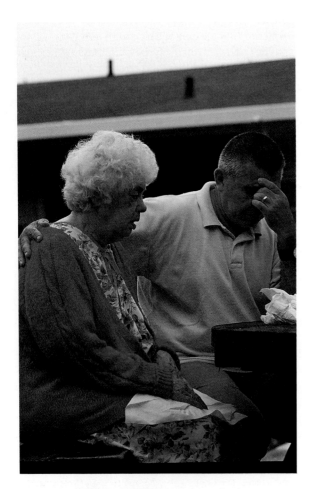

A son talks with his 91-year-old mother, who has dementia of the Alzheimer's type. Considerable stress can occur in family members of individuals having this disorder.

progressive brain damage and how much is due to embarrassment over their failing abilities. The DSM-IV diagnostic criteria for **dementia of the Alzheimer's type** are listed in Table 15.6.

A definitive diagnosis of Alzheimer's disease can be made only after an autopsy determines whether certain characteristic types of damage are present in the brain, although currently clinicians are accurate in identifying this condition approximately 90% of the time (Tierney et al., 1988). The characteristic dysfunctions associated with dementia of the Alzheimer's type include language difficulties (aphasia), coordination problems that usually develop later in the progression of this disorder, failure to recognize common objects (agnosia), and deficits in planning, organizing, and abstracting information.

Dementia of the Alzheimer's type progresses gradually. Cognitive deterioration is slow during the early and later stages of the disorder but more rapid during the middle stages (Stern et al., 1994). The average survival time for this disorder is estimated to be about 8 years (Trèves, 1991). The onset can occur relatively early in life—in a person's 40s or 50s (sometimes referred to as *presenile dementia*)—but more commonly appears in the 60s or 70s (Trèves, 1991). Approximately 50% of the cases of dementia are ultimately found to be the result of Alzheimer's disease (Loebel et al., 1993).

More than 4 million Americans are believed to have dementia of the Alzheimer's type (Edwards, 1994). Some research on prevalence suggests that it may be found more often in people who are less educated (Fratiglioni et al., 1991; Korczyn, Kahana, & Galper,

Table 15.6   DSM-IV Diagnostic Criteria for Dementia of the Alzheimer's Type

A. The development of multiple cognitive deficits manifested by both
   1. Memory impairment (impaired ability to learn new information or to recall previously learned information)
   2. One (or more) of the following cognitive disturbances:
       a. aphasia (language disturbance)
       b. apraxia (impaired ability to carry out motor activities despite intact motor function)
       c. agnosia (failure to recognize or identify objects despite intact sensory function)
       d. disturbance in executive functioning (i.e., planning, organizing, sequencing, abstracting)

B. The cognitive deficits in Criteria A1 and A2 each cause significant impairment in social or occupational functioning and represent a significant decline from a previous level of functioning.

C. The course is characterized by gradual onset and continuing cognitive decline.

D. The cognitive deficits in Criteria A1 and A2 are not due to any of the following:
   1. Other central nervous system conditions that cause progressive deficits in memory and cognition (e.g., cerebrovascular disease, Parkinson's disease, Huntington's disease, subdural hematoma, normal-pressure hydrocephalus, brain tumor)
   2. Systemic conditions that are known to cause dementia (e.g., hypothyroidism, vitamin B_{12} or folic acid deficiency, niacin deficiency, hypercalcemia, neurosyphilis, HIV infection)
   3. Substance-induced conditions

E. The deficits do not occur exclusively during the course of a delirium.

F. The disturbance is not better accounted for by another Axis I disorder (e.g., Major Depressive Disorder, Schizophrenia).

With Early Onset: if onset is at age 65 years or below
   With Delirium: if delirium is superimposed on the dementia
   With Delusions: if delusions are the predominant feature
   With Depressed Mood: if depressed mood (including presentations that meet full symptom criteria for a Major Depressive Episode) is the predominant feature. A separate diagnosis of Mood Disorder Due to a General Medical Condition is not given.
   Uncomplicated: if none of the above predominates in the current clinical presentation

With Late Onset: if onset is after age 65 years
   With Delirium: if delirium is superimposed on the dementia
   With Delusions: if delusions are the predominant feature
   With Depressed Mood: if depressed mood (including presentations that meet full symptom criteria for a Major Depressive Episode) is the predominant feature. A separate diagnosis of Mood Disorder Due to a General Medical Condition is not given.
   Uncomplicated: if none of the above predominates in the current clinical presentation

Specify if:
   With Behavioral Disturbance

Source: DSM-IV, APA, 1994.

1991). This finding could mean that there is a much earlier onset of brain impairment among these people and that Alzheimer's disease causes intellectual dysfunction that interferes with educational efforts. Or there could be something about intellectual achievement that prevents or delays the onset or identification of this disorder. To address these issues, Stern, Gurland, and others (1994) examined the incidence of Alzheimer's type dementia to learn whether educational levels affected who would and who would not be diagnosed with the disorder. They found that those who had received the least amount of formal education were more likely to develop dementia than those who had higher levels of formal education. It is important that the researchers were able to study the subjects before they were identified as having dementia, making their's a prospective study; they were thus able to rule out many

alternative explanations for their results, such as a possible bias in assessment tests toward identifying one group over another. Stern and his colleagues concluded that educational attainment may somehow create a "reserve" or a learned set of skills that helps one cope longer with the cognitive deterioration that marks the beginning of dementia. Just as we saw with Diana's mother, who made copious notes and maps to help her function despite the cognitive deterioration she was probably experiencing, some people may adapt to and cope with these cognitive changes more successfully than others and thus escape detection longer. This conclusion suggests that the brain deterioration is comparable for both groups, but that better-educated individuals are able to function successfully on a day-to-day basis for a longer period of time. This tentative hypothesis about the observed differences in

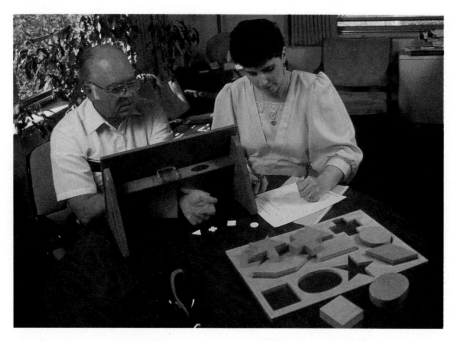

Alzheimer's disease can affect the ability to recognize common objects.

dementia among people of differing educational backgrounds may prove useful in designing treatment strategies to help all people cope with these disruptive changes in their abilities, especially in the early stages of this disorder.

Vascular Dementia: Description and Statistics

Vascular dementia is a progressive brain disorder that is second only to Alzheimer's disease as a cause of dementia (Stuss & Cummings, 1990). The word *vascular* refers to the blood vessels that provide the brain with oxygen and other nutrients by carrying blood. Vascular dementia is primarily the result of vascular insults to the brain; in other words, the blood vessels in the brain become blocked or damaged so that blood does not reach certain areas of the brain and tissue damage results. We learned that MRI scans of Diana Friel McGowin's brain revealed a number of damaged areas—called *multiple infarctions*—left after a stroke she had experienced several years earlier, and that this was one probable cause of her dementia. Because the damaged areas can occur in multiple sites of the brain, the profile of degeneration—the particular skills that are impaired—differs from person to person. DSM-IV lists memory and other cognitive disturbances for vascular dementia that are identical to those described previously for dementia of the Alzheimer's

PET scans of the brains of a person with Alzheimer's disease (*left*) and a person without the disease (*right*). The patchy appearance of the PET scan of the brain with Alzheimer's indicates degeneration in brain tissue.

Simple signs can be used as memory aids for people with dementia.

type. In addition, certain neurological signs that indicate brain tissue damage such as gait or walking abnormalities and weakness in the limbs are also observed in many people with this type of dementia but not in the early stages in people with dementia of the Alzheimer's type. DSM-IV criteria for vascular dementia are shown in Table 15.7.

Relative to the research on dementia of the Alzheimer's type, there are fewer studies on vascular dementia, perhaps because of its lower incidence rates. One study on the incidence of this disorder among people living in a city in Sweden suggests the lifetime risk of having vascular dementia as 4.7% among men and 3.8% among women (Hagnell et al., 1992). The

Table 15.7 DSM-IV Diagnostic Criteria for Vascular Dementia

A. The development of multiple cognitive deficits manifested by both
   1. Memory impairment (impaired ability to learn new information or to recall previously learned information)
   2. One (or more) of the following cognitive disturbances:
      a. aphasia (language disturbance)
      b. apraxia (impaired ability to carry out motor activities despite intact motor function)
      c. agnosia (failure to recognize or identify objects despite intact sensory function)
      d. disturbance in executive functioning (i.e., planning, organizing, sequencing, abstracting)

B. The cognitive deficits in Criteria A1 and A2 each cause significant impairment in social or occupational functioning and represent a significant decline from a previous level of functioning.

C. Focal neurological signs and symptoms (e.g., exaggeration of deep tendon reflexes, extensor plantar response, pseudobulbar palsy, gait abnormalities, weakness of an extremity) or laboratory evidence indicative of cerebrovascular disease (e.g., multiple infarctions involving cortex and underlying white matter) that are judged to be etiologically related to the disturbance.

D. The deficits do not occur exclusively during the course of a delirium.

With Delirium: if delirium is superimposed on the dementia
With Delusions: if delusions are the predominant feature
With Depressed Mood: if depressed mood (including presentations that meet full symptom criteria for a Major Depressive Episode) is the predominant feature. A separate diagnosis of Mood Disorder Due to a General Medical Condition is not given.
Uncomplicated: if none of the above predominates in the current clinical presentation

Specify if:
  With Behavioral Disturbance

Source: DSM-IV, APA, 1994.

higher incidence among men is typical for this disorder and contrasts with the relatively equal rates between men and women for Alzheimer's type dementia (Kay, 1991). The relatively high rate of cardiovascular disease among men in general may account for their increased risk of vascular dementia. We saw that the onset of dementia of the Alzheimer's type is gradual; in contrast, the onset of vascular dementia is typically more sudden. The rapid onset is probably due to the way the disorder begins—through a stroke, which causes damage immediately, rather than through a slow process of deterioration as in dementia of the Alzheimer's type. The outcome, however, is similar for people with both types: Ultimately, they will require formal nursing care until they succumb to a variety of infectious diseases such as pneumonia.

Dementia Due to Other General Medical Conditions: Description and Statistics

In addition to Alzheimer's disease and vascular damage, a number of other neurological and biochemical processes can lead to dementia. DSM-IV lists several other types with specific causes including *dementia due to HIV disease, dementia due to head trauma, dementia due to Parkinson's disease, dementia due to Huntington's disease, dementia due to Pick's disease,* and *dementia due to Creutzfeldt-Jakob disease.* Each of these is discussed here. Other medical conditions that can lead to dementia include normal pressure hydrocephalus (having excessive water in the

cranium, due to brain shrinkage), hypothyroidism (an underactive thyroid gland), brain tumor, and vitamin B_{12} deficiency. The areas of cognitive ability affected make these disorders comparable to the other forms of dementia we have discussed so far; the criteria are listed in Table 15.8.

A recent discovery is that HIV can cause dementia. The human immunodeficiency virus-type-1 (*HIV-1*) is the virus that causes AIDS (acquired immunodeficiency syndrome) (Perry, 1993). Among the other consequences of this disease—which include making the individual vulnerable to infections and tumors—is cognitive impairment of the type we have been describing. This impairment seems to be independent of the other infections that accompany HIV; in other words, the HIV infection itself seems to be responsible for the neurological impairment (Price & Brew, 1988). The early symptoms of dementia due to HIV are cognitive slowness, impaired attention, and forgetfulness. Affected individuals also tend to be clumsy, to show repetitive movements—tremors, leg weakness—and to become apathetic and socially withdrawn (Navia, 1990).

People with HIV seem particularly susceptible to these cognitive impairments in the later stages of HIV infection, although recent evidence suggests that significant impairment of cognitive abilities can occur even in the earlier stages (Heaton et al., 1994). Such cognitive impairments are observed in 29% to 87% of people with AIDS, and approximately one-third of the infected people will ultimately meet the criteria for dementia due

Table 15.8 DSM-IV Diagnostic Criteria for Dementia Due to Other General Medical Conditions

A. The development of multiple cognitive deficits manifested by both
  1. Memory impairment (impaired ability to learn new information or to recall previously learned information)
  2. One (or more) of the following cognitive disturbances:
     a. aphasia (language disturbance)
     b. apraxia (impaired ability to carry out motor activities despite intact motor function)
     c. agnosia (failure to recognize or identify objects despite intact sensory function)
     d. disturbance in executive functioning (i.e., planning, organizing, sequencing, abstracting)

B. The cognitive deficits in Criteria A1 and A2 each cause significant impairment in social or occupational functioning and represent a significant decline from a previous level of functioning.

C. There is evidence from the history, physical examination, or laboratory findings that the disturbance is the direct physiological consequence of one of the general medical conditions listed below.

D. The deficits do not occur exclusively during the course of a delirium.

Dementia Due to HIV Disease
Dementia Due to Head Trauma
Dementia Due to Parkinson's Disease
Dementia Due to Huntington's Disease
Dementia Due to Pick's Disease
Dementia Due to Creutzfeldt-Jakob Disease
Dementia Due to [Indicate the General Medical Condition not listed above]
  For example, normal-pressure hydrocephalus, hypothyroidism, brain tumor, vitamin B_{12} deficiency, intracranial radiation

Source: DSM-IV, APA, 1994.

Table 15.9   Characteristics of Dementias

Characteristic	Dementia of the Alzheimer's Type	Subcortical Dementias
Language	Aphasia (difficulties with articulating speech)	No aphasia
Memory	Both recall and recognition are impaired	Recall is impaired; recognition is normal or less impaired than recall
Visuospatial skills	Impaired	Impaired
Mood	Less severe depression and anxiety	More severe depression and anxiety
Motor speed	Normal	Slowed
Coordination	Normal until late in the progression	Impaired

Source: Adapted from Cummings, 1990.

to HIV disease (Day et al., 1992; Price & Brew, 1988). HIV disease accounts for a relatively small percentage of people with dementia compared to Alzheimer's disease and vascular causes, but its presence complicates an already devastating and ultimately fatal set of conditions.

Dementia resulting from HIV, like that from Parkinson's disease, Huntington's disease, and several other causes, is sometimes referred to as *subcortical dementia,* meaning that these diseases affect primarily the inner areas of the brain, below the outer layer called the *cortex* (Cummings, 1990). The distinction between "cortical" (which would include dementia of the Alzheimer's type) and "subcortical" is important because of the different expressions of dementia in these two categories. Table 15.9 outlines some of the differences between these two types of dementia. Language skills in the form of *aphasia* are impaired among people with dementia of the Alzheimer's type while this skill is unaffected among people with subcortical dementia. In contrast, people with subcortical dementia are more likely to experience severe depression and anxiety than those with dementia of the Alzheimer's type. In general, motor skills including speed and coordination are impaired early on among those with subcortical dementia. The differing patterns of impairment can be attributed to the different areas of the brain affected by these disorders.

Head trauma, injury to the head and therefore the brain that is typically caused by accidents such as crashes in cars or motorcycles, can also lead to cognitive impairments. Memory is the most common impairment observed, and both children and adults can be affected (Capruso & Levin, 1992).

Parkinson's disease is a degenerative brain disorder that affects about 1 out of every 1,000 people worldwide (Freedman, 1990). Motor problems are characteristic among people with Parkinson's disease; they tend to have a stooped posture, slow body movements (called *bradykinesia*), tremors, and a jerki-

ness in walking. The voice is also affected; these individuals will speak very softly and in a monotone. The changes in motor movements are the result of damage to neurons that involve primarily the neurotransmitter dopamine. Because dopamine is involved in complex movement, a reduction in this neurotransmitter causes increasing inability among the affected individuals in controlling their muscle movements, leading to the tremors and muscle weakness observed in them.

Although not true for everyone, a portion of people with Parkinson's develop dementia (La Rue, 1992). Conservative estimates place the rate of dementia in people with Parkinson's at twice that found in the general population (Gibb, 1989). The pattern of impairments for these individuals fits the general pattern of subcortical dementia (Table 15.9).

Huntington's disease is a genetic disorder that initially affects motor movements, typically in the form of *chorea* or involuntary limb movements (Folstein, Brandt, & Folstein, 1990). People with Huntington's can live for 20 years after the first signs of the disease appear, although skilled nursing care is often required during the last stages. Just as with Parkinson's disease, only a portion of persons with Huntington's disease go on to display dementia—somewhere between 20% and 80%—although some researchers believe that all Huntington's patients would eventually display dementia if they lived long enough (Edwards, 1994). Dementia due to Huntington's disease follows the subcortical pattern.

The search for the gene that is responsible for Huntington's disease reads like a detective story. For some time researchers have known that the disease is inherited as an autosomal dominant disorder, meaning that approximately 50% of the offspring of an adult with this disorder will inherit the disease. Since 1979, behavioral scientist Nancy Wexler and a team of researchers have been studying the largest known extended family in the world afflicted by Huntington's disease, located in small villages in Venezuela. The villagers have cooperated with the research, in part because Wexler herself lost her mother, three uncles, and her maternal grandfather to Huntington's, and she too may have the disorder (Turkington, 1994). Using genetic linkage analysis techniques (see Chapter 4), these researchers had previously mapped the deficit to an area on chromosome 4 (Gusella et al., 1983), and, just recently, Wexler's group, using data from the Venezuelan villagers, identified this elusive gene (Huntington's Disease Collaborative Research Group, 1993). Finding one gene as the cause of a disease—in this case Huntington's—is an exception; research on other inherited mental disorders typically points to multiple gene influences (polygenic influences).

Pick's disease is a very rare neurological condition that produces dementia similar to that of Alzheimer's disease (cortical dementia). The course of this disease is believed to last from 5 to 10 years, although its cause is as yet unknown (McDaniel, 1990). Like dementia due to Huntington's disease, this dementia usually occurs relatively early in life—during a person's 40s or 50s—and is therefore considered an

example of presenile dementia. An even rarer condition, **Creutzfeldt-Jakob disease,** also produces dementia and is believed to affect only one in every million individuals (Edwards, 1994).

Substance-Induced Persisting Dementia: Description and Statistics

Prolonged drug use, perhaps in combination with poor diet, can result in damage to the brain and in some circumstances can also lead to dementia. As many as 10% of individuals who are dependent on alcohol meet the criteria for dementia (Horvath, 1975). DSM-IV identifies several drugs that can lead to symptoms of dementia, including alcohol, inhalants (such as glue or gasoline, which some people inhale for the euphoric feeling they produce), and the sedative, hypnotic, or anxiolytic drugs (see Chapter 12). These drugs pose a threat because of their ability to create dependency, making it difficult for the person to stop ingesting them. The brain damage resulting from use of these and other drugs can be permanent and can cause the same symptoms seen in dementia of the Alzheimer's type (Parsons & Nixon, 1993). The DSM-IV criteria for

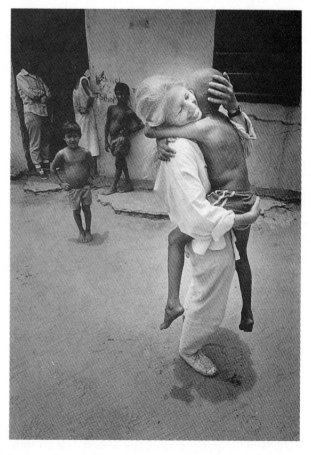

Scientist Nancy Wexler headed the team of researchers who found the gene for Huntington's disease.

substance-induced persisting dementia are listed in Table 15.10.

Causes of Dementia: Biological Influences

The brain can be compromised in many ways, with adverse effects on cognitive abilities. Dementia can be caused by a number of processes: Alzheimer's disease, Huntington's disease, Parkinson's disease, head trauma, substance use, and others. The most common cause of dementia—Alzheimer's disease—is also the most mysterious. As a result of its prevalence as well as our relative ignorance about the factors responsible for it, Alzheimer's disease has occupied the energies of a great many researchers trying to find the cause and ultimately a treatment or cure for this devastating condition. These concerns justify our paying extended attention here to Alzheimer's disease and its etiology.

Looking at this research, we note that findings from this area seem to appear almost daily. We should be cautious when interpreting the output of this fast-paced and competitive field of research; too often, as we have seen in other areas, findings are heralded prematurely as conclusive and important. Remember how "discoveries" of a single gene for bipolar disorder, schizophrenia, and alcoholism were later shown to be overly simplistic accounts of research results. Similarly, findings from Alzheimer's research are sometimes too quickly sanctioned as accepted truths before they have been replicated, a process that is essential for validating new research findings. Several recent examples illustrate this tendency to accept conclusions too quickly.

In 1991, several papers were published proporting to have found strains of mice that developed brain abnormalities similar to the types of damage observed in the brains of patients with Alzheimer's disease (Kawabata, Higgins, & Gordon, 1991; Wirak et al., 1991). If true, this would be an important advance because it would give researchers a way to study this degenerative process directly without having to wait until people with the disorder died and then examine their brains. In less than a year, however, two of the reports were retracted by their authors because errors were found that threatened the validity of their results (Rennie, 1992). In other words, they may have been too quick to declare a major discovery. Researchers are still trying to develop such a strain of mice because of its potential for the study of this disease; as yet, however, they have not been successful (Mar, 1993; Quon et al., 1991).

In a more influential line of research, a number of researchers have for over a decade studied the link between aluminum and Alzheimer's disease. Several studies have reported elevated levels of aluminum in the brains of people with Alzheimer's disease and researchers have hypothesized that this metal may be one cause of the degenerative disorder (for example, Candy et al., 1986). On the other hand, others have argued that the presence of aluminum may be a consequence of the disease and not its cause (Alfrey, 1986). The concern over aluminum was reported in the popular press, and as a result, many people became fearful that the water they drank, the food they ate or the way it was cooked (in aluminum pots and pans), or even the aluminum in their antacids or antiperspirants could be putting them at risk for Alzheimer's disease (Edwards, 1994; Kolata, 1992). Recently, another study has suggested that the aluminum observed in the neuritic plaques—small areas of damaged nerve terminals that are found in the brains of people with Alzheimer's disease—may simply be a lab contaminant: metal from the air and from the chemicals used to prepare the tissue for observation (Landsberg, McDonald, & Watt, 1992). Of course, this is only one study

Table 15.10 DSM-IV Diagnostic Criteria for Substance-Induced Persisting Dementia

A. The development of multiple cognitive deficits manifested by both
  1. Memory impairment (impaired ability to learn new information or to recall previously learned information)
  2. One (or more) of the following cognitive disturbances:
    a. aphasia (language disturbance)
    b. apraxia (impaired ability to carry out motor activities despite intact motor function)
    c. agnosia (failure to recognize or identify objects despite intact sensory function)
    d. disturbance in executive functioning (i.e., planning, organizing, sequencing, abstracting)

B. The cognitive deficits in Criteria A1 and A2 each cause significant impairment in social or occupational functioning and represent a significant decline from a previous level of functioning.

C. The deficits do not occur exclusively during the course of a delirium and persist beyond the usual duration of Substance Intoxication or Withdrawal.

D. There is evidence from the history, physical examination, or laboratory findings that the deficits are etiologically related to the persisting effects of substance use (e.g., a drug of abuse, a medication).

Source: DSM-IV, APA, 1994.

and we must be careful about accepting *its* findings prematurely. It serves as a reminder, however, of the importance of confirming every result of research in order to avoid accepting false conclusions.

Finally, one more lesson in caution comes from research that demonstrates a negative correlation between cigarette smoking and Alzheimer's disease (Brenner et al., 1993). In other words, the study found that smokers are less likely than nonsmokers to develop Alzheimer's disease. Does this mean smoking has a protective effect, shielding a person against the development of this disease? Examined more closely, the finding may instead be the result of the differential survival rates of those who do and those who do not smoke. In general, people who do not smoke tend to live longer, thereby being more likely to develop Alzheimer's disease, which appears later in life. In fact, some believe that the relative inability of cells to repair themselves, a factor that may be more pronounced among people with Alzheimer's disease, may interact with cigarette smoking to shorten the lives of people who are at risk for Alzheimer's and who smoke (Riggs, 1993). Put another way, smoking may exacerbate the degenerative process of Alzheimer's disease, causing people with the disease who also smoke to die much earlier than nonsmokers who have Alzheimer's. These types of studies and the conclusions drawn from them should make readers sensitive to the complicated nature of the disorders we study.

What do we know about Alzheimer's disease, the most common cause of dementia? After the death of the patient he described as having a "strange disease of the cerebral cortex," Alois Alzheimer performed an autopsy on her and found an unusual pattern of damage in the brain, which contained large numbers of tangled, strandlike filaments (referred to as *neurofibrillary tangles*). This type of damage is common in all people with Alzheimer's disease, although we do not know what causes this pattern of deterioration. A second type of degeneration involves the dendrites, or branches, of the neurons, which deteriorate to the point that the neuron itself can no longer function properly. These dead neurons are found in clusters and are called *neuritic plaques*. Both types of damage accumulate over the years and are believed to produce the characteristic cognitive disorders we have been describing.

These two types of degeneration are extremely small and can be detected only by a microscopic examination of the brain. Even today's sophisticated brain-scan techniques are not yet powerful enough to observe these changes in the brain, which is why a definitive diagnosis of Alzheimer's disease requires an autopsy. In addition to the neurofibrillary tangles and neuritic plaques, over time the brains of people with Alzheimer's disease often shrink or atrophy to a greater extent than would be expected through normal aging

(La Rue, 1992). Because many of the causes of dementia produce brain shrinkage, however, only through observing the tangles and plaques can a diagnosis of Alzheimer's be properly made.

Some attention is being paid to a neurochemical that appears to be deficient in people with Alzheimer's disease: *acetylcholine (ACh)*. Acetylcholine is found throughout the nervous system and appears to contribute to movement, attention, arousal, and memory processes. Researchers suspect that the cells responsible for generating acetylcholine are damaged in persons with Alzheimer's, leaving them with abnormally low levels of this neurotransmitter (Allen, Dawbarn, & Wilcock, 1988). The memory loss associated with Alzheimer's disease is believed to result from this deficiency in acetylcholine. We do not know, however, what causes these cells to die and therefore why this neurotransmitter is observed at such low levels. Other recent findings also point to alterations in the neurotransmitters noradrenalin and serotonin in Alzheimer's disease.

One additional theory holds that the immune system, in a misguided attack on healthy brain cells, may be responsible for the neuron degeneration (Pasinetti et al, 1992; Rogers et al., 1992). This process may combine with the destructive presence of amyloid proteins, discussed below, to facilitate the deterioration seen in Alzheimer's disease. To date, this theory is supported by relatively little research, although it may hold clues to the processes that lead to dementia among individuals with this disorder.

The neuritic plaques found in the brains of people with Alzheimer's disease may also hold a clue to the origins of this condition. In the core of these plaques is a solid waxy protein substance called *amyloid protein*. Just as cholesterol buildup on the walls of blood vessels chokes off the blood supply, deposits of amyloid proteins are believed by some researchers to cause the cell death associated with Alzheimer's (Hardy, Mann, Wester, & Winblad, 1986). An important question, then, is how does this protein build up in the brain cells of Alzheimer's patients but not in the brains of people without the disorder.

Two mechanisms that may account for amyloid protein buildup are currently being studied. In the first, researchers have looked at a substance called *amyloid precursor protein (APP)*, a large protein that is eventually broken down into the amyloid protein found in the neuritic plaques. Important new work has located the gene responsible for producing APP on chromosome 21 (Tanzi et al., 1987). This finding may help to integrate two observations about Alzheimer's disease: (a) APP produces the amyloid protein found in the neuritic plaques; (b) Down syndrome, which is associated with an extra 21st chromosome, also results in a higher incidence of Alzheimer's disease. These findings in combination suggest that the gene responsible for producing APP, and ultimately amyloid protein, may be responsible for at least some forms of Alzheimer's disease—in this case, the relatively infrequent early-onset form of the disease. Also, the location of the gene that produces this protein on the 21st chromosome could explain why people with Down syndrome—who have an extra one of these chromosomes and therefore an extra APP gene—are much more likely than the general population to develop Alzheimer's disease.

A second, more indirect way that amyloid protein may build up in brain cells is through another substance called *apolipoprotein E (apoE)*. This protein normally helps to transport cholesterol—amyloid protein being one type of cholesterol—through the bloodstream. We know that there are at least three different forms of this transporter protein: apoE-2, apoE-3, and apoE-4. The last version—apoE-4—seems to be associated with Alzheimer's disease. Specifically, individuals who have late-onset Alzheimer's, the most common form, are likely to carry the gene associated with apoE-4, located on chromosome 19. Researchers have found that about 80% of people with Alzheimer's disease who also have a family history of the disease will have at least one gene for apoE-4 (Saunders et al., 1993; Strittmatter et al., 1993). In contrast, approximately 64% of the individuals with Alzheimer's who have no family history of the disease have at least one gene for apoE-4, and only 31% of nonaffected individuals have the gene. Having two genes for apoE-4 (one on each of the pairs of chromosome 19) increases one's risk for having this disease: One study found that as many as 90% of people with both genes developed Alzheimer's disease (Corder et al., 1993). In addition to increasing the risk of having the disease itself, having two of the apoE-4 genes also seemed to decrease the mean age of onset from 84 years of age to 68 years. These results suggest that apoE-4 may be responsible for late-onset Alzheimer's disease and that a gene on chromosome 19 is responsible for synthesizing this transporter protein. What is still not completely understood is how apoE-4 causes amyloid proteins to build up in the neurons of people who ultimately exhibit Alzheimer's disease and whether this process is responsible for the disease itself.

Another intriguing question that faces researchers trying to understand the mechanisms involved with Alzheimer's disease is how amyloid protein causes brain cell death. In a potentially important study, a group of researchers found that amyloid protein may induce these cells to self-destruct through a natural process called *apoptosis* (Loo et al., 1993). When the brain of a fetus is developing, it has more cells than it needs to work efficiently. As the brain becomes more developed it improves efficiency by "killing off" unnecessary cells through the process known as apopto-

sis. Loo and his colleagues found that when they put amyloid protein with central nervous system neurons that they cultured in the laboratory, the neurons died in a manner resembling the self-destructive process of apoptosis. The researchers hypothesized that this process may produce Alzheimer's disease in two ways. First, cell death and the resulting neuritic plaques occur when amyloid protein comes in contact with the neurons. In a sense, it is as if the amyloid protein is signaling the neuron that it is no longer useful. Second, even when amyloid protein occurs in nonlethal doses, its presence may still weaken the cell and make it more susceptible to other stressors that occur in the brain, such as glucose deprivation. This theory has intuitive appeal because it could explain why some individuals display Alzheimer's disease while others do not, even though they may both have factors (such as the apoE-4 gene) that would make them vulnerable to the disease. Psychological and biological stressors may interact with these physiological processes to produce Alzheimer's disease.

We opened the section with a word of caution, and it is appropriate at this point to repeat the caveat. Many of the findings just reviewed are considered controversial. It is possible, for example, that the neuritic plaques being studied as a cause of Alzheimer's disease may instead be simply a by-product of the deterioration caused by other processes. In addition, the genetic findings, as we have seen with other disorders, should also be viewed cautiously. The apoE-4 gene on chromosome 19 may itself not be responsible for Alzheimer's disease, but may instead be only a marker for a nearby gene that contributes to the condition. We are clearly learning more about Alzheimer's disease, but many questions remain to be answered about this destructive condition.

Causes of Dementia: Psychological and Social Influences

For the most part, research has focused on the biological influences affecting dementia. And while few would argue that psychosocial influences *directly* cause the type of brain deterioration seen in people with dementia, these influences may help to determine the onset and the course of this disorder. For example, a person's life-style may bring him or her into contact with factors that can cause dementia. We saw, for instance, that substance abuse can lead to dementia, and as we discussed previously (see Chapter 12), whether a person abuses drugs is determined by a combination of biological and psychosocial factors. In the case of vascular dementia, a person's biological vulnerability to vascular disease will influence his or her chances of experiencing the strokes that can lead to this form of dementia. At the same time, we also know that life-style issues such as diet, exercise, and stress can influence cardiovascular disease, and can influence who does and does not ultimately experience vascular dementia.

Cultural factors may also have an impact on this process. For example, hypertension and strokes are more prevalent among African-Americans and certain Asian-Americans (Cruickshank & Beevers, 1989), which may explain why vascular dementia is more often observed in members of these cultural groups (de la Monte, Hutchins, & Moore, 1989). In an extreme example, exposure to a viral infection can lead to dementia through a condition known as Kuru. This virus is passed on through a ritualistic form of cannibalism that is practiced in Papua New Guinea as a part of mourning (Gajdusek, 1977). Dementia caused by head trauma and malnutrition are relatively more prevalent in preindustrial and less urbanized societies (Lin, 1986; Westermeyer, 1989), an observation suggesting that social engineering in the form of occupational safety and economic conditions influencing diet will also affect the prevalence of certain forms of dementia. It is apparent that psychosocial factors may help influence who does and who does not develop certain forms of dementia. Brain deterioration is a biological process, but as we have seen throughout this text, even biological processes are influenced by psychosocial factors.

Psychosocial factors can also influence the course of dementia. Recall that a person's level of educational attainment may affect the onset of dementia (Fratiglioni et al., 1991; Korczyn et al., 1991). Having learned certain skills may help some people cope better than others with the early stages of dementia. As we saw earlier, Diana Friel McGowin's mother was able to carry on her day-to-day activities by making maps and using other "tricks" to help her compensate for her failing abilities. Here again, culture can influence the unfolding of this cognitive disorder. For instance, the early stages of confusion and memory loss may be better tolerated in cultures that have lowered expectations for the independence of older adults. Certain cultures—such as the Chinese—expect younger people to take over the demands of work and care from older adults after a certain age (Ikels, 1991). Dementia may go undetected for years in these types of societies.

An Integration

Much remains unknown about the cause and course of most types of dementia. Certain genetic factors—as we saw in Alzheimer's and Huntington's disease—make some individuals vulnerable to progressive cognitive deterioration. In addition, brain trauma, some diseases, and exposure to certain drugs such as alcohol, inhalants, and the sedative, hypnotic, and anxiolytic drugs can cause this characteristic decline in cognitive abilities. We also noticed that psychosocial factors can help determine who will come in contact

with some of these causes, and how people will ultimately cope with these conditions. Looking at dementia from this integrative perspective should help us view treatment approaches in a more optimistic light. It may be possible to prevent people from encountering conditions that lead to dementia, and it is also possible to provide support to individuals who must deal with the devastating consequences of this disorder. We next review attempts to help such people from both biological and psychosocial perspectives.

Treatment of Dementia: An Overview

For many of the disorders we have described and discussed in this textbook, the prospects for treatment are fairly good. Clinicians have been able to combine biological and psychosocial intervention strategies to reduce significantly the suffering of people with a variety of disorders. Even in cases where treatment has not led to expected improvements, mental health professionals have for the most part been able to stop the progression of problems and keep them from getting worse. This is not the case in the treatment of dementia.

One of the factors acting against any major advances in the treatment of dementia is the nature of the damage caused by this disorder. The brain contains billions of neurons, many more than we use. Damage to a portion of these neurons can be compensated for by others, a concept known as *plasticity*. However, there is a limit to how many (and where) these neurons can be destroyed before vital functioning is disrupted. And a neuron that is destroyed is irreplaceable. Therefore, with extensive brain damage, no known treatment process is capable of bringing back abilities that may be lost forever. The goals of treatment therefore become (a) trying to prevent people from contacting certain conditions that may bring on dementia (for instance, preventing substance abuse), (b) trying to stop the brain damage from spreading and becoming worse, and (c) attempting to help these individuals and their caregivers cope with their advancing deterioration. Most of the efforts in dementia have focused on the second and third goals, with biological treatments aimed at stopping the cerebral deterioration and psychosocial treatments directed at assisting patients and caregivers to deal with this disorder.

There is a troubling statistic that goes beyond the already tragic circumstances for the individual with dementia: It has been estimated that over half the caregivers of people with dementia—usually spouses, children, or other relatives—eventually become clinically depressed (Cohen & Eisdorfer, 1988). Compared with the general public, these caregivers tend to use more psychotropic medications and to report stress symptoms at three times the normal rate (George,

1984). Caring for people with dementia—especially in its later stages—is a trying experience.

Treatment of Dementia: Biological Treatments

Dementia due to known infectious diseases, nutritional deficiencies, and depression can be treated if caught early in the development of the cognitive symptoms. Unfortunately, however, for most of the different types of dementia that are responsible for the vast majority of cases, there is no known treatment. Dementia due to such conditions as HIV, Parkinson's disease, and Huntington's disease are not currently treatable because there is no effective treatment for the primary disorder. Most of the current attention on treatment, as we saw in the case of etiology, is focused on a treatment for dementia of the Alzheimer's type, primarily because it affects so many people. Here too, however, intervention efforts have been unsuccessful for the majority of individuals treated.

Most of the work in this area has been directed at medically enhancing the cognitive abilities of people with dementia of the Alzheimer's type by using a variety of drugs. Many of the attempts seem to be effective initially, but long-term improvements have not been observed in placebo-controlled studies (Loebel et al., 1993). Recently, one drug has been shown to have a modest impact on cognitive abilities in some patients. This drug—*tacrine hydrochloride* (trade name Cognex)—is the first of its kind to receive Food and Drug Administration approval for use with people having Alzheimer's disease. Tacrine is an acetylcholinesterase inhibitor, a drug that prevents the breakdown of the neurotransmitter acetylcholine, which is the neurochemical found to be deficient in people with Alzheimer's disease. By preventing the breakdown of this neurotransmitter, tacrine allows the brain to have more acetylcholine available for its use. Research on the use of this drug suggests that people's cognitive abilities improve in an amount equivalent to moving them back 6 months in time (Knapp et al., 1994). But the gain is not permanent. Even people who respond positively to this drug do not stabilize but continue to experience the cognitive decline associated with Alzheimer's disease. In addition, if they stop taking the drug—and almost three-quarters of the patients do because of negative side effects such as liver damage and nausea—they lose even that 6-month gain (Winker, 1994). This drug and the testing that is required to accompany it can cost over $250 per month, so the affected person and his or her family must decide whether the cost is worth the temporary turnback of time for the 6 months that is provided by the drug. To date, no drugs are available that directly treat and therefore stop the progression of the conditions that cause the cerebral damage in Alzheimer's disease.

Treatment of Dementia: Psychosocial Treatments

Psychosocial treatments have for the most part not focused on improving or restoring cognitive abilities but instead have looked to enhancing the lives of the person with dementia and his or her family. One way that people with dementia can be helped is to be taught skills to compensate for their lost abilities. Recall that Diana's mother learned on her own to make maps to help her get from place to place. Diana herself began making lists so she would not forget important things. Some researchers have evaluated more formal adaptations to help people in the early stages of dementia. Bourgeois (1992, 1993) has used "memory wallets" to help people with dementia carry on conversations. These are white index cards inserted into a plastic wallet on which are printed declarative statements such as "My husband John and I have 3 children," or "I was born on January 6, 1911, in Pittsburgh, PA." The goal of these memory wallets is to help individuals who have word-finding problems—not being able to find the right words to express themselves—to converse with other people more easily. In one of her studies, Bourgeois (1992) found that six adults with dementia could, with minimal training, use this memory aid to improve their conversations with others. Three of the adults used their memory wallets with people who had initially not been involved in the training, such as with their children and grandchildren. One of the participants withdrew from the training after several weeks, which seemed to coincide with a substantial decline in her cognitive abilities during that time. Other researchers have used similar memory aids to assist people in orienting themselves in time and place, another of the abilities that becomes disrupted as a consequence of dementia (Hanley, 1986; Hanley & Lusty, 1984). Teaching adaptations such as these not only helps individuals in their ability to communicate with others and remain aware of their surroundings, but it can also help reduce the frustration that comes with the awareness of their own inability to carry on these functions by themselves.

Individuals who have advanced dementia are not able to feed, bathe, or dress themselves. They lose the ability to communicate with others and to recognize even familiar family members. They may wander away from home and become lost. Because they are no longer aware of the social stigma, they may engage in public displays of sexual behavior such as masturbation. They may be frequently agitated or even physically violent. To help both the person with dementia and the caregiver, researchers have explored interventions for dealing with these consequences of the disorder (Fisher & Carstensen, 1990).

Of great concern to caregivers is the tendency of people with dementia to wander. Sometimes they become lost or go to places or situations that are potentially harmful (for instance, stairwells, the street). Often, a response to wandering is to restrain the person by tying him or her to a chair or bed, or to sedate the individual to prevent roaming. Unfortunately, physically or medically restraining people has its own risks, including additional medical complications; it also adds greatly to the feelings of loss of control and independence that already plague the person with dementia. Psychological treatment as an alternative to restraint sometimes involves providing cues for people to help them safely navigate around their home or other areas (Hussian & Brown, 1987). Colored arrows and grids on the floor are used to indicate "safe" and "dangerous" areas. These cues allow people more freedom to ambulate and they free up caregivers from the necessity of constant monitoring.

The individual with dementia can become agitated and sometimes verbally and physically aggressive. This behavior understandably creates a great deal of stress in people trying to provide care. In these situations, medical intervention is often used, although frequently with only modest results (Loebel et al., 1993). Often, assertiveness training is provided to caregivers as a way to deal with these types of behaviors. As you can see in Table 15.11, caregivers are taught to respond in a calm and assertive way to potential problem situations (Edwards, 1994). Caregivers frequently respond either by passively accepting all criticism inflicted by the person with dementia, which can cause increased stress, or by becoming angry and aggressive in return. This last response is of particular concern because of the potential for what is called *elder abuse*. Abuse of older adults in the form of withholding food or medication, or by inflicting physical abuse, is more common among the elderly who have cognitive deficits

(Sachs & Cassel, 1989). It is important to provide caregivers with ways of dealing with these stressful circumstances so that they do not escalate into potentially abusive situations. There is, at present, not a great deal of objective evidence supporting the usefulness of this type of assertiveness training for reducing caregiver stress, and we await research on these procedures to help guide future efforts. In general, families of people with dementia can benefit from supportive counseling to help them deal with their feelings of frustration, guilt, and loss, which take a heavy emotional toll.

Overall, the outlook for stopping the cognitive decline characteristic of dementia is not good, and we have no sense that a research breakthrough is imminent. The best available medication—tacrine—provides people with dementia of the Alzheimer's type some recovery of function, but it does not stop their progressive deterioration. Psychological interventions may help people cope more effectively with the loss of cognitive abilities, especially in the earlier stages of this disorder, but for now, more success may be possible in helping the caregivers—the other victims of dementia—deal with the increasing demands being placed on them as the person they care for continues to decline.

Amnestic Disorder

Say these three words—apple, bird, roof—to yourself, try to remember them, then count backward from 100 by threes. After about 15 seconds of counting, can you still recall the three words? Probably so. However, people with amnestic disorder will not remember them, even after such a short period of time (Butters & Cermak, 1980). The loss of this type of memory that we described as a primary characteristic of dementia

Table 15.11 Examples of Assertive Responses

Patient Behavior	Assertive Response
	Calmly but firmly say:
1. The patient refuses to eat, bathe, or change clothes	"We agreed to do this at this time so that we will be able to (give specific activity or reward)."
2. The patient says she/he wants to go home	"I know you miss some of the places we used to be. This is our home now and together we are safe and happy here."
3. The patient demands immediate gratification	"It's not possible to have everything we want. As soon as I've finished (describe your task or actions), we can discuss other things we want to do."
4. The patient accuses the caregiver of taking his or her possessions	"We both enjoy our own things. I'll help you look for (specific item missing) so you can enjoy it just as soon as I have finished (describe specific task or action)."
5. The patient is angry and/or rebellious	"I like to be treated fairly just as you do. Let's discuss what's bothering you so we can go back to our usual good relationship."

Source: Adapted from Edwards, 1994.

"I still have a pretty major memory problems, which has since brought about a divorce and which I now have a new girlfriend, which helps very much. I even call her . . . my new brain or my new memory . . . If I want to know something, besides relying on this so-called memory notebook, which I jot notes down in constantly and have it every day dated, so I know what's coming up or what's for that day. She also helps very very much with the memory. My mother types up the pages for this notebook, which has each half hour down and the date, the day and the date, which anything coming within an hour or two or the next day or the next week, I can make a note of it so that when that morning comes, and I wake up, I right away, one of the first things, is look at the notebook. What have I got to do today?"

can occur by itself in certain individuals—in other words, without the loss of other high-level cognitive functions. When this happens, it is referred to as **amnestic disorder.** The main deficit appears to be the inability to transfer information—such as the list we just described—into long-term memory, which can involve a time frame of minutes, hours, or years. This disturbance in memory is due either to the physiological effects of some medical condition, such as head trauma, or to the effects of a drug of abuse or a medication, an impact that continues after the substance is no longer ingested. Consider the following case.

The Case of S. T.

S. T., a 67-year-old white woman, suddenly fell, without loss of consciousness. She appeared bewildered and anxious but oriented to person and place yet not to time. Language functioning was normal. She was unable to recall her birthplace, the ages of her children, or any recent presidents of the United States. She could not remember 3 objects for 1 minute, nor recall what she had eaten for her last meal. She could not name the color of any object shown to her but could correctly name the color related to certain words—for example, "grass," "sky." Object nam-

ing was normal. [Examined] one year later, she could repeat 5 digits forward and backward but could not recall her wedding day, the cause of her husband's death, or her children's ages. She did not know her current address or phone number and remembered 0 out of 3 objects after 5 minutes. While she was described by her family as extremely hard-working prior to her illness, after hospitalization she spent most of her time sitting and watching television. She was fully oriented, displayed normal language function, and performed simple calculations without error. (Cole, Winkelman, Morris, Simon, & Boyd, 1992, pp. 63–64)

The DSM-IV criteria for amnestic disorder are listed in Table 15.12. The woman we just described was diagnosed with a type of amnestic disorder called *Korsakoff syndrome,* which is caused by damage to the thalamus—a small region deep inside the brain that acts as a relay station for many other parts of the brain. In her case, the damage to the thalamus was believed due to a stroke that caused vascular damage. Another common cause of Korsakoff syndrome is chronic and heavy alcohol use. As you read in the description of this woman, she had pronounced difficulty recalling infor-

Table 15.12   DSM-IV Diagnostic Criteria for Amnestic Disorder Due to . . . [Indicate the General Medical Condition]

A. The development of memory impairment as manifested by impairment in the ability to learn new information or the inability to recall previously learned information.

B. The memory disturbance causes significant impairment in social or occupational functioning and represents a significant decline from a previous level of functioning.

C. The memory disturbance does not occur exclusively during the course of a delirium or a dementia.

D. There is evidence from the history, physical examination, or laboratory findings that the disturbance is the direct physiological consequence of a general medical condition (including physical trauma).

Specify if:
 Transient: if memory impairment lasts for 1 month or less
 Chronic: if memory impairment lasts for more than 1 month

Source: DSM-IV, APA, 1994.

mation presented just minutes before. While she could repeat a series of numbers, she couldn't remember three objects presented to her moments earlier. As with other people with amnestic disorder, despite these obvious deficits with her memory, her language was fine and she could carry on her simple chores. Yet these individuals are often significantly impaired in social or vocational functioning because of the importance that memory plays in such activities.

As with the other forms of cognitive disorders, a wide range of insults to the brain can cause amnestic disorders. In the woman we described who had vascular damage, and for others with Korsakoff syndrome due to alcohol abuse, this condition is irreversible.

Summary

- The definition of mental retardation has three parts: significantly subaverage intellectual functioning, concurrent deficits or impairments in present adaptive functioning, and an onset before the age of 18.

- DSM-IV groups the learning disorders as reading, mathematics, and written expression disorders. All are defined by a significant decrement in performance compared to expectations based on intelligence and school preparation.

- Delirium is a temporary state of confusion and disorientation that can be caused by brain trauma, intoxication by drugs or poisons, surgery, or a variety of other stressful conditions, especially among older adults.

- Dementia is a progressive and degenerative condition marked by gradual deterioration of a broad range of cognitive abilities—including memory; language; and planning, organizing, sequencing, and abstracting information.

- Alzheimer's disease is the leading cause of dementia, affecting approximately 4 million Americans; there is currently no known cause or cure for this disease.

- To date, there is no effective treatment for the irreversible dementias caused by Alzheimer's disease, Parkinson's disease, Huntington's disease, and the various other less common conditions that produce this progressive cognitive impairment. Treatment often focuses on helping the patient cope with the continuing loss of cognitive skills, and helping caregivers deal with the stress of caring for the affected individuals.

- Amnestic disorders involve a dysfunction in the ability to recall recent and past events, the most common of which is Korsakoff syndrome, a memory disorder usually associated with chronic alcohol abuse.

Key Terms

amnestic disorder (635)

amniocentesis (607)

Creutzfeldt-Jakob disease (628)

cultural/familial retardation (609)

delirium (616)

dementia (619)

dementia of the Alzheimer's type [Alzheimer's disease] (622)

disorder of written expression (614)

Down syndrome (606)

fragile X syndrome (608)

Huntington's disease (627)

Klinefelter's syndrome (609)

learning disorders (613)

mathematics disorder (614)

mental retardation (598)

Parkinson's disease (627)

Pick's disease (628)

reading disorder (614)

Turner's syndrome (609)

vascular dementia (624)

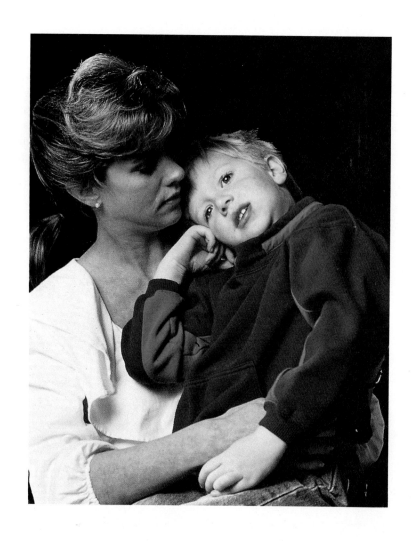

People were forever saying that I had no friends. In fact my world
was full of them. They were far more magical, reliable, predictable,
and real than other children, and they came with guarantees.
It was a world of my own creation where I didn't need to control myself
or the objects, animals, and nature which were simply being *in my presence.*
I had two other friends who did not belong to this physical world: the wisps,
and a pair of green eyes named Willie that hid under my bed.

Donna Williams
Nobody Nowhere

16

Developmental Disorders: Social, Motor, and Speech/Language Impairments

A number of difficulties and, indeed, distinct disorders begin in childhood. In certain disorders, some children are fine except for their ability to talk. Others have problems relating to their peers. Still other children have a combination of conditions that significantly hinder their development, as illustrated by the following case.

The Case of Timmy

Timmy was born with the umbilical cord wrapped around his neck, so he had been without oxygen for an unknown period of time. Nonetheless, he was a beautiful, blond baby who appeared to be normal. His mother would later relate that he was a very good baby and would rarely cry, although she was concerned that he didn't like to be picked up and cuddled. His family became worried about his development when he was 2 years old and didn't talk as his older sister had at that age. They also noticed that he didn't play with other children; he spent most of his time alone, spinning plates on the floor, waving his hands in front of his face, and lining up blocks in a certain order.

The family's pediatrician assured them that Timmy was just developing at a different rate and that he would "grow out of it." When at age 3 Timmy's behavior persisted, his parents consulted a second pediatrician. Neurological examinations revealed nothing unusual, but based on Timmy's delays in learning basic skills such as talking and feeding himself, this pediatrician concluded that Timmy had mild mental retardation.

Timmy's mother did not accept this diagnosis, and over the next few years she consulted numerous other professionals and received a host of varying diagnoses (including childhood schizophrenia, childhood psychosis, and developmental delay). By age 7, Timmy still didn't speak; he didn't play with other children, and he was developing aggressive and self-injurious behaviors. His parents brought him to a clinic that specializes in working with children with severe disabilities. Here, Timmy was diagnosed as having autism.

The clinic recommended a comprehensive educational program of intensive behavioral intervention to help Timmy with his language and social delays as well as to deal with his increasing tendency to engage in tantrums. The work, which continued for approximately 10 years, involved efforts both at the clinic and at home. Over the 10 years of daily therapy, Timmy learned to say only three words: "soda," "cookie," and "Mama." Socially, he appeared to like other people (especially adults), but his interest seemed to center on their ability to get him something he wanted, such as a favorite food or drink. Timmy would become disruptive and violent to the point of hurting himself if his surroundings were changed in even a minor way; to minimize his self-injurious behavior, the family took care to ensure that his surroundings stayed the same as much as possible. However, no real progress was made toward eliminating his violent behavior and as he grew bigger and stronger, he became increasingly difficult to work with; he physically hurt his mother on several occasions. Despite her guilt over the decision, she institutionalized Timmy when he was 17.

As clinicians have grown to appreciate the far-reaching effects of problems in childhood—on the children themselves and on their families—as well as the importance of early intervention in treating disorders of almost any type, they have become more interested in understanding the diversity of severe problems experienced in early life. Timmy was diagnosed with autism in the early 1970s. Two decades later, we know more—though still not enough—about dealing with children who have autism. Who can say what the prognosis for Timmy might be today, especially if he were diagnosed correctly at age 2½ instead of at age 7?

Not too many years ago, a diagnosis of severe problems in children was limited to one broad category: *schizophrenia, childhood type.* It included children with a great variety of abilities in areas such as communication skills, learning capability, and their interactions with others. Clearly, this situation was not ideal for it did not recognize the diversity of severe problems and intervention needs in the area of childhood disorders. Today that situation has changed. In DSM-IV, four categories now exist for severe disabilities, known as *pervasive developmental disorders;* we will look at each of them in this chapter. In addition, we will look at other disorders that involve disruptions in early development, including *attention deficit/hyperactivity disorder* (which involves characteristics of inattention and/or hyperactivity and impulsivity), *tic disorders* (which involve involuntary motor movements and vocalizations), and several *communication disorders,* including *selective mutism* (failure to speak in certain social situations), *stuttering* (speech that is

characterized by frequent repetitions or prolongation of sounds), and *expressive language disorder* (impairment in spoken speech).

We did not include a specific chapter on childhood disorders because to do so would have created the false impression that only *some* disorders have their origins in childhood. As illustrated throughout our discussions of the disorders, most can be present in some form before adulthood. To take schizophrenia as an example, we saw in Chapter 14 that children show subtle signs such as differences in affect before experiencing the major symptoms of hallucinations or delusions as adults. If this observation is found to be reliable, does it mean that the disorder is present in a different and less psychotic form in childhood? Although we do not yet have the answer to this question, viewing disorders from a life-span developmental perspective is an important consideration in psychopathology because it can describe the characteristic course of disorders and point to possible etiological factors and treatment possibilities. For these reasons we placed most of the disorders that are sometimes considered peculiar to childhood—including separation anxiety, eating disorders, mental retardation, and learning disorders—in chapters where these disorders are discussed across the life span. The remaining disorders are described in this chapter on developmental disorders, although here too we characterize their presentation in children, adolescents, and adults.

The Nature of Development: What Is Normal and What Is Abnormal?

Before we turn to our discussion of specific disorders, we need to address the broad topic of development as it relates to disorders usually first diagnosed in infancy, childhood, or adolescence. What can we learn about people such as Timmy, and what effect do very early disruptions in their skills have on their lives at a later time? Does it matter when in the developmental period certain problems arise? Are disruptions in development permanent, thus making any hope for treatment doubtful?

Recall that we described developmental psychopathology as the study of how disorders arise and change with time (Chapter 2). Childhood is considered to be a particularly important time because the brain goes through significant developmental changes for several years after birth; this is also a time when critical developments occur in social, emotional, cognitive, and other important competency areas. These changes, for the most part, follow a pattern, with the child developing one skill before acquiring the next. This pattern of change—although only one aspect of development—is an important concept for us at this point because it implies that any disruption in the development of early skills will, by the very nature of this sequential process, also disrupt the development of later skills. As an example, some researchers believe that people with autism suffer from a disruption in early social development and that this prevents them from developing important social relationships, even with their parents. There can be serious consequences, from a developmental perspective, of not having early and meaningful social relationships. One outcome might be that these children will have a more difficult time learning to communicate because their motivation to interact with others is disrupted. In other words, they may not want to learn to speak to other people if other people are not important to them. We don't know whether a disruption in communication skills—which is present in people with autism—is a direct outcome of the disorder or a by-product of disrupted early social development. Researchers are beginning to explore how developmental influences such as these interact with other biological and psychosocial influences in the developmental disorders.

Understanding this type of developmental relationship is important for several reasons. Knowing what skills are disrupted by a disorder will help us understand the disorder better and may lead to more appropriate intervention strategies. With autism, it may be important to identify affected children at an early age so their social deficits can be addressed before they begin to affect other skill domains, such as language and communication.

Too often people see early and pervasive disruptions in developmental skills, such as we saw with Timmy, and expect the prognosis to be negative, with the problems predetermined and unavoidable. However, it is important to remember that biological and psychosocial influences continuously interact with each other. Therefore, even for disorders such as autism that have clear biological bases, the presentation of the disorder for each individual will be different, depending on how this biological-psychosocial interaction develops. Changes in this system at the biological or the psychosocial level may prove useful in reducing the impact of the disorder in the lives of these individuals.

One note of caution is appropriate here. There is real concern in the profession, especially among developmental psychologists, that some workers in the field may be viewing aspects of normal development as "symptoms" of abnormality. For example, one form of speech that involves repeating the speech of others—called *echolalia*—was once thought to be a sign of autism. However, when you study the development of speech in children without disorders, you see that their

repeating what someone else says is an intermediate step in their language development. In children with autism, therefore, echolalia is just a sign of their relatively delayed language skills and not a symptom of their disorder (Durand & Carr, 1988). Here again, knowledge of development is important for understanding the nature of psychological disorders. With that caveat in mind, we now examine several of the disorders usually diagnosed first in infancy, childhood, or adolescence.

Pervasive Developmental Disorders

Autistic disorder, Rett's disorder, Asperger's disorder, and childhood disintegrative disorder are considered types of **pervasive developmental disorders.** People with these disorders all experience problems with development; they have trouble progressing in areas such as language, socialization, and cognition. The use of the word *pervasive* means that these are not relatively minor problems of development (such as in learning disabilities), but ones that significantly affect how individuals will live. There is general agreement that you can identify a child with a pervasive developmental disorder fairly easily based on the delays you see in his or her daily functioning. Picking out Timmy from his nondisabled peers, for example, didn't require a great deal of diagnostic sophistication. His lack of speech at age 3 and his problems interacting with others were obvious quite early. What is not so easily agreed on, however, is how we should divide this general category (Waterhouse, Wing, Spitzer, & Siegel, 1992).

Most workers in this area agree that the category of autism should remain separate, and this conclusion is based on a considerable amount of research. There is less agreement, however, on whether Asperger's disorder, Rett's disorder, or childhood disintegrative disorder are distinctly different conditions. Some believe that these three—especially Asperger's disorder and autistic disorder—describe different points on a continuum of the same disorder. Others believe that there are important differences, and that the disorders should be separated to improve research on each one. Michael Rutter and Eric Schopler, summarizing the research differentiating these disorders, said, "The answer is a pretty straightforward 'yes' in the case of Rett, a 'probably' in the case of disintegrative disorders, and an uncertain 'maybe' in the case of Asperger syndrome" (Rutter & Schopler, 1992, p. 471). To appreciate this disagreement, you should note that, as late as 1987, DSM-III-R combined these disorders in a category called *Pervasive Developmental Disorder Not Otherwise Specified* (or PDDNOS). With the recent introduction of DSM-IV, the field has formally recognized them as different from each other, and we therefore review them separately here.

Autistic Disorder

Autistic disorder, or autism, is a childhood disorder that is characterized by significant impairment in social interactions and communication, and restricted patterns of behavior, interest, and activities. Individuals with this disorder, although rare, have a puzzling array of symptoms. Consider the following two cases, both of whom are diagnosed with autistic disorder.

The Case of Amy

Amy, 3 years old, spends much of her day picking up pieces of lint. She drops the lint in the air, and then watches intently as it falls to the floor. She also licks the back of her hands and stares at the saliva. She hasn't spoken yet and can't feed or dress herself. Several times a day, she screams so loudly that the neighbors at first thought she was being abused. She doesn't seem to be interested in her mother's love and affection but will take her mother's hand to lead her to the refrigerator. Amy likes to eat butter—whole pats of it, several at a time. Her mother uses the pats of butter that you get at some restaurants to help Amy learn and to keep her well behaved. If Amy helps with dressing herself, or if she sits quietly for several minutes, her mother will give her some butter. Amy's mother knows that the butter isn't good for her, but it is the only thing that seems to get through to the child. The family's pediatrician has been concerned about Amy's developmental delays for some time and has recently suggested that she be evaluated by specialists in this field. The pediatrician feels that Amy may have autism and that the child and her family will probably need extensive support.

The Case of John

At the age of 45, John lives alone in a clean if not luxurious apartment. He has never married, has never had a girlfriend, and does not socialize outside of work. He bags groceries at the local supermarket; he also retrieves carts from the parking lot and does other odd jobs around the store. His head is always down, and he will not make eye contact, even with fellow employees. He rarely speaks.

John came to this country from Puerto Rico with his family almost 25 years ago. Details of his life before coming to the United States are sketchy, but it appears that he lived at home, and was cared for by his extended family. On arriving in this country, counselors in the Department of Social Services recommended that John be placed in an institution to, as they put it, "spare his parents the inevitable burden of caring for him." However, this was unthinkable to his family, who, despite his obvious disabilities, included John as a full member of the family unit. His brother and cousin spent a great deal of time working with John, and over the years he learned daily routines that helped him become more independent. Today, a member of his family visits him in his apartment several times a week to help with bill paying and any other necessary tasks. John seems to be very proud of his home and his job. John has many of the characteristics of people with autism.

Timothy is a 12-year-old first-generation Chinese boy— a gifted piano and violin player who also has autism. Autistic disorder is observed in people from all cultures.

He also shows how far someone with autism can go in life if given the proper help from others. In his case, his family came together to help him learn skills that allowed him to hold a job and live a productive life.

Description of Autistic Disorder

> Since 1938, there have come to our attention a number of children whose condition differs so markedly and uniquely from anything reported so far, that each case merits—and, I hope, will eventually receive—a detailed consideration of its fascinating peculiarities. (Kanner, 1943, p. 217)

So begins Leo Kanner's portrayal of the condition known as *autistic disorder.* Kanner, a noted child psychiatrist, observed 11 cases of children who, like Timmy, Amy, and John, responded in unusual ways to people and to the environment around them. As we saw in these cases, people with this disorder display characteristic problems with social relationships as well as language skills. A father of one of the children Kanner observed described his son in this way:

> He seems to be self-satisfied. He has no apparent affection when petted. He does not observe the

fact that anyone comes or goes, and never seems glad to see father or mother or any playmate. He seems almost to draw into his shell and live within himself. (Kanner, 1943, p. 218)

The three major characteristics of autism are expressed as DSM-IV criteria in Table 16.1 and discussed in the following sections.

Impairment in Social Interactions

One of the defining criteria of people with autistic disorder is that they do not develop the types of social relationships expected for their age. Timmy, Amy, or John never made any friends among their peers and would often limit their contact with adults to using them as tools—taking the adult's hand to reach for something they wanted. For many people with autism, the problems they experience with social interactions may be more *qualitative* than *quantitative.* They may have about the same rate of contact with others as you or your friends, but the way they make contact is unusual. Timmy, for instance, seemed to like to sit on his mother's lap, but he would always sit facing away from her rather than sitting face-to-face, which is typical of most children. Children with autism will sit near their mothers rather than strangers after being left alone for a short period of time. Although they do not make eye contact and smile at their

Sammy, a boy with autism, plays alone in the corner of his room.

Table 16.1   DSM-IV Diagnostic Criteria for Autistic Disorder

A. A total of six (or more) items from (1), (2), and (3), with at least two from (1), and one each from (2) and (3):

  1. Qualitative impairment in social interaction, as manifested by at least two of the following:

     a. marked impairment in the use of multiple nonverbal behaviors such as eye-to-eye gaze, facial expression, body postures, and gestures to regulate social interaction
     b. failure to develop peer relationships appropriate to developmental level
     c. a lack of spontaneous seeking to share enjoyment, interests, or achievements with other people (e.g., by a lack of showing, bringing, or pointing out objects of interest)
     d. lack of social or emotional reciprocity

  2. Qualitative impairments in communication as manifested by at least one of the following:

     a. delay in, or total lack of, the development of spoken language (not accompanied by an attempt to compensate through alternative modes of communication such as gesture or mime)
     b. in individuals with adequate speech, marked impairment in the ability to initiate or sustain a conversation with others
     c. stereotyped and repetitive use of language or idiosyncratic language
     d. lack of varied, spontaneous make-believe play or social imitative play appropriate to developmental level

  3. Restricted repetitive and stereotyped patterns of behavior, interests, and activities, as manifested by at least one of the following:

     a. encompassing preoccupation with one or more stereotyped and restricted patterns of interest that is abnormal either in intensity or focus
     b. apparently inflexible adherence to specific, nonfunctional routines or rituals
     c. stereotyped and repetitive motor mannerisms (e.g., hand or finger flapping or twisting, or complex whole-body movements)
     d. persistent preoccupation with parts of objects

B. Delays or abnormal functioning in at least one of the following areas, with onset prior to age 3 years: (1) social interaction, (2) language as used in social communication, or (3) symbolic or imaginative play.

C. The disturbance is not better accounted for by Rett's Disorder or Childhood Disintegrative Disorder.

Source: DSM-IV, APA, 1994.

mothers like children without autism, they still recognize the difference between their mothers and strangers and prefer to be near their mothers in stressful situations (Sigman & Ungerer, 1984). This research suggests that people with autism are not totally unaware of others as we once thought; however, for some reason we do not yet fully understand, they may not enjoy or have the ability to develop meaningful relationships with others.

Impairment in Communication

People with autism nearly always have severe problems in communicating. About 50% of the persons labeled with autism are like Timmy and never acquire useful speech (Lovaas, 1977; Rutter, 1978). In those with some speech, much of their communication is unusual. Some of them repeat the speech of others, a pattern we referred to before as a sign of delayed speech development, called *echolalia*. If you say "Hello," they will say "Hello." If you then follow with "My name is Eileen, what's yours?" they will repeat all or part of what you said, "Eileen, what's yours?" And often, not only are the words repeated, but so is the intonation, or way they are said. John's inability or unwillingness to carry on conversations with others is another sign of this speech disturbance.

Restricted Behavior, Interests, and Activities

One of the more striking characteristics displayed by children and adults with autism is their *restricted patterns of behavior, interest, and activities.* As we saw with Timmy, he appeared to like having things stay the same and became extremely upset if even a small change was introduced (such as a living room chair that was moved a few inches). This intense preference for the "status quo" has been called *maintenance of sameness.* One parent related that her son, who had autism, liked one particular helicopter from a toy set, and that she had contacted the manufacturer and obtained over 50 of these helicopters for her son. He would spend hours lining them up, and his mother reported that he could immediately tell if even one of the 50 was removed.

Often, people with autism will spend countless hours in *stereotyped and ritualistic behaviors.* It is common for these people to make stereotyped movements such as spinning around in circles, waving their hands in front of their eyes with their heads cocked to one side, or biting their hands. Amy would spend hours watching lint fall to the floor. The rituals can often be complex: Some people must touch each door as they walk down a hall; others touch each desk in a classroom. If they are interrupted or prevented from

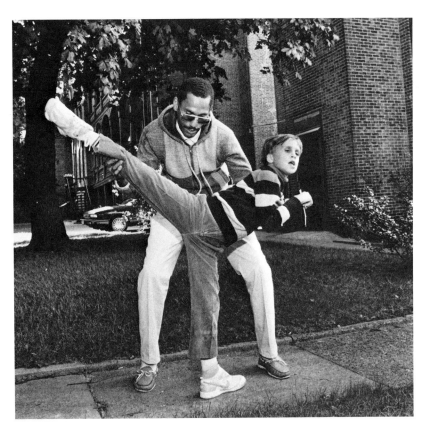

A child with autism being helped with his gymnastic moves. Notice that he continues to play with a stick he picked up off the ground.

completing the ritual, they will sometimes have a severe tantrum.

What must it be like to have autism? Is it an exquisite solitude, divorced from the stressors of modern life? Or is it an oppressive state of anxiety, with a need to try constantly to maintain sameness in a chaotic world? Such fundamental questions about this disorder have led some researchers to interview the few rare individuals who have both autism and good verbal abilities. They hope that by interviewing such people they can gain a better understanding of this disorder and perhaps aid those who have it.

One example of such a firsthand account is an extensive interview with a 27-year-old man named Jim who was diagnosed during his preschool years as having autism (Cesaroni & Garber, 1991). Jim showed all the characteristics we have discussed, including stereotypic movements, resistance to change, repetitive play, and social impairments. Because of these unusual behaviors, a psychiatrist had recommended that he be placed in an institution when he was about 9 years old. Despite these obstacles, Jim acquired sufficient skills to complete high school, and at the time the interview was published, he was completing graduate studies in developmental psychology!

During his interview, Jim explained how he views the world and talked about his own behavior. In describing his sensory impressions, he noted that his sensory processing often gets mixed up: "Sometimes the channels get confused, as when sounds come through as color. Sometimes I know that something is coming in somewhere, but I can't tell right away what sense it's coming through" (p. 305).

He observed that not only do his senses sometimes become switched (hearing sounds and interpreting this as seeing colors) but that sometimes they overlap and become distracting: "I have caught myself turning off the car radio while trying to read a road sign, or turning off the kitchen appliances so that I could taste something" (p. 306).

As he was growing up, Jim engaged in a number of different types of stereotyped behaviors, including rocking back and forth, twirling around, and swinging his limbs from side to side. He continued to behave this way on a limited basis even into adulthood. He has difficulty explaining why he does these things:

> Stereotyped movements aren't things I decide to do for a reason; they're things that happen by themselves when I'm not paying attention to my body. If I'm not monitoring them because I'm worn out, distracted, overwhelmed,

intensely focused on something else, or just relaxed and off-guard, then stereotyped movements will occur.

> People who are close enough for me to be relaxed and off-guard with can expect to see me acting "weird," while people who only see me in my "public display" mode don't see such behavior. (Cesaroni & Garber, 1991, p. 309)

The area of social relationships seems to have given Jim the most trouble, and he reports putting in a tremendous amount of effort to improve these. He felt that he had succeeded in establishing meaningful relationships with others, but at great cost. For example, it wasn't until he was 23 that he allowed people to touch him.

Jim's recollections and responses to having this disorder may illustrate what it is like for most people who have autism or may tell us only what is unique to him. However, to hear about such experiences is enlightening and helps us gain some insight into the disorder. His account makes us wonder whether the abnormal sensory experiences are responsible for disrupted social development, for instance. As we gain access to more of these accounts, our understanding of autism should grow, allowing us to offer greater assistance to those with this disorder.

Statistics and Course for Autistic Disorder

Autism is a relatively rare disorder, although the exact estimates of its occurrence vary. Early research placed the prevalence of this condition at approximately 2 to 5 per 10,000 people (Lotter, 1966). However, recent estimates, using more contemporary definitions of autistic disorder, have lowered this to about 2 per 10,000 people (Gillberg, 1984). Sex differences for autism vary depending on the IQ level of the person affected. Autism is more prevalent among females with IQs under 35 but more prevalent among males in the higher IQ range. We do not know the reason for these sex–IQ differences (Volkmar, Szatmari, & Sparrow, 1993). Autistic disorder appears to be a universal phenomenon, having been identified in every part of the world including Sweden (Gillberg, 1984), Japan, (Sugiyama & Abe, 1989), Russia (Lebedinskaya & Nikolskaya, 1993), and China (Chung, Luk, & Lee, 1990). The vast majority of people with autism developed the behaviors associated with this disorder prior to the age of 36 months (DSM-IV, 1994).

Until people with autistic disorder begin to behave in unusual ways, they often seem to have no particular problem. Their average appearance is part of the enigma of this disorder and has prompted some to suggest that these individuals were all of average or superior intelligence (Kanner, 1943). We now know,

however, that people with autism fall on a continuum of IQ scores. As we saw with Timmy, he showed all the classic signs of autism but also seemed to have the cognitive delays characteristic of people with mental retardation. Three out of every four people with autism are like Timmy and have some form of mental retardation. Almost half these individuals would fall in the severe to profound range of mental retardation (IQ less than 50), about a quarter would test in the mild to moderate range (IQ of 50–70), and the remaining people would display abilities in the borderline to average range (IQ greater than 70) (Waterhouse, Wing, & Fein, 1989).

These measures of IQ have been used to determine prognosis: The higher these children score on IQ tests, the less likely they are to need extensive support by family members or by people in the helping professions. Conversely, if young children with autistic disorder score poorly on IQ tests, they are more likely to be severely delayed in their communication skills and will need a great deal of educational and social support as they grow older. Usually, language abilities and IQ scores are better predictors of how children with autistic disorder will fare later in life: The better the language skills and IQ test performance, the better the prognosis.

Causes of Autistic Disorder

Much research has been done on the causes of this disorder but to date it has provided little conclusive data. Autism is a puzzling condition, so we should not be surprised to find numerous theories for why autistic behaviors develop. One generalization from the research is that autistic disorder probably does not have a single cause (Rutter, 1978). Instead, there may be a number of biological conditions that contribute to it and which, in combination with psychosocial influences, result in the unusual behaviors people with autism display. Because historical context is important in the research on the causes of this disorder, it is helpful to examine past as well as more recent theories of autism, along with the research supporting them. To do this, we are departing from our usual format of providing biological dimensions first.

Psychological and Social Dimensions

What could cause a child to reject her parents' affection but show an intense interest in waving her hand in front of her eyes? Could child-rearing practices go so terribly wrong as to produce such a serious and lasting effect on a child? Do we need to warn parents about the way they hold, feed, or play with their children in order to avoid having a child develop autism? These questions arose from early thinking about the etiology of autism. Part of this concern came from

The ups and downs of a typical day for Sammy, a young boy with autism

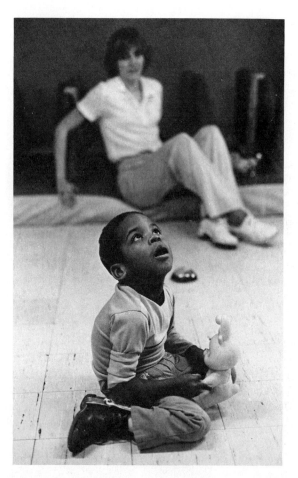

A young boy with autism is fixated on the overhead light.

Kanner's (1943) first portrait of children with autism, which included descriptions of their parents. He noticed that all the parents of the 11 children he studied were highly intelligent, and most were professionals. Nine of the 11 mothers were college graduates, a rather unusual finding for women as a group in the 1940s. All but three of the families had been written up in *Who's Who in America* or in *American Men of Science.* Kanner commented that the very detailed diaries many of the families kept about their unusual children were "obsessive," suggesting that as a group the families tended to be cold and unfeeling.

To his credit, Kanner didn't automatically conclude from his observations that the parents were at fault for their children's problems. He noted that because the "aloneness" exhibited by these children seemed to be present from birth, their problems must be a result of some biological predisposition (Kanner, 1943).

Other researchers, however, were intrigued by the possibility of a psychological cause for autism and wrote extensively on the subject. These theorists worked within very different theoretical perspectives, but all came to a tragic—and we now know incorrect—

conclusion: that autism was caused by psychological factors, specifically faulty interactions with parents. Probably the most famous of these theorists was Bruno Bettelheim, a therapist trained in Vienna as a psychoanalyst. Bettelheim, remembering his early experiences as a Jew in a Nazi concentration camp, noted similarities between the prisoners and the children with whom he was working (Bettelheim, 1967). He believed that the observed dramatic social deficits in the children resulted when their parents blocked the children's attempts to reach out to the world. Just as the concentration camp prisoners were prevented from having any amount of autonomy, children with autism, he said, were being frustrated by their families in their attempts to gain control over their environment. The children were either smothered by too much assistance (not being allowed to pick up their own toys, in their example) or dismissed through parental inattention. Because of the behavior of their parents, children with autism withdrew from contacts with the outside world, or so Bettelheim concluded.

While Bettelheim took a psychoanalytic view of what he saw as the development of autism in children, Charles Ferster (1961) explained the phenomenon from a behavioral perspective. Ferster believed that, by examining the early reinforcement histories of interactions between children with autistic disorder and their parents, he could observe the development of the unusual behaviors seen in autism. He theorized that parents of these children, by not attending to them, extinguished many of their early attempts at social and communicative behaviors. The children would not learn to relate to others because their parents didn't encourage such behaviors. To explain why parents of these children would so grossly ignore them, Ferster offered reasons such as parental depression, drug addiction, or illnesses, suggesting that these factors could affect parents in such a devastating way as to make them almost totally disinterested in their children.

Another psychological view of autism was proposed by two *ethologists* (Tinbergen & Tinbergen, 1983). Niko and Elisabeth Tinbergen, borrowing observations from the "imprinting" research that had won Niko Tinbergen a Nobel Prize, suggested that children with autism engage in unusual social reactions because of a breakdown in the normal motivational conflicts experienced by all children. According to their theory, children approach adults with a combination of social or bonding tendencies and fear of these contacts. Under normal circumstances, the timidity or fear gives way to positive social contacts. For children with autism, however, this process is not resolved in a positive way, and they fail to establish important social bonds. The Tinbergens theorized that this consequence results from a combination of a child's genetic predisposition toward being overtimid and early failed attempts by parents to connect socially with the child. They suggested that children with autism "are the victims of our modern, urbanised, crowded, rationalised and stressful environment—a 'problem environment' in which even healthy, normal parental behaviour may misfire" (Tinbergen & Tinbergen, 1972, p. 34). Although few in the field currently accept this view of autism, it is one of the rare theories that combines both psychological and biological aspects to explain the disorder.

The psychoanalytic views of Bettelheim, the behavioral views of Ferster, and the ethological approach of the Tinbergens are similar in many ways. From each perspective, the origins of autistic disorder are seen as arising from failed parenting. These views of autism were devastating to a generation of parents of these children, making them feel guilty and responsible for their children's problems. Imagine being accused of being so cold toward your own child as to cause him or her to have serious and permanent disabilities throughout life! We now have a great deal of evidence that points to the biological origins of autistic disorder. How, then, could these earlier theories of autism come about and be received with such credibility?

Historically, mothers and fathers of children with autism have been characterized as being perfectionistic, cold, and aloof (Kanner, 1949), having a relatively high socioeconomic status (Allen, DeMyer, Norton, Pontius, & Yang, 1971; Cox, Rutter, Newman, & Bartak, 1975), and possessing higher IQs than the general population (Kanner, 1943). Descriptions such as these have enticed some to theorize that the parents were responsible for their children's unusual behaviors. More contemporary research, however, contradicts these studies and suggests that on a variety of personality measures the parents of individuals with autism may not differ substantially from parents of children without disabilities (Koegel, Schreibman, O'Neill, & Burke, 1983; McAdoo & DeMyer, 1978).

In attempting to account for these contradictory findings, Lorna Wing (1980) conducted an epidemiological study of children in southeast London. Her findings suggest that something as simple as mistakes in *sampling* may have contributed to the accusatory attitude toward parents and, ultimately, to the development of some of the psychological theories of the origins of autistic disorder. She found no socioeconomic differences among the parents of groups of children with autism, schizophrenia, and mental retardation. She did find that fathers of children with autism from higher socioeconomic levels were more likely than poorer fathers to seek out clinical services and to become members of the National Association for Autistic Children. This is an important observation because many previous studies took their samples of parents from clinics and/or national organizations. The Wing study suggests that many previous studies of the

parents of children with autism may have been biased by sampling parents of relatively high socioeconomic status. Such a seemingly innocuous sampling error seems likely to have resulted in a view of autism that had far-reaching negative implications for the parents of these children.

Other theories about the origins of this disorder have arisen from the unusual speech evidenced by some individuals with autism, namely, their tendency to avoid first-person pronouns such as "I" and "me" and to use "he" and "she" instead. For example, if you asked a child with autism, "Do you want something to drink?" he might say, "He wants something to drink" (meaning "I want something to drink"). This observation led some theorists to wonder whether autism involved a lack of self-awareness (Goldfarb, 1963; Mahler, 1952). Imagine, if you can, not understanding that you exist separate from the outside world. There is no *you,* only *them*! Such a debilitating view of the world was used as an explanation for the unusual ways people with autism behaved. These theories suggested that the withdrawal seen among people with autistic disorder was attributable to the lack of awareness that they existed.

An intriguing question arises from this theory. How would you learn whether someone was self-aware? Obviously, this is a particular problem for people with communication difficulties because you can't just ask them. One way researchers have tried to assess the self-awareness of people with autism is to place a colored mark on their faces without their knowledge. The researchers then place them in front of a mirror and observe whether they reach up to their own faces when they see the mark. If they do, the researchers can assume that each individual recognizes the image as himself or herself and not just some other person. If, however, he or she reacts to this novelty (the face with the color red on it) by reaching toward the mirror to touch it, the researchers assume that the person does not see the image as representing his or her face. Results have shown that some people with autistic disorder do seem to have self-awareness (Dawson & McKissick, 1984; Spiker & Ricks, 1984), and this ability seems to follow a developmental progression. Just as in children without a disability, those with cognitive abilities below the level expected for a child of 18–24 months show little or no self-recognition, while people with more advanced abilities do demonstrate self-awareness. Self-concept may be lacking because some people with autism also have cognitive disabilities or delays, and not because of the disorder of autism. This issue of self-awareness and the previously mentioned concern about the affected person's possible lack of attachment again point to the importance of studying disorders from a developmental perspective. Knowing more about how people *without* autistic disorder change over time will help us understand better the people with this disorder.

Because of the importance placed on the socialization problems of people with autism, another more recent theory that has emerged concerns what's called the *Theory of Mind*. Put simply, this theory suggests that the severe social deficits observed among people with autism are a result of their inability to attribute mental states to others and themselves (Leslie, 1987). In other words, the problems these people have relating to others is a result of a cognitive deficit that prevents them from "getting inside the head" of others and explaining and predicting their behavior. This theory is controversial because it suggests that the individuals' social problems are secondary to their cognitive deficits. According to this view, the deficiency results from their lack of Theory of Mind, which in turn leads to social problems. Although this theory is intriguing, recent studies suggest that the social problems of children with autism may occur *before* the development of the skills needed for Theory of Mind (Klin, Volkmar, & Sparrow, 1992). The importance of theories such as these may be in their ability to focus our attention on why people with autism have such unusual reactions to others.

Four-year-old Sammy, who has received the diagnosis of autism

There is a mythology about people with autism that is encouraged when the idiosyncracies of the disorder are highlighted. These perceptions are furthered by portrayals of autism such as the one in *Rainman* by Dustin Hoffman—whose character could, for instance, instantaneously and accurately count hundreds of toothpicks falling to the floor. It is important always to separate myth from reality and to be aware that such portrayals do not represent the full range of manifestations of this very complex disorder.

It is also important when we study developmental disorders such as autism to distinguish between problems that are a result of delays in development and problems that are a result of autism. We have already mentioned some of these efforts—for example, the work on attachment showed that individuals with autism do acquire some form of attachment to others, although the way it is expressed may be different from the way a typical child would show it.

Another area that was once thought to be unique to autism is a phenomenon known as *stimulus overselectivity*. Some people with autism will respond to a small number of sometimes irrelevant cues when they are learning. It would not be unusual for a child with autism to learn a new skill such as pointing to a picture of food to communicate "I'm hungry," then later stop pointing to the picture when it's placed on the right side of the table rather than the left. In this case, the child seems to overselect the cue of position (left side versus right side) rather than the picture itself. It's as if the child learns the particular side of the table means "hungry," and not that the picture itself means "hungry." Only after comparing this type of learning between younger normal children and children with mental retardation did researchers realize that it was common among children at an early stage of cognitive development and was not an oddity unique to autism (Schover & Newsom, 1976).

The phenomenon of *echolalia*, or repeating a word or phrase spoken by another person, was at one time seen as an unusual characteristic of this disorder and was included in DSM-III as one of its defining characteristics. Subsequent work in developmental psychopathology, however, has demonstrated that repeating the speech of others is part of the normally developing language skills observed in most young children (Prizant & Wetherby, 1989). Even a behavior as disturbing as the self-injurious behavior sometimes seen in people with autism is observed in milder forms such as in head banging among infants (de Lissovoy, 1961). This type of research has helped workers isolate the facts from the myths about autism and to clarify the role of development in this disorder. Primarily, it appears that the features predominant among people with autism that clearly distinguish them from others are the social deficiencies.

To date, few workers in the field of autism believe that psychological or social influences play a major role in the development of this disorder. The deficits in such skills as socialization and communication appear to be the outgrowth of biological processes that somehow disrupt development of these skills. To the relief of many families, it is now clear that poor parenting is not responsible for autism. Biological theories about the origins of autism, examined next, have received much empirical support.

Biological Dimensions

If parents don't create autism in their offspring, how do these children come to behave in such unusual ways? A great deal of biologically based research has focused on answering this question. A number of medical conditions have been associated with autism—including congenital rubella (German measles), hypsarrhythmia, tuberose sclerosis, cytomegalovirus, and difficulties during pregnancy and labor—suggesting that autism may result from a number of different disease and biological conditions. Note, for instance, that although a small percentage of mothers exposed to the rubella virus will have a child with autism, most often no autism is present. We still don't know why these medical conditions result in autism *sometimes* but not always.

Genetic Influences

Despite the early theories that implicated the behavior of parents in the cause of autism, it is now clear that this disorder has a *genetic component* (Smalley, 1991). If genetic factors contribute to the development of autistic disorder, it should occur in families at a high rate. A difficulty with looking at family studies in this case, however, is that people with autism seldom marry or have children, making it almost impossible to examine the children or grandchildren of these individuals. We do know, however, that families who have one child with autism have a 3% to 5% risk of having another child with the disorder. When compared to the incidence rate of autism of approximately 0.0002% to 0.0005% in the general population, this rate offers some evidence for a genetic component in the disorder (Falconer, 1965).

Several twin studies have been conducted to assess genetic influences on autistic disorder, although the disorder is so rare that finding large enough groups of people with whom to do valid research is extremely difficult. Susan Folstein and Michael Rutter (1977) studied 11 people with autism who had an identical (or monozygotic [MZ]) twin, and 10 people with autism who had a fraternal (or dizygotic [DZ]) twin. They found a concordance rate of 36% for the monozygotic twins, with 4 of the 11 twin pairs both having autism. In contrast, they found that none of the dizygotic twin pairs were concordant for autism. Folstein and Rutter

also examined these twins for the presence of other developmental and/or cognitive problems and found that the concordance rate increased to 82% for the monozygotic group and to 10% for the dizygotic group. In other words, when they looked at developmental disorders in general, they found that, if one of the monozygotic twins had autism, the other twin was highly likely to have autism or some other cognitive/developmental problem.

An important twin study was recently conducted in the Nordic countries of Denmark, Finland, Iceland, Norway, and Sweden (Steffenburg et al., 1989). Twenty-one pairs of twins (11 monozygotic and 10 dizygotic) and one set of identical triplets were examined across these five countries. The researchers tried to control for some of the limitations of the Folstein and Rutter study by using more contemporary diagnostic criteria for autism and more sophisticated methods for identifying twins as being either monozygotic or dizygotic. In the Nordic study, researchers found a much higher concordance rate for autism: 91% in monozygotic twins and 0% in the dizygotic twins. These studies and others (Ritvo, Freeman, Mason-Brothers, Mo, & Ritvo, 1985) are important because they strongly suggest that autism is an inherited disorder.

Like so many of the disorders we have examined, the exact nature of the genetic influence on autism is not yet clear to researchers. What we can be sure of is that the genetic mechanism (how autism is inherited) is not simple and may involve more than one gene. Current thinking about the genetics of autism suggests an *autosomal recessive inheritance* (Smalley, 1991). This model proposes that the inheritance involves a recessive gene (or genes) on 1 of the 22 non-sex chromosomes. A problem with this theory is the relatively large percentage of male children with autism. Why would males be more likely to be affected if the problem gene is not on one of the sex chromosomes? One reason may be that genetic heterogeneity is indicated in autism. We discussed in Chapter 2 the principle of equifinality and how there can be different causes for the same disorder. Perhaps different genetic abnormalities can result in what we call autism. For example, approximately 10% or more of the people with autism have an X-linked disorder called fragile X (see Chapter 15) or a dominant genetic disorder named *tuberous sclerosis*. The presence of these companion disorders suggests that, although the basis for autism is genetic, different abnormalities in genes may account for the autism in different people. As we continue to discuss this disorder, we will see that there is considerable heterogeneity among the people who share the label of autism.

Neurobiological Influences

Evidence that autism is associated with some form of organic or brain damage comes from a number of different areas. The most obvious hint of this involvement comes from the prevalence data showing that three of every four people with autism also have some level of mental retardation. In addition, it has been estimated that between 30% and 75% of these people display some neurological abnormality such as clumsiness and abnormal posture or gait (Tsai & Ghaziuddin, 1992). These observations provide suggestive but only correlational evidence that autism has a physical origin.

Bernard Rimland in 1964 was among the first to provide a neurobiological model of this disorder. Rimland believed that autism was a cognitive disorder resulting from malfunctioning systems in the brain stem (Rimland, 1964). Subsequent research has provided very little evidence for the involvement of the brain stem in autism, but his theory inspired others to look at the brain for explanations of the unusual behaviors observed among people with the disorder.

Only a handful of cases using postmortem brain examinations have been completed among people with autism. Although the initial studies indicated no specific structural differences in these individuals, more recent work has shown that damage in the cerebellum may be common. Edward Ritvo and his colleagues at UCLA found, in autopsies of four people with autism, that each individual had abnormalities in the cerebellum; specifically, they had fewer Purkinje cells—a particular type of cell present in this area of the brain (Ritvo, Freeman, Scheibel et al., 1986). Although their exact function is not clearly understood, the

Purkinje cells are believed to inhibit the action of other cells and may be sensitive to GABA, a major inhibitory neurotransmitter.

With the recent advent of modern brain-imaging and scanning technologies, a clearer picture of the possible neurological dysfunctions in people with autism may soon be available. One finding that also seems to support the postmortem reports just reviewed is the recent work with computerized axial tomography (CAT) and magnetic resonance imaging (MRI). If you recall from Chapter 2, these are two imaging processes that allow us to view brain structure directly without surgery or autopsy. Researchers using CAT and MRI technologies have found abnormalities in the cerebellum among people with autism; more specifically, they have observed reductions in cerebellar size. In one study, Eric Courchesne and his colleagues at the University of California at San Diego examined the brain of a 21-year-old man who had a diagnosis of autism but no other neurological disorders and a tested IQ score in the average range of intelligence (Courchesne, Hesselink, Jernigan, & Yeung-Courchesne, 1987). He was selected as a subject because he did not have the severe cognitive deficits seen in three-quarters of people with autism. Hence, the researchers could presume that he was free of any brain damage associated with mental retardation but not necessarily with autism. After obtaining the informed consent of this man and his parents, they conducted an MRI scan of his brain. Figure 16.1 shows a picture of the MRI scan of a person without autism on the left and the subject

Normal

Patient with autism

Figure 16.1 MRIs from two individuals: The person on the left has no neurological disorders, whereas the person on the right has autism. Note especially the cerebellum (lower right portion of the brain), which is noticeably smaller in the person with autism (adapted from Courchesne et al., 1987).

of Courchesne's study on the right. The most striking finding was the abnormally small cerebellum of the subject compared with that of a person without autism. Although this observation of cerebellar abnormality has not been found in every study using brain imaging, it appears to be one of the more reliable findings of brain involvement in autism to date (Courchesne, 1991). These findings may point out an important subtype of people with autism.

An Integration

There are currently few comprehensive and generally accepted models of autism that take into account the biological as well as the psychosocial influences we have discussed. Part of the reason for this lack of integration is that considerable controversy continues to exist about the definition of autism, the nature of the brain involvement, and the importance each of the deficits plays in this disorder. Proponents of the Theory of Mind model see cognitive deficits as central to the problems faced by people with this disorder. In contrast, others view problems with arousal, especially in social situations, as the root of later problems (Dawson & Lewy, 1989). In other words, their neurological deficits somehow cause these individuals to be particularly sensitive to social interactions, which make them uncomfortable. This discomfort results in their social withdrawal and difficulties in language development. As you can imagine, you wouldn't want to learn to communicate with other people if you found being around them to be excruciatingly unpleasant. The field of autism is relatively young and still awaits an integrative theory. It is likely, however, that further research will uncover the biological mechanisms that can ultimately explain the social aversion experienced by many people with the disorder. In addition, the psychological and social factors that very early in life interact with the biological influences, producing deficits in socialization and communication as well as the characteristic unusual behaviors, will need to be outlined.

Treatment of Autistic Disorder

One generalization that can be made about autism is that there is no effective treatment for it per se. We have not been successful in eliminating the social problems experienced by people with this disorder. Rather, like the approach taken with individuals having mental retardation, most efforts at treatment for people with autism focus on enhancing their communication and daily living skills and reducing problem behaviors such as tantrums and self-injury (Durand & Carr, 1988). Some of these approaches are described next, including new work on early intervention for young children with autism.

Psychosocial Treatments

Initially, psychosocial treatment efforts were more psychodynamic, encouraging ego development in individuals with autism (Bettelheim, 1967). These approaches were based on the belief that autism was the result of improper parenting. Given our current understanding about the nature of the disorder, we should not be surprised to learn that treatments based solely on ego development have not had a positive impact on the lives of people with autism (Kanner & Eisenberg, 1955). Greater success has been achieved with behavioral approaches that focus on skill building and behavioral treatment of problem behaviors. The origins of this approach to treatment are in the early work of Charles Ferster and Ivar Lovaas.

Although Ferster's view of the origins of autism is now generally discounted, he provided a valuable perspective by showing that children with this disorder responded to simple behavioral procedures (Ferster & DeMyer, 1961). Ferster used basic, single-case experimental designs and patterned his work with these children after the pigeon and rat learning experiments of B. F. Skinner. He found that he could teach children with autism very simple responses, such as putting coins in their proper slots, by reinforcing them with food (Ferster, 1961). Ivar Lovaas at UCLA took Ferster's approach further by demonstrating the clinical importance of these findings. He reasoned that if people with autism responded to reinforcers and punishers in the same way as everyone else, we should be able to use these techniques to help them communicate with us, to help them become more social, and to help them with their behavior problems. Although much refinement of this work has occurred over the past 30 years, the basic premise—that people with autism can learn and that they can be taught some of the skills they lack—remains central in the treatment of these individuals. There is a great deal of overlap between the treatment of the problems associated with autism and the treatment of problems experienced by people with mental retardation, discussed in Chapter 15. With that in mind, rather than review all the treatment work of this type, we will highlight here several areas important for people with autism, including communication and socialization.

Communication

Problems with communication and language have been among the defining characteristics of this disorder. As we saw in Timmy's case, people with autism often do not acquire meaningful speech, having either very limited speech or unusual patterns of speech, such as echolalia. Teaching people to speak in a useful way can be difficult. Think about how we teach languages: It mostly involves imitation. Imagine how you would teach a young girl to say the word *spaghetti*. You could wait for several days until she said a word that sounded something like spaghetti (maybe *confetti*), then reinforce her. You could then spend several weeks trying to "shape" this sound (confetti) into something closer to spaghetti. Or, you could just begin by making the statement, "Say 'spaghetti.'" Fortunately, most children can imitate and can learn to communicate very efficiently. But what if you are working with a child who has autism and can't or won't imitate?

In the mid 1960s Lovaas and his colleagues took a monumental first step toward addressing the difficulty of getting children with autism to respond. They used the basic behavioral procedures of *shaping* and *discrimination training* to teach these nonspeaking children to imitate others verbally (Lovaas, Berberich, Perloff, & Schaeffer, 1966). The first skill the researchers taught them was to imitate other people's speech. They would begin by reinforcing a child with food and praise for making any sound while watching the teacher. After the child mastered that step, they would reinforce the child only if she made a sound after the teacher made a request—such as the phrase, "Say 'ball'" (the procedure known as discrimination training). Once the child reliably made some sound after the teacher's request, the teacher would reinforce only

approximations of the requested sound (shaping), such as the sound of the letter "b." Sometimes the teacher would help the child by prompting her physically—in this case by gently holding her lips together to help her make the sound of "b." Once the child responded successfully, a second word was introduced—such as "mama"—and the procedure was repeated. This continued until the child could correctly respond to multiple requests, thereby demonstrating imitation (copying the words or phrases made by the teacher). Once the children could imitate, teaching them speech became easier, and progress was made in teaching some of them to use labels, plurals, sentences, and other more complex forms of language (Lovaas, 1977). Despite the success of some children in learning speech, other children have not responded to this training, and workers have sometimes used alternatives to vocal speech such as sign language and devices that have vocal output (see Chapter 15).

Socialization

One of the most striking features of people with autism is their unusual reactions to other people. One study compared rates of interacting with peers

---

Box 16.1   Facilitated Communication

Facilitated Communication:
Window on Autism, or Ouija Board?

Several years ago, Rosemary Crossley from Australia reported that she had broken the barrier between people with autism and the rest of the world with her new technique for teaching communication (Crossley, 1988). She claimed that by gently supporting their arms, she could get people to type out their innermost thoughts and fears—this from people who previously seemed to ignore the outside world. She called her technique *facilitated communication*. Think for a moment about what this could mean. What if these children and adults have struggled for years to communicate with us, but could not do so because of their disability. Now, just by having their arms supported as they type, they might be able finally to tell us all those things that have been locked up inside them. What would they tell us about themselves and about a society that tends to isolate them from the rest of the world?

Douglas Biklen, a professor of special education at Syracuse University, observed Ms. Crossley's work and decided to promote her technique in the United States. The six basic elements of facilitated communication include the following (Biklen, 1990; Crossley, 1988):

1. *Physical support.* The facilitator is taught to assist the student by stabilizing his or her hand or arm during typing. The facilitator is not instructed to help the student choose what to type, only to help him or her with the act of typing. The student's hand is pulled back from the keyboard after each selection, slowing down the movements.
2. *Initial training/introduction.* Students are given simple questions at first (for example, "What's your name?"), progressing to open-ended conversation (for instance, "How does it feel to have autism?").
3. *Maintaining focus.* The facilitator assists the student to attend to the keyboard. Prompts are given if the student looks away or if he or she is disruptive during the training.
4. *Avoid testing for competence.* Emotional support and encouragement are highlighted, and facilitators are taught to treat the student as if he or she is fully competent to communicate in a sophisticated way. Built into this aspect of facilitated communication is a deliberate restraint from any effort to determine whether it is the student or the facilitator who is responsible for what is typed. Such testing is said to cast doubt on the student's

Box 16.1   Facilitated Communication (*continued*)

ability to communicate, thereby violating the trust between the student and the facilitator.

5. *Generalizing.* Students with autism are encouraged to use their new communication skills with more than one facilitator, in an effort to generalize their ability beyond just one person.

6. *Fading.* Finally, efforts are made to encourage the students to communicate without the use of a facilitator.

Biklen watched 21 people with autism and reported that, following training in facilitated communication, all could type single words or sentences (Biklen, 1992). For example, one first grader with whom Biklen worked typed the following with his facilitator.

I AI DONT WANT TO BE AUTISTIC. NOBODY REALLY ZUNDERSTANDS WHAT IT FEELS LIKE. IT IS VERY LONELY AND I OFTEN FEEL LOUSY. MY MOOD IS BAD A LOT. I FEEL LESS LONELI WHEN I AM WITH KIDS.

i am autistic and ssick of iut because i cando anything if i am nnot autisttic. i know it is always going to be there (Biklen, 1992)

Such accounts, with their often poignant messages, misspellings, and grammatical errors, have galvanized support for facilitated communication nationwide. Because this technique can be easily applied, and because of the potential to finally "get through" to people with autism, the use of facilitated communication has spread throughout the autism community with unprecedented speed.

On the other hand, facilitated communication has also aroused the ire and indignation of those in the field who do not believe the claims made by its proponents. Two particular elements of facilitated communication have caused a great deal of concern and have fueled the controversy over this technique. First, having the facilitator hold the hand or arm of the student has caused some to liken this technique to using a "Ouija board." In other words, there is some skepticism as to whether the person with autism is really the one directing what is typed; in many cases, the facilitator is believed to influence the messages unknowingly. Could well-meaning therapists, who desperately want to reach these people, inadvertently be leading the person with autism to type out messages that instead come from the minds of the facilitator?

To answer this question one must examine the process closely and determine empirically who is producing these messages. However, there is a problem. Remember from point four that defenders of facilitated communication say it can-

not be tested empirically. Because supporters of facilitated communication "avoid testing for competence," the evidence for success of facilitated communication has come mainly from stories of "breakthroughs" with specific individuals, reported in the popular media.

If you work in this field, you are likely to be stuck in a bit of a dilemma. Do you trust facilitated communication as working, or do you wait until there is research to support its use? At first glance there may not seem to be a dilemma. Could it hurt to try to teach people with autism to communicate in this way? In some cases, it may. Along with the stories of success using facilitated communication have come some disturbing accounts, such as the case of Jerry Gherardi and his son Matthew. Seventeen-year-old Matthew has a diagnosis of autism and was introduced to facilitated communication at his New Hampshire school. During the first few weeks using this technique with his school facilitator, Matthew typed out two pages of obscenities, including the charge that he was being sexually abused by his father. Within days, an arrest warrant was issued for Matthew's father Jerry.

To test the validity of these claims, Stephen Calculator of the University of New Hampshire spent 6 hours evaluating Matthew with his facilitator. He had the facilitator wear headphones and sometimes played a distracting sound called "white noise." When Matthew was asked a question and the facilitator could also hear it, Matthew typed out the correct answer. When he was asked a question that the facilitator could not hear because of the white noise, Matthew answered incorrectly. Calculator's conclusion was that Matthew was typing only what the facilitator wanted him to type and provided no input on his own.

A growing number of claims of abuse like that against Matthew's father are emerging from people using facilitated communication, but researchers are beginning to test the validity of the claims being made by proponents of this technique. We may soon know if it is a panacea for all people with autism, or if it holds promise for an as yet unknown subgroup (Regal, Rooney, & Wandas, 1994; Smith, Haas, & Belcher, 1994). This phenomenon and the surrounding controversy highlight the importance of validating our techniques empirically. Just as people who go to physicians expect that the medical treatments they are prescribed have been demonstrated to be safe and effective, people who use the services of mental health professionals deserve the same level of accountability. We discuss this issue in more detail in Chapter 17.

Ivar Lovaas, a psychologist at UCLA, who has conducted groundbreaking work on the behavioral treatment of children with autism.

among adolescents with autism, those with Down syndrome, and those developing normally; the researchers found that the adolescents with autism showed significantly fewer interactions with their peers (Attwood, Frith, & Hermelin, 1988). Although deficits in socialization seem to be among the more obvious problems experienced by people with autism, limited progress has been achieved toward improving these skills. Some success has been observed with using behavioral procedures to increase the *rate* or frequency of behaviors such as playing with toys or with peers, although there appear to be problems in trying to improve the *quality* of these interactions (Durand & Carr, 1988). In other words, behavioral clinicians have had more difficulty teaching people with autism the more subtle social skills that are important for interactions with peers—including how to initiate and maintain social interactions that lead to meaningful relationships such as friendships.

Timing and Settings for Treatment

Lovaas and his colleagues at UCLA have recently reported on their early intervention efforts with very young children (Lovaas, 1987). One group received intensive behavioral treatment for their communication and social skills problems for 40 hours or more per week. A second group of these very young (under 3½ years of age) children with autism received less intensive behavioral treatment, averaging 10 hours or fewer of one-on-one treatment per week.

After more than 2 years of this treatment, the children were followed up to assess their progress as they entered school. The researchers reported that 47% of the group receiving the intensive treatment (40 or more hours per week) achieved normal intellectual and educational functioning and were doing well in regular first grade classes. In contrast, none of the children in the less intensive treatment group achieved this level of improvement. The 47% who improved so dramatically tended to be those children with a higher mental age at the start of treatment. A more recent follow-up of these children, who are now 11 years old, indicated that these improvements were long-lasting (McEachin, Smith, & Lovaas, 1993). These studies have created considerable interest as well as controversy, with some critics questioning the research on practical as well as experimental grounds: They claimed that providing one-on-one therapy for 40 hours per week was too expensive and time-consuming, and also criticized the studies for having no proper control group. Despite the controversy, however, the results suggest that early intervention with this disorder is promising.

Among the findings reported by Lovaas to support the improvements made by the children was school placement. He found that the children who improved most were likely to have been placed in regular classrooms in their schools, and children not doing as well were placed in separate special education classes. As we saw in the chapter on mental retardation, children with even the most severe disabilities are now being taught in regular classrooms. The current trend is away from separating children because of their disabilities. In addition, *inclusion*—the term used for the move from segregation to integration—applies not only to schools but to all aspects of life. Many different models are being used to integrate people with autism in part because of the philosophy of "normalizing" their experiences. For instance, community homes are being encouraged rather than separate residential settings, including the use of specialized foster care programs (Smith, 1992). And supported employment options are being tested to let individuals with autism work in regular jobs. The behavioral interventions discussed to this point have proven to be essential in order to ease this transition to fully integrated settings.

Biological Treatments

Just as with behavioral interventions, no one medical treatment has been documented to "cure" autism. In fact, medical intervention has produced little success in treating this disorder. A variety of pharmacological treatments have been tried to remediate some of the \problems experienced by people with autism; but, as we saw with facilitated communication, some medical treatments have been introduced and heralded as effective before research has validated their use.

The use of vitamins and dietary changes has been promoted as one approach to treating autism. One of the better studied of these nutritional approaches is the use of megavitamin therapy, with an emphasis on vitamin B_6 (pyridoxine). Although initial reports were very optimistic, with parents reporting great improvements in their children when using vitamin B_6 (Rimland, Callaway, & Dreyfus, 1978), subsequent research found little support for significant improvements in children with autism (Holm & Varley, 1989). Another of the B vitamins, folate, has been tried in a limited way as a treatment for those with autism who also have the fragile X syndrome, primarily because this vitamin has been reported to decrease the number of fragile X cells in boys with the syndrome. This research is only in its initial phase so we cannot draw any conclusions just yet, but it does show that researchers are trying to find subgroups of people with autism like those with fragile X and evaluate treatments separately in these groups (Hagerman et al., 1986).

Fenfluramine is a drug that has recently been investigated as a treatment for autism. It lowers serotonin levels in the brain and is commonly found in diet pills because it also suppresses appetite. This medication was tried with people having autism because some researchers had observed that they have elevated serotonin levels. To date, a number of studies have used this drug, including a well-controlled study across several medical centers that used the same definition of autism, the same drug dose, and the same evaluation measures (Ritvo et al., 1986). Only minor improvements on measures such as IQ and social relatedness have been observed in these studies, and usually with only a small subgroup of people. The drug appears to help some of these people by reducing hyperactivity and increasing their attention span (Groden et al., 1987), but most of the beneficial effects seem to wear off after a few months of use, making it ineffective for long-term treatment (Holm & Varley, 1989).

Because autism may result from a variety of different deficits, it is unlikely that one drug will be found to significantly improve the lives of all people with this disorder. Much of the current work is focused on finding pharmacological treatments for specific behaviors or symptoms associated with the disorder.

Integrating Treatments

The treatment of choice for people with autism involves a combination of approaches to address the many facets of this disorder. For children, most of the "therapy" is conducted in the form of education at school in combination with special psychological supports for their problems with communication and socialization. Behavioral approaches have been most helpful and most clearly documented to benefit chil-

dren in this area. Pharmacological treatments can help some of them on a temporary basis. Parents also need support because of the great demands and stressors involved in living with and caring for such children. As children with autism grow older, intervention becomes focused on efforts to integrate them into the community, often with supported living arrangements and work settings. Because the range of abilities of people with autism is so great, however, the nature of these efforts can differ dramatically. As we saw with John, he was able to live in his own apartment with only minimal support from his family. Others, who may have more severe forms of mental retardation, will require more extensive efforts to support them in their communities.

Asperger's Disorder

Asperger's disorder is characterized by impairments in social relationships and restricted or unusual behaviors or activities, but without the language delays seen in people with autism. First described by the Austrian physician Hans Asperger in 1944, this disorder has only recently received the type of scrutiny given to other pervasive developmental disorders such as autism. The inclusion of this disorder is new to DSM-IV and is controversial. Consider the following case.

The Case of Rachel

Rachel, 20 years old, is enrolled in a local community college. She is very interested in America's past and is a history major. She likes writing and is proud of some of the essays she has written for her courses. Her mother will sometimes goad her to show off her writing talents, and she happily obliges by pulling out a notebook filled with articles. As she reads, you are at once impressed with her intensity. Her eyes are wide and she smiles slightly as she presents her prose.

It's her voice that begins to reveal something different. She speaks a little too loudly, and her pitch increases to almost a screech. You get the feeling as you watch and listen to her that she isn't reading to an outside audience, *she* is her audience.

Rachel was given a diagnosis of autism some years ago because of her lack of interest in others. She never showed much interest in her peers, and her sometimes odd manner of speaking would set her apart from her classmates. Recently, a psychologist suggested that she might have a disorder known as Asperger's disorder because her language skills were not delayed.

Her scores on IQ tests have always fallen in the average range, at about 110. Despite her social difficulties, and with the encouragement of her parents, Rachel succeeded in graduating from high school and is a solid "C" student in college. She is looking forward to getting an apartment and moving out of the house. Her parents worry about what will happen to her outside their protection.

Did Rachel have autism? She seems to fit more closely another of the pervasive developmental disorders—*Asperger's disorder*. One of the concerns about this disorder is that it may be a milder form of autism rather than a separate disorder in itself. In other words, if you look at the disorder of autism on a continuum from most severe to least severe, some believe that people with Asperger's disorder are on the less severe end of the continuum. Lorna Wing in the early 1980s recommended that Asperger's disorder be reconsidered as a separate problem, with an emphasis on the unusual and circumscribed interests displayed by these individuals (Wing, 1981). The DSM-IV criteria for Asperger's disorder are listed in Table 16.2

Asperger's disorder seems to be even less frequent in the population than autism, with a prevalence rate estimated at 1 per 10,000 population. This disorder is seen more often in boys than in girls,

although accurate numbers are not yet available (Volkmar & Cohen, 1991). As we saw with Rachel, people with this disorder tend to have few cognitive impairments, and their IQ scores are usually within the average range. Rachel could converse with us, but the more subtle aspects of speech like her intonation and gestures were unusual. People with Asperger's disorder also tend to have unusual and circumscribed interests; they will engage in such activities as closely following airline schedules, memorizing ZIP codes, or listing fountains found in all parts of the world. In addition, they often exhibit clumsiness and poor coordination.

Problems with social relationships demonstrated by people with Asperger's disorder lead to comparisons between them and people with autism. Although their ability to communicate with others on a factual level is usually fine, individuals with Asperger's disorder have an unusual obsession with such things as clocks and timetables; they are generally preoccupied with these items or activities to such an extent as to exclude social interactions. Like others with this disorder, Rachel seemed to interact well with her mother but she was never able to make friends with her peers and seemed disinterested in the typical social interactions that occur between acquaintances.

The cause of this disorder is currently unclear. One reason for our relative lack of knowledge about Asperger's is that it has historically been included under the category of autism. Recently, however, researchers have begun to examine people with the diagnosis of

Table 16.2 DSM-IV Diagnostic Criteria for Asperger's Disorder

A. Qualitative impairment in social interaction, as manifested by at least two of the following:

1. Marked impairment in the use of multiple nonverbal behaviors such as eye-to-eye gaze, facial expression, body postures, and gestures to regulate social interaction
2. Failure to develop peer relationships appropriate to developmental level
3. A lack of spontaneous seeking to share enjoyment, interests, or achievements with other people (e.g., by a lack of showing, bringing, or pointing out objects of interest to other people)
4. Lack of social or emotional reciprocity

B. Restricted repetitive and stereotyped patterns of behavior, interests, and activities, as manifested by at least one of the following:

1. Encompassing preoccupation with one or more stereotyped and restricted patterns of interest that is abnormal either in intensity or focus
2. Apparently inflexible adherence to specific, nonfunctional routines or rituals
3. Stereotyped and repetitive motor mannerisms (e.g., hand or finger flapping or twisting, or complex whole-body movements)
4. Persistent preoccupation with parts of objects

C. The disturbance causes clinically significant impairment in social, occupational, or other important areas of functioning.

D. There is no clinically significant general delay in language (e.g., single words used by age 2 years, communicative phrases used by age 3 years).

E. There is no clinically significant delay in cognitive development or in the development of age-appropriate self-help skills, adaptive behavior (other than in social interaction), and curiosity about the environment in childhood.

F. Criteria are not met for another specific Pervasive Developmental Disorder or Schizophrenia.

Source: DSM-IV, APA, 1994.

Asperger's as a separate group, and this focus has led to interesting findings. For example, some evidence has been uncovered to suggest that Asperger's may be more prevalent among family members than in the general population, suggesting a possible genetic contribution (Volkmar & Cohen, 1991). Two researchers have also reported on a possible etiological link between Asperger's disorder and bipolar affective disorder (manic depression). Robert DeLong and Judith Dwyer (1988) conducted a family history study and found that the incidence of bipolar affective disorder was higher among family members of people with Asperger's disorder than would be expected in the general population. To date, no psychosocial theories have been proposed to explain the development of this disorder. Further exploration is still needed to probe the causes of Asperger's disorder and to determine whether the indications of a genetic basis can be validated.

Very little treatment research has been carried out with people diagnosed with Asperger's disorder. In general, they need the same types of support in school, at home, and later at work that we have described for people with autism. Because of their communication skills, they will have fewer difficulties academically and vocationally than will people with more severe cases of autism. Rachel is a good example of someone who was able to use the skills that she had (writing and logical thinking) to help her succeed in school. Although she needed a great deal of support from her mother, she was successful in graduating from high school and in keeping a part-time job in the school library.

Rett's Disorder

Rett's disorder is a progressive neurological disorder, primarily affecting girls, that is characterized by constant handwringing, mental retardation, and impaired motor skills (Van Acker, 1991) (see Table 16.3). These problems appear after a person has had an apparently normal start in development. The disorder has been known for only a short time, first being described by Andreas Rett in 1966. However, it was 17 years later that a published report of this disorder among 35 girls from France, Portugal, and Sweden brought Rett's disorder to the attention of the world (Hagberg, Aicardi, Dias, & Ramos, 1983). Consider the following case.

The Case of Laurie

Laurie was 9 years old, although she easily could have passed for a 4-year-old. Her big brown eyes and ever-present grin endeared her to all who worked with her. Despite her charm, Laurie didn't appear to understand much of what she heard (although her hearing was fine), and she had been assessed to have severe to profound mental retardation. Laurie didn't speak, and would breathe heavily (hyperventilation) and grind her teeth (bruxism) constantly. One of the more noticeable things about her was that she constantly moved her hands, wringing them like silent movie actors did during tense moments in old films. Neurological examinations showed that, as she grew older, she experienced increasing seizure activity. In recent years she had been having more and more difficulty walking. To help her with her balance, Laurie would walk with her legs apart, moving from side to side.

In combination with her hyperventilation, Laurie's handwringing often gave the impression that she was impatient with what was going on around her. On one occasion when she was 7, Laurie slipped and almost fell to the floor. While apparently trying to regain her balance, she reached up and grabbed her hair and pulled it. Thereafter, Laurie would not only wring her hands but would also pull her own hair. The hair

Table 16.3 DSM-IV Diagnostic Criteria for Rett's Disorder

A. All of the following:

1. Apparently normal prenatal and perinatal development
2. Apparently normal psychomotor development through the first 5 months after birth
3. Normal head circumference at birth

B. Onset of all of the following after the period of normal development:

1. Deceleration of head growth between ages 5 and 48 months
2. Loss of previously acquired purposeful hand skills between ages 5 and 30 months with the subsequent development of stereotyped hand movements (e.g., handwringing or hand washing)
3. Loss of social engagement early in the course (although often social interaction develops later)
4. Appearance of poorly coordinated gait or trunk movements
5. Severely impaired expressive and receptive language development with severe psychomotor retardation

Source: DSM-IV, APA, 1994.

pulling increased until she had pulled out much of the hair on one side of her head.

Laurie's condition continued to worsen. She needed more and more help walking, and the pace of her physical growth seemed to slow down. Her ability to understand others or to communicate with them never improved. On the positive side, she seemed to respond to some of the efforts to get her to become more social, at least to the point of looking at adults and other children more.

Much of the therapy Laurie received in her early years came before there was widespread knowledge about the disorder she had—Rett's disorder. No one knew then that her problems with walking would likely get worse, no matter how much physical therapy she received. We now know that, over time, people with Rett's disorder tend to improve in areas such as eye contact, and that she probably would have done so without intensive training. To put it simply, all the work with Laurie to improve her walking and social skills during this time probably did very little to help her overcome the problems she was experiencing. Despite the behavioral interventions being used with her, she followed the typical developmental course of Rett's disorder.

As we saw with Laurie, the pattern of skill development among girls with Rett's disorder is uneven. Their motor skills, such as walking and using their hands, and their cognitive skills seem to deteriorate progressively over time. Their social skills, however, seem to develop normally from birth, then decline between the ages of 1 and 3, then partially improve after that time. Like autism and Asperger's disorder, Rett's disorder is also relatively rare, occurring in approximately 1 per 12,000–15,000 live female births. Unlike

the other two disorders, however, Rett's disorder is observed almost exclusively in females. To date, only three cases of what appears to be Rett's disorder have been observed among males (Coleman, 1990; Philippart, 1990).

The developmental changes that occur among these females are fairly rapid and dramatic. Table 16.4 shows the different stages they experience in childhood in motor, social, and cognitive skills. Just as we saw with Laurie, there is a general deterioration in many motor functions, such as walking, that begins after the first 6 months or so of life. Loss of the ability to walk is the most serious of these. Handwringing, which is one of the more striking characteristics of these girls, also begins during this period. Although some skills seem to develop normally during these early months, the skills begin to decline sometime after the first year. Descriptions of the disorder note that social interaction improves at about the time the girls reach 2 years of age. In Laurie's case, her eye contact improved although there was no general increase in more sophisticated social interactions. Finally, the girls' cognitive skills also decline during their childhood to a level of severe to profound mental retardation.

No one has yet tried to explain the development of Rett's disorder in terms of psychological or sociocultural influences. It seems unlikely, given the pervasive and rapid deterioration of skills seen with this disorder, that psychological influences play a strong role in the etiology of this disorder. In fact, the behaviors associated with it are not readily responsive to social interventions. The affected girls do not appear to be greatly influenced by what is going on around them.

Because this disorder appears almost exclusively in females, researchers have hypothesized that it may be a genetic disorder involving the X chromosome. The disorder is quite rare, however, and relatively new to workers in this field; therefore no extensive studies of the genetics of Rett's disorder have been done. Research on the organic involvement with this disorder

Table 16.4 Stages of Rett's Disorder

Stages	Motor Development	Social Development	Cognitive Development
Stage 1 (6–18 months)	General deterioration or slowing of motor development; appearance of some hand patting, waving		
Stage 2 (1–3 years)	Loss of purposeful hand use; development of spasticity	Rapidly declining social interaction	Loss of speech and other cognitive skills
Stage 3 (2–10 years)	Progressive spasticity or rigidity with jerky movements	Improved social interaction	Severe to profound mental retardation
Stage 4 (over 10 years)	Progressive muscle deterioration; reduced mobility	Improved eye contact and attentiveness	Little expressive or receptive language

Source: Adapted from Van Acker, 1991.

has shown decreased brain weight, and CAT scans often pick up mild brain atrophy in affected girls (Volkmar & Cohen, 1991).

In retrospect, the efforts to treat Laurie's problems seem particularly ironic. Not knowing that her problems with walking were likely to become worse over time, the people who tried to help her improve were particularly frustrated by their lack of success. As we discussed earlier, treatment of pervasive developmental disorders involves addressing the skills and deficits of each person and trying to assist each one with skills training. Because these people also have severe to profound mental retardation, treatment often focuses on teaching them self-help skills and communication skills and efforts to reduce their problem behaviors (Van Acker, 1991). Despite the progressive nature of the disorder, active efforts are made to help the girls maintain some of the motor skills they do have and to help them use their abilities to the fullest.

Childhood Disintegrative Disorder

Childhood disintegrative disorder involves severe regression in language, adaptive behavior, and motor skills after a period of normal development for approximately 2 to 4 years. We saw that Rett's disorder involved a developmental regression after a period of early normal development. More than 80 years ago, Theodor Heller reported his observations of six children who experienced severe regression after developing normally for several years—with deterioration coming much later than in Rett's. The disorder Heller identified has had a variety of names over the years, including *dementia infantilis, Heller's syndrome, disintegrative psychosis,* and the current, *childhood disintegrative disorder.* This disorder, too, is new to DSM-IV and is probably the least understood of the disorders we have examined so far. Estimates of its prevalence suggest that it is very rare, occurring once in approximately every 100,000 births (Kurita, Kita, & Miyake, 1992). It also may occur more often in boys than in girls.

The DSM-IV criteria illustrated in Table 16.5 suggest that these children develop normally for at least the first 2 years of life, although researchers have noted that some have minor developmental delays early on. The regression or loss of skills experienced by people with childhood disintegrative disorder can occur in a number of areas, including the loss of speech and play skills. Because of the problems they face in social situations, these individuals behave very much like children with autism. They also have mental retardation, with some indication that their cognitive skills may be more seriously impaired than in people having autism. A recent survey in Japan found that approximately 80% of the children with this disorder showed some recovery of their lost skills after age 4, although they continued to have severe disabilities (Kurita, Kita, & Miyake, 1992).

Several factors suggest that childhood disintegrative disorder has a neurological origin. Brain activity, as measured by EEG, appears to be abnormal in almost half the cases of this disorder. The incidence of seizures is about 10% and may rise to almost one-quarter of the cases in the teenage years (Hill & Rosenbloom, 1986). Currently, no specific cause has been identified for childhood disintegrative disorder. As with the other pervasive developmental disorders, treatment of this

Table 16.5 DSM-IV Diagnostic Criteria for Childhood Disintegrative Disorder

A. Apparently normal development for at least the first 2 years after birth as manifested by the presence of age-appropriate verbal and nonverbal communication, social relationships, play, and adaptive behavior.

B. Clinically significant loss of previously acquired skills (before age 10 years) in at least two of the following areas:

    1. Expressive or receptive language
    2. Social skills or adaptive behavior
    3. Bowel or bladder control
    4. Play
    5. Motor skills

C. Abnormalities of functioning in at least two of the following areas:

    1. Qualitative impairment in social interaction (e.g., impairment in nonverbal behaviors, failure to develop peer relationships, lack of social or emotional reciprocity)
    2. Qualitative impairments in communication (e.g., delay or lack of spoken language, inability to initiate or sustain a conversation, stereotyped and repetitive use of language, lack of varied make-believe play)
    3. Restricted, repetitive, and stereotyped patterns of behavior, interests, and activities, including motor stereotypes and mannerisms

D. The disturbance is not better accounted for by another specific Pervasive Developmental Disorder or by Schizophrenia.

Source: DSM-IV, APA, 1994.

one typically involves the use of behavioral interventions, to teach affected individuals the skills they have lost, and behavioral and pharmacological treatments, to help reduce their behavior problems.

Attention Deficit/Hyperactivity Disorder

Do you know someone who "flits" from activity to activity, who starts many tasks but never finishes them, who has trouble concentrating, and who doesn't seem to be paying attention when others speak to him? If this describes someone you know, this person may have **attention deficit/hyperactivity disorder.** The primary characteristics of such people include a pattern of inattention—such as not paying attention to school or work-related tasks—and/or displaying hyperactivity-impulsivity. This pattern of deficits can significantly disrupt academic efforts as well as social relationships. Consider the following case.

The Case of Michael

Michael was a handsome 9-year-old boy who was referred to us because of his difficulties at school and at home. Michael had a great deal of energy and loved playing most sports, especially baseball. Academically, he performed adequately, although his teacher reported that his performance was worsening and she believed he would do better if he paid more attention in class. Michael would rarely spend more than a few minutes on a task without some interruption; he would get up out of his seat, rifle through his desk, or constantly ask the teacher questions. His peers were frustrated with him because he would be equally impulsive during their interactions; he never finished a game, or when playing some sport, he would try to play *all* the positions simultaneously.

At home, Michael was considered by his parents to be a "handful." His room was a constant mess because he would become engaged in some game or activity only to drop it and initiate something else. Michael's parents reported that they often scolded him for not carrying out some task, although the reason seemed to be that he would forget what he was doing rather than that he was deliberately trying to defy them. They also said that, out of their own frustration, they would sometimes grab him by the shoulders and yell "Slow down!" because his hyperactivity would drive them crazy.

Michael has many of the characteristics of attention deficit/hyperactivity disorder (ADHD), one of the most common reasons children are referred for mental health services in the United States (Frick, Strauss, Lahey, & Christ, 1993). Like Michael, people with this disorder have a great deal of difficulty sustaining their attention on a task or activity. As a result, their tasks are frequently unfinished and these individuals often seem not to be listening when someone else is speaking. In addition to this serious disruption in attention, some people with ADHD also display motor hyperactivity. Children with this disorder are often described as being fidgety in school, not being able to sit still for more than a few minutes. Michael displayed this restlessness in his classroom, which was a considerable source of concern for his teacher. It was also apparent in his interactions with his playmates, who were frustrated with his lack of patience. In addition to hyperactivity and problems sustaining attention, impulsivity—seeming to act without thinking—is a common complaint made about people with ADHD. For instance, during team meetings for his baseball team, Michael would often shout out responses to his coach's questions even before the coach had a chance to finish his sentence. The DSM-IV criteria for ADHD are listed in Table 16.6.

The symptoms of inattention, hyperactivity, and impulsivity often cause other problems that appear secondary to ADHD. Academic performance tends to suffer, especially as the child progresses in school. The cause of this poor performance is not known. It could be a result of the problems with attention and impulsivity characteristic of ADHD, or it might be caused by factors such as brain impairment that may be responsible for the disorder itself (Frick, Strauss, Lahey, & Christ, 1993). Children with ADHD are likely to be unpopular and rejected by their peers (Carlson, Lahey, & Neeper, 1984). Here, however, the difficulty appears to be directly related to the behaviors symptomatic of ADHD, as their problems of inattention, impulsivity, and hyperactivity get in the way of their establishing and maintaining friendships. Their problems with peers in combination with frequent negative feedback from parents and teachers over their behavior often result in low self-esteem among these children (Johnston, Pelham, & Murphy, 1985).

Attention deficit/hyperactivity disorder is estimated to occur in about 3% of all children (Barkley, 1981), with males outnumbering females roughly 6 to 1 (Whalen & Henker, 1980). Children with ADHD are first identified as being different from their peers around the ages of 3 and 4 years, with parents describing them as being very active, mischievous, slow to toilet train, and oppositional (Barkley, 1989). The symptoms of inattention, impulsivity, and hyperactivity become obvious during the school years. Despite the perception that

Table 16.6 DSM-IV Diagnostic Criteria for Attention Deficit/Hyperactivity Disorder

A. Either (1) or (2):

1. Six (or more) of the following symptoms of **inattention** have persisted for at least 6 months to a degree that is maladaptive and inconsistent with developmental level:

   Inattention
   a. often fails to give close attention to details or makes careless mistakes in schoolwork, work, or other activities
   b. often has difficulty sustaining attention in tasks or play activities
   c. often does not seem to listen when spoken to directly
   d. often does not follow through on instructions and fails to finish schoolwork, chores, or duties in the workplace (not due to oppositional behavior or failure to understand instructions)
   e. often has difficulty organizing tasks and activities
   f. often avoids, dislikes, or is reluctant to engage in tasks that require sustained mental effort (such as schoolwork or homework)
   g. often loses things necessary for tasks or activities (e.g., toys, school assignments, pencils, books, or tools)
   h. is often easily distracted by extraneous stimuli
   i. is often forgetful in daily activities

2. Six (or more) of the following symptoms of **hyperactivity/impulsivity** have persisted for at least 6 months to a degree that is maladaptive and inconsistent with developmental level:

   Hyperactivity
   a. often fidgets with hands or feet or squirms in seat
   b. often leaves seat in classroom or in other situations in which remaining seated is expected
   c. often runs about or climbs excessively in situations in which it is inappropriate (in adolescents or adults, may be limited to subjective feelings of restlessness)
   d. often has difficulty playing or engaging in leisure activities quietly
   e. is often "on the go" or often acts as if "driven by a motor"
   f. often talks excessively

   Impulsivity
   g. often blurts out answers before questions have been completed
   h. often has difficulty awaiting turn
   i. often interrupts or intrudes on others (e.g., butts into conversations or games)

B. Some hyperactive–impulsive or inattentive symptoms that caused impairment were present before age 7 years.

C. Some impairment from the symptoms is present in two or more settings (e.g., at school [or work] and at home).

D. There must be clear evidence of clinically significant impairment in social, academic, or occupational functioning.

E. The symptoms do not occur exclusively during the course of a Pervasive Developmental Disorder, Schizophrenia, or other Psychotic Disorder and are not better accounted for by another mental disorder (e.g., Mood Disorder, Anxiety Disorder, Dissociative Disorder, or a Personality Disorder).

Source: DSM-IV, APA, 1994.

children with ADHD "grow out" of this disorder, their problems continue, with 75% of adolescents with ADHD having ongoing difficulties at school and at home (Weiss & Hechtman, 1986). Little research on adults with this disorder is currently available, although it appears that 60% of children diagnosed with ADHD will continue to have symptoms as adults, such as difficulties concentrating (Barkley, 1989). It appears that, although the manifestations of this disorder may change as people grow older, their problems persist.

Numerous theories about the causes of ADHD have arisen over the years, but only recently has hard evidence become available on the etiology of this disorder. Research on the heritability of ADHD—including twin and adoption studies—suggests that the disorder is influenced by genetic factors (Stevenson, 1992). In one recent study, 140 probands (children with ADHD) and 120 normal controls were identified along with their first-degree relatives; the results showed that

the relatives of children with ADHD were more likely to have ADHD themselves than would be expected in the general population (Biederman et al., 1992). As with many of the other disorders, we are just beginning to explore the genetics of ADHD, and we await more detailed analyses of the mechanisms involved in this disorder.

For several decades, ADHD has been thought to involve brain damage, and this notion is reflected in the previous use of labels such as "minimal brain damage" or "minimal brain dysfunction" (Ross & Pelham, 1981). However, only in recent years has our scanning technology permitted a sophisticated assessment of the validity of this assumption. Two areas of the brain, the frontal cortex (found in the outer portion of the brain) and the basal ganglia (located deep within the brain), have recently been implicated in ADHD; specifically, a relative lack of activity in these areas of the brain has been observed among people with ADHD

(Zametkin et al., 1990). Other evidence suggests that portions of the right hemisphere may be malfunctioning among people with this disorder (Riccio, Hynd, Cohen, & Gonzalez, 1993). Researchers have yet to outline precisely the neurological mechanisms underlying the basic symptoms of ADHD, and we await further breakthroughs in this area in the years to come.

A variety of toxins, such as allergens and food additives, have been advanced as possible causes of ADHD over the years, although very little evidence supports these theories. One such theory—that food additives such as artificial colors, flavorings, and preservatives are responsible for the symptoms of ADHD—has had a substantial impact over the years. Proposed by Feingold (1975), this view was presented along with recommendations for eliminating these substances as a treatment for ADHD, referred to as the Feingold diet. Hundreds of thousands of families have put their children on this diet over the intervening years, despite evidence that it has little or no effect on the symptoms of ADHD (Barkley, 1989).

Psychological and social dimensions of ADHD have been discussed as influences on this disorder. Specifically, the negative responses by parents, teachers, and peers to the affected child's impulsivity and hyperactivity have been hypothesized to contribute to his or her feelings of low self-esteem and rejection by peers (Barkley, 1989). Years of constant reprimands by teachers and parents to behave, sit quietly, and pay attention may create a negative self-image in these children, which in turn can have a negative impact on their ability to make friends. Thus, the possible biological influences on impulsivity, hyperactivity, and attention may interact with attempts by caregivers to control these children, leading to their rejection and poor self-image. Research on the psychological and social dimensions of ADHD is currently in its infancy.

Treatment for the disorder has proceeded on two fronts: biological and psychosocial interventions. Typically, biological treatments have been used to try to reduce the children's impulsivity and hyperactivity and to improve their attentional skills. Psychosocial treatments have generally focused on broader issues such as improving their academic performance, decreasing their disruptive behavior, and improving their social skills. Although these two lines of work have typically developed independently of each other, more recent efforts have combined them to have a broader impact on people with ADHD.

Since the use of stimulant medication with children having ADHD was first described (Bradley, 1937), hundreds of studies have documented the effectiveness of this medication in reducing the "core" symptoms of the disorder. Drugs such as methylphenidate (Ritalin), d-amphetamine (Dexedrine), and pemoline (Cylert) have proven to be helpful for approximately 75% of cases in at least temporarily reducing hyperactivity and impulsivity and improving concentration on tasks (Swanson et al., 1993). In addition, these drugs seem to improve compliance and decrease negative behaviors in many of these children. On the other hand, stimulant medication does not appear to produce substantial improvement in learning and academic performance, and its effects are usually not successful over the long term.

We don't know why these stimulant medications help people with ADHD. We do know that these medications do not have a "paradoxical effect" on people with this disorder. Taking the same, low doses, children and adults with and without ADHD react in the same way to these medications. Although considerable controversy exists over the use of stimulant medications, especially for children, most clinicians recommend their temporary use, in combination with psychosocial interventions to help improve children's social and academic skills.

A portion of children with ADHD do not respond to stimulant medications, and most children who do respond do not show gains in the important areas of academics and social skills. Because of these findings and concerns over the side effects of medication (disturbed sleep and reduced appetite), researchers have applied behavioral interventions to help these children. A number of approaches have been attempted to help children both at home and in school (Fiore, Becker, & Nero, 1993). In general, the programs identify targets of intervention such as increasing the amount of time the child stays in his seat, increasing the number of math papers he completes, or increasing his appropriate play skills with peers. Reinforcement programs are then designed to reward the child for improvements, and at times to punish the child with loss of rewards for misbehavior. Although many children have benefited from these types of programs, others have not, and there is no way to predict which children will respond positively (Fiore, Becker, & Nero, 1993). In sum, both medication and behavioral interventions have shortcomings that limit their benefits for children with ADHD. Most clinicians typically recommend a combination of approaches designed to individualize treatments for children with ADHD, targeting both short-term management issues (decreasing hyperactivity and impulsivity) and long-term concerns (preventing and reversing academic decline and improving social skills). Currently, however, children with ADHD continue to pose a considerable challenge to their families as well as to the educational system.

Tic Disorders

Tics are involuntary motor movements, such as head twitching, or vocalizations, such as grunts, that often occur in rapid succession, come on suddenly, and happen in very idiosyncratic or stereotyped ways. You may be surprised to learn that between 12% and 24% of all children show some tics during their growing years, after which time most tend to disappear (Ollendick & Ollendick, 1990).

Perhaps the most startling of the tic disorders is **Tourette's disorder,** described by Gilles de la Tourette in 1885. It involves both motor and vocal manifestations. The vocal tics can be the most dramatic symptom, with the person emitting grunting noises, yelps, and sniffs. Some of the affected individuals engage in **coprolalia,** or the involuntary repetition of obscenities. Table 16.7 lists the DSM-IV criteria for Tourette's disorder. It is more commonly observed among males, and tics usually develop before the age of 14.

Oliver Sachs (1987) describes several cases of people with Tourette's disorder. An excerpt from the case of one of these individuals is included below.

Witty Ticcy Ray

When I first saw Ray he was 24 years old and almost incapacitated by multiple tics of extreme violence coming in volleys every few seconds. He had been subject to these since the age of 4 and severely stigmatised by the attention they aroused, though his high intelligence, his wit, his strength of character and sense of reality enabled him to pass successfully through school and college and to be valued and loved by a few friends and his wife. Since leaving college, however, he had been fired from a dozen jobs—always because of tics, never for incompetence—was continually in crises of one sort and another, usually caused by his impatience, his pugnacity, and his coarse, brilliant "chutzpah," and had found his marriage threatened by involuntary cries of "Fuck!" "Shit!," and so on, which would burst from him in times of sexual excitement. He was (like many Touretters) remarkably musical and could scarcely have survived—emotionally or economically—had he not been a weekend jazz drummer of real virtuosity, famous for his sudden and wild extemporisations, which would arise from a tic or a sudden compulsive hitting of a drum and would instantly be made the nucleus of a wild and wonderful improvisation, so that the "sudden intruder" would be turned to brilliant advantage. His Tourette's was also of advantage in various games, especially ping pong, at which he excelled, partly in consequence of his abnormal quickness of reflex and reaction, but especially, again, because of "improvisations," "very sudden, nervous, *frivolous* shots" (in his words), which were so unexpected and startling as to be virtually unanswerable. The only time he was free from tics was in post-coital quiescence or in sleep; or when he swam or sang or worked, evenly and rhythmically, and found "a kinetic melody," a play, which was tension-free, tic-free and free. (Sachs, 1987, p. 97)

When Gilles de la Tourette originally wrote about the cases he observed with this disorder, he also commented on the association between the tics and obsessive-compulsive behavior. He wrote about one woman whose vocal tics bothered her a great deal: "The more revolting these [vocal] explosions are, the more tormented she becomes by the fear that she will say them again; and this obsession forces these words into her mind and to the tip of her tongue" (Tourette, cited in Pauls, Towbin, Leckman, Zahner, & Cohen, 1986, p. 1180). Almost one century later, researchers have discovered that Tourette may have noted an important instance of comorbidity or coexistence of two disorders: Tourette's disorder and obsessive-compulsive disorder (see Chapter 5 for a discussion

Table 16.7 DSM-IV Diagnostic Criteria for Tourette's Disorder

A. Both multiple motor and one or more vocal tics have been present at some time during the illness, although not necessarily concurrently. (A *tic* is a sudden, rapid, recurrent, nonrhythmic, stereotyped motor movement or vocalization.)

B. The tics occur many times a day (usually in bouts) nearly every day or intermittently throughout a period of more than 1 year, and during this period there is never a tic-free period of more than 3 consecutive months.

C. The disturbance causes marked distress or significant impairment in social, occupational, or other important areas of functioning.

D. The onset is before age 18 years.

E. The disturbance is not due to the direct physiological effects of a substance (e.g., stimulants) or a general medical condition (e.g., Huntington's disease or postviral encephalitis).

Source: DSM-IV, APA, 1994.

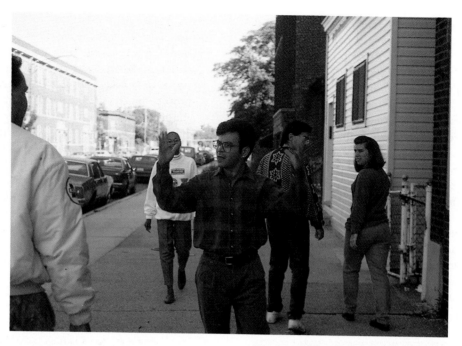

Young man with Tourette's disorder swearing and engaging in motor tics in public

of this disorder). Several studies have found increased rates of obsessive-compulsive disorder among people with Tourette's disorder as well as in their relatives (Pauls et al., 1986). The role of genetics in the etiology of Tourette's disorder is also supported by recent research suggesting that the mode of inheritance may be through a dominant gene or genes (Bowman & Nurnberger, 1993).

Both behavioral and pharmacological treatments have been used with people displaying Tourette's disorder. For a number of years one particular drug—haloperidol—has been used with some success. Haloperidol is a dopamine-blocking agent, and its success in reducing the tics associated with this disorder has led to speculation that the dopamine system is somehow involved in Tourette's disorder. Recently, two new drugs, pimozide and clonidine, have also shown some effectiveness with people experiencing this disorder, and they seem to produce fewer unpleasant side effects than haloperidol (Cohen, Riddle, & Leckman, 1992).

Clinicians have expressed some skepticism about using behavioral interventions for Tourette's disorder because of its presumed biological origins. However, some have achieved a degree of success with treatments based on behavioral principles. In a recent study, Alan Peterson and Nate Azrin used a single-case experimental design (see Chapter 4) to compare the use of three different treatments on the tics displayed by six males with Tourette's disorder (Peterson & Azrin, 1992). The ages of these males ranged from 10 years to 40 years. The re-searchers used *self-monitoring,* teaching people how to be aware of their tics; *relaxation training,* showing them how to relax the muscles involved in the tics; and *habit reversal,* having them practice a competing response to replace the tic when it occurs. Peterson and Azrin found that tics were reduced, although not eliminated, with each of these techniques. The subjects' response also varied with different treatments; some of them did better with habit reversal, while others found self-monitoring or relaxation more helpful.

Although research on using a combination of pharmacological and behavioral techniques has not yet been attempted, it seems like an obvious next step. Behavioral interventions might allow clinicians to reduce the medication needed, thereby limiting its negative side effects. Finally, because Tourette's disorder is also associated with obsessive-compulsive behaviors as well as attentional and social skills problems, combining strategies is necessary to assist these people in their daily lives.

Communication Disorders

Communication disorders appear deceptively benign, yet their presence early in life can cause wide-ranging problems later on. Several of these disorders of communication are discussed in this chapter, including *expressive language disorder, stuttering,* and *selective mutism.*

Selective Mutism

Selective mutism is a rare and puzzling disorder that involves a person's persistent failure to speak in very specific situations—such as in school—even though he or she is able to speak, and in fact does so in other situations, such as at home. Consider the following case.

The Case of Grace

Two weeks after Grace started first grade, her parents were at school, attending a meeting with her teacher and the school's social worker. Everyone was very polite and they chatted for a few minutes about the weather and the new school gym, until Grace's first grade teacher cleared her throat and began to look very concerned. "Grace doesn't talk in class," her teacher began, looking directly at Grace's mother. Her parents knew Grace tended to be shy with people she didn't know. They tried to reassure the teacher and the social worker. "She usually doesn't talk much in front of strangers," her parents said in unison. The social worker took a deep breath and tried to be tactful. "It's not that she doesn't talk *much*, it's that she doesn't talk *at all*! Not a word since she's been in this class. And, this is a little embarrassing, but we also talked to Grace's kindergarten teacher, and she doesn't remember if Grace spoke in her class either."

Grace's parents and the school staff met for several hours that afternoon to try to untangle what was happening to Grace in school and why there might be a problem. Her parents admitted that, at relatives' homes or at stores in town, they often spoke for Grace. If someone gave her something or complimented her, the parents would say thank you for her. Grace would talk to her parents in public, but often in a whisper in an apparent attempt not to let others hear what she had to say. They hadn't been too concerned about her behavior because they felt that she would "grow out of it" as she got older.

Consultation with one of us determined that Grace's problem with talking in school fit the criteria for the disorder known as *selective mutism* because she was capable of talking but chose not to do so in school. Her reticence to talk in school seemed to be part of her overall anxiety about interacting with people other than her immediate family. Grace's teacher reported that attempts to get her to speak in class by rewarding her were unsuccessful because she could "wait out" any of these efforts. Her teacher was told not to try to force her to speak in class. Instead, she gave her a pad of paper with questions and answers written on it—for example, "I need help," "May I go to the bathroom?" "Yes," "No." This system was to be used by Grace to communicate with her teacher and the rest of the class. She seemed to accept this method of communication and used it regularly. Within a few weeks, her teacher noted that Grace would say some words as she pointed to them on her pad. As instructed, the teacher did not call attention to this speech but did comment on occasion on how happy she was with Grace. By mid-semester, Grace was talking more and using her pad less, and by the end of the school year, she no longer used the pad at all.

Why would a little girl like Grace, who otherwise was a bright and likable youngster, refuse to speak? This is the puzzle of *selective mutism,* a disorder that involves a person's refusal to speak despite having the ability to do so. This problem in children was identified as early as 1877 and was first called *aphasic voluntaria* or voluntary mutism (Labbe & Williamson, 1984). We don't know how prevalent selective mutism is among all children, but estimates are that less than 1% of children referred to clinics for psychological problems have this particular disorder (Fundudis, Kolvin, & Garside, 1979). It also appears to be more prevalent among girls than boys (Frick et al., 1993), and seems to occur most often between the ages of 5 and 7 (Wilkins, 1985). Table 16.8 shows the DSM-IV criteria for this disorder.

Grace's case raises an interesting question of sexism: Did the fact that she was a girl contribute to the kindergarten teacher's failure to report her problem? Would her teacher have been more alarmed if a boy hadn't talked at school? It may well be that sexism delayed help for Grace.

Because it is rare, not much is known about selective mutism. Observations of these children have led some clinicians to assume that selective mutism is related to anxiety. Many of these children are also shy and prone to excessive crying, an observation that points to anxiety as one possible cause (Wilkins, 1985). Because the rarity of this disorder makes its study difficult, some time may elapse before we have more definitive information about the cause of selective mutism.

Research on treatment of selective mutism is usually carried out using single-case experimental designs, primarily because the disorder is so rare. In one notable exception, Calhoun and Koenig (1973) as-

Table 16.8 DSM-IV Diagnostic Criteria for Selective Mutism

A. Consistent failure to speak in specific social situations (in which there is an expectation for speaking, such as, at school) despite speaking in other situations.

B. The disturbance interferes with educational or occupational achievement or with social communication.

C. The duration of the disturbance is at least 1 month (not limited to the first month of school).

D. The failure to speak is not due to a lack of knowledge of, or comfort with, the spoken language required in the social situation.

E. The disturbance is not better accounted for by a Communication Disorder (e.g., Stuttering) and does not occur exclusively during the course of a Pervasive Developmental Disorder, Schizophrenia, or other Psychotic Disorder.

Source: DSM-IV, APA, 1994.

sessed the treatment of selective mutism among four children and compared the results with four other children in a no-treatment control group. The treatment they used with these children—*contingency management*—is commonly used in cases of this disorder. It involves giving children praise and other more tangible reinforcers for speaking while at the same time ignoring their attempts to communicate in other ways, such as by pointing or simply mouthing words. They found that the treated group improved after treatment, but they also observed some moderate improvement in the untreated children 1 year later. Perhaps some of the children with this disorder will improve on their own, possibly because their peers and teachers encourage their speech without formally conducting a "treatment."

In a more recent study, Edward and Marya Pecukonis (1991) treated the selective mutism of one 7-year-old African-American boy. They first encouraged him to attend to his teacher by reinforcing him with praise and tokens that he could trade for things he liked. They used the same strategy to encourage him to imitate them, saying single words such as "dog," and later to answer open-ended questions such as "How do you take care of your dog?" This

young boy successfully increased his attention and his speech once training had begun. There appears to be very little pharmacological research in this area. Most of the research involves the types of behavioral treatments just described.

Note that some children refuse to speak only in school while others may have problems with particular people or other particular places. Additionally, refusal to speak may occur because of the child's anxiety or for other reasons such as the positive attention he or she receives from friends and teachers for withdrawing.

Stuttering

Stuttering—a disturbance in speech fluency—has been recognized throughout history (Brady, 1991). People who stutter have a number of problems with speech, such as repeating syllables or words, prolonging certain sounds, making obvious pauses in speech, or substituting words to replace ones that are difficult to articulate. The DSM-IV criteria for stuttering are described in Table 16.9.

Table 16.9 DSM-IV Diagnostic Criteria for Stuttering

A. Disturbance in the normal fluency and time patterning of speech (inappropriate for the individual's age), characterized by frequent occurrences of one or more of the following:

1. Sound and syllable repetitions
2. Sound prolongations
3. Interjections
4. Broken words (e.g., pauses within a word)
5. Audible or silent blocking (filled or unfilled pauses in speech)
6. Circumlocutions (word substitutions to avoid problematic words)
7. Words produced with an excess of physical tension
8. Monosyllabic whole-word repetitions (e.g., "I-I-I see him")

B. The disturbance in fluency interferes with academic or occupational achievement or with social communication.

C. If a speech-motor or sensory deficit is present, the speech difficulties are in excess of those usually associated with these problems.

Source: DSM-IV, APA, 1994.

We know that stuttering occurs twice as frequently among boys as among girls and begins most often in children under the age of 3 (Yairi & Ambrose, 1992); 98% of the cases of stuttering occur before the age of 10 (Mahr & Leith, 1992). The developmental course of stuttering is important in selecting treatment. In general, approximately 80% of children who stutter before they are school age will no longer stutter after they have been in school a year or so (Yairi & Ambrose, 1992). This observation has important implications for treatment, as intervention may not be necessary for many preschool children who stutter.

Ann Landers, the advice columnist, once responded to a letter from someone who stuttered (she used the term "stammer") in the following way: "Stammering is not a sickness. It is a speech problem often caused by an unresolved emotional problem" (*Washington Post,* March 1, 1991). Her comments about stuttering reflect the view that many laypersons have about this problem. People who stutter are seen as anxiety-ridden individuals who are so troubled that they can't get their words to come out right. Although anxiety has played a major role in theories of stuttering, recent research refutes anxiety as a causal factor. Research conducted in the Netherlands found stutterers to be less anxious than a comparable group of people with social phobias (Kraaimaat, Janssen, & Van Dam-Baggen, 1991). A study by Susan Miller and Ben Watson, which looked at both male and female stutterers ranging in age from 16 to 68, also found that stuttering was not related to anxiety (Miller & Watson, 1992). The researchers found that the subjects' anxiety was limited to those times when they needed to communicate. In other words, anxiety didn't make them stutter, but stuttering made them anxious—a rational response to an often negative experience.

Family studies of stuttering typically show that this speech problem runs in families, suggesting that something in the family life could contribute to stuttering or that genetics plays a role in the disorder. A recent report suggests that genetics accounts for 71% of the cause of stuttering, with 29% being the result of the environment (Andrews, Morris-Yates, Howie, & Martin, 1991).

Attitudes of people toward stuttering can determine whether they seek treatment. In a cross-cultural study of attitudes toward speech disorder, Linda Bebout and Bradford Arthur (1992) questioned people from various cultures about their views of stuttering. They found that people from Asian cultures, more than their North American counterparts, tended to view stuttering as something that should be controlled by the people with the disorder. Figure 16.2 shows the responses of various groups to the statement, "Severe adult stutterers could stutter less if they tried hard." Bebout and Arthur also found that people from cultures outside of North America were more likely to say that people who stuttered were being punished by God and were emotionally disturbed. Depending on the culture, treatment may not be offered; if available, the focus of treatment may vary greatly from one culture to another.

A number of drugs have been tried to help people control their stuttering. Haloperidol, the drug used for people with Tourette's disorder, seemed to be somewhat successful initially. However, its negative side effects—which include dizziness, feeling "drugged," and more serious problems with motor control—outweigh any benefit it offers. There have

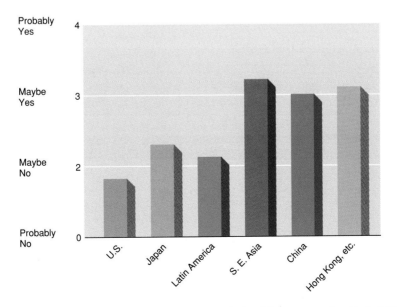

Figure 16.2   The ratings of people across six cultures about their beliefs of the causes of stuttering. Their responses to the statement, "Severe adult stutterers could stutter less if they tried hard" are presented (from Bebout & Arthur, 1992).

been recent reports that a drug called verapamil—a medication used to treat cardiac arrhythmia—may decrease the severity of stuttering in some individuals (Brady, 1991).

Psychological treatments are commonly used for people who stutter. One frequently recommended approach has been to counsel parents about how they talk to their children who stutter. They are usually taught to speak to their children more slowly, to use shorter and less complex sentences, and to allow more time for conversations. The assumption underlying this strategy is that speaking too quickly and in a more complex way can worsen children's stuttering (Conture, 1990). Recent work, however, seems to suggest that treatments based on this philosophy may have no positive impact on children's stuttering (Ratner, 1992).

One behavioral treatment that may hold more promise as an aid to stutterers is called the *regulated-breathing method.* In this technique, developed by Azrin and Nunn (1974), the person is instructed to stop speaking when a stuttering episode occurs and then to take a deep breath (exhale then inhale) before proceeding. A recent evaluation of this technique using single-case experimental designs suggested that it could greatly reduce stuttering among children (Gagnon & Ladouceur, 1992).

Although stuttering is relatively common among children and can persist into adulthood with very negative consequences for affected people, there are relatively few well-controlled treatment studies of this disorder. Because of the possible negative side effect of drugs, psychological treatments are most often recommended. Stuttering, however, continues to be difficult to treat (Ingham, 1990).

Expressive Language Disorder

The selective mutism that we saw illustrated by our case description of Grace involved the lack of speech in some situations but not in others. Children who have **expressive language disorder,** by comparison, have very limited speech in *all* situations. These children do not seem to have the types of cognitive deficits that lead to language problems in people with mental retardation or one of the pervasive developmental disorders. In fact, one of the defining characteristics of this disorder is that, **expressive language** of these children (what they say) is significantly below their usually average **receptive language** (what they understand). A 2½-year-old boy with this disorder, for example, might understand and respond to everything his parents say to him, but may use only four words to communicate with others. These children are delayed in learning to talk. Criteria for expressive language disorder are shown in Table 16.10.

Approximately 2.2% of the population of 3-year-olds are estimated to have expressive language disorder (Silva, 1980). Boys are almost five times as likely as girls to have this problem, and the affected children may be more likely to have other types of behavior problems such as aggressiveness and noncompliance (Whitehurst et al., 1988).

The etiology of the disorder has been recently studied in a number of ways. One *psychological* explanation for these language problems is that the children's parents may not speak to them enough, or may not require them to speak in complex ways, such as in complete sentences, with the resulting delays observed in these children. In one study, Russ Whitehurst and his colleagues (1988) studied the verbal interactions of families who had a child with expressive language disorder. They compared them with families having children of the same age but with no language problems and families with younger children who had expressive language abilities similar to those of the children with expressive language disorder. The researchers found that the parents changed the way they spoke to their children depending on their children's abilities. If their child spoke using only a few words, the parents tended to simplify their own speech. This was true for both the families with a child who had the

---

Table 16.10 DSM-IV Diagnostic Criteria for Expressive Language Disorder

A. The scores obtained from standardized individually administered measures of expressive language development are substantially below those obtained from standardized measures of both nonverbal intellectual capacity and receptive language development. The disturbance may be manifest clinically by symptoms that include having a markedly limited vocabulary, making errors in tense, or having difficulty recalling words or producing sentences with developmentally appropriate length or complexity.

B. The difficulties with expressive language interfere with academic or occupational achievement or with social communication.

C. Criteria are not met for Mixed Receptive-Expressive Language Disorder or a Pervasive Developmental Disorder.

D. If Mental Retardation, a speech-motor or sensory deficit, or environmental deprivation is present, the language difficulties are in excess of those usually associated with these problems.

Source: DSM-IV, APA, 1994.

disorder and the families who had younger children. The researchers concluded that the problems these children have with speech is *not* brought on by the way their parents speak to them. It seems that, although the parents adapt to their children's speech, the children are not changing the way they speak because of their parents (Whitehurst et al., 1988).

One *biological* theory of expressive language disorder involves the role of *otitis media* (middle ear infection). By the age of 3, approximately two-thirds of all children have had at least one episode of this illness. Because this type of infection can lead to temporary or chronic hearing problems, it can also result in delays in language development. Recent longitudinal research has followed children with expressive language disorder and has examined the incidence in them of otitis media (Lonigan, Fischel, Whitehurst, Arnold, & Valdez-Menchaca, 1992). The researchers found that in some children, having had otitis media during a crucial point in language development (between 12 and 18 months) seemed to contribute to the disorder, but this group also seemed to improve rapidly. In other words, the ear infection could have led to delays in language development, but once the infection was over, the children rapidly caught up in their speech development. A second group of children with the disorder did not appear to be directly affected by otitis media. This group was also *less* likely to improve their language abilities over time. This research points to the role of one biological factor—middle ear infection—as a contributory cause of expressive language disorder in some children.

In the case of expressive language disorder, it may be important to ask *whether* children with this problem should be treated before we ask *how* it should be done. The reason for this change in focus comes from an elegant series of studies conducted over several years with children having expressive language disorder (Whitehurst, Fischel, Arnold, & Lonigan, 1992). In this research, a home-based parent training package was used whereby the parent served as the therapist to help improve the child's expressive speech. The inter-

vention was initially successful in improving the speech of the children in the study. The researchers followed these children several years later and found that by 5½ years of age, children with expressive language disorder had improved *regardless of whether they had received treatment*. In effect, expressive language disorder may be "self-correcting" and may not require special intervention. It is not clear yet whether the children who did receive early intervention benefited in some way that was not measured. However, this type of research again points to the importance of studying disorders and the effects of treatments over time in order to understand the developmental course of the disorder. It may not always be necessary to invest large amounts of time and money on treatments for problems that may simply reflect differences in development and that may resolve themselves on their own.

Conclusions

Research on children and their disorders over the past decade has accelerated, as has our understanding of these developmental disorders. Despite the advances, however, integrative work on the etiology of, and treatment for, many of these disorders lags behind work on the other disorders we have reviewed in this text. Although there are probably many reasons for this situation, it fits with a larger pattern of neglect of childhood disorders in the past. Typically, research on the problems of children has not received the attention or the money comparable to that devoted to research on adult disorders and has therefore not advanced as quickly. This situation is particularly disturbing when we consider that working with children who have problems can often eliminate or at least reduce the negative impact of these problems in later years. We hope that greater emphasis will be placed on studying *all* the disorders as they are manifested in childhood as well as efforts at early intervention for these conditions.

Summary

- Developmental psychopathology is the study of how disorders arise and change with time. These changes, for the most part, follow a pattern, with the child developing one skill before acquiring the next. This pattern of change—although only one aspect of development—is an important concept because it implies that any disruption in the development of early skills will, by the very nature of the developmental process, also disrupt the development of later skills.

- Autistic disorder, Rett's disorder, Asperger's disorder, and childhood disintegrative disorder are considered types of *pervasive developmental disorders*. People with these conditions all experience problems with development; namely, they have trouble progressing in areas such as language, socialization, and cognition. The use of the word *pervasive* means that these are not relatively minor problems of development (as learning disabilities are), but are conditions that significantly affect how individuals will live.

• *Autistic disorder,* or autism, is a childhood disorder characterized by significant impairment in social interactions, gross and significant impairment in communication, and restricted patterns of behavior, interest, and activities.

• Autistic disorder probably does not have a single cause; instead, a number of biological conditions may contribute to this disorder, and these, in combination with psychosocial influences, result in the unusual behaviors displayed by people with autism.

• *Asperger's disorder* is characterized by impairments in social relationships and restricted or unusual behaviors or activities, but it does not present the language delays observed in people with autism.

• *Rett's disorder,* almost exclusively observed in females, is a progressive neurological disorder that is characterized by constant handwringing, mental retardation, and impaired motor skills.

• *Childhood disintegrative disorder* involves severe regression in language, adaptive behavior, and motor skills after a period of normal development for approximately 2 to 4 years.

• The primary characteristics of people with *attention deficit/hyperactivity disorder* are a pattern of inattention—such as not paying attention to school or work related tasks—and/or hyperactivity–impulsivity. These deficits can significantly disrupt academic efforts as well as social relationships.

• *Tics* are involuntary motor movements, such as head twitching, or vocalizations, such as grunts, that often occur in rapid succession, come on suddenly, and happen in very idiosyncratic or stereotyped ways.

• *Tourette's disorder,* a variety of tic disorder, involves both motor and vocal forms. The most dramatic symptom is the vocal tics, such as grunting noises, yelps, and sniffs. Some of the affected individuals engage in *coprolalia,* or the involuntary repetition of obscenities.

• *Selective mutism* is a disorder that involves a person's refusal to speak despite having the ability to do so.

• *Stuttering* is a disturbance in speech fluency.

• Children who have *expressive language disorder* have very limited speech in *all* situations. These children do not seem to have the types of cognitive deficits that lead to language problems in people with mental retardation or one of the pervasive developmental disorders.

Key Terms

Asperger's disorder (657)

attention deficit/hyperactivity
  disorder (662)

autistic disorder (642)

childhood disintegrative disorder
  (661)

coprolalia (665)

expressive language (670)

expressive language disorder (670)

pervasive developmental disorders
  (641)

receptive language (670)

Rett's disorder (659)

selective mutism (667)

stuttering (668)

tics (664)

Tourette's disorder (665)

Everyone's future is, in reality, an urn full
of unknown treasures from which all
may draw unguessed prizes.
Lord Dunsany
"Nothing is Final"

17

Mental Health Services and Society: Legal, Ethical, and Professional Issues Affecting Research and Practice

In Chapter 14 we introduced Arthur—the young man who suddenly experienced the delusion that he could "save the world" and who had *brief psychotic disorder.* If you remember, Arthur's family was devastated by the drastic changes he was going through, including his delusions of grandeur and his plan to break into the German embassy; they desperately sought help for him. They contacted a local mental health facility, described Arthur's condition, and asked that he be admitted. His family was astonished to learn that, despite his marked psychotic state and the possibility that he might hurt himself or hurt someone else in trespassing on embassy property, the hospital would not pick Arthur up or even admit him involuntarily. The family was told that, because Arthur had not in actuality hurt himself or someone else, he had to seek help on his own before the hospital would give him any assistance, even though everyone involved realized that such action on his part was very unlikely. This response by the mental health system added one more layer of helplessness to the family's already desperate emotional state.

Why wouldn't the mental health facility admit Arthur, who was clearly out of touch with reality and in need of help? Why couldn't his own family give permission for the mental health facility to act? What would have happened if Arthur had entered the German embassy and hurt someone, or worse yet, killed someone? Would he have gone to jail, or would he have received help then from the mental health community? Would Arthur have been held responsible for hurting other people while he was in this delusionary condition? These are just a few of the many issues that surface when you try to balance the rights of people who have psychological disorders and the responsibilities of society and the mental health profession to provide care for these individuals.

Mental health professionals daily face questions such as those above. Not only must practitioners try to understand psychological disorders and develop effective treatments for people who have them; they must also consider individual and societal rights and responsibilities. As we describe how systems of ethics and legal concepts have arisen over the years, remember that these concepts *change* with time and with changing societal perspectives on mental illness. How we treat people with psychological disorders is in part a function of how society views these individuals. For example, are people with mental illness in need of help and protection, or is society in need of protection from them? As public opinion of people with mental illness changes, so too do the laws affecting them. We therefore should be reminded of the evolving nature of these concepts as we explore current societal views.

Different cultures vary considerably in their treatment of people with severe mental illness. This "mental hospital" in Somaliland houses people with mental illness for life.

In this chapter, consistent with the scientist-practitioner approach to abnormal behavior that we have adopted throughout this text, we address legal and ethical issues that have an effect on both research and practice. As you will see, many times the issues affecting research and practice are complementary. For instance, the protections important for a person who is the subject of a research study are similar to the protections required for a person who is receiving psychological services. In just one example, confidentiality—the protection of a person's identity as a participant in a research study or as a patient seeking help for a psychological disorder—is an important concern for both the researcher and the practitioner. And because people receiving mental health services are often simultaneously participants in research studies, the concerns of both constituencies are important for us to consider.

We start with a discussion of legal concerns that have an effect on people with mental illness, beginning with those first introduced with Arthur, as his family tried to get help for him despite his denial of a need for assistance. We then discuss issues that arise when people with psychological disorders also commit criminal offenses—including how to assess a person's competency to stand trial and the use of the insanity defense. The discussion of legal issues is followed by ethical concerns facing scientist-practitioners, such as the nature of their relationships with subjects or patients. Finally, we discuss an important contemporary issue: The major changes occurring in the practice of psychotherapy. These discussions are presented to show how societal concerns interact with the work we have outlined throughout the previous chapters.

Legal and Ethical Issues

The legal system, for better or for worse, exercises significant influence over the mental health system. Laws have been enacted over the years to provide protection for people displaying abnormal behavior as well as for society as a whole. Often, achieving this protection is a delicate balancing act, sometimes thought to be tipped in favor of the rights of people with psychological disorders and at other times in favor of society at large. For example, laws concerning civil commitment, described next, protected Arthur from being forced into a mental health facility involuntarily, but they also potentially put him and others at risk by not compelling him to get help. La Fond and Durham (1992) have argued that two clear trends in mental health law are evident in the recent history of the United States. According to these authors, a "liberal era" occurred from 1960 to 1980, a period characterized by a commitment to individual rights and fairness. In contrast, 1980 to the present has been a "neoconservative era," partly as a reaction to the liberal reforms of the 1960s and 1970s, and has focused on majority concerns as well as law and order. Simply put, in the liberal era, the rights of people with mental illness dominated; in the neoconservative era, these rights have been limited to provide greater protection to society. As we discuss legal precedents that affect people with mental illness, remember that the political and social climate influences how the rights of individuals are interpreted by our society and that these rights have changed and will continue to change over time.

Professional behavior is dictated by laws developed at both the state and federal levels as well as by ethical principles outlined by professional organizations such as the American Psychological Association and the American Psychiatric Association. Several of the issues we discuss in this section are not addressed by the legal system but nonetheless require our attention and careful consideration. Included here are the proper behavior of mental health professionals in such roles as expert witnesses and the way people are treated in treatment and as subjects in research. We review these ethical concerns as well as legal issues next.

Civil Commitment

Fearing that Arthur might harm himself or others, his family tried to have him involuntarily committed to a mental health facility. Hospital officials, however, decided that because he was not in imminent danger of hurting himself or others Arthur could not be committed against his will. This decision wasn't an arbitrary one; in fact, each state has what are called **civil commitment laws**—laws that determine the conditions under which

a person is certified legally to have a mental illness and therefore should be placed in a hospital, sometimes in conflict with the person's own wishes. In a second type of commitment, **criminal commitment,** people who are accused of committing a crime are held in a mental health facility for assessment to determine whether they are fit to participate in legal proceedings against them; also this is the procedure used to detain those who have been determined to be not guilty of a crime by reason of insanity.

Civil commitment laws in the United States date back to the late 19th century. Before this time, almost all people with severe mental illness were cared for at home by family members or the community at large, or were left to care for themselves. A major change in caring for people with mental disorders came about in the latter half of the 19th century with the development of a large public hospital system devoted to providing treatment for such individuals. Unfortunately, with the availability of these hospitals came an alarming trend—involuntary commitment of people for reasons that were unrelated to mental illness (La Fond & Durham, 1992). There were even instances in which women were committed to psychiatric hospitals by their husbands simply for holding differing personal or political views. One such woman, Mrs. E. P. W. Packard, crusaded for better civil commitment laws after being involuntarily confined to a psychiatric hospital for 3 years (Weiner & Wettstein, 1993). Although all of us would probably agree that committing people to a mental health facility because of differing beliefs would

Here a woman faced with an unwanted pregnancy contemplates suicide. Sometimes it is not so clear when a person is in imminent danger of doing harm to themselves or others.

A man with schizophrenia being held in a high security prison. The criminal justice system is often ill prepared to deal with people who have severe mental illness.

be inappropriate, we would also agree that careful consideration should be made in determining whether or when people should be held in these institutions against their will.

Historically, states have permitted commitment when several conditions have been met: (a) The person has a "mental illness" and is in need of treatment, (b) the person is dangerous to himself or herself or others, and/or (c) the person is unable to care for himself or herself, a situation referred to as having a "grave disability." The way these conditions are interpreted has varied over the years and has always been controversial. It is important to see how the government justifies its right to act against the wishes of an individual—in this case, to commit someone to a mental health facility. The state takes on this control of its citizens under two types of authority: police power and *parens patriae* ("parent of the country") power. Under police power, the government takes responsibility for protecting the public health, safety, and welfare, and can create laws and regulations to ensure this protection. Criminal offenders are held in custody under this authority if they are a threat to society. The state also applies *parens patriae* power in circumstances in which citizens are not likely to act in their own best interest. This principle is used by the state to assume custody of children who have no living parents. Similarly, it is used to commit individuals with severe mental illness to mental health facilities in certain situations: when it is believed that they might be harmed because their mental state interferes with their ability to secure the basic necessities of life (such as food, shelter)—a condition labeled grave disability—or because they do not recognize their need for treatment (Brakel, Parry, & Weiner, 1985). Under *parens patriae*

power, the state acts as a surrogate parent, presumably acting in the best interests of a person who needs help because of his or her disturbed mental state.

Always, a person in need of help can voluntarily request to be admitted to a mental health facility; and after an evaluation by a mental health professional, he or she may be accepted for treatment. However, when an individual does not voluntarily seek this type of help, but friends, relatives, or others feel that treatment or protection is necessary, a formal process of civil commitment can be initiated. The specifics of this process differ from state to state, but it usually begins with a petition by a relative or mental health professional to a judge. The court may then request that an examination of the person be conducted to assess his or her psychological status, ability to care for himself or herself, need for treatment, and potential for harm. The judge then takes this information into consideration and decides on the appropriateness of commitment. This process is similar to other legal proceedings, and the person under question has all the rights and protections provided by the law. In most states the person can even request that a jury hear the evidence and make a determination of commitment. In all cases, the person must be notified that the civil commitment proceedings are taking place, must be present during the trial, must have representation by an attorney, and can examine the witnesses and request an independent evaluation. These safeguards are built into the civil commitment process to guarantee the rights of the person being examined and to ensure that no one is involuntarily committed to a psychiatric facility for other than legitimate reasons.

In emergency situations, when it is clear that the person or others are in immediate danger, there can be a short-term commitment without the formal proceedings required of a civil commitment. Family members, or sometimes police officers, certify that the person is presenting a clear and present danger to himself or to others (Weiner & Wettstein, 1993). In Arthur's case, his family was unsuccessful in having him admitted on an emergency basis because it was not clear that anyone was in immediate danger, only that someone *might* be hurt. Again, decisions about what is a "clear and present danger" sometimes require a great deal of subjective judgment from the court and mental health professionals.

The Definition of Mental Illness

The term *mental illness* figures prominently in this discussion of civil commitment, and it's important to define the concept in the legal system. Mental illness is not synonymous with psychological disorder; in other words, receiving a DSM-IV diagnosis does not necessarily mean that a person fits the *legal* definition of mental illness. Each state has its own definition of mental illness, usually meant to include people with severe disturbances that negatively affect their health and safety. For example, New York's Mental Hygiene Law states: "'Mental illness' means an affliction with a mental disease or mental condition which is manifested by a disorder or disturbance in behavior, feeling, thinking, or judgment to such an extent that the person afflicted requires care, treatment and rehabilitation" (New York Mental Hygiene Law, 1992). In contrast, Connecticut's law states: " 'Mentally ill person' means a person who has a mental or emotional condition which

has substantial adverse effects on his or her ability to function and who requires care and treatment, and specifically excludes a person who is an alcohol-dependent person or a drug-dependent person" (Connecticut Gen. Stat. Ann., 1992). Many states exclude mental retardation or substance-related disorders from the definition of mental illness. Overall, there is considerable ambiguity in these definitions about what constitutes a "mental condition" or what are "adverse effects on his or her ability to function." This ambiguity allows for some flexibility in making decisions on an individual basis, but it also leaves open the possibility of subjective impression and bias as influences on these outcomes.

Dangerousness

We have used the phrase "dangerous to others" a number of times throughout this discussion of civil commitment, and it is important to call attention to the controversy surrounding this concept. One related issue involves whether people with mental illness are themselves more dangerous or more prone to violent behavior than is the general population. The popular media often depict these individuals as more violent but the justification for doing so can be questioned. Such portrayals are important for the issue of civil commitment because they could bias any determination of **dangerousness,** unfairly linking dangerousness with having a severe mental illness. Put another way, people could be presumed violent solely on the basis of their mental status. Research on this question is mixed, with some studies showing no unusual association between mental illness and violence (Steadman & Ribner, 1980;

Larry Hogue, a homeless man who was involuntarily committed to Creedmor Psychiatric Hospital, has terrorized a particular New York City neighborhood for several years. On the left is Mr. Hogue under the influence of drugs threatening his neighbors; on the right is the same man off drugs and able to control his outbursts.

Teplin, 1985) and others finding a slightly greater risk for violence among people with mental illness (Lindquist & Allebeck, 1990). One difficulty with interpreting the results of these studies is that they often use varying definitions of mental illness, so it is not clear whether people with a specific disorder or symptoms are or are not at greater risk for violence. Recently this concern was addressed in a rare prospective study of 728 randomly selected male jail detainees (Teplin, Abram, & McClelland, 1994). The researchers assessed individuals who were being held for violent crimes between November 1983 and November 1984 and then collected arrest data on them over the next 6 years. They found that among the whole population arrested for violent crimes, nearly half were rearrested during the intervening 6 years. However, they also found that having mental illness did not increase the likelihood of a person's being arrested again for violent crimes, casting suspicion on previous findings of such an association.

One explanation for the discrepancy comes from a more detailed analysis of the data from the Teplin study. The researchers found that although having a mental illness in general did not increase the likelihood of future violence—defined as rearrest for a violent crime—specific symptoms did slightly increase the rate of violence. Specifically, persons suffering from hallucinations and delusions were more likely than others in the study population to have a higher number of arrests. This study suggests that even previously violent individuals with mental illness are not necessarily going to commit violent crimes after they are released, although having certain symptoms may increase the risk.

Returning to the general issue of dangerousness, how do you determine whether a person is dangerous to others? How accurate are mental health professionals at predicting who will and who will not later be violent? The answers to these questions bear directly on the process of civil commitment—and as we will see later, on criminal commitment—as well as protection for society against potentially dangerous individuals. If we can't accurately predict dangerousness, how can we justify involuntary commitment?

A series of studies conducted in the 1970s further compounds the dilemma. Even among individuals with characteristics suggesting future violence, such as having violent histories, only about 20% to 40% were identified later as engaging in violent acts (Cocozza & Steadman, 1976; Ennis & Litwack, 1974). These findings were used to suggest that dangerousness could not be reliably predicted because 60% to 80% of the people would register as false positives—people who would be inaccurately identified as being at risk for committing violent acts when they would not later do so (Grisso & Appelbaum, 1992). However, the courts do not require absolute certainty that a person will commit a violent act; there is often a great deal of leeway in determining

dangerousness. As an example, civil commitment in the state of Massachusetts requires a "likelihood of serious harm" defined as a "substantial risk of physical harm" (Massachusetts General Laws, Ch. 123, Sec. 1). In other words, something less than 100% certainty is required to judge someone dangerous, although the degree of certainty is not absolutely clear.

Research suggests that we are better at assessing relative risk—the information required of the legal system—than determining dangerousness on a case-by-case basis (Grisso & Appelbaum, 1992). Stated in another way, mental health professionals are able to identify groups of people who are at greater risk than the general population for being violent—such as having both a previous history of violence and drug or alcohol dependence—and can advise the court system about this risk. What we cannot do at the present time is predict with certainty whether a particular person will or will not be violent in the future.

The points discussed thus far should show clearly that there are significant problems with the process of civil commitment. In particular, deciding whether a person has a mental illness and/or is dangerous requires considerable subjective judgment, and because of varying legal language, this determination can be different from state to state. These problems have resulted in a number of significant legal developments. We next describe how the difficulties in this process have been addressed over the years and show that changes in the civil commitment procedures have resulted in significant economic and social consequences, including the impact on one of our more important social problems—homelessness.

The Supreme Court and Civil Commitment

In 1957, the parents of Kenneth Donaldson had him committed, under civil commitment procedures, to the Florida State Hospital for treatment of paranoid schizophrenia. Donaldson was not considered dangerous, and although he had repeated offers to be placed in a halfway house or with a friend, Dr. O'Connor, the superintendent of the hospital, refused to release him for almost 15 years, during which time he received virtually no treatment (Donaldson, 1976). Donaldson successfully sued Dr. O'Connor for damages, winning $48,500. In deciding the case, the Supreme Court found that "a State cannot constitutionally confine . . . a nondangerous individual who is capable of surviving safely in freedom by himself or with the help of willing and responsible family and friends" (*O'Connor v. Donaldson*, 1975).

With this and a subsequent decision known as *Addington v. Texas* (1979), the Supreme Court said that more than just a promise of improving one's quality of life is required to commit someone involuntarily. If nondangerous persons can survive in the community with the help of others, they should not be detained against their will. The effect of this decision was to limit substantially the government's ability to commit individuals unless they were dangerous (La Fond & Durham, 1992). Being in need of treatment or having grave disability was not sufficient to involuntarily commit someone with a mental illness.

Criminalization of the Mentally Ill

With tightened restrictions on involuntary commitment—a philosophy that prevailed in the 1970s and 1980s—there was a concern that many people who would normally have been committed to mental health facilities for treatment were now instead being handled by the criminal justice system. In other words, people with severe mental illness were now living in the community, but many were not receiving the mental health services they needed and would eventually run afoul of the legal system because of their behavior. This "criminalization" of the mentally ill was of great concern, because the criminal justice system was not prepared to care for these individuals (Teplin, 1984). Family members were increasingly frustrated that they couldn't obtain help for their loved ones— because, as in Arthur's case, mental health facilities were reluctant to commit these people involuntarily

except under the most extreme circumstances—and the families worried that these individuals were instead languishing in jail without the services they needed.

Deinstitutionalization and Homelessness Among the Mentally Ill

In addition to concerns about criminalization, two other trends also began to emerge at this time: the increase in the number of people who were homeless and the movement of people with severe mental illness out of institutions (**deinstitutionalization**). Homelessness, although not exclusively a problem of the mentally ill, is affected by society's changing views of people with mental illness. Ronald Reagan, former president of the United States, once remarked, "The homeless are homeless, you might say, by choice" (Bassuk, 1984). Obviously, few people living in our society would choose to be homeless, but it is difficult to evaluate people who are homeless accurately because of the transient nature of this population. Rough estimates place their numbers at between 250,000 and 3 million in the United States today (Morse, 1992). We know that people who are homeless are a diverse group, having arrived at this state by a variety of routes.

A combination of factors, such as economic conditions, drug use, and mental health status, account for the alarmingly high number of homeless persons in the United States.

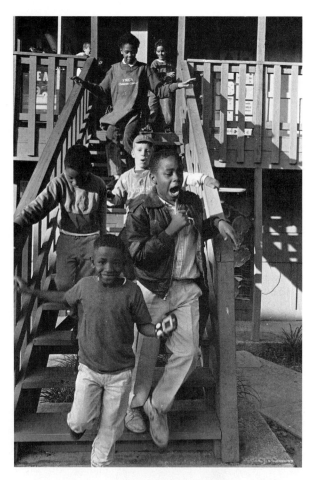

At this Jacksonville, Florida facility, homeless mothers and their families are provided with job training and day care.

In one recent study of 248 persons in the St. Louis area, about 20% of those surveyed were characterized as primarily alcohol dependent, with another 16.5% of the group seen as having mental health needs (Morse & Calsyn, 1992). Most studies find that about 25% of people who are homeless have a previous history of hospitalization for mental health problems (Robertson, 1986) and about 30% are considered severely mentally ill (Koegel, Burnam, & Farr, 1988).

Information on the characteristics of people who are homeless is important because it provides us with clues about why people become homeless, and it dispels the notion that *all* homeless people have mental health problems. The idea that all homeless people have severe mental illness was used for a time to blame the strict civil commitment criteria and deinstitutionalization as the sole causes of homelessness in this country (Torrey, 1988). In other words, policies to severely limit who can be involuntarily committed to a psychiatric hospital, along with the concurrent closing of large psychiatric hospitals and placing of limits on the stays of people with severe mental illness, were thought

to be responsible for the substantial increase in homelessness in the 1980s. Although a sizable portion among the homeless population does have mental illness, the rise in homelessness is also attributed to economic factors such as an increase in unemployment and a shortage of low-income housing (Morse, 1992). Yet the *perception* that civil commitment restrictions and deinstitutionalization caused homelessness resulted in movements to change commitment procedures.

Reforms in civil commitment—making it more difficult to commit someone involuntarily—occurred at the same time the policy of deinstitutionalization was closing large psychiatric hospitals (Turkheimer & Parry, 1992). Deinstitutionalization had two goals: (a) to close the large state mental hospitals and (b) to create a network of community mental health centers where the released individuals could be treated in their communities. Although the first goal appears to have been substantially accomplished, with about a 75% decrease in the number of patients in these hospitals (Kiesler & Sibulkin, 1987), the second goal—to provide alternative community care for these individuals, which was an essential part of the plan—appears not to have been attained. Instead, there was **transinstitutionalization** or the movement of people with severe mental illness from large psychiatric hospitals to nursing homes or other group residences, many of which provide only marginal services (Bachrach, 1987, Sharfstein, 1987). Because of the deterioration in care for many people previously served by the mental hospital system, deinstitutionalization is largely considered a failure. Although many praise the ideal of providing community care for people with severe mental illness, the support needed to provide this type of care outside the hospital was not available for the majority of people in need of assistance.

Reaction to Strict Civil Commitment Procedures

Arthur's psychotic reaction and his family's travails in trying to get him help all occurred in the mid 1970s. This time was characterized by more concern with individual freedom than with society's rights and a belief that people with mental illness were not being properly served by forcing them into treatment. Others, however, especially family members, felt that, by not coercing some individuals into getting treatment, the system was sanctioning their mental decline and placing them at grave risk of harm. The culmination of a number of factors—such as the lack of success with deinstitutionalization, the rise in homelessness, and the criminalization of people with severe mental illness—gave rise to a backlash against their perceived causes, including the strict civil commitment laws. The case of

Joyce Brown captures this clash of concerns between individual freedoms for people with mental illness and society's concerns with treating these individuals.

The Case of Joyce Brown

During a 1988 winter emergency in New York City, then Mayor Ed Koch ordered that all people living on the street who appeared to be mentally ill should be involuntarily committed to a mental health facility for their protection. He used the legal principle of *parens patriae,* citing the need to protect these individuals from the cold and from themselves to justify this action. One of the people who was taken off the streets, the 40-year-old Joyce Brown, was picked up against her will and admitted to Bellevue Hospital, where she received a diagnosis of paranoid schizophrenia. For some time she had been living on the street, swearing at people as they walked by; at one point she adopted the name Billy Boggs after the New York television personality Bill Boggs, with whom she fantasized a relationship. She, along with the New York Civil Liberties Union, contested her commitment and she was released after 3 months (Kasindorf, 1988).

This case is important because it illustrates the conflicting interests at play over civil commitment. Joyce Brown's family had for some time been concerned over her well-being and had tried unsuccessfully to have her involuntarily committed. Although she had never hurt anyone or tried to commit suicide, they were afraid that living on the streets of New York City was too dangerous and they feared for her welfare. New York City officials expressed concern for Brown and others like her, especially during a dangerously cold winter, although some more cynically thought that this was an excuse to remove people with disturbing behavior from the streets of the more affluent sections of New York (Kasindorf, 1988). At the same time, Brown chose not to seek treatment and resisted efforts to place her in alternative settings. At times she could be quite articulate and could make a case for her own freedom of choice. Only weeks after she was released from the hospital, she was again living on the streets. To illustrate the ongoing nature of this dilemma, Brown was involuntarily committed to a mental health facility again in 1994, and by February of that year, she was once more attempting to be released from the hospital (*New York Times,* Feb. 2, 1994).

Rulings such as *O'Connor v. Donaldson* and *Addington v. Texas* had argued for criteria of mental illness plus dangerousness as justifications for invol-

untary commitment. However, because of cases like that of Joyce Brown and concerns about homelessness and criminalization, a movement has emerged calling for a return to more broadly drafted civil commitment procedures that would permit commitment not only of those who showed dangerousness to self or others, but also of individuals who were not dangerous but were in need of treatment, or those with grave disability. Groups such as the National Alliance for the Mentally Ill (NAMI), a coalition of family members of people with mental illness, argued for legal reform to make involuntary commitment easier—an emotional response that we saw illustrated in the case of Arthur and his family. Several states in the late 1970s and early 1980s began to change their civil commitment laws in an attempt to address these concerns. In one example, the state of Washington revised its laws in 1979 to allow commitment of people who were judged to be in need of treatment. This law produced a 91% increase in the number of involuntary commitments in the first year it was in effect (Durham & La Fond, 1985). There was essentially no change in the size of the hospital population at this time, only the status under which patients were committed (La Fond & Durham, 1992). Whereas people were previously detained because of violence, they were now admitted under *parens patriae* powers; also, whereas most admissions previously would have been voluntary, now they were involuntary. This change occurred because hospitals began to fill up (because of longer stays and repeated admissions) and began accepting only involuntary admissions. Therefore, the result of easing the procedure for involuntarily committing people with mental illness was only to change the authority under which the mentally ill were admitted.

Overview of Civil Commitment

What should the criteria be for involuntarily committing someone with severe mental illness to a mental health facility? Should imminent danger to oneself or others be the only justification, or should society adopt a more paternalistic attitude and coerce people who appear to be in distress and in need of asylum or a safe place to live? How do we address the concerns of families such as Arthur's, who see their loved ones overcome by their psychological problems? And what of society's need not to be harassed by people such as Joyce Brown? When do these rights take precedence over the rights of an individual to be free from unwanted incarceration? It is tempting to look at the legal system and conclude that it has failed to address these issues. The shift from the liberal attitude of the courts, which focused on individual rights, to the neoconservative movements of late may give the impression that the system does not work and reacts only to the political whims of the times.

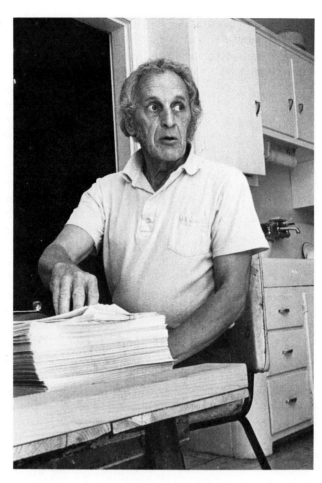

Kenneth Donaldson looks over the extensive files he compiled in the 18 years he was involuntarily confined to a Florida mental hospital. Donaldson was successful in his suit against the superintendent of the hospital.

However, another view of the legal system and its handling of people with severe mental illness suggests that the periodic changing of laws is a sign of a healthy system that is responsive to limitations of previous decisions. The reactions by the Supreme Court in the 1970s to the coercive and arbitrary nature of civil commitment were as understandable as are more recent attempts to make it easier to commit people in obvious need of help. As the consequences of these changes become apparent—as in the Washington State civil commitment laws—the system responds to correct injustices. Although these changes may seem excruciatingly slow and may not always correctly address the issues in need of reform, the fact that the legal system can be changed should serve as a source of optimism for ultimately addressing through the courts the varying needs of individuals as well as society.

Criminal Commitment

Arthur was not involuntarily committed to the local mental health facility because it wasn't clear that he was dangerous to himself or others. But what would have

happened if he had been arrested for trespassing on embassy grounds or, worse yet, if he had hurt or killed someone in his effort to present his plan for saving the world? Would he have been held responsible for his actions, given his obvious disturbed mental state? How would a jury have responded to him when he seemed fine just several days later? Was he not responsible for his behavior then, as he seems so normal now?

These questions are of enormous importance to us today as our society is now debating whether people should be held responsible for their criminal behavior—despite the possible presence of mental illness. Cases such as that of Lyle and Eric Menendez, who admit to murdering their parents but who claim they were driven to it by the abusiveness of their father, have people wondering whether the laws have gone too far in absolving people of responsibility for criminal behavior. Remember that **criminal commitment** is the process by which people are held for two reasons: (a) They have been accused of committing a crime and are detained in a mental health facility until they can be determined as fit or unfit to participate in legal proceedings against them; or (b) they have been found not guilty of a crime by reason of insanity. In the next section we examine how the criminal justice system addresses issues of mental illness, with particular attention to the insanity defense and the way people are determined to be competent to stand trial.

The Insanity Defense

The purpose of our criminal justice system is to protect our life, our liberty, and our pursuit of happiness. Laws have been developed over the years to shield citizens from harm and to punish those who act in ways that threaten our safety. But not all people are punished for criminal behavior. The law recognizes that, under certain circumstances, people are not responsible for their behavior and that it would be unfair, and perhaps ineffective, to try to punish these individuals. Current views of criminal behavior committed by people with mental illness originate from a case recorded over 150 years ago in England. Daniel M'Naghten was a person who today might have received the diagnosis of paranoid schizophrenia. M'Naghten held the delusion that the English Tory party was persecuting him, and he set out to kill the British prime minister—although he mistook the man's secretary for the prime minister himself and killed the secretary instead. In what has become known as the *M'Naghten* rule, the English court decreed that people are not responsible for their criminal behavior if they do not know what they are doing, or if they don't know that what they are doing is wrong (see Table 17.1). For over 100 years, this rule was the test used to determine culpability when a person's mental state was in question.

In the intervening years, other standards have been introduced to modify the *M'Naghten* rule because many critics felt that simply relying on an accused person's knowledge of right or wrong was too limiting and that a broader definition was needed (Guttmacher & Weihofen, 1952). Mental illness alters not only a person's cognitive abilities (for instance, knowing right from wrong) but also other important aspects, such as emotional functioning, and mental health professionals believed that the entire range of functioning should be taken into account when a person's responsibility for his or her behavior was determined. One influential decision, referred to as the *Durham* rule, was initiated in 1954 by Judge David Bazelon of the Federal Circuit Court of Appeals for the District of Columbia based on the case *Durham v. United States*. The *Durham* rule broadened the criteria for responsibility from a knowledge of right or wrong to the presence of a "mental disease or defect" (see Table 17.1). This decision was initially hailed by mental health professionals because it allowed them to present to a judge or jury a complete picture of the person with mental illness. Unfortunately, it soon became apparent that mental health professionals did not have the expertise to reliably assess whether a person's mental illness *caused* the criminal behavior

Table 17.1   Important Concepts in the Evolution of the Insanity Defense

The *M'Naghten* Rule	1843	[I]t must be clearly proved that at the time of committing the act, the party accused was labouring under such a defect of reason, from disease of the mind, as not to know the nature and quality of the act he was doing; or if he did know it, that he did not know he was doing what was wrong. [101 Cl. & F. 200, 8 Eng. Rep. 718 (H.L. 1843)]
The *Durham* Rule	1954	An accused is not criminally responsible if his unlawful act was the product of mental disease or mental defect. [*Durham v. United States*, 214 F.2d 862, 876 (D.C. Cir. 1954)]
American Law Institute (ALI) Rule	1962	1. A person is not responsible for criminal conduct if at the time of such conduct as a result of mental disease or defect he lacks substantial capacity either to appreciate the criminality (wrongfulness) of his conduct or to conform his conduct to the requirements of law. 2. As used in the Article, the terms "mental disease or defect" do not include an abnormality manifested only by repeated criminal or otherwise antisocial conduct. [American Law Institute (1962). *Model penal code: Proposed official draft*. Philadelphia: Author.]
Diminished Capacity	1978	Evidence of abnormal mental condition would be admissible to affect the degree of crime for which an accused could be convicted. Specifically, those offenses requiring intent or knowledge could be reduced to lesser included offenses requiring only reckless or criminal neglect. [New York State Department of Mental Hygiene (1978). *The insanity defense in New York*. New York: New York Department of Mental Hygiene.]
American Psychiatric Association	1982	A person charged with a criminal offense should be found not guilty by reason of insanity if it is shown that, as a result of mental disease or mental retardation, he was unable to appreciate the wrongfulness of his conduct at the time of his offense. (American Psychiatric Association, 1982, p. 685)

in question, and therefore decisions were being based on unscientific opinions (Arens, 1974). Although the *Durham* rule is no longer used, its effect was to cause a reexamination of the criteria used in the **insanity defense.**

An influential study of this question was conducted around the same time as the *Durham* decision by a group of attorneys, judges, and law scholars who belonged to the American Law Institute (ALI). Their challenge, to develop criteria for determining whether a person's mental competence makes him or her answerable for criminal behavior, was articulated by the ALI:

> No problem in the drafting of a penal code presents larger intrinsic difficulty than that of determining when individuals whose conduct otherwise would be criminal ought to be exculpated on the ground that they were suffering from mental disease or defect when they acted as they did. (*Model Penal Code and Commentaries,* 1962, pp. 164–165)

Taking on this challenge, the ALI first reaffirmed the importance of distinguishing the behavior of people with mental illness from that of people without mental disorders. They pointed out that the threat of punishment was unlikely to deter someone who had severe mental illness; their position was that these individuals should instead be treated, and when they have improved, they should be released. This concept of providing treatment instead of punishment is discussed further when we examine recent developments and criticisms of the insanity defense. The ALI concluded that people were not responsible for their criminal behavior if, because of their mental illness, they either lacked the cognitive ability to recognize the inappropriateness of their behavior or they lacked the ability to control their behavior (American Law Institute, 1962). These criteria, shown in Table 17.1, are referred to as the *ALI test*. They stipulate that the person must either be unable to distinguish right from wrong—as set forth in the *M'Naghten* rule—or be unable to control himself or herself. Thus, either a person's lack of knowledge of the inappropriateness of criminal behavior or lack of will to control his or her behavior was sufficient to shield the person from legal consequences.

Also included in the writings of the ALI were provisions for the concept of **diminished capacity** (see Table 17.1), which held that people's ability to understand the nature of their behavior and therefore their criminal intent could be lessened by their mental illness. The theory of criminal intent—otherwise called *mens rea* or having a "guilty mind"—is an important legal principle because it is required for conviction of a crime. To convict someone of a crime there must be proof of the physical act (*actus rea*) and the mental state

(*mens rea*) of the person committing the act (Weiner & Wettstein, 1993). For example, if a woman accidentally hits someone who steps in front of her car and the person subsequently dies, the woman would not be held criminally responsible; although a person was killed, there was no criminal intent—the driver didn't deliberately hit the person and attempt murder. The diminished capacity concept proposes that a person with mental illness who commits a criminal offense may not, because of his or her mental illness, have criminal intent and therefore cannot be held responsible for his or her behavior. By the mid 1970s, approximately 25 states had adopted the concept of diminished capacity as a way to assess the responsibility of persons with mental illness, in part because it is a concept that softens the strict requirements of the *M'Naghten* rule (Lewin, 1975).

Reaction to the Insanity Defense

The primary thrust of judicial rulings through the 1960s and 1970s regarding criminal responsibility parallels our previous discussion of civil commitment. During this time there was an effort to focus on the needs of the offender, providing mental health treatment instead of punishment for people with mental illness who also broke the law. However, just as we saw with civil commitment, the successful use of concepts such as insanity or diminished capacity in criminal cases began to alarm large segments of the population. For instance, in 1979 a man successfully pleaded not guilty by reason of insanity after being arrested for writing bad checks. His case was based on the testimony of an expert witness that he suffered from *pathological gambling,* a disorder characterized by persistent and recurrent gambling, and he therefore could not distinguish right from wrong (*State v. Campanaro,* 1980). Other new defenses that were successfully presented using more liberal definitions of insanity included the use of disorders included in the DSM, such as *posttraumatic stress disorder,* as well as those that are not in this system, including "battered wife syndrome."

Without question, the case that has prompted the most anger and outrage against the use of the insanity defense, as well as calls for its abolishment, is that of John W. Hinckley, Jr. (Simon & Aaronson, 1988). On March 31, 1981, then President Ronald Reagan was walking out of the Washington Hilton Hotel after a speech when John Hinckley fired several shots, hitting and wounding President Reagan and a Secret Service agent, and seriously wounding James Brady, the president's press secretary. In an instant, Secret Service agents hurried the president into a waiting limousine, and simultaneously tackled and disarmed Hinckley. Hinckley later was shown to have been obsessed with actress Jodie Foster and claimed he tried to kill the president to impress her. Hinckley was judged by a jury

John Hinckley, Jr., whose successful plea of not guilty by reason of insanity in the attempted murder of President Reagan resulted in a widespread negative reaction to the use of this plea.

to be not guilty by reason of insanity (NGRI)—using the American Law Institute standard—sending shock waves throughout the country and legal community (Rogers, 1987). One of the many consequences of this event was the emergence of James and Sarah Brady (the seriously wounded press secretary and his wife) as advocates for stricter gun control laws and the ultimate passage of the "Brady Law."

Although criticism of the insanity defense existed prior to the Hinckley case, one study found that, following Hinckley's verdict, more than half the states considered abolishing it as a defense (Keilitz & Fulton, 1984). As we have seen before, often such decisions are based more on emotion than fact. Highly publicized cases such as those of Hinckley, Charles Manson, and Jeffrey Dahmer along with the characterization of people with mental illness in the media as excessively violent have resulted in an unfavorable public perception of the insanity defense. One telephone survey study found that 91% of people who responded agreed with the statement that "judges and juries have a hard time telling whether the defendants are really sane or insane" (Hans, 1986). Almost 90% agreed that the "insanity plea is a loophole that allows too many guilty people to go free." In a similar study, 90% of people agreed that "the insanity plea is used too much. Too many people escape responsibilities for crimes by pleading insanity" (Pasewark & Seidenzahl, 1979). Is there justification with hard evidence for this fear that the insanity defense is used too often?

A recent study examined the public's impression of the insanity defense and compared it to the actual use of the defense and its outcomes (Silver, Cirincione, & Steadman, 1994). As Table 17.2 shows, the general public grossly overestimates how often the insanity defense is used. While the public's perception is that this defense is used in 37% of all felony cases, the actual figure is less than 1%. In addition, the public overestimates how often this defense is successful as well as how often people judged NGRI are set free. People tend to underestimate the length of hospitalization of people who are successfully acquitted with the insanity defense. This last issue is important: In contrast to the perceptions of the general public, the length of time a person is confined to a hospital after being judged NGRI may *exceed* the time the person would have spent in jail had he or she been convicted of the crime (Steadman, 1985). John Hinckley, for example, has been a patient in St. Elizabeth's Hospital for the last 12 years. People with mental illness apparently do not often "beat the rap" as a result of being judged NGRI.

Despite evidence that the insanity defense is not used excessively and does not result in widespread early release of dangerous individuals, major changes were made in the criteria for the insanity defense after the Hinckley verdict. Both the American Psychiatric Association (1983) and the American Bar Association (1984) recommended modifications in the insanity criteria, moving back toward *M'Naghten*-like definitions (see Table 17.1). Shortly afterward, Congress

Table 17.2   Comparison of Public Perceptions with the Actual Operation of the Insanity Defense

	Public	Actual
A. Use of the insanity defense		
Percentage of felony indictments resulting in an insanity plea	37%	0.9%
Percentage of insanity pleas resulting in acquittal	44%	26%
B. Disposition of insanity acquittees		
Percentage of insanity acquittees sent to a mental hospital	50.6%	84.7%
Percentage of insanity acquittees set free	25.6%	15.3%
Conditional Release		11.6%
Outpatient		2.6%
Release		1.1%
C. Length of confinement of insanity acquittees (in months)		
All crimes	21.8	32.5
Murder		76.4

Source: Silver, Cirincione, & Steadman, 1994.

passed the Insanity Defense Reform Act of 1984, which incorporated these suggestions, making successful use of the insanity defense more difficult.

Another attempt at reforming the insanity plea has been to replace "not guilty by reason of insanity" (NGRI) with "guilty but mentally ill" (GBMI) as a verdict for a crime committed by a person with mental illness (Callahan, McGreevy, Cirincione, & Steadman, 1992). Although there are several versions of the GBMI verdict, the major premise of all these is that the consequences for a person ruled GBMI are different from those for a person who is NGRI. People who are found to be NGRI are not sent to prison but are evaluated to determine whether they are currently mentally ill and dangerous. If a person is found to be mentally ill, he or she is sent to a psychiatric facility until such time as he or she is judged ready for release. If a person is determined no longer to be mentally ill, the person must be released. Going back to Arthur's case, if he had committed a crime and was found NGRI, because his *brief psychotic disorder* was quickly resolved, he would probably have been released immediately. In contrast, one version of the GBMI verdict in theory allows the system both to treat and to punish the individual. If the person is found guilty, he or she is given a prison term just as would be done if there were no question of mental illness. A determination of whether to send him or her to prison or to a mental health facility is made by legal authorities. Then, if the person is found no longer to be mentally ill before the duration of the sentence has

passed, he or she can be confined in prison for the maximum length of the prison term. Returning to Arthur's case, if he were found GBMI under this system, he could serve a full prison sentence, even though his mental illness had been resolved. This version of GBMI has, as of 1992, been adopted by 11 states (La Fond & Durham, 1992).

The second version of GBMI is even harsher for the mentally ill offender. Individuals convicted with this verdict are imprisoned and the prison authorities *may* provide mental health services if such are available. The verdict itself is simply a declaration by the jury that the person was mentally ill at the time the crime was committed and does not result in differential treatment for the perpetrator. Currently, three states—Idaho, Montana, and Utah—have abandoned the insanity defense altogether and have adopted this version of GBMI (La Fond & Durham, 1992). The Supreme Court recently upheld the constitutionality of Montana's abolition of the insanity defense in *Cowan v. Montana* (DeAngelis, 1994).

As noted, the GBMI verdict was a reaction to the perceived loophole provided by the insanity defense. It has been in use in several states for over 15 years, and there is now research available with which to judge its effects. Two studies have shown that persons receiving the GBMI verdict in states with this provision of the law are more likely to be imprisoned and are more likely to receive longer sentences than people pleading insanity for similar offenses in other states (Callahan et al., 1992; Keilitz, 1987). Research also indicates that individuals receiving GBMI verdicts are no more likely to receive treatment for their mental illness than are others who have mental illness and who are in the prison system (Keilitz, 1987; Smith & Hall, 1982).

Early on our system recognized the need to identify people who commit crimes but who may not be in control of their behavior and who may not benefit from simple incarceration. One difficulty with identifying these individuals has been in trying to do what may be impossible: getting into the mind of a person *at the time the crime was committed* and determining whether the person knew what he or she was doing, knew what was right and wrong, and could control his or her behavior. Mental health professionals do not have the technology or expertise to assess mental health *retrospectively*. An additional dilemma is the desire on the one hand to provide care and treatment to people with mental illness while on the other to provide consequences that treat them also as responsible individuals. Finally, we must resolve the simultaneous and conflicting interests between wanting to assist people with mental illness and wanting to be protected from them. By evaluating the effects of these differing ways of dealing with people with mental illness, science can help to resolve some of these issues. The findings, however, must then be used by the legal system. Also, we must reach a national consensus about the basic value of people with mental illness to help decide how they should be dealt with in the legal system. We hope that the recent trend of placing concern with law and order over the rights of people with mental illness can be mitigated to provide attention to both concerns.

Competency to Stand Trial

Before people can be tried for a criminal offense, they must be able to understand the charges against them and to assist with their own defense. These are the criteria that must be met for a person to be considered *competent to stand trial,* a prerequisite outlined by the Supreme Court in *Dusky v. United States* (1960). Thus, in addition to determining a person's state of mind during the criminal act, those involved in the legal system must also determine his or her state of mind during the subsequent legal proceedings. A person could be ruled not guilty by reason of insanity based on his or her mental illness at the time of the criminal act yet still be competent to stand trial—a situation that would have occurred in Arthur's case if he had committed a crime.

Determining that a person is incompetent to stand trial typically leads to the removal of decision-making authority from the individual and results in commitment. Because a determination of **competency** comes before the trial, most people with obvious and severe impairments who commit crimes never go to trial. Some observers estimate that for every person who receives a verdict of NGRI, 45 others are committed to a mental health facility based on a diagnosis of severe mental illness (Steadman, 1979). The length

of stay in these facilities is determined by the time it takes the committed person to regain his or her competency. However, because this can be a protracted period of time, the courts have ruled that it cannot be indefinite, and that, after a reasonable amount of time, the person must be found competent, set free, or civilly committed—a decision made in the case of *Jackson v. Indiana* (1972). Note that courts are often not precise in their language—with the phrase "reasonable amount of time" open to a great deal of interpretation.

A final issue relates to the legal concept of *burden of proof*—or the weight of evidence needed to win a case. In decisions of competency to stand trial, a recent ruling placed responsibility on the defendant to provide the burden of proof, meaning that the person to be put on trial—through his or her legal counsel—is required to prove that he or she is incompetent to stand trial (*Medina v. California,* 1992). Again, public concern that dangerous individuals with mental illness are routinely acquitted and let loose on society after committing multiple violent offenses flies in the face of the facts. The more realistic scenario is of a person with mental illness who commits a nonviolent crime and receives treatment through legal actions, such as the competency proceedings just described.

A Duty to Warn

Do mental health professionals have any responsibility for the behavior of the people they serve? This is especially important when you consider the dangerous behavior exhibited by a minority of people with severe mental illness. What are the responsibilities of profes-

The murder of 20-year-old Tatiana Tarasoff by fellow student Prosenjit Poddar, who revealed his murderous intentions to his therapist, has served as the basis for court decisions regulating when a therapist has a duty to warn others about patients.

sionals who suspect that someone with whom they are working may hurt or possibly kill another person? Do they need to contact the appropriate authority or the person who may be harmed, or are they forbidden to discuss information disclosed during therapy sessions?

These issues are the subject of a tragic case known as *Tarasoff v. Regents of the University of California* (1974/1976). In 1969, a graduate student at the University of California named Prosenjit Poddar killed a fellow student, Tatiana Tarasoff, who had previously rejected his romantic advances. At the time, he was being seen by two therapists at the University Health Center and had received a diagnosis of paranoid schizophrenia. At his last therapy session, Poddar hinted that he was going to kill Tarasoff. His therapist believed this was a serious threat and contacted the campus police, who investigated the incident and received assurances from Poddar that he would leave Tarasoff alone. Weeks later, after repeated attempts to contact her, Poddar shot and stabbed Tarasoff until she died.

After learning of the therapist's role in the case, Tatiana Tarasoff's family sued the university, the therapists, and the university police, saying that they should have warned Tatiana of the danger she was in. The court agreed, and the *Tarasoff* case has been used as a standard for therapists concerning their **duty to warn**

potential victims of their clients. Since the original case, a number of other related cases have further defined the role of the therapist to warn others (Kermani & Drob, 1987). For example, courts have generally ruled that the threats have to be specific. In *Thompson v. County of Alameda* (1980), the California Supreme Court ruled that a therapist does not have a duty to warn if a person makes nonspecific threats against nonspecific people. These types of cases make it difficult for therapists to know their exact responsibilities for protecting third parties from their clients. Good clinical practice dictates that any time therapists are in doubt about their responsibilities in these cases, they should consult with colleagues about their best course of action. A second opinion can be just as helpful to the therapist as to a client.

Mental Health Professionals as Expert Witnesses

Judges and juries often have to rely on individuals who have specialized knowledge—**expert witnesses**—to assist them in making decisions (Melton, Petrila, Poythress, & Slobogin, 1987). We have alluded to several instances in which mental health professionals serve in such a capacity, such as providing information about dangerousness or the ability of a person to understand

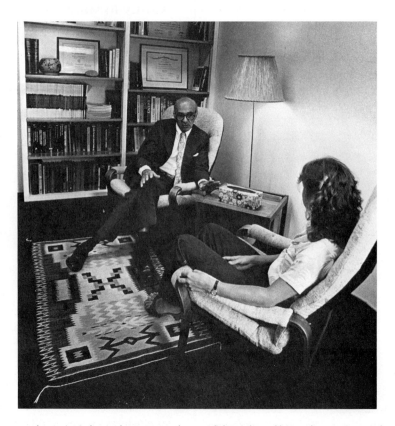

Under most circumstances, a therapist is bound to protect the confidentiality of his or her patient. When must the therapist reveal information from therapy?

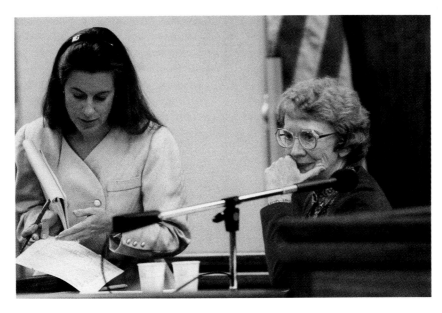

Deputy District Attorney Pamela Bozanich discusses evidence with mental health expert Ann Wolbert Burgess during the Erik and Lyle Menendez murder trial.

and participate in the defense. Unfortunately, the public's perception of expert witnesses seems to be characterized by ambivalence. On one hand, they see the value of persuasive expert testimony in educating a jury; on the other, they see expert witnesses as "hired guns" whose opinions match whichever side pays their bills (Hollien, 1990). It is important to ask at this point, how accurate and reliable are mental health professionals in helping to make these decisions?

We've already discussed one of the tasks faced by mental health professionals: assessing dangerousness. In deciding whether someone should be civilly committed, for instance, the assessor must determine the person's potential for future violence. Research suggests that mental health professionals can make reliable predictions of dangerousness over the short term—for a period of 2 to 20 days after the evaluation (Lidz, Mulvey, Appelbaum, & Cleveland, 1989; McNiel & Binder, 1991). However, they have not been able to make reliable predictions of violence after longer periods of time (Monahan, 1984). A second area in which mental health professionals are frequently asked to provide consultation is in assigning a diagnosis. In Chapter 3 we discussed the development of diagnostic systems and earlier concerns over the lack of reliability of diagnoses. Recent revisions of diagnostic criteria, most notably DSM-III-R and the current DSM-IV, have addressed this issue directly, thus helping clinicians to make diagnoses that are generally more reliable. Remember, however, that the legal definition of mental illness is not matched by a comparable disorder in DSM-IV. Therefore, statements about whether some-

one has a "mental illness" reflect determinations made by the judge or jury and not a mental health professional.

Areas in which mental health professionals do appear to have expertise are in assessing the presence of malingering and in assessing competence. **Malingering** is the label assigned to faking or grossly exaggerating symptoms—usually done in order to be absolved from blame. For example, a person might claim that she was actively hallucinating at the time she committed a crime, and therefore was not responsible for her behavior. Evidence suggests that, at least in some cases, mental health professionals are capable of detecting malingering. Research using the Minnesota Multiphasic Personality Inventory (MMPI) indicates that this test is almost 90% accurate in revealing malingering in people claiming to have posttraumatic stress disorder (PTSD) (McCaffrey & Bellamy-Campbell, 1989). And last, mental health professionals do appear to be capable of providing reliable information about a person's ability to understand and assist with a defense (competency) (Melton et al., 1987). Overall, mental health professionals can provide judges and juries with reliable and useful information in certain specific areas (Garb, 1992).

The research described here addresses how accurate expert testimony *can* be, but it does not tell us directly how accurate expert testimony actually *is* under everyday conditions. In other words, under the right circumstances, experts can make accurate determinations of the short-term risk that a person will commit an act of violence, of whether a person is "faking" certain symptoms, of whether a person is competent to stand trial, and of what diagnosis a person should be given. Yet during trials, other factors conspire to influence expert testimony. Personal and professional opinions about certain issues that go beyond the competence of the expert witness can influence what information is or is not presented, and how this information is relayed to the court (Hollien, 1990). For instance, if the expert witness believes in general that people should not be involuntarily committed to mental health facilities, this opinion will likely influence how the witness presents clinical information in civil commitment court proceedings.

Testimony can also be influenced by how the expert witness perceives himself or herself in this process. The differing roles of the expert witness have been categorized by Schultz-Ross (1993) as including the "adversarial model," the "objective model," and the "hired gun." The adversarial model applies to experts who become involved in cases in which they hold strong opinions and make the best case for that position. Some have argued that this approach to providing counsel to the court is unethical because it allows unbalanced information and has the potential for misleading judges and juries (Stone, 1984). The objective model, in contrast, seeks to have expert witnesses who are not aligned to any particular view but simply provide impartial information to the court. This approach has advantages over the adversarial model, but judges and juries might not find purely objective information useful without the benefit of some subjective interpretation.

Finally, the hired gun model describes an expert whose opinions are determined by the side that hires him or her. This person provides equally convincing arguments regardless of the position that needs to be taken. Although hired guns are viewed with some scorn by the mental health profession, they do provide the best available case, a concept that is essential for legal defense (Schultz-Ross, 1993). These models show the ways in which bias can enter the expert witness process. Ethical behavior by expert witnesses requires them to know the limits of what they can testify to (for example, short-term versus long-term risk of violence) and to have sufficient training in the areas of mental health and mental law to provide accurate information. Purely objective testimony may not be possible at this point, so potential experts are alerted to these possible sources of influence on their testimony.

Patients' Rights

Until about 20 years ago, people who received care in mental health facilities were accorded few rights. What treatment they received and whether they could make phone calls, send and receive mail, or have visitors was typically decided by hospital personnel; rarely did these people consult with the patient. However, abuses of this authority led to legal action and subsequent rulings by the courts concerning the rights of people in these facilities. We next discuss a number of rights that are now guaranteed by the courts as well as ongoing controversies in this area.

The Right to Treatment

One of the most fundamental of the rights of people in mental health facilities, and one that may at first seem obvious, is the right to treatment. For too many and for too long, conditions were poor and treatment was lacking in numbers of the large mental health facilities. Starting in the early 1970s, a series of class action lawsuits (lawsuits filed on behalf of many individuals—in this case, people residing in institutions) helped establish the rights of people with mental illness and mental retardation. A landmark case, *Wyatt v. Stickney* (1972), grew out of a lawsuit filed by the employees of large institutions in Alabama who were being fired because of funding difficulties. The case established for the first time the minimum standards that facilities had to meet in relation to the people who were hospitalized. Among the standards set by *Wyatt v. Stickney* were minimum staff/patient ratios and requirements for the physical makeup of the facilities such as a certain number of showers and toilets for a given number of residents. The case mandated that positive efforts be made by these facilities to attain treatment goals for their patients.

Wyatt v. Stickney went further and expanded on a concept called the "least restrictive alternative," indicating that, wherever possible, people should be provided with care and treatment in the least confining and limiting environment. For example, the court noted the following for those with mental retardation:

> Residents shall have a right to the least restrictive conditions necessary to achieve the purpose of habilitation. To this end the institution shall make every attempt to move residents from (1) more to less structured living; (2) large to smaller facilities; (3) large to smaller living units; (4) group to individual residences; (5) segregated from the community to integrated into the community living; (6) dependent to independent living.

With this movement toward securing treatment for people in mental health facilities, a gap was left as to what constituted proper treatment. Another case, *Youngberg v. Romeo* (1982), reaffirmed the need to treat people in nonrestrictive settings but essentially left to professionals the decision about the type of treatment to be provided. This move caused some concern among patient advocates because, historically, leaving treatment to professional judgment has not always resulted

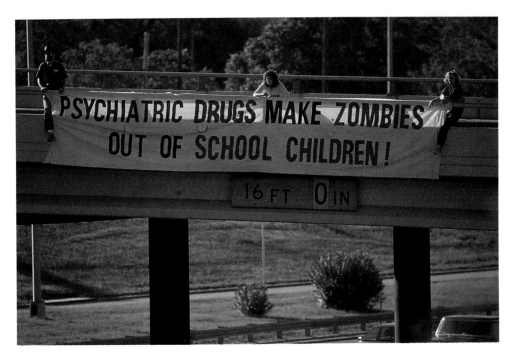

Treatments for psychological disorders—especially psychotropic medication—can elicit strong reactions from patients and their families.

in the intended end for the people in need of this help. In 1986, Congress provided a number of safeguards by passage of the Protection and Advocacy for Mentally Ill Individuals Act (Woodside & Legg, 1990). This act established a series of protection and advocacy agencies in each state, with the mission of investigating allegations of abuse and neglect and of acting as legal advocates. This layer of protection has resulted in a balance between professional concerns and the needs and rights of patients in mental health facilities.

The Right to Refuse Treatment

One of the most controversial issues in mental health today is the right of people, especially those with severe mental illness, to refuse treatment. In recent times, the thrust of the argument has centered around the use of psychotropic medications. On one side of this issue is often the mental health professional, who believes that, under certain circumstances, people with severe mental illness may not be capable of making a decision in their own best interest, and that the clinician therefore has the responsibility of providing treatment despite the protestations of the person affected. On the other hand, patients and their advocates would argue that all people have a fundamental right to make decisions about their own treatment, even if doing so is not in their own best medical interests.

Although not yet completely resolved, a recent court case has responded to a related question: Can people be "forced" to become competent to stand trial?

This question presents an interesting dilemma: If people facing criminal charges are delusional or are having such frequent and severe hallucinations that they cannot fully participate in the legal proceedings, can they be forced against their will to take psychotropic medication that may reduce these symptoms, thereby making them competent to stand trial? A recent Supreme Court ruling, *Riggins v. Nevada* (1992), has stated that, because of the potential for negative side effects (such as tardive dyskinesia) from using these medications, people cannot be forced to take psychotropic medication to make them competent to enter legal proceedings against them. While this decision does not put to rest the issue of refusing treatment, it does indicate the high court's wish to honor individual choice in this issue (Perlin & Dorfman, 1993).

Research Participants' Rights

Throughout this text, we have described research being conducted throughout the world with people who have psychological disorders, and we touched briefly in Chapter 4 on the issue of the rights of these individuals. In general, people who participate in research have the following rights:

1. To be informed about the purpose of the research study,
2. The right to privacy,
3. The right to be treated with respect and dignity,

4. The right to be protected from physical and mental harm,

5. The right to choose to participate or to refuse to participate without prejudice or reprisals,

6. The right to anonymity in the reporting of results, and

7. The right to the safeguarding of their records (American Psychological Association, 1992).

These concerns are particularly important for people with psychological disorders because they may not be able to understand these rights fully. One of the most important concepts in research is that those who participate must be fully informed of the study—its risks and benefits. And simple consent is not sufficient; it must be **informed consent,** or formal agreement by the subject to participate after being fully apprised of all important aspects of the study, including any possibility of harm. A recent case underlines the importance of informed consent and the sometimes gray areas that exist in applied research.

The Case of Greg Aller

In 1988, 23-year-old Greg Aller signed a consent form agreeing to participate in a treatment study at the University of California at Los Angeles (UCLA) Neuropsychiatric Institute (Willwerth, 1993). During the previous year, Greg had experienced vivid and frightening hallucinations and delusions about space aliens. His parents had been concerned about him and had contacted UCLA for assistance. They learned that the university was initiating a new study to evaluate people in the early stages of schizophrenia and to assess which of them would and would not be affected by the withdrawal of medication. Participating meant that Greg could receive extremely expensive drug therapy and counseling free. After taking the drug Prolixin for 3 months as part of the study, he improved dramatically; the hallucinations and delusions were gone. He

Greg Aller, right, with his parents in a UCLA campus garden. Greg suffered a severe relapse of psychotic symptoms while participating in a drug study at UCLA, and he and his family have raised concerns about informed consent for this type of research.

was now able to enroll in college and made the dean's list.

Although overjoyed with the results, Greg's parents were concerned about the second phase of the study, which involved taking him off the medication. They were reassured by the researchers that this was an important and normal part of treatment for people with schizophrenia, and that the potential for negative side effects for taking the drug for too long was great. They were also told that the researchers would put Greg back on the medication if he grew considerably worse without it.

Toward the end of 1989, Greg was slowly taken off the drug, and he soon started having delusions about Ronald Reagan and space aliens. Although his deterioration was obvious to his parents, Greg did not indicate to the researchers that he needed the medication, not telling them of his now continuous hallucinations and delusions. Greg continued to deteriorate, at one point threatening to kill his parents. After several more months, Greg's parents coerced him into asking UCLA for more medication. Although better than he was earlier, Greg has still not returned to the much improved state he achieved following his first round of medication.

This case highlights the conflicts that can arise when researchers attempt to study important questions in psychopathology. Did the UCLA researchers fully inform Greg and his parents of the risks involved in participating in this study, or was their interest in studying relapse after withdrawing medication influencing the information they provided participants? Recently, administrators at the National Institutes of Health have reported that the researchers did not give Greg and his family all the information about the risks and the possibility of other approaches to treatment (Hilts, 1994). Critics of this incident claim that informed consent in this and similar situations is too often not fully met, and that information is frequently colored to assure participation. However, the UCLA researchers note that what they did with Greg was no different from what would have happened outside the research study—namely, attempting to remove him from potentially dangerous psychotropic medication. The controversy emerging from this case should serve as an added warning to researchers about their responsibilities to people who participate in their research and their need to design added safeguards to protect the welfare of their study subjects.

Contemporary Issues in Mental Health

We have discussed a number of legal and ethical issues that are important in practice and research, and now we need to see how science, therapy, the law, and ethics come together for people who study abnormal behavior. We begin with a discussion of recent changes in the provision of mental health services to those in need.

The Future of Mental Health Service Delivery

Major changes are taking place in the delivery of mental health services, particularly mental health treatments involving drugs and psychosocial interventions. In the past, mental health services along with other health services were delivered on a "fee for service" basis. Under this system the patient would choose his or her own health professional such as a family doctor or a child psychologist, usually by referral from another health professional or on the advice of friends. The health professional would then evaluate the problem, treat it using the interventions she thought were most appropriate, and bill the patient or the patient's health insurance company at the "going rate." The going rate was whatever most health care professionals in the community were charging for that service. The patient or the health insurance company (or more usually a combination of the two) would then pay the bill.

As the years have gone by several problems have arisen with this system. First, health care costs in the United States increased greatly. One cause of the increase was the substantial technical advances in the delivery of health care, including sophisticated and expensive new equipment and procedures. But another cause was that hospitals and health care professionals were free to charge whatever they wanted for the service and could expect to be paid by the health insurance companies. Since most patients didn't "shop" for doctors or hospitals based on price, costs tended to increase very quickly.

Second, a great deal of variability existed in the types of services delivered, sometimes for the same condition. For example, someone with atherosclerosis (clogged arteries) might be advised to have either surgery or treatment with drugs depending on the physician he happened to visit since some physicians favored one approach over the other. Similarly, someone with panic disorder visiting a mental health professional might be treated with psychoanalysis, behavior therapy, or any of a number of psychosocial interventions, or with one of 8 or 10 different drugs, depending on the approach favored by the mental health professional to whom she had been referred.

Greatly escalating costs, wide variability in services (including on occasion the delivery of ineffective or even harmful interventions), and the growing recognition that every citizen has a right to receive adequate health and mental health care have led to significant and yet controversial developments in the delivery of health care services.

Some of these developments have focused on controlling costs. As a cost control measure, *health maintenance organizations (HMOs)* are now common around the country and you or your family may belong to one. In these groups, your family and/or your family's employer and everyone else enrolled in the organization pays a preset fee per year. The health maintenance organization in turn agrees to provide all your medical and mental health care for that fee and hires a group of health care professionals to provide the care. You pay the same fee regardless of whether you and your family needed any services throughout the year. The health care professional is paid a straight salary rather than a separate fee for each service. The federal government is strongly encouraging HMOs and similar forms of service delivery in an attempt to control costs. The rationale for support is that the health maintenance organization makes a profit by keeping their enrollees healthy rather than by treating them when they are sick, as in the fee for service system. Some have questioned whether HMOs actually reduce costs and, if so, whether they accomplish this by cutting back on important health care services that their patients need.

Another development is the establishment within the health system of the *managed care* industry. While this concept has many variations (with HMOs being one of the variations), managed care companies usually contract with large groups of people, such as the employees of a big corporation (or many small corporations banding together), to provide all their health services at a reasonably low cost. The company then contracts with groups of health and mental health service providers, to whom all patients who have signed up with a managed care company are referred. Another name for the arrangement is "Preferred Provider Organization" (PPO). The health service provider still operates on a fee for service basis but the managed care company very closely monitors the health care professionals to assure that they are providing what the companies define as adequate care at the lowest possible cost. Often health service providers must request authorization to perform certain services, particularly expensive services, in advance and receive permission from the managed care company before delivering and being reimbursed for the service. The monitoring process is called *utilization review*. Natu-

rally, psychologists, physicians, and other health care providers often object strongly to being told how to do their job. Managed care companies, on the other hand, accuse health care professionals of delivering lengthy or unnecessarily expensive treatments and not wanting to update their services.

This is just a sampling of recent innovations in the delivery of health and mental health services. We are sure to see more of these types of efforts as the United States government moves toward a national health care plan that would ensure full access for every one of its citizens to the health and mental health system—while at the same time controlling costs. Many states have already adopted some of these innovations.

Clinical Practice Guidelines

Controlling costs will be of little use to the government or its citizens if treatments delivered in the health care system are not effective. This concern has led the government to greater interest in ascertaining whether treatments delivered are safe and effective. The United States has long had an agency—the Food and Drug Administration (FDA)—to evaluate the safety and efficacy of pharmacological agents before allowing their prescription in this country. The FDA is one of the toughest regulatory agencies on drugs in the world, but it is uncertain if we will see an FDA for psychosocial interventions soon because of the inherent differences between these treatments and drugs. Drugs are manufactured in a factory to preset specifications. The job of the clinician is to monitor the effects of the pill very closely. Psychosocial treatments, on the other hand, are delivered in the context of a continual interplay between the clinician and patient and therefore require somewhat more flexibility and less structure than drug treatments. Nevertheless, recognizing the wide variability that exists around the country in treating the same disorder and the increasing demand of managed care companies for knowledge of appropriate and effective treatments, the government has stepped in. In 1989 legislation was passed establishing a new branch of the government called the Agency for Health Care Policy and Research (AHCPR). The purpose of this agency is to begin establishing more uniformity in the delivery of effective health and mental health care and to communicate to health and mental health practitioners throughout the country the latest developments in treating certain disorders effectively. This agency is also responsible for research into improving systems for the delivery of health and mental health services.

To accomplish their goals, the AHCPR began developing and publishing *clinical practice guidelines* for specific disorders. The purpose of the guidelines is to provide a broad outline of the approaches or interventions that are likely to be effective for a specific disorder. Thus far the AHCPR has published guidelines for a number of disorders or conditions, such as sickle cell disease, management of cancer pain, unstable angina, and depression in primary care settings. Through their promulgation the government hopes not only to reduce costs by eliminating unnecessary or ineffective treatments but also to facilitate the dissemination of effective interventions based on the latest research evidence. Treating people effectively— alleviating their pain and distress—is ultimately the most important way to reduce health care costs, since these individuals will no longer remain in the health care system requesting one treatment after another in an unending search for relief from their suffering.

Recognizing the importance of this trend and the necessity that these clinical practice guidelines be constructed in a sound and valid manner, a task force of the American Psychological Association is writing a template, or set, of principles for constructing and evaluating guidelines for clinical interventions for both psychological disorders and psychosocial aspects of physical disorders. These principles currently exist in draft form. They are necessary to ensure that future clinical practice guidelines will be comprehensive and consistent. As envisioned by the task force creating the template, the guidelines developed from it should help both the practitioner and the patient make decisions about appropriate treatment interventions for cognitive, emotional, and behavioral disorders and dysfunctions as well as psychosocial aspects of physical disorders. Guidelines based on these principles should also ideally restrain administrators of health care plans from sacrificing or proscribing effective treatment or limiting the amount of clinician time necessary to deliver treatment in order to save costs. The task force also felt that guidelines for psychosocial interventions could never be strict since they must allow for the individual issues that arise in treating people with psychological disorders.

In writing this template, the task force decided that clinical practice guidelines for specific disorders should be constructed on the basis of two simultaneous considerations or "axes." The first axis is a thorough consideration of the scientific evidence to determine whether the intervention in question is effective. This evidence would answer the question, "Is the treatment effective when compared to an alternative treatment or to no treatment in a controlled clinical research context?" That is, what is the **clinical efficacy** of the treatment? (Clinical efficacy is the name given to this axis.) In Chapter 4, we reviewed the various research strategies used to determine whether an intervention is effective. As you will remember, there are many reasons a treatment might seem to be effective when it is not effective at all. For instance, patients might improve on their own while being treated simply because of the passage of time or the natural healing process; the treatment would have little to do with the improve-

ment. Or it is possible that nonspecific effects of the treatment—perhaps just meeting with a health professional who is a caring person—would be enough to make someone feel better without any contribution from the particular treatment technique used by the mental health practitioner. Another label describing the process to determine whether an intervention is truly effective is *internal validity:* Can we attribute the effects of the intervention to the treatment itself and not to a variety of other factors that may be ongoing in the treatment setting? To determine clinical efficacy or internal validity we rely on randomized control trials (RCTs) as described in Chapter 4. These clinical experiments might determine whether the intervention in question is better than no therapy, better than a nonspecific therapy, or better than some alternative therapy. The latter finding provides the highest level of evidence for a treatment's effectiveness. We might also rely on information on the effects of treatment collected from various clinics where a large number of clinicians or mental health practitioners are actually treating the disorder in question. If these clinicians collect systematic data on the outcomes of their patients, they can ascertain how many are "cured," how many improve somewhat without recovering totally, and how many fail to respond to the intervention. Such data are referred to as quantified clinical observations or clinical replication series. These observations can also contribute to determining whether a treatment is efficacious. Finally, a clinical consensus of leading experts is also a valuable source of information, although not as valuable as data from quantified clinical observations or randomized control trials. Suggested guidelines for evaluating evidence on this treatment efficacy axis are presented in Table 17.3.

The second consideration, or axis, is concerned with the effectiveness of the intervention in the practice setting in which it is to be applied regardless of research evidence on its efficacy. In other words, will an intervention with proven efficacy in a research setting also be effective in the various frontline clinical settings in which it will be most frequently utilized? Also, is application of the intervention in the settings where it is needed feasible and cost effective? The name of this axis is **clinical utility.** Another label would be *external validity* or the extent to which an internally valid intervention is effective in different settings or under different circumstances from those where it was tested.

The first major issue to consider on the clinical utility axis is feasibility. Will patients accept the intervention and comply with its requirements, and is the intervention relatively easy for a mental health practitioner to administer? As noted in Chapter 7, electroconvulsive therapy (ECT) is an effective treatment for very severe depression in many cases but it is extremely frightening to patients, many of whom refuse it. The

Table 17.3 Selected Guidelines for Evaluating the Clinical Efficacy (Internal Validity) of Psychological Interventions

Guideline 1.0—All interventions should be subject to empirical confirmation. Such confirmation is necessary regardless of the theoretical derivation of the intervention. At present, many empirically based investigations have been completed or are underway to test the efficacy of psychotherapeutic and pharmacological interventions.

Guideline 2.0—Efforts should be made to generate systematic compilations of clinical consensus by sampling opinions across recognized interdisciplinary groups of experts. Such efforts probably inspire greater confidence than unsystematic clinical opinion but still fall short of judgments based on carefully controlled evaluation.

Guideline 3.0—Each intervention should be subjected to an increasingly stringent set of methodologies designed to enhance confidence in the efficacy of that intervention. Panels developing recommendations for specific interventions should consider the level of technological advancement in the research producing the available data base.

Guideline 3.1—Quantified clinical observation represents an initial step in the systematic evaluation of treatment efficacy. In this procedure, sometimes referred to as clinical replication series, the extent of the clinical efficacy of an intervention is "tested" with a series of patients. The intervention is applied in the practice setting and quantifiable observations are made in regard to clinical efficacy of the intervention across a large number of diverse patients with a given disorder. These clinical observations may then form the basis for further systematic evaluation.

Guideline 3.2—Randomized controlled trials represent another means of evaluating treatment efficacy. In essence, patients are randomly assigned to conditions so as to reduce the likelihood that the groups differ prior to treatment with respect to characteristics that could influence subsequent status.

Source: U.S. Department of Health and Human Services, Draft 5/13/94.

treatment also requires sophisticated procedures and close supervision by medical personnel, usually in a hospital setting. Therefore, it is not particularly feasible. Suggested guidelines for evaluating the feasibility of an intervention are listed in Table 17.4.

A second issue on the clinical utility axis is generalizability, which refers to the extent to which an intervention is effective across patients of different backgrounds—ethnicity, age, or sex—as well as across different settings—inpatient, outpatient, community— or across different therapists. Once again an intervention could be very effective in a research setting with one group of patients but generalize very poorly across different ethnic groups. Suggested guidelines to consider when evaluating the generalizability of an intervention are also listed in Table 17.5. Both axes are presented in Table 17.6.

In reading through the disorder chapters you will have noted that we now have a number of effective treatments, both psychosocial and drug, for the various disorders. However, most of these treatments are still in a preliminary stage of development. In the future, we will see a great deal of research to establish both the clinical efficacy and the clinical

Table 17.4 Selected Guidelines for Evaluating the Feasibility of Psychological Interventions as Part of the Clinical Utility (External Validity) of These Interventions

Guideline 4.0—The Panel should evaluate the acceptability of the intervention to patients who will receive the service. There are many reasons patients would prefer not to receive some treatments regardless of demonstrated efficacy. These reasons may include such factors as pain, cost, duration, fear, side effects, and adverse reactions.

Guideline 4.1—In the context of relatively equal efficacy, patient choice is an important factor in recommending one intervention over the other. There is some evidence that patient choice will increase the clinical utility of a given intervention. In addition, patient unacceptability may preclude the administration of an intervention, regardless of efficacy.

Guideline 4.2—The Panel should evaluate evidence on the likelihood of compliance with an intervention by the patients who will receive the service. Interventions require in and out of session activity on the part of the patient. If the patients are unable or unwilling to comply with treatment requirements despite the best efforts of the therapist, the intervention will not be effective. Examples of this concern include the patient's unwillingness to self-monitor activities, to engage in new behaviors, or to take medications regularly, when these are integral parts of treatment.

Guideline 5.0—The Panel should evaluate the ease of dissemination of the intervention.

Guideline 5.1—The Panel should evaluate the availability of practitioners who possess satisfactory competence in the administration of the intervention. Interventions require differing levels of training and skill to achieve optimal effects. Clinical utility may be affected if the availability of competent practitioners is severely limited. Therefore, the Panel should take into account the requirements for training as well as the availability of opportunities to reach a level of satisfactory competence with the intervention.

Guideline 5.2—The Panel should take into account the cost of administering the intervention. Some interventions require costly technology or the support of additional personnel or resources.

Source: U.S. Department of Health and Human Services, Draft 5/13/94.

Table 17.5 Selected Guidelines for Evaluating the Generalizability of Psychological Interventions as Part of the Clinical Utility (External Validity) of These Interventions

Guideline 6.0—The Panel should take into account the breadth of patient variables when evaluating patient characteristics in the intervention. Variability in responding among broadly defined groups of patients may contribute to knowledge of patient-to-treatment matchings, which is an important consideration in clinical settings.

Guideline 6.1—The Panel should be guided by research and cultural expertise in addressing issues regarding the cultural background of the patient when evaluating the intervention. Interventions that are of demonstrable efficacy with one ethnic group may not be equally applicable to patients from other ethnic or cultural groups. In the absence of relevant research, caution must be exercised in generalizing to patients with varied cultural backgrounds. Provisions should be made for cultural input whenever treatment guidelines are applied to diverse populations.

Guideline 6.2—The Panel should consider research addressing the issue of the sex (biological characteristics) and gender (social characteristics) of the patient. Interventions that are of demonstrable efficacy with male patients may not be applicable to female patients in the absence of an equivalent data base. For example, men and women often have different thresholds for entering treatment for alcoholism (because of greater perceived stigma for women). Males and females metabolize drugs in different ways.

Guideline 6.3—The Panel should evaluate research concerning the developmental level of the patient. Interventions that are of demonstrable efficacy with middle-aged patients may not be equally applicable with children or geriatric patients. For example, interventions that require complex verbal behavior are not appropriate for most young children.

Guideline 6.4—The Panel should consider whether data exist on other relevant patient characteristics when evaluating the intervention. Patient characteristics such as, but not limited to, SES, geographical location, sexual orientation, and physical condition may play an important role in determining the clinical utility of an intervention.

Guideline 7.0—The Panel should evaluate the efficacy of treatment when administered by therapists who differ on a number of relevant dimensions, such as, but not limited to, training, skill, ethnicity, or sex.

Guideline 8.0—The Panel should evaluate evidence pertaining to treatment robustness. A well-designed efficacy study often makes use of a highly structured approach to treatment, such as adherence to a manual, whereas treatment as offered in the practice setting rarely conforms to this high level of structure. A treatment's clinical utility may vary with alterations in administration from the specified treatment protocol. Data relevant to issues such as adhering to a protocol, differing time frames for delivering treatment, and the possibility of interrupting treatment to address family crises should be addressed.

Source: U.S. Department of Health and Human Services, Draft 5/13/94.

Table 17.6 Overview of Template (Draft) for Constructing Psychological Intervention Guidelines

Clinical Efficacy (Internal Validity)
1. Better than alternative therapy (randomized controlled trials RCTs)
2. Better than nonspecific therapy (RCTs)
3. Better than no therapy (RCTs)
4. Quantified clinical observations
5. Clinical consensus
   Strongly positive
   Mixed
   Strongly negative
6. Contradictory evidence

Note: Confidence in treatment efficacy is based on both (a) the absolute and relative efficacy of the treatment and (b) the quality and replicability of the studies on which this judgment is made.

Clinical Utility (External Validity)
1. Feasibility
   A. Patient acceptability (cost, pain, duration, side effects, etc.)
   B. Patient choice in face of relatively equal efficacy
   C. Probability of compliance
   D. Ease of dissemination—number of practitioners with competence, requirements for training, opportunities for training, need for costly technologies or additional support personnel, etc.
2. Generalizability
   A. Patient characteristics
      (1) Cultural background issues
      (2) Gender issues
      (3) Developmental level issues
      (4) Other relevant patient characteristics
   B. Therapist characteristics
   C. Issues of robustness when applied in practice settings with different time frames, etc.
   D. Contextual factors regarding setting in which treatment is delivered
3. Costs and benefits
   A. Costs of delivering intervention to individual and society
   B. Costs of withholding intervention to individual and society

Note: Confidence in clinical utility as reflected on these three dimensions should be based on systematic and objective methods and strategies for assessing these characteristics of treatment as they are applied in actual practice. In some cases, randomized controlled trials will exist. More often, data will be in the form of quantified clinical observations (clinical replication series) or other strategies such as health economic calculations.

Source: U.S. Department of Health and Human Services, Draft 5/13/94.

utility of various interventions for psychological disorders.

In Chapter 1, we reviewed various activities that make up the role of the scientist-practitioner in the mental health professions. In this role, mental health professionals take a scientific approach to their clinical work in order to provide the most effective assessment procedures and interventions for people suffering from psychological disorders. Changes in the delivery of mental health services are likely to be accompanied by considerable disruption, as would occur any time there are changes in a major system that affects millions of people. But there will also be opportunities during a period of change. Specifically, the institution of clinical practice guidelines and the continual development and refinement of new guidelines will provide an opportunity for scientist-practitioners to contribute to the process of guideline development in several ways. For example, as attempts are made to assess the clinical utility or external validity of interventions, immense value can be derived from the collected experience of mental health professionals acting as scientist-practitioners seeing thousands of diverse patients of different ages and ethnic backgrounds in different locations. Clinical researchers can use the information collected by these

practitioners to evaluate the generalizability and feasibility of various new treatments. In fact, most of the information relevant to clinical utility or external validity will be collected by these clinicians in the course of their practice. Thus they will be acting as scientists (as many are now) and truly fulfilling the scientist-practitioner role to the benefit of patients in our field.

Conclusions

Therapy and science do not occur in a vacuum. People who study and treat abnormal behavior are responsible not only for knowing the wealth of information we have only touched on in this book, but also for understanding and appreciating their role in society and the world at large. Every facet of life, from the biological to the social, political, and legal, interacts with the other facets; if we are to help people, we must appreciate this complexity. We hope we have given readers a glimpse of the challenges facing workers in the field of mental health and have spurred some to join in this rewarding work.

Summary

- Societal views concerning people with mental illness, and therefore its laws, do not remain static; they change with time. Often these changes are responses to perceived problems with the laws, and changes are effected to improve them. According to La Fond and Durham (1992), two trends in mental health law are evident in the recent history of the United States: A "liberal era" occurred between 1960 and 1980, characterized by a commitment to individual rights and fairness; a "neoconservative era" began in 1980 and continues to the present, focused on majority concerns as well as law and order.

- *Civil commitment laws* determine the conditions under which a person is certified legally to have a mental illness and therefore is placed in a hospital, sometimes in conflict with the person's own wishes. A second type of commitment—*criminal commitment*—is the process by which people are held for two reasons: (a) They have been accused of committing a crime and are detained in a mental health facility until they can be determined as fit or unfit to participate in legal proceedings against them; or (b) they have been found not guilty of a crime by reason of insanity.

- Historically, states have permitted commitment when several conditions have been met: (1) when the person has a "mental illness" and is in need of treatment, (2) when the person is dangerous to himself or herself or to others, and/or (3) when the person is unable to care for himself or herself—otherwise referred to as having a grave disability.

- The state takes control of its citizens under two types of authority: police power—the power to impose on private rights restrictions that are reasonably related to the promotion and maintenance of the health, safety, and welfare of the public—and *parens patriae* ("parent of the country") power—the role of the state as guardian of persons with legally certified disability.

- *Mental illness* as used in legal system language is not synonymous with psychological disorder; each state has its own definition of mental illness, usually meant to include people with very severe disturbances that negatively impact on their health and safety.

• Having a mental illness does not seem to increase the likelihood that a person will commit violent acts in the future, although having symptoms of hallucinations and delusions does seem to put a person at more risk for behaving violently.

• The combination of factors such as the lack of success with deinstitutionalization, the rise in homelessness, and the criminalization of people with severe mental illness led to a backlash against the perceived causes of these factors, including the strict civil commitment laws.

• The *M'Naghten* rule states that people are not responsible for criminal behavior if they do not know what they are doing, or if they do know and they don't know it is wrong. The *Durham* rule broadened the criteria for responsibility from a knowledge of right or wrong to the presence of a "mental disease or defect." The American Law Institute (ALI) criteria concluded that people were not responsible for their criminal behavior if, because of their mental illness, they either lacked cognitive ability to recognize the inappropriateness of their behavior or they lacked the ability to control their behavior.

• The concept of *diminished capacity* holds that people's ability to understand the nature of their behavior and therefore their criminal intent could be lessened by their mental illness.

• Before people can be tried for a criminal offense, they must be *competent to stand trial;* in other words, they must be able to understand the charges against them and must be able to assist with their own defense.

• Individuals who have specialized knowledge and who assist judges and juries in making decisions are called *expert witnesses.*

Key Terms

civil commitment laws (677)
clinical efficacy [axis] (697)
clinical utility [axis] (697)
competency (689)
criminal commitment (677, 684)

dangerousness (679)
deinstitutionalization (681)
diminished capacity (686)
duty to warn (690)
expert witness (690)

informed consent (694)
insanity defense (686)
malingering (691)
transinstitutionalization (682)

Glossary

Prepared by David Santogrossi

Note: Many familiar words have specialized meanings and usage in psychology. A number of these, used in the text, are defined here.

3-methoxy-4-hydroxy-phenylglycol (MHPG) By-product of **norepinephrine.** Depressed patients with lower levels of MHPG respond better to **tricyclic antidepressants** than those with higher levels.

5-hydroxyindoleacetic acid (5-HIAA) By-product of the **neurotransmitter serotonin** in the cerebrospinal fluid, which serves as an indirect measure of serotonin.

abnormal behavior Actions that are unexpected and often evaluated negatively because they differ from typical or usual behavior.

abnormality Deviation from the average or the usual.

acetylcholine (ACh) Neurotransmitter, pervasive throughout the nervous system, that contributes to movement, attention, arousal, and memory. A deficiency of ACh is found in people with Alzheimer's disease.

acute onset Sudden beginning of a disease or disorder.

acute PTSD Posttraumatic stress disorder that is diagnosed one to three months following the traumatic event.

acute stress disorder Severe reaction immediately following a terrifying event, often including amnesia about the event, emotional numbing, and derealization. Many victims later develop **posttraumatic stress disorder.**

addiction Informal term for **substance dependence.**

adoptees' relatives method In genetics research, the evaluation and study of the biological and adoptive families of individuals who display the disorder being investigated. The purpose is to assess genetic and environmental contributions to the disorder.

adoptees' study method In genetics research, the evaluation and study of children who have been adopted by another family and who have a biological parent displaying the disorder in question. The purpose is to assess genetic and environmental contributions to the disorder.

adoption studies In genetics research, the study of first-degree relatives reared in different families and environments. If they share common characteristics, such as a disorder, this finding suggests that those characteristics have a genetic component.

advanced sleep phase type Type of circadian rhythm problem, not a DSM-IV disorder, involving a persistent pattern of early sleep onset and awakening times.

affect Conscious, subjective aspect of an emotion that accompanies an action at a given time.

age normed Standardized by age level; used for test scores.

age of onset Person's age when he or she develops or exhibits symptoms of a disease or condition.

agnosia Inability to recognize and name objects; may be a symptom of dementia or other brain disorders.

agonist Chemical substance that effectively increases the activity of a **neurotransmitter** by imitating its effects.

agonist substitution Replacement of a drug on which a person is dependent with one having a similar chemical makeup, an agonist. Used as a treatment for substance dependence.

agoraphobia Anxiety about being in places or situations from which escape might be difficult.

agreeableness One of the dimensions of the five-factor model of personality and individual differences, involving being warm, kind, and trusting as opposed to hostile, selfish, and mistrustful.

AIDS-related complex (ARC) Group of minor health problems such as weight loss, fever, and night sweats that appears after HIV infection, but prior to development of full-blown AIDS.

akinesia Extrapyramidal symptom involving slow motor activity, an expressionless face, and emotionless speech (see also **extrapyramidal symptoms**).

alcohol By-product of the fermentation of yeasts, sugar, and water; the most commonly used and abused depressant substance.

alcohol dehydrogenase (ADH) Enzyme that helps humans metabolize alcohol. Different levels of its subtypes may account for different susceptibilities to disorders such as **fetal alcohol syndrome.**

alcohol myopia Condition in which a person under the influence of alcohol ignores the long-range consequences of his or her behavior and responds only to the poorly thought-out immediate aspects of a situation.

alcohol-use disorder Cognitive, biological, behavioral, and social problems associated with alcohol use and abuse.

alcohol withdrawal delirium Set of symptoms including body tremors and frightening hallucinations that may result during withdrawal from extended alcohol use. Also known as delirium tremens or the "DTs."

alogia Deficiency in the amount or content of speech, a disturbance often seen in people with schizophrenia.

alpha adrenergic receptors One group of nervous system receptors stimulated by the **neurotransmitter norepinephrine.**

alpha waves Regular pattern of brain-wave voltage changes typical of calm relaxation.

alprazolam High-potency **benzodiazepine** medication (trade-name *Xanax*) for panic disorder that is fast acting but may lead to dependence and addiction.

alter Shorthand term for alter egoes, the different personalities or identities in **dissociative identity disorder.**

altruistic suicide Formalized suicide approved and even expected by some cultures.

ambulatory polysomnography Assessment of sleep disorders with portable electronic metering devices that allow clients sleeping in their natural home environments to be monitored for heart, muscle, respiration, brain wave, and other functions.

amnestic disorder Deterioration in the ability to transfer information from short- to long-term memory, in the absence of other dementia symptoms, as a result of head trauma or drug abuse.

amniocentesis Prenatal medical procedure that allows the detection of abnormalities (e.g., Down syndrome) in the developing fetus. It involves removal and analysis of amniotic fluid from the mother.

amok One of several running disorders seen in non-Western cultures—as in "running amok"—in which the individual enters a trancelike state and may commit violent acts; later he or she will have amnesia about the episode.

amotivational syndrome Impairment reported among heavy marijuana users involving apathy or an unwillingness to carry out long-term plans. Its actual prevalence level is controversial.

amphetamine Stimulant medication used to treat hypersomnia by keeping the person awake during the day, and to treat narcolepsy by suppressing REM sleep, including sudden onset episodes.

amphetamine-use disorder Psychological, biological, behavioral, and social problems associated with amphetamine use and abuse.

amygdala Part of the brain's limbic system that regulates emotions and the ability to learn and control impulses; figures prominently in some psychopathology.

amyloid precursor protein Large protein, controlled by a gene on chromosome 21, that breaks down to contribute to the neuritic plaque characteristic of people with Alzheimer's disease.

amyloid protein Solid waxy substance forming the core of the neuritic plaque characteristic of people with Alzheimer's disease.

analgesic rebound headache Headache, more severe than the original one, that occurs after the medication used to treat headache pain has "worn off."

analogue model Approach to research employing subjects who are similar to clinical clients, allowing replication of a clinical problem under controlled conditions.

anandamide Neurochemical that seems to be a naturally occurring version of the active chemical in marijuana.

angina pectoris Chest pain caused by partial blockage of the arteries that supply blood to the heart.

angulate gyrus Part of the brain's limbic system that regulates emotions and the ability to learn and control impulses; figures prominently in some psychopathology.

anhedonia Inability to experience pleasure, associated with some mood and schizophrenic disorders.

animal phobia Unreasonable, enduring fear of animals or insects that usually develops early in life.

anomic suicide Suicide motivated by loss and confusion caused by a major life disruption.

anorexia nervosa Eating disorder characterized by recurrent food refusal leading to dangerously low body weight.

Antabuse See **disulfiram.**

antagonist In neuroscience, a chemical substance that decreases or blocks the effects of a **neurotransmitter.**

antagonist drugs Medications that block or counteract the effects of psychoactive drugs.

antibodies Highly specific molecules called *immunoglobulins* produced by B cells to combine with and neutralize antigens.

antigens Foreign materials that enter the body, including bacteria and parasites.

antisocial personality disorder Cluster B (dramatic, emotional, or erratic) **personality disorder** involving a pervasive pattern of disregard for and violation of the rights of others. Similar to the non-DSM label **psychopathy** but with greater emphasis on overt behavior rather than personality traits.

anxiety Mood state characterized by marked negative affect and bodily symptoms of tension in which a person apprehensively anticipates future danger or misfortune. Anxiety may involve feelings, behaviors, and physiological responses.

Anxiety Disorders Interview Schedule-IV (ADIS-IV) Specialized, structured interview protocol to assess anxiety and related disorders.

aphasia Impairment or loss of language skills resulting from brain damage caused by stroke, Alzheimer's disease, or other illness or trauma.

apnea Brief interruption in breathing, sometimes occurring during sleep.

apolipoprotein E (apoE) Protein involved in the transport of cholesterol. High concentration of one subtype, controlled by a gene on chromosome 19, is associated with Alzheimer's disease.

apoptosis Naturally occurring process that kills unnecessary nerve cells. It may be induced to occur excessively by amyloid protein and is associated with Alzheimer's disease.

arousal stage Phase of sexual activity featuring sensations of pleasure and physiological

changes including erection of the penis in males and the nipples in females. Women also experience vaginal lubrication and blood pooling in the pelvic region.

arrhythmia Irregular heart beat.

Asperger's disorder Pervasive developmental disorder characterized by impairments in social relationships and restricted or unusual behaviors, but without language delays seen in autism.

assertiveness training Instruction in which an individual learns to cope with stress by rehearsing ways to protect his or her time and personal rights in appropriate ways to avoid being exploited and feeling used. For example, caregivers of people with Alzheimer's disease learn assertion to prevent them from resorting to abuse in frustration.

assessment gender bias Possibility that gender differences in the reported prevalence or diagnosis of certain diagnostic categories may be due to prejudice in the assessment measures or the ways they are used.

associative splitting Separation among basic functions of human personality (e.g., cognition, emotion, perception) that is seen by some as the defining characteristic of schizophrenia.

asylum Safe refuge; specifically, an institution to house mentally disordered people.

atherosclerosis Process by which a fatty substance or plaque builds up inside arteries to form obstructions.

attention-deficit/hyperactivity disorder (ADHD) Developmental disorder featuring maladaptive levels of inattention, excessive activity, and impulsiveness.

atypical depressive episode Depressive episode characterized by some ability to experience interest and pleasure, increased anxiety, overeating, and oversleeping.

auditory hallucinations Psychotic disturbance in perception in which person hears sounds or voices although these are not real or actually present. The voices are often critical, accusatory, or demanding.

augmentative communication strategies Pictures or computer aids to assist people with communication deficits to communicate.

autistic disorder (autism) Pervasive developmental disorder characterized by significant impairment in social interactions and communication, and restricted patterns of behavior, interest, and activity.

autogenic relaxation training Instruction that teaches clients to relax by focusing attention on blood flow and tense muscle groups, and by suggesting to themselves that they are feeling warm and relaxed.

autoimmune disease Condition in which the body's immune system attacks healthy tissue rather than antigens.

autonomic nervous system Part of the **peripheral nervous system** that regulates cardiovascular (heart, blood vessel), endocrine (hormone), and digestive functions. Includes the **sympathetic** and **parasympathetic nervous systems.**

autonomic restrictors Term for people with **generalized anxiety disorder (GAD)** because they show lower heart rate, blood pressure, skin conductance, and respiration rate activity than do people with other anxiety disorders.

avoidant personality disorder Cluster C (anxious or fearful) personality disorder featuring a pervasive pattern of social inhibition, feelings of inadequacy, and hypersensitivity to criticism.

avolition Apathy, or the inability to initiate or persist in important activities.

axes Several dimensions for which information is provided in DSM-IV diagnosis protocols—for example, clinical disorders and medical conditions.

axon Nerve cell branches that transmit outgoing electrochemical impulses to other neurons.

B cells Special type of white blood cells produced in bone marrow. They release molecules in the humoral branch of the immune system that circulate in the blood to seek out, identify, and neutralize antigens.

barbiturates Sedative (and addictive) drugs including Amytal, Seconal, and Nembutal that are used as sleep aids.

basal ganglia Brain area at the base of the telencephalon that seems to control motor behavior and to be involved in obsessive-compulsive disorder.

baseline Measured rate of a behavior before introduction of an intervention that allows comparison and assessment of the effects of the intervention.

behavioral assessment Measuring, observing, and systematically evaluating (rather than inferring) the client's thoughts, feelings and behavior in the actual problem situation or context.

behavioral inhibition system (BIS) Brain circuit in the **limbic system** that responds to threat signals by inhibiting activity and causing anxiety.

behavioral medicine Interdisciplinary approach applying behavioral science to the prevention, diagnosis, and treatment of medical problems.

behavioral model Explanation of human behavior, including dysfunction, based on principles of learning and adaptation derived from experimental psychology.

behavioral rehearsal Behavior therapy technique in which the client practices coping with troublesome or anxiety-arousing situations in a safe and supervised situation.

behavior rating scales Structured assessment instruments used before and during treatment to evaluate the frequency and severity of specific behaviors.

behavior therapy Array of therapy methods based on the principles of behavioral and cognitive science as well as principles of learning as applied to clinical problems. It considers specific behaviors rather than inferred conflict as legitimate targets for change.

Bender Visual-Motor Gestalt Test Neuropsychological test for children in which they copy a variety of lines and shapes.

benzodiazepine-GABA system Chemical benzodiazepines (minor tranquilizers) that facilitate the effects of the **neurotransmitter gamma-aminobutyric acid (GABA)** in reducing anxiety. Such a system suggests the existence of natural benzodiazepines in the nervous system that have not yet been discovered.

benzodiazepines Anti-anxiety drugs including Valium, Xanax, Dalmane, and Halcion also used to treat insomnia. Effective against anxiety (and, at high potency, panic disorder), they show some side effects, such as some cognitive and motor impairment, and may result in dependence and addiction. Relapse rates are extremely high when the drug is discontinued.

beta adrenergic receptors Group of nervous system receptors stimulated by the **neurotransmitter norepinephrine** to increase blood pressure and heart rate. Drugs called beta blockers act at this level to control high blood pressure.

binge Relatively brief episode of uncontrolled, excessive consumption, usually of food or alcohol.

binge-eating disorder (BED) Pattern of eating involving distress-inducing binges not followed by purging behaviors; being considered as a new DSM diagnostic category.

biofeedback Use of physiological monitoring equipment to make individuals aware of their own bodily functions, such as blood pressure or brain waves, that they cannot normally access, with the purpose of controlling these functions.

biological model Explanation of psychological dysfunction that primarily emphasizes brain disorder or illness as the cause.

bipolar mood disorder Mood disorder in which major depressive episodes alternate with manic episodes (*bipolar I disorder*) or with hypomanic episodes (*bipolar II disorder*).

bisexuality Attraction to both same- and opposite-sex sexual partners.

black box Concept of the inner workings of the organism, such as thoughts and feelings that cannot be observed directly.

blind sight Also called **unconscious vision;** phenomenon in which a person is able to perform visual functions while having no awareness or memory of these abilities.

blood-injury-injection phobia Unreasonable fear and avoidance of exposure to blood, injury, or the possibility of an injection. Victims experience fainting and a drop in blood pressure.

body dysmorphic disorder Somatoform disorder featuring a disruptive preoccupation with some imagined defect in appearance ("imagined ugliness").

borderline personality disorder Cluster B (dramatic, emotional, or erratic) personality disorder involving a pervasive pattern of instability of interpersonal relationships, self-image, affects, and control over impulses.

bradykinesia Slowed body movements, as occur in **Parkinson's disease.**

brain circuits Neurotransmitter currents or neural pathways in the brain.

brain stem Ancient lower part of the brain responsible for many life-sustaining automatic functions such as breathing and coordinated movement.

breathalyzer test Measure of alcohol intoxication that uses a breath sample because some consumed alcohol is vaporized in the lungs and exhaled.

breathing-related sleep disorders Sleep disruption leading to excessive sleepiness or insomnia, caused by a breathing problem such as interrupted (**apnea**) or labored (**hypoventilation**) breathing.

Brief Psychiatric Rating Scale Behavior rating scale used to assess the severity of patient problem areas such as guilt feelings and preoccupation with health.

brief psychotic disorder Psychotic disturbance involving delusions, hallucinations, or disorganized speech or behavior, but lasting less than one month; often occurs in reaction to a stressor.

Briquet's syndrome Obsolete term for **somatization disorder.**

bulimia disorder Eating disorder involving recurrent episodes of uncontrolled excessive (binge) eating followed by compensatory actions to remove the food (e.g., deliberate vomiting, laxative abuse, excessive exercise).

caffeine-use disorders Cognitive, biological, behavioral, and social problems associated with the use and abuse of caffeine.

cancer Category of often-fatal medical conditions involving abnormal cell growth and malignancy.

cannabinoids Family of chemicals in marijuana believed to be responsible for its mood- and behavior-altering ability.

carbamazepine Antiseizure medication sometimes effective in treating bipolar disorder.

cardiovascular disease Afflictions in the mechanisms, including the heart, blood vessels, and their controllers, that are responsible for transporting blood to the body's tissues and organs. Psychological factors may play important roles in such diseases and their treatments.

cardiovascular system Heart, blood vessels, and their controlling mechanisms, all of which serve to transport blood and nutrients to the tissues of the body.

case study method Research procedure in which a single person or small group is studied in detail. The method does not allow conclusions about cause and effect relationships, and findings can be generalized only with great caution.

castration anxiety In psychoanalysis, the fear in young boys that they will be mutilated genitally because of their lust for their mothers.

catalepsy Motor movement disturbance seen in people with some psychoses and mood disorders in which body postures are waxy and can be "sculpted," to remain fixed for long periods of time.

cataplexy Sudden loss of muscle tone that accompanies **narcolepsy** (sudden sleep attacks).

catatonia Disorder of movement involving immobility or excited agitation.

catatonic depressive episode (*depressive stupor*) Rare but severe mood disorder depressive episode usually featuring substantial reduction in spontaneous motor movement or, on occasion, agitation or odd mannerisms.

catatonic immobility Disturbance of motor behavior in which the person remains motionless, sometimes in an awkward posture, for extended periods of time.

catatonic type, schizophrenia Type of **schizophrenia** in which motor disturbances (rigidity, agitation, odd mannerisms) predominate.

catecholamine hypothesis Outdated, simplistic theory of mood disorder etiology stating that **norepinephrine** (a catecholamine) excess causes mania, and that low levels of it cause some forms of depression.

catharsis Rapid or sudden release of emotional tension thought to be an important factor in psychoanalytic therapy.

caudate nucleus Brain structure; part of the basal ganglia that controls motor behavior and is implicated in **obsessive-compulsive disorder.**

cellular branch Branch of the immune system using specialized cells to protect the body cells against viral and parasite infections.

central nervous system Brain and spinal cord.

central sleep apnea Brief periods of complete cessation in respiratory activity during sleep that may be associated with central nervous system disorders. Most clients awaken often as a result but do not report sleepiness and may be unaware of any problem.

cerebellum Part of the **hindbrain** in the **brain stem** that controls motor coordination and may be involved in **autism.**

cerebral cortex Largest part of the **forebrain,** divided into two hemispheres; responsible for human functions such as perceiving, reasoning, planning, creating, and remembering.

chemical imbalance Relative excess or deficit in brain chemicals, such as **neurotransmitters,** that may be implicated in some psychological disorders.

Child Behavior Checklist Behavior rating scale completed by parents and teachers to assess the frequency and severity of a range of possible childhood behavior problems.

childhood disintegrative disorder Pervasive developmental disorder involving severe regression in language, adaptive behavior, and motor skills after a two- to four-year period of normal development.

choking phobia Also known as *hypersensitive gag reflex* or *globus hystericus;* the fear and avoidance of swallowing pills, foods, and fluids, which may lead to significant weight loss.

chorea Motor problems characterized by involuntary limb movements.

chronic fatigue syndrome Incapacitating exhaustion following only minimal exertion, accompanied by fever, headaches, muscle and joint pain, depression, and anxiety.

chronic pain Enduring pain that does not decrease over time; may occur in muscles, joints, and the lower back, and may be due to enlarged blood vessels, or degenerating or cancerous tissue. Other significant factors are social and psychological.

chronic PTSD Posttraumatic stress disorder that endures longer than three months and is associated with greater avoidance and a higher likelihood of **comorbidity** with additional disorders.

chronic stage Final of Jellinek's four stages identified in the progression of alcoholism, where the individual's primary daily activities revolve around obtaining and drinking alcohol.

chronological age   Person's age in calendar years.

chronotherapy   Treatment for circadian rhythm sleep disorders that systematically moves bedtime later in intervals (phase delays) until it approaches the desired bedtime.

circadian rhythm sleep disorder   Sleep disturbance resulting in sleepiness or insomnia, caused by the body's inability to synchronize its sleep patterns with the current pattern of day and night.

civil commitment   Legal proceedings that determine a person is mentally disordered and may be hospitalized, even involuntarily.

classical categorical approach   Classification method founded on the assumption of clearcut differences among disorders, each with a different known cause.

classical conditioning   Fundamental learning process first described by Ivan Pavlov. An event that automatically elicits a response is paired with another stimulus event that does not (a neutral stimulus). After repeated pairings, the neutral stimulus becomes a conditioned stimulus that by itself can elicit the desired response.

classification   Assignment of objects or people to categories on the basis of shared characteristics.

clinical assessment   Systematic evaluation and measurement of psychological, biological, and social factors in a person presenting with a possible psychological disorder.

clinical efficacy (axis)   One of a proposed set of guidelines for evaluating clinical interventions on the evidence of their effectiveness.

clinical description   Details of the combination of behaviors, thoughts, and feelings of an individual that make up a particular disorder.

clinical psychologist   Person who has earned a Ph.D. or related degree (e.g., Psy.D.) in psychology and is trained to conduct research into the causes and treatment of severe psychological disorders as well as to diagnose, assess, and treat them.

clinical significance   Degree to which research findings have useful and meaningful applications to real problems.

clinical utility (axis)   One of a proposed set of guidelines for evaluating clinical interventions by whether they can be applied effectively and cost effectively in real clinical settings.

clonidine   Medical treatment for hypertension that is often used to reduce the negative symptoms of withdrawal from **opiates.**

clozapine   One of the newer medications for **schizophrenia,** trade name Clozaril, a weak **dopamine antagonist** that seems effective in some previously untreatable cases and with fewer serious side effects.

cocaine   Derivative of coca leaves used medically as a local anesthetic and narcotic; often a substance of abuse.

cocaine-use disorders   Cognitive, biological, behavioral, and social problems associated with the use and abuse of **cocaine.**

codeine   Opiate; a mild, medical narcotic derived from morphine.

cognitive-behavioral therapy   Group of treatment procedures aimed at identifying and modifying faulty thought processes, attitudes and attributions, and problem be-

haviors; often used synonymously with **cognitive therapy.**

cognitive relaxation   Use of meditation or imagery to combat anxiety that may result from sleeplessness.

cognitive restructuring   Cognitive therapy procedure used to change negative or unrealistic thoughts or attributions.

cognitive science   Field of study that examines how humans and other animals acquire, process, store, and retrieve information.

cognitive therapy   Treatment approach that involves identifying and altering negative thinking styles related to psychological disorders such as depression and anxiety and replacing them with more positive beliefs and attitudes—and, ultimately, more adaptive behavior and coping styles.

cohort   Participants in each age group of a cross-sectional research study.

cohort effect   Observation that people of different age groups also differ in their values and experiences.

collective unconscious   Accumulated wisdom of a culture collected and remembered across generations, a psychodynamic concept introduced by Karl Jung.

communication disorders   Problems in transmitting or conveying information, including **stuttering, selective mutism,** and **expressive language disorder.**

community intervention   Approach to treating and preventing disorders by directing action at the organizational, agency, and community levels rather than at individuals.

comorbidity   The presence of two or more disorders in an individual at the same time.

comparative treatment research   Outcome research that contrasts two or more treatment methods to determine which is most effective.

competency   Ability of legal defendants to participate in their own defense and understand the charges and the roles of the trial participants.

Comprehensive System   Standardized system of administering and scoring the Rorschach inkblot test that seeks to improve its reliability and validity.

compulsions   Repetitive, ritualistic, time-consuming behaviors or mental acts a person feels driven to perform.

computerized axial tomography (CAT) scan   Noninvasive imaging procedure useful in identifying abnormalities in the structure or shape of the brain.

concurrent (descriptive) validity   Condition of testing in which the results from one test correspond to the results of other measures of the same phenomenon.

conditioned response (CR)   Learned reaction, similar to the unconditioned response, that is elicited by a conditioned stimulus following classical conditioning.

conditioned stimulus (CS)   Environmental event that acquires the ability to elicit a learned response as a result of classical conditioning associated with an **unconditioned stimulus.**

conditioning   Process by which behaviors can be learned or modified through interaction with the environment. See **classical** and **operant conditioning.**

confound   Any factor occurring in a research study that makes the results uninterpretable

because its effects cannot be separated from those of the variables being studied.

confusional arousals   Sleep disturbance characterized by bewildered reactions of the sleeper on awakening that may last for several minutes.

conscientiousness   One of the dimensions of the five-factor model of personality and individual differences involving being organized, thorough, and reliable as opposed to careless, negligent, and unreliable.

construct validity   Degree to which signs and symbols used to categorize a disorder relate to each other while differing from those for other disorders.

content validity   Degree to which the characteristics of a disorder are a true sample of the phenomenon in question.

contingency management   Encouragement of reinforcers to promote and maintain desired behaviors, and the removal of those reinforcers that maintain undesired behaviors.

control group   Group of individuals in a research study who are similar to the experimental subjects in every way but are not exposed to the treatment received by the experimental group; their presence allows for a comparison of the differential effects of the treatment.

controlled drinking   Controversial treatment for alcohol abusers that attempts to teach them to drink in moderation rather than requiring them to abstain totally.

conversion disorder   Physical malfunctioning, such as blindness or paralysis, suggesting neurological impairment, but with no organic pathology to account for it.

conversion hysteria   Obsolete term for **conversion disorder** derived from the Freudian notion that physical symptoms represented a conversion of unconscious conflicts into a more acceptable form.

coping procedure   Another term for **defense mechanism,** a pattern of behavior for dealing with anxiety-arousing situations.

coprolalia   Vocal tic characterized by the involuntary repetition of obscenities.

coronary heart disease   Blockage of the arteries supplying blood to the heart muscle, the major cause of death in Western culture, with social and psychological factors involved.

correlation   Degree to which two variables are associated. In a **positive correlation,** the two variables increase or decrease together; in a **negative correlation,** one variable decreases as the other increases.

correlational coefficient   Computed statistic reflecting the strength and direction of any association between two variables. It can range from +1.00 through zero (indicating no association) to−1.00, with the absolute value indicating the strength, and the sign reflecting the direction.

correlational method   Research procedure in which variables are measured and compared to detect any association but are not manipulated. Conclusions about cause-and-effect relationships are not permissible.

cortical immaturity hypothesis   Theory that the behavior and arousal levels of psychopaths result from incomplete development of the cerebral cortex.

corticosteroids Hormones, including cortisol, released by the adrenal gland in response to stressors to activate and, later, to turn off the body's stress response. Also called **stress hormones.**

corticotropin releasing factor (CRF) Neuromodulator hormone secreted into the blood by the **hypothalamus.** It stimulates the pituitary gland as part of a reaction chain called the stress response. It may be implicated in mood disorders as well as physical problems.

cortisol Stress hormone (**corticosteroid**) secreted by the cortex of the adrenal glands as part of the stress response.

counseling psychologist Person who has earned a Ph.D. or related degree in psychology and is trained to study and treat adjustment and vocational issues in relatively healthy people.

countertransference Psychoanalytic concept involving personal issues the therapist brings to professional relationships with clients.

course Pattern of development and change of a disorder over time.

course modifiers Patterns of development in a disorder that help predict its future course. These include recurrence, time sequences, and seasonal patterns.

covert sensitization Cognitive-behavioral intervention to reduce unwanted behaviors by having clients imagine the extremely aversive consequences of the behaviors and establish negative rather than positive associations with them.

crack **Cocaine** in a highly potent, solid, rocklike form.

crack babies Infants who were exposed to cocaine prenatally because of their mothers' use. Their characteristic irritability and high-pitched crying may in fact be due to other abuse or neglect in addition to the cocaine itself.

Creutzfeldt-Jakob disease Extremely rare condition that causes **dementia.**

criminal commitment Legal procedure by which a person who is found not guilty of a crime by reason of insanity must be confined in a psychiatric hospital.

criterion gender bias Possibility that gender differences in the reported prevalence or diagnosis of certain diagnostic categories may be due to prejudice in the defining criteria for the disorder.

criterion validity Extent to which categorization accurately predicts the future course of a disorder, whether treated or untreated; also known as **predictive validity.**

cross-generational effect Limit to the generalizability of longitudinal research because the group under study may differ from others in culture and experience.

cross-sectional research design Methodology to examine a characteristic by comparing different individuals of different ages. Contrast with **longitudinal research design.**

cross-tolerance Condition in which a person may replace addiction to one drug with addiction to the other when the two drugs have similar chemical makeup and act on the same **neurotransmitter receptors.**

crucial stage Third of four of Jellinek's stages identified in the progression of alcoholism,

involving a loss of control of drinking and occasional binges of heavy drinking.

cued, or situationally bound, panic attack Panic attack for which the triggering circumstances are known to the client.

cultural-familial retardation Mild mental retardation which may be caused largely by environmental influences.

cyclothymic disorder Chronic (at least two years) mood disorder characterized by alternating mood elevation and depression levels that are not as severe as manic or major depressive episodes.

dangerousness Tendency to violence which, contrary to popular opinion, is not more likely among mental patients.

deep sleep Sleep stage characterized by slow (**delta**) brain **wave** patterns. A person in deep sleep is difficult to rouse and slow to become alert.

defense mechanisms Common patterns of behavior, often adaptive coping styles when they occur in moderation, observed in response to particular situations. In psychoanalysis, these are thought to be unconscious processes originating in the **ego.**

deinstitutionalization Systematic removal of people with severe mental illness or mental retardation out of institutions like psychiatric hospitals.

delayed-onset PTSD Posttraumatic stress **disorder** with onset more than six months after the traumatic event.

delayed sleep phase type of circadian rhythm sleep disorder A persistent pattern of late sleep onset and awakening time.

delirium Rapid-onset reduced clarity of consciousness and cognition, with confusion, disorientation, and deficits in memory and language.

delta waves Relatively slow and irregular pattern of brain waves typical of the deepest, most relaxed stage of sleep; this is the time when sleeping panic attacks may occur. Delta activity during wakefulness may indicate brain dysfunction.

delusion Psychotic symptom involving disorder of thought content and presence of strong beliefs that are misrepresentations of reality.

delusional disorder Psychotic disorder featuring a persistent belief contrary to reality (delusion) but no other symptoms of **schizophrenia.**

delusion of grandeur Psychotic symptom, a person's unfounded belief that he or she is more famous or important than is true.

delusion of persecution Person's unfounded belief that others seek to harm him or her.

demence precoce French-language form of **dementia praecox.**

dementia Gradual-onset deterioration of brain functioning, involving memory loss, inability to recognize objects or faces, and problems in planning and abstract reasoning. These are associated with frustration and discouragement.

dementia of the Alzheimer's type Gradual onset of cognitive deficits caused by Alzheimer's disease, principally identified by person's inability to recall newly or previously learned material. The most common form of dementia.

dementia praecox Latin term meaning "premature loss of mind," an early label for what is now called schizophrenia, emphasizing the disorder's frequent appearance during adolescence.

dendrite Nerve cell branches that receive incoming electrochemical information for transmission along the neuron.

dependent personality disorder Cluster C (anxious or fearful) personality disorder characterized by a person's pervasive and excessive need to be taken care of, a condition that leads to submissive and clinging behavior and fears of separation.

dependent variable In an experimental research study, the phenomenon that is measured and expected to be influenced.

depersonalization Altering of perception that causes a person temporarily to lose a sense of his or her own reality; most prevalent in people with the dissociative disorders. There is often a feeling of being an outside observer of one's own behavior.

depersonalization disorder Dissociative disorder in which feelings of depersonalization are so severe they dominate the client's life and prevent normal functioning.

depressants Psychoactive substances that result in behavioral sedation, including alcohol and the sedative, hypnotic, and anxiolytic drugs.

depressive cognitive triad Thinking errors in depressed people negatively focused in three areas: themselves, their immediate world, and their future.

depressive personality disorder Pervasive pattern dominated by dejection, self-criticism, and a judgmental stance toward other people; under consideration as a future DSM category.

derailment See **loose associations.**

derealization Situation in which the individual loses his or her sense of the reality of the external world.

desipramine Antidepressant medication that has shown some effectiveness in increasing abstinence rates among cocaine users.

desire phase First stage of sexual activity, when sexual urges, thoughts, or fantasies occur, either in reaction to or even in the absence of a stimulating cue.

developmental psychology Study of changes in behavior that occur over time.

developmental psychopathology Study of changes in abnormal behavior that occur over time.

deviation IQ Intelligence test score that estimates how much a child's school performance will deviate from the average performance of others of the same age.

dexamethasone suppression test (DST) Proposed biological test for depression; the test failed to discriminate depression from other disorders, however.

diagnosis Process of determining whether a presenting problem meets the established criteria for a specific psychological disorder.

***Diagnostic and Statistical Manual,* Fourth Edition (DSM-IV)** Current version of the official classification system for psychological disorders, published by the American Psychiatric Association.

dialectical behavioral therapy Promising treatment for borderline personality disorder that involves exposing the client to stressors in a controlled situation as well as helping the client regulate emotions and cope with stressors that might trigger suicidal behavior.

diastolic blood pressure Blood pressure level when the heart is at rest or between heartbeats.

diathesis-stress model Hypothesis that both an inherited tendency (a **vulnerability**) and specific stressful conditions are required to produce a disorder.

diencephalon Brain structure containing the **thalamus** and **hypothalamus** that serves as a relay between the **forebrain** and the **brain stem.**

dimensional approach Method of categorizing characteristics on a continuum rather than on a binary, either-or, or all-or-none basis.

dimethyltryptamine (DMT) Natural hallucinogen from the bark of trees that grow in Central and South America.

diminished capacity Evidence of an abnormal mental condition in a person that causes criminal charges against him or her requiring intent or knowledge to be reduced to lesser offenses requiring only reckless or criminal neglect.

directionality issue The possibility that, when two variables A and B are correlated, variable A causes variable B, or that B causes A.

discrimination training Arrangement of experiences in which the person or animal learns to respond under certain conditions and not to respond under other conditions.

disease conviction Core feature of **hypochondriasis,** the firm belief that one currently has a disease, based on the misinterpretation of one's own symptoms and sensations.

disease model of dependence View that drug dependence is caused by a physiological disorder. This implies that the user is a blameless victim of an illness.

disorder of written expression Condition in which one's writing performance is significantly below age norms.

disorganized speech Style of talking often seen in people with **schizophrenia,** involving incoherence and a lack of typical logic patterns.

disorganized type, schizophrenia Type of schizophrenia featuring disrupted speech and behavior, disjointed delusions and hallucinations, and flat or silly affect.

displacement Defense mechanism in which a person directs a problem impulse toward a safe substitute.

dispositional optimism Cognitive style involving expectations of positive outcomes; seems to influence physical health in a positive way.

dissociation Detachment or loss of integration between identity or reality and consciousness.

dissociative amnesia Dissociative disorder featuring the inability to recall personal information, usually of a stressful or traumatic nature.

dissociative disorders Disorder in which individuals feel detached from themselves or their surroundings, and reality, experience, and identity may disintegrate.

dissociative fugue Dissociative disorder featuring sudden, unexpected travel away from home, along with an inability to recall one's past, sometimes with assumption of a new identity.

dissociative identity disorder (DID) Formerly known as *multiple personality disorder,* a disorder in which as many as 100 personalities or fragments of personalities coexist within one body and mind.

dissociative trance disorder Altered state of consciousness in which the person believes firmly that he or she is possessed by spirits; considered a disorder only where there is distress and dysfunction.

disulfiram (Antabuse) Chemical used as an aversion treatment for heavy drinking because it causes a buildup in the body of an alcohol by-product, making the person vomit after drinking. Clients must continue taking it for the chemical to remain effective.

dominant gene The one gene of any pair of genes that determines a particular trait.

dopamine Neurotransmitter whose generalized function is to activate other neurotransmitters and to aid in exploratory and pleasure-seeking behaviors (thus balancing **serotonin**). A relative excess of dopamine is implicated in **schizophrenia** (though contradictory evidence suggest the connection is not simple) and its deficit is involved in **Parkinson's disease.**

dopaminergic system Parts of the nervous system activated by the **neurotransmitter dopamine;** involved in many functions including the experience of reward.

dorsal horns of the spinal cord Sections of the spinal cord responsible for transmitting sensory input to the brain. They function as a "gate" that allows transmission of pain sensations if the stimulation is sufficiently intense.

double bind communication According to an obsolete, unsupported theory, the practice of transmitting conflicting messages that was thought to cause **schizophrenia.**

double-blind control Procedure in outcome studies that prevents bias by ensuring that neither the subjects nor the providers of the experimental treatment know who is receiving treatment and who is receiving placebo.

double depression Severe mood disorder typified by major depressive episodes superimposed over a background of **dysthymic disorder.**

Down syndrome Type of mental retardation caused by a chromosomal aberration (chromosome 21) and involving characteristic physical appearance.

dream interpretation Psychoanalytic therapy method in which dream contents are examined as symbolic of **id** impulses and intrapsychic conflicts.

duty to warn Mental health professional's responsibility to break confidentiality and notify the potential victim whom a client has specifically threatened.

dysfunctional attitudes Cognitive errors seen in depressed individuals, who may automatically assume the worst, draw negative conclusions arbitrarily, and treat minor problems as major ones.

dyslexia Learning disability involving problems in reading.

dysmorphophobia Literally, "fear of ugliness," an obsolete term for **body dysmorphic disorder.**

dysphoric manic episode See **mixed manic episode.**

dyssomnias Problems in getting to sleep or in obtaining sufficient quality sleep.

dysthymic disorder Mood disorder involving persistently depressed mood, with low self-esteem, withdrawal, pessimism or despair, present for at least two years, with no absence of symptoms for more than two months.

echolalia Repetition or echoing of the speech of others, a normal intermediate step in the development of speech skills. Originally thought to be a unique symptom of **autism,** it is now seen as evidence of developmental delay involved in that disorder.

echo planar magnetic resonance imaging Experimental version of magnetic resonance imaging that can make rapid multiple sequential images of the brain as it functions.

educable mental retardation Obsolete term referring to level of retardation comparable to the DSM "mild" designation that assumes the individual can learn basic academic skills.

ego In psychoanalysis, the psychical entity responsible for finding realistic and practical ways to satisfy **id** drives.

egoistic suicide Suicide that occurs in the context of diminished social supports, as in the case of some elderly persons who have lost friends and family contacts.

ego psychology Derived from psychoanalysis, this theory emphasizes the role of the **ego** in development and attributes psychological disorders to failure of the ego to manage impulses and internal conflicts.

Electra complex In psychoanalysis, a young girl's intrapsychic desire to replace her mother, possess her father, and acquire a penis. The resolution of this complex results in development of the **superego.**

electrocardiogram Measure of electrical activity generated by heart muscle exertion used to detect and evaluate heart diseases.

electroconvulsive shock therapy (ECT) Biological treatment for severe, chronic depression involving the application of electrical impulses through the brain to produce seizures. The reasons for its effectiveness are unknown.

electrodermal responding Psychophysiological assessment of skin conductance and sweat gland activity as a measure of **autonomic nervous system** responses to stress.

electroencephalogram (EEG) Measure of electrical activity patterns in the brain, taken through electrodes placed on the scalp.

electromyogram (EMG) Measure of muscle movement.

electrooculogram (EOG) Measure of eye muscle movement particularly relevant to detecting dream stages during sleep.

emotion Pattern of action elicited by an external event and a feeling state, accompanied by a characteristic physiological response.

emotional stability One of the dimensions of the five-factor model of personality and individual differences, involving being even-tempered as opposed to nervous, moody, and temperamental.

emotion contagion Situation in which an emotional reaction spreads from one individual to others nearby.

empathy Condition of sharing and understanding the emotions of another person.

empirical criterion keying Selection of test items by their ability to identify people with known characteristics.

endocrine system Network of glands that affect bodily functions by releasing hormones into the bloodstream. Some endocrine activity is implicated in psychological disorders.

endogenous Having internal causes or sources.

endogenous opioids Substances occurring naturally throughout the body that function like **neurotransmitters** to shut down pain sensation even in the presence of marked tissue damage. These may contribute to psychological problems such as eating disorders. Also known as endorphins or enkephalins.

endorphins See **endogenous opioids.**

enkephalins See **endogenous opioids.**

epidemiology Psychopathology research method examining the prevalence, distribution, and consequences of disorders in populations.

episodic course Pattern of a disorder alternating between recovery and recurrence.

equifinality Developmental psychopathology principle that a behavior or disorder may have several different causes.

erotomanic type Type of delusional disorder featuring belief that another person, usually of higher status, is in love with the individual.

erotophobia Learned negative reaction to or attitude about sexual activity, perhaps developed as a result of a negative or even traumatic event such as rape.

essential hypertension High blood pressure with no verifiable physical cause, which makes up the overwhelming majority of high blood pressure cases.

etiology Cause or source of a disorder.

event-related potential (ERP) Also known as **evoked potential;** the brain's electrical reaction to a psychologically meaningful environment event, as measured by the **EEG.**

exhibitionism Sexual gratification attained by exposing one's genitals to unsuspecting strangers.

exorcism Religious ritual that, attributing disordered behavior to possession by demons, seeks to treat the individual by driving the demons from his or her body.

expectancy effect People's response to a substance on the basis of their beliefs about it, even if it contains no active ingredient. This phenomenon demonstrates that cognitive as well as physiological factors are involved in drug reaction and dependence.

experiment Research method that can establish causation by manipulating the variables in question and controlling for other alternative explanations of any observed effects.

expert witness Person who because of special training and experience is allowed to offer opinion testimony in legal trials.

explicit memory Good recollection of actual events. Contrast with **implicit memory.**

expressed emotion The hostility, criticism, and overinvolvement demonstrated by some families toward a family member with a psychological disorder; this can often contribute to the person's relapse.

expressive language Communication with words.

expressive language disorder An individual's problems in spoken communication, as measured by significantly low scores on standardized tests of expressive language relative to nonverbal intelligence test scores. Symptoms may include a markedly limited vocabulary or errors in verb tense.

extensive support retardation Retardation level characterized by the long-term and regular care required for individuals with this degree of disability.

external validity Extent to which research study findings generalize, or apply, to people and settings not involved in the study.

extinction Learning process in which a response maintained by reinforcement in **operant conditioning** or pairing in **classical conditioning** decreases when that reinforcement or pairing is removed. The procedure of removing that reinforcement or pairing is also called **extinction.**

extrapyramidal symptoms Serious side effects of **neuroleptic** medications resembling the motor difficulties of **Parkinson's disease.** Also called parkinsonian symptoms, they include **akinesia** and **tardive dyskinesia.**

extraversion One of the dimensions of the five-factor model of personality and individual differences, involving being talkative, assertive, and active, as opposed to silent, passive, and reserved.

face validity Condition of testing in which test items appear plausible for their intended purposes, even if they are not truly valid discriminators.

facial agnosia Type of **agnosia** characterized by a person's inability to recognize even familiar faces.

facilitated communication Method claimed by proponents to allow autistic individuals to communicate when a facilitator supports their arms and provides encouragement while they type messages on a keyboard. Objective attempts to validate the procedures often find that the communication actually originates with the facilitator.

factitious disorder Nonexistent physical or psychological disorder deliberately faked for no apparent gain except possibly sympathy and attention.

failure to thrive Stunted physical growth and maturation in children, often associated with psychosocial factors such as lack of love and nurturing.

false negative Assessment error in which no pathology is noted (i.e., test results are negative) when it is actually present.

false positive Assessment error in which pathology is reported (i.e., test results are positive) when none is actually present.

family studies Genetic studies that examine patterns of traits and behaviors among relatives.

fatalistic suicide Suicide in the context of a person's hopelessness and loss of the feeling of control over his or her own destiny.

fear Emotion of an immediate alarm reaction to present danger or life-threatening emergencies.

fearlessness hypothesis One of the major theories of the etiology of antisocial personality disorder, stating that psychopaths are less prone to fear and, thus, less inhibited from dangerous or illicit activities.

female orgasmic disorder Recurring delay or absence of orgasm in some women following a normal sexual excitement phase, relative to their prior experience and current stimulation. Also known as **inhibited female orgasm.**

female sexual arousal disorder Recurrent inability in some women to attain or maintain adequate lubrication and swelling sexual excitement responses until completion of sexual activity.

fermentation The decomposition process by which yeasts, water, and sugar form alcohol.

fetal alcohol syndrome (FAS) Pattern of problems including learning difficulties, behavior deficits, and characteristic physical flaws, resulting from heavy drinking by the victim's mother when she was pregnant with the victim.

fetishism Long-term, recurring, intense sexually arousing urges, fantasies, or behavior involving the use of nonliving, unusual objects, which cause distress or impairment in life functioning.

fixation In psychoanalysis, stopping or concentrating at a psychosexual stage because of a lack of appropriate gratification at that stage.

flashback Sudden, intense reexperiencing of a previous, usually traumatic, event.

flat affect Apparently emotionless demeanor (including toneless speech and vacant gaze) when a reaction would be expected.

flight/fight system (FFS) Brain circuit in animals that when stimulated causes an immediate alarm and escape response resembling human panic.

flight or fight response Biological reaction to alarming stressors that musters the body's resources (e.g., blood flow, respiration) to resist or flee the threat.

fluoxetine Trade name *Prozac;* a selective **serotonin reuptake blocker,** that acts on the serotonergic system as a treatment for depression, **obsessive-compulsive disorder,** and **bulimia.**

flurazepam Trade name *Dalmane;* a long-acting medication for insomnia that may cause daytime sleepiness.

forebrain Top section of the brain, also called the **telencephalon,** that includes the **limbic system, basal ganglia, caudate nucleus,** and **cerebral cortex.**

formal observation Structured recording of behaviors that are measurable and well defined.

fragile X syndrome Pattern of abnormality caused by a defect in the **X chromosome** resulting in mental retardation, learning problems, and unusual physical characteristics.

free association Psychoanalytic therapy technique intended to explore threatening material repressed into the unconscious. The patient is instructed to say whatever comes to mind without censoring.

frenzy witchcraft Running frenzy disorder among the Navajo tribe that seems equivalent to **dissociative fugue.**

frontal lobe Forward section of each cerebral hemisphere, most responsible for thinking, reasoning, memory, the experience of reward, and social behavior and, thus, most likely to be involved in a wide range of psychopathology.

frottuerism **Paraphilia** in which the person gains sexual gratification by rubbing against unwilling victims in crowds from which they cannot escape.

functional analysis Careful study of behaviors and the environmental variables that cause or maintain them.

functional communication training Teaching of speech or nonspeech communication skills to replace undesired behavior. The new skills are useful to the person and will be maintained because of the effects they have on others.

GABA Gamma-aminobutyric acid, a neurotransmitter that reduces activity across the synapse and thus inhibits a range of behaviors and emotions, especially generalized anxiety.

gate control theory of pain View that psychological factors can enhance or diminish the sensation and perception of pain by influencing the transmission of pain impulses through the section of the spinal cord that acts as a "gate."

gender identity disorder Psychological dissatisfaction with one's own biological gender, a disturbance in the sense of one's identity as a male or female. The primary goal is not sexual arousal but rather to live the life of the opposite gender.

General adaptation syndrome (GAS) Sequence of reactions to sustained stress described by Hans Selye. These stages are alarm, resistance, and exhaustion, which may lead to death.

generalizability Extent to which research results apply to a range of individuals not included in the study.

generalized amnesia Condition in which one loses memory of all personal information, including one's own identity.

generalized anxiety disorder (GAD) Anxiety disorder characterized by intense, uncontrollable, unfocused, chronic, and continuous worry that is distressing and unproductive accompanied by physical symptoms of tenseness, irritability, and restlessness.

genes Long deoxyribonucleic acid (DNA) molecules, the basic physical units of heredity that appear as locations on chromosomes.

genetic linkage studies Studies that seek to match the inheritance pattern of a disorder to that of a genetic marker; this helps researchers establish the location of the gene responsible for the disorder.

genetic marker Inherited characteristic for which the chromosomal location of the responsible gene is known.

genital herpes Incurable sexually transmitted viral disease with alternating periods of dormancy and activity. The active periods involve pain, liquid discharge, itching, and ulcerative lesions, and their recurrence may be influenced by stress.

genotype Specific genetic makeup of an individual.

gila Disorder reported in Malaysia, similar to **schizophrenia** but different in important

ways that may illuminate details of both disorders.

globus hystericus Sensation of a lump in the throat causing the person difficulty in swallowing, eating, and talking. A **conversion** symptom or part of **choking phobia.**

glutamate system Excitatory neurotransmitter system that may be the avenue by which alcohol affects cognitive abilities.

good premorbid Outdated classification for **schizophrenia,** referring to the quality of social functioning of the individual just prior to the emergence of the disorder.

graduated extinction Monitoring of a desired behavior, such as sleeping or compliance by children, less and less frequently to encourage independence.

grandiose type Type of delusional disorder featuring beliefs of inflated worth, power, knowledge, identity, or special relationship to a deity or famous person.

habit reversal Treatment for tics that requires the person to practice a competing response to replace the tic when it occurs.

hallucinations Psychotic symptoms of perceptual disturbance in which things are seen or heard or otherwise sensed although they are not real or actually present.

hallucinogen Any psychoactive substance such as **LSD** or **marijuana** that can produce delusions, hallucinations, paranoia, and altered sensory perception.

hallucinogen-use disorders Cognitive, biological, behavioral, and social problems associated with the use and abuse of hallucinogenic substances.

Halstead-Reitan Neuropsychological Battery Relatively precise instrument that helps identify and locate organic damage by testing various skills, including rhythm, grip, and tactile performance.

health psychology Subfield of behavioral medicine that studies psychological factors important in health promotion and maintenance.

hebephrenia Silly and immature emotionality, a characteristic of some types of **schizophrenia.**

helper T cells T-type of lymphocyte that enhances the immune system response by signaling B cells to produce **antibodies** and other T cells to destroy **antigens.**

hermaphrodite See **intersex individual.**

heterosexual behavior Sexual activity with members of the opposite gender.

hierarchy of needs Ranking of human necessities from basic food to self-actualization, proposed by Abraham Maslow.

hindbrain Lowest part of the **brain stem;** regulates many automatic bodily functions such as breathing and digestion; includes the **medulla, pons,** and **cerebellum.**

hippocampus Part of the brain's **limbic system** that regulates emotions and the ability to learn and control impulses; figures prominently in some psychopathology.

histrionic personality disorder Cluster B (dramatic, emotional, or erratic) personality disorder involving a pervasive pattern of excessive emotionality and attention seeking.

homosexual behavior Sexual activity with members of the same gender.

Homovanillic acid (HVA) By-product of the **neurotransmitter dopamine** in the cerebrospinal fluid that serves as an indirect measure of dopamine.

human genome project Ongoing scientific attempt to develop a comprehensive map of all human **genes.**

humoral branch One of two main branches of the **immune system;** operates in the blood and other bodily fluids to develop **antibodies** and neutralize **antigens.**

humoral theory Ancient belief that psychological disorders were caused by imbalances in bodily humors or fluids.

humors Bodily fluids (blood, black and yellow bile, and phlegm) that early theorists believed controlled normal and abnormal functioning.

Huntington's disease Genetic disorder marked by involuntary limb movements and progressing to dementia.

hypersomnia Abnormally excessive sleep; a person with this condition will fall asleep several times a day.

hypertension Also known as **high blood pressure;** a major risk factor for stroke and heart and kidney disease that is intimately related to psychological factors.

hypnagogic hallucinations Characteristic of **narcolepsy** involving frightening and vivid experiences during sleep that are visual, tactile, aural, and mobile.

hypoactive sexual desire disorder Apparent lack of interest in sexual activity or fantasy that would be expected considering the person's age and life situation.

hypochondriasis **Somatoform disorder** involving severe anxiety over the belief that one has a disease process without any evident physical cause.

hypofrontality Relative deficiency in activity in the **frontal lobes** of the brains of people with **schizophrenia;** associated with the negative symptoms of the disorder.

hypomanic episode Less severe and less disruptive version of a **manic episode** that is one of the criteria for several mood disorders.

hypothalamic-pituitary-adrenalcortical (HYPAC) axis Brain-endocrine system connection implicated in some psychological disorders.

hypothalamus Part of the **diencephalon** of the brain broadly involved in the regulation of behavior and emotion.

hypothesis Educated guess or statement to be tested by research.

hypoventilation Reduced or labored breathing—for example, during sleep.

id In psychoanalysis, the unconscious psychical entity present at birth representing basic drives.

ideas of reference Person's delusion that the actions, thoughts, laughter, and meaningless activities of others are directed toward or refer to him or her.

idiographic strategy Close and detailed investigation of one individual emphasizing what makes him or her unique (compare with **nomothetic strategy**).

illness phobia Extreme fear of the possibility of contracting a disease (as opposed to the belief that one already has it), combined with irrational behaviors to avoid contracting it.

imaginal exposure Presentation or **systematic exposure** of emotions or fearful or traumatic experiences in the imagination.

imipramine One of the **tricyclic antidepressant** drugs affecting the serotonergic and noradrenergic neurotransmitter systems. It blocks panic attacks but not more generalized anxiety and causes side effects such as dry mouth, dizziness, and, occasionally, sexual dysfunction; effective in some mood and anxiety disorders, as well as other disorders.

immune system Body's means of identifying and eliminating any foreign materials (e.g., bacteria, parasites, even transplanted organs) that enter.

implicit memory Condition of memory in which a person cannot recall past events even though he or she acts in response to them.

inappropriate affect Emotional displays that are improper for the situation.

incest Deviant sexual attraction (**pedophilia**) directed toward one's own family member; often the attraction of a father toward a daughter who is maturing physically.

incidence Number of new cases of a disorder appearing during a specific time period (compare with **prevalence**).

independent variable Phenomenon that is manipulated by the experimenter in a research study and that is expected to influence the dependent variable.

index disorder In genetics research family studies, the particular disorder being investigated.

indoleamine hypothesis Outdated, simplistic theory that low levels of **serotonin** (one of the indoleamines) might cause depression.

inferiority complex Feeling of being inferior to others while striving for superiority.

informal observation Attention paid to behavior but without defining or recording it in any systematic fashion.

information transmission Warnings about the feared object repeated so often that the person develops a phobia solely on the basis of hearing them.

informed consent Ethical requirement whereby research subjects agree to participate in a research study only after they receive full disclosure about the nature of the study and their own role in it.

insanity Legal rather than psychological or medical concept involving both mental disorder and an inability to know or appreciate the wrongfulness of criminal acts.

insanity defense Legal plea that a defendant should not be held responsible for a crime because he or she was mentally ill at the time of the offense.

insidious onset Development of a disorder that occurs gradually over an extended period of time. Contrast with **acute onset**.

insight In psychoanalysis, recognition of the causes of emotional distress.

insomnia, primary Difficulty falling asleep, staying asleep, or feeling rested where there is no apparent medical or psychological cause.

insulin shock therapy A dangerous biological treatment involving the administration of large doses of insulin to induce seizures.

intelligence quotient Score on an intelligence test, abbreviated IQ, estimating a person's deviation from average test performance.

intermittent support retardation Retardation level characterized by the need for only episodic special care—for example, during crises and difficult life changes.

internal validity Extent to which the results of a research study can be attributed to the independent variable after confounding alternative explanations have been ruled out.

interoceptive avoidance Avoidance of situations or activities, such as exercise, that produce internal physical arousal similar to the beginnings of a panic attack.

interpersonal psychotherapy (IPT) Newer brief treatment approach that emphasizes resolution of interpersonal problems and stressors such as role disputes in marital conflict, or forming relationships in marriage or a new job. It has demonstrated effectiveness for such problems as depression.

interpersonal therapy Brief, structured treatment that focuses on teaching a person skills to improve existing relationships or develop new ones.

interrater reliability Degree to which two or more observers make the same ratings or measurements.

intersex individuals (hermaphrodites) People born with ambiguous genitalia and hormonal abnormalities. They are assigned a gender at birth and then often provided hormones and surgery to complete the correspondence.

intrapsychic conflict In psychoanalysis, the struggles among the **id, ego,** and **superego.**

introjection In object relations theory, the process of incorporating memories and values of individuals who are important and close to the person.

introspection Early, nonscientific approach to the study of psychology involving systematic attempts to report thoughts and feelings that specific stimuli evoked.

introversion Tendency to be shy and withdrawn.

inverse agonist Chemical substance that produces effects opposite those of a particular **neurotransmitter.**

ischemia Narrowing of arteries caused by plaque buildup within the arteries.

jealous type Type of delusional disorder featuring delusions that the individual's sexual partner is unfaithful.

jet lag type of circadian rhythm sleep disorder Disorder in which sleepiness and alertness patterns conflict with local time and occur after recent or repeated travel across time zones.

K complexes Brain wave pattern of high-amplitude spikes typical of Stage 2 sleep.

Klinefelter's syndrome Disorder among males caused by an extra **X chromosome,** resulting in physical deformities, infertility, and sometimes mental retardation.

koro In Singapore, a condition of mass hysteria or group delusion in which people believe their genitals are retracting into their bodies.

Korsakoff syndrome Amnestic disorder caused by damage to the **thalamus** resulting from stroke or chronic and heavy alcohol use.

labeling Applying a name to a phenomenon or a pattern of behavior. The label may acquire negative connotations or be applied erroneously to the person rather than his or her behaviors.

la belle indifference Lack of distress shown by some individuals presenting **conversion, somatization,** or **amnestic disorders.**

large fibers Nerve fibers in the **dorsal horns of the spinal cord** that regulate the pattern and intensity of pain sensations. They close the gate, decreasing the transmission of painful stimuli.

lateral ventricles Naturally occurring cavities in the brain filled with cerebrospinal fluid. Some individuals with **schizophrenia** have enlarged ventricles, probably resulting from insufficient development or atrophy of surrounding tissue.

law of effect Thorndike's principle that behaviors are strengthened or weakened by the environmental events that follow them.

learned helplessness Condition that results when humans or animals learn they cannot affect their environment (e.g., solve problems, escape shock) and stop trying to cope in other situations.

learning disorders Reading, mathematics, or written expression performance substantially below levels expected relative to the person's age, IQ, and education.

Lesch-Nyhan syndrome X-linked disorder characterized by **mental retardation,** signs of cerebral palsy, and **self-injurious behavior.**

leukocytes White blood cells of varying types that play specialized roles in the **immune system** to fight viral and parasitic infections.

libido In psychoanalysis, the energy within the **id** that drives people toward life and fulfillment.

life-span developmental psychopathology The study of psychological disorders over the entire age range.

limbic system Part of the **forebrain** involved in emotion, the ability to learn and to control impulses, and the regulation of sex, hunger, thirst, and aggression drives. This system figures prominently in much of psychopathology.

limited support retardation Retardation level characterized by the special care needed on a consistent though time-limited basis—for example, during employment training.

lithium carbonate Common salt used in substantial doses to treat bipolar disorder. Clients often discontinue its use because they enjoy the manic periods, and relapse rates are high. The mechanism for its effects is unknown.

lobotomy Neurosurgery procedure intended to eliminate undesirable behaviors by severing the connections between the **thalamus/ hypothalamus** and the **frontal lobes** of the brain.

localized amnesia Memory loss limited to specific times and events, particularly traumatic events.

locus coeruleus Area in the **hindbrain** that is part of a noradrenergic (norepinephrine-sensitive) circuit. It is involved in emergency and alarm reactions and may be related to panic states.

longitudinal course specifiers Time patterns among mood disorders (e.g., prior dysthymia or cyclothymia rapid cycling, seasonal patterns) that may suggest their course, treatment, and prognosis.

longitudinal research design Systematic study of changes in the same individual or group examined over time.

loose associations Deficits in logical continuity of speech, with abrupt movement between ideas. A characteristic of **schizophrenia** also called derailment.

LSD (d-lysergic acid diethylamide) Most common hallucinogenic drug; a synthetic version of the grain fungus ergot.

Luria-Nebraska Neuropsychological Battery Relatively precise instrument that helps identify and locate organic damage by testing various skills.

lysergic acid amide A naturally occurring hallucinogen found in the seeds of the morning glory plant.

madhouses Pejorative, negative term for asylums, the institutions of refuge for the mentally disordered.

magnetic resonance imaging (MRI) Procedure using radio signals generated in a strong magnetic field and passed through body tissue to produce detailed, even layered, images of its structure.

maintenance of sameness Necessity among people with **autism** that their familiar environments remain unchanged; they become upset when changes are introduced.

maintenance treatment Combination of continued psychosocial treatment and/or medication designed to prevent relapse following therapy.

major depressive disorder Mood disorder involving one (**single episode**) or more (separated by at least two months without depression—**recurrent**) major depressive episodes.

major depressive episode Most common and severe experience of depression, including feelings of worthlessness, disturbances in bodily activities such as sleep, loss of interest, and the inability to experience pleasure, persisting at least two weeks.

male erectile disorder Recurring inability in some men to attain or maintain adequate penile erection until completion of sexual activity.

male orgasmic disorder Recurring delay in or absence of orgasm in some men following a normal sexual excitement phase, relative to age and current stimulation. Also known as **inhibited male orgasm.**

malingering Deliberate faking of a physical or psychological disorder motivated by gain.

mania Period of abnormally excessive elation or euphoria, associated with some **mood disorders.**

manic episode Period of abnormally elevated or irritable mood that may include inflated self-esteem, decreased need for sleep, pressured speech, flight of ideas, agitation, or self-destructive behavior.

marijuana (cannabis sativa) Dried part of the hemp plant, a hallucinogen that is the most widely used illegal substance.

marital therapy Interventions for the relationship problems of couples, whether married or not.

mass hysteria Phenomenon in which people in groups share the same fear, delusion, abnormal behavior, or even physical symptoms as a result of psychological processes and suggestion.

mathematics disorder Mathematics performance significantly below age norms.

medroxyprogesterone Medication that helps stimulate respiration and is used in treatment of **obstructive sleep apnea.**

medulla Part of the **hindbrain,** which regulates such automatic bodily functions as breathing and digestion.

melancholic (endogenous) depressive episode Mood disorder depressive episode associated with more severe somatic disturbances such as **anhedonia,** loss of sex drive, or weight loss.

melatonin Hormone produced by the pineal gland that is activated by darkness to control the body's biological clock and to induce sleep. It is implicated in **seasonal affective disorder** and may be used in treatments for **circadian rhythm sleep disorders.**

memory B cells Specialized lymphocytes created after **antigens** are neutralized to help the **immune system** fight off new invasions by those antigens more rapidly. These account for the effectiveness of inoculations.

mental age (MA) Score a person achieves on an intelligence test representing the highest age-equivalent items he or she passed.

mental disorder Psychological disorder.

mental hygiene movement Mid-19th-century effort to improve care of the mentally disordered by informing the public of their mistreatment.

mental illness Term formerly used to mean psychological disorder but less preferred because it implies that the causes of the disorder can be found in a medical disease process.

mental retardation Significantly subaverage intellectual functioning paired with deficits in adaptive functioning such as self-care or occupational activities, appearing prior to age 18.

mental status exam Relatively coarse preliminary test of a client's judgment, orientation to time and place, and emotional and mental state; typically conducted during an initial interview.

mescaline Naturally occurring hallucinogen found in the peyote cactus plant.

metabolites By-products of **neurotransmitter** activity; their measurement allows study of that activity.

methadone **Opiate agonist** used as a treatment for heroin addiction. It initially provides the analgesic and sedative effects of heroin. After extended use, these effects diminish and tolerance develops. An effective treatment for some when combined with counseling.

methylphenidate Stimulant medication known as Ritalin used to treat **hypersomnia** by keeping the person awake during the day, **narcolepsy** by suppressing REM sleep including that with sudden onset, and attention deficit hyperactivity disorder.

microsleeps Short, seconds-long periods of sleep that occur in people who have been deprived of sleep.

midbrain Section of the brain that coordinates movement with sensory input and contributes to the processes of arousal and tension.

migraine headache Debilitating, throbbing, or pulsing head pain with rapid onset, usually occurring on one side of the head.

mild mental retardation Level of retardation defined by IQ scores between 55 and 70.

Millon Multiaxial Clinical Inventory (MMCI) Standardized measure to identify and assess personality disorders.

Minnesota Multiphasic Personality Inventory (MMPI) Empirically derived standardized personality test that provides scales for assessing such abnormal functioning as depression and paranoia. One of the most widely used and heavily researched assessment instruments.

mixed manic episode Condition in which the individual experiences both elation and depression or anxiety at the same time. Also known as **dysphoric manic episode.**

mixed sleep apnea Combination of obstructive and central sleep apnea, such as brief interruptions in breathing during sleep caused by a blocked air passage and by cessation in respiratory activity.

modeling Learning through observation and imitation of the behavior of other individuals and the consequences of that behavior.

moderate mental retardation Level of retardation defined by IQ scores between 40 and 55.

monoamine oxidase (MAO) inhibitors Medications that treat depression and severe social anxiety by blocking an enzyme that breaks down the **neurotransmitters norepinephrine** and **serotonin.**

mood Enduring period of emotionality.

mood congruent Consistent with the person's emotional level. Hallucinations and delusions may be congruent or incongruent with a depressed person's mood.

mood disorders Group of disorders involving severe and enduring disturbances in emotionality ranging from elation to severe depression.

mood incongruent Not consistent with the person's emotional level. Psychotic symptoms associated with mood disorders may not be congruent with the person's mood.

moral therapy 19th-century psychosocial approach to treatment that involved treating patients as normally as possible in normal environments.

moral weakness model of chemical dependence View that substance abusers should be blamed because their behavior results from lack of self-control, character, or moral fiber.

morphine Opiate medication used as an analgesic (pain reliever) and narcotic that is sometimes a substance of abuse.

multiaxial classification Categorization system, such as in DSM-IV, employing several dimensions or axes, each used for differentiating among the categories.

multiple baseline Single-case experimental research design in which measures are taken on two or more behaviors, or on a single behavior in two or more situations. A particular intervention is introduced for each at different times. If behavior change is coincident with each introduction, this is strong evidence the intervention caused the change.

multiple infarctions More than one area or incident of death to tissue (e.g., in the brain or heart) due to blockage of blood flow.

myocardial infarction Death of heart tissue when its blood supply artery is blocked by plaque or a blood clot.

myocardium Heart muscle.

naltrexone Most widely used **opiate-antagonist** drug; it produces immediate withdrawal and, thus, a great deal of discomfort. It may also contribute to the treatment of alcohol abuse, but is not as successful for either substance as was originally hoped.

narcissistic personality disorder Cluster B (dramatic, emotional, or erratic) **personality disorder** involving a pervasive pattern of grandiosity in fantasy or behavior, need for admiration, and lack of empathy.

narcolepsy Sleep disorder involving sudden and irresistible sleep attacks.

natural-environment phobia Clusters of fears involving situations in nature such as fear of heights, storms, and water. Often such phobias develop at an early age.

necessary condition Circumstance required for a particular phenomenon to occur.

negative affect Emotional symptoms that are part of the definition of both anxiety and depression but are not specific to either of these. Also, the fact that substance abuse may be maintained because the substance causes an escape from unpleasant circumstances, responsibilities, or especially, feelings.

negative correlation An association between two variables in which one increases as the other decreases.

negative schema Automatic, enduring, and stable negative cognitive bias or belief system about some aspect of life.

negative symptoms Less outgoing symptoms, such as flat affect and poverty of speech, displayed by some people with schizophrenia.

negativistic personality disorder Pervasive pattern of resisting routine requests and expectations and adopting a contrary attitude; considered for but not included in DSM-IV. Corresponds to former category known as **passive-aggressive personality disorder.**

nervous breakdown Lay term for a severe psychological upset that actually has no meaning in scientific or professional psychopathology.

neurasthenia Disorder common in the United States in the mid-1800s, although the label is no longer used here (though still prevalent in China). Its symptoms include a lack of energy, a variety of aches and pains, and sometimes fever. This disorder is similar to present-day **chronic fatigue syndrome.**

neuritic plaque Clusters of dead neurons found during autopsy in the brains of people with Alzheimer's disease.

neurofibrillary tangles Brain damage in the form of large numbers of strand-like filaments found during autopsy in people with Alzheimer's disease.

neurohormones Hormones that affect the brain and are increasingly the focus of study in psychopathology.

neuroimaging Sophisticated computer-aided procedures that allow nonintrusive examination of nervous system structure and function.

neuroleptics Major antipsychotic medications, dopamine antagonists, that diminish delusions, hallucinations, and aggressive behavior in psychotic patients but that may also cause serious side effects.

neuromodulators Hormones secreted into the blood to transmit brain messages throughout the body; also known as **neuropeptides.**

neuron Individual nerve cell; responsible for transmitting information.

neuropsychological testing Assessment of brain and nervous system functioning by testing an individual's performance on behavioral tasks.

neuroscience Study of the nervous system and its role in behavior, thoughts, and emotions.

neurosis Obsolete psychodynamic term for psychological disorder thought to result from unconscious conflicts and the anxiety they cause. Plural is **neuroses.**

neurotransmitters Chemicals that cross the **synaptic cleft** between nerve cells to transmit impulses from one **neuron** to the next. Their relative excess or deficiency is involved in several psychological disorders.

nicotine Toxic and addictive substance found in tobacco leaves.

nicotine gum Chewing gum that delivers nicotine to smokers without the carcinogens in cigarette smoke. This substitute may help people stop smoking, especially when combined with counseling.

nicotine patch Patch placed on the skin that delivers nicotine to smokers without the carcinogens in cigarette smoke. Somewhat more successful than nicotine gum because it requires less effort by the user and delivers the drug more consistently; should be coupled with counseling to stop smoking and avoid relapse.

nicotine-use disorders Cognitive, biological, behavioral, and social problems associated with the use and abuse of nicotine.

nightmares Frightening and anxiety-provoking dreams occurring during **rapid eye movement (REM) sleep.** The individual recalls the bad dreams and recovers alertness and orientation quickly.

nocturnal myoclonus Periodic jerky arm and leg motions occurring during sleep.

nocturnal penile tumescence (NPT) Erection of the penis during sleep, usually **REM-stage sleep.** If this normal reaction occurs in a man with erectile problems in the waking state, his problems may be assumed to have psychological origins.

nomenclature In a naming system or **nosology,** the actual labels or names that are applied. In psychopathology these include, for example, mood disorders or eating disorders.

nomothetic strategy Identification and examination of large groups of people with the same disorder to note similarities and develop general laws (compare with **idiographic**).

nondemand pleasuring Procedure to reestablish sexual arousal involving fondling and caressing while intercourse is forbidden. This method avoids the anxiety provoked by the need to perform sexually.

nondisjunction In Down syndrome, the fusing of two of the 21st chromosomes to create one cell with one copy that dies and one cell with three copies that continue to divide.

non-rapid eye movement (NREM) sleep Periods in the sleep cycle, divided into four substages, when the body may be active while the brain is relatively less active and dreaming does not occur.

non-24-hour sleep-wake syndrome Disruptive circadian rhythm problem, not a DSM-IV disorder, in which the person's biological clock does not correspond to a 24-hour cycle, forcing the sleep-wake pattern out of synchrony with this cycle.

norepinephrine Neurotransmitter also known as noradrenaline that is active in the central and peripheral nervous systems controlling heart rate, blood pressure, and respiration, among other functions. Because of its role in the body's alarm reaction, it may also contribute in general and indirectly to panic attacks and other disorders.

nosology Classification and naming system for medical and psychological phenomena.

nucleus accumbens A complex of neurons that is part of the brain's "pleasure pathway" responsible for the experience of reward.

object relations A modern development in psychodynamic theory involving the study of how children incorporate the memories and values of people who are close and important to them.

obsessions Recurrent intrusive thoughts or impulses the client seeks to suppress or neutralize while recognizing they are not imposed by outside forces.

obsessive-compulsive disorder Anxiety disorder involving unwanted, persistent, intrusive thoughts and impulses as well as repetitive actions intended to suppress them.

obsessive-compulsive personality disorder Cluster C (anxious or fearful) **personality disorder** featuring a pervasive pattern of preoccupation with orderliness, perfectionism, and mental and interpersonal control at the expense of flexibility, openness, and efficiency.

obstructive sleep apnea Snoring and brief interruptions in breathing during sleep caused by blockage of the airway.

occipital lobe Section of each cerebral hemisphere that integrates and makes sense of visual inputs.

Oedipus complex In psychoanalysis, the intrapsychic struggle within a young boy between his lust for his mother and his fear of castration because of it. The resolution of this complex results in development of the **superego.**

operant conditioning Fundamental behavioral learning process in which responses are modified by their consequences (reinforcers, punishers, extinction, and so on).

operational definition Delineation of a concept on the basis of the operation used to measure it.

opiates Addictive psychoactive substances such as **heroin, opium,** and **morphine** that cause temporary euphoria and analgesia (pain reduction).

opioid-releasing neurons Nerve cells that release **endogenous opioids** and that play a role in the brain's pleasure pathway controlling the experience of reward.

opioids Family of substances including **opiates** and **endorphins** as well as synthetic variants such as **methadone** that have a narcotic effect.

opioid-use disorders Cognitive, biological, behavioral, and social problems associated with the use and abuse of **opiates** and their synthetic variants.

opium Naturally occurring compound from the poppy plant that is a strong narcotic, having pain-relieving and sleep- and euphoria-inducing effects. Its derivatives include morphine and heroin.

opponent-process theory Explanation of drug tolerance and dependence suggesting that when a person experiences positive feelings these will be followed shortly by negative feelings, and vice versa. Eventually, the motivation for drug taking shifts from a desire for the euphoric high to a need to relieve the increasingly unpleasant feelings that follow drug use. A vicious cycle develops in that the drug that makes a person feel terrible is the one thing that can eliminate the pain.

orgasmic reconditioning Learning procedure to help clients strengthen appropriate patterns of sexual arousal by pairing appropriate stimuli with the pleasurable sensations of masturbation.

orgasm phase Stage of sexual activity involving ejaculation in men and vaginal wall contractions in women. Women are able to experience orgasm again immediately while men are unable to form an erection for a time interval called a refractory period.

oriented times three Patient is aware of, or oriented to, his or her identity, location, and time (person, place, and time).

otitis media Infection of the middle ear, an extremely common childhood problem; the attendant temporary or chronic hearing loss may lead to language development delays.

outcome research Studies examining the effectiveness and results, positive or negative, of treatment procedures.

pain behaviors Observable manifestations of the private experience of pain. These may include wincing or other facial expressions, verbal complaints of distress, and avoidance of activities that increase pain sensations.

pain disorder **Somatoform disorder** featuring true pain but for which psychological factors play an important role in onset, severity, or maintenance.

panic Sudden overwhelming fright or terror.

panic attack Abrupt experience of intense fear or discomfort accompanied by a number of physical symptoms, such as dizziness or heart palpitations.

panic control treatment Cognitive-behavioral treatment for panic attacks, involving gradual exposure to feared somatic sensations and modification of perceptions and attitudes about them.

panic disorder with agoraphobia Fear and avoidance of situations the person believes might induce a dreaded panic attack.

panic disorder without agoraphobia Panic attacks experienced without development of agoraphobia.

papaverine Vasodilating medication used to treat male erectile disorder by dilating blood vessels, increasing blood flow to the penis to form an erection. The medication must be injected and the procedure can be painful; it is also so intrusive it is often declined or discontinued by patients.

paradoxical intention Instructing clients to do the opposite of the desired behavior. Telling an impotent man not to have sex or an insomniac not to sleep reduces anxiety to perform.

paranoia Person's irrational beliefs that he or she is especially important (delusions of grandeur) or that other people are seeking to do him or her harm.

paranoid personality disorder Cluster A (odd or eccentric) **personality disorder** involving pervasive distrust and suspiciousness of others such that their motives are interpreted as malevolent.

paranoid type, schizophrenia Type of schizophrenia in which symptoms primarily involve delusions and hallucinations, while speech, and motor and emotional behavior are relatively intact.

paraphilia Sexual disorders and deviations in which sexual arousal occurs almost exclusively in the context of inappropriate objects or individuals.

parasomnias Abnormal behaviors such as nightmares or sleepwalking that occur during sleep.

parasympathetic nervous system Part of the **autonomic nervous system** that regulates bodily systems (e.g., digestion) while activity level is low and that balances **sympathetic nervous system** activity.

parietal lobe Section of each cerebral hemisphere responsible for recognizing touch sensations.

Parkinson's disease Degenerative brain disorder principally affecting motor performance (e.g., tremors, stooped posture) associated with reduction in dopamine. Dementia may be a result as well.

passive-aggressive personality disorder Former diagnostic category not included in DSM-IV for lack of sufficient research. See a similar category **negativistic personality disorder.**

pathological grief reaction (impacted grief reaction) Extreme reaction to the death of a loved one that involves psychotic features, suicidal ideation, or severe loss of weight or energy, or that persists more than two months.

patient uniformity myth Tendency to consider all members of a category as more similar than they are, ignoring their individual differences.

pedophilia **Paraphilia** (sexual deviation) involving strong sexual attraction toward children.

penile implant Surgical treatment for **male erectile disorder** involving the insertion of a prosthesis that may be a semirigid silicone rod or an inflatable tube.

penile strain gauge Psychophysiological monitoring device that measures male sexual arousal by changes in penis circumference.

performance scales In the Wechsler group of intelligence tests, subtests that assess psychomotor and nonverbal reasoning skills and the ability to learn new relationships.

peripheral nervous system Neural networks outside the brain and spinal cord, including the **somatic nervous system,** which controls muscle movement, and the **autonomic nervous system,** which regulates cardiovascular, endocrine, digestion, and regulation functions.

permissive hypothesis Theory that **neurotransmitter** systems contribute to mood irregularities when low **serotonin** levels permit them to range widely and become unregulated.

personality disorders Enduring maladaptive patterns for relating to the environment and oneself, exhibited in a wide range of contexts that cause significant functional impairment or subjective distress.

personality inventories Self-report questionnaires that assess personal traits by asking respondents to identify descriptions that apply to them.

personality trait Enduring tendency to behave in particular predisposed ways across situations.

person-centered therapy Therapy method in which the client, rather than the counselor, primarily directs the course of discussion, seeking self-discovery and self-responsibility.

pervasive developmental disorders Wide-ranging, significant, and long-lasting dysfunctions that appear before the age of eighteen.

pervasive support retardation Retardation level characterized by the constant, intensive care needed by the individual in all environments.

phantom limb pain Perception of pain in a limb that actually is absent due to amputation. This phenomenon suggests pain is not entirely a physical experience.

phencyclidine (PCP) Dangerous synthetic hallucinogen, also called angel dust, that may cause agitated or violent behavior, disorientation, convulsions, coma, and even death.

phenotype Observable characteristics or behaviors of an individual.

phenylketonuria (PKU) Recessive disorder involving the inability to break down a food chemical whose buildup causes retardation, seizures, and behavior problems. PKU can be detected by infant screening and prevented by a specialized diet.

phii pob Thailand's version of **dissociative trance** states.

phobic avoidance Extreme shunning of feared objects or situations displayed by people with phobias.

phototherapy Treatment of seasonal affective disorder with large doses of exposure to bright light.

pica Eating disorder in infants or individuals with mental retardation characterized by ingesting non-nutritive substances such as paint, dirt, or insects.

Pick's disease Very rare neurological disorder that results in **presenile** (early onset) **dementia.**

pivloktoq Running frenzy disorder among native peoples of the Arctic that seems equivalent to **dissociative fugue.**

placebo control group In an outcome experiment, a control group that does not receive the experimental manipulation but is given a similar procedure with an identical expectation of change, allowing the researcher to assess any placebo effect.

placebo effect Behavior change resulting from the person's expectation of change rather than from the experimental manipulation itself.

plasticity Phenomenon by which damage to neurons sometimes can be compensated for by the action of other neurons.

plateau phase Brief time period immediately before orgasm.

pleasure principle Tendency to seek pleasure and minimize discomfort.

polygenetic abnormality Abnormality whose causes include action by several genes located at different chromosome sites.

polysomnographic (PSG) evaluation Assessment of sleep disorders in which a client sleeping in the lab is monitored for heart, muscle, respiration, brain wave, and other functions.

polysubstance use Use of multiple mind- and behavior-altering substances, such as drugs.

pons Part of the hindbrain that controls such automatic bodily functions as breathing and digestion.

poor premorbid Outdated classification for schizophrenia, referring to the quality of social functioning of the individual just prior to the emergence of the disorder.

positive correlation Association between two variables in which one increases as the other increases.

positive symptoms More overt symptoms, such as delusions and hallucinations, displayed by some people with schizophrenia.

positron emission tomography (PET) scan Imaging procedure in which a radioactive tracer that binds to blood glucose is detected as the glucose is metabolized during brain activity. This allows nonintrusive localization and observation of brain activity.

postpartum onset Disorder that first appears in mothers during the time immediately following childbirth.

posttraumatic stress disorder (PTSD) Enduring, distressing emotional disorder that follows exposure to a severe helplessness- or fear-inducing threat. The victim reexperiences the trauma, avoids stimuli associated with it, and develops a numbing of responsiveness and an increased vigilance and arousal.

prealcoholic stage First of Jellinek's four stages identified in the progression of alcoholism, involving occasional drinking with few serious consequences.

predictive validity Degree to which an assessment instrument accurately predicts a person's future behavior. See **criterion validity.**

premature ejaculation Recurring ejaculation before the person wishes it, with minimal sexual stimulation.

premorbid Individual's level of functioning prior to the development of a disorder. Good and poor premorbid are no longer considered useful distinguishing categories of schizophrenia.

prepared learning Certain associations can be learned more readily than others because this ability has been adaptive for evolution.

presenile dementia Dementia that appears before old age, between ages 40 and 60.

presenting problem Original complaint reported by the client to the therapist. The actual treated problem may sometimes be a modification derived from the presenting problem.

prevalence Number of people displaying a disorder in the total population at any given time (compare with **incidence**).

primary gain Freudian notion that anxiety reduction is the principal reinforcement obtained for the display of psychological symptoms.

primary insomnia Difficulty in initiating, maintaining or gaining from sleep; not related to other medical or psychological problems.

primary process In psychodynamic theory, the **id**'s characteristic mode of thinking, which is emotional, irrational, and preoccupied with sex, aggression, and envy.

proband In genetics research, the individual displaying the trait or characteristic being studied. Also known as **index case.**

process schizophrenia Means of grouping schizophrenia on the basis of slow onset, lack of a precipitating stressor, with associated social skill deficits and flat affect.

prodromal stage Second of Jellinek's four stages identified in the progression of alcoholism, featuring heavy drinking but with few outward signs of a problem.

profound mental retardation Level of retardation defined by IQ scores below 20 and extremely limited communication and self-help skills.

prognosis Predicted future development of a disorder over time.

progressive muscle relaxation Set of exercises to teach people to become aware of and actively counteract muscle tension to induce relaxation or drowsiness.

projective tests Psychoanalytically based measures that present ambiguous stimuli to clients on the assumption that their responses will reveal their unconscious conflicts. Such tests are very inferential and lack high reliability and validity.

prototypal approach System for categorizing disorders using both essential, defining characteristics and a range of variation on other characteristics.

psilocybin Naturally occurring hallucinogen found in certain species of mushrooms.

psychiatric nurse Person with nursing training who specializes in care and treatment of psychiatric patients, usually in a hospital setting.

psychiatric social worker Person who has earned a Master of Social Work (MSW) degree or, occasionally, a Doctor of Social Work (DSW) and is trained to work with social agencies to help psychologically disordered clients and their families.

psychiatrist Person who has earned an M.D. degree and then has specialized in psychiatry during residency training. Psychiatrists are trained to investigate primarily the biological nature and causes of psychiatric disorders, and to diagnose and treat them as well.

psychoactive substances Substances, such as drugs, that alter mood or behavior.

psychoanalysis Psychoanalytic assessment and therapy, which emphasizes exploration of, and insight into, unconscious processes and conflicts, pioneered by Sigmund Freud.

psychoanalyst Therapist who practices psychoanalysis after earning either an M.D. or Ph.D. degree and then receiving additional specialized postdoctoral training.

psychoanalytic model Complex and comprehensive theory originally advanced by Sigmund Freud that seeks to account for the development and structure of personality, as well as the origin of abnormal behavior, based primarily on inferred inner entities and forces.

psychodynamic psychotherapy Contemporary version of psychoanalysis that still emphasizes unconscious processes and conflicts but is briefer and more focused on specific problems.

psychological autopsy Postmortem psychological profile of a suicide victim constructed from interviews with people who knew the person before death.

psychological disorder Psychological dysfunction associated with distress or impairment in functioning that is not a typical or culturally expected response.

psychological model Explanation of human behavior and its dysfunction that emphasizes the influence of the social environment and early experience.

psychomotor retardation Deficits in motor activity and coordination development.

psychoncology Study of psychological factors involved in the course and treatment of cancer.

psychoneuroimmunology (PNI) Study of psychological influences on the neurological responding involved in the body's immune response.

psychopathology Scientific study of psychological disorders.

psychopathy Non-DSM category similar to **antisocial personality disorder** but with less emphasis on overt behavior; indicators include superficial charm, lack of remorse, and other personality characteristics.

psychophysiological assessment Measurement of changes in the nervous system reflecting psychological or emotional events such as anxiety, stress, and sexual arousal.

psychophysiological disorders Outdated term, similar to **psychosomatic medicine,** for the study of psychological and social factors influencing physical disorders. The term is misleading because it falsely implies that other psychological problems such as mood disorders do not also have significant biological components.

psychosexual stages of development In psychoanalysis, the sequence of phases a person passes through during development. Each stage is named for the location on the body where **id** gratification is maximal at that time.

psychosis Group of severe psychological disorders, including **schizophrenia,** featuring **delusions** and **hallucinations.**

psychosocial treatment Treatment practices that focus on social and cultural factors (such as family experience) as well as psychological influences. These approaches include cognitive, behavioral, and interpersonal methods.

psychosomatic medicine See **behavioral medicine.**

psychosurgery Biological treatment involving neurosurgery, such as **lobotomy,** for a psychological disorder. For example, a specific surgical lesion to the cingulate bundle may be an effective last-resort treatment for **obsessive-compulsive disorder.**

psychotic behavior Severe psychological disorder category characterized by hallucinations and loss of contact with reality.

psychotic depressive episode Condition in which psychotic symptoms such as delusions and hallucinations accompany depressive episodes.

psychotic symptoms Delusions and hallucinations that may appear during depressive or manic episodes.

purging techniques In the eating disorder **bulimia nervosa,** the self-induced vomiting or laxative abuse used to compensate for excessive food ingestion.

Purkinje cells Cells in the **cerebellum** that may inhibit the action of other cells and may be sensitive to a major inhibitory **neurotransmitter, GABA.** A deficit of these cells has been noted in some people with **autism.**

quantitative genetics Method of genetics research that examines patterns of genetic control over a wide range of genes, each of which may contribute only a small effect.

randomization Method for placing individuals into research groups that assures each one of an equal chance of being assigned to any group, to eliminate any systematic differences across groups.

rapid cycling pattern Temporal course of a **bipolar disorder** when transitions between mania and depression are quick, occurring four or more times in one year.

rapid eye movement (REM) sleep Periodic intervals of sleep during which the eyes move rapidly from side to side, and dreams occur, but the body is inactive.

rational-emotive therapy **Cognitive-behavioral** treatment approach that seeks to identify and eliminate irrational beliefs that may cause maladaptive emotions and behavior.

rauwolfia serpentina More commonly known as reserpine, an early medication derived from the snakeroot plant that helps control the agitation and aggressiveness of some psychotic patients.

Raynaud's disease Cardiovascular disease involving blockage of blood circulation to the extremities, with resultant pain and cold sensations in the hands and feet.

reactive schizophrenia Means of grouping schizophrenia on the basis of rapid onset, presence of a precipitating stressor, with associated social adequacy and volatile and intense emotional expression.

reactivity Changes in one person's behavior as a result of observing the behavior in another.

reading disorder Reading performance significantly below age norms.

reality principle In psychodynamic theory, the logical reasoning style of the **ego** that ensures that actions are practical and realistic.

rebound insomnia In a person with insomnia, the worsened sleep problems that can occur when medications are used to treat insomnia and then withdrawn.

receptive language Communicated material that is understood.

receptors Locations on nerve cell **dendrites** that receive chemical impulses for transmission through the **neuron.**

recessive gene Gene that must be paired with another recessive gene to determine a trait.

reciprocal gene-environment model Hypothesis that people with a genetic predisposition for a disorder may also have a genetic tendency to create environmental risk factors that promote the disorder.

reexperiencing Careful and systematic visualizing and reliving of traumatic life events to diminish their power and emotional effects as a means of treating **dissociative identity disorder** or **posttraumatic stress disorder.**

regulated breathing Intervention for **stuttering** in which the person is instructed to stop and take a deep breath whenever a stuttering episode begins.

reinforcement In **operant conditioning,** consequences for behavior that strengthen it or increase its frequency. **Positive** reinforcement involves the contingent delivery of a desired consequence, while **negative** reinforcement is the contingent escape from an aversive consequence. Unwanted behaviors may result from their reinforcement, or the failure to reinforce desired behaviors.

relapse Reappearance of or return to problem behaviors after treatment or recovery.

relapse prevention Extending therapeutic progress by teaching the client how to cope with future troubling situations.

relaxation response Active components of meditation methods, including repetitive thoughts of a sound to reduce distracting thoughts, and closing the mind to other intruding thoughts, that decrease the flow of stress **hormones** and **neurotransmitters** and cause a feeling of calm.

relaxation training Intervention for tics in which the person is taught to relax the muscles involved in the tics.

reliability (of measurement) Degree to which a measurement is consistent—for example, over time or among different raters.

replication Confirming the results of a research study by repeating it, often by a separate, independent researcher.

repressed memories Concept involving recollections of traumatic events actively eliminated from memory. Controversy surrounds whether recall that seems to occur years later is real or accurate.

repression In psychoanalytic theory, a process that forces unwanted material from the conscious to the unconscious.

research design Plan of experimentation used to test a hypothesis.

reserpine See **rauwolfia serpentina.**

residual type, schizophrenia Diagnostic category for people who have experienced at least one episode of schizophrenia, and who no longer display its major symptoms but still show some bizarre thoughts or social withdrawal.

resolution phase Decrease in sexual arousal after orgasm, particularly in men. This phase is not involved in sexual dysfunctions.

response prevention Behavioral therapy method to diminish compulsive behavior by prohibiting that behavior in its usual circumstance while the individual learns the dreaded outcome will not occur.

retarded ejaculation Male orgasmic disorder in which ejaculation is delayed so the patient is unable to reach orgasm with his partner, though he is able to ejaculate during masturbation.

reticular activating system (RAS) Section of the **midbrain** responsible for tension and arousal processes, including sleep and wakefulness.

retrograde ejaculation Condition in which ejaculatory fluids travel backward into the bladder, usually as a result of certain drugs or a medical condition. This is not considered a DSM-IV male orgasmic disorder.

retrospective information Literally "the view back," data collected by examining records or recollections of the past. It is limited by the accuracy, validity, and thoroughness of the sources.

retrospective study Research that utilizes retrospective information and shares its limitations.

Rett's disorder Progressive neurological developmental disorder featuring constant hand-wringing, mental retardation, and impaired motor skills.

reuptake Action by which a neurotransmitter is quickly drawn back into the discharging neuron after being released into a synaptic cleft.

reversal design See **withdrawal design.**

rheumatoid arthritis Painful, degenerative disease in which the immune system essentially attacks itself, resulting in stiffness, swelling, and even destruction of the joints. Cognitive-behavioral treatments can help relieve pain and stiffness.

Rhythm Test Subtest of the **Halstead-Reitan Neuropsychological Battery** that asks respondents to compare rhythmic beats to assess sound recognition, attention, and concentration.

Rorschach inkblot test Projective test that uses irregular patterns of ink as its ambiguous stimuli.

rumination disorder Regurgitation and reswallowing of partially digested food, interfering with nutritional intake or weight gain.

sadistic personality disorder Pervasive pattern of deriving pleasure by inflicting pain on others; proposed as a category for DSM-III-R but not included in DSM-IV for lack of research.

Saint Vitus's Dance Instance of mass hysteria in which groups of people experienced a simultaneous compulsion to dance and shout in the streets.

scheduled awakening For children who wake frequently at night, awakening them about an hour before and from a deeper sleep than their usual times to help them learn to fall asleep on their own.

Schedule for Affective Disorders and Schizophrenia (SADS) Specialized semistructured interview protocol that specifically assesses mood and schizophrenic disorders.

schedules of reinforcement In operant conditioning, the pattern of consequences following a behavior, based on the number of responses emitted or the time intervals between them.

schizoaffective disorder Psychotic disorder featuring symptoms of both schizophrenia and major mood disorder.

schizoid personality disorder Cluster A (odd or eccentric) **personality disorder** featuring a pervasive pattern of detachment from social relationships and a restricted range of expression of emotions.

schizophrenia Devastating psychotic disorder that may involve characteristic disturbances in thinking (delusions), perception (hallucinations), speech, emotions, and behavior.

schizophrenia, childhood type Outdated, global category formerly used to cover all severe childhood disorders. It included problems in communication, learning, and social interaction, but ignored the wide variety of needs and disorders of children.

schizophreniform disorder Psychotic disorder involving the symptoms of schizophrenia but lasting less than six months.

schizophrenogenic mother According to an obsolete, unsupported theory, a cold, dominating, and rejecting parent who was thought to cause schizophrenia in her offspring.

schizotypal personality disorder Cluster A (odd or eccentric) **personality disorder** involving a pervasive pattern of interpersonal deficits featuring acute discomfort with, and reduced capacity for, close relationships, as well as by cognitive or perceptual distortions and eccentricities of behavior.

scientist-practitioner model Expectation that mental health professionals will apply scientific methods to their work. They must keep current in the latest research on diagnosis and treatment, they must evaluate their own methods for effectiveness, and they may generate their own research to discover new knowledge of disorders and their treatment.

script theory Theory of sexual functioning that suggests people's sexual behavior and attitudes are guided by scripts reflecting social and cultural expectations. Negative scripts may increase vulnerability to the development of sexual dysfunction.

seasonal affective disorder (SAD) Mood disorder involving a cycling of episodes corresponding to the seasons of the year, typically with depression occurring during winter.

seasonal patterning Temporal course of bipolar or recurrent major depressive disorders in which episodes occur during particular seasons of the year.

secondary gain Additional reinforcers beyond *primary gain* that a person may obtain by the display of symptoms. These may include attention, sympathy, and avoidance of unwanted responsibilities.

selective mutism Developmental disorder characterized by the individual's consistent failure to speak in specific social situations despite speaking in other situations.

selective serotonergic reuptake inhibitors (SSRIs) Class of medications for depression (including *Prozac*) that act on the serotonergic system by inhibiting the **reuptake** of the **neurotransmitter serotonin.**

self-actualizing Process emphasized in humanistic psychology in which people strive to achieve their highest potential against difficult life experiences.

self-defeating personality disorder Pervasive pattern of being overly passive and accepting the pain and suffering imposed by others. A category proposed for DSM-III-R but not included in DSM-IV for lack of research.

self-efficacy Perception that one has the ability to cope with stress or challenges.

self-injurious behavior Dangerous actions, including head-banging and hitting and biting oneself, seen in many children with **autism.**

self-medication Process by which some individuals may abuse substances in attempting to use them to relieve other problems such as anxiety, pain, or sleeplessness.

self-monitoring Action by which clients observe and record their own behaviors as either an assessment of a problem and its change, or a treatment procedure that makes them more aware of their responses.

self-psychology See **ego psychology.**

semistructured interviews Interviews that employ preplanned, standardized questions to elicit information in a consistent way.

sensate focus Sex therapy in which couples concentrate on pleasurable sensations from caressing and fondling. Intercourse is forbidden to prevent focus on sexual performance and the anxiety it may provoke.

sensorium Person's general awareness of the surroundings, including time and place.

sentence-completion method Projective test in which the person is asked to finish a series of incomplete sentences.

separation anxiety disorder Excessive enduring fear in some children that harm will come to them or their parents while they are apart.

septum Part of the **limbic system** that regulates emotions and the ability to learn and control impulses as well as such drives as sex, hunger, thirst, and aggression.

sequential design Combination of the cross-sectional and longitudinal research methods involving repeated study of different cohorts over time.

serotonin Neurotransmitter involved in processing information and coordination of movement as well as inhibition and restraint;

it also assists in the regulation of eating, sexual, and aggressive behaviors, all of which may be involved in different psychological disorders. Its interaction with **dopamine** is implicated in **schizophrenia.**

serotonin reuptake blockers See **selective serotonergic reuptake inhibitors.**

severe mental retardation Level of retardation defined by IQ scores between 20 and 40 and with somewhat limited communication, self-help, social, and vocational skills.

sex ratio Percentage of people with a disorder who are male and female.

sex (or gender) reassignment surgery Surgical procedures to alter a person's physical anatomy to conform to that person's psychological gender identity.

sexual aversion disorder Extreme and persistent dislike of sexual contact or similar activities.

sexual dysfunction Sexual disorder in which the client finds it difficult to function adequately while having sex.

sexual masochism Paraphilia in which sexual arousal is associated with experiencing pain or humiliation.

sexual pain disorder (dyspareunia) Recurring genital pain in either males or females before, during, or after sexual intercourse.

sexual sadism Paraphilia in which sexual arousal is associated with inflicting pain or humiliation.

shaping In operant conditioning, the development of a new response by reinforcing successively more similar versions of that response. Both desirable and undesirable behaviors may be learned in this manner.

shared psychotic disorder (folie à deux) Psychotic disturbance in which an individual develops a delusion similar to that of a person with whom he or she shares a close relationship.

shift work type Circadian rhythm sleep disorder characterized by insomnia during sleep time and sleepiness during wake time due to late-shift work or frequent work shift changes.

silver nitrate Chemical that can be used in gum or lozenges to make subsequent smoking aversive by producing a bad taste in the mouth. Research indicates this treatment approach is not particularly effective.

single-case experimental designs Research tactic in which an independent variable is manipulated for a single individual, allowing cause-and-effect conclusions, but with limited generalizability (contrast with **case study method**).

single photon emission computed tomography (SPECT) Neuroimaging procedure similar to PET scanning, though less accurate, less complex, and less costly.

sinoaortic baroreflex arc Body's mechanism to compensate for sudden blood pressure increases by decreasing pressure. This reaction causes some people to faint and may lead them to develop phobias.

situationally predisposed panic attack Circumstance that increases the likelihood that a panic attack may be triggered.

situational phobia Anxiety involving enclosed places (e.g., claustrophobia) or public transportation (e.g., fear of flying).

sleep apnea Disorder involving brief periods when breathing ceases during sleep.

sleep attacks Unexpected episodes of falling asleep during the day.

sleep efficiency (SE) Percentage of time actually spent sleeping of the total time spent in bed.

sleep enuresis Urination while sleeping.

sleep hygiene Psychological treatment for insomnia that teaches clients to recognize and eliminate environmental obstacles to sleep. These include the use of nicotine, caffeine, certain medications, and alcohol as well as ill-timed exercise.

sleep paralysis Brief and frightening period at the beginning or end of sleep when the individual cannot move or speak; sometimes mistaken for nocturnal panic attack.

sleep restriction Treatment for insomnia that involves limiting time in bed to the actual amount spent sleeping so that the bed is associated with sleep and no other competing activities.

sleep spindles Brief spurts of rapid brain wave activity during Stage 2 sleep.

sleep starts Brief muscle contractions, usually in the legs, just as sleep begins.

sleep state misperception (SSM) Under- or overestimating the amount or quality of sleep one is experiencing.

sleep stress Environmental events, such as ingesting excess caffeine, that can affect sleep negatively.

sleep terrors Episodes of apparent awakening from sleep, accompanied by signs of panic, followed by disorientation and amnesia for the incident. These occur during NREM sleep and so do not involve frightening dreams.

slow wave/delta sleep Slow brain wave activity that characterizes deep sleep.

small fibers Nerve fibers in the **dorsal horns of the spinal cord** that regulate the pattern and intensity of pain sensations. They open the gate, increasing the transmission of painful stimuli.

smooth-pursuit eye movement Also called **eye-tracking;** the ability to follow moving targets visually. Deficits in this skill can be caused by a single gene whose location is known. This problem is associated with **schizophrenia** and, thus, may serve as a genetic marker for this disorder.

social phobia Extreme, enduring, irrational fear and avoidance of social or performance situations.

sociopathic personality disturbances Obsolete term corresponding to the current category **antisocial personality disorder;** it included alcohol and drug abuse because these were considered merely symptoms of other problems.

somatic delusions False and unfounded beliefs about the body—for example, that parts are rotting or turning to stone.

somatic nervous system Part of the **peripheral nervous system** that controls muscle movement.

somatic treatments Biological interventions that include medication, electroconvulsive (shock) therapy, and psychosurgery.

somatization disorder Somatoform disorder involving extreme and long-lasting focus on multiple physical symptoms for which no medical cause is evident.

somatoform disorders Pathological concern of individuals with the appearance or functioning of their bodies, usually in the absence of any identifiable medical condition.

somnambulism Repeated sleepwalking that occurs during NREM sleep and so is not the acting out of a dream. The person is difficult to waken and does not recall the experience.

specific phobia Unreasonable fear of a specific object or situation that markedly interferes with daily life functioning.

specifiers in mood disorders Patterns of characteristics that sometimes accompany major depressive or manic episodes and may help predict their course and prognosis. These include psychotic, melancholic, atypical, catatonic, chronic, and with postpartum onset.

standardization Process of establishing specific norms and requirements for a measurement technique to ensure that it is used consistently across measurement occasions. This includes instructions for administering the measure, evaluating its findings, and comparing these to data for large numbers of people.

Stanford-Binet Early standardized intelligence test designed to identify children who will experience academic difficulties by assessing their attention, perception, reasoning, and comprehension.

statistical significance Probability that obtaining the observed research findings merely by chance is small.

statistics Branch of mathematics concerned with gathering, analyzing, and interpreting data from research.

stimulants Psychoactive substances that elevate mood, activity, and alertness, including amphetamines, caffeine, cocaine, and nicotine.

stimulus control Deliberate arrangement of the environment so that it encourages desired behaviors and discourages problem behaviors. For example, insomnia may be combatted by limiting time in, and associations with, the bed.

stimulus overselectivity Failure to generalize a learned behavior to other stimulus situations. Originally thought to be a characteristic of people with **autism,** it is now seen as a normal early stage of cognitive development, indicating the delays involved in autism.

Strength of Grip Test Subtest of the Halstead-Reitan Neuropsychological Battery that compares the grip strength of the client's right and left hands.

stress Body's physiological response to a stressor, which is any event or change that requires adaptation.

stress hormones Group of hormones including **corticosteroids,** that are involved in the body's physiological stress response.

stress physiology Study of the body's response to stressful events.

stroke (cerebral vascular accident) Temporary blockage of blood vessels supplying the brain, or a rupture of vessels in the brain, resulting in temporary or permanent loss of brain functioning.

Structured Clinical Interview for DSM-III-R (SCID) General, semistructured interview for assessing a wide range of disorders by examining a minimal sample of information about each of the major disorders.

stuttering Disturbance in the fluency and time patterning of speech (e.g., sound and syllable repetitions or prolongations).

subcortical dementia Disease affecting the inner areas of the brain below the cortex that differs from dementia of the Alzheimer's type in that it involves impaired recall but normal recognition, more severe depression and anxiety, slowed motions and impaired coordination, but no **aphasia.**

sublimation Psychodynamic defense mechanism in which the person redirects energy from conflict and anxiety into more constructive outlets, such as work.

substance abuse Pattern of psychoactive substance use leading to significant distress or impairment in social and occupational roles, and in hazardous situations.

substance dependence Maladaptive pattern of substance use characterized by the need for increased amounts to achieve the desired effect, negative physical effects when the substance is withdrawn, unsuccessful efforts to control its use, and substantial effort expended to seek it or recover from its effects.

substance intoxication Physiological reactions, such as impaired judgment and motor ability as well as mood changes, resulting from the ingestion of psychoactive substances.

substance-related disorders Range of problems associated with the use and abuse of drugs such as alcohol, cocaine, heroin, and other substances people use to alter the way they think, feel, and behave. These are extremely costly in human and financial terms.

sufficient condition Circumstance that, by itself, is enough to cause or allow for a particular phenomenon to occur.

suicidal ideation Serious thoughts about committing suicide.

suicide attempts Efforts made to kill oneself.

superego In psychoanalysis, the psychical entity representing the internalized moral standards of parents and society.

supernatural model Explanation of human behavior and its dysfunction that posits important roles for spirits, demons, grace, sin, and so on.

sympathetic nervous system Part of the **autonomic nervous system** that prepares the body for activity or to respond to stressors—by increasing heart rate and blood flow to muscles, for instance.

Symptom Check List-90 Revised (SCL-90 R) Self-report measure in which respondents indicate their degree of distress on 90 physical and psychological symptoms.

symptom substitution Psychodynamic assertion that if overt problem behavior (the "symptom") is treated without eliminating the underlying conflict thought to be causing it, that conflict will reemerge in the form of new, perhaps worse, symptoms.

synaptic cleft Space between nerve cells where chemical transmitters act to move impulses from one neuron to the next.

systematic desensitization Behavioral therapy technique to diminish excessive fears, involving gradual exposure to the feared stimulus paired with a positive coping experience, usually relaxation.

systematic exposure Behavioral therapy method to reduce excessive fears by gradually presenting the feared stimulus until the fear reaction extinguishes.

systemic perspective View that the many contributing causes of abnormal behavior form a *system* involving biology, behavior, cognition, emotion, culture, and society. Each component of the system affects all the others.

systolic blood pressure blood pressure generated when the heart is at work pumping blood.

T cells Lymphocytes produced in bone marrow, developed in the thymus gland, and operating in the cellular branch of the **immune system.** Some attack **antigens** directly while others help regulate the system.

tacrine hydrochloride Medication for patients with Alzheimer's disease that prevents the breakdown of **acetylcholine,** keeping it available for use by the brain. Improvements are small and the drug is expensive and causes serious side effects.

Tactile Performance Test Subtest of the **Halstead-Reitan Neuropsychological Battery** that asks the respondent to insert wooden shapes into a hidden form board, allowing the examiner to assess the subject's learning and memory skills.

taijin phobia Japanese variant of **social phobia.** In many cases individuals avoid social interaction believing they have terrible body or breath odor.

tangentiality Characteristic of the loose cognitive and verbal associations seen in **schizophrenia** in which the person fails to answer questions and quickly moves the conversation to unrelated topics.

Tarantism See **St. Vitus's Dance.**

tardive dyskinesia Extrapyramidal symptom and sometimes irreversible side effect of long-term **neuroleptic** medication, involving involuntary motor movements, especially in the face and tongue.

task analysis Method for evaluating a skill to be learned, breaking it down into its component parts.

taxonomy System of naming and classification (e.g., of specimens) in science.

telencephalon See **forebrain.**

telephone scatologia **Paraphilia** in which the person gains sexual gratification by making obscene phone calls, usually while masturbating.

temporal lobe Section of each cerebral hemisphere associated primarily with sight and sound recognition and with long-term memory storage.

temporal patterning Course modifier for mood disorders describing their time sequences, including recurrence, recovery, and alternation.

tension headaches Bilateral head pain characterized by a dull ache, usually starting at the front or back of the head.

tension reduction Negative reinforcement motivation account for substance abuse, suggesting it is maintained because it allows people to escape anxiety.

testability Ability of a hypothesis, for example, to be subjected to scientific scrutiny and to be accepted or rejected, a necessary condition for the hypothesis to be useful.

test-retest reliability Degree to which results of two administrations of a test to the same person are similar.

tetrahydrocannabinols (THC) Most common active chemicals in **marijuana (cannabis sativa)** responsible for its ability to alter mood and behavior.

thalamus Part of the **diencephalon** of the brain, broadly associated with regulation of behavior and emotion.

thanatos Freudian concept of a human drive toward death and destruction.

Thematic Apperception Test Projective test in which the respondent is asked to tell stories about a series of ambiguous drawings.

tic disorder Disruption in early development involving involuntary motor movements or vocalizations.

tics Sudden, rapid, and recurrent involuntary motor movements or vocalizations.

time-limited course Condition in which a disorder improves on its own in a relatively brief period of time.

time-management training Instruction that teaches one to deal with stress by establishing priorities among activities and demands, and paying less attention to the less important ones.

token economy Social learning behavior modification system in which individuals earn items they can exchange for desired rewards by displaying appropriate behaviors.

tolerance Need for increased amounts of a substance to achieve the desired effect, and a diminished effect with continued use of the same amount.

total sleep time (TST) Actual combined time a person spends sleeping each day.

Tourette's disorder Developmental disorder featuring multiple dysfunctional motor and vocal tics.

trainable mental retardation Obsolete term referring to level of retardation comparable to the DSM "moderate" designation that suggests the individual can learn rudimentary vocational but not academic skills.

transcendental meditation Technique for focusing attention by softly repeating a single syllable (mantra); often accompanied by slow and regular breathing.

transference Psychoanalytic concept suggesting that clients may seek to relate to the therapist as they do to important authority figures, particularly their parents.

transinstitutionalization Movement of people with severe mental illness from large psychiatric hospitals to smaller group residences.

transsexualism Obsolete term for **gender identity disorder.**

transvestic fetishism **Paraphilia** in which individuals, usually males, are sexually aroused or receive gratification by wearing clothing of the opposite sex.

treatment outcome Effects, including success or failure, of clinical interventions.

treatment outcome research Studies of the effectiveness of clinical interventions, including the comparison of competing treatments.

triazolam Short-acting **benzodiazepine** medication known as *Halcion* used to treat insomnia. Possible negative side effects include drowsiness, dependence, short-term memory loss, or rebound.

tricyclic antidepressants Most common treatment for depression, a group of medications including imipramine and amitriptyline that block the **reuptake** of **neurotransmitters,** principally **serotonin** and **norepinephrine,** at the synapse. The drugs are effective for some anxiety disorders and mood disorders. They are also used to treat **obstructive sleep apnea** because they help maintain respiratory muscle tone to assist breathing during REM sleep. Positive effects are delayed, and negative side effects may include dizziness and even death, so close monitoring is required. Relapse rates range from 20% to 50% when the drug is stopped.

tuberous sclerosis Rare dominant gene disorder characterized by bumps on the skin and sometime mental retardation and seizures.

Turner's syndrome Pattern of abnormality involving a missing X chromosome in females that causes mental retardation and physical deformities.

twin studies In genetics research, the comparison of twins with unrelated or less closely related individuals. If twins, particularly monozygotic twins who share identical genotypes, share common characteristics such as a disorder, even if they were reared in different environments, this is strong evidence of genetic involvement in those characteristics.

type A behavior pattern Cluster of behaviors, including excessive competitiveness, time-pressured impatience, accelerated speech and anger, originally thought to promote high risk for heart disease.

type B behavior pattern Cluster of behaviors including a relaxed attitude, indifference to time pressure, and less forceful ambition; originally thought to cause low risk for heart disease.

unconditional positive regard Acceptance by the counselor of the client's feelings and actions without judgment or condemnation.

unconditioned response (UCR) In classical conditioning, the natural or unlearned reaction to the unconditioned stimulus.

unconditioned stimulus (UCS) Environmental event that would elicit a response in almost anyone and requires no learning. In classical conditioning, it is paired with a neutral stimulus that, after training, may become a conditioned stimulus.

unconscious Part of the psychic makeup that is outside the awareness of the person.

unconscious vision Also called **blind sight;** a phenomenon in which a person is able to perform visual functions while having no awareness or memory of these abilities.

underarousal hypothesis Theory of the etiology of **antisocial personality disorder** suggesting psychopaths engage in dangerous or illicit behavior to stimulate the under-aroused cerebral cortex in their brains.

undifferentiated somatoform disorder Somatization disorder with fewer than eight symptoms but still causing distress and impaired functioning.

undifferentiated type schizophrenia Category for individuals who meet the criteria for schizophrenia but not for any one of the defined subtypes.

unexpected or uncued panic attack Panic attack that has no identified triggering circumstance.

unipolar mood disorder Mood disorder characterized by depression or mania, but not both. Most cases involve unipolar depression.

unshared environments Term indicating that even identical twins living in the same home may have different prenatal and family experiences.

vacuum device therapy Mechanical treatment for male erectile disorder that employs a vacuum cylinder to draw blood into the penis, where it is held by a ring placed at the base of the penis.

vaginal photoplethysmograph Light-sensitive psychophysiological monitoring device that measures female sexual arousal reflected by blood flow to the vagina.

vaginismus Recurring involuntary muscle spasms in the outer third of the vagina that interfere with sexual intercourse.

validity Degree to which a technique actually measures what it purports to measure.

variability Degree of change in a phenomenon over time.

vascular Pertaining to the vessels that transport blood and other fluids in the body.

vascular dementia Progressive brain disorder involving loss of cognitive functioning, caused by blockage of blood flow to the brain, that appears concurrently with other neurological signs and symptoms.

vasovagal syncope Fainting due to low blood pressure in the head and brain.

ventral tegmental area The **midbrain** region that includes part of the "pleasure pathway" responsible for the experience of reward.

verbal scales Sections of the Wechsler series of intelligence tests that assess vocabulary, memory, reasoning skills, and information facts.

vinvuza Nigerian variant of **dissociative trance** states.

visuospatial skills Ability to see, recognize, orient within, and negotiate between objects in space.

voyeurism **Paraphilia** in which sexual arousal is derived from observing unsuspecting individuals undressing or naked.

vulnerability Susceptibility or tendency to develop a disorder.

waxy flexibility Characteristic of **catatonia** in which the person remains in bodily postures positioned by another person.

Wechsler Adult Intelligence Scale-Revised (WAIS-R) IQ test for adults, assessing a range of verbal and performance abilities.

Wechsler Intelligence Scale for Children—3rd Edition (WISC-III) IQ test for children assessing a range of verbal and performance abilities.

Wechsler Preschool and Primary Scale of Intelligence—Revised (WPPSI-R) IQ test for young children that measures a range of performance, verbal, and preverbal abilities.

Wernicke's disease Organic brain syndrome resulting from prolonged heavy alcohol use, involving confusion, unintelligible speech, and loss of motor coordination. It may be caused by a deficiency of thiamine, a vitamin that is metabolized poorly by heavy drinkers.

withdrawal Severely negative physiological reaction to removal of a psychoactive substance, which can be alleviated by the same or a similar substance.

withdrawal delirium (delirium tremens, DT's) Frightening hallucinations and body tremors that result when a heavy drinker withdraws from alcohol.

withdrawal design Removing a treatment to note whether it has been effective. In single-case experimental designs, a behavior is measured (**baseline**), an independent variable is introduced (*intervention*), and then the intervention is *withdrawn*. Because the behavior continues to be measured throughout (*repeated measurement*), any effects of the intervention can be noted. Also called **reversal design.**

X chromosome One of the two sex chromosomes that determine gender; females have two and males have one, contributed by the mother. X chromosome abnormalities are implicated in some physical and cognitive problems.

Y chromosome One of the two sex chromosomes that determine gender; its presence, contributed by the father, determines the offspring will be male.

Yerkes-Dodson curve Inverted U-shaped graphical relationship between arousal and performance. Optimal performance occurs at intermediate levels of arousal. Psychopaths may engage in stimulus-seeking behavior to increase their low arousal to more useful levels.

References

ABADINSKY, H. (1993). *Drug abuse: An introduction* (2nd ed.). Chicago: Nelson-Hall Publishers. **(Chap 12)**

ABBEDUTO, L., & ROSENBERG, S. (1992). Linguistic communication in persons with mental retardation. In S. F. Warren & J. Reichle (Eds.), *Causes and effects in communication and language intervention* (pp. 331–359). Baltimore: Paul H. Brookes. **(Chap 15)**

ABBEY, S. E., & GARFINKEL, P. E. (1991). Neurasthenia and chronic fatigue syndrome: The role of culture in the making of a diagnosis. *American Journal of Psychiatry, 148,* 1638–1646. **(Chap 9)**

ABEL, G. G. (1989). Behavioral treatment of child molesters. In A. J. Stunkard & A. Baum (Eds.), *Perspectives in behavioral medicine: Eating, sleeping and sex.* Hillsdale, NJ: Lawrence Erlbaum. **(Chap 11)**

ABEL, G. G., BARLOW, D. H., BLANCHARD, E. B., & GUILD, D. (1977). The components of rapists' sexual arousal. *Archives of General Psychiatry, 34,* 895–903. **(Chap 11)**

ABEL, G. G., BECKER, J. V., CUNNINGHAM-RATHNER, J., MITTELMAN, M., & ROULEAU, J. L. (1988). Multiple paraphilic diagnoses among sex offenders. *Bulletin of the American Academy of Psychiatry and Law, 16,* 153–168. **(Chap 11)**

ABEL, G. G., BECKER, J. V., MITTELMAN, M., CUNNINGHAM-RATHNER, J., ROULEAU, J. L., & MURPHY, W. E. (1987). Self-reported sex crimes of nonincarcerated paraphiliacs. *Journal of Interpersonal Violence, 2,* 3–25. **(Chap 11)**

ABEL, G. G., BLANCHARD, E. B., BARLOW, D. H., & MAVISSAKALIAN, M. (1975). Identifying specific erotic cues in sexual deviations by audiotaped descriptions. *Journal of Applied Behavior Analysis, 8,* 247–260. **(Chap 11)**

ABEL, G. G., LEVIS, D. J., & CLANCY, J. (1970). Aversion therapy applied to taped sequences of deviant behavior in exhibitionism and other sexual deviations: A preliminary report. *Journal of Behavior Therapy and Experimental Psychiatry, 1,* 59–66. **(Chap 11)**

ABRAHAMSON, D. J., BARLOW, D. H., SAKHEIM, D. K., BECK, J. G., & ATHANASIOU, R. (1985). Effects of distraction on sexual responding in functional and dysfunctional men. *Behavior Therapy, 16,* 503–515. **(Chap 11)**

ABRAMOWITZ, S. I. (1986). Psychosocial outcomes of sex reassignment surgery. *Journal of Consulting and Clinical Psychology, 54,* 183–189. **(Chap 11)**

ABRAMSON, L. Y., METALSKY, G. I., & ALLOY, L. B. (1989). Hopelessness depression: A theory-based subtype of depression. *Psychological Review, 96*(2), 358–372. **(Chaps 4, 7)**

ABRAMSON, L. Y., SELIGMAN, M. E. P., & TEASDALE, J. D. (1978). Learned helplessness in humans: Critique and reformulation. *Journal of Abnormal Psychology, 87,* 49–74. **(Chap 2, 7)**

ABSE, D. W. (1987). *Hysteria and related mental disorders: An approach to psychological medicine.* Bristol: Wright. **(Chap 13)**

ABUELO, D. N. (1991). Genetic disorders. In J. L. Matson & J. A. Mulick (Eds.), *Handbook of mental retardation* (2nd ed.), pp. 97–114. Elmsford, NY: Pergamon Press. **(Chap 15)**

ACHENBACH, T. M., & EDELBROCK, C. S. (1983). *Manual for the child behavior checklist and revised child behavior profile.* Burlington: University of Vermont. **(Chap 3)**

ACKERMAN, M. D., D'ATTILIO, J. P., ANTONI, M. H., WEINSTEIN, D., RHAMY, R. K., & POLITANO, V. A. (1991). The predictive significance of patient-reported sexual functioning in rigiscan sleep evaluations. *Journal of Urology, 146,* 1559–1563. **(Chap 11)**

ACKLIN, M. W., MCDOWELL, C. J., & ORNDOFF, S. (1992). Statistical power and the Rorschach: 1975–1991. *Journal of Personality Assessment, 59,* 366–379. **(Chap 3)**

ADAIR, R., BAUCHNER, H., PHILIPP, B., LEVENSON, S., & ZUCKERMAN, B. (1991). Night waking during infancy: Role of parent presence at bedtime. *Pediatrics, 87,* 500–504. **(Chap 10)**

ADAMS, F. (1988). Neuropsychiatric evaluation and treatment of delirium in cancer patients. *Advanced Psychosomatic Medicine, 18,* 26–36. **(Chap 15)**

ADDINGTON V. TEXAS, 99 S. CT. 1804. (1979). **(Chap 17)**

ADER, R., & COHEN, N. (1975). Behaviorally conditioned immunosuppression. *Psychosomatic Medicine, 37,* 333–340. **(Chap 9)**

ADER, R., & COHEN, N. (1993). Psychoneuroimmunology: Conditioning and stress. *Annual Review of Psychology, 44,* 53–85. **(Chap 9)**

ADLER, C. M., COTE, G., BARLOW, D. H., & HILLHOUSE, J. J. (submitted). *Phenomenological relationships between somatoform, anxiety, and psychophysiological disorders.* Unpublished manuscript. **(Chap 6)**

ADLER, P. S. J., FRANCE, C., & DITTO, B. (1991). Baroreflex sensitivity at rest and during stress in individuals with a history of vasovagal syncope. *Journal of Psychosomatic Research, 35*(4), 1–7. **(Chap 2)**

AGBAYEWA, M. O., & COSSETTE, P. (1990). A psychiatric clinic within a geriatric medical day hospital: Descriptive study. *Canadian Journal on Aging, 9*(1), 5–12. **(Chap 15)**

AGRAS, W. S. (1982). Behavioral medicine in the 1980s: Nonrandom connections. *Journal of Consulting and Clinical Psychology, 50,* 797–803. **(Chap 9)**

AGRAS, W. S. (1987). *Eating disorders: Management of obesity, bulimia, and anorexia nervosa.* Elmsford, NY: Pergamon Press. **(Chap 8)**

AGRAS, W. S., BARLOW, D. H., CHAPIN, H. N., ABEL, G. G., & LEITENBERG, H. (1974). Behavior modification of anorexia nervosa. *Archives of General Psychiatry, 30,* 279–286. **(Chap 8)**

AGRAS, W. S., CHAPIN, H. N., & OLIVEAU, D. C. (1972). The natural history of phobia. *Archives of General Psychiatry, 26,* 315–317. **(Chap 5)**

AGRAS, W. S., & KIRKLEY, B. G. (1986). Bulimia: Theories of etiology. In K. D. Brownell & J. P. Foreyt (Eds.), *Handbook of eating disorders: Physiology, psychology, and treatment of obesity, anorexia, and bulimia* (pp. 367–378). New York: Basic Books. **(Chap 8)**

AGRAS, W. S., ROSSITER, E. M., ARNOW, B., SCHNEIDER, J. A., TELCH, C. F., RAEBURN, S. D., BRUCE, B., PERL, M., & KORAN, L. M. (1992). Pharmacologic and cognitive-behavioral treatment for bulimia-nervosa: A controlled comparison. *American Journal of Psychiatry, 149,* 82–87. **(Chap 8)**

AGRAS, W. S., SCHNEIDER, J. A., ARNOW, B., RAEBURN, S. D., & TELCH, C. F. (1989). Cognitive-behavioral and response-prevention treatments for bulimia nervosa. *Journal of Consulting and Clinical Psychology, 57,* 215–221. **(Chap 8)**

AGRAS, W. S., SYLVESTER, D., & OLIVEAU, D. (1969). The epidemiology of common fears and phobia. *Comprehensive Psychiatry, 10,* 151–156. **(Chap 5)**

AHERN, D., GORKIN, L., ANDERSON, J., TIERNEY, C., HALLSTROM, A., EWART, C., CAPONE, R. J., SCHRON, E., KORNFELD, D., HERD, J., RICHARDSON, D., & FOLLICK, M. (1990). Biobehavioral variables and mortality or cardiac arrest in the cardiac arrhythmia pilot study (CAPS). *American Journal of Cardiology, 66,* 59–62. **(Chap 9)**

AHLES, T. A., & MARTIN, J. B. (1989). The relationship of electromyographic and vasomotor activity to MMPI subgroups in chronic headache patients: The use of the original and contemporary MMPI norms. *Headache, 29,* 584–587. **(Chap 9)**

AKBARIAN, S., BUNNEY, W. E., POTKIN, S. G., WIGAL, S. B., HAGMAN, J. O., SANDMAN, C. A., & JONES, E. G. (1993). Altered distribution of nicotinamide-adenine dinucleotide phosphate-diaphorase cells in frontal lobe of schizophrenics implies disturbances of cortical development. *Archives of General Psychiatry, 50,* 169–177. **(Chap 14)**

AKBARIAN, S., VINUELA, A., KIM, J. J., POTKIN, S. G., BUNNEY, W. E., & JONES, E. G. (1993).

Distorted distribution of nicotinamide-adenine dinucleotide phosphate-diaphorase neurons in temporal lobe of schizophrenics implies anomalous cortical development. *Archives of General Psychiatry, 50,* 178–187. **(Chap 14)**

AKISKAL, H. S., KHANI, M. K., & SCOTT-STRAUSS, A. (1979). Cyclothymic temperamental disorders. *Psychiatric Clinics of North America, 2,* 527–554. **(Chap 7)**

AKTAR, S., & BRENNER, I. (1979). Differential diagnosis of fugue-like states. *Journal of Clinical Psychiatry, 40,* 381–385. **(Chap 6)**

ALBANO, A. M., MARTEN, P. A., HEIMBERG, R. G., & BARLOW, D. H. (in press). Children and adolescents: Assessment and treatment. In R. G. Heimberg, M. R. Liebowitz, D. A. Hope, & F. Schneier (Eds.), *Social phobia: Diagnosis, assessment and treatment.* New York: Guilford Press. **(Chap 5)**

ALCOHOLICS ANONYMOUS. (1990). Comments on A.A.'s triennial surveys. New York: Alcoholics Anonymous World Services. **(Chap 12)**

ALDEN, L. (1989). Short-term structured treatment for avoidant personality disorder. *Journal of Consulting and Clinical Psychology, 57,* 756–764. **(Chap 13)**

ALDEN, L., & CAPP, R. (1988). Characteristics predicting social functioning and treatment response in clients impaired by extreme shyness: Age of onset and the public/private shyness distinction. *Canadian Journal of Behavioural Science, 20,* 40–49. **(Chap 13)**

ALDEN, L. E., & CAPREOL, M. J. (1993). Avoidant personality disorder: Interpersonal problems as predictors of treatment response. *Behavior Therapy, 24,* 357–376. **(Chap 13)**

ALEXANDER, F. (1950). *Psychosomatic medicine.* New York: Norton. **(Chap 9)**

ALEXANDER, F. G. (1939). Emotional factors in essential hypertension: Presentation of a tentative hypothesis. *Psychosomatic Medicine, 1,* 175–179. **(Chap 9)**

ALEXANDER F. G., & SELESNICK, S. T. (1966). *The history of psychiatry: An evaluation of psychiatric thought and practice from prehistoric times to the present.* New York: Harper & Row, Publishers. **(Chap 1)**

ALFREY, A. C. (1986). Systemic toxicity of aluminum in man. *Neurobiology of Aging, 7,* 543–545. **(Chap 15)**

ALLEN, J., DEMYER, M., NORTON, J., PONTIUS, W., & YANG, G. (1971). Intellectuality in parents of psychotic, subnormal, and normal children. *Journal of Autism and Childhood Schizophrenia, 1,* 311–326. **(Chap 16)**

ALLEN, J. M., LAM, R. W., REMICK, R. A., & SADOVNICK, A. D. (1993). Depressive symptoms and family history in seasonal and nonseasonal mood disorders. *American Journal of Psychiatry, 150*(3), 443–448. **(Chap 7)**

ALLEN, L. S., & GORSKI, R. A. (1992). Sexual orientation and the size of the anterior commissure in the human brain. *Proceedings of the National Academy of Science, 89,* 7199–7202. **(Chap 11)**

ALLEN, S. J., DAWBARN, D., & WILCOCK, G. K. (1988). Morphometric immunochemical analysis of neurons in the nucleus basalis of Meynert in Alzheimer's disease. *Brain Research, 454,* 275–281. **(Chap 15)**

ALLOY, L. B., CLEMENTS, C., & KOLDEN, G. (1985). The cognitive diathesis-stress theories of depression: Therapeutic implications. In S. Reiss & R. Bootzin (Eds.), *Theoretical issues in behavior therapy* (pp. 379–410). New York: Academic Press. **(Chap 7)**

ALLOY, L. B., KELLY, K. A., MINEKA, S., & CLEMENTS, C. M. (1990). Comorbidity of anxiety and depressive disorders: A helplessness-hopelessness perspective. In J. D. Maser & C. R. Cloninger (Eds.), *Comorbidity of mood and anxiety disorders* (pp. 499–543). Washington, DC: American Psychiatric Press. **(Chap 7)**

ALTHOF, S., TURNER, L. A., LEVINE, S. B., RISEN, C., KURSH, E. D., BODNER, D., & RESNICK, M. (1987). Intracavernosal injection in the treatment of impotence: A prospective study of sexual, psychological and marital functioning. *Journal of Sex and Marital Therapy, 13,* 155–167. **(Chap 11)**

AMERICAN BAR ASSOCIATION, STANDING COMMITTEE ON ASSOCIATION STANDARDS FOR CRIMINAL JUSTICE. (1984). *Criminal justice and mental health standards.* Chicago: Author. **(Chap 17)**

AMERICAN HEART ASSOCIATION REPORT. (1994). *Smoke free society.* Austin, TX: Author. **(Chap 12)**

AMERICAN LAW INSTITUTE. (1962). *Model penal code: Proposed official draft.* Philadelphia: Author. **(Chap 17)**

AMERICAN PSYCHIATRIC ASSOCIATION. (1952). *Diagnostic and statistical manual of mental disorders* (1st ed.). Washington, DC: Author. **(Chap 3)**

AMERICAN PSYCHIATRIC ASSOCIATION. (1968). *Diagnostic and statistical manual of mental disorders* (2nd ed.). Washington, DC: Author. **(Chaps 3)**

AMERICAN PSYCHIATRIC ASSOCIATION. (1980). *Diagnostic and statistical manual of mental disorders* (3rd ed.). Washington, DC: Author. **(Chaps 3, 5, 6, 7)**

AMERICAN PSYCHIATRIC ASSOCIATION. (1982). *American Psychiatric Association statement on the insanity defense.* Washington, DC: Author. **(Chap 17)**

AMERICAN PSYCHIATRIC ASSOCIATION. (1983). American Psychiatric Association statement on the insanity defense. *American Journal of Psychiatry, 140,* 681–688. **(Chap 17)**

AMERICAN PSYCHIATRIC ASSOCIATION. (1987). *Diagnostic and statistical manual of mental disorders* (3rd ed. rev.). Washington, DC: Author. **(Chap 3)**

AMERICAN PSYCHIATRIC ASSOCIATION. (1990). *Benzodiazepine dependence, toxicity, and abuse: A task force report of the American Psychiatric Association.* Washington, DC: Author. **(Chap 12)**

AMERICAN PSYCHIATRIC ASSOCIATION. (1993). Practice guidelines for eating disorders. *American Journal of Psychiatry, 150*(2), 212–228. **(Chap 8)**

AMERICAN PSYCHIATRIC ASSOCIATION. (1994). *Diagnostic and statistical manual of mental disorders* (4th ed.). Washington, DC: Author. **(Chaps 1, 3, 5, 6, 7, 8, 9, 11)**

AMERICAN PSYCHOLOGICAL ASSOCIATION. (1990). Ethical principles of psycholog-

ists. *American Psychologist, 45,* 390–395. **(Chap 7)**

AMERICAN PSYCHOLOGICAL ASSOCIATION. (1992). Ethical principles of psychologists and code of conduct. *American Psychologist, 47,* 1597–1611. **(Chaps 4, 17)**

AMERICAN SLEEP DISORDERS ASSOCIATION. (1990). *The international classification of sleep disorders: Diagnostic and coding manual.* Rochester, MN: Author. **(Chap 10)**

ANASTASI, A. (1988). *Psychological testing* (6th ed.). New York: Oxford University Press. **(Chap 3)**

ANCH, A. M., BROWMAN, C. P., MITLER, M. M., & WALSH, J. K. (1988). *Sleep: A scientific perspective.* Englewood Cliffs, NJ: Prentice-Hall. **(Chap 10)**

ANDERSEN, B. L. (1992). Psychological interventions for cancer patients to enhance the quality of life. Special issue: Behavioral medicine: An update for the 1990s. *Journal of Consulting and Clinical Psychology, 60*(4), 552–568. **(Chap 9)**

ANDERSON, A. E. (1983). Anorexia nervosa and bulimia: A spectrum of eating disorders. *Journal of Adolescent Health Care, 4,* 15–21. **(Chap 8)**

ANDERSON, A. E., & HAY, A. (1985). Racial and socioeconomic influences in anorexia nervosa and bulimia. *International Journal of Eating Disorders, 4*(4), 479–487. **(Chap 8)**

ANDERSON, D. J., NOYES, R., & CROWE, R. R. (1984). A comparison of panic disorder and generalized anxiety disorder. *American Journal of Psychiatry, 141,* 572–575. **(Chap 5)**

ANDERSON, N. B., & JACKSON, J. S. (1987). Race, ethnicity and health psychology: The example of essential hypertension. In C. M. Stone, S. M. Weiss, J. D. Matarazzo, N. E. Miller, J. Rodin, C. D. Belar, M. J. Follick, & J. E. Singer (Eds.), *Health psychology: A discipline and a profession.* Chicago: University of Chicago Press. **(Chap 9)**

ANDRASIK, F., BLANCHARD, E. B., ARENA, J. E., SAUNDERS, N. L., & BARRON, K. D. (1982). Psychophysiology of recurrent headache: Methodological issues and new empirical findings. *Behavior Therapy, 13,* 407–429. **(Chap 9)**

ANDRASIK, F., & HOLROYD, K. A. (1980). A test of specific and nonspecific effects in the biofeedback treatment of tension headache. *Journal of Consulting and Clinical Psychology, 48,* 575–586. **(Chap 9)**

ANDREASEN, N. C. (1979). Thought, language, and communication disorders: I. Clinical assessment, definition of terms, and evaluation of their reliability. *Archives of General Psychiatry, 36,* 1315–1321. **(Chap 14)**

ANDREASEN, N. C. (1987). Creativity and mental illness: Prevalence rates in writers and their first-degree relatives. *American Journal of Psychiatry, 144*(10), 1288–1292. **(Chap 7)**

ANDREASEN, N. C., & BARDACH, J. (1977). Dysmorphophobia: Symptom or disease? *American Journal of Psychiatry, 134,* 673–676. **(Chap 6)**

ANDREASEN, N. C., & CARPENTER, W. T., JR. (1993). Diagnosis and classification of schizophrenia. *Schizophrenia Bulletin, 19,* 199–214. **(Chap 14)**

ANDREASEN, N. C., & FLAUM, M. A. (1990). Schizophrenia and related psychotic disorders. *Hospital and Community Psychiatry, 41,* 954–956. **(Chap 14)**

ANDREASEN, N. C., REZAI, K., ALLIGER, R., SWAYZE, V. W., FLAUM, M., KIRCHNER, P., COHEN, G., & O'LEARY, D. S. (1992). Hypofrontality in neuroleptic-naive patients and in patients with chronic schizophrenia: Assessment with xenon 133 single-photon emission computed tomography with the Tower of London. *Archives of General Psychiatry, 49,* 943–958. **(Chap 14)**

ANDREASEN, N. C., & SWAYZE, V. W. (1993). Neuroimaging. In J. A. Costa e Silva & C. C. Nadelson (Eds.), *International review of psychiatry* (Vol. 1). Washington, DC: American Psychiatric Press. **(Chap 3)**

ANDREASEN, N. C., SWAYZE, V. W., II, FLAUM, M., YATES, W. R., ARNDT, S., & MC-CHESNEY, C. (1990). Ventricular enlargement in schizophrenia evaluated with computed tomographic scanning: Effects of gender, age, and stage of illness. *Archives of General Psychiatry, 47,* 1008–1015. **(Chap 14)**

ANDREWS, G., MORRIS-YATES, A., HOWIE, P., & MARTIN, N. G. (1991). Genetic factors in stuttering confirmed. *Archives of General Psychiatry, 48,* 1034–1035. **(Chap 16)**

ANGST, J. (1981). Course of affective disorders. In H. Van Praag (Ed.), *Handbook of biological psychiatry: Part IV. Brain mechanisms and abnormal behavior-chemistry* (pp. 225–242). New York: Marcel Dekker. **(Chap 7)**

ANISMAN, H. (1984). Vulnerability to depression: Contribution of stress. In R. Post & J. Ballenger (Eds.), *Neurobiology of mood disorders.* Baltimore: Williams & Wilkins. **(Chap 2)**

ANTONI, M. H., BAGGETT, L., IRONSON, G., LAPERRIERE, A., AUGUST, S., KLIMAS, N., SCHNEIDERMAN, N., & FLETCHER, M. A. (1991). Cognitive-behavioral stress management intervention buffers distress responses and immunologic changes following notification of HIV-1 seropositivity. *Journal of Consulting and Clinical Psychology, 59*(6), 906–915. **(Chaps 2, 9)**

ANTONI, M. H., & GOODKIN, K. (in press). The interaction of viral and psychological factors in the promotion of cervical neoplasia. In H. Balner & J. Have (Eds.), *Coping with cancer and beyond: Cancer treatment and mental health.* Amsterdam: Swets and Zeitlinger. **(Chaps 2, 9)**

ANTONY, M. M., BROWN, T. A., CRASKE, M. G., BARLOW, D. H., MITCHELL, W. B., & MEADOWS, E. A. (1993). *Accuracy of heart beat estimation in panic disorder, social phobic and non-anxious controls.* Manuscript submitted for publication. **(Chap 5)**

ANXIETY AND PANIC DISORDER PANEL. (1994). [Draft, 5/13/94] *Template for developing guidelines: Interventions for mental and psychosocial aspects of physical disorders.* Rockville, MD: U.S. Department of Health and Human Services, Public Health Service, Agency for Health Care Policy and Research. **(Chap 17)**

APPELBAUM, K. A., BLANCHARD, E. B., HICKLING, E. J., & ALFONSO, M. (1988). Cognitive behavioral treatment of a veteran population with moderate to severe rheumatoid arthritis. *Behavior Therapy, 19,* 489–502. **(Chap 9)**

ARENA, J. G., BLANCHARD, E. B., ANDRASIK, F., & DUDEK, B. C. (1982). The headache symptom questionnaire: Discriminant classificatory ability and headache syndromes suggested by a factor analysis. *Journal of Behavioral Assessment, 4,* 55–69. **(Chap 9)**

ARENS, R. (1974). *Insanity defense.* New York: Philosophical Library. **(Chap 17)**

ARMSTEAD, C. A., LAWLER, K. A., GORDEN, G., CROSS, J., & GIBBONS, J. (1989). Relationship of racial stressors to blood pressure responses and anger expression in black college students. *Health Psychology, 8,* 541–556. **(Chap 9)**

ARMSTRONG, H. E. (1993). Review of psychosocial treatments for schizophrenia. In D. L. Dunner (Ed.), *Current psychiatric therapy* (pp. 183–188). Philadelphia: W. B. Saunders. **(Chaps 10, 14)**

ARNETZ, B. B., WASSERMAN, J., PETRINI, B., BRENNER, S. O., LEVI, L., ENEROTH, P., SALOVAARA, H., HJELM, R., SALOVAARA, L., THEORELL, T., & PETTERSON, I. L. (1987). Immune function in unemployed women. *Psychosomatic Medicine, 49,* 3–12. **(Chap 9)**

ARNOW, B., KENARDY, J., & AGRAS, W. S. (1992). Binge eating among the obese: A descriptive study. *Journal of Behavioral Medicine, 15*(2), 155–170. **(Chap 8)**

ASBERG, M., NORDSTROM, P., & TRASKMAN-BENDZ, L. (1986). Cerebrospinal fluid studies in suicide: An overview. *Annals of the American Academy of Science, 487,* 243–255. **(Chap 7)**

ASCHOFF, J., & WEVER, R. (1962). Spontanperiodik des Menschen die Ausschluß aller Zeitgeber. *Die Naturwissenschaften, 49,* 337–342. **(Chap 10)**

ASHERSON, P., PARFITT, E., SARGEANT, M., TIDMARSH, S., BUCKLAND, P., TAYLOR, C., CLEMENTS, A., GILL, M., MCGUFFIN, P., & OWEN, M. (1992). No evidence for a pseudoautosomal locus for schizophrenia linkage analysis of multiply affected families. *British Journal of Psychiatry, 161,* 63–68. **(Chap 14)**

ASPINWALL, L. G., KEMENY, M. E., TAYLOR, S. E., SCHNEIDER, S. G., & DUDLEY, J. P. (1991). Psychosocial predictors of gay men's AIDS risk-reduction behavior. *Health Psychology, 10*(6), 432–444. **(Chap 9)**

ATTWOOD, A., FRITH, U., & HERMELIN, B. (1988). The understanding and use of interpersonal gesture by autistic and Down's syndrome children. *Journal of Autism and Developmental Disorders, 18,* 241–258. **(Chap 16)**

AUSABEL, D. P. (1971). Personality disorder is disease. *American Psychologist, 16,* 59–74. **(Chap 1)**

AYLLON, T., & AZRIN, N. H. (1968). *The token economy: A motivational system for therapy and rehabilitation.* New York: Appleton-Century-Crofts. **(Chap 14)**

AZMITIA, E. C. (1978). The serotonin-producing neurons of the midbrain median and dorsal raphe nuclei. In L. Iverson, S. Iverson, & S. Snyder (Eds.), *Handbook of psychopharmacology: Vol. 9. Chemical pathways in the brain* (pp. 233–314). New York: Plenum Press. **(Chap 2)**

AZRIN, N. H., & NUNN, R. C. (1974). A rapid method of eliminating stuttering by a regulated-breathing method. *Behavior Research and Therapy, 12,* 279–286. **(Chap 16)**

BACHRACH, L. L. (1987). Deinstitutionalization in the United States: Promises and prospects. *New Directions for Mental Health Services, 35,* 75–90. **(Chap 17)**

BACHRACH, L. L. (1992). Psychosocial rehabilitation and psychiatry in the care of long-term patients. *American Journal of Psychiatry, 149,* 1455–1463. **(Chap 14)**

BADDELEY, A. D. (1986). *Working memory.* Oxford: Clarendon Press. **(Chap 2)**

BAER, D. M., WOLF, M. M., & RISLEY, T. R. (1968). Some current dimensions of applied behavior analysis. *Journal of Applied Behavior Analysis, 1,* 91–97. **(Chaps 3, 4)**

BAER, J. S., MARLATT, G. A., KIVLAHAN, D. R., FROMME, K., LARIMER, M. E., & WILLIAMS, E. (1992). An experimental test of three methods of alcohol risk reduction with young adults. *Journal of Consulting and Clinical Psychology, 60,* 974–979. **(Chap 12)**

BAILEY, J. M., & BENISHAY, D. S. (1993). Familial aggregation of female sexual orientation. *American Journal of Psychiatry, 150*(2), 272–277. **(Chap 11)**

BAILEY, J. M., & PILLARD, R. C. (1991). A genetic study of male sexual orientation. *Archives of General Psychiatry, 48,* 1089–1096. **(Chap 11)**

BAILEY, J. M., PILLARD, R. C., NEALE, M. C., & AGYEI, Y. (1993). Heritable factors influence sexual orientation in women. *Archives of General Psychiatry, 50,* 217–223. **(Chap 11)**

BAKER, C. D., & DESILVA, P. (1988). The relationship between male sexual dysfunction and belief in Zilbergeld's myths: An empirical investigation. *Sexual and Marital Therapy, 3*(2), 229–238. **(Chap 11)**

BAKER, T. B., MORSE, E., & SHERMAN, J. E. (1987). The motivation to use drugs: A psychobiological analysis of urges. In P. Clayton Rivers (Ed.), *Alcohol and addictive behavior: Nebraska symposium on motivation 1986* (pp. 257–323). Lincoln: University of Nebraska Press. **(Chap 12)**

BALDESSARINI, R. J. (1989). Current status of antidepressants: Clinical pharmacology and therapy. *Journal of Clinical Psychiatry, 50*(4), 117–126. **(Chap 7)**

BALDWIN, J. D., & BALDWIN, J. I. (1989). The socialization of homosexuality and heterosexuality in a non-western society. *Archives of Sexual Behavior, 18,* 13–29. **(Chap 11)**

BALL, J. C., & ROSS, A. (1991). *The effectiveness of methadone maintenance treatment.* New York: Springer-Verlag. **(Chap 12)**

BALLENGER, J. C., BURROWS, G. D., DUPONT, R. L., LESSER, I. M., NOYES, R., PECKNOLD, J. C., RISKIN, A., & SWINSON, R. P. (1988). Alprazolam in panic disorder and agoraphobia: Results from a multi center trial: I. Efficacy in short-term treatment. *Archives of General Psychiatry, 45,* 413–422. **(Chap 5)**

BALTER, M. B., & BAUER, M. L. (1975). Patterns of prescribing and use of hypnotic drugs in the United States. In A. D. Clift (Ed.), *Sleep disturbance and hypnotic drug dependence.* Amsterdam: Excerpta Medica. **(Chap 10)**

BANCROFT, J. (1974). *Deviant sexual behaviour: Modification and assessment.* Oxford: Clarendon Press. **(Chap 11)**

BANCROFT, J. (1989). *Human sexuality and its problems* (2nd ed.). Edinburgh: Churchill Livingstone. **(Chap 11)**

BANCROFT, J. (1994). Homosexual orientation: The search for a biological basis. *British Journal of Psychiatry, 164,* 437–440. **(Chap 11)**

BANDURA, A. (1973). *Aggression: A social learning analysis.* Englewood Cliffs, NJ: Prentice-Hall. **(Chap 2)**

BANDURA, A. (1986). *Social foundations of thought and action: A social cognitive theory.* Englewood Cliffs, NJ: Prentice-Hall. **(Chaps 2, 5, 9)**

BANDURA, A., CIOFFI, D., TAYLOR, C. B., & BROUILLARD, M. E. (1988). Perceived self-efficacy in coping with cognitive stressors and opioid activation. *Journal of Personality and Social Psychology, 55,* 479–488. **(Chap 9)**

BANDURA, A., O'LEARY, A., TAYLOR, C. B., GAUTHIER, J., & GOSSARD, D. (1987). Perceived self-efficacy and pain control: Opioid and nonopioid mechanisms. *Journal of Personality and Social Psychology, 53,* 563–571. **(Chap 9)**

BANSAL, S., WINCZE, J. P., NIRENBERG, T., LIEPMAN, M. J., & ENGLE-FRIEDMAN, M. (1990). *Sex-steroid levels in chronic alcoholic males: Relationship to age and liver functions.* Unpublished manuscript, Brown University. **(Chap 11)**

BARINAGA, M. (1992). Pot, heroin unlock new areas for neuroscience. *Science, 258,* 1882–1884. **(Chap 12)**

BARKLEY, R. A. (1981). *Hyperactive children: A handbook for diagnosis and treatment.* New York: Guilford Press. **(Chap 16)**

BARKLEY, R. A. (1989). Attention deficit-hyperactivity disorder. In E. J. Mash & R. A. Barkley (Eds.), *Treatment of childhood disorders* (pp. 39–72). New York: Guilford Press. **(Chap 16)**

BARLOW, D. H. (1986). Causes of sexual dysfunction: The role of anxiety and cognitive interference. *Journal of Consulting and Clinical Psychology, 54,* 140–148. **(Chap 11)**

BARLOW, D. H. (1988). *Anxiety and its disorders: The nature and treatment of anxiety and panic.* New York: Guilford Press. **(Chaps 1, 3, 5, 7, 9, 11)**

BARLOW, D. H. (1991). Disorders of emotion. *Psychological Inquiry, 2*(1), 58–71. **(Chaps 5, 7)**

BARLOW, D. H. (1993). Covert sensitization for paraphilia. In J. R. Cautela & A. J. Kearney (Eds.), *Covert Conditioning Casebook* (pp. 187–198). Pacific Grove, CA: Brooks/Cole Publishing Company. **(Chap 11)**

BARLOW, D. H., & ABEL, G. G. (1976). Recent developments in assessment and treatment of sexual deviation. In W. E. Craighead, A. E. Kazdin, & M. J. Mahoney (Eds.), *Behavior modification: Principles, issues, and applications* (pp. 337–356). Boston: Houghton Mifflin. **(Chap 11)**

BARLOW, D. H., ABEL, G. G., & BLANCHARD, E. B. (1979). Gender identity change in transsexuals: Follow-up and replications. *Archives of General Psychiatry, 36,* 1001–1007. **(Chap 11)**

BARLOW, D. H., BECKER, R., LEITENBERG, H., & AGRAS, W. S. (1970). A mechanical strain gauge for recording penile circumference change. *Journal of Applied Behavior Analysis, 3,* 73–76. **(Chap 11)**

BARLOW, D. H., BROWN, T. A., & CRASKE, M. G. (1994). Definitions of panic attacks and panic disorder in DSM-IV: Implications for research. *Journal of Abnormal Psychology, 103,* 553–554. **(Chap 5)**

BARLOW, D. H., & CRASKE, M. G. (1989). *Mastery of your anxiety and panic.* Albany, NY: Graywind Publications. **(Chap 5)**

BARLOW, D. H., & CRASKE, M. G. (1994). *Mastery of your anxiety and panic* (MAP II). Albany, NY: Graywind Publications. **(Chap 5)**

BARLOW, D. H., HAYES, S. C., & NELSON, R. O. (1984). *The scientist practitioner: Research and accountability in clinical and educational settings.* Boston: Allyn & Bacon. **(Chap 1)**

BARLOW, D. H., HAYES, S. C., NELSON, R. O., STEELE, D. L., MEELER, M. E., & MILLS, J. R. (1979). Sex role motor behavior: A behavioral checklist. *Behavioral Assessment, 1,* 119–138. **(Chap 11)**

BARLOW, D. H., & HERSEN, M. (1984). *Single case experimental design: Strategies for studying behavior change.* Elmsford, NY: Pergamon Press. **(Chap 4)**

BARLOW, D. H., & RAPEE, R. M. (1991). *Mastering stress: A lifestyle approach.* Dallas, TX: American Health Publishing. **(Chap 9)**

BARLOW, D. H., REYNOLDS, E. J., & AGRAS, W. S. (1973). Gender identity change in a transsexual. *Archives of General Psychiatry, 28,* 569–576. **(Chap 11)**

BARLOW, D. H., SAKHEIM, D. K., & BECK, J. G. (1983). Anxiety increases sexual arousal. *Journal of Abnormal Psychology, 92,* 49–54. **(Chap 11)**

BARLOW, D. H., & WINCZE, J. P. (1980). Treatment of sexual deviations. In S. R. Leiblum & L. A. Pervin (Eds.), *Principles and practice of sex therapy* (pp. 347–375). New York: Guilford Press. **(Chap 11)**

BARLOW, J., BLOUIN, J., BLOUIN, A., & PEREZ, E. (1988). Treatment of bulimia with desipramine: A double-blind crossover study. *Canadian Journal of Psychiatry, 33,* 129–133. **(Chap 8)**

BARNES, D. M. (1988). The biological tangle of drug addiction. *Science, 241,* 415–417. **(Chap 12)**

BARNES, J. (1981). Non-consummation of marriage. *Irish Medical Journal, 74,* 19–21. **(Chap 11)**

BARNES, J., BOWMAN, E. P., & CULLEN, J. (1984). Biofeedback as an adjunct to psychotherapy in the treatment of vaginismus. *Biofeedback and Self-Regulation, 9,* 281–289. **(Chap 11)**

BARNETT, P. A., & GOTLIB, I. H. (1988). Psychosocial functioning and depression: Distinguishing among antecedents, concomitants and consequences. *Psychological Bulletin, 104*(1), 97–126. **(Chap 7)**

BARNETT, P. A., & GOTLIB, I. H. (1990). Cognitive vulnerability to depressive symptoms among men and women. *Cognitive Therapy and Research, 14*(1), 47–61. **(Chap 7)**

BARON, M., GRUEN, R., ASNIS, L., & LORD, S. (1985). Familial transmission of schizotypal and borderline personality disorders. *American Journal of Psychiatry, 142,* 927–934. **(Chap 13)**

BARRETT, J. (1984). Naturalistic change over two years in neurotic depressive disorders (RDC categories). *Comprehensive Psychiatry, 25*(4), 404–418. **(Chap 7)**

BARRETT, J. E., BARRETT, J. A., OXMAN, T. E., & GERBER, P. D. (1988). The prevalence of psychiatric disorders in a primary care practice. *Archives of General Psychiatry, 45,* 1100–1106. **(Chap 3)**

BARSKY, A. J., FRANK, C. B., CLEARY, P. D., WYSHAK, G., & KLERMAN, G. L. (1991). The relation between hypochondriasis and age. *American Journal of Psychiatry, 148,* 923–928. **(Chap 6)**

BARSKY, A. J., & WYSHAK, G. (1990). Hypochondriasis and somatosensory amplification. *British Journal of Psychiatry, 157,* 404–409. **(Chap 6)**

BARSKY, A. J., WYSHAK, G., & KLERMAN, G. L. (1986). Hypochondriasis: An evaluation of the DSM-III criteria in medical outpatients. *Archives of General Psychiatry, 43,* 493–500. **(Chap 6)**

BARSKY, A. J., WYSHAK, G., KLERMAN G. L., & LATHAM, K. S. (1990). The prevalence of hypochondriasis in medical outpatients. *Social Psychiatry & Psychiatric Epidemiology, 25,* 89–94. **(Chap 6)**

BASSETT, A. S. (1989). Chromosome 5 and schizophrenia: Implications for genetic linkage studies, current and future. *Schizophrenia Bulletin, 15,* 393–402. **(Chap 14)**

BASSUK, E. L. (1984). The homelessness problem. *Scientific American, 251,* 40–45. **(Chap 17)**

BATES, M. D., GINGRICH, J. A., SENOGLES, S. E., FALARDEAU, P., & CARON, M. G. (1991). Biochemical characterization of D1 and D2 dopamine receptors. In C. A. Tamminga & S. C. Schulz (Eds.), *Advances in neuropsychiatry and psychopharmacology, Volume 1: Schizophrenia research* (pp. 3–11). New York: Raven Press. **(Chap 14)**

BATESON, G. (1959). Cultural problems posed by a study of schizophrenic process. In A. Auerbach (Ed.), *Schizophrenia: An integrated approach.* New York: Ronald Press. **(Chap 14)**

BAUM, A., DAVIDSON, L. M., SINGER, J. E., & STREET, S. W. (1987). Stress as a psychophysiological process. In A. Baum & J. E. Singer (Eds.), *Handbook of psychology and health: Stress* (Vol. 5). Hillsdale, NJ: Lawrence Erlbaum. **(Chap 9)**

BAXTER, L. R., GUZE, B. H., & REYNOLDS, C. A. (1993). Neuroimaging: Uses in psychiatry. In D. L. Dunner (Ed.), *Current psychiatric therapy.* Philadelphia: W. B. Saunders. **(Chap 3)**

BAXTER, L. R., JR., SCHWARTZ, J. M., BERGMAN, K. S., SZUBA, M. P., GUZE, B. H., MAZZIOTTA, J. C., ALAZRAKI, A., SELIN, C. E., FERNG, H. K., MUNFORD, P., & PHELPS, M. E. (1992). Caudate glucose metabolic rate changes with both drug and behavior therapy for obsessive-compulsive disorder. *Archives of General Psychiatry, 49,* 681–689. **(Chap 2)**

BEACH, S. R. H., SANDEEN, E. E., & O'LEARY, K. D. (1990). Depression in marriage: A model for etiology and treatment. In D. H. Barlow (Ed.), *Treatment manuals for practitioners*. New York: Guilford Press. **(Chap 7)**

BEARD, G. M. (1869). Neurasthenia or nervous exhaustion. *Boston Medical Surgical Journal, 3*, 217–221. **(Chap 9)**

BEARD, J. H., MALAMUD, T. J., & ROSSMAN, E. (1978). Psychiatric rehabilitation and long-term rehospitalization rates: The findings of two research studies. *Schizophrenia Bulletin, 4*, 622–635. **(Chap 14)**

BEARD, J. H., PROPST, R. N., & MALAMUD, T. J. (1982). The Fountain House model of psychiatric rehabilitation. *Psychosocial Rehabilitation Journal, 5*, 47–53. **(Chap 14)**

BEBBINGTON, P. E., BRUGHA, T., MACCAR-THY, B., POTTER, J., STURT, E., WYKES, T., KATZ, R., & MCGUFFIN, P. (1988). The Camberwell Collaborative Depression Study. I. Depressed probands: Adversity and the form of depression. *British Journal of Psychiatry, 152*, 754–765. **(Chap 2)**

BEBOUT, L., & ARTHUR, B. (1992). Cross-cultural attitudes toward speech disorders. *Journal of Speech and Hearing Research, 35*, 45–52. **(Chap 16)**

BECK, A. T. (1967). *Depression: Clinical, experimental and theoretical aspects*. New York: Harper & Row. **(Chap 7)**

BECK, A. T. (1976). *Cognitive therapy and the emotional disorders*. New York: International Universities Press. **(Chaps 2, 7, 9)**

BECK, A. T. (1986). Hopelessness as a predictor of eventual suicide. *Annals of the New York Academy of Science, 487*, 90–96. **(Chap 7)**

BECK, A. T., & EMERY, G. (1985). *Anxiety disorders and phobias*. New York: Basic Books. **(Chaps 1, 2, 5)**

BECK, A. T., EPSTEIN, N., & HARRISON, R. (1983). Cognitions, attitudes and personality dimensions in depression. *British Journal of Cognitive Psychotherapy, 1*(1), 1–16. **(Chap 7)**

BECK, A. T., & FREEMAN, A. (1990). *Cognitive therapy of personality disorders*. New York: Guilford Press. **(Chap 13)**

BECK, A. T., HOLLON, S. D., YOUNG, J. E., BEDROSIAN, R. C., & BUDENZ, D. (1985). Treatment of depression with cognitive therapy and amitriptyline. *Archives of General Psychiatry, 42*, 142–148. **(Chap 7)**

BECK, A. T., STEER, R., KOVACS, M., & GARRISON, B. (1985). Hopelessness and eventual suicide: A 10-year prospective study of patients hospitalized with suicidal ideation. *American Journal of Psychiatry, 142*, 559–563. **(Chap 7)**

BECK, A. T., STEER, R. A., SANDERSON, W. C., & SKEIE, T. M. (1991). Panic disorder and suicidal ideation and behavior: Discrepant findings in psychiatric outpatients. *American Journal of Psychiatry, 148*(9), 1195–1199. **(Chap 5)**

BECK, A. T., & YOUNG, J. E. (1985). Depression. In D. H. Barlow (Ed.), *Clinical handbook of psychological disorders*. New York: Guilford Press. **(Chap 7, 9)**

BECK, J. G. (1993). Vaginismus. In W. O'Donohue & J. H. Geer (Eds.), *Handbook of Sexual Dysfunctions: Assessment and Treat-ment* (pp. 381–397). Boston, MA: Allyn and Bacon. **(Chap 11)**

BECK, J. G., & BARLOW, D. H. (1984). Unraveling the nature of sex roles. In E. A. Blechman (Ed.), *Behavior modification with women* (pp. 34–59). New York: Guilford Press. **(Chap 11)**

BECK, J. G., BARLOW, D. H., SAKHEIM, D. K., & ABRAHAMSON, D. J. (1984). *A cognitive processing account of anxiety and sexual arousal: The role of selective attention, thought content, and affective states*. Paper presented at the annual convention of the American Psychological Association, Toronto. **(Chap 11)**

BECK, J. G., BARLOW, D. H., SAKHEIM, D. K., & ABRAHAMSON, D. J. (1987). Shock threat and sexual arousal: The role of selective attention, thought content and affective states. *Psychophysiology, 24*, 165–172. **(Chap 11)**

BECK, J. G., SAKHEIM, D. K., & BARLOW, D. H. (1983). Operating characteristics of the vaginal photoplethysmograph: Some implications for its use. *Archives of Sexual Behavior, 12*(1), 43–58. **(Chap 11)**

BECKER, J. V. (1989). Impact of sexual abuse on sexual functioning. In S. R. Leiblum & R. C. Rosen (Eds.), *Principles and practice of sex therapy: Update for the 1990s* (2nd ed., pp. 298–318). New York: Guilford Press. **(Chap 11)**

BECKER, J. V. (1990). Treating adolescent sexual offenders. *Professional Psychology: Research and Practice, 21*, 362–365. **(Chap 11)**

BEGLIN, S. J., & FAIRBURN, C. G. (1992). What is meant by the term "Binge"? *American Journal of Psychiatry, 149*, 123–124. **(Chap 8)**

BELITSKY, R., & MCGLASHAN, T. H. (1993). The manifestations of schizophrenia in late life: A dearth of data. *Schizophrenia Bulletin, 19*, 683–685. **(Chap 14)**

BELL, C. C., DIXIE-BELL, D. D., & THOMPSON, B. (1986). Further studies on the prevalence of isolated sleep paralysis in Black subjects. *Journal of the National Medical Association, 75*, 649–659. **(Chap 5)**

BELL, I. R., JASNOSKI, M. L., KAGAN, J., & KING, D. S. (1991). Depression and allergies: Survey of a nonclinical population. *Psychotherapy and Psychosomatics, 55*, 24–31. **(Chap 4)**

BELL, K. E., & STEIN, D. M. (1992). Behavioral treatments for pica: A review of empirical studies. *International Journal of Eating Disorders, 11*, 377–389. **(Chap 8)**

BELLACK, A., & HERSEN, M. (1985). *Dictionary of behavior therapy techniques*. Elmsford, NY: Pergamon Press. **(Chap 13)**

BELLACK, A. S., & MUESER, K. T. (1992). Social skills training for schizophrenia? *Archives of General Psychiatry, 49*, 76. **(Chap 14)**

BELLACK, A. S., & MUESER, K. T. (1993). Psychosocial treatment for schizophrenia. *Schizophrenia Bulletin, 19*, 317–336. **(Chap 14)**

BELLAK, L. (1975). *The thematic apperception test, the children's apperception test, and the senior apperception technique in clinical use* (3rd ed.). New York: Grune & Stratton. **(Chap 3)**

BELLAMY, G. T., RHODES, L. E., MANK, D. M., & ALBIN, J. M. (1988). *Supported employment: A community implementation guide*. Baltimore: Paul H. Brookes. **(Chap 15)**

BELLIS, D. J. (1981). *Heroin and politicians: The failure of public policy to control addiction in America*. Westport, CT: Greenwood Press. **(Chap 12)**

BENCA, R. M., OBERMEYER, W. H., THISTED, R. A., & GILLIN, J. C. (1992). Sleep and psychiatric disorders: A meta-analysis. *Archives of General Psychiatry, 49*, 651–668. **(Chap 10)**

BENNETT, A. H. (1988). Venous arterialization for erectile impotence. *Urologic Clinics of North America, 15*, 111–113. **(Chap 11)**

BENOWITZ, N. L. (1992). Cigarette smoking and nicotine addiction. *Medical Clinics of North America, 76*, 415–437. **(Chap 12)**

BENSON, H. (1975). *The relaxation response*. New York: William Morrow. **(Chap 9)**

BENSON, H. (1984). *Beyond the relaxation response*. New York: Times Books. **(Chap 9)**

BERENBAUM, H., & OLTMANNS, T. F. (1992). Emotional experience and expression in schizophrenia and depression. *Journal of Abnormal Psychology, 101*, 37–44. **(Chap 14)**

BERKMAN, L. F., & SYME, S. L. (1979). Social networks, host resistance, and mortality: A nine-year follow-up study of Alameda county residents. *American Journal of Epidemiology, 109*, 186. **(Chap 2)**

BERLIN, I. N. (1987). Suicide among American Indian adolescents: An overview. *Suicide and Life Threatening Behavior, 17*(3), 218–232. **(Chap 7)**

BERMAN, A. L., & JOBES, D. A. (1991). *Adolescent suicide: Assessment and intervention*. Washington, DC: American Psychological Association. **(Chap 7)**

BERMAN, K. F., & WEINBERGER, D. R. (1990). Lateralization of cortical function during cognitive tasks: Regional cerebral blood flow studies of normal individuals and patients with schizophrenia. *Journal of Neurology, Neurosurgery and Psychiatry, 53*, 150–160. **(Chap 14)**

BERNSTEIN, D. A., & BORKOVEC, T. D. (1973). *Progressive relaxation training: A manual for the helping professions*. Champaign, IL: Research Press. **(Chap 9)**

BERNSTEIN, D. P., USEDA, D., & SIEVER, L. J. (1993). Paranoid personality disorder: Review of the literature and recommendations for DSM-IV. *Journal of Personality Disorders, 7*, 53–62. **(Chap 13)**

BERTELSEN, B., HARVALD, B., & HAUGE, M. (1977). A Danish twin study of manic-depressive disorders. *British Journal of Psychiatry, 130*, 330–351. **(Chap 7)**

BETTELHEIM, B. (1967). *The empty fortress*. New York: Free Press. **(Chap 16)**

BIEDERMAN, J., FARAONE, S. V., KEENAN, K., BENJAMIN, J., KRIFCHER, B., MOORE, C., SPRICH-BUCKMINSTER, S., UGAGLIA, K., JELLINEK, M. S., STEINGARD, R., SPENCER, T., NORMAN, D., KOLODNY, R., KRAUS, I., PERRIN, J., KELLER, M., & TSUANG, M. T. (1992). Further evidence for family-genetic risk factors in attention deficit hyperactivity disorder: Patterns of comorbidity in probands and relatives in psychiatrically and pediatrically referred samples. *Archives of General Psychiatry, 49*, 728–738. **(Chap 16)**

BIEDERMAN, J., MUNIR, K., KNEE, D., ARMEN-TANO, M., AUTOR, S., WATERNAUX, C., & TSUANG, M. (1987). High rate of affective disorders in probands with attention deficit disorder and in their relatives: A controlled family study. *American Journal of Psychiatry, 144*(3), 330–333. **(Chap 7)**

BIGLAN, A., HOPS, H., SHERMAN, L., FRIED-MAN, L. S., ARTHUR, J., & OSTEEN, V. (1985). Problem solving interactions of depressed women and their husbands. *Behavior Therapy, 16*, 431–451. **(Chap 7)**

BIKLEN, D. (1990). Communication unbound: Autism and praxis. *Harvard Educational Review, 60*, 291–314. **(Chap 16)**

BIKLEN, D. (1992). Typing to talk: Facilitated communication. *American Journal of Speech-Language Pathology, 1*, 15–17. **(Chap 16)**

BILLE, B. (1981). Migraine in childhood and its prognosis. *Cephalalgia, 1*, 71–75. **(Chap 9)**

BILLY, J. O. G., TANFER, K., GRADY, W. R., & KLEPINGER, D. H. (1993). The sexual behavior of men in the United States. *Family Planning Perspectives, 25*, 52–60. **(Chap 11)**

BIRLEY, J., & BROWN, G. W. (1970). Crisis and life changes preceding the onset or relapse of acute schizophrenia: Clinical aspects. *British Journal of Psychiatry, 16*, 327–333. **(Chap 14)**

BIRON, M., RISCH, N., HAMBURGER, R., MAN-DEL, B., KUSHNER, S., NEWMAN, M., DRUMER, D., & BELMAKER, R. H. (1987). Genetic linkage between X-chromosome markers and bipolar affective illness. *Nature, 326*, 289–292. **(Chap 4)**

BJORKLUND, D. F. (1989). *Children's thinking: Developmental function and individual differences.* Pacific Grove, CA: Brooks/Cole. **(Chap 3)**

BLACK, D. W., & WINOKUR, G. (1990). Suicide and psychiatric diagnosis. In S. J. Blumenthal & D. J. Kupfer (Eds.), *Suicide over the life cycle: Risk factors, assessment and treatment of suicidal patients.* Washington, DC: American Psychiatric Press. **(Chap 7)**

BLACK, D. W., WINOKUR, G., & NASRALLAH, A. (1987). The treatment of depression: Electroconvulsive therapy vs. antidepressants: A naturalistic evaluation of 1,495 patients. *Comprehensive Psychiatry, 28*(2), 169–182. **(Chap 7)**

BLAKESLEE, S. (1993, AUGUST 3). Mystery of sleep yields as studies reveal immune tie. *New York Times,* C1. **(Chap 10)**

BLANCHARD, C. G., BLANCHARD, E. B., & BECKER, J. V. (1976). The young widow: Depressive symptomatology throughout the grief process. *Psychiatry, 39*, 394–399. **(Chap 7)**

BLANCHARD, E. B. (1987). Long-term effects of behavioral treatment of chronic headache. *Behavior Therapy, 18*, 375–385. **(Chap 9)**

BLANCHARD, E. B. (1992). Psychological treatment of benign headache disorders. Special issue: Behavioral medicine: An update for the 1990s. *Journal of Consulting and Clinical Psychology, 60*(4), 537–551. **(Chaps 3, 9)**

BLANCHARD, E. B., & ANDRASIK, F. (1982). Psychological assessment and treatment of headache: Recent developments and emerging issues. *Journal of Consulting and Clinical Psychology, 50*(6), 859–879. **(Chap 9)**

BLANCHARD, E. B., ANDRASIK, F., AHLES, T. A., TEDERS, S. J., & O'KEEFE, D. (1980). Migraine and tension headache: A meta-analytic review. *Behavior Therapy, 11*, 613–631. **(Chap 9)**

BLANCHARD, E. B., ANDRASIK, F., NEFF, D. F., ARENA, J. G., AHLES, T. A., JURISH, S. E., PALLMEYER, T. P., SAUNDERS, N. L., TEDERS, S. J., BARRON, K. D., & RODICHOK, L. D. (1982). Biofeedback and relaxation training with three kinds of headache: Treatment effects and their prediction. *Journal of Consulting and Clinical Psychology, 50*, 562–575. **(Chap 9)**

BLANCHARD, E. B., APPELBAUM, K. A., RAD-NITZ, C. L., MICHULTKA, D., MORRILL, B., KIRSH, C., HILLHOUSE, J., EVANS, D. D., GUARNIERI, P., ATTANASIO, V., AN-DRASIK, F., JACCARD, J., & DENTINGER, M. P. (1990). Placebo-controlled evaluation of abbreviated progressive muscle relaxation combined with cognitive therapy in the treatment of tension headache. *Journal of Consulting and Clinical Psychology, 58*(2), 210–215. **(Chap 9)**

BLANCHARD, E. B., & EPSTEIN, L. H. (1977). *A biofeedback primer.* Reading, MA: Addison-Wesley. **(Chap 9)**

BLANCHARD, E. B., MARTIN, J. E., & DUBBERT, P. M. (1988). *Non-drug treatments for essential hypertension.* Elmsford, NY: Pergamon Press. **(Chap 3)**

BLANCHARD, E. B., MCCOY, G., BERGER, M., MUSSO, A., PALLMEYER, T., GERARDI, R., GERARDI, M., & PANGBURN, P. (1989). A controlled comparison of thermal biofeedback and relaxation training in the treatment of essential hypertension. IV: Prediction of short term clinical outcome. *Behavior Therapy, 20*, 405–416. **(Chap 9)**

BLANCHARD, J. J., & NEALE, J. M. (1992). Medication effects: Conceptual and methodological issues in schizophrenia research. *Clinical Psychology Review, 12*, 345–361. **(Chap 14)**

BLANCHARD, R., & STEINER, B. W. (1992). *Clinical management of gender identity disorders in children and adults.* Washington, DC: American Psychiatric Press. **(Chap 11)**

BLASHFIELD, R. K., & LIVESLEY, W. J. (1991). Metaphorical analysis of psychiatric classification as a psychological test. *Journal of Abnormal Psychology, 100*(3), 262–270. **(Chap 3)**

BLAZER, D. G. (1989). Current concepts: Depression in the elderly. *New England Journal of Medicine, 320*, 164–166. **(Chap 7)**

BLAZER, D. G., GEORGE, L., & HUGHES, D. (1991). The epidemiology of anxiety disorders: An age comparison. In C. Salzman & B. Liebowitz (Eds.), *Anxiety disorders in the elderly* (pp. 17–30). New York: Springer. **(Chap 5)**

BLAZER, D. G., HUGHES, D., GEORGE, L. K., SWARTZ, M., & BOYER, R. (1991). Generalized anxiety disorder. In L. N. Robins & D. A. Regier (Eds.), *Psychiatric disorders in America* (pp. 180–203). New York: Free Press. **(Chap 5)**

BLEHAR, M. C., & ROSENTHAL, N. E. (1989). Seasonal affective disorder and photo-therapy. *Archives of General Psychiatry, 46*, 469–474. **(Chap 7)**

BLEHAR, M. C., WEISSMAN, M. M., GERSHON, E. S., & HIRSCHFELD, R. M. A. (1988). Family and genetic studies of affective disorders. *Archives of General Psychiatry, 45*, 289–292. **(Chap 7)**

BLEULER, E. (1908). Die Prognose der Dementia praecox (Schizophreniegruppe). *Allgemeine Zeitschrift für Psychiatrie, 65*, 436–464. **(Chap 14)**

BLEULER, E. (1924). *Textbook of psychiatry.* A. A. Brill, Trans. New York: Macmillan. **(Chap 13)**

BLINDER, B. J., GOODMAN, S. L., & GOLD-STEIN, R. (1988). Rumination: A critical review of diagnosis and treatment. In B. J. Blinder, B. F. Chaitin, & R. S. Goldstein (Eds.), *The eating disorders: Medical and psychological bases of diagnosis and treatment* (pp. 315–329). New York: PMA Publishing Corp. **(Chap 8)**

BLISS, E. L. (1984). A symptom profile of patients with multiple personalities including MMPI results. *Journal of Nervous and Mental Diseases, 172*, 197–211. **(Chap 6)**

BLISS, E. L. (1986). *Multiple personality allied disorders and hypnosis.* New York: Oxford University Press. **(Chap 6)**

BLUE, A. V., & GAINES, A. D. (1992). The ethnopsychiatric répertoire: A review and overview of ethnopsychiatric studies. In A. D. Gaines (Ed.), *Ethnopsychiatry: The cultural construction of professional and folk psychiatries* (pp. 397–484). Albany: State University of New York Press. **(Chap 4)**

BLUM, K., NOBLE, E. P., SHERIDAN, P. J., MONTGOMERY, A., RITCHIE, T., JA-GADEESWARAN, P., NOGAMI, H., BRIGGS, A. H., & COHN, J. B. (1990). Allelic association of human dopamine D2 receptor gene in alcoholism. *Journal of the American Medical Association, 263*, 2055–2060. **(Chap 12)**

BLUMENTHAL, S. J. (1990). An overview and synopsis of risk factors, assessment, and treatment of suicidal patients over the life cycle. In S. J. Blumenthal & D. J. Kupfer (Eds.), *Suicide over the life cycle: Risk factors, assessment and treatment of suicidal patients.* Washington, DC: American Psychiatric Press. **(Chap 7)**

BLUMENTHAL, S. J., & KUPFER, D. J. (1988). Clinical assessment and treatment of youth suicide. *Journal of Youth and Adolescence, 17*, 1–24. **(Chap 5)**

BOCKOVEN, J. S. (1963). *Moral treatment in American psychiatry.* New York: Springer Publishing Company. **(Chap 1)**

BOCKTING, W. O., & COLEMAN, E. (1992). A comprehensive approach to the treatment of gender dysphoria. *Journal of Psychology and Human Sexuality, 5*(4), 131–155. **(Chap 11)**

BOGERTS, B. (1993). Images in psychiatry: Alois Alzheimer. *American Journal of Psychiatry, 150*, 1868. **(Chap 15)**

BOHMAN, M., CLONINGER, C. R., VON KNOR-RING, A. L., & SIGVARDSSON, S. (1984). An adoption study of somatoform disorders: III. Cross-fostering analysis and genetic relationship to alcoholism and criminality. *Archives of General Psychiatry, 41*, 872–878. **(Chap 6)**

BOHMAN, M., SIGVARDSSON, S., & CLONINGER, C. R. (1981). Maternal inheritance of alcohol abuse. *Archives of General Psychiatry, 38,* 965–969. **(Chap 12)**

BOLL, T. J. (1985). Developing issues in clinical neuropsychology. *Journal of Clinical and Experimental Neuropsychology, 7*(5), 473–485. **(Chap 3)**

BOND, A., & LADER, M. L. (1979). Benzodiazepines and aggression. In M. Sandler (Ed.), *Psychopharmacology of aggression.* New York: Raven Press. **(Chap 2)**

BOOKER, J. M., & HELLEKSON, C. J. (1992). Prevalence of seasonal affective disorder in Alaska. *American Journal of Psychiatry, 149,* 1176–1182. **(Chap 7)**

BOON, S., & DRAIJER, N. (1991). Diagnosing dissociative disorders in the Netherlands: A pilot study with the Structured Clinical Interview for DSM-III-R dissociative disorders. *American Journal of Psychiatry, 148,* 458–462. **(Chap 6)**

BOOTH-KEWLEY, S., & FRIEDMAN, H. S. (1987). Psychological predictors of heart disease: A quantitative review. *Psychological Bulletin, 101*(3), 343–362. **(Chap 9)**

BOOTZIN, R. R., ENGLE-FRIEDMAN, M., & HAZELWOOD, L. (1983). Sleep disorders and the elderly. In P. M. Lewinson & L. Teri (Eds.), *Clinical geropsychology: New directions in assessment and treatment.* Elmsford, NY: Pergamon. **(Chap 4)**

BOOTZIN, R. R., MANBER, R., PERLIS, M. L., SALVIO, M., & WYATT, J. K. (1993). Sleep disorders. In P. B. Sutker & H. E. Adams (Eds.), *Comprehensive handbook of psychopathology* (2nd ed., pp. 531–561). New York: Plenum Press. **(Chaps 10, 12)**

BOOTZIN, R. R., & NICASSIO, P. M. (1978). Behavioral treatments of insomnia. In M. Hersen, R. Eisler, & P. M. Miller (Eds.), *Progress in behavior modification* (Vol. 6, pp. 1–45). New York: Academic Press. **(Chap 10)**

BORING, E. G. (1950). *A history of experimental psychology.* New York: Appleton-Century-Crofts. **(Chap 3)**

BORKOVEC, T. D., & COSTELLO, E. (1993). Efficacy of applied relaxation and cognitive-behavioral therapy in the treatment of generalized anxiety disorder. *Journal of Consulting and Clinical Psychology, 61*(4), 611–619. **(Chap 5)**

BORKOVEC, T. D., & IIU, S. (1990). The effect of worry on cardiovascular response to phobic imagery. *Behaviour Research and Therapy, 28,* 69–73. **(Chap 5)**

BORKOVEC, T. D., & INZ, J. (1990). The nature of worry in generalized anxiety disorder: A predominance of thought activity. *Behaviour Research and Therapy, 28,* 153–158. **(Chap 5)**

BORKOVEC, T. D., & MATHEWS, A. M. (1988). Treatment of nonphobic anxiety disorders: A comparison of nondirective, cognitive, and coping desensitization therapy. *Journal of Consulting and Clinical Psychology, 56,* 877–884. **(Chap 5)**

BORKOVEC, T. D., SHADICK, R., & HOPKINS, M. (1991). The nature of normal and pathological worry. In R. M. Rapee & D. H. Barlow (Eds.), *Chronic anxiety, generalized anxiety disorder, and mixed anxiety depression.* New York: Guilford Press. **(Chap 5)**

BORNSTEIN, R. F. (1992). The dependent personality: Developmental, social, and clinical perspectives. *Psychological Bulletin, 112,* 3–23. **(Chap 13)**

BORYSENKO, M. (1987). Area review: Psychoneuroimmunology. *Annals of Behavioral Medicine, 9,* 3–10. **(Chap 9)**

BORYSENKO, M., & BORYSENKO, J. (1982). Stress, behavior, and immunity: Animal models and mediating mechanisms. *General Hospital Psychiatry, 4,* 59–67. **(Chap 9)**

BOSKIND-LODAHL, M. (1976). Cinderella's stepsisters: A feminist perspective on anorexia nervosa and bulimia. *Signs, 2,* 342–356. **(Chap 8)**

BOUCHARD, T. J., JR., LYKKEN, D. T., MCGUE, M., SEGAL, N. L., & TELLEGEN, A. (1990). Sources of human psychological differences: The Minnesota study of twins reared apart. *Science, 250,* 223–228. **(Chap 2)**

BOULOS, C., KUTCHER, S., MARTON, P., SIMEON, J., FERGUSON, B., & ROBERTS, N. (1991). Response to desipramine treatment in adolescent major depression. *Psychopharmacology Bulletin, 27*(1), 59–65. **(Chap 7)**

BOURGEOIS, M. S. (1992). Evaluating memory wallets in conversations with persons with dementia. *Journal of Speech and Hearing Research, 35,* 1344–1357. **(Chap 15)**

BOURGEOIS, M. S. (1993). Effects of memory aids on the dyadic conversations of individuals with dementia. *Journal of Applied Behavior Analysis, 26,* 77–87. **(Chap 15)**

BOWDEN, W. D. (1993). First person account: The onset of paranoia. *Schizophrenia Bulletin, 19,* 165–167. **(Chap 14)**

BOWER, G. H. (1981). Mood and memory. *American Psychologist, 36,* 129–148. **(Chap 2)**

BOWLBY, J. (1977). The making and breaking of affectionate bonds. *British Journal of Psychiatry, 130,* 201–210. **(Chap 13)**

BOWMAN, E. S., & NURNBERGER, J. I. (1993). Genetics of psychiatric diagnosis and treatment. In D. L. Dunner (Ed.), Current psychiatric therapy (pp. 46–53). Philadelphia: W. B. Saunders. **(Chap 16)**

BRACHA, H. S., TORREY, E. F., GOTTESMAN, I. I., BIGELOW, L. B., & CUNNIFF, C. (1992). Second-trimester markers of fetal size in schizophrenia: A study of monozygotic twins. *American Journal of Psychiatry, 149,* 1355–1361. **(Chap 14)**

BRADLEY, B. P., & MATHEWS, A. (1988). Memory bias in recovered clinical depressives. Special issue: Information processing and the emotional disorders. *Cognition and Emotion, 2*(3), 235–245. **(Chap 7)**

BRADLEY, L. A., YOUNG, L. D., ANDERSON, K. O., TURNER, R. A., AGUDELO, C. A., MCDANIEL, L. K., PISKO, E. J., SEMBLE, E. L., & MORGAN, T. M. (1987). Effects of psychological therapy on pain behavior of rheumatoid arthritis patients: Treatment outcome and six-month follow-up. *Arthritis and Rheumatism, 30,* 1105–1114. **(Chap 9)**

BRADLEY, W. E., TIMM, G. W., GALLAGHER, J. M., & JOHNSON, B. K. (1985). New method for continuous measurement of nocturnal penile tumescence and rigidity. *Urology, 26,* 4. **(Chap 11)**

BRADLEY, W. (1937). The behavior of children receiving Benzedrine. *American Journal of Psychiatry, 94,* 577–585. **(Chap 16)**

BRADY, J. P. (1991). The pharmacology of stuttering: A critical review. *American Journal of Psychiatry, 148,* 1309–1316. **(Chap 16)**

BRADY, J. P., & LIND, D. L. (1961). Experimental analysis of hysterical blindness. *Archives of General Psychiatry, 4,* 331–339. **(Chap 6)**

BRAKEL, S. J., PARRY, J., & WEINER, B. A. (1985). *The mentally disabled and the law* (3rd ed.). Chicago: American Bar Association. **(Chap 17)**

BRAND, R. (1978). Coronary-prone behavior as an independent risk factor of coronary heart disease. In T. M. Dembroski, S. M. Weiss, J. L. Shields, S. G. Haynes, & M. Feinleib (Eds.), *Coronary-prone behavior.* New York: Springer-Verlag. **(Chap 9)**

BRANDON, S., COWLEY, P., MCDONALD, C., NEVILLE, P., PALMER, R., & WELLSTOOD-EASON, S. (1984). Electroconvulsive therapy: Results in depressive illness from the Leicestershire trial. *British Medical Journal, 288*(6410), 22–25. **(Chap 7)**

BRANDON, T. H., & BAKER, T. B. (1992). The smoking consequences questionnaire: The subjective utility of smoking in college students. *Psychological Assessment: A Journal of Consulting and Clinical Psychology, 3,* 484–491. **(Chap 12)**

BRAUCHI, J. T., & WEST, L. J. (1959). Sleep deprivation. *Journal of the American Medical Association, 171,* 11–14. **(Chap 10)**

BREIER, A. (1993). Paranoid disorder: Clinical features and treatment. In D. L. Dunner (Ed.), *Current psychiatric therapy* (pp. 154–159). Philadelphia: W. B. Saunders. **(Chap 14)**

BREIER, A., BUCHANAN, R. W., KIRKPATRICK, B., DAVIS, O. R., IRISH, D., SUMMERFELT, A., & CARPENTER, W. Y. (1994). Effects of clozapine on positive and negative symptoms in outpatients with schizophrenia. *American Journal of Psychiatry, 151,* 20–26. **(Chap 14)**

BREIER, A., CHARNEY, D. S., & HENINGER, G. R. (1985). The diagnostic validity of anxiety disorders and their relationship to depressive illness. *American Journal of Psychiatry, 142,* 787–797. **(Chap 7)**

BRENNER, D. E., KUKULL, W. A., VAN BELLE, G. BOWEN, J. D., MCCORMICK, W. C., TERI, L., & LARSON, E. B. (1993). Relationship between cigarette smoking and Alzheimer's disease in a population-based case-control study. *Neurology, 43,* 293–300. **(Chap 15)**

BRENT, D. A., KERR, M. M., GOLDSTEIN, C., BOZIGAR, J., WARTELLA, M., & ALLAN, M. J. (1989). An outbreak of suicide and suicidal behavior in a high school. *Journal of the American Academy of Child and Adolescent Psychiatry, 28*(6), 918–924. **(Chap 7)**

BRENT, D. A., & KOLKO, D. J. (1990). The assessment and treatment of children and adolescents at risk for suicide. In S. J. Blumenthal & D. J. Kupfer (Eds.), *Suicide over the life cycle: Risk factors, assessment and treatment of suicidal patients.* Washington, DC: American Psychiatric Press. **(Chap 7)**

BRENT, D. A., PERPER, J. A., GOLDSTEIN, C. E., KOLKO, D. J., ALLAN, M. J., ALLMAN, C. J., & ZELLENAK, J. P. (1988). Risk factors for adolescent suicide: A comparison of adolescent suicide victims with suicidal inpatients. *Archives of General Psychiatry, 45,* 581–588. **(Chap 7)**

BRESLAU, N., KILBEY, M. M., & ANDRESKI, P. (1993). Nicotine dependence and major depression: New evidence from a prospective investigation. *Archives of General Psychiatry, 50,* 31–35. **(Chap 12)**

BREUER, J., & FREUD, S. (1957). *Studies on hysteria.* New York: Basic Books. (Original work published 1895) **(Chaps 1, 2)**

BROADHEAD, W. E., KAPLAN, B. H., & JAMES, S. A. (1983). The epidemiologic evidence for a relationship between social support and health. *American Journal of Epidemiology, 117,* 521–537. **(Chaps 1, 9)**

BROUDE, G. J., & GREENE, S. J. (1980). Cross-cultural codes on 20 sexual attitudes and practices. In H. Barry, III, & A. Schlegel (Eds.), *Cross-cultural samples and codes* (pp. 313–333). Pittsburgh: University of Pittsburgh Press. **(Chap 11)**

BROWN, D. R., & EATON, W. W. (1986). *Racial differences in risk factors for phobic disorders.* Paper presented at the 114th meeting of the American Public Health Association, Las Vegas. **(Chap 5)**

BROWN, D. R., EATON, W. W., & SUSSMAN, L. (1990). Racial differences in prevalence of phobic disorders. *Journal of Nervous and Mental Disease, 178,* 434–441. **(Chap 5)**

BROWN, G. K., & NICASSIO, P. M. (1987). The development of a questionnaire for the assessment of active and passive coping strategies in chronic pain patients. *Pain, 31,* 53–65. **(Chap 9)**

BROWN, G. W. (1959). Experiences of discharged chronic schizophrenic mental hospital patients in various types of living group. *Millbank Memorial Fund Quarterly, 37,* 105–131. **(Chap 14)**

BROWN, G. W. (1989). Depression. In G. W. Brown & T. O. Harris (Eds.), *Life events and illness* (pp. 49–93). New York: Guilford Press. **(Chap 7)**

BROWN, G. W., & BIRLEY, J. L. T. (1968). Crisis and life change and the onset of schizophrenia. *Journal of Health and Social Behavior, 9,* 203–214. **(Chap 14)**

BROWN, G. W., & HARRIS, T. O. (1978). *Social origins of depression: A study of psychiatric disorder in women.* London: Tavistock. **(Chap 7)**

BROWN, G. W., MONCK, E. M., CARSTAIRS, G. M., & WING, J. K. (1962). Influence of family life on the course of schizophrenic illness. *British Journal of Preventive and Social Medicine, 16,* 55–68. **(Chap 14)**

BROWN, J., & FINN, P. (1982). Drinking to get drunk: Findings of a survey of junior and senior high school students. *Journal of Alcohol and Drug Education, 27,* 13–25. **(Chap 4)**

BROWN, T. A., BARLOW, D. H., & LIEBOWITZ, M. R. (1994). The empirical basis of generalized anxiety disorder. *American Journal of Psychiatry, 15*(9), 1272–1280. **(Chap 5)**

BROWNELL, K. D. (1991). Dieting and the search for the perfect body: Where physiology and culture collide. *Behavior Therapy, 22,* 1–12. **(Chap 8)**

BROWNELL, K. D., HAYES, S. C., & BARLOW, D. H. (1977). Patterns of appropriate and deviant sexual arousal: The behavioral treatment of multiple sexual deviations. *Journal*

of *Consulting and Clinical Psychology, 45*(6), 1144–1155. **(Chap 11)**

BROWNELL, K. D., & RODIN, J. (IN PRESS). The dieting maelstrom: Is it possible and advisable to lose weight? *American Psychologist.* **(Chap 8)**

BROWNMILLER, S. (1984). *Femininity.* New York: Ballantine Books. **(Chap 6)**

BRUCE, B., & AGRAS, W. S. (1992). Binge eating in females: A population based investigation. *International Journal of Eating Disorders, 12*(4), 365–373. **(Chap 8)**

BRUCE, M. L., & KIM, K. M. (1992). Differences in the effects of divorce on major depression in men and women. *American Journal of Psychiatry, 149*(7), 914–917. **(Chap 7)**

BRUCH, H. (1973). *Eating disorders: Obesity, anorexia nervosa, and the person within.* New York: Basic Books. **(Chap 8)**

BRUCH, H. (1985). Four decades of eating disorders. In D. M. Garner & P. E. Garfinkel (Eds.), *Handbook of psychotherapy for anorexia nervosa and bulimia* (pp. 7–18). New York: Guilford Press. **(Chap 8)**

BRUCH, H. (1986). Anorexia nervosa: The therapeutic task. In K. D. Brownell & J. P. Foreyt (Eds.), *Handbook of eating disorders: Physiology, psychology, and treatment of obesity, anorexia, and bulimia* (pp. 328–332). New York: Basic Books. **(Chap 8)**

BRUCH, M. A., HEIMBERG, R. G., BERGER, P., & COLLINS, T. M. (1989). Social phobia and perceptions of early parental and personal characteristics. *Anxiety Research, 2,* 57–63. **(Chap 5)**

BRUININKS, R. H., WOODCOCK, R. W., WEATHERMAN, R. F., & HILL, B. K. (1984). *Scales of independent behavior.* Allen, TX: DLM/Teaching Resources. **(Chap 15)**

BRUNNER, H. G., NELEN, M., BREAKEFIELD, X. O., ROPERS, H. H., & VAN OOST, B. A. (1993). Abnormal behavior associated with a point mutation in the structural gene for monoamine oxidase A. *Science, 262,* 578–580. **(Chap 13)**

BRUNNER, H. G., NELEN, M. R., VAN ZANDVOORT, P., ABELING, N. G. G. M., VAN GENNIP, A. H., WOLTERS, E. C., KUIPER, M. A., ROPERS, H. H., & VAN OOST, B. A. (1993). X-linked borderline mental retardation with prominent behavioral disturbance: Phenotype, genetic localization, and evidence for disturbed monoamine metabolism. *American Journal of Human Genetics, 52,* 1032–1039. **(Chap 13)**

BUCHWALD, A. M., & RUDICK-DAVIS, D. (1993). The symptoms of major depression. *Journal of Abnormal Psychology, 102*(2), 197–205. **(Chap 7)**

BUDA, M., & TSUANG, M. T. (1990). The epidemiology of suicide: Implications for clinical practice. In S. J. Blumenthal & D. J. Kupfer (Eds.), *Suicide over the life cycle: Risk factors, assessment and treatment of suicidal patients.* Washington, DC: American Psychiatric Press. **(Chap 7)**

BUEHLER, R. E., PATTERSON, G. R., & FURNISS, J. M. (1966). The reinforcement of behavior in institutional settings. *Behavior, Research, and Therapy, 4,* 157–167. **(Chap 4)**

BUFFUM, J. (1982). Pharmacosexology: The effects of drugs on sexual function—A review. *Journal of Psychoactive Drugs, 14,* 5–44. **(Chap 11)**

BUREAU OF THE CENSUS. (1983). *Statistical Abstract of the United States.* Washington, DC: U.S. Government Printing Office. **(Chap 8)**

BURISH, T. G., CAREY, M. P., KROZELY, M. G., & GRECO, F. A. (1987). Conditioned side effects induced by cancer chemotherapy: Prevention through behavioral treatment. *Journal of Consulting and Clinical Psychology, 55,* 42–48. **(Chap 9)**

BURNETTE, M. M., KOEHN, K. A., KENYON-JUMP, R., HUTTON, K., & STARK, C. (1991). Control of genital herpes recurrences using progressive muscle relaxation. *Behavior Therapy, 22,* 237–247. **(Chap 9)**

BURNS, M. O., & SELIGMAN, M. E. P. (1989). Explanatory style across the life span: Evidence for stability over 52 years. *Journal of Personality and Social Psychology, 56,* 471–477. **(Chap 9)**

BURTON, R. (1977). *Anatomy of melancholy.* (Reprint edition). New York: Random House. **(Chap 1)**

BUSHMAN, B. J. (1993). Human aggression while under the influence of alcohol and other drugs: An integrative research review. *Psychological Science, 2,* 148–152. **(Chap 12)**

BUSHNELL, J. A., WELLS, J. E., HORNBLOW, A. R., OAKLEY-BROWNE, M. A., & JOYCE, P. (1990). Prevalence of three bulimia syndromes in the general population. *Psychological Medicine, 20,* 671–680. **(Chap 8)**

BUTCHER, J. N., & GRAHAM, J. R. (EDS.) (1989). *Topics in MMPI-2 interpretation.* Minneapolis: MMPI-2 Workshops and Symposia. **(Chap 3)**

BUTCHER, J. N., GRAHAM, J. R., WILLIAMS, C. L., & BEN-PORATH, Y. S. (1990). *Development and use of the MMPI-2 content scales.* Minneapolis: University of Minnesota Press. **(Chap 3)**

BUTCHER, J. N., & WILLIAMS, C. L. (1992). *Essentials of the MMPI—An interpretation.* Minneapolis: University of Minnesota Press. **(Chap 3)**

BUTLER, G., & MATHEWS, A. (1983). Cognitive processes in anxiety. *Advances in Behaviour Research and Therapy, 5,* 51–62. **(Chap 5)**

BUTLER, G., CULLINGTON, A., MUNBY, M., AMIES, P., & GELDER, M. (1984). Exposure and anxiety management in the treatment of social phobia. *Journal of Consulting and Clinical Psychology, 52,* 642–650. **(Chap 5)**

BUTLER, J. S. (1887). *Curability of insanity and the individualized treatment of the insane.* New York: G. P. Putnam's Sons. **(Chap 1)**

BUTTERS, N., & CERMAK, L. S. (1980). *Alcoholic Korsakoff's syndrome: An information-processing approach to amnesia.* New York: Academic Press. **(Chap 15)**

BUYSSE, D. J., REYNOLDS, C. F., & KUPFER, D. J. (1993). Classification of sleep disorders: A preview of the DSM-IV. In D. L. Dunner (Ed.), *Current psychiatric therapy* (pp. 360–361). Philadelphia: W. B. Saunders. **(Chap 10)**

BYERLY, W., PLAETKE, R., JENSEN, S., HOLIK, J., HOFF, M., MYLES-WORSLEY, M., WENDER, P., REIMHERR, F., LEPPERT, M., O'CONNELL, P., LALOUEL, J., & WHITE, R. (1991). Linkage analysis of six schizophrenia pedigrees with 150 DNA markers. *Schizophrenia Research, 4* (Special Issue), 274–275. **(Chap 14)**

BYNE, W., & PARSONS, B. (1993). Human sexual orientation: The biologic theories reappraised. *Archives of General Psychiatry, 50,* 228–239. **(Chap 11)**

BYRNE, D., & SCHULTE, L. (1990). Personality dispositions as mediators of sexual responses. *Annual Review of Sex Research, 1,* 93–117. **(Chap 11)**

CADORET, R. J. (1978). Psychopathology in the adopted-away offspring of biologic parents with antisocial behavior. *Archives of General Psychiatry, 35,* 176–184. **(Chap 6)**

CADORET, R. J., O'GORMAN, T., TROUGHTON, E., & HEYWOOD, E. (1987). An adoption study of genetic and environmental factors in drug abuse. *Archives of General Psychiatry, 43,* 1131–1136. **(Chap 12)**

CAIRD, W., & WINCZE, J. P. (1977). *Sex therapy: A behavioral approach.* New York: Harper & Row. **(Chap 11)**

CALHOUN, J., & KOENIG, K. (1973). Classroom modification of elective mutism. *Behavior Therapy, 4,* 700–702. **(Chap 16)**

CALHOUN, K. S., & RESICK, P. A. (1993). Post-traumatic stress disorder. In D. H. Barlow (Ed.), *Clinical handbook of psychological disorders* (2nd ed., pp. 48–98). New York: Guilford Press. **(Chaps 11, 17)**

CALLAHAN, L. A., MCGREEVY, M. A., CIRINCIONE, C., & STEADMAN, H. J. (1992). Measuring the effects of the guilty but mentally ill (GBMI) verdict: Georgia's 1982 GBMI reform. *Law and Human Behavior, 16,* 447–462. **(Chap 17)**

CANDY, J. M., KLINOWSKY, J., PERRY, R. H., PERRY, E. K., FAIRBAIRN, A., OAKLEY, A. E., CARPENTER, T. A., ATACK, J. R., BLESSED, G., & EDWARDSON, J. A. (1986). Aluminosilicates and senile plaque formation in Alzheimer's disease. *Lancet, 335,* 354–357. **(Chap 15)**

CANNON, T. D., BARR, C. E., & MEDNICK, S. A. (1991). Genetic and perinatal factors in the etiology of schizophrenia. In E. F. Walker (Ed.), *Schizophrenia: A life-course developmental perspective* (pp. 9–31). New York: Academic Press. **(Chap 14)**

CANNON, W. B. (1929). *Bodily changes in pain, hunger, fear and rage* (2nd ed.). New York: Appleton-Century-Crofts. **(Chap 2)**

CANNON, W. B. (1942). Voodoo death. *American Anthropologist, 44,* 169–181. **(Chap 2)**

CAPPELL, H., & GREELEY, J. (1987). Alcohol and tension reduction: An update on research and theory. In H. T. Blane & K. E. Leonard (Eds.), *Psychological theories of drinking and alcoholism* (pp. 15–54). New York: Guilford Press. **(Chap 12)**

CAPRUSO, D. X., & LEVIN, H. S. (1992). Cognitive impairment following closed head injury. *Neurologic Clinics, 10,* 879–893. **(Chap 15)**

CARDENA, E., LEWIS-FERNANDEZ, R., BEAR, D., PAKIANATHAN, I., & SPIEGEL, D. (IN PRESS). DSM-IV sourcebook for dissociative disorders. In T. Widiger, A. J. Frances, H. Pincus, M. First, & W. W. David (Eds.), *DSM-IV sourcebook.* Washington, DC.: American Psychiatric Association. **(Chap 6)**

CAREY, G. (1992). Twin imitation for antisocial behavior: Implications for genetic and family environment research. *Journal of Abnormal Psychology, 101,* 18–25. **(Chap 4)**

CAREY, M. P., & BURISH, T. G. (1988). Etiology and treatment of the psychological side effects associated with cancer chemotherapy: A critical review and discussion. *Psychological Bulletin, 104*(3), 307–325. **(Chap 9)**

CARLSON, C. L., LAHEY, B. B., & NEEPER, R. (1984). Peer assessment of the social behavior of accepted, rejected, and neglected children. *Journal of Abnormal Child Psychology, 12,* 189–198. **(Chap 16)**

CARLSON, E. B., & PUTNAM, F. W. (1989). Integrating research on dissociation and hypnotizability: Are there two pathways to hypnotizability? *Dissociation, 2,* 32–38. **(Chap 6)**

CARLSON, G. A., & KASHANI, J. H. (1988). Phenomenology of major depression from childhood through adulthood: Analysis of three studies. *American Journal of Psychiatry, 145*(10), 1222–1225. **(Chap 7)**

CARLSSON, A. (1978). Antipsychotic drugs, neurotransmitters and schizophrenia. *American Journal of Psychiatry, 135,* 164–173. **(Chap 14)**

CARMELLI, D., SWAN, G. E., ROBINETTE, D., & FABSITZ, R. (1992). Genetic influences on smoking—A study of male twins. *New England Journal of Medicine, 327,* 829–833. **(Chap 12)**

CARON, C., & RUTTER, M. (1991). Comorbidity in childhood psychopathology: Concepts, issues, and research strategies. *Journal of Child Psychology and Psychiatry, 32,* 1063–1080. **(Chap 13)**

CARPENTER, W. T. (1992). The negative symptom challenge. Archives of General Psychiatry, 49, 236–237.

CARPENTER, W. T. (1994). The deficit syndrome. *American Journal of Psychiatry, 151,* 327–329.

CARROLL, B. J., FEINBERG, M., GREDEN, J. F., HASKETT, R. F., JAMES, N. M., STEINER, M., & TARIKA, J. (1980). Diagnosis of endogenous depression: Comparison of clinical, research, and neuroendocrine criteria. *Journal of Affective Disorders, 2,* 177–194. **(Chap 7)**

CARROLL, B. J., MARTIN, F. I., & DAVIES, B. (1968). Resistance to suppression by dexamethasome of plasma 11-O.H.C.S. levels in severe depressive illness. *British Medical Journal, 3,* 285–287. **(Chap 7)**

CARROLL, E. M., RUEGER, D. B., FOY, D. W., & DONAHOE, C. P. (1985). Vietnam combat veterans with posttraumatic stress disorder: Analysis of marital and cohabitating adjustment. *Journal of Abnormal Psychology, 94,* 329–337. **(Chap 5)**

CARROLL, K. M. (1992). Psychotherapy for cocaine abuse: Approaches, evidence, and conceptual models. In T. R. Kosten & H. D. Kleber (Eds.), *Clinician's guide to cocaine addiction: Theory, research, and treatment* (pp. 290–313). New York: Guilford Press. **(Chap 12)**

CARSKADON, M. A. (1992). *Sleep: A complex behavioral adaptation.* Grass Instrument Company. **(Chap 10)**

CARSKADON, M. A., & DEMENT, W. C. (1982). The multiple sleep latency test: What does it measure? *Sleep, 5,* 67–72. **(Chap 10)**

CARSKADON, M. A., & DEMENT, W. C. (1989). Normal human sleep: An overview. In M. H.

Kryer, T. Roth, & W. C. Dement (Eds.), *Principles and practice of sleep medicine* (pp. 3–13). Philadelphia: W. B. Saunders. **(Chap 10)**

CARSON, R. C. (1991). Discussion: Dilemmas in the pathway of DSM-IV. *Journal of Abnormal Psychology, 100,* 302–307. **(Chap 3)**

CARSON, R. C., & SANISLOW, C. A. (1993). The schizophrenias. In P. B. Sutker & H. E. Adams (Eds.), *Comprehensive handbook of psychopathology* (pp. 295–333). New York: Plenum Press. **(Chap 14)**

CASPER, R. C. (1982). Treatment principles in anorexia nervosa. *Adolescent Psychiatry, 10,* 431–454. **(Chap 8)**

CASPER, R. C., REDMOND, D. E., KATZ, M. M., SCHAFFER, C. B., DAVIS, J. M., & KOSLOW, S. H. (1985). Somatic symptoms in primary affective disorder: Presence and relationship to the classification of depression. *Archives of General Psychiatry, 42,* 1098–1104. **(Chap 7)**

CASPI, A., ELDER, G. H., JR., & BEM, D. L. (1987). Moving against the world: Life-course patterns of explosive children. *Developmental Psychology, 23,* 308–313. **(Chap 13)**

CAUTELA, J. R. (1966). Treatment of compulsive behavior by covert sensitization. *Psychological Record, 16,* 33–41. **(Chap 12)**

CAUTELA, J. R. (1967). Covert sensitization. *Psychological Reports, 20,* 459–468. **(Chap 11)**

CAVIOR, N., & MARABOTTO, C. M. (1976). Monitoring verbal behaviors in a dyadic interaction: Valence of target behaviors, type, timing, and reactivity of monitoring. *Journal of Consulting and Clinical Psychology, 44,* 68–76. **(Chap 3)**

CECI, S. J., PETERS, D., & PLOTKIN, J. (1985). Human subjects review, personal values, and the regulation of social science research. *American Psychologist, 40,* 994–1002. **(Chap 4)**

CENTERS FOR DISEASE CONTROL. (1980). *Ten leading causes of death in the United States, 1977.* Washington, DC: Government Publishing Office. **(Chap 9)**

CENTERS FOR DISEASE CONTROL. (1988). CDC recommendations for a community plan for the prevention and containment of suicide clusters. *Morbidity and Mortality Weekly Report* (Supplement No. 5-6), *37,* 1–12. **(Chap 7)**

CENTERS FOR DISEASE CONTROL. (1991, DECEMBER). HIV/AIDS surveillance report (through November 30, 1991). Atlanta: Author. **(Chap 9)**

CEPEDA-BENITO, A. (1993). Meta-analytical review of the efficacy of nicotine chewing gum in smoking treatment programs. *Journal of Consulting and Clinical Psychology, 61,* 822–830. **(Chap 12)**

CESARONI, L., & GARBER, M. (1991). Exploring the experience of autism through firsthand accounts. *Journal of Autism and Developmental Disorders, 21,* 303–313. **(Chap 16)**

CHAMBLESS, D. L., CHERNEY, J., CAPUTO, G. C., & RHEINSTEIN, B. J. G. (1987). Anxiety disorders and alcoholism: A study with inpatient alcoholics. *Journal of Anxiety Disorders, 1,* 29–40. **(Chap 5)**

CHAMBLESS, D. L., SULTAN, F. E., STERN, T. E., O'NEILL, C., GARRISON, S., & JACKSON, A. (1984). Effect of pubococcygeal exercise on coital orgasm in women. *Journal of Consulting and Clinical Psychology, 52,* 114–118. **(Chap 11)**

CHAN, C. H., JANICAK, P. G., DAVIS, J. M., & ALTMAN, E. (1987). Response of psychotic and nonpsychotic depressed patients to tricyclic antidepressants. *Journal of Clinical Psychiatry, 48,* 197–200. **(Chap 7)**

CHARLEBOIS, P., LEBLANC, M., GAGNON, C., LARIVEE, S., & TREMBLAY, R. (1993). Age trends in early behavioral predictors of serious antisocial behaviors. *Journal of Psychopathology and Behavioral Assessment, 15,* 23–41. **(Chap 13)**

CHARNEY, D. S., DEUTCH, A. Y., KRYSTAL, J. H., SOUTHWICK, S. M., & DAVIS, M. (1993). Psychobiological mechanisms of posttraumatic stress disorder. *Archives of General Psychiatry, 50,* 294–305. **(Chap 5)**

CHARNEY, D. S., WOODS, S. W., PRICE, L. H., GOODMAN, W. K., GLAZER, W. M., & HENINGER, G. R. (IN PRESS). Noradrenergic dysregulation in panic disorder. In I. Boris-Wollner & R. D. Zimmerman (Eds.), *Neurobiology of panic disorder, frontiers of clinical neuroscience series.* New York: Alan R. Liss. **(Chap 2)**

CHASSIN, L., PILLOW, D. R., CURRAN, P. J., MOLINA, B. S. G., & BARRERA, M. (1993). Relation of parental alcoholism to early adolescent substance use: A test of three mediating mechanisms. *Journal of Abnormal Psychology, 102,* 3–19. **(Chap 12)**

CHESNEY, M. A. (1986, NOVEMBER). *Type A behavior: The biobehavioral interface.* Keynote address presented at the annual meeting of the Association for Advancement of Behavior Therapy, Chicago. **(Chap 2)**

CHESNEY, M. A. (1993). Health psychology in the 21st century: Acquired immunodeficiency syndrome as a harbinger of things to come. *Health Psychology, 12*(4), 259–268. **(Chap 9)**

CHODOFF, P. (1974). The diagnosis of hysteria: An overview. *American Journal of Psychiatry, 131,* 1073–1078. **(Chap 6)**

CHODOFF, P. (1982). Hysteria in women. *American Journal of Psychiatry, 139,* 545–551. **(Chap 13)**

CHOJNACKI, J. T., & WALSH, W. B. (1992). The consistency of scores and configural patterns between the MMPI and MMPI-2. *Journal of Personality Assessment, 59,* 276–289. **(Chap 3)**

CHOR, P. N., MERCIER, M. A., & HALPER, I. S. (1988). Use of cognitive therapy for treatment of a patient suffering from a bipolar affective disorder. *Journal of Cognitive Psychotherapy, 2*(1), 51–58. **(Chap 7)**

CHRISTENSON, R., & BLAZER, D. (1984). Epidemiology of persecutory ideation in an elderly population in the community. *American Journal of Psychiatry, 141,* 1088–1091. **(Chap 13)**

CHRISTIANSEN, B. A., SMITH, G. T., ROEHLING, P. V., & GOLDMAN, M. S. (1989). Using alcohol expectancies to predict adolescent drinking behavior after one year. *Journal of Consulting and Clinical Psychology, 57,* 93–99. **(Chap 12)**

CHUNG, S. Y., LUK, S. L., & LEE, P. W. H. (1990). A follow-up study of infantile autism in Hong Kong. *Journal of Autism and Developmental Disorders, 20,* 221–232. **(Chap 16)**

CICCHETTI, D. (1991). A historical perspective on the discipline of developmental psychopathology. In J. Rolf, A. S. Masten, D. Cicchetti, K. H. Nuechterlein, & S. Weintraub (Eds.), *Risk and protective factors in the development of psychopathology* (pp. 2–28). New York: Cambridge University Press. **(Chap 2)**

CIPANI, E. (1991). Educational classification and placement. In J. L. Matson & J. A. Mulick (Eds.), *Handbook of mental retardation* (2nd ed., pp. 181–191). Elmsford, NY: Pergamon Press. **(Chap 15)**

CLARK, D. M. (1986). A cognitive approach to panic. *Behaviour Research and Therapy, 24,* 461–470. **(Chap 5)**

CLARK, D. M. (1988). A cognitive model of panic attacks. In S. Rachman & J. D. Maser (Eds.), *Panic: Psychological perspectives* (pp. 71–89). Hillsdale, NJ: Lawrence Erlbaum. **(Chap 5)**

CLARK, D. M., SALKOVSKIS, P. M., HACKMANN, A., MIDDLETON, H., ANASTASIADES, P., & GELDER, M. (in press). A comparison of cognitive therapy, applied relaxation and imiprimane in the treatment of panic disorder. *British Journal of Psychiatry.* **(Chap 5)**

CLARK, D. M., & TEASDALE, J. D. (1982). Diurnal variation in clinical depression and accessibility of memories of positive and negative experiences. *Journal of Abnormal Psychology, 91*(2), 87–95. **(Chap 7)**

CLARK, L. A. (1993). *Manual for the Schedule of Nonadaptive and Adaptive Personality.* Minneapolis: University of Minnesota Press. **(Chap 13)**

CLARK, L. A., & WATSON, D. (1991). Tripartite model of anxiety and depression: Psychometric evidence and taxonomic implications. Special issue: Diagnoses, dimensions, and DSM-IV: The science of classification. *Journal of Abnormal Psychology, 100*(3), 316–336. **(Chap 5)**

CLAYTON, P. J., & DARVISH, H. S. (1979). Course of depressive symptoms following the stress of bereavement. In J. E. Barrett (Ed.), *Stress and mental disorder.* New York: Raven. **(Chap 7)**

CLECKLEY, H. M. (1982). *The mask of sanity* (6th ed.). St. Louis: Mosby. **(Chap 13)**

CLEGHORN, J. M., & ALBERT, M. L. (1990). Modular disjunction in schizophrenia: A framework for a pathological psychophysiology. In A. Kales, C. N. Stefanis, & J. A. Talbot (Eds.), *Recent advances in schizophrenia* (pp. 59–80). New York: Springer-Verlag. **(Chap 14)**

CLEGHORN, J. M., FRANCO, S., SZECHTMAN, B., KAPLAN, R. D., SZECHTMAN, H., BROWN, G. M., NAHMIAS, C., & GARNETT, E. S. (1992). Toward a brain map of auditory hallucinations. *American Journal of Psychiatry, 149,* 1062–1069. **(Chap 14)**

CLEMENT, U. (1990). Surveys of heterosexual behavior. *Annual Review of Sex Research, 1,* 45–74. **(Chap 11)**

CLEMENTZ, B. A., & SWEENEY, J. A. (1990). Is eye movement dysfunction a biological marker for schizophrenia? A methodological review. *Psychological Bulletin, 108,* 77–92. **(Chap 14)**

CLONINGER, C. R. (1978). The link between hysteria and sociopathy: An integrative model of pathogenesis based on clinical,

genetic, and neurophysiological observations. In H. S. Akiskal & W. L. Webb (Eds.), *Psychiatric diagnosis: Exploration of biological predictors* (pp. 189–218). New York: Spectrum. **(Chaps 6, 13)**

CLONINGER, C. R. (1986). A unified biosocial theory of personality and its role in the development of anxiety states. *Psychiatric Developments, 3,* 167–226. **(Chap 2)**

CLONINGER, C. R. (1987A). Neurogenetic adaptive mechanisms in alcoholism. *Science, 236,* 410–416. **(Chap 12)**

CLONINGER, C. R. (1987B). A systematic method for clinical description and classification of personality variants: A proposal. *Archives of General Psychiatry, 44,* 573–588. **(Chaps 6, 13)**

CLONINGER, C. R. (1989). Establishment of diagnostic validity in psychiatric illness: Robins and Guze's method revisited. In L. N. Robins & J. E. Barrett (Eds.), *The validity of psychiatric diagnosis* (pp. 9–16). New York: Raven Press. **(Chap 3)**

CLONINGER, C. R. (1991). D2 dopamine receptor gene is associated but not linked with alcoholism. *Journal of the American Medical Association, 266,* 1833–1834. **(Chap 12)**

CLONINGER, C. R. (IN PRESS). Somatization disorder. Literature review for DSM-IV sourcebook. Washington, DC: American Psychiatric Press. **(Chap 6)**

CLONINGER, C. R., BOHMAN, M., & SIGVARDSSON, S. (1981). Inheritance of alcohol abuse. *Archives of General Psychiatry, 38,* 861–868. **(Chap 12)**

CLOSSER, M. H. (1992). Cocaine epidemiology. In T. R. Kosten & H. D. Kleber (Eds.), *Clinician's guide to cocaine addiction: Theory, research, and treatment* (pp. 225–240). New York: Guilford Press. **(Chap 12)**

COATES, T. J. (1990). Strategies for modifying sexual behavior for primary and secondary prevention of HIV disease. *Journal of Consulting and Clinical Psychology, 58*(1), 57–69. **(Chap 9)**

COATES, T. J., MCKUSICK, L., KUNO, R., & STITES, D. P. (1989). Stress management training reduced number of sexual partners but did not improve immune function in men infected with HIV. *American Journal of Public Health, 79,* 885–887. **(Chap 9)**

COBB, S. (1976). Social support as a moderator of life stress. *Psychosomatic Medicine, 38,* 300. **(Chap 2)**

COCHRAN, S. D. (1984). Preventing medical noncompliance in the outpatient treatment of bipolar affective disorders. *Journal of Consulting and Clinical Psychology, 52*(5), 873–878. **(Chap 7)**

COCORES, J. A., MILLER, N. S., POTTASH, A. C., & GOLD, M. S. (1988). Sexual dysfunction in abusers of cocaine and alcohol. *American Journal of Drug and Alcohol Abuse, 14,* 169–173. **(Chap 11)**

COCOZZA, J., & STEADMAN, H. (1976). The failure of psychiatric predictions of dangerousness: Clear and convincing evidence. *Rutgers Law Review, 29,* 1084–1101. **(Chap 17)**

COHEN, A. S., BARLOW, D. H., & BLANCHARD, E. B. (1985). Psychophysiology of relaxation-associated panic attacks. *Journal of Abnormal Psychology, 94,* 96–101. **(Chap 5)**

COHEN, D., & EISDORFER, C. (1988). Depression in family members caring for a relative with Alzheimer's disease. *Journal of the American Geriatrics Society, 36,* 885–889. **(Chap 15)**

COHEN, D. J., RIDDLE, M. A., & LECKMAN, J. F. (1992). Pharmacotherapy of Tourette's syndrome and associated disorders. *Psychiatric Clinics of North America, 15,* 109–129. **(Chap 16)**

COHEN, J. B., & REED, D. (1985). Type A behavior and coronary heart disease among Japanese men in Hawaii. *Journal of Behavioral Medicine, 8,* 343–352. **(Chap 9)**

COHEN, M. S., ROSEN, B. R., & BRADY, T. J. (1992). Ultrafast MRI permits expanded clinical role. *Magnetic Resonance, 2,* 26–37. **(Chap 3)**

COHEN, S., KAPLAN, J. R., CUNNICK, J. E., MANUCK, S. B., & RABIN, B. S. (1992). Chronic social stress, affiliation, and cellular immune response in nonhuman primates. *Psychological Science, 3*(5), 301–304. **(Chap 2)**

COHEN, S., TYRRELL, D. A. J., & SMITH, A. P. (1991). Psychological stress and susceptibility to the common cold. *New England Journal of Medicine, 325,* 606–612. **(Chap 9)**

COHEN, S., TYRRELL, D. A., & SMITH, A. P. (1993). Negative life events, perceived stress, negative affect, and susceptibility to the common cold. *Journal of Personality and Social Psychology, 64*(1), 131–140. **(Chap 9)**

COHEN, S., & WILLS, T. A. (1985). Stress, social support, and the buffering hypothesis. *Psychological Bulletin, 98,* 310–357. **(Chap 7)**

COLE, M., WINKELMAN, M. D., MORRIS, J. C., SIMON, J. E., & BOYD, T. A. (1992). Thalamic amnesia: Korsakoff syndrome due to left thalamic infarction. *Journal of the Neurological Sciences, 110,* 62–67. **(Chap 15)**

COLEMAN, E., BOCKTING, W. O., & GOOREN, L. (1993). Homosexual and bisexual identity in sex-reassigned female-to-male transsexuals. *Archives of Sexual Behavior, 22,* 37–50. **(Chap 11)**

COLEMAN, E., COLGAN, P., & GOOREN, L. (1992). Male cross-gender behavior in Myanmar (Burma): A description of the acault. *Archives of Sexual Behavior, 21*(3), 313–321. **(Chap 11)**

COLEMAN, M. (1990). Is classical Rett syndrome ever present in males? *Brain and Development, 12,* 31–32. **(Chap 16)**

COMAS-DIAZ, L. (1981). Puerto Rican espiritismo and psychotherapy. *American Journal of Orthopsychiatry, 51*(4), 636–645. **(Chap 6)**

CONDELLI, W. S., FAIRBANK, J. A., DENNIS, M. L., & RACHAL, J. V. (1991). Cocaine use by clients in methadone programs: Significance, scope, and behavioral interventions. *Journal of Substance Abuse Treatment, 8,* 203–212. **(Chap 12)**

CONDON, W., OGSTON, W., & PACOE, L. (1969). Three faces of Eve revisited: A study of transient microstrabismus. *Journal of Abnormal Psychology, 74,* 618–620. **(Chap 6)**

CONN. GEN. STAT. ANN. (1992). 319:Part II 17a-495. **(Chap 17)**

CONTURE, E. (1990). *Stuttering* (2nd ed.). Englewood Cliffs, NJ: Prentice-Hall. **(Chap 16)**

COOK, C. C. H., & GURLING, H. M. D. (1991). Genetic factors in alcoholism. In T. N. Pal-

mer (Ed.), *The molecular pathology of alcoholism* (pp. 182–210). New York: Oxford University Press. **(Chap 12)**

COOK, E. W., III, HODES, R. L., & LANG, P. J. (1986). Preparedness and phobia: Effects of stimulus content on human visceral conditioning. *Journal of Abnormal Psychology, 95,* 195–207. **(Chap 2)**

COOK, P. J. (1993). The matter of tobacco use. *Science, 262,* 1750–1751. **(Chap 12)**

COON, P. M. (1986). Treatment progress in 20 patients with multiple personality disorder. *Journal of Nervous and Mental Disease, 174,* 715–721. **(Chap 6)**

COOPER, A. J. (1988). Sexual dysfunction and cardiovascular disease. *Stress Medicine, 4,* 273–281. **(Chap 11)**

COOPER, A. M., & RONNINGSTAM, E. (1992). Narcissistic personality disorder. In A. Tasman & M. B. Riba (Eds.), *Review of psychiatry* (Vol. 11, pp. 80–97). Washington, DC: Psychiatric Press. **(Chap 13)**

COOPER, M. (1957). *Pica.* Springfield, IL: Charles Thomas. **(Chap 8)**

COOPER, M. L., RUSSELL, M., & GEORGE, W. H. (1988). Coping, expectancies, and alcohol abuse: A test of social learning formulations. *Journal of Abnormal Psychology, 97,* 218–230. **(Chap 12)**

COOPER, M. L., RUSSELL, M., SKINNER, J. B., FRONE, M. R., & MUDAR, P. (1992). Stress and alcohol use: Moderating effects of gender, coping, and alcohol expectancies. *Journal of Abnormal Psychology, 101,* 139–152. **(Chap 12)**

COPOLOV, D. L., RUBIN, R. T., MANDER, A. J., SASHIDHARAN, S. P., WHITEHOUSE, A. M., BLACKBURN, I. M., FREEMAN, C. P., & BLACKWOOD, D. H. R. (1986). DSM-III melancholia: Do the criteria accurately and reliably distinguish endogenous pattern depression? *Journal of Affective Disorders, 10,* 191–202. **(Chap 7)**

CORDER, E. H., SAUNDERS, A. M., STRITTMATTER, W. J., SCHMECHEL, D. E., GASKELL, P. C., SMALL, G. W., ROSES, A. D., HAINES, J. L., & PERICAK-VANCE, M. A. (1993). Gene dose of apolipoprotein E type 4 allele and the risk of Alzheimer's disease in late onset families. *Science, 261,* 921–923. **(Chap 15)**

CORYELL, W. (1981). Obsessive-compulsive disorder and primary unipolar depression. Comparisons of background, family history, course and mortality. *Journal of Nervous and Mental Disorders, 169,* 220–224. **(Chap 5, 7)**

CORYELL, W., SCHEFTNER, W., KELLER, M., ENDICOTT, J., MASER, J., & KLERMAN, G. L. (1993). The enduring psychosocial consequences of mania and depression. *American Journal of Psychiatry, 150*(5), 720–727. **(Chap 7)**

CORYELL, W., & TURNER, R. (1985). Outcome with desipramine therapy in subtypes of nonpsychotic major depression. *Journal of Affective Disorders, 9,* 149–154. **(Chap 7)**

CORYELL, W. H., & ZIMMERMAN, M. (1989). Personality disorder in the families of depressed, schizophrenic, and never-ill probands. *American Journal of Psychiatry, 146,* 496–502. **(Chap 13)**

COSTA, E. (1985). Benzodiazepine-GABA interactions: A model to investigate the neurobiology of anxiety. In A. H. Tuma & J. D. Maser (Eds.), *Anxiety and the anxiety disorders.*

Hillsdale, NJ: Lawrence Erlbaum. **(Chap 2)**

COSTA, P. T., JR., & MCCRAE, R. R. (1990). Personality disorders and the five-factor model of personality. *Journal of Personality Disorders, 4,* 362–371. **(Chap 13)**

COTE, G., O'LEARY, T., BARLOW, D. H., & STRAIN, J. (in press). Hypochondriasis: Integrative review. In T. Widiger, A. J. Frances, H. Pincus, M. First, & W. W. Davis (Eds.), *DSM-IV sourcebook.* Washington, DC: American Psychiatric Association. **(Chap 6)**

COURCHESNE, E. (1991). Neuroanatomic imaging in autism. *Pediatrics, 87,* 781–790. **(Chaps 2, 16)**

COURCHESNE, E., HESSELINK, J. R., JERNIGAN, T. L., & YEUNG-COURCHESNE, R. (1987). Abnormal neuroanatomy in a nonretarded person with autism: Unusual findings with magnetic resonance imaging. *Archives of Neurology, 44,* 335–341. **(Chap 16)**

COVI, L., & LIPMAN, R. S. (1987). Cognitive-behavioral group psychotherapy combined with imipramine in major depression. *Psychopharmocology Bulletin, 23,* 173–176. **(Chap 7)**

COX, A., RUTTER, M., NEWMAN, S., & BARTAK, L. (1975). A comparative study of infantile autism and specific developmental receptive language disorder: II. Parental characteristics. *British Journal of Psychiatry, 126,* 146–159. **(Chap 16)**

COYNE, J. C. (1976). Toward an interactional description of depression. *Psychiatry, 39*(1), 28–40. **(Chap 7)**

COYNE, J. C., WORTMAN, C. B., & LEHMAN, D. R. (1988). The other side of support: Emotional overinvolvement and miscarried helping. In B. H. Gottlieb (Ed.), *Marshaling social support: Formats, processes and effects* (pp. 305–330). Newbury Park, CA: Sage. **(Chap 9)**

CRABBE, J. C., MCSWIGAN, J. D., & BELKNAP, J. K. (1985). The role of genetics in substance abuse. In M. Galizio & S. A. Maisto (Eds.), *Determinants of substance abuse: Biological, psychological, and environmental factors* (pp. 13–64). New York: Plenum Press. **(Chap 12)**

CRAIGHEAD, L. W., & AGRAS, W. S. (1991). Mechanisms of action in cognitive-behavioral and pharmacological interventions for obesity and bulimia nervosa. *Journal of Consulting and Clinical Psychology, 59,* 115–125. **(Chap 8)**

CRANSTON-CUEBAS, M. A., & BARLOW, D. H. (1990). Cognitive and affective contributions to sexual functioning. *Annual Review of Sex Research, 1,* 119–161. **(Chap 11)**

CRASKE, M. G. (IN PRESS). Integrated literature review. Simple Phobia Subcommittee of the DSM-IV Anxiety Disorders Work Group. **(Chap 5)**

CRASKE, M. G., & BARLOW, D. H. (1988). A review of the relationship between panic and avoidance. *Clinical Psychology Review, 8,* 667–685. **(Chap 5)**

CRASKE, M. G., & BARLOW, D. H. (1989). Nocturnal panic. *Journal of Nervous and Mental Disease, 177,* 160–167. **(Chap 5)**

CRASKE, M. G., & BARLOW, D. H. (1993). Panic disorder and agoraphobia. In D. H. Barlow (Ed.), *Clinical handbook of psychological disorders* (2nd ed.). New York: Guilford Press. **(Chap 5)**

CRASKE, M. G., BARLOW, D. H., & O'LEARY, T. A. (1992). *Mastery of your anxiety and worry*. Albany, NY: Graywind Publications. **(Chap 5)**

CRASKE, M. G., BROWN, T. A., & BARLOW, D. H. (1991). Behavioral treatment of panic disorder: A two year follow-up. *Behavior Therapy, 22,* 289–304. **(Chap 5)**

CRASKE, M. G., RAPEE, R. M., & BARLOW, D. H. (1988). The significance of panic expectancy for individual patterns of avoidance. *Behavior Therapy, 19,* 577–592. **(Chap 5)**

CRASKE, M. G., STREET, L., & BARLOW, D. H. (1989). Instructions to focus upon or to distract from internal cues during exposure treatment of agoraphobic avoidance. *Behaviour Research and Therapy, 27,* 663–672. **(Chap 5)**

CREESE, I., BURT, D. R., & SNYDER, S. H. (1976). Dopamine receptor binding predicts clinical and pharmacological potencies of antischizophrenic drugs. *Science, 192,* 481–483. **(Chap 14)**

CRISP, A. H., CALLENDER, J. S., HALEK, C., & HSU, L. K. G. (1992). Long-term mortality in anorexia nervosa: A 20-year follow-up of the St. George's and Aberdeen cohorts. *British Journal of Psychiatry, 161,* 104–107. **(Chap 8)**

CROCKER, A. C. (1992). Data collection for the evaluation of mental retardation prevention activities: The fateful forty-three. *Mental Retardation, 30,* 303–317. **(Chap 15)**

CROSSLEY, R. (1988, OCTOBER). *Unexpected communication attainments by persons diagnosed as autistic and intellectually impaired.* Unpublished paper presented at the International Society for Augmentative and Alternative Communication, Los Angeles, CA. **(Chap 16)**

CROSS-NATIONAL COLLABORATIVE GROUP. (1992). The changing rate of major depression: Cross-national comparisons. *Journal of the American Medical Association, 268,* 3098–3105. **(Chap 7)**

CROW, T. J. (1980). Molecular pathology of schizophrenia: More than one dimension of pathology? *British Medical Journal, 280,* 66–68. **(Chap 14)**

CROW, T. J. (1985). The two-syndrome concept: Origins and current status. *Schizophrenia Bulletin, 11,* 471–486. **(Chap 14)**

CROW, T. J. (1988). Sex chromosomes and psychosis: The case for pseudoautosomal locus. *British Journal of Psychiatry, 153,* 675–683. **(Chap 14)**

CROW, T. J., CROSS, A. J., OWEN, D., FERRIER, N., JOHNSTONE, E. C., MACREADIE, R. M., & OWNES, D. G. C. (1981). *Neurochemical studies on post mortem brains in schizophrenia: Changes in the dopamine receptor in relation to psychiatric and neurological symptoms.* Proceedings of the 134th Meeting of the American Psychiatric Association, p. 39. **(Chap 14)**

CROW, T. J., DEAKIN, J. F. W., JOHNSTONE, E. C., ET AL. (1984). The Northwich Park ECT trial. Predictors of response to real and simulated ECT. *British Journal of Psychiatry, 144,* 227–237. **(Chap 7)**

CROWE, L. C., & GEORGE, W. H. (1989). Alcohol and human sexuality: Review and integration. *Psychological Bulletin, 105*(3), 374–386. **(Chap 11)**

CROWE, R. R. (1974). An adoption study of antisocial personality. *Archives of General Psychiatry, 31,* 785–791. **(Chap 13)**

CROWE, R. R. (1984). Electroconvulsive therapy-A current perspective. *New England Journal of Medicine, 311,* 163–167. **(Chap 7)**

CROWLEY, P. H., HAYDEN, T. L., & GULATI, D. K. (1982). Etiology of Down syndrome. In S. M. Pueschel & J. E. Rynders, (Eds.), *Down syndrome: Advances in biomedicine and behavioral sciences* (pp. 89–131). Cambridge, MA: Ware Press. **(Chap 15)**

CRUICKSHANK, J. K., & BEEVERS, D. G. (1989). *Ethnic factors in health and disease.* London: Wright. **(Chap 15)**

CUMMINGS, J. L. (1990). *Subcortical dementia.* New York: Oxford University Press. **(Chap 15)**

CURTIS, G. C., HILL, E. M., & LEWIS, J. A. (1990). *Heterogeneity of DSM-III-R simple phobia and the simple phobia/agoraphobia boundary: Evidence from the ECA study.* Preliminary report to the Simple Phobia subcommittee of the DSM-IV Anxiety Disorders Work Group. **(Chap 5)**

CURTIS, G. C., HIMLE, J. A., LEWIS, J. A., & LEE, Y-J. (1989). *Specific situational phobias: Variant of agoraphobia?* Paper requested by the Simple Phobia subcommittee of the DSM-IV Anxiety Disorders Work Group. **(Chap 5)**

CUTRONA, C. E. (1984). Social support and stress in the transition to parenthood. *Journal of Abnormal Psychology, 93*(4), 378–390. **(Chap 7)**

CUTTING, J. (1985). *The psychology of schizophrenia.* New York: Churchill Livingstone. **(Chap 14)**

CZEISLER, C. A., & ALLAN, J. S. (1989). Pathologies of the sleep-wake schedule. In R. L. Williams, I. Karacan, & C. A. Morre (Eds.), *Sleep disorders: Diagnosis and treatment* (pp. 109–129). New York: John Wiley. **(Chap 10)**

CZEISLER, C. A., ALLAN, J. S., STROGATZ, S. H., RONDA, J. M., SANCHEZ, R., RIOS, C. D., FRIETAG, W. O., & DEMENT, W. (1960). The effect of dream deprivation. *Science, 131,* 1705–1707. **(Chap 10)**

CZEISLER, C. A., ALLAN, J. S., STROGATZ, S. H., RONDA, J. M., SANCHEZ, R., RIOS, C. D., FRIETAG, W. O., RICHARDSON, G. S., & KRONAUER, R. E. (1986). Bright light resets the human circadian pacemaker independent of the timing of the sleep-wake cycle. *Science, 233,* 667–671. **(Chap 10)**

CZEISLER, C. A., RICHARDSON, G. S., COLEMAN, R. M., ZIMMERMAN, J. C., MOORE-EDE, M. C., DEMENT, W. C., & WEITZMAN, E. D. (1981). Chronotherapy: Resetting the circadian clocks of patients with delayed sleep phase insomnia. *Sleep, 4,* 1–21. **(Chap 10)**

DADDS, M. R., SANDERS, M. R., MORRISON, M., & REBGETZ, M. (1992). Childhood depression and conduct disorder: II. An analysis of family interaction patterns in the home. *Journal of Abnormal Psychology, 101*(3), 505–513. **(Chap 7)**

DAHL, A. A. (1993, SPRING). The personality disorders: A critical review of family, twin, and adoption studies. *Journal of Personality Disorders,* Supplement, 86–99. **(Chap 13)**

DALACK, G. W., GLASSMAN, A. H., & COVEY, L. S. (1993). Nicotine use. In D. L. Dunner (Ed.), *Current psychiatric therapy* (pp. 114–118). Philadelphia: W. B. Saunders. **(Chap 12)**

DALTON, K. (1979). *Once a month.* Pomona, CA: Hunter House. **(Chap 3)**

DALY, R. J. (1983). Samuel Pepys and post-traumatic stress disorder. *British Journal of Psychiatry, 143,* 64–68. **(Chap 5)**

D'AMATO, T., CAMPION, D., GORWOOD, P., JAY, M., SABATE, O., PETIT, C., ABBAR, M., MALAFOSSE, A., LEBOYER, M., HILLAIRE, D., CLERGET-DARPOUX, F., FEINGOLD, J., WAKSMAN, G., & MALLET, J. (1992). Evidence for a pseudoautosomal locus for schizophrenia. II: Replication of a non-random segregation of alleles at the DXYS14 locus. *British Journal of Psychiatry, 161,* 59–62. **(Chap 14)**

DARWIN, C. R. (1872). *The expression of emotions in man and animals.* London: John Murray. **(Chaps 1, 5)**

DAVIDSON, J., MILLER, R. D., TURNBULL, C. D., & SULLIVAN, J. L. (1982). Atypical depression. *Archives of General Psychiatry, 39,* 527–534. **(Chap 7)**

DAVIDSON, J., & ROBERTSON, E. (1985). A follow-up study of postpartum illness, 1946–1978. *Acta Psychiatrica Scandinavica, 71*(15), 451–457. **(Chap 7)**

DAVIDSON, J., SWARTZ, M., STORCK, M., KRISHNAN, R. R., & HAMMETT, E. (1985). A diagnostic and family study of posttraumatic stress disorder. *American Journal of Psychiatry, 142,* 90–93. **(Chap 5)**

DAVIDSON, J. R. T., HUGHES, D. L., BLAZER, D. G., & GEORGE, L. K. (1991). Posttraumatic stress in the community: An epidemiological study. *Journal of Psychological Medicine, 21,* 713–721. **(Chap 5)**

DAVIDSON, M., KEEFE, R. S. E., MOHS, R. C., SIEVER, L. J., LOSONCZY, M. F., HORVATH, T. B., & DAVIS, K. L. (1987). L-Dopa challenge and relapse in schizophrenia. *American Journal of Psychiatry, 144,* 934–938. **(Chap 14)**

DAVIS, K. L., KAHN, R. S., KO, G., & DAVIDSON, M. (1991). Dopamine in schizophrenia: A review and reconceptualization. *American Journal of Psychiatry, 148,* 1474–1486. **(Chap 14)**

DAVISON, G. C. (1968). Elimination of a sadistic fantasy by a client-controlled counter-conditioning technique: A case study. *Journal of Abnormal Psychology, 73,* 91–99. **(Chap 11)**

DAWSON, G., & LEWY, A. (1989). Arousal, attention, and the socioemotional impairments of individuals with autism. In G. Dawson (Ed.), *Autism: Nature, diagnosis, and treatment* (pp. 49–74). New York: Guilford Press. **(Chap 16)**

DAWSON, G., & MCKISSICK, F. C. (1984). Self-recognition in autistic children. *Journal of Autism and Developmental Disorders, 14,* 383–394. **(Chap 16)**

DAY, J., GRANT, I., ATKINSON, J. H., BRYSK, L. T., MCCUTCHAN, J. A., HESSELINK, J. R., KEATON, R. K., WEINRICH, J. D., SPECTOR, S. A., & RICHMAN, D. D. (1992). Incidence of AIDS dementia in a 2-year follow-up of AIDS and ARC patients on an initial phase II AZT placebo-controlled study: San Diego cohort. *Journal of Neu-*

ropsychiatry and Clinical Neuroscience, 4, 15–20. **(Chap 15)**

DAY, R., NIELSEN, J. A., KORTEN, A., ERNBERG, G., DUBE, K. C., GEBHART, J., JABLENSKY, A., LEON, C., MARSELLA, A., OLATAWURA, M., SARTORIUS, N., STROMGREN, E., TAKAHASHI, R., WIG, N.; & WYNNE, L. C. (1987). Stressful life events preceding the acute onset of schizophrenia: A cross-national study from the World Health Organization. *Cultural Medicine and Psychiatry, 11,* 123–205. **(Chap 14)**

DE ALMEIDO-FILHO, N., SANATANA, U. S., PINTO, I. M., & DE CARVALHO-NETO, J. A. (1991). Is there an epidemic of drug misuse in Brazil? A review of the epidemiological evidence (1977–1988). *International Journal of the Addictions, 26,* 355–369. **(Chap 12)**

DE ANGELIS, T. (1994). Experts see little impact from insanity plea ruling. *APA Monitor, 25,* 28. **(Chap 17)**

DE KLOET, E. R., ROSENFELD, P., VAN EEKELEN, J. A. M., SUTANTO, W., & LEVINE, S. (1988). Stress, glucocorticoids and development. *Progress in Brain Research, 73,* 101–120. **(Chap 9)**

DE LA MONTE, S. M., HUTCHINS, G. M., & MOORE, G. W. (1989). Racial differences in the etiology of dementia and frequency of Alzheimer lesions in the brain. *Journal of the National Medical Association, 81,* 644–652. **(Chap 15)**

DE LISSOVOY, V. (1961). Head banging in early childhood. *Child Development, 33,* 43–56. **(Chap 16)**

DEAKIN, J. F. W., & GRAEFF, F. G. (1991). Critique: 5-HT and mechanisms of defence. *Journal of Psychopharmacology, 5*(4), 305–315. **(Chap 5)**

DEAN, C., & KENDELL, R. E. (1981). The symptomatology of postpartum illness. *British Journal of Psychiatry, 139,* 128–133. **(Chap 7)**

DEAN, R. R., KELSEY, J. E., HELLER, M. R., & CIARANELLO, R. D. (1993). Structural foundations of illness and treatment: Receptors. In D. L. Dunner (Ed.), *Current psychiatric therapy.* Philadelphia: W. B. Saunders. **(Chap 2)**

DEBACKER, G., KITTEL, F., KORNITZER, M., & DRAMAIX, M. (1983). Behavior, stress, and psychosocial traits as risk factors. *Preventative Medicine, 12,* 32–36. **(Chap 9)**

DEBUONO, B. A., ZINNER, S. H., DAAMEN, M., & MCCORMACK, W. M. (1990). Sexual behavior of college women in 1975, 1986 and 1989. *New England Journal of Medicine, 322*(12), 821–825. **(Chap 11)**

DELONG, G. R., & DWYER, J. T. (1988). Correlation of family history with specific autistic subgroups: Asperger's syndrome and bipolar affective disease. *Journal of Autism and Developmental Disorders, 18,* 593–600. **(Chap 16)**

DEMBROSKI, T. M., & COSTA, P. T., JR. (1987). Coronary prone behavior: Components of the Type A pattern and hostility. *Journal of Personality, 55*(2), 211–235. **(Chap 9)**

DEMBROSKI, T. M., MACDOUGALL, J. M., COSTA, P. T., & GRANDITS, G. A. (1989). Components of hostility as predictors of sudden death and myocardial infarction in the multiple risk factor intervention trial. *Psychosomatic Medicine, 51*(5), 514–522. **(Chap 9)**

DEMENT, W. (1960). The effect of sleep deprivation. *Science, 131,* 1705–1707. **(Chap 10)**

DENZIN, N. K. (1987). *The recovering alcoholic.* Newbury Park, CA: Sage Publications. **(Chap 12)**

DEPRESSION GUIDELINE PANEL. (1993, APRIL). *Depression in primary care: Vol. 1. Detection and diagnosis* (AHCPR Publication No. 93-0550). Clinical practice guideline, No. 5. Rockville, MD: U.S. Department of Health and Human Services, Public Health Service, Agency for Health Care Policy and Research. **(Chap 7)**

DEPTULA, D., & POMARA, N. (1990). Effects of antidepressants on human performance: A review. *Journal of Clinical Psychopharmacology, 10,* 105–111. **(Chap 7)**

DEPUE, R. A. (IN PRESS). *Neurobehavioral systems, personality, and psychopathology.* New York: Springer-Verlag. **(Chap 2)**

DEPUE, R. A., & IACONO, W. G. (1989). Neurobehavioral aspects of affective disorders. *Annual Review of Psychology, 40,* 457–492. **(Chap 7)**

DEPUE, R. A., LUCIANA, M., ARBISI, P., COLLINS, P., & LEON, A. (IN PRESS). Dopamine and the structure of personality: Relation of agonist-induced dopamine activity to positive emotionality. *Journal of Personality and Social Psychology.* **(Chap 2)**

DEPUE, R. A., SLATER, J. F., WOLFSTETTER-KAUSCH, H., KLEIN, D., GOPLERUD, E., & FARR, D. (1981). A behavioral paradigm for identifying persons at risk for bipolar depressive disorder: A conceptual framework and five validation studies. *Journal of Abnormal Psychological Monographs, 90,* 381–437. **(Chap 7)**

DEPUE, R. A., & SPOONT, M. R. (1986). Conceptualizing a serotonin trait: A behavioral dimension of constraint. *Annals of the New York Academy of Sciences, 487,* 47–62. **(Chap 2)**

DEPUE, R. A., & ZALD, D. (1993). Biological and environmental processes in nonpsychotic psychopathology: A neurobehavioral system perspective. In C. Costello (Ed.), *Basic issues in psychopathology.* New York: Guilford Press. **(Chap 2)**

DEROGATIS, L. (1977). *SCL-90-R Manual.* Baltimore: Clinical Psychometrics Research Unit, Johns Hopkins University. **(Chap 3)**

DERSHEWITZ, R. A., & WILLIAMSON, J. W. (1977). Prevention of childhood household injuries: A controlled clinical trial. *American Journal of Public Health, 67,* 1148–1153. **(Chap 9)**

DEVINSKY, O., FELDMAN, E., BURROWES, K., & BROMFIELD, E. (1989). Autoscopic phenomena with seizures. *Archives of Neurology, 46*(10), 1080–1088. **(Chap 6)**

DILALLA, L. F., & GOTTESMAN, I. I. (1991). Biological and genetic contributors to violence—Widom's untold tale. *Psychological Bulletin, 109,* 125–129. **(Chap 13)**

DIMBERG, U., & ÖHMAN, A. (1983). The effects of directional facial cues on electrodermal conditioning to facial stimuli. *Psychophysiology, 20,* 160–167. **(Chap 5)**

DINARDO, P. A. (1991). *MacArthur reanalysis of generalized anxiety disorder.* Unpublished manuscript. **(Chap 5)**

DINARDO, P. A., & BARLOW, D. H. (1990). Syndrome and symptom comorbidity in the anxiety disorders. In J. D. Maser & C. R. Cloninger (Eds.), *Comorbidity of mood and anxiety disorders* (pp. 205–230). Washington, DC: American Psychiatric Press. **(Chap 7)**

DINARDO, P. A., BROWN, T. A., & BARLOW. D. H. (1994). *Anxiety disorders interview schedule for DSM-IV (ADIS-IV).* Albany, NY: Graywind Publications. **(Chap 3)**

DINARDO, P. A., MORAS, K., BARLOW, D. H., RAPEE, R. M., & BROWN, T. A. (1993). Reliability of DSM-III-R anxiety disorder categories: Using the Anxiety Disorders Interview Schedule-Revised (ADIS-R). *Archives of General Psychiatry, 50,* 251–256. **(Chap 3)**

DINARDO, P. A., O'BRIEN, G. T., BARLOW, D. H., WADDELL, M. T., & BLANCHARD, E. B. (1983). Reliability of DSM-III anxiety disorder categories using a new structured interview. *Archives of General Psychiatry, 40,* 1070–1074. **(Chap 3)**

DIOKNO, A. C., BROWN, M. B., & HERZOG, A. R. (1990). Sexual function in the elderly. *Archives of Internal Medicine, 150,* 197–200. **(Chap 11)**

DISHION, T. J., PATTERSON, G. R., & REID, J. R. (1988). Parent and peer factors associated with drug sampling in early adolescence: Implications for treatment. In E. R. Rahdert & J. Gabowski (Eds.), *Adolescent drug abuse: Analyses of treatment research* (NIDA Research Monograph No. 77, DHHS Publication No. ADM88-1523, pp. 69–93). Rockville, MD: National Institute on Drug Abuse. **(Chap 12)**

DIXON, J. C. (1963). Depersonalization phenomena in a sample population of college students. *British Journal of Psychiatry, 109,* 371–375. **(Chap 6)**

DOBSON, K. S. (1985). The relationship between anxiety and depression. *Clinical Psychology Review, 5,* 307–324. **(Chap 7)**

DODD, B., & LEAHY, J. (1989). Facial prejudice. *American Journal on Mental Retardation, 94,* 111. **(Chap 15)**

DOHRENWEND, B. P., & DOHRENWEND, B. S. (1981). Socioenvironmental factors, stress and psychopathology. *American Journal of Community Psychology, 9*(2), 128–164. **(Chap 7)**

DOHRENWEND, B. P., & EGRI, G. (1981). Recent stressful life events and episodes of schizophrenia. *Schizophrenia Bulletin, 7,* 12–23. **(Chap 14)**

DOHRENWEND, B. S., DOHRENWEND, B. P., DODSON, M., & SHROUT, P. E. (1984). Symptoms, hassles, social supports and life events: Problem of confounded measures. *Journal of Abnormal Psychology, 93,* 222–230. **(Chap 7)**

DONALDSON, K. (1976). *Insanity inside out.* New York: Crown. **(Chap 17)**

DOYNE, E. J., OSSIP-KLEIN, D. J., BOWMAN, E. D., OSBORN, K. M., MCDOUGALL-WILSON, I. B., & NEIMEYER, R. A. (1987). Running versus weight lifting in the treatment of depression. Special issue: Eating disorders. *Journal of Consulting and Clinical Psychology, 55*(5), 748–754. **(Chap 7)**

DREVETS, W. C., VIDEEN, T. O., MACLEOD, A. K., HALLER, J. W., & RAICHLE, M. E. (1992). PET images of blood flow changes during anxiety: Correction. *Science, 256,* 1696. **(Chap 5)**

DROTAR, D., & STURM, L. (1991). Psychosocial influences in the etiology, diagnosis, and prognosis of nonorganic failure to thrive. In H. E. Fitzgerald, B. M. Lester, & M. W. Yogman, *Theory and research in behavioral pediatrics.* New York: Plenum Press. **(Chap 2)**

DUBOVSKY, S. L. (1983). Psychiatry in Saudi Arabia. *American Journal of Psychiatry, 140,* 1455–1459. **(Chap 4)**

DULIT, R. A., MARIN, D. B., & FRANCES, A. J. (1993). Cluster B personality disorders. In D. L. Dunner (Ed.), *Current psychiatric therapy* (pp. 405–411). Philadelphia: W. B. Saunders. **(Chap 13)**

DUMAS, J., & WAHLER, R. G. (1983). Predictors of treatment outcome in parent training: Mother insularity and socioeconomic disadvantage. *Behavioral Assessment, 5,* 301–313. **(Chap 13)**

DUNNER, D. D., & FIEVE, R. (1974). Clinical factors in lithium carbonate prophylaxis failure. *Archives of General Psychiatry, 30,* 229–233. **(Chap 7)**

DURAND, V. M. (1990). *Severe behavior problems: A functional communication training approach.* New York: Guilford Press. **(Chap 15)**

DURAND, V. M. (1993). Functional communication training using assistive devices: Effects on challenging behavior and affect. *Augmentative and Alternative Communication, 9,* 168–176. **(Chap 15)**

DURAND, V. M., BLANCHARD, E. B., & MINDELL, J. A. (1988). Training in projective testing: A survey of clinical training directors and internship directors. *Professional Psychology: Research and Practice, 19,* 236–238. **(Chap 3)**

DURAND, V. M., & CARR, E. G. (1988). Autism. In V. B. VanHasselt, P. S. Strain, & M. Hersen (Eds.), *Handbook of developmental and physical disabilities* (pp. 195–214). Elmsford, NY: Pergamon Press. **(Chap 16)**

DURAND, V. M., & CARR, E. G. (1992). An analysis of maintenance following functional communication training. *Journal of Applied Behavior Analysis, 25,* 777–794. **(Chap 4)**

DURAND, V. M., & CRIMMINS, D. B. (1988). Identifying the variables maintaining self-injurious behavior. *Journal of Autism and Developmental Disorders, 18,* 99–117. **(Chap 3)**

DURAND, V. M., & MINDELL, J. A. (1990). Behavioral treatment of multiple childhood sleep disorders. *Behavior Modification, 14,* 37–49. **(Chap 10)**

DURAND, V. M., MINDELL, J., MAPSTONE, E., & GERNERT-DOTT, P. (IN PRESS). Treatment of multiple sleep disorders in children. In C. E. Schaefer (Ed.), *Clinical handbook of sleep disorders in children.* New York: Jason Aronson. **(Chap 10)**

DURHAM, M. L., & LA FOND, J. Q. (1985). The empirical consequences and policy implications of broadening the statutory criteria for civil commitment. *Yale Law and Policy Review, 3,* 395–446. **(Chap 17)**

DURHAM V. UNITED STATES. (1954). 214 F.2d, 862, 874–875 (D.C. Cir.). **(Chap 17)**

DURKHEIM, E. (1951). *Suicide: A study in sociology.* (J. A. Spaulding & G. Simpson, Trans.). New York: Free Press. **(Chap 7)**

DUSKY V. UNITED STATES. (1960), 362, U.S. 402, 4L. ed 2d 824, 80 S. Ct., 788. **(Chap 17)**

DWYER, E. (1992). Attendants and their world of work. In A. D. Gaines (Ed.), *Ethnopsychiatry: The cultural construction of professional and folk psychiatries* (pp. 291–305). Albany: State University of New York Press. **(Chap 4)**

DWYER, J. T., FELDMAN, J. J., SELTZER, C. C., & MAYER, J. (1969). Body image in adolescents: Attitudes toward weight and perception of appearance. *American Journal of Clinical Nutrition, 20,* 1045–1056. **(Chap 8)**

DYKENS, E., LECKMAN, J., PAUL, R., & WATSON, M. (1988). Cognitive, behavioral, and adaptive functioning in fragile X and nonfragile X retarded men. *Journal of Autism and Developmental Disorder, 18,* 41–52. **(Chap 15)**

EAKER, E. D., PINSKY, J., & CASTELLI, W. P. (1992). Myocardial infarction and coronary death among women: Psychosocial predictors from a 20-year follow-up of women in the Framingham study. *American Journal of Epidemiology, 135,* 854–864. **(Chap 9)**

EATON, W. W., DRYMAN, A., & WEISSMAN, M. M. (1991). Panic and phobia. In L. N. Robins & D. A. Regier (Eds.), *Psychiatric disorders in America: The epidemiologic catchment area study* (pp. 155–179). New York: Free Press. **(Chap 5)**

EATON, W. W., HAYWARD, C., & RAM, R. (1992). Schizophrenia and rheumatoid arthritis: A review. *Schizophrenia Research, 6,* 181–192. **(Chap 14)**

EBIGNO, P. (1982). Development of a culture-specific screening scale of somatic complaints indicating psychiatric disturbance. *Culture, Medicine, and Psychiatry, 6,* 29–43. **(Chap 4)**

EBIGNO, P. O. (1986). A cross sectional study of somatic complaints of Nigerian females using the Enugu Somatization Scale. *Culture, Medicine, and Psychiatry, 10,* 167–186. **(Chap 6)**

ECKMAN, T. A., WIRSHING, W. C., MARDER, S. R., LIBERMAN, R. P., JOHNSTON-CRONK, K., ZIMMERMANN, K., & MINTZ, J. (1992). Techniques for training schizophrenic patients in illness self-management: A controlled trial. *American Journal of Psychiatry, 149,* 1549–1555. **(Chap 14)**

EDWARDS, A. J. (1994). *When memory fails: Helping the Alzheimer's and dementia patient.* New York: Plenum Press. **(Chap 15)**

EGELAND, J. A., GERHARD, D. S., PAULS, D. L., SUSSEX, J. N., KIDD, K. K., ALLEN, C. R., HOSTELLER, A. M., & HOUSMAN, D. E. (1987). Bipolar affective disorders linked to DNA markers on chromosome 11. *Nature, 325*(6107), 783–787. **(Chap 7)**

EHLERS, A., & BREUER, P. (1992). Increased cardiac awareness in panic disorder. *Journal of Abnormal Psychology, 101*(3), 371–382. **(Chap 5)**

EHRHARDT, A. A., & MEYER-BAHLBURG, H. F. L. (1981). Effects of prenatal sex hormones on gender-related behavior. *Science, 211,* 1312–1318. **(Chap 11)**

EHRHARDT, A. A., MEYER-BAHLBURG, H. F. L., ROSEN, L. R., FELDMAN, J. F., VERIDIANO, N. P., ZIMMERMAN, I., & MCEWEN, B. S. (1985). Sexual orientation after prenatal exposure to exogenous estrogen. *Archives of Sexual Behavior, 14*(1), 57–77. **(Chap 11)**

EKSTRAND, M. L., & COATES, T. J. (1990). Maintenance of safer sexual behaviors and predictors of risky sex: The San Francisco men's health study. *American Journal of Public Health, 80,* 973–977. **(Chap 9)**

ELKIN, I., SHEA, M. T., WATKINS, J. T., IMBER, S. D., SOTSKY, S. M., COLLINS, J. F., GLASS, D. R., PILKONIS, P. A., LEBER, W. R., DOCHERTY, J. P., FIESTER, S. J., & PARLOFF, M. B. (1989). National Institute of Mental Health Treatment of Depression Collaborative Research Program: General effectiveness of treatments. *Archives of General Psychiatry, 46*(11), 971–982. **(Chap 7)**

ELLICOTT, A. G. (1988). *A prospective study of stressful life events and bipolar illness.* Unpublished doctoral dissertation, University of California, Los Angeles. **(Chap 7)**

ELLIS, A. (1962). *Reason and emotion in psychotherapy.* Secaucus, NJ: Prentice-Hall. **(Chap 2)**

ELLIS, H. (1906). *Studies in the psychology of sex* (7 vols.). New York: Random House. **(Chap 11)**

ELLIS, N. R. (1970). Memory processes in retardates and normals. In N. R. Ellis (Ed.), *International review of research in mental retardation* (Vol. 4, pp. 1–32). New York: Academic Press. **(Chap 15)**

EMERY, R. E. (1982). Interparental conflict and the children of discord and divorce. *Psychological Bulletin, 92,* 310–330. **(Chap 4)**

EMRICK, C. D., TONIGAN, J. S., MONTGOMERY, H., & LITTLE, L. (1993). Alcoholics Anonymous: What is currently known? In B. S. McCrady & W. R. Miler (Eds.), *Research on Alcoholics Anonymous: Opportunities and alternatives* (pp. 41–76). New Brunswick, NJ: Rutgers Center of Alcohol Studies. **(Chap 12)**

ENNIS, B., & LITWACK, T. (1974). Psychiatry and the presumption of expertise: Flipping coins in the courtroom. *California Law Review, 62,* 693–752. **(Chap 17)**

EPPRIGHT, T. D., KASHANI, J. H., ROBISON, B. D., & REID, J. C. (1993). Comorbidity of conduct disorder and personality disorders in an incarcerated juvenile population. *American Journal of Psychiatry, 150,* 1233–1236. **(Chap 13)**

ERIKSON, E. (1982). *The life cycle completed.* New York: Norton. **(Chap 2)**

ESCOBAR, J. I., BURNAM, A., KARNO, M., FORSYTHE, A., & GOLDING, J. M. (1987). Somatization in the community. *Archives of General Psychiatry, 44,* 713–718. **(Chap 6)**

ESCOBAR, J. I., & CANINO, G. (1989). Unexplained physical complaints: Psychopathology and epidemiological correlates. *British Journal of Psychiatry, 154,* 24–27. **(Chap 6)**

ESLINGER, P. J., & DAMASIO, A. R. (1985). Severe disturbance of higher cognition after bilateral frontal lobe ablation: Patient EVR. *Neurology, 35,* 1731–1741. **(Chap 2)**

ETH, S. (1990). Posttraumatic stress disorder in childhood. In M. Hersen & C. G. Last (Ed.), *Handbook of child and adult psychopathology: A longitudinal perspective.* Elmsford, NY: Pergamon Press. **(Chap 5)**

EVANS, D. A., FUNKENSTEIN, H. H., ALBERT, M. S., SCHERR, P. A., COOK, N. R., CHONN, M. J., HEBERT, L. E., HENNEKENS, C. H., & TAYLOR, J. O. (1989). Prevalence of Alzheimer's disease in a community population of older persons. *Journal of the American Medical Association, 262,* 2551–2556. **(Chap 15)**

EVANS, I. M. (1991). Testing and diagnosis: A review and evaluation. In L. H. Meyer, C. A. Peck, & L. Brown (Eds.), *Critical issues in the lives of people with severe disabilities* (pp. 25–44). Baltimore: Paul H. Brookes. **(Chap 15)**

EVANS, J. A., & HAMMERTON, J. L. (1985). Chromosomal anomalies. In A. M. Clarke, A. D. B. Clarke, & J. M. Berg (Eds.), *Mental deficiency: The changing outlook* (4th ed., pp. 213–266). New York: Free Press. **(Chap 15)**

EVANS, M. D., HOLLON, S. D., DERUBEIS, R. J., PINSECKI, J. M., GROVE, W. M., GARVEY, J. J., & TUASON, V. B. (1992). Differential relapse following cognitive therapy and pharmacotherapy for depression. *Archives of General Psychiatry, 49*(10), 802–808. **(Chap 7)**

EXNER, J. E. (1974). *The Rorschach: A comprehensive system* (Vol. 1). New York: John Wiley. **(Chap 3)**

EXNER, J. E. (1978). *The Rorschach: A comprehensive system* (Vol. 2). *Current research and advanced interpretation*. New York: John Wiley. **(Chap 3)**

EXNER, J. E. (1986). *The Rorschach: A comprehensive system* (Vol. 1, 2nd ed.). New York: John Wiley. **(Chap 3)**

EXNER, J. E., & CLARK, B. (1978). The Rorschach. In B. B. Wolman (Ed.), *Clinical diagnosis of mental disorders: A handbook* (pp. 147–178). New York: Plenum. **(Chap 3)**

EXNER, J. E., & WEINER, I. B. (1982). *The Rorschach: A comprehensive system* (Vol 3). *Assessment of children and adolescents*. New York: John Wiley. **(Chap 3)**

EYMAN, R. K., CALL, T. L., & WHITE, J. F. (1991). Life expectancy of persons with Down syndrome. *American Journal on Mental Retardation, 95,* 603–612. **(Chap 15)**

EYSENCK, H. J. (ED.). (1967). *The biological basis of personality*. Springfield, IL: Charles C. Thomas. **(Chap 5)**

EYSENCK, H. J., & EYSENCK, S. B. G. (1975). *Manual for the Eysenck Personality Questionnaire*. London: Hodder & Stoughton. **(Chap 13)**

EYSENCK, H. J., & EYSENCK, S. B. G. (1978). Psychopathy, personality, and genetics. In R. D. Hare & D. Schalling (Eds.), *Psychopathic behaviour: Approaches to research* (pp. 197–223). Chichester, England: John Wiley. **(Chap 13)**

EYSENCK, M. W. (1992). *Anxiety: The cognitive perspective*. Hove, United Kingdom: Lawrence Erlbaum. **(Chaps 2, 5)**

EZZEL, C. (1993). On borrowed time: Long-term survivors of HIV-l infection. *The Journal of NIH Research, 5,* 77–82. **(Chap 9)**

FACKELMANN, K. A. (1993). Marijuana and the brain: Scientists discover the brain's own THC. *Science, 143,* 88–94. **(Chap 12)**

FADEN, R. R. (1987). Health psychology and public health. In G. L. Stone, S. M. Weiss, J. D. Matarazzo, N. E. Miller, J. Rodin, C. D. Belar, M. J. Follick, & J. E. Singer (Eds.), *Health psychology: A discipline and a profession*. Chicago, IL: University of Chicago Press. **(Chap 9)**

FAHRNER, E. M. (1987). Sexual dysfunction in male alcohol addicts: Prevalence and treatment. *Archives of Sexual Behavior, 16*(3), 247–257. **(Chap 11)**

FAIRBURN, C. G. (1985). Cognitive-behavioral treatment for bulimia. In D. M. Garner & P. E. Garfinkel (Eds.), *Handbook of psychotherapy for anorexia nervosa and bulimia* (pp. 160–192). New York: Guilford Press. **(Chap 8)**

FAIRBURN, C. G., AGRAS, W. S., & WILSON, G. T. (1992). The research on the treatment of bulimia nervosa: Practical and theoretical implications. In G. H. Anderson & S. H. Kennedy (Eds.), *The biology of feast and famine: Relevance to eating disorders* (pp. 317–340). New York: Academic Press. **(Chap 8)**

FAIRBURN, C. G., & BEGLIN, S. J. (1990). Studies of the epidemiology of bulimia nervosa. *American Journal of Psychiatry, 147*(4), 401–409. **(Chap 8)**

FAIRBURN, C. G., BEGLIN, S. J., & DAVIES, B. (1992). *Eating habits and disorders amongst young adult women: An interview-based study*. Unpublished manuscript. **(Chap 8)**

FAIRBURN, C. G., & COOPER, P. J. (1984). Rumination in bulimia nervosa. *British Medical Journal, 288,* 826–827. **(Chap 8)**

FAIRBURN, C. G., & COOPER, Z. (in press). The schedule of the eating disorder examination. In C. G. Fairburn & G. T. Wilson (Eds.), *Binge eating: Nature, assessment, and treatment*. New York: Guilford Press. **(Chap 8)**

FAIRBURN, C. G., COOPER, Z., & COOPER, P. J. (1986). The clinical features and maintenance of bulimia nervosa. In K. D. Brownell & J. P. Foreyt (Eds.), *Handbook of eating disorders: Physiology, psychology, and treatment of obesity, anorexia, and bulimia* (pp. 389–404). New York: Basic Books. **(Chap 8)**

FAIRBURN, C. G., HAY, P. J., & WELCH, S. L. (in press). Binge eating and bulimia nervosa: Distribution and determinants. In C. G. Fairburn & G. T. Wilson (Eds.), *Binge eating: Nature, assessment, and treatment*. New York: Guilford Press. **(Chap 8)**

FAIRBURN, C. G., JONES, R., PEVELER, R. C., CARR, S., SOLOMON, R., O'CONNOR, M. E., & HOPE, R. A. (1991). Three psychological treatments for bulimia nervosa: A comparative trial. *Archives of General Psychiatry, 48,* 463–469. **(Chap 8)**

FAIRBURN, C. G., JONES, R., PEVELER, R. C., HOPE, R. A., & O'CONNOR, M. (1993). Psychotherapy and bulimia nervosa: The longer-term effects of interpersonal psychotherapy, behaviour therapy and cognitive behaviour therapy. *Archives of General Psychiatry, 50,* 419–428. **(Chap 8)**

FAIRBURN, C. G., MARCUS, M. D., & WILSON, G. T. (in press). Cognitive behaviour therapy for binge eating and bulimia nervosa: A comprehensive treatment manual. In C. G. Fairburn & G. T. Wilson (Eds.), *Binge eating: Nature, assessment, and treatment*. New York: Guilford Press. **(Chap 8)**

FAIRBURN, C. G., & WILSON, G. T. (in press). Binge eating: Definition and classification. In C. G. Fairburn & G. T. Wilson (Eds.), *Binge eating: Nature, assessment, and treatment*. New York: Guilford Press. **(Chap 8)**

FALCONER, D. S. (1965). The inheritance of liability to certain diseases, estimated from the incidence among relatives. *Annals of Human Genetics, 29,* 51–76. **(Chap 16)**

FALLON, A. (1990). Culture in the mirror: Sociocultural determinants of body image. In T. F. Cash & T. Pruzinsky (Eds.), *Body images: Development, deviance, and change* (pp. 80–109). New York: Guilford Press. **(Chap 6)**

FALLON, A. E., & ROZIN, P. (1985). Sex differences in perceptions of desirable body shape. *Journal of Abnormal Psychology, 94,* 102–105. **(Chap 8)**

FALLOON, I. R. H., BOYD, J. L., MCGILL, C. W., WILLIAMSON, M., RAZANI, J., MOSS, H. B., GILDERMAN, A. M., & SIMPSON, G. M. (1985). Family management in the prevention of morbidity of schizophrenia. *Archives of General Psychiatry, 42,* 887–896. **(Chap 14)**

FALLOON, I. R. H., BROOKER, C., & GRAHAM-HOLE, V. (1992). Psychosocial interventions for schizophrenia. *Behaviour Change, 9,* 238–245. **(Chap 14)**

FARDE, L., WIESEL, F. A., STONE-ELANDER, S., HALLDIN, C., NORDSTROM, A. L., HALL, H., & SEDVALL, G. (1990). D2 dopamine receptors in neuroleptic-naive patients: A positron emission tomography study with [11C] raclopride. *Archives of General Psychiatry, 47,* 213–219. **(Chap 14)**

FAVA, M., COPELAND, P. M., SCHWEIGER, U., & HERZOG, D. B. (1989). Neurochemical abnormalities of anorexia and bulimia nervosa. *American Journal of Psychiatry, 146,* 963–971. **(Chap 8)**

FAVA, M., & ROSENBAUM, J. F. (1991). Suicidality and fluoxetine: Is there a relationship? *Journal of Clinical Psychiatry, 52*(3), 108–111. **(Chap 7)**

FAWZY, F. I., COUSINS, N., FAWZY, N. W., KEMENY, M. E., ELASHOFF, R., & MORTON, D. (1990). A structured psychiatric intervention for cancer patients: I. Changes over time in methods of coping and affective disturbance. *Archives of General Psychiatry, 47,* 720–728. **(Chap 9)**

FAWZY, F. I., FAWZY, N. W., HYUN, C. S., ELASHOFF, R., GUTHRIE, D., FAHEY, J. L., & MORTON, D. L. (1993). Malignant melanoma: Effects of an early structured psychiatric intervention, coping, and affective state on recurrence and survival 6 years later. *Archives of General Psychiatry, 50,* 681–689. **(Chap 9)**

FAWZY, F. I., KEMENY, M. E., FAWZY, N. W., ELASHOFF, R., MORTON, D., COUSINS, N., & FAHEY, J. L. (1990). A structured psychiatric intervention for cancer patients: II. Changes over time in immunological measures. *Archives of General Psychiatry, 47,* 729–735. **(Chap 9)**

FEIN, G., & CALLAWAY, E. (1993). Electroencephalograms and event-related potentials in clinical psychiatry. In D. L. Dunner (Ed.), *Current psychiatric therapy* (pp. 18–26). Philadelphia: W. B. Saunders. **(Chap 3)**

FEINBERG, M., & CARROLL, B. J. (1984). Biological "markers" for endogenous depression: Effect of age, severity of illness, weight loss and polarity. *Archives of General Psychiatry, 41,* 1080–1085. **(Chap 7)**

FEINGOLD, B. F. (1975). *Why your child is hyperactive*. New York: Random House. **(Chap 16)**

FERBER, R. (1985). *Solve your child's sleep problems*. New York: Simon & Schuster. **(Chap 10)**

FERNANDEZ, F., LEVY, J. K., & MANSELL, P. W. A. (1989). Management of delirium in terminally ill AIDS patients. *International Journal of Psychiatry Medicine, 19,* 165–172. **(Chap 15)**

FERSTER, C. B. (1961). Positive reinforcement and behavioral deficits of autistic children. *Child Development, 32,* 437–456. **(Chap 16)**

FERSTER, C. B., & DEMYER, M. K. (1961). The development of performances in autistic children in an automatically controlled environment. *Journal of Chronic Diseases, 13,* 312–345. **(Chap 16)**

FERSTER, C. B., & SKINNER, B. F. (1957). *Schedules of reinforcement.* New York: Appleton-Century-Crofts. **(Chap 1)**

FEUERSTEIN, M., LABBE, E. E., & KUCZMIER-CZYK, A. R. (1986). *Health psychology: A psychobiological perspective.* New York: Plenum Press. **(Chap 9)**

FIELD, T., HEALY, B., GOLDSTEIN, S., PERRY, S., BENDELL, D., SCHANBERG, S., ZIMMERMAN, E. A., & KUHN, C. (1988). Infants of depressed mothers show "depressed" behavior even with nondepressed adults. *Child Development, 59*(6), 1569–1579. **(Chap 7)**

FILS-AIME, M. L. (1993). Sedative-hypnotic abuse. In D. L. Dunner (Ed.), *Current psychiatric therapy* (pp. 124–131). Philadelphia: W. B. Saunders. **(Chap 12)**

FIORE, T. A., BECKER, E. A., & NERO, R. C. (1993). Educational interventions for students with attention deficit disorder. *Exceptional Children, 60,* 163–173. **(Chap 16)**

FISCHER, M. (1971). Psychoses in the offspring of schizophrenic monozygotic twins and their normal co-twins. *British Journal of Psychiatry, 118,* 43–52. **(Chap 14)**

FISH, B. (1977). Neurobiological antecedents of schizophrenia in children: Evidence for an inherited, congenital, neurointegrative defect. *Archives of General Psychiatry, 34,* 1297–1313. **(Chap 14)**

FISH, B. (1987). Infant predictors of the longitudinal course of schizophrenic development. *Schizophrenia Bulletin, 13,* 395 410. **(Chap 14)**

FISHBAIN, D. A., & GOLDBERG, M. (1991). The misdiagnosis of conversion disorder in a psychiatric emergency service. *General Hospital Psychiatry, 13*(3), 177–181. **(Chap 6)**

FISHER, J. E., & CARSTENSEN, L. L. (1990). Behavior management of the dementias. *Clinical Psychology Review, 10,* 611–629. **(Chap 15)**

FISHER, M., & ZEAMAN, D. (1973). An attention-retention theory of retardate discrimination learning. In N. R. Ellis (Ed.), *International review of research in mental retardation* (Vol. 6, pp. 169–256). New York: Academic Press. **(Chap 15)**

FITTS, S. N., GIBSON, P., REDDING, C. A., & DEITER, P. J. (1989). Body dysmorphic disorder: Implications for its validity as a DSM-III-R clinical syndrome. *Psychological Reports, 64,* 655–658. **(Chap 6)**

FLEISCHMAN, M. J. (1981). A replication of Patterson's "Intervention for boys with conduct problems." *Journal of Consulting and Clinical Psychology, 49,* 342–351. **(Chap 13)**

FLEMING, J. E., BOYLE, M. H., & OFFORD, D. R. (1993). The outcome of adolescent depression in the Ontario child health study follow-up. *Journal of the American Academy of Child and Adolescent Psychiatry, 32*(1), 28–33. **(Chap 7)**

FLOR, H., & TURK, D. C. (1988). Chronic back pain and rheumatoid arthritis: Predicting pain and disability from cognitive variables. *Journal of Behavioral Medicine, 11,* 251–265. **(Chap 9)**

FLOR, H., & TURK, D. C. (1989). Psychophysiology of chronic pain: Do chronic pain patients exhibit symptom-specific psychophysiological responses? *Psychological Bulletin, 105,* 215–259. **(Chap 9)**

FLUOXETINE BULIMIA NERVOSA COLLABORATIVE STUDY GROUP. (1992). Fluoxetine in the treatment of bulimia nervosa: A multicenter, placebo-controlled, double-blind trial. *Archives of General Psychiatry, 49,* 139–147. **(Chap 8)**

FOA, E. B., & KOZAK, M. J. (in press). *Report on the DSM-IV field trial for obsessive-compulsive disorder.* In DSM-IV Source book. Washington, DC: American Psychiatric Association. **(Chap 5)**

FOLKS, D. G., FORD, C. U., & REGAN, W. M. (1984). Conversion symptoms in a general hospital. *Psychosomatics, 25*(4), 285–295. **(Chap 6)**

FOLSTEIN, S., & RUTTER, M. (1977). Genetic influences and infantile autism. *Nature, 265,* 726–728. **(Chap 16)**

FOLSTEIN, S. E., BRANDT, J., & FOLSTEIN, M. F. (1990). Huntington's disease. In J. L. Cummings (Ed.), *Subcortical dementia* (pp. 87–107). New York: Oxford University Press. **(Chap 15)**

FORD, C., & BEACH, F. (1951). *Patterns of sexual behavior.* New York: Harper & Row. **(Chap 11)**

FORD, C. V. (1985). Conversion disorders: An overview. *Psychosomatics, 26,* 371–383. **(Chap 6)**

FORD, D. E., & KAMEROW, D. B. (1989). Epidemiologic study of sleep disturbances and psychiatric disorder: An opportunity for prevention? *Journal of the American Medical Association, 262,* 1479–1404. **(Chap 10)**

FORD, M. R., & WIDIGER, T. A. (1989). Sex bias in the diagnosis of histrionic and antisocial personality disorders. *Journal of Consulting and Clinical Psychology, 57,* 301–305. **(Chap 13)**

FORDYCE, W. E. (1976). *Behavioral methods in chronic pain and illness.* St. Louis, MO: Mosby. **(Chap 9)**

FORDYCE, W. E. (1988). Pain and suffering: A reappraisal. *American Psychologist, 43*(4), 276–283. **(Chap 9)**

FOWLES, D. C. (1988). Psychophysiology and psychopathy: A motivational approach. *Psychophysiology, 25,* 373–391. **(Chap 13)**

FOWLES, D. C. (1992A). Motivational approach to anxiety disorders. In D. G. Forgays, T. Sosnowski, & K. Wrzesniewski (Eds.), *Anxiety: Recent developments in cognitive, psychophysiological, and health research* (pp. 181–192). Washington: Hemisphere Publishing Corporation. **(Chap 5)**

FOWLES, D. C. (1992B). Schizophrenia: Diathesis-stress revisited. *Annual Review of Psychology, 43,* 303–336. **(Chap 14)**

FOWLES, D. C. (IN PRESS). A motivational theory of psychopathology. In W. Spaulding (Ed.), *Nebraska symposium on motivation: Integrated views of motivation, cognition and emotion* (Vol. 41). Lincoln: University of Nebraska Press. **(Chaps 5, 6, 11)**

FOXX, R. M., & MARTIN, E. D. (1975). Treatment of scavenging behavior (coprophagy and pica) by overcorrection. *Behavior Research and Therapy, 13,* 153–162. **(Chap 8)**

FOY, D. W., RESNICK, H. S., SIPPRELLE, R. C., & CARROLL, E. M. (1987). Premilitary, military and postmilitary factors in the development of combat related posttraumatic stress disorder. *The Behavior Therapist, 10,* 3–9. **(Chap 5)**

FOY, D. W., SIPPRELLE, R. C., RUEGER, D. B., & CARROLL, E. M. (1984). Etiology of posttraumatic stress disorder in Vietnam veterans: Analysis of premilitary, military, and combat exposure influences. *Journal of Consulting and Clinical Psychology, 52,* 79–87. **(Chap 5)**

FRANCES, A., & BLUMENTHAL, S. J. (1989). Personality disorders and characteristics in youth suicide. In *Alcohol, drug abuse and mental health administration. Report of the Secretary's Task Force on youth suicide: Vol. 12, Risk factors for youth suicide* (DHHS Publication No. ADM89-1622, pp. 172–185). Washington, DC: U.S. Government Printing Office. **(Chap 7)**

FRANCES, A., & WIDIGER, T. A. (1986). Methodological issues in personality disorder diagnosis. In T. Millon & G. Klerman (Ed.), *Contemporary directions in psychopathology.* New York: Guilford Press. **(Chap 3)**

FRANCES, A., & WIDIGER, T. (1987). A critical review of four DSM-III personality disorders: Borderline, avoidant, dependent, and passive aggressive. In G. Tischler (Ed.), *Diagnosis and classification in psychiatry* (pp. 269–289). New York: Cambridge University Press. **(Chap 13)**

FRANCES, R., FRANKLIN, J., & FLAVIN, D. (1986). Suicide and alcoholism. *Annals of the New York Academy of Science, 287,* 316–326. **(Chap 7)**

FRANCIS, G., & HART, K. J. (1992). Depression and suicide. In V. B. Van Hasselt & D. J. Kolko (Eds.), *Inpatient behavior therapy for children and adolescents* (pp. 93–111). New York: Plenum Press. **(Chap 4)**

FRANCIS, G., LAST, C. G., & STRAUSS, C. C. (1987). Expression of separation anxiety disorder: The roles of age and gender. *Child Psychiatry and Human Development, 18,* 82–89. **(Chap 5)**

FRANCIS, J., MARTIN, D., & KAPOOR, W. N. (1990). A prospective study of delirium in hospitalized elderly. *Journal of the American Medical Association, 263,* 1097–1101. **(Chap 15)**

FRANK, E., ANDERSON, C., & RUBINSTEIN, D. (1978). Frequency of sexual dysfunction in "normal" couples. *New England Journal of Medicine, 299,* 111–115. **(Chap 11)**

FRANK, E., KUPFER, D. J., PEREL, J. M., CORNES, C., JARRETT, D. B., MALLINGER, A. G., THASE, M. E., MCEACHRAN, A. B., & GROCHOCINSKI, V. J. (1990). Three year outcomes for maintenance therapies in recurrent depression. *Archives of General Psychiatry, 47*(12), 1093–1099. **(Chap 7)**

FRANK, E., KUPFER, D. J., WAGNER, E. F., MCEACHRAN, A. B., & CORNES, C. (1991). Efficacy of interpersonal psychotherapy as a maintenance treatment for recurrent depression: Contributing factors. *Archives of General Psychiatry, 48,* 1053–1059. **(Chap 7)**

FRANK, G. (1992). The response of African-Americans to the Rorschach: A review of the research. *Journal of Personality Assessment, 59,* 317–325. **(Chap 3)**

FRANKLIN, D. (1990, November/December). Hooked–Not hooked: Why isn't everyone an addict? *Health,* pp. 39–52. **(Chap 12)**

FRASURE-SMITH, N. (1991). In-hospital symptoms of psychological stress as predictors of long-term outcome after acute myocardial infarction in men. *American Journal of Cardiology, 67,* 121–127. **(Chap 9)**

FRASURE-SMITH, N., LESPERANCE, F., & TALAJIC, M. (1993). Depression following myocardial infarction: Impact on 6-month survival. *Journal of the American Medical Association, 270*(15), 1819–1825. **(Chap 9)**

FRATIGLIONI, L., GRUT, M., FORSELL, Y., VIITANEN, M., GRAFSTROM, M., HOLMEN, K., ERICSSON, K., BACKMAN, L., AHLBOM, A., & WINBLAD, B. (1991). Prevalence of Alzheimer's disease and other dementias in an elderly urban population: Relationship with age, sex and education. *Neurology, 41,* 1886–1892. **(Chap 15)**

FREDRIKSON, M., & MATTHEWS, K. A. (1990). Cardiovascular responses to behavioral stress and hypertension: A meta-analytic review. *Annals of Behavioral Medicine, 12*(1), 30–39. **(Chap 9)**

FREEDMAN, M. (1990). Parkinson's disease. In J. L. Cummings (Ed.), *Subcortical dementia* (pp. 108–122). New York: Oxford University Press. **(Chap 15)**

FREEMAN, A., PRETZER, J., FLEMING, B., & SIMON, K. M. (1990). *Clinical applications of cognitive therapy.* New York: Plenum Press. **(Chap 13)**

FREEMAN, L., NIXON, P. G. F., SALLABANK, P., & REAVELEY, D. (1987). Psychological stress and silent myocardial ischemia. *American Heart Journal, 114,* 477–482. **(Chap 9)**

FRENCH-BELGIAN COLLABORATIVE GROUP. (1982). Ischemic heart disease and psychological patterns: Prevalence and incidence studies in Belgium and France. *Advances in Cardiology, 29,* 25–31. **(Chap 9)**

FREUD, A. (1946). *Ego and the mechanisms of defense.* New York: International Universities Press. **(Chap 1)**

FREUD, S. (1894). The neuro-psychoses of defence. In J. Strachey (Ed.), *The complete psychological works* (Vol. 3, pp. 45–62). London: Hogarth Press (1962). **(Chap 6)**

FREUD, S. (1938). *Psychopathology of everyday life.* Harmondsworth: Pelican Books. **(Chap 1)**

FREUD, S. (1957). Mourning and melancholia. In J. Strachey (Ed. and Trans.), *The standard edition of the complete psychological works of Sigmund Freud* (Vol. 14). London: Hogarth Press. (Original work published 1917) **(Chap 7)**

FREUD, S. (1962). *Three essays on the theory of sexuality* (J. Strachey, Trans.). New York: Avon. (Original work published 1905) **(Chap 11)**

FREUD, S. (1963). Introductory lectures on psycho-analysis: Lecture 25. Anxiety. In J. Strachey (Ed. and Trans.), *The standard edi-tion of the complete psychological works of Sigmund Freud* (Vol. 16). London: Hogarth Press. (Original work published 1917) **(Chap 5)**

FREUD, S. (1974). On coca. In R. Byck (Ed.), *Cocaine papers by Sigmund Freud* (pp. 49–73). New York: Stonehill. (Original work published 1885) **(Chap 12)**

FRICK, P. J., STRAUSS, C. C., LAHEY, B. B., & CHRIST, M. A. G. (1993). Behavior disorders of children. In P. B. Sutker & H. E. Adams (Eds.), *Comprehensive handbook of psychopathology* (pp. 765–789). New York: Plenum. **(Chap 16)**

FRIEDLAND, G. H., SALTZMAN, B., VILENE, J., FREEMAN, K., SCHRAGER, L. K., & KLEIN, R. S. (1991). Survival differences in patients with AIDS. *Journal of Acquired Immune Deficiency Syndromes, 4,* 144–153. **(Chap 9)**

FRIEDMAN, A. WEBB, J., & LEWAK, R. (1989). *Psychological assessment with the MMPI.* Hillsdale, NJ: Lawrence Erlbaum Associates. **(Chap 3)**

FRIEDMAN, J. M., & HOGAN, D. R. (1985). Sexual dysfunction: Low sexual desire. In D. H. Barlow (Ed.), *Clinical handbook of psychological disorders* (pp. 417–461). New York: Guilford Press. **(Chap 11)**

FRIEDMAN, M., & ROSENMAN, R. H. (1959). Association of specific overt behavior pattern with blood and cardiovascular findings. *Journal of the American Medical Association, 169,* 1286. **(Chap 9)**

FRIEDMAN, M., & ROSENMAN, R. H. (1974). *Type A behavior and your heart.* New York: Knopf. **(Chap 9)**

FRIEDMAN, M., THORESEN, C. E., GILL, J., POWELL, L. H., ULMER, D., THOMPSON, L., PRICE, V. A., RABIN, D. D., BREALL, W. S., DIXON, T., LEVY, R., & BOURG, E. (1984). Alteration of type A behavior and reduction in cardiac recurrences in post-myocardial infarction patients. *American Heart Journal, 108,* 237–248. **(Chap 9)**

FRIEDMAN, S., JONES, J. C., CHERNEN, L., & BARLOW, D. H. (1992). Suicidal ideation and suicide attempts among patients with panic disorder: A survey of two outpatient clinics. *American Journal of Psychiatry, 149*(5), 680–685. **(Chap 5)**

FROMM-REICHMANN, F. (1948). Notes on the development of treatment of schizophrenics by psychoanalytic psychotherapy. *Psychiatry, 11,* 263–273. **(Chap 14)**

FROST, R. O., SHER, K. J., & GEEN, T. (1986). Psychotherapy and personality characteristics of non-clinical compulsive checkers. *Behaviour Research and Therapy, 24,* 133–143. **(Chap 5)**

FUNDUDIS, T., KOLVIN, I., & GARSIDE, R. (1979). *Speech retarded and deaf children: Their psychological development.* London: Academic Press. **(Chap 16)**

FYER, A., LIEBOWITZ, M., GORMAN, J., COMPEAS, R., LEVIN, A., DAVIES, S., GOETZ, D., & KLEIN, D. (1987). Discontinuation of alprazolam treatment in panic patients. *American Journal of Psychiatry, 144,* 303–308. **(Chap 5)**

FYER, A. J., MANNUZZA, S., CHAPMAN, T. F., LIEBOWITZ, M. R., & KLEIN, D. F. (1993). A direct interview family study of social phobia. *Archives of General Psychiatry, 50,* 286–293. **(Chap 5)**

FYER, A. J., MANNUZZA, S., GALLOPS, M. S., MARTIN, L. Y., AARONSON, C., GORMAN, J. M., LIEBOWITZ, M. R., & KLEIN, D. F. (1990). Familial transmission of simple phobias and fears: A preliminary report. *Archives of General Psychiatry, 47,* 252–256. **(Chap 5)**

GAGNON, J. H. (1977). *Human sexualities.* New York: Scott, Foresman. **(Chap 11)**

GAGNON, J. H. (1990). The explicit and implicit use of the scripting perspective in sex research. *Annual Review of Sex Research, 1,* 1–43. **(Chap 11)**

GAGNON, M., & LADOUCEUR, R. (1992). Behavioral treatment of child stutterers: Replication and extension. *Behavior Therapy, 23,* 113–129. **(Chap 16)**

GAJDUSEK, D. C. (1977). Unconventional viruses and the origin and disappearance of Kuru. *Science, 197,* 943. **(Chap 15)**

GALLANT, S. J., & HAMILTON, J. A. (1988). On a premenstrual psychiatric diagnosis: What's in a name? *Professional Psychology: Research and Practice, 19,* 271–278. **(Chap 3)**

GARB, H. N. (1992). The *trained* psychologist as expert witness. *Clinical Psychology Review, 12,* 451–467. **(Chap 17)**

GARBER, J., WEISS, B., & SHANLEY, N. (1993). Cognitions, depressive symptoms and development in adolescents. *Journal of Abnormal Psychology, 102*(1), 47–57. **(Chap 7)**

GARCIA, J., MCGOWAN, B. K., & GREEN, K. F. (1972). Biological constraints on conditioning. In A. H. Black & W. F. Prokasy (Eds.), *Classical conditioning II: Current research and theory.* New York: Appleton-Century-Crofts. **(Chap 2)**

GARDNER, D. L., & COWDRY, R. W. (1986). Alprazolam-induced dyscontrol in borderline personality disorder. *American Journal of Psychiatry, 143,* 519–522. **(Chap 13)**

GARFINKEL, P. E. (in press). Evidence in support of attitudes to shape and weight as a diagnostic criterion of bulimia nervosa. *International Journal of Eating Disorders.* **(Chap 8)**

GARFINKEL, P. E., & GARNER, D. M. (1982). *Anorexia nervosa: A multidimensional perspective.* New York: Brunner/Mazel. **(Chap 8)**

GARFINKEL, P. E., MOLDOFSKY, H., & GARNER, D. M. (1979). The heterogeneity of anorexia nervosa: Bulimia as a distinct subgroup. *Archives of General Psychiatry, 37,* 1036–1040. **(Chap 8)**

GARLAND, A. F., & ZIGLER, E. (1993). Adolescent suicide prevention: Current research and social policy implications. *American Psychologist, 48*(2), 169–182. **(Chap 7)**

GARMEZY, N., & RUTTER, M. (Eds.). (1983). *Stress, coping and development in children.* New York: McGraw-Hill. **(Chap 2)**

GARNER, D. M., & FAIRBURN, C. G. (1988). Relationship between anorexia nervosa and bulimia nervosa: Diagnostic implications. In D. M. Garner & P. E. Garfinkel (Eds.), *Diagnostic issues in anorexia nervosa and bulimia nervosa.* New York: Brunner/Mazel. **(Chap 8)**

GARNER, D. M., & GARFINKEL, P. E. (Eds.) (1985). *Handbook of psychotherapy for anorexia nervosa and bulimia.* New York: Guilford Press. **(Chap 8)**

GARNER, D. M., GARFINKEL, P. E., & O'SHAUGHNESSY, M. (1985). The validity of the distinction between bulimics with and without anorexia nervosa. *American Journal of Psychiatry, 142,* 581–587. **(Chap 8)**

GARNER, D. M., GARFINKEL, P. E., ROCKERT, W., & OLMSTED, M. P. (1987). A prospective study of eating disturbances in the ballet. Ninth World Congress of the International College of Psychosomatic Medicine, Sydney, Australia. *Psychotherapy and Psychosomatics, 48,* 170–175. **(Chap 8)**

GARNER, D. M., GARFINKEL, P. E., SCHWARTZ, D., & THOMPSON, M. (1980). Cultural expectation of thinness in women. *Psychological Reports, 47,* 483–491. **(Chap 8)**

GARVEY, M., HOLLON, S. D., DERUBEIS, R. J., & EVANS, M. D. (1990A). Does 24-h urinary MHPG predict treatment response to antidepressants? I. A review. *Journal of Affective Disorders, 20*(3), 173–179. **(Chap 7)**

GARVEY, M., HOLLON, S. D., DERUBEIS, R. J., & EVANS, M. D. (1990B). Does 24-h MHPG predict treatment response to antidepressants? II. Association between imipramine response and low MHPG. *Journal of Affective Disorders, 20*(3), 181–184. **(Chap 7)**

GATZ, M., & SMYER, M. A. (1992). The mental health system and older adults in the 1990s. *American Psychologist, 47*(6), 741–751. **(Chap 2)**

GAWIN, F. H. (1991). Cocaine addiction: Psychology and neurophysiology. *Science, 251,* 1580–1586. **(Chap 12)**

GAWIN, F. H., & KLEBER, H. D. (1992). Evolving conceptualizations of cocaine dependence. In T. R. Kosten & H. D. Kleber (Eds.), *Clinician's guide to cocaine addiction: Theory, research, and treatment* (pp. 33–52). New York: Guilford Press. **(Chap 12)**

GAWIN, F. H., KLEBER, H. D., BYCK, R., ROUNSAVILLE, B. J., KOSTEN, T. R., JATLOW, P. I., & MORGAN, C. (1989). Desipramine facilitation of initial cocaine abstinence. *Archives of General Psychiatry, 46,* 117–121. **(Chap 12)**

GAZIANO, J. M., BURING, J. E., BRESLOW, J. L., GOLDHABER, S. Z., ROSNER, B., VANDENBURGH, M., WILLETT, W., & HENNEKENS, C. H. (1993). Moderate alcohol intake, increased levels of high-density lipoprotein and its subfractions, and decreased risk of myocardial infarction. *New England Journal of Medicine, 329,* 1829–1834. **(Chap 12)**

GEER, J. H., & FUHR, R. (1976). Cognitive factors in sexual arousal: The role of distraction. *Journal of Consulting and Clinical Psychology, 44,* 238–243. **(Chap 11)**

GEER, J. H., MOROKOFF, P., & GREENWOOD, P. (1974). Sexual arousal in women: The development of a measurement device for vaginal blood volume. *Archives of Sexual Behavior, 3,* 559–564. **(Chap 11)**

GELLER, B., COOPER, T. B., GRAHAM, D. L., FETAER, H. M., MARSTELLER, F. A., & WELLS, J. M. (1992). Pharmacokinetically designed double blind placebo controlled study of nortriptyline in 6–12 year olds with major depressive disorder: Outcome: Nortriptyline and hydroxy-nortriptyline plasma levels; EKG, BP and side effect measurements. *Journal of the American Academy of Child and Adolescent Psychiatry, 31,* 33–44. **(Chap 7)**

GEORGE, L. K. (1984). *The burden of caregiving: Center reports of advances in research* (Vol. 8). Durham, NC: Duke University Center for the Study of Aging and Human Development. **(Chap 15)**

GEORGE, L. K., LANDOMAN, R., BLAZER, D. G., & ANTHONY, J. C. (1991). Cognitive impairment. In L. N. Robins & D. A. Regier (Eds.), *Psychiatric disorders in America* (pp. 291–327). New York: Free Press. **(Chap 15)**

GERSHON, E. S. (1990). Genetics. In F. K. Goodwin & K. R. Jamison (Eds.), *Manic-depressive illness* (pp. 373–401). New York: Oxford University Press. **(Chap 7)**

GIBB, W. R. G. (1989). Dementia and Parkinson's disease. *British Journal of Psychiatry, 154,* 596–614. **(Chap 15)**

GIBBONS, J. L. (1964). Cortisol secretion rates in depressive illness. *Archives of General Psychiatry, 10,* 572–575. **(Chap 7)**

GIL, K., WILLIAMS, D., KEEFE, F., & BECKHAM, J. (1990). The relationship of negative thoughts to pain and psychological distress. *Behavior Therapy, 21,* 349–362. **(Chap 9)**

GILBERT, H. W., & GINGELL, J. C. (1991). The results of an intracorporeal papaverine clinic. *Sexual and Marital Therapy, 6*(1), 49–56. **(Chap 11)**

GILBERT, R. E. (1993). Travails of the chief: Killer stress plagues the White House. *The Sciences,* 9–12. **(Chap 7)**

GILES, D. E., & BUYSSE, D. J. (1993). Parasomnias. In D. L. Dunner (Ed.), *Current psychiatric therapy* (pp. 361–372). Philadelphia: W. B. Saunders. **(Chap 10)**

GILLBERG, C. (1984). Infantile autism and other childhood psychoses in a Swedish urban region: Epidemiological aspects. *Journal of Child Psychology and Psychiatry, 25,* 35–43. **(Chap 16)**

GILLIGAN, S. G., & BOWER, G. H. (1984). Cognitive consequences of emotional arousal. In C. E. Izard, J. Kagan, & R. B. Zajonc (Eds.), *Emotions, cognition, and behavior.* New York: Cambridge University Press. **(Chap 2)**

GILLIN, J. C. (1993). Clinical sleep-wake disorders in psychiatric practice: Dyssomnias. In D. L. Dunner (Ed.), *Current psychiatric therapy* (pp. 373–380). Philadelphia: W. B. Saunders. **(Chap 10)**

GISLASON, I. L. (1988). Eating disorders in childhood (ages 4 through 11 years). In B. J. Blinder, B. F. Chaitin, & R. S. Goldstein (Eds.), *The eating disorders: Medical and psychological bases of diagnosis and treatment* (pp. 285–293). New York: PMA. **(Chap 8)**

GLADSTONE, M., BEST, C. T., & DAVIDSON, R. J. (1989). Anomalous bimanual coordination among dyslexic boys. *Developmental Psychology, 25,* 236–246. **(Chap 2)**

GLADUE, B. A., GREEN, R., & HELLMAN, R. E. (1984). Neuroendocrine response to estrogen and sexual orientation. *Science, 225,* 1496–1499. **(Chap 11)**

GLASER, R., KENNEDY, S., LAFUSE, W. P., BONNEAU, R. H., SPEICHER, C. E., HILLHOUSE, J., & KIECOLT-GLASER, J. K. (1990). Psychological stress-induced modulation of 1L–2 receptor gene expression and 1L–2 production in peripheral blood leukocytes. *Archives of General Psychiatry, 47,* 707–712. **(Chap 9)**

GLASER, R., KIECOLT-GLASER, J. K., SPEICHER, C. E., & HOLLIDAY, J. E. (1985). Stress, loneliness, and changes in herpes virus latency. *Journal of Behavioral Medicine, 8,* 249–260. **(Chap 9)**

GLASER, R., RICE, J., SHERIDAN, J., FERTEL, R., STOUT, J., SPEICHER, C., PINSKY, D., KOTAR, M., POST, A., BECK, M., & KIECOLT-GLASER, J. K. (1987). Stress-related immune suppression: Health implications. *Brain, Behavior, and Immunity, 1,* 7–20. **(Chap 9)**

GLASSMAN, A. H., & PLATMAN, S. R. (1969). Potentiation of a monamine oxidase inhibitor by tryptophan. *Journal of Psychiatric Research, 7,* 83–88. **(Chap 7)**

GLASSMAN, A. H., & ROOSE, S. P. (1981). Delusional depression: A distinct clinical entity? *Archives of General Psychiatry, 138,* 424–427. **(Chap 7)**

GLATT, A. E., ZINNER, S. H., & MCCORMACK, W. M. (1990). The prevalence of dyspareunia. *Obstetrics and Gynecology, 75,* 433–436. **(Chap 11)**

GODDARD, P., & CARSTENSEN, L. L. (1986). Behavioral treatment of chronic depression in an elderly nursing home resident. *Clinical Gerontologist, 4,* 13–20. **(Chap 7)**

GOEDDE, H. W., & AGARWAL, D. P. (1987). Polymorphism of aldehyde dehydrogenase and alcohol sensitivity. *Enzyme, 37,* 29–44. **(Chap 12)**

GOLD, J., ENDICOTT, J., PARRY, B., SEVERINO, S., STOTLAND, N., & FRANK, E. (in press). DSM-IV literature review: Late luteal phase dysphoric disorder. **(Chap 3)**

GOLD, P. W., GOODWIN, F. K., & CHROUSOS, G. P. (1988). Clinical and biochemical manifestations of depression: Relation to the neurobiology of stress. *New England Journal of Medicine, 319,* 348–353. **(Chap 7)**

GOLDBERG, L. (1993). The structure of phenotypic personality traits. *American Psychologist, 48,* 26–34. **(Chap 13)**

GOLDBERG, S. C., SCHULTZ, C., RESNICK, R. J., HAMER, R. M., & SCHULTZ, P. M. (1987). Differential prediction of response to thiothixene and placebo in borderline and schizotypal personality disorders. *Psychopharmacology Bulletin, 23,* 342–346. **(Chap 13)**

GOLDEN, C. J., HAMMEKE, T. A., & PURISCH, A. D. (1980). *The Luria-Nebraska Battery manual.* Palo Alto, CA: Western Psychological Services. **(Chap 3)**

GOLDFARB, W. (1963). Self-awareness in schizophrenic children. *Archives of General Psychiatry, 8,* 63–76. **(Chap 16)**

GOLDMAN, M. S., & RATHER, B. C. (1993). Substance use disorders: Cognitive models and architecture. In K. S. Dobson & P. C. Kendall (Eds.), *Psychopathology and cognition* (pp. 245–292). New York: Academic Press. **(Chap 12)**

GOLDMAN, S. J., D'ANGELO, E. J., DEMASO, D. R., & MEZZACAPPA, E. (1992). Physical and sexual abuse histories among children with borderline personality disorder. *American Journal of Psychiatry, 149,* 1723–1726. **(Chap 13)**

GOLDSTEIN, A. (1994). *Addiction: From biology to drug policy.* New York: W. H. Freeman. **(Chap 12)**

GOLDSTEIN, G., & SHELLY, C. (1984). Discriminative validity of various intelligence and neuropsychological tests. *Journal of Consulting and Clinical Psychology, 52,* 383–389. **(Chap 3)**

GOLEMAN, D. (1989, OCTOBER 31). Dangerous delusions: When fans are a threat. *New York Times*, pp. C1, C16. **(Chap 14)**

GOOD, B. J., & KLEINMAN, A. M. (1985). Culture and anxiety: Cross-cultural evidence for the patterning of anxiety disorders. In A. H. Tuma & J. D. Maser (Eds.), *Anxiety and the anxiety disorders*. Hillsdale, NJ: Lawrence Erlbaum. **(Chaps 2, 9)**

GOODE, E. (1993). *Drugs in American society* (4th ed.). New York: McGraw-Hill. **(Chap 12)**

GOODWIN, D. S. (1979). Alcoholism and heredity. *Archives of General Psychiatry, 36,* 57–61. **(Chap 12)**

GOODWIN, D. W., & GUZE, S. B. (1984). *Psychiatric diagnosis* (3rd ed). New York: Oxford University Press. **(Chap 6)**

GOODWIN, F. K., & JAMISON, K. R. (1990). *Manic depressive illness*. New York: Oxford University Press. **(Chap 7)**

GOODWIN, J. S., HUNT, W. C., KEY, C. R., & SAMET, J. M. (1987). The effect of marital status on stage, treatment, and survival of cancer patients. *Journal of the American Medical Association, 258,* 3125–3130. **(Chap 9)**

GORDIS, E. (1991). *Alcohol research: Promise for the decade*. Rockville, MD: National Institute of Alcohol Abuse and Alcoholism. **(Chap 12)**

GORENSTEIN, E. E., & NEWMAN, J. P. (1980). Disinhibitory psychopathology: A new perspective and a model for research. *Psychological Review, 87,* 301–315. **(Chap 6)**

GORMAN, J. M., GOETZ, R. R., DILLON, D., LIEBOWITZ, M. R. ET AL. (1990). Sodium d-lactate infusion in panic disorder patients. *Neuropsychopharmacology, 3,* 181–189. **(Chap 5)**

GORMAN, J. M., LIEBOWITZ, M. R., FYER, A. J., & STEIN, J. A. (1989, February). Neuroanatomical hypothesis for panic disorder. *American Journal of Psychiatry, 146,* 148–161. **(Chap 5)**

GOTLIB, I. H. (1984). Depression and general psychopathology in university students. *Journal of Abnormal Psychology, 93,* 19–30. **(Chap 7)**

GOTLIB, I. H., & CANE, P. B. (1989). Self-report assessment of depression and anxiety. In P. C. Kendall & D. Watson (Eds.), *Anxiety and depression: Distinctive and overlapping features* (pp. 131–169). San Diego, CA: Academic Press. **(Chap 7)**

GOTLIB, I. H., WHIFFEN, V. E., WALLACE, P. M., & MOUNT, J. H. (1991). Prospective investigation of postpartum depression: Factors involved in onset and recovery. *Journal of Abnormal Psychology, 100*(2), 122–132. **(Chap 7)**

GOTTESMAN, I. I. (1991). *Schizophrenia genesis: The origins of madness*. New York: W. H. Freeman. **(Chaps 2, 4, 14)**

GOTTESMAN, I. I., & BERTELSEN, A. (1989). Dual mating studies in psychiatry— Offspring of inpatients with examples from reactive (psychogenic) psychoses. *International Review of Psychiatry, 1,* 287–296. **(Chap 14)**

GOTTESMAN, I. I., MCGUFFIN, P., & FARMER, A. E. (1987). Clinical genetics as clues to the "real" genetics of schizophrenia: A decade of modest gains while playing for time. *Schizophrenia Bulletin, 13,* 23–47. **(Chap 14)**

GOTTESMAN, I. I., & SHIELDS, J. A. (1982). *Schizophrenia: The epigenetic puzzle*. New York: Cambridge University Press. **(Chap 14)**

GOULD, M. S. (1990). Suicide clusters and media exposure. In S. J. Blumenthal & D. J. Kupfer (Eds.), *Suicide over the life cycle: Risk factors, assessment and treatment of suicidal patients*. Washington, DC: American Psychiatric Press. **(Chap 7)**

GRAEFF, F. G. (1987). The anti-aversive action of drugs. In T. Thompson, P. B. Dews, & J. Barrett (Eds.), *Advances in behavioral pharmacology* (Vol. 6). Hillsdale, NJ: Lawrence Erlbaum. **(Chap 5)**

GRAF, P., SQUIRE, L. R., & MANDLER, G. (1984). The information that amnesic patients do not forget. *Journal of Experimental Psychology: Learning, Memory, and Cognition, 10,* 164–178. **(Chap 2)**

GRAHAM, J. R. (1990). *MMPI-2: Assessing personality and psychopathology*. New York: Oxford University Press. **(Chap 3)**

GRAHAM, J. R., TIMBROOK, R. E., BENPORATH, Y. S., & BUTCHER, J. N. (1991). Code-type congruence between MMPI and MMPI-2: Separating fact from artifact. *Journal of Personality Assessment, 57,* 264–277. **(Chap 3)**

GRANT, I., PATTERSON, T. L., & YAGER, J. (1988). Social supports in relation to physical health and symptoms of depression in the elderly. *American Journal of Psychiatry, 145*(10), 1254–1258. **(Chaps 2, 7, 9)**

GRAY, J. A. (1982). *The neuropsychology of anxiety*. New York: Oxford University Press. **(Chaps 2, 5, 6)**

GRAY, J. A. (1985). Issues in the neuropsychology of anxiety. In A. H. Tuma & J. D. Maser (Eds.), *Anxiety and the anxiety disorders* (pp. 5–25). Hillside, NJ: Lawrence Erlbaum. **(Chaps 2, 5, 6, 7)**

GRAY, J. A. (1987). *The psychology of fear and stress* (2nd ed.). New York: Cambridge University Press. **(Chaps 12, 13)**

GRAY, J. A. (1991). Fear, panic, and anxiety: What's in a name? *Psychological Inquiry, 2*(1), 72–96. **(Chap 5)**

GRAY, J. A. (in press). Neural systems, emotion and personality. In J. Madden, S. Matthysse, & J. Barchas (Eds.), *Adaptation, learning and affect*. New York: Raven. **(Chap 5)**

GRAY, J. A., & BUFFERY, A. W. H. (1971). Sex differences in emotional and cognitive behavior in mammals including man: Adaptive and neural bases. *Acta Psychologica, 35,* 89–111. **(Chap 6)**

GREEN, B. L., GRACE, M. C., LINDY, J. D., TITCHENER, J. L., & LINDY, J. G. (1983). Levels of functional impairment following a civilian disaster: The Beverly Hills Supper Club fire. *Journal of Consulting and Clinical Psychology, 51,* 573–580. **(Chap 5)**

GREEN, R. (1987). *The "sissy boy syndrome" and the development of homosexuality*. New Haven: Yale University Press. **(Chap 11)**

GREEN, R., & FLEMING, D. T. (1990). Transsexual surgery follow-up: Status in the 1990s. *Annual Review of Sex Research, 1,* 163–174. **(Chap 11)**

GREEN, R., & MONEY, J. (1969). *Transsexualism and sex reassignment*. Baltimore: Johns Hopkins Press. **(Chap 11)**

GREENBERG, M. S., & BECK, A. T. (1989). Depression versus anxiety: A test of the content specificity. *Journal of Abnormal Psychology, 98*(1), 9–13. **(Chap 7)**

GREENBLATT, D. J., & SHADER, R. I. (1978). Pharmacotherapy of anxiety with benzodiazepines and beta-adrenergic blockers. In M. Lipton, A. DiMascio, & F. Killiam (Eds.), *Psychopharmacology: A generation of progress*. New York: Raven. **(Chap 5)**

GREENOUGH, W. T., WITHERS, G. S., & WALLACE, C. S. (1990). Morphological changes in the nervous system arising from behavioral experience: What is the evidence that they are involved in learning and memory? In L. R. Squire & E. Lindenlaub (Eds.), *The biology of memory, Symposia Medica Hoescht 23* (pp. 159–183). Stuttgart/New York: Schattauer Verlag. **(Chap 2)**

GREGOIRE, A. (1992). New treatments for erectile impotence. *British Journal of Psychiatry, 160,* 315–326. **(Chap 11)**

GREIST, J. H. (1990). Treatment of obsessive compulsive disorder: Psychotherapies, drugs, and other somatic treatments. *Journal of Clinical Psychiatry, 51,* 44–50. **(Chap 5)**

GRIFFITH, E. E. H., ENGLISH, T., & MAYFIELD, U. (1980). Possession, prayer and testimony: Therapeutic aspects of the Wednesday night meeting in a black church. *Psychiatry, 43*(5), 120–128. **(Chap 6)**

GRINSPOON, L., & BAKALAR, J. B. (1980). Drug dependence: Non-narcotic agents. In H. I. Kaplan, A. M. Freedman, & B. J. Sadock (Eds.), *Comprehensive textbook of psychiatry* (3rd ed., pp. 1614–1629). Baltimore: Williams and Wilkins. **(Chap 12)**

GRISSO, T., & APPELBAUM, P. S. (1992). Is it unethical to offer predictions of future violence? *Law and Human Behavior, 16,* 621–633. **(Chap 17)**

GRODEN, G., GRODEN, J., DONDEY, M., ZANE, T., PUESCHEL, S. M., & VELICEUR, W. (1987). Effects of fenfluramine on the behavior of autistic individuals. *Research in Developmental Disabilities, 8,* 203–211. **(Chap 16)**

GROSS, J., & ROSEN, J. C. (1988). Bulimia in adolescents: Prevalence and psychosocial correlates. *International Journal of Eating Disorders, 7,* 51–61. **(Chap 8)**

GROSS, R. T., & BORKOVEC, T. D. (1982). Effects of cognitive intrusion manipulation on sleep-onset latency of good sleepers. *Behavior Therapy, 13,* 112–116. **(Chap 10)**

GROSZ, H. J., & ZIMMERMAN, J. (1965). Experimental analysis of hysterical blindness: A follow-up report and new experimental data. *Archives of General Psychiatry, 13,* 255–260. **(Chap 6)**

GROSZ, H. J., & ZIMMERMAN, J. (1970). A second detailed case study of functional blindness: Further demonstration of the contribution of objective psychological laboratory data. *Behavior Therapy, 1,* 115–123. **(Chap 6)**

GROVE, W. M., CLEMENTZ, B. A., IACONO, W. G., & KATSANIS, J. (1992). Smooth pursuit ocular motor dysfunction in schizophrenia: Evidence for a major gene. *American Journal of Psychiatry, 149,* 1362–1368. **(Chap 14)**

GROVE, W. M., & TELLEGEN, A. (1991). Problems in the classification of personality disorders. *Journal of Personality Disorders, 5,* 31–42. **(Chap 13)**

GRUDER, C. L., MERMELSTEIN, R. J., KIRKENDOL, S., HEDEKER, D., WONG, S. C., SCHRECKENGOST, J., WARNECKE, R. B., BURZETTE, R., & MILLER, T. Q. (1993). Effects of social support and relapse prevention training as adjuncts to a televised smoking-cessation intervention. *Journal of Consulting and Clinical Psychology, 61,* 113–120. **(Chap 12)**

GUILLEMINAULT, C. (1989). Clinical features and evaluation of obstructive sleep apnea. In M. H. Kryger, T. Roth, & W. C. Dement (Eds.), *Principles and practice of sleep medicine* (pp. 552–558). Philadelphia: W. B. Saunders. **(Chap 10)**

GUILLEMINAULT, C., & DEMENT, W. C. (1988). Sleep apnea syndromes and related sleep disorders. In R. L. Williams, I. Karacan, & C. A. Moore (Eds.), *Sleep disorders: Diagnosis and treatment* (pp. 47–71). New York: John Wiley. **(Chap 10)**

GUILLEMINAULT, C., & MONDINI, S. (1986). Mononucleosis and chronic daytime sleepiness. *Archives of Internal Medicine, 146,* 1333–1335. **(Chap 10)**

GUNDERSON, J. G. (1992). Diagnostic controversies. In A. Tasman & M. B. Riba (Eds.), *Review of psychiatry* (Vol. 11, pp. 9–24). Washington, DC: American Psychiatric Press. **(Chap 13)**

GUNDERSON, J. G., RONNINGSTAM, E., & SMITH, L. E. (1991). Narcissistic personality disorder: A review of data on DSM-III-R descriptions. *Journal of Personality Disorders, 5,* 167–177. **(Chap 13)**

GUNDERSON, J. G., & SABO, A. N. (1993). The phenomenological and conceptual interface between borderline personality disorder and PTSD. *American Journal of Psychiatry, 150,* 19–27. **(Chap 13)**

GUR, R. E., & PEARLSON, G. D. (1993). Neuroimaging in schizophrenia research. *Schizophrenia Bulletin, 19,* 337–353. **(Chap 14)**

GUSELLA, J. F., WEXLER, N. S., CONNEALLY, P. M., NAYLOR, S. L., ANDERSON, M. A., TANZI, R. E., WATKINS, P. C., OTTINA, K., WALLACE, M. R., SAKAGUCHI, A. Y., YOUNG, A. B., SHOULSON, I., BONILLA, E., & MARTIN, J. B. (1983). A polymorphic DNA marker genetically linked to Huntington's disease. *Nature, 306,* 234–239. **(Chap 15)**

GUTELIUS, M. F., MILLICIN, F. K., & LAYMAN, E. H. (1963). Treatment of pica with a vitamin and mineral supplement. *American Journal of Clinical Nutrition, 12,* 388–393. **(Chap 8)**

GUTTMACHER, M. S., & WEIHOFEN, H. (1952). *Psychiatry and the law.* New York: Norton. **(Chap 17)**

GUYTON, A. (1981). *Textbook of medical physiology.* Philadelphia: W. B. Saunders. **(Chap 9)**

GUZE, S. B. (1976). *Criminality and psychiatric disorders.* New York: Oxford University Press. **(Chap 13)**

GUZE, S. B., CLONINGER, C. R., MARTIN, R. L., & CLAYTON, P. J. (1986). A follow-up and family study of Briquet's syndrome. *British Journal of Psychiatry, 149,* 17–23. **(Chap 6)**

HAAGA, D. A. F., DYCK, M. J., & ERNST, D. (1991). Empirical status of cognitive theory of depression. *Psychological Bulletin, 110*(2), 215–236. **(Chap 7)**

HAAS, A. P., & HENDIN, H. (1987). The meaning of chronic marijuana use among adults: A psychosocial perspective. *Journal of Drug Issues, 17,* 333–348. **(Chap 12)**

HABER, S. N., & BARCHAS, P. R. (1983). The regulatory effect of social rank on behavior after amphetamine administration. In P. R. Barchas (Ed.), *Social hierarchies: Essays toward a sociophysiological perspective* (pp. 119–132). Westport, CT: Greenwood Press. **(Chap 2)**

HACKETT, T. P., & CASSEM, N. H. (1973). Psychological adaptation to convalescence in myocardial infarction patients. In J. P. Naughton, H. K. Hellerstein, & I. C. Mohler (Eds.), *Exercise testing and exercise training in coronary heart disease.* New York: Academic Press. **(Chap 9)**

HAGBERG, B., AICARDI, J., DIAS, K., & RAMOS, O. (1983). A progressive syndrome of autism, dementia, ataxia, and loss of purposeful hand use in girls: Rett syndrome: Report of 35 cases. *Annals of Neurology, 14,* 471–479. **(Chap 16)**

HAGERMAN, R. J., JACKSON, A. W., LEVITAS, A., BRACKEN, M., MCBOGG, P., KEMPER, M., MCGRAVIAN, L., BERRY, R., MATUS, I., & HAGERMAN, P. J. (1986). Oral folic acid versus placebo in the treatment of males with the fragile X syndrome. *American Journal of Medical Genetics, 23,* 241–262. **(Chap 16)**

HAGNELL, O., FRANCK, A., GRASBECK, A., OHMAN, R., OJESJO, L., OTTERBECK, L., & RORSMAN, B. (1992). Vascular dementia in the Lundby study: I. A prospective, epidemiological study of incidence and risk from 1957 to 1972. *Neuropsychobiology, 26,* 43–49. **(Chap 15)**

HALL, S. M., MUNOZ, R. F., & REUS, V. I. (1994). Cognitive-behavioral intervention increases abstinence rates for depressive-history smokers. *Journal of Consulting and Clinical Psychology, 62,* 141–146. **(Chap 12)**

HALL, S. M., MUNOZ, R. F., REUS, V. I., & SEES, K. L. (1993). Nicotine, negative affect, and depression. *Journal of Consulting and Clinical Psychology, 61,* 761–767. **(Chap 12)**

HALMI, K. A., ECKERT, E., LADU, T. J., & COHEN, J. (1986). Anorexia nervosa: Treatment efficacy of cyproheptadine and anitriptyline. *Archives of General Psychiatry, 43,* 177–181. **(Chap 8)**

HAMER, D. H., HU, S., MAGNUSON, V. L., HU, N., & PATTATUCCI, A. M. (1993). A linkage between DNA markers on the X chromosome and male sexual orientation. *Science, 261,* 321–327. **(Chap 11)**

HAMILTON, E. W., & ABRAMSON, L. Y. (1983). Cognitive patterns and major depressive disorders: A longitudinal study in a hospital setting. *Journal of Abnormal Psychology, 92,* 173–184. **(Chap 7)**

HAMMEN, C., BURGE, D., BURNEY, E., & ADRIAN, C. (1990). Longitudinal study of diagnoses in children of women with unipolar and bipolar affective disorder. *Archives of General Psychiatry, 47*(12), 1112–1117. **(Chap 7)**

HAMMEN, C., ELLICOTT, A., GITLIN, M., & JAMISON, K. R. (1989). Sociotropy/autonomy and vulnerability to specific life events in patients with unipolar depression and bipolar disorders. *Journal of Abnormal Psychology, 98,* 154–160. **(Chap 7)**

HAMMEN, C., MARKS, T., MAYOL, A., & DE MAYO, R. (1985). Depressive self-schemas, life stress, and vulnerability to depression. *Journal of Abnormal Psychology, 94,* 308–319. **(Chap 7)**

HANLEY, I. (1986). Reality orientation in the care of the elderly patient with dementia—three case studies. In I. Hanley & M. Gilhooly (Eds.), *Psychological therapies for the elderly* (pp. 65–79). New York: New York University Press. **(Chap 15)**

HANLEY, I. G., & LUSTY, K. (1984). Memory aids in reality orientation: A single-case study. *Behavior Research and Therapy, 22,* 709–712. **(Chap 15)**

HANS, S. L., & MARCUS, J. (1991). Neurobehavioral development of infants at risk for schizophrenia: A review. In E. F. Walker (Ed.), *Schizophrenia: A life-course developmental perspective* (pp. 33–57). New York: Academic Press. **(Chap 14)**

HANS, V. P. (1986). An analysis of public attitudes toward the insanity defense. *Criminology, 4,* 393–415. **(Chap 17)**

HANSON, R. K., STEFFY, R. A., AND GAUTHIER, R. (1993). Long-term recidivism of child molesters. *Journal of Consulting and Clinical Psychology, 61,* 646–652. **(Chap 11)**

HARBERT, T. L., BARLOW, D. H., HERSEN, M., & AUSTIN, J. B. (1974). Measurement and modification of incestuous behavior: A case study. *Psychological Reports, 34,* 79–86. **(Chap 11)**

HARDY, J. A., MANN, D. M., WESTER, P., & WINBLAD, B. (1986). An integrative hypothesis concerning the pathogenesis and progression of Alzheimer's disease. *Neurobiology of Aging, 7,* 489–502. **(Chap 15)**

HARE, R. D. (1970). *Psychopathy: Theory and research.* New York: John Wiley. **(Chap 13)**

HARE, R. D. (1983). Diagnosis of antisocial personality disorder in two prison populations. *American Journal of Psychiatry, 140,* 887–890. **(Chap 13)**

HARE, R. D. (1991). *Manual for the Revised Psychopathy Checklist.* Toronto: Multi-Health Systems. **(Chap 13)**

HARE, R. D. (1993). *Without conscience: The disturbing world of the psychopaths among us.* New York: Pocket Books. **(Chap 13)**

HARE, R. D., MCPHERSON, L. M., & FORTH, A. E. (1988). Male psychopaths and their criminal careers. *Journal of Consulting and Clinical Psychology, 56,* 710–714. **(Chap 13)**

HARRIS, G. T., RICE, M. E., QUINSEY, V. L., CHAPLING, T. C. & EARLS, C. (1992). Maximizing the discriminant validity of phallometric assessment daa. *Psychological Assessment, 4,* 502–511. **(Chap 11)**

HARPUR, T. J., HARE, R. D., & HAKSTIAN, A. R. (1989). Two-factor conceptualization of psychopathy: Construct validity and assessment implications. *Psychological Assessment: A Journal of Consulting and Clinical Psychology, 1,* 6–17. **(Chap 13)**

HART, S. D., FORTH, A. E., & HARE, R. D. (1990). Performance of criminal psychopaths on selected neuropsychological tests. *Journal of Abnormal Psychology, 99,* 374–379. **(Chap 13)**

HASLAM, J. (1809/1976). *Observations on madness and melancholy.* New York: Arno Press. **(Chap 14)**

HATCH, J. P., PRIHODA, T. J., MOORE, P. J., & CYR-PROVOST, M. (1991). A naturalistic study of the relationship among electromyographic activity, psychological stress, and pain in ambulatory tension-type headache patients and headache-free controls. *Psychosomatic Medicine, 53,* 576–584. **(Chap 9)**

HATFIELD, E., CACIOPPO, J. T., & RAPSON, R. L. (1993). Emotional contagion. *Current Directions in Psychological Science, 2*(3), 96–99. **(Chaps 1, 2)**

HATFIELD, E., SPRECHER, S., PILLEMER, J. T., GREENBERGER, D, ET AL. (1988). Gender differences in what is desired in the sexual relationship. *Journal of Psychology and Human Sexuality, 1*(2), 39–52. **(Chap 11)**

HATHAWAY, S. R., & MCKINLEY, J. C. (1943). *Manual for the Minnesota Multiphasic Personality Inventory.* New York: Psychological Corporation. **(Chap 3)**

HAURI, P. (1982). *The sleep disorders* (2nd ed.). Kalamazoo, MI: Upjohn Company. **(Chap 10)**

HAURI, P. J. (1991). Sleep hygiene, relaxation therapy, and cognitive interventions. In P. J. Hauri (Ed.), *Case studies in insomnia* (pp. 65–84). New York: Plenum Medical Books Company. **(Chap 10)**

HAWKINS, R. P. (1979). The functions of assessment: Implications for selection and development of devices for assessing repertoires in clinical, educational, and other settings. *Journal of Applied Behavior Analysis, 12,* 501–516. **(Chap 3)**

HAWTON, K., CATALAN, J., & FAGG, J. (1992). Sex therapy for erectile dysfunction: Characteristics of couples, treatment outcome, and prognostic factors. *Archives of Sexual Behavior, 21*(2), 161–175. **(Chap 11)**

HAY, P. J., & HALL, A. (1991). The prevalence of eating disorders in recently admitted psychiatric in-patients. *British Journal of Psychiatry, 159,* 562–565. **(Chap 8)**

HAYNES, S. G., FEINLEIB, M., & KANNEL, W. B. (1980). The relationship of psychosocial factors to coronary heart disease in the Framingham study: III. Eight-year incidence of coronary heart disease. *American Journal of Epidemiology, 111,* 37–58. **(Chap 9)**

HAYNES, S. G., & MATTHEWS, K. A. (1988). Area review: Coronary-prone behavior: Continuing evolution of the concept: Review and methodologic critique of recent studies on type A behavior and cardiovascular disease. *Annals of Behavioral Medicine, 10*(2), 47–59. **(Chap 9)**

HAYWARD, G., KILLEN, J. D., HAMMER, L. D., LITT, I. F., WILSON, D. M., SIMMONDS, B., & TAYLOR, C. B. (1992). Pubertal stage and panic attack history in sixth- and seventh-grade girls. *American Journal of Psychiatry, 149,* 1239–1243. **(Chap 5)**

HEADACHE CLASSIFICATION COMMITTEE OF THE INTERNATIONAL HEADACHE SOCIETY. (1988). Classification and diagnostic criteria for headache disorders, cranial neuralgias and facial pain. *Cephalalgia, 8*(Suppl. 7), 9–96. **(Chap 9)**

HEATON, R. K. (1988). Introduction to special series. *Journal of Consulting and Clinical Psychology, 56,* 787–788. **(Chap 15)**

HEATON, R. K., VELIN, R. A., MCCUTCHAN, A., GULEVICH, S. J., ATKINSON, J. H., WAALACE, M. R., GODFREY, H. P. D., KIRSON, D. A., & GRANT, I. (1994). Neuropsychological impairment in human immunodeficiency virus-infection: Implications for employment. *Psychosomatic Medicine, 56,* 8–17. **(Chap 15)**

HEIMAN, J. R., & LOPICCOLO, J. (1983). *Effectiveness of daily versus weekly therapy in the treatment of sexual dysfunction.* Unpublished manuscript, State University of New York at Stony Brook. **(Chap 11)**

HEIMAN, J. R., & LOPICCOLO, J. (1988). *Becoming orgasmic: A sexual and personal growth program for women* (rev. ed.). New York: Prentice-Hall. **(Chap 11)**

HEIMBERG, R. G., DODGE, C. S., HOPE, D. A., KENNEDY, C. R., ZOLLO, L., & BECKER, R. E. (1990). Cognitive behavioral group treatment for social phobia: Comparison to a credible placebo control. *Cognitive Therapy and Research, 14,* 1–23. **(Chap 5)**

HEIMBERG, R. G., KLOSKO, J. S., DODGE, C. S., & SHADICK, R. (1989). Anxiety disorders, depression and attributional style: A further test of the specificity of depressive attributions. *Cognitive Therapy and Research, 13*(1), 21–36. **(Chap 7)**

HEIMBERG, R. G., SALZMAN, D. G., HOLT, C. S., & BLENDELL, K. A. (1993). Cognitive-behavioral group treatment for social phobia: Effectiveness at five-year follow up. *Cognitive Therapy and Research, 17,* 325–339. **(Chap 5)**

HELMES, E., & REDDON, J. R. (1993). A perspective on developments in assessing psychopathology: A critical review of the MMPI and MMPI-2. *Psychological Bulletin, 113,* 453–471. **(Chap 3)**

HELZER, J. E., & CANINO, G. (1992). Comparative analyses of alcoholism in 10 cultural regions. In J. Helzer & G. Canino (Eds.), *Alcoholism—North America, Europe and Asia: A coordinated analysis of population data from ten regions* (pp. 131–155). London: Oxford University Press. **(Chap 12)**

HELZER, J. E., ROBINS, L. N., & MCEVOY, L. (1987). Posttraumatic stress disorder in the general population: Findings from the Epidemiologic Catchment Area survey. *New England Journal of Medicine, 317,* 1630–1634. **(Chap 5)**

HERBERT, T. B., & COHEN, S. (1993). Depression and immunity: A meta-analytic review. *Psychological Bulletin, 113*(3), 472–486. **(Chap 9)**

HERDT, G. H. (1987). *The Sambia: Ritual and gender in New Guinea.* New York: Holt, Rinehart and Winston. **(Chap 11)**

HERDT, G. H., & STOLLER, R. J. (1989). Commentary to "The socialization of homosexuality and heterosexuality in a non-western society." *Archives of Sexual Behavior, 18,* 31–34. **(Chap 11)**

HERMAN, J. L., PERRY, C., & VAN DER KOLK, B. A. (1989). Childhood trauma in borderline personality disorder. *American Journal of Psychiatry, 146,* 490–495. **(Chap 13)**

HERSEN, M., & VAN HASSELT, V. B. (1992). Behavioral assessment and treatment of anxiety in the elderly. *Clinical Psychology Review, 12,* 619–640. **(Chap 5)**

HERSEN, M., VAN HASSELT, V. B., & GORECZNY, A. J. (1993). Behavioral assessment of anxiety in older adults. *Behavior Modification, 17*(2), 99–112. **(Chap 5)**

HERZOG, D. B. (1988). Eating disorders. In A. M. Nicoli, Jr. (Ed.), *The new Harvard guide to psychiatry* (pp. 434–445). Boston: Harvard University Press. **(Chap 8)**

HETHERINGTON, E. M., STANLEY-HAGAN, M., & ANDERSON, E. R. (1989). Marital transitions: A child's perspective. *American Psychologist, 44,* 303–312. **(Chap 13)**

HIGGINS, S. T., BUDNEY, A. J., BICKEL, W. K., HUGHES, J. R., FOERG, F., & BADGER, G. (1993). Achieving cocaine abstinence with a behavioral approach. *American Journal of Psychiatry, 150,* 763–769. **(Chap 12)**

HILGARD, E. R. (1992). Divided consciousness and dissociation. *Consciousness & Cognition, 1,* 16–31. **(Chap 2)**

HILL, A. E., & ROSENBLOOM, L. (1986). Disintegrative psychosis of childhood: Teenage follow-up. *Developmental Medicine and Child Neurology, 28,* 34–40. **(Chap 16)**

HILLMAN, E., KRIPKE, D. F., & GILLIN, J. C. (1990). Sleep restriction, exercise, and bright lights: Alternate therapies for depression. In A. Tasman, C. Kaufman, & S. Goldfinger (Eds.), *American Psychiatric Press review of psychiatry: Section I: Treatment of refractory affective disorder.* (R. Post, section ed.) (Vol. 9, pp. 132–144). Washington, DC: American Psychiatric Press. **(Chap 10)**

HILTS, P. J. (1994, MARCH 10). Agency faults a U.C.L.A. study for suffering of mental patients. *New York Times,* A1. **(Chap 17)**

HIMMELFARB, S., & MURRELL, S. A. (1984). The prevalence and correlation of anxiety symptoms in older adults. *Journal of Psychiatry, 116,* 159–167. **(Chap 5)**

HIMMELHOCH, J. M., & THASE, M. E. (1989). The vagaries of atypical depression. In J. E. Havells (Ed.), *Modern perspectives in the psychiatry of depression* (pp. 223–242). New York: Brunner/Mazel. **(Chap 7)**

HINDMARCH, I. (1986). The effects of psychoactive drugs on car handling and related psychomotor ability: A review. In J. F. O'Hanlon & J. J. Gier (Eds.), *Drugs and driving* (pp. 71–79). London: Taylor and Francis. **(Chap 5)**

HINDMARCH, I. (1990). Cognitive impairment with anti-anxiety agents: A solvable problem? In D. Wheatley (Ed.), *The anxiolytic jungle: Where, next?* (pp. 49–61). Chichester, England: John Wiley. **(Chap 5)**

HINSHELWOOD, J. A. (1896). A case of dyslexia: A peculiar form of word-blindness. *Lancet, 2,* 1451–1454. **(Chap 15)**

HIRSCH, S., CRAMER, P., & BOWEN, J. (1992). The triggering hypothesis of the role of life events in schizophrenia. *British Journal of Psychiatry, 161,* 84–87. **(Chap 14)**

HIRSCHFELD, R. M., SHEA, M. T., & WEISE, R. E. (1991). Dependent personality disorder: Perspectives for DSM-IV. *Journal of Personality Disorders, 5,* 135–149. **(Chap 13)**

HITCHCOCK, P. B., & MATHEWS, A. (1992). Interpretation of bodily symptoms in hypochondriasis. *Behaviour Research and Therapy, 30*(3), 223–234. **(Chap 6)**

HODAPP, R. M., & DYKENS, E. M. (1994). Mental retardation's two cultures of behavioral research. *American Journal of Mental Retardation, 98,* 675–687. **(Chap 15)**

HOEHN-SARIC, R. (1982). Neurotransmitters in anxiety. *Archives of General Psychiatry, 39,* 735–742. **(Chap 2)**

HOEHN-SARIC, R., & MASEK, B. J. (1981). Effects of naloxone on normals and chronically anxious patients. *Biological Psychiatry, 16,* 1041–1050. **(Chap 5)**

HOEHN-SARIC, R., MCLEOD, D. R., & ZIMMERLI, W. D. (1989). Somatic manifestations in women with generalized anxiety disorder: Psychophysiological responses to psychological stress. *Archives of General Psychiatry, 46,* 1113–1119. **(Chap 5)**

HOGARTY, G. E., ANDERSON, C. M., REISS, D. J., KORNBLITH, S. J., GREENWALD, D. P., JAVNA, C. D., & MADONIA, M. J. (1986). Family psychoeducation, social skills training, and maintenance chemotherapy in the aftercare treatment of schizophrenia: I. One year effects of a controlled study on relapse and expressed emotion. *Archives of General Psychiatry, 43,* 633–642. **(Chap 14)**

HOGARTY, G. E., ANDERSON, C. M., REISS, D. J., KORNBLITH, S. J., GREENWALD, D. P., ULRICH, R. F., CARTER, M., & THE ENVIRONMENTAL-PERSONAL INDICATORS IN THE COURSE OF SCHIZOPHRENIA (EPICS) RESEARCH GROUP. (1991). Family psychoeducation, social skills training, and maintenance chemotherapy in the aftercare treatment of schizophrenia. *Archives of General Psychiatry, 48,* 340–347. **(Chap 14)**

HOGARTY, G. E., REIS, D., KORNBLITH, S. J., GREENWALD, D., ULRICH, R., & CARTER, M. (1992). In reply. *Archives of General Psychiatry, 49,* 76–77. **(Chap 14)**

HOGE, S. K., APPELBAUM, P. S., LAWLER, T., BECK, J. C., LITMAN, R., GREER, A., GUTHEIL, T. G., & KAPLAN, E. (1990). A prospective, multicenter study of patients' refusal of antipsychotic medication. *Archives of General Psychiatry, 47,* 949–956. **(Chap 14)**

HOKANSON, J. E., RUBERT, M. P., WELKER, R. A., HOLLANDER, G. R., & HEDEEN, C. (1989). Interpersonal concomitants and antecedents of depression among college students. *Journal of Abnormal Psychology, 98*(3), 209–217. **(Chap 7)**

HOLDEN, A. E., & BARLOW, D. H. (1986). Heart rate and heart rate variability recorded in vivo agoraphobics and nonphobics. *Behavior Therapy, 17,* 26–42. **(Chap 3)**

HOLDEN, C. (1993). Wake-up call for sleep research. *Science, 259,* 305. **(Chap 10)**

HOLLAND, A. J., HALL, A., MURRAY, R., RUSSELL, G. F. M., & CRISP, A. H. (1984). Anorexia nervosa: A study of 34 twin pairs and one set of triplets. *British Journal of Psychiatry, 145,* 414–418. **(Chap 8)**

HOLLANDER, E., LIEBOWITZ, M. R., WINCHEL, R., KLUMKER, A., & KLEIN, D. F. (1989). Treatment of body-dysmorphic disorder with serotonin reuptake blockers. *American Journal of Psychiatry, 1989, 146,* 768–770. **(Chap 6)**

HOLLIEN, H. (1990). The expert witness: Ethics and responsibilities. *Journal of Forensic Sciences, 35,* 1414–1423. **(Chap 17)**

HOLLIFIELD, M., KATON, W., SPAIN, D., & PULE, L. (1990). Anxiety and depression in a

village in Lesotho, Africa: A comparison with the United States. *British Journal of Psychiatry, 156,* 343–350. **(Chap 5)**

HOLLIS, J. F., CONNETT, J. E., STEVENS, V. J., & GREENLICK, M. R. (1990). Stressful life events, Type A behavior, and the prediction of cardiovascular and total mortality over six years. *Journal of Behavioral Medicine, 13*(3), 263–280. **(Chap 9)**

HOLLON, S. D. (1993). Review of psychosocial treatments for mood disorders. In D. L. Dunner (Ed.), *Current psychiatric therapy.* Philadelphia: W. B. Saunders. **(Chap 7)**

HOLLON, S. D., & BECK, A. T. (in press). Cognitive and cognitive behavioral therapies. In S. L Garfield & A. E. Bergin (Eds.), *Handbook of psychotherapy and behavior change: An empirical analysis* (4th ed.). New York: John Wiley. **(Chap 7)**

HOLLON, S. D., DERUBEIS, R. J., EVANS, M. D., WIENER, M. J., GARVEY, M. J., GROSE, W. M., & TUASON, V. B. (1992). Cognitive therapy and pharmacotherapy for depression: Singly and in combination. *Archives of General Psychiatry, 49*(10), 772–781. **(Chap 7)**

HOLLON, S. D., KENDALL, P. C., & LUMRY, A. (1986). Specificity of depressotypic cognitions in clinical depression. *Journal of Abnormal Psychology, 95,* 52–59. **(Chap 7)**

HOLLON, S. D., SHELTON, R. C., & LOOSEN, P. T. (1991). Cognitive therapy and pharmacotherapy for depression. *Journal of Consulting and Clinical Psychology, 59*(1), 88–99. **(Chap 7)**

HOLM, V. A., & VARLEY, C. K. (1989). Pharmacological treatment of autistic children. In G. Dawson (Ed.), *Autism: Nature, diagnosis, and treatment* (pp. 386–404). New York: Guilford Press. **(Chap 16)**

HOLROYD, K. A., ANDRASIK, F., & NOBLE, J. (1980). A comparison of EMG biofeedback and a credible pseudotherapy in treating tension headache. *Journal of Behavioral Medicine, 3,* 29–39. **(Chap 9)**

HOLROYD, K. A., NASH, J. M., PINGEL, J. D., CORDINGLEY, G. E., & JEROME, A. (1991). A comparison of pharmacological (amitriptyline HCL) and nonpharmacological (cognitive-behavioral) therapies for chronic tension headaches. *Journal of Consulting and Clinical Psychology, 59*(3), 387–393. **(Chap 9)**

HOLROYD, K. A., & PENZIEN, D. B. (1986). Client variables in the behavioral treatment of current tension headache: A meta-analytic review. *Journal of Behavioral Medicine, 9,* 515–536. **(Chap 9)**

HOLROYD, K. A., PENZIEN, D. B., HURSEY, K. G., TOBIN, D. L., ROGERS, L., HOLM, J. E., MARCILLE, P. J., HALL, J. R., & CHILA, A. G. (1984). Change mechanisms in EMG biofeedback training: Cognitive changes underlying improvements in tension headache. *Journal of Consulting and Clinical Psychology, 52,* 1039–1053. **(Chap 9)**

HOLZMAN, P. S., & LEVY, D. L. (1977). Smooth pursuit eye movements and functional psychoses: A review. *Schizophrenia Bulletin, 3,* 15–27. **(Chap 14)**

HOOK, E. B. (1982). Epidemiology of Down syndrome. In S. M. Pueschel & J. E. Rynders (Eds.), *Down syndrome: Advances in biomedicine and the behavioral sciences* (pp. 11–88). Cambridge: Ware Press. **(Chap 15)**

HOOLEY, J. M. (1985). Expressed emotion: A review of the critical literature. *Clinical Psychology Review, 5,* 119–139. **(Chap 14)**

HOOLEY, J. M., ORLEY, J., & TEASDALE, J. D. (1986). Levels of expressed emotion and relapse in depressed patients. *British Journal of Psychiatry, 148,* 642–647. **(Chap 7)**

HOOLEY, J. M., & TEASDALE, J. D. (1989). Predictors of relapse in unipolar depressives: Expressed emotion, marital distress, and perceived criticism. *Journal of Abnormal Psychology, 98*(3), 229–235. **(Chap 7)**

HOON, P. W., WINCZE, J. P., & HOON, E. F. (1977). A test of reciprocal inhibition: Are anxiety and sexual arousal in women mutually inhibitory? *Journal of Abnormal Psychology, 86,* 65–74. **(Chap 11)**

HOPE, D. A., & HEIMBERG, R. G. (in press). Social phobia. In C. Last & M. Hersen (Eds.), *Adult behavior therapy casebook.* New York: Plenum Press. **(Chap 5)**

HORGAN, M. M., SPARROW, M. D., & BRAZEAU, R. (1986). *Alcoholic beverage taxation and control policies* (6th ed.). Ottawa: Brewers Association of Canada. **(Chap 12)**

HORIKOSHI, H. (1980). Asrama: An Islamic psychiatric institution in West Java. *Social Science and Medicine, 14,* 157–165. **(Chap 4)**

HOROWITZ, G. P., & DUDEK, B. C. (1983). Behavioral pharmacogenetics. In J. L. Fuller & E. C. Simmel (Eds.), *Behavior genetics: Principles and applications* (pp. 117–154). Hillsdale, NJ: Lawrence Erlbaum. **(Chap 12)**

HOROWITZ, M. (1986). *Stress response syndromes.* London: Jason Aronson. **(Chap 5)**

HORVATH, T. B. (1975). Clinical spectrum and epidemiological features of alcohol dementia. In J. G. Rankin (Ed.), *Alcohol, drugs and brain damage* (pp. 1–16). Toronto: Toronto Addiction Center. **(Chap 15)**

HOUSE, J. S., LANDIS, K. R., & UMBERSON, D. (1988). Social relationships and health. *Science, 241,* 540–545. **(Chaps 1, 2, 7)**

HOUSE, J. S., ROBBINS, C., & METZNER, H. M. (1982). The association of social relationships and activities with mortality: Prospective evidence from the Tecumseh community health study. *American Journal of Epidemiology, 116,* 123. **(Chap 2)**

HOUSTON, B. K. (1988). Division 38 survey: Synopsis of results. *Health Psychologist, 10,* 2–3. **(Chap 9)**

HOUSTON, B. K., CHESNEY, M. A., BLACK, G. W., CATES, D. S., & HECKER, M. H. L. (1992). Behavioral clusters and coronary heart disease risk. *Psychosomatic Medicine, 54*(4), 447–461. **(Chap 9)**

HOWARD, R., CASTLE, D., WESSELY, S., & MURRAY, R. (1993). A comparative study of 470 cases of early-onset and late-onset schizophrenia. *British Journal of Psychiatry, 163,* 352–357. **(Chap 14)**

HSER, Y., ANGLIN, M. D., & POWERS, K. (1993). A 24-year follow-up of California narcotics addicts. *Archives of General Psychiatry, 50,* 577–584. **(Chap 12)**

HSIAO, J. K., COLISON, J., BARTKO, J. J., DORAN, A. R., KONICKI, P. E., POTTER, W. Z., & PICKAR, D. (1993). Monoamine neurotransmitter interactions in drug-free and neuroleptic-treated schizophrenics. *Archives of General Psychiatry, 50,* 606–614. **(Chap 14)**

HSU, L. K. G. (1988). The outcome of anorexia nervosa: A reappraisal. *Psychological Medicine, 18,* 807–812. **(Chap 8)**

HSU, L. K. G. (1990). *Eating disorders.* New York: Guilford Press. **(Chap 8)**

HSU, L. K. G., CHESLER, B. E., & SANTHOUSE, R. (1990). Bulimia nervosa in eleven sets of twins: A clinical report. *International Journal of Eating Disorders, 9,* 275–282. **(Chap 8)**

HSU, L. K. G., & ZIMMER, B. (1988). Eating disorders in old age. *International Journal of Eating Disorders, 7,* 133–138. **(Chap 8)**

HSU, L. M. (1989). Random sampling, randomization, and equivalence of contrasted groups in psychotherapy outcome research. *Journal of Consulting and Clinical Psychology, 57,* 131–137. **(Chap 4)**

HUBERT, N. C., JAY, S. M., SALTOUN, M., & HAYES, M. (1988). Approach-avoidance and distress in children undergoing preparation for painful medical procedures. *Journal of Clinical Child Psychology, 17,* 194–202. **(Chap 9)**

HUDSON, J., POPE, H., JONAS, J. M., & YURGELUN-TODD, D. (1983). Family history study of anorexia nervosa and bulimia. *British Journal of Psychiatry, 142,* 133–138. **(Chap 8)**

HUDZINSKI, L. G., & LAWRENCE, G. S. (1988). Significance of EMG surface electrode placement models and headache findings. *Headache, 28,* 30–35. **(Chap 9)**

HUGHES, J. R. (1993). Pharmacotherapy for smoking cessation: Unvalidated assumptions, anomalies, and suggestions for future research. *Journal of Consulting and Clinical Psychology, 61,* 751–760. **(Chap 12)**

HUGHES, J. R., GUST, S. W., SKOOG, K., KEENAN, R. M., & FENWICK, J. W. (1991). Symptoms of tobacco withdrawal: A replication and extension. *Archives of General Psychiatry, 48,* 52–61. **(Chap 12)**

HUMPHREY, L. L. (1986). Structural analysis of parent-child relationships in eating disorders. *Journal of Abnormal Psychology, 95,* 395–402. **(Chap 8)**

HUMPHREY, L. L. (1988). Relationships within subtypes of anorexic, bulimic, and normal families. *Journal of the American Academy of Child and Adolescent Psychiatry, 27,* 544–551. **(Chap 8)**

HUMPHREY, L. L. (1989). Observed family interactions among subtypes of eating disorders using structural analysis of social behavior. *Journal of Consulting and Clinical Psychology, 57,* 206–214. **(Chap 8)**

HUNICUTT, C. P., & NEWMAN, I. A. (1993). Adolescent dieting practices and nutrition knowledge. *Health Values: The Journal of Health Behavior, Education and Promotion, 17*(4), 35–40. **(Chap 8)**

HUNT, W. A. (1980). History and classification. In A. E. Kazdin, A. S. Bellack, & M. Hersen (Eds.), *New perspectives in abnormal psychology.* New York: Oxford University Press. **(Chap 1)**

HUNTINGTON'S DISEASE COLLABORATIVE RESEARCH GROUP. (1993). A novel gene containing a trinucleotide repeat that is expanded and unstable on Huntington's disease chromosomes. *Cell, 72,* 971–983. **(Chap 15)**

HURT, S. W., SCHNURR, P. P., SEVERINO, S. K., FREEMAN, E. W., GISE, L. H., RIVERA-TOVAR, A., & STEEGE, J. F. (1992). Late luteal phase dysphoric disorder in 670 women evaluated for premenstrual complaints. *American Journal of Psychiatry, 149,* 525–530. **(Chap 3)**

HUSSIAN, R. A. & BROWN, D. C. (1987). Use of two dimensional grid patterns to limit hazardous ambulation in demented patients. *Journal of Gerontology, 42,* 558–560. **(Chap 15)**

HUTTON, H. E., MINER, M. H., BLADES, J. R., & LANGFELDT, V. C. (1992). Ethnic differences on the MMPI overcontrolled-hostility scale. *Journal of Personality Assessment, 58,* 260–268. **(Chap 3)**

HYLER, S. E., WILLIAMS, J. B. W., & SPITZER, R. L. (1982). Reliability in the DSM-III field trials: Interview v. case summary. *Archives of General Psychiatry, 39,* 1275–1278. **(Chap 3)**

HYMOWITZ, P., FRANCES, A., JACOBSBERG, L., SICKLES, M., & HOYT, R. (1986). Neuroleptic treatment of schizotypal personality disorder. *Comprehensive Psychiatry, 27,* 267–271. **(Chap 13)**

HYND, G. W., & SEMRUD-CLIKEMAN, M. (1989). Dyslexia and brain morphology. *Psychological Bulletin, 106,* 447–482. **(Chap 15)**

IACONO, W. G. (1988). Eye movement abnormalities in schizophrenic and affective disorders. In C. W. Johnson & F. J. Pirozzolo (Eds.), *Neuropsychology of eye movements* (pp. 115–145). Hillsdale, NJ: Lawrence Erlbaum. **(Chap 14)**

IACONO, W. G., & BEISER, M. (1992). Are males more likely than females to develop schizophrenia? *American Journal of Psychiatry, 149,* 1070–1074. **(Chap 14)**

ICKOVICS, J. R., & RODIN, J. (1992). Women and AIDS in the United States: Epidemiology, natural history, and mediating mechanisms. *Health Psychology, 11*(1), 1–16. **(Chap 9)**

IGUCHI, M. Y., GRIFFITHS, R. R., BICKEL, W. K., HANDELSMAN, L., CHILDRESS, A. R., & MCLELLAN, A. T. (1990). Relative abuse liability of benzodiazepines in methadone maintenance populations in three cities. *Problems of drug dependence* (pp. 364–365). (NIDA Publication Number ADM90-1663). Washington, DC: U.S. Government Printing Office. **(Chap 12)**

IKELS, C. (1991). Aging and disability in China: Cultural issues in measurement and interpretation. *Social Science Medicine, 32,* 649–665. **(Chap 15)**

IMBER, S. D., GLANZ, L. M., ELKIN, I., SOTSKY, S. M., BOYER, J. L., & LEBER, W. R. (1986). Ethical issues in psychotherapy research: Problems in a collaborative clinical trials study. *American Psychologist, 41,* 137–146. **(Chap 4)**

IMPERATO-MCGINLEY, J., PETERSON, R. E., GAUTIER, T., & STURLA, E. (1979). Androgens and the evolution of male-gender identity among male pseudohermaphrodites with 5-alpha-reductase deficiency. *The New England Journal of Medicine, 300,* 1233–1237. **(Chap 11)**

INGHAM, R. J. (1990). Stuttering. In A. S. Bellack, M. Hersen, & A. E. Kazdin (Eds.), *International handbook of behavior modification and therapy* (pp. 599–631). New York: Plenum Press. **(Chap 16)**

THE INSANITY DEFENSE IN NEW YORK: A REPORT TO GOVERNOR HUGH L. CAREY. (1978). New York State Department of Mental Hygiene. **(Chap 17)**

INSEL, T. R. (ED.). (1984). *New findings in obsessive-compulsive disorder.* Washington, DC: American Psychiatric Press. **(Chap 5)**

INSEL, T. R. (1992). Toward a neuroanatomy of obsessive-compulsive disorder. *Archives of General Psychiatry, 49,* 739–744. **(Chap 2)**

INSEL, T. R., CHAMPOUX, M., SCANLAN, J. M., & SUOMI, S. J. (1986, May). *Rearing condition and response to anxiogenic drug.* Paper presented at the annual meeting of the American Psychiatric Association, Washington, DC. **(Chap 2)**

IRONSON, G., TAYLOR, C. B., BOLTWOOD, M., BARTZOKIS, T., DENNIS, C., CHESNEY, M., SPITZER, S., & SEGALL, G. M. (1992). Effects of anger on left ventricular ejection fraction in coronary artery disease. *American Journal of Cardiology, 70,* 281–285. **(Chaps 2, 9)**

IRWIN, M., DANIELS, M., SMITH, T. L., BLOOM, E., & WEINER, H. (1987). Impaired natural killer cell activity during bereavement. *Brain, Behavior, and Immunity, 1,* 98–104. **(Chap 9)**

IZARD, C. E. (1992). Basic emotions, relations among emotions, and emotion-cognition relations. *Psychological Review, 99*(3), 561–565. **(Chap 2)**

JACKSON V. INDIANA, 406 U.S. 715 (1972). **(Chap 17)**

JACOBI, W., & WINKLER, H. (1927). Encephalographische Studien an chronischen Schizophrenen. *Arch. Psychiatr. Nervenk.r, 81,* 299–332. **(Chap 14)**

JACOBS, S. (1993). *Pathologic grief: Maladaptation to loss.* Washington, DC: American Psychiatric Press. **(Chap 7)**

JACOBS, S., HANSEN, F., BERKMAN, L., KASL, S., & OSTFELD, A. (1989). Depressions of bereavement. *Comprehensive Psychiatry, 30*(3), 218–224. **(Chap 7)**

JACOBSON, E. (1938). *Progressive relaxation.* Chicago: University of Chicago Press. **(Chap 9)**

JACOBSON, N. S., DOBSON, K., FRUZZETTI, A. E., SCHMALING, K. B., & SALUSKY, S. (1991). Marital therapy as a treatment for depression. *Journal of Consulting and Clinical Psychology, 59*(4), 547–557. **(Chap 7)**

JACOBSON, N. S., FRUZZETTI, A. E., DOBSON, K., WHISMAN, M., & HOPS, H. (1993). Couple therapy as a treatment for depression: II. The effects of relationship quality and therapy on depressive relapse. *Journal of Consulting and Clinical Psychology, 61*(3), 516–519. **(Chap 7)**

JACOBSON, N. S., & TRUAX, P. (1991). Clinical significance: A statistical approach to defining meaningful change in psychotherapy research. *Journal of Consulting and Clinical Psychology, 59,* 12–19. **(Chap 4)**

JAFFE, J. (1985). *Drug addiction and drug abuse.* In A. Gilman, L. Goodman, T. Rall, & F. Murad (Eds.), *The pharmacological basis of therapeutics* (7th ed.). New York: Macmillan. **(Chap 12)**

JAFFE, J. H. (1991). Opiates. In I. B. Glass (Ed.), *The international handbook of addiction behaviour* (pp. 64–68). London: Tavistock/Routledge. **(Chap 12)**

JAMISON, K. R. (1986). Suicide and bipolar disorders. *Annual New York Academy of Science, 487,* 301–315. **(Chap 7)**

JAMISON, K. R. (1989). Mood disorders and patterns of creativity in British writers and artists. *Psychiatry, 52,* 125–134. **(Chap 7)**

JAMISON, R. N., & VIRTS, K. L. (1990). The influence of family support on chronic pain. *Behaviour Research and Therapy, 28*(4), 283–287. **(Chap 9)**

JAMNER, L. D., SHAPIRO, D., GOLDSTEIN, I. B., & HUG, R. (1991). Ambulatory blood pressure and heart rate in paramedics: Effects of cynical hostility and defensiveness. *Psychosomatic Medicine, 53,* 393–406. **(Chap 9)**

JANOFSKY, M. (1993, December 6). On cigarettes, health and lawyers. *New York Times,* D8. **(Chap 12)**

JASPERS, K. (1963). *General psychopathology* (J. Hoenig & M. W. Hamilton, Trans.). Manchester, England: Manchester University Press. **(Chap 14)**

JAY, S. M., ELLIOTT, C. H., OZOLINS, M., OLSON, R. A., & PRUITT, S. D. (1985). Behavioral management of childrens' distress during painful medical procedures. *Behaviour Research and Therapy, 23*(5), 513–520. **(Chap 9)**

JELLINEK, E. M. (1946). Phases in the drinking histories of alcoholics. *Quarterly Journal of Studies on Alcohol, 7,* 1–88. **(Chap 12)**

JELLINEK, E. M. (1952). Phases of alcohol addiction. *Quarterly Journal of Studies on Alcohol, 13,* 673–684. **(Chap 12)**

JELLINEK, E. M. (1960). *The disease concept of alcohol.* New Brunswick, NJ: Hillhouse Press. **(Chap 12)**

JENIKE, M. A., BAER, L., BALLANTINE, H. T., MARTUZA, R. L., TYNES, S., GIRIUNAS, I., BUTTOLPH, M. L., & CASSEM, N. H. (1991). Cingulotomy for refractory obsessive-compulsive disorder: A long-term follow-up of 33 patients. *Archives of General Psychiatry, 48,* 548–555. **(Chaps 2, 5)**

JENIKE, M. A., BAER, L., & MINICHIELLO, W. E. (EDS.). (1986). *Obsessive-compulsive disorders: Theory and management.* Littleton, MA: PSG Publishing. **(Chap 5)**

JENKINS, C. D., ZYZANSKI, S. J., & ROSENMAN, R. H. (1976). Risk of new myocardial infarction in middle-age men with manifest coronary heart disease. *Circulation, 53,* 342–347. **(Chap 9)**

JENKINS, J. H., & KARNO, M. (1992). The meaning of expressed emotion: Theoretical issues raised by cross-cultural research. *American Journal of Psychiatry, 149,* 9–21. **(Chap 14)**

JENKINS, J. H., KLEINMAN, A., & GOOD, B. J. (1990). Cross-cultural studies of depression. In J. Becker & A. Kleinman (Eds.), *Psychosocial aspects of depression.* Hillsdale, NJ: Lawrence Erlbaum. **(Chap 7)**

JENSEN, E. J., SCHMIDT, E., PEDERSEN, B., & DAHL, R. (1991). Effect on smoking cessation of silver acetate, nicotine and ordinary chewing gum. *Psychopharmacology, 104,* 470–474. **(Chap 12)**

JENSEN, G. B., & PAKKENBERG, B. (1993). Do alcoholics drink their neurons away? *Lancet, 342,* 1201–1204. **(Chap 12)**

JENSEN, M. P., KAROLY, P., & HAGER, R. (1987). The development and preliminary validation of an instrument to assess patients' attitudes toward pain. *Journal of Psychosomatic Research, 31,* 393–400. **(Chap 9)**

JENSEN, M. P., TURNER, J. A., ROMANO, J. M., & KAROLY, P. (1991). Coping with chronic pain: A critical review of the literature. *Pain, 47,* 249–283. **(Chap 9)**

JILEK, W. G. (1982). Altered states of consciousness in North American Indian ceremonials. *Ethos, 10*(4), 326–343. **(Chap 6)**

JOHANNESSEN, D. J., COWLEY, D. S., WALKER, R. D., JENSEN, C. F., & PARKER, L. (1989). Prevalence, onset and clinical recognition of panic states in hospitalized male alcoholics. *American Journal of Psychiatry, 146,* 1201–1203. **(Chap 5)**

JOHNS, M. B. ET AL. (1987). Primary care and health promotion: A model for preventive medicine. *American Journal of Preventive Medicine, 3* **(Chap 9)**

JOHNSON, A. M., WADSWORTH, J., WELLINGS, K., BRADSHAW, S., & FIELD, J. (1992). Sexual lifestyles and HIV risk. *Nature, 360,* 410–412. **(Chap 11)**

JOHNSON, B. A. (1991). Cannabis. In I. B. Glass (Ed.), *International handbook of addiction behaviour* (69–76). London: Tavistock/Routledge. **(Chap 12)**

JOHNSON, D. L. (1989). Schizophrenia as a brain disease: Implications for psychologists and families. *American Psychologist, 44,* 553–555. **(Chap 14)**

JOHNSON, J., & WEISSMAN, M. M. (N.D.). *E.C.A. data reanalysis.* A review commissioned by the Panel on Depression, Agency for Health Care Policy and Research, Public Health Service, Department of Health and Human Services. Unpublished manuscript. **(Chap 7)**

JOHNSON, J., WEISSMAN, M. M., & KLERMAN, G. L. (1990). Panic disorder, comorbidity and suicide attempts. *Archives of General Psychiatry, 47,* 805–808. **(Chap 5)**

JOHNSON, J. L., & MCCOWN, W. G. (1993). Addictive behaviors and substance abuse: An overview. In P. B. Sutker & H. E. Adams (Eds.), *Comprehensive handbook of psychopathology* (2nd ed., pp. 437–450). New York: Plenum Press. **(Chap 12)**

JOHNSON, R. E., NAHMIAS, A. J., MAGDER, L. S., LEE, F. K., BROOKS, C. A., & SNOWDEN, C. B. (1989). A seroepidemiologic survey of the prevalence of herpes simplex virus type 2 infection in the United States. *New England Journal of Medicine, 321,* 7–12. **(Chap 9)**

JOHNSTON, C., PELHAM, W. E., & MURPHY, H. A. (1985). Peer relationships in ADHD and normal children: A developmental analysis of peer and teacher ratings. *Journal of Abnormal Child Psychology, 13,* 89–100. **(Chap 16)**

JONES, B. E., & GRAY, B. A. (1986). Problems in diagnosing schizophrenia and affective disorders in Blacks. *Hospital and Community Psychiatry, 37,* 61–65. **(Chap 14)**

JONES, D. J., FOX, M. M., BABIGAN, H. M., & HUTTON, H. E. (1980). Epidemiology of anorexia nervosa in Monroe County, New York: 1960–1976. *Psychosomatic Medicine, 42,* 551–558. **(Chap 8)**

JONES, J. C., & BARLOW, D. H. (1990). The etiology of posttraumatic stress disorder. *Clinical Psychology Review, 10,* 299–328. **(Chap 5)**

JONES, K. L., & SMITH, D. W. (1973). Recognition of the Fetal Alcohol Syndrome in early infancy. *Lancet, 2,* 999–1001. **(Chap 12)**

JONES, M. C. (1924A). The elimination of children's fears. *Journal of Experimental Psychology, 7,* 383–390. **(Chap 1)**

JONES, M. C. (1924B). A laboratory study of fear. The case of Peter. *Pedagogical Seminary, 31,* 308–315. **(Chap 1)**

JONES, R. T., & HANEY, J. I. (1984). A primary preventive approach to the acquisition and maintenance of fire emergency responding: Comparison of external and self-instruction strategies. *Journal of Community Psychology, 12*(2), 180–191. **(Chap 9)**

JONES, R. T., & KAZDIN, A. E. (1980). Teaching children how and when to make emergency telephone calls. *Behavior Therapy, 11*(4), 509–521. **(Chap 9)**

JUELS-JENSEN, B. E. (1973). Herpes simplex and zoster. *British Medical Journal, 1,* 406–410. **(Chap 9)**

KAGAN, J., REZNICK, J. S., & SNIDMAN, N. (1988A). Biological bases of childhood shyness. *Science, 240,* 167–171. **(Chaps 5, 13)**

KAGAN, J., REZNICK, J. S., & SNIDMAN, N. (1988B). The physiology and psychology of behavioral inhibition in children. *Annual Progress in Child Psychiatry and Child Development,* 102–127. **(Chap 2)**

KAGAN, J., & SNIDMAN, N. (1991). Infant predictors of inhibited and uninhibited profiles. *Psychological Science, 2,* 40–44. **(Chap 5)**

KAHN, R. S., DAVIDSON, M., KNOTT, P., STERN, R. G., APTER, S., & DAVIS, K. L. (1993). Effect of neuroleptic medication on cerebrospinal fluid monoamine metabolite concentrations in schizophrenia: Serotonin-dopamine interactions as a target for treatment. *Archives of General Psychiatry, 50,* 599–605. **(Chap 14)**

KALANT, H. (1989). The nature of addiction: An analysis of the problem. In A. Goldstein (Ed.), *Molecular and cellular aspects of the drug addictions* (pp. 1–28). New York: Springer-Verlag. **(Chap 12)**

KALES, A., & KALES, J. D. (1974). Sleep disorders: Recent findings in the diagnosis and treatment of disturbed sleep. *New England Journal of Medicine, 290,* 487. **(Chap 10)**

KALES, J. D., KALES, A., SOLDATOS, C. R., CALDWELL, A. B., CHARNEY, D. S., & MARTIN, E. D. (1980). Night terrors: Clinical characteristics and personality patterns. *Archives of General Psychiatry, 37,* 1406–1410. **(Chap 10)**

KALES, A., SOLDATOS, C. R., BIXLER, E. O., LADDA, R. L., CHARNEY, D. S., WEBER, G., & SCHWEITZER, P. K. (1980). Hereditary factors in sleepwalking and night terrors. *British Journal of Psychiatry, 137,* 111–118. **(Chap 10)**

KALES, A., SOLDATOS, C. R., CALDWELL, A., KALES, J., HUMPHREY, F., CHARNEY, D., & SCHWEITZER, P. (1980). Somnambulism: Clinical characteristics and personality patterns. *Archives of General Psychiatry, 37,* 1406–1410. **(Chap 10)**

KALLMANN, F. J. (1938). *The genetics of schizophrenia.* New York: Augustin. **(Chap 14)**

KALUS, O., BERNSTEIN, D. P., & SIEVER, L. J. (1993). Schizoid personality disorder: A review of current status and implications for DSM-IV. *Journal of Personality Disorders, 7,* 43–52. **(Chap 13)**

KANDEL, E. R. (1983). From metapsychology to molecular biology: Explorations into the nature of anxiety. *American Journal of Psychiatry, 140,* 1277–1293. **(Chap 2)**

KANE, J., HONIGFELD, G., SINGER, J., & MELTZER, H. Y. (1988). Clozapine for the treatment resistant schizophrenic. *Archives of General Psychiatry, 45,* 789–796. **(Chap 14)**

KANE, J. M., & MARDER, S. R. (1993). Psychopharmacologic treatment of schizophrenia. *Schizophrenia Bulletin, 19,* 287–302. **(Chap 14)**

KANIGEL, R. (1988, October/November). Nicotine becomes addictive. *Science Illustrated,* pp. 12–14, 19–21. **(Chap 12)**

KANNER, L. (1943). Autistic disturbances of affective contact. *Nervous Child, 2,* 217–250. **(Chap 16)**

KANNER, L. (1949). Problems of nosology and psychodynamics of early infantile autism. *American Journal of Orthopsychiatry, 19,* 416–426. **(Chap 16)**

KANNER, L., & EISENBERG, L. (1955). Notes on the follow-up studies of autistic children. In P. Hoch & J. Zubin (Eds.), *Psychopathology of childhood* (pp. 227–239). New York: Grune & Stratton. **(Chap 16)**

KAPLAN, H. S. (1979). *Disorders of sexual desire.* New York: Brunner/Mazel. **(Chap 11)**

KAPLAN, H. S. (1987). *Sexual aversion, sexual phobias, and panic disorder.* New York: Brunner/Mazel. **(Chap 11)**

KAPLAN, M. (1983). A woman's view of DSM-III. *American Psychologist, 38,* 786–792. **(Chap 13)**

KAPLAN, N. M. (1980). The control of hypertension: A therapeutic breakthrough. *American Scientist, 68,* 537–545. **(Chap 9)**

KARACAN, I. (1988). Parasomnias. In R. L. Williams, I. Karacan, & C. A. Moore (Eds.), *Sleep disorders: Diagnosis and treatment* (pp. 131–144). New York: John Wiley. **(Chap 10)**

KARNO, M., & GOLDING, J. M. (1991). Obsessive-compulsive disorder. In L. N. Robins & D. A. Regier (Eds.), *Psychiatric disorders in America: The epidemiologic catchment area study* (pp. 204–219). New York: Free Press. **(Chap 5)**

KASHANI, J. H., HOEPER, E. W., BECK, N. C., & CORCORAN, C. M. (1987). Personality, psychiatric disorders, and parental attitude among a community sample of adolescents. *Journal of the American Academy of Child and Adolescent Psychiatry, 26*(6), 879–885. **(Chap 7)**

KASHANI, J. H., MCGEE, R. O., CLARKSON, S. E. A., WALTON, L. A., WILLIAMS, S., SILVA, P. A., ROBINS, A. J., CYTRYN, L., & MCKNEW, D. H. (1983). Depression in a sample of 9-year-old children: Prevalence and associated characteristics. *Archives of General Psychiatry, 40,* 1217–1223. **(Chap 7)**

KASINDORF, J. (1988, MAY 2). The real story of Billie Boggs: Was Koch right—Or the civil libertarians? *New York,* 36–44. **(Chap 17)**

KASS, D. J., SILVERS, F. M., & ABRAMS, G. M. (1972). Behavioral group treatment of hysteria. *Archives of General Psychiatry, 26,* 42–50. **(Chap 13)**

KASTNER, T., NATHANSON, R., & FRIEDMAN, D. L. (1993). Mortality among individuals with mental retardation living in the community. *American Journal on Mental Retardation, 98,* 285–292. **(Chap 15)**

KATON, W. (1993). Somatization disorder, hypochondriasis, and conversion disorder. In D. L. Dunner (Ed.), *Current psychiatric therapy*

(pp. 314–320). Philadelphia: W. B. Saunders. **(Chap 6)**

KATON, W., LIN, E., VON KORFF, M., RUSSO, J., LIPSCOMB, P., & BUSH, T. (1991). Somatization: A spectrum of severity. *American Journal of Psychiatry, 148,* 34–40. **(Chap 6)**

KATON, W., & ROY-BYRNE, P. P. (1991). Mixed anxiety and depression. *Journal of Abnormal Psychology, 100*(3), 337–345. **(Chap 3)**

KATZ, I. R. (1993). Delirium. In D. L. Dunner (Ed.), *Current psychiatric therapy* (pp. 65–73). Philadelphia: W. B Saunders. **(Chap 15)**

KATZ, I. R., LESHEN, E., KLEBAN, M., & JETHANANDANI, V. (1989). Clinical features of depression in the nursing home. *International Psychogeriatrics, 1,* 5–15. **(Chap 7)**

KATZ, J. L., WEINER, H., GALLAGHER, T. F., & HELLMAN, I. (1970). Stress, distress, and ego defenses: Psychoendocrine response to impending breast tumor biopsy. *Archives of General Psychiatry, 23,* 131–142. **(Chap 9)**

KATZ, S., & KRAVETZ, S. (1989). Facial plastic surgery for persons with Down syndrome: Research findings and their professional and social implications. *American Journal on Mental Retardation, 94,* 101–110. **(Chap 15)**

KAWABATA, S., HIGGINS, G. A., & GORDON, J. W. (1991). Amyloid plaques, neurofibrillary tangles and neuronal loss in brains of transgenic mice overexpressing a C-terminal fragment of human amyloid precursor protein. *Nature, 354,* 476–478. **(Chap 15)**

KAY, D. W. K. (1991). The epidemiology of dementia: A review of recent work. *Review of Clinical Gerontology, 1,* 55–66. **(Chap 15)**

KAYE, W. H., WELTZIN, T. E., HSU, L. K. G., MCCONAHA, C. W., & BOLTON, B. (1993). Amount of calories retained after binge eating and vomiting. *American Journal of Psychiatry, 150*(6), 969–971. **(Chap 8)**

KAZDIN, A. E. (1979). Unobtrusive measures in behavioral assessment. *Journal of Applied Behavior Analysis, 12,* 713–724. **(Chap 3)**

KAZDIN, A. E. (1981). Drawing valid inferences from case studies. *Journal of Consulting and Clinical Psychology, 49,* 183–192. **(Chap 4)**

KAZDIN, A. E. (1983). Hopelessness, depression, and suicidal intent among psychiatrically disturbed inpatient children. *Journal of Consulting and Clinical Psychology, 51*(4), 504–510. **(Chap 7)**

KAZDIN, A. F., MAZURICK, J. L., & BASS, D. (1993). Risk for attrition in treatment of antisocial children and families. *Journal of Child Clinical Psychology, 22,* 2–16. **(Chap 13)**

KEEFE, F. J., CRISSON, J., URBAN, B. J., & WILLIAMS, D. A. (1990). Analyzing chronic low back pain: The relative contribution of pain coping strategies. *Pain, 40,* 293–301. **(Chap 9)**

KEEFE, F. J., DUNSMORE, J., & BURNETT, R. (1992). Behavioral and cognitive-behavioral approaches to chronic pain: Recent advances and future directions. Special issue: Behavioral medicine: An update for the 1990s. *Journal of Consulting and Clinical Psychology, 60*(4), 528–536. **(Chap 9)**

KEILITZ, I. (1987). Researching and reforming the insanity defense. *Rutgers Law Review, 39,* 289–322. **(Chap 17)**

KEILITZ, I., & FULTON, J. P. (1984). *The insanity defense and its alternatives: A guide for*

policymakers. Williamsburg, VA: National Center for State Courts. **(Chap 17)**

KEITH, S. J., & MATTHEWS, S. M. (1993). The implications of criteria changes for DSM-IV schizophrenia. In D. L. Dunner (Ed.), *Current psychiatric therapy* (pp. 139–142). Philadelphia: W. B. Saunders. **(Chap 14)**

KELLER, M. B. (1988). Diagnostic issues and clinical cause of unipolar illness. In A. J. Frances & R. E. Hales (Eds.), *Review of psychiatry* (Vol. 7, pp. 188–212). Washington, DC: American Psychiatric Press. **(Chap 7)**

KELLER, M. B., BAKER, L. A., & RUSSELL, C. W. (1993). Classification and treatment of dysthymia. In D. L. Dunner (Ed.), *Current psychiatric therapy.* Philadelphia: W. B. Saunders. **(Chap 7)**

KELLER, M. B., & LAVORI, P. W. (1984). Double depression, major depression, and dysthymia: Distinct entities or different phases of a single disorder? *Psychopharmacology Bulletin, 20*(3), 399–402. **(Chap 7)**

KELLER, M. B., LAVORI, P. W., ENDICOTT, J., CORYELL, W., & KLERMAN, G. L. (1983). "Double depression": Two year follow-up. *American Journal of Psychiatry, 140*(6), 689–694. **(Chap 7)**

KELLER, M. B., & SHAPIRO, R. W. (1982). Double depression: Superimposition of acute depressive episodes on chronic depressive disorders. *American Journal of Psychiatry, 139*(4), 438–442. **(Chap 7)**

KELLER, M. B., & WUNDER, J. (1990). Bipolar disorder in childhood. In M. Hersen & C. G. Last (Eds.), *Handbook of child and adult psychopathology: A longitudinal perspective.* Elmsford, NY: Pergamon Press. **(Chap 7)**

KELLETT, J. M. (1991). Sexuality of the elderly. *Sexual and Marital Therapy, 6,* 147–155. **(Chap 11)**

KELLNER, R. (1985). Functional somatic symptoms and hypochondriasis: A survey of empirical studies. *Archives of General Psychiatry, 42,* 821–833. **(Chap 6)**

KELLNER, R. (1986). *Somatization and hypochondriasis.* New York: Praeger-Greenwood. **(Chap 6)**

KELLNER, R. (IN PRESS). *Diagnosis and treatments of hypochondriacal syndromes.* Unpublished manuscript. **(Chap 6)**

KELLNER, R., HERNANDEZ, J., & PATHAK, D. (1992). Hypochondriacal fears and beliefs, anxiety, and somatization. *British Journal of Psychiatry, 160,* 525–532. **(Chap 6)**

KELLY, J. A., & MURPHY, D. A. (1992). Psychological interventions with AIDS and HIV: Prevention and treatment. *Journal of Consulting and Clinical Psychology, 60*(4), 576–585. **(Chap 9)**

KELLY, J. A., ST. LAWRENCE, J. S., HOOD, H. V., & BRASFIELD, T. L. (1989). Behavioral intervention to reduce AIDS risk activities. *Journal of Consulting and Clinical Psychology, 57*(1), 60–67. **(Chap 9)**

KELLY, M. P., STRASSBERG, D. S., & KIRCHER, J. R. (1990). Attitudinal and experiential correlates of anorgasmia. *Archives of Sexual Behavior, 19*(2), 165–177. **(Chap 11)**

KELSOE, J. R., GINNS, E. I., EGELAND, J. A., GERHARD, D. S., GOLDSTEIN, A. M., BALE, S. J., PAULS, D. J., LONG, R. T., KIDD, K. K., CONTE, G., HOUSMAN, D. E., & PAUL, S. M. (1989). Reevaluation of the linkage relationship between chromosome 11p loci and the gene for bipolar affective disorder in the Old Order Amish. *Nature, 342,* 238–243. **(Chap 7)**

KEMENY, M. E., COHEN, F., ZEGANS, L. S., & CONANT, M. A. (1989). Psychological and immunological predictors of genital herpes recurrence. *Psychosomatic Medicine, 51,* 195–208. **(Chap 9)**

KEMP, S. (1990). *Medieval psychology.* New York: Greenwood Press. **(Chap 1)**

KENDALL, P. C., & WATSON, D. (Eds.). (1989). *Anxiety and depression: Distinctive and overlapping features.* San Diego: Academic Press. **(Chap 7)**

KENDELL, R. (1985). Emotional and physical factors in the genesis of puerperal mental disorders. *Journal of Psychosomatic Research, 29,* 3–11. **(Chap 7)**

KENDLER, K. S. (1982). Demography of paranoid psychosis (delusional disorder): A review and comparison with schizophrenia and affective illness. *Archives of General Psychiatry, 39,* 890–902. **(Chap 14)**

KENDLER, K. S., & DIEHL, S. R. (1993). The genetics of schizophrenia: A current, genetic-epidemiologic perspective. *Schizophrenia Bulletin, 19,* 261–285. **(Chap 14)**

KENDLER, K. S., & GRUENBERG, A. M. (1982). Genetic relationship between paranoid personality disorder and the "schizophrenic spectrum" disorders. *American Journal of Psychiatry, 139,* 1185–1186. **(Chap 13)**

KENDLER, K. S., HEATH, A. C., MARTIN, N. G., & EAVES, L. J. (1987). Symptoms of anxiety and symptoms of depression: Same genes, different environments? *Archives of General Psychiatry, 44*(5), 451–457. **(Chap 7)**

KENDLER, K. S., HEATH, A. C., NEALE, M. C., KESSLER, R. C., & EAVES, L. J. (1992). A population-based twin study of alcoholism in women. *Journal of the American Medical Association, 268,* 1877–1882. **(Chap 12)**

KENDLER, K. S., KESSLER, R. C., NEALE, M. C., HEATH, A. C., & EAVES, L. J. (1993). The prediction of major depression in women: Toward an integrated etiologic model. *American Journal of Psychiatry, 150,* 1139–1148. **(Chap 4)**

KENDLER, K. S., MACLEAN, C., NEALE, M., KESSLER, R., HEATH, A., & EAVES, L. (1991). The genetic epidemiology of bulimia nervosa. *American Journal of Psychiatry, 148*(12), 1627–1637. **(Chap 8)**

KENDLER, K. S., NEALE, M. C., KESSLER, R. C., HEATH, A. C., & EAVES, L. J. (1992A). Generalized anxiety disorder in women: A population-based twin study. *Archives of General Psychiatry, 49,* 267–272. **(Chap 5)**

KENDLER, K. S., NEALE, M. C., KESSLER, R. C., HEATH, A. C., & EAVES, L. J. (1992B). Major depression and generalized anxiety disorder: Same genes, (partly) different environments? *Archives of General Psychiatry, 49,* 716–722. **(Chap 7)**

KENDLER, K. S., NEALE, M. C., MACLEAN, C. J., HEATH, A. C., EAVES, L. J., & KESSLER, R. C. (1993). Smoking and major depression: A causal analysis. *Archives of General Psychiatry, 50,* 36–43. **(Chap 12)**

KERMANI, E. J., & DROB, S. L. (1987). *Tarasoff* decision: A decade later dilemma still faces psychotherapists. *American Journal of Psychotherapy, 41,* 271–285. **(Chap 17)**

KERNS, R., SOUTHWICK, S., GILLER, E., HAYTHORNWAITE, J., JACOB, M., & ROSENBERG, R. (1991). The relationship between reports of pain-related social interactions and expressions of pain and affective distress. *Behavior Therapy, 22,* 101–111. **(Chap 9)**

KERNS, R. D., HAYTHORNWAITE, J., SOUTHWICK, S., & GILLER, E. L., JR. (1990). The role of marital interaction in chronic pain and depressive symptom severity. *Journal of Psychosomatic Research, 34,* 401–408. **(Chap 9)**

KERTZNER, R. M., & GORMAN, J. M. (1992). Psychoneuroimmunology and HIV infection. In A. Tashan & M. B. Riba (Eds.), *Review of psychiatry* (Vol. 11). Washington, DC: American Psychiatric Press. **(Chap 9)**

KESSLER, R. C., MCGONAGLE, K. A., ZHAO, S., NELSON, C. B., HUGHES, M., ESHLEMAN, S., WITTCHEN, H. U., & KENDLER, K. S. (In press). Lifetime and 12-month prevalence of DSM-III-R psychiatric disorders among persons aged 15–54 in the United States: Results from the national comorbidity survey. *Archives of General Psychiatry.* **(Chap 5)**

KETY, S. S. (1990). Genetic factors in suicide: Family, twin, and adoption studies. In S. J. Blumenthal & D. J. Kupfer (Eds.), *Suicide over the life cycle: Risk factors, assessment and treatment of suicidal patients* (pp. 127–133). Washington, DC: American Psychiatric Press. **(Chap 7)**

KETY, S. S., ROSENTHAL, D., WENDER, P. H., SCHULSINGER, F., & JACOBSEN, B. (1978). The biological and adoptive families of adoptive individuals who become schizophrenic. In L. C. Wynne, R. L. Cromwell, & S. Matthysse (Eds.), *The nature of schizophrenia* (pp. 25–37). New York: John Wiley. **(Chap 14)**

KEYS, A., BROZEK, J., HENSCHEL, A., MICHELSON, O., & TAYLOR, H. L. (1950). *The biology of human starvation* (Vol. 1). Minneapolis: University of Minnesota Press. **(Chap 8)**

KHANTZIAN, E. J., GAWIN, F., KLEBER, H. D., & RIORDAN, C. E. (1984). Methylphenidate (Ritalin) treatment of cocaine dependence: A preliminary report. *Journal of Substance Abuse Treatment, 1,* 107–112. **(Chap 12)**

KIECOLT-GLASER, J. K., FISHER, L., OGROCKI, P., STOUT, J. C., SPEICHER, C. E., & GLASER, R. (1987). Marital quality, marital disruption, and immune function. *Psychosomatic Medicine, 49,* 13–34. **(Chap 9)**

KIECOLT-GLASER, J. K., & GLASER, R. (1987). Chronic stress and immunity in family caregivers of Alzheimer's disease victims. *Psychosomatic Medicine, 49*(5), 523–535. **(Chap 9)**

KIECOLT-GLASER, J. K., & GLASER, R. (1992). Psychoneuroimmunology: Can psychological interventions modulate immunity? Special issue: Behavioral medicine: An update for the 1990s. *Journal of Consulting and Clinical Psychology, 60*(4), 569–575. **(Chap 9)**

KIESLER, C. A., & SIBULKIN, A. E. (1987). *Mental hospitalization: Myths and facts about a national crisis.* Beverly Hills, CA: Sage. **(Chap 17)**

KIESLER, D. J. (1966). Some myths of psychotherapy research and the search for a para-

digm. *Psychological Bulletin, 65,* 110–136. **(Chap 4)**

KIHLSTROM, J. F. (1992). Dissociation and dissociations: A commentary on consciousness and cognition. *Consciousness & Cognition, 1,* 47–53. **(Chap 2)**

KIHLSTROM, J. F., BARNHARDT, T. M., & TATARYN, D. J. (1992). The psychological unconscious: Found, lost, and regained. *American Psychologist, 47*(6), 788–791. **(Chap 2)**

KILPATRICK, D. G., BEST, C. L., VERONEN, L. J., AMICK, A. E., VILLEPONTEAUX, L. A., & RUFF, G. A. (1985). Mental health correlates of criminal victimization: A random community survey. *Journal of Consulting and Clinical Psychology, 53,* 866–873. **(Chap 5)**

KIMBLE, R., WILLIAMS, J. G., & AGRAS, S. (1975). A comparison of two methods of diagnosing hysteria. *American Journal of Psychiatry, 134,* 1020–1025. **(Chap 6)**

KING, A. C., TAYLOR, C. B., ALBRIGHT, C. A., & HASKELL, W. L. (1990). The relationship between repressive and defensive coping styles and blood pressure responses in healthy, middle-aged men and women. *Journal of Psychosomatic Research, 34,* 461–471. **(Chap 9)**

KING, N. J., GULLONE, E., & TONGE, B. J. (1991). Childhood fears and anxiety disorders. *Behaviour Change, 8,* 124–135. **(Chap 5)**

KING, S. A., & STRAIN, J. J. (1991). *Pain disorders: A proposed classification for DSM-IV.* Paper presented at the 144th annual meeting of the American Psychiatric Association, New Orleans. **(Chap 6)**

KINSELLA, J. E., FRANKEL, E., GERMAN, B., & KANNER, J. (1993). Possible mechanisms for the protective role of antioxidants in wine and plant foods. *Food Technology, 47,* 85–89. **(Chap 12)**

KINSEY, A. C., POMEROY, W. B., & MARTIN, C. E. (1948). *Sexual behavior in the human male.* Philadelphia: W. B. Saunders. **(Chap 11)**

KINSEY, A. C., POMEROY, W. B., MARTIN, C. E., & GEBHARD, P. H. (1953). *Sexual behavior in the human female.* Philadelphia: W. B. Saunders. **(Chap 11)**

KINZIE, J. D., LEUNG, P. K., BOEHNLEIN, J., & MATSUNAGA, D. (1992). Psychiatric epidemiology of an Indian village: A 19-year replication study. *Journal of Nervous and Mental Disease, 180*(1), 33–39. **(Chap 7)**

KIRCH, D. G. (1993). Infection and autoimmunity as etiologic factors in schizophrenia: A review and reappraisal. *Schizophrenia Bulletin, 19,* 355–370. **(Chap 14)**

KIRK, J. (1993). Two generations illustrate changes in options and opinions. *The Special Edge, 7,* 16. **(Chap 15)**

KIRKLEY, B. A., KOLOTKIN, R. L., HERNANDEZ, J. T., & GALLAGHER, P. N. (1992). A comparison of binge-purgers, obese binge eaters and obese nonbinge eaters on the MMPI. *International Journal of Eating Disorders, 12*(2), 221–228. **(Chap 8)**

KIRMAYER, L. J. (1991). The place of culture in psychiatric nosology: Taijin kyōfushō and DSM-III-R. *Journal of Nervous and Mental Disease, 179,* 19–28. **(Chap 5)**

KIRMAYER, L. J., & ROBBINS, J. M. (1991). Three forms of somatization in primary care: Prevalence, co-occurrence, and sociodemographic characteristics. *Journal of Nervous and Mental Disease, 179,* 647–655. **(Chap 6)**

KIRMAYER, L. J., & WEISS, M. (1993). *On cultural considerations for somatoform disorders in the DSM-IV.* In cultural proposals and supporting papers for DSM-IV. Submitted to the DSM-IV Task Force by the Steering Committee, NIMH-Sponsored Group on Culture and Diagnosis. **(Chap 6)**

KLEIN, D. F. (1964). Delineation of two drug responsive anxiety syndromes. *Psychopharmacologia, 5,* 397–408. **(Chap 5)**

KLEIN, D. F. (1989). The pharmacological validation of psychiatric diagnosis. In L. Robins & J. Barrett (Eds.), *Validity of psychiatric diagnosis.* New York: Raven Press. **(Chap 7)**

KLEIN, D. N., TAYLOR, E. B., DICKSTEIN, S., & HARDING, K. (1988). The early-late onset distinction in DSM-III-R dysthymia. *Journal of Affective Disorders, 14*(1), 25–33. **(Chap 7)**

KLEINMAN, A. (1982). Neurasthenia and depression: A study of somatization and culture in China. *Culture, Medicine, and Psychiatry, 6,* 117–190. **(Chap 4)**

KLEINMAN, A. (1986). *Social origins of distress and disease: Depression neurasthenia, and pain in modern China.* New Haven, CT: Yale University Press. **(Chap 9)**

KLERMAN, G. L. (1988). Depression and related disorders of mood (affective disorders). In A. M. Nicholi, Jr. (Ed.), *The new Harvard guide to psychiatry.* Cambridge, MA: Harvard University Press. **(Chap 7)**

KLERMAN, G. L., & WEISSMAN, M. M. (1989). Increasing rates of depression. *Journal of the American Medical Association, 261,* 2229–2235. **(Chap 7)**

KLERMAN, G. L., & WEISSMAN, M. M. (1992). The course, morbidity, and costs of depression. *Archives of General Psychiatry, 49*(10), 831–834. **(Chap 7)**

KLERMAN, G. L., WEISSMAN, M. M., ROUNSAVILLE, B. J., & CHEVRON, E. S. (1984). *Interpersonal psychotherapy of depression.* New York: Basic Books. **(Chaps 2, 7, 8)**

KLIN, A., VOLKMAR, F. R., & SPARROW, S. S. (1992). Autistic social dysfunction: Some limitations of the Theory of Mind hypothesis. *Journal of Child Psychology and Psychiatry, 33,* 861–876. **(Chap 16)**

KLOSKO, J. S., BARLOW, D. H., TASSINARI, R., & CERNY, J. A. (1990). A comparison of alprazolam and behavior therapy in treatment of panic disorder. *Journal of Consulting and Clinical Psychology, 58,* 77–84. **(Chap 5)**

KLUFT, R. P. (1984). Treatment of multiple personality disorder. *Psychiatric Clinics of North America, 7,* 9–29. **(Chap 6)**

KLUFT, R. P. (1991). Multiple personality disorder. In A. Tasman, & S. W. Goldinger (Eds.), *Review of psychiatry* (Vol. 10). Washington, DC: American Psychiatric Press. **(Chap 6)**

KNAPP, M. J., KNOPMAN, D. S., SOLOMON, P. R., PENDLEBURY, W. W., DAVIS, C. S., & GRACON, S. I. (1994). A 30-week randomized controlled trial of high-dose tacrine in patients with Alzheimer's disease. *Journal of the American Medical Association, 271,* 985–991. **(Chap 15)**

KNIGHT, R. A., & PRENTKY, R. A. (1990). Classifying sexual offenders: The develop-ment and corroboration of taxonomic models. In W. L. Marshall, D. R. Laws, & H. E. Barbaree (Eds.), *Handbook of sexual assault: Issues, theories and treatment of the offender* (pp. 23–52). New York: Plenum Press. **(Chap 11)**

KNOTT, V. J. (1988). Dynamic EEG changes during cigarette smoking. *Neuropsychobiology, 19,* 54–60. **(Chap 12)**

KOCSIS, O. H., CROUGHAN, J. L., KATZ, M. M., BUTLER, T. P., SECUNDA, S., BOWDEN, C. L., & DAVIS, J. M. (1990). Response to treatment with antidepressants of patients with severe or moderate nonpsychotic depression and of patients with psychotic depression. *American Journal of Psychiatry, 147,* 621–624. **(Chap 7)**

KOEGEL, P., BURNAM, M. A., & FARR, R. K. (1988). The prevalence of specific psychiatric disorders among homeless individuals in the inner city of Los Angeles. *Archives of General Psychiatry, 45,* 1085–1092. **(Chap 17)**

KOEGEL, R. L., SCHREIBMAN, L., O'NEILL, R. E., & BURKE, J. C. (1983). The personality and family interaction characteristics of parents of autistic children. *Journal of Consulting and Clinical Psychology, 51,* 683–692. **(Chap 16)**

KOHUT, H. (1971). *The analysis of self.* New York: International Universities Press. **(Chap 13)**

KOHUT, H. (1977). *The restoration of the self.* New York: International Universities Press. **(Chap 13)**

KOLATA, G. (1992, NOVEMBER 10). New Alzheimer's study questions link to metal. *New York Times,* C2. **(Chap 15)**

KOOB, G. F. (1992). Drugs of abuse: Anatomy, pharmacology and function of reward pathways. *Trends in Pharmacological Sciences, 13,* 177–184. **(Chap 12)**

KORCZYN, A. D., KAHANA, E., & GALPER, Y. (1991). Epidemiology of dementia in Ashkelon, Israel. *Neuroepidemiology, 10,* 100. **(Chap 15)**

KORENMAN, S. G., & BARCHAS, J. D. (1993). *Biological basis of substance abuse.* New York: Oxford University Press. **(Chap 12)**

KOTSAFTIS, A., & NEALE, J. M. (1993). Schizotypal personality disorder I: The clinical syndrome. *Clinical Psychology Review, 13,* 451–472. **(Chap 13)**

KOVACS, M., GATSONIS, C., PAULAUSKAS, S. L., & RICHARDS, C. (1989). Depressive disorders in childhood: IV. A longitudinal study of comorbidity with and risk for anxiety disorders, 46*(9), 776–782. **(Chap 7)**

KOVACS, M., GOLDSTON, D., & GATSONIS, C. (1993). Suicidal behaviors and childhood-onset depressive disorders: A longitudinal investigation. *Journal of the American Academy of Child and Adolescent Psychiatry, 32,* 8–20. **(Chap 7)**

KOVACS, M., RUSH, A. J., BECK, A. T., & HOLLON, S. D. (1981). Depressed outpatients treated with cognitive therapy or pharmacotherapy: A one-year follow-up. *Archives of General Psychiatry, 38*(1), 33–39. **(Chap 7)**

KRAAIMAAT, F. W., JANSSEN, P., & VAN DAMBAGGEN, R. (1991). Social anxiety and stuttering. *Perceptual and Motor Skills, 72,* 766. **(Chap 16)**

KRAEPELIN, E. (1898). *The diagnosis and prognosis of dementia praecox.* Paper presented at the 29th Congress of Southwestern German Psychiatry, Heidelberg. **(Chap 14)**

KRAEPELIN, E. (1899). *Kompendium der Psychiatrie* (6th ed.). Leipzig: Abel. **(Chap 14)**

KRAEPELIN, E. (1913). *Psychiatry: A textbook.* Leipzig: Barth. **(Chap 1, 3)**

KRAEPELIN, E. (1919). *Dementia praecox and paraphrenia.* (R. M. Barclay & G. M. Robertson, Trans.). New York: R. E. Krieger.

KRAMER, M. (1969). *Applications of mental health statistics.* Geneva: World Health Organization. **(Chap 15)**

KRANTZ, D. S., & DECKEL, A. W. (1983). Coping with coronary heart disease and stroke. In T. G. Burish, & L. A. Bradley (Eds.), *Coping with chronic disease: Research and applications.* New York: Academic Press. **(Chap 9)**

KRASSOIEVITCH, M., PEREZ-RINCON, H., & SUAREZ, P. (1982). Correlation entre les hallucinations visuelles et auditives dans une population de schophrenes Mexicains. *Confrontations Psychiatriques, 15,* 149–162. **(Chap 14)**

KRAUSE, J., HERTH, T., MAIER, W., STEIGER, A., SCHONEICH, S., & BENKERT, O. (1991). An interdisciplinary study towards a multiaxial classification of male sexual dysfunction. *Acta Psychiatrica Scandinavica, 84*(2), 130–136. **(Chap 11)**

KRISHNAN, K. R., DORAISWAMY, P. M., VENKATARAMAN, S., REED, D., & RICHIE, J. C. (1991). Current concepts in hypothalamo-pituitary-adrenal axis regulation. In J. A. McCubbin, P. G. Kaufmann, & C. B. Nemeroff (Eds.), *Stress, neuropeptides, and systemic disease* (pp. 19–35). San Diego: Academic Press. **(Chap 9)**

KUDROW, L. (1982). Paradoxical effects of frequent analgesic use. In M. Critchley, A. Friedman, S. Gorini, & F. Sicuteri (Eds.), *Headache: Physiopathological and clinical concepts: Advances in Neurology* (Vol. 33). New York: Raven Press. **(Chap 9)**

KUECHENMEISTER, C. A., LINTON, P. H., MUELLER, T. V., & WHITE, H. B. (1977). Eye tracking in relation to age, sex, and illness. *Archives of General Psychiatry, 34,* 578–579. **(Chap 14)**

KUHN, R. (1957). Über die Behandlung depressive Zustande mit einem Iminodibenzylderivat (G22355) [Treatment of depressive states with an iminodibenzyl derivative (G22355)]. *Schweizerische Medizinische Wochenschrift, 87,* 1135–1140. **(Chap 7)**

KUIPER, B., & COHEN-KETTENIS, P. (1988). Sex reassignment surgery: A study of 141 Dutch transsexuals. *Archives of Sexual Behaviour, 17,* 439–457. **(Chap 11)**

KUPFER, D. J., FRANK, E., PEREL, J. M., CORNES, C., MALLINGER, A. G., THASE, M. E., MCEACHRAN, A. B., & GRONCHOCINSKI, V. J. (1992). Five-year outcome for maintenance therapies in recurrent depression. *Archives of General Psychiatry, 49,* 769–773. **(Chap 7)**

KUPFER, D. J., REYNOLDS, C. F., III, GROCHOCINSKI, V. J., ULRICH, R. F., & MCEACHRAN, A. (1986). Aspects of short REM latency in affective states: A revisit. *Psychiatry Research, 17,* 49–59. **(Chap 7)**

KURITA, H., KITA, M., & MIYAKE, Y. (1992). A comparative study of development and symptoms among disintegrative psychosis and infantile autism with and without speech loss. *Journal of Autism and Developmental Disorders, 22,* 175–188. **(Chap 16)**

LABBE, E. E., & WILLIAMSON, D. A. (1984). Behavioral treatment of elective mutism: A review of the literature. *Clinical Psychology Review, 4,* 273–292. **(Chap 16)**

LACEY, J. H. (1992). The treatment demand for bulimia: A catchment area report of referral rates and demography. *Psychiatric Bulletin, 16,* 203–205. **(Chap 8)**

LACKS, P., & MORIN, C. M. (1992). Recent advances in the assessment and treatment of insomnia. *Journal of Consulting and Clinical Psychology, 60,* 586–594. **(Chap 10)**

LADEE, G. A. (1966). *Hypochondriacal syndromes.* New York: Elsevier. **(Chap 6)**

LADER, M. H. (1975). *The psychophysiology of mental illness.* London: Routledge & Kegan Paul. **(Chap 2)**

LADER, M., & SARTORIUS, N. (1968). Anxiety in patients with hysterical conversion symptoms. *Journal of Neurology, Neurosurgery, and Psychiatry, 31,* 490–495. **(Chap 6)**

LADER, M. H., & WING, L. (1964). Habituation of the psycho-galvanic reflex in patients with anxiety states and in normal subjects. *Journal of Neurology, Neurosurgery, and Psychiatry, 27,* 210–218. **(Chap 5)**

LA FOND, J. Q., & DURHAM, M. L. (1992). *Back to the asylum: The future of mental health law and policy in the United States.* New York: Oxford University Press. **(Chap 17)**

LAING, R. D. (1967). *The politics of experience.* New York: Pantheon. **(Chap 14)**

LAKIN, M. M., MONTAGUE, D. K., VANDERBRUG MEDENDORP, S., TESAR, L., & SCHOVER, L. R. (1990). Intracavernous injection therapy: Analysis of results and complications. *Journal of Urology, 143,* 1138–1141. **(Chap 11)**

LAMBERT, M. C., WEISZ, J. R., KNIGHT, F., DESROSIERS, M., OVERLY, K., & THESIGER, C. (1992). Jamaican and American adult perspectives on child psychopathology: Further explorations of the threshold model. *Journal of Consulting and Clinical Psychology, 60,* 146–149. **(Chap 4)**

LAMBERT, M. J., SHAPIRO, D. A., & BERGIN, A. E. (1986). The effectiveness of psychotherapy. In S. L. Garfield & A. E. Bergin (Eds.), *Handbook of psychotherapy and behavior change* (3rd ed.). New York: John Wiley. **(Chap 4)**

LANDIS, S. E., EARP, J. L., & KOCH, G. G. (1992). Impact of HIV testing and counseling on subsequent sexual behavior. *AIDS Education and Prevention, 4*(1), 61–70. **(Chap 9)**

LANDRY, D. W., ZHAO, K., YANG, G. X. Q., GLICKMAN, M., & GEORGIADIS, T. M. (1993). Antibody-catalyzed degradation of cocaine. *Science, 259,* 1899–1901. **(Chap 12)**

LANDSBERG, J. P., MCDONALD, B., & WATT, F. (1992). Absence of aluminum in neuritic plaque cores in Alzheimer's disease. *Nature, 360,* 65–68. **(Chap 15)**

LANG, P. J. (1979). A bio-informational theory of emotional imagery. *Psychophysiology, 16,* 495–512. **(Chap 2)**

LANG, P. J. (1985). The cognitive psychophysiology of emotion: Fear and anxiety. In A. H.

Tuma & J. D. Maser (Eds.), *Anxiety and the anxiety disorders.* Hillsdale, NJ: Lawrence Erlbaum. **(Chap 2)**

LANYON, R. I. (1986). Theory and treatment in child molestation. *Journal of Consulting and Clinical Psychology, 54,* 176–182. **(Chap 11)**

LA PERRIERE, A. R., ANTONI, M. H., SCHNEIDERMAN, N., IRONSON, G., & KLIMAS, N. (1990). Exercise intervention attenuates emotional distress and natural killer cell decrements following notification of positive serologic status for HIV-1. *Biofeedback and Self-Regulation, 15,* 229–242. **(Chap 9)**

LA RUE, A. (1992). *Aging and neuropsychological assessment.* New York: Plenum Press. **(Chap 15)**

LASCH, C. (1978). *The culture of narcissism: American life in an age of diminishing expectations.* New York: W. W. Norton. **(Chap 13)**

LAST, C. G., HERSEN, M., KAZDIN, A. E., FINKELSTEIN, R., & STRAUSS, C. C. (1987). Comparison of DSM-III separation anxiety and overanxious disorders: Demographic characteristics and patterns of comorbidity. *Journal of the American Academy of Child and Adolescent Psychiatry, 26,* 527–531. **(Chap 5)**

LAWRENCE, R. C., HOCHBERG, M. C., KELSEY, J. L., MCDUFFIE, F. C., MEDSGER, T. A., FELTS, W. R., & SCHULMAN, L. E. (1989). Estimates of the prevalence of selected arthritic and musculo-skeleto diseases in the U.S. *Journal of Rheumatology, 16,* 427–441. **(Chap 9)**

LAWS, D. R. (Ed.). (1989). *Relapse prevention with sex offenders.* New York: Guilford Press. **(Chap 11)**

LAXENAIRE, M., GANNE-VEVONEC, M. O., & STREIFF, O. (1982). Les problemes d'identité chez les enfants des migrants. *Annales Medico-Psychologiques, 140,* 602–605. **(Chap 13)**

LAXOVA, R., RIDLER, M. A. C., & BOWENBRAVERY, M. (1977). An etiological survey of the severely retarded Hertfordshire children who were born between January 1, 1965 and December 31, 1967. *American Journal of Medical Genetics, 1,* 75–86. **(Chap 15)**

LAZARE, D. (1989, OCTOBER 18–24). Drugs 'R' Us. *In These Times,* pp. 12–13. **(Chap 12)**

LAZARUS, R. A., & FOLKMAN, S. (1984). *Stress, appraisal, and coping.* New York: Springer. **(Chap 9)**

LAZARUS, R. S. (1968). Emotions and adaptation: Conceptual and empirical relations. In W. J. Arnold (Ed.), *Nebraska Symposium on Motivation* (Vol. 16). Lincoln: University of Nebraska Press. **(Chap 2)**

LAZARUS, R. S. (1991). Progress on a cognitive-motivational relational theory of emotion. *American Psychologist, 46*(8), 819–834. **(Chap 2)**

LEBEDINSKAYA, K. S., & NIKOLSKAYA, O. S. (1993). Brief report: Analysis of autism and its treatment in modern Russian defectology. *Journal of Autism and Developmental Disorders, 23,* 675–697. **(Chap 16)**

LECCESE, A. P. (1991). *Drugs and society: Behavioral medicines and abusable drugs.* Englewood Cliffs, NJ: Prentice-Hall. **(Chap 12)**

LECKMAN, J. F., WEISSMAN, M. M., MERIKAN-GAS, K. R., PAULS, D. L., & PRUSOFF, B. A. (1983). Panic disorder and major depression. *Archives of General Psychiatry, 40,* 1055–1060. **(Chap 7)**

LEE, C. K. (1992). Alcoholism in Korea. In J. Helzer & G. Canino (Eds.), *Alcoholism—North America, Europe and Asia: A coordinated analysis of population data from ten regions* (pp. 247–262). London: Oxford University Press. **(Chap 12)**

LEE, K. (1992). Pattern of night waking and crying of Korean infants from 3 months to 2 years old and its relation with various factors. *Journal of Developmental & Behavioral Pediatrics, 13,* 326–330. **(Chap 10)**

LEE, S., HSU, L. K. G., & WING, Y. K. (1992). Bulimia nervosa in Hong Kong Chinese patients. *British Journal of Psychiatry, 161,* 545–551. **(Chap 8)**

LEE, S., LEUNG, C. M., WING, Y. K., CHIU, H. F. ET AL. (1991). Acne as a risk factor for anorexia nervosa in Chinese. *Australian and New Zealand Journal of Psychiatry, 25*(1), 134–137. **(Chap 8)**

LEE, T., & TANG, S. W. (1984). Lozapine and clozapine decrease serotonin (S2) but do not elevate dopamine (D2) receptor numbers in the rat brain. *Psychiatry Research, 12,* 277–285. **(Chap 14)**

LEFRANCOIS, G. R. (1990). *The lifespan* (3rd ed.). Belmont, CA: Wadsworth Publishing. **(Chap 4)**

LEHRER, P. M., & MURPHY, A. I. (1991). Stress reactivity and perception of pain among tension headache sufferers. *Behaviour Research and Therapy, 29*(1), 61–69. **(Chap 9)**

LEIBLUM, S. R., & ROSEN, R. C. (EDS.). (1988). *Sexual desire disorders.* New York: Guilford Press. **(Chap 11)**

LEITENBERG, H., DETZER, M. J., & SREBNIK, D. (1993). Gender differences in masturbation and the relation of masturbation experience in preadolescence and/or early adolescence to sexual behavior and sexual adjustment in young adulthood. *Archives of Sexual Behavior, 22*(2), 87–98. **(Chap 11)**

LEJEUNE, J., GAUTHIER, M., & TURPIN, R. (1959). Étude des chromosomes somatiques de neuf enfants mongoliens. *Comptes Rendus Hebdomadaires des Seances de l'Academie des Sciences. D: Sciences Naturelles (Paris), 248,* 1721–1722. **(Chap 15)**

LEMOINE, P., HAROUSSEAU, H., BORTEYRU, J. P., & MENUET, J. C. (1968). Les enfants de parents alcooliques: Anomalies observées. Á propos de 127 cas [Children of alcoholic parents: Anomalies observed in 127 cases]. *Quest Medicine, 21,* 476–482. **(Chap 12)**

LENKE, R. R., & LEVY, H. (1980). Maternal phenylketonuria and hyperphenylalanemia: An international survey of the outcome of untreated and treated pregnancies. *New England Journal of Medicine, 303,* 1202–1208. **(Chap 15)**

LEO, J. (1983, AUGUST 15). Take me out to the ballgame. *Time,* p. 72. **(Chap 5)**

LESLIE, A. M. (1987). Pretense and representation: The origins of "Theory of Mind." *Psychological Review, 94,* 412–426. **(Chap 16)**

LEVAY, S. (1991). A difference in hypothalamic structure between heterosexual and homosexual men. *Science, 253,* 1034–1037. **(Chap 11)**

LEVIN, A., & HYLER, S. (1986). DSM-III personality diagnosis in bulimia. *Comprehensive Psychiatry, 27,* 47. **(Chap 13)**

LEVINE, M. N., GUYATT, G. H., GENT, M., DEPAUW, S., GOODYEAR, M. D., HRYNIUK, W. M., ARNOLD, A., FINDLAY, B., SKILLINGS, J. R., BRAMWELL, V. H., LEVIN, L., BUSH, H., ABU-ZAHRA, H., & KOTALIK, J. (1988). Quality of life in stage II breast cancer: An instrument for clinical trials. *Journal of Clinical Oncology, 6,* 1798–1810. **(Chap 9)**

LEVINE, S. B., & YOST, M. A. (1976). Frequency of sexual dysfunction in a general gynecological clinic: An epidemiological approach. *Archives of Sexual Behavior, 5,* 229–238. **(Chap 11)**

LEVY, S. M., & WISE, B. D. (1987). Psychosocial risk factors, natural immunity, and cancer progression: Implications for intervention. Special issue: Health psychology. *Current Psychology Research and Reviews, 6*(3), 229–243. **(Chap 9)**

LEWIN, T. H. D. (1975). Psychiatric evidence in criminal cases for purposes other than the defense of insanity. *Syracuse Law Review, 26,* 1051–1115. **(Chap 17)**

LEWINSOHN, P. M., & CLARKE, G. N. (1984). Group treatment of depressed individuals: The "coping with depression" course. *Advances in Behaviour Research and Therapy, 6*(2), 99–114. **(Chap 7)**

LEWINSOHN, P. M., CLARKE, G. N., HOPS, H., & ANDREWS, J. (1990). Cognitive behavioral treatment for depressed adolescents. *Behavior Therapy, 21,* 385–401. **(Chap 7)**

LEWINSOHN, P. M., HOBERMAN, H. M., & ROSENBAUM, M. (1988). A prospective study of risk factors for unipolar depression. *Journal of Abnormal Psychology, 97,* 251–264. **(Chap 7)**

LEWINSOHN, P. M., HOPS, H., ROBERTS, R. E., SEELEY, J. R., & ANDREWS, J. A. (1993). Adolescent psychopathology: I. Prevalence and incidence of depression and other DSM-III-R disorders in high school students. *Journal of Abnormal Psychology, 102*(1), 133–144. **(Chap 7)**

LEWINSOHN, P. M., ROHDE, P., & SEELEY, J. R. (1993). Psychosocial characteristics of adolescents with a history of suicide attempt. *Journal of the American Academy of Child and Adolescent Psychiatry, 32*(1), 60–68. **(Chap 7)**

LEWINSOHN, P. M., ROHDE, P., SEELEY, J. R., & FISCHER, S. A. (1993). Age-cohort changes in the lifetime occurrence of depression and other mental disorders. *Journal of Abnormal Psychology, 102*(1), 110–120. **(Chap 7)**

LEWINSOHN, P. M., & ROSENBAUM, M. (1987). Recall of parental behavior by acute depressives, remitted depressives and nondepressives. *Journal of Personality and Social Psychology, 52*(3), 611–619. **(Chap 7)**

LEWINSOHN, P. M., STEINMETZ, J. L., LARSON, D. W., & FRANKLIN, J. (1981). Depression-related cognitions: Antecedent or consequences? *Journal of Abnormal Psychology, 90,* 213–219. **(Chap 7)**

LEWIS, G., CROFT-JEFFREYS, C., & ANTHONY, D. (1990). Are British psychiatrists racist? *British Journal of Psychiatry, 157,* 410–415. **(Chap 14)**

LEWIS, G., DAVID, A., ANDREASSON, S., & ALLSBECK, P. (1992). Schizophrenia and city life. *Lancet, 340,* 137–140. **(Chap 2, 14)**

LEWY, A. J. (1993). Seasonal mood disorders. In D. L. Dunner (Ed.), *Current psychiatric therapy* (pp. 220–225). Philadelphia: W. B. Saunders. **(Chap 7)**

LEWY, A. J., KERN, H. E., ROSENTHAL, N. E., & WEHR, T. A. (1982). Bright artificial light treatment of a manic-depressive patient with a seasonal mood cycle. *American Journal of Psychiatry, 139,* 1496–1498. **(Chap 7)**

LIBERMAN, R. P., DERISI, W. D., & MUESER, K. T. (1989). *Social skills training for psychiatric patients.* Boston, MA: Allyn & Bacon. **(Chap 14)**

LIDDELL, H. S. (1949). The role of vigilance in the development of animal neurosis. In P. Hoch & J. Zubin (Eds.), *Anxiety.* New York: Grune & Stratton. **(Chap 5)**

LIDZ, C. W., MULVEY, E. P., APPELBAUM, P. S., & CLEVELAND, S. (1989). Commitment: The consistency of clinicians and the use of legal standards. *American Journal of Psychiatry, 146,* 176–186. **(Chap 17)**

LIEBERMAN, J. A., JODY, D., ALVIR, J. M. J., ASHTARI, M., LEVY, D. L., BOGERTS, B., DEGREEF, G., MAYEROFF, D. I., & COOPER, T. (1993). Brain morphology, dopamine, and eye-tracking abnormalities in first-episode schizophrenia. *Archives of General Psychiatry, 50,* 357–368. **(Chap 14)**

LIEBESKIND, J. (1991). Pain *can* kill. *Pain, 44,* 3–4. **(Chap 9)**

LIEBOWITZ, M. R., SCHNEIER, F., CAMPEAS, R., HOLLANDER, E., HATTERER, J., FYER, A., GORMAN, J., PAPP, L., DAVIES, S., GULLY, R., & KLEIN, D. F. (1992). Phenelzine vs. atenolol in social phobia: A placebo controlled comparison. *Archives of General Psychiatry, 49,* 290–300. **(Chap 5)**

LIEBOWITZ, S. F. (1983). Hypothalamic catecholamine systems controlling eating behavior: A potential model for anorexia nervosa. In P. L. Darby, P. E. Garfinkel, D. M. Garner, & D. V. Corsica (Eds.), *Anorexia nervosa: Recent developments in research* (pp. 221–229). New York: Alan R. Liss. **(Chap 8)**

LIEBOWITZ, S. F. (1985). Brain neurotransmitters and appetite regulation. *Psychopharmacology Bulletin, 21,* 415. **(Chap 8)**

LIGGETT, J. (1974). *The human face.* New York: Stein and Day. **(Chap 6)**

LILIENFELD, S. O. (1992). The association between antisocial personality and somatization disorders: A review and integration of theoretical models. *Clinical Psychology Review, 12,* 641–662. **(Chaps 6, 13)**

LILIENFELD, S. O., VANVALKENBURG, C., LARNTZ, K., & AKISKAL, H. S. (1986). The relationship of histrionic personality to antisocial personality and somatization disorders. *American Journal of Psychiatry, 143,* 718–722. **(Chap 13)**

LIN, K. M. (1986). Psychopathology and social disruption in refugees. In C. L. Williams & J. Westermeyer (Eds.), *Refugee mental health in resettlement countries* (pp. 61–73). Washington, DC: Hemisphere Publishing Corp. **(Chap 15)**

LIN, N., & ENSEL, W. M. (1984). Depression-mobility and its social etiology: The role of life events and social support. *Journal of Health and Social Behavior, 25*(2), 176–188. **(Chap 7)**

LINDESAY, J. (1991). Phobic disorders in the elderly. *British Journal of Psychiatry, 159,* 531–541. **(Chap 5)**

LINDQUIST, P., & ALLEBECK, P. (1990). Schizophrenia and crime: A longitudinal follow-up of 644 schizophrenics in Stockholm. *British Journal of Psychiatry, 157,* 345–350. **(Chap 17)**

LINDSEY, K. P., & PAUL, G. L. (1989). Involuntary commitments to public mental institutions: Issues involving the overrepresentation of blacks and assessment of relevant functioning. *Psychological Bulletin, 106,* 171–183. **(Chap 14)**

LINEHAN, M. M. (1987). Dialectical behavior therapy for borderline personality disorder: Theory and method. *Bulletin of the Menninger Clinic, 51,* 261–276. **(Chap 13)**

LINEHAN, M. M., ARMSTRONG,, H. E., SUAREZ, A., ALLMON, D., & HEARD, H. L. (1991). Cognitive-behavioral treatment of chronically parasuicidal borderline patients. *Archives of General Psychiatry, 48,* 1060–1064. **(Chap 13)**

LINEHAN, M. M., HEARD, H. L., & ARMSTRONG, H. E. (1992). *Naturalistic follow-up of a behavioral treatment for chronically parasuicidal borderline patients.* Unpublished manuscript, University of Washington, Seattle. **(Chap 13)**

LINEHAN, M. M., & KEHRER, C. A. (1993). Borderline personality disorder. In D. H. Barlow (Ed.), *Clinical handbook of psychological disorders: A step by step treatment manual.* New York: Guilford Press. **(Chaps 7, 13)**

LINKS, P. S., STEINER, M., BOIAGO, I., & IRWIN, D. (1990). Lithium therapy for borderline patients: Preliminary findings. *Journal of Personality Disorders, 4,* 173–181. **(Chap 13)**

LINKS, P., STEINER, M., & HUXLEY, G. (1988). The occurrence of borderline personality disorder in families of borderline patients. *Journal of Personality Disorders, 2,* 14–20. **(Chap 13)**

LIPOWSKI, Z. J. (1983). Transient cognitive disorders (delirium, acute confusional states) in the elderly. *American Journal of Psychiatry, 140,* 1426–1436. **(Chap 15)**

LIPOWSKI, Z. J. (1990). *Delirium: Acute confusional states.* New York: Oxford University Press. **(Chap 15)**

LIPSKA, B. K., JASKIW, G. E., & WEINBERGER, D. R. (1993). Postpubertal emergence of hyperresponsiveness to stress and to amphetamine after neonatal excitotoxic hippocampal damage: A potential animal model of schizopherenia. *Neuropsychopharmacology, 9,* 67–75.

LISSPERS, J., & ÖST, L. (1990). Long-term follow-up of migraine treatment: Do the effects remain up to six years? *Behaviour Research and Therapy, 28,* 313–322. **(Chap 9)**

LITZ, B. T., PENK, W. E., WALSH, S., HYER, L., BLAKE, D. D., MARX, B., KEANE, T. M., & BITMAN, D. (1991). Similarities and differences between MMPI and MMPI-2 applications to the assessment of posttraumatic stress disorder. *Journal of Personality Assessment, 57,* 238–253. **(Chap 3)**

LIVESLEY, W. J., SCHROEDER, M. L., JACKSON, D. N., & JANG, K. L. (1994). Categorical distinctions in the study of personality disorder: Implications for classification. *Journal of Abnormal Psychology, 103,* 6–17. **(Chap 13)**

LOEBEL, J. P., DAGER, S. R., & KITCHELL, M. A. (1993). Alzheimer's disease. In D. L. Dunner (Ed.), *Current psychiatric therapy* (pp. 59–65). Philadelphia: W. B. Saunders. **(Chap 15)**

LOEBER, R. (1982). The stability of antisocial and delinquent child behavior: A review. *Child Development, 53,* 1431–1446. **(Chap 13)**

LOEWENSTEIN, R. J. (1991). Psychogenic amnesia and psychogenic fugue: A comprehensive review. *Annual Review of Psychiatry, 10,* 223–247. **(Chap 6)**

LONIGAN, C. J., FISCHEL, J. E., WHITEHURST, G. J., ARNOLD, D. S., & VALDEZ-MENCHACA, M. C. (1992). The role of otitis media in the development of expressive language disorder. *Developmental Psychology, 28,* 430–440. **(Chap 16)**

LOO, D. T., COPANI, A., PIKE, C. J., WHITTEMORE, E. R., WALENCEWICZ, A. J., & COTMAN, C. W. (1993). Apoptosis is induced by B-amyloid in cultured central nervous system neurons. *Proceedings of the National Academy of Sciences, 90,* 7951–7955. **(Chap 15)**

LOPICCOLO, J., & FRIEDMAN, J. M. (1988). Broad spectrum treatment of low sexual desire: Integration of cognitive, behavioral, and systemic therapy. In S. R. Leiblum & R. C. Rosen (Eds.), *Sexual desire disorders* (pp. 107–144). New York: Guilford Press. **(Chap 11)**

LOPICCOLO, J., HEIMAN, J. R., HOGAN, D. R., & ROBERTS, C. W. (1985). Effectiveness of single therapists versus cotherapy teams in sex therapy. *Journal of Consulting and Clinical Psychology, 53*(3), 287–294. **(Chap 11)**

LOPICCOLO, J., & STEGER, J. C. (1974). The sexual interaction inventory: A new instrument for assessment of sexual dysfunction. *Archives of Sexual Behavior, 3,* 585 595. **(Chap 11)**

LOPICCOLO, J., & STOCK, W. E. (1987). Sexual function, dysfunction and counseling in gynecological practice. In Z. Rosenwaks, F. Benjamin, & M. L. Stone (Eds.), *Gynecology.* New York: Macmillan. **(Chap 11)**

LOTTER, V. (1966). Epidemiology of autistic conditions in young children: I. Prevalence. *Social Psychiatry, 1,* 124–137. **(Chap 16)**

LOVAAS, O. I. (1977). *The autistic child: Language development through behavior modification.* New York: Irvington. **(Chap 16)**

LOVAAS, O. I. (1987). Behavioral treatment and normal educational and intellectual functioning in young autistic children. *Journal of Consulting and Clinical Psychology, 55,* 3–9. **(Chap 16)**

LOVAAS, O. I., BERBERICH, J. P., PERLOFF, B. F., & SCHAEFFER, B. (1966). Acquisition of imitative speech by schizophrenic children. *Science, 151,* 705–707. **(Chap 16)**

LOWING, P. A., MIRSKY, A. F., & PEREIRA, R. (1983). The inheritance of schizophrenic spectrum disorders: A reanalysis of the Danish adoptee study data. *American Journal of Psychiatry, 140,* 1167–1171. **(Chap 14)**

LUCAS, A. R., BEARD, C. M., O'FALLON, W. M., & KURLAN, L. T. (1991). 50-year trends in the incidence of anorexia nervosa in Rochester, Minn.: A population-based study. *American Journal of Psychiatry, 148,* 917–922. **(Chap 8)**

LUCKASSON, R., COULTER, D. L., POLLOWAY, E. A., REISS, S., SCHALOCK, R. L., SNELL, M. E., SPITALNIK, D. M., & STARK, J. A. (1992). *Mental retardation: Definition, classification, and systems of supports.* Washington, DC: American Association on Mental Retardation. **(Chaps 3, 15)**

LUDWIG, A. M. (1985). Cognitive processes associated with "spontaneous" recovery from alcoholism. *Journal of Studies on Alcohol, 46,* 53–58. **(Chap 12)**

LUDWIG, A., BRANDSMA, J., WILBUR, C., BENDFELDT, F., & JAMESON, D. (1972). The objective study of a multiple personality. *Archives of General Psychiatry, 26,* 298–310. **(Chap 6)**

LUNDSTROM, B., PAULY, I., & WALINDER, J. (1984). Outcome of sex reassignment surgery. *Acta Psychiatrica Scandinavica, 70,* 289–294. **(Chap 11)**

LUNDY, A. (1985). The reliability of the thematic apperception test. *Journal of Personality Assessment, 49,* 141–145. **(Chap 3)**

LYKKEN, D. T. (1957). A study of anxiety in the sociopathic personality. *Journal of Abnormal and Social Psychology, 55,* 6–10. **(Chap 13)**

LYKKEN, D. T. (1982). Fearfulness: Its carefree charms and deadly risks. *Psychology Today, 16,* 20–28. **(Chap 13)**

MACDONALD, P. T., WALDORF, D., REINARMAN, C., & MURPHY, S. (1988). Heavy cocaine use and sexual behavior. *Journal of Drug Issues, 18,* 437–455. **(Chap 11)**

MACDOUGALL, J. M., DEMBROSKI, T. M., DIMSDALE, J. E., & HACKETT, T. P. (1985). Components of Type A, hostility, and anger-in: Further relationships to angiographic findings. *Health Psychology, 4*(2), 137–152. **(Chap 2)**

MACE, C. J. (1992). Hysterical conversion II: A critique. *British Journal of Psychiatry, 161,* 378–389. **(Chap 6)**

MACLEOD, C., & MATHEWS, A. M. (1991). Cognitive-experimental approaches to the emotional disorders. In P. R. Martin (Ed.), *Handbook of behavior therapy and psychological science: An integrative approach* (pp. 116–150). Elmsford, NY: Pergamon Press. **(Chap 5)**

MACLEOD, C., MATHEWS, A., & TATA, P. (1986). Attentional bias in emotional disorders. *Journal of Abnormal Psychology, 95,* 15–20. **(Chap 5)**

MACMILLAN, D. L., GRESHAM, F. M., & SIPERSTEIN, G. N. (1993). Conceptual and psychometric concerns about the 1992 AAMR definition of mental retardation. *American Journal of Mental Retardation, 98,* 325–335. **(Chap 15)**

MAGNE-INGVAR, U., OJEHAGEN, A., & TRASKMAN-BENDZ, L. (1992). The social network of people who attempt suicide. *Acta Psychiatrica Scandinavica, 86,* 153–158. **(Chap 7)**

MAHER, B. A., & MAHER, W. B. (1985A). Psychopathology: I. From ancient times to the eighteenth century. In G. A. Kimble & K. Schlesinger (Eds.), *Topics in the history of psychology* (pp. 251–294). Hillsdale, NJ: Lawrence Erlbaum. **(Chap 1)**

MAHER, B. A., & MAHER, W. B. (1985B). Psychopathology: II. From the eighteenth century to modern times. In G. A. Kimble & K. Schlesinger (Eds.), *Topics in the history of psychology* (pp. 295–329). Hillsdale, NJ: Lawrence Erlbaum. **(Chap 1)**

MAHER, M. (1952). On childhood psychosis and schizophrenia: Autistic and symbiotic infantile psychosis. *Psychoanalytic Study of the Child, 7,* 286–305. **(Chap 16)**

MAHR, G., & LEITH, W. (1992). Psychogenic stuttering of adult onset. *Journal of Speech and Hearing Research, 35,* 283–286. **(Chap 16)**

MALATESTA, V. J., & ADAMS, H. E. (1984). The sexual dysfunctions. In H. E. Adams & P. B. Sutker (Eds.), *Comprehensive handbook of psychopathology* (pp. 725–775). New York: Plenum Press. **(Chap 11)**

MALETZKY, B. M. (1991). *Treating the sexual offender.* Newbury Park, CA: Sage. **(Chap 11)**

MALPASS, R. S., & POORTINGA, Y. H. (1986). Strategies for design and analysis. In W. J. Lonner & J. W. Berry (Eds.), *Field methods in cross-cultural research* (pp. 47–83). Beverly Hills, CA: Sage. **(Chap 4)**

MANDALOS, G. E., & SZAREK, B. L. (1990). Dose-related paranoid reaction associated with fluoxetine. *Journal of Nervous and Mental Disease, 178*(1), 57–58. **(Chap 7)**

MANDEL, J. L., MONACO, A. P., NELSON, D. L., SCHLESSINGER, D., & WILLARD, H. (1992). Genome analysis and the human X chromosome. *Science, 258,* 103–109. **(Chap 4)**

MANDELL, A. J., & KNAPP, S. (1979). Asymmetry and mood, emergent properties of seratonin regulation: A proposed mechanism of action of lithium. *Archives of General Psychiatry, 36*(8), 909–916. **(Chap 7)**

MANIC STATES IN AFFECTIVE DISORDERS OF CHILDHOOD AND ADOLESCENCE. (1979). *British Medical Journal, 27,* 214–215. **(Chap 7)**

MANN, J. M. (1991). Global AIDS: Critical issues for prevention in the 1990's. *International Journal of Health Sciences, 21*(3), 553–559. **(Chap 9)**

MANSON, S. M., & GOOD, B. J. (1993, January). *Cultural considerations in the diagnosis of DSM-IV mood disorders.* Cultural proposals and supporting papers for DSM-IV. Submitted to the DSM-IV Task Force by the Steering Committee, NIMH-Sponsored Group on Culture and Diagnosis. **(Chap 7)**

MAR, J. (1993). New lead to an Alzheimer's mouse? *Science, 261,* 1520. **(Chap 15)**

MARCOPULOS, B. A., & GRAVES, R. E. (1990). Antidepressant effect on memory in depressed older persons. *Journal of Clinical and Experimental Neuropsychology, 12*(5), 655–663. **(Chap 7)**

MARCUS, M. D., SMITH, D., SANTELLI, R., & KAYE, W. (1992). Characterization of eating disordered behavior in obese binge eaters. *International Journal of Eating Disorders, 12,* 249–255. **(Chap 8)**

MARCUS, M. D., WING, R. R., EWING, L., KEERN, E., GOODING, W., & MCDERMOTT, M. (1990). Psychiatric disorders among obese binge eaters. *International Journal of Eating Disorders, 9,* 69–77. **(Chap 8)**

MARCUS, M. D., WING, R. R., & HOPKINS, J. (1988). Obese binge eaters: Affect, cognitions, and response to behavioral weight control. *Journal of Consulting and Clinical Psychology, 3,* 433–439. **(Chap 8)**

MARGO, A., HEMSLEY, D. R., & SLADE, P. D. (1981). The effects of varying auditory input on schizophrenic hallucinations. *British Journal of Psychiatry, 139,* 122–127. **(Chap 14)**

MARKS, I. M. (1969). *Fears and phobias.* London: Heineman. **(Chap 3)**

MARKS, I. M. (1985). Behavioural treatment of social phobia. *Psychopharmacology Bulletin, 21,* 615–618. **(Chap 5)**

MARKS, I. M. (1988). Blood-injury phobia: A review. *American Journal of Psychiatry, 145,* 1207–1213. **(Chap 2)**

MARLATT, G. A. (1985). Relapse prevention: Theoretical rationale and overview of the model. In G. A. Marlatt & J. R. Gordon (Eds.), *Relapse prevention: Maintenance strategies in the treatment of addictive behaviors* (pp. 3–70). New York: Guilford Press. **(Chap 12)**

MARLATT, G. A., & GORDON, J. R. (1980). Determinants of relapse: Implications for the maintenance of behavior change. In P. O. Davidsen & S. M. Davidsen (Eds.), *Behavioral medicine: Changing health life-styles* (pp. 474–482). New York: Brunner/Mazel. **(Chap 12)**

MARLATT, G. A., & GORDON, J. R. (Eds.) (1985). *Relapse prevention: Maintenance strategies in the treatment of addictive behaviors.* New York: Guilford Press. **(Chap 12)**

MARLATT, G. A., LARIMER, M. E., BAER, J. S., & QUIGLEY, L. A. (1993). Harm reduction for alcohol problems: Moving beyond the controlled drinking controversy. *Behavior Therapy, 24,* 461–504. **(Chap 12)**

MARRAZZI, M. A., & LUBY, E. D. (1986). An auto-addiction model of chronic anorexia nervosa. *International Journal of Eating Disorders, 5,* 191–208. **(Chap 8)**

MARSDEN, C. D. (1986). Hysteria—a neurologist's view. *Psychological Medicine, 16,* 277–288. **(Chap 6)**

MARSHALL, P. S. (1993). Allergy and depression: A neurochemical threshold model of the relation between the illnesses. *Psychological Bulletin, 113,* 23–43. **(Chap 4)**

MARSHALL, W. L, BARBAREE, H. E., & CHRISTOPHE, D. (1986). Sexual offenders against femaile children: Sexual preferences for age of victims and type of behavior. *Canadian Journal of Behavioral Science, 18,* 424–439. **Chap 11)**

MARSHALL, W. L., ECCLES, A., & BARBAREE, H. E. (1991). The treatment of exhibitionists: A focus on sexual deviance versus cognitive and relationship features. *Behavior Research and Therapy, 29,* 129–135. **(Chap 11)**

MARSHALL, W. L., JONES, R., WARD, T., JOHNSTON, P., & BARBAREE, H. E. (1991). Treatment outcome with sex offenders. *Clinical Psychology Review, 11,* 465–485. **(Chap 11)**

MARTEN, P. A., BROWN, T. A., BARLOW, D. H., BORKOVEC, T. D., SHEAR, M. K., & LYDIARD, M. B. (In press). Evaluation of the ratings comprising the associated symptom criterion of DSM-III-R generalized anxiety disorder. *Journal of Nervous and Mental Disease.* **(Chap 5)**

MARTIN, I. (1983). Human classical conditioning. In A. Gale & J. A. Edward (Eds.), *Physiological correlates of human behavior: Vol. 2. Attention and performance.* London: Academic Press. **(Chaps 2, 5)**

MARTIN, I., & LEVEY, A. B. (1985). Conditioning, evaluations and cognitions: An axis of integration. *Behaviour Research and Therapy, 23,* 167–175. **(Chap 2)**

MARTIN, P. R. (1993). *Psychological management of chronic headaches.* New York: Guilford Press. **(Chap 9)**

MARTIN, P. R., MARIE, G. V., & NATHAN, P. R. (1992). Psychophysiological mechanisms of chronic headaches: Investigation using pain induction and pain reduction procedures. *Journal of Psychosomatic Research, 36,* 137–148. **(Chap 9)**

MARTIN, S. L., RAMEY, C. T., & RAMEY, S. L. (1990). The prevention of intellectual impairment in children of impoverished families: Findings of a randomized trial of educational daycare. *American Journal of Public Health, 80,* 844–847. **(Chap 15)**

MASER, J. D. (1985). List of phobias. In A. H. Tuma & J. D. Maser (Eds.), *Anxiety and the anxiety disorders.* Hillsdale, NJ: Lawrence Erlbaum. **(Chap 5)**

MASER, J. D., & GALLUP, G. G. (1974). Tonic immobility in the chicken: Calalepsy potentiation by uncontrollable shock and alleviation by imipramine. *Psychosomatic Medicine, 36,* 199–205. **(Chap 2)**

MASER, J. D., KAELBER, C., & WEISE, R. E. (1991). International use and attitudes toward DSM-III and DSM-III-R: Growing consensus in psychiatric classification. *Journal of Abnormal Psychology, 100*(3), 271–279. **(Chap 3)**

MASTERS, W. H., & JOHNSON, V. E. (1966). *Human sexual response.* Boston: Little, Brown. **(Chap 11)**

MASTERS, W. H., & JOHNSON, V. E. (1970). *Human sexual inadequacy.* Boston: Little, Brown. **(Chap 11)**

MATHEWS, A., RICHARDS, A., & EYSENCK, M. (1989). Interpretation of homophones related to threat in anxiety states. *Journal of Abnormal Psychology, 98,* 31–34. **(Chap 5)**

MATSUMOTO, D. (1994). *People: Psychology from a cultural perspective.* Pacific Grove, CA: Brooks/Cole. **(Chap 12)**

MATTHEWS, K. A. (1988). Coronary heart disease and Type A behaviors: Update on and alternative to the Booth-Kewley and Friedman (1987) quantitative review. *Psychological Bulletin, 104*(3), 373–380. **(Chap 9)**

MATTHEWS, K. A., & HAYNES, S. G. (1986). Type A behavior pattern and coronary risk: Update and critical evaluation. *American Journal of Epidemiology, 123,* 923–960. **(Chap 9)**

MAY, P. A., & HYMBAUGH, K. J. (1983). A pilot project of fetal alcohol syndrome among American Indians. *Alcohol Health and Research World, 7,* 3–9. **(Chap 12)**

MAYS, V. M., & COCHRAN, S. D. (1988). Issues in the perception of AIDS risk and risk reduction activities by black and Hispanic/Latino women. *American Psychologist, 43*(11), 949–957. **(Chap 9)**

MCADOO, W. G., & DEMYER, M. K. (1978). Research related to family factors in autism. *Journal of Pediatric Psychology, 2,* 162–166. **(Chap 16)**

MCCAFFREY, R. J., & BELLAMY-CAMPBELL, R. (1989). Psychometric detection of fabricated symptoms of combat-related posttraumatic stress disorder: A systematic replication. *Journal of Clinical Psychology, 45,* 76–79. **(Chap 17)**

MCCAFFREY, R. J., GOETSCH, V. L., ROBINSON, J., & ISAAC, W. (1986). Differential responsivity of the vasomotor response system to a "novel" stressor. *Headache, 26,* 240–242. **(Chap 9)**

MCCALL, W. V., EDINGER, J. E., & ERWIN, C. W. (1989). Clinical utility of cassette polysomnography in sleep and sleep-related disorders. In J. S. Ebersole (Ed.), *Ambulatory EEG monitoring* (pp. 267–275). New York: Raven Press. **(Chap 10)**

MCCANN, U. D., ROSSITER, E. M., KING, R. J., & AGRAS, W. S. (1991). Nonpurging bulimia: A distinct subtype of bulimia nervosa. *International Journal of Eating Disorders, 10,* 679–687. **(Chap 8)**

MCCAUGHRIN, W. B. (1988). *Longitudinal trends of competitive employment for developmentally disabled adults: A benefit-cost analysis.* Unpublished doctoral dissertation, University of Illinois at Urbana-Champaign. **(Chap 15)**

MCCREERY, J. M., & WALKER, R. D. (1993). Alcohol problems. In D. L. Dunner (Ed.), *Current psychiatric therapy* (pp. 92–98). Philadelphia: W. B. Saunders. **(Chaps 4, 12)**

MCDANIEL, K. (1990). Thalmic degeneration. In J. L. Cummings (Ed.), *Subcortical dementia* (pp. 132–144). New York: Oxford University Press. **(Chap 15)**

MCEACHIN, J. J., SMITH, T., & LOVAAS, O. I. (1993). Long-term outcome for children with autism who received early intensive behavioral treatment. *American Journal on Mental Retardation, 97,* 359–372. **(Chap 16)**

MCELROY, S. L., & KECK, P. E. (1993). Rapid cycling. In D. L. Dunner (Ed.), *Current psychiatric therapy* (pp. 226–231). Philadelphia: W. B. Saunders. **(Chap 7)**

MCELROY, S. L., KECK, P. E., POPE, H. G., HUDSON, J. I., FAEDDA, G. L., & SWANN, A. C. (1992). Clinical and research implications of the diagnosis of dysphoric or mixed mania or hypomania. *American Journal of Psychiatry, 149*(12), 1633–1644. **(Chap 7)**

MCGILLIVRAY, B. C., BASSETT, A. S., LANGLOIS, S., PANTZAR, T., & WOOD, S. (1990). Familial 5q11.2-q13.3 segmental duplication cosegregating with multiple anomalies, including schizophrenia. *American Journal of Medical Genetics, 35,* 10–13. **(Chap 14)**

MCGLASHAN, T. H., & FENTON, W. S. (1991). Classical subtypes for schizophrenia: Literature review for DSM-IV. *Schizophrenia Bulletin, 17,* 609–623. **(Chap 14)**

MCGOWIN, D. F. (1993). *Living in the labyrinth: A personal journey through the maze of Alzheimer's.* New York: Delacorte Press. **(Chap 15)**

MCGRATH, P. A., & DEVEBER, L. L. (1986). The management of acute pain evoked by medical procedures in children with cancer.

Journal of Pain and Symptom Management, 1, 145–150. **(Chap 9)**

MCGUE, M., & LYKKEN, D. T. (1992). Genetic influence on risk of divorce. *Psychological Science, 3*(6), 368–373. **(Chaps 2, 4)**

MCGUE, M., PICKENS, R. W., & SVIKIS, D. S. (1992). Sex and age effects on the inheritance of alcohol problems: A twin study. *Journal of Abnormal Psychology, 101,* 3–17. **(Chaps 4, 12)**

MCGUFFIN, P., & KATZ, R. (1989). The genetics of depression and manic-depressive disorder. *British Journal of Psychiatry, 155,* 294–304. **(Chap 7)**

MCGUFFIN, P., KATZ, R., ALDRICH, J., & BEBBINGTON, P. (1988). The Camberwell Collaborative Depression Study. II. Investigation of family members. *British Journal of Psychiatry, 152,* 766–774. **(Chap 2)**

MCGUFFIN, P., KATZ, R., & BEBBINGTON, P. (1988). The Camberwell Collaborative Depression Study. III. Depression and adversity in the relatives of depressed probands. *British Journal of Psychiatry, 152,* 775–782. **(Chap 2)**

MCGUFFIN, P., & REICH, T. (1984). Psychopathology and genetics. In H. E. Adams & P. B. Sutker (Eds.), *Comprehensive handbook of psychopathology.* New York: Plenum Press. **(Chap 5)**

MCGUIRE, P. K., SHAH, G. M. S., & MURRAY, R. M. (1993). Increased blood flow in Broca's area during auditory hallucinations in schizophrenia. *Lancet, 342,* 703–706. **(Chap 14)**

MCKENZIE, S. J., WILLIAMSON, D. A., & CUBIC, B. A. (1993). Stable and reactive body image disturbances in bulimia nervosa. *Behavior Therapy, 24,* 195–207. **(Chap 8)**

MCKEON, P., & MURRAY, R. (1987). Familial aspects of obsessive-compulsive neuroses. *British Journal of Psychiatry, 151,* 528–534. **(Chap 13)**

MCKIM, W. A. (1991). *Drugs and behavior: An introduction to behavioral pharmacology* (2nd ed.). Englewood Cliffs, NJ: Prentice-Hall. **(Chap 12)**

MCKINNON, W., WEISSE, C. S., REYNOLDS, C. P., BOWLES, C. A., & BAUM, A. (1989). Chronic stress, leukocyte subpopulations, and hormonal response to latent viruses. *Health Psychology, 8,* 399–402. **(Chap 9)**

MCKNIGHT, D. L., NELSON-GRAY, R. O., & BARNHILL, J. (1992). Dexamethasone suppression test and response to cognitive therapy and antidepressant medication. *Behavior Therapy, 23*(1), 99–111. **(Chap 7)**

MCLAREN, J., & BRYSON, S. E. (1987). Review of recent epidemiological studies of mental retardation: Prevalence, associated disorders, and etiology. *American Journal of Mental Retardation, 92,* 243–254. **(Chap 15)**

MCLEAN, P., & TAYLOR, S. (1992). Severity of unipolar depression and choice of treatment. *Behaviour Research and Therapy, 30*(5), 443–451. **(Chap 7)**

MCLEOD, J. D., KESSLER, R. C., & LANDIS, K. R. (1992). Speed of recovery from major depressive episodes in a community sample of married men and women. *Journal of Abnormal Psychology, 101*(2), 277–286. **(Chap 7)**

MCNALLY, R. M. (1989). *On the distinction between traumatic simple phobia and post-traumatic stress disorder.* Paper requested by the Simple Phobia subcommittee of the DSM-IV Anxiety Disorders Work Group. **(Chap 5)**

MCNEIL, E. B. (1970). *Neuroses and personality disorders.* Englewood Cliffs, NJ: Prentice-Hall. **(Chap 13)**

MCNEIL, T. F. (1987). Perinatal influences in the development of schizophrenia. In H. Helmchen & F. A. Henn (Eds.), *Biological perspectives of schizophrenia* (pp. 125–138). New York: John Wiley. **(Chap 14)**

MCNIEL, D. E., & BINDER, R. L. (1987). Clinical assessment of the risk of violence among psychiatric inpatients. *American Journal of Psychiatry, 148,* 1317–1321. **(Chap 17)**

MEDINA VS. CALIFORNIA. (1992). 112 S. Ct. 2572. **(Chap 17)**

MEDNICK, S. A., GABRIELLI, W. F., JR., & HUTCHINGS, B. (1987). Genetic factors in the etiology of criminal behavior. In S. A. Mednick, T. E. Moffitt, & S. A. Stack (Eds.), *The causes of crime: New biological approaches* (pp. 74–91). Cambridge, England: Cambridge University Press. **(Chap 13)**

MEDNICK, S. A., & SCHULSINGER, F. (1965). A longitudinal study of children with a high risk for schizophrenia: A preliminary report. In S. Vandenberg (Ed.), *Methods and goals in human behavior genetics* (pp. 255–296). New York: Academic Press. **(Chap 14)**

MEDNICK, S. A., & SCHULSINGER, F. (1968). Some premorbid characteristics related to breakdown in children with schizophrenic mothers. *Journal of Psychiatric Research, 6,* 267–291. **(Chap 14)**

MEEHAN, P. J., LAMB, J. A., SALTZMAN, L. E., & O'CARROLL, P. W. (1992). Attempted suicide among young adults: Progress toward a meaningful estimate of prevalence. *American Journal of Psychiatry, 149*(1), 41–44. **(Chap 7)**

MEEHL, P. E. (1945). The dynamics of "structured" personality tests. *Journal of Clinical Psychology, 1,* 296–303. **(Chap 3)**

MEEHL, P. E. (1962). Schizotaxia, schizotypy, schizophrenia. *American Psychologist, 17,* 827–838. **(Chaps 13, 14)**

MEEHL, P. E. (1989). Schizotaxia revisited. *Archives of General Psychiatry, 46,* 935–944. **(Chap 3)**

MEISLER, A. W., & CAREY, M. P. (1990). A critical reevaluation of nocturnal penile tumescence monitoring in the diagnosis of erectile dysfunction. *Journal of Nervous and Mental Disease, 178,* 78–89. **(Chap 11)**

MELAMED, B. G., & SIEGEL, L. J. (1975). Reduction of anxiety in children facing hospitalization and surgery by use of filmed modeling. *Journal of Consulting and Clinical Psychology, 43*(4), 511–521. **(Chap 9)**

MELLINGER, G. D., BALTER, M. B., & UHLENHUTH, E. H. (1985). Insomnia and its treatment: Prevalence and correlates. *Archives of General Psychiatry, 42,* 225–232. **(Chaps 4, 10)**

MELTON, G. B., PETRILA, J., POYTHRESS, N. G., & SLOBOGIN, C. (1987). *Psychological evaluations for the courts.* New York: Guilford. **(Chap 17)**

MELTZER, E. S., & KUMAR, R. (1985). Puerperal mental illness, clinical features and classification: A study of 142 mother-and-baby admissions. *British Journal of Psychiatry, 147,* 647–654. **(Chap 7)**

MELZACK, R., & WALL, P. D. (1965). Pain mechanisms: A new theory. *Science, 150,* 971–979. **(Chap 9)**

MELZACK, R., & WALL, P. D. (1982). *The challenge of pain.* New York: Basic Books. **(Chap 9)**

MENDLEWICZ, J., & RAINER, J. D. (1977). Adoption study supporting genetic transmission in manic-depressive illness. *Nature, 268*(5618), 327–329. **(Chap 7)**

METALSKY, G. I., HALBERSTADT, L. J., & ABRAMSON, L. Y. (1987). Vulnerability to depressive mood reactions: Toward a more powerful test of the diathesis-stress and causal mediation components of the reformulated theory of depression. *Journal of Personality and Social Psychology, 52*(2), 386–393. **(Chap 7)**

MEYER, A. J., NASH, J. D., MCALISTER, A. L., MACCOBY, M., & FARQUHAR, J. W. (1980). Skills training in a cardiovascular health education campaign. *Journal of Consulting and Clinical Psychology, 2,* 129–142. **(Chap 9)**

MEYER, J. K., & RETER, D. J. (1979). Sex reassignment: Follow up. *Archives of General Psychiatry, 36,* 1010–1015. **(Chap 11)**

MEYER, L. H., PECK, C. A., & BROWN, L. (1991). *Critical issues in the lives of people with severe disabilities.* Baltimore: Paul H. Brookes. **(Chap 15)**

MEYEROWITZ, B. E. (1983). Postmastectomy coping strategies and quality of life. *Health Psychology, 2,* 117–132. **(Chap 9)**

MEYERS, A. (1991). Biobehavioral interactions in behavioral medicine. *Behavior Therapy, 22,* 129–131. **(Chap 9)**

MEZZICH, J. E., GOOD, B. J., LEWIS-FERNANDEZ, R., GUARNACCIA, P., LIN, K. M., PARRON, D., O'NELL, T., MANSON, S., FLEMING, C., WEISS, M., & HUGHES, C. (1993, SEPTEMBER). *Cultural formulation guidelines.* Revised cultural proposals for DSM-IV. Submitted to the DSM-IV Task Force by the Steering Committee, NIMH-Sponsored Group on Culture and Diagnosis. **(Chap 3)**

MEZZICH, J. E., KLEINMAN, A., FABREGA, H., JR., GOOD, B., JOHNSON-POWELL, G., LIN, K. M., MANSON, S., & PARRON, D. (1992). *Cultural proposals for DSM-IV.* Submitted to the DSM-IV Task Force by the Steering Committee, NIMH-Sponsored Group on Culture and Diagnosis. **(Chap 6)**

MICHULTKA, D. M., BLANCHARD, E. B., APPELBAUM, K. A., JACCARD, J., & DENTINGER, M. P. (1989). The refractory headache patient. II. High medication consumption (analgesic rebound) headache. *Behaviour Research and Therapy, 27,* 411–420. **(Chap 9)**

MIKLOWITZ, D. J., & GOLDSTEIN, M. J. (1990). Behavioral family treatment for patients with bipolar affective disorder. *Behavior Modification, 14,* 457–489. **(Chap 7)**

MIKLOWITZ, D. J., SIMONEAU, T. L., SACHS-ERICSSON, N., WARNER, R., & SUDDATH, R. (In press). Family risk indicators in the course of bipolar affective disorder. In C. Mundt (Ed.), *Interpersonal factors in origin and course of affective disorders.* London: Royal College of Psychiatrists. **(Chap 7)**

MILBY, J. B., WILLIAMS, V., HALL, J. N., KHUDER, S., MCGILL, T., & WOOTEN, V. (1993). Effectiveness of combined triazolam-behavior therapy for primary insomnia. *American Journal of Psychiatry, 150,* 1259–1260. **(Chap 10)**

MILLER, I. W., KEITNER, G. I., EPSTEIN, N. B., BISHOP, D. S., & RYAN, C. E. (1991). *Families of bipolar patients: Dysfunction, course of illness, and pilot treatment study.* Paper presented at the annual meeting of the Association for the Advancement of Behavior Therapy, New York. **(Chap 7)**

MILLER, I. W., KEITNER, G. I., WHISMAN, M. A., RYAN, C. E., EPSTEIN, N. B., & BISHOP, D. S. (1992). Depressed patients with dysfunctional families: Description and course of illness. *Journal of Abnormal Psychology, 101*(4), 637–646. **(Chap 7)**

MILLER, I. W., & NORMAN, W. H. (1979). Learned helplessness in humans: A review and attribution-theory model. *Psychological Bulletin, 86*(1), 93–118. **(Chaps 2, 7)**

MILLER, I. W., NORMAN, W. H., KEITNER, G. I., BISHOP, S. B., & DOWN, M. G. (1989). Cognitive-behavioral treatment of depressed inpatients. *Behavior Therapy, 20*(1), 25–47. **(Chap 7)**

MILLER, N. E. (1969). Learning of visceral and glandular responses. *Science, 163,* 434–445. **(Chap 9)**

MILLER, N. E. (1987). Education for a lifetime of learning. In G. C. Stone, S. M. Weiss, J. D. Matarazzo, N. E. Miller, J. Rodin, C. D. Belar, M. J. Follick, & J. E. Singer (Eds.), *Health psychology: A discipline and a profession.* Chicago: IL: University of Chicago Press. **(Chap 9)**

MILLER, N. S., GOLD, M. S., & POTTASH, A. C. (1989). A 12-step treatment approach for marijuana (cannabis) dependence. *Journal of Substance Abuse Treatment, 6,* 241–250. **(Chap 12)**

MILLER, P. M., SMITH, G. T., & GOLDMAN, M. S. (1990). Emergence of alcohol expectancies in childhood: A possible critical period. *Journal of Studies on Alcohol, 51,* 343–349. **(Chap 12)**

MILLER, P. P., ALBANO, A. M., & BARLOW, D. H. (1992). *Sibling modeling in the treatment of PTSD.* Paper presented at the annual meeting of the Association for the Advancement of Behavior Therapy, Boston, MA. **(Chap 5)**

MILLER, S., & WATSON, B. C. (1992). The relationship between communication attitude, anxiety, and depression in stutterers and nonstutterers. *Journal of Speech and Hearing Research, 35,* 789–798. **(Chap 16)**

MILLER, S. D. (1989). Optical differences in cases of multiple personality disorder. *Journal of Nervous and Mental Disease, 177*(8), 480–486. **(Chap 6)**

MILLER, W. R. (1985). Motivation for treatment: A review with special emphasis on alcoholism. *Psychological Bulletin, 98,* 84–107. **(Chap 12)**

MILLER, W. R., & HESTER, R. K. (1986). Inpatient alcoholism treatment: Who benefits? *American Psychologist, 41,* 794–805. **(Chap 12)**

MILLER, W. R., & MCCRADY, B. S. (1993). The importance of research on Alcoholics Anonymous. In B. S. McCrady & W. R. Miller (Eds.), *Research on Alcoholics Anonymous: Opportunities and alternatives* (pp. 3–11).

New Brunswick, NJ: Rutgers Center of Alcohol Studies. **(Chap 12)**

MILLON, T. (1981). *Disorders of personality: DSM-III, Axis II.* New York: John Wiley. **(Chap 13)**

MILLON, T. (1986A). Schizoid and avoidant personality disorders in DSM-III. *American Journal of Psychiatry, 143,* 1321–1322. **(Chap 13)**

MILLON, T. (1986B). The MCMI and DSM-III: Further commentaries. *Journal of Personality Assessment, 50,* 205–207. **(Chap 3)**

MILLS, J. L., HOLMES, L. B., AARONS, J. H., SIMPSON, J. L., BROWN, Z. A., JOVANOVIC-PETERSON, L. G., CONLEY, M. R., GRAUBARD, B. I., KNOPP, R. H., & METZGER, B. E. (1993). Moderate caffeine use and the risk of spontaneous abortion and intrauterine growth retardation. *Journal of the American Medical Association, 269,* 593–597. **(Chap 12)**

MINDELL, J. A. (1993). Sleep disorders in children. *Health Psychology, 12,* 152–163. **(Chap 10)**

MINDELL, J. A., & ANDRASIK, F. (1987). Headache classification and factor analysis with a pediatric population. *Headache, 27,* 96–101. **(Chap 9)**

MINEKA, S. (1985A). Animal models of anxiety based disorders: Their usefulness and limitations. In A. H. Tuma & J. D. Maser (Eds.), *Anxiety and the anxiety disorders.* Hillsdale, NJ: Lawrence Erlbaum. **(Chap 5)**

MINEKA, S. (1985B). The frightful complexity of the origins of fears. In F. R. Bruch & J. B. Overmier (Eds.), *Affect, conditioning, and cognition: Essays on the determinants of behavior.* Hillsdale, NJ: Lawrence Erlbaum. **(Chaps 2, 5)**

MINEKA, S., DAVIDSON, M., COOK, M., & KEIR, R. (1984). Observational conditioning of snake fear in rhesus monkeys. *Journal of Abnormal Psychology, 93,* 355–372. **(Chap 5)**

MINEKA, S., GUNNAR, M., & CHAMPOUX, M. (1986). Control and early socioemotional development: Infant rhesus monkeys reared in controllable versus uncontrollable environments. *Child Development, 57,* 1241–1256. **(Chap 2)**

MINEKA, S., & KELLY, K. A. (1989). The relationship between anxiety, lack of control and loss of control. In A. Steptoe & A. Appels (Eds.), *Stress, personal control and worker health.* New York: John Wiley. **(Chap 7)**

MINGDAO, Z., & ZHENYI, X. (1990). Delivery systems and research for schizophrenia in China. In A. Kales, C. N. Stefanis, & J. A. Talbott (Eds.), *Recent advances in schizophrenia* (pp. 373–395). New York: Springer-Verlag. **(Chap 14)**

MINTZ, J., MINTZ, L. I., ARUDA, M. J., & HWANG, S. S. (1992). Treatments of depression and the functional capacity to work. *Archives of General Psychiatry, 49*(10), 761–768. **(Chap 7)**

MINUCHIN, S., ROSMAN, B. L., & BAKER, L. (1978). *Psychosomatic families.* Cambridge, MA: Harvard University Press. **(Chap 8)**

MIRANDA, J., & PERSONS, J. B. (1988). Dysfunctional attitudes are mood-state dependent. *Journal of Abnormal Psychology, 97*(1), 76–79. **(Chap 7)**

MITCHELL, J. E., & PYLE, R. L. (1988). The diagnosis and clinical characteristics of bulimia. In B. J. Blinder, B. F. Chaitin, & R. S. Goldstein (Eds.), *The eating disorders: Medical and psychological bases of diagnosis and treatment* (pp. 267–273). New York: PMA. **(Chap 8)**

MITCHELL, J. E., PYLE, R. L., ECKERT, E. D., HATSUKAMI, D., POMEROY, C., & ZIMMERMAN, R. (1990). A comparison study of antidepressants and structured intensive group psychotherapy in the treatment of bulimia nervosa. *Archives of General Psychiatry, 47,* 149–157. **(Chap 8)**

MODEL PENAL CODE AND COMMENTARIES. (1962). 4.01, 164–165. **(Chap 17)**

MOGG, K., MATHEWS, A., & WEINMAN, J. (1989). Selective processing of threat cues in anxiety states: A replication. *Behaviour Research and Therapy, 27,* 317–323. **(Chap 5)**

MOGIL, J. S., STERNBERG, W. F., KEST, B., MAREK, P., & LIEBESKIND, J. C. (1993). Sex differences in the antagonism of swim stress-induced analgesia: Effects of gonadectomy and estrogen replacement. *Pain, 53,* 17–25. **(Chap 9)**

MOHLER, H., & OKADA, T. (1977). Benzodiazepine receptor: Demonstration in the central nervous system. *Science, 198,* 849. **(Chap 2)**

MOHR, D. C., & BEUTLER, L. E. (1990). Erectile dysfunction: A review of diagnostic and treatment procedures. *Clinical Psychology Review, 10*(1), 123–150. **(Chap 11)**

MONAHAN, J. (1984). The prediction of violent behavior: Toward a second generation of theory and policy. *American Journal of Psychiatry, 141,* 10–15. **(Chap 17)**

MONEY, J. (1992). *The Kaspar Hauser syndrome of "psychosocial dwarfism": Deficient statural, intellectual, and social growth induced by child abuse.* Buffalo: Prometheus Books. **(Chap 2)**

MONEY, J., ANNECILLO, C., & HUTCHISON, J. W. (1985). Forensic and family psychiatry in abuse dwarfism: Munchausen's Syndrome by proxy, atonement, and addiction to abuse. *Journal of Sex and Marital Therapy, 11*(1), 30–40. **(Chap 2)**

MONEY, J., & EHRHARDT, A. (1972). *Man and woman, boy and girl.* Baltimore: Johns Hopkins University Press. **(Chap 11)**

MONK, T. H., & MOLINE, M. L. (1989). The timing of bedtime and waketime decisions in free-running subjects. *Psychophysiology, 26,* 304–310. **(Chap 10)**

MONROE, S. M., BROMET, E. J., CONNELL, M. M., & STEINER, S. C. (1986). Social support, life events, and depressive symptoms: A 1 year prospective study. *Journal of Consulting and Clinical Psychology, 54*(4), 424–431. **(Chap 7)**

MONROE, S. M., IMHOFF, D. F., WISE, B. D., & HARRIS, J. E. (1983). Prediction of psychological symptoms under high-risk psychosocial circumstances: Life events, social support, and symptom specificity. *Journal of Abnormal Psychology, 92*(2), 338–350. **(Chap 7)**

MONROE, S. M., KUPFER, D. J., & FRANK, E. (1992). Life stress and treatment course of recurrent depression: I. Response during index episode. *Journal of Consulting and Clinical Psychology, 60*(5), 718–724. **(Chap 7)**

MONROE, S. M., & ROBERTS, J. E. (1990). Conceptualizing and measuring life stress: Problems, principles, procedures, progress. Special issue: II–IV. Advances in measuring life stress. *Stress Medicine, 6*(3), 209–216. **(Chap 7)**

MONROE, S. M., THASE, M. E., & SIMONS, A. D. (1992). Social factors and the psychobiology of depression: Relations between life stress and rapid eye movement sleep latency. *Journal of Abnormal Psychology, 101*(3), 528–537. **(Chap 7)**

MOONEY, J. J., SCHATZBERG, A. F., COLE, J. O., & SAMSON, J. A. (1991). Urinary 3-methoxy-4-hydroxyphenylglycol and the depression-type score as predictors of differential responses to antidepressants. *Journal of Clinical Psychopharmacology, 11*(6), 339–343. **(Chap 7)**

MOORE, R. Y. (1973). Retinohypothalamic projection in mammals: A comparative study. *Brain Research, 49,* 403–409. **(Chap 2)**

MOREAU, D., & WEISSMAN, M. M. (1992). Panic disorder in children and adolescents: A review. *American Journal of Psychiatry, 149,* 1306–1314. **(Chap 5)**

MOREL, B. A. (1852). *Traite des maladies mentales.* Paris: Masson. **(Chap 14)**

MORELLI, G. A., ROGOFF, B., OPPENHEIM, D., & GOLDSMITH, D. (1992). Cultural variation in infants' sleeping arrangements: Questions of independence. *Developmental Psychology, 28,* 604–613. **(Chap 10)**

MOREY, L. C. (1988). Personality disorders in DSM-III and DSM-III-R: Convergence, coverage, and internal consistency. *American Journal of Psychiatry, 145,* 573–577. **(Chap 13)**

MOREY, L. C. (1991). Classification of mental disorder as a collection of hypothetical constructs. *Journal of Abnormal Psychology, 100*(3), 289–293. **(Chap 3)**

MOREY, L. C., & KURTZ, J. E. (1989). *The place of neurasthenia in the DSM-IV.* Unpublished report to the DSM-IV subgroup on generalized anxiety disorder and mixed anxiety depression. **(Chap 9)**

MOREY, L. C., & OCHOA, E. S. (1989). An investigation of adherence to diagnostic criteria: Clinical diagnosis of the DSM-III personality disorders. *Journal of Personality Disorders, 3*(3), 180–192. **(Chap 3)**

MORGAN, H. W. (1981). *Drugs in America: A social history, 1800–1980.* Syracuse, NY: Syracuse University Press. **(Chap 12)**

MORGENSTERN, H., & GLAZER, W. M. (1993). Identifying risk factors for tardive dyskinesia among long-term outpatients maintained with neuroleptic medications: Results of the Yale tardive dyskinesia study. *Archives of General Psychiatry, 50,* 723–733. **(Chap 14)**

MORGENSTERN, M., & KLASS, E. (1991). Standard intelligence tests and related assessment techniques. In J. L. Matson & J. A. Mulick (Eds.), *Handbook of mental retardation* (2nd ed., pp. 195–210). Elmsford, NY: Pergamon Press. **(Chap 15)**

MORIN, C. (1993). *Psychological management of insomnia.* New York: Guilford Press. **(Chap 10)**

MORIN, C. M. (1993). *Insomnia: Psychological assessment and management.* New York: Guilford Press. **(Chap 10)**

MORIN, C. M., & AZRIN, N. H. (1988). Behavioral and cognitive treatments of geriatric insomnia. *Journal of Consulting and Clinical Psychology, 56,* 748–753. **(Chap 10)**

MORIN, C. M., KOWATCH, R. A., BARRY, T., & WALTON, E. (1993). Cognitive-behavior therapy for late-life insomnia. *Journal of Consulting and Clinical Psychology, 61,* 137–146. **(Chap 10)**

MORIN, C. M., STONE, J., TRINKLE, D., MERCER, J., & REMSBERG, S. (IN PRESS). Dysfunctional beliefs and attitudes about sleep among older adults with and without insomnia complaints. *Psychology and Aging.* **(Chap 10)**

MOROKOFF, P. J. (1993). Female sexual arousal disorder. In W. O'Donohue & J. H. Geer (Eds.), *Handbook of sexual dysfunctions: Assessment and treatment* (pp. 157–199). Boston: Allyn & Bacon. **(Chap 11)**

MOROKOFF, P. J., & HEIMAN, J. R. (1980). Effects of erotic stimuli on sexually functional and dysfunctional women: Multiple measures before and after sex therapy. *Behaviour Research and Therapy, 18,* 127–137. **(Chap 11)**

MORRIS, D. (1985). *Body watching: A field guide to the human species.* New York: Crown. **(Chap 6)**

MORRIS, M., LACK, L., & DAWSON, D. (1990). Sleep-onset insomniacs have delayed temperature rhythms. *Sleep, 13,* 1–14. **(Chap 10)**

MORRIS, R. J., & KRATOCHWILL, T. R. (1983). *Treating children's fears and phobias: A behavioral approach.* Elmsford, NY: Pergamon Press. **(Chap 5)**

MORRISON, J., & KRIEGER, R. (1970). *People are strange.* New York: Electra Records. **(Chap 13)**

MORROW, G. R. (1986). Behavioral management of chemotherapy-induced nausea and vomiting in the cancer patient. *The Clinical Oncologist, 113,* 11–14. **(Chap 9)**

MORROW, G. R., & DOBKIN, P. L. (1988). Anticipatory nausea and vomiting in cancer patients undergoing chemotherapy treatment: Prevalence, etiology, and behavioral interventions. *Clinical Psychology Review, 8,* 517–556. **(Chaps 1, 9)**

MORSE, G. A. (1992). Causes of homelessness. In M. J. Robertson & M. Greenblatt (Eds.), *Homelessness: A national perspective* (pp. 3–17). New York: Plenum Press. **(Chap 17)**

MORSE, G. A., & CALSYN, R. J. (1992). Mental health and other human service needs of homeless people. In M. J. Robertson & M. Greenblatt (Eds.), *Homelessness: A national perspective* (pp. 117–130). New York: Plenum Press. **(Chap 17)**

MORTON, A. (1992). *Diana: Her true story.* New York: Pocket Books. **(Chap 8)**

MOSHER, D. L., & SIRKIN, M. (1984). Measuring a macho personality constellation. *Journal of Research in Personality, 18,* 150–163. **(Chap 13)**

MOSS, A. R., & BACCHETTI, P. (1989). Natural history of HIV infection. *AIDS, 3,* 55–61. **(Chap 9)**

MOWRER, O. H. (1950). *Learning theory and the personality dynamics.* New York: Arnold Press. **(Chap 5)**

MUCHA, T. F., & REINHARDT, R. F. (1970). Conversion reactions in student aviators. *American Journal of Psychiatry, 127,* 493–497. **(Chap 6)**

MUEHLENHARD, C. L., JULSONNET, S., CARLSON, M. I., & FLARITY-WHITE, L. A. (1989). A cognitive-behavioral program for preventing sexual coercion. *The Behavior Therapist, 12,* 211–214. **(Chap 11)**

MUESER, K. T., BELLACK, A. S., WADE, J. H., SAYERS, S. L., TIERNEY, A., & HAAS, G. (1993). Expressed emotion, social skill, and response to negative affect in schizophrenia. *Journal of Abnormal Psychology, 102,* 339–351. **(Chap 14)**

MUESER, K. T., LIBERMAN, R. P., & GLYNN, S. M. (1990). Psychosocial interventions in schizophrenia. In A. Kales, C. N. Stefanis, & J. A. Talbott (Eds.), *Recent advances in schizophrenia* (pp. 213–235). New York: Springer-Verlag. **(Chap 14)**

MULLANEY, J. A., & TRIPPETT, C. J. (1979). Alcohol dependence and phobias: Clinical description and relevance. *British Journal of Psychiatry, 135,* 565–573. **(Chap 5)**

MUNCK, A., GUYRE, P. M., & HOLBROOK, N. J. (1984). Physiological functions of glucocorticoids in stress and their relation to pharmacological actions. *Endocrine Reviews, 5*(1), 25–44. **(Chap 9)**

MUNJACK, D. J. (1984). The onset of driving phobias. *Journal of Behavior Therapy and Experimental Psychiatry, 15,* 305–308. **(Chap 5)**

MUNOZ, R. F. (1993). The prevention of depression: Current research and practice. *Applied and Preventative Psychology, 2,* 21–33. **(Chap 7)**

MURPHY, A., LEHRER, P., & JURISH, S. (1990). Cognitive coping skills training and relaxation training as treatments for tension headaches. *Behavior Therapy, 21,* 89–98. **(Chap 9)**

MURPHY, G. E., SIMONS, A. D., WETZEL, R. D., & LUSTMAN, P. J. (1984). Cognitive therapy and pharmacotherapy, singly and together in the treatment of depression. *Archives of General Psychiatry, 41,* 33–41. **(Chap 7)**

MURRAY, M. E., KEELE, D. K., & McCARVER, J. W. (1976). Behavioral treatment of rumination. *Clinical Pediatrics, 15,* 591–596. **(Chap 8)**

MUSTAFA, G. (1990). Delivery systems for the care of schizophrenic patients in Africa—Sub-Sahara. In A. Kales, C. N. Stefanis, & J. A. Talbot (Eds.), *Recent advances in schizophrenia* (pp. 353–371). New York: Springer-Verlag. **(Chap 14)**

MUSTO, D. F. (1992). America's first cocaine epidemic: What did we learn? In T. R. Kosten & H. D. Kleber (Eds.), *Clinician's guide to cocaine addiction: Theory, research, and treatment* (pp. 3–15). New York: Guilford Press. **(Chap 12)**

MYERS, J. K., WEISSMAN, M. M., TISCHLER, C. E., HOLZER, C. E., III, ORVASCHEL, H., ANTHONY, J. C., BOYD, J. H., BURKE, J. D., JR., KRAMER, M., & STOLTZMAN, R. (1984). Six-month prevalence of psychiatric disorders in three communities. *Archives of General Psychiatry, 41,* 959–967. **(Chap 3)**

NADIG, P. W., WARE, J. C., & BLUMOFF, R. (1986). Noninvasive device to produce and maintain an erection-like state. *Urology, 27,* 126–131. **(Chap 11)**

NAGEL, D. B. (1991). Psychotherapy of schizophrenia: 1900–1920. In J. G. Howells (Ed.), *The concept of schizophrenia: Historical perspectives* (pp. 191–201). Washington, DC: American Psychiatric Press. **(Chap 14)**

NASSER, M. (1986). Comparative study of the prevalence of abnormal eating attitudes among Arab female students of both London and Cairo universities. *Psychological Medicine, 16,* 621–625. **(Chap 8)**

NASSER, M. (1988). Eating disorders: The cultural dimension. *Social Psychiatry and Psychiatric Epidemiology, 23,* 184–187. **(Chap 8)**

NATHAN, P. E. (1993). Alcoholism: Psychopathology, etiology, and treatment. In P. B. Sutker & H. E. Adams (Eds.), *Comprehensive handbook of psychopathology* (pp. 451–476). New York: Plenum Press. **(Chap 12)**

NATHAN, P. W. (1976). The gate-control theory of pain: A critical review. *Brain, 99,* 123–158. **(Chap 9)**

NATIONAL FOUNDATION FOR BRAIN RESEARCH. (1992). *The care of disorders of the brain.* Washington, DC: National Foundation for Brain Research. **(Chap 14)**

NATIONAL INSTITUTE ON DRUG ABUSE. (1991). *National household survey on drug abuse, population estimates, 1991* (DHHS Publication No. ADM 91-1732). Washington, DC: U.S. Government Printing Office. **(Chap 12)**

NAVIA, B. A. (1990). The AIDS dementia complex. In J. L. Cummings (Ed.), *Subcortical dementia* (pp. 181–198). New York: Oxford University Press. **(Chap 15)**

NDETEI, D. M., & SINGH, A. (1983). Hallucinations in Kenyan schizophrenic patients. *Acta Psychiatrica Scandinavica, 67,* 144–147. **(Chap 14)**

NDETEI, D. M., & VADHER, A. (1984). A cross-cultural study of the frequencies of Schneider's first rank symptoms of schizophrenia. *Acta Psychiatrica Scandinavica, 70,* 540–544. **(Chap 14)**

NEAL, A. M., & TURNER, S. M. (1991). Anxiety disorders research with African Americans: Current status. *Psychological Bulletin, 109*(3), 400–410. **(Chap 5)**

NEIGHBORS, H. W., JACKSON, J. S., CAMPBELL, L., & WILLIAMS, D. (1989). The influence of racial factors on psychiatric diagnosis: A review and suggestions for research. *Community Mental Health Journal, 25*(4), 301–311. **(Chap 7)**

NELLES, W. B. N., & BARLOW, D. H. (1988). Do children panic? *Clinical Psychology Review, 8*(4), 359–372. **(Chap 5)**

NELSON, R. O., & BARLOW, D. H. (1981). Behavioral assessment: Basic strategies and initial procedures. In D. H. Barlow (Ed.), *Behavioral assessment of adult disorders.* New York: Guilford Press. **(Chap 3)**

NESTADT, G., ROMANOSKI, A. J., CHAHAL, R., MERCHANT, A., FOLSTEIN, M. F., GRUENBERG, E. M., & MCHUGH, P. R. (1990). An epidemiological study of histrionic personality disorder. *Psychological Medicine, 20,* 413–422. **(Chap 13)**

NEWLIN, D. B. (1989). The skin-flushing response: Autonomic, self-report, and conditioned responses to repeated administrations of alcohol in Asian men. *Journal of Abnormal Psychology, 98,* 421–425. **(Chap 12)**

NEWLIN, D. B., & THOMSON, J. B. (1990). Alcohol challenge with sons of alcoholics: A critical review and analysis. *Psychological Bulletin, 108,* 383–402. **(Chap 12)**

NEWMAN, J. P., PATTERSON, C. M., & KOSSON, D. S. (1987). Response perseveration in psychopaths. *Journal of Abnormal Psychology, 96,* 145–148. **(Chap 13)**

NEWMAN, J. P., & WALLACE, J. F. (1993). Psychopathy and cognition. In K. S. Dobson & P. C. Kendall (Eds.), *Psychopathology and cognition* (pp. 293–349). New York: Academic Press. **(Chap 13)**

NEWMAN, J. P., WIDOM, C. S., & NATHAN, S. (1985). Passive-avoidance in syndromes of disinhibition: Psychopathy and extraversion. *Journal of Personality and Social Psychology, 50,* 624–630. **(Chap 6)**

NEW YORK MENTAL HYGIENE LAW. (1992). 1.03 (20). **(Chap 17)**

NEW YORK TIMES. (1994, February 2). **(Chap 17)**

NGUI, P. W. (1969). The koro epidemic in Singapore. *Australian and New Zealand Journal of Psychiatry, 3,* 263–266. **(Chap 1)**

NICHOLSON, N. L., BLANCHARD, E. B., & APPELBAUM, K. A. (1990). Two studies of the occurrence of psychophysiological symptoms in chronic headache patients. *Behaviour Research and Therapy, 28*(3), 195–203. **(Chap 9)**

NIHIRA, K., FOSTER, R., SHELLHAAS, M., & LELAND, H. (1974). *Adaptive behavior scales.* Washington, DC: American Association on Mental Deficiency. **(Chap 15)**

NISBETT, R. E., & ROSS, L. (1980). *Human inference: Strategies and shortcomings in social judgement.* New York: Century. **(Chap 4)**

NOFZINGER, E. A., SCHWARTZ, C. F., REYNOLDS, C. F., THASE, M. E., JENNINGS, J. R., FRANK, E., FASICZKA, A. L., GARAMONI, G. L., & KUPFER, D. J. (1994). Affect intensity and phasic REM sleep in depressed men before and after treatment with cognitive-behavior therapy. *Journal of Consulting and Clinical Psychology, 62,* 83–91. **(Chap 10)**

NOLEN-HOEKSEMA, S. (1987). Sex differences in unipolar depression: Evidence and theory. *Psychological Bulletin, 101*(2), 259–282. **(Chap 7)**

NOLEN-HOEKSEMA, S. (1990). *Sex differences in depression.* Stanford, CA: Stanford University Press. **(Chap 7)**

NOLEN-HOEKSEMA, S., GIRGUS, J. S., & SELIGMAN, M. E. P. (1992). Predictors and consequences of childhood depressive symptoms: A 5-year longitudinal study. *Journal of Abnormal Psychology, 101*(3), 405–422. **(Chaps 4, 7)**

NOLL, R. B., ZUCKER, R. A., & GREENBERG, G. S. (1990). Identification of alcohol by smell among preschoolers: Evidence for early socialization about drugs occurring in the home. *Child Development, 61,* 1520–1527. **(Chap 12)**

NORMAN, W. H., MILLER, I. W., & DOW, M. G. (1988). Characteristics of depressed patients with elevated levels of dysfunctional cognitions. *Cognitive Therapy and Research, 12,* 39–51. **(Chap 7)**

NORTON, G. R., HARRISON, B., HAUCH, J., & RHODES, L. (1985). Characteristics of people with infrequent panic attacks. *Journal of Abnormal Psychology, 94,* 216–221. **(Chap 5)**

NOYES, R., CLARKSON, C., CROWE, R. R., YATES, W. R., & MCCHESNEY, C. M. (1987). A family study of generalized anxiety disorder. *American Journal of Psychiatry, 144,* 1019–1024. **(Chap 5)**

NOYES, R., GARVEY, M. J., COOK, B., & SUELZER, M. (1991). Controlled discontinuation of benzodiazepine treatment for patients with panic disorder. *American Journal of Psychiatry, 148,* 517–523. **(Chap 5)**

NOYES, R., HOENK, P., KUPERMAN, S., & SLYMEN, D. (1977). Depersonalization in accident victims and psychiatric patients. *Journal of Nervous and Mental Disease, 164,* 401–407. **(Chap 6)**

NOYES, R., & KLETTI, R. (1977). Depersonalization in response to life-threatening danger. *Comprehensive Psychiatry, 18,* 375–384. **(Chap 6)**

NOYES, R., WOODMAN, C., GARVEY, M. J., COOK, B. L., SUELZER, M., CLANCY, J., & ANDERSON, D. J. (1992). Generalized anxiety disorder vs. panic disorder: Distinguishing characteristics and patterns of comorbidity. *Journal of Nervous and Mental Disease, 180,* 369–379. **(Chap 5)**

NURNBERG, H. G., RASKIN, M., LEVINE, P. E., POLLACK, S., SIEGEL, O., & PRINCE, R. (1991). The comorbidity of borderline personality and other DSM-III-R Axis II personality disorders. *American Journal of Psychiatry, 148,* 1371–1377. **(Chap 13)**

NURNBERGER, J. I., JR., BERRETTINI, W., TAMARKIN, L., HAMOVIT, J., NORTON, J., & GERSHON, E. S. (1988). Supersensitivity to melatonin suppression by light in young people at high risk for affective disorder: A preliminary report. *Neuropsychopharmacology, 1,* 217–223. **(Chap 7)**

NURNBERGER, J. I., & GERSHON, E. S. (1992). Genetics. In E. S. Paykel (Ed.), *Handbook of affective disorders* (pp. 126–145). New York: Guilford Press. **(Chap 7)**

NUTT, D., & LAWSON, C. (1992). Panic attacks: A neurochemical overview of models and mechanisms. *British Journal of Psychiatry, 160,* 165–178. **(Chap 5)**

NYHAN, W. L. (1978). The Lesch-Nyhan syndrome. *Developmental Medicine and Child Neurology, 20,* 376–387. **(Chap 15)**

OADES, R. D. (1985). The role of noradrenaline in tuning and dopamine in switching between signals in the CNS. *Neuroscience and Biobehavioral Reviews, 9,* 261–282. **(Chap 2)**

OATLEY, K., & JENKINS, J. M. (1992). Human emotions: Function and dysfunction. *Annual Review of Psychology, 43,* 55–85. **(Chap 2)**

O'BRIEN, M. M., TRESTMAN, R. L., & SIEVER, L. J. (1993). Cluster A personality disorders. In D. L. Dunner (Ed.), *Current psychiatric therapy* (pp. 399–404). Philadelphia: W. B. Saunders. **(Chap 13)**

O'CALLAGHAN, E., SHAM, P., TAKEI, N., GLOVER, G., & MURRAY, R. M. (1991). Schizophrenia after prenatal exposure to 1957 A2 influenza epidemic. *Lancet, 337,* 1248–1250. **(Chap 14)**

O'CARROLL, P. W. (1990). Community strategies for suicide prevention and intervention. In S. J. Blumenthal & D. J. Kupfer (Eds.), *Suicide over the life cycle: Risk factors, assessment and treatment of suicidal patients.* Washington, DC: American Psychiatric Press. **(Chap 7)**

O'CONNOR V. DONALDSON. (1975). 95 S. Ct. 2486. **(Chap 17)**

OGATA, S. N., SILK, K. R., GOODRICH, S., LOHR, N. E., WESTEN, D., & HILL, E. M. (1990). Childhood sexual and physical abuse in adult patients with borderline personality disorder. *American Journal of Psychiatry, 147,* 1008–1013. **(Chap 13)**

OGLOFF, J. P. R., WONG, S., & GREENWOD, A. (1990). Treating criminal psychopaths in a therapeutic community program. *Sciences and the Law, 8,* 81–90. **(Chap 13)**

O'HAGAN, S. (1992, February 22). Raving madness. *The Times Saturday Review,* pp. 10–12. **(Chap 12)**

O'HANLON, J. F., HAAK, J. W., BLAAUW, G. J., & RIEMERSMA, J. B. J. (1982). Diazepam impairs lateral position control in highway driving. *Science, 27,* 79–81. **(Chap 5)**

O'HARA, M. W. (1986). Social support, life events and depression during pregnancy and the puerperium. *Archives of General Psychiatry, 43*(6), 569–575. **(Chap 7)**

O'HARA, M. W., REHM, L. P., & CAMPBELL, S. B. (1982). Predicting depressive symptomatology: Cognitive-behavioral models and postpartum depression. *Journal of Abnormal Psychology, 91,* 457–461. **(Chap 7)**

O'HARA, M. W., ZEKOSKI, E. M., PHILIPPS, L. H., & WRIGHT, E. J. (1990). Controlled prospective study of postpartum mood disorders: Comparison of child bearing and nonbearing women. *Journal of Abnormal Psychology, 99*(1), 3–15. **(Chap 7)**

ÖHMAN, A. (1986). Face the beast and fear the face: Animal and social fears as prototypes for evolutionary analyses of emotion. *Psychophysiology, 23,* 123–145. **(Chap 5)**

ÖHMAN, A., & DIMBERG, U. (1978). Facial expressions as conditioned stimuli for electrodermal responses: A case of preparedness? *Journal of Personality and Social Psychology, 36*(11), 1251–1258. **(Chap 5)**

OLDS, J. (1956). Pleasure centers in the brain. *Scientific American, 195,* 105–116. **(Chap 12)**

OLDS, J., & MILNER, P. M. (1954). Positive reinforcement produced by electrical stimulation of septal area and other regions of rat brain. *Journal of Comparative and Physiological Psychology, 47,* 419–427. **(Chap 12)**

O'LEARY, A. (1990). Stress, emotion, and human immune function. *Psychological Bulletin, 108*(3), 363–382. **(Chap 9)**

O'LEARY, A. (1992). Self-efficacy and health: Behavioral and stress-physiological mediation. *Cognitive Therapy and Research, 16*(2), 229–245. **(Chap 9)**

O'LEARY, A., SHOOR, S., LORIG, K., & HOLMAN, H. R. (1988). A cognitive-behavioral treatment for rheumatoid arthritis. *Health Psychology, 7*(6), 527–544. **(Chap 9)**

O'LEARY, A., TEMOSHOK, L., JENKINS, S. R., & SWEET, D. M. (1989). *Autonomic reactivity and immune function in men with AIDS.* Paper presented at the annual meeting of the Society for Psychophysiological Research. New Orleans, LA. **(Chap 9)**

O'LEARY, K. D., & BEACH, S. R. (1990). Marital therapy: A viable treatment for depression and marital discord. *American Journal of Psychiatry, 147*(2), 183–186. **(Chap 7)**

OLIVER, M. B., & HYDE, J. S. (1993). Gender differences in sexuality: A meta-analysis. *Psychological Bulletin, 114*(1), 29–51. **(Chap 11)**

OLLENDICK, T. H., & HUNTZINGER, R. M. (1990). Separation anxiety disorder in childhood. In M. Hersen & C. G. Last (Eds.),

Handbook of child and adult psychopathology: A longitudinal perspective. Elmsford, NY: Pergamon Press. **(Chap 5)**

OLLENDICK, T. H., & OLLENDICK, D. G. (1990). Tics and Tourette syndrome. In A. M. Gross & R. S. Drabman (Eds.), *Handbook of clinical behavioral pediatrics* (pp. 243–252). New York: Plenum Press. **(Chap 16)**

O'MALLEY, S. S., JAFFE, A. J., CHANG, G., SCHOTTENFELD, R. S., MEYER, R. E., & ROUNSAVILLE, B. J. (1992). Naltrexone and coping skills therapy for alcohol dependence: A controlled study. *Archives of General Psychiatry, 49,* 881–887. **(Chap 12)**

ONSTAD, S., SKRE, I., TORGERSEN, S., & KRINGLEN, E. (1991). Twin concordance for DSM-III-R schizophrenia. *Acta Psychiatrica Scandinavica, 83,* 395–401. **(Chap 14)**

OPJORDSMOEN, S. (1989). Delusional disorders. I. Comparative long-term outcome. *Acta Psychiatrica Scandia, 80,* 603–612. **(Chap 14)**

ORITIZ, A., & MEDICNA-MORA, M. E. (1988). Research on drugs in Mexico: Epidemiology of drug abuse and issues among Native American populations. In Community Epidemiology Work Group Proceedings, December, 1987. Contract No. 271-87-8321. Washington, DC: U.S. Government Printing Office. **(Chap 12)**

ORNE, M. T., DINGES, D. F., & ORNE, E. C. (1984). On the differential diagnosis of multiple personality in the forensic context. *International Journal of Clinical and Experimental Hypnosis, 32,* 118–169. **(Chap 6)**

ORTONY, A., & TURNER, T. J. (1990). What's basic about basic emotions? *Psychological Review, 97,* 315–331. **(Chap 2)**

OSSIP-KLEIN, D. J., DOYNE, E. J., BOWMAN, E. D., OSBORN, K. M., MCDOUGALL-WILSON, I. B., & NEIMEYER, R. A. (1989). Effects of running or weight lifting on self-concept in clinically depressed women. *Journal of Consulting and Clinical Psychology, 57*(1), 158–161. **(Chap 7)**

ÖST, L. G. (1985). Mode of acquisition of phobias. *Acta Universitatis Uppsaliensis (Abstracts of Uppsala Dissertations from the Faculty of Medicine), 529,* 1–45. **(Chap 5)**

ÖST, L. G. (1987). Age at onset in different phobias. *Journal of Abnormal Psychology, 96,* 223–229. **(Chap 5)**

ÖST, L. G. (1989). *Blood phobia: A specific phobia subtype in DSM-IV.* Paper requested by the Simple Phobia subcommittee of the DSM-IV Anxiety Disorders Work Group. **(Chap 5)**

ÖST, L. G. (1992). Blood and injection phobia: Background and cognitive, physiological, and behavioral variables. *Journal of Abnormal Psychology, 101*(1), 68–74. **(Chaps 2, 5)**

ÖST, L. G., & STERNER, U. (1987). Applied tension: A specific behavioural method for treatment of blood phobia. *Behaviour Research and Therapy, 25,* 25–30. **(Chap 5)**

ÖST, L. G. (In press). Integrated literature review. Simple Phobia subcommittee of the DSM-IV Anxiety Disorders Work Group. **(Chap 5)**

OSTERBERG, E. (1986). Alcohol-related problems in cross-national perspectives: Results of the ISACE study. Special issue: Alcohol and culture: Comparative perspectives from

Europe and America (T. Babot, Ed.). *Annals of the New York Academy of Sciences, 472,* 10–20. **(Chap 12)**

O'SULLIVAN, K. (1979). Observations on vaginismus in Irish women. *Archives of General Psychiatry, 36,* 824–826. **(Chap 11)**

OVERALL, J. E., & HOLLISTER, L. E. (1982). Decision rules for phenomenological classification of psychiatric patients. *Journal of Consulting and Clinical Psychology, 50,* 535–545. **(Chap 3)**

OVUGA, E. B. L. (1992). Murder during sleepwalking. *East Africa Medical Journal, 69,* 533–534. **(Chap 10)**

OWENS, M. J., & NEMEROFF, C. B. (In press). The role of CRF in the pathophysiology of affective and anxiety disorders: Laboratory and clinical studies. In *Corticotropin-releasing factor,* Ciba Foundation Symposium. **(Chap 7)**

OYAMA, O., & ANDRASIK, F. (1992). Behavioral strategies in the prevention of disease. In S. M. Turner, K. S. Calhoun & H. E. Adams (Eds.), *Handbook of clinical behavior therapy* (2nd ed., pp. 397–413). New York: John Wiley. **(Chap 9)**

PAGE, G. G., BEN-ELIYAHU, S., YIRMIYA, R., & LIEBESKIND, J. C. (1993). Morphine attenuates surgery-induced enhancement of metastatic colonization in rats. *Pain, 54*(1), 21–28. **(Chap 9)**

PAHL, J. J., SWAYZE, V. W., & ANDREASEN, N. C. (1990). Diagnostic advances in anatomical and functional brain imaging in schizophrenia. In A. Kales, C. N. Stefanis, & J. A. Talbott (Eds.), *Recent advances in schizophrenia* (pp. 163–189). New York: Springer-Verlag. **(Chap 14)**

PALACE, E. M., & GORZALKA, B. B. (1990). The enhancing effects of anxiety on arousal in sexually dysfunctional and functional women. *Journal of Abnormal Psychology, 99*(4), 403–411. **(Chap 11)**

PALMBLAD, J., PETRINI, B., WASSERMAN, J., & AKERSTEDT, T. (1979). Lymphocyte and granulocyte reactions during sleep deprivation. *Psychosomatic Medicine, 41,* 273–278. **(Chap 10)**

PAPILLO, J. F., & SHAPIRO, D. (1990). The cardiovascular system. In J. T. Cacioppo & L. G. Tassinaryo (Eds.), *Principles of psychophysiology: Physical, social, and inferential elements.* New York: Cambridge University Press. **(Chap 9)**

PARKER, G., & HADZI-PAVLOVIC, D. (1990). Expressed emotion as a predictor of schizophrenic relapse: An analysis of aggregated data. *Psychological Medicine, 20,* 961–965. **(Chap 14)**

PARKES, J. D., & BLOCK, C. (1989). Genetic factors in sleep disorders. *Journal of Neurology, Neurosurgery, and Psychiatry, 52,* 101–108. **(Chap 10)**

PARKINSON, L., & RACHMAN, S. (1981A). Intrusive thoughts: The effects of an uncontrived stress. *Advances in Behaviour Research and Therapy, 3,* 111–118. **(Chap 5)**

PARKINSON, L., & RACHMAN, S. (1981B). Speed of recovery from an uncontrived stress. *Advances in Behaviour Research and Therapy, 3,* 119–123. **(Chap 5)**

PARLOFF, M. B. (1986). Placebo controls in psychotherapy research: A sine qua non or a placebo for research problems? *Journal of*

Consulting and Clinical Psychology, 54, 79–87. **(Chap 4)**

PARSONS, O. A., & NIXON, S. J. (1993). Behavioral disorders associated with central nervous system dysfunction. In P. B. Sutker & H. E. Adams (Eds.), *Comprehensive handbook of psychopathology* (pp. 689–733). New York: Plenum Press. **(Chap 15)**

PASEWARK, R. A., & SEIDENZAHL, D. (1979). Opinions concerning the insanity plea and criminality among mental patients. *Bulletin of the American Academy of Psychiatry and Law, 7,* 199–202. **(Chap 17)**

PASINETTI, G. M., JOHNSON, S. A., ROZOVSKY, I., LAMPETETCHELLS, M., MORGAN, D. G., GORDON, M. N., WILLOUGHBY, D., & FINCH, C. E. (1992). Complement Clqb-messenger RNA & C4 messenger RNA responses to lesioning in rat brain. *Experimental Neurology, 118,* 117–125. **(Chap 15)**

PATAKI, C. S., & CARLSON, G. A. (1990). Major depression in childhood. In M. Hersen & C. Last (Eds.), *Handbook of child and adult psychopathology: A longitudinal perspective.* Elmsford, NY: Pergamon Press. **(Chap 7)**

PATO, M. T., ZOHAR-KADOUCH, R., ZOHAR, J., & MURPHY, D. L. (1988). Return of symptoms after discontinuation of clomipramine in patients with obsessive-compulsive disorder. *American Journal of Psychiatry, 145,* 1521–1525. **(Chap 5)**

PATTERSON, G. R. (1982). *Coercive family process.* Eugene, OR: Castalia Publishing Company. **(Chaps 4, 13)**

PATTERSON, G. R. (1986). Performance models for antisocial boys. *American Psychologist, 41,* 432–444. **(Chap 13)**

PATTERSON, G. R., CHAMBERLAIN, P., & REID, J. B. (1982). A comparative evaluation of a parent-training program. *Behavior Therapy, 13,* 638–650. **(Chap 13)**

PATTERSON, G. R., COBB, J. A., & RAY, R. S. (1972). Direct intervention in the classroom: A set of procedures for the aggressive child. In F. Clark, D. Evans, & L. Hamerlynck (Eds.), *Implementing behavioral programs for schools and clinics.* Champaign, IL: Research Press. **(Chap 4)**

PATTERSON, G. R., DEBARYSHE, B. D., & RAMSEY, E. (1989). A developmental perspective on antisocial behavior. *American Psychologist, 44,* 329–335. **(Chap 13)**

PATTERSON, G. R., & FLEISCHMAN, M. J. (1979). Maintenance of treatment effects: Some considerations concerning family systems and follow-up data. *Behavior Therapy, 10,* 168–185. **(Chap 4)**

PATTON, G. C. (1988). Mortality in eating disorders. *Psychological Medicine, 18*(4), 947–951. **(Chap 8)**

PATTON, G. C., JOHNSON-SABINE, E., WOOD, K., MANN, A. H., & WAKELING, A. (1990). Abnormal eating attitudes in London school girls—a prospective epidemiological study: Outcome at twelve month follow-up. *Psychological Medicine, 20,* 383–394. **(Chap 8)**

PAUL, G. L., & LENTZ, R. J. (1977). *Psychosocial treatment of chronic mental patients: Milieu versus social learning programs.* Cambridge, MA: Harvard University Press. **(Chap 14)**

PAUL, S. M., & SKOLNICK, P. (1978). Rapid changes in brain benzodiazepine receptors after experimental seizures. *Science, 202,* 892–894. **(Chap 2)**

PAUL, S. M., & SKOLNICK, P. (1981). Benzodiazepine receptors and psychopathological states: Towards a neurobiology of anxiety. In D. F. Klein & J. Rabkin (Eds.), *Anxiety: New research and changing concepts.* New York: Raven Press. **(Chap 2)**

PAULS, D. L., TOWBIN, K. E., LECKMAN, J. F., ZAHNER, G. E. P., & COHEN, D. J. (1986). Gilles de la Tourette's syndrome and obsessive-compulsive disorder. *Archives of General Psychiatry, 43,* 1180–1182. **(Chap 16)**

PAYKEL, E. S., BRAYNE, C., HUPPERT, F. A., GILL, C., BARKLEY, C., GEHLHAAR, E., BEARDSALL, L., GIRLING, D. M., POLLITT, P., & O'CONNOR, D. (1994). Incidence of dementia in a population older than 75 years in the United Kingdom. *Archives of General Psychiatry, 51,* 325–332. **(Chap 15)**

PAYKEL, E. S., HOLLYMAN, J. A., FREELING, P., & SEDGWICH, P. (1988). Predictor of therapeutic benefit from amitriptyline in mild depression: A general practice placebo-controlled trial. *Journal of Affective Disorders, 14,* 83–95. **(Chap 7)**

PAYKEL, E. S., MYERS, J. K., DIENELT, M. N., KLERMAN, G. L., LINDENTHAL, J. J., & PEPPER, M. P. (1969). Life events and depression: A controlled study. *Archives of General Psychiatry, 21,* 753–760. **(Chap 7)**

PAYKEL, E. S., & WEISSMAN, M. M. (1973). Social adjustment and depression: A longitudinal study. *Archives of General Psychiatry, 28,* 659–663. **(Chap 7)**

PECUKONIS, E. V., & PECUKONIS, M. T. (1991). An adapted language training strategy in the treatment of an electively mute male child. *Journal of Behavior Therapy and Experimental Psychiatry, 22,* 9–21. **(Chap 16)**

PENDERY, M. L., MALTZMAN, I. M., & WEST, L. J. (1982). Controlled drinking by alcoholics? New findings and a reevaluation of a major affirmative study. *Science, 217,* 169–175. **(Chap 12)**

PENNINGTON, B. F., & SMITH, S. D. (1988). Genetic influences on learning disabilities: An update. *Journal of Consulting and Clinical Psychology, 56,* 817–823. **(Chap 15)**

PERLIN, M. L., & DORFMAN, D. A. (1993). Sanism, social science, and the development of mental disability law jurisprudence. *Behavioral Sciences and the Law, 11,* 47 66. **(Chap 17)**

PEROUTKA, S. J., & SNYDER, S. H. (1980). Relationship of neuroleptic drug effects at brain dopamine, serotonin, alpha-adrenergic, and histamine receptors to clinical potence. *American Journal of Psychiatry, 137,* 1518–1522. **(Chap 14)**

PERRY, J. C. (1993). Longitudinal studies of personality disorders. *Journal of Personality Disorders, 7,* 63–85. **(Chap 13)**

PERRY, S. (1993). Psychiatric treatment of adults with human immunodeficiency virus infection. In D. L. Dunner (Ed.), *Current psychiatric therapy* (pp. 475–482). Philadelphia: W. B. Saunders. **(Chap 15)**

PETERS, C. P. (1991). Concepts of schizophrenia after Kraepelin and Bleuler. In J. G. Howells (Ed.), *The concept of schizophrenia: Historical perspectives* (pp. 93–107). Washington, DC: American Psychiatric Press. **(Chap 14)**

PETERSEN, A. C., COMPAS, B. E., BROOKS-GUNN, J., STEMMLER, M., EY, S., & GRANT, K. E. (1993). Depression in adolescence. *American Psychologist, 48*(2), 155–168. **(Chap 7)**

PETERSON, A. L., & AZRIN, N. H. (1992). An evaluation of behavioral treatments for Tourette Syndrome. *Behaviour Research and Therapy, 30,* 167–174. **(Chap 16)**

PETERSON, D. R. (1968). *The clinical study of social behavior.* New York: Appleton-Century-Crofts. **(Chap 3)**

PETERSON, L., FARMER, J., & KASHANI, J. H. (1990). Parental injury prevention endeavors: A function of health beliefs? *Health Psychology, 9*(2), 177–191. **(Chap 9)**

PETERSON, L., & ROBERTS, M. C. (1992). Complacency, misdirection, and effective prevention of children's injuries. *American Psychologist, 47*(8), 1040–1044. **(Chap 9)**

PETERSON, L., SELIGMAN, M. E. P., & VAILLANT, G. E. (1988). Pessimistic explanatory style is a risk factor for physical illness: A thirty-five-year longitudinal study. *Journal of Personality and Social Psychology, 55,* 23–27. **(Chap 9)**

PETERSON, L., & THIELE, C. (1988). Home safety at school. *Child and Family Behavior Therapy, 10*(1), 1–8. **(Chap 9)**

PETURSSON, H., & LADER, M. H. (1981). Withdrawal from long-term benzodiazepine treatment. *British Medical Journal, 283,* 643–645. **(Chap 5)**

PFOHL, B. (1991). Histrionic personality disorder: A review of available data and recommendations for DSM-IV. *Journal of Personality Disorders, 5,* 150–166. **(Chap 13)**

PFOHL, B. (1993). Proposed DSM-IV criteria for personality disorders. In D. L. Dunner (Ed.), *Current psychiatric therapy* (pp. 397–399). Philadelphia: W. B. Saunders. **(Chap 13)**

PHELPS, L., & GRABOWSKI, J. (1992). Fetal alcohol syndrome: Diagnostic features and psychoeducational risk factors. *School Psychology Quarterly, 7,* 112–128. **(Chap 12)**

PHIBBS, C. S., BATEMAN, D. A., & SCHWARTZ, R. M. (1991). The neonatal costs of maternal cocaine use. *Journal of the American Medical Association, 266,* 1521–1526. **(Chap 12)**

PHIFER, J. F., & MURRELL, S. A. (1986). Etiologic factors in the onset of depressive symptoms in older adults. *Journal of Abnormal Psychology, 95,* 282–291. **(Chap 7)**

PHILIPPART, M. (1990). The Rett syndrome in males. *Brain and Development, 12,* 33–36. **(Chap 16)**

PHILIPS, H. C. (1987A). Avoidance behavior and its role in sustaining chronic pain. *Behaviour Research and Therapy, 25,* 273–279. **(Chap 9)**

PHILIPS, H. C. (1987B). The effects of behavioural treatment on chronic pain. *Behaviour Research and Therapy, 25,* 365–377. **(Chap 9)**

PHILIPS, H. C., & GRANT, L. (1991). Acute back pain: A psychological analysis. *Behaviour Research and Therapy, 29,* 429–434. **(Chap 9)**

PHILLIPS, K. A. (1991). Body dysmorphic disorder: The distress of imagined ugliness. *American Journal of Psychiatry, 148,* 1138–1149. **(Chap 6)**

PHILLIPS, K. A., MCELROY, S. L., KECK, P. E., JR., POPE, H. G., JR., & HUDSON, J. I. (1993). Body dysmorphic disorder: 30 cases of imagined ugliness. *American Journal of Psychiatry, 150,* 302–308. **(Chap 6)**

PICKENS, R. W., SVIKIS, D. S., MCGUE, M., LYKKEN, D. T., HESTON, L. L., & CLAYTON, P. J. (1991). Heterogeneity in the inheritence of alcoholism. *Archives of General Psychiatry, 48,* 19–28. **(Chap 12)**

PIHL, R. O., PETERSON, J. B., & LAU, M. A. (1993). A biosocial model of the alcohol-aggression relationship. *Journal of Studies on Alcohol,* Supplement No. 11, 128–139. **(Chap 12)**

PIKE, K. M., & RODIN, J. (1991). Mothers, daughters, and disordered eating. *Journal of Abnormal Psychology, 100*(2), 198–204. **(Chap 8)**

PILOWSKY, I. (1970). Primary and secondary hypochondriasis. *Acta Psychiatrica Scandinavica, 46,* 273–285. **(Chap 6)**

PINEL, P. (1801/1962). *A treatise on insanity.* New York: Hafner. **(Chap 14)**

PINEL, P. (1962). *A treatise on insanity* (D. D. Davis, Trans.). New York: Published under the auspices of the Library of the New York Academy of Medicine by Hafner Publishing Company. (Original work published in 1801) **(Chap 13)**

PINEL, P. H. (1809). *Traite medico-philosophique sur l'alienation mentale.* Paris: Chez J. Ant Brosson. **(Chap 14)**

PIRKE, K. M., SCHWEIGER, U., & FICHTER, M. M. (1987). Hypothalamic-pituitary-ovarian axis in bulimia. In J. I. Hudson & H. G. Pope (Eds.), *The psychobiology of bulimia* (pp. 15–28). Washington, DC: American Psychiatric Press. **(Chap 8)**

PITHERS, W. D., MARTIN, G. R., & CUMMING, G. F. (1989). Vermont treatment program for sexual aggressors. In D. R. Laws (Ed.), *Relapse prevention with sex offenders* (pp. 292–310). New York: Guilford Press. **(Chap 11)**

PLOMIN, R. (1990). The role of inheritance in behavior. *Science, 248,* 183–188. **(Chaps 2, 4, 14)**

POLICH, J., POLLOCK, V. E., & BLOOM, F. E. (1994). Meta-analysis of P300 amplitude from males at risk for alcoholism. *Psychological Bulletin, 115,* 55–73. **(Chap 12)**

POLIVY, J. M., & HERMAN, C. P. (1993). Etiology of binge eating: Psychological mechanisms. In C. G. Fairburn & G. T. Wilson (Eds.), *Binge eating: Nature, assessment, and treatment.* New York: Guilford Press. **(Chap 8)**

POLLACK, C., & ANDREWS, G. (1989). Defense styles associated with specific anxiety disorders. *American Journal of Psychiatry, 146,* 1500–1502. **(Chap 1)**

POLLACK, M. H., BROTMAN, A. W., & ROSENBAUM, J. F. (1989). Cocaine abuse and treatment. *Comprehensive Psychiatry, 30,* 31–44. **(Chap 12)**

POLLITT, J., & YOUNG, J. (1971). Anxiety state or masked depression? A study based on the action of monoamine oxidase inhibitors. *British Journal of Psychiatry, 119,* 143–149. **(Chap 7)**

POLLOWAY, E. A., SCHEWEL, R., & PATTON, J. R. (1992). Learning disabilities in adulthood: Personal perspectives. *Journal of Learning Disabilities, 25,* 520–522. **(Chap 15)**

POPE, H. G., & HUDSON, J. I. (1984). *New hope for binge-eaters: Advances in the understanding and treatment of bulimia.* New York: Harper & Row. **(Chap 8)**

POPE, H. G., HUDSON, J. I., JONAS, J. M., & YURGELUN-TODD, D. (1983). Bulimia treated with imipramine: A placebo-controlled, double-blind study. *American Journal of Psychiatry, 140,* 554–558. **(Chap 8)**

POPE, H. G., IONESCU-PIOGGIA, M., AIZLEY, H. G., & VARMA, D. K. (1990). Drug use and life style among college undergraduates in 1989: A comparison with 1969 and 1978. *American Journal of Psychiatry, 147,* 998–1001. **(Chap 12)**

POST, R. M. (1992). Transduction of psychosocial stress into the neurobiology of recurrent affective disorder. *American Journal of Psychiatry, 149*(8), 999–1010. **(Chap 7)**

POST, R. M., RUBINOW, D. R., UHDE, T. W., ROY-BYRNE, P. P., LINNOILA, M., ROSOFF, A., & COWDRY, R. (1989). Dysphoric mania: Clinical and biological correlates. *Archives of General Psychiatry, 46,* 353–358. **(Chap 7)**

POTKIN, S. G., ALBERS, L. J., & RICHMOND, G. (1993). Schizophrenia: An overview of pharmacological treatment. In D. L. Dunner (Ed.), *Current psychiatric therapy* (pp. 142–154). Philadelphia: W. B. Saunders. **(Chap 14)**

POTTER, W. Z. (1984). Psychotherapeutic drugs and biogenic amines: Current concepts and therapeutic implications. *Drugs, 28,* 127–143. **(Chap 7)**

POTTER, W. Z., & MANJI, H. K. (1993). Are monoamine metabolites in cerebral spinal fluid worth measuring? *Archives of General Psychiatry, 50,* 653–656. **(Chap 14)**

POTTER, W. Z., RUDORFER, M. V., & GOODWIN, F. K. (1987). Biological findings in bipolar disorders. In R. E. Hales & A. J. Francis (Eds.), *American Psychiatric Association Annual Review,* (Vol. 6, 32–60). Washington, DC: American Psychiatric Press. **(Chap 7)**

POZNANSKI, E. O., ISRAEL, M. C., & GROSSMAN, J. A. (1984). Hypomania in a four year old. *Journal of the American Academy of Child Psychiatry, 23*(1), 105–110. **(Chap 7)**

PRESLEY, C. A., & MEILMAN, P. W. (1992). *Alcohol and drugs on American college campuses: A report to college presidents.* Carbondale: Southern Illinois University Press. **(Chap 12)**

PRICE, R., & BREW, B. (1988). The AIDS dementia complex. *Journal of Infectious Diseases, 158,* 1079–1083. **(Chap 15)**

PRIEN, R. F., & GELENBERG, A. J. (1989). Alternatives to lithium for preventive treatment of bipolar disorder. *American Journal of Psychiatry, 146*(7), 840–848. **(Chap 7)**

PRIEN, R. F., & KUPFER, D. J. (1986). Continuation drug therapy for major depressive episodes: How long should it be maintained? *American Journal of Psychiatry, 143*(1), 18–23. **(Chap 7)**

PRIEN, R. F., KUPFER, D. J., MANSKY, P. A., SMALL, J. G., TUASON, V. B., VOSS, C. B., & JOHNSON, W. E. (1984). Drug therapy in the prevention of recurrences in unipolar and bipolar affective disorders: Report of the NIMH collaborative study group comparing lithium carbonate, imipramine and a lithium carbonate-imipramine combination. *Ar-*

chives of General Psychiatry, 41, 1096–1104. **(Chap 7)**

PRIEN, R. F., & POTTER, W. Z. (1993). Maintenance treatment for mood disorders. In D. L. Dunner (Ed.), *Current psychiatric therapy* (pp. 255–260). Philadelphia: W. B. Saunders. **(Chap 7)**

PRINCE, M. (1906–1907). Hysteria from the point of view of dissociated personality. *Journal of Abnormal Psychology, 1,* 170–187. **(Chap 6)**

PRIZANT, B. M., & WETHERBY, A. M. (1989). Enhancing language and communication in autism: From theory to practice. In G. Dawson (Ed.), *Autism: Nature, diagnosis, and treatment* (pp. 282–309). New York: Guilford Press. **(Chap 16)**

PRUDIC, J., SACKEIM, H. A., & DEVANAND, D. P. (1990). Medication resistance and clinical response to electroconvulsive therapy. *Psychiatry Research, 31,* 287–296. **(Chap 7)**

PRUZINSKY, T. (1988). Collaboration of plastic surgeon and medical psychotherapist: Elective cosmetic surgery. *Medical Psychotherapy, 1,* 1–13. **(Chap 6)**

PUESCHEL, S. M., & GOLDSTEIN, A. (1991). Genetic counseling. In J. L. Matson & J. A. Mulick (Eds.), *Handbook of mental retardation* (2nd ed., pp. 279–291). Elmsford, NY: Pergamon Press. **(Chap 15)**

PUESCHEL, S. M., & THULINE, H. C. (1991). Chromosome disorders. In J. L. Matson & J. A. Mulick (Eds.), *Handbook of mental retardation* (2nd ed., pp. 115–138). Elmsford, NY: Pergamon Press. **(Chap 15)**

PUGLIESE, M. T., WEYMAN-DAUN, M., MOSES, N., & LIFSHITZ, F. (1987). Parental health beliefs as a cause of nonorganic failure to thrive. *Pediatrics, 80,* 175–182. **(Chap 8)**

PUIG-ANTICH, J. (1982). Major depression and conduct disorder in prepuberty. *Journal of the American Academy of Child Psychiatry, 21,* 118–128. **(Chap 7)**

PUIG-ANTICH, J., & RABINOVICH, H. (1986). Relationship between affective and anxiety disorders in childhood. In R. G. Helman (Ed.), *Anxiety disorders of childhood* (pp. 136–156). New York: John Wiley. **(Chap 7)**

PURDIE, F. R., HAREGINAN, B., & ROSEN, P. (1981). Acute organic brain syndrome: A review of 100 cases. *Annual of Emergency Medicine, 10,* 455–461. **(Chap 15)**

PURDY, D., & FRANK, E. (1993). Should postpartum mood disorders be given a more prominent or distinct place in DSM-IV? *Depression, 1,* 59–70. **(Chap 7)**

PUTNAM, F. W. (1989). *Diagnosis and treatment of multiple personality disorder.* New York: Guilford Press. **(Chap 6)**

PUTNAM, F. W. (1991). Dissociative phenomena. In A. Tasman & S. M. Goldinger (Eds.), *American Psychiatric Press Review of Psychiatry* (Vol. 10). Washington, DC: American Psychiatric Press. **(Chap 6)**

PUTNAM, F. W. (1992). Altered states: Peeling away the layers of a multiple personality. *Sciences, 32*(6), 30–36. **(Chap 6)**

PUTNAM, F. W., GUROFF, J. J., SILBERMAN, E. K., BARBAN, L., & POST, R. M. (1986). The clinical phenomenology of multiple personality disorder: Review of 100 recent cases. *Journal of Clinical Psychiatry, 47,* 285–293. **(Chap 6)**

PYLE, R. L., NEUMAN, P. A., HALVORSON, P. A., & MITCHELL, J. E. (1991). An ongoing cross-sectional study of the prevalence of eating disorders in freshman college students. *International Journal of Eating Disorders, 10,* 667–677. **(Chap 8)**

QUALITY ASSURANCE PROJECT (1990). Treatment outlines for paranoid, schizotypal and schizoid personality disorders. *Australian and New Zealand Journal of Psychiatry, 24,* 339–350. **(Chap 13)**

QUAY, H. C. (1965). Psychopathic personality as pathological stimulation seeking. *American Journal of Psychiatry, 122,* 180–183. **(Chap 13)**

QUAY, H. C. (1993). The psychobiology of undersocialized aggressive conduct disorder: A theoretical perspective. *Development and Psychopathology, 5,* 165–180. **(Chap 13)**

QUITKIN, F. M., HARRISON, W., STEWART, J. W., MCGRATH, P., TRICAMO, E., OCEPEK-WELIKSON, K., RABKIN, J. G., WAGER, S. G., NUNES, E., & KLEIN, D. F. (1991). Response to pheneizine and imipramine in placebo nonresponders with atypical depression: A new application of the crossover design. *Archives of General Psychiatry, 48,* 319–323. **(Chap 7)**

QUITKIN, F. M., STEWART, J. W., MCGRATH, P. J., LIEBOWITZ, M. R., HARRISON, W. M., TRICAMO, E., KLEIN, D. F., RABKIN, J. G., MARKOWITZ, J. S., & WAGER, S. G. (1988). Pheneizine versus imipramine in the treatment of probable atypical depression: Defining syndrome boundaries of selective MAOI responders. *American Journal of Psychiatry, 145,* 306–311. **(Chap 7)**

QUON, D., WANG, Y., CATALANO, R., SCARDINA, J. M., MURAKAMI, K., & CORDELL, B. (1991). Formation of B-amyloid protein deposits in brains of transgenic mice. *Nature, 352,* 239–241. **(Chap 15)**

RACHMAN, S. (1978). *Fear and courage.* San Francisco: W. H. Freeman. **(Chap 5)**

RACHMAN, S. (1991). Neo-conditioning and the classical theory of fear acquisition. *Clinical Psychology Review, 11,* 155–173. **(Chap 5)**

RACHMAN, S., & HODGSON, R. (1968). Experimentally induced "sexual fetishism": Replication and development. *Psychological Record, 18*(1), 25–27. **(Chap 11)**

RADNITZ, C. L., APPELBAUM, K. A., BLANCHARD, E. B., ELLIOTT, L., & ANDRASIK, F. (1988). The effect of self-regulatory treatment on pain behavior in chronic headache. *Behaviour Research and Therapy, 26,* 253–260. **(Chap 9)**

RADO, S. (1962). Theory and therapy: The theory of schizotypal organization and its application to the treatment of decompensated schizotypal behavior. In S. Rado (Ed.), *Psychoanalysis of behavior* (Vol. 2, pp. 127–140). New York: Grune & Stratton. **(Chap 13)**

RAGLAND, D. R., & BRAND, R. J. (1988). Type A behavior and mortality from coronary heart disease. *New England Journal of Medicine, 318,* 65–69. **(Chap 9)**

RAICH, R. M., ROSEN, J. C., DEUS, J., PEREZ, O., REQUIENA, A., & GROSS, J. (1992). Eating disorder symptoms among adolescents in the United States and Spain: A comparative study. *International Journal of Eating Disorders, 11,* 63–72. **(Chap 8)**

RAINE, A., VENABLES, P. H., & WILLIAMS, M. (1990). Relationships between central and autonomic measures of arousal at age 15 years and criminality at age 24 years. *Archives of General Psychiatry, 47,* 1003–1007. **(Chap 13)**

RAMACHANDRAN, V. S. (1993). Filling in the gaps in perception II: Scotomas and phantom limbs. *Current Directions in Psychological Science, 2,* 56–65. **(Chap 9)**

RAMEY, C. T., & RAMEY, S. L. (1992). Effective early intervention. *Mental retardation, 30,* 337–345. **(Chap 15)**

RAPEE, R. M. (1991). The conceptual overlap between cognition and conditioning in clinical psychology. *Clinical Psychology Review, 11,* 193–203. **(Chap 2)**

RAPKIN, A. J., CHANG, L. C., & READING, A. E. (1989). Mood and cognitive style in premenstrual syndrome. *Obstetrics and Gynecology, 74,* 644–649. **(Chap 3)**

RAPP, S. R., PARISI, S. A., & WALLACE, C. E. (1991). Comorbid psychiatric disorders in elderly medical patients: A l-year prospective study. *Journal of the American Geriatrics Society, 39*(2), 124–131. **(Chap 7)**

RASMUSSEN, S. A., & EISEN, J. L. (1990). Epidemiology of obsessive-compulsive disorder. *Journal of Clinical Psychiatry, 51,* 10–14. **(Chap 5)**

RASMUSSEN, S. A., & TSUANG, M. T. (1984). The epidemiology of obsessive-compulsive disorder. *Journal of Clinical Psychiatry, 45,* 450–457. **(Chap 5)**

RASMUSSEN, S. A., & TSUANG, M. T. (1986). Clinical characteristics and family history in DSM-III obsessive-compulsive disorder. *American Journal of Psychiatry, 143,* 317–322. **(Chap 5)**

RAST, J., JOHNSTON, J. M., LUBIN, D., & ELLINGER-ALLEN, J. (1988). Effects of pre-meal chewing on ruminative behavior. *American Journal of Mental Retardation, 93*(1), 67–74. **(Chap 8)**

RATNASURIYA, R. H., EISLER, I., SZMUHTER, G. I., & RUSSELL, G. F. (1991). Anorexia nervosa: Outcome and prognostic factors after 20 years. *British Journal of Psychiatry, 158,* 495–502. **(Chap 8)**

RATNER, N. B. (1992). Measurable outcomes of instructions to modify normal parent-child verbal interaction: Implications for indirect stuttering therapy. *Journal of Speech and Hearing Research, 35,* 14–20. **(Chap 16)**

RAY, W. A., GURWITZ, J., DECKER, M. D., & KENNEDY, D. L. (1992). Medications and the safety of the older driver: Is there a basis for concern? Special issue: Safety and mobility of elderly drivers: II. *Human Factors, 34*(1), 33–47. **(Chap 5)**

RAZRAN, G. (1961). The observable unconscious and the inferable conscious in current Soviet psychophysiology: Interoceptive conditioning, semantic conditioning, and the orienting reflex. *Psychological Review, 68,* 81–150. **(Chap 5)**

RECHTSCHAFFEN, A., & FOULKES, D. (1965). Effect of visual stimuli on dream content. *Perceptual and Motor Skills, 20,* 1149–1160. **(Chap 10)**

REDD, W. H., ANDREASON, G. V., & MINAGAWA, R. Y. (1982). Hypnotic control of anticipatory emesis in patients receiving cancer chemotherapy. *Journal of Consult-ing and Clinical Psychology, 50,* 14–19. **(Chap 9)**

REDD, W. H., & ANDRYKOWSKI, M. A. (1982). Behavioral intervention in cancer treatment: Controlling aversion reactions to chemotherapy. *Journal of Consulting and Clinical Psychology, 50,* 1018–1029. **(Chap 1)**

REDMOND, D. E., JR. (1977). Alterations in the function of the nucleus locus coeruleus: A possible model for studies of anxiety. In I. Hanin & E. Usdin (Eds.), *Animal models in psychiatry and neurology.* Elmsford, NY: Pergamon Press. **(Chap 2)**

REDMOND, D. E., JR. (1979). New and old evidence for the involvement of a brain norepinephrine system in anxiety. In W. E. Fann, I. Karacan, A. D. Pokorny, & R. L. Williams (Eds.), *Phenomenology and treatment of anxiety.* Hillsdale, NJ: Lawrence Erlbaum. **(Chap 2)**

REEVE, R. E., & KAUFFMAN, J. M. (1988). Learning disabilities. In V. B. Van Hasselt, P. S. Strain, & M. Hersen (Eds.), *Handbook of developmental and physical disabilities* (pp. 316–335). Elmsford, NY: Pergamon Press. **(Chap 15)**

REGAL, R. A., ROONEY, J. R., & WANDAS, T. (1994). Facilitated communication: An experimental evaluation. *Journal of Autism and Developmental Disorders, 24,* 345–355. **(Chap 16)**

REGIER, D. A., FARMER, M. E., RAE, D. S., LOCKE, B. Z., KEITH, S. J., JUDD, L. L., & GOODWIN, F. K. (1990). Comorbidity of mental disorders with alcohol and other drug abuse. *Journal of the American Medical Association, 264,* 2511–2518. **(Chap 12)**

REHM, L. P., KASLOW, N. J., & RABIN, A. S. (1987). Cognitive and behavioral targets in a self-control therapy program for depression. *Journal of Consulting and Clinical Psychology, 55*(1), 60–67. **(Chap 7)**

REICH, J. (1987). Sex distribution of DSM-III personality disorders in psychiatric outpatients. *American Journal of Psychiatry, 144,* 485–488. **(Chap 13)**

REICH, J., YATES, W., & NDUAGUBA, M. (1989). Prevalence of DSM-III personality disorders in the community. *Social Psychiatry and Psychiatric Epidemiology, 24,* 12–16. **(Chap 13)**

REICHLE, J., MIRENDA, P., LOCKE, P., PICHE, L., & JOHNSTON, S. (1992). Beginning augmentative communication systems. In S. F. Warren & J. Reichle (Eds.), *Causes and effects in communication and language intervention* (pp. 131–156). Baltimore: Paul H. Brookes. **(Chap 15)**

REID, D. H., WILSON, P. G., & FAW, G. D. (1991). Teaching self-help skills. In J. L. Matson & J. A. Mulick (Eds.), *Handbook of mental retardation* (2nd ed., pp. 436–450). Elmsford, NY: Pergamon Press. **(Chap 15)**

REID, L. D. (1985). Endogenous opioid peptides and the regulation of drinking and feeding. *American Journal of Clinical Nutrition, 42,* 1099–1132. **(Chap 8)**

REID, W. J., & CRISAFULLI, A. (1990). Marital discord and child behavior problems: A meta-analysis. *Journal of Abnormal Child Psychology, 18,* 105–117. **(Chap 4)**

REIK, T. (1964). *Pagan rites in Judaism.* New York: Farrar, Strauss. **(Chap 3)**

REIMAN, E. M., RAICHLE, M. E., ROBINS, E., BUTLER, F. K., HERSCOVITCH, P., FOX, P., &

PERLMUTTER, J. (1986). The application of positron emission tomography to the study of panic disorder. *American Journal of Psychiatry, 143,* 469–476. **(Chap 5)**

REISS, A. L. (1985). Developmental manifestations in a boy with prepubertal bipolar disorder. *Journal of Clinical Psychiatry, 46*(10), 441–443. **(Chap 7)**

REITAN, R. M., & DAVISON, I. A. (1974). *Clinical neuropsychology: Current status and applications.* Washington, DC: V. H. Winston. **(Chap 3)**

RENDE, R., & PLOMIN, R. (1992). Diathesis-stress models of psychopathology: A quantitative genetic perspective. *Applied & Preventive Psychology, 1,* 177–182. **(Chap 2)**

RENNEBERG, B., GOLDSTEIN, A. J., PHILLIPS, D., & CHAMBLESS, D. L. (1990). Intensive behavioral group treatment of avoidant personality disorder. *Behavior Therapy, 21,* 363–377. **(Chap 13)**

RENNIE, J. (1992). The mice that missed: Two models for Alzheimer's disease are retracted. *Scientific American, 267,* 20–26. **(Chap 15)**

RENSHAW, D. C. (1988). Profile of 2,376 patients treated at Loyola Sex Clinic between 1972 and 1987. *Sexual and Marital Therapy, 3,* 111–117. **(Chap 11)**

REPP, A. C., & SINGH, N. N. (1990). *Perspectives on the use of nonaversive and aversive interventions for persons with developmental disabilities.* Sycamore, IL: Sycamore Publishing. **(Chap 15)**

RESCHLY, D. J., & WARD, S. M. (1991). Use of adaptive behavior measures and overrepresentation of black students in programs for students with mild mental retardation. *American Journal of Mental Retardation, 96,* 257–268. **(Chap 15)**

RESCORLA, R. A. (1988). Pavlovian conditioning: It's not what you think it is. *American Psychologist, 43*(3), 151–160. **(Chaps 1, 2)**

RESNER, J., & HARTOG, J. (1970). Concepts and terminology of mental disorders among Malays. *Journal of Cross-Cultural Psychology, 1,* 369–381. **(Chap 4)**

REYNOLDS, C. F., KUPFER, D. J., TASKA, L. S., HOCH, C. C., SEWITCH, D. W., & SPIKER, D. G. (1985). The sleep of healthy seniors: A revisit. *Sleep, 8,* 20–29. **(Chap 10)**

RICCIO, C. A., HYND, G. W., COHEN, M. J., & GONZALEZ, J. J. (1993). Neurological basis of attention deficit hyperactivity disorder. *Exceptional Children, 60,* 118–124. **(Chap 16)**

RICE, D. P., & MACKENZIE, E. J. (1989). *Cost of injury in the United States: A report to Congress.* San Francisco: University of California and Injury Prevention Center, Institute for Health and Aging, and the Johns Hopkins University. **(Chap 9)**

RICE, M. E., HARRIS, G. T., & QUINSEY, V. L. (1990). A follow-up of rapists assessed in a maximum security psychiatric facility. *Journal of Interpersonal Violence, 4,* 435–448. **(Chap 13)**

RICHARDS, R., KINNEY, D. K., LUNDE, I., BENET, M., & MERZEL, A. P. C. (1988). Creativity in manic depressives, cyclothymes, their normal relatives, and control subjects. *Journal of Abnormal Psychology, 97*(3), 281–288. **(Chap 7)**

RICHARDSON, S. A., KATZ, M., & KOLLER, H. (1986). Sex differences in number of children administratively classified as mildly mentally retarded: An epidemiological review. *American Journal of Mental Deficiency, 91,* 250–256. **(Chap 15)**

RICHEIMER, S. H. (1987). Psychological intervention in delirium: An important component of management. *Postgraduate Medicine, 81,* 173–180. **(Chap 15)**

RICKELS, K., SCHWEIZER, E., CASE, W. G., & GREENBLATT, D. J. (1990). Long-term therapeutic use of benzodiazepines. I. Effects of abrupt discontinuation. *Archives of General Psychiatry, 47,* 899–907. **(Chap 5)**

RIDING, A. (1992, November 17). New catechism for Catholics defines sins of modern world. *New York Times,* A14. **(Chap 12)**

RIGGINS V. NEVADA. (1992). 112 S. Ct. 1810. **(Chap 17)**

RIGGS, D. S., & FOA, E. B. (1993). Obsessive compulsive disorder. In D. H. Barlow (Ed.), *Clinical handbook of psychological disorders* (2nd ed.). New York: Guilford Press. **(Chap 5)**

RIGGS, J. E. (1993). Smoking and Alzheimer's disease: Protective effect or differential survival bias? *Lancet, 342,* 793–794. **(Chap 15)**

RIMLAND, B. (1964). *Infantile autism: The syndrome and its implications for a neural theory of behavior.* New York: Appleton-Century-Crofts. **(Chap 16)**

RIMLAND, B., CALLAWAY, E., & DREYFUS, P. (1978). The effects of high doses of vitamin B_6 on autistic children. A double-blind crossover study. *American Journal of Psychiatry, 135,* 472–475. **(Chap 16)**

RITENBAUGH, C., SHISSTAK, C., TEUFEL, N., LEONARD-GREEN, T. K., & PRINCE, R. (1993). Eating disorders: A cross-cultural review in regard to DSM-IV. In J. E. Mezzich, A. Kleinman, H. Fabrega, B. Good, G. Johnson-Powell, K. M. Lin, S. Manson, & D. Parron (Eds.), *Cultural proposals and supporting papers for DSM-IV.* **(Chap 8)**

RITVO, E. R., FREEMAN, B. J., MASON BROTHERS, A., MO, A., & RITVO, A. M. (1985). Concordance for the syndrome of autism in 40 pairs of afflicted twins. *American Journal of Psychiatry, 142,* 74–77. **(Chap 16)**

RITVO, E. R., FREEMAN, B. J., SCHEIBEL, A. B., DUONG, T., ROBINSON, H., GUTHRIE, D., & RITVO, A. (1986). Lower Purkinje cell counts in the cerebella of four autistic subjects: Initial findings of the UCLA-NSAC autopsy research report. *American Journal of Psychiatry, 143,* 826–866. **(Chap 16)**

RITVO, E. R., FREEMAN, B. J., YUWILER, A., GELLER, E., SCHROTH, P., YOKOTA, A., MASON-BROTHERS, A., AUGUST, G. J., KLYKYLO, W., LEVENTHAL, B., LEWIS, K., PIGGOTT, L., REALMUTO, G., STUBBS, E. G., & UMANSKY, R. (1986). Fenfluramine treatment of autism: UCLA collaborative study of 81 patients at nine medical centers. *Psychopharmacology Bulletin, 22,* 133–140. **(Chap 16)**

RIVERA-TOVAR, A. D., & FRANK, E. (1990). Late luteal phase dysphoric disorder in young women. *American Journal of Psychiatry, 147,* 1634–1636. **(Chap 3)**

RIVERA-TOVAR, A. D., PILKONIS, P., & FRANK, E. (1992). Symptom patterns in late luteal-phase dysphoric disorder. *Journal of Psychopathology and Behavioral Assessment, 14,* 189–199. **(Chap 3)**

ROBERTS, G. A. (1991). Delusional belief and meaning in life: A preferred reality? *British Journal of Psychiatry, 159,* 20–29. **(Chap 14)**

ROBERTS, J., & ROWLAND, M. (1981). *Hypertension in adults 25–74 years of age.* United States, 1971–1975 (Series II No. 221). Washington, DC: U.S. Department of Health, Education, and Welfare, National Center for Health Statistics. **(Chap 9)**

ROBERTSON, M. J. (1986). Mental disorder among homeless people in the United States: An overview of recent empirical literature. *Administration in Mental Health, 4,* 14–27. **(Chap 17)**

ROBERTSON, N. (1988). *Getting better: Inside Alcoholics Anonymous.* New York: William Morrow. **(Chap 12)**

ROBINS, C. J., BLOCK, P., & PESELOW, E. D. (1990). Endogenous and non-endogenous depressions: Relations to life events, dysfunctional attitudes and event perceptions. *British Journal of Clinical Psychology, 29,* 201–207. **(Chap 7)**

ROBINS, L. N. (1966). *Deviant children grown up: A sociological and psychiatric study of sociopathic personality.* Baltimore: Williams & Wilkins. **(Chap 13)**

ROBINS, L. N. (1978). Sturdy childhood predictors of adult antisocial behavior: Replications from longitudinal studies. *Psychological Medicine, 8,* 611–622. **(Chap 13)**

ROBINS, L. N., HELZER, J. E., & DAVIS, D. H. (1975). Narcotic use in Southeast Asia and afterwards. *Archives of General Psychiatry, 32,* 955–961. **(Chap 12)**

ROCKNEY, R. M., & LEMKE, T. (1992). Casualties from a junior-senior high school during the Persian Gulf war: Toxic poisoning or mass hysteria? *Developmental and Behavioral Pediatrics, 13*(5), 339–342. **(Chap 1)**

ROCKWOOD, K., STOLEE, P., & BRAHIM, A. (1991). Outcomes of admission to a psychogeriatric service. *Canadian Journal of Psychiatry, 36*(4), 275–279. **(Chap 7)**

RODIN, J., & SALOVEY, P. (1989). Health psychology. *Annual Review of Psychology, 40,* 533–579. **(Chap 9)**

ROEHRICH, L., & KINDER, B. N. (1991). Alcohol expectancies and male sexuality: Review and implications for sex therapy. *Journal of Sex and Marital Therapy, 17*(1), 45–54. **(Chap 11)**

ROFFMAN, R. A., & BARNHART, R. (1987). Assessing need for marijuana dependence treatment through an anonymous telephone interview. *International Journal of the Addictions, 22,* 639–651. **(Chap 12)**

ROFFMAN, R. A., & STEPHENS, R. S. (1993). Cannabis dependence. In D. L. Dunner (Ed.), *Current psychiatric therapy* (pp. 105–109). Philadelphia: W. B. Saunders. **(Chap 12)**

ROFFWARG, H. P., MUZIO, J. N., & DEMENT, W. C. (1966). Ontogenetic development of the human sleep-dream cycle. *Science, 152,* 604–619. **(Chap 10)**

ROGERS, C. R. (1961). *On becoming a person.* Boston: Houghton Mifflin. **(Chap 1)**

ROGERS, D., STRATTON, P., VICTOR, J., KENNEDY, B., & ANDRES, M. (1992). Chronic regurgitation among persons with mental retardation: A need for combined medical and interdisciplinary strategies. *American Journal on Mental Retardation, 96*(5), 522–527. **(Chap 8)**

ROGERS, J., COOPER, N., WEBSTER, S., SCHULTZ, J., MCGEER, P., STYREN, S., CIVIN, W., BRACHOVA, L., BRADT, B., WARD, P., & LIEBERBURG, I. (1992). Complement activation by B-amyloid in Alzheimer disease. *Proceedings of the National Academy of Sciences, 89,* 10016–10020. **(Chap 15)**

ROGERS, R. (1987). APA's position on the insanity defense: Empiricism versus emotionalism. *American Psychologist, 42,* 840–848. **(Chap 17)**

ROITT, I. (1988). *Essential immunology* (6th ed.). Oxford, England: Blackwell. **(Chap 9)**

ROOM, R. (1993). Alcoholics Anonymous as a social movement. In B. S. McCrady & W. R. Miller (Eds.), *Research on Alcoholics Anonymous: Opportunities and alternatives* (pp. 167–187). New Brunswick, NJ: Rutgers Center of Alcohol Studies. **(Chap 12)**

RORABAUGH, W. J. (1991, FALL). Alcohol in America. *OAH Magazine of History,* pp. 17–19. **(Chap 12)**

RORSCHACH, H. (1951). *Psychodiagnostics.* New York: Grune & Stratton. (Original work published 1921) **(Chap 3)**

RORSMAN, B., HAGNELL, O., & LANKE, J. (1986). Prevalence and incidence of senile and multi-infarct dementia in the Lundby Study: A comparison between the time periods 1947–1957 and 1957–1974. *Neuropsychobiology, 15,* 122–129. **(Chap 15)**

ROSEN, J. C., & LEITENBERG, H. (1985). Exposure plus response prevention treatment of bulimia. In D. M. Garner & P. E. Garfinkel (Eds.), *Handbook of psychotherapy for anorexia nervosa and bulimia* (pp. 193–209). New York: Guilford Press. **(Chap 8)**

ROSEN, J. C., LEITENBERG, H., FISHER, C., & KHAZAM, C. (1986). Binge-eating episodes in bulimia nervosa: The amount and type of food consumed. *International Journal of Eating Disorders, 5,* 255–267. **(Chap 8)**

ROSEN, L. W., SHAFER, C. L., DUMMER, G. M., CROSS, L. K., DEUMAN, G. W., & MALMBERG, S. R. (1988). Prevalence of pathogenic weight-control behaviors among Native American women and girls. *International Journal of Eating Disorders, 7*(6), 807–811. **(Chap 8)**

ROSEN, R. C., & BECK, J. G. (1988). *Patterns of sexual arousal: Psychophysiological processes and clinical applications.* New York: Guilford Press. **(Chap 11)**

ROSENBERG, H. (1993). Prediction of controlled drinking by alcoholics and problem drinkers. *Psychological Bulletin, 113,* 129–139. **(Chap 12)**

ROSENGREN, A., TIBBLIN, G., & WILHELMSEN, L. (1991). Self-perceived psychological stress and incidence of coronary artery disease in middle-aged men. *American Journal of Cardiology, 68,* 1171–1175. **(Chap 9)**

ROSENMAN, R. H., BRAND, R. J., JENKINS, C. D., FRIEDMAN, M., STRAUS, R., & WURM, M. (1975). Coronary heart disease in the Western Collaborative Group Study: Final follow-up experience of 8½ years. *Journal of the American Medical Association, 233,* 872–877. **(Chap 9)**

ROSENTHAL, D. (ED.). (1963). *The genain quadruplets: A case study and theoretical analysis of heredity and environment in schizophrenia.* New York: Basic Books. **(Chap 14)**

ROSENTHAL, D., WENDER, P. H., KETY, S. S., SCHULSINGER, F., WELNER, J., & OSTERGAARD, L. (1968). Schizophrenics' offspring reared in adoptive homes. In D. Rosenthal & S. S. Kety (Eds.), *The transmission of schizophrenia* (pp. 377–391). Oxford: Pergamon Press. **(Chap 14)**

ROSENTHAL, P. A., & ROSENTHAL, S. (1984). Suicidal behavior by preschool children. *American Journal of Psychiatry, 141,* 520–525. **(Chap 7)**

ROSOWSKY, E., & GURIAN, B. (1992). Impact of borderline personality disorder in late life on systems of care. *Hospital and Community Psychiatry, 43,* 386–389. **(Chap 13)**

ROSS, A. O., & PELHAM, W. E. (1981). Child psychopathology. *Annual Review of Psychology, 32,* 243–278. **(Chap 16)**

ROSS, C. A. (1989). *Multiple personality disorder: Diagnosis, clinical features, and treatment.* New York: John Wiley. **(Chap 6)**

ROSS, C. A., HEBER, S., ANDERSON, G., NORTON, G. R., ET AL. (1989). Differentiating multiple personality disorder and complex partial seizures. *General Hospital Psychiatry, 11*(1), 54–58. **(Chap 6)**

ROSS, C. A., MILLER, S. D., REAGOR, P., BJORNSON, L., FRASER, G. A., & ANDERSON, G. (1990). Structured interview data on 102 cases of multiple personality disorder from four centers. *American Journal of Psychiatry, 147,* 596–601. **(Chap 6)**

ROSS, M. W., WALINDER, J., LUNDSTROM, B., & THUWE, I. (1981). Cross-cultural approaches to transsexualism: A comparison between Sweden and Australia. *Acta Psychiatrica Scandinavica, 63,* 75–82. **(Chap 11)**

ROTHENBERG, R., WOEFEL, M., STONEBURNER, R., MILBERG, J., PARKER, R., & TRUMAN, B. (1987). Survival with the acquired immunodeficiency syndrome. *New England Journal of Medicine, 317,* 1297–1302. **(Chap 9)**

ROTTER, J. B., & RAFFERTY, J. E. (1950). *Manual: The Rotter incomplete sentences blank.* New York: Psychological Corporation. **(Chap 3)**

ROUNSAVILLE, B. J., SHOLOMSKAS, D., & PRUSOFF, B. A. (1988). Chronic mood disorders in depressed outpatients: Diagnosis and response to pharmacotherapy. *Journal of Affective Disorders, 2,* 72–88. **(Chap 7)**

ROWELL, E. A., & ROWELL, R. (1939). *On the trail of marihuana: The weed of madness.* Mountain View, CA: Pacific Press Publishing Association. **(Chap 12)**

ROZANSKI, A., BAIREY, N., KRANTZ, D., FRIEDMAN, J., RESSER, K., MORELL, M., HILTON-CHAFER, S., HESTRIN, L., BIETENDORF, J., & BERMAN, D. S. (1988). Mental stress and the induction of silent myocardial ischemia in patients with coronary artery disease. *New England Journal of Medicine, 318,* 1005–1012. **(Chap 9)**

RUBIN, R. T. (1982). Koro (Shook Yang): A culture-bound psychogenic syndrome. In C. T. H. Friedmann & R. A. Fauger (Eds.), *Extraordinary disorders of human behavior* (pp. 155–172). New York: Plenum Press. **(Chap 6)**

RUBIN, R., & BALOW, B. (1971). Learning and behavior disorders: A longitudinal study. *Exceptional Children, 38,* 293–299. **(Chap 15)**

RUSH, A. J., ERMAN, M. K., GILES, D. E., SCHLESSER, M. A., CARPENTER, G., VASAVADA, N., & ROFFWARG, H. P. (1986). Polysomnographic findings in recently drug-free and clinically remitted depressed patients. *Archives of General Psychiatry, 43,* 878–884. **(Chap 7)**

RUSH, B. (1812). *Medical inquiries and observations upon the diseases of the mind.* Philadelphia: Kimber and Richardson. **(Chap 7)**

RUSH, J. A. (1993). Mood disorders in DSM-IV. In D. L. Dunner (Ed.), *Current psychiatric therapy* (pp. 189–195). Philadelphia: W. B. Saunders. **(Chap 7)**

RUSSELL, G. F. M. (1979). Bulimia nervosa: An ominous variant of anorexia nervosa. *Psychological Medicine, 9,* 429–448. **(Chap 8)**

RUSSELL, G. F. M., SZMUKLER, G. I., DARE, C., & EISLER, I. (1987). An evaluation of family therapy in anorexia nervosa and bulimia nervosa. *Archives of General Psychiatry, 44,* 1047–1056. **(Chap 8)**

RUTTER, M. (1978). Diagnosis and definition. In M. Rutter & E. Schopler (Eds.), *Autism: A reappraisal of concepts and treatments* (pp. 1–26). New York: Plenum Press. **(Chap 16)**

RUTTER, M., & GILLER, H. (1984). *Juvenile delinquency: Trends and perspectives.* New York: Guilford Press. **(Chap 4)**

RUTTER, M., MACDONALD, H., LE COUTEUR, A., HARRINGTON, R., BOLTON, P., & BAILY, A. (1990). Genetic factors in child psychiatric disorders—II. Empirical findings. *Journal of Child Psychology and Psychiatry, 31,* 39–83. **(Chap 4)**

RUTTER, M., & SCHOPLER, E. (1992). Classification of pervasive developmental disorders: Some concepts and practical considerations. *Journal of Autism and Developmental Disorders, 22,* 459–482. **(Chap 16)**

RYAN, W. D. (1992). The pharmacologic treatment of child and adolescent depression. *Psychiatric Clinics of North America, 15,* 29–40. **(Chap 7)**

RYGH, J. L., & BARLOW, D. H. (1986, November). *Treatment of simple phobias with panic management techniques.* Paper presented at the annual meeting of the Association for Advancement of Behavior Therapy, Chicago. **(Chap 5)**

SAAB, P. G., LLABRE, M. M., HURWITZ, B. E., FRAME, C. A., REINEKE, I., FINS, A. I., MCCALLA, J., CIEPLY, L. K., & SCHNEIDERMAN, N. (1992). Myocardial and peripheral vascular responses to behavioral challenges and their stability in Black and White Americans. *Psychophysiology, 29*(4), 384–397. **(Chap 9)**

SACHS, G. A., & CASSEL, C. K. (1989). Ethical aspects of dementia. *Neurologic Clinics, 7,* 845–858. **(Chap 15)**

SACK, R. L., & LEWY, A. J. (1993). Human circadian rhythms: Lessons from the blind. *Annals of Medicine, 25,* 303–305. **(Chap 10)**

SACKEIM, H. A., & DEVANAND, D. P. (1991). Dissociative disorders. In M. Hersen & S. M. Turner (Eds.), *Adult psychopathology & diagnosis* (2nd ed., pp. 279–322). New York: John Wiley. **(Chap 6)**

SACKEIM, H. A., NORDLIE, J. W., & GUR, R. C. (1979). A model of hysterical and hypnotic blindness: Cognition, motivation and awareness. *Journal of Abnormal Psychology, 88,* 474–489. **(Chap 6)**

SAIGH, P. A. (1984). Pre- and postinvasion anxiety in Lebanon. *Behavior Therapy, 15,* 185–190. **(Chap 5)**

SAJWAJ, T., LIBET, J., & AGRAS, S. (1974). Lemon-juice therapy: The control of life threatening rumination in a six-month old infant. *Journal of Applied Behavior Analysis, 7*(4), 557–563. **(Chap 8)**

SAKEL, M. (1958). *Schizophrenia.* New York: Philosophical Library Inc. **(Chap 1)**

SAKHEIM, D. K., BARLOW, D. H., ABRAHAMSON, D. J., & BECK, J. G. (1987). Distinguishing between organogenic and psychogenic erectile dysfunction. *Behaviour Research and Therapy, 25,* 379–390. **(Chap 11)**

SAKHEIM, D. K., & DEVINE, S. E. (EDS.). (1992). *Out of darkness: Exploring satanism and ritual abuse.* New York: Lexington Books. **(Chap 6)**

SALGE, R. A., BECK, J. G., & LOGAN, A. (1988). A community survey of panic. *Journal of Anxiety Disorder, 2,* 157–167. **(Chap 5)**

SALKOVSKIS, P. M. (1985). Obsessional compulsive problems: A cognitive behavioral analysis. *Behaviour Research and Therapy, 23,* 571–577. **(Chap 5)**

SALKOVSKIS, P. M., ATHA, C., & STORER, D. (1990). Cognitive-behavioural problem solving in the treatment of patients who repeatedly attempt suicide: A controlled trial. *British Journal of Psychiatry, 157,* 871–876. **(Chap 7)**

SALKOVSKIS, P. M., & CAMPBELL, P. (1994). Thought suppression induces intrusion in naturally occurring negative intrusive thoughts. *Behaviour Research and Therapy, 32*(1), 1–8. **(Chap 5)**

SALKOVSKIS, P. M., WARWICK, H. M. C., & CLARK, D. M. (1990). *Hypochondriasis, illness phobia, and other anxiety disorders.* Paper requested by the Simple Phobia and Panic Disorder subcommittees of the DSM-IV Anxiety Disorders Work Group. **(Chaps 5, 6)**

SALZMAN, C. (1991). Pharmacologic treatment of the anxious elderly patient. In C. Salzman & B. D. Lebowitz (Eds.), *Anxiety in the elderly: Treatment and research* (pp. 149–173). New York: Springer. **(Chap 5)**

SAMEROFF, A. J., & SEIFER, R. (1990). Early contributors to developmental risk. In J. Rolf, A. S. Masten, D. Cicchetti, K. H. Nuechterlein, & S. Weintrab (Eds.), *Risk and protective factors in the development of psychopathology* (pp. 52–66). Cambridge: Cambridge University Press. **(Chap 4)**

SAMSON, J. A., MIRIN, S. M., HAUSER, S. T., FENTON, B. T., & SCHILDKRAUT, J. J. (1992). Learned helplessness and urinary MHPG levels in unipolar depression. *American Journal of Psychiatry, 149*(6), 806–809. **(Chap 7)**

SANDERS, M. R. (1992). Enhancing the impact of behavioural family intervention with chil-

dren: Emerging perspectives. *Behaviour Change, 9,* 115–119. **(Chap 13)**

SANDERS, M. R., DADDS, M. R., JOHNSTON, B. M., & CASH, R. (1992). Childhood depression and conduct disorder: I. Behavioral, affective and cognitive aspects of family problem solving interactions. *Journal of Abnormal Psychology, 101*(3), 495–504. **(Chap 7)**

SANDERSON, W.C., & BARLOW, D. H. (1986, November). *A description of the subcategories of the DSM-III-Revised category of panic disorder: Characteristics of 100 patients with different levels of avoidance.* Poster session at the 20th annual convention of the Association for the Advancement of Behavior Therapy. Chicago, Illinois. **(Chap 5)**

SANDERSON, W. C., & BARLOW, D. H. (1990). A description of patients diagnosed with DSM-III-R generalized anxiety disorder. *Journal of Nervous and Mental Disease, 178,* 588–591. **(Chap 5)**

SANDERSON, W. C., DINARDO, P. A., RAPEE, R. M., & BARLOW, D. H. (1990). Syndrome comorbidity in patients diagnosed with a DSM-III-R anxiety disorder. *Journal of Abnormal Psychology, 99,* 308–312. **(Chaps 5, 7)**

SANSBURY, L. L., & WAHLER, R. G. (1992). Pathways to maladaptive parenting with mothers and their conduct disordered children. *Behavior Modification, 16,* 574–592. **(Chap 13)**

SAPER, J. R. (1989). Chronic headache syndromes. *Neurologic Clinics, 7,* 387–411. **(Chap 9)**

SAPOLSKY, R. M. (1990, JANUARY). Stress in the wild. *Scientific American,* 116–123. **(Chap 9)**

SAPOLSKY, R. M., & MEANEY, M. J. (1986). Maturation of the adrenal stress response: Neuroendocrine control mechanisms and the stress hyporesponsive period. *Brain Research Review, 11,* 65–76. **(Chap 9)**

SAPOLSKY, R., & RAY, J. C. (1989). Styles of dominance and their endocrine correlates among wild, live baboons. *American Journal of Primatology, 18*(1), 1–13. **(Chap 9)**

SARBIN, T., & MANCUSO, J. (1980). *Schizophrenia: Medical diagnosis or moral verdict?* Elmsford, NY: Pergamon Press. **(Chap 14)**

SARREL, P. M., & MASTERS, W. H. (1982). Sexual molestation of men by women. *Archives of Sexual Behavior, 11,* 117–131. **(Chap 11)**

SATEL, S. (1992). Craving for and fear of cocaine: A phenomenologic update on cocaine craving and paranoia. In T. R. Kosten & H. D. Kleber (Eds.), *Clinician's guide to cocaine addiction: Theory, research, and treatment* (pp. 172–192). New York: Guilford Press. **(Chap 12)**

SAUNDERS, A. M., STRITTMATTER, W. J., SCHMECHEL, D., ST. GEORGE-HYSLOP, P. H., PERICAK-VANCE, M. A., JOO, S. H., ROSI, B. L., GUSELLA, J. F., CRAPPER-MACLACHLAN, D. R., ALBERTS, M. J., HULETTE, C., CRAIN, B., GOLDGABER, D., & ROSES, A. D. (1993). Association of apolipoprotein E allele e4 with late-onset familial and sporadic Alzheimer's disease. *Neurology, 43,* 1467–1472. **(Chap 15)**

SAXENA, S., & PRASAD, K. (1989). DSM-III subclassifications of dissociative disorders applied to psychiatric outpatients in India.

American Journal of Psychiatry, 146, 261–262. **(Chap 6)**

SCHACHT, T. E. (1985). DSM-III and the politics of truth. *American Psychologist, 40,* 513–521. **(Chap 3)**

SCHAFER, J., & BROWN, S. A. (1991). Marijuana and cocaine effect expectancies and drug use patterns. *Journal of Consulting and Clinical Psychology, 59,* 558–565. **(Chap 12)**

SCHEERENBERGER, R. C. (1983). *A history of mental retardation.* Baltimore: Paul H. Brookes. **(Chap 15)**

SCHEIBEL, A. B., & CONRAD, A. S. (1993). Hippocampal dysgenesis in mutant mouse and schizophrenic man: Is there a relationship? *Schizophrenia Bulletin, 19,* 21–33. **(Chap 14)**

SCHEIER, M. F., & CARVER, C. S. (1987). Dispositional optimism and physical well-being: The influence of generalized outcome expectancies on health. Special issue: Personality and physical health. *Journal of Personality, 55*(2), 169–210. **(Chap 9)**

SCHEIER, M. F., MATTHEWS, K. A., OWENS, J. F., MAGOVERN, G. J., SR., LEFEBVRE, R. C., ABBOTT, R. A., & CARVER, C. S. (1989). Dispositional optimism and recovery from coronary artery bypass surgery: The beneficial effects on physical and psychological well-being. *Journal of Personality and Social Psychology, 57*(6), 1024–1040. **(Chap 9)**

SCHEMO, D. J. (1992, December 14). A matchmaker's niche: Mentally ill couples. *New York Times,* **(Chap 14)**

SCHENK, L., & BEAR, D. (1981). Multiple personality and related dissociative phenomena in patients with temporal lobe epilepsy. *American Journal of Psychiatry, 138,* 1311–1316. **(Chap 6)**

SCHIAVI, R. C. (1990). Chronic alcoholism and male sexual dysfunction. *Journal of Sex and Marital Therapy, 16,* 23–33. **(Chap 11)**

SCHILDKRAUT, J. J. (1965). The catecholamine hypothesis of affective disorders: A review of supporting evidence. *American Journal of Psychiatry, 122,* 509–522. **(Chaps 2, 7)**

SCHLEIFER, S. J., KELLER, S. E., BOND, R. N., COHEN, J., & STEIN, M. (1989). Major depressive disorder and immunity: Role of age, sex, severity, and hospitalization. *Archives of General Psychiatry, 46,* 81–87. **(Chap 9)**

SCHLEYER, B., AARONSON, C., MANNUZZA, S., MARTIN, L. Y., & FYER, A. J. (November, 1990). *Schedule for affective disorders and schizophrenia—Lifetime anxiety version* (rev. ed.). New York: Anxiety Disorders Clinic, New York State Psychiatric Institute. **(Chap 3)**

SCHLUNDT, O. G., & JOHNSON, W. G. (1990). *Eating disorders: Assessment and treatment.* Boston: Allyn & Bacon. **(Chap 8)**

SCHLUTTER, L. C., GOLDEN, C. J., & BLUME, H. G. (1980). A comparison of treatments for prefrontal muscle contraction headache. *British Journal of Medical Psychology, 53,* 47–52. **(Chap 9)**

SCHNEIDERMAN, N., ANTONI, M. H., IRONSON, G., LAPERRIERE, A., & FLETCHER, M. A. (1992). Applied psychological science and HIV-1 spectrum disease. *Applied and Preventive Psychology, 1,* 67–82. **(Chaps 2, 9)**

SCHNEIER, F. R., JOHNSON, J., HORNIG, C. D., LIEBOWITZ, M. R., & WEISSMAN, M. M. (1992). Social phobia: Comorbidity and morbidity in an epidemiologic sample. *Archives of General Psychiatry, 49,* 282–288. **(Chap 5)**

SCHNEIER, F. R., LIEBOWITZ, M. R., BEIDEL, D. C., FYER, A. J., GEORGE, M. S., HEIMBERG, R. G., HOLT, C. S., KLEIN, D. F., LEVIN, A. P., LYDIARD, R. B., MANNUZZA, S., MARTIN, L. Y., NARDI, A. E., ROSCOW, D. B., SPITZER, R. L., TURNER, S. M., UHDE, T. W., VASCONCELOS, I. L., & VERSIANI, M. (in press). Social phobia. *DSM-IV sourcebook.* Washington, DC: American Psychiatric Association. **(Chap 5)**

SCHOENBACH, V. J., KAPLAN, B. H., FREDMAN, L., & KLEINBAUM, D. G. (1986). Social ties and mortality in Evans County, Georgia. *American Journal of Epidemiology, 123,* 577. **(Chap 2)**

SCHOENEMAN, T. J. (1977). The role of mental illness in the European witchhunts of the sixteenth and seventeenth centuries: An assessment. *Journal of the History of the Behavioral Sciences, 13,* 337–351. **(Chap 1)**

SCHOVER, L. R. (1981). Unpublished data. Cited by Schover, L. R. & Jensen, S. B. (1988). *Sexuality and chronic illness: A comprehensive approach* (pp. 59–60, 126, 130–135). New York: Guilford Press. **(Chap 11)**

SCHOVER, L. R., & JENSEN, S. B. (1988). *Sexuality and chronic illness: A comprehensive approach.* New York: Guilford Press. **(Chap 11)**

SCHOVER, L. R., & NEWSOM, C. D. (1976). Overselectivity, developmental level, and overtraining in autistic and normal children. *Journal of Abnormal Child Psychology, 4,* 289–298. **(Chap 16)**

SCHREIBER, F. R. (1973). *Sybil.* Chicago: Regnery. **(Chap 6)**

SCHREINER-ENGEL, P., & SCHIAVI, R. C. (1986). Lifetime psychopathology in individuals with low sexual desire. *Journal of Nervous and Mental Disease, 174,* 646–651. **(Chap 11)**

SCHROEDER, M. L., WORMWORTH, J. A., & LIVESLEY, W. J. (1993). Dimensions of personality disorder and the five-factor model of personality. In P. T. Costa, Jr., & T. A. Widiger (Eds.), *Personality disorders and the five-factor model of personality* (pp. 117–127). Washington, DC: American Psychological Association. **(Chap 13)**

SCHUBERT, D. S., BURNS, R., PARAS, W., & SIOSON, E. (1992). Increase of medical hospital length of stay by depression in stroke and amputation patients: A pilot study. *Psychotherapy and Psychosomatics, 57*(1–2), 61–66. **(Chap 7)**

SCHUCKIT, M. A. (1993). Keeping current with the DSMs and substance use disorder. In D. L. Dunner (Ed.), *Current psychiatric therapy* (pp. 89–91). Philadelphia: W. B. Saunders. **(Chap 12)**

SCHUCKIT, M. A. (1994). Low level of response to alcohol as a predictor of future alcoholism. *American Journal of Psychiatry, 151,* 184-189. **(Chap 12)**

SCHUCKIT, M. A., SMITH, T. L., ANTHENELLI, R., & IRWIN, M. (1993). Clinical course of alcoholism in 636 male inpatients. *American Journal of Psychiatry, 150,* 786–792. **(Chap 12)**

SCHULSINGER, F., KETY, S. S., & ROSENTHAL, D. (1979). A family study of suicide. In M. Schou & E. Stromgren (Eds.), *Origin, prevention, and treatment of affective disorders.* New York: Academic Press. **(Chap 7)**

SCHULTZ-ROSS, R. A. (1993). Ethics and the expert witness. *Hospital and Community Psychiatry, 44,* 388–389. **(Chap 17)**

SCHWALBERG, M. D., BARLOW, D. H., ALGER, S. A., & HOWARD, L. J. (1992). Comparison of bulimics, obese binge eaters, social phobics, and individuals with panic disorder or comorbidity across DSM-III-R anxiety. *Journal of Abnormal Psychology, 101,* 675–681. **(Chap 8)**

SCHWARTZ, A. J., & WHITAKER, L. C. (1990). Suicide among college students: Assessment, treatment, and intervention. In S. J. Blumenthal & D. J. Kupfer (Eds.), *Suicide over the life cycle: Risk factors, assessment and treatment of suicidal patients.* Washington, DC: American Psychiatric Press. **(Chap 7)**

SCHWARTZ, G. E., & WEISS, S. M. (1978). Behavioral medicine revisited: An amended definition. *Journal of Behavioral Medicine, 1,* 249–252. **(Chap 9)**

SCHWARTZ, I. M. (1993). Affective reactions of American and Swedish women to the first premarital coitus: A cross-cultural comparison. *Journal of Sex Research, 30*(1), 18–26. **(Chap 11)**

SCHWEIZER, E., RICKELS, K., CASE, W. G., & GREENBLATT, D. J. (1990). Long-term use of benzodiazepines. II. Effects of gradual taper. *Archives of General Psychiatry, 47,* 908–915. **(Chap 5)**

SCOTT, K. G., & CARRAN, D. T. (1987). The epidemiology and prevention of mental retardation. *American Psychologist, 42,* 801–804. **(Chap 15)**

SEDGWICK, P. (1982). *Psycho politics.* New York: Harper & Row. **(Chap 1)**

SEDLMEIER, P., & GIGERENZER, G. (1989). Do studies of statistical power have an effect on the power of studies? *Psychological Bulletin, 105,* 309–316. **(Chap 4)**

SEEMAN, P., LEE, T., CHAU WONG, M. & WONG, K. (1976). Antipsychotic drug doses and neuroleptic/dopamine receptors. *Nature, 261,* 717–719. **(Chap 14)**

SEGAL, J. H. (1989). Erotomania revisited: From Kraepelin to DSM-III-R. *American Journal of Psychiatry, 146,* 1261–1266. **(Chap 14)**

SEGAL, S. (1978). Attitudes toward the mentally ill: A review. *Social Work, 23,* 211–217. **(Chap 3)**

SEGAL, Z. V., HOOD, J. E., SHAW, B. F., & HIGGINS, E. (1988). A structural analysis of the self-schema construct in major depression. *Cognitive Therapy and Research, 12*(5), 471–485. **(Chap 7)**

SEGAL, Z. V., SHAW, B. F., & VELLA, D. D. (1989). Life stress and depression: A test of the congruency hypothesis for life event content and depressive subtype. Special issue: Clinical depression. *Canadian Journal of Behavioural Science, 21*(4), 389–400. **(Chap 7)**

SEGRAVES, K. B., & SEGRAVES, R. T. (1991). Multiple-phase sexual dysfunction. *Journal of Sex Education and Therapy, 17*(3), 153–156. **(Chap 11)**

SEGRAVES, R. T. (1988). Drugs and desire. In S. R. Leiblum & R. C. Rosen (Eds.), *Sexual desire disorders* (pp. 313–347). New York: Guilford Press. **(Chap 11)**

SELBY, G., & LANCE, J. W. (1960). Observations on 500 cases of migraine and allied vascular headache. *Journal of Neurology, Neurosurgery and Psychiatry, 23,* 23–32. **(Chap 9)**

SELIGMAN, M. E. P. (1971). Phobias and preparedness. *Behavior Therapy, 2,* 307–320. **(Chap 2)**

SELIGMAN, M. E. P. (1975). *Helplessness: On depression, development and death.* San Francisco: W. H. Freeman. **(Chaps 7, 9)**

SELYE, H. (1936). A syndrome produced by diverse noxious agents. *Nature, 138,* 32. **(Chap 9)**

SELYE, H. (1950). *The physiology and pathology of exposure to stress.* Montreal: Acta. **(Chap 9)**

SEMANS, J. H. (1956). Premature ejaculation: A new approach. *Southern Medical Journal, 49,* 353–358. **(Chap 11)**

SEVERINO, S. K., & MOLINE, M. L. (1989). *Premenstrual syndrome: A clinician's guide.* New York: Guilford Press. **(Chap 3)**

SEXTON, M. M. (1979). Behavioral epidemiology. In O. F. Pomerleau & J. P. Brady (Eds.), *Behavioral medicine: Theory and practice* (pp. 3–21). Baltimore: Williams & Wilkins. **(Chap 9)**

SHABECOFF, P. (1987, October 14). Stress and the lure of harmless remedies. *New York Times,* p. 12. **(Chap 12)**

SHAFFER, D. R. (1993). *Developmental psychology: Childhood and adolescence* (3rd ed.). Pacific Grove, CA: Brooks/Cole. **(Chap 2)**

SHAFFER, D., GARLAND, A., GOULD, M., FISHER, P., & TRAUTMEN, P. (1988). Preventing teenage suicide: A critical review. *Journal of the American Academy of Child and Adolescent Psychiatry, 27,* 675–687. **(Chap 7)**

SHAFFER, D., GARLAND, A., VIELAND, V., UNDERWOOD, M., & BUSNER, C. (1991). The impact of curriculum based suicide prevention programs for teenagers. *Journal of the American Academy of Child and Adolescent Psychiatry, 30*(4), 588–596. **(Chap 7)**

SHAPIRO, D. (1965). *Neurotic styles.* New York: Basic Books. **(Chap 13)**

SHAPIRO, D. (1974). Operant-feedback control of human blood pressure: Some clinical issues. In P. A. Obrist, A. H. Black, J. Brener, & L. V. DiCara (Eds.), *Cardiovascular psychophysiology: Current issues in response mechanisms, biofeedback, and methodology.* Chicago: Aldine. **(Chap 9)**

SHAPIRO, E. S., & LENTZ, F. E. (1991). Vocational-technical programs: Follow-up of students with learning disabilities. *Exceptional Children, 58,* 47–59. **(Chap 15)**

SHARFSTEIN, S. S. (1987). Reimbursement resistance to treatment and support for the long-term mental patient. *New Directions for Mental Health Services, 33,* 75–85. **(Chap 17)**

SHARPE, M. (1992). Fatigue and chronic fatigue syndrome. *Current Opinion in Psychiatry, 5,* 207–212. **(Chap 9)**

SHARPE, M. (1993). *Chronic fatigue syndrome* (pp. 298–317). Chichester, England: John Wiley. **(Chap 9)**

SHEA, M. T., ELKIN, I., IMBER, S. D., SOTSKY, S. M., WATKINS, J. T., COLLINS, J. F.,

PILKONIS, P. A., BECKHAM, E., GLASS, D. R., DOLAN, R. T., & PARLOFF, M. B. (1992). Course of depressive symptoms over follow-up: Findings from the National Institute of Mental Health Treatment of Depression Collaborative Research Program. *Archives of General Psychiatry, 49* (10), 782–787. **(Chap 7)**

SHEA, M. T., PILKONIS, P. A., BECKHAM, E., COLLINS, J. F., ELKIN, I. SOTSKY, S. M., & DOCHERTY, J. P. (1990). Personality disorders and treatment outcome in the NIMH treatment of depression collaborative research program. *American Journal of Psychiatry, 147,* 711–718. **(Chap 13)**

SHEAFFER, R. (1986). *The UFO verdict: Examining the evidence.* Buffalo, NY: Prometheus. **(Chap 10)**

SHEIKH, J. I. (1992). Anxiety and its disorders in old age. In J. E. Birren, K. Sloan, & G. D. Cohen (Eds.), *Handbook of mental health and aging* (pp. 410–432). New York: Academic Press. **(Chap 5)**

SHNEIDMAN, E. S. (1989). Approaches and commonalities of suicide. In R. F. W. Diekstra, R. Mariss, S. Platt, A. Schmidtke, & G. Sonneck (Eds.), *Suicide and its prevention: The role of attitude and imitation. Advances in Suicidology* (Vol. 1). Leiden, Netherlands: E. J. Brill. **(Chap 7)**

SHNEIDMAN, E. S., FARBEROW, N. L., & LITMAN, R. E. (EDS.) (1970). *The psychology of suicide.* New York: Science House. **(Chap 7)**

SHORE, J. H., TATUM, E. L., & VOLLMER, W. M. (1986). Evaluation of mental health effects of disaster. *American Journal of Public Health, 76,* 76–83. **(Chap 4)**

SHOW, M. (1985). Practical problems of lithium maintenance treatment. *Advances in Biochemical Psychopharmacology, 40,* 131–138. **(Chap 7)**

SHROUT, P. E., LINK, B. G., DOHRENWEND, B. P., SKODOL, A. E., STUEVE, A., & MIROTZNIK, J. (1989). Characterizing life events as risk factors for depression: The role of fateful loss events. *Journal of Abnormal Psychology, 98,* 460–467. **(Chap 7)**

SIBLEY, D. C., & BLINDER, B. J. (1988). Anorexia nervosa. In B. J. Blinder, B. F. Chaitin, & R. S. Goldstein (Eds.), *The eating disorders: Medical and psychological bases of diagnosis and treatment* (pp. 247–258). New York: PMA Publishing Corp. **(Chap 8)**

SIECK, W. A., & MCFALL, R. M. (1976). Some determinants of self-monitoring effects. *Journal of Consulting and Clinical Psychology, 44,* 958–965. **(Chap 3)**

SIEVER, L. J. (1992). Schizophrenia spectrum personality disorders. In A. Tasman & M. B. Riba (Eds.), *Review of psychiatry* (Vol. 11, pp. 25–42). Washington, DC: American Psychiatric Press. **(Chap 13)**

SIEVER, L. J., BERNSTEIN, D. P., & SILVERMAN, J. M. (1991). Schizotypal personality disorder: A review of its current status. *Journal of Personality Disorders, 5,* 178–193. **(Chap 13)**

SIEVER, L. J., DAVIS, K. L., & GORMAN, L. K. (1991). Pathogenesis of mood disorders. In K. Davis, H. Klar, & J. T. Coyle, *Foundations of psychiatry.* Philadelphia: W. B. Saunders. **(Chap 2)**

SIFFRE, M. (1964). *Beyond time.* (H. Briffault, Ed. and Trans.) New York: McGraw-Hill. **(Chap 10)**

SIGMAN, M., & UNGERER, J. A. (1984). Attachment behaviors in autistic children. *Journal of Autism and Developmental Disorders, 14,* 231–244. **(Chap 16)**

SIGVARDSSON, S., CLONINGER, C. R., BOHMAN, M., & VON-KNORRING, A. L. (1982). Predisposition to petty criminality in Swedish adoptees. *Archives of General Psychiatry, 39,* 1248–1253. **(Chap 13)**

SILLANPAA, M. (1976). Prevalence of migraine and other headaches in Finnish children starting school. *Headache, 16,* 288–290. **(Chap 9)**

SILVA, P. A. (1980). The prevalence, stability and significance of developmental language delay in preschool children. *Developmental Medicine and Child Neurology, 22,* 768–777. **(Chap 16)**

SILVER, E., CIRINCIONE, C., & STEADMAN, H. J. (1994). Demythologizing inaccurate perceptions of the insanity defense. *Law and Human Behavior, 18,* 63–70. **(Chap 17)**

SILVERMAN, K., EVANS, S. M., STRAIN, E. C., & GRIFFITHS, R. R. (1992). Withdrawal syndrome after the double-blind cessation of caffeine consumption. *New England Journal of Medicine, 327,* 1109–1114. **(Chap 12)**

SILVERSTONE, T. (1985). Dopamine in manic depressive illness: A pharmacological synthesis. *Journal of Affective Disorders, 8*(3), 225–231. **(Chap 7)**

SIMON, R. J., & AARONSON, D. E. (1988). *The insanity defense: A critical assessment of law and policy in the post-Hinckley era.* New York: Praeger Press. **(Chap 17)**

SIMONS, A. D., MURPHY, G. E., LEVINE, J. L., & WETZEL, R. D. (1986). Cognitive therapy and pharmacotherapy for depression: Sustained improvement over one year. *Archives of General Psychiatry, 43*(1), 43–48. **(Chap 7)**

SIMPSON, G. M., PI, E. H., GROSS, L., BARON, D., & NOVEMBER, M. (1988). Plasma levels and therapeutic response with trimipramine treatment of endogenous depression. *Journal of Clinical Psychiatry, 49,* 113–116. **(Chap 7)**

SINGH, N. N., MANNING, P. J., & ANGELL, M. J. (1982). Effects of an oral hygiene punishment on chronic rumination and collateral behaviors in monozygotic twins. *Journal of Applied Behavioral Analysis, 15,* 309–314. **(Chap 8)**

SINGH, N. N., & WINTON, A. S. W. (1984). Effects of a screening procedure on pica and collateral behaviors. *Journal of Behavior Therapy and Experimental Psychiatry, 15,* 59–65. **(Chap 8)**

SINGHI, S., SINGHI, P., & ADWANI, G. B. (1981). Role of psychosocial stress in the cause of pica. *Clinical Pediatrics, 20,* 783–785. **(Chap 8)**

SIRIS, S. G. (1993). The treatment of schizoaffective disorder. In D. L. Dunner (Ed.), *Current psychiatric therapy* (pp. 160–165). Philadelphia: W. B. Saunders. **(Chap 14)**

SISSON, R. W., & AZRIN, N. H. (1989). The community reinforcement approach. In R. K. Hester & W. R. Miller (Eds.), *Handbook of alcohol treatment approaches: Effective alternatives.* Elmsford: NY: Pergamon Press. **(Chap 12)**

SKHIRI, D., ANNABI, S., BI, S., & ALLANI, D. (1982). Enfants d'immigrés: Facteurs de liens ou de rupture? *Annales Medico-Psychologiques, 140,* 597–602. **(Chap 13)**

SKINNER, B. F. (1938). *The behavior of organisms.* New York: Appleton-Century-Crofts. **(Chap 1)**

SKINNER, B. F. (1948). *Walden two.* New York: Macmillan. **(Chap 1)**

SKINNER, B. F. (1971). *Beyond freedom and dignity.* New York: Knopf. **(Chap 1)**

SMAIL, P., STOCKWELL, T., CANTER, S., & HODGSON, R. (1984). Alcohol dependence and phobic anxiety states: I. A prevalence study. *British Journal of Psychiatry, 144,* 53–57. **(Chap 5)**

SMALL, G. W. (1991). Recognition and treatment of depression in the elderly. The clinician's challenge: Strategies for treatment of depression in the 1990's. *Journal of Clinical Psychiatry, 52,* 11–22. **(Chap 7)**

SMALLEY, S. L. (1991). Genetic influences in autism. *Psychiatric Clinics of North America, 14,* 125–139. **(Chap 16)**

SMITH, C., & LAPP, L. (1991). Increases in number of REMS and REM density in humans following an intensive learning period. *Sleep, 14,* 325–330. **(Chap 10)**

SMITH, D. E., MARCUS, M. D., & KAYE, W. (1992). Cognitive-behavioral treatment of obese binge eaters. *International Journal of Eating Disorders, 12,* 257–262. **(Chap 8)**

SMITH, G. A., & HALL, J. A. (1982). Evaluating Michigan's guilty but mentally ill verdict: An empirical study. *Journal of Law Reform, 16,* 75–112. **(Chap 17)**

SMITH, G. R., MONSON, R. A., & RAY, D. B. (1986). Psychiatric consultation in somatization disorder. *New England Journal of Medicine, 314,* 1407–1413. **(Chap 6)**

SMITH, J. E., & KREJCI, J. (1991). Minorities join the majority: Eating disturbances among Hispanic and Native American youth. *International Journal of Eating Disorders, 10,* 179–186. **(Chap 8)**

SMITH, M. D. (1992). Community integration and supported employment. In D. E. Berkell (Ed.), *Autism: Identification, education, and treatment* (pp. 253–271). Hillsdale, NJ: Lawrence Erlbaum. **(Chap 16)**

SMITH, M. D., HAAS, P. J., & BELCHER, R. G. (1994). Facilitated communication: The effects of facilitator knowledge and level of assistance on output. *Journal of Autism and Developmental Disorders, 24,* 357–367. **(Chap 16)**

SMITH, R. J. (1991). Somatization disorder: Defining its role in clinical medicine. *Journal of General Internal Medicine, 6,* 168–175. **(Chap 6)**

SMITH, S. E. (1993). Cognitive deficits associated with fragile X syndrome. *Mental Retardation, 31,* 279–283. **(Chap 15)**

SMITH, S. S., & NEWMAN, J. P. (1990). Alcohol and drug abuse-dependence disorders in psychopathic and nonpsychopathic criminal offenders. *Journal of Abnormal Psychology, 99,* 430–439. **(Chap 13)**

SMITH, S. S., O'HARA, B. F., PERSICO, A. M., GORELICK, D. A., NEWLIN, D. B., VLAHOV, D., SOLOMON, L., PICKENS, R., & UHL, G. R. (1992). Genetic vulnerability to drug abuse:

The D2 dopamine receptor Taq B1 restriction fragment length polymorphism appears more frequently in polysubstance abusers. *Archives of General Psychiatry, 49,* 723–727. **(Chap 12)**

SMITH, T. W. (1992). Hostility and health: Current status of a psychosomatic hypothesis. *Health Psychology, 11*(3), 139–150. **(Chap 9)**

SNYDER, F. (1971). Psychophysiology of human sleep. *Clinical Neurosurgery, 18,* 503–536. **(Chap 10)**

SNYDER, S. H. (1976). The dopamine hypothesis of schizophrenia: Focus on the dopamine receptor. *American Journal of Psychiatry, 133,* 197–202. **(Chap 2)**

SNYDER, S. H. (1981). Opiate and benzodiazepine receptors. *Psychosomatics, 22*(11), 986–989. **(Chap 2)**

SNYDER, S. H. (1984). Adenosine as a mediator of the behavioral effects of caffeine. In P. B. Dews (Ed.), *Caffeine: Perspectives from recent research* (pp. 129–141). Berlin: Springer-Verlag. **(Chap 12)**

SNYDER, S. H., BURT, D. R., & CREESE, I. (1976). Dopamine receptor of mammalian brain: Direct demonstration of binding to agonist and antagonist states. *Neuroscience Symposia, 1,* 28–49. **(Chap 2)**

SOBELL, M. B., & SOBELL, L. C. (1978). *Behavioral treatment of alcohol problems.* New York: Plenum Press. **(Chap 12)**

SOBELL, M. B., & SOBELL, L. C. (1993). *Problem drinkers: Guided self-change treatment.* New York: Guilford Press. **(Chap 12)**

SOCIETY FOR RESEARCH IN CHILD DEVELOPMENT, COMMITTEE FOR ETHICAL CONDUCT IN CHILD DEVELOPMENT RESEARCH. (1990, Winter). SRCD ethical standards for research with children. *SRCD Newsletter,* Chicago. **(Chap 4)**

SOLOFF, P. H., GEORGE, A., NATHAN, R. S., SCHULZ, P. M., CORNELIUS, J. R., HERRING, J., & PEREL, J. M. (1989). Amitrityline versus haloperidol in borderlines: Final outcomes and predictors of response. *Journal of Clinical Psychopharmacology, 9,* 238–246. **(Chap 13)**

SOLOMON, K., & HART, R. (1978). Pitfalls and prospects in clinical research on antianxiety drugs: Benzodiazepines and placebos. *Journal of Clinical Psychiatry, 39,* 823–831. **(Chap 5)**

SOLOMON, R. L. (1980). The opponent-process theory of acquired motivation: The costs of pleasure and the benefits of pain. *American Psychologist, 35,* 691–712. **(Chap 12)**

SOLOMON, R. L., & CORBIT, J. D. (1974). An opponent process theory of motivation: I. Temporal dynamics of affect. *Psychological Review, 81,* 119–145. **(Chap 12)**

SOMBER NEWS FROM THE AIDS FRONT. (1993). *Science, 260,* 1712–1713. **(Chap 2)**

SOMERS, V. K., DYKEN, M. E., MARK, A. L., & ABBAD, F. M. (1993). Sympathetic nerve activity during sleep in normal subjects. *New England Journal of Medicine, 328*(5), 303–307. **(Chap 10)**

SONNANDER, K., EMANUELSSON, I., & KEBBON, L. (1993). Pupils with mild mental retardation in regular Swedish schools: Prevalence, objective characteristics, and subjective evaluations. *American Journal on Mental Retardation, 97,* 692–701. **(Chap 15)**

SOUTHWICK, S. M., KRYSTAL, J. H., & CHARNEY, D. S. (1991). *Yohimbine in PTSD* (Abstract No. NR478). New research abstracts of the American Psychiatric Association 143rd annual meeting. **(Chap 5)**

SOUTHWICK, S. M., KRYSTAL, J. H., JOHNSON, D. R., & CHARNEY, D. S. (1992). Neurobiology of posttraumatic stress disorder. In A. Tasman & M. B. Riba (Eds.), *Review of psychiatry* (Vol. 11, pp. 347–367). Washington, DC: American Psychiatric Press. **(Chap 5)**

SPANOS, N. P., CROSS, P. A., DICKSON, K., & DUBREUIL, S. C. (1993). Close encounters: An examination of UFO experiences. *Journal of Abnormal Psychology, 102,* 624–632. **(Chap 10)**

SPANOS, N. P., JAMES, B., & DE GROOT, H. P. (1990). Detection of simulated hypnotic amnesia. *Journal of Abnormal Psychology, 99*(2), 179–182. **(Chap 6)**

SPANOS, N. P., WEEKS, J. R., & BERTRAND, L. D. (1985). Multiple personality: A social psychological perspective. *Journal of Abnormal Psychology, 92,* 362–376. **(Chap 6)**

SPARROW, S. S., BALLA, D. A., & CICCHETTI, D. V. (1984). *Vineland adaptive behavior scales.* Circle Pines, MN: American Guidance Service. **(Chap 15)**

SPECTOR, I. P., & CAREY, M. P. (1990). Incidence and prevalence of the sexual dysfunctions: A critical review of the empirical literature. *Archives of Sexual Behavior, 19*(4), 389–408. **(Chap 11)**

SPEER, D. C. (1992). Clinically significant change: Jacobson and Truax (1991) revisited. *Journal of Consulting and Clinical Psychology, 60,* 402–408. **(Chap 4)**

SPENCE, D. W., GALANTINO, M. L., MOSSBERG, K. A., & ZIMMERMAN, S. O. (1990). Progressive resistance exercise: Effect on muscle function and anthropometry of a select AIDS population. *Archives of Physical Medicine and Rehabilitation, 71,* 644–648. **(Chap 9)**

SPIEGEL, D., BLOOM, J. R., KRAMER, H. C., & GOTHEIL, E. (1989). Effect of psychosocial treatment on survival of patients with metastatic breast cancer. *Lancet, 14,* 888–891. **(Chap 9)**

SPIEGEL, D., & CARDENA, E. (1991). Disintegrated experience: The dissociative disorders revisited. *Journal of Abnormal Psychology, 100*(3), 366–378. **(Chap 6)**

SPIELBERGER, C. D., & FRANK, R. G. (1992). Injury control: A promising field for psychologists. *American Psychologist, 47*(8), 1029–1030. **(Chap 9)**

SPIELMAN, A. J., & GLOVINSKY, P. (1991). The varied nature of insomnia. In P. J. Hauri (Ed.), *Case studies in insomnia* (pp. 1–15). New York: Plenum Press. **(Chap 10)**

SPIKER, D., & RICKS, M. (1984). Visual self-recognition in autistic children: Developmental relationships. *Child Development, 55,* 214–225. **(Chap 16)**

SPIKER, D. G., WEISS, J. C., DEALY, R. S., GRIFFIN, S. J., HANIN, I., NEIL, J. F., PEREL, J. M., ROSSI, A. J., & SOLOFF, P. H. (1985). The pharmacological treatment of delusional depression. *American Journal of Psychiatry, 142,* 430–436. **(Chap 7)**

SPIRA, A., BAJOS, N., BEJIN, A., BELTZER, N., BOZON, M., DUCOT, M., DURANDEAU, A., FERRAND, A., GIAMI, A., GILLOIRE, A.,

GIRAUD, M., LERIDON, H., MESSIAH, A., LUDWIG, D., MOATTI, J., MOUNNIER, L., OLOMUCKI, H., POPLAVSKY, J., RIADNEY, B., SPENCER, B., SZTALRYD, J., & TOUZARD, H. (1992). AIDS and sexual behavior in France. *Nature, 360,* 407–409. **(Chap 11)**

SPITZER, R. L. (1991). An outsider-insider's views about revising the DSMs. *Journal of Abnormal Psychology, 100*(3), 294–296. **(Chap 3)**

SPITZER, R. L., DEVLIN, M. J., WALSH, B. T., HASIN, D., WING, R., MARCUS, M. D., MITCHELL, J., & NONAS, C. (1991). Binge eating disorder: To be or not to be in DSM-IV. *International Journal of Eating Disorders, 10,* 627–629. **(Chap 8)**

SPITZER, R. L., DEVLIN, M. J., WALSH, B. T., HASIN, D., WING, R., MARCUS, M. D., STUNKARD, A., WADDEN, T., YANOVSKI, S., AGRAS, S., MITCHELL, J., & NONAS, C. (1992). Binge eating disorder: A multisite field trial of the diagnostic criteria. *International Journal of Eating Disorders, 11,* 191–203. **(Chap 8)**

SPITZER, R. L., FORMAN, J. B. W., & NEE, J. (1979). DSM-III field trials: I. Initial interrater diagnostic reliability. *American Journal of Psychiatry, 136,* 815–817. **(Chap 3)**

SPITZER, R. L., WILLIAMS, J., GIBBON, M., & FIRST, J. (1989). *Structured clinical interview for DSM-III-R.* New York: New York State Psychiatric Institute. **(Chap 3)**

SPOONT, M. R. (1992). Modulatory role of serotonin in neural information processing: Implications for human psychopathology. *Psychological Bulletin, 112*(2), 330–350. **(Chaps 2, 7, 11)**

SPREEN, O. (1988). Prognosis of learning disability. *Journal of Consulting and Clinical Psychology, 56,* 836–842. **(Chap 15)**

SQUIRES, R. F., & BRAESTRUP, C. (1970). Benzodiazepine receptors in rat brain. *Nature* (London), *266,* 732–734. **(Chap 2)**

STALL, R., MCKUSICK, L., WILEY, J., COATES, T. J., & OSTROW, D. G. (1986). Alcohol and drug use during sexual activity and compliance with safe sex guidelines for AIDS. *Health Education Quarterly, 13,* 359–371. **(Chap 9)**

STAM, H., & STEGGLES, S. (1987). Predicting the onset or progression of cancer from psychological characteristics: Psychometric and theoretical issues. *Journal of Psychosocial Oncology, 5*(2), 35–46. **(Chap 9)**

STATE V. CAMPANARO. (1980). Nos. 632–79, 1309–79, 1317–79, 514–80, & 707–80 (Supreme Court of New Jersey Criminal Division, Union County). **(Chap 17)**

STEADMAN, H. J. (1979). *Beating a rap: Defendents found incompetent to stand trial.* Chicago: University of Chicago Press. **(Chap 17)**

STEADMAN, H. J. (1985). Empirical research on the insanity defense. *Annals of the American Academy of Political and Social Sciences, 477,* 58–71. **(Chap 17)**

STEADMAN, H. J., & RIBNER, S. A. (1980). Changing perceptions of the mental health needs of inmates in local jails. *American Journal of Psychiatry, 137,* 1115–1116. **(Chap 17)**

STEEGE, J. F., STOUT, A. L., & CARSON, C. C. (1986). Patient satisfaction in Scott and Small carrion penile implant recipients: A study of 52 patients. *Archives of Sexual Behavior, 15,* 393–399. **(Chap 11)**

STEELE, C. M., & JOSEPHS, R. A. (1990). Alcohol myopia: Its prized and dangerous effects. *American Psychologist, 45*(8), 921–933. **(Chap 12)**

STEFFENBURG, S., GILLBERG, C., HELLGREN, L., ANDERSSON, L., GILLBERG, I. C., JAKOBSSON, G., & BOHMAN, M. (1989). A twin study of autism in Denmark, Finland, Iceland, Norway, and Sweden. *Journal of Child Psychology and Psychiatry, 30,* 405–416. **(Chap 16)**

STEIN, M. I. (1978). Thematic apperception test and related methods. In B. B. Wolman (Ed.), *Clinical diagnosis of mental disorders: A handbook* (pp. 179–235). New York: Plenum Press. **(Chap 3)**

STEIN, R. M., & ELLINWOOD, E. H. (1993). Stimulant use: Cocaine and amphetamine. In D. L. Dunner (Ed.), *Current psychiatric therapy* (pp. 98–105). Philadelphia: W. B. Saunders. **(Chap 12)**

STEINBERG, M. (1991). The spectrum of depersonalization: Assessment and treatment. *Annual Review of Psychiatry, 10,* 223–247. **(Chap 6)**

STEINGLASS, P., WEISSTUB, E., & KAPLAN DE-NOUR, A. K. (1988). Perceived personal networks as mediators of stress reactions. *American Journal of Psychiatry, 145,* 1259–1264. **(Chap 2)**

STEPHENS, R. S., ROFFMAN, R. A., & SIMPSON, E. E. (1994). Treating adult marijuana dependence: A test of the relapse prevention model. *Journal of Consulting and Clinical Psychology, 62,* 92–99. **(Chap 12)**

STERN, R. G., MOHS, R. C., DAVIDSON, M., SCHMEIDLER, J., SILVERMAN, J., KRAMER-GINSBERG, E., SEARCEY, T., BIERER, L., & DAVIS, K. L. (1994). A longitudinal study of Alzheimer's disease: Measurement, rate, and predictors of cognitive deterioration. *American Journal of Psychiatry, 151,* 390–396. **(Chap 15)**

STERN, Y., GURLAND, B., TATEMICHI, T. K., TANG, M. X., WILDER, D., & MAYEUX, R. (1994). Influence of education and occupation on the incidence of Alzheimer's disease. *Journal of the American Medical Association, 271,* 1004–1010. **(Chap 15)**

STERNBERG, R. J. (1988). Intellectual development: Psychometric and information-processing approaches. In M. H. Bornstein & M. E. Lamb (Eds.), *Developmental psychology: An advanced textbook* (2nd ed.). Hillsdale, NJ: Lawrence Erlbaum. **(Chap 3)**

STEVENS, J. (1987). *Storming heaven: LSD and the American dream.* New York: Atlantic Monthly Press. **(Chap 12)**

STEVENSON, J. (1992). Evidence for a genetic etiology in hyperactivity in children. *Behavior Genetics, 22,* 337–344. **(Chap 16)**

STEWART, J. W., RABKIN, J. G., QUITKIN, F. M., MCGRATH, P. J., & KLEIN, D. F. (1993). Atypical depression. In D. L. Dunner (Ed.), *Current psychiatric therapy.* Philadelphia: W. B. Saunders. **(Chap 7)**

STOCK, W. (1993). Inhibited female orgasm. In W. O'Donohue & J. H. Geer (Eds.), *Handbook of Sexual Dysfunctions: Assessment and Treatment* (pp. 253–277). Boston, MA: Allyn and Bacon. **(Chap 11)**

STOLLER, R. J. (1976). Two feminized male American Indians. *Archives of Sexual Behavior, 5,* 529–538. **(Chap 11)**

STOLLER, R. J. (1982). Transvestism in women. *Archives of Sexual Behavior, 11,* 99–115. **(Chap 11)**

STONE, A. A. (1984). The ethical boundaries of forensic psychiatry: A view from the ivory tower. *Bulletin of the American Academy of Psychiatry and the Law, 12,* 209–219. **(Chap 17)**

STONE, A. B., PEARLSTEIN, T. B., & BROWN, W. A. (1991). Fluoxetine in the treatment of late luteal phase dysphoric disorder. *Journal of Clinical Psychiatry, 52*(7), 290–293 **(Chap 3)**

STONE, G. C. (1987). The scope of health psychology. In G. C. Stone, S. M. Weiss, J. D. Matarazzo, N. E. Miller, J. Rodin, C. D. Belar, M. J. Follick, & J. E. Singer (Eds.), *Health psychology: A discipline and a profession.* Chicago, IL: University of Chicago Press. **(Chap 9)**

STONE, M. (1983). Psychotherapy with schizotypal borderline patients. *Journal of the American Academy of Psychoanalysis, 11,* 87–111. **(Chap 13)**

STONE, M. H. (1986). Borderline personality disorder. In A. M. Cooper, A. J. Frances, & M. H. Sacks (Eds.), *The personality disorders and neuroses* (pp. 203–217). New York: Basic Books. **(Chap 13)**

STONE, M. H. (1989). The course of borderline personality disorder. In A. Tasman, R. E. Hales, & A. J. Frances (Eds.), *Annual Review of Psychiatry* (Vol. 8, pp. 103–122). Washington, DC: American Psychiatric Press. **(Chap 13)**

STONE, M. H. (1993). Cluster C personality disorders. In D. L. Dunner (Ed.), *Current psychiatric therapy* (pp. 411–417). Philadelphia: W. B. Saunders. **(Chap 13)**

STONE, R. (1992). HHS "violence initiative" caught in crossfire. *Science, 258,* 212–213. **(Chap 17)**

STONE, R. (1994). Reefer madness at FDA. *Science, 263,* 599. **(Chap 12)**

STOUT, C. W., & BLOOM, L. J. (1986). Genital herpes and personality. *Journal of Human Stress, 12,* 119–124. **(Chap 9)**

STRASSBERG, D. S., KELLY, M. P., CARROLL, C., & KIRCHER, J. C. (1987). The psychophysiological nature of premature ejaculation. *Archives of Sexual Behavior, 16,* 327–336. **(Chap 11)**

STRAUS, S. E. (1988). The chronic mononucleosis syndrome. *Journal of Infectious Disease, 157,* 405–412. **(Chap 9)**

STRAUS, S. E., TOSATO, G., ARMSTRONG, G., LAWLEY, T., PREBLE, O. T., HENLE, W., DAVEY, R., PEARSON, G., EPSTEIN, J., BRUS, I., & BLAESE, R. M. (1985). Persisting illness and fatigue in adults with evidence of Epstein Barr virus infection. *Annals of Internal Medicine, 102,* 7–16. **(Chap 9)**

STRAUSS, J., CARPENTER, W. T., JR., & BARTKO, J. (1974). The diagnosis and understanding of schizophrenia: Part III. Speculations on the processes that underlie schizophrenic symptoms and signs. *Schizophrenia Bulletin, 1,* 61–69. **(Chap 14)**

STRAVYNSKI, A., ELIE, R., & FRANCHE, R. L. (1989). Perception of early parenting by patients diagnosed avoidant personality dis-

order: A test of the overprotection hypothesis. *Acta Psychiatrica Scandinavica, 80,* 415–420. **(Chap 13)**

STRAVYNSKI, A., LESAGE, A., MARCOUILLER, M., & ELIE, R. (1989). A test of the therapeutic mechanism in social skills training with avoidant personality disorder. *Journal of Nervous and Mental Disease, 177,* 739–744. **(Chap 13)**

STRICKLAND, B. R. (1992). Women and depression. *Current Directions in Psychological Science, 1*(4), 132–135. **(Chap 7)**

STRIEGAL-MOORE, R. H., SILBERSTEIN, L. R., & RODIN, J. (1986). Toward an understanding of risk factors for bulimia. *American Psychologist, 3,* 246–263. **(Chap 8)**

STRIEGAL-MOORE, R. H., SILBERSTEIN, L. R., & RODIN, J. (1993). The social self in bulimia nervosa: Public self-consciousness, social anxiety, and perceived fraudulence. *Journal of Abnormal Psychology, 102*(2), 297–303. **(Chap 8)**

STRITTMATTER, A. M. SAUNDERS, A. M., SCHMECHEL, D., PERICAK-VANCE, EN-GHILD, J., SALVESEN, G. S., & ROSES, A. D. (1993). Apolipoprotein E: High-avidity binding to B-amyloid and increased frequency of type 4 allele in late-onset familial Alzheimer disease. *Proceedings of the National Academy of Sciences, 90,* 1977–1981. **(Chap 15)**

STROBER, M., & HUMPHREY, L. L. (1987). Familial contributions to the etiology and course of anorexia nervosa and bulimia. Special Issue: Eating disorders. *Journal of Consulting and Clinical Psychology, 55*(5), 654–659. **(Chap 8)**

STUNKARD, A., SORENSEN, T. & SCHULSINGER, F. (1980). Use of the Danish adoption register for the study of obesity and thinness. In S. Kety (Ed.), *The genetics of neurological and psychiatric disorders.* New York: Raven Press. **(Chap 8)**

STUSS, D. T., & CUMMINGS, J. L. (1990). Subcortical vascular dementias. In J. L. Cummings (Ed.), *Subcortical dementia* (pp. 145–163). New York: Oxford University Press. **(Chap 15)**

STYRON, W. (1990). *Darkness visible: A memoir of madness.* New York: Vintage Books. **(Chap 12)**

SU, Y., BURKE, J., O'NEILL, F. A., MURPHY, B., NIE, L., KIPPS, B., BRAY, J., SHINKWIN, R., NI NUALLAIN, M., MACLEAN, C. J., WALSH, D., DIEHL, S. R., & KENDLER, K. S. (1993). Exclusion of linkage between schizophrenia and D2 dopamine receptor gene region of chromosome 11q in 112 Irish multiplex families. *Archives of General Psychiatry, 50,* 205–211. **(Chap 14)**

SUDDATH, R. L., CHRISTISON, G. W., TORREY, E. F., CASANOVA, M. F., & WEINBERGER, D. R. (1990). Anatomical abnormalities in the brains of monozygotic twins discordant for schizophrenia. *New England Journal of Medicine, 322,* 789–794. **(Chap 14)**

SUGIYAMA, T., & ABE, T. (1989). The prevalence of autism in Nagoya, Japan: A total population study. *Journal of Autism and Developmental Disorders, 19,* 87–96. **(Chap 16)**

SULLOWAY, F. (1979). *Freud, biologist of the mind.* London: Burnett. **(Chap 6)**

SULTZER, D. L., LEVIN, H. S., MAHLER, M. E., HIGH, W. M., & CUMMINGS, J. L. (1993). A comparison of psychiatric symptoms in vascular dementia and Alzheimer's disease. *American Journal of Psychiatry, 150,* 1806–1812. **(Chap 15)**

SUPPES, T., BALDESSARINI, R. J., FAEDDA, G. L., & TOHEN, M. (1991). Risk of recurrence following discontinuation of lithium treatment in bipolar disorder. *Archives of General Psychiatry, 48*(12), 1082–1088. **(Chap 7)**

SUTHERLAND, G. R., & RICHARDS, R. I. (1994). Dynamic mutations. *American Scientist, 82,* 157–163. **(Chap 15)**

SUTKER, P. B., BUGG, F., & WEST, J. A. (1993). Antisocial personality disorder. In P. B. Sutker & H. E. Adams (Eds.), *Comprehensive handbook of psychopathology* (2nd. ed., pp. 337–369). New York: Plenum Press. **(Chap 13)**

SWANSON, J. M., MCBURNETT, K., WIGAL, T., PFIFFNER, L. J., LERNER, M. A., WILLIAMS, L., CHRISTIAN, D. L., TAMM, L., WILLCUT, E., CROWLEY, K., CLEVENGER, W., KHOUZAM, N., WOO, C., CRINELLA, F. M., & FISHER, T. D. (1993). Effect of stimulant medication on children with attention deficit disorder: A "review of reviews." *Exceptional Children, 60,* 154–162. **(Chap 16)**

SWARTZ, M., BLAZER, D., GEORGE, L., & LANDERMAN, R. (1986). Somatization disorder in a community population. *American Journal of Psychiatry, 143,* 1403–1408. **(Chap 6)**

SWARTZ, M., BLAZER, D., GEORGE, L., & LANDERMAN, R. (1988). Somatization disorder in a southern community. *Psychiatric Annals, 18,* 335–339. **(Chap 6)**

SWARTZ, M., BLAZER, D., WOODBURY, M., GEORGE, L., & LANDERMAN, R. (1986). Somatization disorder in a U.S. southern community: Use of a new procedure for analysis of medical classification. *Psychological Medicine, 16,* 595–609. **(Chap 6)**

SWARTZ, M., LANDERMAN, R., GEORGE, L. K., BLAZER, D. G., & ESCOBAR, J. (1991). Somatization disorder. In L. N. Robins & D. A. Regier (Eds.), *Psychiatric disorders in America: The epidemiologic catchment area study* (pp. 220–257). New York: Free Press. **(Chap 6)**

SWINSON, R. P., & COX, B. J. (1993). Diagnostic validity in genetics research on generalized anxiety disorder. *Archives of General Psychiatry, 50,* 916. **(Chap 5)**

SZASZ, T. (1961). *The myth of mental illness: Foundations of a theory of personal conduct.* New York: Hoeber-Harper. **(Chap 14)**

SZMUKLER, G. I., EISLER, I., GILLIS, C., & HAYWOOD, M. E. (1985). The implications of anorexia nervosa in a ballet school. *Journal of Psychiatric Research, 19,* 177–181. **(Chap 8)**

TALBOTT, J. A. (1990). Current perspectives in the United States on the chronically mentally ill. In A. Kales, C. N. Stefanis, & J. A. Talbott (Eds.), *Recent advances in schizophrenia* (pp. 279–295). New York: Springer-Verlag. **(Chap 14)**

TAN, E. S. (1969). The symptomatology of anxiety in West Malaysia. *Australian and New Zealand Journal of Psychiatry, 3,* 271–276. **(Chap 1)**

TAN, E. S. (1980). Transcultural aspects of anxiety. In G. D. Burrows & B. Davies (Eds.), *Handbook of studies on anxiety.* Amsterdam: Elsevier/North-Holland. **(Chaps 2, 5)**

TANZI, R. E., GUSELLA, F., WATKINS, P. C., BRUNS, G. A. P., ST. GEORGE-HYSLOP, P., VAN KEUNEN, M. L., PATTERSON, D., PAGAN, S., KURNIT, D. M., & NEVE, R. L. (1987). Amyloid B protein gene: cDNA, mRNA distribution, and genetic linkage near the Alzheimer locus. *Science, 235,* 880–884. **(Chap 15)**

TARASOFF V. REGENTS OF UNIVERSITY OF CALIFORNIA ("TARASOFF I"), 529 P.2D 553 (CAL. SUP. CT. 1974); ("TARASOFF II"), 551 P.2D 334 (CAL. SUP. CT. 1976). **(Chap 17)**

TAYLOR, C. B., SHEIKH, J., AGRAS, W. S., ROTH, W. T., MARGRAF, J., EHLERS, A., MADDOCK, R. J., & GOSSARD, D. (1986). Self-report of panic attacks: Agreement with heart rate changes. *American Journal of Psychiatry, 143,* 478–482. **(Chap 5)**

TAYLOR, H. G. (1988). Learning disabilities. In E. J. Mash & L. G. Terdal (Eds.), *Behavioral assessment of childhood disorders* (2nd ed.). New York: Guilford Press. **(Chap 15)**

TAYLOR, M. A., & ABRAMS, R. (1981). Early and late-onset bipolar illness. *Archives of General Psychiatry, 38*(1), 58–61. **(Chap 7)**

TAYLOR, R. (1993). Sex surveys help map AIDS risk. *Journal of NIH Research, 5*(2), 31–32. **(Chap 11)**

TAYLOR, S. (1991). *Health psychology* (2nd ed.). New York: McGraw-Hill. **(Chap 9)**

TEASDALE, J. D. (1993). Emotion and two kinds of meaning: Cognitive therapy and applied cognitive science. *Behaviour Research and Therapy, 31*(4), 339–354. **(Chap 2)**

TEASDALE, J. D., FENNELL, J. J., HIBBERT, G. A., & AMIES, P. L. (1984). Cognitive therapy for major depressive disorder in primary care. *British Journal of Psychiatry, 144,* 400–406. **(Chap 7)**

TEICHER, M. H., GLOD, C., & COLE, J. O. (1990). Emergence of intense suicidal preoccupation during fluoxetine treatment. *American Journal of Psychiatry, 147*(1), 207–210. **(Chap 7)**

TELCH, C. F., & AGRAS, W. S. (1993). The effects of a very low calorie diet on binge eating. *Behavior Therapy, 24,* 177–193. **(Chap 8)**

TELCH, C. F., AGRAS, W. S., & ROSSITER, E. M. (1988). Binge eating increases with increasing adiposity. *International Journal of Eating Disorders, 7,* 115–119. **(Chap 8)**

TELCH, M. J. (1988). Combined pharmacologic and psychological treatments for panic sufferers. In S. Rachman & J. D. Maser (Eds.), *Panic: Psychological perspectives.* Hillsdale, NJ: Lawrence Erlbaum. **(Chap 5)**

TELCH, M. J., LUCAS, J. A., & NELSON, P. (1989). Nonclinical panic in college students: An investigation of prevalence and symptomatology. *Journal of Abnormal Psychology, 98,* 300–306. **(Chap 5)**

TELCH, M. J., TEARNAN, B. H., & TAYLOR, C. B. (1983). Antidepressant medication in the treatment of agoraphobia. A critical review. *Behaviour Research and Therapy, 21,* 505–527. **(Chap 5)**

TELLEGEN, A. (1978). *Manual for the Multidimensional Personality Questionnaire.* Unpublished manuscript, University of Minnesota, Minneapolis. **(Chap 13)**

TELLEGEN, A. (1985). Structures of mood and personality and their relevance to assessing anxiety, with an emphasis on self-report. In A. H. Tuma & J. D. Maser (Eds.), *Anxiety and the anxiety disorders* (pp. 681–706). Hillsdale, NJ: Lawrence Erlbaum. **(Chaps 5, 7)**

TEPLIN, L. A. (1984). Criminalizing mental disorder: The comparative arrest rate of the mentally ill. *American Psychologist, 39,* 794–803. **(Chap 17)**

TEPLIN, L. A. (1985). The criminality of the mentally ill: A dangerous misconception. *American Journal of Psychiatry, 142,* 593–599. **(Chap 17)**

TEPLIN, L. A., ABRAM, K. M., & MCCLELLAND, G. M. (1994). Does psychiatric disorder predict violent crime among released jail detainees? A six-year longitudinal study. *American Psychologist, 49,* 335–342. **(Chap 17)**

TERMAN, M. (1988). On the question of mechanism in phototherapy for seasonal affective disorder: Considerations of clinical efficacy and epidemiology. *Journal of Biological Rhythms, 3*(2), 155–172. **(Chap 7)**

THACKWRAY, D. E., SMITH, M. C., BODFISH, J. W., & MEYERS, A. (1993). A comparison of behavioral and cognitive-behavioral interventions for bulimia nervosa. *Journal of Consulting and Clinical Psychology, 61*(4), 639–645. **(Chap 8)**

THASE, M. E. (1990). Relapse and recurrence in unipolar major depression: Short-term and long-term approaches. *Journal of Clinical Psychiatry, 51*(6, Suppl.), 51–57. **(Chap 7)**

THASE, M. E., SIMONS, A. D., MCGEARY, J., CAHALANE, J. F., HUGHES, C., HARDEN, T., & FREIDMAN, E. (1992). Relapse after cognitive behavior therapy of depression: Potential implications for longer courses of treatment. *American Journal of Psychiatry, 149*(8), 1046–1052. **(Chap 7)**

THEANDER, S. (1985). Outcome and prognosis in anorexia nervosa and bulimia: Some results of previous investigations, compared with those of the Swedish long-term study. *Journal of Psychiatric Research, 19,* 493–508. **(Chap 8)**

THOMPSON V. COUNTY OF ALAMEDA, 614 P.2d 728 (Cal. Sup. Ct. 1980). **(Chap 17)**

THOMPSON-POPE, S. K., & TURKAT, I. D. (1993). Schizotypal, schizoid, paranoid, and avoidant personality disorders. In P. B. Sutker & H. E. Adams (Eds.), *Comprehensive handbook of psychopathology* (2nd ed., pp. 411–434). New York: Plenum Press. **(Chap 13)**

THORESEN, C. E., & POWELL, L. H. (1992). Type A behavior pattern: New perspectives on theory, assessment and intervention. Special issue: Behavioral medicine: An update for the 1990s. *Journal of Consulting and Clinical Psychology, 60*(4), 595–604. **(Chap 9)**

THORNDIKE, R. L., HAGEN, E. P., & SATTLER, J. M. (1986). *The Stanford-Binet Intelligence Scale: Fourth edition. Guide for administering and scoring.* Chicago: Riverside Publishing Co. **(Chap 3)**

THORPE, G. L., & BURNS, L. E. (1983). *The agoraphobic syndrome.* New York: John Wiley. **(Chap 5)**

THORPY, M., & GLOVINSKY, P. (1987). Parasomnias. *Psychiatric Clinics of North America, 10,* 623–639. **(Chap 10)**

THURSTONE, L. L. (1934). The vectors of mind. *Psychological Review, 41,* 1–32. **(Chap 13)**

THYER, B. A. (1993). Childhood separation anxiety disorder and adult-onset agoraphobia: Review of evidence. In C. Last (Ed.), *Anxiety across the lifespan: A developmental perspective* (pp. 128–145). New York: Springer. **(Chap 5)**

THYER, B. A., HIMLE, J., & CURTIS, G. C. (1985). Blood-injury-illness phobia: A review. *Journal of Clinical Psychology, 41,* 451–459. **(Chap 2)**

TIENARI, P. (1991). Interaction between genetic vunerability and family environment: The Finnish adoptive family study of schizophrenia. *Acta Psychiatrica Scandinavica, 84,* 460–465. **(Chap 14)**

TIENARI, P. (1992). Implications of adoption studies on schizophrenia. *British Journal of Psychiatry, 161,* 52–58. **(Chap 14)**

TIERNEY, M. C., FISHER, R. H., LEWIS, A. J., ZORZITTO, M. L., SNOW, W. G., REID, D. W., & NIEUWSTRATEN, P. (1988). The NINCDS-ADRDA work group criteria for the clinical diagnosis of probable Alzheimer's disease: A clinicopathologic study of 57 cases. *Neurology, 38,* 359–364. **(Chap 15)**

TIFFANY, S. T. (1990). A cognitive model of drug urges and drug-use behavior: Role of automatic and nonautomatic processes. *Psychological Review, 97,* 147–168. **(Chap 12)**

TINBERGEN, E. A., & TINBERGEN, N. (1972). *Early childhood autism: An ethological approach.* Berlin: Paul Parey. **(Chap 16)**

TINBERGEN, N., & TINBERGEN, E. A. (1983). *Autistic children: New hope for a cure.* Winchester, MA: Allen & Unwin. **(Chap 16)**

TINGELSTAD, J. B. (1991). The cardiotoxicity of the tricyclics. *Journal of the American Academy of Child and Adolescent Psychiatry, 30,* 845–846. **(Chap 7)**

TJIO, J. H., & LEVAN, A. (1956). The chromosome number of man. *Hereditas, 42,* 1–6. **(Chap 15)**

TOLLEFSON, G. D. (1993). Major depression. In D. L. Dunner (Ed.), *Current psychiatric therapy.* Philadelphia: W. B. Saunders. **(Chap 7)**

TORGERSEN, S. (1983). Genetic factors in anxiety disorders. *Archives of General Psychiatry, 40,* 1085–1089. **(Chap 5)**

TORGERSEN, S. (1986). Genetics of somatoform disorder. *Archives of General Psychiatry, 43,* 502–505. **(Chap 6)**

TORGERSEN, S., ONSTAD, S., SKRE, I., EDVARDSEN, J., & KRINGLEN, E. (1993). "True" schizotypal personality disorder: A study of co-twins and relatives of schizophrenic probands. *American Journal of Psychiatry, 150,* 1661–1667. **(Chap 13)**

TORREY, E. F. (1988A). *Nowhere to go: The tragic odyssey of the homeless mentally ill.* New York: Harper & Row. **(Chap 17)**

TORREY, E. F. (1988B). Stalking the schizovirus. *Schizophrenia Bulletin, 14,* 223–229. **(Chap 14)**

TORREY, E. F., BOWLER, A. E., TAYLOR, E. H., & GOTTESMAN, I. I. (1994). *Schizophrenia and manic-depressive disorder: The biological roots of mental illness as revealed by the landmark study of identical twins.* New York: Basic Books.

TORREY, E. F., RAWLINGS, R., & WALDMAN, I. (1988). Schizophrenic births and viral diseases in two states. *Schizophrenia Research, 1,* 73–77. **(Chap 14)**

TREBBE, A. (1979, SEPTEMBER 15). Ideal is body beautiful and clean cut. *USA Today,* pp. 1–2. **(Chap 8)**

TREVES, T. A. (1991). Epidemiology of Alzheimer's disease. *The Psychiatric Clinics of North America, 14,* 251–265. **(Chap 15)**

TRIMBELL, M. R. (1981). *Neuropsychiatry.* Chichester, England: John Wiley. **(Chap 6)**

TRUE, W. R., RICE, J., EISEN, S. A., HEATH, A. C., GOLDBERG, J., LYONS, M. J., & NOWAK, J. (1993). A twin study of genetic and environmental contributions to liability for posttraumatic stress symptoms. *Archives of General Psychiatry, 50,* 257–264. **(Chap 5)**

TSAI, L. Y., & GHAZIUDDIN, M. (1992). Biomedical research in autism. In D. E. Berkell (Ed.), *Autism: Identification, education, and treatment* (pp. 53–74). Hillsdale, NJ: Lawrence Erlbaum. **(Chap 16)**

TSUANG, D., & CORYELL, W. (1993). An 8-year follow-up of patients with DSM-III-R psychotic depression, schizoaffective disorder, and schizophrenia. *American Journal of Psychiatry, 150,* 1182–1188.

TUCHMAN, B. (1978). *A distant mirror.* New York: Ballantine Books. **(Chap 1)**

TUCKER, G. J. (1993). DSM-IV: Organic disorders. In D. L. Dunner (Ed.), *Current psychiatric therapy* (pp. 57–59). Philadelphia: W. B. Saunders. **(Chap 15)**

TUCKER, G. J., FERRELL, R. B., & PRICE, T. R. P. (1984). The hospital treatment of schizophrenia. In A. S. Bellack (Ed.), *Schizophrenia: Treatment, management, and rehabilitation* (pp. 175–191). New York: Grune & Stratton. **(Chap 14)**

TUCKER, G., POPKIN, M., CAINE, E., FOLSTEIN, M., & GRANT, I. (1990). Reorganizing the "organic" disorders. *Hospital and Community Psychiatry, 41,* 722–724. **(Chap 15)**

TUKAT, I. D., & MAISTO, S. A. (1985). Personality disorders: Applications of the experimental method to the formulation and modification of personality disorders. In D. H. Barlow (Ed.), *Clinical handbook of psychological disorders.* New York: Guilford Press. **(Chap 13)**

TUPES, E. C., & CHRISTAL, R. E. (1992). Recurrent personality factors based on trait ratings. *Journal of Personality, 60,* 225–251. **(Chap 13)**

TURK, D. C., MEICHENBAUM, D., & GENEST, M. (1983). *Pain and behavioral medicine: A cognitive-behavioral perspective.* New York: Guilford Press. **(Chap 9)**

TURK, D. C., MEICHENBAUM, D., & GENEST, M. (1987). *Pain and behavioral medicine: A cognitive-behavioral perspective.* New York: Guilford Press. **(Chap 9)**

TURKHEIMER, E., & PARRY, C. D. H. (1992). Why the gap? Practice and policy in civil commitment hearings. *American Psychologist, 47,* 646–655. **(Chap 17)**

TURKINGTON, C. (1994, January). Wexler wins Lasker award for her work on Huntington's. *APA Monitor,* pp. 20–21. **(Chap 15)**

TYLER, D. B. (1955). Psychological changes during experimental sleep deprivation. *Diseases of the Nervous System, 16,* 293–299. **(Chap 10)**

TYNES, L. L., WHITE, K., & STEKETEE, G. S. (1990). Toward a new nosology of obsessive-compulsive disorder. *Comprehensive Psychiatry, 31,* 465–480. **(Chap 6)**

TYRER, P. J., & OWEN, R. (1984). Anxiety in primary care: Is short-term drug treatment appropriate? *Journal of Psychiatric Research, 18,* 73–79. **(Chap 5)**

UDDO, M., MALOW, R., & SUTKER, P. B. (1993). Opioid and cocaine abuse and dependence disorders. In P. B. Sutker & H. E. Adams (Eds.), *Comprehensive handbook of psychopathology* (pp. 477–503). New York: Plenum Press. **(Chap 12)**

U.S. BUREAU OF THE CENSUS. (1989). *Projections of the population of the United States by age, sex and race: 1988 to 2080* (Current Population Report, Sexes P-25, No. 1018). Washington, DC: U.S. Government Printing Office. **(Chap 2)**

U.S. CONGRESS, OFFICE OF TECHNOLOGY ASSESSMENT. (1992, September). *The biology of mental disorders,* OTA-BA-538. Washington, DC: U.S. Government Printing Office. **(Chap 7)**

U.S. DEPARTMENT OF HEALTH AND HUMAN SERVICES. (1982). *The health consequences of smoking. Cancer: A report of the Surgeon General.* Washington, DC: U.S. Government Printing Office. **(Chap 9)**

U.S. DEPARTMENT OF HEALTH AND HUMAN SERVICES. (1988). *The health consequences of smoking—nicotine addiction: A report of the surgeon general* (DHHS Publication No. CDC 88-8406). Washington, DC: U.S. Government Printing Office. **(Chap 12)**

U.S. DEPARTMENT OF HEALTH AND HUMAN SERVICES. (1989). *Reducing the health consequences of smoking: 25 years of progress. A report of the Surgeon General, Executive summary* (DHHS Publication No. CDC 89-8411). Washington, DC: U.S. Goverment Printing Office. **(Chap 12)**

U.S. DEPARTMENT OF HEALTH AND HUMAN SERVICES. (1990). *Seventh annual report to the U.S. Congress on alcohol and health from the Secretary of Health and Human Services.* Rockville, MD: National Institute on Alcohol Abuse and Alcoholism. **(Chaps 4, 12)**

U.S. DEPARTMENT OF HEALTH AND HUMAN SERVICES. (1991). *Health and behavior research.* National Institutes of Health: Report to Congress. **(Chap 9)**

U.S. SURGEON GENERAL. (1979). *Healthy people.* Washington, DC: Government Printing Office. **(Chap 9)**

VAILLANT, G. E. (1976). Natural history of male psychological health V: The relation of choice of ego mechanisms of defense to adult adjustment. *Archives of General Psychiatry, 33,* 535–545. **(Chap 1)**

VAILLANT, G. E. (1979). Natural history of male psychological health. *New England Journal of Medicine, 301,* 1249–1254. **(Chap 9)**

VAILLANT, G. (1983). *The natural history of alcoholism.* Cambridge, MA: Harvard University Press. **(Chap 12)**

VAILLANT, G. E., BOND, M., & VAILLANT, C. D. (1986). An empirically validated hierarchy of defense mechanisms. *Archives of General Psychiatry, 43,* 786–794. **(Chap 1)**

VAN ACKER, R. (1991). Rett syndrome: A review of current knowledge. *Journal of Autism and Developmental Disorders, 21,* 381–406. **(Chap 16)**

VAN DER MOLEN, G. M., VAN DEN HOUT, M. A., VAN DIEREN, A. C., & GRIEZ, E. (1989). Childhood separation anxiety and adult-onset panic disorders. *Journal of Anxiety Disorders, 3,* 97–106. **(Chap 5)**

VANDER PLATE, C., ARAL, S. O., & MAGDER, L. (1988). The relationship among genital herpes simplex virus, stress, and social support. *Health Psychology, 7,* 159–168. **(Chap 9)**

VAN KAMMEN, D. P., DOCHERTY, J. P., & BUNNEY, W. E. (1982). Prediction of early relapse after pimozide discontinuation by response to d-amphetamine during pimozide treatment. *Biological Psychiatry, 17,* 223–242. **(Chap 14)**

VANKAMMEN, W. B., LOEBER, R., & STOUTHAMER-LOEBER, M. (1991). Substance use and its relationship to conduct problems and delinquency in young boys. *Journal of Youth and Adolescence, 20,* 399–413. **(Chap 13)**

VAN PRAAG, H. M., & KORF, J. (1975). Central monamine deficiency in depressions: Causative of secondary phenomenon? *Pharmakopsychiatr Neuropsychopharmakol, 8,* 322–326. **(Chap 7)**

VENTURA, J., NUECHTERLEIN, K. H., LUKOFF, D., & HARDESTY, J. P. (1989). A prospective study of stressful life events and schizophrenia relapse. *Journal of Abnormal Psychology, 98,* 407–411. **(Chap 14)**

VINKEN, P. J., & BRUYN, G. W. (1972). The phakomatoses. In P. J. Vinken & G. W. Bruyn (Eds.), *Handbook of clinical neurology* (Vol. 14). New York: Elsevier. **(Chap 15)**

VIOLENCE RESEARCH COMES UNDER ATTACK. (1992, DECEMBER). *APA Monitor,* p. 1. **(Chap 17)**

VOLKMAR, F. R., & COHEN, D. J. (1991). Nonautistic pervasive developmental disorders. In R. Michels (Ed.), *Psychiatry* (pp. 201–210). Philadelphia: J. B. Lippincott. **(Chap 16)**

VOLKMAR, F. R., SZATMARI, P., & SPARROW, S. S. (1993). Sex differences in pervasive developmental disorders. *Journal of Autism and Developmental Disorders, 23,* 579–591. **(Chap 16)**

VOLPICELLI, J. R., ALTERMAN, A. I., HAYASHIDA, M., & O'BRIEN, C. P. (1992). Naltrexone in the treatment of alcohol dependence. *Archives of General Psychiatry, 49,* 876–880. **(Chap 12)**

VON KNORRING, A. L., CLONINGER, C. R., BOHMAN, M., & SIGVARDSSON, S. (1983). An adoption study of depressive disorders and substance abuse. *Archives of General Psychiatry, 40,* 943–950. **(Chap 7)**

VON KRAFFT-EBING, R. (1965). *Psychopathia sexualis.* New York: Bell Publishing. (First published 1886) **(Chap 11)**

VUCHINICH, S., BANK, L., & PATTERSON, G. R. (1992). Parenting, peers, and the stability of antisocial behavior in preadolescent boys. *Developmental Psychology, 28,* 510–521. **(Chap 13)**

WAGNER, A. W., & LINEHAN, M. M. (1994). Relationship between childhood sexual abuse and topography of parasuicide among women with borderline personality disorder. *Journal of Personality Disorders, 8,* 1–9. **(Chap 13)**

WAGNER, M. (1990, APRIL). *The school programs and school performance of secondary students classified as learning disabled: Findings from the National Longitudinal Transition Study of special education students.* Paper presented at Division G, American Educational Research Association Annual Meeting, Boston. **(Chap 15)**

WAKEFIELD, J. C. (1992). The concept of mental disorder: On the boundary between biological facts and social values. *American Psychologist, 47,* 373–388. **(Chap 1)**

WALKER, E. (1991). Research on life-span development in schizophrenia. In E. F. Walker (Ed.), *Schizophrenia: A life-course developmental perspective* (pp. 1–6). New York: Academic Press. **(Chap 14)**

WALKER, E. F., GRIMES, K. E., DAVIS, D. M., & SMITH, A. J. (1983). Childhood precursors of schizophrenia: Facial expressions of emotion. *American Journal of Psychiatry, 150* 1654–1660.

WALLACE, J., & O'HARA, M. W. (1992). Increases in depressive symptomatology in the rural elderly: Results from a cross-sectional and longitudinal study. *Journal of Abnormal Psychology, 101*(3), 398–404. **(Chaps 4, 7)**

WALSH, B. T. (1991). Fluoxetine treatment of bulimia nervosa. *Journal of Psychosomatic Research, 35,* 471–475. **(Chap 8)**

WALSH, B. T., HADIGAN, C. M., DEVLIN, M. J., GLADIS, M., & ROOSE, S. P. (1991). Long-term outcome of antidepressant treatment of bulimia nervosa. *Archives of General Psychiatry, 148,* 1206–1212. **(Chap 8)**

WARD, M. M., SWAN, G. E., & CHESNEY, M. A. (1987). Arousal-reduction treatments for mild hypertension: A meta-analysis of recent studies. *Handbook of hypertension, 9,* 285–302. **(Chap 9)**

WARE, J. C. (1988). Sleep and anxiety. In R. L. Williams, I. Karacan, & C. A. Moore (Eds.), *Sleep disorders: Diagnosis and treatment* (pp. 189–214). New York: John Wiley. **(Chap 10)**

WARHEIT, G. J., HOLZER, C. E., & AREY, S. (1975). Race and mental health: An epidemiologic update. *Journal of Health and Social Behavior, 16,* 243–256. **(Chap 5)**

WARNEKE, L. B. (1991). Benzodiazepines: Abuse and new use. *Canadian Journal of Psychiatry, 36,* 194–205. **(Chap 12)**

WARNER, P., VANCROFT, J., & MEMBERS OF EDINBURGH HUMAN SEXUALITY GROUP. (1987). A regional service for sexual problems: A three-year study. *Sexual and Marital Therapy, 2,* 115–126. **(Chap 11)**

WARREN, S. F., & REICHLE, J. (1992). *Causes and effects in communication and language intervention.* Baltimore: Paul H. Brookes. **(Chap 15)**

WARWICK, H. M. C., & SALKOVSKIS, P. M. (1990). Hypochondriasis. *Behaviour Research and Therapy, 28,* 105–117. **(Chap 6)**

WATERHOUSE, L., WING, L., & FEIN, D. (1989). Re-evaluating the syndrome of autism in light of empirical research. In G. Dawson (Ed.), *Autism: Nature, diagnosis and treatment* (pp. 263–281). New York: Guilford Press. **(Chap 16)**

WATERHOUSE, L., WING, L., SPITZER, R., & SIEGEL, B. (1992). Pervasive developmental disorders: From DSM-III to DSM-III-R. *Journal of Autism and Developmental Disorders, 22,* 525–549. **(Chap 16)**

WATERS, B. G. H. (1979). Early symptoms of bipolar affective psychosis: Research and clinical implications. *Canadian Psychiatric Association Journal, 2,* 55–60. **(Chap 7)**

WATSON, D., CLARK, L. A., & CAREY, G. (1988). Positive and negative affectivity and their relation to anxiety and depressive disorders. *Journal of Abnormal Psychology, 97*(3), 346–353. **(Chap 7)**

WATSON, D., CLARK, L. A., & HARKNESS, A. R. (1994). Structures of personality and their relevance to psychopathology. *Journal of Abnormal Psychology, 103,* 18–31. **(Chap 13)**

WATSON, D., & KENDALL, P. C. (1989). Common and differentiating features of anxiety and depression: Current findings and future directions. In P. C. Kendall & D. Watson (Eds.), *Anxiety and depression: Distinctive and overlapping features* (pp. 493–508). San Diego, CA: Academic Press. **(Chap 7)**

WATSON, G. C., & BURANEN, C. (1979). The frequency and identification of false positive conversion reactions. *Journal of Nervous and Mental Disease, 167,* 243–247. **(Chap 6)**

WATSON, J. B. (1913). Psychology as a behaviorist views it, *Psychology Review, 20,* 158–177. **(Chap 1)**

WEAVER, D. R., RIVKEES, S. A., & REPPERT, S. M. (1992). D1-dopamine receptors activate c-fos expression in the fetal suprachiasmatic nuclei. *Proceedings of the National Academy of Science, 89,* 9201–9204. **(Chap 12)**

WECHSLER, D. (1989). *Manual for the Wechsler Preschool and Primary Scale of Intelligence* (rev. ed.). New York: Psychological Corporation. **(Chap 3)**

WECHSLER INTELLIGENCE SCALE FOR CHILDREN (3RD ED.). (1991). San Antonio: Psychological Corporation. **(Chap 3)**

WEHR, T., & GOODWIN, F. K. (1979). Rapid cycling in manic-depressives induced by tricyclic antidepressants. *Archives of General Psychiatry, 36,* 555–559. **(Chap 7)**

WEHR, T. A., GOODWIN, F. K., WIRZ-JUSTICE, A., BREITMEIER, J., & CRAIG, C. (1982). Forty-eight-hour sleep-wake cycles in manic-depressive illness: Naturalistic observations and sleep-deprivation experiments. *Archives of General Psychiatry, 39,* 559–565. **(Chap 7)**

WEHR, T. A., & SACK, D. A. (1988). The relevance of sleep research to affective illness. In W. P. Koella, F. Obal, H. Schulz, & P. Visser, *Sleep '86* (pp. 207–211). New York: Gustav Fischer Verlag. **(Chap 7)**

WEHR, T., SACK, D., ROSENTHAL, N. E., & COWDRY, R. W. (1988). Rapid cycling affective disorder: Contributing factors and treatment response on 51 patients. *American Journal of Psychiatry, 145,* 179–184. **(Chap 7)**

WEIDEN, P. J., DIXON, L., FRANCES, A., APPELBAUM, P., HAAS, G., & RAPKIN, B. (1991). In C. A. Tamminga & S. C. Schulz (Eds.), *Advances in neuropsychiatry and psychopharmacology, Volume 1: Schizophrenia research* (pp. 285–296). New York: Raven Press. **(Chap 14)**

WEINBERGER, D. R. (1987). Implications of normal brain development for the pathogenesis of schizophrenia. *Archives of General Psychiatry, 44,* 660–669. **(Chap 14)**

WEINBERGER, D. R., BERMAN, K. F., & CHASE, T. N. (1988). Mesocortical dopaminergic function and human cognition. *Annals of the New York Academy of Sciences, 537,* 330–338. **(Chap 14)**

WEINBERGER, D. R., BERMAN, K. F., SUDDATH, R., & TORREY, E. F. (1992). Evidence of dysfunction of a prefrontal-limbic network in schizophrenia: A magnetic resonance imaging and regional cerebral blood flow study of discordant monozygotic twins. *American Journal of Psychiatry, 149,* 890–897. **(Chap 14)**

WEINER, B. A., & WETTSTEIN, R. M. (1993). *Legal issues in mental health care.* New York: Plenum Press. **(Chap 17)**

WEINER, D. B. (1979). The apprenticeship of Philippe Pinel: A new document, "Observations of Citizen Pussin on the insane." *American Journal of Psychiatry, 136,* 1128-1134. **(Chap 1)**

WEISKRANTZ, L. (1980). Varieties of residual experience. *Quarterly Journal of Experimental Psychology, 32,* 365–386. **(Chap 6)**

WEISKRANTZ, L. (1992, September/October). Unconscious vision: The strange phenomenon of blindsight. *The Sciences,* 23–28. **(Chap 2)**

WEISS, B., WEISZ, J. R., & BROMFIELD, R. (1986). Performance of retarded and nonretarded persons on information-processing tasks: Further tests of the similar structure hypothesis. *Psychological Bulletin, 100,* 157–175. **(Chap 15)**

WEISS, G., & HECHTMAN, L. (1986). *Hyperactive children grown up.* New York: Guilford Press. **(Chap 16)**

WEISSE, C. S. (1992). Depression and immunocompetence: A review of the literature. *Psychological Bulletin, 111*(3), 475–489. **(Chap 9)**

WEISSE, C. S., PATO, C. W., MCALLISTER, C. G., LITTMAN, R., & BREIER, A. (1990). Differential effects of controllable and uncontrollable acute stress on lymphocyte proliferation and leukocyte percentages in humans. *Brain, Behavior, and Immunity, 4,* 339–351. **(Chap 9)**

WEISSMAN, M. (1985). The epidemiology of anxiety disorders: Rates, risks, and familial patterns. In A. H. Tuma & J. D. Maser (Eds.), *Anxiety and the anxiety disorders.* Hillsdale, NJ: Lawrence Erlbaum. **(Chap 7)**

WEISSMAN, M. M. (1993). The epidemiology of personality disorders: A 1990 update. *Journal of Personality Disorders,* Supplement, Spring, 44–62. **(Chap 13)**

WEISSMAN, M. M. (IN PRESS). *Mastery of your depression through interpersonal psychotherapy.* Albany, NY: Graywind Publications. **(Chap 7)**

WEISSMAN, M. M., BRUCE, M. L., LEAF, P. J., FLORIO, L. P., & HOLZER, C. (1991). Affective disorders. In L. N. Robins & D. A. Regier (Eds.), *Psychiatric disorders of America: The epidemiologic catchment area study* (pp. 53–80). New York: Free Press. **(Chap 7)**

WEISSMAN, M. M., & KLERMAN, G. L. (1977). Sex differences and the epidemiology of depression. *Archives of General Psychiatry, 34,* 98–111. **(Chap 7)**

WEISSMAN, M. M., KLERMAN, G. L., MARKOW-ITZ, J. S., & OUELLETTE, R. (1989). Suicidal ideation and suicide attempts in panic disorder and attacks. *New England Journal of Medicine, 321,* 1209–1214. **(Chap 5)**

WEISSMAN, M. M., PRUSOFF, B. A., DIMASCIO, A., NEU, C., GOKLANEY, M., & KLERMAN, G. L. (1979). The efficacy of drugs and psychotherapy in the treatment of acute depressive episodes. *American Journal of Psychiatry, 136,* 555–558. **(Chap 7)**

WELLER, E. B., & WELLER, R. A. (1988). Neuroendocrine changes in affectively ill children and adolescents. *Endocrinology and Metabolism Clinics of North America, 17,* 41–53. **(Chap 7)**

WELLS, K. B., STEWART, A., HAYS, R. D., BURNAM, M. A., ROGERS, W., DANIELS, M., BERRY, S., GREENFIELD, S., & WARE, J. (1989). The functioning and well-being of depressed patients: Results from the medical outcomes study. *Journal of the American Medical Association, 262*(7), 914–919. **(Chap 3)**

WENDER, P. H., KETY, S. S., ROSENTHAL, D., SCHLUSINGER, F., ORTMANN, J., & LUNDE, I. (1986). Psychiatric disorders in the biological and adoptive families of adopted individuals with affective disorders. *Archives of General Psychiatry, 43,* 923–929. **(Chap 7)**

WESTERMEYER, J. (1989). *Mental health for refugees and other migrants: Social and preventive approach.* Illinois: C. C. Thomas. **(Chap 15)**

WESTPHAL, C. (1871). Die Agoraphobia: Eine neuropathische Eischeinung. *Archives für Psychiatrie und Nervenkrankheiten, 3,* 384–412. **(Chap 5)**

WHALEN, C. K., & HENKER, B. (1980). *Hyperactive children: The social ecology of identification and treatment.* New York: Academic Press. **(Chap 16)**

WHIFFEN, V. E. (1992). Is postpartum depression a distinct diagnosis? *Clinical Psychology Review, 12*(5), 485–508. **(Chap 7)**

WHIFFEN, V. E., & GOTLIB, I. H. (1989). Stress and coping in maritally distressed and non-distressed couples. *Journal of Social and Personal Relationships, 6*(3), 327–344. **(Chap 7)**

WHIFFEN, V. E., & GOTLIB, I. H. (1993). Comparison of postpartum and nonpostpartum depression: Clinical presentation, psychiatric history, and psychosocial functioning. *Journal of Consulting and Clinical Psychology, 61*(3), 485–494. **(Chap 7)**

WHITE, J. L., MOFFITT, T. E., & SILVA, P. A. (1989). A prospective replication of the protective effects of IQ in subjects at high risk for juvenile delinquency. *Journal of Consulting and Clinical Psychology, 57,* 719–724. **(Chap 13)**

WHITEHURST, G. J., FISCHEL, J. E., ARNOLD, D. S., & LONIGAN, C. J. (1992). Evaluating outcomes with children with expressive language delay. In S. F. Warren & J. Reichle (Eds.), *Causes and effects in communication and language intervention* (pp. 277–313). Baltimore: Brookes Publishing. **(Chap 16)**

WHITEHURST, G. J., FISCHEL, J. E., LONIGAN, C. J., VALDEZ-MENCHACA, M. C., DEBARY-SHE, B. D., & CAULFIELD, M. B. (1988). Verbal interaction in families of normal and expressive-language-delayed children. *Developmental Psychology, 24,* 690–699. **(Chap 16)**

WHITNAM, F. L., DIAMOND, M., & MARTIN, J. (1993). Homosexual orientation in twins: A report on 61 pairs and three triplet sets. *Archives of Sexual Behavior, 22*(3), 187–206. **(Chap 11)**

WICKRAMARATNE, P. J., WEISSMAN, M. M., LEAF, D. J., & HOLFORD, T. R. (1989). Age, period and cohort effects on the risk of major depression: Results from five United States communities. *Journal of Clinical Epidemiology, 42,* 333–343. **(Chap 7)**

WIDIGER, T. A. (1991). Personality disorder dimensional models proposed for the DSM-IV. *Journal of Personality Disorders, 5,* 386–398. **(Chap 13)**

WIDIGER, T. A., & FRANCES, A. (1985). The DSM-III personality disorders: Perspectives from psychology. *Archives of General Psychiatry, 42,* 615–623. **(Chap 13)**

WIDIGER, T., & FRANCES, A. (1989). Epidemiology, diagnosis, and comorbidity of borderline personality disorder. In A. Tasman, R. Hales, & A. Frances (Eds.), *Review of psychiatry* (Vol. 8, pp. 8–24). Washington, DC: American Psychiatric Press. **(Chap 13)**

WIDIGER, T. A., & ROGERS, J. H. (1989). Prevalence and comorbidity of personality disorders. *Psychiatry Annual, 19,* 132. **(Chap 13)**

WIDIGER, T. A., & SPITZER, R. L. (1991). Sex bias in the diagnosis of personality disorders: Conceptual and methodological issues. *Clinical Psychology Review, 11,* 1–22. **(Chap 13)**

WIDIGER, T. A., & TRULL, T. J. (1993). Borderline and narcissistic personality disorders. In P. B. Sutker & H. E. Adams (Eds.), *Comprehensive handbook of psychopathology* (2nd ed., pp. 371–394). New York: Plenum Press. **(Chap 13)**

WIDIGER, T. A., & WEISSMAN, M. M. (1991). Epidemiology of borderline personality disorder. *Hospital and Community Psychiatry, 42,* 1015–1021. **(Chap 13)**

WIDOM, C. S. (1977). A methodology for studying noninstitutionalized psychopaths. *Journal of Consulting and Clinical Psychology, 45,* 674–683. **(Chap 13)**

WIDOM, C. S. (1984). Sex roles, criminality, and psychopathology. In C. S. Widom (Ed.), *Sex roles and psychopathology* (pp. 183–217). New York: Plenum Press. **(Chap 6)**

WILFLEY, D. E., AGRAS, W. S., TELCH, C. F., ROSSITER, E. M., SCHNEIDER, J. A., COLE, A. G., SIFFORD L., & RAEBURN, S. D. (1993). Group cognitive-behavioral therapy and group interpersonal psychotherapy for the nonpurging bulimic individual: A controlled comparison. *Journal of Consulting and Clinical Psychology, 61*(2), 296–305. **(Chap 8)**

WILKINS, R. (1985). A comparison of elective mutism and emotional disorders in children. *British Journal of Psychiatry, 146,* 198–203. **(Chap 16)**

WILLI, J., & GROSSMAN, S. (1983). Epidemiology of anorexia nervosa in a defined region of Switzerland. *American Journal of Psychiatry, 140,* 564–567. **(Chap 8)**

WILLIAMS, R. B., JR., HANEY, T. L., LEE, K. L., KONG, V., & BLUMENTHAL, J. A. (1980). Type A behavior, hostility, and coronary atherosclerosis. *Psychosomatic Medicine, 42,* 529–538. **(Chap 2)**

WILLMUTH, M. E., LEITENBERG, H., ROSEN, J. C., & CADO, S. (1988). A comparison of purging and nonpurging normal weight bulimics. *International Journal of Eating Disorders, 7,* 825–835. **(Chap 8)**

WILLWERTH, J. (1993, August 30). Tinkering with madness. *Time,* pp. 40–42 **(Chap 17)**

WILSON, G. T. (1977). Alcohol and human sexual behavior. *Behaviour Research and Therapy, 15,* 239–252. **(Chap 11)**

WILSON, G. T. (1987). Cognitive studies in alcoholism. *Journal of Consulting and Clinical Psychology, 55,* 325–331. **(Chap 12)**

WILSON, G. T. (1991). The addiction model of eating disorders: A critical analysis. *Advances in Behavior Research and Therapy, 13,* 27–72. **(Chap 8)**

WILSON, G. T. (1993). Psychological and pharmacological treatments of bulimia nervosa: A research update. *Applied and Preventive Psychology, 2,* 35–42. **(Chap 8)**

WILSON, G. T., & PIKE, K. M. (in press). *Eating disorders.* **(Chap 8)**

WINCHEL, R. M., STANLEY, B., & STANLEY, M. (1990). Biochemical aspects of suicide. In S. J. Blumenthal & D. J. Kupfer (Eds.), *Suicide over the life cycle: Risk factors, assessment and treatment of suicidal patterns* (pp. 97–126). Washington, DC: American Psychiatric Press. **(Chap 7)**

WINCZE, J. P., & BANSAL, S. (1993). *Effects of antihypertensive medication on sexual functioning in males.* Poster presentation at the 19th Annual Meeting of the International Academy of Sex Research, Pacific Grove, California. **(Chap 11)**

WINCZE, J. P., & CAREY, M. P. (1991). *Sexual dysfunction: A guide for assessment and treatment.* New York: Guilford Press. **(Chap 11)**

WINDGASSEN, K. (1992). Treatment with neuroleptics: The patient's perspective. *Acta Psychiatrica Scandinavica, 86,* 405–410. **(Chap 14)**

WING, J. K., COOPER, J. E., & SARTORIUS, N. (1974). *The measurement and classification of psychiatric symptoms.* Cambridge, England: Cambridge University Press. **(Chap 3)**

WING, L. (1980). Childhood autism and social class: A question of selection? *British Journal of Psychiatry, 137,* 410–417. **(Chap 16)**

WING, L. (1981). Asperger's syndrome: A clinical account. *Psychological Medicine, 11,* 115. **(Chap 16)**

WINKER, M. A. (1994). Tacrine for Alzheimer's disease: Which patient, what dose? *Journal of the American Medical Association, 271,* 1023–1024. **(Chap 15)**

WINOKUR, G. (1985). Familial psychopathology in delusional disorder. *Comprehensive Psychiatry, 26,* 241–248. **(Chap 14)**

WINOKUR, G., CORYELL, W., ENDICOTT, J., & AKISKAL, H. (1993). Further distinctions between manic-depressive illness (bipolar disorder) and primary depressive disorder (unipolar depression). *American Journal of Psychiatry, 150,* 1176–1181. **(Chap 7)**

WINOKUR, G., PFOHL, B., & TSUANG, M. (1987). A 40-year follow-up of hebephrenic-catatonic schizophrenia. In N. Miller & G. Cohen (Eds), *Schizophrenia and aging* (pp. 52–60). New York: Guilford Press.

WIRAK, D. O., BAYNEY, R., RAMABHADRAN, T. V., FRACASSO, R. P., HART, J. T., HAUER, P. E., HSIAU, P., PEKAR, S. K., SCANGOS, G. A., TRAPP, B. D., & UNTERBECK, A. J. (1991). Deposits of amyloid B protein in the central nervous system of transgenic mice. *Science, 253,* 323–325. **(Chap 15)**

WISE, R. A. (1988). The neurobiology of craving: Implications for the understanding and treatment of addiction. *Journal of Abnormal Psychology, 97,* 118–132. **(Chap 12)**

WISEMAN, C. V., GRAY, J. J., MOSIMANN, J. E., & AHRENS, A. H. (1992). Cultural expectations of thinness in women: An update. *International Journal of Eating Disorders, 11,* 85–89. **(Chap 8)**

WISOCKI, P. A. (1988). Worry as a phenomenon relevant to the elderly. *Behavior Therapy, 19,* 369–379. **(Chap 5)**

WISOCKI, P. A., HANDEN, B., & MORSE, C. K. (1986). The Worry Scale as a measure of anxiety among homebound and community active elderly. *The Behavior Therapist, 5,* 91–95. **(Chap 5)**

WITHERINGTON, R. (1988). Suction device therapy in the management of erectile impotence. *Urologic Clinics of North America, 15,* 123–128. **(Chap 11)**

WOLANIN, M. O., & PHILLIPS, L. R. F. (1981). *Confusion.* St. Louis: C. V. Mosby. **(Chap 15)**

WOLF, M. M. (1978). Social validity: The case for subjective measurement or how applied behavior analysis is finding its heart. *Journal of Applied Behavior Analysis, 11,* 203–214. **(Chap 4)**

WOLFE, D. A. (1991). *Preventing physical and emotional abuse of children.* New York: Guilford Press. **(Chap 3)**

WOLFF, S., TOWNSHED, R., MCGUIRE, R. J., & WEEKS, D. J. (1991). "Schizoid" personality in childhood and adult life II: Adult adjustment and continuity with schizotypal personality disorder. *British Journal of Psychiatry, 159,* 615–620. **(Chap 13)**

WOLKIN, A., SANFILIPO, M., WOLF, A. P., ANGRIST, B., BRODIE, J. D., & ROTROSEN, J. (1992). Negative symptoms and hypofrontality in chronic schizophrenia. *Archives of General Psychiatry, 49,* 959–965. **(Chap 14)**

WOLPE, J. (1958). *Psychotherapy by reciprocal inhibition.* Stanford, CA: Stanford University Press. **(Chaps 1, 4)**

WOOD, J. M., BOOTZIN, R. R., ROSENHAN, D., NOLEN-HOEKSEMA, S., & JOURDEN, F. (1992). Effects of the 1989 San Francisco earthquake on frequency and content of nightmares. *Journal of Abnormal Psychology, 101,* 219–224. **(Chap 10)**

WOODS, N. S., EYLER, F. D., BEHNKE, M., & CONLON, M. (1992). Cocaine use during pregnancy: Maternal depressive symptoms and infant neurobehavior over first month. *Infant Behavior and Development, 16,* 83–98. **(Chap 12)**

WOODSIDE, M. R., & LEGG, B. H. (1990). Patient advocacy: A mental health perspective. *Journal of Mental Health Counseling, 12,* 38–50. **(Chap 17)**

WOOTEN, V. (1990). Evaluation and management of sleep disorders in the elderly. *Psychiatric Annals, 20,* 466–473. **(Chap 10)**

WORELL, J., & REMER, P. (1992). *Feminist perspectives in therapy: An empowerment model for women.* New York: John Wiley. **(Chap 3)**

WORLD HEALTH ORGANIZATION. (1969). *International classification of diseases and related health problems* (8th rev.). Geneva. **(Chap 3)**

WORLD HEALTH ORGANIZATION. (1973). *The international pilot study of schizophrenia.* Geneva. **(Chap 14)**

WORLD HEALTH ORGANIZATION. (1993). *International classification of diseases and related health problems* (10th rev.). Geneva. **(Chap 3)**

WURTMAN, J. (1984). The involvement of brain serotonin in excessive carbohydrate snacking by obese subjects. *Journal of the American Dietetic Association, 84,* 1004–1007. **(Chap 8)**

WYATT V. STICKNEY, 344 F. Supp. 373 (Ala. 1972). **(Chap 17)**

YAIRI, E., & AMBROSE, N. (1992). Onset of stuttering in preschool children: Selected factors. *Journal of Speech and Hearing Research, 35,* 782–788. **(Chap 16)**

YAMAMOTO, J., SILVA, A., SASAO, T., WANG, C., & NGUYEN, L. (1993). Alcoholism in Peru. *American Journal of Psychiatry, 150,* 1059–1062. **(Chap 12)**

YEATON, W. H., & BAILEY, J. S. (1978). Teaching pedestrian safety skills to young children: An analysis and one-year follow-up. *Journal of Applied Behavior Analysis, 11,* 315–329. **(Chap 9)**

YERKES, R. M., & DODSON, J. D. (1908). The relation of strength of stimulus to rapidity of habit-formation. *Journal of Comprehensive Neurologic and Psychology, 18,* 459–482. **(Chap 5)**

YOSHIDA, A., HUANG, I-Y., & IKAWA, M. (1984). Molecular abnormality of an inactive aldehyde dehydrogenase variant commonly found in Orientals. *Proceedings of the National Academy of Sciences, 81,* 258–261. **(Chap 12)**

YOUNG, A. M., & HERLING, S. (1986). Drugs as reinforcers: Studies in laboratory animals. In S. R. Goldberg & I. P. Stolerman (Eds.), *Behavioral analysis of drug dependence* (pp. 9–67). Orlando, FL: Academic Press. **(Chap 12)**

YOUNG, J. E., BECK, A. T., & WEINBERGER, A. (1993). Depression. In D. H. Barlow (Ed.), *Clinical handbook of psychological disorders* (2nd ed., pp. 240–277), New York: Guilford Press. **(Chap 7)**

YOUNG, L. D. (1992). Psychological factors in rheumatoid arthritis. Special issue: Behavioral medicine: An update for the 1990s. *Journal of Consulting and Clinical Psychology, 60*(4), 619–627. **(Chap 9)**

YOUNGBERG V. ROMEO, 457 U.S. 307 (1982). **(Chap 17)**

ZAJECKA, J., FAWCETT, J., SCHAFF, M., JEFFRIESS, H., & GUY, C. (1991). The role of serotonin in sexual dysfunction: Fluoxetine-associated orgasm dysfunction. *Journal of Clinical Psychiatry, 52,* 66–68. **(Chap 11)**

ZAJONC, R. B. (1984). On the primacy of affect. *American Psychologist,* 117–123. **(Chap 2)**

ZAKOWSKI, S. M., HALL, H., & BAUM, A. (1992). Stress, stress management, and the immune system. *Applied and Preventative Psychology, 1,* 1–13. **(Chap 9)**

ZAKOWSKI, S. M., MCALLISTER, C. G., DEAL, M., & BAUM, A. (in press). Stress, reactivity and immune function. *Health Psychology.* **(Chap 9)**

ZAMETKIN, A. J., NORDAHL, T., GROSS, M., KING, A. C., SEMPLE, W. E., RUMSEY, J., HAMBURGER, S., & COHEN, R. M. (1990). Cerebral glucose metabolism in adults with hyperactivity of childhood onset. *New England Journal of Medicine, 323,* 1361–1366. **(Chap 16)**

ZANARINI, M., GUNDERSON, J., MARINO, M., SCHWARTZ, E., & FRANKENBURG, F. (1988). DSM-III disorders in the families of borderline outpatients. *Journal of Personality Disorders, 2,* 292–302. **(Chap 13)**

ZIGLER, E., & BALLA, D. (1982). *Mental retardation: The developmental-difference controversy.* Hillsdale, NJ: Lawrence Erlbaum. **(Chap 15)**

ZIGLER, E., & CASCIONE, R. (1984). Mental retardation: An overview. In E. S. Gollin (Ed.), *Malformations of development: Biological and psychological sources and consequences* (pp. 69–90). New York: Academic Press. **(Chap 15)**

ZIGLER, E., & HODAPP, R. M. (1986). *Understanding mental retardation.* Cambridge: Cambridge University Press. **(Chap 15)**

ZIGLER, E., TAUSSIG, C., & BLACK, K. (1992). Early childhood intervention: A promising preventative for juvenile delinquency. *American Psychologist, 47,* 997–1006. **(Chap 13)**

ZIGLER, E. F., & STEVENSON, M. F. (1993). *Children in a changing world: Development and social issues* (2nd ed.). Pacific Grove, CA: Brooks/Cole Publishing. **(Chap 15)**

ZILBERGELD, B. (1992). *The new male sexuality.* New York: Bantam Books. **(Chap 11)**

ZILBOORG, G., & HENRY, G. (1941). *A history of medical psychology.* New York: W. W. Norton. **(Chap 1)**

ZILLMANN, D. (1983). Arousal and aggression. In R. G. Geen & E. Donnerstein (Eds.), *Aggression: Theoretical and empirical reviews* (Vol. 1). New York: Academic Press. **(Chap 9)**

ZIMMERMAN, M., & CORYELL, W. (1989). DSM-III personality disorder diagnoses in a nonpatient sample. *Archives of General Psychiatry, 46,* 682–689. **(Chap 13)**

ZIMMERMAN, M., & CORYELL, W. (1990). Diagnosing personality disorders in the community: A comparison of self-report and interview measures. *Archives of General Psychiatry, 47,* 527–531. **(Chap 13)**

ZIMMERMAN, M., & SPITZER, R. L. (1989). Melancholia: From DSM-III to DSM-III-R. *American Journal of Psychiatry, 146,* 20–28. **(Chap 7)**

ZINBARG, R. E., & BARLOW, D. H. (in press). The structure of anxiety and the DSM-III-R anxiety disorders: A hierarchical model. *Journal of Abnormal Psychology.* **(Chap 7)**

ZINBARG, R. E., BARLOW, D. H., LIEBOWITZ, M., STREET, L., BROADHEAD, E., KATON, W., ROY-BYRNE, P., LEPINE, J. P., TEHERANI, M., RICHARDS, J., BRANTLEY, P. J., & KRAEMER, H. (1994). The DSM-IV field trial for mixed anxiety depression. *American Journal of Psychiatry, 151,* 1153–1162. **(Chaps 3, 7)**

ZUBIN, J., STEINHAUER, S. R., & CONDRAY, R. (1992). Vulnerability to relapse in schizophrenia. *British Journal of Psychiatry, 161,* 13–18. **(Chap 14)**

Name Index

Subject Index

Credits

End Papers: Axis reprinted with permission from the American Psychiatric Association *Diagnostic and Statistical Manual of Mental Disorders, Fourth Edition.* Washington D.C., American Psychiatric Association, 1994.

Chapter 1: 27: Table 1.1 reprinted with permission from the American Psychiatric Association *Diagnostic and Statistical Manual of Mental Disorders, Fourth Edition.* Washington D.C., American Psychiatric Association, 1994.

Chapter 2: 56: Figure 2.8 adapted from "A United Biosocial Theory of Personality and Its Role in the Development of Anxiety States," by C. R. Cloninger, 1986, *Psychiatric Developments, 3,* 167-226. Copyright 1986 by Oxford University Press. Adapted by permission of Oxford University Press.

Chapter 3: 77: Excerpt from "Behavioral Assessment: Basic Strategies and Initial Procedures," by R. O. Nelson, and D. H. Barlow. In D. H. Barlow (Ed.), *Behavioral Assessment of Adult Disorders,* 1981. Copyright 1981 by Guilford Press. Reprinted by permission. **85:** Table 3.1 adapted from *Anxiety Disorders Interview Schedule for DSM-IV (ADIS-IV),* by P. A. DiNardo, T. A. Brown, and D. H. Barlow. Copyright 1994 by Graywind Publications Incorporated. Reprinted by permission. **87:** Table 3.2 from *Schedule for Affective Disorders and Schizophrenia - Lifetime Anxiety Version, Revised* by B. Schleyer, C. Aaronson, C. Mannuzza, L. Y. Martin, and A. J. Fyer, November, 1990, Anxiety Disorders Clinic, New York State Psychiatric Institute, New York. Reprinted by permission. The SADS-LA is a modification of the original SADS-L (Life-time Version) by R. Spitzer and J. Endicott, New York State Psychiatric Institute, 1979. **96:** Figure 3.7 from Minnesota Multiphasic Personality Inventory (MMPI). Copyright © the University of Minnesota 1942, 1943 (renewed 1970). This profile form 1948, 1976, 1982. Reproduced by permission of the University of Minnesota Press. **102:** Figure 3.8 from "Heart Rate and Heart Rate Variability Recorded in Vivo in Agoraphobics and Nonphobics," by A. E. Holden and D. H. Barlow, 1986, *Behavior Therapy,* 17, 26-42. Copyright 1986 by the Association for Advancement of Behavior Therapy. Reprinted by permission. **111:** Excerpt from *Cultural Formulation Guidelines,* by J. E. Mezzich, B. J. Good, R. Lewis-Fernandez, P. Guarnaccia, K. M. Lin, D. Parron, T. O'Nell, S. Manson, C. Fleming, M. Weiss, and C. Hughes, September, 1993, p. 166. Revised Cultural Proposals for DSM-IV. Submitted to the DSM-IV Task Force by the Steering Committee, NIMH-Sponsored Group on Culture and Diagnosis.

Chapter 4: 135: Figure 4.3 from "An Analysis of Maintenance Following Functional Communication Training," by V. M. Durand and E. G. Carr, 1992, Journal of Applied Behavior Analysis, 25, 777-794. Copyright 1992 by the *Journal of Applied Behavior Analysis.* Reprinted by permission. **136:** Illustration from "Genetics: The Future is Now," by Nigel Holmes in *Time Magazine,* January 17, 1994, pp. 50-51. Reprinted by permission of Time, Inc.

Chapter 5: 155: Table 5.1 reprinted with permission from the American Psychiatric Association *Diagnostic and Statistical Manual of Mental Disorders, Fourth Edition.* Washington D.C., American Psychiatric Association, 1994. **156:** Figure 5.1 from "The Psychophysiology of Relaxation-Associated Panic Attacks," by A. S. Cohen, D. H. Barlow, and E. B. Blanchard, 1985, *Journal of Abnormal Psychology, 94,* 96-101. Copyright 1985 by the American Psychological Association. Reprinted by permission. **160:** Table 5.2 reprinted with permission from the American Psychiatric Association *Diagnostic and Statistical Manual of Mental Disorders, Fourth Edition.* Washington D.C., American Psychiatric Association, 1994. **161:** Figure 5.2 from "Domains of Worry Within the DSM-III-R Generalized Anxiety Disorder Catagory Reliability and Description," by W. C. Sanderson, and D. H. Barlow, November, 1986. Paper presented at the annual meeting of the Association for Advancement of Behavior Therapy, Chicago. **166:** Table 5.3 reprinted with permission from the American Psychiatric Association *Diagnostic and Statistical Manual of Mental Disorders, Fourth Edition.* Washington D.C., American Psychiatric Association, 1994. **167:** Table 5.4 from *Mastery of Your Anxiety and Panic II,* by D. H. Barlow, and M. G. Craske, 1994. Albany, NY: Graywind Publications Incorporated. Reprinted by permission. **168:** Table 5.5 from *Mastery of Your Anxiety and Panic II,* by D. H. Barlow, and M. G. Craske, 1994. Albany, NY: Graywind Publications Incorporated. Reprinted by permission. **171:** Figure 5.4 from *Anxiety and Its Disorders: The Nature and Treatment of Anxiety and Panic,* by D. H. Barlow. Copyright © 1988 Guilford Press. Reprinted by permission. **175:** Table 5.6 from *Mastery of Your Anxiety and Panic II,* by D. H. Barlow, and M. G. Craske, 1994. Albany, NY: Graywind Publications Incorporated. Reprinted by permission. **175:** Table 5.7 from *Mastery of Your Anxiety and Panic II,* by D. H. Barlow, and M. G. Craske, 1994. Graywind Publications Incorporated. Reprinted by permission. **176:** Figure 5.5 adapted from "A Comparison of Alprazolam and Behavior Therapy in Treatment of Panic Disorder," by J. S. Klosko, D. H. Barlow, R. Tassinari, and J. A. Cerny, 1990, *Journal of Consulting and Clinical Psychology, 58,* 77-84. Copyright 1990 by the American Psychological Association. Reprinted by permission. **177:** Table 5.8 reprinted with permission from the American Psychiatric Association *Diagnostic and Statistical Manual of Mental Disorders, Fourth Edition.* Washington D.C., American Psychiatric Association, 1994. **178:** Table 5.9 from "List of Phobias," by J. D. Maser, p. 805. In A. H. Tuma and J. D. Maser (Eds.), *Anxiety and the Anxiety Disorders,* 1985. Copyright 1985 by Lawrence Erlbaum Associates. Reprinted by permission. **180:** Table 5.10 adapted from "The Epidemiology of Common Fears and Phobia," by S. Agras, D. Sylvester, & D. Oliveau, 1969, *Comprehensive Psychiatry, 10,* 151-156. Copyright 1969 by Grune & Stratton. Adapted by permission of W. B. Saunders Co. **183:** Figure 5.6 from *Anxiety and Its Disorders: The Nature and Treatment of Anxiety and Panic,* by D. H. Barlow. Copyright © 1988 Guilford Press. Reprinted by permission. **186:** Table 5.12 reprinted with permission from the American Psychiatric Association *Diagnostic and Statistical Manual of Mental Disorders, Fourth Edition.* Washington D.C., American Psychiatric Association, 1994. **188:** Figure 5.7 from *Anxiety and Its Disorders: The Nature and Treatment of Anxiety and Panic,* by D. H. Barlow. Copyright © 1988 Guilford

Press. Reprinted by permission. **190:** Table 5.13 reprinted with permission from the American Psychiatric Association *Diagnostic and Statistical Manual of Mental Disorders, Fourth Edition.* Washington D.C., American Psychiatric Association, 1994. **191:** Table 5.14 from "Sibling Modeling in the Treatment of PTSD," by P. P. Miller, A. M. Albano, and D. H. Barlow, 1992. Paper presented at the annual meeting of the Association for the Advancement of Behavior Therapy, Boston, MA. **193:** Table 5.15 from "Mental Health Correlates of Criminal Victimization: A Random Community Survey," by D. G. Kilpatrick, C. L. Best, L. J. Veronen, A. E. Amick, L. A. Villeponteaux, and G. A. Ruff, 1985, *Journal of Consulting Psychology, 53,* 866-873. Copyright 1985 by the American Psychological Association. Reprinted by permission. **194:** Table 5.16 from "Neurobiology of Posttraumatic Stress Disorder," by S. M. Southwick, J. H. Krystal, D. R. Johnson, and D. S. Charney, 1992, *Review of Psychiatry, 11,* 347-367. Copyright 1992 by the American Psychiatric Press. Reprinted by permission. **195:** Figure 5.8 from *Anxiety and Its Disorders: The Nature and Treatment of Anxiety and Panic,* by D. H. Barlow. Copyright © 1988 Guilford Press. Reprinted by permission. **195:** Table 5.17 from "Sibling Modeling in the Treatment of PTSD," by P. P. Miller, A. M. Albano, and D. H. Barlow, 1992. Paper presented at the annual meeting of the Association for the Advancement of Behavior Therapy, Boston, MA. **197:** Table 5.18 reprinted with permission from the American Psychiatric Association *Diagnostic and Statistical Manual of Mental Disorders, Fourth Edition.* Washington D.C., American Psychiatric Association, 1994. **199:** Figure 5.9 from *Anxiety and Its Disorders: The Nature and Treatment of Anxiety and Panic,* by D. H. Barlow. Copyright © 1988 Guilford Press. Reprinted by permission.

Chapter 6: 205: Table 6.1 reprinted with permission from the American Psychiatric Association *Diagnostic and Statistical Manual of Mental Disorders, Fourth Edition.* Washington D.C., American Psychiatric Association, 1994. **210:** Table 6.2 reprinted with permission from the American Psychiatric Association *Diagnostic and Statistical Manual of Mental Disorders, Fourth Edition.* Washington D.C., American Psychiatric Association, 1994. **214:** Table 6.3 reprinted with permission from the American Psychiatric Association *Diagnostic and Statistical Manual of Mental Disorders, Fourth Edition.* Washington D.C., American Psychiatric Association, 1994. **215:** Table 6.4 reprinted with permission from the American Psychiatric Association *Diagnostic and Statistical Manual of Mental Disorders, Fourth Edition.* Washington D.C., American Psychiatric Association, 1994. **218:** Table 6.5 reprinted with permission from the American Psychiatric Association *Diagnostic and Sta-*

tistical Manual of Mental Disorders, Fourth Edition. Washington D.C., American Psychiatric Association, 1994. **219:** Table 6.6 reprinted with permission from the American Psychiatric Association *Diagnostic and Statistical Manual of Mental Disorders, Fourth Edition.* Washington D.C., American Psychiatric Association, 1994. **220:** Table 6.7 from "Body Dysmorphic Disorder: 30 Cases of Imagined Ugliness," by K. A. Phillips, S. L. McElroy, P. E. Keck, Jr., H. G. Pope, Jr., and J. I. Hudson, 1993, *American Journal of Psychiatry, 150,* 302-308. Copyright 1993 by the American Psychiatric Association. Reprinted by permission. **224:** Table 6.8 reprinted with permission from the American Psychiatric Association *Diagnostic and Statistical Manual of Mental Disorders, Fourth Edition.* Washington D.C., American Psychiatric Association, 1994. **225:** Table 6.9 reprinted with permission from the American Psychiatric Association *Diagnostic and Statistical Manual of Mental Disorders, Fourth Edition.* Washington D.C., American Psychiatric Association, 1994. **226:** Table 6.10 reprinted with permission from the American Psychiatric Association *Diagnostic and Statistical Manual of Mental Disorders, Fourth Edition.* Washington D.C., American Psychiatric Association, 1994. **227:** Table 6.11 reprinted with permission from the American Psychiatric Association *Diagnostic and Statistical Manual of Mental Disorders, Fourth Edition.* Washington D.C., American Psychiatric Association, 1994. **229:** Table 6.12 reprinted with permission from the American Psychiatric Association *Diagnostic and Statistical Manual of Mental Disorders, Fourth Edition.* Washington D.C., American Psychiatric Association, 1994.

Chapter 7: 241: Table 7.1 reprinted with permission from the American Psychiatric Association *Diagnostic and Statistical Manual of Mental Disorders, Fourth Edition.* Washington D.C., American Psychiatric Association, 1994. **242:** Table 7.2 reprinted with permission from the American Psychiatric Association *Diagnostic and Statistical Manual of Mental Disorders, Fourth Edition.* Washington D.C., American Psychiatric Association, 1994. **244:** Table 7.3 reprinted with permission from the American Psychiatric Association *Diagnostic and Statistical Manual of Mental Disorders, Fourth Edition.* Washington D.C., American Psychiatric Association, 1994. **245:** Table 7.4 reprinted with permission from the American Psychiatric Association *Diagnostic and Statistical Manual of Mental Disorders, Fourth Edition.* Washington D.C., American Psychiatric Association, 1994. **246:** Table 7.5 adapted and reprinted with the permission of The Free Press, an imprint of Simon & Schuster from "Affective Disorders," by M. M. Weissman, M. L. Bruce, P. J. Leaf, L. P. Fiorio, and C. Holzer, in *Psychiatric Disorders in America: The Epidemiologic*

Catchment Area Study, by Lee N. Robins, Ph.D. and Darrel A. Regier, M.D. Copyright © 1991 by Lee N. Robins and Darrel A. Regier. **247:** Figure 7.1 adapted from "The Changing Rate of Major Depression: Cross-National Comparisons," by the Cross-National Collaborative Group, 1992, *Journal of the American Medical Association, 268,* 3098-3105. Copyright 1992 by the American Medical Association. Reprinted by permission. **248:** Figure 7.2 adapted and reprinted with the permission of The Free Press, an imprint of Simon & Schuster from "Affective Disorders," by M. M. Weissman, M. L. Bruce, P. J. Leaf, L. P. Fiorio, and C. Holzer, in *Psychiatric Disorders in America: The Epidemiologic Catchment Area Study,* by Lee N. Robins, Ph.D. and Darrel A. Regier, M.D. Copyright © 1991 by Lee N. Robins and Darrel A. Regier. **250:** Table 7.6 reprinted with permission from the American Psychiatric Association *Diagnostic and Statistical Manual of Mental Disorders, Fourth Edition.* Washington D.C., American Psychiatric Association, 1994. **251:** Table 7.7 reprinted with permission from the American Psychiatric Association *Diagnostic and Statistical Manual of Mental Disorders, Fourth Edition.* Washington D.C., American Psychiatric Association, 1994. **251:** Table 7.8 adapted and reprinted with the permission of The Free Press, an imprint of Simon & Schuster from "Affective Disorders," by M. M. Weissman, M. L. Bruce, P. J. Leaf, L. P. Fiorio, and C. Holzer, in *Psychiatric Disorders in America: The Epidemiologic Catchment Area Study,* by Lee N. Robins, Ph.D. and Darrel A. Regier, M.D. Copyright © 1991 by Lee N. Robins and Darrel A. Regier. **256:** Table 7.9 from "Prevalence of Seasonal Affective Disorder in Alaska," by J. M. Booker, and C. J. Hellekson, 1992, *American Journal of Psychiatry, 149,* 1176-1182. Copyright 1992 by the American Psychiatric Association. Reprinted by permission. **257:** Table 7.10 adapted and reprinted with the permission of The Free Press, an imprint of Simon & Schuster from "Affective Disorders," by M. M. Weissman, M. L. Bruce, P. J. Leaf, L. P. Fiorio, and C. Holzer, in *Psychiatric Disorders in America: The Epidemiologic Catchment Area Study,* by Lee N. Robins, Ph.D. and Darrel A. Regier, M.D. Copyright © 1991 by Lee N. Robins and Darrel A. Regier. **259:** Table 7.11 from "Phenomenology of Major Depression from Childhood Through Adulthood: Analysis of Three Studies," by G. A. Carlson, and J. H. Kashani, 1988, *American Journal of Psychiatry, 145*(10), 1222-1225. Copyright 1988 by the American Psychiatry Association. Reprinted by permission. **262:** Table 7.12 from *Manic-Depressive Illness* by Frederick K. Goodwin and Kay Redfield Jamison, p. 347. Copyright © 1990 by Oxford University Press, Inc. Reprinted by permission. **263:** Table 7.13 adapted from "The DSM-IV Field Trial for Mixed Anxiety Depression," by R. E. Zinbarg, D. H. Barlow, M.

Liebowitz, L. Street, E. Broadhead, W. Katon, P. Roy-Byrne, J. P. Lepine, M. Teherani, J. Richards, P. J. Brantley, and H. Kraemer, (in press), *The American Journal of Psychiatry*. **265:** Table 7.14 adapted from "Genetics," by E. S. Gershon, 1990. In Frederick K. Goodwin and Kay Redfield Jamison (Eds.), *Manic-Depressive Illness*. Copyright © 1990 by Oxford University Press. Reprinted by permission. **266:** Figure 7.4 adapted from "A Danish Twin Study of Manic-Depressive Disorders," by A. Bertelsen, B. Harvald, and M. Hauge, 1977, *British Journal of Psychiatry, 130*, 330-351. Reprinted by permission. **271:** Figure 7.5 from "Life Events and Measurement," by G. W. Brown, 1989. In G. W. Brown and T. O. Harris (Eds.), *Life Events and Illness*. Copyright © 1989 by The Guilford Press. Reprinted by permission. **272:** Table 7.15 from "Depression," by G. W. Brown, 1989. In G. W. Brown and T. O. Harris (Eds.), *Life Events and Illness*, p. 56. Copyright © 1989 by The Guilford Press. Reprinted by permission. **283:** Excerpt from "Depression," by J. E. Young, A. T. Beck, and A. Weinberger, 1993. In D. H. Barlow (Ed.), *Clinical Handbook of Psychological Disorders*, 2nd Edition, pp. 34-35. Copyright 1993 by Guilford Press. Reprinted by permission. **287:** Table 7.17 from "Cognitive Therapy and Pharmacotherapy for Depression: Singly and in Combination," by S. D. Hollon, R. J. DeRubeis, M. D. Evans, M. J. Wiemer, M. J. Garvey, W. M. Grove, and V. B. Tuason, 1992, *Archives of General Psychiatry, 49*, 774-781. Copyright 1992 by the American Medical Association. Reprinted by permission. **288:** Figure 7.8 from "Differential Relapse Following Cognitive Therapy and Pharmacotherapy for Depression," by M. D. Evans, S. D. Hollon, R. J. DeRubeis, J. M. Piasecki, W. M. Grove, M. J. Garvey, and V. B. Tuason, 1992, *Archives of General Psychiatry, 49*, 802-808. Copyright 1992 by the American Medical Association. Reprinted by permission. **290:** Figure 7.9 adapted from "Families of Bipolar Patients: Dysfunction, Course of Illness, and Pilot Treatment Study," by I. W. Miller, G. I. Keitner, N. B. Epstein, D. S. Bishop, and C. E. Ryan, 1991. Paper presented at the annual meeting of the Association for the Advancement of Behavior Therapy, New York. Adapted by permission. **291:** Figure 7.10 from "The Epidemiology of Suicide: Implications for Clinical Practice," by M. Buda, and M. T. Tsuang, 1990. In S. J. Blumenthal and D. J. Kupfer (Eds.), *Suicide Over the Life Cycle: Risk Factors, Assessment, and Treatment of Suicidal Patients*, pp. 17-37. Copyright 1990 by the American Psychiatric Press, Inc. Reprinted by permission. **292:** Figure 7.11 from "The Epidemiology of Suicide: Implications for Clinical Practice," by M. Buda, and M. T. Tsuang, 1990. In S. J. Blumenthal and D. J. Kupfer (Eds.), *Suicide Over the Life Cycle: Risk Factors, Assessment, and Treatment of Suicidal Patients*, pp. 17-37. Copyright 1990 by

the American Psychiatric Press, Inc. Reprinted by permission. **295:** Figure 7.12 from "Clinical Assessment and Treatment of Youth Suicide," by S. J. Blumenthal, and D. J. Kupfer, 1988, *Journal of Youth and Adolescence, 17*, 1-24. Copyright 1988 by Plenum Publishing Corporation. Reprinted by permission.

Chapter 8: 300: Figure 8.1 from "Relationship Between Anorexia Nervosa and Bulimia Nervosa: Diagnostic Implications," by D. M. Garner and C. G. Fairburn, 1988, p. 60. In D. M. Garner and P. E. Garfinkel (Eds.), *Diagnostic Issues in Anorexia Nervosa and Bulimia Nervosa*. Copyright 1988 by Brunner/Mazel, Inc. Reprinted with permission from Brunner/Mazel, Inc. **303:** Table 8.1 reprinted with permission from the American Psychiatric Association *Diagnostic and Statistical Manual of Mental Disorders, Fourth Edition*. Washington D.C., American Psychiatric Association, 1994. **305:** Table 8.2 reprinted with permission from the American Psychiatric Association *Diagnostic and Statistical Manual of Mental Disorders, Fourth Edition*. Washington D.C., American Psychiatric Association, 1994. **311:** Figure 8.2 from "The Genetic Epidemiology of Bulimia Nervosa," by K. S. Kendler, C. Maclean, M. Neale, R. Kessler, A. Heath, and L. Evans, 1991, *American Journal of Psychiatry, 148*(12), 1627-1637. Copyright © 1991 by the American Psychiatric Association. Reprinted by permission. **312:** Figure 8.3 from "Cultural Expectations of Thinness in Women: An Update," by C. V. Wiseman, J. J. Gray, J. E. Mosimann, and A. H. Ahrens, 1992, *International Journal of Eating Disorders, 11*(1), 85-89. Copyright © 1992 by John Wiley & Sons. Reprinted by permission of John Wiley & Sons, Inc. **313:** Figure 8.4 from "Cultural Expectations of Thinness in Women: An Update," by C. V. Wiseman, J. J. Gray, J. E. Mosimann, and A. H. Ahrens, 1992, *International Journal of Eating Disorders, 11*(1), 85-89. Copyright © 1992 by John Wiley & Sons. Reprinted by permission of John Wiley & Sons, Inc. **324:** Figure 8.7 from "Psychotherapy and Bulimia Nervosa: The Longer-Term Effects of Interpersonal Psychotherapy, Behaviour Therapy and Cognitive Behaviour Therapy," by C. G. Fairburn, R. Jones, R. C. Peveler, R. A. Hope, and M. O'Connor, 1993, *Archives of General Psychiatry*. Copyright 1993 by the American Medical Association. Reprinted by permission. **324:** Table 8.3 from L. K. G. Hsu, *Eating Disorders*, p. 136, 1990. Copyright 1990 by Guilford Press. Reprinted by permission. **325:** Figure 8.8 from "Behavior Modification of Anorexia Nervosa," by W. S. Agras, D. H. Barlow, H. N. Chapin, G. G. Abel, H. Leitenberg, 1974, *Archives of General Psychiatry, 30*, 279-286. Copyright 1974 by the American Medical Association. Reprinted by permission.

Chapter 9: 330: Figure 9.1 adapted from "Control of Genital Herpes Recurrences Using Progressive Muscle Relaxation," by M. M. Burnette, K. A. Koehn, R. Kenyon-Jump, and C. Stark, 1991, *Behavior Therapy, 22*, 237-247. Copyright 1991 by the Association for Advancement of Behavior Therapy. Reprinted by permission of the publisher and author. **339:** Figure 9.2 from "Styles of Dominance and Their Endocrine Correlates Among Wild, Live Baboons," by R. Sapolsky, and J. C. Ray, 1989, *American Journal of Primatology, 18*(1), 1-13. Copyright 1989 by Wiley-Liss, Inc. Reprinted by permission of John Wiley & Sons. **340:** Figure 9.3 after *Mastering Stress: A Lifestyle Approach* by D. H. Barlow and R. M. Rapee, 1991. Copyright 1991 by American Health Publishing Co. Reprinted by permission. **347:** Figure 9.5 adapted from "Effect of Psychosocial Treatment on Survival of Patients with Metastatic Breast Cancer," by D. Spiegel, J. R. Bloom, H. C. Kramer, and E. Gotheil, 1989, Lancet, 14, 888-891. © by The Lancet Ltd. 1989. Reprinted by permission. **352:** Figure 9.6 adapted from "In-Hospital Symptoms of Psychological Stress as Predictors of Long-Term Outcome After Acute Myocardial Infarction in Men," by N. Frasure-Smith, 1991, *The American Journal of Cardiology, 67*, 121-127. Copyright 1991 by Cahners Publishing Company. Reprinted by permission. **359:** Table 9.1 from "Classification and Diagnostic Criteria for Headache Disorder, Cranial Neuralgias, and Facial Pain," by the Headache Classification Committee of the International Headache Society, 1988, *Cephalagia, 8*(Supplement 7), 9-96. Reprinted by permission. **361:** Table 9.2 adapted from "Neurasthenia and Chronic Fatigue Syndrome: The Role of Culture in the Making of a Diagnosis," by S. E. Abbey, and P. E. Garfinkel, 1991, *American Journal of Psychiatry, 148*, 1638-1646. Copyright 1991 by American Psychiatric Association. Reprinted by permission. **364:** Figure 9.7 adapted from "A Test of Specific and Nonspecific Effects in the Biofeedback Treatment of Tension Headache," by F. Andrasik, and K. A. Holroyd, 1980, *Journal of Consulting and Clinical Psychology, 48*, 575-586. Copyright 1980 by the American Psychological Association. Reprinted by permission. **365:** Excerpts from *Mastering Stress: A Lifestyle Approach* by D. H. Barlow, and R. M. Rapee, 1991. Copyright 1991 by the American Health Publishing. Reprinted by permission. **366:** Figure 9.8 from *Mastering Stress: A Lifestyle Approach* by D. H. Barlow, and R. M. Rapee, 1991. Copyright 1991 by the American Health Publishing. Reprinted by permission. **367:** Table 9.3 from *Mastering Stress: A Lifestyle Approach* by D. H. Barlow, and R. M. Rapee, 1991. Copyright 1991 by the American Health Publishing. Reprinted by permission. **369:** Table 9.4 from "Primary Care and Health Promotion: A Model for Preventive Medicine," by M. B. Johns et al, 1987, *Ameri-*

can *Journal of Preventive Medicine,* *3*(6), 351. Copyright 1987 American Journal of Preventive Medicine. Reprinted by permission. **371:** Table 9.5 from "Strategies for Modifying Sexual Behavior for Primary and Secondary Prevention of HIV Disease," by T. J. Coates, 1990, *Journal of Consulting and Clinical Psychology, 58*(1), 57-69. Copyright 1990 by the American Psychological Association. Reprinted by permission. **372:** Table 9.6 from "Women and AIDS in the United States: Epidemiology, Natural History, and Mediating Mechanisms," by J. R. Ickovics, and J. Rodin, 1992, *Health Psychology, 11*(1), 1-16. Copyright 1992 by the American Psychological Association. Reprinted by permission. **374:** Figure 9.9 from "Skills Training in a Cardiovascular Health Education Campaign," by A. J. Meyer, J. D. Nash, A. L. McAlister, N. Maccoby, and J. W. Farquhar, 1980, *Journal of Consulting and Clinical Psychology, 48,* 129-142. Copyright 1980 by the American Psychological Association. Reprinted by permission.

Chapter 10: 378: Figure 10.1 from "Ontogenetic Development of the Human Sleep-Dream Cycle," by H. P. Roffwarg, J. N. Muzio, and W. C. Dement, 1966, *Science, 152,* 604-619. Copyright 1966 by the AAAS. Revised since publication by the authors. Used by permission of the authors. **380:** Figure 10.2 from *The Sleep Disorder,* 2nd Edition, by P. Hauri, 1982. Copyright 1982 by The Upjohn Company. Reprinted by permission. **381:** Figure 10.3 from "Sleep Disorders: Recent Findings in the Diagnosis and Treatment of Disturbed Sleep," by A. Kales and J. D. Kales, 1974, *New England Journal of Medicine, 290,* 487. Copyright 1974 by the Massachusetts Medical Society. Reprinted by permission. **385:** Table 10.2 reprinted with permission from the American Psychiatric Association *Diagnostic and Statistical Manual of Mental Disorders, Fourth Edition.* Washington D.C., American Psychiatric Association, 1994. **390:** Table 10.3 reprinted with permission from the American Psychiatric Association *Diagnostic and Statistical Manual of Mental Disorders, Fourth Edition.* Washington D.C., American Psychiatric Association, 1994. **391:** Figure 10.5 from "The Multiple Sleep Latency Test as an Evaluation for Excessive Somnolence," by M. M. Mitler, in C. Guilleminault, *Sleeping and Waking Disorders: Indications and Techniques,* 1982. Copyright 1982 by Addison-Wesley. Reprinted by permission of Butterworth Publishers. **392:** Table 10.4 reprinted with permission from the American Psychiatric Association *Diagnostic and Statistical Manual of Mental Disorders, Fourth Edition.* Washington D.C., American Psychiatric Association, 1994. **394:** Table 10.5 reprinted with permission from the American Psychiatric Association *Diagnostic and Statistical Manual of Mental Disorders, Fourth Edition.* Washington D.C., American Psychiatric Association,

1994. **395:** Table 10.6 reprinted with permission from the American Psychiatric Association *Diagnostic and Statistical Manual of Mental Disorders, Fourth Edition.* Washington D.C., American Psychiatric Association, 1994. **396:** Figure 10.6 from the *New York Times,* November 3, 1992, Science News Section, page C-12. Copyright © 1992 by the New York Times Company. Reprinted by permission. **398:** Figure 10.7 adapted from "Chronotherapy: Resetting the Circadian Clocks of Patients with Delayed Sleep Phase Insomnia," by C. A. Czeisler, G. S. Richardson, R. M. Coleman, J. C. Zimmerman, M. C. Moore-Ede, W. C. Dement, and E. D. Weitzman, *Sleep,* 1981, 4(1), 1-21. Reprinted by permission of the journal, Sleep. **401:** Table 10.9 from "Classification of Sleep Disorders: A Preview of the DSM-IV," by D. J. Buysse, C. F. Reynolds, & D. J. Kupfer, 1993. In D. L. Dunner (Ed.), *Current Psychiatric Therapy,* pp. 360-361. Copyright 1993 by W. B. Saunders Company. Reprinted by permission. **402:** Table 10.10 reprinted with permission from the American Psychiatric Association *Diagnostic and Statistical Manual of Mental Disorders, Fourth Edition.* Washington D.C., American Psychiatric Association, 1994. **403:** Table 10.11 reprinted with permission from the American Psychiatric Association *Diagnostic and Statistical Manual of Mental Disorders, Fourth Edition.* Washington D.C., American Psychiatric Association, 1994. **404:** Table 10.12 reprinted with permission from the American Psychiatric Association *Diagnostic and Statistical Manual of Mental Disorders, Fourth Edition.* Washington D.C., American Psychiatric Association, 1994.

Chapter 11: 410: Figure 11.2 from "Sex Surveys Help Map AIDS Risk," by Robert Taylor, February 1993, *The Journal of NIH Research, 5*(2), 31-32. Copyright ©1994 The Journal of NIH Research, Washington DC. Reprinted with permission. **411:** Table 11.1 from "Sexual Behavior of College Women in 1975, 1986 and 1989," by B. A. DeBuono, S. H. Zinner, M. Daamen, and W. M. McCormack, 1990, *The New England Journal of Medicine, 322*(12), 821-825. Copyright 1990 by the Massachusetts Medical Society. Reprinted with permission from The New England Journal of Medicine. **411:** Table 11.2 from "Gender Differences in Masturbation and the Relation of Masturbation Experience in Preadolescence and/or Early Adolescence to Sexual Behavior and Sexual Adjustment," by H. Leitenberg, M. J. Detzer, and D. Srebnik, 1993, *Archives of Sexual Behavior, 22,* 87-98. Copyright 1993 by Plenum Press. Reprinted by permission. **413:** Table 11.3 from "Affective Reactions of American and Swedish Women to Their First Premarital Coitus: A Cross Comparison," by I. M. Schwartz, 1993, *The Journal of Sex Research, 30,* 18-26. Copyright 1993 by the Society for the Scientific Study of Sex. Reprinted by permission. **415:** Table

11.4 from "Sexual Function in the Elderly," by A. C. Diokno, M. B. Brown, and A. R. Herzog, 1990, *Archives of Internal Medicine, 150,* 197-200. Copyright 1990 by the American Medical Association. Reprinted by permission. **415:** Table 11.5 from "Sexual Function in the Elderly," by A. C. Diokno, M. B. Brown, and A. R. Herzog, 1990, *Archives of Internal Medicine, 150,* 197-200. Copyright 1990 by the American Medical Association. Reprinted by permission. **417:** Table 11.6 reprinted with permission from the American Psychiatric Association *Diagnostic and Statistical Manual of Mental Disorders, Fourth Edition.* Washington D.C., American Psychiatric Association, 1994. **422:** Table 11.7 from *Sexual Dysfunction: A Guide for Assessment and Treatment,* by J. P. Wincze and M. P. Carey, 1991. Copyright 1991 by Guilford Press. Reprinted by permission. **423:** Table 11.8 reprinted with permission from the American Psychiatric Association *Diagnostic and Statistical Manual of Mental Disorders, Fourth Edition.* Washington D.C., American Psychiatric Association, 1994. **424:** Table 11.9 reprinted with permission from the American Psychiatric Association *Diagnostic and Statistical Manual of Mental Disorders, Fourth Edition.* Washington D.C., American Psychiatric Association, 1994. **426:** Table 11.10 reprinted with permission from the American Psychiatric Association *Diagnostic and Statistical Manual of Mental Disorders, Fourth Edition.* Washington D.C., American Psychiatric Association, 1994. **428:** Table 11.11 reprinted with permission from the American Psychiatric Association *Diagnostic and Statistical Manual of Mental Disorders, Fourth Edition.* Washington D.C., American Psychiatric Association, 1994. **429:** Table 11.12 reprinted with permission from the American Psychiatric Association *Diagnostic and Statistical Manual of Mental Disorders, Fourth Edition.* Washington D.C., American Psychiatric Association, 1994. **429:** Figure 11.3 from "A Regional Service for Sexual Problems: A Three Year Study," by P. Warner, J. Bancroft, & Members of the Edinburgh Human Sexuality, 1987, *Sexual and Marital Therapy, 2,* 115-126. Published by Carfax Publishing Company, P. O. Box 25, Abingdon, Oxfordshire, 0X14 3UE, UK. Reprinted by permission. **430:** Table 11.13 reprinted with permission from the American Psychiatric Association *Diagnostic and Statistical Manual of Mental Disorders, Fourth Edition.* Washington D.C., American Psychiatric Association, 1994. **436:** Figure 11.4 from "Anxiety Increases Sexual Arousal," by D. H. Barlow, D. K. Sakheim, and J. G. Beck, 1983, *Journal of Abnormal Psychology, 92,* 49-54. Copyright 1983 by the American Psychological Association. Reprinted by permission. **437:** Figure 11.5 adapted from "Causes of Sexual Dysfunction: The Role of Anxiety and Cognitive Interference, 1986, *Journal of Consulting and Clinical Psychology, 54,*

140-148. Copyright 1986 by the American Psychological Association. Reprinted by permission. **439:** Left side of Table 11.14 from the book, *Becoming Orgasmic: A Sexual and Personal Growth Program for Women,* Rev. Ed., by Julia R. Heiman, Ph.D. and Joseph LoPiccolo, Ph.D., © 1976,1988. Used by permission of the publisher, Prentice Hall Press/A Division of Simon & Schuster, New York. **439:** Right side of Table 11.14 from *The New Male Sexuality,* by Bernie Zilbergeld, Ph.D. Copyright © 1992 by Bernie Zilbergeld, Ph.D. Used by permission of Bantam Books, a division of Bantam Doubleday Dell Publishing Group, Inc. **445:** Table 11.15 reprinted with permission from the American Psychiatric Association *Diagnostic and Statistical Manual of Mental Disorders, Fourth Edition.* Washington D.C., American Psychiatric Association, 1994. **446:** Table 11.16 reprinted with permission from the American Psychiatric Association *Diagnostic and Statistical Manual of Mental Disorders, Fourth Edition.* Washington D.C., American Psychiatric Association, 1994. **447:** Table 11.17 reprinted with permission from the American Psychiatric Association *Diagnostic and Statistical Manual of Mental Disorders, Fourth Edition.* Washington D.C., American Psychiatric Association, 1994. **449:** Table 11.18 reprinted with permission from the American Psychiatric Association *Diagnostic and Statistical Manual of Mental Disorders, Fourth Edition.* Washington D.C., American Psychiatric Association, 1994. **450:** Figure 11.6 from "The Components of Rapists' Sexual Arousal," by G. G. Abel, D. H. Barlow, E. B. Blanchard, and D. Guild, 1977, *Archives of General Psychiatry, 34,* p. 900. Copyright 1977 by the American Medical Association. Reprinted by permission. **451:** Figure 11.7 from "The Components of Rapists' Sexual Arousal," by G. G. Abel, D. H. Barlow, E. B. Blanchard, and D. Guild, 1977, *Archives of General Psychiatry, 34,* 895-903. Copyright 1977 by the American Medical Association. Reprinted by permission. **452:** Table 11.19 reprinted with permission from the American Psychiatric Association *Diagnostic and Statistical Manual of Mental Disorders, Fourth Edition.* Washington D.C., American Psychiatric Association, 1994. **454:** Table 11.20 reprinted with permission from the American Psychiatric Association *Diagnostic and Statistical Manual of Mental Disorders, Fourth Edition.* Washington D.C., American Psychiatric Association, 1994. **457:** Figure 11.9 from "Identifying Specific Erotic Cues in Sexual Deviations by Audiotaped Descriptions," by G. G. Abel, E. B. Blanchard, D. H. Barlow, and M. Mavissakalian, 1975, *Journal of Applied Behavior Analysis, 8,* 247-260. Copyright 1975 by Journal of Applied Behavior Analysis. Reprinted by permission. **458:** Excerpt reproduced with permission of authors and publisher from Harbert, T. L. , Barlow, D. H., Hersen, M., and Austin,

J. B., "Measurement and Modification of Incestuous Behavior: A Case Study." *Psychological Reports,* 1974, 34, 79-86. Copyright Psychological Reports 1974. **459:** Figure 11.11 reproduced with permission of authors and publisher from Harbert, T. L. , Barlow, D. H., Hersen, M., and Austin, J. B., "Measurement and Modification of Incestuous Behavior: A Case Study." *Psychological Reports,* 1974, 34, 79-86. Copyright Psychological Reports 1974. **459:** Table 11.21 from "Data Generated By An Outpatient Sexual Abuse Clinic," by B. M. Maletzky, in *Treating the Sexual Offender,* p. 257. Copyright 1991 by Sage Publications. Reprinted by permission of Sage Publications, Inc.

Chapter 12: 466: Table 12.1 reprinted with permission from the American Psychiatric Association *Diagnostic and Statistical Manual of Mental Disorders, Fourth Edition.* Washington D.C., American Psychiatric Association, 1994. **466:** Table 12.2 reprinted with permission from the American Psychiatric Association *Diagnostic and Statistical Manual of Mental Disorders, Fourth Edition.* Washington D.C., American Psychiatric Association, 1994. **467:** Table 12.3 reprinted with permission from the American Psychiatric Association *Diagnostic and Statistical Manual of Mental Disorders, Fourth Edition.* Washington D.C., American Psychiatric Association, 1994. **470:** Figure 12.1 from the sidebar "Is Everything Addictive," researched by Valerie Fahey, *In Health,* January/February 1990. Reprinted from *In Health,* © 1990 by permission. **471:** Figure 12.2 from the sidebar "Easy to Get Hooked On, Hard to Get Off," researched by John Hastings, *In Health,* November/December 1990, p. 37. Reprinted from *In Health,* © 1990. **472:** Table 12.4 reprinted with permission from the American Psychiatric Association *Diagnostic and Statistical Manual of Mental Disorders, Fourth Edition.* Washington D.C., American Psychiatric Association, 1994. **477:** Figure 12.6 from *Alcoholic Beverage Taxation and Control Policies* (8th ed.), by Ron Brazeau and Nancy Burr, 1992. Copyright by the Brewers Association of Canada. Reprinted by permission. **481:** Table 12.5 reprinted with permission from the American Psychiatric Association *Diagnostic and Statistical Manual of Mental Disorders, Fourth Edition.* Washington D.C., American Psychiatric Association, 1994. **484:** Table 12.6 reprinted with permission from the American Psychiatric Association *Diagnostic and Statistical Manual of Mental Disorders, Fourth Edition.* Washington D.C., American Psychiatric Association, 1994. **485:** Table 12.7 reprinted with permission from the American Psychiatric Association *Diagnostic and Statistical Manual of Mental Disorders, Fourth Edition.* Washington D.C., American Psychiatric Association, 1994. **487:** Table 12.8 from "The Anatomy of a High," by William Booth,

The Washington Post National Weekly Edition, March 26-April 1, 1990, p. 38. © 1990 The Washington Post. Reprinted with permission. **488:** Table 12.8 reprinted with permission from the American Psychiatric Association *Diagnostic and Statistical Manual of Mental Disorders, Fourth Edition.* Washington D.C., American Psychiatric Association, 1994. **489:** Figure 12.9 adapted from "Nicotine Becomes Addictive," by R. Kanigel, 1988, *Science Illustrated,* October/November, pp. 12-14, 19-21. Copyright 1988 Science Illustrated. Reprinted by permission. **489:** Figure 12.10 adapted from "Nicotine Becomes Addictive," by R. Kanigel, 1988, *Science Illustrated,* October/November, pp. 12-14, 19-21. Copyright 1988 Science Illustrated. Reprinted by permission. **491:** Table 12.9 reprinted with permission from the American Psychiatric Association *Diagnostic and Statistical Manual of Mental Disorders, Fourth Edition.* Washington D.C., American Psychiatric Association, 1994. **491:** Table 12.10 reprinted with permission from the American Psychiatric Association *Diagnostic and Statistical Manual of Mental Disorders, Fourth Edition.* Washington D.C., American Psychiatric Association, 1994. **492:** Figure 12.11 from "A 24-Year Follow-Up of California Narcotics Addicts," by Y. Hser, M. D. Anglin, and K. Powers, 1993, *Archives of General Psychiatry, 50,* 577-584. Copyright 1993 by the American Medical Association. Reprinted by permission. **493:** Table 12.11 reprinted with permission from the American Psychiatric Association *Diagnostic and Statistical Manual of Mental Disorders, Fourth Edition.* Washington D.C., American Psychiatric Association, 1994. **495:** Table 12.12 reprinted with permission from the American Psychiatric Association *Diagnostic and Statistical Manual of Mental Disorders, Fourth Edition.* Washington D.C., American Psychiatric Association, 1994. **497:** Table 12.13 adapted from "A Population-Based Twin Study of Alcoholism in Women," by K. S. Kendler, A. C. Heath, M. C. Neale, R. C. Kessler, and L. J. Eaves, 1992, *Journal of the American Medical Association, 268,* 1877-1882. Copyright 1992 by the American Medical Association. Reprinted by permission. **508:** Table 12.14, *The Twelve Steps* are reprinted with permission of Alcoholics Anonymous World Services, Inc. Permission to reprint this material does not mean that AA has reviewed or approved the contents of this publication, nor that AA agrees with the views expressed herein. AA is a program of recovery from alcoholism only - use of the Twelve Steps in connection with programs and acitivites which are patterned after AA, but which address other problems, does not imply otherwise.

Chapter 13: 520: Figure 13.1 from "Sex Bias in the Diagnosis of Histrionic and Antisocial Personality Disorders," by M. R. Ford, and T. A. Widiger, 1989, *Journal of Consulting and Clinical Psychology,*

TO THE OWNER OF THIS BOOK:

We hope that you have enjoyed *Abnormal Psychology: An Integrative Approach* as much as we have enjoyed writing it. We'd like to know your thoughts and experiences about the book as a student. In what ways did it help you, and how can we make it better for future readers?

School and address: _____

Department: _____

Instructor's name: _____

1. What did you like most about *Abnormal Psychology: An Integrative Approach?*

_____

_____

2. What did you like least about the book?_____

_____

_____

3. Were all of the chapters assigned for you to read? _____

   If not, which ones weren't?_____

4. What was your reaction to the cases provided in the book? _____

_____

5. Did your instructor use the accompanying video: *Abnormal Psychology: Inside Out?*_____

   Do you have any suggestions for improving it in the future? _____

6. In the space below, or on a separate letter, please let us know any additional reactions that you may have. (For example, did you find any of the chapters particularly difficult?) We'd be delighted to hear from you!

_____

_____

_____

_____

_____

_____

Optional:

Your name: _____ Date: _____

May Brooks/Cole quote you, either in promotion for *Abnormal Psychology: An Integrative Approach*, or in future publishing ventures?

Yes: _____ No: _____

Best Regards,

David H. Barlow, Ph.D.
V. Mark Durand, Ph.D.

FOLD HERE

FOLD HERE

DSM-IV Classification: Axes I and II

DISORDERS USUALLY FIRST DIAGNOSED IN INFANCY, CHILDHOOD, OR ADOLESCENCE

Learning Disorders (Academic Skills Disorders)
Reading Disorder (Developmental Reading Disorder)/Mathematics Disorder (Developmental Arithmetic Disorder)/Disorder of Written Expression (Developmental Expressive Writing Disorder)

Motor Skills Disorder
Developmental Coordination Disorder

Pervasive Developmental Disorders
Autistic Disorder/Rett's Disorder/Childhood Disintegrative Disorder/Asperger's Disorder

Disruptive Behavior and Attention-Deficit Disorders
Attention-Deficit/Hyperactivity Disorder/Oppositional Defiant Disorder/Conduct Disorder

Feeding and Eating Disorders of Infancy or Early Childhood Pica/Rumination
Disorder/Feeding Disorder of Infancy or Early Childhood

Tic Disorders
Tourette's Disorder/Chronic Motor or Vocal Tic Disorder/ Transient Tic Disorder

Communication Disorders
Expressive Language Disorder (Developmental Expressive Language Disorder)/Mixed Receptive/Expressive Language Disorder (Developmental Receptive Language Disorder)/Phonological Disorder (Developmental Articulation Disorder)/Stuttering

Elimination Disorders
Encopresis/Enuresis

Other Disorders of Infancy, Childhood, or Adolescence
Separation Anxiety Disorder/Selective Mutism (Elective Mutism)/Reactive Attachment Disorder of Infancy or Early Childhood/Stereotypic Movement Disorder (Stereotypy/Habit Disorder)

DELIRIUM, DEMENTIA, AMNESTIC AND OTHER COGNITIVE DISORDERS

Deliria
Delirium Due to a General Medical Condition/Substance-Induced Delirium/Delirium Due to Multiple Etiologies

Dementias
Dementia of the Alzheimer's Type; With Early Onset: if onset at age 65 or below; With Late Onset: if onset after age 65/ Vascular Dementia/Dementias Due to Other General Medical Conditions/Substance-Induced Persisting Dementia/Dementia Due to Multiple Etiologies

Amnestic Disorders
Amnestic Disorder Due to a General Medical Condition/Substance-Induced Persisting Amnestic Disorder (refer to specific Substance for code)

SUBSTANCE-RELATED DISORDERS

Alcohol Use Disorders
Amphetamine (or Related Substance) Use Disorders
Caffeine Use Disorders
Cannabis Use Disorders
Cocaine Use Disorders
Hallucinogen Use Disorders
Inhalant Use Disorders
Nicotine Use Disorders
Opioid Use Disorders
Phencyclidine (or Related Substance) Use Disorders
Sedative, Hypnotic, or Anxiolytic Substance Use Disorders
Polysubstance Use Disorder
Sedative, Hypnotic, or Anxiolytic Related Disorder Not Otherwise Specified

SCHIZOPHRENIA AND OTHER PSYCHOTIC DISORDERS

Schizophrenia
Paranoid Type/Disorganized Type/Catatonic Type/Undifferentiated Type/Residual Type

Schizophreniform Disorder
Schizoaffective Disorder
Delusional Disorder
Brief Psychotic Disorder
Shared Psychotic Disorder (Folie à Deux)
Psychotic Disorder Due to a General Medical Condition
With Delusions/With Hallucinations/Substance-Induced Psychotic Disorder
Psychotic Disorder Not Otherwise Specified

MOOD DISORDERS

Depressive Disorders
Major Depressive Disorder/Dysthymic Disorder/Depressive Disorder Not Otherwise Specified

Bipolar Disorders
Bipolar I Disorder/Bipolar II Disorder (Recurrent Major Depressive Episodes with Hypomania)/Bipolar Not Otherwise Specified/Cyclothymic Disorder

Mood Disorder Due to a General Medical Condition
Substance-Induced Mood Disorder
Mood Disorder Not Otherwise Specified

ANXIETY DISORDERS

Panic Disorder
Without Agoraphobia/With Agoraphobia

Agoraphobia without History of Panic Disorder
Specific Phobia (Simple Phobia)
Social Phobia (Social Anxiety Disorder)
Obsessive-Compulsive Disorder
Posttraumatic Stress Disorder
Acute Stress Disorder
Generalized Anxiety Disorder (Includes Overanxious Disorder of Childhood)
Anxiety Disorder Due to a General Medical Condition
Substance-Induced Anxiety Disorder
Anxiety Disorder Not Otherwise Specified

SOMATOFORM DISORDERS

Somatization Disorder
Conversion Disorder